¡Ven conmigo!®

Your passport to proficiency

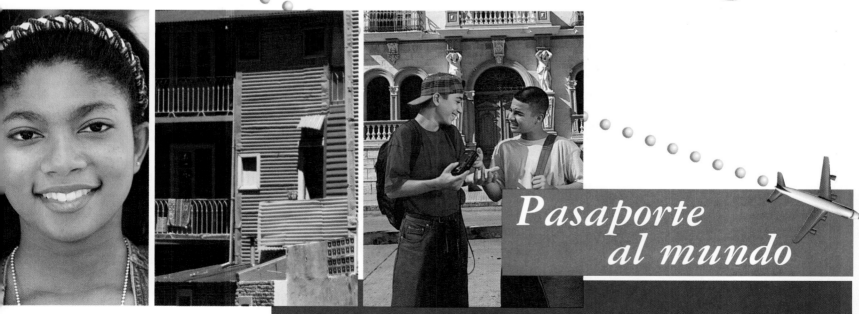

Pasaporte al mundo

Plan your itinerary for success

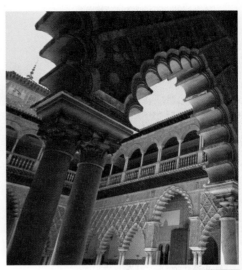

What's your **Destination?**

Communication!

¡Ven conmigo! takes

your classroom there.

It's even possible that

"What's next?"

becomes your

students' favorite

question!

Communication
and culture in context

The clear structure of each chapter makes it easy to present, practice, and apply language skills—all in the context of the location where the chapter takes place!

Grammar support and
practice in every lesson

¡Ven conmigo! builds a proven communicative approach on a solid foundation of grammar and vocabulary so students become proficient readers, writers, and speakers of Spanish. With the Cuaderno de gramática, Grammar Tutor, and the CD-ROM and DVD Tutors, students can practice the way they learn best.

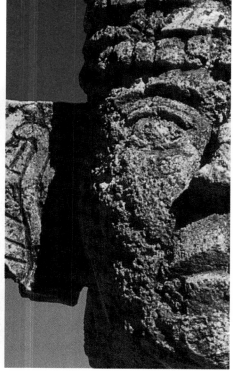

Technology that takes you there

Bring the world into your classroom with integrated audio, video, CD-ROM, DVD, and Internet resources that immerse students in authentic language and culture.

Assessment for state and national standards

To help you incorporate standardized test practice, the Standardized Assessment Tutor provides reading, writing, and math tests in Spanish that target the skills students need. The ¡Lee conmigo! Reader and Reading Strategies and Skills Handbook offer additional reading practice and reading skills development.

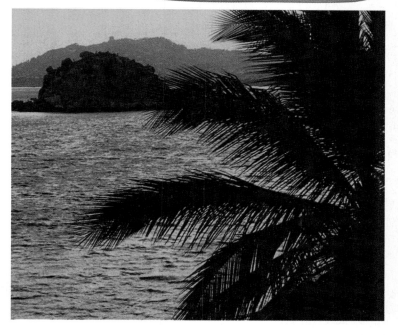

Easy lesson planning for all learning styles

Planning lessons has never been easier with a Lesson Planner with Substitute Teacher Lesson Plans, an editable One-Stop Planner® CD-ROM, and a Student Make-Up Assignments with Alternative Quizzes resource.

Travel a balanced program that's easy to navigate.

¡El mundo a su alcance!

The *¡Ven conmigo!* family

or

Program components
¡Ven conmigo! Levels 1-3

Texts
- Pupil's Edition
- Teacher's Edition

Planning and Presenting
- One-Stop Planner CD-ROM with Test Generator
- Exploratory Guide
- Lesson Planner with Substitute Teacher Lesson Plans
- Student Make-Up Assignments with Alternative Quizzes
- Teaching Transparencies

Native Speakers
- Cuaderno para hispanohablantes

Grammar
- Cuaderno de gramática
- Grammar Tutor for Students of Spanish

Reading and Writing
- Reading Strategies and Skills Handbook
- ¡Lee conmigo! Reader
- Cuaderno de actividades

Listening and Speaking
- Audio CD Program
- Listening Activities
- Activities for Communication
- TPR Storytelling Book (Levels 1 and 2)

Assessment
- Testing Program
- Alternative Assessment Guide
- Student Make-Up Assignments with Alternative Quizzes
- Standardized Assessment Tutor

Technology
- One-Stop Planner CD-ROM with Test Generator
- Audio CD Program
- Interactive CD-ROM Tutor
- Video Program
- Video Guide
- DVD Tutor (Levels 1 and 2)

Internet
- go.hrw.com
- www.hrw.com
- www.hrw.com/passport

¡Ven conmigo!®

HOLT SPANISH

LEVEL 3

HOLT, RINEHART AND WINSTON

A Harcourt Classroom Education Company

Austin • New York • Orlando • Atlanta • San Francisco • Boston • Dallas • Toronto • London

Requests for permission to make copies of any part of the work should be mailed to the following address: Permissions Department, Holt, Rinehart and Winston, 10801 N. MoPac Expressway, Building 3, Austin, Texas 78759.

In the *Annotated Teacher's Edition:*

Acknowledgements
For permission to reprint copyrighted material, grateful acknowledgment is made to the following source: National Standards in Foreign Language Education Project: "National Standards Report" from *Standards for Foreign Language Learning: Preparing for the 21st Century.* Copyright © 1996 by National Standards in Foreign Language Education Project.

Photography Credits
Abbreviations used: (b) bottom, (c) center, (l) left, (r) right, (bkgrd) background.
All photographs belong to Holt, Rinehart and Winston except:
Front cover: bkgd, James Blank/Stock Boston; teens, Steve Ewert/HRW Photo; Back cover: James Blank/Stock Boston; frame, ©1998 Image Farm Inc. 3D, Patrick Ward/CORBIS; 33D, Eye Ubiquitous/CORBIS; 93D, ©Chris Sharp; 189D, Suzanne Murphy-Larronde/D. Donne Bryant Photography; 219D, book cover, Algonquin Books of Chapel Hill; Julia Álvarez, Daniel Cima; 251D, Pablo Corral Vega/CORBIS; 281D, Jeremy Horner/CORBIS; 345D, Courtesy the Ramona Pageant Association; 157D, © Digital Vision; 315D, Corbis Images.

Acknowledgments continued on page R105, which is an extension of the copyright page.

¡Ven conmigo! Level 3 Annotated Teacher's Edition

CONTRIBUTING WRITERS

Dr. Marjorie Artzer
Northern Kentucky University
Highland Heights, KY
Dr. Artzer contributed to Chapters 10 and 12.

Dena Bachman
Lafayette High School
St. Joseph, MO
Ms. Bachman contributed to Chapter 11, and to several chapters' Games, Projects, and **Vamos a escribir.**

Letitia Blalock
Austin, TX
Ms. Blalock contributed to Chapters 3, 4, 7, and 9.

Brenda Boyd
Parkland Elementary
El Paso, TX
Ms. Boyd contributed to Chapters 2 and 6.

Mildred Cancel-García
Santurce, PR
Ms. Cancel-García contributed answers for all chapters.

Mariana Colten
Frankfort, KY
Ms. Colten contributed to Chapters 1 and 8.

María Franco
Pflugerville High School
Pflugerville, TX
Ms. Franco contributed to Chapter 3.

Sharon Heller
Austin, TX
Ms. Heller contributed modality and Thinking Critically suggestions.

María Lado
Austin, TX
Ms. Lado wrote material for the Traditions in Chapters 3–12 and provided recipes for Chapters 1–12.

Laura Mau
Austin, TX
Ms. Mau contributed to Games and Projects.

Mary Nichols
Austin High School
Austin, TX
Ms. Nichols contributed to various sections of several chapters.

Peggy Patterson
The University of Texas at Austin
Ms. Patterson wrote the Location Opener on Guadalajara.

Cindy Proctor
Montgomery Central High School
Clarksville, TN
Ms. Proctor contributed to the **Panorama cultural** sections.

Amy Propps
Austin, TX
Ms. Propps wrote the Location Opener on Galicia.

Dana Slawsky
Melrose, MA
Ms. Slawsky wrote material for the Internet Connection in Chapters 1–12.

Elizbia Tamez
Austin High School
Austin, TX
Ms. Tamez contributed to the Games and Projects.

Marcia Tugendhat
Austin, TX
Ms. Tugendhat wrote material for the Traditions in Chapters 1–2.

Mayanne Wright
Austin, TX
Ms. Wright wrote Lesson Plans for Chapters 1–12 and the Location Openers on Caracas, Buenos Aires, New York City, and Costa Rica. She also contributed to Chapter 5.

FIELD TEST PARTICIPANTS

We express our appreciation to the teachers and students who participated in the field test. Their comments were instrumental in the development of this program. Please see a list of their names and affiliations on page T8.

REVIEWERS

Dr. Edward Allen
Ohio State University
Columbus, OH

Elida M. Bonet
Eanes Elementary School
Austin, TX

Renato Cervantes
Pacific High School
San Bernardino, CA

Dr. Lynn Rice Cortina
North Miami Senior High School
North Miami, FL

Rubén Garza
Bowie High School
Austin, TX

Joseph N. Harris
Poudre School District
Fort Collins, CO

Dr. Lina Lee
State University of New York
Plattsburgh, NY

Stephen L. Levy
Roslyn Public Schools
Roslyn, NY

Patricia Rossett
Austin High School
Austin, TX

Dr. Yolanda Russinovich Solé
The University of Texas
Austin, TX

Brian A. Souza
Plymouth South High School
Plymouth, MA

Elena Steele
Clark County School District
Las Vegas, NV

Carol Villalobos
Hazelwood Central High School
St. Louis, MO

Dora Villani
John F. Kennedy High School
New York, NY

Natalie Walters
Monrovia Schools
Monrovia, IN

PROFESSIONAL ESSAYS

Bringing Standards into the Classroom
Paul Sandrock
Foreign Language Consultant
Department of Public Instruction
Madison, WI

Reading Strategies and Skills
Nancy A. Humbach
Miami University
Oxford, OH

Using Portfolios in the Language Classroom
JoAnne S. Wilson
J. Wilson Associates
Glen Arbor, MI

Learning Styles and Multi-Modality Teaching
Mary B. McGehee
Louisiana State University
Baton Rouge, LA

New Perspectives for Native Speakers
Cecilia Rodríguez-Pino
New Mexico State University
Las Cruces, NM

Multi-Level Classrooms
Dr. Joan H. Manley
The University of Texas
El Paso, TX

To the Teacher

Principles and Practices

As nations become increasingly interdependent, the need for effective communication and sensitivity to other cultures becomes more important. Today's youth must be culturally and linguistically prepared to participate in a global society. At Holt, Rinehart and Winston, we believe that proficiency in more than one language is essential to meeting this need.

The primary goal of the Holt, Rinehart and Winston World Languages programs is to help students develop linguistic proficiency and cultural sensitivity. By interweaving language and culture, our programs seek to broaden students' communication skills while at the same time deepening their appreciation of other cultures.

We believe that all students can benefit from foreign language instruction. We recognize that not everyone learns at the same rate or in the same way; nevertheless, we believe that all students should have the opportunity to acquire language proficiency to a degree commensurate with their individual abilities.

Holt, Rinehart and Winston's World Languages programs are designed to accommodate all students by appealing to a variety of learning styles.

We believe that effective language programs should motivate students. Students deserve an answer to the question they often ask: "Why are we doing this?" They need to have goals that are interesting, practical, clearly stated, and attainable.

Holt, Rinehart and Winston's World Languages programs promote success. They present relevant content in manageable increments that encourage students to attain achievable functional objectives.

We believe that proficiency in another language is best nurtured by programs that encourage students to think critically and to take risks when expressing themselves in the language. We also recognize that students should strive for accuracy in communication. While it is imperative that students have a knowledge of the basic structures of the language, it is also important that they go beyond the simple manipulation of forms.

Holt, Rinehart and Winston's World Languages programs reflect a careful progression of activities that guide students from comprehensible input of authentic language through structured practice to creative, personalized expression. This progression, accompanied by consistent re-entry and spiraling of functions, vocabulary, and structures, provides students with the tools and the confidence to express themselves in their new language.

Finally, we believe that a complete program of language instruction should take into account the needs of teachers in today's increasingly demanding classrooms.

At Holt, Rinehart and Winston, we have designed programs that offer practical teacher support and provide resources to meet individual learning and teaching styles.

We have seen significant advances in modern language curriculum practices:

1. a redefinition of the objectives of foreign language study involving a commitment to the development of proficiency in the four skills and in cultural awareness;

2. a recognition of the need for longer sequences of study;

3. a new student-centered approach that redefines the role of the teacher as facilitator and encourages students to take a more active role in their learning;

4. the inclusion of students of all learning abilities.

The new Holt, Rinehart and Winston World Languages programs take into account not only these advances in the field of foreign language education but also the input of teachers and students around the country.

ANNOTATED TEACHER'S EDITION
Contents

Pacing and Planning

Traditional Schedule

Days of instruction: 180		
Location Opener	2 days per Location Opener	
	x 6 Location Openers	12 days
Chapter	13 days per chapter	
	x 12 chapters	156 days
		168 days

If you are teaching on a traditional schedule, we suggest following the plan above and spending 13 days per chapter. A complete set of lesson plans in the interleaf provides detailed suggestions for each chapter. For more suggestions, see the **Lesson Planner with Substitute Teacher Lesson Plans.**

Block Schedule

Blocks of instruction: 90		
Location Opener	1/2 block per Location Opener	
	x 6 Location Openers	3 blocks
Chapter	7 blocks per chapter	
	x 12 chapters	84 blocks
		87 blocks

If you are teaching on a block schedule, we suggest following the plan above and spending seven blocks per chapter. A complete set of lesson plans in the interleaf provides detailed suggestions for each chapter. For more suggestions, see the **Lesson Planner with Substitute Teacher Lesson Plans.**

 One-Stop Planner CD-ROM

Use the **One-Stop Planner CD-ROM with Test Generator** to aid in lesson planning and pacing.

- Editable lesson plans with direct links to teaching resources
- Printable worksheets from resource books
- Direct launches to the HRW Internet activities
- Video and audio segments
- Test Generator
- Clip Art for vocabulary items

 Pacing Tips

At the beginning of each chapter, you will find a Pacing Tip to help you plan your lessons.

Articulation Across Levels

CHAPTER 12
Review of Level 1

- **gustar** and **encantar**
- **e** to **ie** and **o** to **ue** stem-changing verbs
- Uses of verbs **ser** and **estar**
- Present progressive
- Uses of the preterite
- Verbs followed by an infinitive
- Discussing what you would like to do on vacation
- Making future plans
- Saying where you went and what you did on vacation
- Talking about what you do and like to do every day

The following chart shows how topics are repeated across levels in *¡Ven conmigo!* from the end of Level 1 to the beginning of Level 3.

- In each level, the last chapter is a review chapter.
- In Levels 2 and 3, the first two chapters review the previous level.

LEVEL 2

CHAPTER 1
Review of Level 1

- Adjective agreement
- Future tense with **ir**
- **gustar**
- Indirect object pronouns
- Present tense of regular verbs
- Present tense of **salir, venir, hacer, ver, ir, tener**
- Describing people
- Introducing yourself and others
- Saying what you like and don't like
- Talking about what you and others do

CHAPTER 2

- The verb **estar**
- Preterite of **-ar** verbs
- Present tense of **querer** and **poder**
- Asking for and offering help
- Clothing
- Describing your city or town
- Places around town
- Making suggestions and responding
- Saying if something has already been done
- Talking about how you are feeling

CHAPTER 12
Review of Level 2

- Imperfect tense
- Regular and irregular verbs in the preterite tense
- Subjunctive mood
- Describing places
- Exchanging the latest news
- Saying how you feel about people
- Saying when you're going to do something
- Talking about where you went and what you did
- Telling when something happened

LEVEL 3

CHAPTER 1
Review of Level 2

- Adjectives
- Stem-changing verbs in the present tense
- The present tense
- The preterite
- Question formation
- **saber** vs. **conocer**
- **y** and **o** before vowels
- Asking for information
- Describing yourself and others
- Expressing interest, indifference, and displeasure
- Sports and hobbies

CHAPTER 2

- Informal commands
- Irregular informal commands
- Present progressive
- Reflexive verbs
- The imperfect
- Uses of the imperfect
- Asking for and giving advice
- Parts of the body
- Talking about taking care of yourself

CHAPTER 12
Review of Level 3

- Future tense and **ir a +** infinitive
- Personal **a** before certain pronouns
- Preterite and imperfect
- The past subjunctive
- The subjunctive
- Giving advice and making recommendations about work
- Talking about former jobs and goals
- Talking about future career plans

¡Ven conmigo! Spanish Level 1
Scope and Sequence

FUNCTIONS	GRAMMAR	VOCABULARY	CULTURE	RE-ENTRY
CAPÍTULO PRELIMINAR ¡Adelante!, *Pages xxx–11*				
• **Frases útiles**		• **Nombres comunes** • **El alfabeto** • **Colores y números** • **Para mejor aprender el español**	• **El mapa del mundo hispanohablante** • **El español—¿Por qué?** • **¿Sabías...?** • **¿Los conoces?**	

España

FUNCTIONS	GRAMMAR	VOCABULARY	CULTURE	RE-ENTRY
CAPÍTULO 1 ¡Mucho gusto!, *Pages 16–45*				
• Saying hello and goodbye • Introducing people and responding to an introduction • Asking how someone is and saying how you are • Asking and saying how old someone is • Asking where someone is from and saying where you're from • Talking about likes and dislikes	• Spanish punctuation marks • Pronouns **yo** and **tú** • Use of **ser** for origin • Forming questions with **¿cómo?, ¿cuántos?, ¿de dónde?** • Singular definite articles: **el, la** • Noun gender and agreement	• Numbers 0–30 • Names of some Spanish-speaking countries • Sports • Musical genres • Classes at school • Foods	• Greetings and goodbyes • First names and saint's days • **¿De dónde eres?** • **la distancia interpersonal**	• Accent marks • Numbers 0–30

España

FUNCTIONS	GRAMMAR	VOCABULARY	CULTURE	RE-ENTRY
CAPÍTULO 2 ¡Organízate!, *Pages 46–73*				
• Talking about what you want and need • Describing the contents of your room • Talking about what you need and want to do	• Indefinite articles **un, una, unos, unas** • Making nouns plural • Agreement of **mucho** and **cuánto** with nouns • Subject pronouns **él** and **ella** • The three types of infinitives: **-ar, -er, -ir**	• School supplies • The contents of your room • Things you do • Numbers 31–199	• The school day in Spain and Latin America • **¿Qué necesitas para el colegio?** • Apartments in Spain • Spanish currency	• Subject pronouns **yo** and **tú** • Talking about likes and dislikes • Forming questions with **¿cuántos?**

FUNCTIONS	GRAMMAR	VOCABULARY	CULTURE	RE-ENTRY

México

CAPÍTULO 3 Nuevas clases, nuevos amigos, *Pages 78–107*

FUNCTIONS	GRAMMAR	VOCABULARY	CULTURE	RE-ENTRY
• Talking about class schedules and sequencing events • Telling time • Telling at what time something happens • Talking about being late or in a hurry • Describing people and things • Talking about things you like and explaining why	• Plural definite articles **los, las** • Using **ser** to tell time • Forms of **ser** • Adjective agreement • Tag questions • Possession with **de**	• School subjects • Words that describe people and things • Free-time activities and things you like • Words that refer to time	• Grade scales • **¿Cómo es un día escolar típico?** • Student course loads • **hora latina** • Entertainment guide	• Present tense of **tener** • Numbers 0–199 • Forming questions • Noun-adjective agreement • Forms of **necesitar, querer**

México

CAPÍTULO 4 ¿Qué haces esta tarde? *Pages 108–135*

FUNCTIONS	GRAMMAR	VOCABULARY	CULTURE	RE-ENTRY
• Talking about what you like to do • Discussing what you and others do during free time • Telling where people and things are • Talking about where you and others go during free time	• Present tense of regular **-ar** verbs • Present tense of **jugar** • The contraction **al** • **con, conmigo, contigo** • Use of **que** • Present tense of **estar** • Subject pronouns • Present tense of **ir** • Use of **el** and **los** with days of the week	• Places in town and their location • The days of the week • Things you like to do • Talking about where you and others go	• Popular sports in Spanish-speaking countries • Use of **tú** and **usted** • **el paseo** • School-sponsored activities	• Subject pronouns: **yo, tú, él, ella** • Present tense of **ser** and **tener** • Telling time

Florida

CAPÍTULO 5 El ritmo de la vida, *Pages 140–167*

FUNCTIONS	GRAMMAR	VOCABULARY	CULTURE	RE-ENTRY
• Discussing how often you do things • Talking about what you and your friends like to do together • Talking about what you do during a typical week • Giving today's date • Talking about the weather	• Negation • **¿quién?** and **¿quiénes?** • **les** and **a ustedes, a ellos, a ellas** • Regular **-er** and **-ir** verbs • Giving the date in Spanish	• Weekend activities • The seasons and the months • Weather expressions • Frequency terms	• Getting together with friends • **¿Cómo es una semana típica?** • Seasons in South America	• Gender • Subject pronouns with **-er** and **-ir** verbs • Days of the week

	FUNCTIONS	GRAMMAR	VOCABULARY	CULTURE	RE-ENTRY
Florida	**CAPÍTULO 6 Entre familia,** *Pages 168–197*				
	• Describing a family • Describing people • Discussing things a family does together • Discussing problems and giving advice	• Possessive adjectives • Present tense of **hacer** and **salir** • Present tense of **deber** • Present tense of **poner** • Understanding "personal **a**"	• Members of the family • Words that describe people • Household chores	• **el compadrazgo** • Privacy in Hispanic culture • **la familia** • Diminutives	• **hay** • Possessive adjectives • Colors • Descriptions of people • Pastimes/hobbies • **¿con qué frecuencia?** • Forming questions
Ecuador	**CAPÍTULO 7 ¿Qué te gustaría hacer?,** *Pages 202–229*				
	• Talking on the telephone • Extending and accepting invitations • Making plans • Talking about getting ready • Turning down an invitation and explaining why	• **e** to **ie** stem-changing verbs • **pensar** + infinitive • **ir** + **a** + infinitive • Reflexive verbs • Expressions with **tener**	• Places and events • Words used to extend and accept invitations • Telephone vocabulary • Personal chores	• Common telephone expressions • Getting around without a car • **¿Qué haces para conocer a una persona?** • Party invitation	• **gustar** • Days of the week • **pensar** and **ir** • Future expressions
Ecuador	**CAPÍTULO 8 ¡A comer!,** *Pages 230–259*				
	• Talking about meals and food • Commenting on food • Making polite requests • Ordering dinner in a restaurant • Asking for and paying the bill in a restaurant	• Present tense of **encantar** and indirect object pronouns • Use of **estar** to talk about how things taste • **ser** and **estar** • **o** to **ue** stem-changing verbs • Expressions with **tener** • The forms of **otro**	• The table setting • Food and drink items for breakfast, lunch, and dinner • Words to describe food • Restaurant vocabulary	• **la comida de las Américas** • Breakfast in Spanish-speaking countries • Lunch in Spanish-speaking countries • Dinner in Spanish-speaking countries • **¿Cuál es un plato típico de tu país?** • Table manners in Spanish-speaking countries • Common Andean dishes • Latin American and Spanish tortillas	• **e** to **ie** stem-changing verbs • Numbers 200–100,000 • Expressing likes and dislikes • Expressions with **tener** • **estar** and **ser**

FUNCTIONS	GRAMMAR	VOCABULARY	CULTURE	RE-ENTRY

Texas

CAPÍTULO 9 ¡Vamos de compras!, *Pages 264–291*

FUNCTIONS	GRAMMAR	VOCABULARY	CULTURE	RE-ENTRY
• Discussing gift suggestions • Asking for and giving directions downtown • Commenting on clothes • Making comparisons • Expressing preferences • Asking about prices and paying for something	• Indirect object pronouns: **le, les** • **es/son** + **de** + material or pattern • Comparisons: **más... que, menos... que, tan... como** • Demonstrative adjectives	• Gift suggestions • Stores downtown • Words describing clothes • Vocabulary for shopping	• Specialty stores in Spain • **¿Estás a la moda?** • Catalog page with clothing • *Tamalada* • Currency in some Spanish-speaking countries, the **euro**	• **ir** + **a** + infinitive • Talking about locations • Describing family • Numbers 0–100,000

Texas

CAPÍTULO 10 Celebraciones, *Pages 292–321*

FUNCTIONS	GRAMMAR	VOCABULARY	CULTURE	RE-ENTRY
• Talking about what you're doing right now • Asking for and giving an opinion • Asking for help and responding to requests • Telling a friend what to do • Talking about past events	• Present progressive • Informal commands • Preterite tense of regular **-ar** verbs • Direct object pronouns **lo** and **la**	• Festivals and holidays • Preparations for a party • Expressions for times in the past	• **día del santo** • **¿Qué hacen ustedes para celebrar?** • **la fiesta de quinceañera** • **¿Cómo se celebra una boda?** • **las piñatas**	• **estar** • **tú** versus **usted** • Dates, months, seasons • Extending, accepting, and turning down invitations • **¿quién?, ¿quiénes?**

Puerto Rico

CAPÍTULO 11 Para vivir bien, *Pages 326–355*

FUNCTIONS	GRAMMAR	VOCABULARY	CULTURE	RE-ENTRY
• Making suggestions and expressing feelings • Talking about moods and physical condition • Saying what you did • Talking about where you went and when	• The verb **sentirse** • The verb **doler** with **me, te,** and **le** • The verbs **ir** and **jugar** in the preterite	• Fitness activities • Words to describe moods and physical conditions • The human body • Locations for sports events	• Questionnaire about living well • Baseball in Spanish-speaking countries • **¿Qué deporte practicas?** • Magazine article on relieving stress • American football vs. soccer, **jai alai** • **remedios caseros**	• **estar** + condition • Stem-changing verbs • The preterite • Food vocabulary • Sports

Puerto Rico

CAPÍTULO 12 Las vacaciones ideales, *Pages 356–383*

REVIEW CHAPTER

FUNCTIONS	GRAMMAR	VOCABULARY	CULTURE	RE-ENTRY
• Talking about what you do and like to do every day • Making future plans • Discussing what you would like to do on vacation • Saying where you went and what you did on vacation	• **e** to **ie** and **o** to **ue** stem-changing verbs • Verbs followed by an infinitive • Uses of verbs **ser** and **estar** • Uses of the preterite	• Vacation activities and objects • Wilderness activities	• **¿Adónde vas y qué haces en las vacaciones?** • Spain's **paradores** • Spanish colloquialisms	• Chapter 12 is a global review of Chapters 1–11.

¡Ven conmigo! Spanish Level 2
Scope and Sequence

	FUNCTIONS	GRAMMAR	VOCABULARY	CULTURE	RE-ENTRY

Andalucía — **CAPÍTULO 1 Mis amigos y yo,** *Pages 4–33*

REVIEW CHAPTER	FUNCTIONS	GRAMMAR	VOCABULARY	CULTURE	RE-ENTRY
	• Introducing yourself and others • Describing people • Talking about what you and others do • Saying what you like and don't like	• Present tense of **tener** • Adjective agreement • Present tense of regular verbs • Indirect object pronouns with verbs like **gustar**	• Nationalities • Numbers • Colors • Family members	• Description of appearance of Hispanics • **¿Qué es el euro?** • Planning evening activities in Spain • **¿Qué es un buen amigo?** • **cafeterías** • **¡Soy así!**	• Chapter 1 reviews Spanish taught in *¡Ven conmigo!* Level 1.

Andalucía — **CAPÍTULO 2 Un viaje al extranjero,** *Pages 34–61*

REVIEW CHAPTER	FUNCTIONS	GRAMMAR	VOCABULARY	CULTURE	RE-ENTRY
	• Talking about how you're feeling • Making suggestions and responding to them • Saying if something has already been done • Asking for and offering help • Describing your city or town	• The verb **estar** • Preterite of **-ar** verbs • Present tense of **querer** and **poder**	• Calendar expressions • Places around town • Weather expressions • Clothing	• Extended family living together • **¿En dónde te gustaría vivir?** • Celsius vs. Fahrenheit • Barcelona	• Chapter 2 reviews Spanish taught in *¡Ven conmigo!* Level 1.

Valle de México — **CAPÍTULO 3 La vida cotidiana,** *Pages 66–93*

	FUNCTIONS	GRAMMAR	VOCABULARY	CULTURE	RE-ENTRY
	• Talking about your daily routine • Talking about responsibilities • Complaining • Talking about hobbies and pastimes • Saying how long something has been going on	• Reflexive verbs and pronouns • **e** to **i** stem change in **vestirse** • Adverbs ending in **-mente** • Direct object pronouns: **lo, la, los, las** • **hace** + quantity of time + **que** + present tense	• Daily activities • Chores • Hobbies and pastimes	• **¿Cuál es tu profesión?** • Household chores • Expressions of agreement • Popular free-time activities among teenagers • **¿Estás aburrido/a de tu rutina?**	• Verbs of personal grooming • Adverbs of time and place • Vocabulary of household chores in Spain • Asking for help, responding to requests • Giving explanations • Vocabulary of hobbies and pastimes • Question formation

Valle de México

CAPÍTULO 4 ¡Adelante con los estudios! *Pages 94–123*

FUNCTIONS	GRAMMAR	VOCABULARY	CULTURE	RE-ENTRY
• Asking for and giving opinions • Giving advice • Talking about things and people you know • Making comparisons • Making plans	• **deberías** vs. **debes** • **ser** + adjective to describe people • **estar** + adjective to describe location • Present tense of the verb **conocer** • Direct object pronouns	• Classroom activities • School and computer terms • Describing people • Activities around town	• School levels in Mexico • Cost of university education in Latin America • **¿Qué haces después del colegio?** • **¿Quién es americano?**	• School subjects • **para** (in order to) + infinitive • **ser** vs. **estar** • Comparisons: **más... que, menos... que** • **ir** + **a** + infinitive

Texas

CAPÍTULO 5 ¡Ponte en forma!, *Pages 128–157*

FUNCTIONS	GRAMMAR	VOCABULARY	CULTURE	RE-ENTRY
• Talking about staying fit and healthy • Telling someone what to do and not to do • Giving explanations	• Preterite of the verb **dormir** • Preterite of regular **-er** and **-ir** verbs • Informal commands • Irregular informal commands • Preterite of **poder** • Reflexives with verbs of emotion	• Sports • Fitness activities • Health and fitness terms • Body parts • Injuries and explanations	• **¿Sanos o no?** • Student responses about health habits in Spanish-speaking countries • Snack foods in Spanish-speaking countries • **Garnachas, antojitos y bocadillos** • **¿Qué haces para mantenerte en forma?** • Flyers and radio ads	• Preterite of regular **-ar** verbs • Informal commands • Spelling changes in verbs that end in **-car, -gar, -zar** • Reflexive verbs

Texas

CAPÍTULO 6 De visita en la ciudad, *Pages 158–185*

FUNCTIONS	GRAMMAR	VOCABULARY	CULTURE	RE-ENTRY
• Asking for and giving information • Relating a series of events • Ordering in a restaurant	• Present tense of **saber** • **saber** vs. **conocer** • Preterite forms of **pedir, servir, traer**	• In the city • Places in the city • In the train station • In a restaurant	• San Antonio • **¿Cómo llegas al colegio?** • Birthday celebrations • **El festival de la música tejana**	• Direct object pronouns • **poder** • The preterite for listing events • Food vocabulary

El Caribe — CAPÍTULO 7 ¿Conoces bien tu pasado?, *Pages 190–219*

FUNCTIONS	GRAMMAR	VOCABULARY	CULTURE	RE-ENTRY
• Talking about what you used to do • Saying what you used to like and dislike • Describing what people and things were like • Using comparisons to describe people	• The imperfect tense of **-ar, -er, -ir** verbs • The imperfect tense of **ir** and **ver** • Spelling change of **o** to **u** and **y** to **e** to avoid vowel repetition • Imperfect of **ser** to describe people and things • The imperfect of **hay** • **tan** + adjective/adverb + **como**	• Childhood activities • Describing people • Describing places • Conveniences	• **Lo mejor de lo antiguo** • Public services in Latin American cities • **dichos** • **¿De quién es esta estatua?** • **el merengue**	• The preterite • Talking about likes and dislikes using the preterite • Comparisons: **más/menos** + adjective + **que** • Complaining • Descriptive adjectives

El Caribe — CAPÍTULO 8 Diversiones, *Pages 220–247*

FUNCTIONS	GRAMMAR	VOCABULARY	CULTURE	RE-ENTRY
• Describing a past event • Saying why you couldn't do something • Reporting what someone said	• Adjectives with **-ísimo/a** • Superlatives • Verbs with prepositions • Using **mientras** in the past • Preterite of **decir**	• In the zoo, the amusement park, and movie theater • Running errands • At a festival	• **El Yunque** and **el coquí** • **¿Cuáles son las fiestas más importantes de tu ciudad o país?** • Holidays and festivals in Spanish-speaking countries • **Ponce es Ponce**	• Describing things • Describing what you did • The imperfect tense • Imperfect of **hay** • The preterite

Los Andes — CAPÍTULO 9 ¡Día de mercado!, *Pages 252–281*

FUNCTIONS	GRAMMAR	VOCABULARY	CULTURE	RE-ENTRY
• Asking for and giving directions • Asking for help in a store • Talking about how clothes look and fit • Bargaining in a market	• Formal commands with **usted, ustedes**	• Giving directions • In a clothing store • In a market	• **En la ventanilla tres, por favor** • Clothing/shoe sizes • **¿Dónde compras tu comida?** • Expressions for shopping • Mural art • **el mercado de Otavalo**	• Numbers • **ser** + **de** + material • Comparisons • Clothing material and pattern • Direct and indirect objects

FUNCTIONS	GRAMMAR	VOCABULARY	CULTURE	RE-ENTRY

Los Andes · **CAPÍTULO 10** ¡Cuéntame!, *Pages 282–311*

FUNCTIONS	GRAMMAR	VOCABULARY	CULTURE	RE-ENTRY
• Setting the scene for a story • Continuing and ending a story • Talking about the latest news • Reacting to news	• The preterite vs. the imperfect • Preterite of **oír, creer, leer, caerse** • The preterite and the imperfect to tell a story • Preterite of **tener**	• Weather • Accidents, mishaps, and daily events • Science fiction and fairy tales • The latest news	• Weather map of Bolivia • **¿Te sabes algún cuento?** • A Chilean folk tale • An Ecuadorean legend • **La Llorona**	• Reflexive verbs • Preterite of **ser** • Weather expressions

California · **CAPÍTULO 11** Nuestro medio ambiente, *Pages 316–345*

FUNCTIONS	GRAMMAR	VOCABULARY	CULTURE	RE-ENTRY
• Describing a problem • Talking about consequences • Expressing agreement and disagreement • Talking about obligations and solutions	• Negative words • **si** clauses in present tense • **nosotros** commands	• Environmental problems • Animals • Protecting the environment • Materials and resources	• The rain forest • **El Yunque** • **¿Qué haces para el medio ambiente?** • Environmental programs • **el medio ambiente** • San Diego and Tijuana	• Affirmative and negative words • Giving an opinion • Cognates • Informal commands • Preterite of **decir**

California · **CAPÍTULO 12** Veranos pasados, veranos por venir, *Pages 346–371*

	FUNCTIONS	GRAMMAR	VOCABULARY	CULTURE	RE-ENTRY
REVIEW CHAPTER	• Exchanging the latest news • Talking about where you went and what you did • Telling when something happened • Saying how you feel about people • Describing places • Saying when you're going to do something	• Review of regular and irregular verbs in the preterite tense • The subjunctive mood • Review of the imperfect tense	• Writing a letter • Vacation activities • Describing places	• Baja California • **¿Cómo celebran el fin de cursos?** • Interviews: **¡Nos llevamos muy bien!** • **viaje de curso**	• Chapter 12 is a global review of Chapters 1–11, *Level 2.*

¡Ven conmigo! Spanish Level 3
Scope and Sequence

FUNCTIONS	GRAMMAR	VOCABULARY	CULTURE	RE-ENTRY

La Coruña — CAPÍTULO 1 ¡Qué bien lo pasé este verano!, Pages 4–31

REVIEW CHAPTER

FUNCTIONS	GRAMMAR	VOCABULARY	CULTURE	RE-ENTRY
• Expressing interest, indifference, and displeasure • Asking for information • Describing yourself and others	• Stem-changing verbs in the present tense • The present tense • The preterite • **y** and **o** before vowels • Adjectives • **saber** vs. **conocer**	• Names of sports • Names of hobbies • Words and expressions to describe people	• Vacation activities of students from Costa Rica, Spain, and Miami • Seafood in Spain	• Chapters 1 and 2 are a global review of *¡Ven conmigo!* Levels 1 and 2.

La Coruña — CAPÍTULO 2 Por una vida sana, Pages 32–61

REVIEW CHAPTER

FUNCTIONS	GRAMMAR	VOCABULARY	CULTURE	RE-ENTRY
• Asking for and giving advice • Talking about taking care of yourself	• Informal commands • Irregular informal commands • Reflexive verbs • The imperfect	• Expressions to tell how you are feeling today • Words and expressions to talk about stress • Expressions to talk about how to relieve stress	• Regional languages of Spain • Work schedules in Spain • Health habits of people in Spain and Latin America • Socializing with friends in Spain	• Chapters 1 and 2 are a global review of *¡Ven conmigo!* Levels 1 and 2.

Caracas — CAPÍTULO 3 El ayer y el mañana, Pages 66–95

FUNCTIONS	GRAMMAR	VOCABULARY	CULTURE	RE-ENTRY
• Talking about what has happened • Expressing and supporting a point of view • Using conversational fillers • Talking about future events • Talking about responsibilities	• The present perfect • **lo que** • The future tense	• Words and expressions related to technology • Words and expressions to talk about changes in the city • Things that may protect the environment	• Today's technology in the Spanish-speaking world • The role of oil in the Venezuelan economy • The benefits of technology for Venezuela	• Electrical appliances • Object pronouns • **todavía, ya, alguna vez** • Affirmatives and negatives • Comparisons of equality and inequality • **vamos a** + infinitive • Supporting opinions

Caracas

CAPÍTULO 4   Alrededor de la mesa, *Pages 96–123*

FUNCTIONS	GRAMMAR	VOCABULARY	CULTURE	RE-ENTRY
• Talking about how food tastes • Talking about unintentional events • Asking for help and requesting favors	• **se** with unintentional events • **por** and **para** • Double object pronouns	• Salads, meat, seafood, fruit, and desserts • Food stores • Repair shops	• The **sobremesa** • Ways of getting assistance from emergency service personnel • Foods and holiday dishes of Venezuela • Favorite foods of typical students from Miami, Quito, and Caracas • **causa picante**	• Ordering a meal • Giving explanations • Commands • Pronouns with commands • The suffix **-ísimo**

Guadalajara

CAPÍTULO 5   Nuestras leyendas, *Pages 128–155*

FUNCTIONS	GRAMMAR	VOCABULARY	CULTURE	RE-ENTRY
• Expressing qualified agreement and disagreement • Reporting what others say and think • Talking about hopes and wishes	• Impersonal **se** • The subjunctive to express hopes and wishes • Subjunctive of **ir, ser, dar, estar**	• Words and expressions to talk about war and peace	• la **"leyenda negra"** • Aztec pictographs • The legends **"La Llorona"** and **"La carreta sin bueyes"** • The legend of **Quetzalcóatl** • The legend **"El Quetzal"**	• Verbs followed by an infinitive

Guadalajara

CAPÍTULO 6   El arte y la música, *Pages 156–185*

FUNCTIONS	GRAMMAR	VOCABULARY	CULTURE	RE-ENTRY
• Introducing and changing a topic of conversation • Expressing what needs to be done • Expressing an opinion • Making suggestions and recommendations • Turning down an invitation	• Gender of some words ending in **-a** and **-o** • The subjunctive after expressions of need • The subjunctive mood with recommendations • **nosotros** commands	• Words related to the arts • Words and expressions to describe works of art	• The murals of Orozco • The role of murals in Mexico • How some Hispanic students express themselves through art • Musical instruments • Mexican pop music star Luis Miguel • Life and works of Frida Kahlo	• The use of the infinitive vs. the subjunctive • Formation of the subjunctive • **dar, estar, ir,** and **ser** in the present subjunctive • Comparisons

FUNCTIONS	GRAMMAR	VOCABULARY	CULTURE	RE-ENTRY

Buenos Aires   **CAPÍTULO 7**   **Dime con quién andas,** *Pages 190–219*

FUNCTIONS	GRAMMAR	VOCABULARY	CULTURE	RE-ENTRY
• Expressing happiness and unhappiness • Comforting someone • Making an apology • Describing an ideal relationship	• The subjunctive with expressions of feelings • Reflexive verbs for reciprocal actions • The present perfect subjunctive • The subjunctive with the unknown or nonexistent • The present subjunctive of **saber**	• Words and expressions to talk about friendship • Things that friends might do	• The use of **vos** • Cafés • The Organization of American States • The popularity of movies • The popularity of soccer • How Spanish-speaking teenagers solve interpersonal problems	• The use of the infinitive vs. the subjunctive • Irregular subjunctive • Past participle forms • Affirmative and negative words • Subjunctive forms

Buenos Aires   **CAPÍTULO 8**   **Los medios de comunicación,** *Pages 220–247*

FUNCTIONS	GRAMMAR	VOCABULARY	CULTURE	RE-ENTRY
• Expressing doubt and disbelief • Expressing certainty • Talking about possibility and impossibility • Expressing surprise	• The subjunctive after expressions of doubt and disbelief • **por** in fixed expressions • The subjunctive after impersonal expressions	• Words to talk about television • Words and expressions to talk about information • Sections of a newspaper	• The use of the Internet in Argentina • How commercials affect our attitudes and behavior • Newsstands in Buenos Aires	• Uses of **se**

Nueva York   **CAPÍTULO 9**   **Las apariencias engañan,** *Pages 252–279*

FUNCTIONS	GRAMMAR	VOCABULARY	CULTURE	RE-ENTRY
• Talking about your emotional reaction to something • Expressing disagreement • Expressing an assumption • Making hypothetical statements	• More on preterite versus imperfect • The preterite of **estar, ponerse, querer, saber,** and **sentirse** • The subjunctive with expressions of denial and disagreement • The conditional	• Words to describe people's behavior • Words and expressions to talk about prejudice and stereotypes	• Hispanics in the United States • Impressions Spanish-speaking people have of the United States • Spanish-language media in New York	• The subjunctive

FUNCTIONS	GRAMMAR	VOCABULARY	CULTURE	RE-ENTRY

Nueva York — **CAPÍTULO 10 La riqueza cultural,** *Pages 280–309*

• Talking about accomplishments • Talking about future plans • Expressing cause and effect • Expressing intention and purpose	• The subjunctive with certain conjunctions • Verbs after prepositions • The subjunctive with **para que**	• Words and expressions to talk about achievements and future plans • Words and expressions to talk about your background and ambitions	• Hispanics in New York City • How Spanish-speaking students view themselves • **La Sociedad Hispánica de América** • **El Ballet Hispánico de Nueva York**	• The present perfect • Reflexive pronouns • The subjunctive

Costa Rica — **CAPÍTULO 11 El mundo en que vivimos,** *Pages 314–341*

• Pointing out problems and their consequences • Talking about how you would solve a problem • Talking about hypothetical situations	• The past subjunctive	• Today's problems	• Environmental issues facing North and Central America • Literacy in Costa Rica • Political stability in Costa Rica • Conservation in Costa Rica	• Impersonal **se** • Talking about consequences • The conditional • The preterite

Costa Rica — **CAPÍTULO 12 Mis planes para el futuro,** *Pages 342–371*

REVIEW CHAPTER

• Talking about former jobs and goals • Talking about future career plans • Giving advice and making recommendations about work	• Preterite and imperfect • Future tense and **ir a** + infinitive • The subjunctive • Personal **a** before certain pronouns • The past subjunctive	• Names of professions • Words and expressions to talk about employment	• Universities in Costa Rica • Plans some Hispanic students have for the future • Employment in Costa Rica • Ecotourism in Costa Rica • Formality in the Spanish-speaking world	• Chapter 12 is a global review of Chapters 1–11, Level 3.

Pupil's Edition

¡Ven conmigo! offers an integrated approach to language learning. Presentation and practice of functional expressions, vocabulary, and grammar structures are interwoven with cultural information, language learning tips, and realia to facilitate both learning and teaching. The technology, audiovisual materials, and additional print resources are integrated throughout each chapter.

¡Ven conmigo! Level 3

¡Ven conmigo! *Level 3* consists of twelve instructional chapters. Chapters 1 and 2 are a review of **¡Ven conmigo!** Level 2. To facilitate articulation from one level to the next, Chapter 11 introduces minimal new material and Chapter 12 is a review chapter.

Following is a description of the various features in **¡Ven conmigo!** and suggestions on how to use them in the classroom.

Starting Out...

Location Opener In **¡Ven conmigo!,** chapters · · · · · are arranged in groups of two, with each pair of chapters set in a different Spanish-speaking location. Each new location is introduced by four pages of colorful photos and information about the region.

Chapter Opener These two pages provide a · · · · · · · · · · · · · · · visual introduction to the theme of the chapter and include a list of objectives students will be expected to achieve.

Setting The Scene...

Language instruction begins with **De antemano** and **¡Adelante!:** the comprehensible input that models language in a culturally authentic setting. Whether presented on video or as a reading accompanied by the audio CD recording, the highly visual presentation ensures success as students practice their receptive skills and begin to recognize some of the new functions and vocabulary they will encounter in the chapter. Following **De antemano** and **¡Adelante!** is a series of activities to check comprehension.

Building Proficiency Step By Step...

Primer paso and **Segundo paso** are the two core instructional sections where most language acquisition will take place. The communicative goals in each chapter center on the functional expressions presented in **Así se dice** boxes. These expressions are supported by material in the **Vocabulario, Gramática,** and **Nota gramatical** sections. Activities following the above features are designed to practice recognition or to provide closed-ended practice. Activities then progress from controlled to open-ended practice where students are able to express themselves in meaningful communication.

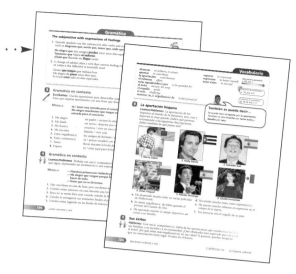

Discovering the People and the Culture...

There are also two major cultural features to help students develop an appreciation and understanding of the cultures of Spanish-speaking countries.

Panorama cultural presents interviews conducted throughout the Spanish-speaking world on a topic related to the chapter theme. The interviews may be presented on video or done as a reading supplemented by the compact disc recording. Culminating activities on this page verify comprehension and encourage students to think critically about the target culture as well as their own.

Encuentro cultural invites students to compare and contrast other cultures with their own.

También se puede decir... helps students become familiar with the linguistic richness of the Spanish-speaking world by presenting regional alternatives for the vocabulary introduced in the chapter.

Nota cultural helps students gain knowledge and understanding of other cultures.

> **También se puede decir...**
> También se puede decir **tremendo** en vez de **magnífico:** Rufino Tamayo me parece un artista **tremendo.** Pero ¡hay que tener cuidado! **Un niño tremendo** es un niño muy mal educado (*ill-mannered*).

Nota cultural

Los argentinos, como los estadounidenses, son muy aficionados a los deportes. El fútbol es el deporte más popular. Hay mucha competencia entre los equipos de los barrios de las ciudades grandes. El tenis es muy popular en parte debido a jugadores como Guillermo Vilas y Gabriela Sabatini. Hay mucho interés en los deportes ecuestres también. ¿Participan tú y tus amigos(as) en equipos o ligas locales?

Understanding Authentic Documents...

Vamos a leer presents reading strategies that help students understand authentic Spanish documents and literature presented in each chapter. The accompanying prereading, reading, and postreading activities develop students' overall reading skills and challenge their critical thinking abilities.

Vamos a escribir presents writing strategies that help students develop their writing skills. The strategies are integrated with prewriting, writing, and postwriting tasks designed to develop students' expressive and creative writing abilities in Spanish.

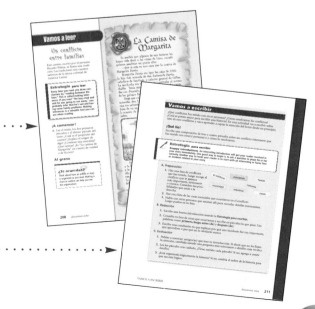

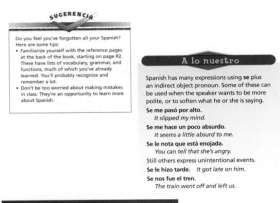

A lo nuestro

Spanish has many expressions using **se** plus an indirect object pronoun. Some of these can be used when the speaker wants to be more polite, or to soften what he or she is saying.

Se me pasó por alto.
It slipped my mind.

Se me hace un poco absurdo.
It seems a little absurd to me.

Se le nota que está enojada.
You can tell that she's angry.

Still others express unintentional events.

Se le hizo tarde.   *It got late on him.*

Se nos fue el tren.
The train went off and left us.

Vocabulario extra

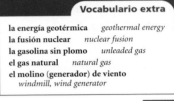

la energía geotérmica	*geothermal energy*
la fusión nuclear	*nuclear fusion*
la gasolina sin plomo	*unleaded gas*
el gas natural	*natural gas*
el molino (generador) de viento	
	windmill, wind generator

¿Se te ha olvidado?
irregular future stems
Ver la página 265

¿Te acuerdas?
One way to talk about what's happening right now is to use the present progressive. It's formed with **estar + -ando/-iendo**. It corresponds to the English *-ing* form in sentences like: **Estamos esperando a Marta.** *(We're waiting for Marta.)*

Cuaderno de gramática, p. 13, Acts. 7–8   Más práctica gramatical, p. 55, Act. 5

Targeting Students' Needs...

In each **Paso** several special features may be used to enhance language learning and cultural appreciation.

Sugerencia suggests effective ways for students to learn a foreign language.

A lo nuestro provides students with tips for speaking more natural-sounding Spanish.

Vocabulario extra presents optional vocabulary related to the chapter theme.

¿Te acuerdas? is a re-entry feature that lists and briefly explains previously learned vocabulary, functions, and grammar that students might need to review at the moment.

¿Se te ha olvidado? is a handy page reference to either an earlier chapter where material was presented or to a reference section in the back of the book.

Wrapping It All Up...

Más práctica gramatical provides additional practice on the grammar concepts presented in the chapter.

Repaso gives students the opportunity to review what they have learned and to apply their skills in new communicative contexts. Focusing on all four language skills as well as cultural awareness, the **Repaso** can help you determine whether students are ready for the Chapter Test.

A ver si puedo... is a checklist that students can use on their own to see if they have achieved the goals stated on the Chapter Opener.

Vocabulario presents the chapter vocabulary grouped by **Paso** and arranged according to function or theme.

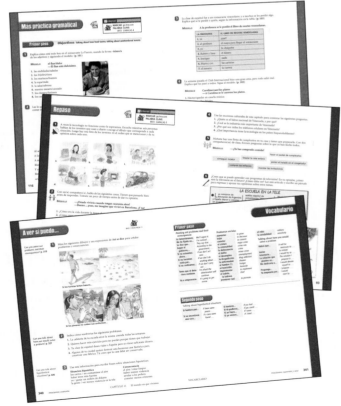

Technology Resources

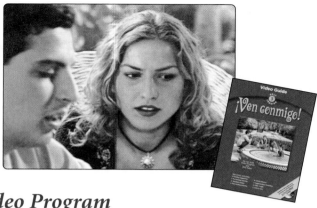

Video Program

The *Video Program* provides the following video support:

- **Location Opener** documentaries
- **De antemano, ¡Adelante,** and **Contigo en la distancia** dramatic episodes
- **Panorama cultural** interviews on a variety of cultural topics
- **Videoclips** which present authentic footage from target cultures

The *Video Guide* contains background information, suggestions for presentation, and activities for all portions of the *Video Program*.

Interactive CD-ROM Tutor

The *Interactive CD-ROM Tutor* offers:

- a variety of supporting activities correlated to the core curriculum of *¡Ven conmigo!* and targeting all five skills

- a Teacher Management System (TMS) that allows teachers to view and assess students' work, manage passwords and records, track students' progress as they complete the activities, and activate English translations

- features such as a grammar reference section and a glossary to help students to complete the activities

Internet Connection

Keywords in the *Pupil's Edition* provide access to two types of online activities:

- **Juegos interactivos** are directly correlated to the instructional material in the textbook. They can be used as homework, extra practice, or assessment.

- **Actividades Internet** provide students with selected Web sites in Spanish-speaking countries and activities related to the chapter theme. A printable worksheet in PDF format includes pre-surfing, surfing, and post-surfing activities that guide students through their research.

For easy access, see the keywords provided in the *Pupil's* and *Teacher's Editions*. For chapter-specific information, see the F page of the chapter interleaf.

One-Stop Planner CD-ROM with Test Generator

The *One-Stop Planner CD-ROM* is a convenient tool to aid in lesson planning and pacing.

Easy navigation through menus or through lesson plans allows for a quick overview of available resources. For each chapter the *One-Stop Planner* includes:

- Editable lesson plans with direct links to teaching resources

- Printable worksheets from resource books

- Direct launches to the HRW Internet activities

- Video and audio segments

- Test Generator

- Clip Art for vocabulary items

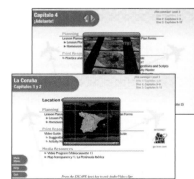

Ancillary Program

The *¡Ven conmigo!* Spanish program offers a comprehensive ancillary package that addresses the concerns of today's teachers and is relevant to students' lives.

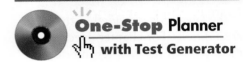
Lesson Planning

One-Stop Planner with Test Generator

- editable lesson plans
- printable worksheets from the resource books
- direct link to HRW Internet activities
- entire video and audio programs
- Test Generator
- Clip Art for vocabulary items

Lesson Planner with Substitute Teacher Lesson Plans

- complete lesson plans for every chapter
- block scheduling suggestions
- correlations to Standards for Foreign Language Learning
- a homework calendar
- chapter-by-chapter lesson plans for substitute teachers
- lesson plan forms for customizing lesson plans

Student Make-Up Assignments

- diagnostic information for students who are behind in their work
- copying masters for make-up assignments

Listening and Speaking

Listening Activities

- print material associated with the *Audio Program*
- Student Response Forms for all *Pupil's Edition* listening activities
- Additonal Listening Activities
- scripts, answers
- lyrics to each chapter's song

Audio Compact Discs

Listening activities for the *Pupil's Edition*, the Additional Listening Activities, and the *Testing Program*

Activities for Communication

- Communicative activities for partner work based on an information gap
- Situation Cards to practice interviews and role-plays
- Realia: reproductions of authentic documents

Grammar

Cuaderno de gramática

- re-presentations of major grammar points
- additional focused practice
- *Teacher's Edition* with overprinted answers

Grammar Tutor for Students of Spanish

- presentations of grammar concepts in English
- re-presentations of Spanish grammar concepts
- discovery and application activities

Reading and Writing

Reading Strategies and Skills Handbook
- explanations of reading strategies
- copying masters for application of strategies

¡Lee conmigo!
- readings on familiar topics
- cultural information
- additional vocabulary
- interesting and engaging activities

Cuaderno de actividades
- activities for practice
- *Teacher's Edition* with overprinted answers

Teaching Transparencies
Colorful transparencies that help present and practice vocabulary, grammar, culture, and a variety of communicative functions

- **Más práctica gramatical** Answers
- **Cuaderno de gramática** Answers

Native Speaker Activity Book
- a diagnostic test
- grammar and spelling exercises
- reading and listening comprehension exercises
- explanations of variances in vocabulary and pronunciation
- *Teacher's Edition* with an answer key

Assessment

Testing Program
- Grammar and Vocabulary quizzes
- **Paso** quizzes that test the four skills
- Chapter Tests
- Speaking Tests
- Midterm and Final Exams
- Score sheets, scripts, answers

Alternative Assessment Guide
- Suggestions for oral and written Portfolio Assessment
- Performance Assessment
- CD-ROM Assessment
- rubrics, portfolio checklists, and evaluation forms

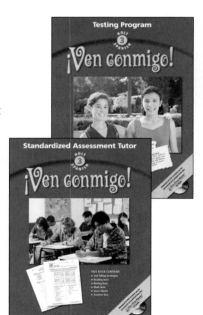

Student Make-Up Assignments
Alternative Grammar and Vocabulary quizzes for students who missed class and have to make up the quiz

Standardized Assessment Tutor
Reading, writing, and math tests in a standardized, multiple-choice format

Annotated Teacher's Edition

Using the Chapter Interleaf

Each chapter of the *¡Ven conmigo! Annotated Teacher's Edition* includes the following interleaf pages to help you plan, teach, and expand your lessons.

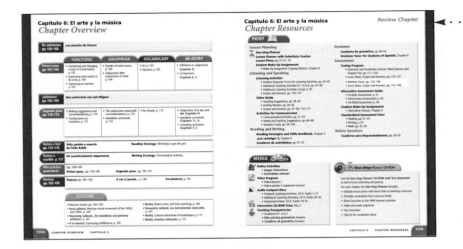

Chapter Overview

The Chapter Overview chart outlines at a glance the functions, grammar, vocabulary, re-entry, and culture featured in the chapter. You will also find a list of corresponding print and audiovisual resources organized by listening, speaking, reading, and writing skills, grammar, and assessment.

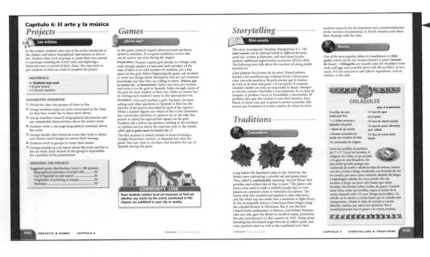

Projects/Games/ Storytelling/Traditions

Projects allow students to personalize and expand on the information from the chapter. Games reinforce the chapter content. In the Storytelling feature, you will find a story related to a *Teaching Transparency*. The Traditions feature concentrates on a unique aspect of the culture of the region. A recipe typical of the region accompanies this feature.

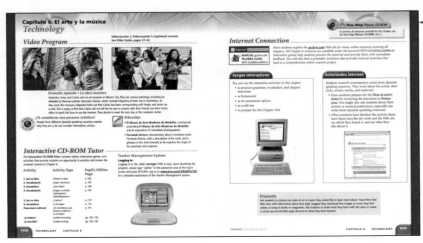

Technology

These pages assist you in integrating technology into your lesson plans. The Technology pages provide a detailed list of video, CD-ROM, and Internet resources for your lesson. You will also find an Internet research project in each chapter.

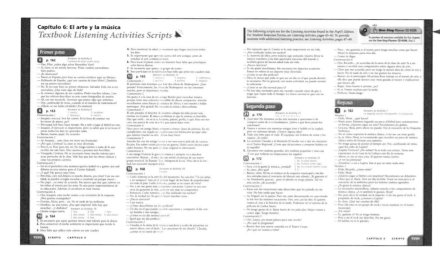

Textbook Listening Activities Scripts
Textbook Listening Activities Scripts provide the scripts of the chapter listening activities for reference or for use in class. The answers to each activity are provided below each script for easy reference.

Suggested Lesson Plans— 50-Minute Schedule
This lesson plan is used for classes with 50-minute schedules. Each lesson plan provides a logical sequence of instruction along with homework suggestions.

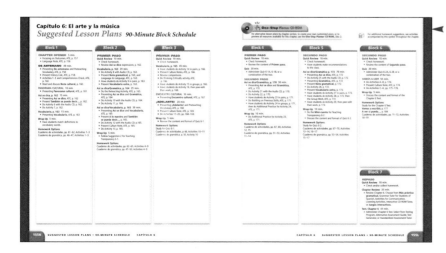

Suggested Lesson Plans— 90-Minute Schedule
This lesson plan is used for classes with 90-minute schedules. Each lesson plan provides a logical sequence of instruction along with homework suggestions.

Using the Wrap-Around Teacher Text

Teaching Resources
pp. 9–13

PRINT
- Lesson Planner, p. 3
- Listening Activities, pp. 3–4, 7–8
- Activities for Communication, pp. 1–2, 51, 53, 89–90
- Cuaderno de gramática, pp. 1–5
- Grammar Tutor for Students of Spanish, Chapter 1
- Cuaderno de actividades, pp. 2–5
- Cuaderno para hispanohablantes, pp. 1–5
- Testing Program, pp. 1–4
- Alternative Assessment Guide, p. 30
- Student Make-Up Assignments, Chapter 1

MEDIA
- One-Stop Planner
- Audio Compact Discs, CD 1, Trs. 3–5, 19–21, 15
- Teaching Transparencies 1-1; **Más práctica gramatical** Answers; Cuaderno de gramática Answers
- Interactive CD-ROM Tutor, Disc 1

Resource boxes provide a quick list of all the resources you can use for each chapter section.

Presenting
Gramática de repaso

The preterite tense Model proper use of the preterite by relating what you did yesterday. Emphasize pronunciation and proper stress. Remind students that stressed final vowels must carry a written accent.

Presenting boxes offer useful suggestions for presenting new material.

Answers

14 *Sample answer:*
Josefina vio a un chico en la playa. Luego lo conoció en la fiesta de una amiga que se llama Teresa. Empezaron a hablar y vieron que tenían mucho en común. Él le dijo que la reconoció de la playa. Se hicieron amigos inmediatamente.

Gramática de repaso

The preterite tense

The preterite is used to talk about what happened on a particular occasion or within a certain period of time in the past. The **yo** forms of verbs ending in **-car, -gar,** and **-zar** have spelling changes: **toqué, jugué, comencé.**

PASAR	COMER	ESCRIBIR
pasé	comí	escribí
pasaste	comiste	escribiste
pasó	comió	escribió
pasamos	comimos	escribimos
pasasteis	comisteis	escribisteis
pasaron	comieron	escribieron

Más práctica gramatical, p. 25, Act. 5

Cuaderno de actividades, pp. 4–5, Acts. 8, 10

Cuaderno de gramática, pp. 4–5, Acts. 7–11

13 Gramática en contexto Script and answers on p. 3G.

Escuchemos Vas a escuchar a Luisita conversar por teléfono con Miguel. Para cada verbo que sigue, indica si están hablando del **presente** o del **pasado.**

1. escuchar la radio
2. ir a la playa
3. nadar en el mar
4. practicar el esquí acuático
5. pasear en velero
6. jugar a las cartas
7. leer el periódico
8. ir al concierto

CD 1 Tr. 5

14 Gramática en contexto See sample answer below.

Hablemos/Escribamos Con un(a) compañero(a), haz un resumen de lo que escribió Josefina. Luego digan dónde y cuándo conocieron Uds. a su mejor amigo(a). ¿De qué hablaron la primera vez que se conocieron?

¿Se te ha olvidado?
irregular preterite
Ver la página R56

Querido diario, 2 de septiembre

Hoy conocí a un tipo increíble. Fui a la playa Riazor esta tarde y vi al chico de mis sueños pero me pareció que él no me vio a mí. Bueno, por la noche hubo una fiesta en casa de Teresa. De veras no quería ir, pero fui... y ¿sabes qué? ¡El chico de la playa estaba allí! Resulta que es amigo de Teresa. Pues, ella me lo presentó y empezamos a hablar. Se llama Joaquín y es de La Coruña. Hablamos tres horas sin parar y nos dimos cuenta de que tenemos mucho en común. Y no puedo creer lo que me dijo... ¡que me reconoció de la playa! Me gustaría hablar más con él pero mañana vuelvo a Madrid. ¡Qué lata que no puedo quedarme!

SUGERENCIA

Do you feel you've forgotten all your Spanish? Here are some tips:
- Familiarize yourself with the reference pages at the back of the book, starting on page R2. These have lists of vocabulary, grammar, and functions, much of which you've already learned. You'll probably recognize and remember a lot.
- Don't be too worried about making mistakes in class. They're an opportunity to learn more about Spanish.

Communication for All Students

Slower Pace
13 Have the class conjugate the given verbs in both the present indicative and preterite tenses before listening to the recording.

Auditory Learners
15 After the writing exercise, have the students role-play the same content using telephones.

Cooperative Learning
15 Have students work together in groups of three to prepare a skit about a couple on a date. Assign one student to be the scribe and two to be the performers. Each group should agree on the correct sequence of events mentioned in Activity 15. The students assigned to perform may use cue cards when performing for the class.

STANDARDS: 1.1, 1.2, 1.3, 4.1

Communication for All Students Under this head you will find helpful suggestions for students with different learning styles and abilities.

Correlations to the Standards for Foreign Language Learning are provided for your reference.

15 Una cita Answers will vary.

Escribamos Imagina que pasaste un fin de semana fenomenal con un grupo de amigos. ¿Qué hicieron? ¿Adónde fueron? Escribe un párrafo con los siguientes verbos u otros. También puedes usar palabras como **primero, luego, después** y **por fin**.

regresar   pasar
ir   montar
esquiar
jugar   hacer

Nota cultural

¿Acaso come tu familia percebes (barnacles) en casa? Pues, la gente de Galicia y de Asturias come muchos pescados y mariscos. Por ejemplo, comen bacalao (cod), mejillones, vieiras (scallops), sardinas (sardines), calamares, anguilas, centollo y almejas. Hasta se come el pulpo (octopus), que se cocina en ollas (pots) grandes en las fiestas. ¿Te gustan los mariscos?

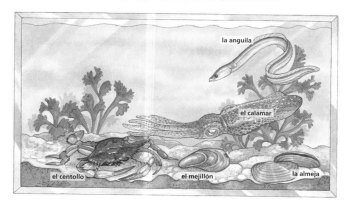

la anguila
el calamar
el centollo   el mejillón   la almeja

16 ¿Qué tal las vacaciones? Answers will vary.

Hablemos/Escribamos Pregúntale a un(a) compañero(a) qué hizo en sus vacaciones de verano. Escribe después un párrafo sobre sus experiencias y preséntalo a la clase.

Connections and Comparisons

Health Link
Fish and shellfish (both important sources of protein, B vitamins, and Omega-3 fatty acids, which reduce the risk of heart disease) are an important part of the Spanish diet. Have students research the role of the different food groups in the everyday diet of Spaniards. As a starting point, you might have them refer to the **platos típicos** listed on page 1. Ask them to find out what other foods are commonly eaten in Galicia or elsewhere in Spain and to discuss whether they represent a nutritionally balanced diet. You might suggest that they use the Internet to search for this information; a cookbook of Spanish dishes would also be a good resource.

Primer paso

CAPÍTULO 1

Writing Assessment

16 Have students write a letter to a friend in which they relate what they did over the summer, including sports or other pastimes that they spent time doing. They should also use the **Así se dice** functions on page 9 to talk about their current interests. You may wish to assess this assignment using the following rubric.

Writing Rubric	Points			
	4	3	2	1
Content (Complete– Incomplete)				
Comprehensibility (Comprehensible– Incomprehensible)				
Accuracy (Accurate– Seldom accurate)				
Organization (Well organized– Poorly organized)				
Effort (Excellent–Minimal)				

18–20: A	14–15: C	Under
16–17: B	12–13: D	12: F

Teaching Suggestion
Nota cultural Ask students to name the most exotic seafood they have eaten. How often do they eat seafood? Have students name restaurants in their town or city where seafood is served.

Assess
▸ Testing Program, pp. 1–4
  Quiz 1-1A, Quiz 1-1B
  Audio CD 1, Tr. 15

▸ Student Make-Up Assignments,
  Chapter 1, Alternative Quiz

▸ Alternative Assessment Guide,
  p. 30

The Annotated Teacher's Edition Wrap-Around Text offers helpful suggestions and information at point-of-use. You will also find annos, cultural information, correlations to the Standards for Foreign Language Learning, and references to other ancillaries.

Assessment
At the end of every **Paso** and again at the end of the chapter, you will find references to all the assessment material available for that section of the chapter.

Connections and Comparisons
Under this head you will find helpful information for connecting with other disciplines and developing insight into the nature of language and culture.

Bringing Standards into the Classroom

by Paul Sandrock, Foreign Language Consultant, Wisconsin Department of Public Education

The core question that guided the development of the National Standards and their accompanying goals was simply: what matters in instruction?

Each proposed standard was evaluated. Did the standard target material that will have application beyond the classroom? Was the standard too specific or not specific enough? Teachers should be able to teach the standard and assess it in multiple ways. A standard needs to provide a target for instruction and learning throughout a student's K–12 education.

In the development of standards, foreign languages faced other unique challenges. The writers could not assume a K–12 sequence available to all students. In fact, unlike other disciplines, they could not guarantee that all students would experience even any common sequence.

From this context, the National Standards in Foreign Language Education Project's task force generated the five C's, five goals for learning languages: communication, cultures, connections, comparisons, and commu-

nities. First presented in 1995, the standards quickly became familiar to foreign language educators across the U.S., representing our professional consensus and capturing a broad view of the purposes for learning another language.

To implement the standards, however, requires a shift from emphasizing the means to focusing on the ends. It isn't a matter of grammar versus communication, but rather how much grammar is needed to communicate. Instead of teaching to a grammatical sequence, teaching decisions become based on what students need to know to achieve the communicative goal.

The Focus on Communication

The first standard redefined communication, making its purpose **interpersonal**, **interpretive**, and **presentational** communication. Teaching to the purpose of interpersonal communication takes us away from memorized dialogues to spontaneous, interactive conversation, where the message is most important

and where meaning needs to be negotiated between the speakers. Interpretive communication is not an exercise in translation, but asks beginners to tell the gist of an authentic selection that is heard, read, or viewed, while increasingly advanced learners tell deeper and deeper levels of detail and can interpret based on their knowledge of the target culture. In the presentational mode of communication, the emphasis is on the audience, requiring the speaker or writer to adapt language to fit the situation and to allow for comprehension without any interactive negotiation of the meaning.

Standards challenge us to refocus many of the things we've been doing all along. The requirements of speaking and our expectation of how well students need to speak change when speaking is for a different purpose. This focus on the purpose of the communication changes the way we teach and test the skills of listening, speaking, reading, and writing.

Standards help us think about how to help students put the pieces of language to work in meaningful ways. Our

Standards for Foreign Language Learning

Communication Communicate in Languages Other than English	**Standard 1.1** Students engage in conversations, provide and obtain information, express feelings and emotions, and exchange opinions.
	Standard 1.2 Students understand and interpret written and spoken language on a variety of topics.
	Standard 1.3 Students present information, concepts, and ideas to an audience of listeners or readers on a variety of topics.
Cultures Gain Knowledge and Understanding of Other Cultures	**Standard 2.1** Students demonstrate an understanding of the relationship between the practices and perspectives of the culture studied.
	Standard 2.2 Students demonstrate an understanding of the relationship between the products and perspectives of the culture studied.
Connections Connect with Other Disciplines and Acquire Information	**Standard 3.1** Students reinforce and further their knowledge of other disciplines through the foreign language.
	Standard 3.2 Students acquire information and recognize the distinctive viewpoints that are only available through the foreign language and its cultures.
Comparisons Develop Insight into the Nature of Language and Culture	**Standard 4.1** Students demonstrate understanding of the nature of language through comparisons of the language studied and their own.
	Standard 4.2 Students demonstrate understanding of the concept of culture through comparisons of the cultures studied and their own.
Communities Participate in Multilingual Communities at Home and Around the World	**Standard 5.1** Students use the language both within and beyond the school setting.
	Standard 5.2 Students show evidence of becoming life-long learners by using the language for personal enjoyment and enrichment.

standards answer *why* we are teaching various components of language, and we select *what* we teach in order to achieve those very standards.

The 5 C's

Originally the five C's were presented as five equal circles. During the years since the National Standards were printed, teachers implementing and using the standards to write curriculum, texts, and lesson plans have come to see that communication is at the core, surrounded by four C's that influence the context for teaching and assessing.

The four C's surrounding our core goal of **Communication** change our classrooms by bringing in real-life applications for the language learned:

- **Cultures:** Beyond art and literature, learning occurs in the context of the way of life, patterns of behavior, and contributions of the people speaking the language being taught.

- **Connections:** Beyond content limited to the culture of the people speaking the target language, teachers go out to other disciplines to find topics and ideas to form the context for language learning.

- **Comparisons:** Foreign language study is a great way for students to learn more about native language and universal principles of language and culture by comparing and contrasting their own to the target language and culture.

- **Communities:** This goal of the standards adds a broader motivation to the context for language learning. The teacher makes sure students use their new language beyond the class hour, seeking ways to experience the target culture.

Implementation at the Classroom Level: Assessment and Instruction

After the publication of the standards, states developed more specific performance standards that would provide evidence of the application of the national content standards. Standards provide the organizing principle for teaching and assessing. The standards-oriented teacher, when asked what she's teaching, cites the standard "students will sustain a conversation." With that clear goal in mind, she creates lessons to teach various strategies to ask for clarification and to practice asking follow-up questions that explore a topic in more depth.

Textbook writers and materials providers are responding to this shift. Standards provide our goals; the useful textbooks and materials give us an organization and a context. Standards provide the ends; textbooks and materials can help us practice the means. Textbooks can bring authentic materials into the classroom, real cultural examples that avoid stereotypes, and a broader exposure to the variety of people who speak the language being studied. Textbooks can model the kind of instruction that will lead students to successful demonstration of the knowledge and skill described in the standards.

To really know that standards are the focus, look at the assessment. If standards are the target, assessment won't consist only of evaluation of the means (grammatical structures and vocabulary) in isolation. If standards are the focus, teachers will assess students' use of the second language in context. The summative assessment of our target needs to go beyond the specific and include open-ended, personalized tasks. Regardless of how the students show what they can do, the teacher will be able to gauge each student's progress toward the goal.

Assessment is like a jigsaw puzzle. If we test students only on the means, we just keep collecting random puzzle pieces. We have to test, and students have to practice, putting the pieces together in meaningful and purposeful ways. In order to learn vocabulary that will help students "describe themselves," for example, students may have a quiz on Friday with an expectation of close to 100% accuracy. But if that is all we ever do with those ten words, they will quickly be gone from students' memory, and we will only have collected a puzzle piece from each student. It is absolutely essential to have students use those puzzle pieces to complete the puzzle to provide evidence of what they "can do" with the language.

During this period of implementing our standards, we've learned that the standards provide a global picture, the essence of our goals. But they are not curriculum, nor are they lesson plans. The standards influence how we teach, but do not dictate one content nor one methodology. How can we implement the standards in our classrooms? Think about the targets; think about how students will show achievement of those targets through our evaluation measures; then think about what we need to teach and how that will occur in our classrooms. Make it happen in your classroom to get the results we've always wanted: students who can communicate in a language other than English.

¡Ven conmigo!

supports the Standards for Foreign Language Learning in the following ways:

THE PUPIL'S EDITION

▶ Encourages students to take responsibility for their learning by providing clearly defined objectives at the beginning of each chapter.

▶ Provides a variety of pair- and group-work activities to give students an opportunity to use the target language in a wide range of settings and contexts.

▶ Offers culture-related activities and poses questions that develop students' insight and encourage them to develop observational and analytical skills.

THE ANNOTATED TEACHER'S EDITION

▶ Provides a broad framework for developing a foreign language program and offers specific classroom suggestions for reaching students with various learning styles.

▶ Offers ideas for multicultural and multidisciplinary projects as well as community and family links that encourage students to gain access to information both at school and in the community.

THE ANCILLARY PROGRAM

▶ Provides students with on-location video footage of native speakers interacting in their own cultural and geographic context.

▶ Includes multiple options for practicing new skills and assessing performance.

▶ Familiarizes students with the types of tasks they will be expected to perform on exit exams.

Reading Strategies and Skills

by Nancy A. Humbach, Miami University

Reading is the most enduring of the language skills. Long after a student ceases to study the language, the ability to read will continue to provide a springboard to the renewal of the other skills. We must consider all the ways in which our students will read and address the skills needed for those tasks.

How can we accomplish this goal? How can we, as teachers, present materials, encourage students to read, and at the same time foster understanding and build the student's confidence and interest in reading?

Selection of Materials

Reading material in the foreign language classroom should be relevant to students' backgrounds and at an accessible level of difficulty; i.e., at a level of difficulty only slightly above the reading ability of the student.

Authentic materials are generally a good choice. They provide cultural context and linguistic authenticity seldom found in materials created for students, and the authentic nature of the language provides a window on a new world. The problem inherent in the selection of authentic materials at early levels is obvious: the level of difficulty is frequently beyond the skill of the student. At the same time, however, readers are inspired by the fact that they can understand materials designed to be read by native speakers.

Presenting a Selection/ Reading Strategies

We assume that students of a second language already have a reading knowledge in their first language and that many of the skills they learned in their "reading readiness" days will serve them well. Too

often, however, students have forgotten such skills as activating background knowledge, skimming, scanning, and guessing content based on context clues. Helping students to reactivate these skills is part of helping them become better readers.

Teachers should not assume their students' ability to transfer a knowledge set from one reading to another. Students use these skills on a regular basis, but often do not even realize they are doing so. To help students become aware of these processes, they need to be given strategies for reading. These strategies offer students a framework for the higher-level skills they need to apply when reading. Strategies also address learners of different learning styles and needs.

Advance Organizers

One way to activate the student's background knowledge is through advance organizers. They also serve to address the student's initial frustrations at encountering an unfamiliar text.

Advance organizers call up pertinent background knowledge, feelings, and experiences that can serve to focus the attention of the entire group on a given topic. In addition, they provide for a sharing of information among the students. Background information that includes cultural references and cultural information can reactivate in students skills that will help them with a text and provide for them clues to the meaning of the material.

A good advance organizer will provide some information and guide students to think about the scenarios being presented. An advance organizer might include photographs, drawings, quotations, maps, or information about the area where the story takes

place. It might also be posed as a question, for example, "What would you do if you found yourself in….?" Having students brainstorm in advance, either as a whole class or in small groups, allows them to construct a scenario which they can verify as they read.

Prereading Activities

Prereading activities remind students of how much they really know and can prepare students in a number of ways to experience the language with less frustration. While we know that we must choose a reading selection that is not far beyond students' experience and skill level, we also know that no group of students reads at the same level. In the interest of assisting students to become better language learners, we can provide them with opportunities to work with unfamiliar structures and vocabulary ahead of time.

Preparing students for a reading selection can include a number of strategies that may anticipate but not dwell on potential problems to be encountered by students. Various aspects of grammar, such as differences in the past tenses and the meanings conveyed, can also cause problems. Alerting students to some of the aspects of the language allows them to struggle less, understand more quickly, and enjoy a reading selection to a greater degree.

Grouping vocabulary by category or simply choosing a short list of critical words for a section of reading is helpful. Providing an entire list of vocabulary items at one time can be overwhelming. With a bit of organization, the task becomes manageable to the point where students begin to master words they will find repeated throughout the selection.

Having students skim for a particular piece of information or scan for words, phrases, indicators of place or time, and names, and then asking them to write a sentence or two about the gist of a paragraph or story, gives them a sense of independence and success before they begin to read.

Getting into the Assignment

Teachers can recount the times they have assigned a piece of reading for homework, only to find that few students even attempted the work. Therefore, many teachers choose to complete the reading in class. Homework assignments should then be structured to have the student return to the selection and complete a assignment that requires critical thinking and imagination.

During class, several techniques assist students in maintaining interest and attention to the task. By varying these techniques, the teacher can provide for a lively class, during which students realize they *are* able to read. Partners can read passages to each other or students can take turns reading in small groups. The teacher might pose a question to be answered during that reading. Groups might also begin to act out short scenes, reading only the dialogue. Students might read a description of a setting and then draw what they imagine it to be. Of course, some selections might be silent reading with a specific amount of time announced for completion.

Reading aloud for comprehension and reading aloud for pronunciation practice are two entirely unrelated tasks. We can all recall classes where someone read aloud to us from weary lecture notes. Active engagement of the readers, on the other hand, forces them to work for comprehension, for the development of thought processes, and for improvement of language skills.

Postreading Activities

It is important to provide students with an opportunity to expand the knowledge

they have gained from the reading selection. Students should apply what they have learned to their own personal experiences. How we structure activities can provide students more opportunities to reflect on their reading and learn how much they have understood. We often consider a written test the best way to ensure comprehension; however, many other strategies allow students to keep oral skills active. These might include acting out impromptu scenes from the story and creating dialogues that do not exist in a story, but might be imagined, based on other information. Consider the possibility of debates, interviews, TV talk show formats, telephone dialogues, or a monologue in which the audience hears only one side of the conversation.

Written assignments are also valid assessment tools, allowing students to incorporate the vocabulary and structures they have learned in the reading. Students might be encouraged to write journal entries for a character, create a new ending, or retell the story from another point of view. Newspaper articles, advertisements, and other creations can also be a means of following up. Comparisons with other readings require students to keep active vocabulary and structures they have studied previously. Encourage students to read their creations aloud to a partner, to a group, or to the class.

Conclusion

Reading can be exciting. The combination of a good selection that is relevant and rates high on the interest scale, along with good preparation, guidance, and post reading activities that demonstrate to the students the level of success attained, can encourage them to continue to read. These assignments also allow for the incorporation of other aspects of language learning, and incorporate the Five C's of the National Standards. Communication and culture are obvious links, but so are connections (advance organizers, settings, and so on), comparisons (with other works in the

heritage or target language), and communities (learning why a type of writing is important in a culture).

¡Ven conmigo!

offers reading practice and develops reading skills and strategies in the following ways:

THE PUPIL'S EDITION

▶ Provides an extensive reading section in each chapter called **Vamos a leer.** Each **Vamos a leer** section offers a strategy students apply to an authentic text, as well as activities to guide understanding and exploration of the text.

THE ANNOTATED TEACHER'S EDITION

▶ Provides teachers with additional activities and information in every **Vamos a leer** section. Additional suggestions are provided for Pre-reading, Reading, and Postreading activities.

THE ANCILLARY PROGRAM

▶ *¡Lee conmigo!* This component offers reading selections of various formats and difficulty levels. Each chapter has a prereading feature, a reading selection with comprehension questions, and two pages of activities.

▶ The *Reading Strategies and Skills Handbook* offers useful strategies that can be applied to reading selections in the *Pupil's Edition*, *¡Lee conmigo!*, or a selection of your choosing.

▶ The *Cuaderno de actividades* contains a reading selection tied to the chapter theme, and reading activities for each chapter in *¡Ven conmigo!*

▶ The *Cuaderno para hispano-hablantes* offers reading selections and comprehension activities correlated to chapters in the *Pupil's Edition.*

Using Portfolios in the Language Classroom

by JoAnne S. Wilson

Portfolios offer a more realistic and accurate way to assess the process of language teaching and learning.

The communicative, whole-language approach of today's language instruction requires assessment methods that parallel the teaching and learning strategies in the proficiency-oriented classroom. We know that language acquisition is a process. Portfolios are designed to assess the steps in that process.

What Is a Portfolio?

A portfolio is a purposeful, systematic collection of a student's work. A useful tool in developing a student profile, the portfolio shows the student's efforts, progress, and achievements for a given period of time. It may be used for periodic evaluation, as the basis for overall evaluation, or for placement. It may also be used to enhance or provide alternatives to traditional assessment measures, such as formal tests, quizzes, class participation, and homework.

Why Use Portfolios?

Portfolios benefit both students and teachers because they:

- **Are ongoing and systematic.** A portfolio reflects the real-world process of production, assessment, revision, and reassessment. It parallels the natural rhythm of learning.

- **Offer an incentive to learn.** Students have a vested interest in creating the portfolios, through which they can showcase their ongoing efforts and tangible achievements. Students select the works to be included and have a chance to revise, improve, evaluate, and explain the contents.

- **Are sensitive to individual needs.** Language learners bring varied abilities to the classroom and do not acquire skills in a uniformly neat and orderly fashion. The personalized, individualized assessment offered by portfolios responds to this diversity.

- **Provide documentation of language development.** The material in a portfolio is evidence of student progress in the language learning process. The contents of the portfolio make it easier to discuss their progress with the students as well as with parents and others.

- **Offer multiple sources of information.** A portfolio presents a way to collect and analyze information from multiple sources that reflects a student's efforts, progress, and achievements in the language.

Portfolio Components

The language portfolio should include both oral and written work, student self-evaluation, and teacher observation, usually in the form of brief, nonevaluative comments about various aspects of the student's performance.

The Oral Component

The oral component of a portfolio might be an audio- or videocassette. It may contain both rehearsed and extemporaneous monologues and conversations. For a rehearsed speaking activity, give a specific communicative task that students can personalize according to their individual interests (for example, ordering a favorite meal in a restaurant). If the speaking activity is extemporaneous, first acquaint students with possible topics for discussion or even the specific task they will be expected to perform. (For example, tell them they will be asked to discuss a picture showing a sports activity or a restaurant scene.)

The Written Component

Portfolios are excellent tools for incorporating process writing strategies into the language classroom. Documentation of various stages of the writing process—brainstorming, multiple drafts, and peer comments—may be included with the finished product.

Involve students in selecting writing tasks for the portfolio. At the beginning levels, the tasks might include some structured writing, such as labeling or listing. As students become more proficient, journals, letters, and other more complicated writing tasks are valuable ways for them to monitor their progress in using the written language.

Student Self-Evaluation

Students should be actively involved in critiquing and evaluating their portfolios and monitoring their own progress.

The process and procedure for student self-evaluation should be considered in planning the contents of the portfolio. Students should work with you and their peers to design the exact format. Self-evaluation encourages them to think about what they are learning (content), how they learn (process), why they are learning (purpose), and where they are going in their learning (goals).

Teacher Observation

Systematic, regular, and ongoing observations should be placed in the portfolio after they have been discussed with the student. These observations provide feedback on the student's progress in the language learning process.

Teacher observations should be based on an established set of criteria that has been developed earlier with input from the student. Observation techniques may include the following:

- Jotting notes in a journal to be discussed with the student and then placed in the portfolio

- Using a checklist of observable behaviors, such as the willingness to take risks when using the target language or staying on task during the lesson

- Making observations on adhesive notes that can be placed in folders

- Recording anecdotal comments, during or after class, using a cassette recorder.

Knowledge of the criteria you use in your observations gives students a framework for their performance.

Electronic Portfolios

Technology can provide help with managing student portfolios. Digital or computer-based portfolios offer a means of saving portfolios in an electronic format. Students can save text, drawings, photographs, graphics, audio or video recordings, or any combination of multimedia information. Teachers can create their own portfolio templates or consult one of the many commercial software programs available to create digital portfolios. Portfolios saved on videotapes or compact discs provide a convenient way to access and store students' work. By employing technology, this means of alternative assessment addresses the learning styles and abilities of individual students. Additionally, electronic portfolios can be shared among teachers, and parents have the ability to easily see the students' progress.

Logistically, the hypermedia equipment and software available for students' use determine what types of entries will be included in the portfolios. The teacher or a team of teachers and students may provide the computer support.

How Are Portfolios Evaluated?

The portfolio should reflect the process of student learning over a specific period of time. At the beginning of that time period, determine the criteria by which you will assess the final product and convey them to the students. Make this evaluation a collaborative effort by seeking students' input as you formulate these criteria and your instructional goals.

Students need to understand that evaluation based on a predetermined standard is but one phase of the assessment process; demonstrated effort and growth are just as important. As you consider correctness and accuracy in both oral and written work, also consider the organization, creativity, and improvement revealed by the student's portfolio over the time period. The portfolio provides a way to monitor the growth of a student's knowledge, skills, and attitudes and shows the student's efforts, progress, and achievements.

How to Implement Portfolios

Teacher-teacher collaboration is as important to the implementation of portfolios as teacher-student collaboration. Confer with your colleagues to determine, for example, what kinds of information you want to see in the student portfolio, how the information will be presented, the purpose of the portfolio, the intended purposes (grading, placement, or a combination of the two), and criteria for evaluating the portfolio. Conferring among colleagues helps foster a departmental cohesiveness and consistency that will ultimately benefit the students.

The Promise of Portfolios

The high degree of student involvement in developing portfolios and deciding how they will be used generally results in renewed student enthusiasm for learning and improved achievement. As students compare portfolio pieces done early in the year with work produced later, they can take pride in their progress as well as reassess their motivation and work habits.

¡Ven conmigo!
supports the use of portfolios in the following ways:

THE PUPIL'S EDITION

▸ Includes numerous oral and written activities that can be easily adapted for student portfolios, such as **En mi cuaderno, Vamos a escribir**, and **Situación.**

THE ANNOTATED TEACHER'S EDITION

▸ Suggests activities in the Portfolio Assessment feature that may serve as portfolio items.

THE ANCILLARY PROGRAM

▸ Includes criteria in the *Alternative Assessment Guide* for evaluating portfolios.

▸ Provides Speaking Tests in the *Testing Program* for each chapter that can be adapted for use as portfolio assessment items.

▸ Offers several oral and written scenarios on the *Interactive CD-ROM Tutor* that students can develop and include in their portfolios.

Learning Styles and Multi-Modality Teaching

by Mary B. McGehee, Louisiana State University

Incorporating a greater variety of activities to accommodate the learning styles of all students can make the difference between struggle and pleasure in the foreign language classroom.

The larger and broader population of students who are enrolling in foreign language classes brings a new challenge to foreign language educators, calling forth an evolution in teaching methods to enhance learning for all our students. Educational experts now recognize that every student has a preferred sense for learning and retrieving information: visual, auditory, or kinesthetic. Incorporating a greater variety of activities to accommodate the learning styles of all students can make the difference between struggle and pleasure in the foreign language classroom.

Accommodating Different Learning Styles

A modified arrangement of the classroom is one way to provide more effective and enjoyable learning for all students. Rows of chairs and desks must give way at times to circles, semicircles, or small clusters. Students may be grouped in fours or in pairs for cooperative work or peer teaching. It is important to find a balance of arrangements, thereby providing the most comfort in varied situations.

Since visual, auditory, and kinesthetic learners will be in the class, and because every student's learning will be enhanced by a multi-sensory approach, lessons must be directed toward all three learning styles. Any language lesson content may be presented visually, aurally, or kinesthetically.

Visual presentations and practice may include the chalkboard, charts, posters, television, overhead projectors, books, magazines, picture diagrams, flash cards, bulletin boards, films, slides, or videos. Visual learners need to see what they are to learn. Lest the teacher think he or she will never have the time to prepare all those visuals, Dickel and Slak (1983) found that visual aids generated by students are more effective than ready-made ones.

Auditory presentations and practice may include stating aloud the requirements of the lesson, oral questions and answers, paired or group work on a progression of oral exercises from repetition to communication, tapes, CDs, dialogues, and role-playing. Jingles, catchy stories, and memory devices using songs and rhymes are good learning aids. Having students record themselves and then listen as they play back the cassette allows them to practice in the auditory mode.

Kinesthetic presentations entail the students' use of manipulatives, chart materials, gestures, signals, typing, songs, games, and role-playing. These lead the students to associate sentence constructions with meaningful movements.

A Sample Lesson Using Multi-Modality Teaching

A multi-sensory presentation on greetings might proceed as follows:

For Visual Learners
As the teacher begins oral presentation of greetings and introductions, he or she simultaneously shows the written forms on transparencies, with the formal expressions marked with an adult's hat, and the informal expressions marked with a baseball cap.

The teacher then distributes cards with the hat and cap symbols representing the formal and informal expressions. As the students hear taped mini-dialogues, they hold up the appropriate card to indicate whether the dialogues are formal or informal. On the next listening, the students repeat the sentences they hear.

For Auditory Learners
A longer taped dialogue follows, allowing the students to hear the new expressions a number of times. They write from dictation several sentences containing the new expressions. They may work in pairs, correcting each other's work as they "test" their own understanding of the lesson at hand. Finally, students respond to simple questions using the appropriate formal and informal responses cued by the cards they hold.

For Kinesthetic Learners
For additional kinesthetic input, members of the class come to the front of the room, each holding a hat or cap symbol. As the teacher calls out situations, the students play the roles, using gestures and props appropriate to the age group they are portraying. Non-cued, communicative role-playing with props further enables the students to "feel" the differences between formal and informal expressions.

Helping Students Learn How to Use Their Preferred Mode

Since we require all students to perform in all language skills, part of the assistance we must render is to help them develop strategies within their preferred learning modes to carry out an assignment in another mode. For example, visual students hear the teacher assign an oral exercise and visualize what they must do. They must see themselves carrying out the assignment, in effect watching themselves as if there were a movie going on in their heads. Only then can they also hear themselves saying the right things. Thus, this assignment will be much easier for the visual learners who have been taught this process, if they have not already figured it out for themselves. Likewise, true auditory students, confronted with a reading/writing assignment, must talk themselves through it, converting the entire process into sound as they plan and prepare their work. Kinesthetic students presented with a visual or auditory task must first break the assignment into tasks and then work their way through them.

Students who experience difficulty because of a strong preference for one mode of learning are often unaware of the degree of preference. In working with these students, I prefer the simple and direct assessment of learning styles offered by Richard Bandler and John Grinder in their book *Frogs into Princes*, which allows the teacher and student to quickly determine how the student learns. In an interview with the student, I follow the assessment with certain specific recommendations of techniques to make the student's study time more effective.

It is important to note here that teaching students to maximize their study does not require that the teacher give each student an individualized assignment. It does require that each student who needs it be taught how to prepare the assignment using his or her own talents and strengths. This communication between teacher and student, combined with teaching techniques that reinforce learning in all modes, can only maximize pleasure and success in learning a foreign language.

References

Dickel, M.J. and S. Slak. "Imaging Vividness and Memory for Verbal Material." *Journal of Mental Imagery* 7, i (1983):121–126.

Bandler, Richard, and John Grinder. *Frogs into Princes*. Real People Press, Moab, UT. 1978.

¡Ven conmigo!
accommodates different learning styles in the following ways:

THE PUPIL'S EDITION

▸ Presents basic material in audio, video, and print formats.

▸ Includes role-playing activities and a variety of multi-modal activities, including an extensive listening strand and many art-based activities.

THE ANNOTATED TEACHER'S EDITION

▸ Provides suggested activities for visual, auditory, and kinesthetic learners as well as suggestions for slower-paced learning and challenge activities.

▸ Includes Total Physical Response activities.

THE ANCILLARY PROGRAM

▸ Provides additional reinforcement activities for a variety of learning styles.

▸ Presents a rich blend of audiovisual input through the *Video Program, Audio Program, Interactive CD-ROM Tutor, Teaching Transparencies*, and blackline masters.

New Perspectives for Native Speakers

by Cecilia Rodríguez-Pino, New Mexico State University

Spanish teachers often simultaneously teach two groups of students whose learning needs are markedly different. The first group, the majority, for whom most curricula are developed, are English-proficient but at a beginner's level in Spanish. The second group consists of students whose proficiency in English varies but who already speak Spanish, often quite proficiently. From their own experience they already understand a great deal about the Spanish language and the cultures of Spanish speakers. Many schools have not yet set up Spanish for Native Speakers (SNS) sections with specialized curricula that would build on these students' linguistic and cultural strengths. As a result, in some schools native speakers who want to study Spanish are enrolled in courses where Spanish is taught as a foreign language. Addressing their learning needs thus becomes the particular challenge of the teacher, who must create and implement supplemental classroom materials.

Types of Native Spanish Speakers

The greatest number of native Spanish speakers in the classroom are Spanish-speaking immigrants and American students of Hispanic descent. Many immigrants have been uprooted from their native countries and find themselves in a new and foreign environment without the skills to communicate. Often they must struggle to adapt to mainstream sociocultural norms and values. Psychological adjustment, cultural integration, and the acquisition of new communicative skills are daily concerns for them. Building teacher-student and peer-peer learning relationships may be harder for such students.

American students of Hispanic descent are often bilingual. Some are highly proficient in both written and oral Spanish, but many are proficient to varying degrees, depending on the circumstances, topics, tasks, and informal situations. These students reflect the various socioeconomic classes of society and speak a wide range of Spanish dialects. Research indicates that the dialect they speak affects how they are viewed at school. When they speak a "standard" variety of Spanish and are from an educated class, as are many Cuban Americans in Florida, reactions to them are usually positive. But when Spanish speakers are from a rural background, speak a "nonstandard" dialect, or come from a nonliterate background, reactions in school are often negative. Attempting to modify their dialect can be detrimental to their linguistic and social development.

Linguistic Needs

Native Spanish speakers need to retrieve any Spanish they may have lost, maintain the competency they already have, and expand their knowledge and skills in Spanish.

The problem of native language loss is receiving much attention in the profession. Children appear to lose production skills more quickly than they lose comprehension ability. Thus retrieval efforts should focus on production. Rapid changes in society and in the patterns by which Spanish is transmitted from one generation to the next account for much of students' language loss. Word borrowing and code switching to English may also account for language loss. These practices are not unique to bilingual students in the United States; they are common linguistic phenomena, observed wherever languages are in contact. A native speaker may switch from Spanish to English when referring to activities generally associated with the dominant culture—even when the speaker is perfectly familiar with the relevant Spanish vocabulary. Efforts to eradicate code switching may harm students' linguistic and social development.

Affective Needs

Native Spanish-speaking students bring to class much valuable cultural and linguistic experience. Cultural opportunities need to be provided for them through which they can express their knowledge of their own particular Spanish-speaking culture and gain a greater overview of other Spanish-speaking communities and countries. They need to understand that their heritage, language, culture, dialect, and individual abilities are valuable to society. As teachers we must respect and value the different languages and dialects our students speak, and we must create an instructional context in which students will develop positive attitudes toward their own ethnic group and their own ethnic identity.

An SNS Program Approach

A task-based, whole-language approach is recommended. Receptive and productive skills can be developed through culturally meaningful activities whose contexts are community, school, home, and self. These activities can be carried out in conjunction with textbook thematic units. Such an approach creates a student-centered classroom in which the teacher acts as a facilitator connecting students to the bilingual community.

Expanding Receptive Skills

Students should perform activities in which they listen to their native language in a broad range of formal and informal contexts, from simple topics to complex ones. Audio- or videotaped versions of stories, songs, documentaries, speeches, or debates can be adapted for class assignments. Guest speakers from the community are extremely valuable resources for presentations or interviews on the chapter topic.

Students should have access to diverse, authentic reading materials from the popular culture as well as from more formal subject areas. Chicano, Cuban, Dominican, Colombian, Nicaraguan, Honduran, Panamanian, and Puerto Rican writings—which are underrepresented in the mainstream literary canon—can play an important role in instilling in students a sense of pride and awareness of their cultural heritage. Students relate well to literature written by contemporary Hispanic authors who have had experiences similar to the students' in the United States. For example, they might read the short story "Desde que se fue," from the collection *Madreselvas en flor* by literary prize-winning Chicano author Ricardo Aguilar-Melantzón, about growing up in a bilingual setting.

Developing Productive Skills

Oral history projects, ethnographic interviews, sociolinguistic surveys, dialogue journals, letter writing, and other purposeful authentic activities are effective techniques that focus on interactions among students, teacher, and community. These kinds of activities give students the opportunity to develop individual strengths and to explore their language and culture in a community context.

Classroom Environment

We can change the classroom space itself to create an environment that recognizes the prestige of the students' language and cultural heritage. Using a brief questionnaire, the teacher can find out the students' backgrounds and then display relevant posters, travel brochures, art, literature, or historical information. Students can contribute captioned photographs depicting cultural events and family traditions, so that the bulletin board reflects their personal view of the Spanish-speaking world rather than just the teacher's perspective.

Individual Assessment and Evaluation

Individual assessment at the beginning of the year should be based primarily on content so that students' errors are not the main focus. Use content, organization, and language as criteria for evaluating speaking and writing. In evaluating students' work for the year, take into account how students have broadened their functional range. This requires students to be responsible for the concepts that are essential to comprehension and production. A writing portfolio is a valuable component of the evaluation process. Oral presentations of ethnographic and sociolinguistic projects are contextualized activities for evaluating speaking.

¡Ven conmigo!

supports native speakers' continued development of Spanish in the following ways:

THE PUPIL'S EDITION

▸ Promotes pride and awareness of cultural heritage through Location Openers on U.S. Spanish-speaking areas, as well as cultural features, interviews with native speakers, and literary selections by U.S. and non-U.S. native speakers.

▸ Validates the use of regionally specific vocabulary and authentic expression in the **También se puede decir** and **A lo nuestro** features.

▸ Fosters the student's self-concept by encouraging individual expression in journal entries and other authentic tasks, such as letter writing.

THE ANNOTATED TEACHER'S EDITION

▸ Includes specific suggestions for activities to be performed by native speakers, both independently and with other students.

▸ Provides the teacher with additional vocabulary suggestions and language notes that validate regional variants.

▸ Suggests family and community links that strengthen students' ties to the wider bilingual community via family and community interviews and ethnographic reports.

THE ANCILLARY PROGRAM

▸ Offers a *Cuaderno para hispanohablantes* with a diagnostic instrument and, chapter by chapter, additional reading practice based on authentic literature on topics of interest to native speakers. In addition, this book addresses issues of formal usage and pronunciation and provides additional writing and speaking practice.

▸ Provides a **Para hispanohablantes** writing feature in each chapter of the *Interactive CD-ROM Tutor.*

Multi-Level Classrooms

by Joan H. Manley

There are positive ways, both psychological and pedagogical, to make this situation work for you and your students.

So you have just heard that your third-period class is going to include both Levels 2 and 3! While this is never the best news for a foreign language teacher, there are positive ways, both psychological and pedagogical, to make this situation work for you and your students.

Relieving student anxieties

Initially, in a multi-level class environment, it is important to relieve students' anxiety by orienting them to their new situation. From the outset, let all students know that just because they "did" things the previous year, such as learn how to conjugate certain verbs, they may not yet be able to use them in a meaningful way. Students should not feel that it is demeaning or a waste of time to recycle activities or to share knowledge and skills with fellow students. Second-year students need to know they are not second-class citizens and that they can benefit from their classmates' greater experience with the language. Third-year students may achieve a great deal of satisfaction and become more confident in their own language skills when they have opportunities to help or teach their second-year classmates. It is important to reassure third-year students that you will devote time to them and challenge them with different assignments.

Easing your own apprehension

When you are faced with both Levels 2 and 3 in your classroom, remind yourself that you teach students of different levels in the same classroom every year, although not officially. After one year of classroom instruction, your Level 2 class will never be a truly homogeneous group. Despite being made up of students with the same amount of "seat time," the class comprises multiple layers of language skills, knowledge, motivation, and ability. Therefore, you are constantly called upon to make a positive experience out of a potentially negative one.

Your apprehension will gradually diminish to the extent that you are able to . . .

- make students less dependent on you for the successful completion of their activities.
- place more responsibility for learning on the students.
- implement creative group, pair, and individual activities.

How can you do this? Good organization will help. Lessons will need to be especially well-planned for the multi-level class. The following lesson plan is an example of how to treat the same topic with students of two different levels.

Teaching a lesson in a multi-level classroom

Lesson objectives

Relate an incident in the past that you regret.

Level 2: Express surprise and sympathy.

Level 3: Offer encouragement and make suggestions.

Lesson plan

1. **Review and/or teach the past tense.** Present the formation of the past tense. Model its use for the entire class or call upon Level 3 students to give examples.

2. **Practice the past tense.** Have Level 3 students who have mastered the past tense teach it to Level 2 students in pairs or small groups. Provide the Level 3 student instructors with several drill and practice activities they may use for this purpose.

3. **Relate your own regrettable past experience.** Recount a personal regrettable incident—real or imaginary—to the entire class as a model. For example, you may have left your automobile lights on, and when you came out of school, the battery was dead and you couldn't start your car. Or you

may have scolded a student for not doing the homework and later discovered the student had a legitimate reason for not completing the assignment.

4. Prepare and practice written and oral narratives. Have Level 2 students pair off with Level 3 students. Each individual writes about his or her experience, the Level 3 partner serving as a resource for the Level 2 student. Partners then edit each other's work and listen to each other's oral delivery. You might choose to have students record their oral narratives.

5. Present communicative functions.
   A. Ask for a volunteer to recount his or her own regrettable incident for the entire class.
   B. Model reactions to the volunteer's narrative.
      (1) Express surprise and sympathy
          (for Level 2): "Really! That's too bad!"
      (2) Offer encouragement and make suggestions
          (for Level 3): "Don't worry. You can still..."

6. Read narratives and practice communicative functions. Have Level 2 students work together in one group or in small groups, listening to classmates' stories and reacting with the prescribed communicative function. Have Level 3 students do the same among themselves. Circulate among the groups, listening, helping, and assessing.

7. Assess progress. Repeat your personal account for the entire class and elicit reactions from students according to their level. Challenge students to respond with communicative functions expected of the other level if they can.

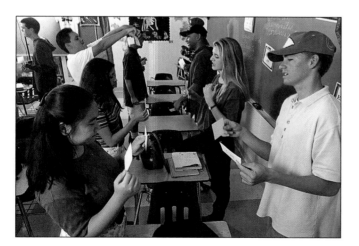

Every part of the above lesson plan is important. Both levels have been accommodated. The teacher has not dominated the lesson. Students have worked together in pairs and small groups, while Level 3 students have helped their Level 2 classmates. Individual groups still feel accountable, both within their level and across levels.

Any lesson can be adapted in this way. It takes time and effort, but the result is a student-centered classroom where students share and grow, and the teacher is the facilitator.

¡Ven conmigo!
facilitates work in a multi-level classroom
in the following ways:

THE PUPIL'S EDITION
▸ Provides creative activities for pair and group work that allow students at different levels to work together and learn from one another.

THE ANNOTATED TEACHER'S EDITION
▸ Offers practical suggestions for Projects and Cooperative Learning that engage students of different levels.

▸ Provides Communication for All Students teaching suggestions throughout the program. Second-year students will benefit from the Slower Pace activities, while third-year students will take advantage of the Challenge exercises.

▸ Provides a clear, comprehensive outline of the functions, vocabulary, and grammar that are recycled in each chapter. The Chapter Overview of each chapter is especially helpful to the teacher who is planning integrated or varied lessons in the multi-level classroom.

THE ANCILLARY PROGRAM
▸ Provides a variety of materials and activities to accommodate different levels in a multi-level classroom.

▸ Facilitates collective learning so that groups of students at different learning levels may work together, pacing an activity according to their specific abilities.

Professional References

This section provides information about resources that can enrich your Spanish class. Included are addresses of Spanish and Latin American government offices, pen pal organizations, subscription agencies, and many others. Since addresses change frequently, you may want to verify them before you send your requests.

PEN PAL ORGANIZATIONS

For the names of pen pal groups other than those listed below, contact your local chapter of AATSP. There are fees involved, so be sure to write for information.

Student Letter Exchange (League of Friendship)
211 Broadway, Suite 201
Lynbrook, NY 11563
(516) 887-8628

World Pen Pals
1694 Como Avenue
St. Paul, MN 55108
(612) 647-0191

EMBASSIES AND CONSULATES

Addresses and phone numbers of embassies and consulates for Spanish-speaking countries are available in most U.S. city telephone directories. All are available in the directory for Washington, D.C.

PERIODICALS

Subscriptions to the following cultural materials are available through some larger bookstores or directly from the publishers. See also the section on Subscription Services.

- *El País,* a major Spanish newspaper
- *GeoMundo,* a cultural and environmental magazine
- *Hispanic,* an English-language magazine about Hispanics in the U.S.
- *El Nuevo Día,* a Puerto Rican newspaper
- *La Prensa,* a major daily paper in Argentina
- *Tú internacional,* a magazine for teens published in several Spanish-speaking countries
- *México desconocido,* a cultural and environmental magazine about Mexico

CULTURAL AGENCIES

For historical and tourist information about Spanish-speaking regions, contact:

Greater Miami Convention and Visitors Bureau
701 Brickell Ave., Suite 2700
Miami, FL 33131
(800) 283-2707

Mexican Government Tourism Office
10440 West Office Drive
Houston, TX 77042
(800) 446-3942

Tourist Office of Spain
666 Fifth Avenue
New York, NY 10022
(212) 265-8822

INTERCULTURAL EXCHANGE

CIEE Student Travel Services
205 East 42nd St.
New York, NY 10017
(888) 268-6245

American Field Service
198 Madison, 8th Floor
New York, NY 10016
(212) 299-9000

PROFESSIONAL ORGANIZATIONS

The American Council on the Teaching of Foreign Languages (ACTFL)
6 Executive Plaza
Yonkers, NY 10701
(914) 963-8830

American Association of Teachers of Spanish and Portuguese (AATSP)
Butler-Hancock Hall, Room 210
University of Northern Colorado
Greeley, CO 80639
(970) 351-1090

SUBSCRIPTION SERVICES

Spanish-language magazines can be obtained through subscription agencies in the United States. The following companies are among the many which can provide your school with subscriptions:

EBSCO Subscription Services
P.O. Box 1943
Birmingham, AL 35201-1943
(205) 991-6600

Continental Book Company
8000 Cooper Ave., Bldg. 29
Glendale, NY 11385
(718) 326-0560

MISCELLANEOUS

Educational Resources Information Center (ERIC)
2277 Research Blvd.
Rockville, MD 20852
(800) 538-3742

U.S. Department of Education
400 Maryland Ave., SW
Washington, D.C. 20202-0498
(800) USA-LEARN
- Information and resource center; publications and videos available

The International Film Bureau
332 South Michigan Ave.
Chicago, IL 60604-4382
(312) 427-4545
- Foreign language videos for sale and/or rent

Américas
Organization of American States
17th and Constitution Ave. NW
Room #307
Washington, D.C. 20006
(202) 458-3000
- Magazine available in English or Spanish text

A Bibliography for the Spanish Teacher

This bibliography is a compilation of resources available for professional enrichment.

SELECTED AND ANNOTATED LIST OF READINGS

I. Methods and Approaches

Cohen, Andrew D. *Assessing Language Ability in the Classroom,* 2/e. Boston, MA: Heinle, 1994.
- Assessment processes, oral interviews, role-playing situations, dictation, portfolio assessment and computer-based testing.

Hadley, Alice Omaggio. *Teaching Language in Context,* 2/e. Boston, MA: Heinle, 1993.
- Overview of the proficiency movement and a survey of past language teaching methods and approaches; application of the five skills in language education; includes sample activities, teaching summaries, and references.

Lafayette, R. (Ed.). *National Standards: A Catalyst for Reform.* Lincolnwood, IL: National Textbook Co., 1996.
- Outline and implications of the National Standards for the modern language classroom, addresses technology, teacher training, materials development, and the changing learning environment.

Lee, James F., and Bill VanPatten. *Making Communicative Language Teaching Happen.* New York: McGraw-Hill, 1995.
- Task-based approach to language education, includes activities and test sections to encourage communicative interaction in the classroom.

II. Second-Language Theory

Brown, H. Douglas. *Principles of Language Learning and Teaching* (3rd. ed.). Englewood Cliffs, NJ: Prentice Hall Regents, 1994.
- Addresses the cognitive, psychological, and sociocultural factors influencing the language learning process; also includes theories of learning, styles and strategies, motivation, and culture; as well as an introduction to assessment, error analysis, communicative competence and theories of acquisition.

Ellis, Rod. *The Study of Second Language Acquisition.* Oxford: Oxford University Press, 1994.
- Provides an overview of second language acquisition: error analysis, acquisition orders, social factors, affective variables, individual differences, and the advantages and disadvantages of classroom instruction.

Krashen, Stephen. *The Power of Reading.* New York: McGraw-Hill, 1994.
- Updates Optimal Input Theory by incorporating the reading of authentic texts.

Liskin-Gasparro, Judith. *A Guide to Testing and Teaching for Oral Proficiency.* Boston, MA: Heinle, 1990.
- Oral proficiency through interview techniques and speech samples.

III. Technology-Enhanced Instruction

Bush, Michael D., and Robert M. Terry, (Eds.), in conjunction with ACTFL. *Technology Enhanced Language Learning.* Lincolnwood, IL: National Textbook Co., 1997.
- Articles deal with the application of technology in the modern language classroom, including: computer-mediated communication, electronic discussions, hyper-media, the Internet, multimedia, videos, and the WWW.

Muyskens, Judith Ann. (Ed.). *New Ways of Learning and Teaching: Focus on Technology and Foreign Language Education.* Boston: Heinle and Heinle, 1997.
- Compilation of articles on the use of technology in the classroom; techniques for applying technology tools to the four skills and culture; also discusses implementation, teacher training, and language laboratories.

Steen, Douglas R., Mark R. Roddy, Derek Sheffield, and Michael Bryan Stout. *Teaching With the Internet: Putting Teachers before Technology.* Bellevue, WA: Resolution Business Press, Inc., 1995.
- Designed for K–12 teachers and based on educational theory, provides tips and strategies for using the Internet in and out of the classroom, cites specific case studies; topics include the Internet, e-mail, mailing lists, news-groups, the WWW, creating a Web page, and other research services.

IV. Teaching Native Speakers

Merino, Barbara J., Henry T. Trueba, and Fabián A. Samaniego. *Language and Culture in Learning: Teaching Spanish to Native Speakers of Spanish.* London, England: Falmer Press, 1993.

Rodríguez-Pino, Cecilia, and Daniel Villa. "A Student-Centered Spanish for Native Speakers Program: Theory, Curriculum Design and Outcome Assessment." In *Faces in a Crowd: The Individual Learner in Multisection Courses.* Edited by Carol A. Klee. American Association of University Supervisors Series. Boston, MA: Heinle, 1994.

Valdés, Guadalupe. "The Role of the Foreign Language Teaching Profession in Maintaining Non-English Languages in the United States." In *Northeast Conference Reports: Languages for a Multicultural World in Transition.* Edited by Heidi Byrnes. Lincolnwood, IL: National Textbook, 1992.

¡Ven conmigo!®

HOLT SPANISH

LEVEL 3

HOLT, RINEHART AND WINSTON

A Harcourt Classroom Education Company

Austin • New York • Orlando • Atlanta • San Francisco • Boston • Dallas • Toronto • London

ASSOCIATE DIRECTOR
Barbara Kristof

SENIOR EDITORS
Lynda Cortez
Janet Welsh Crossley
Jean Miller
Beatriz Malo Pojman
Paul Provence
Douglas Ward

MANAGING EDITOR
Chris Hiltenbrand

EDITORIAL STAFF
Hubert Bays
Nancy Bundy
Jeff Cole
Milagros Escamilla
Catherine Gavin
Martha Lashbrook
Carmen de la Morena
Zahydée Minnick
Jorge Muñoz
Todd Phillips
Brent Turnipseed
Todd Wolf
J. Elisabeth Wright
Mark Eells, *Editorial Coordinator*

EDITORIAL PERMISSIONS
Ann B. Farrar, *Senior Permissions Editor*
Yuri Muñoz, *Interpreter-Translator*

ART, DESIGN, & PHOTO
BOOK DESIGN
Richard Metzger, *Design Director*
Marta L. Kimball, *Design Manager*
Mary Wages, *Senior Designer*
Andrew Lankes
Alicia Sullivan
Ruth Limon

IMAGE SERVICES
Joe London, *Director*
Jeannie Taylor, *Photo Research Supervisor*
Diana Suthard
Michelle Rumpf, *Art Buyer Supervisor*
Coco Weir

DESIGN NEW MEDIA
Susan Michael, *Design Director*
Amy Shank, *Design Manager*
Kimberly Cammerata, *Design Manager*
Czeslaw Sornat, *Senior Designer*
Grant Davidson

MEDIA DESIGN
Curtis Riker, *Design Director*
Richard Chavez

GRAPHIC SERVICES
Kristen Darby, *Manager*
Linda Wilbourn
Jane Dixon
Dean Hsieh

COVER DESIGN
Richard Metzger, *Design Director*
Candace Moore, *Senior Designer*

PRODUCTION
Amber McCormick, *Production Supervisor*

MANUFACTURING
Shirley Cantrell, *Supervisor, Inventory & Manufacturing*
Deborah Wisdom, *Senior Inventory Analyst*

NEW MEDIA
Jessica Bega, *Senior Project Manager*
Elizabeth Kline, *Senior Project Manager*

VIDEO PRODUCTION
Video materials produced by Edge Productions, Inc., Aiken, S.C.

COVER PHOTOGRAPHY CREDITS

FRONT COVER: bkgd, Mireille Vautier/Woodfin Camp & Associates; teens, Steve Ewert/HRW Photo.

BACK COVER: Rob Crandall/Stock Boston; frame, © 1998 Image Farm Inc.

Acknowledgments appear on page R106, which is an extension of the copyright page.

¡VEN CONMIGO! is a trademark licensed to Holt, Rinehart and Winston registered in the United States of America and/or other jurisdictions.

Printed in the United States of America

ISBN 0-03-056592-8

1 2 3 4 5 6 7 032 06 05 04 03 02

AUTHORS

Nancy A. Humbach
Miami University
Oxford, Ohio
Ms. Humbach collaborated in the development of the scope and sequence and created activities.

Dr. Oscar Ozete
University of Southern Indiana
Evansville, Indiana
Dr. Ozete collaborated in the development of the scope and sequence and wrote grammar explanations.

CONTRIBUTING WRITERS

Kristin Boyer
McPherson, KS
Ms. Boyer wrote activities for several chapters.

Jean R. Miller
The University of Texas at Austin
Ms. Miller wrote activities for several chapters.

Abby Kanter
Dwight Englewood High School
Englewood, NJ
Ms. Kanter wrote the material for **De antemano** and **¡Adelante!** for several chapters.

Corliss Figueroa
Orlando, FL
Ms. Figueroa wrote activities for several chapters.

Susan Peterson
The Ohio State University
Columbus, OH
Mrs. Peterson was responsible for developing reading activities.

Barbara Sawhill
Noble and Greenough School
Dedham, MA
Ms. Sawhill wrote activities for several chapters.

CONSULTANTS

John DeMado
John DeMado Language Seminars, Inc.
Washington, CT

Dr. Ingeborg R. McCoy
Southwest Texas State University
San Marcos, TX

Jo Anne S. Wilson
J. Wilson Associates
Glen Arbor, MI

REVIEWERS

These educators reviewed one or more chapters of the Pupil's Edition.

Silvia Alemany
Native speaker reviewer
Austin, TX

O. Lynn Bolton
Nathan Hale High School
West Allis, WI

Juanita Carfora
Central Regional High School
Bayville, NJ

Renato Cervantes
Pacific High School
San Bernadino, CA

Dr. Lynn Cortina
North Miami High School
North Miami, FL

Dr. Rodolfo Cortina
Florida International University
Miami, FL

Lucila Dorsett
Native speaker reviewer
Round Rock, TX

Dr. Barbara González-Pino
The University of Texas at San Antonio

Dr. C. Gail Guntermann
Arizona State University
Tempe, AZ

Dr. Audrey Heining-Boynton
The University of North Carolina at Chapel Hill

Dr. Dianne Hobbs
Virginia Polytechnic Institute and State University
Blacksburg, VA

Rose Kent
Finneytown High School
Cincinnati, OH

Stephen Levy
Roslyn Public Schools
Roslyn, NY

Miranda Manners
Jordan High School
Los Angeles, CA

Dr. Cristóbal Pera
The University of Texas at Austin

Dr. Francisco Perea
Native speaker reviewer
Austin, TX

John Piermani
Carlisle High School
Carlisle, PA

Edward Quijada
Native speaker reviewer

Carmen Reyes
Jonesboro High School
Jonesboro, GA

Dr. Yolanda Russinovich Solé
The University of Texas at Austin

Carol A. Villalobos
Hazelwood Central High School
St. Louis, MO

Dora Villani
John F. Kennedy High School
New York City, NY

Isabel de Weil
Native speaker reviewer
Miami, FL

FIELD TEST PARTICIPANTS

We express our appreciation to the teachers and students who participated in the field.

Bill Braden
South Junior High School
Boise, ID

Paula Critchlow
Indian Hills Middle School
Sandy, UT

Frances Cutter
Convent of the Visitation School
St. Paul, MN

Carlos Fernández
Sandy Creek High School
Tyrone, GA

Jan Holland
Lovejoy High School
Lovejoy, GA

Gloria Holmstrom
Emerson Junior High School
Yonkers, NY

Nancy Holmes
Marian Catholic High School
Chicago Heights, IL

K. A. Lagana
Ponus Ridge Middle School
Norwalk, CT

Michelle Mistric
Iowa High School
Iowa, LA

Rubén Moreno
Aycock Middle School
Greensboro, NC

Maureen Nelligan
Marian Catholic High School
Chicago Heights, IL

Fred Pratt
San Marcos High School
San Marcos, TX

Regina Salvi
Museum Junior High School
Yonkers, NY

Lorraine Walsh
Lincoln Southeast High School
Lincoln, NE

TO THE STUDENT

Some people have the opportunity to learn a new language by living in another country.
Most of us, however, begin learning another language and getting acquainted with a foreign
culture in a classroom with the help of a teacher, classmates, and a textbook.
To use your book effectively, you need to know how it works.

¡Ven conmigo! *(Come along!)* is organized to help you learn Spanish and become familiar
with the cultures of people who speak Spanish. There are six Location Openers and
twelve chapters.

Location Opener Six four-page
photo essays called Location
Openers introduce different
Spanish-speaking places. You can
also see these locations on video
and on CD-ROM.

Chapter Opener The Chapter
Opener pages tell you the chapter
theme and goals.

De antemano *(Getting started)*
and **¡Adelante!** *(Moving ahead)*
show you Spanish-speaking
people in real-life situations, as
well as stories and legends from
the Spanish-speaking world.
These features model the
language you'll learn in the
chapter.

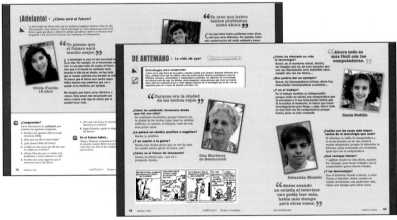

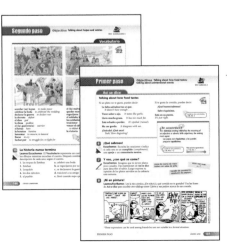

Primer and **Segundo paso** *(First and Second part)*
The chapter is divided into two sections called **Pasos**.
Within the **Paso** are **Así se dice** *(Here's how you say it)*
boxes that contain the Spanish expressions you'll need
to communicate and **Vocabulario** and **Gramática/Nota
gramatical** boxes that give you the Spanish words and
grammatical structures you'll need to know. Activities in
each **Paso** enable you to develop your skills in listening,
reading, speaking, and writing.

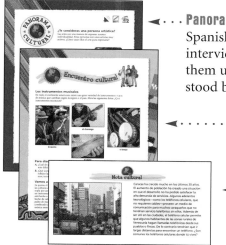

Panorama cultural *(Cultural panorama)* On this page are interviews with Spanish-speaking people from around the world. You can watch these interviews on video or listen to them on audio CD. You can also watch them using the *CD-ROM Tutor;* then check to see how well you understood by answering some questions about what the people say.

Encuentro cultural *(Cultural encounter)* This section, found in six of the chapters, gives you a firsthand encounter with some aspect of a Spanish-speaking culture.

Nota cultural *(Culture note)* In each chapter, there are notes with more information about the cultures of Spanish-speaking people.

Vamos a leer *(Let's read)* The reading section follows the two **Pasos.** The selections are related to the chapter themes and will help you develop your reading skills in Spanish.

Vamos a escribir *(Let's write)* will develop your writing skills. Each chapter will guide you to write a composition related to the themes of the chapter.

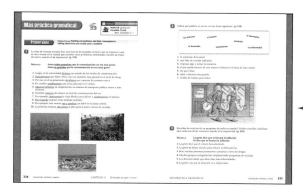

Más práctica gramatical *(Additional grammar practice)* You will find four pages of activities that provide additional practice with the grammar concepts you learned in the chapter.

Repaso *(Review)* The activities on these pages practice what you've learned in the chapter and help you improve your listening, reading, and communication skills. You'll also review what you've learned about culture.

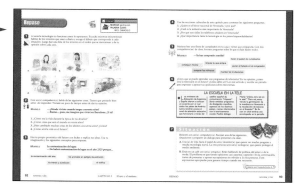

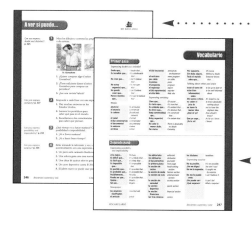

A ver si puedo... *(Let's see if I can . . .)* This page at the end of each chapter contains a series of questions and short activities to help you see if you've achieved the chapter goals.

Vocabulario *(Vocabulary)* In the Spanish-English vocabulary list on the last page of the chapter, the words are grouped by **Paso.** These words and expressions will be on the quizzes and tests.

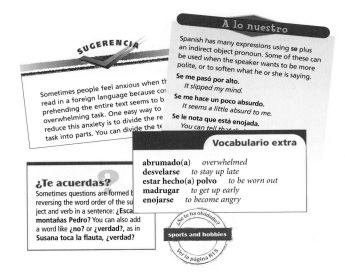

SUGERENCIA

Sometimes people feel anxious when th...
read in a foreign language because co...
prehending the entire text seems to b...
overwhelming task. One easy way to...
reduce this anxiety is to divide the re...
task into parts. You can divide the te...

A lo nuestro

Spanish has many expressions using **se** plus an indirect object pronoun. Some of these can be used when the speaker wants to be more polite, or to soften what he or she is saying.

Se me pasó por alto.
It slipped my mind.

Se me hace un poco absurdo.
It seems a little absurd to me.

Se le nota que está enojada.
You can tell that sh...

Vocabulario extra

abrumado(a)	*overwhelmed*
desvelarse	*to stay up late*
estar hecho(a) polvo	*to be worn out*
madrugar	*to get up early*
enojarse	*to become angry*

¿Se te ha olvidado?
sports and hobbies
Ver la página R15

¿Te acuerdas?
Sometimes questions are formed b...
reversing the word order of the su...
ject and verb in a sentence: ¿Esca...
montañas Pedro? You can also add
a word like ¿**no?** or ¿**verdad?**, as in
Susana toca la flauta, ¿verdad?

You'll also find special features in each chapter that provide extra tips and reminders.

Sugerencia *(Suggestion)* offers study hints to help you succeed in a foreign language class.

¿Te acuerdas? *(Do you remember?)* reminds you of expressions, grammar, and vocabulary you may have forgotten.

A lo nuestro *(Our way)* gives you additional expressions to add more color to your speech.

Vocabulario extra *(Extra vocabulary)* lists extra words you might find helpful. These words will not appear on the quizzes and tests unless your teacher chooses to include them.

¿Se te ha olvidado? *(Have you forgotten?)* tells you where you can look up grammar or vocabulary you may have forgotten.

You'll also find Spanish-English and English-Spanish vocabulary lists at the end of the book. The words you'll need to know for the quizzes and tests are in boldface type.

At the end of your book, you'll find more helpful material, such as:
- a summary of the expressions you'll learn in the **Así se dice** boxes
- a summary of the grammar you'll study
- additional vocabulary words you might want to use
- a grammar index to help you find where structures are presented.

¡Ven conmigo! Come along on an exciting trip to new cultures and a new language.

¡Buen viaje!

Explanation of Icons in *¡Ven conmigo!*

Throughout ¡Ven conmigo!, you'll see these symbols, or icons, next to activities and presentations. The following key will help you understand them.

 Video Whenever this icon appears, you'll know there is a related segment in the *¡Ven conmigo! Video Program.*

 Listening Activities This icon indicates a listening activity.

 Pair Work/Group Work Activities Activities with these icons are to be completed with a partner or with a small group of classmates.

 Writing Activities You'll see this icon next to writing activities.

 CD-ROM Activities Whenever this icon appears, you'll know there is a related activity on the *¡Ven conmigo! Interactive CD-ROM Tutor.*

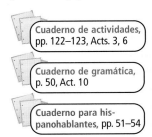

Cuaderno de actividades,
pp. 122–123, Acts. 3, 6

Cuaderno de gramática,
p. 50, Act. 10

Cuaderno para hispanohablantes, pp. 51–54

Más práctica gramatical,
pp. 334–335, Acts. 4–6

Practice Activities These icons tell you which activities from the *Cuaderno de actividades, Cuaderno de gramática,* and *Cuaderno para hispanohablantes* practice the material presented.

Más práctica gramatical This reference tells you where you can find related additional grammar practice in the review section of the chapter.

 Internet Activities This icon provides the keyword you'll need to access related online activities at **go.hrw.com.**

¡Ven conmigo!

Contents

Come along—to a world of new experiences!

¡Ven conmigo! offers you the opportunity to learn the language spoken by millions of people in the many Spanish-speaking countries around the world. Let's find out about the countries, the people, and the Spanish language.

¡VEN CONMIGO A

La Coruña!

LOCATION FOR CAPÍTULOS 1, 2 1

CAPÍTULO 1

¡Qué bien lo pasé este verano! 4

CAPÍTULO 2

Por una vida sana.....32

¡VEN CONMIGO A

Caracas!

LOCATION FOR CAPÍTULOS 3, 4.....62

CAPÍTULO 3

El ayer y el mañana.....66

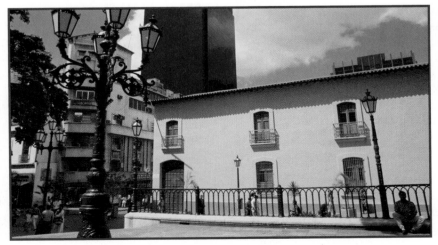

CAPÍTULO 4

Alrededor de la mesa 96

Guadalajara!

CAPÍTULO 5

Nuestras leyendas 128

CAPÍTULO 6

El arte y la música 156

CAPÍTULO 7

Dime con quién andas.....190

CAPÍTULO 8

Los medios de comunicación.....220

Nueva York!

CAPÍTULO 9

Las apariencias engañan.....252

CAPÍTULO 10

La riqueza cultural 280

¡VEN CONMIGO A

Costa Rica!

CAPÍTULO 11

El mundo en que vivimos.....314

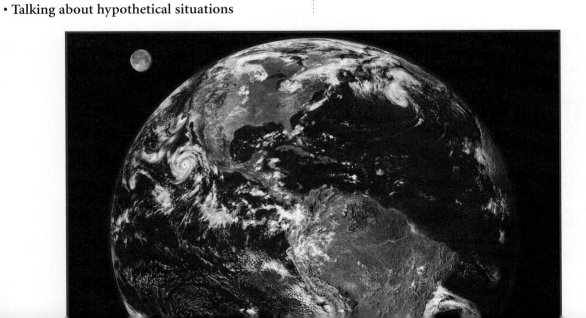

CAPÍTULO 12

Mis planes para el futuro.....342

Cultural References

Page numbers referring to material in the Pupil's Edition appear in regular type.
For material located in the Annotated Teacher's Edition, page numbers appear in boldface type.

La Península Ibérica

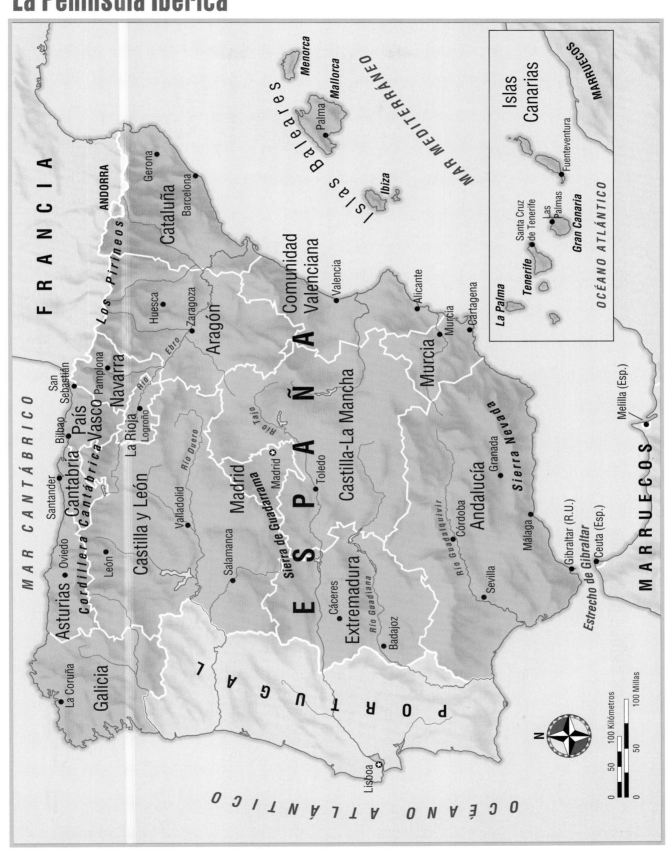

FRANCIA

ANDORRA

MAR CANTÁBRICO

Los Pirineos

Cataluña

Gerona

Barcelona

Huesca

Zaragoza

Aragón

San Sebastián

Bilbao

Santander

País Vasco

Pamplona

Navarra

Cordillera Cantábrica

La Rioja

Logroño

Río Ebro

Río Duero

Oviedo

Asturias

Cantabria

León

Castilla y León

Valladolid

Salamanca

Galicia

La Coruña

Comunidad Valenciana

Valencia

Alicante

Río Tajo

Madrid

Sierra de Guadarrama

ESPAÑA

Toledo

Castilla-La Mancha

Murcia

Cartagena

Murcia

Cáceres

Extremadura

Badajoz

Río Guadiana

Córdoba

Andalucía

Granada

Sierra Nevada

Río Guadalquivir

Sevilla

Málaga

Gibraltar (R.U.)

Estrecho de Gibraltar

Ceuta (Esp.)

MARRUECOS

Melilla (Esp.)

PORTUGAL

Lisboa

OCÉANO ATLÁNTICO

Islas Baleares

MAR MEDITERRÁNEO

Menorca

Mallorca

Palma

Ibiza

Islas Canarias

La Palma

Tenerife

Santa Cruz de Tenerife

Las Palmas

Gran Canaria

Fuerteventura

MARRUECOS

OCÉANO ATLÁNTICO

N

100 Kilómetros

50

100 Millas

50

0

0

América Central y las Antillas

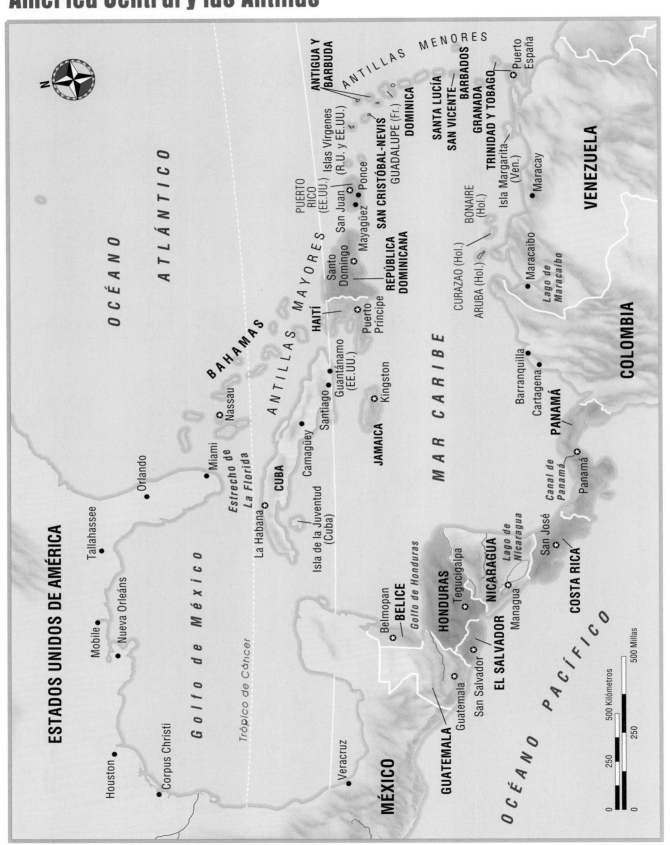

ANTILLAS MENORES

ESTADOS UNIDOS DE AMÉRICA

OCÉANO ATLÁNTICO

Houston
Corpus Christi
Mobile
Nueva Orleáns
Tallahassee
Orlando
Miami

Golfo de México

Trópico de Cáncer

MÉXICO

Veracruz

Estrecho de La Florida

La Habana
Isla de la Juventud (Cuba)
CUBA
Camagüey
Santiago

BAHAMAS
Nassau

ANTILLAS MAYORES

Guantánamo (EE.UU.)
Kingston
JAMAICA

HAITÍ
Puerto Príncipe

Santo Domingo
REPÚBLICA DOMINICANA

PUERTO RICO (EE.UU.)
San Juan
Mayagüez
Ponce
Islas Vírgenes (R.U. y EE.UU.)
SAN CRISTÓBAL-NEVIS
GUADALUPE (Fr.)
DOMINICA

ANTIGUA Y BARBUDA

SANTA LUCÍA
SAN VICENTE
BARBADOS
GRANADA
TRINIDAD Y TOBAGO

Puerto España
Maracay
Isla Margarita (Ven.)

BONAIRE (Hol.)
CURAZAO (Hol.)
ARUBA (Hol.)

Maracaibo
Lago de Maracaibo

VENEZUELA

COLOMBIA

MAR CARIBE

Barranquilla
Cartagena

PANAMÁ
Panamá
Canal de Panamá

GUATEMALA
Guatemala
San Salvador
EL SALVADOR

BELICE
Belmopan
Golfo de Honduras

HONDURAS
Tegucigalpa

NICARAGUA
Managua
Lago de Nicaragua

COSTA RICA
San José

OCÉANO PACÍFICO

500 Millas
500 Kilómetros
250
250
0
0

México

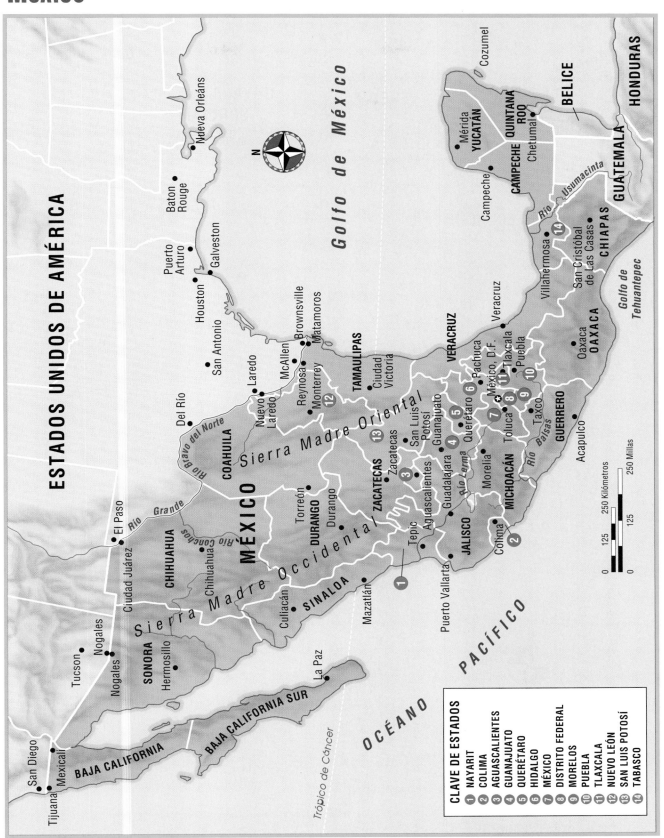

ESTADOS UNIDOS DE AMÉRICA

Nueva Orleáns

Baton Rouge

Galveston

Puerto Arturo

Houston

San Antonio

Brownsville
Matamoros

Laredo
McAllen
Nuevo Laredo
Reynosa
Monterrey

Ciudad Victoria

Del Río

TAMAULIPAS

VERACRUZ

Golfo de México

N

Cozumel

Mérida
YUCATÁN

Chetumal

Campeche
CAMPECHE

QUINTANA
ROO

BELICE

HONDURAS

Río Usumacinta

Villahermosa

San Cristóbal
de Las Casas

GUATEMALA

CHIAPAS

Golfo de
Tehuantepec

Pachuca
México, D.F.
Veracruz

Tlaxcala
Puebla

Oaxaca
OAXACA

COAHUILA

Sierra Madre Oriental

Río Bravo del Norte

MÉXICO

San Luis
Potosí
Guanajuato

Querétaro

Toluca

Taxco

GUERRERO

Acapulco

El Paso

Ciudad Juárez

Río Grande

Río Conchos

Chihuahua

CHIHUAHUA

Torreón

Durango

DURANGO

Zacatecas
ZACATECAS

Aguascalientes

Guadalajara

Río Lerma

JALISCO

Morelia

MICHOACÁN

Río Balsas

Tucson

Nogales
Nogales

SONORA

Hermosillo

Culiacán

SINALOA

Tepic

Colima

Mazatlán

Puerto Vallarta

PACÍFICO

Trópico de Cáncer

La Paz

San Diego

Tijuana
Mexicali

BAJA CALIFORNIA

BAJA CALIFORNIA SUR

OCÉANO

250 Kilómetros

250 Millas

0   125   250

0   125   250

CLAVE DE ESTADOS

1 NAYARIT
2 COLIMA
3 AGUASCALIENTES
4 GUANAJUATO
5 QUERÉTARO
6 HIDALGO
7 MÉXICO
8 DISTRITO FEDERAL
9 MORELOS
10 PUEBLA
11 TLAXCALA
12 NUEVO LEÓN
13 SAN LUIS POTOSÍ
14 TABASCO

Sierra Madre Occidental

T75

América del Sur

MAR DE LAS ANTILLAS

OCÉANO

ATLÁNTICO

América Central

Cartagena
Maracaibo
Caracas
VENEZUELA
Orinoco
GUYANA
SURINAM
Medellín
Ciudad
Bolívar
Georgetown
Cayena
COLOMBIA
Paramaribo
GUAYANA
FRANCESA
Bogotá
Río Putumayo
Cordillera
Ecuador
Islas
Galápagos
(Ecuador)
Quito
Río
Manaus
Belén
ECUADOR
Amazonas
Guayaquil
Cuenca
de
los
BRASIL
Recife
PERÚ
Andes
Salvador
Lima
Cuzco
Brasilia
Lago
Titicaca
La Paz
BOLIVIA
Sucre
OCÉANO
Cordillera
de
los
PARAGUAY
Paraná
Río de Janeiro
San Pablo
Asunción
Trópico de Capricornio
Río
Tucumán
CHILE
PACÍFICO
ARGENTINA
Córdoba
URUGUAY
Valparaíso
Mendoza
Montevideo
Santiago
Buenos Aires
Río de la Plata
N
OCÉANO
Bariloche
ATLÁNTICO
Cordillera de los
0   500   1.000 Kilómetros
0   500   1.000 Millas
Andes
Estrecho de Magallanes
Islas
Malvinas
(R.U.)
Punta Arenas
Tierra del Fuego
Cabo de
Hornos

Estados Unidos de América

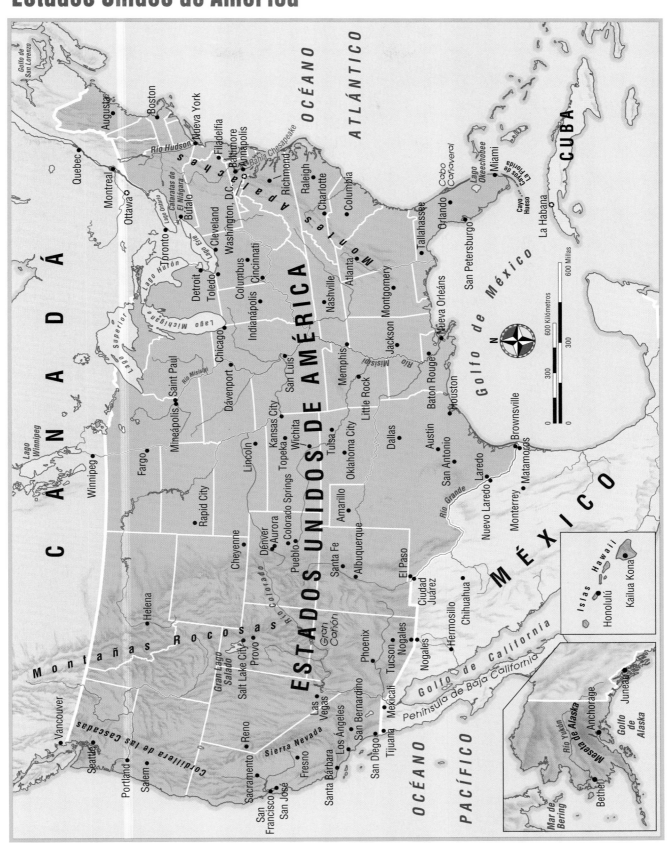

CANADÁ

OCÉANO ATLÁNTICO

Golfo de San Lorenzo

Quebec
Montreal
Ottawa
Toronto
Augusta
Boston
Nueva York
Filadelfia
Baltimore
Annapolis
Washington, D.C.
Río Hudson
Cataratas de El Niágara
Buffalo
Cleveland
Lago Ontario
Lago Erie
Bahía Chesapeake
Richmond
Raleigh
Charlotte
Columbia

Lago Superior
Lago Michigan
Lago Hurón
Detroit
Toledo
Columbus
Cincinnati
Indianápolis
Chicago
Saint Paul
Mineápolis
Dávenport
Río Misisipi

Montes Apalaches

ESTADOS UNIDOS DE AMÉRICA

Nashville
Atlanta
Montgomery
Jackson
Memphis
Little Rock
Río Misisipi

Tallahassee
Orlando
Cabo Cañaveral
Lago Okeechobee
Miami
Cayos de la Florida
Cayo Hueso

CUBA
La Habana
San Petersburgo

Nueva Orleáns
Baton Rouge
Houston

Golfo de México

Winnipeg
Lago Winnipeg
Fargo
Rapid City
Lincoln
Kansas City
Topeka
Wichita
Tulsa
Oklahoma City
Amarillo
Colorado Springs
Pueblo
Dénver
Aurora
Cheyenne
San Luis
Dallas
Austin
San Antonio
Laredo
Nuevo Laredo
Brownsville
Matamoros
Monterrey

MÉXICO

N
600 Kilómetros
600 Millas
300
300
0
0

Helena
Montañas Rocosas
Gran Lago Salado
Salt Lake City
Provo
Río Colorado
Gran Cañón
Santa Fe
Albuquerque
El Paso
Ciudad Juárez
Chihuahua
Hermosillo
Phoenix
Tucson
Nogales
Nogales
Mexicali
Tijuana
San Diego

Islas Hawaii
Honolulú
Kailua Kona

Vancouver
Seattle
Portland
Salem
Cordillera de las Cascadas
Sierra Nevada
Reno
Sacramento
San Francisco
San José
Fresno
Santa Bárbara
Los Ángeles
San Bernardino
Las Vegas

Golfo de California
Península de Baja California

OCÉANO PACÍFICO

Río Yukón
Meseta de Alaska
Anchorage
Juneau
Golfo de Alaska
Bethel
Mar de Bering

T77

El mundo

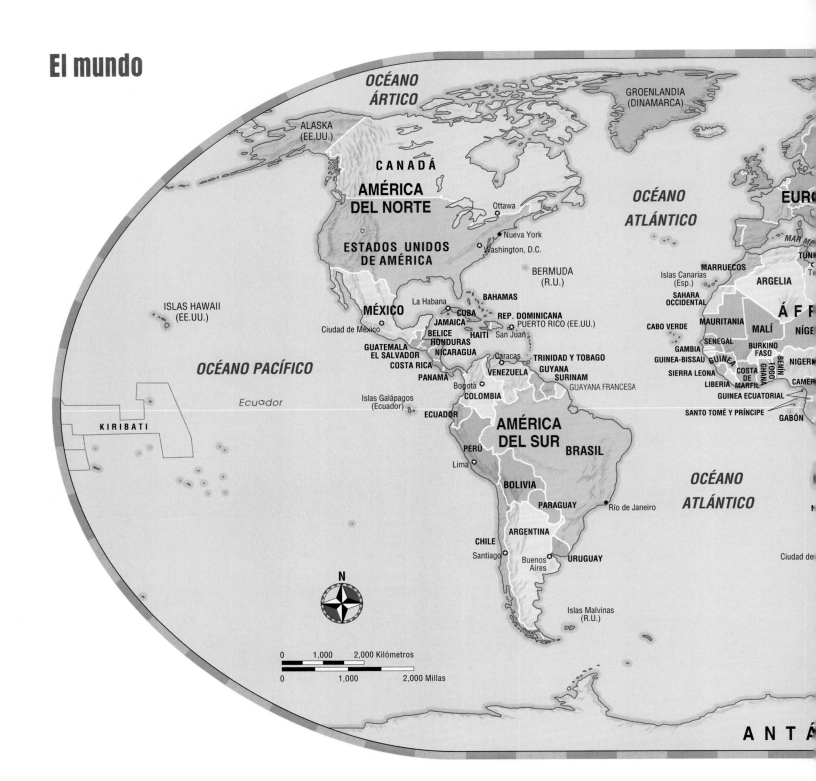

OCÉANO ÁRTICO

GROENLANDIA (DINAMARCA)

ALASKA (EE.UU.)

CANADÁ

AMÉRICA DEL NORTE

OCÉANO ATLÁNTICO

EURO

Ottawa

Nueva York

Washington, D.C.

ESTADOS UNIDOS DE AMÉRICA

BERMUDA (R.U.)

Islas Canarias (Esp.)

MAR ME

TÚN

MARRUECOS

ARGELIA

ISLAS HAWAII (EE.UU.)

MÉXICO

La Habana

BAHAMAS

SAHARA OCCIDENTAL

ÁFR

Ciudad de México

CUBA

REP. DOMINICANA

PUERTO RICO (EE.UU.)

CABO VERDE

MAURITANIA

MALÍ

NÍGE

JAMAICA

BELICE

HAITÍ

San Juan

GAMBIA

SENEGAL

BURKINO FASO

GUATEMALA

HONDURAS

GUINEA-BISSAU

GUINEA

BENÍN

TOGO

NIGER

EL SALVADOR

NICARAGUA

SIERRA LEONA

COSTA DE MARFIL

GHANA

OCÉANO PACÍFICO

COSTA RICA

Caracas

TRINIDAD Y TOBAGO

LIBERIA

CAMER

PANAMÁ

VENEZUELA

GUYANA

SURINAM

GUINEA ECUATORIAL

Bogotá

GUAYANA FRANCESA

SANTO TOMÉ Y PRÍNCIPE

GABÓN

Ecuador

Islas Galápagos (Ecuador)

COLOMBIA

ECUADOR

AMÉRICA DEL SUR

KIRIBATI

PERÚ

BRASIL

Lima

BOLIVIA

OCÉANO ATLÁNTICO

PARAGUAY

Río de Janeiro

ARGENTINA

CHILE

Santiago

Buenos Aires

URUGUAY

Ciudad de

N

Islas Malvinas (R.U.)

0   1,000   2,000 Kilómetros

0   1,000   2,000 Millas

ANTÁ

RUSIA

KAZAJSTÁN

MONGOLIA

GEORGIA
ARMENIA

ASIA

Pekín

COREA
DEL NORTE
Seúl
COREA
DEL SUR

JAPÓN
Tokio

UZBEKISTÁN
TURKMENISTÁN
AZERBAIYÁN
ara
JRQUÍA
ANO SIRIA
Teherán
IRAQ
nasco
Bagdad
JORDANIA
ARABIA
SAUDITA
BAHREIN
UNIÓN DE
EMIRATOS
ÁRABES
OMÁN

KIRGUIZISTÁN
TAJIKISTÁN
AFGANISTÁN
IRÁN
KUWAIT
PAKISTÁN
QATAR

CHINA

BHUTÁN

Nueva
Delhi
NEPAL

INDIA

BANGLADESH

MYANMAR

OCÉANO PACÍFICO

Taipei
TAIWAN

DÁN
ERITREA
YEMEN
YIBUTI

ETIOPÍA

SOMALIA

LAOS

TAILANDIA
CAMBOYA

VIETNAM

SRI
LANKA

Manila
FILIPINAS

GUAM
(EE.UU.)

ANDA
KENIA
Nairobi

Ecuador

MALASIA

KIRIBATI

SEYCHELLES

NAURÚ

TANZANIA

OCÉANO
ÍNDICO

INDONESIA

PAPÚA
NUEVA GUINEA

ISLAS
SALOMÓN

ISLAS
TUVALU

MALAWI
COMORES

ABWE
MADAGASCAR
MAURICIO

VANUATU

NUEVA
CALEDONIA
(Fr.)

ISLAS
FIDJI

MOZAMBIQUE

SWAZILANDIA
LESOTHO

AUSTRALIA

Canberra

Wellington

NUEVA
ZELANDA

PAÍS	CAPITAL
1 REPÚBLICA CHECA	Praga
2 REPÚBLICA ESLOVACA	Bratislava
3 ESLOVENIA	Liubliana
4 CROACIA	Zagreb
5 BOSNIA Y HERZEGOVINA	Sarajevo
6 MACEDONIA	Skopje
7 YUGOSLAVIA	Belgrado
8 LITUANIA	Vilna
9 LETONIA	Riga
10 ESTONIA	Tallin
11 LIECHTENSTEIN	Vaduz
12 LUXEMBURGO	Luxemburgo

Europa

OCÉANO ÁRTICO

ISLANDIA
Reikiavik

NORUEGA

SUECIA

FINLANDIA

Helsinki

Oslo
Estocolmo

San Petersburgo

RUSIA

10

9

Moscú

REINO
UNIDO

DINAMARCA
Copenhague

8

Minsk

Dublín

HOLANDA
Ámsterdam

Varsovia

BIELORRUSIA

Londres
Berlín

ALEMANIA

POLONIA

Kiev

IRLANDA

BÉLGICA
Bruselas

1

UCRANIA
Kishinev

París

12

Viena

2

OCÉANO
ATLÁNTICO

SUIZA

11

AUSTRIA HUNGRÍA

MOLDAVIA

FRANCIA

Berna

3

RUMANIA

Bucarest

4

5

7

Sofía

PORTUGAL

Madrid

ANDORRA

Roma

Tirana

6

BULGARIA

MAR NEGRO

Lisboa

ESPAÑA

ITALIA

ALBANIA

Atenas

TURQUÍA

MAR MEDITERRÁNEO

GRECIA

MALTA

CHIPRE

D A

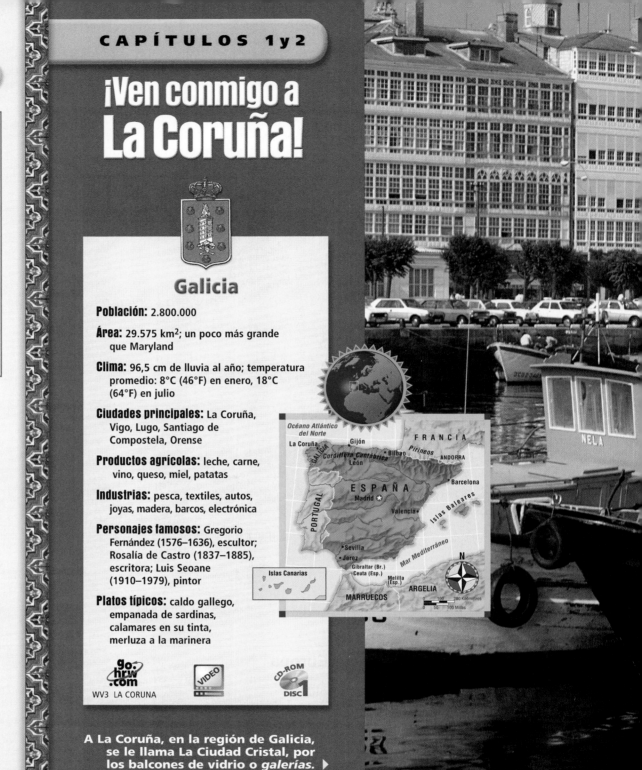

¡Ven conmigo a La Coruña!

Teaching Resources
pp. T80–3

PRINT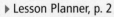
▸ Lesson Planner, p. 2
▸ Video Guide, pp. 1–2

MEDIA
▸ One-Stop Planner
▸ Video Program, Videocassette 1, 01:10–02:41
▸ Interactive CD-ROM Tutor, Disc 1
▸ Map Transparency 1

 go.hrw.com
WV3 LA CORUNA

 Using the Almanac and Map

Terms in the Almanac

- **Industrias:** Galicia's long coastline, **rías** *(estuaries)*, and inland waterways have made fishing a principal industry of the region. Most restaurants offer a wide array of local seafood.

- **Personajes famosos:** The works of Baroque sculptor Gregorio Fernández are seen in convents and cathedrals around Spain. Rosalía de Castro is perhaps Galicia's most famous poet. Her poems, written in both Spanish and Galician, span her life experiences.

- **Platos típicos: caldo gallego:** a soup of **grelos** (a green similar to collard greens), potatoes, chorizo sausage, pork, and beef; **empanada de sardinas:** a thin pie of sardines and red bell peppers; **calamares en su tinta:** whole squid cooked in a squid ink broth flavored with onions; **merluza a la marinera:** hake in a sauce of tomatoes, onions, and olive oil.

Galicia

Población: 2.800.000

Área: 29.575 km²; un poco más grande que Maryland

Clima: 96,5 cm de lluvia al año; temperatura promedio: 8°C (46°F) en enero, 18°C (64°F) en julio

Ciudades principales: La Coruña, Vigo, Lugo, Santiago de Compostela, Orense

Productos agrícolas: leche, carne, vino, queso, miel, patatas

Industrias: pesca, textiles, autos, joyas, madera, barcos, electrónica

Personajes famosos: Gregorio Fernández (1576–1636), escultor; Rosalía de Castro (1837–1885), escritora; Luis Seoane (1910–1979), pintor

Platos típicos: caldo gallego, empanada de sardinas, calamares en su tinta, merluza a la marinera

go.hrw.com
WV3 LA CORUNA

A La Coruña, en la región de Galicia, se le llama La Ciudad Cristal, por los balcones de vidrio o *galerías.* ▸

Cultures and Communities

 Culture Note
Galicia boasts many prominent contemporary and historical figures. José de San Martín (founding father of Argentina), Simón Bolívar (liberator of Spanish-speaking South America), Gabriel García Márquez (Colombian winner of the Nobel Prize for Literature), and Carlos Saavedra Lamas (winner of the Nobel Peace Prize) are all of Galician descent.

Background Information
- La Coruña, a major port, is built on a small peninsula surrounded by gently rolling hills and forests of pine and eucalyptus.
- The **galerías** or **miradores** seen in the photo are floor-to-ceiling, glassed-in porches that insulate the waterfront homes.

MAPQUEST.COM

**HRW
Atlas Interactivo
Mundial**

Have students use the interactive atlas at **go.hrw.com** to find out more about the geography of Galicia and complete the Map Activities below.

Map Activities

Have students use the map on page T73 (Pupil's Edition page xxiii) to identify Galicia's natural and political boundaries. (the Atlantic Ocean to the north and west, Portugal to the south, Asturias and Castilla y León to the east) You may want to have them find a detailed map of Galicia in an atlas or guidebook and locate its major cities, **rías,** and rivers.

CNNenEspañol.com

Have students check the **CNN en español** Web site for news on Galicia. The **CNN en español** site is also a good source of timely, high-interest readings for Spanish students.

Connections and Comparisons

Geography Links

• Have students find Galicia on a world map (pages T78–T79; *Pupil's Edition* pages xxviii–xxix) and trace its latitude line (43°) to North America. Which cities have a similar latitude? (Concord, NH; Buffalo, NY; Grand Rapids, MI; Madison, WI; Sioux Falls, SD; Boise, ID; Coos Bay, OR)

• Have students search the Internet for information on the climate of Galicia and compare it with the climate of at least two regions in the United States at the same latitude. Also have them research the causes of the relatively mild climate of Western European coastal lands. (the Gulf Stream, warm ocean currents from the Gulf of Mexico)

Using the Photo Essay

1 La costa gallega The **Rías Bajas** of the northwest coast open to a jagged coastline that is often referred to as the **Costa de la Muerte.** Many annual festivals celebrate the coast's legendary history. One such festival features a re-enactment of the landing of the Vikings from a replica of a drakar ship.

2 Hermosa vista de la catedral de Santiago Tell students that **Santiago** means Saint James and that the name **Compostela** is believed to be derived from the Latin *campus stellae,* which means *field of the star.* St. James is the patron saint of Galicia. It is said that St. James preached in Spain and was later martyred in Jerusalem. His followers brought his body back to Spain and buried it somewhere in Galicia. Legend has it that when the shrine's whereabouts were revealed by a star centuries later, the city of Santiago de Compostela was built there. The cathedral of Santiago de Compostela is the best-known destination in Spain for Christian pilgrims from around the world.

3 El monumento más antiguo de La Coruña The five-story **Torre de Hércules** was first used as a lighthouse in the second century. Many renovations have been made to the weathered building over the years. The square tower of 242 stairs was redesigned and renovated in the 18th century.

Galicia

Con sus bonitas bahías y playas y la verdura de su paisaje montañoso, Galicia es una de las regiones más preciosas de toda España. Los romanos llamaron a Galicia *Finis Terrae*, el fin del mundo, porque era el punto más occidental de su imperio. Galicia le ofrece al visitante un fuerte contraste entre lo antiguo y lo moderno. Presenta al mismo tiempo un pasado céltico y romano y un amplio panorama de industrias y tecnologías modernas. Es un centro artístico de primera categoría. Galicia tiene algo para todos.

🖅 internet

go.hrw.com
MARCAR: go.hrw.com
PALABRA CLAVE:
WV3 LA CORUNA

1 La costa gallega
Galicia tiene 386 kilómetros de costa. Las rías de Galicia son como los fiordos de Noruega. Su belleza es extraordinaria.

2 Hermosa vista de la catedral de Santiago
Se dice que el Apóstol Santiago está enterrado en Santiago de Compostela. Durante la Edad Media muchos peregrinos de todas partes de Europa hacían el viaje a Santiago de Compostela a pie cada año. La catedral de Santiago existe desde el siglo XI, y hoy en día llegan muchos turistas para verla.

3 El monumento más antiguo de La Coruña
El faro de La Coruña, la Torre de Hércules, es el único faro romano en el mundo que todavía se usa. Hay tres leyendas sobre quién lo construyó: el Hércules de los mitos de Grecia y de Roma, el legendario jefe céltico Breogán o los romanos.

Cultures and Communities

Culture Note
Galicians celebrate their patron saint with an elaborate festival each year. The feast of St. James begins on July 25 and ends 10 days later. When the 25th falls on a Sunday, the whole year is declared a Holy Year, or **Año Santo.** During such years there are many special commemorative events celebrating the history of the pilgrimage and of the city.

Language Note
Tell students that Galician, or **gallego,** the regional language of Galicia, is spoken by about 85 percent of Galicians. Children study Galician in school from the second grade through high school. Galicians also speak Spanish, but a Spanish that has traces of **gallego.** Most street signs in Galicia are printed in both Spanish and Galician.

4 Presente y pasado se mezclan
La Plaza de María Pita en La Coruña es un hermoso ejemplo de cómo La Coruña combina elementos de lo antiguo y lo moderno.

5 Turismo náutico
El mar, que es tan importante para la economía de Galicia, también ofrece muchas oportunidades para el recreo. Galicia tiene algunos de los lugares más bonitos para los deportes acuáticos como el buceo y la vela ligera.

En los capítulos 1 y 2,

vas a conocer a algunas personas de Galicia. La larga historia de Galicia se refleja en su arquitectura, música, danza, literatura y en su lengua propia. Además del español, muchos gallegos también hablan el gallego, otro idioma derivado del latín. Aunque son de una región fuertemente tradicional, vas a ver que los gallegos tal vez no sean tan distintos de ti en sus maneras de pasar el tiempo y en sus actitudes hacia la salud.

6 La música céltica
El instrumento tradicional de Galicia es la gaita y el baile tradicional es la muñeira. Estas dos tradiciones muestran la influencia céltica. Los celtas poblaron esta región hace muchos siglos, mucho antes que los romanos.

4 Presente y pasado se mezclan The **Plaza de María Pita** is the site of the **Palacio Municipal,** an elaborate building with a wide, arcaded façade and three cupolas. The **Palacio,** built in the early 20th century, is quite new compared to others in the city—some date from the 12th century.

5 Turismo náutico Galicia's proximity to the sea makes it an ideal spot for those who love the outdoors. The region's coastal waters are the site of world-famous sailing regattas. Water-skiing is also popular. Galicia is widely known for its fishing and hunting and for its spas. People come from all over Europe to bask in the region's natural spas, many of which were first used by the Romans.

6 La música céltica Galician bagpipes **(gaita gallega)** are not unlike the Scottish bagpipes familiar to North American students. While the Highland pipes were developed as a military instrument in the 18th century, the Galician bagpipes are primarily used for folk music. Students may want to research the famous **gaitero gallego** Carlos Núñez, a master of Galician, Scottish, and Irish bagpipes.

Connections and Comparisons

Art Link
Tell students that the ornate façade of the cathedral of Saint James (photo 2) is an example of baroque architecture. Explain that baroque was an artistic style used widely in Europe from about 1550 until the early 1700s. Ask them to research the baroque style. (It is typified by ornate scrolls, curves, and other symmetrical ornamentation.)

Multicultural Link
The **Torre de Hércules** is a landmark of the city of La Coruña. Have students list famous towers around the world (Seattle, WA—Space Needle; Washington, D.C.—Washington Monument; Paris, France—Eiffel Tower; Pisa, Italy—Leaning Tower of Pisa) and have them research the history of one of them.

Capítulo 1: ¡Qué bien lo pasé este verano! *Review Chapter*

Chapter Overview

De antemano pp. 6–8	*Una carta de Amparo*

	FUNCTIONS	**GRAMMAR**	**VOCABULARY**	**RE-ENTRY**
Primer paso pp. 9–13	• Expressing interest, indifference, and displeasure, p. 9	• Present tense of stem-changing verbs, p. 11 • The present tense, p. 11 • The preterite tense, p. 12	• Sports and hobbies, p. 10	• Chapters 1 and 2 are a global review of *¡Ven conmigo!* Levels 1 and 2.

¡Adelante! pp. 14–15	*Una carta a Miguel*

Segundo paso pp. 16–18	• Asking for information, p. 16 • Describing yourself and others, p. 17	• Word order in questions, p. 16 • **saber** vs. **conocer**, p. 18 • Changing **o** and **y** before vowels, p. 18	• Describing people, p. 17	• Chapters 1 and 2 are a global review of *¡Ven conmigo!* Levels 1 and 2.

Vamos a leer pp. 20–22	**La tortuga** and **Biografía de Pablo Neruda**	**Reading Strategy:** Background knowledge

Vamos a escribir p. 23	**Tu pasatiempo favorito**	**Writing Strategy:** Know your audience

Más práctica gramatical	**pp. 24–27** **Primer paso,** pp. 24–25	**Segundo paso,** pp. 26–27

Review pp. 28–31	**Repaso,** pp. 28–29	**A ver si puedo...,** p. 30	**Vocabulario,** p. 31

CULTURE

- **Nota cultural,** Seafood in Galicia, p. 13
- **Realia,** Tira cómica, p. 13
- **Realia,** Tira cómica, p. 16
- **Panorama cultural, ¿Qué hiciste en las últimas vacaciones?,** p. 19

Capítulo 1: ¡Qué bien lo pasé este verano! **Review Chapter**
Chapter Resources

 **PRINT**

Lesson Planning

One-Stop Planner

Lesson Planner with Substitute Teacher

Lesson Plans, pp. 2–6, 65

Student Make-Up Assignments
- Make-Up Assignment Copying Masters, Chapter 1

Listening and Speaking

Listening Activities
- Student Response Forms for Listening Activities, pp. 3–5
- Additional Listening Activities 1-1 to 1-6, pp. 7–9
- Additional Listening Activities (song), p. 10
- Scripts and Answers, pp. 100–105

Video Guide
- Teaching Suggestions, pp. 3–5
- Activity Masters, pp. 6–8
- Scripts and Answers, pp. 86–88, 114

Activities for Communication
- Communicative Activities, pp. 1–4
- Realia and Teaching Suggestions, pp. 51–53
- Situation Cards, pp. 89–90

Reading and Writing

Reading Strategies and Skills Handbook, Chapter 1

¡Lee conmigo! 3, Chapter 1

Cuaderno de actividades, pp. 1–12

Grammar

Cuaderno de gramática, pp. 1–9

Grammar Tutor for Students of Spanish, Chapter 1

Assessment

Testing Program
- Grammar and Vocabulary Quizzes, **Paso** Quizzes, and Chapter Test, pp. 1–14
- Score Sheet, Scripts and Answers, pp. 15–21

Alternative Assessment Guide
- Portfolio Assessment, p. 16
- Performance Assessment, p. 30
- CD-ROM Assessment, p. 44

Student Make-Up Assignments
- Alternative Quizzes, Chapter 1

Standardized Assessment Tutor
- Reading, pp. 1–3
- Writing, p. 4
- Math, pp. 25–26

Native Speakers

Cuaderno para hispanohablantes, pp. 1–5

 **MEDIA**

 Online Activities
- Juegos interactivos
- Actividades Internet

 Video Program
- Videocassette 1
- Videocassette 5 (captioned version)

Audio Compact Discs
- Textbook Listening Activities, CD 1, Tracks 1–14
- Additional Listening Activities, CD 1, Tracks 19–25
- Assessment Items, CD 1, Tracks 15–18

 Interactive CD-ROM Tutor, Disc 1

 Teaching Transparencies
- Situations 1-1 to 1-2
- **Más práctica gramatical** Answers
- **Cuaderno de gramática** Answers

  One-Stop Planner CD-ROM

Use the **One-Stop Planner CD-ROM** with **Test Generator** to aid in lesson planning and pacing.

For each chapter, the **One-Stop Planner** includes:

- Editable lesson plans with direct links to teaching resources
- Printable worksheets from resource books
- Direct launches to the HRW Internet activities
- Video and audio segments
- Test Generator
- Clip Art for vocabulary items

Capítulo 1: ¡Qué bien lo pasé este verano!

Projects

TEACHER NOTE

Some activities suggested in the *Annotated Teacher's Edition* ask students to contact various people, businesses, and organizations in the community. It is advisable to first request parental permission and permission from the parties the students will be asked to contact.

When giving assignments that entail the disclosure of personal information, keep in mind that some students and their families may consider such matters private. You may want to give an alternative assignment in which students discuss a make-believe individual or family.

Itinerario

In this activity, students create a week-long itinerary for a group of Spanish exchange students.

MATERIALS

✂ **Students may need**
- Plain white paper
- Brochures or pictures of their city
- Scissors
- Glue or tape

SUGGESTED SEQUENCE

1. Tell students they are in charge of creating an itinerary for a group of Spanish high-school students visiting their city for a week during summer vacation. Their itineraries should include fun, useful information about their city.

2. Assign students to groups of three or four to work on each itinerary.

3. Students work together to write the itinerary in the form of a daily schedule. They should plan several activities, meals, and free times throughout each day.

4. When students have created the itinerary, they should copy it onto plain white paper and illustrate it with pictures from local brochures, personal pictures, or drawings.

GRADING THE PROJECT

Suggested point distribution: (total = 100 points)

Content	30
Language use	30
Creativity/Originality	20
Appearance	20

Games

¿Cómo te diré?

This game will help your students develop the skill of circumlocution. Explain that they will learn to paraphrase, use synonyms, and apply key phrases to communicate.

Materials To play this game, you will need index cards.

Preparation Make a list of related vocabulary words. Write one word on each index card. Arrange four desks so that two sets of partners face each other. Place the cards face down. On the board or on a transparency, write the following key phrases:

Es un(a) cosa, persona, animal que...

Es alto(a), bajo(a), viejo(a), nuevo(a).

Es parecido(a) a...

Es lo contrario de...

Es un lugar donde...

Tiene...

Está hecho de plástico, metal, madera, vidrio...

Se usa para...

Procedure Divide the class into two teams and appoint a scorekeeper and a timekeeper. Have two players from each team sit at the four desks. A player from Team A takes a card and shows it to one of the players from Team B. Using circumlocution, the Team A player describes the word to his or her partner without saying the word itself. If the partner guesses the word, Team A receives five points. If not, the Team B player gives a clue to his or her partner. If the partner guesses correctly, Team B receives four points. Play alternates between the two teams, with the points earned dropping by one after each incorrect guess. Announce the answer if no one guesses correctly.

COMMUNITY LINK

You might have students contact the local Chamber of Commerce to find out what sights and activities the organization recommends to Spanish-speaking visitors.

Storytelling

Mini-cuento

This story accompanies Teaching Transparency 1-1. The **mini-cuento** *can be told and retold in different formats, acted out, written as dictation, and read aloud to give students additional opportunities to practice all four skills. The following story tells about people at a hobbies and pastimes exhibition.*

¿Qué pasatiempo te gusta?

Muchas personas están muy emocionadas porque hoy empieza la Feria de los Deportes y los Pasatiempos. Lolita y Rosa tienen un grupo musical. Ellas son aficionadas a la música y pasaron el tiempo tocando la batería y el clarinete. Pedro también está loco por la música y le gustaría tocar el piano eléctrico. Fue con su maestro de música. Su maestro sabe que el piano más pequeño es mejor y que tiene mejor sonido. Pedro piensa comprarlo. Ernesto y Carlos son fanáticos del patinaje sobre ruedas. Ernesto ya está imaginando que va a invitar a sus amigos a patinar al parque esta tarde. En la feria hay también exhibiciones de tiras cómicas, sellos, equitación, fotografía, videojuegos, montañismo y buceo.

¡Es una exhibición muy interesante para todos!

Traditions

Rapa das bestas

Every summer for at least the last two hundred years, towns and villages around Galicia have celebrated the ritual of the **rapa das bestas,** or *horsesharing.* Wild Galician ponies (**caballos gallegos de monte**) are rounded up in the mountains and brought down to enclosures called **curros,** an activity referred to in **gallego** as **baixa das bestas.** Once enclosed in the **curros,** the ponies' manes are cut. The hair of the manes has traditionally been used for making brushes. Some of the horses are bought and sold, and the rest are set free again. Surrounding the **rapa das bestas** is a **romería,** or popular festival, as villagers and tourists alike celebrate one of the oldest Galician traditions. Ask students to learn more about this tradition, and research one other Galician festival such as the **Romería vikinga,** or the **Fiesta de María Pita.**

Receta

No trip to Galicia, and especially to Santiago de Compostela, would be complete without tasting the **tarta de Santiago.** *Its most outstanding feature is the cross of St. James, which is put on each* **tarta** *using a paper template and then sprinkling the top generously with powdered sugar. Santiago is the Spanish name for the apostle St. James, who is believed to be buried in a crypt under the main altar in the cathedral. The* **tarta de Santiago** *is eaten as a dessert in Galicia, but it is more like a tea cake.*

TARTA DE SANTIAGO

para 8 personas

4 huevos

1 taza de azúcar

la piel rallada de un limón

2 tazas de almendras finamente molidas (como harina)

mantequilla para untar el molde

azúcar en polvo, para espolvorear

un molde de tarta de 10" con fondo desprendible

Unte el molde con mantequilla y espolvoréelo con harina. Bata los huevos y el azúcar hasta que queden cremosos. Añada la piel de limón rallada y las almendras molidas. Ponga la mezcla en el molde y cocínela en un horno precalentado a 350° por 30–35 minutos. Deje enfriar la tarta. Quite los lados del molde. Ponga el patrón de la cruz de Santiago encima, espolvoree la tarta con el azúcar en polvo, quite el patrón y sírvala.

Technology

Video Program ....

Videocassette 1, Videocassette 5 (captioned version)
See Video Guide, pages 3–8.

Dramatic episode • ¿Qué hicisteis en México?
Javier and Sergio, two high school students from Seville, Spain, have just returned from Mexico, where they spent the summer. At an outdoor cafe, Javier's sister Zoraida is waiting for them, and she is dying to know more about their trip. Javier and Sergio describe their new Mexican friends, Carlos, Alejandra, and Irene. Javier really misses Alejandra but doesn't want anyone to know.

¿Qué hiciste en las últimas vacaciones?
Teenagers from various Spanish-speaking countries tell what they did during summer vacation.

Videoclips
- **Cantabria:** commercial promoting the region of Cantabria, Spain, as rich in nature and culture
- **La escalada deportiva:** minidocumentary about a rock-climbing competition in Spain. A Spanish rock climber explains how she trains for the sport.

Interactive CD-ROM Tutor ....

The **Interactive CD-ROM Tutor** contains videos, interactive games, and activities that provide students an opportunity to practice and review the material covered in Chapter 1.

Activity	Activity Type	Pupil's Edition Page
1. Así se dice	¿Cuál es?	p. 9
2. Gramática	¿Qué falta?	p. 11
3. Gramática	¡Atrévete!	p. 12
4. Así se dice	Imagen y sonido ¡Exploremos! ¡Identifiquemos!	p. 17
5. Vocabulario	¡Super memoria!	p. 17
6. Gramática	¡Presta el oído!	p. 18
Panorama cultural	¿Qué hiciste en las últimas vacaciones? ¡A escoger!	p. 19
¡A hablar!	*Guided recording*	pp. 24–25
¡A escribir!	*Guided writing*	pp. 24–25

Teacher Management System
Logging In
Logging in to the *¡Ven conmigo!* TMS is easy. Upon launching the program, simply type "admin" in the password area of the log-in screen and press RETURN. Log on to **www.hrw.com/CDROMTUTOR** for a detailed explanation of the Teacher Management System.

One-Stop Planner CD-ROM

To preview all resources available for this chapter, use the **One-Stop Planner CD-ROM,** Disc 1.

Internet Connection

MARCAR: go.hrw.com
PALABRA CLAVE:
WV3 LA CORUNA-1

*Have students explore the **go.hrw.com** Web site for many online resources covering all chapters. All Chapter 1 resources are available under the keyword **WV3 LA CORUNA-1.** Interactive games help students practice the material and provide them with immediate feedback. You will also find a printable worksheet that provides Internet activities that lead to a comprehensive online research project.*

Juegos interactivos

You can use the interactive activities in this chapter

- to practice grammar, vocabulary, and chapter functions
- as homework
- as an assessment option
- as a self-test
- to prepare for the Chapter Test

Actividades Internet

Students plan sports- and fitness-themed vacations to Spanish-speaking countries. They do online research about appropriate places for skiing, diving, and mountaineering, and suggest activities to do in each destination.

- To prepare students for the **Hoja de actividades,** have them review the vocabulary in **Primer paso.** You might also ask them what activities they might enjoy on an adventure vacation.
- After students have finished the activity sheet, have them promote the vacations as a television travel show would, by describing the destination, the activities, and the quality of the conditions.

Proyecto

Have students create a Web site promoting a vacation for travelers who want to see or take part in sporting events around the world. Ask them to find three sports or activities played in three different Spanish-speaking countries. Students should describe those activities and other tourist attractions in those places.

Textbook Listening Activities Scripts 🔊

Primer paso

6 p. 9

MIGUEL	Oye, Laura, ¿te gusta el tenis?
LAURA	Ay, Miguel, a mí no me interesa el tenis para nada.
MIGUEL	Dime, Juan, ¿qué piensas del fútbol?
JUAN	Hombre, tú sabes que estoy loco por el fútbol.
MIGUEL	Beatriz, tú coleccionas revistas, ¿no?
BEATRIZ	¿Coleccionar revistas? Ay, Miguel, ¡eso me parece aburridísimo!
MIGUEL	Oye, Roberto, ¿qué tal si jugamos a los videojuegos después de clases?
ROBERTO	Me da lo mismo si jugamos hoy o mañana.
MIGUEL	Dime, Pilar, ¿eres aficionada a los deportes?
PILAR	Soy gran aficionada al baloncesto. Así es, Miguel.
MIGUEL	Mónica, sé que eres fanática de la música rock. ¿Qué tal si asistimos al concierto mañana?
MÓNICA	Lo siento, Miguel, pero estoy harta de ir a conciertos. ¿Por qué no vamos a un museo?
MIGUEL	Mercedes, ¿prefieres ver una película o quedarte en casa esta noche?
MERCEDES	En realidad, me da igual. ¿Qué prefieres tú?
MIGUEL	Luis, tienes una gran colección de adhesivos, ¿verdad?
LUIS	¿Yo? ¡No, señor! Coleccionar adhesivos me parece un rollo.

Answers to Activity 6
1. Laura, aversión
2. Juan, interés
3. Beatriz, aversión
4. Roberto, indiferencia
5. Pilar, interés
6. Mónica, aversión
7. Mercedes, indiferencia
8. Luis, aversión

8 p. 10

1. Bueno, no me interesa tanto nadar, yo prefiero bucear. Hay cosas maravillosas en el mar.

2. Estoy loco por los deportes, sobre todo por el ciclismo; es mi deporte favorito. Es mucho más divertido que patinar en línea.

3. A mi novio y a mí nos gusta muchísimo jugar a las cartas. Nos gusta más que jugar a los videojuegos.

4. Me gusta más leer revistas que tiras cómicas porque aprendo más sobre lo que pasa en el mundo.

5. Me la paso coleccionando adhesivos. Pero coleccionar sellos me parece un rollo.

6. Muchas veces me gusta simplemente tocar la guitarra con mis amigos. No me interesa para nada tocar otros instrumentos.

Answers to Activity 8
1. bucear
2. ciclismo
3. jugar a las cartas
4. leer revistas
5. coleccionar adhesivos
6. tocar la guitarra

13 p. 12

MIGUEL	¿Luisita? Habla Miguel. ¿Cómo estás? ¿Qué estás haciendo?
LUISITA	Estoy escuchando la radio y limpiando mi cuarto.
MIGUEL	¿Cómo pasaste el verano?
LUISITA	De maravilla. Mi familia y yo fuimos a la playa y regresamos la semana pasada.
MIGUEL	¿De veras?
LUISITA	Sí, mi hermana Marisela y yo nadamos en el mar y practicamos el esquí acuático. Los demás pasearon en velero.
MIGUEL	¿Cómo están todos en tu casa?
LUISITA	Todos aquí están bien. Mi hermano está jugando a las cartas con Marisela y mi mamá está leyendo el periódico.
MIGUEL	Oye, Luisita, ¿te acuerdas del año pasado cuando tu hermano vino de visita y fuimos todos juntos al concierto de U2?
LUISITA	Claro que sí. ¡Estuvo fantástico!
MIGUEL	Bueno, tengo que irme ahora. Quizás podamos asistir a otro concierto este año. Hasta luego.
LUISITA	Vale. ¡Chao!

Answers to Activity 13
escuchar la radio — presente
ir a la playa — pasado
nadar en el mar — pasado
practicar el esquí acuático — pasado
pasear en velero — pasado
jugar a las cartas — presente
leer el periódico — presente
ir al concierto — pasado

The following scripts are for the listening activities found in the *Pupil's Edition*. For Student Response Forms, see *Listening Activities*, pages 3–5. To provide students with additional listening practice, see *Listening Activities*, pages 7–10.

One-Stop Planner CD-ROM

To preview all resources available for this chapter, use the **One-Stop Planner CD-ROM**, Disc 1.

20   p. 15

1. — ¿Verónica, qué hiciste este verano?

— Bueno, tomé una clase de fotografía y saqué muchas fotos.

2. — ¿Qué hizo Joaquín?

— Hizo una vuelta en bicicleta con su hermano por el campo y lo pasaron muy bien. Pasearon en bicicleta por varios días.

3. — Y tú, Benjamín, ¿paseaste en velero?

— Sí, mi primo tiene un velero y paseamos mucho durante las vacaciones. Fue fenomenal. La próxima vez te invito.

4. — ¿Qué hicieron tus hermanas este verano?

— Ellas fueron al Festival de Cine en Gijón. Tú sabes como les encantan las películas.

5. — Concha, ¿adónde fuiste de vacaciones?

— Fui a un parque nacional e hice camping con un grupo de amigos. ¡Fue increíble!

6. — Y tu novia, Víctor, ¿lo pasó bien este verano?

— Sí, gracias. Lo más interesante fue cuando montó a caballo. Hizo una excursión por un fin de semana. ¿Quieres ver las fotos?

Answers to Activity 20
1. Amparo	3. Miguel	5. Amparo
2. Miguel	4. Amparo	6. Amparo

Segundo paso

22   p. 16

1. — ¿Qué tal, Amparo, cómo estás?

— Voy a la playa este fin de semana. ¿Y tú? ¿Adónde vas?

2. — Hiciste camping con tu familia, ¿no? ¿Adónde fuisteis?

— Fuimos al parque nacional de Covadonga. Es maravilloso—tienes que verlo.

3. — Amparo, ¿con quién fuiste al concierto?

— Fuimos el sábado por la noche. No llegué a casa hasta muy tarde. ¡Estuvo excelente!

4. — Oye, Amparo, ¿por qué no me llamaste el otro día? Íbamos a estudiar juntos para el examen, ¿no?

— Ay, Javier, ¡me olvidé por completo de llamarte! ¿Te parece bien si estudiamos juntos mañana?

5. — Amparo, ¿cuándo vas a montar a caballo? Me encantaría ir contigo.

— ¡Perfecto! Pienso ir este domingo por la tarde. Yo te llamo el sábado y te doy más detalles.

6. — Paloma me dice que vosotros fuisteis al cine ayer. ¿Qué película visteis?

— Sí, salimos con Ignacio y su primo. Pero la película estuvo aburridísima; no nos gustó para nada.

7. — Oye, Amparo, ¿qué tal te gustan tus clases este año?

— Bueno, tengo seis clases en total y además, estoy tomando clases particulares de piano en mi casa.

8. — Ya conoces al novio de Eva María, ¿verdad?

— Sí, claro que sí. Lo conocí el mes pasado en la casa de Eva María.

Answers to Activity 22
1. ilógica	3. ilógica	5. lógica	7. ilógica
2. lógica	4. lógica	6. ilógica	8. lógica

Repaso

1   p. 28

1. — Oye, Francisco, pienso ir a la playa con Hilaria el sábado. ¿Quieres venir con nosotras?

— Gracias, pero ya tengo planes. Pienso montar a caballo con unos amigos.

2. — Y tú, Beatriz, ¿ya tienes planes para el sábado?

— Sí, dan dos películas que me gustaría ver y Paco ya me invitó a verlas.

3. — Jorge, ¿por qué no nos acompañas a la playa este sábado?

— Me gustaría pero no puedo. Los sábados practico la guitarra con mi banda.

4. — Natalia, por favor, no me digas que no. Ven con nosotras a la playa.

— Ay, Amparo, lo siento, pero no. Me parece aburrido pasar horas y horas en el sol. Y además, tengo mi clase de fotografía.

5. — Catalina, acompáñanos a la playa este fin de semana, ¿quieres?

— Lo siento, no puedo. Carmen y yo vamos a patinar sobre ruedas este fin de semana.

Answers to Repaso Activity 1
1. d	3. no corresponde	5. c
2. b	4. a	

Capítulo 1: ¡Qué bien lo pasé este verano! *Review Chapter*

Suggested Lesson Plans *50-Minute Schedule*

Day 1

CHAPTER OPENER 5 min.
- Focusing on Outcomes, ATE, p. 5
- Present Language-to-Language, Culture Note, and Geography Link, ATE, pp. 4–5.

DE ANTEMANO 40 min.
- Presenting **De antemano** and Preteaching Vocabulary, ATE, p. 6
- Present Culture Note, ATE, p. 7.
- Activities 1–5 and Comprehension Check, ATE, p. 8

Wrap-Up 5 min.
- Do Additional Practice Activity, ATE, p. 8.

Homework Options
Cuaderno de actividades, p. 1, Activities 1–2

Day 2

PRIMER PASO
Quick Review 5 min.
- Check homework.
- Bell Work, ATE, p. 9

Así se dice, p. 9 20 min.
- Presenting **Así se dice**, ATE, p. 9
- Do Activity 6 with the Audio CD, p. 9.
- Do Activity 7, p. 9.

Vocabulario, p. 10 20 min.
- Presenting **Vocabulario**, ATE, p. 10
- Present **También se puede decir...**, p. 10.
- Do Activity 8 with the Audio CD, p. 10.

Wrap-Up 5 min.
- Have students say how they feel about each of the activities you mime.

Homework Options
Cuaderno de actividades, pp. 2–3, Activities 3–6
Cuaderno de gramática, p. 1, Activities 1–2

Day 3

PRIMER PASO
Quick Review 10 min.
- Check homework.
- Use Teaching Transparency 1-1 to review **Vocabulario**, p. 10, and **Así se dice**, p. 9.

Vocabulario, p. 10 15 min.
- Do Activity 9, then Visual/Auditory Learners, ATE, p. 10.
- Have students do Activity 10 in pairs, p. 10.

Gramática de repaso, p. 11 20 min.
- Presenting **Gramática de repaso**, ATE, p. 11
- Do Activity 11, p. 11.
- Have students do Activity 12 in groups, p. 11.

Wrap-Up 5 min.
- Follow the Career Path Suggestion, ATE, p. 11.

Homework Options
Cuaderno de actividades, p. 4, Activity 7
Cuaderno de gramática, pp. 2–3, Activities 3–6

Day 4

PRIMER PASO
Quick Review 5 min.
- Check homework.

Gramática de repaso, p. 12 40 min.
- Presenting **Gramática de repaso**, p. 12
- Do Activity 13 with the Audio CD, p. 12.
- Have students do Activity 14 in pairs, p. 12.
- Have students do Activity 15, p. 13, then peer-edit their work.
- Follow the Teaching Suggestion, ATE, p.13.
- Read and discuss the Health Link, ATE, p. 13.
- Do Activity 16, p. 13.

Wrap-Up 5 min.
- Ask students if they did the activities from the **Paso** last week.
- Discuss the content and format of Quiz 1-1.

Homework Options
Study for Quiz 1-1.
Cuaderno de actividades, pp. 4–5, Activities 8–10
Cuaderno de gramática, pp. 4–5, Activities 7–11

Day 5

PRIMER PASO
Quick Review 5 min.
- Check homework.
- Review **Primer paso**.

Quiz 20 min.
- Administer Quiz 1-1A, 1-1B, or a combination of the two.

¡ADELANTE! 20 min.
- Presenting **¡Adelante!** and Preteaching Vocabulary, ATE, p. 14
- Do Activities 17–21, p. 15

Wrap-Up 5 min.
- Have students compare Amparo's letter with Miguel's.

Homework Options
Cuaderno de actividades, p. 6, Activities 11–12

Day 6

SEGUNDO PASO
Quick Review 5 min.
- Check homework.
- Bell Work, ATE, p. 16

Así se dice, p. 16 20 min.
- Presenting **Así se dice**, ATE, p. 16
- Review **¿Te acuerdas?**, p. 16.
- Do Activity 22 with the Audio CD, p. 16.
- Have students do Activity 23 in pairs, p. 16.

Así se dice/Vocabulario, p. 17 20 min.
- Presenting **Así se dice** and **Vocabulario**, ATE, p. 17
- Present **También se puede decir...**, p. 17.
- Do Activity 24, p. 17.

Wrap-Up 5 min.
- Have students describe the people in Teaching Transparency 1-2.

Homework Options
Cuaderno de actividades, pp. 7–10, Activities 13–14, 16–18
Cuaderno de gramática, pp. 6–7, Activities 12–15

One-Stop Planner CD-ROM

For alternative lesson plans by chapter section, to create your own customized plans, or to preview all resources available for this chapter, use the **One-Stop Planner CD-ROM,** Disc 1.

 For additional homework suggestions, see activities accompanied by this symbol throughout the chapter.

Day 7

SEGUNDO PASO

Quick Review 5 min.
- Check homework.

Vocabulario, p. 17 20 min.
- Do Activity 25 in groups, then follow the suggestion in History Link, ATE, p. 17.

Gramática de repaso, p. 18 20 min.
- Presenting **Gramática de repaso,** ATE, p. 18
- Do **Más práctica gramatical,** p. 27, Activity 8.
- Have students do Activity 26 in pairs and Activity 27 in groups, p. 18.

Wrap-Up 5 min.
- Ask students questions about who and what they know.

Homework Options
Cuaderno de actividades, pp. 8, 10, Activities 15, 19–20
Cuaderno de gramática, p. 8, Activities 16–18

Day 8

SEGUNDO PASO

Quick Review 10 min.
- Check homework.
- Describe a celebrity and have students guess who it is.

Nota gramatical, p. 18 20 min.
- Presenting **Nota gramatical,** p. 18
- **Más práctica gramatical,** p. 26, Activity 7
- Have students do Activity 28, p. 18, then peer-edit their work.

PANORAMA CULTURAL 15 min.
- Presenting **Panorama cultural,** ATE, p. 19
- Present the Culture and Language Note, ATE, p. 19.

Wrap-Up 5 min.
- Discuss the content and format of Quiz 1-2.

Homework Options
Study for Quiz 1-2.
Cuaderno de gramática, p. 9, Activities 19–21

Day 9

SEGUNDO PASO

Quick Review 5 min.
- Check homework.
- Review **Segundo paso.**

Quiz 20 min.
- Administer Quiz 1-2A, 1-2B, or a combination of the two.

VAMOS A LEER 20 min.
- Read and discuss the **Estrategia,** p. 20.
- Do Activities A–C, following the Prereading Suggestion, ATE, p. 20.

Wrap-Up 5 min.
- Discuss the Biology and Science Links, ATE, p. 20.
- Discuss Culture Note, ATE, p. 21.

Homework Options
Assign Activities D–E, p. 21

Day 10

VAMOS A LEER
Quick Review 10 min.
- Check homework.
- Using Prior Knowledge, ATE, p. 21

VAMOS A LEER 20 min.
- Using Context Clues, ATE, p. 21.
- Read ¿**Te acuerdas?,** then do Activities F–G, p. 22.

VAMOS A ESCRIBIR 15 min.
- Read and discuss the **Estrategia,** p. 23
- Have students do Activity A and begin Activity B, p. 23.

Wrap-Up 5 min.
- Have students comment on what their partners have written so far.

Homework Options
Finish **Vamos a escribir,** p. 23.
Cuaderno de actividades, pp. 11–12, Activities 21–23

Day 11

VAMOS A ESCRIBIR
Quick Review 5 min.
- Check homework and collect **Vamos a escribir,** p. 23.

REPASO 35 min.
- Do Activity 1 with the Audio CD, p. 28.
- Do Activities 2–3 and 5, pp. 28–29. Check.
- Have students do Activities 4 and 7 in pairs, p. 29.
- Have students do Activity 6, p. 29, then exchange papers for peer-editing.

Wrap-Up 10 min.
- Have students read letters from Activity 7, p. 29. Then have the class vote on who deserves to be honored.

Homework Options
A ver si puedo..., p. 30

Day 12

REPASO
Quick Review 5 min.
- Check homework.

Chapter Review 40 min.
- Review Chapter 1. Choose from **Más práctica gramatical,** Grammar Tutor for Students of Spanish, Activities for Communication, Listening Activities, Interactive CD-ROM Tutor, or **Juegos interactivos.**

Wrap-Up 5 min.
- Discuss the content of the Chapter 1 Test and provide sample questions.

Homework Options
Study for the Chapter 1 Test.

Assessment

Quick Review 5 min.
- Answer any last-minute questions.

Test, Chapter 1 45 min.
- Administer Chapter 1 Test. Select from Testing Program, Alternative Assessment Guide, Test Generator, or Standardized Assessment Tutor.

Capítulo 1: ¡Qué bien lo pasé este verano! *Review Chapter*

Suggested Lesson Plans 90-Minute Block Schedule

Block 1

CHAPTER OPENER 5 min.
- Focusing on Outcomes, ATE, p. 5
- Present Language-to-Language, Culture Note, and Geography Link, ATE, pp. 4–5

DE ANTEMANO 40 min.
- Presenting **De antemano** and Preteaching Vocabulary, ATE, p. 6
- Present Culture Note, ATE, p. 7.
- Activities 1–5 and Comprehension Check, ATE, p. 8

Así se dice, p. 9 20 min.
- Presenting **Así se dice**, ATE, p. 9
- Do Activity 6 with the Audio CD, p. 9.
- Do Activity 7, p. 9.

Vocabulario, p. 10 20 min.
- Presenting **Vocabulario**, ATE, p. 10
- Present **También se puede decir...**, p. 10.
- Do Activity 8 with the Audio CD, p. 10.

Wrap-Up 5 min.
- Have students say how they feel about each of the activities you mime.

Homework Options
Cuaderno de actividades, pp. 1–3, Activities 1–6
Cuaderno de gramática, p. 1, Activities 1–2

Block 2

PRIMER PASO
Quick Review 10 min.
- Check homework.
- Use Teaching Transparency 1-1 to review **Así se dice**, p. 10, and **Vocabulario**, p. 9.

Vocabulario, p. 10 15 min.
- Do Activity 9, p. 10, then do Visual/Auditory Learners, ATE, p. 10.
- Have students do Activity 10 in pairs, p. 10.

Gramática de repaso, p. 11 20 min.
- Presenting **Gramática de repaso**, ATE, p. 11
- Do Activity 11, p. 11.
- Have students do Activity 12 in groups, p. 11.

Gramática de repaso, p. 12 40 min.
- Presenting **Gramática de repaso**, ATE, p. 12
- Activity 13 with the Audio CD, p. 12.
- Have students do Activity 14 in pairs, p. 12.
- Have students do Activity 15, p. 13, then peer-edit.
- Follow the Teaching Suggestion, ATE, p. 13.
- Read and discuss the Health Link, ATE, p. 13.
- Do Activity 16, p. 13.

Wrap-Up 5 min.
- Ask students if they did the activities from the **Paso** last week.
- Discuss the content and format of Quiz 1-1.

Homework Options
Study for Quiz 1-1.
Cuaderno de actividades, pp. 4–5, Activities 7–10
Cuaderno de gramática, pp. 2–5, Activities 3–11

Block 3

PRIMER PASO
Quick Review 10 min.
- Check homework.
- Review **Primer paso**.

Quiz 20 min.
- Administer Quiz 1-1A, 1-1B, or a combination of the two.

¡ADELANTE! 20 min.
- Presenting **¡Adelante!** and Preteaching Vocabulary, ATE, p. 14
- Do Activities 17–21, p. 15

SEGUNDO PASO
Así se dice, p. 16 20 min.
- Presenting **Así se dice**, ATE, p. 16
- Review **¿Te acuerdas?**, p. 16.
- Do Activity 22 with the Audio CD, p. 16.
- Have students do Activity 23 in pairs, p. 16.

Así se dice/Vocabulario, p. 17 15 min.
- Presenting **Así se dice** and **Vocabulario**, ATE, p. 17
- Present **También se puede decir...**, p. 17.

Wrap-Up 5 min.
- Describe a celebrity or someone in the class for students to guess.

Homework Options
Cuaderno de actividades, pp. 6–7, Activities 11–14
Cuaderno de gramática, pp. 6–7, Activities 12–15

One-Stop Planner CD-ROM

For alternative lesson plans by chapter section, to create your own customized plans, or to preview all resources available for this chapter, use the **One-Stop Planner CD-ROM,** Disc 1.

For additional homework suggestions, see activities accompanied by this symbol throughout the chapter.

Block 4

SEGUNDO PASO
Quick Review 10 min.
- Check homework.
- Have students ask questions based on a statement you make.

Vocabulario, p. 17 25 min.
- Review adjectives using Teaching Transparency 1-2.
- Do Activity 24, p. 17.
- Do Activity 25 in groups, then follow the suggestion in History Link, ATE, p. 17.

Gramática de repaso, p. 18 35 min.
- Presenting **Gramática de repaso,** ATE, p. 18
- **Más práctica gramatical,** p. 27, Activity 8
- Have students do Activity 26 in pairs and Activity 27 in groups, p. 18.
- Presenting **Nota gramatical,** p. 18
- **Más práctica gramatical,** p. 26, Activity 7
- Have students do Activity 28, p. 18, then peer-edit their work.

PANORAMA CULTURAL 15 min.
- Presenting **Panorama cultural,** ATE, p. 19
- Present the Culture and Language Note, ATE, p. 19.

Wrap-Up 5 min.
- Discuss the content and format of Quiz 1-2.

Homework Options
Study for Quiz 1-2.
Cuaderno de actividades, pp. 8–10, Activities 15–20
Cuaderno de gramática, pp. 8–9, Activities 16–21

Block 5

SEGUNDO PASO
Quick Review 10 min.
- Check homework.
- Review **Segundo paso.**

Quiz 20 min.
- Administer Quiz 1-2A, 1-2B, or a combination of the two.

VAMOS A LEER 55 min.
- Read and discuss the **Estrategia,** p. 20.
- Do Activities A–C, following the Prereading Suggestion, ATE, p. 20.
- Discuss the Biology and Science Links, ATE, p. 21.
- Discuss Culture Note, ATE, p. 21.
- Do Activities D–E, p. 21.

Wrap-Up 5 min.
- Using Context Clues, ATE, p. 21

Homework Options
Assign Activity F, p. 22.
Cuaderno de actividades, pp. 11–12, Activities 21–23

Block 6

VAMOS A LEER
Quick Review 5 min.
- Check and discuss the homework.

VAMOS A LEER 10 min.
- Have students do Activity G in pairs, p. 22.

VAMOS A ESCRIBIR 35 min.
- Read and discuss the **Estrategia,** p. 23.
- Have students do Activity A and Activity B, then follow the Teaching Suggestion, ATE, p. 23.

REPASO 35 min.
- Do Activity 1 with the Audio CD, p. 28.
- Do Activities 2–3 and 5, pp. 28–29. Check.
- Have students do Activities 4 and 7 in pairs, p. 29.
- Have students do Activity 6, p. 29, then peer-edit.

Wrap-Up 5 min.
- Discuss the content of the Chapter 1 Test and provide sample questions.

Homework Options
Study for Chapter 1 Test.
Assign part C of **Vamos a escribir,** p. 23.
A ver si puedo..., p. 30

Block 7

REPASO
Quick Review 5 min.
- Check homework and collect **Vamos a escribir,** p. 23.

Chapter Review 40 min.
- Review Chapter 1. Choose from **Más práctica gramatical,** Grammar Tutor for Students of Spanish, Activities for Communication, Listening Activities, Interactive CD-ROM Tutor, or **Juegos interactivos.**

Test, Chapter 1 45 min.
- Administer Chapter 1 Test. Select from Testing Program, Alternative Assessment Guide, Test Generator, or Standardized Assessment Tutor.

Chapter Opener

CAPÍTULO 1

  One-Stop Planner CD-ROM

For resource information, see the **One-Stop Planner**, Disc 1.

Pacing Tips
Chapters 1 and 2 are a global review of *¡Ven conmigo!* Levels 1 and 2. Be sure to balance speaking practice and cultural notes while still leaving time for **Gramática de repaso.** See Suggested Lesson Plans, pp. 3I–3L.

Meeting the Standards

Communication
• Expressing interest, indifference, and displeasure, p. 9
• Asking for information, p. 16
• Describing yourself and others, p. 17

Cultures
• Culture Note, p. 7
• Culture Note, p. 11
• Nota cultural, p. 13
• Culture Note, p. 15
• Panorama cultural, p. 19
• Language Note, p. 19

Connections
• Geography Link, p. 5
• Health Link, p. 13
• Biology Link, p. 20

Comparisons
• Language-to-Language, p. 4
• Culture Note, p. 19

Communities
• Career Path, p. 11

Connections and Comparisons

Language-to-Language
Six of Spain's self-governing regions (**comunidades autónomas**) are officially bilingual. In Catalonia and the Balearic Islands, **catalán,** a Romance language, is widely spoken; **valenciano,** a variant of Catalan, is spoken in Valencia. **Gallego,** similar to Portuguese, is spoken in Galicia, while in the Basque Country and Navarre many speak Basque, or **euskera** (a non-Indo-European language of unknown origin). The cultural and political identity of these six regions is closely tied to their languages. Have students name places in the United States where languages other than English are widely spoken. (South Texas, South Florida, Southern California, New Mexico, Louisiana, Northern Maine) What effect does bilingualism have on an individual or a community?

CAPÍTULO

1
¡Qué bien lo pasé este verano!

Objectives

In this chapter you will review and practice how to

Primer paso

- **express interest, indifference, and displeasure**

Segundo paso

- **ask for information**
- **describe yourself and others**

🔲 internet

go.hrw.com
MARCAR: go.hrw.com
PALABRA CLAVE:
WV3 LA CORUNA-1

◀ **¿Cuándo aprendiste a bucear?**

Photo Flash!
Water sports may be enjoyed throughout the world. Ask students if they have ever snorkeled or dived. Are these sports among their favorites?

Focusing on Outcomes
In this chapter students will practice expressing interest, indifference, and displeasure. They will describe themselves and their hobbies. Point out the purpose of describing people and asking others for information. You might follow up by asking students to describe what they did over their summer vacations.

Cultures and Communities

Culture Note
Spain is one of the leading fishing countries in Europe. Its rivers and lakes are home to carp, eel, pike, and trout, while the Mediterranean and Atlantic yield anchovies, cod, octopus, sardines, squid, tuna, and mussels. The Bay of Biscay off the northern coast, known to Spaniards as the **Mar Cantábrico,** has always been an especially rich fishing area.

Geography Link
During the study of this chapter ask students to collect information on good locations for diving. You may wish to have them do an Internet search for such information. Have students identify the similarities among these locations.

Teaching Resources
pp. 6–8

PRINT
▸ Lesson Planner, p. 3
▸ Video Guide, pp. 3–4, 6
▸ Cuaderno de actividades, p. 1

MEDIA
▸ One-Stop Planner
▸ Video Program
Contigo en la distancia
Videocassette 1, 02:42–07:59
Videocassette 5 (captioned version), 00:45–06:02
▸ Audio Compact Discs, CD 1, Trs. 1–2

Presenting
De antemano

Have students read and discuss **Estrategia para comprender.** Then play the Audio CD once, while students look at the photos and read the letters. Next, present the Preteaching Vocabulary. Ask students to identify phrases used to describe themselves and their pastimes.

DE ANTEMANO ▪ *Una carta a Amparo*

Cuaderno de actividades, p. 1, Acts. 1–2

CD 1
Trs. 1–2

Estrategia **para comprender**
Miguel Pereira es un muchacho de La Coruña. Le escribió una carta a Amparo Pedregal, una nueva amiga en la ciudad de Gijón. En su carta le dice cómo es, qué hizo de vacaciones este verano y qué deportes y pasatiempos le gustan.

CURSOS DE VELA LIGERA
El Club de Vela
ofrece cursos de vela ligera para jóvenes de 9 a 18 años durante los meses de junio, julio y agosto. Cada curso dura tres semanas.
Horario:
11.00 a 15.00 horas.

27 de agosto

El mes de julio tomé cursos de vela en el Club de Vela. También tomé clases de tenis y jugué mucho.

Querida Amparo,

¡Hola! Encantado de conocerte, aunque sea por carta. Me llamo Miguel y tengo dieciséis años. Soy alto, moreno y atlético. Vivo en La Coruña con mis padres y mi hermano menor, Jorge, que tiene diez años.

Soy un gran aficionado a los deportes, sobre todo al remo, a la vela y al tenis. Me encanta el baloncesto y me gusta mucho bucear. Realmente me interesa casi todo menos ver televisión—¡eso me parece un rollo! Me gustan las tiras cómicas y los videojuegos.

Yo pasé un verano estupendo. Normalmente mi familia viaja durante el verano. El año pasado fuimos a Barcelona y mi madre insistió en visitar

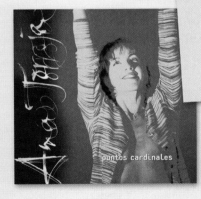

Me encanta la música de Ana Torroja. La vi cuando estaba con el grupo Mecano.

Preteaching Vocabulary

Guessing Words from Context
Ask students what types of expressions they would use in a letter to a pen pal. Have students identify expressions in **De antemano** that describe people and the sports and pastimes they enjoy. Then point out the following phrases: **aunque sea por carta; soy un gran aficionado; me encanta; me interesa; me parece un rollo; ¡qué paliza!; estaba harto; hay tanto que hacer; sobre todo.** Have students use context to determine the meanings of these phrases.

STANDARDS: 1.2, 2.1, 3.2

Me la paso coleccio-
nando adhesivos y
leyendo tiras cómicas.

todos los museos. Puedo apreciar la cultura, pero
¡qué paliza! Estaba harto de tantos museos. Este
año decidimos quedarnos aquí en La Coruña. Me
da igual si no viajamos. Es más, prefiero estar
aquí porque hay tanto que hacer, ¡sobre todo los
deportes!

Un amigo mío de Nueva York, Josh, pasó el mes
de agosto con mi familia. Lo pasamos super bien.
Escuchamos música, jugamos al baloncesto y
salimos con amigos.

Trato de imaginarme cómo eres. ¿Cuántos años
tienes? ¿Eres alta o baja? ¿Rubia o morena?
¿Tienes hermanos? ¿Cómo pasaste el verano?
¿Tocas algún instrumento? (Yo no). Espero
recibir una carta tuya dentro de poco.
¡Escríbeme pronto!

Saludos,

Miguel

**Mi amigo Josh—es un
poco tímido pero muy
divertido. Fuimos varias
veces a la playa Riazor
para nadar. Le enseñé a
bucear y pasear en velero.**

**El verano que viene voy a dar
una vuelta ciclista rumbo a
Francia. Vamos a pasar un día en
Gijón y podemos conocernos.
¡Qué suerte!**

Using the Captioned Video

As an alternative, you might want to
show the captioned version of *Contigo
en la distancia: ¿Qué hicisteis en México?*
on Videocassette 5. Some students may benefit
from seeing the written words as they listen to
the target language and watch the gestures and
actions in context. This visual reinforcement of
vocabulary and functions will facilitate students'
comprehension and help reduce their anxiety
before they are formally introduced to the new
language in the chapter.

CAPÍTULO 1

Visual/Tactile Learners
Have students create an annotated
collage about what they did during
their summer vacations.

Challenge
Have students work in small groups
to come up with other greetings,
closings, and ways of introducing
themselves to another person.

Culture Note
Ana Torroja was the lead
singer of Mecano, a
Spanish pop music group popular all
over the Spanish-speaking world.
The group was also known for its
keen awareness of environmental
and social issues, and their work
to help stop the depletion of the
rainforest. You may wish to use one
of their songs for a listening activity.

Thinking Critically
Synthesizing Have students write
a response to Miguel from Amparo,
answering all of Miguel's questions.

Contigo en la distancia
You may choose to show students
Episode 1: *¿Qué hicisteis en
México?* now or wait until later
in the chapter. Javier and Sergio
have just returned to Seville from
Mexico, where they spent the
summer. Javier's sister Zoraida
wants to hear all about the trip,
especially the new friends they
have made, Carlos, Alejandra, and
Irene. Javier misses Alejandra but
does not want to admit it. Before
showing the video, have students
predict which chapter functions
and/or vocabulary they think they
will hear in the episode.

1 **¿Cierto o falso?** See answers below.

Indica si cada oración es **cierta** o **falsa**. Si es falsa, corrígela.

1. Miguel es alto y rubio.
2. A Miguel le encantan los deportes.
3. Miguel tenía ganas de visitar más museos.
4. Amparo pasó el mes de agosto con Miguel.
5. Ana Torroja es la cantante favorita de su amigo de Nueva York.
6. La Coruña está al lado del mar.
7. A Miguel le gusta mucho ver televisión.
8. Miguel sabe bucear.
9. Miguel le enseñó a Josh a remar.

2 **Busca la expresión** See answers below.

¿Qué expresiones usa Miguel para...?

1. preguntarle a Amparo qué edad tiene
2. describirse a sí mismo físicamente; describir a Josh
3. expresar su entusiasmo por los deportes y sus pasatiempos
4. decir que algo no le importa
5. decir que algo no le gusta

3 **Ponlo en orden** See answers below.

 Con un(a) compañero(a), pon en orden estas oraciones según lo que escribió Miguel.

1. Miguel toma cursos de vela en el Club de Vela.
2. Miguel da una vuelta ciclista rumbo a Francia.
3. Josh, el amigo de Miguel, viene a visitarlo.
4. Miguel va a Barcelona con su familia.

4 **¿Comprendiste?** See answers below.

Contesta las siguientes preguntas en español.

1. ¿Dónde pasó Miguel el verano este año?
2. ¿Dónde lo pasó Miguel el año pasado?
3. ¿Qué tipo de vacaciones prefiere él?
4. ¿Por qué quiere quedarse en La Coruña?
5. ¿Quién vino *(came)* a visitar a Miguel?
6. ¿Qué deportes acuáticos se pueden practicar en La Coruña?
7. ¿Cuándo van a tener la oportunidad de verse Miguel y Amparo?

5 **Ahora te toca a ti**

Mira otra vez las fotos que le manda Miguel a Amparo. ¿Qué deporte o pasatiempo te interesa más a ti? ¿Crees que te gustaría visitar La Coruña? ¿Por qué sí o por qué no?

Answers

1
1. falsa; Miguel es alto y moreno.
2. cierta.
3. falsa; Estaba harto de los museos.
4. falsa; Josh pasó el mes de agosto con Miguel.
5. falsa; Ana Torroja es la cantante favorita de Miguel.
6. cierta.
7. falsa; Le interesa todo menos ver televisión.
8. cierta.
9. falsa; Miguel le enseñó a bucear y pasear en velero.

2
1. ¿Cuántos años tienes?
2. Miguel: Soy alto y moreno. Josh: Es tímido pero divertido.
3. Soy un gran aficionado de los deportes; Me interesa...; Me gustan...; Me la paso...; Me encanta...
4. Me da igual si no viajamos.
5. Eso me parece un rollo. Estaba harto de...

3 4,1,3,2

4
1. Pasó el verano en La Coruña.
2. Lo pasó en Barcelona.
3. Prefiere hacer deportes en sus vacaciones.
4. Quiere quedarse en La Coruña porque hay tanto que hacer.
5. Su amigo Josh vino a visitarlo.
6. Se puede nadar, remar, bucear y pasear en velero.
7. Van a tener la oportunidad de verse el verano que viene en Gijón.

Comprehension Check

Challenge

2 Divide the class into small groups. Have students talk about themselves, using the expressions employed by Miguel.

Slower Pace

3 Before students break into pairs, have them locate the parts of Miguel's letter that are summarized by the four sentences.

Additional Practice

4 After students have completed the excercise in writing, give them a moment to look over their answers. Then have them put their papers away and answer the questions orally as you call upon them.

Así se dice

Expressing interest, indifference, and displeasure

Cuando algo te interesa puedes decir:

Soy un(a) gran aficionado(a) a los deportes.
Soy un(a) fanático(a) de...
Estoy loco(a) por...
Me la paso coleccionando adhesivos.

I spend my time . . .

© Billiken

Cuando algo no te importa puedes decir:

Me da igual.
Me da lo mismo. } *It's all the same to me.*

No me importa. *It doesn't matter to me.*
Como quieras. *Whatever (you want).*

Para decir que algo no te gusta puedes decir:

Ver televisión **me parece un rollo.**
A mí **no me interesa para nada** ver televisión.
¡Qué paliza! Estoy harto(a) de tantos museos.
What a drag! I'm fed up with . . .

Cuaderno de actividades, pp. 2–3, Acts. 4, 6

6 Como quieras Script and answers on p. 3G.

Escuchemos En una hoja de papel, escribe **interés, indiferencia** y **aversión** en tres columnas. Escucha las siguientes conversaciones. Luego, escribe en la categoría apropiada el nombre de la persona que expresa cada emoción.

CD 1 Tr. 3

7 ¿Qué dicen ellos? See possible answers below.

Escribamos ¿Qué crees que están pensando las personas en estos dibujos? ¿Les gusta el deporte o pasatiempo? Usa las frases de **Así se dice** para expresar sus pensamientos.

¿Quieres ver una película o ir a un concierto?

Adriana　　**Beto**　　**Ken**　**Marcos**　**Charo**　**Gonzalo**

Communication for All Students

Native Speakers
Have pairs of students make a list of their top five interests or pastimes. Students then take turns naming items on their lists as their partner tells how he or she feels about each one.

Auditory Learners
Have students listen to the video (Videocassette 1, Episode 1) without watching the screen. Ask them to clap their hands when they hear a positive phrase from **Así se dice,** hit their desks when they hear a negative phrase, and raise their hands when they hear a neutral phrase.

Primer paso

CAPÍTULO 1

Teaching Resources
pp. 9–13

PRINT
▶ Lesson Planner, p. 3
▶ Listening Activities, pp. 3–4, 7–8
▶ Activities for Communication, pp. 1–2, 51, 53, 89–90
▶ Cuaderno de gramática, pp. 1–5
▶ Grammar Tutor for Students of Spanish, Chapter 1
▶ Cuaderno de actividades, pp. 2–5
▶ Cuaderno para hispanohablantes, pp. 1–5
▶ Testing Program, pp. 1–4
▶ Alternative Assessment Guide, p. 30
▶ Student Make-Up Assignments, Chapter 1

MEDIA
▶ One-Stop Planner
▶ Audio Compact Discs, CD 1, Trs. 3–5, 19–21, 15
▶ Teaching Transparencies 1-1; **Más práctica gramatical** Answers; Cuaderno de gramática Answers
▶ Interactive CD-ROM Tutor, Disc 1

Bell Work
Have students write answers to these questions: **¿Cómo eres? ¿Cómo es tu mejor amigo(a)? ¿Qué les gusta hacer a Uds. los fines de semana?**

Presenting
Así se dice
Model the expressions for students by telling what does and does not interest you. Have students respond to what you say.

Answers
7 *Possible answers:*
1. Estoy loca por el tenis.
2. ¡Qué paliza! Me encanta coleccionar adhesivos.
3. Me da igual. Como tú quieras.
4. Soy un gran fanático del remo.

Teaching Resources
pp. 9–13

PRINT
▶ Lesson Planner, p. 3
▶ Listening Activities, pp. 3–4, 7–8
▶ Activities for Communication, pp. 1–2, 51, 53, 89–90
▶ Cuaderno de gramática, pp. 1–5
▶ Grammar Tutor for Students of Spanish, Chapter 1
▶ Cuaderno de actividades, pp. 2–5
▶ Cuaderno para hispanohablantes, pp. 1–5
▶ Testing Program, pp. 1–4
▶ Alternative Assessment Guide, p. 30
▶ Student Make-Up Assignments, Chapter 1

MEDIA
▶ One-Stop Planner
▶ Audio Compact Discs, CD 1, Trs. 3–5, 19–21, 15
▶ Teaching Transparencies 1-1; **Más práctica gramatical** Answers; Cuaderno de gramática Answers
▶ Interactive CD-ROM Tutor, Disc 1

Presenting
Vocabulario

Display *Teaching Transparency 1-1* and model pronunciation of the vocabulary. Then present the new and review vocabulary with photos clipped from magazines, narrating what someone did on their last vacation.

---

la escalada deportiva

la vela
pasear en velero

la equitación
montar a caballo

practicar ciclismo

patinar en línea

¿Qué deporte practicas?
el montañismo (escalar montañas)
el esquí acuático (hacer esquí acuático)
el patinaje (patinar sobre ruedas/hielo)
el remo (remar)
el buceo (bucear)

¿Qué pasatiempo te gusta más?
escuchar música
leer tiras cómicas/revistas
ir a la playa
coleccionar adhesivos/sellos
tocar un instrumento (la flauta/la batería/el clarinete/el saxofón)
la fotografía (sacar fotos)
jugar (ue) a los video-juegos/las cartas

Más práctica gramatical, p. 24, Act. 1

Cuaderno de gramática, p. 1, Acts. 1–2   Cuaderno de actividades, pp. 2–3, Acts. 3, 5

También se puede decir...

Puedes decir **alpinismo** por **montañismo**. En Latinoamérica también se usa **andinismo**. Puedes usar **submarinismo** por **buceo**, **tomar fotos** por **sacar fotos** y **calcomanías** por **adhesivos**.

Script and answers on p. 3G.

8 **Una entrevista**

Escuchemos Una periodista está entrevistando a varios jóvenes sobre qué pasatiempos y deportes les gustan. Vas a escuchar seis frases. ¿Qué deporte o pasatiempo le gusta a cada persona?

CD 1
Tr. 4

¿Se te ha olvidado?
sports and hobbies
Ver la página R15

9 **¡Estoy harto del fútbol!**

Escribamos Escribe oraciones que expresen interés, indiferencia o aversión con el deporte o pasatiempo indicado. Usa expresiones de **Así se dice** en la página 9.

1. la escalada deportiva   4. el patinaje   7. el montañismo
2. la fotografía   5. dibujar   8. el esquí acuático
3. la natación   6. leer tiras cómicas   9. escuchar música

10 **Es tu turno**

Hablemos Trabaja con un(a) compañero(a). Usen expresiones de **Así se dice** para comparar sus reacciones a los deportes y pasatiempos en la Actividad 9. ¿Qué deporte o pasatiempo les gusta a los (las) dos?

Communication for All Students

Challenge
Give students a closed-book dictation, having them check their spelling when done. (**Mi hermano y su esposa son aficionados a las actividades al aire libre. El verano pasado fueron a España y visitaron los Pirineos donde practicaron la escalada deportiva. También practicaron ciclismo en Barcelona. Luego pasearon en velero en Andalucía.**)

Visual/Auditory Learners
After students have completed the writing assignment, have them draw faces on index cards representing **interés**, **indiferencia**, and **aversión**. Ask volunteers to read their sentences aloud while the rest of the class guesses the emotion they depicted by holding up the appropriate card.

Gramática de repaso

Present tense of stem-changing verbs

Here is a review of stem-changing verbs in the present tense. Notice that the endings are regular. The verb **jugar** changes **u → ue** in all present-tense forms except **nosotros** and **vosotros**.

CD-ROM DISC 1

	e → ie	o → ue	e → i
yo	emp**ie**zo	p**ue**do	p**i**do
tú	emp**ie**zas	p**ue**des	p**i**des
él, ella, Ud.	emp**ie**za	p**ue**de	p**i**de
nosotros(as)	empezamos	podemos	pedimos
vosotros(as)	empezáis	podéis	pedís
ellos, ellas, Uds.	emp**ie**zan	p**ue**den	p**i**den

Más práctica gramatical, pp. 24–25, Acts. 2–4

Cuaderno de gramática, pp. 2–3, Acts. 3–5

Cuaderno de actividades, pp. 4–5, Acts. 7, 9

11 **Gramática en contexto** See answers below.

Leamos/Escribamos El horario de Rafael está muy lleno. Completa las oraciones con las formas correctas del presente de los verbos.

Mi día ___1___ (comenzar) a las seis de la mañana. Siempre ___2___ (empezar) con un buen desayuno. Mis padres nunca ___3___ (querer) que salga de la casa sin comer. Aprovecho una hora por la mañana para practicar ciclismo antes de las siete y media, cuando ___4___ (comenzar) las clases. Después de las clases, mis amigos me ___5___ (pedir) que vaya a pasar el rato con ellos o a remar en el río. Pero, no ___6___ (poder) porque ___7___ (empezar) a trabajar a las dos. Le pido a Dios que ponga más horas en el día.

¿Se te ha olvidado?

present tense

Ver la página R35

Cuaderno de gramática, p. 3, Act. 6

12 **¿Qué pasatiempo te gusta?**

Hablemos/Escribamos Prepara un cuestionario para investigar los deportes y pasatiempos que prefieren cinco compañeros de clase. Después, decide cuál de los amigos por correspondencia es más apropiado para cada estudiante.

- -

Nombre: Liliana Aguilar
Edad: 15 años
Pasatiempos: Practicar deportes, ir a la playa, coleccionar estampillas de distintos países, escuchar música y leer.

- -

Nombre: Antonio Villa
Edad: 16 años
Pasatiempos: Montar en bicicleta, ir al cine, sacar fotos, pintar, escribir poemas, tocar la guitarra.

- -

Nombre: Laura Espinoza
Edad: 16 años
Pasatiempos: Patinar en línea, hablar por teléfono con mis amigos, coleccionar carteles de mis artistas favoritos, bailar, escuchar música, leer revistas.

- -

Nombre: Francisco Andrade
Edad: 17 años
Pasatiempos: ir a conciertos, practicar deportes, coleccionar postales, tocar la batería, ver televisión, jugar videojuegos.

Cultures and Communities

Culture Note
Traditional sports in the Basque Country include the game of **pelota vasca** (jai alai) and tests of strength—tossing tree trunks, lifting boulders, and woodcutting. Bullfighting is popular all over Spain. Winter sports are popular, as are mountain climbing and hang-gliding. Soccer is by far the favorite sport.

Career Path
Ask students to think about careers in the travel industry. Some areas of the United States are very popular destinations for Spanish-speaking tourists. Ask students to think of tourism industry jobs where their knowledge of Spanish would be useful. (travel agent, hotel manager, tour operator, tour guide, airline employee, retail business owner)

Teaching Resources
pp. 9–13

PRINT

▸ Lesson Planner, p. 3
▸ Listening Activities, pp. 3–4, 7–8
▸ Activities for Communication, pp. 1–2, 51, 53, 89–90
▸ Cuaderno de gramática, pp. 1–5
▸ Grammar Tutor for Students of Spanish, Chapter 1
▸ Cuaderno de actividades, pp. 2–5
▸ Cuaderno para hispanohablantes, pp. 1–5
▸ Testing Program, pp. 1–4
▸ Alternative Assessment Guide, p. 30
▸ Student Make-Up Assignments, Chapter 1

MEDIA

▸ One-Stop Planner
▸ Audio Compact Discs, CD 1, Trs. 3–5, 19–21, 15
▸ Teaching Transparencies 1-1; **Más práctica gramatical** Answers; Cuaderno de gramática Answers
▸ Interactive CD-ROM Tutor, Disc 1

Presenting
Gramática de repaso

The preterite tense Model proper use of the preterite by relating what you did yesterday. Emphasize pronunciation and proper stress. Remind students that stressed final vowels must carry a written accent.

Answers

14 *Sample answer:*
Josefina vio a un chico en la playa. Luego lo conoció en la fiesta de una amiga que se llama Teresa. Empezaron a hablar y vieron que tenían mucho en común. Él le dijo que la reconoció de la playa. Se hicieron amigos inmediatamente.

Gramática de repaso

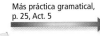

The preterite tense

The preterite is used to talk about what happened on a particular occasion or within a certain period of time in the past. The **yo** forms of verbs ending in **-car**, **-gar**, and **-zar** have spelling changes: **toqué, jugué, comencé.**

PASAR	COMER	ESCRIBIR
pas**é**	com**í**	escrib**í**
pas**aste**	com**iste**	escrib**iste**
pas**ó**	com**ió**	escrib**ió**
pas**amos**	com**imos**	escrib**imos**
pas**asteis**	com**isteis**	escrib**isteis**
pas**aron**	com**ieron**	escrib**ieron**

Más práctica gramatical, p. 25, Act. 5

Cuaderno de actividades, pp. 4–5, Acts. 8, 10

Cuaderno de gramática, pp. 4–5, Acts. 7–11

13 **Gramática en contexto** Script and answers on p. 3G.

Escuchemos Vas a escuchar a Luisita conversar por teléfono con Miguel. Para cada verbo que sigue, indica si están hablando del **presente** o del **pasado.**

CD 1 Tr. 5

1. escuchar la radio
2. ir a la playa
3. nadar en el mar
4. practicar el esquí acuático
5. pasear en velero
6. jugar a las cartas
7. leer el periódico
8. ir al concierto

14 **Gramática en contexto**   See sample answer below.

Hablemos/Escribamos Con un(a) compañero(a), haz un resumen de lo que escribió Josefina. Luego digan dónde y cuándo conocieron Uds. a su mejor amigo(a). ¿De qué hablaron la primera vez que se conocieron?

¿Se te ha olvidado?
irregular preterite
Ver la página R36

> **Querido diario,**   2 de septiembre
>
> Hoy conocí a un tipo increíble. Fui a la playa Riazor esta tarde y vi al chico de mis sueños pero me pareció que él no me vio a mí. Bueno, por la noche hubo una fiesta en casa de Teresa. De veras no quería ir, pero fui... y ¿sabes qué? ¡El chico de la playa estaba allí! Resulta que es amigo de Teresa. Pues, ella me lo presentó y empezamos a hablar. Se llama Joaquín y es de La Coruña. Hablamos tres horas sin parar y nos dimos cuenta de que tenemos mucho en común. Y no puedo creer lo que me dijo... ¡que me reconoció de la playa! Me gustaría hablar más con él pero mañana vuelvo a Madrid. ¡Qué lata que no puedo quedarme!

SUGERENCIA

Do you feel you've forgotten all your Spanish? Here are some tips:

• Familiarize yourself with the reference pages at the back of the book, starting on page R2. These have lists of vocabulary, grammar, and functions, much of which you've already learned. You'll probably recognize and remember a lot.
• Don't be too worried about making mistakes in class. They're an opportunity to learn more about Spanish.

Communication for All Students

Slower Pace

13 Have the class conjugate the given verbs in both the present indicative and preterite tenses before listening to the recording.

Auditory Learners

15 After the writing exercise, have the students role-play the same content using telephones.

Cooperative Learning

15 Have students work together in groups of three to prepare a skit about a couple on a date. Assign one student to be the scribe and two to be the performers. Each group should agree on the correct sequence of events mentioned in Activity 15. The students assigned to perform may use cue cards when performing for the class.

15 **Una cita** Answers will vary.

Escribamos Imagina que pasaste un fin de semana fenomenal con un grupo de amigos. ¿Qué hicieron? ¿Adónde fueron? Escribe un párrafo con los siguientes verbos u otros. También puedes usar palabras como **primero, luego, después** y **por fin.**

regresar · pasar · ir · montar · esquiar · jugar · hacer

Nota cultural

¿Acaso come tu familia percebes *(barnacles)* en casa? Pues, la gente de Galicia y de Asturias come muchos pescados y mariscos. Por ejemplo, comen bacalao *(cod)*, mejillones, vieiras *(scallops)*, sardinas *(sardines)*, calamares, anguilas, centollo y almejas. Hasta se come el pulpo *(octopus)*, que se cocina en ollas *(pots)* grandes en las fiestas. ¿Te gustan los mariscos?

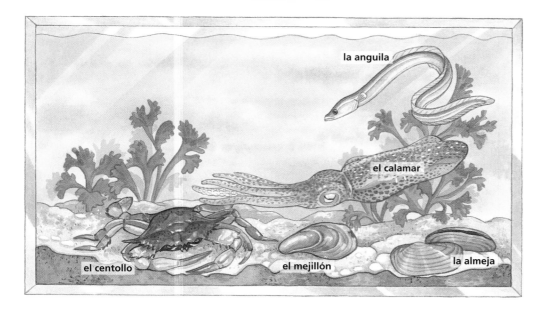

la anguila · el calamar · el centollo · el mejillón · la almeja

16 **¿Qué tal las vacaciones?** Answers will vary.

Hablemos/Escribamos Pregúntale a un(a) compañero(a) qué hizo en sus vacaciones de verano. Escribe después un párrafo sobre sus experiencias y preséntalo a la clase.

© Watterson Dist. by Universal Press Syndicate. Reprinted with permission. All rights reserved.

Connections and Comparisons

Health Link

Fish and shellfish (both important sources of protein, B vitamins, and Omega-3 fatty acids, which reduce the risk of heart disease) are an important part of the Spanish diet. Have students research the role of the different food groups in the everyday diet of Spaniards. As a starting point, you might have them refer to the **platos típicos** listed on page 1. Ask them to find out what other foods are commonly eaten in Galicia or elsewhere in Spain and to discuss whether they represent a nutritionally balanced diet. You might suggest that they use the Internet to search for this information; a cookbook of Spanish dishes would also be a good resource.

Primer paso

CAPÍTULO 1

Writing Assessment

16 Have students write a letter to a friend in which they relate what they did over the summer, including sports or other pastimes that they spent time doing. They should also use the **Así se dice** functions on page 9 to talk about their current interests. You may wish to assess this assignment using the following rubric.

Writing Rubric	Points			
	4	3	2	1
Content (Complete–Incomplete)				
Comprehensibility (Comprehensible–Incomprehensible)				
Accuracy (Accurate–Seldom accurate)				
Organization (Well organized–Poorly organized)				
Effort (Excellent–Minimal)				

18–20: A   14–15: C   Under
16–17: B   12–13: D   12: F

Teaching Suggestion

Nota cultural Ask students to name the most exotic seafood they have eaten. How often do they eat seafood? Have students name restaurants in their town or city where seafood is served.

Assess

▸ Testing Program, pp. 1–4 Quiz 1-1A, Quiz 1-1B Audio CD 1, Tr. 15

▸ Student Make-Up Assignments, Chapter 1, Alternative Quiz

▸ Alternative Assessment Guide, p. 30

Presenting
¡Adelante!

Play the Audio CD while students look at the photos and read the captions and Amparo's letter. Next, present the Preteaching Vocabulary. Ask students to use the photos and captions to describe what Amparo is like.

Contigo en la distancia

As an alternative or in addition to **¡Adelante!,** you may wish to show Episode 1 of **Contigo en la distancia.** For suggestions and activities, see the *Video Guide.*

Cuaderno de actividades, p. 6, Acts. 11–12

¡Adelante! · *Una carta a Miguel*

CD 1
Trs. 6–7

Amparo recibió la carta de Miguel y le respondió. Ella es de Gijón, una ciudad en la región de Asturias. Amparo le cuenta cuáles son sus pasatiempos y deportes favoritos. Lee su carta para saber más de ella.

HOMBRES EN LA LUNA
y Los Pasotes
Viernes 18 Julio
21,30 h
Sala Peñas
Precio Único 2.500 pts [IVA incl.]

Lo mejor del verano fue el concierto de Hombres en la Luna. Fui al concierto con mis amigos.

Hice una excursión a caballo en junio. En julio mi familia y yo hicimos camping en el Parque Nacional de Covadonga. ¡Qué belleza!

Querido Miguel,
                                                3 de septiembre
        ¡Gracias por tu carta! Yo también tengo 16 años.
Soy baja y rubia, y mis amigas dicen que soy simpática
aunque Isabel, mi hermana menor, piensa que soy la persona
más pesada del mundo. Ella tiene 10 años y es muy traviesa.
        Me gustan también los deportes, pero prefiero los
deportes individuales, y no de equipo. Practico el montañismo en los Picos de Europa y sé montar a caballo. También me
gusta mucho esquiar. Una vez mi familia y yo fuimos a
Valgrande-Pajares a esquiar, un lugar de esquí fenomenal en
Asturias. Además, también me interesan la fotografía y las
películas.
        Yo también lo pasé muy bien este verano. Hice cam-
ping con mi familia en Covadonga, un parque nacional. ¡Me
gustaría conocerte el próximo año! Quiero saber más de ti.
¿Te llevas bien con tu hermanito, o a veces es tan pesado
como mi hermana? ¿Cómo sabes practicar tantos deportes?
¿Cuándo aprendiste a bucear? ¿Dónde conociste a tu amigo
de Nueva York?
        Bueno, es todo por ahora.

                                        Saludos, *Amparo*

EXCURSIONES A CABALLO

• Turismo ecuestre de un día, un fin de semana o una semana completa, por los ríos y las montañas de Asturias
• No es necesario tener experiencia

Centro De Equitación "La Granja"

Preteaching Vocabulary

Activating Prior Knowledge

Point out that in **¡Adelante!,** Amparo is respond-ing to Miguel's letter. How might she respond to his questions about what she likes to do? Based on Spanish expressions students already know, can they guess what Amparo means when she says that her sister thinks she is **la persona más pesada del mundo?** What does Amparo mean when she asks Miguel if his brother is **tan pesado como mi hermana?** Amparo says that she enjoys **deportes individuales.** Of the sports that students currently know, which ones would they classify as individual sports? Which would they classify as team sports?

17 **¿Cómo es Amparo?** See answers below.

Completa las siguientes oraciones según la carta de Amparo.

1. Según sus amigas, Amparo es una persona...
2. Según su hermana menor, Amparo es...
3. A ella le gustan los deportes pero prefiere los...
4. Practica el montañismo en...
5. Una vez esquió en...
6. A ella le gustan...
7. Amparo fue al concierto de...
8. Ella hizo camping en...
9. Amparo piensa que su hermana es...

18 **¿Qué palabras se usan?** See answers below.

¿Qué palabras usa Amparo para...?

1. describirse a sí misma
2. hacerle preguntas a Miguel sobre los deportes
3. hablar de lo que hizo en sus vacaciones
4. hablar de lo que le interesa

19 **¿Comprendiste?** See answers below.

Contesta las siguientes preguntas.

1. ¿Qué tienen en común Miguel y Amparo?
2. ¿Qué tipo de deportes prefiere Amparo? ¿Cuáles son?
3. ¿Cuáles son sus pasatiempos?
4. Según Amparo, ¿cuál fue la mejor experiencia del verano?
5. ¿Qué hizo ella en junio?
6. ¿Adónde fue Amparo con su familia en julio? ¿Qué hicieron allí?
7. ¿Crees que Miguel y Amparo son compatibles como amigos? ¿Por qué sí o por qué no?

20 **¿Qué tienen en común?** Script and answers on p. 3H.

Vas a escuchar a seis compañeros de Amparo hablar de lo que hicieron durante el verano. Después de escuchar las frases, indica si tienen más en común con Amparo o con Miguel.

21 **Ahora te toca a ti**

Lee la carta y mira las fotos de Amparo otra vez. ¿Qué tienes en común con Amparo? ¿Qué deporte o pasatiempo te interesa más? ¿Crees que te gustaría visitar Asturias? ¿Por qué sí o por qué no?

FESTIVAL INTERNACIONAL DE CINE DE GIJON

¡ADELANTE!

CAPÍTULO 1

Culture Note
Have students look at the **Hombres en la Luna** concert ticket stub. The letters **IVA** stand for **impuesto sobre el valor añadido** (known as the VAT, or value-added tax, in English). This sales tax is included in the price of most goods and services within the European Union.

Answers

17 1. simpática
2. la persona más pesada del mundo
3. deportes individuales
4. los Picos de Europa
5. Valgrande-Pajares
6. la fotografía y las películas
7. Hombres en la Luna
8. el Parque Nacional de Covadonga
9. pesada

18 1. baja, rubia
2. ¿Cómo sabes practicar tantos deportes? ¿Cuándo aprendiste a bucear?
3. Fui al concierto. Hice una excursión a caballo. Mi familia y yo hicimos camping.
4. Me gusta mucho esquiar. Me interesan la fotografía y las películas.

19 1. Miguel y Amparo tienen 16 años. Son aficionados a los deportes.
2. Amparo prefiere los deportes individuales, como el montañismo y el esquí.
3. Le interesan la fotografía y las películas.
4. La mejor experiencia del verano fue el concierto de Hombres en la Luna.
5. Hizo una excursión a caballo.
6. Fue al Parque Nacional de Covadonga. Ella y su familia hicieron camping allí.
7. *Answers will vary.*

Comprehension Check

Slower Pace

17 Before completing the activity, have the class work together to locate the information in the text necessary to answer each question.

Additional Practice

19 Have pairs of students rewrite questions two through six so that the questions will be about them. Then ask students to take turns answering the questions with their partners.

Thinking Critically

Comparing and Contrasting Have students compare Amparo's letter to Miguel's. In what ways are Amparo and Miguel alike? How are they different? Have groups of students chart their answers and report them to the class.

Objectives Asking for information; describing yourself and others

WV3 LA CORUNA-1

Teaching Resources
pp. 16–18

PRINT
- Lesson Planner, p. 4
- Listening Activities, pp. 4, 8–9
- Activities for Communication, pp. 3–4, 52–53, 89–90
- Cuaderno de gramática, pp. 6–9
- Grammar Tutor for Students of Spanish, Chapter 1
- Cuaderno de actividades, pp. 7–10
- Cuaderno para hispanohablantes, pp. 1–5
- Testing Program, pp. 5–8
- Alternative Assessment Guide, p. 30
- Student Make-Up Assignments, Chapter 1

MEDIA
- One-Stop Planner
- Audio Compact Discs, CD 1, Trs. 9, 22–24, 16
- Teaching Transparencies 1-2; **Más práctica gramatical** Answers; Cuaderno de gramática Answers
- Interactive CD-ROM Tutor, Disc 1

 Bell Work

Have students write answers to the following questions: **¿A qué deporte eres aficionado(a)? ¿De qué deporte estás harto(a)? ¿Qué pasatiempo te gusta más?**

Presenting
Así se dice

Review the question words by asking students basic questions: **¿Cómo te llamas? ¿Qué hiciste anoche?** Then have students read the cartoon, paying special attention to the questions.

Así se dice

Asking for information

Para hacer una pregunta en español puedes usar palabras interrogativas como **¿Quién?, ¿Por qué?** y **¿De dónde?** Mira los ejemplos:

¿Cuántos años tienes?

¿Qué te gusta hacer en tus ratos libres?

¿Cómo sabes practicar tantos deportes?

¿Cuándo aprendiste a bucear?

¿Dónde conociste a tu amigo de Nueva York?

Más práctica gramatical, p. 26, Act. 6

Cuaderno de actividades, p. 7, Acts. 13–14

Cuaderno de gramática, p. 6, Acts. 12–13

22 **¿Me oíste?** Script and answers on p. 3H.

Escuchemos Amparo está hablando con varios amigos en una fiesta. No responde bien a las preguntas porque la música está muy alta y no oye bien. Escucha las siguientes conversaciones e indica si las respuestas son **lógicas** o **ilógicas.**

CD 1
Tr. 9

23 **¿Cuál es la pregunta?** See possible answers below.

 Hablemos/Escribamos Mira otra vez la información cultural en las páginas 1, 2 y 3. Con un(a) compañero(a), escribe preguntas apropiadas para las siguientes respuestas. Puede haber *(There can be)* más de una pregunta.

1. Galicia es una región muy verde y fresca.
2. Muchos peregrinos cristianos iban a Santiago de Compostela durante la Edad Media.
3. Galicia tiene un área de 29.575 kilómetros cuadrados *(square).*
4. La Coruña se llama La Ciudad Cristal porque tiene galerías o balcones de vidrio.
5. Rosalía de Castro fue una escritora famosa de Galicia.
6. Galicia tiene unos 2.800.000 de habitantes.
7. Los celtas poblaron Galicia mucho antes que los romanos.
8. La gaita es un instrumento tradicional de Galicia.
9. El único faro romano que todavía se usa es la Torre de Hércules.
10. Galicia tiene 386 kilómetros de costa.

¿Te acuerdas?

Sometimes questions are formed by reversing the word order of the subject and verb in a sentence: **¿Escala montañas Pedro?** You can also add a word like **¿no?** or **¿verdad?**, as in **Susana toca la flauta, ¿verdad?**

Communication for All Students

Challenge

Have pairs of students write creative answers to each of Calvin's questions. Then ask volunteers to read their answers to the other students who will guess which question is being answered.

Group Work

23 Ask groups of three students to look at the Location Opener on pages 2–3 and write six questions based on the information presented there. Then have groups trade papers and answer each others' questions. Ask for a volunteer from each group to report the information to the class.

STANDARDS: 1.2, 2.2

Así se dice

Describing yourself and others

Noor es muy simpática e inteligente. Es alta, morena y muy guapa, ¿no crees?

Si quieres describir el aspecto físico de una persona, puedes decir:

El Sr. Montálvez **tiene bigote y barba,** y es calvo.
. . . *has a moustache and a beard* . . .

Mi prima Julia **es pelirroja y tiene el pelo rizado.**

Patricio **es de estatura mediana y lleva gafas.**

Si quieres describir la personalidad de una persona también, puedes decir:

La profesora Minguillón **es seria pero es muy buena gente.**

Florencio es **pesado; ¡no hay quien lo aguante!**

Esteban es **un tío estupendo.**
. . . *a great guy.*

Mi novio es muy **abierto y tiene un buen sentido del humor.**

Cuaderno de actividades, pp. 8–10, Acts. 16–17, 20

También se puede decir...

En Latinoamérica se usan las palabras **anteojos, lentes** y **espejuelos** por **gafas.**

---

24 **Amigos nuevos** Possible answers below.

✏️ **Escribamos** Escribe descripciones de las siguientes personas. Usa expresiones de **Así se dice.**

a.

b.

c.

d.

Vocabulario

abierto(a)	*open*	**no hay quien lo (la) aguante**	*nobody can stand him (her)*
buena gente	*nice*	**pesado(a)**	*annoying*
fenomenal	*great*		
una gran persona	*a great person*		
un gran tipo	*a great guy*		
majo(a)	*nice (Spain)*		

Cuaderno de gramática, p. 7, Acts. 14–15   Cuaderno de actividades, p. 10, Act. 18

---

25 **¿En quién piensas?**

👥 **Hablemos** Con dos compañeros de clase, describe a cuatro personas famosas para ver si pueden adivinar quiénes son. Intercambien papeles.

¿Se te ha olvidado?
adjectives
Ver las páginas R79–98

Connections and Comparisons

History Link

25 Have the class play **Veinte preguntas** in which one student thinks of a historical figure while the rest of the class tries to guess his or her identity by asking yes-or-no questions in a round-robin fashion. If the student does not know the answer to a question, he or she can say **Eso no lo sé.** The student who identifies the person then thinks of another famous person from history and answers the class's questions. Ask one student to end each round at 20 questions and to keep track of how many questions are necessary to arrive at the correct answer. Have students create posters of the people who were most difficult to identify.

STANDARDS: 1.1, 1.3, 3.1, 5.1, 5.2

Presenting
Así se dice, Vocabulario
Describe people familiar to students using the different physical traits and personality types presented. Ask for a volunteer to read the description under the photo of Noor. Ask the class if they agree with the description; if not, have them change it to reflect their opinion. Ask students to name people who match the descriptions in **Así se dice.**

Answers

23 *Possible answers:*
1. ¿Cómo es Galicia?
2. ¿Adónde iban los peregrinos cristianos en la Edad Media?
3. ¿Qué área tiene Galicia?
4. ¿Por qué La Coruña se llama la Ciudad Cristal?
5. ¿Quién fue Rosalía de Castro?
6. ¿Cuántos habitantes tiene Galicia?
7. ¿Cuándo llegaron los celtas a Galicia?
8. ¿Qué es la gaita?
9. ¿Cuál es el único faro romano que todavía se usa?
10. ¿Cuántos kilómetros de costa tiene Galicia?

24 *Possible answers:*
a. Lleva anteojos. Es un poco serio pero tiene buen sentido del humor.
b. Es moreno y toca el clarinete.
c. Es mayor y pelirroja y es buena gente.
d. Es alto, y tiene barba y bigote. Es muy abierto.

Presenting
Gramática de repaso

saber vs. conocer To model usage of **saber** and **conocer**, relate facts about people and places with which you and the students are familiar. **(Yo sé que Bismarck es la capital de Dakota del Norte. Conozco bien la ciudad de Santiago.)** Tell students to write five sentences using a different form of **conocer** in each. They should do the same with **saber**. Then go over the sentences with the students, checking for comprehension.

Presenting
Nota gramatical

o to **u; y** to **e** Display *Teaching Transparency 1–2* and describe it orally. Ask students to note each use of **u** or **e** in your description.

Assess
▶ Testing Program, pp. 5–8
Quiz 1-2A, Quiz 1-2B
Audio CD 1, Tr. 16

▶ Student Make-Up Assignments, Chapter 1, Alternative Quiz

▶ Alternative Assessment Guide, p. 30

Answers
26 1. Conoces
2. Sabes
3. Sabes
4. Conoces
5. Sabes
6. Sabes
7. Conoces

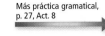

Gramática de repaso

saber vs. conocer

Both **saber** and **conocer** mean *to know.*

1. **Conocer** means *to know, to meet or see for the first time,* or *to be familiar with* a person or a place. Remember to use the "personal **a**" when referring to a person.

   ¿Dónde **conociste a** tu amigo de Nueva York?
   ¿**Conoces** las playas de Galicia?

   > Más práctica gramatical, p. 27, Act. 8

2. **Saber** means *to know* a fact or *to have information about* something or someone. It also means to *know how* to do something when used with an infinitive.

   Quiero **saber** más de ti.
   Amparo **sabe** hablar francés.

   > Cuaderno de actividades, pp. 8–10, Acts. 15, 19

   > Cuaderno de gramática, p. 8, Acts. 16–18

---

26 ### Gramática en contexto   See answers below.

Leamos/Hablemos Con un(a) compañero(a), decide entre **sabes** o **conoces** para las siguientes preguntas. Después, contesten las preguntas.

1. ¿_____ a una persona muy inteligente?
2. ¿_____ el nombre del rey de España?
3. ¿_____ tocar algún instrumento?
4. ¿_____ al presidente de Estados Unidos?
5. ¿_____ remar?
6. ¿_____ cuál es la flor oficial de tu estado?
7. ¿_____ a alguien que practique ciclismo?

27 ### Gramática en contexto

Leamos/Hablemos Con unos compañeros, lee las siguientes oraciones e indica si son **ciertas** o **falsas**. Luego cambien las oraciones falsas para reflejar la realidad de su grupo.

MODELO   Todos sabemos patinar.
—Falso. Dos personas saben patinar pero una no.

1. Nadie en nuestro grupo conoce a ninguna persona de otro país.
2. Dos personas en nuestro grupo saben hacer el esquí acuático.
3. Todos sabemos tres idiomas.
4. Todos conocemos a un adulto pesado.
5. Una persona en nuestro grupo sabe bucear.
6. Todos conocemos Escocia e Inglaterra.

Nota gramatical

In Spanish, **o** *(or)* changes to **u** before a word that begins with **o-** or **ho-**.

El viaje a La Coruña es de siete u ocho horas.

In the same way, **y** *(and)* changes to **e** before a word that begins with **i-** or **hi-**.

Sergio e Hilaria van a bucear.

> Cuaderno de gramática, p. 9, Acts. 19–21

> Más práctica gramatical, p. 26, Act. 7

---

28 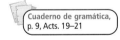 Del colegio al trabajo

Escribamos Imagina que eres el(la) director(a) de un programa de intercambio en España. Tienes que preparar preguntas para entrevistar a los estudiantes que quieren participar. Incluye datos personales (edad, dónde vives, etc.), los deportes y pasatiempos que les gustan o que no les gustan y por qué desean ir. Escribe las preguntas en una hoja de papel.

Communication for All Students

Native Speakers
Have students list all the words they know that begin with **o-, ho-, i-,** and **hi-**. Then have pairs of students write five sentences in which **o** would become **u** and **y** would become **e**. Ask students to read one of their sentences to the class, omitting the conjunction for volunteers to fill in.

Additional Practice
26 Ask students to look at the Location Opener on pages 2–3 and write six questions based on the information presented there. In three of their questions they should use **saber** and in the remaining three they should use **conocer**. Have students ask their questions to a partner or to the class as a whole.

¿Qué hiciste en las últimas vacaciones?

CD 1
Trs. 10–13

¿Qué piensas que hacen de vacaciones los muchachos hispanohablantes? ¿Tienes algo en común con estos tres jóvenes?

Teaching Resources
p. 19

PRINT
▶ Video Guide, pp. 3–5, 7
▶ Cuaderno de actividades, p. 12
▶ Cuaderno para hispanohablantes, pp. 1–5

MEDIA
▶ One-Stop Planner
▶ Video Program, Videocassette 1, 08:00–10:19
▶ Audio Compact Discs, CD 1, Trs. 10–13
▶ Interactive CD-ROM Tutor, Disc 1

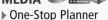

Yoni Antonio
Barba de Heredia, Costa Rica   CD 1 Tr. 11

"Bueno, me quedé ayudándole a mi padre a hacer trabajos allí en la casa y por ratillos ir a practicar deporte: la montañera o jugar basquetbol".

CD 1 Tr. 12
Begonia
Madrid, España

"Fui a Cataluña. Me lo pasé muy bien y me bañé, visité monumentos... fui de compras... compré cosas para la playa".

CD 1 Tr. 13
Vivian
Miami, Florida

"Estuve en Nueva York con mi mamá y con mi hermana y con una amiga mejor allí. Fuimos a pasear, ... de compras".

Presenting
Panorama cultural

Have students read the captions, then play the audio or video recording. Discuss the questions in **Para pensar y hablar...** Play the recording again and have students answer the **Preguntas.**

Para pensar y hablar...

A. Escribe en una hoja de papel qué hiciste durante las últimas vacaciones. Compara tu respuesta con las de las personas entrevistadas.

B. Barba de Heredia is a small town. Imagine that Yoni Antonio went to Madrid for vacation. What kinds of activities could he do in Madrid that he probably couldn't do in his hometown? If Begonia were to travel to Barba de Heredia, what could she do there that she probably couldn't do in Madrid?

Cuaderno para hispanohablantes, pp. 1–5

Preguntas
1. **¿Qué deportes practicaba Yoni Antonio?** (la montañera y el básquetbol)
2. **¿Adónde fue Begonia?** (Fue a Cataluña.)
3. **¿Con quiénes estuvo Vivian en Nueva York?** (Estuvo con su mamá, su hermana y una amiga.)
4. **¿A quién ayudaba Yoni Antonio?** (Ayudaba a su padre.)
5. **¿Qué hizo Vivian en Nueva York?** (Fue a pasear y a hacer compras.)

Cultures and Communities

Culture Note
Yoni Antonio is the only student to mention work, and he works at home with his father. Have students compare this to their own experience. In Spanish-speaking countries middle and upper-income young people rarely seek employment outside the home during vacation periods. They live at home until marriage, school, or work obliges them to move.

Language Note
Point out that both Begonia and Vivian use the idiomatic expression **ir de compras.** What other idioms can students recognize in the interviews?

CAPÍTULO 1

Teaching Resources
pp. 20–22

PRINT
▸ Lesson Planner, p. 5
▸ Cuaderno de actividades, p. 11
▸ Cuaderno para hispanohablantes, pp. 1–5
▸ Reading Strategies and Skills Handbook, Chapter 1
▸ ¡Lee conmigo! 3, Chapter 1
▸ Standardized Assessment Tutor, Chapter 1

MEDIA
▸ One-Stop Planner

Prereading
Activities A, B, and C

Using Text Structures
Before students read **"La tortuga,"** you might choose a poem in English to read together. Ask whether what you have read is poetry or prose and discuss what characteristics distinguish the two. (Poetry is more concise; each word is chosen for its visual and auditory effect; it is often characterized by its use of rhyme and rhythm.) Then ask them how they would expect to see turtles described in the poem. Do they expect to see complete sentences? (Poetry can take liberties with traditional prose syntax.) Have students try to determine some kind of organization in the poem, first scanning for adjectives and then for verbs.

Answers

A *Possible answers:*
Turtles are reptiles with a distinctive protective shell. They may be land- or sea-dwelling. They may live to be very old.

B *Possible answers:*
date and place of birth and death; education; occupation; accomplishments

C *Possible answers:*
shelter, protection, slowness, age

Pablo Neruda

Vas a leer un poema de Pablo Neruda, seguido por una biografía del poeta chileno.

Estrategia **para leer**
Use background knowledge as you read the poem and the poet's biography. Think about what you already know about the topic of the poem. Look for the poem's symbolic meaning by considering other ideas or experiences that might be represented by the topic. When reading about the poet, think about what information is usually conveyed in a biography. This will help you to predict the content.

¡A comenzar!

A. Read the title of the poem. Make a list of what you already know about turtles. What are they like? Where do they live? What do they do? See possible answers below.

B. Take a look at the biography on page 22. Think about the types of information that usually go into a biography. List three things that you expect to find in this reading. See possible answers below.

C. Get together with a partner and go over your lists about turtles. Think about the different symbolic meanings of a turtle. Besides what you normally think of, what else can a turtle represent? See possible answers below.

Connections and Comparisons

Biology Link
There are five species of sea turtles, and all are listed as endangered. Sea turtles may live for more than a century, and can swim up to 300 miles in a single day! They spend most of their lives in water and have flippers instead of feet. When they are ready to lay eggs, female sea turtles return to the beach where they were hatched.

Science Link
Have students do research about the species of turtles that live in the area. Students should find out how long these turtles live, what they eat, and what their natural predators are. Students can present their findings to the class with a poster or a simple poem describing the life of a local turtle.

STANDARDS: 1.2, 2.2, 3.1

La tortuga

Pablo Neruda

La tortuga que
anduvo
tanto tiempo
y tanto vio
con
sus
antiguos
ojos,
la tortuga
que comió
aceitunas
del más profundo
mar,
la tortuga que nadó
siete siglos
y conoció
siete
mil
primaveras,
la tortuga
blindada
contra
el calor
y el frío,
contra
los rayos y las olas,

la tortuga
amarilla
y plateada,
con severos
lunares
ambarinos
y pies de rapiña,
la tortuga
se quedó
aquí
durmiendo,
y no lo sabe.
De tan vieja
se fue
poniendo dura,
dejó
de amar las olas
y fue rígida
como una plancha
de planchar.
Cerró
los ojos que
tanto
mar, cielo, tiempo y
tierra
desafiaron,
y se durmió
entre las otras
piedras.

Vamos a leer

CAPÍTULO 1

Reading
Activities D, E, and F

¿Te acuerdas?
Use context to guess the meaning of unknown words. Make logical guesses by using the words and phrases that surround the unknown word.

Al grano

D. Scan the poem and try to understand how the poet describes the turtle. What images or ideas come to mind? Read the following sentences and indicate whether each one is **cierto** o **falso.**

1. La tortuga vive muchos años. cierto

2. A la tortuga le afecta mucho el clima. falso

3. La tortuga tiene mucha energía. falso

4. La tortuga ha visto *(has seen)* mucho. cierto

5. La tortuga parece dormir. cierto

E. Now read the following questions. Read the poem again more carefully. Keep these questions in mind as you read. Answers will vary.

1. What does **"...dejó de amar las olas"** mean?

2. What is the poet referring to with the following simile: **"...y fue rígida como una plancha de planchar"**? A simile is a phrase that compares one thing to another to create an image. For example, "The stars were like jewels in the night sky."

3. Neruda ends the poem with **"...y se durmió entre las otras piedras."** What is the metaphor in this phrase? What does it stand for? Remember that a metaphor refers to a thing or idea as something else. For example, "The jewels of the night sky shone brightly." In this case, the word "jewels" is a metaphor for "stars".

Using Prior Knowledge
Ask students what is unusual about the way in which the poem is arranged on the page. (Many lines consist of only one word.) Ask what effect this arrangement has on the reader. (slows the poem's pace; gives individual words and phrases added significance; enhances the poem's contemplative tone) Ask how the form of the poem relates to its topic. (suggests the length and pace of the turtle's life) Ask students if they know of other poems whose form and content are closely related. (Shelley's "To a Skylark"; e.e. cummings's "in Just-")

Using Context Clues
At first, students may have difficulty using context to determine meaning in this poem.

- Remind students to pay close attention to the words they recognize in the poem, and suggest that they look up some of the words they do not know in a dictionary. (You can make this a class activity.) Looking up a few key words will help them build the context they need for understanding more of the poem.

- Encourage them to look at the poem's structure to find context for unfamiliar words. For instance, each time the phrase **la tortuga** is used, it is followed by modifiers.

Cultures and Communities

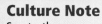

Culture Note
Sea turtle eggs are a popular food in parts of Mexico and Central America, and sales can be quite profitable. In an effort to save the endangered species from both human and natural predators, Tortuguero National Park in Costa Rica was established to protect 22 miles of nesting beach for the turtles.

Group Work
The ancient Greek writer Aesop wrote perhaps the most famous story about a tortoise (a land turtle) in his fable "The Tortoise and the Hare." Have groups of students create a children's adaptation of the story in Spanish with illustrations. Students can then share their stories with elementary students.

CAPÍTULO 1

Teaching Resources
pp. 20–22

PRINT
▸ Lesson Planner, p. 5
▸ Cuaderno de actividades, p. 11
▸ Cuaderno para hispanohablantes, pp. 1–5
▸ Reading Strategies and Skills Handbook, Chapter 1
▸ ¡Lee conmigo! 3, Chapter 1
▸ Standardized Assessment Tutor, Chapter 1

MEDIA
▸ One-Stop Planner

Postreading

Activity G

Making Inferences

Have students reread the biography of Neruda and organize elements of the text. They should list all of the places where Neruda lived, his publications, and how old he was at various important times.

Answers

G *Sample answer:*
The variety of experiences in Neruda's life is reflected in what he reveals about the turtle. Just as the turtle "saw" many things that hardened it, Neruda was toughened by what he saw during his career, especially during the Spanish Civil War. As the turtle defied its environment (sea, sky, time, and earth), Neruda rebelled against social and political conventions. But just as the turtle eventually left the sea that had both nourished it and challenged it for so long, Neruda moved away from the controversial literary style that brought him fame.

¿Te acuerdas?

Use cognates to guess the meaning of new words. Cognates are words that look alike and have similar meanings in two languages.

F. Read the biography of Pablo Neruda. Then look at the following groups of sentences and, for each group, decide which sentence best summarizes the narrative.

1. a. Neruda began writing and publishing poems in his later years.
   b. Pablo Neruda first experimented with writing poetry during his teenage years and published his first book before he was twenty.
   c. Neruda began to write poetry after his experiences in the Spanish Civil War.

2. a. After spending a long and productive life in Chile, Neruda won the Nobel Prize for Literature.
   b. The hardships he experienced from spending his whole life in the frontier town of Temuco were the only factor that affected his poetry.
   c. Neruda's writing was deeply affected by political events and by his life in other countries.

G. Now get together with a partner and discuss **La tortuga** again based on what you know about the poet's life. What experiences do you think motivated him to write this poem? Why? See sample answer below.

Cuaderno de actividades, p. 11, Act. 21

Cuaderno para hispanohablantes, pp. 1–5

Pablo Neruda (1904–1973)

Pablo Neruda, cuyo nombre verdadero fue Neftalí Reyes, nació en Parral, Chile, y es considerado uno de los poetas latinoamericanos más importantes del siglo veinte. Cuando tenía tres años se fue con su familia a Temuco, un pueblito fronterizo en el sur. Las duras condiciones de la región más tarde tendrían una gran influencia en su poesía. A los trece años Neruda publicó un artículo en un periódico local donde, poco después, lo pusieron a cargo de la página literaria.

En 1920 se fue a Santiago a estudiar en la Universidad de Chile. Cuando uno de sus poemas ganó el primer premio en un concurso literario, los patrocinadores le publicaron su primera colección de versos, *La canción de la fiesta* (1921). Ese volumen y el próximo, *Crepusculario* (1923), son de tema romántico y de estructura tradicional.

La publicación de *Veinte poemas de amor y una canción desesperada* (1924) lo consagró como un importante poeta nacional.

Neruda entró en el terreno político cuando lo nombraron cónsul honorario en Rangún, Birmania, y poco después en Ceilán y Java. Neruda se sentía frustrado en el Lejano Oriente cuando comenzó a componer *Residencia en la tierra*.

La vida y obra de Neruda se vieron profundamente afectadas por la Guerra Civil Española que estalló en 1936. Neruda empezó a escribir poesía y prosa a favor de un cambio social. Uno de sus mayores logros literarios, *Canto general de Chile* (1946), es una obra épica sobre la historia cultural y política de Chile, al mismo tiempo que una exploración de la lucha por la justicia en las Américas.

Neruda huyó de Chile en 1949 tras haber criticado severamente al presidente de la nación. En 1953 se le permitió regresar. Durante los veinte años siguientes escribió con un estilo simple y claro y volvió a temas más introspectivos y personales. En su poesía sobre el amor y la naturaleza, Neruda examina las cosas cotidianas con cuidado y atención. En 1971 ganó el Premio Nóbel de Literatura.

Communication for All Students

Slower Pace
Encourage students to approach the biographical reading by thinking about paragraph structure. Remind them that each paragraph conveys one main idea, usually stated in the first sentence, and that this "topic sentence" is supported by those that follow.

Challenge
To help students understand the range of Neruda's poetry, have them read one or more of his odes. Ask students to look for similarities and differences in form and tone. Ask students to write a brief **oda** to a common, everyday thing, expressing its importance and utility.

Vamos a escribir

¿Alguna vez has intentado explicarle a alguien uno de tus pasatiempos? Para explicarle a alguien un pasatiempo que desconoce, hay que tener cuidado con las palabras que se usan. En esta actividad, le escribirás a un amigo sobre algún pasatiempo que le interese y aprenderás una manera de organizar tu escritura.

Tu pasatiempo favorito

Imagina que tienes un(a) amigo(a) que quiere saber más sobre tu pasatiempo o deporte favorito. Escríbele una carta para describírselo, cómo se practica, qué equipo se necesita, las precauciones necesarias, etc. Toma en cuenta lo que tu amigo(a) ya sabe de tu pasatiempo.

Estrategia para escribir

Know your audience Before you write, think about who you're writing to and the reason you're writing. Write using words your reader could be expected to understand, and use an appropriate tone. For example, you'd describe a hobby differently depending on whether you were writing to your grandmother or to a child.

A. Preparación

Antes de escribir tu descripción, considera las siguientes preguntas.

1. ¿Por qué escribes esta carta?

2. ¿Para quién escribes? ¿Es niño(a) o adulto(a)? ¿Debes usar **tú** o **usted?**

3. ¿Cuánto ya sabe esta persona de tu pasatiempo o deporte?

4. ¿Qué detalles necesitas incluir para describirlo bien?

5. ¿Necesitas incluir fotos o dibujos para hacer una buena descripción?

B. Redacción

1. Escribe tu carta. Pon la fecha y una introducción para preguntar cómo está tu amigo(a), qué pasa donde vive, etc.

2. Escribe otros párrafos para describir tu pasatiempo o deporte. Usa el vocabulario y los detalles adecuados. Si la persona que va a leer esta carta es de tu edad, usa las formas de **tú.**

3. Escribe una conclusión adecuada. Si quieres, puedes resumir *(sum up)* los detalles más importantes de tu descripción.

4. Incluye fotos o dibujos si son adecuados.

C. Evaluación

1. ¿Usaste un tono adecuado? Si no, puedes hacerlo más formal o más informal.

2. Mira bien las palabras que usaste. ¿Crees que tu amigo(a) puede comprenderlas? Si no, usa otras.

3. ¿Escribiste bien todas las palabras? Si no, corrige las palabras mal escritas.

4. Si usaste fotos o dibujos, ¿qué piensas de ellos? Si no apoyan la presentación, omítelos o busca otros.

Apply and Assess

Postwriting

Pair Work

Once papers are written, have students pair up for peer-editing. They may use the Peer Editing Rubric in the *Alternative Assessment Guide,* page 8. Remind students that peer evaluation should focus on content and organization as well as spelling and grammar. Partners should point out both strengths and weaknesses and make specific suggestions to help the writer improve the text. You may want to consider grading students on their editing as well as their writing.

Teaching Resources
p. 23

PRINT
▶ Lesson Planner, p. 5
▶ Cuaderno de actividades, pp. 145–156
▶ Cuaderno para hispanohablantes, pp. 1–5
▶ Alternative Assessment Guide, p. 16
▶ Standardized Assessment Tutor, Chapter 1

MEDIA
▶ One-Stop Planner, Disc 1
  ⚡ Test Generator,
  ✍ Chapter 1
▶ Interactive CD-ROM Tutor, Disc 1

Process Writing

Prewriting

Slower Pace

A. Have students first think of a topic. Then have them work in small groups and share their topics with the group. The group will brainstorm and make suggestions regarding the content of each student's letter. Each member will take notes on the group's suggestions to help write his or her individual letter.

Writing

Have students reread Miguel's letter to Amparo in **De antemano,** and her reply in **¡Adelante!** What words and expressions do they use to greet each other? How do they close their letters to each other? You may want to review formatting, phrasing and punctuation of letters in Spanish before students write their final draft.

For **Más práctica gramatical** Answer Transparencies, see the *Teaching Transparencies* binder.

Más práctica gramatical

Primer paso

Objective Expressing interest, indifference, and displeasure

1 ¿Qué pasatiempos les gustan a todos? Combina los verbos de la primera columna con las palabras correspondientes de la segunda para formar las expresiones del **Vocabulario** en la página 10. Usa cada palabra sólo una vez. **(p. 10)**

1. hacer	**a.** a caballo
2. escalar	**b.** en línea
3. patinar	**c.** fotos
4. pasear	**d.** adhesivos
5. montar	**e.** montañas
6. sacar	**f.** esquí acuático
7. coleccionar	**g.** en velero

2 Lee lo que escribe Joaquín sobre los pasatiempos de sus amigos y su familia, y completa su descripción con el tiempo presente de los verbos **pensar** y **preferir**. **(p. 11)**

Yo ___1___ (pensar) que los videojuegos son aburridísimos. En mi

tiempo libre, ___2___ (preferir) escuchar música o tocar la batería.

Mis amigos Germán y Sergio están locos por los deportes. Ellos ___3___

(preferir) el fútbol y el baloncesto, pero ___4___ (pensar) que casi todos los

deportes son interesantes. Mi hermana y yo vamos mucho al cine. Nosotros

___5___ (preferir) las películas de ciencia ficción y de horror. Y también

___6___ (pensar) que las películas de Alfred Hitchcock son fabulosas. En

cambio, a mamá no le interesa el cine. Ella ___7___ (pensar) que es un rollo

hacer cola. En su tiempo libre, ___8___ (preferir) leer novelas o ver videos

en casa. ¿Y tú? ¿Qué pasatiempos ___9___ (preferir)? ¿Tú ___10___ (pensar)

hacer algo interesante este fin de semana?

Answers

1
1. f
2. e
3. b
4. g
5. a
6. c
7. d

2
1. pienso
2. prefiero
3. prefieren
4. piensan
5. preferimos
6. pensamos
7. piensa
8. prefiere
9. prefieres
10. piensas

Grammar Resources for Chapter 1

The **Más práctica gramatical** activities are designed as supplemental activities for the grammatical concepts presented in the chapter. You might use them as additional practice, for review, or for assessment.

For more grammar presentation, review, and practice, refer to the following:
• Cuaderno de gramática
• Grammar Tutor for Students of Spanish

• Grammar Summary on pp. R25–R46
• Cuaderno de actividades
• Grammar and Vocabulary quizzes (Testing Program)
• Test Generator on the One-Stop Planner CD-ROM
• Interactive CD-ROM Tutor
• **Juegos interactivos** at <u>go.hrw.com</u>

3 Explica a qué deportes u otras actividades juegan todos por la tarde, y a qué hora vuelven a casa. Usa el tiempo presente de los verbos **jugar** y **volver**. Sigue el modelo. **(p. 11)**

MODELO **Marisol/jugar a los videojuegos/volver a casa/4:30**
—Marisol juega a los videojuegos. Vuelve a casa a las cuatro y media.

1. (yo)/jugar al voleibol/volver a casa/6:00
2. mi abuelo/jugar al dominó/volver a casa/5:30
3. mi hermanito/jugar un juego de mesa/volver a casa/3:30
4. Patricia y Lourdes/jugar al tenis/volver a casa/6:30
5. Fernando y yo/jugar al baloncesto/volver a casa/5:00
6. ¿(tú)/jugar al fútbol o al béisbol?/¿volver a casa/4:00 o 4:30?

4 Para Alicia y su familia, ¿qué es el regalo ideal? Escribe lo que todos quieren este año. Consulta la tabla y usa el tiempo presente del verbo **pedir**. (p. 11)

MODELO **Suso/guitarra eléctrica**
—Suso pide una guitarra eléctrica.

SUSO	GUITARRA ELÉCTRICA
1. yo	caballo
2. mis hermanitos	perro
3. mi hermana	velero
4. papá	cámara
5. mamá y tía Inés	viaje al Caribe
6. Suso y yo	clases de buceo

5 Teresa y su club de montañismo pasaron el fin de semana en un campamento. Completa la descripción de la excursión con el pretérito de los verbos entre paréntesis. (p. 12)

¡Qué bien lo pasé este fin de semana! Yo __1__ (llegar) al campamento el viernes por la tarde. Nélida y Fran __2__ (buscar) leña y Ricardo y yo __3__ (preparar) la cena. Nosotros __4__ (comer) hamburguesas, perros calientes y galletas de chocolate. Después, Fran __5__ (tocar) la guitarra y nuestro instructor nos __6__ (explicar) qué íbamos a hacer al día siguiente. El sábado, todos __7__ (levantarse) temprano. Pasamos el día practicando la escalada deportiva. ¡Yo __8__ (escalar) el cerro Gordo cuatro veces! Nuestro instructor me __9__ (ayudar) bastante y yo __10__ (aprender) muchísimo. Yo __11__ (sacar) muchas fotos de todo el grupo. Esa noche, todos estábamos cansados y __12__ (dormir) como lirones. El domingo por la mañana, yo __13__ (nadar) con Nélida por un rato, y Fran y Ricardo __14__ (montar) a caballo. Después, nosotros __15__ (quitar) las tiendas de campaña, limpiamos el campamento y __16__ (volver) a casa.

CAPÍTULO 1

3 Answers
1. Juego al voleibol. Vuelvo a casa a las seis.
2. Abuelo juega al dominó. Vuelve a casa a las cinco y media.
3. Mi hermanito juega un juego de mesa. Vuelve a casa a las tres y media.
4. Patricia y Lourdes juegan al tenis. Vuelven a casa a las seis y media.
5. Fernando y yo jugamos al baloncesto. Volvemos a casa a las cinco.
6. ¿Juegas al fútbol o al béisbol? ¿Vuelves a casa a las cuatro o a las cuatro y media?

4
1. Pido un caballo.
2. Mis hermanitos piden un perro.
3. Mi hermana pide un velero.
4. Papá pide una cámara.
5. Mamá y tía Inés piden un viaje al Caribe.
6. Suso y yo pedimos unas clases de buceo.

5
1. llegué
2. buscaron
3. preparamos
4. comimos
5. tocó
6. explicó
7. nos levantamos/se levantaron
8. escalé
9. ayudó
10. aprendí
11. saqué
12. dormimos
13. nadé
14. montaron
15. quitamos
16. volvimos

Communication for All Students

Challenge
3 Have pairs of students write two questions that would generate the responses for each item. (**¿A qué juega el abuelo? ¿A qué hora vuelve a casa?**) Then have all students close their books as various students ask their questions. Students should attempt to answer from memory.

Native Speakers
5 Have students write a paragraph in the third person describing a camping trip in which Teresa did not have a good time. Students should turn all of Teresa's experiences into negative ones and explain why they were unpleasant. The paragraph should close with what Teresa will do differently on the next trip.

STANDARDS: 1.2, 1.3 **MÁS PRÁCTICA GRAMATICAL**   **VEINTICINCO** **25**

For **Más práctica gramatical** Answer Transparencies, see the *Teaching Transparencies* binder.

Segundo paso

Objectives Asking for information; describing yourself and others

6 Amalia le está haciendo muchas preguntas a Robert, un estudiante de intercambio. Completa sus preguntas con la palabra interrogativa correcta. **(p. 16)**

> ¿quién? ¿qué? ¿de dónde? ¿por qué?
>
> ¿cuántos? ¿cuál? ¿cuándo? ¿cómo?

1. Buenos días, Robert. ¿ ═══ eres originalmente?
2. ¿ ═══ años tienes?
3. Robert, hablas muy bien el español. ¿ ═══ empezaste a estudiarlo?
4. Éste es tu primer año aquí, ¿verdad? ¿ ═══ te parece nuestro colegio?
5. ¿ ═══ clases tienes este año?
6. ¿ ═══ es tu profesor favorito?
7. Háblame un poco de tu familia. ¿ ═══ son tus padres y tus hermanos?
8. ¿ ═══ es tu deporte favorito?
9. Pues, gracias otra vez, Robert. Oye, ¿te gusta el helado? ¿ ═══ no vamos a tomar un helado después de clases hoy?

7 Completa lo que dicen todos sobre sus planes para el fin de semana con la palabra correcta: **y, e, o, u. (p. 18)**

1. El sábado quiero descansar (y/e) ir a la playa. Si hace mal tiempo, pienso leer (o/u) ver un video en casa.
2. Leticia, ¿tienes clase de baile mañana? ¿Es a las diez (o/u) a las once?
3. Raimundo nunca quiere salir con nosotros. Siempre dice que está cansado (o/u) ocupado.
4. Manuel no va a salir este fin de semana—el lunes tiene exámenes de química (y/e) inglés. ¡Qué paliza!
5. Me gustaría salir con Isa y Óscar. Voy a llamarlos (y/e) invitarlos a cenar conmigo el domingo.
6. Siempre invitamos a Lalo a salir, ¡pero el tipo está tan distraído! O llega tarde (o/u) olvida la cita o deja el dinero en casa.
7. Teresa quería hacer algo con nosotros esta noche, (y/e) iba a venir a mi casa, pero ahora no puede. Se enfermó su hermanito (y/e) ella tiene que cuidarlo.

Answers

6
1. De dónde
2. Cuántos
3. Cuándo
4. Qué
5. Qué
6. Quién
7. Cómo
8. Cuál
9. Por qué

7
1. e, o
2. o
3. u
4. e
5. e
6. u
7. e, y

Communication for All Students

Group Work

6 Bring in various items and photos of people and things that might be hard to identify. Divide the class into groups of three or four and give each group an item or photo. Ask students to write as many questions as possible that would elicit information about the item. Other students answer the questions creatively.

Slower Pace

7 Have pairs of students write a survey of five questions about personal preferences (food, pastimes, clothing) in which **e** and **u** replace **y** and **o**. Students then ask their questions to classmates and keep track of responses. Students can report the results of their surveys to the class.

8 Jaime le escribió una carta a Thomas, su amigo por correspondencia. Completa la carta con las formas correctas de **saber** o **conocer**. Usa la **a** personal si es necesario. (p. 18)

Querido Thomas,

Dices que quieres ___1___ más de mis pasatiempos. En mi tiempo libre, practico la escalada deportiva. Algún día, quiero ___2___ los parques nacionales de tu país y escalar las Montañas Rocosas. ¿Tú ___3___ bien el oeste de los Estados Unidos? ¿___4___ cuáles son los mejores lugares para la escalada deportiva?

También me interesa el esquí acuático, pero todavía no ___5___ hacerlo muy bien. Yo ___6___ un chico en mi clase de arte que me va a dar unas clases de esquí acuático este verano. Él y yo ___7___ un lugar bonito donde podemos nadar, bucear y pasear en velero. Nosotros también ___8___ muy bien muchos otros lagos y ríos que hay por aquí.

Mis hermanas dicen que los deportes son aburridos, pero ellas no ___9___ nada. Se la pasan tocando el piano. Ellas ___10___ tocar muy bien el piano, eso sí.

Bueno, amigo, es todo por ahora. Me gustaría ___11___ más de tu vida allí. ¿Qué deportes practicas? ¿___12___ tocar un instrumento musical? ¿___13___ alguien de mi país allí?

¡Escríbeme pronto!

Review and Assess

You may wish to assign the **Más práctica gramatical** activities as additional practice or homework after presenting material throughout the chapter. Assign Activity 1 after **Vocabulario** (p. 10), Activities 2–4 after **Gramática de repaso** (p. 11), Activity 5 after **Gramática de repaso** (p. 12), Activity 6 after **Así se dice** (p. 16), Activity 7 after **Nota gramatical** (p. 18), and Activity 8 after **Gramática de repaso** (p. 18). To prepare students for the **Paso** Quizzes and Chapter Test, have them do the **Más práctica gramatical** activities in the following order: complete Activities 1–5 before taking Quiz 1-1A or 1-1B; Activities 6–8 before taking Quiz 1-2A or 1-2B.

Answers
8
1. saber
2. conocer
3. conoces
4. Sabes
5. sé
6. conozco a
7. conocemos
8. conocemos
9. saben
10. saben
11. saber
12. Sabes
13. Conoces a

Repaso

CAPÍTULO 1

The **Repaso** reviews all four skills and culture in preparation for the Chapter Test.

internet

MARCAR: go.hrw.com
PALABRA CLAVE:
WV3 LA CORUNA-1

Teaching Resources
pp. 28–29

PRINT
▶ Lesson Planner, p. 6
▶ Listening Activities, p. 5
▶ Video Guide, pp. 3, 5, 8
▶ Grammar Tutor for Students of Spanish, Chapter 1
▶ Cuaderno para hispanohablantes, pp. 1–5
▶ Standardized Assessment Tutor, Chapter 1

MEDIA
▶ One-Stop Planner
▶ Video Program, Videocassette 1, 10:20–14:57
▶ Audio Compact Discs, CD 1, Tr. 14
▶ Interactive CD-ROM Tutor, Disc 1

Teaching Suggestion

3 As a prewriting activity, you may wish to have students list the areas and activities pictured on pages 2–3, their favorite sports and pastimes among those in the **Vocabulario** on page 10, and their favorite seafood among those mentioned in the **Nota cultural** on page 13.

Answers

2 *Sample answers:*
¿Adónde fuiste? ¿Con quién?
¿A quiénes conociste? ¿Cómo lo pasaste? ¿Cuándo regresaste?
¿Sacaste fotos?

3 *Possible answers:*
En Galicia, comí mucho pescado y muchos mariscos, nadé y caminé por la playa y visité todos los pueblos de la región.

1 Amparo está invitando a varios amigos a acompañarla a la playa, ¡pero todos ya tienen planes! Escucha las siguientes conversaciones e indica qué dibujo corresponde a cada conversación. Una de las conversaciones no corresponde a ningún dibujo. Script and answers on p. 3H.

CD 1
Tr. 14

a.

b.

c.

d.

2 Imagina que un(a) amigo(a) volvió ayer de unas vacaciones en La Coruña. Escribe una lista de preguntas que puedes hacerle sobre sus vacaciones. Usa algunas de estas palabras. See sample answers below.

leer   montar a caballo   tener   sacar fotos

bucear   conocer   ir   remar   jugar   venir

3 Imagina que pasaste un verano en Galicia. Usa la información cultural que aprendiste de Galicia en este capítulo. En un párrafo breve describe qué actividades hiciste, qué comiste, qué deportes practicaste y qué lugares conociste. See possible answers below.

Apply and Assess

Additional Practice

1 Have students tell their own plans in response to Amparo's invitation. Call on students randomly as they volunteer. They should respond with activities different from those mentioned in the exercise, and not repeat what a classmate says.

Challenge

1 Have pairs of students create a narrative description for one of the drawings. Then have volunteers present their descriptions to the class.

Slower Pace

2 Review the question words with flashcards and ask questions of the students using new material from this chapter.

4 Con un(a) compañero(a), compara estos deportes o pasatiempos. Indiquen si a Uds. les interesan, si no les interesan tanto o si no les gustan para nada.

5 Imagina que eres la persona que entrevistó a la joven alpinista del artículo. ¿Qué preguntas le hiciste para averiguar la siguiente información? See possible answers below.

1. su nombre
2. su edad
3. el monte que escaló
4. la persona que la entrenó
5. su edad cuando aprendió a esquiar
6. la ubicación del monte

SUPERNIÑA ALPINISTA

La alpinista más joven que haya escalado el Monte Blanco es la genovesa Valerie Schwartz, de siete años. La niña hizo la ascensión con sus padres y un guía. Su papá la entrenó durante dos años. Valerie esquía desde los dos años y está acostumbrada a caminar en terrenos difíciles. El Monte Blanco, de 4.810 metros, es el más alto de Europa. Está en los Alpes.

6 Escoge a un(a) amigo(a) por correspondencia de la Actividad 12 en la página 11 y escríbele una carta para presentarte a él o a ella. Descríbele cómo eres (físicamente y tu personalidad) y pregúntale acerca de su personalidad, de sus pasatiempos y de sus deportes favoritos. Answers will vary.

7 **Situación**

A. Imagina que conoces a un(a) estudiante hispanohablante en una fiesta de tu colegio. Uds. hablan de los deportes y pasatiempos que les interesan.

B. El (La) director(a) de tu colegio quiere honrar al mejor estudiante del colegio. Piensas que tu mejor amigo(a) merece (*deserves*) este honor. Escribe una carta en la que describas a tu amigo(a). Indica por qué él o ella merece este honor y menciona las cosas importantes que hizo este año.

Apply and Assess

Additional Practice

6 Have students exchange their letters with a partner and write responses based on the information given on page 11. The responses should also include questions to elicit further information about what each student said in the original letter.

Native Speakers

7 Have pairs of students write the acceptance speech for the winner of the award in **Situación B.** The speech should specify the student's motivations to excel and outline his or her plans for the future.

STANDARDS: 1.1, 1.2, 1.3, 5.1

Repaso

CAPÍTULO 1

Culture Note
Tell students that Europe is not the only place where people enjoy mountain climbing. In Latin America tourists can climb **Pico Bolívar** in Venezuela, **Cerro Aconcagua** in Argentina, or the **Torres del Paine** in Chile.

Teaching Suggestion
5 After students read the article, divide them into pairs and have them ask each other comprehension questions. They need to use each of the interrogatives at least once.

Portfolio
6 **Written** Your students may want to consider including this assignment in their written Portfolios. For an additional written Portfolio suggestion, *see Alternative Assessment Guide,* page 16.

Answers
5 *Possible answers:*
1. ¿Cómo te llamas?
2. ¿Cuántos años tienes?
3. ¿Qué monte escalaste?
4. ¿Quién te entrenó?
5. ¿Cuántos años tenías cuando aprendiste a esquiar?
6. ¿Dónde está el monte?

Teacher Note
This page is intended to help students prepare for the Chapter Test. It is a brief checklist of the major points covered in the chapter. The students should be reminded that this is only a checklist and does not necessarily include everything that will appear on the Chapter Test.

Answers

1 *Possible answers:*
1. Me parecen un rollo los videojuegos.
2. Sí, cómo no. Soy un(a) gran aficionado(a) a las cartas.
3. Como quieras.
4. ¡Qué paliza! Estoy harto de montar en bicicleta.
5. Estoy loca por la playa.
6. Me da igual.

2
1. ¿De dónde eres?
2. ¿Cuándo llegaste a esta ciudad?
3. ¿Cuántos hermanos tienes? ¿Y cuántas hermanas?
4. ¿Qué pasatiempos tienes?
5. ¿Cómo llegas al colegio?
6. ¿Por qué estudias aquí?

3 *Answers will vary.*

4 *Possible answers:*
1. La conozco. Es buena gente.
2. Todavía no los conozco, pero sé que son estrictos.
3. Los conozco. Sé que les gusta el fútbol.
4. Conozco al alcalde. Sé que es bajo.
5. La conozco. Es muy abierta.
6. No lo conozco pero sé que es profesor de inglés.

A ver si puedo...

WV3 LA CORUNA-1

Can you express interest, indifference, and displeasure? p. 9

1 Tu mejor amigo(a) te sugiere cosas que Uds. pueden hacer este fin de semana. Responde a cada una de las ideas de tu amigo(a). See possible answers below.
1. ¿Por qué no jugamos videojuegos?
2. ¿Qué te parece si jugamos a las cartas en mi casa?
3. ¡Vamos a escalar la Montaña Encantada!
4. Va a hacer buen tiempo. Podemos montar en bicicleta.
5. ¿Qué te parece si vamos a la playa?
6. Podemos tomar una clase de patinaje.

Can you ask for information? p. 16

2 Un amigo te presenta a Mónica, una estudiante nueva. ¿Qué preguntas le haces para averiguar la siguiente información? See answers below.
1. su lugar de origen
2. la fecha cuando llegó
3. el número de hermanos y hermanas que tiene
4. lo que le gusta hacer
5. el medio de transporte que usa para llegar al colegio
6. sus motivos para estudiar en los Estados Unidos

3 ¿Cómo le preguntarías a un(a) compañero(a) lo que hizo ayer después de clases? Usa las siguientes sugerencias.

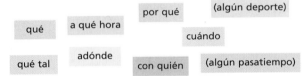

qué   a qué hora   por qué   (algún deporte)   cuándo   qué tal   adónde   con quién   (algún pasatiempo)

Can you describe yourself and others? p. 17

4 Indica si conoces a las siguientes personas y qué sabes de cada una. See possible answers below.

MODELO   mi prima Julia
—Sí, la conozco y sé que es pelirroja y que tiene el pelo rizado.

1. el (la) gobernador(a) de tu estado
2. el padre o la madre de tu mejor amigo(a)
3. tus primos(as)
4. el alcalde o la alcaldesa de tu ciudad
5. el (la) profesor(a) de español
6. el (la) entrenador(a) del equipo de baloncesto

Review and Assess

Group Work
Divide students into groups of three or four. Have them develop a conversation using the following situation: You and a friend are going to the movies. You stop to buy a newspaper to see what is playing at the theater. Some classmates happen by and want to join you. You have trouble agreeing on a movie because some of you like horror movies and some do not. Express your opinions to each other, ask for information about different movies and showing times, come to a consensus, and choose a movie. Give students an in-class time limit for preparation and do not allow any written script.

Vocabulario

Primer paso

Expressing interest

Estoy loco(a) por...	I'm crazy about . . .
Me la paso...	I spend my time . . .
Soy un(a) fanático(a) de...	I'm a big fan of . . .
Soy un(a) gran aficionado(a) a...	I'm a big fan of . . .

Expressing indifference

Como quieras.	Whatever (you want).
Me da igual.	It's all the same to me.
Me da lo mismo.	It's all the same to me.
No me importa.	It doesn't matter to me.

Expressing displeasure

Estoy harto(a) de...	I am fed up with . . .
Me parece un rollo.	It seems really boring to me.
No me interesa para nada.	It doesn't interest me at all.

Sports

¡Qué paliza!	What a drag!
bucear	to go scuba diving
el buceo	scuba diving
la equitación	horseback riding
la escalada deportiva	rock climbing
escalar montañas	to go mountain climbing
el esquí acuático	water skiing
hacer esquí acuático	to water-ski
el montañismo	mountain climbing
montar a caballo	to go horseback riding
pasear en velero	to go sailing
el patinaje	skating
patinar en línea	to go inline skating
patinar sobre hielo	to ice-skate
patinar sobre ruedas	to roller-skate
practicar ciclismo	to be a cyclist
remar	to row

el remo	rowing
la vela	sailing

Hobbies

coleccionar adhesivos/sellos	to collect stickers/stamps
escuchar música	to listen to music
la fotografía	photography
ir a la playa	to go to the beach
jugar (ue) a las cartas	to play cards
jugar (ue) a los videojuegos	to play video games
leer tiras cómicas	to read comics
sacar fotos	to take pictures
tocar un instrumento	to play an instrument

Musical instruments

la batería	the drums
el clarinete	the clarinet
la flauta	the flute
el saxofón	the saxophone

Segundo paso

Asking for information, See p. 16.

Describing yourself and others

abierto(a)	open
alto(a)	tall
la barba	beard
el bigote	moustache
buena gente	nice
de estatura mediana	of medium height
fenomenal	great
las gafas	glasses

una gran persona	a great person
un gran tipo	a great guy
guapo(a)	good-looking
llevar gafas	to wear glasses
majo(a)	nice (Spain)
moreno(a)	dark-haired, dark-skinned
No hay quien lo (la) aguante.	Nobody can stand him (her).

pelirrojo(a)	red-headed
pesado(a)	annoying
rizado(a)	curly
serio(a)	serious
tener un buen sentido del humor	to have a good sense of humor
un(a) tío(a) estupendo(a)	a great guy/girl

CAPÍTULO 1

 Circumlocution
Give pairs of students two or three words in English for things used in the sports and hobbies in this chapter. Tell students to imagine that they are looking for these things in a hobby, music, or sporting goods store in a Spanish-speaking country. They must describe them. Some possible words: *oar, mitt, water ski, climbing boots, rope, saddle, oxygen tank, photographic lens, (stereo) speaker, tuba, joystick.* Each pair reads its descriptions to the class. The class guesses the thing being described.

Additional Practice
Ask students to complete all open-ended phrases on this page in an original way. (expressing interest, expressing indifference, expressing displeasure)

Chapter 1 Assessment

▸ **Testing Program**
Chapter Test, pp. 9–14
 Audio Compact Discs, CD 1, Trs. 17–18
Speaking Test, p. 295

▸ **Alternative Assessment Guide**
Portfolio Assessment, p. 16
Performance Assessment, p. 30
CD-ROM Assessment, p. 44

▸ **Interactive CD-ROM Tutor, Disc 1**
 ¡A hablar!
¡A escribir!

▸ **Standardized Assessment Tutor**
Chapter 1

▸ **One-Stop Planner, Disc 1**
Test Generator
Chapter 1

Review and Assess

 Game

MÍMICA DE DEPORTES Y PASATIEMPOS
Have students write the Spanish words for sports and hobbies (page 10) on slips of paper and put them in a bag. Then divide the class into groups of three to four students, having each group draw one slip of paper. All the group members must pantomime the activity for the other groups to guess. The group that guesses correctly within a set amount of time receives a point. Total the points after all the groups have pantomimed their words. To continue the game, have each group draw another slip of paper.

Capítulo 2: Por una vida sana

Chapter Overview

De antemano pp. 34–36	*Una vida equilibrada*

	FUNCTIONS	GRAMMAR	VOCABULARY	RE-ENTRY
Primer paso pp. 37–40	• Asking for and giving advice, p. 37	• Informal commands, p. 38 • Irregular informal commands, p. 38 • Present progressive, p. 39	• Emotional states, pp. 38–39	• Chapters 1 and 2 are a global review of *¡Ven conmigo!* Levels 1 and 2.

¡Adelante! pp. 42–43	*¡Nos cuidamos mucho!*

Segundo paso pp. 44–49	• Talking about taking care of yourself, p. 44	• Reflexive verbs, p. 45 • Imperfect tense, p. 47	• Healthy living, p. 46	• Chapters 1 and 2 are a global review of *¡Ven conmigo!* Levels 1 and 2.

Vamos a leer pp. 50–52	**Cómo aliviar el estrés: 10 cosas esenciales** and **Cómo lograr el balance en tu vida**	**Reading Strategy:** Using background information to activate vocabulary and ideas
Vamos a escribir p. 53	**¡No lo aguanto más!**	**Writing Strategy:** Listing and clustering ideas about the writing topic
Más práctica gramatical	**pp. 54–57** **Primer paso,** pp. 54–55	**Segundo paso,** pp. 56–57
Review pp. 58–61	**Repaso,** pp. 58–59	**A ver si puedo...,** p. 60 **Vocabulario,** p. 61

CULTURE

- **Nota cultural,** Language of Spain, p. 36
- **Nota cultural,** Spanish business hours, p. 40
- **Panorama cultural, ¿Cómo te cuidas?,** p. 41
- **Nota cultural,** Spanish health habits, p. 46
- **Nota cultural,** Socializing with friends in Spain, p. 47
- **Realia, Tira Cómica,** p. 49

Capítulo 2: Por una vida sana

Chapter Resources

PRINT

Lesson Planning

One-Stop Planner

Lesson Planner with Substitute Teacher Lesson Plans, pp. 7–11, 66

Student Make-Up Assignments
- Make-Up Assignment Copying Masters, Chapter 2

Listening and Speaking

Listening Activities
- Student Response Forms for Listening Activities, pp. 11–13
- Additional Listening Activities 2-1 to 2-6, pp. 15–17
- Additional Listening Activities (song), p. 18
- Scripts and Answers, pp. 106–110

Video Guide
- Teaching Suggestions, pp. 10–11
- Activity Masters, pp. 12–14
- Scripts and Answers, pp. 88–89, 114–115

Activities for Communication
- Communicative Activities, pp. 5–8
- Realia and Teaching Suggestions, pp. 54–56
- Situation Cards, pp. 91–92

Reading and Writing

Reading Strategies and Skills Handbook, Chapter 2

¡Lee conmigo! 3, Chapter 2

Cuaderno de actividades, pp. 13–24

Grammar

Cuaderno de gramática, pp. 10–18

Grammar Tutor for Students of Spanish, Chapter 2

Assessment

Testing Program
- Grammar and Vocabulary Quizzes, **Paso** Quizzes, and Chapter Test, pp. 23–36
- Score Sheet, Scripts and Answers, pp. 37–43

Alternative Assessment Guide
- Portfolio Assessment, p. 17
- Performance Assessment, p. 31
- CD-ROM Assessment, p. 45

Student Make-Up Assignments
- Alternative Quizzes, Chapter 2

Standardized Assessment Tutor
- Reading, pp. 5–7
- Writing, p. 8
- Math, pp. 25–26

Native Speakers

Cuaderno para hispanohablantes, pp. 6–10

MEDIA

 Online Activities
- Juegos interactivos
- Actividades Internet

 Video Program
- Videocassette 1
- Videocassette 5 (captioned version)

 Audio Compact Discs
- Textbook Listening Activities, CD 2, Tracks 1–19
- Additional Listening Activities, CD 2, Tracks 24–30
- Assessment Items, CD 2, Tracks 20–23

 Interactive CD-ROM Tutor, Disc 1

Teaching Transparencies
- Situations 2-1 to 2-2
- **Más práctica gramatical** Answers
- **Cuaderno de gramática** Answers

  One-Stop Planner CD-ROM

Use the **One-Stop Planner CD-ROM with Test Generator** to aid in lesson planning and pacing.

For each chapter, the **One-Stop Planner** includes:
- Editable lesson plans with direct links to teaching resources
- Printable worksheets from resource books
- Direct launches to the HRW Internet activities
- Video and audio segments
- Test Generator
- Clip Art for vocabulary items

Projects

Te aconsejo

In groups, students write and present (live or on video) a five- to ten-minute skit dealing with a health issue. (diet, exercise, substance abuse, chronic illness, or disability)

SITUATION

Tell students to pretend that they work for a production company. They've been hired to make an educational video similar to those in *¡Ven conmigo!* for a Spanish-language high-school health class.

MATERIALS

✂ **Students may need**
- Video camera
- Videotape
- Costumes
- Scenery
- Props

SUGGESTED SEQUENCE

1. Groups of four to five students choose a health issue that interests them. You might want to have them use the Internet to research the issue they have chosen. Tell students to get your approval for topics before beginning the project. You may also want to check with parents before proceeding. Have each group brainstorm about a story around which to write a script. They may divide the tasks among them, but every student should have a speaking role in the skit.

2. Students submit a draft of their script for teacher correction and approval.

3. Students rehearse their skit and then perform it for the class, or they videotape it and show the tape to the class.

GRADING THE PROJECT

Suggested point distribution: (total = 100 points)
Organization..10
Creativity..20
Oral presentation (individual grade) 30
Vocabulary and language usage 40

Games

Buenos consejos

*In this game, to be played after **Primer paso,** students compete to give informal commands promoting healthy behavior.*

Preparation Write a series of sentences that use elements of the chapter to describe healthy and unhealthy habits.

Procedure Divide the class into two teams. The **consejos afirmativos** team must give affirmative commands promoting healthy behavior, and the **consejos negativos** team must give negative commands that also encourage healthy behavior. A representative of each team listens as you read one of the sentences that you wrote in Preparation. (e.g., **Duermo cuatro horas cada noche.**) The first to raise his or her hand tries to respond with an affirmative or negative command. (**Duerme más. No te acuestes tarde.**) An appropriate response earns a point; an inappropriate one means the opposing team gets a try. The team earning the most points in the time allotted wins.

Descifra las frases

*In this game, teams unscramble sentences built from **Así se dice** and **Vocabulario.** It should be played at the end of the chapter.*

Preparation Write sentences from **Así se dice** or create new ones using the chapter **Vocabulario** in each sentence. Write each word of the sentence on a separate card large enough to be easily visible to the class. Make two identical sets of cards.

Procedure Divide the class into two teams. Give each team one set of cards for the same sentence. The first team to reconstruct the sentence correctly wins a point. The completed sentence must be held up in the correct order.

COMMUNITY LINK

Students might contact a local organization concerned with the health issue they research to get further information. They might also invite a representative of that organization to class to watch the skits.

Storytelling

Mini-cuento

This story accompanies Teaching Transparency 2-1. The **mini-cuento** *can be told and retold in different formats, acted out, written as a dictation, and read aloud to give students additional opportunities to practice all four skills. The following story tells about people at the doctor's office.*

Elena, Antonio y Ciro están en la oficina del doctor Zaldívar. Ellos tienen un problema en común; tienen mala salud a causa del estrés. Ellos llevan vidas muy agitadas, no hacen mucho ejercicio y tienen mala alimentación. Elena mira el reloj y piensa que va a llegar tarde a la escuela. Dice que no tiene tiempo para relajarse. Antonio siempre está rendido. Tenía que hacer la tarea ayer pero comió mucho y miró la televisión toda la tarde. Ahora tiene que terminarla mientras espera ver al doctor. Ciro no se siente muy bien. No pudo dormir anoche y también sufre de presiones en la escuela. La enfermera le recomienda tomar las cosas con calma. ¿Qué les va a aconsejar el doctor a Elena y a Antonio? ¡Que se cuiden!

Traditions

Música céltica

The popularity of Celtic music worldwide has brought attention to the Celtic musical traditions of Galicia. Among the traditional instruments, the best known is the **gaita,** or bagpipe. Other instruments, such as the **zanfona** (a type of lute), various kinds of drums, and the **pandeireta,** or tambourine, also represent this ancient musical tradition. A number of **escolas de gaitas** have been established around Spain to teach and preserve these musical traditions. Have students research Galician music on the Internet. Ask them to prepare a presentation for the class comparing one or two Galician Celtic tunes to music from other Celtic lands.

Receta

Empanadas *are typical of Galicia. Made of pork, chicken, sardines, tuna, even* **anguilas** *(eels), they are very large, baked pies. Latin American* **empanadas** *are small half-moon-shaped pies, fried or baked, with meat or fruit.*

EMPANADAS

para 6 personas

1 cebolla grande, picada

1 pimiento verde, picado

2 dientes de ajo, picados

1 pollo de 2 libras (o muslos de pollo), cocinado y deshuesado

1 lata (16 onzas) de tomates, sin líquido, picados

un poco de azafrán

1 hoja de laurel

sal y pimienta al gusto

aceite de oliva para freír

2 paquetes de *prepared pie crust*

2 moldes para *pies*

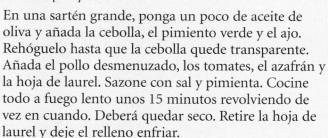

En una sartén grande, ponga un poco de aceite de oliva y añada la cebolla, el pimiento verde y el ajo. Rehóguelo hasta que la cebolla quede transparente. Añada el pollo desmenuzado, los tomates, el azafrán y la hoja de laurel. Sazone con sal y pimienta. Cocine todo a fuego lento unos 15 minutos revolviendo de vez en cuando. Deberá quedar seco. Retire la hoja de laurel y deje el relleno enfriar.

Unte los moldes con un poco de grasa y coloque una masa de *pie* en el fondo de cada uno de forma que los bordes sobresalgan del recipiente. Divida el relleno entre los dos moldes. Tape cada empanada con otra masa. Cierre los bordes, como un *pie*. Haga unos pequeños cortes en la tapa. Ponga las empanadas al horno a 350° unos 30 minutos, o hasta que la masa esté dorada. Córtela y sírvala caliente o fría.

Video Program

Videocassette 1, Videocassette 5 (captioned version)
See Video Guide, pages 9–14.

Dramatic episode • Desde que se fueron los muchachos…

In Mexico, Alejandra calls her best friend Irene and tells her that she can't stop thinking about Sergio. Irene suggests that she call him, but Alejandra is too shy. Early the next morning, the girls go jogging and then meet Carlos, who is on his way to a computer design class at the university. They decide to eat a healthy breakfast at the university cafeteria. Alejandra also decides to confide in Carlos, telling him about her feelings for Sergio.

¿Cómo te cuidas?

People from five Spanish-speaking countries talk about what they do for their health.

Videoclips

- **Alimentos de España:** advertisement encouraging people to get their vitamins by consuming more lemons

- **La salud:** minidocumentary about two basic types of exercise, aerobic and anaerobic

Interactive CD-ROM Tutor

The **Interactive CD-ROM Tutor** contains videos, interactive games, and activities that provide students an opportunity to practice and review the material covered in Chapter 2.

Activity	Activity Type	Pupil's Edition Page
1. Gramática	¡Atrévete!	p. 38
2. Vocabulario	¿Cuál es?	p. 39
3. Gramática (**¿Te acuerdas?**)	¿Qué falta?	p. 39
4. Así se dice	¡Super memoria!	p. 44
5. Gramática	Imagen y sonido ¡Exploremos! ¡Identifiquemos!	p. 45
6. Gramática	Patas arriba	p. 47
Panorama cultural	¿Cómo te cuidas? ¡A escoger!	p. 41
¡A hablar!	*Guided recording*	pp. 54–55
¡A escribir!	*Guided writing*	pp. 54–55

Teacher Management System

Logging In

Logging in to the *¡Ven conmigo!* TMS is easy. Upon launching the program, simply type "admin" in the password area of the log-in screen and press RETURN. Log on to **www.hrw.com/CDROMTUTOR** for a detailed explanation of the Teacher Management System.

One-Stop Planner CD-ROM

To preview all resources available for this chapter, use the **One-Stop Planner CD-ROM**, Disc 1.

Internet Connection

MARCAR: go.hrw.com
PALABRA CLAVE:
WV3 LA CORUNA-2

*Have students explore the **go.hrw.com** Web site for many online resources covering all chapters. All Chapter 2 resources are available under the keyword **WV3 LA CORUNA-2** Interactive games help students practice the material and provide them with immediate feedback. You will also find a printable worksheet that provides Internet activities that lead to a comprehensive online research project.*

Juegos interactivos

You can use the interactive activities in this chapter

- to practice grammar, vocabulary, and chapter functions
- as homework
- as an assessment option
- as a self-test
- to prepare for the Chapter Test

Actividades Internet

Students write a magazine column about healthful activities around Spain. They highlight scenarios in which people have specific objectives, such as relieving stress or being outdoors.

- In preparation for the **Hoja de actividades**, ask students what they recall about the climate, topography and culture of Spain. What sports and activities would they expect people to do in the different regions?
- After completing the activity sheet, have students post their column to a personal Web site. They should download any free images they can find to illustrate the activities and events they found.

Proyecto

Have students write two more scenarios like the ones in Activity C of the **Hoja de actividades**. Then have them exchange scenarios with a partner. The partner should answer the questions in the first student's scenarios with facts learned from online research.

De antemano

2 p. 36

1. ¡Iván salió con cuatro chicas la semana pasada y dice que quiere casarse con todas!

2. Moisés es simpático pero casi nunca habla con la gente. Muchas veces se queda solo en casa, escuchando música.

3. A Gabriela le encanta su nuevo trabajo, pero ahora sólo piensa en ganar dinero y comprar más y más.

4. Nadie quiere invitar a Marcos a fiestas. Siempre habla mal de todos y es muy pesimista.

5. Isabel es muy bonita e inteligente pero tiene un defecto muy grande: ¡piensa que es perfecta!

Answers to Activity 2
1. b   3. d   5. c
2. e   4. a

Primer paso

7 p. 38

1. — ¡Qué lío! Mi mejor amiga habla mucho y a veces le cuenta mis secretos a otra gente.

— Entonces, ¡no le cuentes tus secretos! Sería buena idea buscar una nueva amiga.

2. — No tengo muchos amigos y me siento muy solitario.

— Bueno, no te quedes en casa. Te recomiendo participar en un club. Es divertido y es una buena forma de conocer a más gente.

3. — Quiero bajar de peso. Estoy un poco gordo.

— Bueno, come más postre y toma más refrescos.

4. — Quiero mejorar mis notas.

— No estudies mucho y ve televisión todo el día.

5. — ¡Qué aburrida es la vida! No sé qué hacer.

— Hombre, ¡hay mucho que hacer! Haz ejercicio o lee un libro. ¿Por qué no montas en bici?

6. — Nunca tengo dinero y siempre les estoy pidiendo dinero a mis padres.

— Oye, deberías gastar más dinero. ¡Cómprate ropa y una bicicleta nueva!

7. — Tengo un examen este viernes y estoy tan nerviosa que no puedo estudiar.

— No debes ponerte tan nerviosa. Estudia conmigo esta noche.

Answers to Activity 7
1. buen consejo   5. buen consejo
2. buen consejo   6. mal consejo
3. mal consejo   7. buen consejo
4. mal consejo

13 p. 40

Tengo un problema no muy grave pero me molesta mucho y no sé cómo resolverlo. Soy demasiado tímido. Tengo pocos amigos porque es muy difícil para mí hablar con gente que no conozco muy bien. Hay personas en mi escuela y en mi barrio que me caen bien pero no sé de qué hablar ni cómo empezar una conversación. Muchas personas piensan que soy aburrido o, lo que es peor, arrogante ¡pero no es así! ¿Qué hago? ¿Me puedes dar algún consejo?

Answers to Activity 13
Possible answers:
Deberías participar en un club. Te recomiendo estudiar con otro estudiante o participar en un proyecto con otros estudiantes y hablar con ellos. Sería bueno hacerles preguntas personales a otras personas. A muchas personas les gusta hablar de ellas mismas.

Segundo paso

21 p. 45

1. Trabajo cada día de las cinco de la mañana hasta las tres de la tarde. Por eso prefiero acostarme tarde.

2. Juego para el equipo de baloncesto de mi universidad, así que necesito mantenerme en forma. Me levanto temprano para correr y hacer ejercicio aeróbico.

3. Me encantan las frutas y tomo mucha agua. Trato de hacer ejercicio tres veces por semana.

4. Trabajo en un restaurante. Siempre me lavo las manos antes de preparar la comida.

5. Cuando voy a la playa, me quito la camisa para broncearme. No me gustan las cremas protectoras.

6. Me siento bastante bien. Estoy un poco agobiada por las tensiones de la vida a veces pero siempre trato de compartir mis problemas con mis amigos.

Answers to Activity 21
1. no saludable   4. saludable
2. saludable   5. no saludable
3. saludable   6. saludable

One-Stop Planner CD-ROM

To preview all resources available for this chapter, use the **One-Stop Planner CD-ROM**, Disc 1.

23 p. 46

1. Celina hizo mucho ejercicio esta mañana y se cansó. Por eso se durmió durante la cena.
2. ¡Qué lío! ¡Rafa se lavó los dientes con el champú y se lavó el pelo con la pasta de dientes!
3. Esa Lupita no cuida el peso; por eso está gordita.
4. Teresa se acostó a las diez pero se quedó despierta hasta muy tarde.

Answers to Activity 23
1. b
2. a
3. d
4. c

26 p. 47

1. Cuando estaba en el colegio, me mantenía en buena forma. Siempre hacía ejercicios y jugaba a muchos deportes.
2. Comía sólo comida sana y veía poca televisión. Cuando podía, pasaba tiempo hablando con mis amigos.
3. Iba todos los días a las canchas de tenis para practicar, y jugaba con el equipo del colegio.
4. Un día un hombre me vio jugar y me invitó a jugar para la Universidad Central.
5. Cuando no jugaba al tenis, estudiaba. Siempre me importaba sacar buenas notas.
6. Durante mi último año en el colegio, hice un viaje a Europa con unos amigos. Después de regresar, comencé en la universidad.

Answers to Activity 26
1. habitual
2. habitual
3. habitual
4. no habitual
5. habitual
6. no habitual

29 p. 49

Ahora llevo una vida agitada. Sin embargo, antes tenía más tiempo para mantenerme en forma y descansar. Cuando estaba en la escuela secundaria, me cuidaba mucho más. Comía comida sana como frutas y verduras, y hacía ejercicio casi todos los días. Por ejemplo, jugaba al tenis o hacía ejercicio aeróbico. Me encantaba leer novelas y tenía muchos libros. Tocaba la guitarra pero no muy bien porque casi nunca practicaba. Me encantaba escuchar la radio y pasaba horas cantando en mi cuarto.

Answers to Activity 29
1. She has cookies in her room, not fruits and vegetables.
2. She has a basketball, not a tennis racket.
3. She's dancing to music videos on TV, not singing along with the radio.

Repaso

1 p. 58

¡Mi vida es un desastre a veces! Anoche me acosté muy tarde por estar hablando con mi mejor amiga. No me acordaba de que tenía un examen de biología hoy. Quería levantarme hoy a las cinco para estudiar un poco más para el examen, pero no me desperté hasta las siete. Me duché y me vestí rápidamente, y mientras comía el desayuno, intenté estudiar un poco. Cuando entré en el salón de clase, me sentía abrumada por la presión. Me puse muy nerviosa durante el examen. Ahora, estoy sufriendo de muchísimo estrés. Me preocupa mucho la nota que voy a sacar.

Answers to Repaso Activity 1
b, d, c, a

Capítulo 2: Por una vida sana

Suggested Lesson Plans *50-Minute Schedule*

Day 1

CHAPTER OPENER 5 min.
- Focusing on Outcomes, ATE, p. 33
- Culture Note, ATE, p. 32

DE ANTEMANO 40 min.
- Presenting **De antemano** and Preteaching Vocabulary, ATE, p. 34
- Present Using the Captioned Video, ATE, p. 35.
- Activities 1–5 and Comprehension Check, ATE, p. 36
- Read and discuss **Nota cultural,** p. 36.

Wrap-Up 5 min.
- Do the Thinking Critically activity, ATE, p. 35.

Homework Options
Cuaderno de actividades, p. 13, Activity 1

Day 2

PRIMER PASO
Quick Review 5 min.
- Check homework.
- Bell Work, ATE, p. 37

Así se dice, p. 37 15 min.
- Presenting **Así se dice,** ATE, p. 37
- Have students do Activity 6, p. 37, and Pair Work, ATE, p. 37.

Gramática de repaso, p. 38 25 min.
- Presenting **Gramática de repaso,** ATE, p. 38
- Review **¿Te acuerdas?,** p. 38.
- Do Activity 7 with the Audio CD, p. 38, then Thinking Critically, ATE, p. 38.
- Do Activity 8, p. 38.
- Have students do Activity 9 in pairs, p. 38.

Wrap-Up 5 min.
- Discuss Family Link, ATE, p. 38.

Homework Options
Cuaderno de gramática, pp. 10–11, Activities 1–2
Más práctica gramatical, p. 54, Activities 1–3

Day 3

PRIMER PASO
Quick Review 5 min.
- Check homework.
- Have students give advice for different situations.

Vocabulario, p. 38 5 min.
- Presenting **Vocabulario,** ATE, p. 38

Vocabulario, p. 39 35 min.
- Presenting **Vocabulario,** ATE, p. 39
- Review **¿Te acuerdas?,** then do Activity 10, p. 39.
- **Más práctica gramatical,** p. 55, Activities 4–5
- Present **Vocabulario extra,** p. 39.
- Have students do Activity 11, then Activity 12 in groups, p. 39.

Wrap-Up 5 min.
- Do the Kinesthetic Learners activity, ATE, p. 39.

Homework Options
Cuaderno de actividades, pp. 14–15, Activities 2–4
Cuaderno de gramática, pp. 11–13, Activities 3–8

Day 4

PRIMER PASO
Quick Review 10 min.
- Check homework.
- Have students give advice to the people depicted in Teaching Transparency 2-1.

Vocabulario, p. 39 20 min.
- Do Activity 13 with the Audio CD, p. 40.
- Read and discuss the **Nota cultural,** p. 40.
- Present Language Note, ATE, p. 40.
- Have students do Activity 14 in groups, p. 40.

PANORAMA CULTURAL 15 min.
- Presenting **Panorama cultural,** ATE, p. 41
- Present the Language Note and discuss Thinking Critically, ATE, p. 41.
- Discuss **Para pensar y hablar...,** p. 41.

Wrap-Up 5 min.
- Discuss the content and format of Quiz 2-1.

Homework Options
Study for Quiz 2-1.
Cuaderno de actividades, pp. 16–17, Activities 5–8

Day 5

PRIMER PASO
Quick Review 5 min.
- Check homework.
- Review **Primer paso.**

Quiz 20 min.
- Administer Quiz 2-1A, 2-1B, or a combination of the two.

¡ADELANTE! 20 min.
- Presenting **¡Adelante!** and Preteaching Vocabulary, ATE, p. 42
- Do Activities 15–19, p. 43

Wrap-Up 5 min.
- Have students come up with additional solutions to the health problems listed in **¡Adelante!**

Homework Options
Cuaderno de actividades, p. 18, Activities 9–10

Day 6

SEGUNDO PASO
Quick Review 5 min.
- Check homework.
- Bell Work, ATE, p. 44

Así se dice, p. 44 15 min.
- Presenting **Así se dice,** ATE, p. 44
- Present **También se puede decir...,** p. 44
- Do Activity 20 and the Pair Work activity, ATE, p. 44.

Gramática de repaso, p. 45 25 min.
- Presenting **Gramática de repaso,** ATE, p. 45
- Present **¿Te acuerdas?,** and do Group Work and Pair Work activities, ATE, p. 45.
- Do Building on Previous Skills, ATE, p. 45.
- Do Activity 21 with the Audio CD, p. 45.
- Do Activity 22, p. 45.

Wrap-Up 5 min.
- Have students tell what they do to take care of themselves.

Homework Options
Cuaderno de gramática, pp. 14–16, Activities 9–13
Más práctica gramatical, p. 56, Activities 6–7

One-Stop Planner CD-ROM

For alternative lesson plans by chapter section, to create your own customized plans, or to preview all resources available for this chapter, use the **One-Stop Planner CD-ROM**, Disc 1.

 For additional homework suggestions, see activities accompanied by this symbol throughout the chapter.

Day 7

SEGUNDO PASO
Quick Review 10 min.
- Check homework.
- Ask students about their daily routine yesterday.

Vocabulario, p. 46 25 min.
- Presenting **Vocabulario**, ATE, p. 46
- Read and discuss the **Nota cultural**, p. 46.
- Do Activity 23 with the Audio CD, p. 46.
- Have students do Activities 24–25 in pairs, pp. 46–47.

Gramática de repaso, p. 47 10 min.
- Presenting **Gramática de repaso**, ATE, p. 47

Wrap-Up 5 min.
- Ask students to list three bad habits they used to have.

Homework Options
Cuaderno de actividades, pp. 19–22, Activities 11–17
Cuaderno de gramática, pp. 16–18, Activities 14–18

Day 8

SEGUNDO PASO
Quick Review 10 min.
- Check homework.
- Review the imperfect tense.

Gramática de repaso, p. 47 35 min.
- **Más práctica gramatical**, p. 57, Activities 8–9
- Do Activity 26 with the Audio CD, p. 47.
- Read the **Nota cultural**, p. 47, then do the Thinking Critically activity, ATE, p. 47.
- Do Activities 27–28, p. 48.
- Do Activity 29 with the Audio CD, p. 49.

Wrap-Up 5 min.
- Discuss the content and format of Quiz 2-2.

Homework Options
Study for Quiz 2-2.
Assign Activity 32, p. 49.

Day 9

SEGUNDO PASO
Quick Review 10 min.
- Have students peer-edit their homework (Activity 32, p. 49).
- Review **Segundo paso**.

Gramática de repaso, p. 47 15 min.
- Have students do Activity 30 in pairs, p. 49.
- Have students do Activity 31, p. 49, then peer-edit their work.

Quiz 20 min.
- Administer Quiz 2-2A, 2-2B, or a combination of the two.

Wrap-Up 5 min.
- Have students name five things they have done to stay healthy.

Homework Options
Cuaderno de actividades, p. 146

Day 10

VAMOS A LEER
Quick Review 5 min.
- Check homework for completion.

VAMOS A LEER 40 min.
- Read the **Estrategia para leer,** then do Activities A–C, p. 50.
- Review **¿Te acuerdas?**, p. 51, then do Activities D–E, pp. 51–52.
- Follow the suggestions in Paraphrasing and Distinguishing Fact from Opinion, ATE, p. 52, and do Activities F–G, p. 52.

Wrap-Up 5 min.
- Do the Thinking Critically activity, ATE, p. 50.

Homework Options
Cuaderno de actividades, pp. 23–24, Activities 18–20

Day 11

VAMOS A LEER
Quick Review 5 min.
- Check homework.

REPASO 30 min.
- Do Activity 1 with the Audio CD, p. 58.
- Do Activities 3–4 and 6, pp. 58–59.
- Have students do Activities 2, 5, and 7 in pairs, pp. 58–59.

VAMOS A ESCRIBIR 10 min.
- Read the **Estrategia para escribir,** then have students do Activity A, p. 53.

Wrap-Up 5 min.
- Review the steps in **Vamos a escribir.** Discuss the concepts and vocabulary from the chapter they will use in the letters.

Homework Options
Complete **Vamos a escribir**, p. 53.
A ver si puedo..., p. 60

Day 12

REPASO
Quick Review 5 min.
- Check homework. Collect **Vamos a escribir,** p. 53.

Chapter Review 40 min.
- Review Chapter 2. Choose from **Más práctica gramatical,** Grammar Tutor for Students of Spanish, Activities for Communication, Listening Activities, Interactive CD-ROM Tutor, or **Juegos interactivos.**

Wrap-Up 5 min.
- Discuss the content of the Chapter 2 Test and provide sample questions.

Homework Options
Study for the Chapter 2 Test.

Assessment

Quick Review 5 min.
- Answer any last-minute questions.

Test, Chapter 2 45 min.
- Administer Chapter 5 Test. Select from Testing Program, Alternative Assessment Guide, Test Generator, or Standardized Assessment Tutor.

Capítulo 2: Por una vida sana

Suggested Lesson Plans 90-Minute Block Schedule

Block 1

CHAPTER OPENER 5 min.
- Focusing on Outcomes, ATE, p. 33
- Culture Note, ATE, p. 32

DE ANTEMANO 40 min.
- Presenting **De antemano** and Preteaching Vocabulary, ATE, p. 34
- Present Multicultural Link, ATE, p. 36.
- Activities 1–5 and Comprehension Check, ATE, p. 36
- Read and discuss the **Nota cultural**, p. 36.

PRIMER PASO
Así se dice, p. 37 15 min.
- Presenting **Así se dice**, p. 37
- Have students do Activity 6, p. 37, and Pair Work, ATE, p. 37.

Gramática de repaso, p. 38 25 min.
- Presenting **Gramática de repaso**, ATE, p. 38
- Review **¿Te acuerdas?**, p. 38.
- Do Activity 7 with the Audio CD, p. 38, then the Thinking Critically, ATE, p. 38.
- Do Activity 8, p. 38.
- Have students do Activity 9 in pairs, p. 38.

Wrap-Up 5 min.
- Discuss Family Link, ATE, p. 38.

Homework Options
Cuaderno de actividades, p. 13, Activity 1
Cuaderno de gramática, pp. 10–11, Activities 1–2
Más práctica gramatical, p. 54, Activities 1–3

Block 2

PRIMER PASO
Quick Review 10 min.
- Check homework.
- Have students give advice for different situations.

Vocabulario, p. 38 5 min.
- Presenting **Vocabulario**, ATE, p. 38

Vocabulario, p. 39 55 min.
- Presenting **Vocabulario**, ATE, p. 39
- Review **¿Te acuerdas?**, then do Activity 10, p. 39.
- **Más práctica gramatical**, p. 55, Activities 4–5
- Present **Vocabulario extra**, p. 39.
- Have students do Activity 11, then Activity 12 in groups, p. 39.
- Do Activity 13 with the Audio CD, p. 40.
- Read and discuss the **Nota cultural**, p. 40.
- Present Language Note, ATE, p. 40.
- Have students do Activity 14 in groups, p. 40.

PANORAMA CULTURAL 15 min.
- Presenting **Panorama cultural**, ATE, p. 41
- Present the Language Note and discuss Thinking Critically, ATE, p. 41.
- Discuss **Para pensar y hablar...**, p. 41.

Wrap-Up 5 min.
- Have students give advice to the people depicted in Teaching Transparency 2-1.
- Discuss the content and format of Quiz 2-1.

Homework Options
Study for Quiz 2-1.
Cuaderno de actividades, pp. 14–17, Activities 2–8
Cuaderno de gramática, pp. 11–13, Activities 3–8

Block 3

PRIMER PASO
Quick Review 10 min.
- Check homework.
- Review **Primer paso**.

Quiz 20 min.
- Administer Quiz 2-1A, 2-1B, or a combination of the two.

¡ADELANTE! 25 min.
- Presenting **¡Adelante!** and Preteaching Vocabulary, ATE, p. 42
- Do Activities 15–19, p. 43.
- Do the Additional Practice activity, ATE, p. 43.

SEGUNDO PASO
Así se dice, p. 44 15 min.
- Presenting **Así se dice**, ATE, p. 44
- Present **También se puede decir...**, p. 44.
- Do Activity 20 and the Pair Work activity, ATE, p. 44.

Gramática de repaso, p. 45 15 min.
- Presenting **Gramática de repaso**, p. 45
- Present **¿Te acuerdas?** and do Group Work and Pair Work activities, ATE, p. 45.

Wrap-Up 5 min.
- Have students tell what they do to take care of themselves.

Homework Options
Cuaderno de actividades, p. 18, Activities 9–10
Cuaderno de gramática, pp. 14–16, Activities 9–13

One-Stop Planner CD-ROM

For alternative lesson plans by chapter section, to create your own customized plans, or to preview all resources available for this chapter, use the **One-Stop Planner CD-ROM,** Disc 1.

For additional homework suggestions, see activities accompanied by this symbol throughout the chapter.

Block 4

SEGUNDO PASO

Quick Review 5 min.
- Check homework.
- Ask students how they take care of themselves.

Gramática de repaso, p. 45 20 min.
- Do Building on Previous Skills, ATE, p. 45.
- **Más práctica gramatical,** p. 56, Activities 6–7
- Do Activity 21 with the Audio CD, p. 45.
- Do Activity 22, p. 45.

Vocabulario, p. 46 25 min.
- Presenting **Vocabulario,** ATE, p. 46
- Read and discuss the **Nota cultural,** p. 46.
- Do Activity 23 with the Audio CD, p. 46.
- Have students do Activities 24–25 in pairs, pp. 46–47.

Gramática de repaso, p. 47 35 min.
- Presenting **Gramática de repaso,** ATE, p. 47
- **Más práctica gramatical,** p. 57, Activities 8–9
- Do Activity 26 with the Audio CD, p. 47.
- Read the **Nota cultural,** p. 47, then do Thinking Critically, ATE, p. 47.
- Do Activities 27–28, p. 48.

Wrap-Up 5 min.
- Ask students to list three bad habits they used to have.

Homework Options
Assign Activity 32, p. 49.
Cuaderno de actividades, pp. 19–22, Activities 11–17
Cuaderno de gramática, pp. 16–18, Activities 14–18

Block 5

SEGUNDO PASO

Quick Review 10 min.
- Check homework. Check Activity 32 for completion, p. 49.
- Have students describe the habits of students in Teaching Transparency 2-2.

Gramática, p. 47 20 min.
- Do Activity 29 with the Audio CD, p. 49.
- Have students do Activity 30 in pairs, p. 49.
- Have students do Activity 31, p. 49, then peer-edit their work.

VAMOS A LEER 40 min.
- Read the **Estrategia para leer,** then do Activities A–C, p. 50.
- Review **¿Te acuerdas?,** then do Activities D–E, pp. 51–52.
- Follow the suggestions in Paraphrasing and Distinguishing Fact from Opinion, ATE, p. 52, and do Activities F–G, p. 52.

VAMOS A ESCRIBIR 10 min.
- Read the **Estrategia para escribir,** then have students do Activity A, p. 53.

Wrap-Up 10 min.
- Review steps in **Vamos a escribir.** Discuss chapter concepts and vocabulary to be used in the letters.
- Discuss the content and format of Quiz 2-2.

Homework Options
Study for Quiz 2-2.
Complete draft of **Vamos a escribir,** p. 53.
Cuaderno de actividades, pp. 23–24, Activities 18–20

Block 6

SEGUNDO PASO

Quick Review 10 min.
- Check homework.
- Review **Segundo paso.**

Quiz 20 min.
- Administer Quiz 2-2A, 2-2B, or a combination of the two.

VAMOS A ESCRIBIR 20 min.
- Do the Postwriting activity, ATE, p. 53, then have students rewrite letters, p. 53.

REPASO 30 min.
- Do Activity 1 with the Audio CD, p. 58.
- Do Activities 3–4 and 6, pp. 58–59.
- Have students do Activities 2, 5, and 7 in pairs, pp. 58–59.

Wrap-Up 10 min.
- Play **Riesgo,** p. 61
- Discuss the content and format of the Chapter 2 Test.

Homework Options
Study for the Chapter 2 Test.
A ver si puedo..., p. 60

Block 7

REPASO

Quick Review 5 min.
- Check homework.

Chapter Review 40 min.
- Review Chapter 2. Choose from **Más práctica gramatical,** Grammar Tutor for Students of Spanish, Activities for Communication, Listening Activities, Interactive CD-ROM Tutor, or **Juegos interactivos.**

Test, Chapter 2 45 min.
- Administer Chapter Test. Select from Testing Program, Alternative Assessment Guide, Test Generator, or Standardized Assessment Tutor.

CAPÍTULO 2

One-Stop Planner CD-ROM

For resource information, see the **One-Stop Planner,** Disc 1.

Pacing Tips
The first and second **Pasos** present new vocabulary and functions with a review of the grammar learned in *¡Ven conmigo!* Levels 1 and 2, so you might want to allot extra time for speaking practice with the new material. For more tips on pacing, see Suggested Lesson Plans, pp. 31I–31L.

Meeting the Standards

Communication
- Asking for and giving advice, p. 37
- Talking about taking care of yourself, p. 44

Cultures
- Multicultural Link, p. 36
- Nota cultural, p. 40
- Panorama cultural, p. 41
- Nota cultural, p. 46
- Nota cultural, p. 47

Connections
- Language Note, p. 41

Comparisons
- Nota cultural, p. 36
- Language Note, p. 40
- Native Speakers, p. 40
- Thinking Critically, p. 47

Communities
- Career Path, p. 43
- Community Link, p. 49

Cultures and Communities

Culture Note
Public parks are popular places where people relax and picnic. In Spain, lunch is eaten about 2:00 p.m., and dinner often begins after 10:00 p.m. Ask students if they think this schedule is healthy. why or why not? Do students keep regular, healthy eating habits?

Language Note
The word **sano** comes from the Latin *sanus,* meaning *sane* or *sensible.* The expression **sano y salvo** corresponds to the English *safe and sound,* while **cortar por lo sano** means "to settle matters in the most expedient way." Other common Spanish words from the same root are **sanar, sanatorio, sanitario,** and **malsano.**

2
Por una vida sana

Objectives

In this chapter you will review and practice how to

Primer paso

• ask for and give advice

Segundo paso

• talk about taking care of yourself

 internet

go.hrw.com
MARCAR: go.hrw.com
PALABRA CLAVE:
WV3 LA CORUNA-2

◀ Tomo las cosas con calma remando
por el estanque en el Parque del Retiro
de Madrid.

Chapter Opener

CAPÍTULO 2

Photo Flash!
El Parque del Retiro is the largest and most popular park in central Madrid. **Madrileños** enjoy the boating lake with its monument of Alfonso XII.

Focusing on Outcomes
Ask students what they would advise a friend to do to maintain a healthy lifestyle. Then ask students to think of situations in which they would talk about taking care of themselves.

Communication for All Students

Building on Previous Skills
Divide students into groups of three. Write several categories on the board or on a transparency **(comida sana, el ejercicio, buenos hábitos)** and ask groups to write as many words as they can, during a set period of time, that belong in each category. When time is called, have students compare their lists for each category to see who has the most entries. That group reads its list out loud while the rest of the class checks to see how many of the same words they have written.

Teaching Resources
pp. 34–36

PRINT
▶ Lesson Planner, p. 8
▶ Video Guide, pp. 9–10, 12
▶ Cuaderno de actividades, p. 13

MEDIA
▶ One-Stop Planner
▶ Video Program
  Contigo en la distancia
  Videocassette 1, 15:12–21:05
  Videocassette 5 (captioned version), 06:08–12:01
▶ Audio Compact Discs, CD 2, Trs. 1–4

Presenting
De antemano

First play the Audio CD or read the test aloud, pausing to check for comprehension. Next, present the Preteaching Vocabulary. Then have students work in small groups to read the test and write their answers, which they then compare to the key on page 35.

DE ANTEMANO · *Una vida equilibrada*

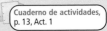
Cuaderno de actividades, p. 13, Act. 1

CD 2
Trs. 1–3

> **Estrategia para comprender**
> Los amigos, la familia, los estudios, las fiestas, el trabajo... la vida está llena de actividades y diversiones y a veces, estrés. ¡No te preocupes! Este "test" te va a ayudar a entender cómo organizas tu tiempo.

¿Equilibrado o descontrolado?   TEST

La vida es un gran pastel con muchas rebanadas: los amigos, la familia, los estudios, las fiestas, el trabajo. ¿Qué tal andas tú en distribuir tu tiempo? Aquí tienes una prueba para saberlo. Tómala y sin trampas.

1 Los sábados en la mañana estás:
a. en casa de tu mejor amigo(a).
b. haciendo las compras o cualquier otra tarea doméstica.
c. esperando la llamada de tu novio(a).
d. trabajando para ganar dinero.
e. en la cama, durmiendo.

2 Si despiertas a medianoche y no puedes dormir, estás pensando en:
a. buscar otro(a) novio(a).
b. ganar dinero.
c. cómo sacar buenas notas en los exámenes.
d. un problema familiar.
e. lo que te vas a poner para la fiesta del viernes.

3 Cuando tienes tiempo para hacer lo que te gusta:
a. sales con tu novio(a).
b. vas a un concierto de rock o a un evento deportivo.
c. descansas.
d. practicas tu deporte o actividad favorita.
e. te cortas el pelo o te haces la permanente.

4 Cuando te sientes cansado(a), es porque:
a. pasaste toda la noche de fiesta.
b. hablaste toda la noche con tus papás.
c. estudiaste toda la noche.
d. fuiste de compras todo el día.
e. trabajaste demasiadas horas extra.

5 Tu mejor amigo(a) te describe como:
a. un "trabajo-hólico(a)".
b. un cerebro.
c. divertido(a).
d. muy unido(a) a tu familia.
e. víctima de la moda.

6 Tu peor enemigo(a) dice que eres:
a. super-engreído(a).
b. antipatiquísimo(a).
c. solitario(a).
d. codicioso(a).
e. enamoradizo(a).

7 Para relajarte:
a. compartes una pizza con tus amigos(as).
b. prefieres ir al parque para mirar a los (las) chicos(as).
c. escuchas música tranquila o lees en tu cuarto.
d. hablas con tu mamá.
e. haces ejercicio.

Preteaching Vocabulary

Identifying Keywords
Ask students to guess the context of **De antemano.** (a personality test) Then have them use the pie chart graphic to identify words or phrases that give them information about the main categories of the survey. (**amor, familia,** **ejercicio, amigos, diversión, estudios**) They should then look at the questions and answers to identify words or phrases from each category. (**novio** in the **amor** category)

8 **Tus fantasías del futuro son:**
a. casarte con tu chico(a).
b. conseguir un buen trabajo.
c. ir a la universidad.
d. tener una fiesta de graduación enorme.
e. ser actor o actriz.

d. no estás con tus amigos(as).
e. no tienes ni trabajo ni dinero.

9 **A veces sufres del estrés cuando:**
a. no tienes tiempo para descansar.
b. no tienes tiempo para estudiar lo suficiente.
c. no estás con tu familia.

10 **El trabajo que te gusta es:**
a. maestro(a) o vendedor(a).
b. escritor(a) o investigador(a).
c. trabajador(a) social, consejero(a) o ministro(a).
d. profesor(a) de universidad, artista, atleta profesional.
e. diseñador(a) de moda o estilista de cabello.

amor
familia
ejercicio
estudios
diversión
amigos

CONFIDENCIAL

P. Querida Consuelo, ¡Socorro! Estoy agobiado por las presiones de mi vida. Tengo muchísimo que hacer en casa, en el colegio y en el trabajo. Quiero tener una vida social también. ¿Qué me aconsejas hacer?
Ansioso en
La Coruña

R: Querido Ansioso, ¡No te pongas ansioso! Es posible resolver tus problemas. Primero, deberías organizar tu tiempo. Pídeles ayuda a tus padres, profesores y compañeros de clase. Te recomiendo dedicar tiempo todas las semanas a las cosas que te interesan y hacerlas con gente que te gusta. Descansa y duerme bien. ¡Cuídate mucho!
Consuelo

Puntuación
¡Ahora te llegó el momento de la verdad! Compara tus respuestas con las de abajo. ¿Cómo pasas el tiempo?
Amigos, diversión: 1a, 3b, 4a, 5c, 7a, 8d, 9d, 10a
Los (Las) chicos(as), tu novio(a): 1c, 2a, 3a, 6e, 7b, 8a
Estudios o proyectos especiales: 2c, 3d, 4c, 5b, 6b, 8c, 9b, 10d
La casa, la familia: 1b, 2d, 4b, 5d, 7d, 9c, 10c
El trabajo: 1d, 2b, 4e, 5a, 6d, 8b, 9e
Pasatiempos o relajamiento: 1e, 3c, 6c, 7c, 9a, 10b
La moda y tu apariencia física: 2e, 3e, 4d, 5e, 6a, 7e, 8e, 10e

DE ANTEMANO

CAPÍTULO 2

Thinking Critically
Synthesizing How would students interpret the scores for this test? Have students assign a point system for each answer and then offer a piece of advice to someone whose score falls into that range.

Additional Practice
You may want to have your students exchange **Querida Consuelo** letters with another class. Have students write letters to Consuelo asking for advice. Put these letters in a container and have students from another class take one and respond to it as if they were Consuelo. This may be done with another Level 3 class or with a class from another school. Or you might wish to have a Level 2 class write the letters and a Level 3 class answer them.

 Contigo en la distancia

You may choose to show students Episode 2: ***Desde que se fueron los muchachos...,*** now or wait until later in the chapter. In the video, Alejandra calls her best friend Irene to tell her that she cannot stop thinking about Sergio. Irene suggests she call him and tell him, but Alejandra is too timid. She does confide in their mutual friend Carlos, whom both girls meet for breakfast the following morning. Have students write down the chapter vocabulary they hear used in the video.

Using the Captioned Video

As an alternative, you might want to show the captioned version of ***Contigo en la distancia: Desde que se fueron los muchachos...*** on Videocassette 5. Some students may benefit from seeing the written words as they listen to the target language and watch the gestures and actions in context. This visual reinforcement of vocabulary and functions will facilitate students' comprehension and help reduce their anxiety before they are formally introduced to the new language in the chapter.

CAPÍTULO 2

Teaching Suggestion

Nota cultural You may want to provide students with copies of the map of Spain. (See *Map Transparency 1* and its blackline master or the map on page T73, or *Pupil's Edition*, page xxiii.) Have students fill in the names of the **comunidades autónomas** *(autonomous regions)* of Spain and the languages spoken in each one.

 Multicultural Link
Have students research a country that has more than one widely-spoken language. (Switzerland, Canada, Belgium, India, China, many countries in Latin America and Africa) What languages are spoken? Who speaks them? How are the languages represented geographically? You may choose to have your students use the Internet to conduct their research. They might include written samples of the languages spoken in the country they are researching.

Answers

1 1. falsa; El problema de Ansioso es que está agobiado porque tiene mucho que hacer.
2. falsa; Dice que quiere tener una vida social también.
3. cierta
4. cierta
5. falsa; Le aconseja descansar y dormir.

4 1. Estoy agobiado por las presiones de mi vida.
2. ¿Qué me aconsejas hacer?
3. deberías organizar tu tiempo, Te recomiendo dedicar tiempo todas las semanas..., No te pongas ansioso, Pídeles ayuda..., Descansa y duerme bien.

These activities check for comprehension only. Students should not yet be expected to produce language modeled in **De antemano.**

1 **Los problemas de "Ansioso"** See answers below.
Indica si cada oración es **cierta** o **falsa**. Si es falsa, corrígela.
1. El problema más grande de "Ansioso" es que no tiene nada que hacer.
2. "Ansioso" sale mucho con sus amigos.
3. Le escribe a Consuelo para pedirle consejos y resolver sus problemas.
4. Según ella, "Ansioso" debe dedicar tiempo a las actividades interesantes.
5. Consuelo le aconseja trabajar más.

2 **¿Cómo los describes?** Script and answers on p. 31G.
Escucha las siguientes descripciones e indica cuál de los consejos corresponde mejor a cada situación.
CD 2
Tr. 4
a. Debe ser más optimista.
b. Debe pasar más tiempo con menos chicos(as).
c. Debe ser más honesto(a) con sus amigos y también consigo mismo(a).
d. Debe ser menos egoísta.
e. Debe tratar de ser más extrovertido(a).

3 **Personalidades**
Con un(a) compañero(a), escribe descripciones de siete personas imaginarias. Sigan el modelo.

MODELO   **A Elisa le encantan los estudios de moda y quiere ser modista.**

familia · moda o apariencia física · amigos · amor · estudios · diversión o relajamiento · trabajo

4 **¿Qué palabras se usan?** See answers below.
1. ¿Qué expresión usa "Ansioso" para decir que tiene muchas presiones?
2. ¿Cómo le pide consejos a Consuelo?
3. Busca por lo menos tres expresiones que usa Consuelo para darle consejos.

5 **¿Cuáles son tus prioridades?**
Compara los resultados de la prueba con los de un(a) compañero(a). ¿Cuáles son las prioridades de cada persona?

Nota cultural
Aunque el idioma nacional de España es el español, algunas regiones de España tienen sus propias lenguas. Por ejemplo, en Cataluña se habla **catalán** y los vascos hablan una lengua llamada **euskera**, que no es similar a ningún idioma conocido. En Galicia se habla el **gallego**. El gallego es similar al portugués y al español. Por ejemplo **tienda** es *tenda* en gallego, **primero(a)** es *primeiro(a)*, **mujer** es *muller* y **llorar** es *chorar*. ¿Qué idiomas se hablan en Estados Unidos además del inglés?

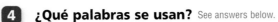

Comprehension Check

Slower Pace
1 Have students read the letters from Ansioso and Consuelo in pairs. Then tell them to list the problems that Ansioso faces and the advice that Consuelo offers.

Visual Learners
3 Ask students to draw one of the imaginary people they listed in the activity. They should be sure to represent visually all of the adjectives used.

Challenge
Have students work in groups of four to write their own test.

Así se dice

Asking for and giving advice

Aquí tienes algunas frases que puedes usar para pedirle y darle consejos a otra persona.

¿Qué me aconsejas hacer?

¿Qué me recomiendas hacer?

¿Puedes darme algún consejo?

¿Qué debo hacer?

Te aconsejo comer bien.

Te recomiendo hacer más ejercicio.

Sería bueno expresar tus emociones.

Deberías descansar más.

No debes preocuparte tanto.

Cuaderno de actividades, p. 17, Acts. 7–8

 6 **¿Qué me aconsejas?** Answers may vary, but best answers are: C and B.

Leemos/Hablemos Con un(a) compañero(a) de clase, indica qué consejo es el mejor para cada problema que sigue.

"Me encanta la comida italiana, sobre todo si tiene ajo. Y cuando cocino, cocino con mucho ajo. El problema es que a mi novia no le gusta para nada y no me quiere hablar si lo como. ¿Puedes darme algún consejo?"

"Tengo 16 años y soy muy independiente para mi edad pero mis papás no me permiten hacer nada después de las nueve de la noche. Si llego tarde, no me permiten salir con amigos, ir a fiestas ni hablar por teléfono por una semana. ¡No es justo! ¿Qué me aconsejas?"

A. ¡Deberías comer lo que te gusta! Si tu novia te quiere, te va a aceptar tal como eres.

B. Sería bueno dejar de comer ajo por completo. Tu novia tiene razón, el ajo es horrible. No debes hacerla sufrir.

C. ¡Hay una solución! Puedes cocinar con ajo pero sólo una vez por semana.

A. Deberías buscar un apartamento y vivir sola. Tus padres no son razonables.

B. Te recomiendo hablar con tus padres para buscar una solución. Tal vez te permitan salir hasta las diez o las once sólo los sábados. Y si no, pues dentro de unos años puedes hacerlo.

C. Te aconsejo seguir las reglas de tus padres. Eres muy joven para salir de noche.

Communication for All Students

Pair Work

6 Have students work in pairs to write a problem and three possible solutions. Pairs exchange their papers with another pair, which then chooses one of the solutions listed or provides an original one.

Visual Learners

6 Have students look at the pictures before reading the paragraph and make hypotheses as to what the problem might be. Ask them to explain their predictions based on the clues in the photos.

Primer paso

CAPÍTULO 2

Teaching Resources
pp. 37–40

PRINT
▶ Lesson Planner, p. 8
▶ Listening Activities, pp. 11, 15–16
▶ Activities for Communication, pp. 5–6, 54, 56, 91–92
▶ Cuaderno de gramática, pp. 10–13
▶ Grammar Tutor for Students of Spanish, Chapter 2
▶ Cuaderno de actividades, pp. 14–17
▶ Cuaderno para hispanohablantes, pp. 6–10
▶ Testing Program, pp. 23–26
▶ Alternative Assessment Guide, p. 31
▶ Student Make-Up Assignments, Chapter 2

MEDIA
▶ One-Stop Planner
▶ Audio Compact Discs, CD 2, Trs. 5–6, 24–26, 20
▶ Teaching Transparencies 2-1; **Más práctica gramatical** Answers; Cuaderno de gramática Answers
▶ Interactive CD-ROM Tutor, Disc 1

Bell Work
On the board or on a transparency, write the following: **¿Cuándo es necesario aconsejarle a alguien?** Students should give one or two short answers in Spanish.

Presenting
Así se dice

Model pronunciation of the phrases in **Así se dice**. Then present a problem to a student and ask him or her for advice. The student should answer using a phrase from **Así se dice** and any appropriate vocabulary.

Teaching Resources
pp. 37–40

PRINT
▶ Lesson Planner, p. 8
▶ Listening Activities, pp. 11, 15–16
▶ Activities for Communication, pp. 5–6, 54, 56, 91–92
▶ Cuaderno de gramática, pp. 10–13
▶ Grammar Tutor for Students of Spanish, Chapter 2
▶ Cuaderno de actividades, pp. 14–17
▶ Cuaderno para hispanohablantes, pp. 6–10
▶ Testing Program, pp. 23–26
▶ Alternative Assessment Guide, p. 31
▶ Student Make-Up Assignments, Chapter 2

MEDIA
▶ One-Stop Planner
▶ Audio Compact Discs, CD 2, Trs. 5–6, 24–26, 20
▶ Teaching Transparencies 2-1; **Más práctica gramatical** Answers; Cuaderno de gramática Answers
▶ Interactive CD-ROM Tutor, Disc 1

Presenting
Gramática de repaso

Informal commands Give several students commands and have them act out what you have told them to do. After students have successfully pantomimed these tasks, tell the same students to stop what they are doing, using negative commands.

Vocabulario

Using the pictures as reference, ask students ¿Cómo estás hoy? Students answer with one of the vocabulary words. You might follow up by asking why he or she feels this way.

Gramática de repaso

Informal commands

1. Affirmative informal commands have the same form as the **él/ella/usted** present indicative form of the verb.

   ¡**Come** las verduras!   **Duerme** bien.   **Descansa** más.

2. For negative forms, start with the **yo** form of the verb in the present indicative and drop the **-o**. Then add **-es** for **-ar** verbs, and **-as** for **-er** and **-ir** verbs.

   mirar → miro → no mires
   No mires el sol.
   comer → como → no comas
   No comas tantos dulces.
   escribir → escribo → no escribas
   No escribas en la pared.

3. For a more complete review of the **tú** commands, see page R39.

Más práctica gramatical, p. 54, Acts. 1, 3

Cuaderno de gramática, pp. 10–11, Acts. 1–3

7 ¿Buen consejo? Script and answers on p. 31G.
Escuchemos Escucha los siguientes problemas y consejos. Si te parece bueno el consejo, escribe **buen consejo** en una hoja de papel. Si te parece malo, escribe **mal consejo.**
CD 2 Tr. 5

8 Gramática en contexto
Escribamos Imagina que tu mejor amigo(a) se peleó con otro(a) amigo(a) y ahora necesita tus consejos. Usa los siguientes verbos o frases en forma positiva o negativa para darle consejos: **perdonar, ser abierto(a), hablar, ser impaciente, decirle cómo te sientes, preocuparte.**

9 Gramática en contexto See sample answers below.
Hablemos Pablo necesita tu ayuda. Se despertó tarde hoy y tiene un examen en su primera clase. Con un(a) compañero(a) de clase, dale cinco consejos sobre lo que debe hacer para no llegar demasiado tarde al colegio y cinco consejos sobre lo que no debe hacer.

¿Te acuerdas?
Here are some informal commands that have irregular forms:
decir **di**   salir **sal**
hacer **haz**   ser **sé**
ir **ve**   tener **ten**
poner **pon**   venir **ven**

Más práctica gramatical, p. 54, Act. 2

Vocabulario

¿Cómo estás hoy?

 agotada  histérico  agobiado  ansiosa

---

Cultures and Communities

Family Link
Have students interview two older family members about the type of commands they heard as teenagers. Ask volunteers to use words they already know to express three of the commands and present them to the class. Other students will categorize the advice as **un buen consejo** or **un mal consejo.**

Thinking Critically
Evaluation Have partners create a prioritized list of ten commands they would give to new students on how to be successful and avoid stress at their school. Encourage students to submit their lists to the school newspaper for publication.

¿Qué causa el estrés?

estar rendido(a)   *to be worn out*
llevar una vida agitada   *to lead a hectic life*
ponerse nervioso(a)   *to get nervous*
sufrir de presiones   *to be under pressure*
sufrir de tensiones   *to suffer from tension*

¿Qué alivia el estrés?

cuidarse   *to take care of oneself*
reírse (í, i)   *to laugh*
relajarse   *to relax*
resolver (ue) un problema   *to solve a problem*
tomar las cosas con calma   *to take things calmly*

CD-ROM DISC 1

Cuaderno de actividades, pp. 14–16, Acts. 2–6
Cuaderno de gramática, pp. 11–12, Acts. 4–6
Más práctica gramatical, p. 55, Act. 4

---

10 **¡No lo aguanto mas!** See sample answers below.

Escribamos Mira el dibujo e indica de qué tensiones sufre Yolanda y qué puede hacer para aliviar el estrés. ¿Alguna vez estuviste tan ocupado(a) como ella? ¿Por qué?

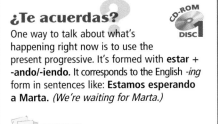

¿Te acuerdas?

One way to talk about what's happening right now is to use the present progressive. It's formed with **estar + -ando/-iendo**. It corresponds to the English *-ing* form in sentences like: **Estamos esperando a Marta.** *(We're waiting for Marta.)*

CD-ROM DISC 1

Cuaderno de gramática, p. 13, Acts. 7–8
Más práctica gramatical, p. 55, Act. 5

---

11 **¿Cómo te sientes cuando...?**

Leamos/Hablemos ¿Cómo te sientes o cómo reaccionas en las siguientes situaciones?

1. Hablas con el presidente del país.
2. Un amigo te cuenta un chiste.
3. Corres 10 kilómetros.
4. Pasas un fin de semana en la playa.
5. Tienes muchísima tarea.
6. Es el primer día de clases en un nuevo colegio.
7. Escuchas tu canción favorita.
8. Tienes cuatro exámenes en un día.

---

12 **¿Cómo alivio el estrés?**

Hablemos En grupos, comparen sus respuestas de la Actividad 11. Dales consejos a tus compañeros(as) sobre las cosas que les causan estrés. Luego piensa en los consejos que te dieron tus compañeros(as). ¿Cuáles van a ser difíciles de seguir? ¿Por qué?

Vocabulario extra

abrumado(a)   *overwhelmed*
desvelarse   *to stay up late*
estar hecho(a) polvo   *to be worn out*
madrugar   *to get up early*
enojarse   *to become angry*

Communication for All Students

Auditory Learners

You may want to suggest to your students that they memorize the irregular **tú** commands as a jingle: **Ten, ven, pon, sal, di, ve, haz y sé.**

Group Work

Divide the class into groups of four. Give groups fifteen minutes to prepare a skit in which one student is ill, a friend gives him or her advice, and a third takes the friend to the hospital where the doctor or nurse also gives advice. You may want to assign different ailments to ensure variety.

Presenting Vocabulario

Pantomime the new words and phrases. As you say **Estoy rendido(a),** sink into a chair or wipe your hand across your forehead. As you say **Me pongo nervioso(a),** look "jumpy" and fiddle with something. Then ask students **¿Qué causa el estrés en tu vida?** They should answer with one of the new expressions, pantomiming how they feel. As a follow-up, ask students **¿Qué alivia el estrés?** Encourage them to act out their responses.

Thinking Critically

10 **Analyzing** Have pairs of students discuss stress. Ask them to list some of its physical manifestations. (release of adrenalin, increased heart rate and blood pressure) What situations are most stressful? (loss of a close friend or relative, failing a test) What are some ways to cope with stress? (exercise, proper nutrition, rest) How can stress benefit someone? (can fuel ambition or healthy competition)

Kinesthetic Learners

Including the descriptive vocabulary here and from page 38, have a student act out one of the emotional conditions while the rest of the class tries to guess the word being portrayed. The student who guesses correctly acts out the next condition.

Answers

9 *Possible answers:*
Corre rápido. Come cereal para el desayuno. Ve al colegio en autobús. Vístete rápido. Sal de casa a tiempo. No vayas a pie. No prepares huevos. No te bañes. No hables por teléfono.

10 *Possible answers:*
Sufre de presiones porque lleva una vida agitada. Está muy ocupada en su oficina hoy. Está rendida porque pasa mucho tiempo tratando de resolver los problemas del trabajo.

13 **Consejero en la radio** Script and answers on p. 31G.

Escuchemos/Escribamos Imagina que trabajas para una emisora. Recibes llamadas de gente que necesita tu ayuda. Escucha la siguiente llamada y toma apuntes sobre el problema. Escucha otra vez y luego escribe una respuesta que le da consejos. Menciona por lo menos tres consejos.

CD 2
Tr. 6

Nota cultural

Muchos estadounidenses creen que los españoles tienen horarios de trabajo muy relajados. Todavía existen muchos lugares donde los empleados se echan la siesta por la tarde, pero la situación va cambiando. Con su entrada a la Unión Europea, España tiene cada año más negocio con los otros países de Europa. Muchas personas creen que para competir en el mercado mundial, los españoles deben adoptar horas de trabajo semejantes a las de otros países europeos. ¿Qué ventajas y desventajas encuentras tú en el horario de trabajo tradicional? ¿en el horario moderno?

14 **Mi escape favorito** See sample answers below.

Leamos/Escribamos En grupos de tres o cuatro estudiantes, lean el artículo sobre los escapes favoritos de Susy, Beto y Patricia. ¿Qué hacen ellos para aliviar el estrés? Escriban un párrafo sobre los "escapes" favoritos de cada miembro de su grupo.

MODELO El escape favorito de Susy es ir a la playa...

MI "ESCAPE" FAVORITO...

¿Abrumado con las presiones del día a día? ¿Echas humo de la tensión? ¡No estalles! Tres lectores comparten contigo su "escape" predilecto:

✳ **Susy**, 17 años: "La playa me serena. Me gusta sentarme frente al mar y concentrarme en el ir y venir de las olas. Me basta con media hora para sentirme como nueva. Si por algún motivo no puedo ir a la playa, contemplo un rato las nubes. Es que a mí me relaja mucho la naturaleza..."

✳ **Beto**, 18 años: "Para poner mi mente en piloto automático, me gustan los crucigramas y los juegos de palabras. La concentración me hace olvidar los otros problemas. Además, mejoro mi vocabulario..."

✳ **Patricia**, 15 años: "A mí me relaja la actividad física. Nadar, correr, hacer ejercicios aeróbicos... Todo eso me saca de mis problemas en un 'tilín'..."

Communication for All Students

Native Speakers

13 Have native speakers find three **refranes** (sayings) that give advice for dealing with stress and share these with the rest of the class. For example, **A las diez, en la cama estés, y si es antes, mejor que después.** Point out that the nearest English equivalent is not a direct translation: *Early to bed, early to rise, makes a man healthy, wealthy, and wise.*

CD 2
Trs. 7–10

¿Cómo te cuidas?

¿Crees que los jóvenes de España y los países de Latinoamérica se cuidan de la misma manera que tú? ¿Sufren ellos del estrés también? Entrevistamos a varios jóvenes para preguntarles qué hacen. ¿Qué tienes en común con ellos?

Teaching Resources
p. 41

PRINT
▸ Video Guide, pp. 9–10, 13
▸ Cuaderno de actividades, p. 24
▸ Cuaderno para hispanohablantes, pp. 6–10

MEDIA
▸ One-Stop Planner
▸ Video Program, Videocassette 1, 21:06–23:54
▸ Audio Compact Discs, CD 2, Trs. 7–10
▸ Interactive CD-ROM Tutor, Disc 1

Gloriela
San Antonio, Texas

"Yo me cuido la salud CD 2 Tr. 8 por comer bien, no como tanto, no como tanto también en la noche y como cosas como verduras, frutas y no tanto dulce".

Érica
San José, Costa Rica

"Bueno, yo hago CD 2 Tr. 9 ejercicios, voy a La Sabana, corro, juego un rato con mi esposo, con mi familia, eso es lo que hago".

Alberto
Caracas, Venezuela

"Para mantener la CD 2 Tr. 10 salud hago deporte, hago una rutina diaria de fisicoculturismo y trato de estar al día en todo lo que se respecta al estado de la forma".

Presenting
Panorama cultural

Play the video or audio recording. Have students read the interview responses aloud. Then replay the recording and have students compare their pronunciation with that of the interviewees.

Para pensar y hablar...

A. ¿Qué haces tú para mantener la buena salud? Lee con atención las respuestas de Alberto y Érica y compáralas. ¿Cuál de los dos prefiere hacer ejercicios en el parque y en grupo y quién lo hace individualmente?

B. En tu opinión, ¿por qué es importante hacer ejercicio y tener una dieta balanceada? ¿Cómo te afecta la inactividad? ¿Cómo te afecta comer demasiado?

Cuaderno para hispanohablantes, pp. 9–10

Preguntas
1. **¿Quién no come mucho por la noche?** (Gloriela)
2. **¿A quién le gusta correr?** (Érica)
3. **¿Quiénes hacen deporte?** (Alberto y Érica)
4. **¿Adónde va Érica para hacer ejercicio?** (La Sabana)
5. **¿Quién tiene la rutina más sana? ¿Por qué?** (Answers will vary.)

Connections and Comparisons

Thinking Critically
Evaluation La Sabana (The Savannah) was once an airport but has been converted into a park. On weekends it fills with people playing tennis or basketball, running, swimming, and playing soccer. How do recreational facilities affect the well-being of urban dwellers? Do students regularly make use of such public places? Why or why not?

Language Note
Ask your students if they can guess from the context of Alberto's interview what he is referring to when he speaks of his **rutina diaria de fisicoculturismo** (daily body-building routine). Physical culture is seldom used in English nowadays, but Webster's Third International Dictionary calls it "the systematic care and development of the physique."

Teaching Resources
pp. 42–43

PRINT
▸ Lesson Planner, p. 9
▸ Video Guide, pp. 9–10, 12
▸ Cuaderno de actividades, p. 18

MEDIA
▸ One-Stop Planner
▸ Video Program
   Contigo en la distancia
   Videocassette 1, 15:12–21:05
   Videocassette 5 (captioned version), 06:08–12:01
▸ Audio Compact Discs, CD 2, Trs. 11–14

Presenting
¡Adelante!

Play the Audio CD once while students look at the photos and read the text. Next, present the Preteaching Vocabulary and check for comprehension.

 Contigo en la distancia

As an alternative or in addition to **¡Adelante!,** you may wish to show Episode 2 of **Contigo en la distancia.** For suggestions and activities, see the *Video Guide.*

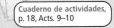
Cuaderno de actividades, p. 18, Acts. 9–10

¡Adelante! ▪ *¡Nos cuidamos mucho!*

CD 2
Trs. 11–14

Pilar, Carlos y Elena hablan de los buenos hábitos. ¿Tienes algo en común con ellos?

Normalmente los padres les enseñan a los hijos los buenos hábitos de alimentación y salud. Pero en mi familia no es así. Cuando mi madre era niña, la gente no sabía mucho sobre los peligros por los que nos preocupamos hoy en día. Por ejemplo, mi madre siempre se bronceaba sin crema protectora y a veces se quemaba. Le hablé del peligro y ahora ella se pone crema protectora. También, ella siempre le echaba mucha sal y aceite a la comida. Ahora sabemos que el uso excesivo de sal y aceite contribuye a los problemas de salud. ¡Nos cuidamos mucho!

Pilar

Antes tenía problemas en hacer amigos porque era bastante reservado. Muchas veces me quedaba en casa, no salía con amigos y no hablaba mucho con mis papás ni con mis amigos. Francamente, me interesaban más las cosas que las personas. Nunca compartía mis problemas con nadie y me sentía muy solo. Un día decidí que tenía que cambiar mi modo de ser. Ahora sé que las personas son más importantes que las cosas. Cuando algo me molesta o si estoy agobiado por las tensiones de la vida, trato de compartirlo con alguien, por ejemplo, con mi familia o con amigos. Comparto las buenas cosas también. Así las cosas negativas no parecen tan graves y ¡las cosas positivas son mejores!

Carlos

Mi amiga Marianela siempre estaba a dieta para bajar de peso. Quería ser tan delgada como las modelos de las revistas. Está bien cuidarse el peso, pero al mismo tiempo yo me preocupaba por ella: no comía lo suficiente, estaba delgadísima y se pesaba dos veces al día. Estaba tan delgada que se cansaba fácilmente. Afortunadamente, sus padres se dieron cuenta del problema y la llevaron a ver a un doctor. Ahora ella está mejorando y subiendo de peso poco a poco. Estoy muy contenta ahora pues es mi mejor amiga y me importa mucho.

Elena

Preteaching Vocabulary

Recognizing Cognates
¡Adelante! contains several words that students will recognize as cognates. Have students find these words and guess what Pilar, Carlos, and Elena are saying about habits: **hábitos, crema protectora, problemas, reservado, personas, decidí, tensiones, negativas, positivas, dieta, modelos, suficiente, problema, doctor.**

These activities check for comprehension only. Students should not yet be expected to produce language modeled in ¡Adelante!

15 **Correcciones** See answers below.

Indica si la frase es **cierta** o **falsa.** Si es falsa, corrígela.

1. En el pasado, Carlos hablaba con sus papás o amigos cuando tenía estrés en su vida.
2. La mamá de Carlos nunca se ponía crema protectora cuando salía al sol.
3. Pilar y su familia ahora se cuidan mucho.
4. Ahora Elena se preocupa por su amiga porque todavía quiere bajar de peso.
5. La amiga de Elena está mejor ahora.

16 **Un resumen** See possible answers below.

Con un(a) compañero(a), haz un resumen de cada párrafo que leyeron en la página 42. ¿Cuál era el problema de cada persona? ¿Cómo resolvió cada persona su problema o el problema de otro?

17 **¿Quién lo dijo?** See answers below.

Identifica cuál de los tres estudiantes habló de cada problema.

1. Su amiga se pesaba dos veces al día.
2. Su familia le echaba mucha sal y aceite a la comida.
3. Nunca compartía sus problemas con nadie.
4. Su mamá se bronceaba sin crema protectora.
5. No hablaba mucho ni con sus papás ni con sus amigos.
6. Una amiga suya estaba tan delgada que se cansaba fácilmente.

18 **Entre amigos** See sample answers below.

Las siguientes personas tienen malos hábitos de salud. Con un(a) compañero(a), dales buenos consejos. Usa frases como **Deberías** o **No deberías** más el vocabulario de las páginas 38 y 39.

1. Anita no habla de sus problemas con nadie.
2. Armando va mucho a la playa y no usa crema protectora.
3. Ignacio sólo come carne y pollo frito.
4. Yusef trabaja 20 horas al día.
5. Florencia toma refrescos todo el día.
6. Andrés se siente muy solo pero no habla con nadie.

LA SALUD ES TODO

Por una vida más sana come sólo lo mejor

"La nutrición es nuestra especialidad"

COMESTIBLES NUTRITEC S.A.

19 **Ahora te toca a ti**

Describe tus hábitos de salud: lo que comes, si hablas con tus amigos y familiares cuando sufres de tensiones y si haces ejercicio.

Using the Captioned Video

Additional Practice

19 Have pairs or small groups create a skit in which a client goes to a counselor for advice. First, groups brainstorm about some problems and appropriate advice for each. They should then use these ideas as a basis for a simple script and perform their skits. After each skit, the class may give further advice to the client.

Challenge

Ask students to discuss in small groups an anonymous friend who has had to break old habits. Challenge students to think about why this person developed bad habits and what factors led him or her to break the habit. (**Mi amigo empezó a fumar porque muchos de sus amigos fumaban. Ya no fuma porque sabe que es malo para la salud.**)

CAPÍTULO 2

Career Path
Have students brainstorm about health-related careers. (clinical or field health-care worker, dietician, social worker, personal trainer, day-care worker, mental health professional, home health-care provider) Ask how the knowledge of a second language might be useful. (increased customer base, better understanding of clients' needs, access to information published in other languages)

Answers

15 1. falsa; No hablaba mucho con sus papás.
   2. falsa; La mamá de Pilar no se ponía crema protectora.
   3. cierta
   4. falsa; Su amiga está subiendo de peso ahora.
   5. cierta

16 *Possible answers:*
   Pilar: Su mamá se bronceaba sin ponerse crema protectora. Le echaba mucha sal y aceite a la comida. Pilar habló con su mamá de los peligros.
   Carlos: Era muy reservado y solitario. Ahora cuando algo le molesta se comunica más.
   Elena: Su amiga bajaba de peso y estaba muy delgada. Se preocupaba mucho por su peso. Sus papás le hablaron del problema y ahora come mejor.

17 1. Elena
   2. Pilar
   3. Carlos
   4. Pilar
   5. Carlos
   6. Elena

18 *Sample answers:*
   1. Te aconsejo hablar con un(a) amigo(a).
   2. Te recomiendo usar crema protectora.
   3. Te recomiendo comer más verduras.
   4. No deberías trabajar tanto.
   5. Deberías tomar más agua y jugo.
   6. Deberías hablar más.

Bell Work
Have students write three problems and some advice for each one. They should use affirmative and negative **tú** commands in their suggestions.

Presenting
Así se dice
Read statements from the **no te cuidas mucho** column and check for comprehension. Ask several students to counter what you say with a statement from the **te cuidas mucho** column.

Así se dice

Talking about taking care of yourself

Para decir que no te cuidas mucho, puedes decir:

Siempre **le echo mucha sal a la comida.** Casi nunca **hago ejercicio. Me quedo frente a la tele** por horas.

Nunca **duermo lo suficiente.**

Siempre **estoy a dieta. Me peso** dos veces al día.

Nunca **comparto** mis problemas **con nadie** y **me siento muy solo(a).**

Para decir que te cuidas mucho, puedes decir:

Tengo buenos hábitos de alimentación.

Como comida sana con poca **grasa.**

Para no broncearme, me pongo crema protectora.

Me mantengo en forma. Hago ejercicio aeróbico tres veces por semana.

Cuaderno de actividades, pp. 20–22, Acts. 13–17

20 **¡Suerte, Li!** See answers below.
Leamos/Escribamos Lee este artículo y luego contesta las preguntas que siguen.
1. ¿De dónde es Li Fapin?
2. ¿Por qué se entrena?
3. ¿Qué tiene de especial el caso de Li?
4. ¿Cómo piensa Li que va a resultar el maratón?
5. ¿Cómo se siente Li ahora?
6. ¿Cómo se mantiene en forma?

También se puede decir...
Algunas personas dicen **estar a régimen** por **estar a dieta.**

¿Se te ha olvidado?
parts of the body
Ver páginas R79–98

Cuaderno de gramática, p. 14, Act. 9

"MARATÓN A LOS 80"

● Li Fapin sueña con convertirse en un chino famoso. ¿Cómo? ¡Corriendo! Li se entrena todos los días para participar en un maratón internacional de 10.000 metros. Y, por supuesto, piensa llevarse los laureles. Lo sorprendente del caso es que tiene 80 años, una salud excelente y energía para cien años más. Mantiene una estricta disciplina. Se acuesta temprano y es un gran madrugador; su dieta es vegetariana y toma vino en raras ocasiones. ¡Suerte, Li!

Communication for All Students

Pair Work
Have students work in pairs. One partner makes a statement about not taking care of him- or herself, and the other responds by saying what he or she does to lead a healthy life. (**—Siempre le echo mucha sal a la comida. —Bueno, yo tengo buenos hábitos de alimentación.**) Students can explain or justify their habits and then switch roles.

Group Work
Have groups of students create posters for a **Semana de la Salud** that educate the public about good and bad health habits. You may wish to review the imperative before students begin. Students should include illustrations on their posters for display in an appropriate place in the school.

Gramática de repaso

Reflexive verbs

1. To conjugate a reflexive verb like **levantarse** *(to get up)*, remember to use the appropriate reflexive pronoun with the verb:

me levanto	nos levantamos
te levantas	os levantáis
se levanta	se levantan

2. When using a reflexive verb in the infinitive form with another conjugated verb, the reflexive pronoun may be attached to the infinitive or placed in front of the conjugated verb:

   Voy a **acostarme** a las diez y media.   **Me** voy a **acostar** a las diez y media.

3. Attach the reflexive pronoun to the end of an affirmative command and place it before a negative command:

   ¡Cuídate mucho!   No **te acuestes** muy tarde.

Cuaderno de gramática, pp. 14–16, Acts. 10–13   Más práctica gramatical, p. 56, Acts. 6–7

---

21 **¿Buenos hábitos?** Script and answers on p. 31G.

Escuchemos Escucha lo que dicen las siguientes personas. Luego indica si cada persona tiene hábitos saludables o no.

CD 2 Tr. 15

22 **Gramática en contexto** See sample answer below.

Escribamos La familia Suárez siempre está muy ocupada. La señora trabaja durante el día pero su esposo trabaja de noche. Describe lo que hace cada persona.

¿Te acuerdas?

acostarse	levantarse
bañarse	ponerse
despertarse	vestirse
lavarse	

MODELO   **El señor Suárez se quita los zapatos.**

Communication for All Students

Group Work
Divide the class into groups of three. One student presents a problem that might elicit a response with a reflexive verb. **(Tengo mucho calor.)** One member of the group will give advice with an affirmative command, and the other student will give a negative command. **(¡Quítate la chaqueta! ¡No te pongas el suéter!)**

Pair Work
Have pairs of students describe their daily routines at the age of seven. **(Me despertaba a las siete y me vestía rápidamente.)** You might review the imperfect tense before beginning. Partners should ask each other questions to obtain more details.

Building on Previous Skills
Play TIC-TAC-TOE to review reflexive verbs. Make 3 x 3 tic-tac-toe grids. In each square, write an infinitive in parentheses followed by a sentence with the verb deleted. **(bañarse) Es necesario que yo _____ después de hacer ejercicio.** Distribute copies to groups of three. One student acts as judge. The other partners take turns saying the correct form of the verb. If the judge verifies that the verb form is correct, that person puts an X or an O in the corresponding square.

Presenting
Gramática de repaso

Reflexive verbs Ask several students questions to which they must respond with a reflexive verb. Then make statements about an unhealthy lifestyle using reflexive verbs. **(Yo me levanto tarde y nunca puedo desayunar.)** Ask a student to give you an informal command, solving your problem. **(Levántate más temprano.)** Ask another student to make a different suggestion, using a negative command with a reflexive verb. **(No te acuestes tan tarde.)**

Answers
20 1. Es de China.
2. Quiere participar en un maratón internacional.
3. Tiene 80 años.
4. Piensa llevarse los laureles (ganar).
5. Tiene muy buena salud y mucha energía.
6. Se acuesta temprano, se levanta temprano, es vegetariano y casi no toma vino.

22 Sample answer:
Una hija se baña. Otra se lava los dientes. En la habitación, otra hija se viste mientras su hermana se despierta. El papá se quita los zapatos. Va a acostarse pronto. La mamá se pone la chaqueta.

 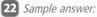

Presenting
Vocabulario

On the board or on a transparency, write the captions of the four pictures. Ask students which of the remaining vocabulary words they associate with each caption. Write the words under each caption and have students make statements about each photo using the appropriate vocabulary.

Vocabulario

alimentarse bien/mal   ducharse   pesarse   ponerse crema protectora

la alimentación *nutrition*	**dormirse (ue, u)** *to fall asleep*
broncearse *to suntan*	**el peligro** *danger*
contribuir *to contribute*	**la piel** *skin*
cuidarse el peso *to watch one's weight*	**quemarse** *to get a sunburn*
darse cuenta de *to realize*	**subir de peso** *to gain weight*

Más práctica gramatical, p. 57, Act. 8

Cuaderno de actividades, pp. 19–20, Acts. 11–12

Cuaderno de gramática, pp. 16–17, Acts. 14–15

23 **¡Qué lío!** Script and answers on p. 31H.

 CD 2 Tr. 16

Escuchemos Escucha las descripciones e indica a qué dibujos corresponden.

a.

b.

c.

d.

Nota cultural

Los españoles tienen buenos hábitos de salud por lo general. Por ejemplo, comen más fruta y vegetales frescos que el estadounidense típico. También caminan mucho más que los estadounidenses. Esto se debe a que las ciudades españolas fueron construidas cuando no había coches. Por eso no es tan necesario usar el coche. Las personas pueden ir de compras o ir al trabajo a pie porque todo les queda más cerca. ¿Caminas mucho tú?

24 **¿Se cuidan?**

Hablemos/Escribamos Compara tus hábitos de salud con los de unos(as) compañeros(as). ¿Se cuidan Uds. o no? ¿A qué hora se levantan? ¿Qué comen normalmente para el desayuno? Hagan una lista de los buenos y malos hábitos que comparten. ¿Qué consejos puede dar el uno al otro?

Communication for All Students

Group Work

Have groups of three to four students create a five-question survey addressing one aspect of health-related habits. (food, sleeping, exercise, skin care) Then allow students to conduct their survey in class, calculate percentages of good and bad habits, and present the findings to the class.

Visual Learners

25 Have students prepare a series of drawings illustrating the events of Carlos's day.

25 **¡Tantos errores!** See sample answer below.

Leamos/Escribamos Carlos se despierta muy cansado todas las mañanas. Por eso, comete varios errores durante el día. Lee el párrafo que describe lo que le pasó hoy. Corrige las oraciones ilógicas. Luego con un(a) compañero(a) de clase, escribe un párrafo tan ilógico como éste. ¡Usen la imaginación! Intercambien su párrafo con otro equipo de compañeros(as) y escriban una versión lógica.

> Carlos se levantó a las seis de la mañana, muy cansado. Fue al baño y se lavó los dientes con el peine. Después, se duchó y se lavó el pelo con pasta de dientes. Después se vistió: se puso un traje de baño, sandalias y un abrigo. Salió de la casa y fue al colegio con su mochila. Regresó a casa, vio la radio unas horas y luego se acostó en el baño a las nueve.

Gramática de repaso

The imperfect

The imperfect tense is used to talk about actions in progress in the past and about what happened in the past on a regular or habitual basis. These are the endings for -**ar**, -**er**, and -**ir** verbs as well as the irregular verbs **ver**, **ser**, and **ir**.

CD-ROM DISC 1

-**ar** verbs	-**er** verbs	-**ir** verbs	VER	SER	IR
llev**aba**	corr**ía**	dorm**ía**	ve**ía**	**era**	**iba**
llev**abas**	corr**ías**	dorm**ías**	ve**ías**	**eras**	**ibas**
llev**aba**	corr**ía**	dorm**ía**	ve**ía**	**era**	**iba**
llev**ábamos**	corr**íamos**	dorm**íamos**	ve**íamos**	**éramos**	**íbamos**
llev**abais**	corr**íais**	dorm**íais**	ve**íais**	**erais**	**ibais**
llev**aban**	corr**ían**	dorm**ían**	ve**ían**	**eran**	**iban**

Cuaderno de gramática, pp. 17–18, Acts. 16–18

Más práctica gramatical, p. 57, Act. 9

26 **Gramática en contexto** Script and answers on p. 31H.

Escuchemos Ricardo, estudiante en la Universidad Central, habla de sus años en el colegio. Escucha cada frase e indica si habla de **acciones habituales** o **no habituales.**

CD 2 Tr. 17

¿Se te ha olvidado?
uses of the imperfect
Ver la página R36

Nota cultural

A muchos jóvenes españoles les gusta salir por la noche para caminar y ver a sus amigos en las calles y en los cafés. Cuando una persona sale con sus amigos en España, hay mucha flexibilidad social. No es obligatorio asociarte sólo con el grupo con el que saliste. Es común andar con gente de varios grupos durante una noche. ¿Ocurre lo mismo en Estados Unidos?

Connections and Comparisons

Thinking Critically
Comparing and Contrasting After students have read the **Nota cultural**, have them compare the Spanish style of socializing with what students are familiar with. Do they go out in big or small groups? If they go out with one group of people, do they spend the evening with the same people or do they socialize with different groups throughout the evening?

Segundo paso

CAPÍTULO 2

Presenting
Gramática de repaso

The imperfect Review the endings for regular verbs in the imperfect and for **ver, ser,** and **ir.** Then make a statement explaining how you have changed a habit either for better or for worse. (**Antes, yo corría cuatro veces por semana, pero ahora sólo corro de vez en cuando.**) In pairs, have one student make a statement with one of the verbs in the imperfect. (**Antes, mi hermano y yo no veíamos mucho a nuestros abuelos.**) His or her partner then brings the first student's statement into the present, indicating a change in behavior. (**Ahora, tú y tu hermano ven a los abuelos con más frecuencia.**)

Answers
25 *Paragraphs may vary.*
Sample logical answer:
Se lavó los dientes con el cepillo. Se lavó el pelo con champú. Se puso ropa como pantalones y una camisa para ir al colegio. Vio la tele. Se acostó en la cama. *Group paragraphs will also vary.*

Teaching Resources
pp. 44–49

PRINT
▸ Lesson Planner, p. 9
▸ Listening Activities, pp. 12–13, 16–17
▸ Activities for Communication, pp. 7–8, 55–56, 91–92
▸ Cuaderno de gramática, pp. 14–18
▸ Grammar Tutor for Students of Spanish, Chapter 2
▸ Cuaderno de actividades, pp. 19–22
▸ Cuaderno para hispanohablantes, pp. 6–10
▸ Testing Program, pp. 27–30
▸ Alternative Assessment Guide, p. 31
▸ Student Make-Up Assignments, Chapter 2

MEDIA
▸ One-Stop Planner
▸ Audio Compact Discs, CD 2, Trs. 15–18, 27–29, 21
▸ Teaching Transparencies 2-2; **Más práctica gramatical** Answers; Cuaderno de gramática Answers
▸ Interactive CD-ROM Tutor, Disc 1

Answers

27 1. Se preocupaba por el clima porque su familia tenía una finca. A veces se sentía rendido por los estudios.
2. Hablaban, leían y se reían.
3. *Answers will vary.*
4. *Answers will vary.*

28 *Possible answers:*
En aquel entonces, Francisco veía televisión y jugaba con sus juguetes. Le pedía dinero a su mamá para comprar helado. Se acostaba temprano. Hoy en día, estudia mucho y trabaja para ganar su dinero. Se acuesta más tarde.

---

27 **En aquel entonces** See answers below.

Leamos/Escribamos Carolina quiere hablar con su abuelo sobre su vida cuando era niño. Lee su conversación y contesta las siguientes preguntas.

1. ¿De qué tipo de presiones sufría el abuelo?
2. ¿Cómo se divertían el abuelo y su familia?
3. En tu opinión, ¿cómo era la niñez del abuelo?
4. ¿Cómo se compara la niñez del abuelo con tu niñez?

CAROLINA	Abuelo, ¿cómo era tu niñez? ¿Era muy diferente de la mía?
ABUELO	Bueno, en algunas cosas sí, en otras no. Por ejemplo, de niño yo me levantaba a las cuatro y media de la mañana, porque vivíamos en el campo y tenía que ayudar con las labores de la finca. Tú no te levantas hasta las siete.
CAROLINA	¿Sufrías de muchas presiones?
ABUELO	No sufría del estrés de la vida urbana como ahora, pero sí había presiones. Nos preocupábamos por el clima, por ejemplo. Si no llovía, la finca no producía lo suficiente. Y claro, asistía a la escuela como tú y a veces me sentía rendido por los estudios.
CAROLINA	Y entre familia, ¿se divertían ustedes bastante?
ABUELO	Ah, ¡pues claro! Dedicábamos mucho tiempo a las actividades para toda la familia, hablábamos y leíamos por la tarde y nos reíamos mucho. En general, yo fui muy feliz de niño.

28 **¡Vaya diferencia!** See possible answers below.

Escribamos Mira los dibujos de Francisco. La primera serie de dibujos muestra la vida de Francisco cuando tenía seis años. La segunda muestra su vida ahora. Describe las diferencias entre la primera y la segunda serie de dibujos.

En aquel entonces

Hoy en día

Communication for All Students

Slower Pace

28 Have students work in pairs to list the vocabulary and constructions they will need to describe the situation in the photos. They can make a two-column chart with **En aquel entonces** and **Hoy en día** as column heads, and separate the words into nouns and verbs.

Group Work

28 Ask students to bring in baby pictures of themselves and a current photograph. Divide students into groups of four. Have each student write two or three sentences describing his or her own photos. Remind them to use the imperfect to describe themselves as children. Students then edit each other's descriptions.

29 **¿Qué está mal en este dibujo?**

Escuchemos/Escribamos Mira el dibujo de Ana Patricia cuando era joven. Luego escucha lo que dice sobre su vida en la escuela secundaria. Hay tres errores en el dibujo. ¿Cuáles son?

CD 2
Tr. 18

Script and answers on p. 31H.

 30

 Del colegio al trabajo

Hablemos/Escribamos Imagina que eres enfermero(a) en una escuela secundaria. Habla con un(a) estudiante acerca de su vida hace tres años y su vida ahora. ¿Cómo se cuidaba? ¿Sufría mucho del estrés? ¿Por qué? ¿Cómo era su horario? ¿Cómo es su vida ahora? Haz una lista de cinco recomendaciones para mejorar su vida actual *(present)*. Intercambien papeles.

 31 **A la hora de cenar** Answers will vary.

Leamos/Escribamos Lee la tira cómica de Calvin. Después, haz una de las siguientes actividades.

1. Escribe un diálogo entre Calvin y su mamá o una continuación de la tira cómica en el que cada uno defiende sus opiniones. La mamá explica por qué es importante comer bien y Calvin explica por qué no quiere comer verduras.

2. Escribe un párrafo que compare tu niñez con la de Calvin. ¿En qué eran diferentes? ¿Qué tenían en común? ¿Cómo eran tus padres en comparación con los de Calvin?

 32 **En mi cuaderno**

Escribamos Ahora escoge una de las siguientes actividades.

a. Entrevista a una persona mayor de tu familia, de tu colegio o de tu barrio y pregúntale cómo era la vida cuando él o ella era joven. Escribe un diálogo o párrafo como el de Carolina y su abuelo en la Actividad 27.

b. Imagina que ya tienes 75 años y estás hablando con tus nietos. Escribe un diálogo o párrafo y describe cómo era la escuela cuando eras joven.

Connections and Comparisons

Thinking Critically

Comparing and Contrasting Ask students to find cartoons or comic strips from Spain or Latin America dealing with young children and food. Students can compare what they find with the strip in Activity 31. How are the presentation and message similar or different? Ask students to create a comic strip expressing their own perspective on the same theme.

Community Link

27 Have students interview older members of their community about what their life was like when they were teenagers. How did they spend their free time? What were their main concerns or worries at that time? Ask volunteers to share the responses with the class.

Segundo paso

CAPÍTULO 2

Writing Assessment

30 Have students write a journal entry in which they describe what they do to stay healthy. Have them compare their health habits now to what they were three years ago. (exercise, food, health goals) Remind students that they may write fictitious responses. You may wish to evaluate their entry using the following rubric.

Writing Rubric	Points			
	4	3	2	1
Content (Complete– Incomplete)				
Comprehensibility (Comprehensible– Incomprehensible)				
Accuracy (Accurate– Seldom accurate)				
Organization (Well organized– Poorly organized)				
Effort (Excellent–Minimal)				

18–20: A	14–15: C	Under
16–17: B	12–13: D	12: F

Assess
▸ Testing Program, pp. 27–30
 Quiz 2-2A, Quiz 2-2B
 Audio CD 2, Tr. 21

▸ Student Make-Up Assignments, Chapter 2, Alternative Quiz

▸ Alternative Assessment Guide, p. 31

Vamos a leer

Teaching Resources
pp. 50–52

PRINT
▸ Lesson Planner, p. 10
▸ Cuaderno de actividades, p. 23
▸ Cuaderno para hispanohablantes, pp. 6–10
▸ Reading Strategies and Skills Handbook, Chapter 2
▸ ¡Lee conmigo! 3, Chapter 2
▸ Standardized Assessment Tutor, Chapter 2

MEDIA
▸ One-Stop Planner

Prereading
Activities A, B, and C

Drawing on Your Experience
Ask students to list the number of areas into which their lives are divided, and to rank them from most to least stressful. Ask for volunteers to share their results. Then have students identify the seven subtitles of the second article, and rank them from most to least stressful for them individually. Ask if they would have ranked these items in the same order two years ago. Has their outlook on life and its stressors changed? Why and how?

Una vida balanceada

Do you ever feel so busy that some activities in your life, like just relaxing and having fun, are crowded out? These articles are about achieving a balance and managing stress.

Estrategia para leer
Pause and think about the topic. What comes to mind when you read the titles? What do the pictures remind you of? What do you think the articles might be about? Thinking about your background knowledge activates pertinent vocabulary and ideas in your mind.

¡A comenzar! Answers will vary.

A. Lee el título del primer artículo. ("Cómo aliviar el estrés..."). Reflexiona sobre las preguntas. ¿En qué áreas sientes más estrés? ¿Qué puedes hacer para controlarlo? Anota tus respuestas.

B. Lee el título del segundo artículo. ("Cómo lograr el balance..."). Piensa en las preguntas y después escribe tus respuestas: ¿Cuáles son las áreas más importantes de tu vida? ¿Qué tipo de balance puedes establecer entre estas áreas?

C. Júntate con un(a) compañero(a) para comparar lo que escribieron en las Actividades A y B.

¿Te acuerdas?
Scan to find specific information. Locate specific information quickly by searching for key words.

Cómo aliviar el estrés: 10 cosas esenciales

1 Piensa bien en lo que comes. Una dieta balanceada es importante para una buena salud y te protege contra el estrés. Evita la grasa, sal y azúcar. Come alimentos ricos en vitamina B: granos germinados, huevos y nueces. Y en vitamina C: frutas y vegetales verdes, que ayudan a evitar el estrés.

2 Duerme lo suficiente, de 7 a 8 horas cada noche. Si duermes bastante y si te acuestas y te levantas a la misma hora, puedes alargar tu vida y controlar el estrés.

3 Haz ejercicio, porque el ejercicio consistente fortalece el corazón, mejora la circulación, disminuye el colesterol, controla el peso, reduce la hipertensión y ayuda a controlar el estrés.

4 Busca buenas amistades. Una persona de confianza es un apoyo y una ayuda. Conversa con esta persona, cuéntale tus alegrías y tristezas. Un(a) buen(a) amigo(a) puede aliviar el estrés con sólo estar presente.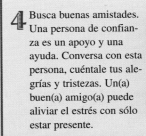

Connections and Comparisons

Thinking Critically
Analyzing After they have read the first article, ask students to list reasons why they might not follow the ten recommendations to reduce stress. Are there people, events, or issues that keep them from following these recommendations consistently? (e.g., Friends keep each other out late at night.)

Health Link
Have students find out about five vitamins that are most important for good health and in which foods they are found. Students can then prepare a sample daily diet that would insure adequate consumption according to currently accepted minimum daily requirements.

5 Analiza las emociones de furia, malgenio, ansiedad y depresión porque llevan al agotamiento. Reprimirlas puede disminuir la resistencia al estrés. Expresa estas emociones. Sé positivo(a) y comunica tus sentimientos a otros.

6 Resuelve los conflictos familiares cada día, no los aplaces. El equipo familiar hace la vida más fácil. Habla con los tuyos con claridad, abiertamente y con respeto.

7 Organiza bien tu tiempo. "El tiempo es como un trozo de oro, pero con todo el oro del mundo no puede comprarse un trozo de tiempo" (proverbio chino). Identifica, entonces, qué es para ti lo fundamental.

8 Conserva tu peso a un nivel saludable. Si tienes exceso de peso disminuye la grasa y el dulce, y come alimentos saludables.

9 Expresa el cariño: las personas alegres y cariñosas viven más y mejor. Expresa el amor con un abrazo y un beso y con palabras tiernas. Demuestra que es mejor dar que recibir.

10 Cultiva el optimismo para evitar complicaciones mentales y síquicas. Las personas optimistas poseen personalidades más fuertes.

Al grano See possible answers below.

¿Te acuerdas?

An excellent way to understand and remember what you read is to make an outline of the structure of what you're reading.

D. Completa los siguientes esquemas que resumen los dos artículos. Puedes hacerlo al leer la lectura o después.

1. Cómo aliviar el estrés: 10 cosas esenciales
   1. Piensa bien en lo que comes.
   2. _____
   3. Haz ejercicio consistente.
   4. _____
   5. _____
   6. Resuelve los conflictos con tu familia.
   7. _____
   8. _____
   9. Expresa el cariño y amor. Sé generoso(a).
   10. _____

2. Cómo lograr el balance en tu vida
   a. _____
   b. Pásalo bien con o sin novio(a).
   c. No seas víctima de la moda.
   d. _____
   e. No te encierres en tu familia.
   f. Ten prioridades acerca del dinero y el trabajo.
   g. _____

E. En el primer artículo, cada sección tiene un consejo y las razones que explican por qué seguir el consejo. Haz una lista de las razones para cada sección.

Vamos a leer

CAPÍTULO 2

Reading
Activities D and E

Determining the Main Idea
Point out to students that the two outlines they are being asked to complete are the supporting details that the writer uses to develop the main idea. Once students complete the outlines, ask if they can determine what the main idea is.

Answers

D *Possible answers:*
1 2. Duerme lo suficiente.
   4. Busca buenas amistades.
   5. Expresa tus emociones y comunica tus sentimientos.
   7. Organiza bien tu tiempo.
   8. Conserva tu peso a un nivel saludable.
   10. Cultiva el optimismo.
2 a. Ten cuidado con la presión del grupo.
   d. No te limites a los estudios.
   g. Ten en cuenta que relajarte es tan importante como cumplir con tus responsabilidades.

E *Sample answers:*
1. Una dieta balanceada es importante para la buena salud y para prevenir el estrés.
2. Dormir lo suficiente es necesario para controlar el estrés y para tener una vida más larga.
3. El ejercicio consistente y regular fortalece el corazón, mejora la circulación, disminuye el colesterol, controla el peso, reduce la hipertensión y ayuda a controlar el estrés.
4. Una persona de confianza es un apoyo y puede aliviar el estrés con sólo estar presente.
5. Reprimir las emociones puede disminuir la resistencia al estrés.
6. El equipo familiar hace la vida más fácil.
7. El tiempo es como un trozo de oro, tiene mucho valor.
8. Un peso normal es bueno para conservar la salud.
9. Las personas alegres y cariñosas viven mejor.
10. Las personas optimistas poseen personalidades más fuertes.

Communication for All Students

Native Speakers
Have native speakers choose one subject **(la nutrición, los estudios, el ejercicio)** and write a short advice column basing their paragraph on the ones seen here. Ask them to think about their lives or their friends and family as they write their columns.

Slower Pace
Have students skim the article for cognates to prepare for a second reading. As students read more carefully for content, ask them to pause after each paragraph to write one or two words that identify the general topic. On the third reading, students should try to guess the meaning of unfamiliar words or expressions.

Teaching Resources
pp. 50–52

PRINT
▸ Lesson Planner, p. 10
▸ Cuaderno de actividades, p. 23
▸ Cuaderno para hispanohablantes, pp. 6–10
▸ Reading Strategies and Skills Handbook, Chapter 2
▸ ¡Lee conmigo! 3, Chapter 2
▸ Standardized Assessment Tutor, Chapter 2

MEDIA
▸ One-Stop Planner

Reading
Activity F

Paraphrasing
Have student partners alternate between reading a section of the article aloud and paraphrasing what their partner has read. For example, while one student is reading aloud the section **Los amigos, la diversión,** his or her partner is concentrating on its meaning in order to paraphrase. Students switch roles to read the next section. Encourage pairs to question and help each other if the meaning of the reading is unclear to them.

Postreading
Activity G

Distinguishing Fact from Opinion
Divide students into small groups and have them look at both articles to determine which statements are facts and which are opinions in each. Do students think differently about the articles once they have determined this? Have students discuss the opinions they formed as they reread each article.

Answers will vary.

F. Imagina que un(a) amigo(a) te pide estos consejos de cómo lograr el balance en su vida. Contesta sus preguntas según la información en el segundo artículo.

1. ¿Qué hay de malo en la presión del grupo?
2. ¿Cómo me ayuda tener un trabajo?
3. Si tengo problemas con la familia, ¿adónde puedo ir por ayuda?
4. Si estoy desesperado(a) por no tener novio(a), ¿qué tiene que ver con mi autoestima?
5. Aparte de mi "look", ¿qué más debo cuidar?
6. ¿Qué pasa si no presto atención a mis estudios?

G. Do you agree or disagree with the advice given in these two articles? Get together with two or three classmates and discuss the following questions. (Use as much Spanish as possible!)

1. In the first article, which suggestions do you agree with most?
2. Do you think any of the advice was unwise or not very important?
3. What other suggestions would you include?
4. In the second article, which ideas or suggestions were most useful?
5. Would you change anything if you were to rewrite the article?
6. Which article did you like better and why?

Cuaderno para hispanohablantes, pp. 6–8

Cuaderno de actividades, p. 23, Acts. 18–19

Cómo lograr el balance en tu vida

LOS AMIGOS, LA DIVERSIÓN Te encanta la gente. ¡Tu debilidad es compartir con tus amigos! Claro, todo con medida. Quizás usas las salidas para escapar de tus problemas. Podrías ser muy susceptible a la presión del grupo, lo cual te metería en muchos problemas. Recomendación: cultiva tu mundo interior.

LOS CHICOS/LAS CHICAS Si tu vida se reduce a la búsqueda y captura del sexo opuesto, es señal de que tu nivel de autoestima está muy bajo. Es que sientes que no eres nadie sin un(a) chico(a) a tu lado. Busca otras amistades, envuélvete en diferentes actividades. De esa forma, con o sin novio(a), lo pasarás súper.

TU "LOOK" Vives para la apariencia física. Eres lo que se dice una "víctima" de la moda. Esmerarse en el físico no es malo, si no se convierte en una obsesión o llegas a pensar que lo único que cuenta es la fachada. Nutre tu mente, tu espíritu; busca la compañía de gente interesante. Comparte ideas, gustos y actividades. Es bien importante ser lindo por dentro.

ESTUDIOS Definitivamente, estudiar está muy bien, pero si es tu obsesión... ¿Es que sientes que las buenas calificaciones son lo único que tienes que ofrecer? No te limites a nutrir tu cabecita: llena tu vida de gente y cosas lindas.

LA FAMILIA Si la familia es la base de tu vida, es bueno que mejores las relaciones, pero ¡no te encierres en ella! Si existen problemas, busca ayuda de un(a) consejero(a) o un(a) adulto(a) de confianza. Fíjate: mami, papi y tus hermanos no pueden ser la suma de tu vida social.

EL TRABAJO No hay dudas, trabajar es bueno, porque te enseña a ser responsable, a tener disciplina y a concentrarte. Pero... ¡OJO! ¿Vives para hacer plata? Eso está mal. Tienes que tener prioridades: ¿trabajas para ahorrar dinero para los estudios... o para coleccionar toneladas de discos compactos? Hum. Sé muy cauteloso(a).

EL "RELAX" Relajarte y dedicarte a tus pasatiempos es tan importante como cumplir con tus deberes, porque si no... ¡te quemas! Pero si descuidas tus estudios, el trabajo o tus relaciones por pasarla bien, estás creando un desbalance peligroso en tu vida. ¡Equilíbrate!

Connections and Comparisons

Culture Notes
• Students in Spanish-speaking countries have different schedules and obligations than do students in the United States. Students in other countries generally do not have an after-school job, and schools do not sponsor team sports. Have students find foreign schools' curricula on the Internet and compare them with their own schedules. What similarities and differences do students see?

• Have students find the Web sites of department stores or online catalogs in Spain or Latin America. Ask them to look at the selection of clothes for people their age. Is the "look" very different or similar?

Vamos a escribir

Si alguien que te importa te escribe para pedirte un consejo sobre algo importante, ¿sabrías qué decirle? Antes de escribir la respuesta, debes pensar en lo que ya sabes acerca del tema y en cómo debes organizar la información.

¡No lo aguanto más!

Imagina que tu mejor amiga Lucía se ha mudado a otra ciudad. Te escribe para decirte que está sufriendo de mucho estrés. Lee su carta, escríbele y dale unos consejos sobre cómo controlar su estrés.

Estrategia para escribir

Listing and clustering Before writing, put your ideas about the topic on paper. First, list everything you know about a topic as quickly as you can. Then draw diagrams using circles and lines to help you visualize how those ideas are related.

A. Preparación

1. Pon las ideas de tu lista en un orden lógico con diagramas.

2. Haz una lista de detalles que puedes mencionar bajo cada idea en tu lista.

3. Decide qué conceptos y detalles son más importantes. Vas a mencionar estos detalles en tu carta.

B. Redacción

1. Escribe una introducción. Pregúntale a tu amiga cómo está, qué pasa en su vida, etcétera.

2. Menciona las presiones de las que tu amiga está sufriendo. Luego, escríbele tus consejos. Escribe un párrafo por cada idea básica.

3. Termina la carta con conclusiones generales.

C. Evaluación

1. Lee bien la carta. ¿Contiene toda la información que quieres mencionar? Si no, incluye más información de tu lista de temas. Puedes agregar más ideas a tu lista si quieres.

2. ¿Está bien organizada? Puedes usar tus diagramas para organizarla mejor. Si es necesario, haz diagramas nuevos.

> Hola.
>
> Parece imposible pero aquí estoy en mi nueva ciudad. Y tengo que decirte la verdad... ¡no quiero vivir aquí! La gente parece simpática pero no lo es conmigo. Nadie me invita a fiestas ni a actividades de la escuela. No sé si es que no me están haciendo caso o que no me quieren. Estoy frustradísima. Mi vida no es más que clases y tarea. No quiero salir porque no conozco a nadie. Me la paso mirando la tele y comiendo. Estoy cansada todo el tiempo y a veces lloro hasta que me duerma. ¿Qué debo hacer? Las cosas van de mal en peor. Escríbeme lo antes posible.
>
> Un abrazo de tu amiga,
> Lucía

Apply and Assess

Postwriting

Have students skip lines as they write. After students have evaluated their own papers, they should exchange papers with each other and peer-edit on the blank lines. Remind students that peer evaluation should focus on content and organization as well as spelling and grammar. Partners should point out both strengths and weaknesses and make specific suggestions to help the writer improve the text. Have them consult the Peer Editing Rubric, found on page 8 of the *Alternative Assessment Guide*, for a proofreader's checklist.

Teaching Resources
p. 53

PRINT
▸ Lesson Planner, p. 10
▸ Cuaderno de actividades, pp. 145–156
▸ Cuaderno para hispanohablantes, pp. 8–9
▸ Alternative Assessment Guide, p. 17
▸ Standardized Assessment Tutor, Chapter 2

MEDIA
▸ One-Stop Planner, Disc 1
▸ Test Generator, Chapter 2
▸ Interactive CD-ROM Tutor, Disc 1

Process Writing

Prewriting
Motivating Activity
Write the headings **Preparación, Redacción,** and **Evaluación** on the board or on a transparency. Under each heading, students list the ideas they think are most important to remember when doing that aspect of writing. Then ask students to rank them in order of descending importance, starting with the most important first. Leave the information on the board for student reference.

Writing
Slower Pace
A. Before beginning this activity, have students refer back to **Vamos a leer,** pages 50–52, as they brainstorm about ideas to pass along to their friend. Write their ideas on the board or on a transparency.

Más práctica gramatical

CAPÍTULO 2

For **Más práctica gramatical** Answer Transparencies, see the *Teaching Transparencies* binder.

Answers

1.
1. Dedica media hora al día al ejercicio.
2. Aprende un deporte nuevo.
3. Respira profundamente.
4. Duerme lo suficiente.
5. Sigue una dieta sana.
6. Toma mucha agua.
7. No fumes.
8. No añadas sal a la comida.
9. No comas muchos dulces.
10. No tomes bebidas con cafeína.
11. No trabajes demasiado.
12. No aumentes de peso.

2.
1. ve
2. pon
3. dile
4. Ten
5. sé
6. haz
7. ven

3.
1. No, no las pongas allí. Ponlas aquí.
2. No, no las mandes hoy. Mándalas mañana.
3. No, no los busques esta tarde. Búscalos ahora mismo.
4. Sí, cómpralas esta mañana.
5. No, no los hagas esta mañana. Hazlos esta tarde.
6. Sí, escríbelas en el calendario ahora.

Más práctica gramatical

Primer paso

Objective Asking for and giving advice

1 Tu clase hizo un cartel con consejos para vivir mejor. Escribe lo que aconsejan los estudiantes de tu clase. Usa mandatos informales y la información de la tabla. **(p. 38)**

MODELO   **dedicar media hora al día al ejercicio**
—**Dedica media hora al día al ejercicio.**

POR UNA VIDA SANA...	
SÍ	**NO**
1. dedicar media hora al día al ejercicio	7. fumar
2. aprender un deporte nuevo	8. añadir sal a la comida
3. respirar profundamente	9. comer muchos dulces
4. dormir lo suficiente	10. tomar bebidas con cafeína
5. seguir una dieta sana	11. trabajar demasiado
6. tomar mucha agua	12. aumentar de peso

2 Hoy es el primer día de clases para Ana. Completa los consejos de su mamá con los mandatos informales de los verbos entre paréntesis. **(p. 38)**

Ana, ___1___ (ir) a la parada de autobuses temprano todas las mañanas. Antes de salir de casa, ___2___ (poner) todos tus libros y cuadernos en la mochila. Y cuando llegues al colegio, ___3___ (decirle) "¡Buenos días!" a la maestra. ___4___ (Tener) mucho cuidado al subirte y bajarte del autobús. Y para sacar buenas notas, ___5___ (ser) aplicada y ___6___ (hacer) la tarea todos los días. Cuando terminen las clases, ___7___ (venir) directamente a casa.

3 Jimena is nervous about her new job and asks her boss a lot of questions. Write the answers her boss gives to Jimena's questions. Use informal commands and the correct object pronouns in your answers, and follow the cues in parentheses. **(p. 38)**

MODELO   **¿Debo buscar los apuntes de la reunión? (sí)**
—**Sí, búscalos, por favor.**

¿Debo leer este artículo ahora? (no/más tarde)
—**No, no lo leas ahora. Léelo más tarde.**

1. ¿Puedo poner mis cosas allí? (no/aquí)
2. ¿Debo mandar estas cartas hoy? (no/mañana)

Grammar Resources for Chapter 2

The **Más práctica gramatical** activities are designed as supplemental activities for the grammatical concepts presented in the chapter. You might use them as additional practice, for review, or for assessment.

For more grammar presentation, review, and practice, refer to the following:
- Cuaderno de gramática
- Grammar Tutor for Students of Spanish

- Grammar Summary on pp. R25–R46
- Cuaderno de actividades
- Grammar and Vocabulary quizzes (Testing Program)
- Test Generator on the One-Stop Planner CD-ROM
- Interactive CD-ROM Tutor
- **Juegos interactivos** at **go.hrw.com**

3. ¿Debo buscar esos números de teléfono esta tarde? (no/ahora mismo)
4. ¿Debo comprar las estampillas esta mañana? (sí)
5. ¿Debo hacer los otros mandados esta mañana? (no/esta tarde)
6. ¿Debo escribir las fechas en el calendario ahora? (sí)

4 Sandra está preocupada por su amigo Diego. Usa la lista de palabras para completar lo que ella dice sobre Diego y sus problemas. **(pp. 38–39)**

aliviar	tomar	agitada	histérico	resolver	sufre	relajarse
reírse	tensiones		se cuida		agobiado	ansiosa

La verdad es que estoy bastante ___1___ por Diego. ¡Pobrecito!

Últimamente en el colegio ___2___ de mucha presión. Siempre está

___3___ porque entre sus clases, su trabajo, los quehaceres y las demás

actividades, lleva una vida ___4___. Ahora parece que sufre de muchas

___5___ en sus clases—tiene tres exámenes esta semana. Me dijo que

estaba casi ___6___ porque no sabía cuándo podía estudiar. No hace

ejercicio, no come bien ni ___7___ en general porque no tiene tiempo.

Le digo que necesita ___8___ las cosas con calma y tratar de ___9___

los problemas uno por uno. También le digo que es necesario ___10___ y

___11___ todos los días. Pero para realmente ___12___ el estrés que siente,

creo que Diego necesita cambiar su estilo de vida.

5 Hoy es sábado, y todo el mundo está tratando de relajarse. Explica qué están haciendo todos en este momento para sentirse mejor. Usa el presente progresivo. **(p. 39)**

MODELO   Sonia/correr por el parque
—Sonia está corriendo por el parque.

1. (yo)/leer una novela
2. Marcos y Fermín/dar una caminata por el bosque
3. el profesor/trabajar en el jardín
4. Teresa/comer pizza con sus amigos
5. Alicia y Pati/hacer yoga
6. la profesora/asistir a un concierto de música clásica
7. todos nosotros/tomar las cosas con calma
8. ¿(tú)/descansar también?

Communication for All Students

Pair Work

4 Have pairs of students role-play a scene in which Diego talks about his hectic life to a school counselor. One student plays Diego and explains his stressful schedule to the partner, who gives advice and commands to help alleviate the problem.

Kinesthetic Learners

Play a game of charades. Divide the class into two teams. A student from one team acts out one of the verbs for his or her team to guess. Students must guess using the present progressive. If the team can guess the word in a set amount of time, it receives a point. If not, the other team has a chance to guess and then plays out another verb.

Answers

4
1. ansiosa
2. sufre
3. agobiado
4. agitada
5. tensiones
6. histérico
7. se cuida
8. tomar
9. resolver
10. reírse/relajarse
11. relajarse/reírse
12. aliviar

5
1. Estoy leyendo una novela.
2. Marcos y Fermín están dando una caminata por el bosque.
3. El profesor está trabajando en el jardín.
4. Teresa está comiendo pizza con sus amigos.
5. Alicia y Pati están haciendo yoga.
6. La profesora está asistiendo a un concierto de música clásica.
7. Todos nosotros estamos tomando las cosas con calma.
8. ¿Tú estás descansando también?

Más práctica gramatical

CAPÍTULO 2

For **Más práctica gramatical** Answer Transparencies, see the *Teaching Transparencies* binder.

Más práctica gramatical

WV3 LA CORUNA-2

Segundo paso   Objective **Talking about taking care of yourself**

6 En la familia de Yoli, todos siguen una rutina diferente por la mañana. Escribe lo que dice Yoli sobre su rutina y las de su hermano y sus padres. Usa las formas correctas de los verbos reflexivos y la información de la tabla. (p. 45)

MODELO   **despertarse**
—**Me despierto a las siete y media. Mi hermano se despierta a las siete y cuarto. Papá y Mamá se despiertan a las siete.**

	Yo	MI HERMANO	PAPÁ Y MAMÁ
despertarse	7:30	7:15	7:00
1. levantarse	7:45	7:45	7:10
2. bañarse	8:00	8:45	7:15 y 7:30
3. cepillarse los dientes	8:10	8:55	7:25 y 7:40
4. secarse el pelo	8:15	9:00	7:30 y 7:45
5. vestirse	8:30	9:10	8:00

7 Margarita está cuidando a sus sobrinos Pablo y Susi hoy. Escribe los mandatos que les da a los niños. Usa mandatos informales. No te olvides de poner el pronombre reflexivo en el lugar correcto. (p. 45)

MODELO   **Pablo/vestirse ahora**
—**Pablo, vístete ahora.**

1. Susi/levantarse inmediatamente
2. Pablo/no irse al parque sin pedir permiso
3. Susi/cepillarse los dientes
4. Pablo/no quitarse la chaqueta
5. Susi/ponerse los zapatos
6. Pablo/irse a dormir
7. Susi/no bañarse con el perro
8. Pablo/lavarse las manos antes de comer
9. Susi/no acostarse tarde

Answers

6 1. Mi hermano y yo nos levantamos a las ocho menos cuarto. Papá y mamá se levantan a las siete y diez.
2. Me baño a las ocho. Mi hermano se baña a las nueve menos cuarto. Papá y mamá se bañan a las siete y cuarto y las siete y media.
3. Me cepillo los dientes a las ocho y diez. Mi hermano se cepilla los dientes a las nueve menos cinco. Papá y mamá se cepillan los dientes a las siete y veinticinco y a las ocho menos veinte.
4. Me seco el pelo a las ocho y cuarto. Mi hermano se seca el pelo a las nueve. Papá y mamá se secan el pelo a las siete y media y a las ocho menos cuarto.
5. Me visto a las ocho y media. Mi hermano se viste a las nueve y diez. Papá y mamá se visten a las ocho.

7 1. Susi, levántate inmediatamente.
2. Pablo, no te vayas al parque sin pedir permiso.
3. Susi, cepíllate los dientes.
4. Pablo, no te quites la chaqueta.
5. Susi, ponte los zapatos.
6. Pablo, vete a dormir.
7. Susi, no te bañes con el perro.
8. Pablo, lávate las manos antes de comer.
9. Susi, no te acuestes tarde.

Cultures and Communities

Family Link

6 Have students create a chart for their own families' morning schedule. Students can ask their family members which daily task they most dislike. Students may choose to create an imaginary family for this activity and can share their information with a partner.

Challenge

7 Ask students to find advertisements for personal care products in Spanish-language magazines or on the Internet. Students can present their ads to the class, making use of commands and reflexive verbs.

8 Lourdes escribió cómo le va con su nuevo régimen. Completa su descripción con las palabras que faltan. Usa cada palabra sólo una vez. (**p. 46**)

> bienestar   ducharme   me pesé
>
> estoy bajando de peso   me duermo
>
> alimentarme   me doy cuenta de

20 de octubre

¡No pude creer lo que vi cuando ___1___ esta mañana como lo hago todos los lunes! ¡60 kilos! Ahora ___2___ que mi nueva dieta es mejor que la que seguía antes. Aunque mis hermanos se rían de mí cuando como mis ensaladas y ellos sus papas fritas, me siento bien con mi nueva vida y ___3___. También contribuye a mi nuevo ___4___ el hecho de que corra en la pista del gimnasio cinco veces por semana. Ya sé que el ___5___ bien me da más energía. Pero después de asistir a clases, hacer la tarea, dar un paseo con mi novio, cenar con mi familia, preparar la ropa para mañana y ___6___, me siento cansadísima. Muchas veces ___7___ tempranísimo, y me siento mal cuando los amigos me llaman por la noche y ¡ya estoy dormida!

9 Ahora que es mayor, Javier pasa los veranos trabajando o estudiando. Pero recuerda cómo eran los veranos cuando era niño. Completa lo que dice sobre los veranos pasados con las formas correctas de los verbos en el imperfecto. (**p. 47**)

Cuando yo ___1___ (ser) niño, nunca sufría de presiones como ahora. ___2___ (Ir) a la casa de mis primos casi siempre y pasaba las vacaciones con ellos. Ellos ___3___ (vivir) en el campo, donde ___4___ (tener) una finca pequeña con vacas y caballos. Por la mañana, nosotros ___5___ (levantarse) temprano para ayudar a mi tío Rafael con los animales. Después, casi todos los días ___6___ (hacer) excursiones. ___7___ (Dar) caminatas, montábamos a caballo y explorábamos las cuevas. A mí me ___8___ (encantar) ir al lago. Allí ___9___ (pasear) en velero o nadaba mientras mis primos tomaban el sol o ___10___ (jugar) a las cartas. Contábamos chistes y ___11___ (reírse) mucho. Muchas veces mi tía Elenita nos ___12___ (preparar) un almuerzo para llevar al campo. ¡Qué tiempos ___13___ (ser) aquéllos! Yo ___14___ (llevar) una vida mucho menos agitada en aquel entonces.

Answers

8
1. me pesé
2. me doy cuenta de
3. estoy bajando de peso
4. bienestar
5. alimentarme
6. ducharme
7. me duermo

9
1. era
2. Iba
3. vivían
4. tenían
5. nos levantábamos
6. hacíamos
7. Dábamos
8. encantaba
9. paseaba
10. jugaban
11. nos reíamos
12. preparaba
13. eran
14. llevaba

Review and Assess

You may wish to assign the **Más práctica gramatical** activities as additional practice or homework after presenting material throughout the chapter. Assign Activities 1–3 after **Gramática de repaso** (p. 38), Activity 4 after **Vocabulario** (pp. 38–39), Activity 5 after **¿Te acuerdas?** (p. 39), Activities 6–7 after **Gramática de repaso** (p. 45),

Activity 8 after **Vocabulario** (p. 46), and Activity 9 after **Gramática de repaso** (p. 47). To prepare students for the **Paso** Quizzes and Chapter Test, have them do the **Más práctica gramatical** activities in the following order: complete Activities 1–5 before taking Quiz 2-1A or 2-1B; Activities 6–9 before taking Quiz 2-2A or 2-2B.

Repaso

CAPÍTULO 2

The **Repaso** reviews all four skills and culture in preparation for the Chapter Test.

Teaching Resources
pp. 58–59

PRINT
▶ Lesson Planner, p. 11
▶ Listening Activities, p. 13
▶ Video Guide, pp. 9, 11, 14
▶ Grammar Tutor for Students of Spanish, Chapter 2
▶ Cuaderno para hispanohablantes, pp. 6–10
▶ Standardized Assessment Tutor, Chapter 2

MEDIA
▶ One-Stop Planner
▶ Video Program, Videocassette 1, 23:55–25:37
▶ Audio Compact Discs, CD 2, Tr. 19
▶ Interactive CD-ROM Tutor, Disc 1

internet

MARCAR: go.hrw.com
PALABRA CLAVE:
WV3 LA CORUNA-2

1 Escucha la descripción del día de Gloria. En una hoja de papel, escribe las letras de las fotos en el orden en que ocurrieron. Script and answers on p. 31H.

CD 2
Tr. 19

b.

d.

a.

c.

2 ¿Sufres mucho del estrés? ¿Tienes dificultades académicas, familiares o de salud? Con un(a) compañero(a), habla de tus problemas y de cómo se pueden resolver.

3 Usa las frases que siguen para decir cómo eras de niño(a). Escribe por lo menos ocho oraciones usando el tiempo imperfecto. Luego escribe ocho oraciones más en las que dices cómo eres hoy en día.

comer dulces	mirar la televisión
montar en bicicleta	hablar con amigos
jugar en casa	cuidarse el peso
ver a mis abuelos	llevar una vida agitada
reírse mucho	

4 Completa las frases con información cultural de este capítulo. See answers below.
1. El descanso tradicional durante el día de trabajo se llama ========.
2. España tiene cada día más contacto con Europa porque participa ahora en ========.
3. La dieta de los españoles es generalmente más rica en ======== que la dieta de los estadounidenses.
4. Los españoles por lo general pueden caminar al trabajo porque ========.
5. Muchos creen que los horarios de trabajo en España deben cambiar para ========.

Apply and Assess

Slower Pace

2 Before students pair up with a partner, have them make a list of difficulties that they have. Remind students that they may choose to list fictitious difficulties.

Additional Practice

3 Have students take a class survey on the health habits in this activity. Tell them to find out how many classmates used to do these things and how many do them now. How many students still need to improve?

Group Work

Have students make a radio commercial. The commercial should warn people of a problem and offer advice or a solution to the problem.

Answers
4 1. la siesta
2. la Unión Europea
3. frutas y verduras
4. todo queda más cerca
5. ser más similares a los otros países europeos

STANDARDS: 1.1, 1.2, 1.3, 2.1

5 Lee los consejos de los dos artículos. ¿Estás de acuerdo con lo que dicen? ¿Qué más debes hacer para tener una vida sana? Con un(a) compañero(a), explica por qué sí o por qué no estás de acuerdo y qué más se debe hacer.

UNA VIDA SALUDABLE

El ejercicio, los alimentos y el agua son necesarios para tener una vida saludable. Además, ésa es la imagen actual. Fortalece tu figura haciendo gimnasia un par de horas al día, tres veces por semana. Toma agua por barriles y balancea tu alimentación. Duerme, descansa, ejercítate y relájate.

REÍR ES BUENO

Si usted ríe fácilmente con cualquier chiste o frecuentemente y toma la vida con humor, no sólo será una persona más feliz sino más sana. Nuevos hallazgos en la materia han demostrado las capacidades curativas de la risa. Por ejemplo, 20 segundos de carcajadas equivalen a 3 minutos de extenuante ejercicio. Reír acelera el ritmo cardíaco y el respiratorio y hace trabajar los músculos del estómago; además, refuerza el sistema inmunitario.

 6 Lee las dos cartas y escríbele algunos consejos a cada persona. See sample answer below.

Ramón
¿Qué me aconsejas hacer? Hay una chica en mi clase y quiero conocerla mejor. Pero me pongo muy nervioso cuando trato de hablarle. Me siento muy ansioso y casi no puedo hablar. Ella no se da cuenta de que me cae bien y cree que soy muy tímido. Por eso nunca me habla.

Fernanda
¿Puedes darme algún consejo? Hay un chico en mi clase que me gusta. Pero él no siente lo mismo. No me habla; no trata de conocerme. Estoy muy nerviosa en su presencia y él cree que soy una esnob. Pero es que no me puedo relajar. Me preocupo mucho porque no sé cómo resolver esta situación.

7 ## Situación

Lee lo que dicen Pilar, Carlos y Elena en **¡Adelante!** en la página 42. Luego tú y un(a) compañero(a) toman los papeles de Pilar y su madre, Carlos y un amigo, o Elena y Marianela. Una persona empieza la conversación mencionando de una forma diplomática el problema que la otra persona tiene. La otra persona defiende sus acciones o hábitos. La primera persona le da consejos y la segunda al fin acepta esos consejos y describe cómo va a cambiar.

Cuaderno para hispanohablantes, p. 10

Apply and Assess

Pair Work

6 Have pairs of students write a description of a problem like the ones presented in this activity. The problem can deal with health or relationship issues and should use vocabulary from this chapter. Pairs then trade their descriptions with another pair and write a response with advice and commands.

Additional Practice

Ask students to give advice to the people in the pictures (see Building on Previous Skills, above) who were described as feeling **agotado, histérica, agobiada** and **ansioso.** (Patricia, la chica en tu foto debe hacer algo divertido antes de estudiar más. Puede hacer su tarea y divertirse también.)

Repaso

CAPÍTULO 2

📁 **Portfolio**

5 **Oral** You may want to have students record their answers as a part of their oral Portfolio. For Portfolio suggestions, see *Alternate Assessment Guide,* p. 17.

Building on Previous Skills
Students clip magazine pictures representing adjectives, such as: **agotado(a), histérico(a), agobiado(a),** and **ansioso(a).** Ask students to share their pictures with the class and explain why each picture was chosen to represent the adjective. **(La chica en la foto se ve agotada porque parece que se acostó muy tarde anoche.)**

Answers
6 *Sample answer:*
Ramón y Fernanda deberían relajarse un poco y empezar a hablar. Les aconsejo tomar las cosas con calma y no ponerse nerviosos. Sería buena idea estudiar juntos o participar en las mismas actividades para empezar a conocerse mejor.

A ver si puedo

Teaching Resources
p. 60

PRINT
▶ Grammar Tutor for Students of Spanish, Chapter 2

MEDIA
▶ Interactive CD-ROM Tutor, Disc 1
▶ Online self-test

 go.hrw.com
WV3 LA CORUNA-2

Teacher Note

This page is intended to prepare students for the Chapter Test. It is a brief checklist of the major points covered in the chapter. The students should be reminded that it is only a checklist and does not necessarily include everything that will appear on the Chapter Test.

Answers

1 *Possible answers:*
1. Tengo tres exámenes mañana y me siento agobiado(a). ¿Qué me aconsejan hacer Uds.?
2. Quiero bajar de peso. ¿Qué debo hacer?
3. Estoy agobiado(a) por las presiones de los estudios. ¿Pueden darme algún consejo?
4. Sufro del estrés porque mis clases son difíciles. ¿Qué me recomienda?

3 *Sample answers:*
1. Cristina, deberías salir.
2. Jorge, sería bueno estudiar con un(a) amigo(a).
3. Mamá, te aconsejo tomar las cosas con calma y descansar más.
4. Ellos te quieren. Deberías ser honesta con ellos.

4 *Sample answer:*
Se broncea sin ponerse crema protectora. Ella tiene buenos hábitos de salud porque hace ejercicio aeróbico. Él no tiene buenos hábitos de salud porque come mal y ve mucha televisión.

5 *Answers will vary.*

A ver si puedo...

Can you ask for and give advice? p. 37

Answers will vary. See possible answers below.

1 Imagina que tienes los siguientes problemas. Pídeles consejos a las personas indicadas. Explica el problema y cómo te sientes.
1. tienes tres exámenes el mismo día / tus profesores
2. quieres bajar de peso / tu amigo o amiga
3. estás agobiado(a) por las presiones / tus padres
4. sufres de muchísimo estrés en la escuela / un(a) consejero(a)

2 Ahora llevas una vida mucho más agitada que la de hace cinco años. Imagina que hablas con un(a) amigo(a). ¿Puedes contarle cómo era tu vida hace cinco años y cómo es ahora? ¿Puedes pedirle consejos?

3 Tus amigos y tu familia siempre te piden consejos. Lee sus problemas y dales consejos a todos.
1. Tu amiga Cristina siempre está aburrida y nunca sabe qué hacer.
2. Tu amigo Jorge, un chico inteligente, saca malas notas porque no dedica suficiente tiempo a los estudios.
3. Tu mamá sufre mucho del estrés en su trabajo.
4. Tu hermanita tiene miedo de decirles a sus padres que sacó una mala nota en su último examen.

Can you talk about taking care of yourself? p. 44

4 ¿Qué buenos o malos hábitos de salud tienen las siguientes personas? Si son malos hábitos de salud, ¿qué pueden hacer para mejorarlos?

5 ¿Qué haces para cuidarte? Contesta las preguntas.
1. ¿Qué haces para aliviar el estrés todos los días?
2. ¿Qué haces todos los días para no enfermarte?
3. ¿Qué es lo más importante que haces todos los días para cuidarte?

Review and Assess

Extension

1 After students have finished the activity, ask them to play the role of the people to whom they have been speaking. Students can respond using phrases like **Sería bueno...** and **Te aconsejo...**, as well as affirmative and negative commands.

Pair Work

5 Have pairs of students turn this activity into an interview with a doctor. One student is the reporter and asks the questions listed and three other questions. The other student plays the doctor and responds giving examples of good and bad health habits, as well as what people should do to be healthy.

Vocabulario

Primer paso

Asking for and giving advice

Deberías + inf.	You should . . .
No debes + inf.	You shouldn't . . .
¿Puedes darme algún consejo?	Can you give me any advice?
¿Qué debo hacer?	What should I do?
¿Qué me aconsejas hacer?	What do you advise me to do?
¿Qué me recomiendas hacer?	What do you recommend that I do?
Sería bueno + inf.	It would be a good idea for you to . . .
Te aconsejo + inf.	I advise you to . . .
Te recomiendo + inf.	I recommend that you . . .

Talking about stress

agobiado(a)	worn out, overwhelmed
agotado(a)	exhausted
aliviar el estrés	to relieve stress
ansioso(a)	anxious
causar el estrés	to cause stress
cuidarse	to take care of oneself
estar rendido(a)	to be worn out
histérico(a)	stressed out
llevar una vida agitada	to lead a hectic life
ponerse nervioso(a)	to get nervous
reírse (i, i)	to laugh

relajarse	to relax
resolver (ue) un problema	to solve a problem
sufrir de presiones	to be under pressure
sufrir de tensiones	to suffer from tension
tomar las cosas con calma	to take things calmly

Segundo paso

Talking about taking care of yourself

la alimentación	nutrition
alimentarse bien	to eat well
alimentarse mal	to eat poorly
broncearse	to suntan
comer comida sana	to eat healthy food
compartir con alguien	to share with someone
contribuir	to contribute
cuidarse el peso	to watch one's weight
darse cuenta de	to realize
dormir (ue, u) lo suficiente	to get enough sleep

dormirse (ue, u)	to fall asleep
ducharse	to take a shower
echarle mucha sal a la comida	to put a lot of salt on food
estar a dieta	to be on a diet
la grasa	fat
hacer ejercicio (aeróbico)	to (do aerobic) exercise
mantenerse (ie) en forma	to stay in shape
el peligro	danger
pesarse	to weigh oneself
la piel	skin

ponerse crema protectora	to put on sunscreen
quedarse frente a la tele	to stay in front of the TV
quemarse	to get a sunburn
sentirse (ie, i) muy solo(a)	to feel very lonely
subir de peso	to gain weight
tener (ie) buenos hábitos de alimentación	to have good eating habits

---

Vocabulario

CAPÍTULO 2

Teaching Suggestions

- Ask students to work in pairs to make flash cards and review the new material with them.

- Ask students to work with a partner. Each partner writes five to ten vocabulary items from this page. Students then take turns asking each other questions using the words from their list, one word per question.

 Circumlocution

Have the class play **¿Cómo te diré?** (page 3C) to practice health-related vocabulary. Ask students to describe conditions other than those they have learned in Chapter 2. Some suggestions: **el insomnio, la obesidad, la depresión, el cáncer, la desnutrición**

Chapter 2 Assessment

▶ **Testing Program**
Chapter Test, pp. 31–36
 Audio Compact Discs, CD 2, Trs. 22–23
Speaking Test, p. 295

▶ **Alternative Assessment Guide**
Portfiolio Assessment, p. 17
Performance Assessment, p. 31
CD-ROM Assessment, p. 45

▶ **Interactive CD-ROM Tutor, Disc 1**
 ¡A hablar!
¡A escribir!

▶ **Standardized Assessment Tutor**
Chapter 2

▶ **One-Stop Planner, Disc 1**
Test Generator
Chapter 2

Review and Assess

Game

RIESGO In this game you provide the answer **(Es un plato típico de La Coruña.)** and students must come up with an appropriate question. **(¿Qué es el caldo gallego?)** On the board, label the columns of a four-by-four grid with categories **(cultura, salud, pasatiempos, comida).** For each category, prepare four answer cards. Write the answer on one side of the card and an assigned point value (25, 50, 75 . . .) on the other. Tape the cards in the grid squares, number side up. Divide the class into teams. Teams take turns selecting a grid square. Remove the card and read the answer. If the team formulates a reasonable question within a set time limit, they earn the points. The team with the highest score wins.

Teaching Resources
pp. 62–65

PRINT
▶ Lesson Planner, p. 12
▶ Video Guide, pp. 15–16
   Videocassette 1, 25:50–27:41

MEDIA
▶ Interactive CD-ROM Tutor, Disc 1
▶ Map Transparency 4

 go.hrw.com
WV3 CARACAS

 Using the Almanac and Map

Terms in the Almanac

- **Ciudades principales:** Roughly 85% of the population of Venezuela lives in cities. About one-sixth of the population lives in the metropolitan area of Caracas.

- **Industrias:** Venezuela's crude oil reserves are more than double those of the U.S.

- **Personajes famosos:** Luis Aparicio was elected to the National Baseball Hall of Fame in 1984. Carolina Herrera is an internationally known designer. María Conchita Alonso has appeared in the movies *Vampire's Kiss, Colors,* and *Moscow on the Hudson.*

- **Platos típicos: Pabellón criollo** consists of beef, rice, black beans, and plantains. **Arepas** are small, flat, round, baked or fried corn meal cakes. **Tequeños** are sticks of cheese wrapped in dough and fried. **Cachapas** are thick corn pancakes. **Hallacas** are similar to Mexican tamales.

¡Ven conmigo a Caracas!

Venezuela

Población: Caracas: 2.785.000 (zona metropolitana: 4,5 millones); Venezuela: 22.311.000

Área: Venezuela, 912.050 km²; Caracas, 78 km²

Ciudades principales: Caracas, Maracaibo, Valencia, Barquisimeto

Productos agrícolas: arroz, maíz, plátanos, café, cacao, caña de azúcar, algodón

Industrias: petróleo, productos comestibles, acero, aluminio

Personajes famosos: Simón Bolívar (1783–1830), libertador; Luis Aparicio (n. 1934), jugador de béisbol; Carolina Herrera (n. 1939), diseñadora de moda; María Conchita Alonso (n. 1957), actriz y cantante

Platos típicos: pabellón criollo, arepas, tequeños, cachapas, hallacas

WV3 CARACAS

▶ Caracas, la capital de Venezuela, es una ciudad moderna y cosmopolita. ▶

Cultures and Communities

Background Information

Caracas is located in a valley about seven miles south of the Caribbean coast and approximately 3,000 feet above sea level. Diego de Losada founded the city in 1567 and named it **Santiago de León de Caracas** in honor of St. James (patron saint of Spain), Ponce de León (the area's provincial governor), and the indigenous people of Caracas. It became a provincial capital in 1577 and survived earthquakes and English pirate attacks and became the capital of Venezuela in 1829. Caracas began to boom in the 1930s, after the discovery of oil beneath Lake Maracaibo. The city is still growing today as a result of immigration and, especially, internal migration.

MAPQUEST.COM™

go.hrw.com

HRW Atlas Interactivo Mundial

Have students use the interactive atlas at <u>go.hrw.com</u> to find out more about the geography of Venezuela and to complete the Map Activities below.

Map Activities

- Using the maps on pages xxiv and xxvi, have students identify the countries that border Venezuela. Ask them what language is spoken in each. (Colombia—Spanish; Brazil—Portuguese; Guyana—English. Islands just offshore include Trinidad and Tobago—English; Aruba and the Netherlands Antilles' Curaçao and Bonaire—Dutch and Papiamento)

- Ask students what major river flows through Venezuela. (the Orinoco)

CNNenEspañol.com

Have students check the **<u>CNN en español</u>** Web site for news on Venezuela. The **<u>CNN en español</u>** site is also a good source of timely, high-interest readings for Spanish students.

Connections and Comparisons

History Link

Have students research the life of Simón Bolívar and report their findings to the class. [Born in Caracas, educated in Europe. Participated in several unsuccessful attempts to drive Spain from northern South America before liberating Colombia in 1819. Oversaw establishment of the republic of **Gran Colombia,** which later included Venezuela (liberated 1821) and Ecuador (1822). Liberated Peru (1823) and Bolivia (1825). Bolivia was named after him. Bolívar envisioned a continent of federated republics with a common military and hemispheric representative assembly. However, civil war broke out in **Gran Colombia** in 1826, and Venezuela seceded in 1829.]

Motivating Activity

Have students look at the photos of Venezuela on pages 64–65. Ask them what their first impressions are of Venezuela, based on the photos: What kind of climate do they think it has? Does Caracas look like a new or old city? Do they see evidence of both old and new styles in the buildings shown in the photos? Ask them which places shown in the photos they would like to visit and why.

Using the Photo Essay

❶ El salto de agua más alto del mundo El Salto del Ángel is the highest waterfall in the world. Named for Jimmy Angel, a pilot from Missouri who crash-landed his plane nearby in 1937, the falls were made famous by W. H. Hudson's book *Green Mansions*.

❷ Lugar de recreación para muchos caraqueños El Parque del Este was designed by contemporary Brazilian landscape architect Roberto Burle Marx. On Sundays more than 80,000 people use its facilities. The park contains playgrounds, an outdoor theater, rock gardens, and nine artificial lakes. It is an escape into nature for city-weary **caraqueños.**

❸ El arte moderno de Jesús Soto This colorful sculpture by Jesús Soto marks **Sabana Grande,** one of Caracas's most popular outdoor venues. The mile-long avenue is closed to vehicular traffic so that pedestrians may shop at vendors' tables, stroll along the tree-lined street, or relax in one of many cafés and restaurants. Friends and business people meet, artists and musicians give lessons, and chess **aficionados** play for hours along **Sabana Grande.**

Venezuela

Venezuela, cuyo nombre quiere decir "Pequeña Venecia", es un país de contrastes, un país a la vez andino, caribeño, amazónico y urbano. Caracas, su capital, es un núcleo de energía y diversidad. Durante los últimos cien años, encima del viejo centro colonial se ha levantado la Caracas moderna: la Caracas de rascacielos impresionantes y un sistema de metro entre los mejores del mundo. Desde la nieve del Pico Bolívar, el punto más alto de Venezuela, hasta las playas de Isla de Margarita, Venezuela es un país único e inolvidable.

📶 internet

go.hrw.com MARCAR: go.hrw.com
PALABRA CLAVE:
WV3 CARACAS

❶ El salto de agua más alto del mundo
El Salto Ángel, la catarata más alta del mundo, presenta una imagen espectacular. Las aguas del Salto Ángel caen unos 979 metros. La catarata está en la Gran Sabana en el oriente de Venezuela.

❷ Lugar de recreación para muchos caraqueños
Una tarde de sol en el Parque del Este de Caracas. Los caraqueños disfrutan de un clima agradable y templado, ya que Caracas tiene una altura de casi 1000 metros sobre el nivel del mar.

❸ El arte moderno de Jesús Soto
Esta escultura cinética, creación del escultor venezolano Jesús Soto (nacido en 1923), está en la calle peatonal de Sabana Grande, al salir del metro en la estación Chacaíto. La zona es un mosaico de música caribeña y de escaparates llenos de perfumes y artesanías venezolanas.

Cultures and Communities

Science Link

Have students research the climate of Venezuela. (Venezuela's climate is tropical, but temperature and precipitation vary according to altitude, season, and exposure to wind. Maracaibo, at sea level, averages 82°F (28°C), whereas Mérida, in the Andean Highlands, averages only 66°F (19°C).

The Perijá Mountains west of Lake Maracaibo receive 120 inches of rain per year, while La Guaira, the port near Caracas, receives only 11 inches per year.) Ask students to report their findings to the class.

5 Torres petroleras
Estas grúas petroleras están en el lago Maracaibo. En 1922 se descubrió un depósito inmenso de petróleo debajo de este lago, el más grande de Sudamérica. Hoy en día, la explotación del petróleo forma la base de la economía venezolana.

4 Un país multicultural About two-thirds of Venezuela's inhabitants are mestizos, people of both European and indigenous ancestry. About one-fifth are of European ancestry. Ten percent are of African ancestry, and 2 percent of Venezuelans are from families entirely indigenous to the region.

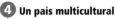

4 Un país multicultural
La población de Venezuela refleja las tradiciones indígenas, europeas y africanas que formaron la corriente étnica y cultural principal de Sudamérica.

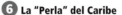

6 La "Perla" del Caribe
La Isla de Margarita, con sus kilómetros de playas preciosas, es donde pasan sus vacaciones miles de venezolanos. Margarita es la más grande de las islas caribeñas venezolanas.

5 Torres petroleras Lake Maracaibo is roughly 130 miles long, 75 miles wide, and 160 feet deep. The offshore oil-drilling techniques used throughout the world today were pioneered on Lake Maracaibo.

6 La Perla del Caribe The island of Margarita is Venezuela's most popular Caribbean holiday destination. It has pristine beaches, fishing villages, and Restinga Lagoon National Park. At its largest, Margarita is about 20 miles from north to south and 42 miles from east to west. Tourists flock to the island's beaches and shopping areas (the island is a duty-free zone), while ecotourists seek out Restinga Lagoon's mangrove swamp with its shellfish and many water birds, including scarlet ibises.

En los capítulos 3 y 4,
vas a conocer a varias personas de Caracas. Vas a aprender de ellos algo del carácter nacional venezolano, que incorpora fuertes elementos del individualismo, la diversidad y el entusiasmo por todo lo moderno. Caracas es el centro de comercio, educación e industria de Venezuela.

7 La escultura ecuestre del caudillo The Plaza Bolívar, although no longer the geographic center of Caracas, nonetheless remains the official center of the downtown area. Over the years, the plaza has been the site of parades, political meetings, bullfights, and outdoor markets. Today one can sit by the statue of **El Libertador** and search the trees for the squirrels and three-toed sloths that live there.

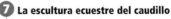

7 La escultura ecuestre del caudillo
En la Plaza Bolívar de Caracas, se encuentra esta escultura del héroe nacional de Venezuela, Simón Bolívar, El Libertador. Con la ayuda de un ejército compuesto de europeos y americanos, Bolívar liberó los territorios de Colombia, Bolivia, Ecuador, Perú y Venezuela del dominio español en 1824.

Cultures and Communities

Culture Note
The regions of Venezuela vary in population and culture. Most of the major cities are found along the coast. The population is black, mulatto, mestizo, and white. In the Andes Mountains people have maintained indigenous agricultural practices as well as traditional music and culture. The center of the country is primarily composed of **llanos** *(plains)*, fed by the Orinoco River and its tributaries and has a largely agricultural economy. In the southeast, **La Gran Sabana,** a high plateau region in the Amazon jungle, is home to indigenous tribes, including the Yanomami. Have students use the Internet to research one of these geographical areas.

Capítulo 3: El ayer y el mañana
Chapter Overview

De antemano pp. 68–70	*La vida de ayer*

	FUNCTIONS	**GRAMMAR**	**VOCABULARY**	**RE-ENTRY**
Primer paso pp. 71–75	• Talking about what has happened, p. 72 • Expressing and supporting a point of view, p. 74 • Using conversational fillers, p. 75	• The present perfect, p. 72 • **Lo que**, p. 74	• Modern day life, p. 71 • City issues, p. 73	• Object pronouns (**Capítulo 2**, II) • Affirmatives and negatives (**Capítulo 11**, II) • **todavía (Capítulo 5**, I) **ya (Capítulo 2**, I)

¡Adelante! pp. 76–77	*¿Cómo será el futuro?*

Segundo paso pp. 78–82	• Talking about future events, p. 78 • Talking about responsibilities, p. 81	• The future tense, p. 79	• The future, p. 81	• Comparisons of equality (**Capítulo 7**, II) • **vamos a** + infinitive (**Capítulo 7**, I) • Supporting opinions (**Capítulo 10**, I)

Vamos a leer pp. 84–86	**El monopolio de la moda**	**Reading Strategy:** Analyzing tone

Vamos a escribir p. 87	**Inventos importantes**	**Writing Strategy:** Listing in order of importance

Más práctica gramatical	**pp. 88–91** **Primer paso,** pp. 88–90	**Segundo paso,** pp. 90–91	

Review pp. 92–95	**Repaso,** pp. 92–93	**A ver si puedo...,** p. 94	**Vocabulario,** p. 95

CULTURE

• **Nota cultural,** The oil boom in Venezuela, p. 74
• **Nota cultural,** Cellular phones in Caracas, p. 78
• **Panorama cultural, ¿Cómo te afecta la tecnología?,** p. 83

Capítulo 3: El ayer y el mañana
Chapter Resources

 **PRINT**

Lesson Planning
One-Stop Planner

Lesson Planner with Substitute Teacher Lesson Plans, pp. 12–16, 67

Student Make-Up Assignments
- Make-Up Assignment Copying Masters, Chapter 3

Listening and Speaking
Listening Activities
- Student Response Forms for Listening Activities, pp. 19–21
- Additional Listening Activities 3-1 to 3-6, pp. 23–25
- Additional Listening Activities (song), p. 26
- Scripts and Answers, pp. 111–115

Video Guide
- Teaching Suggestions, pp. 18–19
- Activity Masters, pp. 20–22
- Scripts and Answers, pp. 90–92, 115

Activities for Communication
- Communicative Activities, pp. 9–12
- Realia and Teaching Suggestions, pp. 57–59
- Situation Cards, pp. 93–94

Reading and Writing
Reading Strategies and Skills Handbook, Chapter 3

¡Lee conmigo! 3, Chapter 3

Cuaderno de actividades, pp. 25–36

Grammar
Cuaderno de gramática, pp. 19–27

Grammar Tutor for Students of Spanish, Chapter 3

Assessment
Testing Program
- Grammar and Vocabulary Quizzes, **Paso** Quizzes, and Chapter Test, pp. 45–58
- Score Sheet, Scripts and Answers, pp. 59–65

Alternative Assessment Guide
- Portfolio Assessment, p. 18
- Performance Assessment, p. 32
- CD-ROM Assessment, p. 46

Student Make-Up Assignments
- Alternative Quizzes, Chapter 3

Standardized Assessment Tutor
- Reading, pp. 9–11
- Writing, p. 12
- Math, pp. 25–26

Native Speakers
Cuaderno para hispanohablantes, pp. 11–15

 **MEDIA**

 Online Activities
- Juegos interactivos
- Actividades Internet

 Video Program
- Videocassette 1
- Videocassette 5 (captioned version)

 Audio Compact Discs
- Textbook Listening Activities, CD 3, Tracks 1–16
- Additional Listening Activities, CD 3, Tracks 21–27
- Assessment Items, CD 3, Tracks 17–20

 Interactive CD-ROM Tutor, Disc 1

 Teaching Transparencies
- Situations 3-1 to 3-2
- **Más práctica gramatical** Answers
- **Cuaderno de gramática** Answers

  One-Stop Planner CD-ROM

Use the **One-Stop Planner CD-ROM with Test Generator** to aid in lesson planning and pacing.

For each chapter, the **One-Stop Planner** includes:
- Editable lesson plans with direct links to teaching resources
- Printable worksheets from resource books
- Direct launches to the HRW Internet activities
- Video and audio segments
- Test Generator
- Clip Art for vocabulary items

Capítulo 3: El ayer y el mañana

Projects

La vida en el porvenir

In this activity students prepare and perform a videotaped skit about everyday life in the future. They practice much of the vocabulary presented in Chapter 3. Students work in small groups on this project. It should be done at the end of the chapter.

MATERIALS

✂ Students may need
- Video camera
- Blank videocassette
- Bilingual dictionary
- Costumes
- Props
- Poster board

SUGGESTED SEQUENCE

1. Divide students into groups of three to five.

2. Groups brainstorm about topics for their skit. Encourage them to use their imagination and to present futuristic situations. For example, what might a future teenager do on his or her first date with someone from another planet? How would people do household chores when their robots are on strike (**los robots están en huelga**)? How would students learn history in virtual schools (**colegios virtuales**)? What problems might someone face babysitting for the aliens next door (**cuidar a los niños extraterrestres**)? What would living under the ocean (**vivir bajo el mar**) be like?

3. Encourage students to use the present perfect and future tenses in their skit. This might be done by talking about how things have been in the recent past or how they will be in the future.

4. To explain actions that cannot be shown, suggest that students write what is happening in large letters on poster board and show it to the audience. (**Ya he volado a Júpiter.**) Poster board signs could also be used to identify the characters or to represent props such as spaceships. Encourage students to use costumes in their skits.

5. Students rehearse their skits once before filming them.

6. Students perform and record their skits.

GRADING THE PROJECT

Suggested point distribution: (total = 100 points)

Creativity	25
Use of Spanish	30
Props	20
Group organization	25

Games

¡Dibújalo!

This is a fast, fun way to review vocabulary at any time.

Preparation Have students make preliminary sketches of vocabulary items so they will be ready to draw them on the board when called.

Procedure Divide the class into two teams. Ask the first player from Team 1 to go to the board. Show the student a vocabulary word. The student draws a picture of the word and Team 1 has one minute to guess the word, including the article, before the opposing team may try. The team who guesses correctly gets a point. Repeat with the other team.

¡A charlar!

This game reviews question formation, vocabulary, grammar, and functions. It should be played upon completion of the chapter.

Preparation Ask students to create a large grid of four-by-four squares on a sheet of paper. In each square they write a question using the functions and vocabulary from the chapter.

Procedure Have students work their way around the room in search of a different classmate to answer each question. A student asks the question of a classmate, who, after answering, jots down his or her answer and signs the questioner's grid in the appropriate square. You may want to play rounds for different winners. (e.g., the first to get four squares signed vertically, horizontally, diagonally, or to complete the whole grid) As a follow-up activity, have individuals report on their classmates' answers.

¿Crees que vale la pena desarrollar la energía solar?	¿Has practicado un deporte acuático alguna vez? ¿Cuál?	¿Cuál es la mejor película que has visto?	¿Cuál es la peor película que has visto?
Sí	*Sí, esquiar*	*Titanic*	*Space Jam*
¿...?	¿...?	¿...?	¿...?
¿...?	¿...?	¿...?	¿...?
¿...?	¿...?	¿...?	¿...?

Storytelling

Mini-cuento

This story accompanies Teaching Transparency 3-1. The **mini-cuento** *can be told and retold in different formats, acted out, written as dictation, and read aloud to give students additional opportunities to practice all four skills. The following story is about technological advances.*

¡Cómo ha cambiado la vida!

Las personas del pasado no tuvieron los adelantos que tenemos hoy en día. Las personas escribían con dibujos, tocaban música sin electricidad y leían muchos libros. ¡No tenían televisión ni computadoras! La vida era más tranquila aunque tal vez menos cómoda. Ahora en la vida moderna los adelantos en la tecnología han cambiado la vida bastante. Hoy las personas tienen teléfonos celulares, satélites, computadoras, contestadoras y muchas cosas más. Es cierto que hay muchas ventajas con tantos inventos, pero la verdad es que también hay mucho estrés en la vida moderna. ¿Alguna vez has pensado cómo sería ahora la vida diaria sin la tecnología? ¿Cómo piensas que será el mundo en el futuro? ¿Habrá más inventos que nos harán la vida más fácil?

Traditions

La Navidad en Venezuela

Venezuela has many Christmas traditions. Elaborate **pesebres,** or nativity scenes, are displayed in homes and churches. On Christmas Eve, **la Nochebuena** *midnight mass* is followed by a huge family dinner. In some areas, people celebrate **la paradura del niño,** when a statue of the baby Jesus is carried from house to house on a large silk cloth, the corners of which are held by people also carrying candles. Children receive gifts on January 6. They leave straw for the camels of **los tres**

Reyes Magos *the Three Wise Men* and when children awaken, the straw has been replaced with the gifts from the Magi. Have students describe some holiday traditions with which they are familiar. How are these customs like or unlike Venezuelan celebrations?

Receta

Rice was brought to Latin America by the Spaniards and is grown along the coastal regions. Latin Americans love rice, which has become a staple of their diet. Rice can be used as a main dish with beans or chicken, in soups and stews, and even in making drinks, such as **horchata**. *One of the most popular dishes in Venezuela, and throughout Latin America and the Caribbean, is* **arroz con leche**. *It is a refreshing dessert that is served cold.*

ARROZ CON LECHE

para 5 personas

1 taza de arroz	2 tazas de azúcar
2 tazas de agua	1/2 cucharadita de sal
7 tazas de leche	
cáscara rallada de un limón	
2 palitos de canela	
canela en polvo	

Cocine el arroz en el agua y hiérvalo unos siete minutos hasta que se ablande un poco y hasta que el agua casi se haya evaporado. Agregue la leche, los palitos de canela y la cáscara de limón. Cocine a fuego moderado hasta el punto de hervir, y después de diez minutos, saque los palitos de canela y la cáscara. Cocine por unos cinco o seis minutos más, revolviendo con una cuchara de madera, hasta que el arroz esté blando. Agregue el azúcar y cocine todo 30 minutos más, a fuego lento, revolviendo frecuentemente. Agregue la sal y cocine uno o dos minutos más. Retire la mezcla del fuego y póngala en un recipiente hondo. Espolvoree el arroz con leche con la canela en polvo y coloque el recipiente en el refrigerador. Se sirve frío en platitos individuales.

Capítulo 3: El ayer y el mañana
Technology

Video Program

Videocassette 1, Videocassette 5 (captioned version)
See Video Guide, pages 17–22.

Dramatic episode • El mundo es un balón de fútbol
Javier and Sergio head to school to get their teacher's permission to use the Internet. They plan to do a research project for a sociology class that would involve the collaboration of their Mexican friends. With Zoraida's help, they get online and find Alejandra's e-mail address, as well as a site that addresses the current problems of Mexico City.

De antemano • La vida de ayer
People from Caracas, Venezuela, explain how their city has changed and how technology has affected their lives. They also talk about the advantages and disadvantages of each and what they think the future will be like.

¿Cómo te afecta la tecnología?
People from different countries talk about technology and how it has affected their lives, their workplaces, and their schools.

Videoclip
- **Empresas públicas de Medellín:** public service message that raises awareness of the services of **Empresas públicas de Medellín**.

Interactive CD-ROM Tutor

The **Interactive CD-ROM Tutor** contains videos, interactive games, and activities that provide students an opportunity to practice and review the material covered in Chapter 3.

Activity	Activity Type	Pupil's Edition Page
1. Vocabulario	¡Super memoria!	p. 71
2. Gramática	¿Qué falta?	p. 72
3. Vocabulario	Imagen y sonido ¡Exploremos! ¡Identifiquemos!	p. 73
4. Así se dice	¡Atrévete!	p. 74
5. Gramática	¿Cuál es?	p. 79
6. Vocabulario	Patas arriba	p. 81
Panorama cultural	¿Cómo te afecta la tecnología? ¡A escoger!	p. 83
¡A hablar!	*Guided recording*	pp. 92–93
¡A escribir!	*Guided writing*	pp. 92–93

Teacher Management System
Logging In
Logging in to the *¡Ven conmigo!* TMS is easy. Upon launching the program, simply type "admin" in the password area of the log-in screen and press RETURN. Log on to **www.hrw.com/CDROMTUTOR** for a detailed explanation of the Teacher Management System.

One-Stop Planner CD-ROM

To preview all resources available for this chapter, use the **One-Stop Planner CD-ROM**, Disc 1.

Internet Connection

internet

go.hrw.com
MARCAR: go.hrw.com
PALABRA CLAVE:
WV3 CARACAS-3

*Have students explore the **go.hrw.com** Web site for many online resources covering all chapters. All Chapter 3 resources are available under the keyword **WV3 CARACAS-3**. Interactive games help students practice the material and provide them with immediate feedback. You will also find a printable worksheet that provides Internet activities that lead to a comprehensive online research project.*

Juegos interactivos

You can use the interactive activities in this chapter

- to practice grammar, vocabulary, and chapter functions
- as homework
- as an assessment option
- as a self-test
- to prepare for the Chapter Test

Actividades Internet

Students research air pollution, waste, and other environmental problems common in large cities. They also research whether various cities have plans to take care of those problems.

- As preparation for the **Hoja de actividades**, ask students to list environmental problems in their city. Also have them review the **Primer paso** vocabulary and the dramatic episode.
- After students have completed the activity sheet, have them take out their list of their city's environmental problems. Are the issues similar to those in other places? Does their city have a plan to solve the problems?

Proyecto

Ask students to post their opinions about a current environmental issue to a class message board or Web site. Then ask them to respond to their classmates' postings. The objective is to generate various points of view and explore students' ideas for solving environmental problems.

Textbook Listening Activities Scripts

Primer paso

7   **p. 72**

Hace sesenta y cinco años que vivo en Caracas. Claro que la ciudad ha cambiado muchísimo. Y es cierto que la población ha crecido bastante. Por ejemplo, mucha gente ha venido aquí de otros lugares desde que yo era niña. Y puesto que cada quien tiene su carro, la contaminación del aire ha empeorado mucho. Otra cosa es que cuando era niña escuchábamos la radio o conversábamos. Hoy día todos vamos muy de prisa y la familia ya no tiene tiempo para hablar. Pero algunas cosas no son muy diferentes. He notado que hay cosas que regresan una y otra vez. La moda es un buen ejemplo. Yo he visto a las jóvenes con unos zapatos que yo usaba hace treinta años.

Answers to Activity 7
1. la ciudad
2. la población
3. la contaminación del aire
4. algunas cosas: la moda, por ejemplo

11   **p. 74**

Felipe   ¿Sabes lo que me parece ridículo? Que después de tantos adelantos tecnológicos no vivamos mejor. La vida es más complicada y hay más estrés que nunca.

Daniela   Bueno, no sé si la situación es tan grave como dices. De todos modos, se me hace que la vida moderna tiene ciertas ventajas. Muchos tienen teléfono celular en el carro y pueden llamar cuando estén atrasados por el tráfico.

Felipe   ¡Ajá! Ya te dije que esta vida no es nada normal. El tráfico es horrible y la contaminación del agua y del aire nos está sofocando poco a poco.

Daniela   Es cierto que hay problemas, pero tienes que adaptarte a la vida moderna. Deberías pensar en los aspectos positivos. Por ejemplo, cuando tengo hambre y poco tiempo, preparo algo en el microondas. Además, si quiero saber lo que está pasando en otro país, pongo la radio o la tele y en seguida me puedo informar.

Felipe   Sí, gracias a las telecomunicaciones puedes saber casi al instante que hubo otro accidente nuclear.

Daniela   ¡Hombre, qué cínico eres! Ten en cuenta que como estudiante la tecnología te ayuda mucho. Con la computadora no tienes que pasar horas escribiendo tus trabajos como antes. ¡Y con el contestador nunca pierdes tus llamadas importantes, como las de Anabel!

Answers to Activity 11
1. Felipe
2. Daniela
3. Felipe
4. Daniela
5. Daniela

Segundo paso

21   **p. 79**

Bárbara   Oye, Ernesto, ¿tienes el periódico de hoy? ¡Sólo encuentro el de la semana pasada!

Ernesto   Lo estoy leyendo ahora. ¿Qué quieres saber?

Bárbara   Bueno, quiero saber a qué hora empieza el concierto de guitarra.

Ernesto   Empezará a las ocho de la noche.

Bárbara   ¿Y la exhibición de arte de Siqueiros?

Ernesto   Ya terminó la exhibición de Siqueiros pero la semana que viene empieza la exhibición de Jesús Soto.

Bárbara   ¡Qué lástima! Bueno, este, me encantaría ver esa película de María Conchita Alonso y—

Ernesto   No, ya no están dando esa película pero el viernes viene una de Meryl Streep que dicen que es buenísima.

Bárbara   Oye, Pavarotti ya vino, ¿no?

Ernesto   Cantará el sábado. Tal vez estás pensando en Plácido Domingo que dio un concierto excelente ayer.

Bárbara   ¿¡Ayer?! ¡No puedo creer que me lo perdí!

Answers to Activity 21
1. pasará
2. ya pasó
3. pasará
4. ya pasó
5. pasará
6. pasará
7. ya pasó

The following scripts are for the listening activities found in the *Pupil's Edition*. For Student Response Forms, see *Listening Activities*, pages 19–21. To provide students with additional listening practice, see *Listening Activities*, pages 23–25.

One-Stop Planner CD-ROM

To preview all resources available for this chapter, use the **One-Stop Planner CD-ROM**, Disc 1.

26   p. 81

Amigos y amigas, tenemos que pensar en el futuro de nuestro mundo. Hay muchos problemas que afectan nuestras vidas como, por ejemplo, el medio ambiente y el crimen. Somos nosotros los que debemos hacer un plan para resolverlos. Aunque no son problemas que los miembros de nuestro club pueden resolver solos, hay cosas que todos pueden hacer, tanto los adultos como los jóvenes. Por ejemplo todos podemos reducir nuestro uso de recursos y de energía, y todos podemos aprender a reciclar productos hechos de madera, de metal y de plástico. No debemos esperar... ¡empecemos hoy!

Answers to Activity 26
1. Cierta
2. Falsa; dice que nos toca a nosotros resolver los problemas.
3. Falsa; Maricarmen dice que hay muchos problemas con el medioambiente y el crimen.
4. Cierta
5. Falsa; según Maricarmen no hay tiempo para esperar.

Repaso

1   p. 92

1. Se me hace que lo bueno de tener este invento es que puedes ir rápidamente de un lado de la ciudad al otro. Claro que lo malo es que todos los demás tratan de hacerlo también y luego tenemos problemas con el tránsito.

2. El sábado pasado queríamos alquilar una película, pero ¡qué crees que sucedió! La videocasetera se descompuso y destruyó el video.

3. Vale la pena tener este invento en casa porque de vez en cuando tengo que cenar en unos pocos minutos cuando tengo un compromiso por la noche. Cocino, ceno y salgo corriendo para llegar a tiempo.

4. ¡Qué invento más pesado! Me da rabia estar con alguien que no me hace caso porque pasa todo el tiempo hablando con otros. Qué egoístas, ¿verdad?

5. Lo que me encanta es estar afuera al aire libre escribiendo trabajos. No tengo que pasar hora tras hora enfrente de una máquina de escribir como antes.

6. Este invento a veces trae buenas y a veces malas noticias. Depende de los recados que me hayan dejado, pero la verdad es que lo encuentro muy útil.

Answers to Repaso Activity 1
1. f
2. a
3. e
4. c
5. d
6. b

Capítulo 3: El ayer y el mañana
Suggested Lesson Plans 50-Minute Schedule

Day 1

CHAPTER OPENER 5 min.
- Focusing on Outcomes, ATE, p. 67
- Present Science Link, Language Note or Thinking Critically, ATE, pp. 66–67.

DE ANTEMANO 40 min.
- Presenting **De antemano** and Preteaching Vocabulary, ATE, p. 68
- Present Background Information, ATE, p. 69.
- Activities 1–5 and Comprehension Check, ATE, p. 70

Wrap-Up 5 min.
- Discuss responses to Activity 5, p. 70.

Homework Options
Cuaderno de actividades, p. 25, Activities 1–2

Day 2

PRIMER PASO
Quick Review 5 min.
- Check homework.
- Bell Work, ATE, p. 71

Vocabulario, p. 71 40 min.
- Presenting **Vocabulario**, ATE, p. 71
- Present **También se puede decir...**, p. 71.
- Review object pronouns.
- Do Activity 6, p. 71.
- **Más práctica gramatical**, p. 88, Activity 1

Wrap-Up 5 min.
- Have students write advantages and disadvantages of the technology in Teaching Transparency 3-1.

Homework Options
Cuaderno de actividades, p. 26, Activity 3
Cuaderno de gramática, pp. 19–21, Activities 1–6

Day 3

PRIMER PASO
Quick Review 5 min.
- Check homework.

Así se dice/Gramática, p. 72 30 min.
- Presenting **Así se dice** and **Gramática**, ATE, p. 72
- Follow suggestions in the Language Note, ATE, p. 72.
- Do Activity 7 with the Audio CD, p. 72.
- Review **¿Te acuerdas?**, p. 72.
- Review affirmatives and negatives.
- Do Activity 8, p. 73.
- Have students do Activity 9 in pairs, p. 73.

Vocabulario, p. 73 10 min.
- Presenting **Vocabulario**, ATE, p. 73
- Do Activity 10, p. 73.

Wrap-Up 5 min.
- Do the Additional Practice, ATE, p. 73.

Homework Options
Cuaderno de actividades, pp. 26–27, Activities 4–6
Cuaderno de gramática, pp. 22–23, Activities 7–11

Day 4

PRIMER PASO
Quick Review 5 min.
- Check homework.

Así se dice/Nota gramatical, p. 74 25 min.
- Presenting **Así se dice, Nota gramatical**, ATE, p. 74
- Do Slower Pace Activity, ATE, p. 74. Then do Activity 11 with the Audio CD, p. 74.
- Have students do Activity 12 in groups, p. 74.
- Read **Nota cultural**, p. 74.

Así se dice, p. 75 15 min.
- Presenting **Así se dice**, ATE, p. 75
- Do Activity 13, p. 75.
- Have students do Activity 14 in pairs, p. 75.

Wrap-Up 5 min.
- Discuss the content and format of Quiz 3-1.

Homework Options
Study for Quiz 3-1.
Cuaderno de actividades, pp. 28–29, Activities 7–9

Day 5

PRIMER PASO
Quick Review 10 min.
- Check homework.
- Review the content of **Primer paso.**

Así se dice, p. 75 15 min.
- Have students do Activity 15, then peer-edit their work, p. 75.

Quiz 20 min.
- Administer Quiz 3-1A, 3-1B, or a combination of the two.

Wrap-Up 5 min.
- **Mini-cuento** for Teaching Transparency 3-1

Homework Options
Cuaderno de actividades, pp. 29, 36, Activities 10 and 23

Day 6

PRIMER PASO
Quick Review 5 min.
- Check homework.

¡ADELANTE! 25 min.
- Presenting **¡Adelante!** and Preteaching Vocabulary, ATE, p. 76
- Do Thinking Critically Activity, ATE, p. 77.
- Do Activities 16–18, pp. 76–77.
- Follow Teaching Suggestion for **Tira cómica**, ATE, p. 77, then have students do Activity 19 in pairs, p. 77.

SEGUNDO PASO
Así se dice, p. 78 15 min.
- Presenting **Así se dice**, ATE, p. 78
- Do Activity 20, p. 78.
- Read **Nota cultural**, p. 78, then follow Group Work suggestion, ATE, p. 79.

Wrap-Up 5 min.
- Have students list technology that will be better in the future.

Homework Options
Cuaderno de actividades, p. 30, Activities 11–12

One-Stop Planner CD-ROM

For alternative lesson plans by chapter section, to create your own customized plans, or to preview all resources available for this chapter, use the **One-Stop Planner CD-ROM,** Disc 1.

 For additional homework suggestions, see activities accompanied by this symbol throughout the chapter.

Day 7

SEGUNDO PASO
Quick Review 5 min.
- Check homework.
- Ask students what they are going to accomplish this year.

Gramática, p. 79 40 min.
- Presenting **Gramática,** ATE, p. 79
- Present the Language Note, ATE, p. 79.
- Do Activity 21 with the Audio CD, p. 79.
- Do Activity 22, p. 79.
- Review **¿Te acuerdas?** Follow Pair Work suggestion, ATE, p. 80.
- Do Activities 23–24, p. 80.
- Have students do Activity 25 in groups, p. 80.

Wrap-Up 5 min.
- Discuss lists from Activity 25 with the class, p. 80.

Homework Options
Cuaderno de actividades, pp. 31–33, Activities 14–16
Cuaderno de gramática, pp. 24–26, Activities 12–17

Day 8

SEGUNDO PASO
Quick Review 10 min.
- Check homework.
- Ask students what they will be doing in 10 years.

Así se dice, p. 81 15 min.
- Presenting **Así se dice,** ATE, p. 81
- Review **¿Te acuerdas?,** p. 81.
- Do Activity 26 with the Audio CD, p. 81.

Vocabulario, p. 81 20 min.
- Presenting **Vocabulario,** ATE, p. 81
- Present **Vocabulario extra,** p. 81.
- Do Activity 27, p. 81.

Wrap-Up 5 min.
- Follow Suggestion 2 for Teaching Transparency 3-2.

Homework Options
Cuaderno de actividades, pp. 31, 33–34, Activities 13, 17–19
Cuaderno de gramática, p. 27, Activities 18–19

Day 9

SEGUNDO PASO
Quick Review 10 min.
- Check homework.
- Follow Suggestion 1 for Teaching Transparency 3-2.

Vocabulario, p. 81 25 min.
- Have students do Activity 28 in pairs and Activity 29 in groups, p. 82.
- Have students do Activity 30, then peer-edit their work, p. 82.

PANORAMA CULTURAL 10 min.
- Presenting **Panorama cultural,** ATE, p. 83

Wrap-Up 5 min.
- Discuss the content and format of Quiz 3-2.

Homework Options
Study for Quiz 3-2.

Day 10

SEGUNDO PASO
Quick Review 5 min.
- Review the content of **Segundo paso.**

Quiz 20 min.
- Administer Quiz 3-2A, 3-2B, or a combination of the two.

VAMOS A LEER 20 min.
- Read the **Estrategia,** then do Activities A–B, pp. 84–85.
- Review **¿Te acuerdas?,** then do Activity C, p. 85.

Wrap-Up 5 min.
- Discuss the Slower Pace Activity, ATE, p. 85.

Homework Options
Assign **Vamos a leer** Activities D–E, pp. 85–86.

Day 11

VAMOS A LEER
Quick Review 5 min.
- Check and discuss homework.

VAMOS A LEER 20 min.
- Do the Thinking Critically Activity, ATE, p. 86.
- Have students do Activities F–G in pairs, p. 86.

REPASO 20 min.
- Do Activity 1 with the Audio CD, p. 92.
- Have students do Activity 2 in pairs, p. 92.
- Do Activities 3–4, pp. 92–93.
- Do Activity 5 in groups, p. 93.

Wrap-Up 5 min.
- Have students list concepts and culture from Chapter 3.

Homework Options
Assign **Vamos a escribir,** p. 87.
A ver si puedo, p. 94
Cuaderno de actividades, pp. 35–36, Activities 20–22

Day 12

REPASO
Quick Review 5 min.
- Check homework and collect **Vamos a escribir,** p. 87.

Chapter Review 40 min.
- Review Chapter 3. Choose from **Más práctica gramatical,** Grammar Tutor for Students of Spanish, Activities for Communication, Listening Activities, Interactive CD-ROM Tutor, or **Juegos interactivos.**

Wrap-Up 5 min.
- Discuss the format of the Chapter 3 Test.

Homework Options
Study for the Chapter 3 Test.

Assessment

Quick Review 5 min.
- Answer any last-minute questions.

Test, Chapter 3 45 min.
- Administer Chapter 3 Test. Select from Testing Program, Alternative Assessment Guide, Test Generator, or Standardized Assessment Tutor.

Capítulo 3: El ayer y el mañana
Suggested Lesson Plans 90-Minute Block Schedule

Block 1

CHAPTER OPENER 5 min.
- Focusing on Outcomes, ATE, p. 67
- Present Science Link, Language Note or Thinking Critically, ATE, pp. 66–67.

DE ANTEMANO 40 min.
- Presenting **De antemano** and Preteaching Vocabulary, ATE, p. 68
- Present Background Information, ATE, p. 69.
- Activities 1–5 and Comprehension Check, ATE, p. 70

Vocabulario, p. 71 40 min.
- Presenting **Vocabulario**, ATE, p. 71
- Present **También se puede decir...**, p. 71.
- Review object pronouns.
- Do Activity 6, p. 71.
- **Más práctica gramatical**, p. 88, Activity 1

Wrap-Up 5 min.
- Have students write advantages and disadvantages for the technology in Teaching Transparency 3-1.

Homework Options
Cuaderno de actividades, pp. 25–26, Activities 1–3
Cuaderno de gramática, pp. 19–21, Activities 1–6

Block 2

PRIMER PASO
Quick Review 10 min.
- Check homework.

Así se dice/Gramática, p. 72 30 min.
- Presenting **Así se dice** and **Gramática**, ATE, p. 72
- Follow suggestions in the Language Note, ATE, p. 72.
- Do Activity 7 with the Audio CD, p. 72.
- Review **¿Te acuerdas?**, p. 72.
- Review affirmatives and negatives.
- Do Activity 8, p. 73.
- Have students do Activity 9 in pairs, p. 73.

Vocabulario, p. 73 15 min.
- Presenting **Vocabulario**, ATE, p. 73
- Do Activity 10, p. 73.

Así se dice/Nota gramatical, p. 74 25 min.
- Presenting **Así se dice, Nota gramatical,** ATE, p. 74
- Do Activity 11 with the Audio CD, p. 74.
- Have students do Activity 12 in groups, p. 74.
- Read **Nota cultural**, p. 74, then present Culture Note, ATE, p. 75.

Wrap-Up 10 min.
- Suggestion 3 and **Mini-cuento** for Teaching Transparency 3-1

Homework Options
Cuaderno de actividades, pp. 26–29, Activities 4–7 and 9
Cuaderno de gramática, pp. 22–23, Activities 7–11

Block 3

PRIMER PASO
Quick Review 10 min.
- Check homework.
- Have students describe how things have changed in their lifetimes.

Así se dice, p. 75 30 min.
- Presenting **Así se dice**, ATE, p. 75
- Do Activity 13, p. 75.
- Have students do Activity 14 in pairs, p. 75.
- Have students do Activity 15, then peer-edit their work, p. 75.

¡ADELANTE! 25 min.
- Presenting **¡Adelante!** and Preteaching Vocabulary, ATE, p. 76
- Do the Thinking Critically Activity, ATE, p. 77.
- Do Activities 16–18, pp. 76–77.
- Follow Teaching Suggestion for **Tira cómica**, ATE, p. 77, then have students do Activity 19 in pairs, p. 77.

SEGUNDO PASO
Así se dice, p. 78 15 min.
- Presenting **Así se dice**, ATE, p. 78
- Do Activity 20, p. 78.
- Present **Nota cultural**, p. 78.

Wrap-Up 10 min.
- Have students talk about what they are going to accomplish this year.
- Discuss the content and format of Quiz 3-1.

Homework Options
Study for Quiz 3-1.
Cuaderno de actividades, pp. 28–30, Activities 8, 10–12

 **One-Stop** Planner CD-ROM

For alternative lesson plans by chapter section, to create your own customized plans, or to preview all resources available for this chapter, use the **One-Stop Planner CD-ROM,** Disc 1.

 For additional homework suggestions, see activities accompanied by this symbol throughout the chapter.

Block 4

PRIMER PASO
Quick Review 10 min.
- Check homework.
- Review the content of **Primer paso.**

Quiz 20 min.
- Administer Quiz 3-1A, 3-1B, or a combination of the two.

SEGUNDO PASO
Gramática, p. 79 40 min.
- Presenting **Gramática,** ATE, p. 79
- Present the Language Note, ATE, p. 79.
- Do Activity 21 with the Audio CD, p. 79.
- Do Activity 22, p. 79.
- Review **¿Te acuerdas?,** p. 80.
- Do Activities 23–24, p. 80.
- Have students do Activity 25 in groups, p. 80.

Así se dice, p. 81 15 min.
- Presenting **Así se dice,** ATE, p. 81
- Review **¿Te acuerdas?,** p. 81.
- Do Activity 26 with the Audio CD, p. 81.

Wrap-Up 5 min.
- Have students describe what the world will be like in 100 years.

Homework Options
Cuaderno de actividades, pp. 31–33, Activities 14–17
Cuaderno de gramática, pp. 24–27, Activities 12–18

Block 5

SEGUNDO PASO
Quick Review 10 min.
- Check homework.
- Follow Suggestion 1 for Teaching Transparency 3-2.

Vocabulario, p. 81 40 min.
- Presenting **Vocabulario,** ATE, p. 81
- Present **Vocabulario extra,** p. 81.
- Do Activity 27, p. 81.
- Have students do Activity 28 in pairs and Activity 29 in groups, p. 82.
- Have students do Activity 30, then peer-edit their work, p. 82.

PANORAMA CULTURAL 15 min.
- Presenting **Panorama cultural,** ATE, p. 83

VAMOS A ESCRIBIR 15 min.
- Have students do Activity A and begin Activity B, p. 87.

Wrap-Up 10 min.
- Do the Thinking Critically/Analysis, ATE, p. 86.
- Discuss the content and format of Quiz 3-2.

Homework Options
Study for Quiz 3-2.
Finish **Vamos a escribir,** p. 87.
Cuaderno de actividades, pp. 31, 34, Activities 13, 18–19
Cuaderno de gramática, p. 27, Activity 19

Block 6

SEGUNDO PASO
Quick Review 10 min.
- Check homework and collect **Vamos a escribir,** p. 87.
- Review the content of **Segundo paso.**

Quiz 20 min.
- Administer Quiz 3-2A, 3-2B, or a combination of the two.

VAMOS A LEER 55 min.
- Do Activities A–C, pp. 84–85.
- Do Activities D–E, pp. 85–86.
- Have students do Activities F–G in pairs, p. 86.

Wrap-Up 5 min.
- Discuss the content and format of the Chapter 3 Test.

Homework Options
Study for the Chapter 3 Test.
Assign **Repaso** Activities 3, 4, and 6, pp. 92–93.
A ver si puedo, p. 94
Cuaderno de actividades, pp. 35–36, Activities 20–23

Block 7

REPASO
Quick Review 10 min.
- Check homework.

Chapter Review 35 min.
- Review Chapter 3. Choose from **Más práctica gramatical,** Grammar Tutor for Students of Spanish, Activities for Communication, Listening Activities, Interactive CD-ROM Tutor, or **Juegos interactivos.**

Test, Chapter 3 45 min.
- Administer Chapter 3 Test from Testing Program, Alternative Assessment Guide, Test Generator, or Standardized Assessment Tutor.

Chapter Opener

CAPÍTULO 3

One-Stop Planner CD-ROM

For resource information, see the **One-Stop Planner**, Disc 1.

Pacing Tips
The **Primer paso** has a great deal of vocabulary as well as new functions. You might want to add extra time to allow students to thoroughly practice the new material. For lesson plans and timing suggestions, see pages 65I–65L.

Meeting the Standards

Communication
- Talking about what has happened, p. 72
- Expressing and supporting a point of view, p. 74
- Using conversational fillers, p. 75
- Talking about future events, p. 78
- Talking about responsibilities, p. 81

Cultures
- Nota cultural, p. 78
- Panorama cultural, p. 83

Connections
- Science Link, p. 66
- Science Link, p. 78
- Literature Link, p. 84

Comparisons
- Language Note, p. 79

Communities
- Career Path, p. 70
- Community Link, p. 78
- Family Link, p. 83

Connections and Comparisons

Science Link
Ask students if they see a connection between the theme of this chapter (technology) and the significance of petroleum industries in Venezuela. Most high-tech apparatuses are made of metals and plastics, down to the tiny circuits and wires. Without petroleum processing, plastics would not exist. Have students research petroleum industries to get an idea of how extensively we use this resource.

Language Note
Point out to students the masculine form of **mañana** in the title of this chapter. The word **mañana,** while feminine when it means *tomorrow* or *morning,* is masculine when it denotes the future or *tomorrow* in a poetic sense.

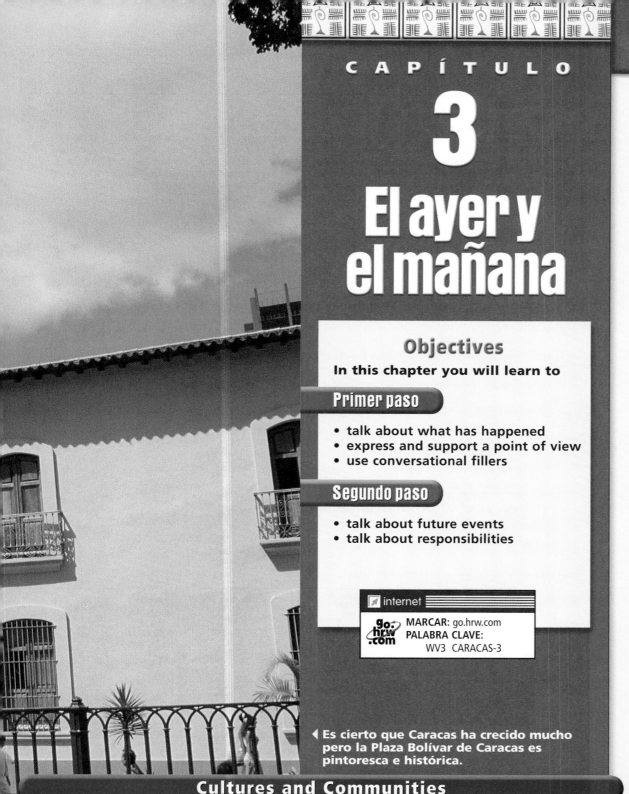

CAPÍTULO

3
El ayer y el mañana

Objectives

In this chapter you will learn to

Primer paso

- talk about what has happened
- express and support a point of view
- use conversational fillers

Segundo paso

- talk about future events
- talk about responsibilities

internet

go.
hrw
.com

MARCAR: go.hrw.com
PALABRA CLAVE:
    WV3 CARACAS-3

◀ **Es cierto que Caracas ha crecido mucho pero la Plaza Bolívar de Caracas es pintoresca e histórica.**

Chapter Opener

CAPÍTULO 3

Photo Flash!
Although earthquakes in 1755 and 1812 almost completely destroyed Caracas, buildings from the colonial era survive in the area surrounding the Plaza Bolívar. This city hub has shops, restaurants, and office buildings. The Santa Teresa church, the municipal council building, the Ministry of Foreign Affairs, and the old cathedral that is now the archbishop's residence are among the most distinctive buildings in the area.

Focusing on Outcomes
In this chapter, students will learn to talk about past and future events, responsibilities, and how to express and support a point of view. They will also use conversational fillers in their discussions. To begin a discussion, ask students whether a person who is concerned about saving the Earth would focus more attention on past events or on expectations for the future.

Cultures and Communities

Thinking Critically
Analyzing Have students use the information they have learned about the geography of Venezuela and their knowledge about the effect of latitude and altitude on climate to develop inferences about lifestyles around the country. How might climate influence how houses are built in Caracas? How might the wardrobes of people who live in San Rafael de Mucuchies, high in the Andes, differ from those who live in Margarita? (Houses in Caracas generally have neither heating nor cooling. People in San Rafael need sweaters and coats year round, whereas those in Margarita wear light clothing all year.)

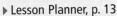

Teaching Resources
pp. 68–70

PRINT
▶ Lesson Planner, p. 13
▶ Video Guide, pp. 17–21
▶ Cuaderno de actividades, p. 25

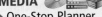

MEDIA
▶ One-Stop Planner
▶ Video Program
Contigo en la distancia
Videocassette 1, 27:42–33:04
Videocassette 5 (captioned version), 12:06–17:28
De antemano
Videocassette 1, 33:05–36:45
▶ Audio Compact Discs, CD 3, Trs. 1–4

Presenting
De antemano

Have students answer the questions in **Estrategia para comprender.** Then have students watch **Contigo en la distancia** and listen for verbs in the imperfect. Present the Preteaching Vocabulary. Then have students read **De antemano,** noting verbs that they did not identify in the video.

De antemano
People from Caracas, Venezuela, explain how technology has affected their lives.

DE ANTEMANO ▪ *La vida de ayer*

Cuaderno de actividades, p. 25, Acts. 1–2

CD 3
Trs. 1–4

Estrategia para comprender
¿Cómo era la vida diaria de tus padres y abuelos cuando eran jóvenes? Bastante diferente de la tuya, ¿verdad? Claro que los últimos años han traído muchos avances tecnológicos, como los teléfonos celulares, contestadores y computadoras avanzadas. Los adelantos en la tecnología nos afectan cada día más. Les hicimos varias preguntas a unas personas que viven en Caracas sobre cómo ha cambiado el país y sobre algunos aspectos de la tecnología hoy en día. Lee sus respuestas para ver si estás de acuerdo con ellos o no.

"Caracas era la ciudad de los techos rojos."

¿Cómo ha cambiado Venezuela desde que Ud. era niña?
Ha cambiado muchísimo, porque Caracas era la ciudad de los techos rojos. Aquí no existían edificios, ni ranchos, ni bloques, nada de eso; eran puras casas.

¿Le parece un cambio positivo o negativo?
Bueno, sí, positivo.

¿Y en cuanto a la gente?
Bueno, hay mucha gente que no son de aquí. Ha venido mucha gente de fuera, ¿no?

¿Cómo ve el futuro de Venezuela?
Bueno, yo pienso que... que va a prosperar mucho.

Ilda Martínez de Betencouth

Preteaching Vocabulary

Guessing Words from Context
Ask students what types of expressions they would use to describe life when their parents were young. Have students identify expressions in **De antemano** that describe events in the past. Then point out the following phrases: **Caracas era la ciudad de los techos rojos; Aquí no existían edificios...; ...antes no existía una computado**ra que te procesara una información básica que necesitas al momento; ...tenías que hacer investigaciones; Antes cuando no existía el televisor uno podía leer más, había más tiempo para otras cosas. Have students use context to determine the meanings.

¿Cómo ha afectado su vida la tecnología?

Bueno, en el momento actual, ahorita, me imagino que no, sin esos aparatos que uno usa diariamente sería imposible sacar, cumplir uno con sus tareas....

¿Nos podría dar un ejemplo?

Bueno, las fotocopiadoras incluso; ahora hay demasiadas fotocopiadoras avanzadas....

¿Y en el trabajo?

En el trabajo también es indispensable porque antes no existía una computadora que te procesara a ti una información básica que tú necesitas al momento, tú tenías que hacer investigaciones para llegar a algo. Ahora todo es más fácil con las computadoras porque bueno, pues, es más avanzado.

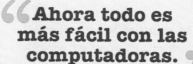

❝Ahora todo es más fácil con las computadoras.❞

Dania Padilla

Sebastián Mozetic

❝Antes cuando no existía el televisor uno podía leer más, había más tiempo para otras cosas.❞

¿Cuáles son las cosas más importantes de la tecnología que usas?

El televisor, la radio, la computadora y si no los tuviera, no sé, me costaría mucho adaptarme, porque la televisión te informa, estás conectado con el mundo, igual que con la computadora.

¿Qué ventajas tienen?

Y agilizan mucho la vida diaria, ayudan. Por ejemplo, para hacer trabajos con la computadora ganas mucho tiempo.

¿Y las desventajas?

Que el televisor tiende a atarte, a estar frente al televisor. Antes cuando no existía el televisor uno podía leer más, había más tiempo para otras cosas.

Background Information

Caracas is a cosmopolitan city with immigrants and residents from many countries. Many **caraqueños** are of European origin. (Spanish, Portuguese, German, Italian, British) A large number of Colombians also reside in the city. Immigrants from Cuba, Argentina, Uruguay, and the Caribbean islands, together with people from the Middle East and the Far East, have further diversified the cultural and racial mix of Caracas. More than 15,000 United States citizens live there as legal residents.

 Contigo en la distancia

You may choose to show students Episode 3: *El mundo es un balón de fútbol* now or wait until later in the chapter. In the video, Javier and Sergio get permission to use the Internet for a research project for a sociology class that would involve the collaboration of their Mexican friends. With Zoraida's help, they find Alejandra's school's Web site, as well as a site on the current problems in Mexico City. Before students view the video, have them predict which chapter functions and vocabulary they will hear used in the episode.

Using the Captioned Video

As an alternative, you might want to show the captioned version of *Contigo en la distancia: El mundo es un balón de fútbol* on Videocassette 5. Some students may benefit from seeing the written words as they listen to the target language and watch the gestures and actions in context. This visual reinforcement of vocabulary and functions will facilitate students' comprehension and help reduce their anxiety before they are formally introduced to the new language in the chapter.

DE ANTEMANO

CAPÍTULO 3

Career Path

Have students brainstorm about careers in the energy industry. (electrical, chemical, civil, and mechanical engineers; nuclear technicians; geologists and soil scientists) Ask students how knowing Spanish might be helpful in this field of work. (When developing nations, including those in Latin America, lack the technological expertise they need, they often recruit experienced personnel from more industrialized countries to help train or supervise local people. Also, increasing development in such countries means rising energy demand, and greater interest in new, cleaner technologies such as solar and wind energy.)

Answers

1 1. Ilda
2. Dania
3. Sebastián
4. Sebastián
5. Dania

2 1. bueno..., yo pienso que...
2. bueno..., sería imposible, es indispensable, porque
3. [Venezuela] ha cambiado muchísimo

3 1. Caracas era una ciudad con casas de techos rojos sin edificios, sin ranchos sin bloques.
2. Sebastián usa el televisor, la radio y la computadora.
3. La señora Betencouth cree que el futuro de Venezuela va a ser muy próspero.
4. Según Dania, las computadoras hacen el trabajo más fácil.
5. Sebastián piensa que el televisor toma demasiado tiempo en la vida de la gente.

4 *Possible answers:*
contestadores, computadoras personales, fotocopiadoras, televisor y radio

---

These activities check for comprehension only. Students should not yet be expected to produce language modeled in **De antemano**.

1 **¿Quién lo expresó?** See answers below.

Todas las siguientes oraciones son parecidas a frases de las entrevistas. Lee cada una e indica quién expresó el concepto — Sebastián, Ilda o Dania.

1. La población de Caracas ha crecido *(has grown)* mucho.
2. ¿La tecnología? Bueno, en el trabajo ahora me parece algo esencial.
3. Antes, la gente salía de noche o leía. Hoy día se queda en casa viendo la tele.
4. Las telecomunicaciones nos mantienen informados.
5. Sin la tecnología es más difícil cumplir con tus tareas.

2 **Pienso que...** See answers below.

Busca las palabras que usan Ilda, Dania y Sebastián para...
1. ganarse tiempo para pensar.
2. expresar opiniones.
3. hablar de los cambios en Caracas.

3 **¿Comprendes?** See answers below.

Contesta las siguientes preguntas.
1. ¿Cómo era Caracas cuando la señora Betencouth era niña?
2. Nombra tres aparatos tecnológicos que usa Sebastián.
3. ¿Cómo ve el futuro de Venezuela la señora Betencouth?
4. ¿Qué cosas hacen el trabajo más fácil, según Dania?
5. ¿Qué preocupación tiene Sebastián acerca del televisor?

4 **¿Y qué más hay?** See possible answers below.

Lee la lista de adelantos *(advances)* que cambiaron nuestras vidas. Luego, con un(a) compañero(a), haz una lista de los adelantos mencionados en **De antemano**.

5 **Ahora te toca a ti**

Piensa en el pueblo o ciudad donde vives. ¿Cómo es ahora? ¿Cómo era cuando eras pequeño(a)? Si no conoces bien el pasado de tu pueblo o ciudad, pregúntale a alguien cómo era. En tu opinión, ¿cuáles de estos cambios son positivos? ¿Cuáles son negativos?

SUGERENCIA

Sometimes people feel anxious when they read in a foreign language because comprehending the entire text seems to be an overwhelming task. One easy way to reduce this anxiety is to divide the reading task into parts. You can divide the text into small sections and concentrate your attention on one section at a time.

5 adelantos tecnológicos que han cambiado nuestras vidas

- **El DVD**
  los últimos años de los 90
- **El teléfono celular**
  los años 90
- **El disco compacto**
  los años 80
- **La computadora personal**
  los años 80
- **El fax**
  los años 80

Comprehension Check

Additional Practice

1 After students identify who expresses each concept, have them point out the statement in the **De antemano** text that justifies their answer.

Challenge

4 Tell students to imagine that they are doing this activity 100 years ago. Have them research inventions that caused great changes in people's lives at that time. (telephone, invented in 1876; gasoline-powered automobile, 1885; radio, 1901) They might also research devices that had already become parts of people's daily lives. (steam engine, telegraph, sewing machine)

Objectives Talking about what has happened; expressing and supporting a point of view; using conversational fillers

WV3 CARACAS-3

Vocabulario

CD-ROM DISC 1

- la antena parabólica
- manejar por la autopista
- el tráfico
- cocinar en el horno de microondas
- hablar por teléfono celular
- la fotocopiadora (a colores)
- el rascacielos
- mandar un fax
- enviar una carta electrónica
- el contestador

a la vez	*at the same time*	
adaptarse	*to adapt*	
los adelantos	*advances*	
la computadora	*computer*	
la desventaja	*disadvantage*	
empeorar	*to get worse*	
en seguida	*right away, immediately*	
hacer trabajos	*to write papers*	

hoy (en) día	*nowadays*
informar	*to inform*
navegar por Internet	*to surf the Internet*
el siglo	*century*
la tecnología	*technology*
la ventaja	*advantage*
la vida diaria	*daily life*

la videocasetera
videocassette player

Más práctica gramatical, p. 88, Act. 1

Cuaderno de actividades, pp. 26–27, Acts. 3, 6

Cuaderno de gramática, pp. 19–20, Acts. 1–3

6 La tecnología See answers below.

Leamos/Escribamos Completa las siguientes oraciones con el nuevo vocabulario.

1. Puedes preparar la cena en seguida con...
2. No debes manejar un carro mientras hablas por...
3. Si sales con frecuencia y la gente te quiere llamar por teléfono, es bueno tener...
4. La gente se enoja cuando hay demasiado tráfico en...
5. El mundo cambia cada día más, por eso hay que...
6. Si quieres ver un video en televisión, necesitas...
7. Si quieres buscar información rápidamente, puedes...

También se puede decir...

Se puede decir **la contestadora** y **la máquina de contestar** por **el contestador**. Otra palabra que significa **tráfico** es **tránsito**. En España dicen **el ordenador** en vez de **la computadora**.

¿Se te ha olvidado?
object pronouns
Ver la página R27

Cuaderno de gramática, pp. 20–21, Acts. 4–6

Communication for All Students

Native Speakers
Divide the class into two groups. One group lists the advantages of technological advancement while the second group lists the disadvantages. Then have groups compare lists and discuss any differences. Students can do the same for specific vocabulary items.

Pair Work
Have pairs of students write the script for a video to be included in a time capsule that will be opened in 100 years. Students should talk about the state of technology today and describe useful items that have become household fixtures. If possible, ask students to film their presentations, making use of visual aids, to show to the class.

CAPÍTULO 3

Teaching Resources
pp. 71–75

PRINT
- Lesson Planner, p. 13
- Listening Activities, pp. 19, 23–24
- Activities for Communication, pp. 9–10, 57, 59, 93–94
- Cuaderno de gramática, pp. 19–23
- Grammar Tutor for Students of Spanish, Chapter 3
- Cuaderno de actividades, pp. 26–29
- Cuaderno para hispanohablantes, pp. 11–15
- Testing Program, pp. 45–48
- Alternative Assessment Guide, p. 32
- Student Make-Up Assignments, Chapter 3

MEDIA
- One-Stop Planner
- Audio Compact Discs, CD 3, Trs. 5–6, 21–23, 17
- Teaching Transparencies 3-1; **Más práctica gramatical** Answers; Cuaderno de gramática Answers
- Interactive CD-ROM Tutor, Disc 1

Bell Work
Write: **Escribe cinco mandatos informales negativos y cinco mandatos informales afirmativos.**

Presenting
Vocabulario

Tell students about traffic problems in your city. Ask them questions using vocabulary items. Urge them to repeat the vocabulary in their answers.

Answers
6.
1. el microondas
2. teléfono celular
3. un contestador
4. la autopista
5. adaptarse
6. una videocasetera
7. navegar por Internet

Teaching Resources
pp. 71–75

PRINT
▶ Lesson Planner, p. 13
▶ Listening Activities, pp. 19, 23–24
▶ Activities for Communication, pp. 9–10, 57, 59, 93–94
▶ Cuaderno de gramática, pp. 19–23
▶ Grammar Tutor for Students of Spanish, Chapter 3
▶ Cuaderno de actividades, pp. 26–29
▶ Cuaderno para hispanohablantes, pp. 11–15
▶ Testing Program, pp. 45–48
▶ Alternative Assessment Guide, p. 32
▶ Student Make-Up Assignments, Chapter 3

MEDIA
▶ One-Stop Planner
▶ Audio Compact Discs, CD 3, Trs. 5–6, 21–23, 17
▶ Teaching Transparencies 3-1; **Más práctica gramatical** Answers; Cuaderno de gramática Answers
▶ Interactive CD-ROM Tutor, Disc 1

Presenting
Así se dice, Gramática

The present perfect Model the phrases in **Así se dice** by talking about what has happened in your area, using the script for Activity 7 as a guide (see p. 65G). Check comprehension by asking yes-or-no questions.

Así se dice

Talking about what has happened

Si quieres hablar de lo que ha pasado *(has happened)*, puedes decir:

Caracas **ha cambiado mucho.**
   . . . *has changed a lot.*

Mucha gente **ha venido de fuera.**
   Many people have come from outside.

La contaminación del aire **ha empeorado bastante.**
   . . . *has gotten quite a bit worse.*

7   **El pasado se repite**   Script and answers on p. 65G.

CD 3
Tr. 5

Escuchemos/Escribamos Escucha mientras una señora de Caracas cuenta cómo la vida ha cambiado desde que era niña. Luego completa las siguientes oraciones.

1. ...ha cambiado mucho.
2. ...ha crecido bastante.
3. ...ha empeorado.
4. ...ha regresado.

Gramática

The present perfect

The present perfect tense tells what has or has not happened. It's formed by combining the present tense of **haber** and the past participle of a verb.

1. To form past participles of regular verbs, drop the **-ar**, **-er**, or **-ir** of the infinitive and add these endings:

-ar verbs: -ado		-er/-ir verbs: -ido	
he bailado	hemos bailado	he comido	hemos comido
has bailado	habéis bailado	has comido	habéis comido
ha bailado	han bailado	ha comido	han comido

2. Here are some irregular past participles:

abrir: **abierto**
decir: **dicho**
descubrir: **descubierto**
escribir: **escrito**
hacer: **hecho**

morir: **muerto**
poner: **puesto**
romper: **roto**
ver: **visto**
volver: **vuelto**

3. Forms of **haber** and the past participle form a unit that cannot be separated by any other words:

¿Has visto a Teresa?
No, no la he visto todavía.

Más práctica gramatical, pp. 88–89, Acts. 2–4

Cuaderno de gramática, pp. 22–23, Acts. 7–9

Cuaderno de actividades, pp. 26–27, 29, Acts. 4–5, 10

¿Te acuerdas?

Cuaderno de gramática, p. 23, Act. 10

Some expressions you are familiar with — **todavía no** *(not yet),* **ya** *(already, yet),* and **alguna vez** *(ever)* — are often used with the present perfect tense. **Todavía no** is used for actions that haven't taken place yet: **Todavía no he leído el periódico. Ya** is used for actions that have already happened: **¿La nueva película de Spielberg? Ya la he visto. ¿Alguna vez has ido a la playa?** means *Have you ever been to the beach?*

Connections and Comparisons

Language Note

Emphasize that when a past participle functions as an adjective with **estar (Las ventanas están abiertas),** it must agree in gender and number with the noun it modifies. However, when it accompanies the auxiliary verb **haber** in the present perfect, it always ends with the letter **-o.** Point out to students that **todavía no** *(not yet),* **ya** *(already),* and **alguna vez** *(ever)* assume the present moment as the point of reference, as do their counterparts in English. *(As of the present moment he still has not done it. He has not done it yet. He has already done it. Has he ever done it?)*

8 Gramática en contexto
Answers will vary.

Escribamos Haz una lista de cinco cosas que ya has hecho y cinco cosas que todavía no has hecho pero que te gustaría hacer.

MODELO Ya he aprendido a manejar un carro.
Todavía no he viajado a Hawaii.

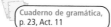

¿Se te ha olvidado?
affirmatives & negatives
Ver la página R29

Cuaderno de gramática, p. 23, Act. 11

9 Gramática en contexto

Hablemos Usa las siguientes preguntas para entrevistar a un(a) compañero(a). Luego responde mientras él o ella te entrevista.

1. ¿Has practicado un deporte acuático alguna vez?
2. ¿Alguna vez has sufrido mucha presión? ¿Por qué?
3. ¿Adónde has viajado con tu familia?
4. ¿Cuál es la mejor película que has visto? ¿la peor?
5. ¿Qué inventos tecnológicos has usado durante la última semana?

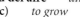

Vocabulario

el ayuntamiento   *town hall*
el basurero   *trash can*
la calidad del aire   *air quality*
crecer (zc)   *to grow*
establecer (zc) una zona peatonal
    to set up a pedestrian zone
la fábrica   *factory*
mejorar   *to improve*
sembrar (ie)   *to plant*

CD-ROM DISC 1

Cuaderno de actividades, p. 29, Act. 9

Más práctica gramatical, p. 91, Act. 7

10 ¡Ha cambiado bastante!
See possible answers below.

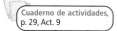

Escribamos Mira los dos dibujos. Luego escribe cinco oraciones que describan los cambios que notas. ¿Qué ha cambiado?

Communication for All Students

Slower Pace

8 Ask students to work in pairs. Have each student read his or her list to the other student. The other student should listen very closely and repeat his or her partner's list using the **tú** form. If he or she cannot repeat it exactly, the first student reads the list again.

Auditory/Kinesthetic Learners

9 Divide the class into pairs or small groups and have them write and perform skits in which one student plays an authority figure (parent, teacher, boss, guidance counselor) who asks the other students about what they have or have not done.

Presenting Vocabulario

Model correct usage of the vocabulary items in a description of your area. You may want to have students make flashcards of these and other chapter vocabulary items, with pictures on one side and the written words on the other. When comprehension is high, ask several students to add to your description using the new vocabulary.

Teaching Suggestion

10 Have students write five sentences describing what has happened. Then have them work with a partner to peer-edit each other's work and to come up with a final description, noting as many changes as possible.

Additional Practice

Ask students to write their own sets of interview questions using the present perfect, and then have them interview each other in pairs.

Answers
10 *Possible answers:*
1. Los carros y las fábricas ya no contaminan el aire.
2. Han establecido una zona peatonal.
3. La calidad del aire ha mejorado.
4. Han sembrado flores.
5. El tráfico ha mejorado.

Teaching Resources
pp. 71–75

PRINT 📖
▸ Lesson Planner, p. 13
▸ Listening Activities, pp. 19, 23–24
▸ Activities for Communication, pp. 9–10, 57, 59, 93–94
▸ Cuaderno de gramática, pp. 19–23
▸ Grammar Tutor for Students of Spanish, Chapter 3
▸ Cuaderno de actividades, pp. 26–29
▸ Cuaderno para hispanohablantes, pp. 11–15
▸ Testing Program, pp. 45–48
▸ Alternative Assessment Guide, p. 32
▸ Student Make-Up Assignments, Chapter 3

MEDIA 💿📹💻
▸ One-Stop Planner
▸ Audio Compact Discs, CD 3, Trs. 5–6, 21–23, 17
▸ Teaching Transparencies 3-1; **Más práctica gramatical** Answers; Cuaderno de gramática Answers
▸ Interactive CD-ROM Tutor, Disc 1

Presenting
Así se dice, Nota gramatical

Model the phrases from **Así se dice** in original sentences in which you express and support your own opinions on a topic. Then write a list of five topics on the board or on a transparency. **(las pruebas, la tarea, el matrimonio, la censura** censorship, **la edad para sacar el permiso de conducir** the age for getting a driver's license, and so on.**)** Tell students to use the new phrases to write one sentence supporting an opinion about each topic.

Así se dice

Expressing and supporting a point of view

Hay varias formas de expresar y apoyar tu punto de vista.

Son buenos los adelantos tecnológicos pero **ten en cuenta que** la tecnología no lo resuelve todo.
   . . . keep in mind that . . .

Me imagino que los adelantos nos ayudan mucho.

Lo que noto es que ahora hay más estrés en la vida.
   What I notice is that . . .

Me parece que los adelantos mejoran la calidad de nuestra vida.

Se me hace que tenemos que usar el transporte público más.
   It seems to me . . .

Lo que es importante es tener cuidado con la tecnología.

Creo que vale la pena encontrar nuevas tecnologías.
   I think it's worth it . . .

Es cierto que hay ventajas, **pero por otro lado** hay desventajas también.
   It's true that . . . but on the other hand . . .

> Cuaderno de actividades, p. 28, Act. 7

11 La vida moderna   Script and answers on p. 65G.

Escuchemos Daniela y Felipe están hablando sobre el progreso tecnológico. Escucha su conversación y luego indica cuál de los dos está de acuerdo con las siguientes ideas.

CD 3
Tr. 6

1. Lo que noto es que hay más estrés que nunca.
2. La vida moderna es un poco más complicada pero ten en cuenta que tiene algunas ventajas.
3. Se me hace que la contaminación del agua y del aire está afectando nuestra salud.
4. Por otro lado se puede cocinar rápidamente y saber las noticias casi al instante.
5. Creo que vale la pena tener un contestador porque siempre sabes si alguien te llamó.

12 Gramática en contexto

Hablemos En un grupo de dos o tres, hablen de sus puntos de vista sobre estos temas. Usen expresiones de **Así se dice**.

1. Es una ventaja vivir cerca de la autopista.
2. Alguien que ve mucha televisión no estudia lo suficiente.
3. Alguien que usa mucho la tecnología es perezoso.
4. La videocasetera fue el mejor adelanto del siglo XX.
5. Algún día vamos a hacer todas nuestras compras por Internet.

Nota gramatical

Lo que means *what*, when *what* is not asking a question but rather implies *the thing that.* **¿Escuchaste lo que dijo la profesora?** means *Did you listen to what the professor said?*

> Más práctica gramatical, p. 90, Act. 5

Nota cultural

El petróleo no les interesaba mucho a los indios ni a los exploradores españoles. Los indios lo usaban para arreglar sus canoas. Esa actitud cambió cuando comenzó el boom petrolero en 1922. Muchas compañías vinieron a extraer el petróleo, y se construyeron muchos caminos, casas y puertos. Después de nacionalizar el petróleo en 1971, Venezuela volvió a permitir la inversión y exploración petrolera por compañías extranjeras en 1995. Venezuela produce aproximadamente 2,5 millones de barriles de petróleo diariamente.

Communication for All Students

Slower Pace

11 Before playing the recording, have volunteers read each sentence aloud. Ask questions to check comprehension before the listening task. **(¿Creen que hay más estrés que nunca? ¿Por qué?)**

12 Ask students to outline their opinions about each of the topics individually, before having them divide into groups.

Kinesthetic Learners

13 Have students act out the conversation between Alberto Flojo and the teacher. Encourage them to use facial expressions and body language to emphasize emotions.

STANDARDS: 1.1, 1.2, 2.2, 3.2, 5.2

Using conversational fillers

Cuando estás hablando y no sabes qué decir, puedes ganarte un poco de tiempo al usar algunas palabras muy útiles. Si alguien te pregunta, **¿Cuáles son los inventos más importantes de las últimas décadas?,** puedes responder:

Bueno, me parece que son...

Este... no sé.

La verdad es que... hay tantos inventos.

A ver, el DVD es un invento muy chévere.

Pues, los aparatos que usamos todos los días son maravillosos.

Eh... la fotocopiadora a colores es una maravilla.

Bueno, a ver...

Cuaderno de actividades, p. 28, Act. 8

13 Este, pues... See answers below.

Leamos/Escribamos Pon las siguientes frases en orden para formar una conversación entre Alberto Flojo y su maestra. Ella quiere saber por qué Alberto no hizo su tarea.

a. Bueno, sí, este... es que mi perro se lo comió.

b. Sí, puedes empezar.

c. Pero, ¿qué te pasó? ¿No has hecho tu informe todavía?

d. A ver, Alberto, empecemos con tu informe sobre algunas soluciones al problema de la contaminación del aire.

e. Pues, en verdad no puedo.

f. Eh... ¿yo? ¿de primero?

14 La verdad es que...

Hablemos/Escribamos Todas estas personas no saben qué decir. Con un(a) compañero(a), usa las expresiones de **Así se dice** y crea oraciones adecuadas para cada dibujo.

a.　　　　　　　　　　b.　　　　　　　　　　c.

15 Cuando mamá era joven Answers will vary.

Escribamos ¿Cuántos adelantos tecnológicos han aparecido desde que tus padres y abuelos tenían tu edad? Resume los cambios que han ocurrido.

Presenting
Así se dice

Play both sides of a dialogue between a parent who has just noticed a dent in his or her car and a teenager who is searching for the words to confess. **(Este, pues... es que no vi el árbol grande que había en el... bueno, en el camino...)** Then have students take turns asking and answering questions regarding the dented car. (Helpful vocabulary: **la abolladura** *dent,* **chocar con** *to run into)*

Assess

▸ Testing Program, pp. 45–48
   Quiz 3-1A, Quiz 3-1B
   Audio CD 3, Tr. 17

▸ Student Make-Up Assignments, Chapter 3, Alternative Quiz

▸ Alternative Assessment Guide, p. 32

Cultures and Communities

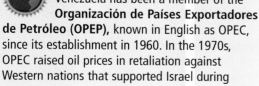

Culture Note

Venezuela has been a member of the **Organización de Países Exportadores de Petróleo (OPEP),** known in English as OPEC, since its establishment in 1960. In the 1970s, OPEC raised oil prices in retaliation against Western nations that supported Israel during the Yom Kippur War in 1973. The higher oil prices led to fuel shortages and inflation in many countries. During the 1980s, these nations began campaigns to conserve energy and to explore alternative fuels to reduce reliance on OPEC oil.

Answers
13 d, f, b, e, c, a

Teaching Resources
pp. 76–77

PRINT
▶ Lesson Planner, p. 14
▶ Video Guide, pp. 17–18, 20
▶ Cuaderno de actividades, p. 30

MEDIA
▶ One-Stop Planner
▶ Video Program
Contigo en la distancia
Videocassette 1, 27:42–33:04
Videocassette 5 (captioned version), 12:06–17:28
▶ Audio Compact Discs, CD 3, Trs. 7–9

Presenting
¡Adelante!

Play the Audio CD once while students look at the photos and read the text. Ask students to name developments or inventions that are mentioned. Then have students list problems that are mentioned. Present the Preteaching Vocabulary and check for comprehension.

 Contigo en la distancia

As an alternative to ¡Adelante!, you may wish to show Episode 3 of *Contigo en la distancia.* For suggestions and activities, see the *Video Guide.*

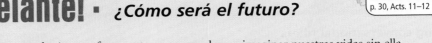

 CD 3 Trs. 7–9

La tecnología nos afecta tanto que no podemos imaginar nuestras vidas sin ella. ¿Has pensado cómo afecta tu vida la tecnología? ¿Y cómo piensas que será en el futuro, igual que ahora o diferente? ¿Mejor que ahora o peor? Les hicimos estas preguntas a dos jóvenes de Caracas. Sus respuestas son interesantes.

**Ofelia Fontés
18 años**

❝Yo pienso que el futuro será mucho mejor.❞

La tecnología es para mí una necesidad en la vida. Por ejemplo, sin el microondas no vivo. Lo uso para todo. En cuanto al futuro... creo que si el mundo ha cambiado tanto durante la vida de mi abuela, no hay duda que el mundo cambiará más durante mi vida. Yo pienso que el futuro será mucho mejor. Habrá muchos más adelantos que van a ayudar en la medicina, por ejemplo.

Me imagino que habrá carros eléctricos o solares. Todo estará más mecanizado que ahora y habrá todo tipo de robots que te puedan hacer todo.

These activities check for comprehension only. Students should not yet be expected to produce language modeled in **¡Adelante!**

16 **¿Comprendes?** See answers below.

Usa la información de **¡Adelante!** para contestar las siguientes preguntas.

1. Nombra tres aparatos eléctricos que menciona Ofelia.
2. ¿Para qué usa ella el microondas?
3. ¿Qué piensa Ofelia del futuro?
4. ¿Cuáles son dos cosas que ella dice que va a haber en el futuro?
5. ¿Piensa Eduardo que va a haber más problemas o menos durante su vida?
6. Nombra dos cosas negativas que él menciona acerca del futuro.
7. ¿Por qué cree él que la comunicación mejorará en el futuro?
8. Según Eduardo, ¿quién es responsable del futuro?

17 **En el futuro habrá...** See answers below.

Ofelia y Eduardo compararon el futuro con el presente cuando dieron sus puntos de vista. Haz una lista de las comparaciones que hicieron.

Preteaching Vocabulary

Activating Prior Knowledge

Point out that in **¡Adelante!**, Ofelia and Eduardo are talking about what they think the future is going to be like. Based on Spanish expressions students already know, can they guess what Ofelia means when she says **Habrá muchos más adelantos que van a ayudar...?** What is she predicting when she says **habrá carros eléctricos o solares** and **Todo estará más mecanizado que ahora y habrá todo tipo de robots?** What types of predictions does Eduardo make? (**habrá más contaminación del medio ambiente y menos recursos naturales, más especies de animales estarán en peligro de extinción, la comunicación entre países mejorará porque todos hablaremos más idiomas**)

**Eduardo Pantoja
16 años**

"**Yo creo que habrá tantos problemas como ahora.**"

Creo que habrá tantos problemas como ahora, sólo que serán diferentes. Por ejemplo, habrá más contaminación del medio ambiente y menos recursos naturales. Más especies de animales estarán en peligro de extinción. Por eso tenemos que trabajar juntos para protegerlos. Y no sé cómo estará la situación del empleo. Por otro lado, creo que la comunicación entre países mejorará porque todos hablaremos más idiomas. ¿Quién sabe exactamente cómo será? En fin, me parece que nos toca a nosotros los jóvenes mejorar el mundo.

Pair Work

17 Have students work in pairs to create a dialogue in which Ofelia persuades Eduardo that the world will get better, or in which Eduardo persuades Ofelia that problems will only get worse.

Additional Practice

19 **Tira cómica** Have students read the cartoon, then ask: **¿Quién está de acuerdo con Calvin: Eduardo u Ofelia?** (Eduardo)

Answers

16 1. Menciona microondas, carros eléctricos o solares y robots.
2. Ella usa el microondas para todo.
3. Ella piensa que el futuro será mejor.
4. Habrá carros eléctricos o solares y robots.
5. Piensa que habrá tantos como ahora.
6. Habrá más contaminación y muchas especies de animales estarán en peligro de extinción.
7. La gente hablará más idiomas.
8. Los jóvenes son responsables del futuro.

17 Ofelia: el futuro va a ser mejor, la medicina será mejor con los adelantos que habrá, todo estará más mecanizado que ahora.
Eduardo: habrá más contaminación que ahora, más animales estarán en peligro, la comunicación entre países mejorará y todos hablaremos más idiomas.

18 1. Ofelia
2. Eduardo
3. Ofelia
4. Ofelia
5. Eduardo

18 **¿Quién será?** See answers below.

Lee las oraciones e indica quién estaría de acuerdo con la idea—Ofelia o Eduardo.

1. Vivir en el futuro va a ser más fácil porque va a haber más adelantos tecnológicos.
2. La vida en el futuro va a ser más difícil para los animales.
3. En el futuro los niños van a tener un robot que les va a ayudar con la tarea.
4. No van a usar la estufa en el futuro. Van a usar el microondas nada más.
5. Nadie sabe cómo va a ser el futuro.

19 **Ustedes, ¿qué piensan?** Answers will vary.

 Lee la tira cómica. Luego, con un(a) compañero(a), contesten las preguntas. ¿Están de acuerdo los dos?

1. Entre Ofelia Fontés, Eduardo Pantoja y el autor de la tira cómica, ¿quién parece sentirse más pesimista acerca del futuro? ¿Quién es más optimista en sus predicciones del futuro?
2. ¿Cuál de los tres puntos de vista es el más parecido al tuyo *(yours)*? ¿Y al de tu compañero(a)? Explica.

Comprehension Check

Thinking Critically
Analyzing Ask students whether or not they think that the opinions expressed by Ofelia and Eduardo contradict each other. (They do not. Although Eduardo does not share Ofelia's optimism for the future, the two of them discuss different aspects of future life, and neither of their predictions precludes the other's.)

Visual Learners
19 Instruct students to create one or two more frames for the cartoon in which Calvin and Hobbes come up with a solution to their problem. Ask: **¿Crees que es demasiado tarde para Calvin o todavía puede hacer algo para salvar el bosque?** Students should illustrate the frames and write captions in Spanish.

Objectives Talking about future events; talking about responsibilities

WV3 CARACAS-3

Teaching Resources
pp. 78–82

PRINT
▶ Lesson Planner, p. 14
▶ Listening Activities, pp. 20, 24–25
▶ Activities for Communication, pp. 11–12, 58–59, 93–94
▶ Cuaderno de gramática, pp. 24–27
▶ Grammar Tutor for Students of Spanish, Chapter 3
▶ Cuaderno de actividades, pp. 31–34
▶ Cuaderno para hispanohablantes, pp. 11–15
▶ Testing Program, pp. 49–52
▶ Alternative Assessment Guide, p. 32
▶ Student Make-Up Assignments, Chapter 3

MEDIA
▶ One-Stop Planner
▶ Audio Compact Discs, CD 3, Trs. 10–11, 24–26, 18
▶ Teaching Transparencies 3-2; **Más práctica gramatical** Answers; Cuaderno de gramática Answers
▶ Interactive CD-ROM Tutor, Disc 1

Bell Work
On the board or a transparency, write: **Escribe diez cosas que piensas hacer en el futuro.**

Presenting
Así se dice
Model sentences describing what you think the next year will be like. Ask students to point out the part of each sentence that indicates the future.

Answers
20 estarán jugando, practicando, van a reciclar, va a haber, recogemos, sembramos, va a hablar, quedará, desperdiciando, mejorará, vamos a resolver, habrá, cambiará, van a decir

Así se dice

Talking about future events

Cuando quieres hablar de algo que va a pasar en el futuro, puedes decir:

El futuro **va a ser** mucho mejor.

Va a haber carros eléctricos o solares.

Todo **va a estar** más mecanizado que ahora.

Mañana **recogemos** basura en el parque.

La comunicación entre países **mejorará** porque todo el mundo **hablará** más idiomas.

Más gente **va a usar** teléfonos celulares.

> Cuaderno de actividades, pp. 32–33, Acts. 15–16

20 **¿Cómo será?** See answers below.

Leamos/Escribamos Lee el siguiente artículo e identifica cada verbo o frase que se refiere al futuro.

> Este fin de semana muchos jóvenes estarán jugando a los videojuegos o practicando deportes, pero Adriana y Raimundo Guzmán van a reciclar latas como parte del esfuerzo por cuidar la Tierra. —También va a haber otras oportunidades para ayudar—explica Raimundo. —Mañana recogemos basura y sembramos árboles en una nueva zona peatonal. Y por la tarde Adriana va a hablar en una conferencia de cómo quedará el mundo si seguimos desperdiciando los recursos naturales.
> ¿Creen que vale la pena? ¿que la situación mejorará? Adriana contesta: —Pues, sé que no vamos a resolver todos los problemas en un día. Y siempre habrá gente que no cambiará su estilo de vida. Pero, ¿qué nos van a decir nuestros hijos si no hacemos nada hoy?

Nota cultural

Caracas ha crecido mucho en los últimos 30 años. El aumento de población ha creado una situación en que el desarrollo no ha podido satisfacer la alta demanda de servicios. Algunos adelantos tecnológicos—como los teléfonos celulares, que no requieren cables—proveen un medio de comunicación para muchos caraqueños que no tendrían servicio telefónico sin ellos. Además de ser útil en las ciudades, el teléfono celular permite que algunos habitantes de las zonas rurales de Venezuela hagan llamadas telefónicas desde sus pueblos o fincas. De lo contrario tendrían que ir largas distancias para encontrar un teléfono. ¿Son comunes los teléfonos celulares donde tú vives?

Connections and Comparisons

Science Link
Have students do research on other advantages and disadvantages of cellular phones. Point out that cellular phone technology is heavily reliant on orbiting satellites. These satellites are very vulnerable to cosmic phenomena such as solar flares and meteor showers. Such events can disrupt telecommunications for extended periods of time.

Community Link
After reading the **Nota cultural,** have students discuss the role that cellular phones play in their own community. Are they widespread? What reasons do people have for using them? How have cellular phones changed everyday life? Have students interview three people in the commmunity about cell phones.

STANDARDS: 1.2, 2.2, 3.1, 4.2, 5.1

The future tense

1. The future tense is formed by taking the future stem and adding the future endings, which all have an accent mark, except the **nosotros(as)** form. The infinitive serves as the future stem for most verbs.

-é	-emos	viajar**é**	viajar**emos**
-ás	-éis	viajar**ás**	viajar**éis**
-á	-án	viajar**á**	viajar**án**

Más práctica gramatical,
p. 90, Act. 6

2. The future stems of some verbs in Spanish are irregular:

decir: **dir-**	querer: **querr-**	poder: **podr-**	tener: **tendr-**
haber: **habr-**	saber: **sabr-**	poner: **pondr-**	valer: **valdr-**
hacer: **har-**	salir: **saldr-**	venir: **vendr-**	

Cuaderno de actividades,
p. 31, Act. 14

3. The future tense form corresponds to *will* + verb in English:

Luis vendrá el martes.   *Luis will come on Tuesday.*

Cuaderno de gramática,
pp. 24–25, Acts. 12–15

21 Gramática en contexto   Scripts and answers on p. 65G.

Escuchemos Escucha a Bárbara y Ernesto hablar sobre varias funciones *(events)* culturales. Luego indica si la función **ya pasó** o si **pasará** en el futuro.

CD 3
Tr. 10

1. el concierto de guitarra
2. la exhibición de arte de Siqueiros
3. la exhibición de arte de Soto
4. la película de María Conchita Alonso

5. la película de Meryl Streep
6. el concierto de Luciano Pavarotti
7. el concierto de Plácido Domingo

22 Gramática en contexto

Escribamos Julián está mirando las fotos de sus compañeros(as) de colegio en el anuario *(yearbook)*. Según las fotos, ¿qué piensas que harán en el futuro?

Presenting
Gramática

The Future Tense Write the present perfect conjugation of **viajar** on the board in traditional paradigm form. Tell the class **No he viajado nunca a Hawaii, pero algún día en el futuro viajaré a Hawaii.** As you say **viajaré,** change the first person form in the paradigm from the present perfect to the future by erasing the **he** and changing the **-do** to **-ré.** Use this visual transformation as you give examples for the other forms in the paradigm, emphasizing **el futuro** as you demonstrate the new verb forms. Finally, point out the irregular future stems.

Language Note

You might point out to the students that the future tense endings are the present tense forms of **haber** minus the **h.** In Old Spanish, which students may encounter in literature, the present tense of **haber de** + infinitive was used to express the future. (**He de hablar.**) A simplification of the same basic structure was infinitive + the present tense of **haber.** (**Hablar he.**) Eventually, the silent **h** was dropped in writing, forming a simple tense from the complex one. (**Hablaré.**)

Communication for All Students

Group Work

22 Allow students to work in groups of four to discuss what they think they will be doing in ten years. Then ask each student to make a brief oral presentation about one of their group member's plans. They should not say the person's name. The class should try to guess whom each student is describing.

Native Speakers

Have pairs of students make predictions about life on Earth 200 years in the future. How and where will people live? What will be the state of technology, the environment, and culture? Students can present their ideas to the class with illustrations or in the form of a skit.

Answers

23 *Sample answers:*

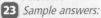

1. me divertiré... trabajaré
2. estudiaré tanto como mi hermano
3. reciclaré más y botaré menos
4. trabajaré tanto como en la escuela
5. practicaré más deportes que ahora
6. trabajaré más y estudiaré menos

24 1. En el año 2067

2. En el Japón
3. En Georgia, Estados Unidos
4. canciones de los Beatles, libros en todos los idiomas actuales, más películas, videos, juguetes, máquinas, etc.

¿Te acuerdas?

To compare people or things that are the same or equal, use:

tan + adjective/adverb + **como**
(as . . . as).

To compare equal amounts, use:

tanto(a)(os)(as) + noun + **como**
(as much/as many . . . as).

To express inequalities use:

más/menos ... que.

Cuaderno de gramática, p. 26, Acts. 16–17

---

23 Gramática en contexto See sample answers below.

Leamos/Escribamos ¿Tienes planes para mejorar tu vida? Completa las siguientes oraciones. Usa los verbos en el tiempo futuro.

1. Yo... más y... menos que ahora.
2. Para mejorar mis notas, yo...
3. Quiero proteger el medio ambiente. Por eso...
4. En mi casa yo...
5. Durante mi tiempo libre...
6. Necesito más dinero. El próximo verano...

ABRIR EN EL AÑO 3502

24 La cápsula de información See answers below.

Leamos/Escribamos Lee el siguiente artículo sobre cápsulas de información *(time capsules)* y luego contesta las siguientes preguntas.

1. ¿En qué año mirarán las cosas en la cápsula en Montreal?
2. ¿En qué país se abrirá la cápsula en el año 6970?
3. ¿Dónde instalaron una habitación subterránea?
4. ¿Qué cosas encontrarán las futuras generaciones?

Historia del Siglo XX

Para que los arqueólogos del futuro no tengan tanto trabajo cuando quieran estudiar el siglo XX, se ha "sembrado" el planeta con cápsulas de información. Se ha hecho un plan de apertura de esas cápsulas (que quién sabe si se cumplirá). En el año 2067 se abrirá una en Montreal, Canadá, enterrada en 1967. Pero hay fechas más ambiciosas. En el 6939, si todos los países siguen estando donde están, hay que abrir una cápsula en la ciudad de Nueva York. En el 6970, la que está en Osaka, Japón. Y en el 8113 se abrirá una habitación subterránea instalada en Georgia, Estados Unidos, en 1940. ¿Qué encontrarán en estos "paquetes"? Desde canciones de Los Beatles hasta libros en todos los idiomas actuales, más películas, videos, juguetes, máquinas, etc. Todo lo que nosotros, los antiguos del siglo XX, amamos, usamos, vimos, leímos e inventamos.

25 ¿Qué pondrás en la cápsula?

Hablemos/Escribamos Imagina que tu escuela va a depositar una cápsula. En grupos de tres o cuatro estudiantes, hagan una lista de lo que pondrán Uds. en ella y expliquen por qué incluirán esas cosas.

Communication for All Students

Pair Work

23 Have students complete the sentences in writing and then work with a partner to compare their sentences. Next, ask them to write at least three original sentences telling what they both will do to improve themselves.

Challenge

25 Ask students to imagine that the class is going to bury a time capsule. Have each student propose an item to be included and have them justify their choice. Have the students select the items they feel would offer the most accurate picture of their lives to those who will find the capsule.

Así se dice

Talking about responsibilities

Lo que hacemos hoy afecta el futuro. ¿Qué debemos hacer para garantizar un futuro mejor?

Hay que buscar soluciones.
It's necessary . . .

Nos toca a nosotros salvar la tierra.
It's up to us . . .

Tanto los jóvenes como los mayores **deben** pensar en el porvenir.

Es nuestra responsabilidad encontrar nuevas formas de energía.
It's our responsibility . . .

Estamos obligados a proteger los animales en peligro de extinción.

Es nuestro deber mejorar el mundo.
It's our duty . . .

Cuaderno de actividades, pp. 33–34, Acts. 17–19

26 **El club de voluntarios** Script and answers on p. 65H.

CD 3
Tr. 11

Escuchemos/Escribamos Escucha lo que dice Maricarmen, la presidenta del club de voluntarios, en una reunión. Luego indica si las siguientes oraciones son **ciertas** o **falsas.** Corrige las oraciones falsas.

1. Maricarmen cree que hay que pensar en el futuro ahora.
2. Dice que le toca al gobierno resolver los problemas.
3. Maricarmen dice que hay muchos problemas con la educación.
4. Le parece que es nuestra responsabilidad aprender a reciclar varios productos.
5. Según Maricarmen, no habrá más problemas mañana.

¿Te acuerdas?

One way of saying *let's* + verb is to use **vamos a** + *infinitive.*

Let's go eat a sandwich.
Vamos a comer un sándwich.

Cuaderno de gramática, p. 27, Act. 18

Vocabulario

el aparato eléctrico	*electrical appliance*	**la energía nuclear** *nuclear energy*
botar	*to throw out*	**la energía solar** *solar energy*
el carro eléctrico	*electric car*	**el porvenir** *future*
desarrollar	*to develop*	
descubrir	*to discover*	
destruir	*to destroy*	

Más práctica gramatical, p. 91, Act. 7

Cuaderno de actividades, p. 31, Act. 13

Cuaderno de gramática, p. 27, Act. 19

27 **Adelantos tecnológicos** See answers below.

Leamos/Escribamos Completa las siguientes oraciones con una palabra del **Vocabulario.** Usa la forma adecuada.

1. Es necesario ▭ nuevos medios de transporte en las ciudades grandes.
2. Hay que usar ▭ en nuestros coches porque produce menos contaminación.
3. Creo que en el ▭ usaremos más formas alternativas de energía como ▭.
4. Mis papás quieren comprar un ▭ porque no usa gasolina. Pero los precios están altos todavía.
5. Tenemos que ▭ la basura; ¿dónde está el basurero?

Vocabulario extra

la energía geotérmica	*geothermal energy*
la fusión nuclear	*nuclear fusion*
la gasolina sin plomo	*unleaded gas*
el gas natural	*natural gas*
el molino (generador) de viento	*windmill, wind generator*

Cultures and Communities

Community Link

Have students research local initiatives that promote alternative energy sources. Then ask students to work alone or in groups and write a paragraph in which they define their responsibilities in the community regarding energy sources and usage. Students can explain the advantages and disadvantages of nuclear, solar, wind, or geothermal energy. Students should end their paragraph by identifying what they can do to promote sensible energy usage.

Career Path

Ask students to list careers and fields of study that deal with the environment and energy issues. In which of these professions might one use Spanish? Have students research energy-related career options on the Internet or talk with a guidance counselor.

Speaking Assessment

29 Before students begin their interviews for Activity 29, review the criteria listed in the following rubric and have them rate each other's performance as they complete the activity. Have them present their findings to the class and evaluate their performance, using the same rubric.

Speaking Rubric	Points			
	4	3	2	1
Content (Complete– Incomplete)				
Comprehension (Total–Little)				
Comprehensibility (Comprehensible– Incomprehensible)				
Accuracy (Accurate– Seldom accurate)				
Fluency (Fluent–Not fluent)				

18–20: A	14–15: C	Under
16–17: B	12–13: D	12: F

Assess

▶ Testing Program, pp. 49–52
  Quiz 3-2A, Quiz 3-2B
  Audio CD 3, Tr. 18

▶ Student Make-Up Assignments, Chapter 3, Alternative Quiz

▶ Alternative Assessment Guide, p. 32

Answers

28 *Sample answers:*
Problemas: la destrucción de la Tierra, la contaminación, no reciclar, maltratar los animales y las plantas

Soluciones: ser optimista, trabajar juntos, desarrollar carros solares, reciclar

---

28 **Las soluciones** See sample answers below.

Leamos/Escribamos Lee las cartas de tres jóvenes en la revista *Nueva voz*. Haz una lista de los problemas que expresan y las soluciones que recomiendan. ¿Cuál de las cartas se parece más a tus propias ideas?

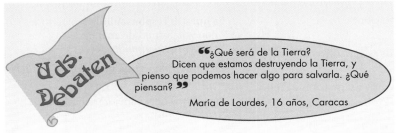

66 ¿Qué será de la Tierra? Dicen que estamos destruyendo la Tierra, y pienso que podemos hacer algo para salvarla. ¿Qué piensan? 99

María de Lourdes, 16 años, Caracas

66 Debemos ser optimistas. Aunque es cierto que las cosas están peor cada día, creo que hay mucho que podemos hacer. Si todos trabajamos juntos podemos encontrar soluciones. Por ejemplo, los chicos de mi escuela están desarrollando un carro solar. El carro va a correr en una carrera de carros solares. Tal vez una compañía quiera fabricar el carro que gane la carrera. Usando nuestra creatividad, podemos buscar soluciones a los problemas de la contaminación. 99

Felipe, 15 años, Nueva York

66 ¡Podemos y debemos hacer algo por la Tierra! Botamos muchísima basura innecesariamente. Por eso, debemos reciclar. ¿Soluciones? Es nuestro deber reciclar, cuidar la Tierra: no botar papeles, no maltratar plantas ni animales... 99

Rosario, 16 años, San José

29 **Del colegio al trabajo** Answers will vary.

 Hablemos Imagina que eres asistente en el laboratorio de computadoras de lenguas de tu escuela y que tu compañero(a) de clase es el (la) jefe(a). Tu jefe(a) te está preguntando qué trabajos has completado. Responde diciéndole que terminarás el trabajo e indica cuándo lo harás.

MODELO —¿Has enviado una carta electrónica al director de la escuela?
—No. Enviaré una carta electrónica al director mañana.

30 **En mi cuaderno**

Escribamos Escribe un párrafo con tus predicciones para el futuro y tus ideas para mejorar el mundo. ¿Cómo crees que será el mundo dentro de diez años? Escoge un tema como la educación, el crimen, tu comunidad u otro tema.

¿Se te ha olvidado?
supporting opinions
Ver la página 74

Creo que el futuro será...

Lo bueno/malo es que...

Una cosa que cambiará mucho es... porque...

A los jóvenes les toca...

Communication for All Students

Kinesthetic Learners

28 Have students write a skit about the problems they discussed in this activity and the solutions they proposed. Then invite students to present their skits to the class.

Slower Pace

30 Before students begin writing, suggest that they organize their thoughts in the following manner. Have them create a list of five predictions and choose the best three. Students should then jot down three possible solutions or consequences for each prediction and choose the best two. Students now have the basic content of their paragraphs and can begin writing.

PANORAMA CULTURAL

¿Cómo te afecta la tecnología?

CD 3
Trs. 12–15

Para unos la tecnología es la solución y para otros...
¡es el problema! Estas tres personas nos contaron lo
que ellos piensan de la tecnología.

Alberto
Quito, Ecuador

"Bueno, la tecnología   CD 3 Tr. 13
que va avanzando poco a
poco aquí en el Ecuador
es muy importante, ya
que cada uno de nosotros
utilizamos la tecnología
prácticamente para
todo... Por ejemplo, en el
colegio, los microscopios
electrónicos; en la casa,
... el microondas, la televisión... Las computado-
ras facilitan el trabajo de
una persona, pero poco a
poco me parece que va a
ir teniendo sus desventa-
jas, de que puede ser que
después de algunos años
los robots reemplacen a
los hombres".

Geralberto
Ponce, Puerto Rico

"Nosotros hemos ido   CD 3 Tr. 14
adaptando la tecnología
en nuestro sistema
educativo, y en cierta
medida nos ha ido...
facilitando el trabajo a
los maestros, ya que,
pues, las clases se nos
hacen un poco más
fácil... Por ejemplo,
nosotros tenemos aquí...
computadoras".

Para pensar y hablar...

A. ¿Cuáles son las ventajas y las desventajas de la tecnología
según los entrevistados? ¿Con quién(es) estás de acuerdo?

B. ¿Qué efecto ha tenido la tecnología en tu vida? ¿Cómo
cambiará tu vida en el futuro?

Jennifer
San Diego, California

"Las computadoras y   CD 3 Tr. 15
mi cámara porque... ya
están poniendo que las
fotos estén en computa-
doras, entonces, yo no
voy a saber cómo hacer
las cosas... Tengo que
aprender cómo hacerlo
diferente cada día más...
¿Ventajas?, sería más
rápido para hacer las
cosas; ¿desventajas?, sería
más tiempo aprenderlo,
cómo hacerlo".

Cuaderno para
hispanohablantes,
pp. 14–15

Teaching Resources
p. 83

PRINT
▸ Video Guide, pp. 17, 19, 22
▸ Cuaderno de actividades, p. 36
▸ Cuaderno para hispanohablantes,
pp. 14–15

MEDIA
▸ One-Stop Planner
▸ Video Program,
Videocassette 1, 36:46–40:58
▸ Audio Compact Discs, CD 3,
Trs. 12–15
▸ Interactive CD-ROM Tutor, Disc 1

Presenting
Panorama cultural
Tell students to read the questions. Then play the video. Have
students answer the **Para pensar y hablar...** questions. Play
the video again and have students answer the **Preguntas.**

Preguntas

1. **¿Qué aspecto de la tecnología
mencionan todos los entrevistados?** (la computadora)

2. **¿Cuál de los entrevistados no
menciona ninguna desventaja?**
(Geralberto)

3. **¿Quién habla de la importancia
de la tecnología tanto en la
casa como en el colegio?**
(Alberto)

4. **¿Qué piensa Alberto de los
robots?** (que van a reemplazar a
los hombres)

Connections and Comparisons

Family Link
Have students make a list of all the ways they
use technology in a typical week. (cooking with
a microwave oven, listening to CDs, playing
videogames, using a computer or calculator)
Encourage them to ask parents or older relatives
how much of the technology on the list existed
when they were in high school. For technology

that was not available then, students should ask
the adults how they managed without it.

Thinking Critically
Analyzing Have students research problems
caused by some technological advances. (cars and
pollution, waste and contamination of ground
water) What problems does the local community
face and what is being done to solve them?

Prereading
Activities A, B, and C

Determining a Writer's Purpose
Make a list of some satirical comic strips, books, or television shows. *(Road Runner and Coyote, Peanuts, Doonesbury,* books by Dave Barry) Talk about why these are examples of satire. (They use exaggeration, irony, and other devices to make fun of human situations.)

Vamos a leer

La sátira

Vas a leer un cuento muy corto de Luis Britto García, un autor venezolano nacido en Caracas en 1940.

Estrategia para leer
As you read, think about the tone and purpose of the story. Stories are often meant to entertain, but they can have a serious, humorous, sad, mysterious, or sarcastic tone. The tone reveals the author's attitude toward the topic, the characters, and the audience. In addition to being entertaining, stories can reveal the author's views of society.

¡A comenzar!

A. La sátira se burla de las debilidades *(weaknesses)* humanas para inducir cambio social. El autor de una sátira usa el humor, la exageración y la ironía para llegar a su meta. Lee las oraciones que siguen. ¿Cuál de cada par crees que usaría el autor de una sátira?

1. a. La semana pasada trabajé mucho y no tuve oportunidad de pasar el rato con mis hijos.
  b. La semana pasada, salí a trabajar el lunes a las cinco de la mañana, dejando mi gato en el cuido del perro, y regresé el viernes a las cinco.

2. a. Me encanta esperar el autobús por media hora en la lluvia.
  b. El autobús llegó tarde y me cansé de esperar.

3. a. El pobre jefe estaba tan cansado de estar sentado en su oficina que echó una siesta a las diez, a las doce, a las dos y a las cuatro.

El monopolio de la moda

Luis Britto García

Ahora reposa y siéntate. Dentro de un instante entrará un vendedor a explicarte que tu televisor está pasado de moda y que debes comprar el nuevo modelo. En pocos minutos convendrás con él las condiciones del crédito, lograrás que te acepten el viejo modelo en el diez por ciento del precio y te dirás que en verdad una mañana de uso ya es suficiente. Al encender el nuevo aparato lo primero que notarás será que las modas del mediodía han cedido el paso a las modas de las dos de la tarde y que una tempestad de insultos te espera si sales a la calle con tus viejas corbatas de la una y veinticinco. Así atrapado, debes llamar por teléfono a la tienda para arreglar el nuevo crédito, a cuyos efectos intentarás dar en garantía el automóvil. El computador de la tienda registrará que el modelo es del día pasado y por lo tanto inaceptable.
Lo mejor que puedes hacer es llamar al

Connections and Comparisons

Literature Link
Luis Britto García (b. 1940, Caracas) studied law at the **Universidad Central de Venezuela.** He says: **"La biblioteca me promovió de indigente a potentado. Navegué entre ficheros con la misma irresponsabilidad con que hoy se deambula por las redes mediáticas".** *(The library took me from indigent to potentate. I navigated the card catalogue with the same abandon with which students today roam the communication networks.;* from "El Nacional On Line", *Cultura,* 12 de octubre de 1997.) Students may want to research Britto García in the library and on the Internet, and compare how much biographical material they are able to find in each place.

concesionario y
preguntarle sobre
los nuevos modelos de esta
mañana. El concesionario
te preguntará qué haces
llamándolo por ese teléfono
de modelo anticuado, y
le dirás es cierto, pero ya
desde hace media hora estás
sobregirado y no puedes cambiar de
mobiliario. No hay más
remedio que llamar al
Departamento de
Crédito, el cual acce-
derá a recibir el viejo
modelo por el uno
porciento de su precio a
condición de que constituyas
la garantía sobre los mobilia-
rios nuevos de las dos de la
tarde para así recibir el modelo
que elijas, de las diez, de las
once, de las doce, de la una, de las
dos y aun de las tres y media, éste
el más a la moda pero desde

b. El jefe estaba agobiado con
sus responsabilidades y se
sentía cansado.

B. Trabaja con un(a) compañero(a).
Hablen de sus respuestas de la
Actividad A. ¿Están de acuerdo
tú y tu compañero(a)? ¿Por qué
sí o por qué no?

¿Te acuerdas?

Use your background knowledge.
Think about what you know about a
topic to help you understand the
reading.

C. Lee el título del cuento. Usando
lo que sabes del tema, completa
las oraciones que siguen.
1. La moda...
   a. se queda igual de año en
   año
   (b.) cambia todo el tiempo
   c. cambia cada siete años
2. La palabra *monopolio* en el
título significa...
   (a.) el control exclusivo sobre
   algo
   b. un juego de mesa
   c. una ciudad

Al grano   See answers below.
D. Read the story quickly, keeping
the following questions in mind.
1. Who is the main character?
   a. the author
   b. the author's friend
   (c.) the reader
2. In general terms, what is the
story about?
   a. the main character's trip to
   the mall
   (b.) the need to keep up with
   changing fashions because
   of social expectations
   c. the character's eagerness to
   find out what the new fashions are

Reading
Activities D and E

Monitoring Comprehension
D. Have students work in groups of
three to read the story through for
the first time and get a general sense
of the meaning of each paragraph.
(Different groups can be assigned to
evaluate different paragraphs.) List
the results on the board and discuss
them briefly. Ask students if they can
tell that the story is a satire. If so,
how? (The author uses exaggeration
to create a humorous effect.)

Monitoring Reading
E. Assign a careful reading of **El
monopolio de la moda** for homework at the end of the first discussion period. During the second class
discussion, ask students to list clues
from the reading that convinced
them that the story is a satire, and
that told them what is being sati-
rized. (The author uses **nuevo** repeat-
edly throughout the piece. This
repetition satirizes consumerism.)

Communication for All Students

Slower Pace
In addition to analyzing tone, students should be
encouraged to use the reading tools they have
already developed: looking for context clues and
cognates, skimming, scanning, and looking at pictures. For example, students may not know exactly
what **concesionario** means, but they can guess by
looking at the surrounding words that it is a
noun that stands for a person in an official capac-
ity. The word **aparato** is close to *apparatus;* and
automóvil looks a lot like *automobile;* these are
cognates. Skimming, scanning, and looking at pictures will help students figure out that Britto
García is satirizing consumerism in an age of fast-
paced technological developments.

Postreading
Activities F and G

Appreciating a Writer's Craft

Why is satire a good vehicle for criticism? (Because its humor distances the reader from the judgment, which can be harsh; it is like a bitter pill with a sugar coating. In this way, the writer gets past the reader's defenses and is able to make his or her point effectively.)

Answers

E *Possible answers:*
1. de la una y veinticinco: Es exageración. ¡Una corbata que compraste hoy no puede estar pasada de moda!
2. garantizados todos hasta las cinco: Una garantía debe durar más de unas pocas horas.
3. de las…: Estas frases sugieren que hay modelos de algo para cada hora del día.

F *Possible answers:*
1. El lector tendrá que trabajar el resto de su vida para pagar la deuda.
2. No, no termina alegremente.
3. El problema está resuelto, pero la gente no se escapa del consumerismo.

G *Possible answers:*
1. humorístico
2. He makes a hypothetical reader his main character, to make the point that runaway consumerism affects everyone.
3. Consumerism. Britto García's point seems to be that we don't really need to buy the latest version of everything.
4. It is a witty yet critical commentary on a human phenomenon. It uses exaggeration and irony to accomplish its purpose.
5. Yes. His criticism is a good reminder to modern people that technology doesn't solve all our problems and, in fact, it creates some of its own.

E. Ahora lee el cuento con más cuidado. Con un(a) compañero(a), lean las frases e indiquen las palabras que expresan ironía, exageración o sátira. Expliquen sus selecciones.

   1. …una tempestad de insultos te espera si sales a la calle con tus viejas corbatas de la una y veinticinco.

   2. …cuando, a las cuatro, lleguen tu mujer y tus hijos cargados con los nuevos trajes y los nuevos juguetes, y tras ellos el nuevo vestuario y el nuevo automóvil y el nuevo teléfono y la nueva cocina, garantizados todos hasta las cinco…

   3. …para así recibir el modelo que elijas, de las diez, de las once, de las doce, de la una, de las dos y aun de las tres y media…

F. Trabaja con un(a) compañero(a).

   1. ¿Cómo termina el cuento?

   2. ¿Termina alegremente?

   3. ¿Resuelve el narrador el problema?

G. Work with a partner. Look at the story again, as needed, to answer the following questions.

   1. Which of the following words best describes the tone of the story? **serio, humorístico, romántico, misterioso**

   2. What reasons might the author have had for choosing this main character?

   3. What aspects of society do you think Luis Britto García criticizes in this story? What is his purpose in writing this story?

   4. What about this story makes it a satire?

   5. Do you agree with Britto García's observations about modern culture? Why or why not? See sample answers below.

> **Cuaderno para hispanohablantes,** pp. 11–14

> **Cuaderno de actividades,** p. 35, Acts. 20–21

---

luego al doble del precio aunque la inversión bien lo vale. Calculas que eso te da tiempo para llamar a que vengan a cambiar el congelador y la nevera, pero otra vez el maldito teléfono anticuado no funciona y minuto tras minuto el cuarto se va haciendo inhóspito y sombrío. Adivinas que ello se debe al indetenible cambio de los estilos y el pánico te irá ganando, e inútil será que en una prisa frenética te arranques la vieja corbata e incineres los viejos trajes y los viejos muebles de ayer y las viejas cosas de hace una hora, aún de sus cenizas fluye su irremediable obsolencia, el líquido pavor del que sólo escaparás cuando, a las cuatro, lleguen tu mujer y tus hijos cargados con los nuevos trajes y los nuevos juguetes, y tras ellos el nuevo vestuario y el nuevo automóvil y el nuevo teléfono y los nuevos muebles y el nuevo televisor y la nueva cocina, garantizados todos hasta las cinco, y el nuevo cobrador de ojos babosos que penetra sinuosamente en el apartamento, rompe tu tarjeta de crédito y te notifica que tienes comprometido tu sueldo de cien años, y que ahora pasas a los trabajos forzados perpetuos que corresponden a los deudores en los sótanos del Monopolio de la Moda.

Communication for All Students

Thinking Critically

Analyzing Encourage students to discuss what they think the tone of the story is. (satirical, humorous) Follow up with a discussion of types of satire. Satire ranges from mildly critical commentary to black humor. What sort of satire is the Britto García piece? Students may have differing opinions that make for a good class discussion.

In Activity G, some students may have said the tone was **serio** instead of **humorístico**. Examine reasons for the difference. (Satire often makes fun of quite serious situations. Students may have been struck more by the seriousness of the problem than by the humor.)

Vamos a escribir

¿Alguna vez has pensado que entendiste bien un tema, pero no pudiste encontrar una manera de organizar la información en la página? Con frecuencia, el tema mismo te sugerirá el orden en que debes presentar lo que ya sabes. En esta actividad, escribirás acerca de los adelantos tecnológicos que han afectado nuestras vidas, y aprenderás una manera sencilla de arreglar la información lógicamente.

Inventos importantes

Escribe una composición corta sobre los inventos que han afectado mucho nuestras vidas, e indica por qué estos inventos han sido importantes. Considera inventos que han tenido impacto en las siguientes áreas:

transporte   comunicaciones   educación   medicina   cocina   trabajo   ciencias

Estrategia para escribir

Listing in order of importance An easy way to write about inventions that have mattered in your life is to list them in the order of their importance. This gives your reader a clear idea of how you value each item. You can list things from the most to the least important or vice versa.

A. Preparación

1. Haz una lista preliminar de inventos que han afectado nuestras vidas.

2. Piensa en detalles interesantes sobre cada invento y apúntalos.

3. Al lado de cada uno, escribe tus impresiones del invento (por qué es importante, cómo ha cambiado nuestras vidas).

4. Busca, si quieres, una foto de cada invento.

B. Redacción

1. Escoge los ocho inventos más importantes de tu lista y escribe sobre ellos en orden de importancia. No te olvides de explicar por qué escogiste cada invento.

2. Incluye las fotos para hacer más interesante la presentación.

C. Evaluación

1. Lee lo que escribiste. ¿Está claro por qué escogiste cada invento? Si no, incluye más detalles.

2. ¿Escribiste correctamente todas las palabras? Búscalas en un diccionario para estar seguro(a). Si están incorrectas, corrígelas.

3. ¿Son visualmente impresionantes las fotos? ¿Ayudan tu descripción? Si no, omítelas o busca otras fotos más interesantes.

Apply and Assess

Postwriting

Additional Practice
Ask students to imagine that they have just produced one of the inventions they discussed in their paper. Have them prepare a short oral presentation on why they invented it and how it will benefit society. Encourage them to use the present perfect and future tenses.

Group Work
Have students write a skit about an inventor who has just invented a solar car that is less expensive to buy than any car on the market. Then have them present it to the class. They should include what the car looks like and how they were able to produce it so inexpensively.

Teaching Resources
p. 87

PRINT
▶ Lesson Planner, p. 15
▶ Cuaderno de actividades, pp. 145–156
▶ Cuaderno para hispanohablantes, p. 14
▶ Alternative Assessment Guide, p. 18
▶ Standardized Assessment Tutor, Chapter 3

MEDIA
▶ One-Stop Planner, Disc 1
  Test Generator, Chapter 3
▶ Interactive CD-ROM Tutor, Disc 1

Process Writing

Prewriting
Motivating Activity
Ask students to list and then discuss several important inventions that have affected the world in the last 50 years.

Writing
Slower Pace
Help students clarify what they are writing about by using their list to formulate a thesis statement.

Thinking Critically
Drawing Inferences Point out that many products today are invented by groups of people rather than individuals. Ask students why they think this is so. (Often a new invention requires the expertise of specialists in different areas. Also, research often involves expensive equipment that is beyond the means of just one person.)

Más práctica gramatical

CAPÍTULO 3

For **Más práctica gramatical**
Answer Transparencies, see the
Teaching Transparencies binder.

Primer paso **Objectives** Talking about what has happened; expressing and supporting a point of view; using conversational fillers

1 Graciela completó una encuesta *(poll)* sobre la tecnología y la vida diaria. Explica con qué frecuencia ella usa las cosas mencionadas en la encuesta. Basa tus respuestas en la información de la tabla, e incluye el complemento directo correcto. **(p. 71)**

MODELO   el microondas
—Lo usa todos los días.

	TODOS LOS DÍAS	A VECES	NUNCA
el microondas	✔		
1. el teléfono celular			✔
2. la computadora	✔		
3. el carro		✔	
4. la videocasetera		✔	
5. la máquina de fax			✔
6. la cámara		✔	
7. las autopistas		✔	
8. el transporte público	✔		
9. el contestador	✔		

2 Alberto está preparando un discurso *(speech)* sobre varios problemas ambientales. Escribe los lemas *(slogans)* que piensa usar. Usa la primera persona del plural del presente perfecto. **(p. 72)**

MODELO   contaminar las playas
—¡Hemos contaminado las playas!

1. tirar productos químicos a los ríos
2. no proteger las especies en peligro
3. no preocuparse por la capa de ozono
4. destruir las selvas tropicales
5. no conservar energía
6. desperdiciar los recursos naturales
7. no cuidar los bosques

Answers

1 1. No lo usa nunca./Nunca lo usa.
2. La usa todos los días.
3. Lo usa a veces.
4. La usa a veces.
5. No la usa nunca./Nunca la usa.
6. La usa a veces.
7. Las usa a veces.
8. Lo usa todos los días.
9. Lo usa todos los días.

2 1. ¡Hemos tirado productos químicos en los ríos!
2. ¡No hemos protegido las especies en peligro!
3. ¡No nos hemos preocupado por la capa de ozono!
4. ¡Hemos destruido las selvas tropicales!
5. ¡No hemos conservado energía!
6. ¡Hemos desperdiciado los recursos naturales!
7. ¡No hemos cuidado los bosques!

Grammar Resources for Chapter 3

The **Más práctica gramatical** activities are designed as supplemental activities for the grammatical concepts presented in the chapter. You might use them as additional practice, for review, or for assessment.

For more grammar presentation, review, and practice, refer to the following:

• Cuaderno de gramática

• Grammar Tutor for Students of Spanish

• Grammar Summary on pp. R25–R46
• Cuaderno de actividades
• Grammar and Vocabulary quizzes (Testing Program)
• Test Generator on the One-Stop Planner CD-ROM
• Interactive CD-ROM Tutor
• **Juegos interactivos** at <u>go.hrw.com</u>

STANDARDS: 1.2

3 Explica qué han hecho todos para ayudar a resolver los problemas ambientales. Usa el presente perfecto y sigue el modelo. **(p. 72)**

MODELO   **Sara/tomar el metro con más frecuencia**
           —Sara ha tomado el metro con más frecuencia.

1. (Yo)/comprar menos productos empacados
2. Mi club de ecología/poner muchos carteles en el colegio
3. Miguel/escribir un artículo para la revista *Ecoverde*
4. Los tíos de Miguel/abrir un restaurante vegetariano
5. ¿(Tú)/empezar a reciclar latas y periódicos?
6. Mis padres/usar el carro con menos frecuencia
7. Mis hermanos y yo/bañarnos rápidamente esta semana
8. Mi hermanito/ver un programa sobre la naturaleza en la tele

4 Jimena necesita escribir un trabajo sobre los problemas ambientales. Explica qué ha hecho ya, y qué no ha hecho todavía. Usa el presente perfecto y la información de la tabla. **(p. 72)**

MODELO   **Ya ha hablado con la directora del centro de reciclaje.**

	YA	TODAVÍA NO
hablar con la directora del centro de reciclaje	✔	
1. escribirles cartas a las organizaciones ambientales		✔
2. ver un video sobre el Amazonas	✔	
3. leer artículos sobre las especies en peligro	✔	
4. hacerle más preguntas al profesor de biología		✔
5. volver a la biblioteca por más libros	✔	
6. organizar sus ideas		✔
7. buscar más información en Internet	✔	

Answers

3 1. He comprado menos productos empacados.
2. Mi club de ecología ha puesto muchos carteles en el colegio.
3. Miguel ha escrito un artículo para la revista *Ecoverde*.
4. Los tíos de Miguel han abierto un restaurante vegetariano.
5. ¿Has empezado a reciclar latas y periódicos?
6. Mis padres han usado el carro con menos frecuencia.
7. Mis hermanos y yo nos hemos duchado rápidamente esta semana.
8. Mi hermanito ha visto un programa sobre la naturaleza en la tele.

4 1. Todavía no les ha escrito cartas a las organizaciones ambientales.
2. Ya ha visto un video sobre el Amazonas.
3. Ya ha leído artículos sobre las especies en peligro.
4. Todavía no le ha hecho más preguntas al profesor de biología.
5. Ya ha vuelto a la bibioteca por más libros.
6. Todavía no ha organizado sus ideas.
7. Ya ha buscado más información con la computadora.

Communication for All Students

Kinesthetic Learners

4 Have students stand in circles of ten students with one student always in the center. That student says something he or she has never done. **(Nunca he comido sushi. Nunca he visitado Puerto Rico.)** Those students in the circle who have done that action, as well as the person who said it, must find another place in the circle. One student will be left in the center and he or she then makes a similar statement.

For **Más práctica gramatical** Answer Transparencies, see the *Teaching Transparencies* binder.

Más práctica gramatical

5 Susi tiene tres años y siempre hace preguntas sobre qué son las cosas y cómo se usan. Escribe unas respuestas para Susi. Usa **lo que** para combinar las dos partes de las oraciones y sigue el modelo. **(p. 74)**

MODELO   **el teléfono celular/usar/para hablar por teléfono fuera de casa**
—**El teléfono celular es lo que usamos para hablar por teléfono fuera de casa.**

1. el contestador/usar/para dejar un recado
2. el televisor/poner/para ver programas
3. el aire acondicionado/poner/cuando tenemos calor
4. la calefacción/poner/cuando tenemos frío
5. la autopista/usar/cuando vamos en carro y tenemos prisa
6. el horno/usar/para preparar la cena
7. la luz/poner/para leer cuando es de noche
8. la computadora/usar/para...
9. la radio/poner/para...

Segundo paso   Objectives Talking about future events; talking about responsibilities

6 Tu clase de español hizo una lista de predicciones para el año 2030. Completa la lista de tus predicciones con el futuro de los verbos entre paréntesis. **(p. 79)**

1. Todos nosotros ══════ (saber) hablar tres o cuatro idiomas.
2. La gente ══════ (hacer) su trabajo en casa por Internet.
3. Muchos países ══════ (usar) energía solar para todo.
4. Y todos ══════ (tener) carros eléctricos.
5. Yo ══════ (inventar) un carro hecho de latas recicladas.
6. Por lo tanto, no ══════ (haber) problemas de contaminación.
7. Algunos de mis amigos ══════ (vivir) en otros planetas o en la Luna.
8. Ellos ══════ (ir) y ══════ (venir) de allí con unas naves espaciales super-rápidas.
9. Mi familia y yo ══════ (estar) aquí en la Tierra. Nosotros ══════ (tener) una casa subterránea.
10. Pero la distancia geográfica entre las personas ya no ══════ (ser) un problema.
11. La gente ══════ (poder) hablarse y verse instantáneamente con unos teléfonos-televisores especiales.

Answers

5
1. El contestador es lo que usamos para dejar un recado.
2. El televisor es lo que ponemos para ver programas.
3. El aire acondicionado es lo que ponemos cuando tenemos calor.
4. La calefacción es lo que ponemos cuando tenemos frío.
5. La autopista es lo que usamos cuando vamos en carro y tenemos prisa.
6. El horno es lo que usamos para preparar la cena.
7. La luz es lo que ponemos para leer cuando es de noche.
8. La computadora es lo que usamos para escribir composiciones.
9. La radio es lo que ponemos para escuchar música.

6
1. sabremos
2. hará
3. usarán
4. tendrán
5. inventaré
6. habrá
7. vivirán
8. irán, vendrán
9. estaremos, tendremos
10. será
11. podrá

Communication for All Students

Challenge
5 Have students come up with a list of verbs dealing with computer terminology that students might not know in Spanish. (to download, to surf, to click, to highlight, to crash, to save) Then have students use circumlocution to express these functions with **lo que.** The class will guess what is being described.

Pair Work
6 Divide the class into pairs. One student says something that the class has or has not done this year. (**Hemos aprendido mucho vocabulario.**) The partner then makes some type of response with the same verb in the future tense. (**Pero el próximo año aprenderemos mucho más.**)

7 Busca la palabra o frase que corresponde a cada definición. (pp. 73, 81)

a. crecer	**i.** la energía solar
b. descubrir	**j.** los aparatos eléctricos
c. la zona peatonal	**k.** el ayuntamiento
d. botar	**l.** el aire
e. el basurero	**m.** mejorar
f. el porvenir	**n.** sembrar
g. los carros eléctricos	**o.** crear
h. la fábrica	

1. la parte de la ciudad donde no se permiten carros
2. un medio de transporte que no usa gasolina
3. los contestadores, microondas y videocaseteras
4. la energía que se produce con la ayuda de la estrella más cercana a nuestro planeta
5. hacer o desarrollar
6. el futuro
7. lo que hacen las plantas y los niños
8. el lugar donde producen cosas como zapatos, carros o computadoras
9. lo que hacemos con las semillas y las plantas
10. lo que la gente hace con la basura
11. hacer cambios positivos
12. la acción de ver o aprender algo por primera vez
13. el lugar donde tiramos la basura
14. lo que respiramos
15. el edificio, que típicamente se encuentra en el centro, donde trabajan los funcionarios de la ciudad

Review and Assess

You may wish to assign the **Más práctica gramatical** activities as additional practice or homework after presenting material throughout the chapter. Assign Activity 1 after **Vocabulario** (p. 71), Activities 2–4 after **Gramática** (p. 72), Activity 5 after **Nota gramatical** (p. 74), Activity 6 after **Gramática** (p. 79), and Activity 7 after **Vocabulario** (p. 81). To prepare students for the **Paso** Quizzes and Chapter Test, have them do the **Más práctica gramatical** activities in the following order: complete Activities 1–5 before taking Quiz 3-1A or 3-1B and Activities 6–7 before taking Quiz 3-2A or 3-2B.

Answers
7
1. c
2. g
3. j
4. i
5. o
6. f
7. a
8. h
9. n
10. d
11. m
12. b
13. e
14. l
15. k

internet

MARCAR: go.hrw.com
PALABRA CLAVE:
WV3 CARACAS-3

CAPÍTULO 3

The **Repaso** reviews and integrates all four skills and culture in preparation for the Chapter Test.

Teaching Resources
pp. 92–93

PRINT
▶ Lesson Planner, p. 16
▶ Listening Activities, p. 21
▶ Video Guide, pp. 17, 19, 22
▶ Grammar Tutor for Students of Spanish, Chapter 3
▶ Cuaderno para hispanohablantes, pp. 11–15
▶ Standardized Assessment Tutor, Chapter 3

MEDIA
▶ One-Stop Planner
▶ Video Program, Videocassette 1, 40:59–41:48
▶ Audio Compact Discs, CD 3, Tr. 16
▶ Interactive CD-ROM Tutor, Disc 1

Teaching Suggestion

2 Before students answer the questions, have them decide whether each question is asking about past, present, or future events.

1 A veces la tecnología no funciona como lo esperamos. Escucha mientras seis personas hablan de los inventos que usan a diario y escoge el dibujo que corresponde a cada situación. Luego haz una lista de los inventos en el orden que se mencionan y da tu opinión sobre cada uno. Scripts and answers on p. 65H.

CD 3
Tr. 16

a.

b.

c.

d.

e.

f.

2 Con un(a) compañero(a), habla de las siguientes cosas. Tienen que pensarlo bien antes de responder. Tómate un poco de tiempo antes de dar tu opinión.

MODELO　　—¿Dónde vivirás cuando tengas cuarenta años?
　　　　　　—Bueno..., pues, me imagino que viviré en Barcelona. ¿Y tú?

1. ¿Cómo era la vida durante la época de tus abuelos?
2. ¿Cómo crees que será el mundo en 20 años?
3. ¿Han cambiado muchas cosas en los últimos 50 años? ¿Cómo?
4. ¿Cómo será la vida en el futuro?

3 Haz tu propio pronóstico del futuro con fechas y explica tus ideas. Usa tu imaginación y los siguientes conceptos para empezar.

MODELO　　La contaminación del agua
　　　　　　—No habrá contaminación del agua en el año 2525 porque...

| la contaminación del aire | los animales en peligro de extinción |
| los trenes y autobuses | el tráfico |

Apply and Assess

Auditory Learners
1 Encourage a group or class discussion about students' own frustrating or humorous experiences with technological devices. **¿Has tenido alguna vez un problema frustrante con la tecnología?** You may want to share an experience that you have had as well.

Additional Practice
3 Ask students to rewrite their sentences as though the events took place in the past.
(No ha habido contaminación del agua desde el año 2525.)

STANDARDS: 1.1, 1.2, 3.1

4 Usa las secciones culturales de este capítulo para contestar las siguientes preguntas.

1. ¿Quién es el héroe nacional de Venezuela, y por qué?
2. ¿Cuál es la industria más importante de Venezuela?
3. ¿Por qué son útiles los teléfonos celulares en Venezuela?
4. ¿Qué importancia tiene la tecnología en los países hispanohablantes?

See answers below.

 5 Mañana hay una fiesta de cumpleaños en tu casa y tienes que prepararla. Con dos compañeros(as) de clase, formen preguntas sobre lo que ya han hecho todos.

MODELO   —¿Ya has comprado comida?

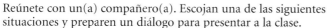

hacer el pastel de cumpleaños

conseguir música   limpiar la casa entera

poner el helado en el congelador

comprar los refrescos

mandar las invitaciones

6 ¿Crees que se puede aprender con programas de televisión? En tu opinión, ¿cómo será la televisión en el futuro? ¿Cómo debe ser? Lee este artículo y escribe un párrafo para expresar y apoyar tus opiniones sobre estos temas.

LA ESCUELA EN LA TELE

Los ministros de Educación de Argentina y España dieron a conocer un acuerdo por el cual todos los países de América Latina tendrán acceso al canal de televisión educativa que funcionará a través del satélite español de comunicación "Hispasat". Serán emitidos programas de divulgación científica, aspectos de los distintos países y temas relacionados con lo estrictamente escolar. Posible diálogo: Mamá: "¡Nene, otra vez en la tele!" "Pero má, estoy viendo la germinación de la mandioca en Venezuela y la recolección de bananas en el Ecuador!" En fin, con un click tendrás una enciclopedia en la pantalla.

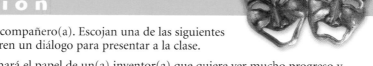
7 ## Situación

Reúnete con un(a) compañero(a). Escojan una de las siguientes situaciones y preparen un diálogo para presentar a la clase.

A. Uno(a) de Uds. hará el papel de un(a) inventor(a) que quiere ver mucho progreso y mucha tecnología nueva. La otra persona será un(a) ecólogo(a) que quiere proteger el medio ambiente.

B. Estás en un café con un(a) amigo(a). Están hablando de política, del amor o de la moda. El problema es que tienen opiniones casi opuestas *(opposite)*. En la conversación, traten de presentar y apoyar sus opiniones sin ofender a la otra persona. Usen expresiones adecuadas para ganarse tiempo cuando sea necesario.

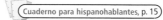 Cuaderno para hispanohablantes, p. 15

Apply and Assess

Group Work

4 Have students work in small groups to prepare an oral report in Spanish summarizing the cultural information presented in this chapter. You may want to refer them to the Location Opener on pages 62–65 for additional cultural information.

Pair Work

6 Have students peer-edit each other's paragraphs, first checking grammar and spelling. Then students reread to determine whether or not the writer has clearly expressed his or her opinions. Students can rewrite their paragraphs after discussing their peer editor's comments.

Teaching Suggestions

5 Instruct students to ask their two partners the questions. Their partners always answer negatively, saying they will do the task later.

7 Suggest to students that they look over all of the information in the chapter on culture and the environment. For Part A, you might suggest that they refer to their **Vamos a escribir** assignment to refresh their memory about inventions.

📁 Portfolio

6 **Written** You may want to have students include their paragraphs in their Portfolios. For Portfolio suggestions, see *Alternative Assessment Guide,* page 18.

Answers

4 1. Simón Bolívar es el héroe nacional porque liberó el país de los españoles en 1821.
2. El petróleo
3. Es un medio de comunicación para la gente que no tiene otro servicio telefónico.
4. *Sample answer:* Contribuye a los adelantos en muchos aspectos de la vida y mejora la calidad de vida.

A ver si puedo...

Teacher Note
This page is intended to help students prepare for the Chapter Test. It is a brief checklist of the major points covered in the chapter. The students should be reminded that this is only a checklist and does not necessarily include everything that will appear on the Chapter Test.

Can you talk about what has happened? p. 72

1 Mira estas fotos de Caracas de la década de 1920. Compáralas con las fotos en las páginas 78 y 91. Explica cómo ha cambiado Caracas. *See answers below.*

Can you express and support a point of view? p. 74

2 Mañana en la clase de español habrá una reunión para hablar de los siguientes temas. Expresa y apoya tus opiniones para estar bien preparado(a). *Answers will vary.*

1. programas de televisión violentos
2. teléfonos celulares
3. automóviles solares o eléctricos
4. preparar toda la comida en el microondas
5. la contaminación del aire en las ciudades grandes

Can you use conversational fillers? p. 75

3 A veces no sabes qué decir y tienes que usar palabras como **este, eh, bueno...** ¿Cómo respondes tú en estas situaciones? *Answers will vary.*

1. Tu hermanito te pide tu nuevo disco compacto.
2. Tu mejor amigo quiere tu opinión sobre su nueva chaqueta.
3. La maestra de física te pregunta si puedes explicar la Teoría de la Relatividad.
4. Quieres invitar a salir a alguien y estás nerviosísimo(a).

Can you talk about future events? p. 78

4 Haz pronósticos sobre tus familiares, tus compañeros y la gente famosa. *Answers will vary.*

1. ¿Cuántas horas tendrán que estudiar tú y tus compañeros(as) para sacar buenas notas?
2. ¿Cuántas horas dormirán tus padres esta noche?
3. ¿Adónde viajará tu cantante favorito(a) durante sus próximas vacaciones?
4. ¿Trabajarás o estudiarás después de terminar la secundaria?
5. ¿Te casarás pronto? ¿Nunca te casarás?

Can you talk about responsibilities? p. 81

5 Crea lemas para un club ecológico. Piensa en tres lemas para inspirar a la gente a mejorar el medio ambiente, a salvar la tierra y a cuidar la ciudad. *Answers will vary.*

MODELO ¡Nos toca a nosotros salvar las ballenas!

Review and Assess

Family Link

1 Have students interview older family members or friends about the changes that have taken place in the community in their lifetime. Students can present their findings to the class using old family photos or drawings to illustrate the changes.

Visual Learners

5 Have groups of students plan an environmental campaign and create three posters that illustrate and explain their **lemas.** Display students' work in an appropriate place in the school.

Answers
1 *Sample answer:*
Caracas ha crecido mucho. Han construido muchos rascacielos. El tráfico ha empeorado y también la contaminación. Ya no hay tantos techos rojos, pero sí hay muchas antenas parabólicas. Es una ciudad más moderna.

Primer paso

Advantages and disadvantages of modern life

a la vez	at the same time
adaptarse	to adapt
los adelantos	advances
la antena parabólica	satellite dish
la autopista	freeway, highway
la computadora	computer
el contestador	answering machine
la desventaja	disadvantage
empeorar	to get worse
en seguida	right away, immediately
enviar una carta electrónica	to send an e-mail
la fotocopiadora (a colores)	(color) photocopier
hacer trabajos	to write papers
cocinar en el horno de microondas	to cook in the microwave oven
hoy (en) día	nowadays
informar	to inform
manejar	to drive
navegar por Internet	to surf the Internet
el rascacielos	skyscraper
el siglo	century
la tecnología	technology
el teléfono celular	cellular phone
el tráfico	traffic
la ventaja	advantage
la vida diaria	daily life
la videocasetera	videocassette player

Talking about what has happened

...ha cambiado mucho.	... has changed a lot.
...ha empeorado bastante.	... has gotten quite a bit worse.
Mucha gente ha venido de fuera.	Many people have come from outside.

Around town

el ayuntamiento	town hall
el basurero	trash can
la calidad del aire	air quality
crecer (zc)	to grow

establecer (zc) una zona peatonal	to set up a pedestrian zone
la fábrica	factory
mejorar	to improve
sembrar (ie)	to plant

Expressing and supporting a point of view

Creo que vale la pena...	I think it's worth it ...
Es cierto que...	It's true that ...
Lo que es importante es...	What's important is ...
Lo que noto es que...	What I notice is that ...
Me imagino que...	I imagine that ...
Me parece que...	It seems to me that ...
pero por otro lado...	but on the other hand ...
Se me hace que...	It seems to me ...
Ten en cuenta que...	Keep in mind that ...

Using conversational fillers, See p. 75.

Segundo paso

Talking about future events, See p. 78.

Technology

el aparato eléctrico	electrical appliance
botar	to throw out
el carro eléctrico	electric car
desarrollar	to develop
descubrir	to discover
destruir	to destroy
la energía nuclear	nuclear energy
la energía solar	solar energy
el porvenir	future

Talking about responsibilities

Deben...	They should ...
Es nuestra responsabilidad...	It's our responsibility ...
Es nuestro deber...	It's our duty ...
Estamos obligados a...	We're obligated to ...
Hay que...	It's necessary ...
Nos toca a nosotros...	It's up to us ...

Vocabulario

CAPÍTULO 3

 Circumlocution
Have students work in pairs. List the technology-related vocabulary from Chapter 3, and have one student from each pair choose a word. The other student tries to find out what it is by asking questions. **Estoy pensando en una cosa. / ¿Es una cosa para cocinar? / (Sí.)... / ¿Es el horno de microondas? / ¡Sí! / Or: ¿Te ayuda a contestar el teléfono? / (Sí.)... / ¿Es el contestador? / ¡Sí!** Encourage students to go over the words on the list and make vocabulary notes if they wish. Once a correct guess is made, partners should switch roles.

Chapter 3 Assessment

▸ **Testing Program**
Chapter Test, pp. 53–58
 Audio Compact Discs, CD 3, Trs. 19–20
Speaking Test, p. 296

▸ **Alternative Assessment Guide**
Portfolio Assessment, p. 18
Performance Assessment, p. 32
CD-ROM Assessment, p. 46

▸ **Interactive CD-ROM Tutor, Disc 1**
 ¡A hablar!
¡A escribir!

▸ **Standardized Assessment Tutor**
Chapter 3

▸ **One-Stop Planner, Disc 1**
Test Generator
Chapter 3

Review and Assess

Game
CEREBRO On a transparency, draw a large square and divide it evenly into a grid of 64 squares, eight to a side. Write the letters A–H along one side, and the numbers 1–8 along the other. Write 32 chapter vocabulary items in 32 randomly selected squares. Write the English equivalents in the remaining squares, selecting them at random as well. Cover each square with a small square of heavy construction paper. Students take turns trying to match up Spanish and English equivalent pairs. If a student identifies the squares containing a pair, give him or her the paper squares. If the items revealed do not match, cover them again and move on to the next student. The student with the most squares at the end of the game wins.

Capítulo 4: Alrededor de la mesa
Chapter Overview

De antemano pp. 98–100	*El anillo*			

	FUNCTIONS	**GRAMMAR**	**VOCABULARY**	**RE-ENTRY**
Primer paso pp. 101–104	• Talking about how food tastes, p. 101 • Talking about unintentional events, p. 103	• **se** + indirect object pronoun, p. 103	• Food items, p. 102	• **-ísimo(a)** with adjectives and adverbs (**Capítulo 8, II**) • Indirect object pronouns (**Capítulo 9, I**) • Expressions for making excuses (**Capítulo 5, II**)

¡Adelante! pp. 106–107	*Platos favoritos*			

Segundo paso pp. 108–110	• Asking for help and requesting favors, p. 108	• **por** and **para**, p. 108 • Double object pronouns, p. 110	• Specialty shops, p. 109	• Informal commands (**Capítulo 5, II**) • Formal commands (**Capítulo 9, II**)

Vamos a leer pp. 112–114	**Una causa picante**	**Reading Strategy:** Identifying chronological information
Vamos a escribir p. 115	**Tu receta favorita**	**Writing Strategy:** Making a writing plan

Más práctica gramatical	**pp. 116–119** **Primer paso,** pp. 116–117	**Segundo paso,** pp. 118–119	
Review pp. 120–123	**Repaso,** pp. 120–121	**A ver si puedo...,** p. 122	**Vocabulario,** p. 123

CULTURE

• **A lo nuestro,** Common expressions with **se** + indirect object pronoun, p. 103
• **Nota cultural, La sobremesa,** p. 104
• **Encuentro cultural, Personal que presta servicios,** p. 105

• **Nota cultural,** Traditional Venezuelan foods, p. 108
• **Nota cultural,** Holiday foods in Venezuela, p. 109
• **Panorama cultural, ¿Cuál es tu plato favorito?,** p. 111
• **Tiras cómicas,** pp. 101, 104

Capítulo 4: Alrededor de la mesa
Chapter Resources

Lesson Planning

 One-Stop Planner

Lesson Planner with Substitute Teacher Lesson Plans, pp. 17–21, 68

Student Make-Up Assignments
- Make-Up Assignment Copying Masters, Chapter 4

Listening and Speaking

Listening Activities
- Student Response Forms for Listening Activities, pp. 27–29
- Additional Listening Activities 4-1 to 4-6, pp. 31–33
- Additional Listening Activities (song), p. 34
- Scripts and Answers, pp. 116–120

Video Guide
- Teaching Suggestions, pp. 24–25
- Activity Masters, pp. 26–28
- Scripts and Answers, pp. 93–94, 115–116

Activities for Communication
- Communicative Activities, pp. 13–16
- Realia and Teaching Suggestions, pp. 60–62
- Situation Cards, pp. 95–96

Reading and Writing

Reading Strategies and Skills Handbook, Chapter 4

¡Lee conmigo! 3, Chapter 4

Cuaderno de actividades, pp. 37–48

Grammar

Cuaderno de gramática, pp. 28–36

Grammar Tutor for Students of Spanish, Chapter 4

Assessment

Testing Program
- Grammar and Vocabulary Quizzes, **Paso** Quizzes, and Chapter Test, pp. 67–80
- Score Sheet, Scripts and Answers, pp. 81–87

Alternative Assessment Guide
- Portfolio Assessment, p. 19
- Performance Assessment, p. 33
- CD-ROM Assessment, p. 47

Student Make-Up Assignments
- Alternative Quizzes, Chapter 4

Standardized Assessment Tutor
- Reading, pp. 13–15
- Writing, p. 16
- Math, pp. 25–26

Native Speakers

Cuaderno para hispanohablantes, pp. 16–20

 Online Activities
- Juegos interactivos
- Actividades Internet

 Video Program
- Videocassette 2
- Videocassette 5 (captioned version)

 Audio Compact Discs
- Textbook Listening Activities, CD 4, Tracks 1–18
- Additional Listening Activities, CD 4, Tracks 23–28
- Assessment Items, CD 4, Tracks 19–22

Interactive CD-ROM Tutor, Disc 1

Teaching Transparencies
- Situations 4-1 to 4-2
- **Más práctica gramatical** Answers
- **Cuaderno de gramática** Answers

 One-Stop Planner CD-ROM

Use the **One-Stop Planner CD-ROM with Test Generator** to aid in lesson planning and pacing.

For each chapter, the **One-Stop Planner** includes:
- Editable lesson plans with direct links to teaching resources
- Printable worksheets from resource books
- Direct launches to the HRW Internet activities
- Video and audio segments
- Test Generator
- Clip Art for vocabulary items

Capítulo 4: Alrededor de la mesa

Projects

Una degustación de comida venezolana

In this project students plan a tasting party of Venezuelan dishes (degustación de comida venezolana). They prepare dishes at home and sample them in class. During the party, students may speak only Spanish.

MATERIALS

✂ **Students may need**

- Paper plates
- Paper napkins
- Paper cups
- Poster board
- Plastic utensils
- Markers

RECIPES

Venezuela's national dish, **pabellón criollo,** is a main course of shredded beef, or **carne mechada,** served with rice, beans, **arepas,** and **plátanos fritos.**

SUGGESTED SEQUENCE

1. Students work in groups of four. Each group selects a recipe to prepare for the class. They might consult an international cookbook or use the Internet.

2. Students divide the responsibilities for preparing their dish and decide how they will accomplish the shopping, preparation, and cooking. Dishes are to be prepared outside of class. Students need to make only enough for everyone to have a taste. Make sure everyone does not bring the same dish.

3. Each group also makes a small sign indicating the name of its dish.

4. At the **degustación,** each group serves its dish and answers questions about how it is made and what is in it. Students sample different dishes and discuss them with classmates.

5. If possible, videotape the **degustación** and play the tape later for the class.

6. Students straighten up the classroom after they have finished.

GRADING THE PROJECT

Suggested point distribution: (total = 100 points)
Preparing food...50
Use of Spanish at the **degustación** 50

Games

Un cuento

In this game students create a story while they practice specific grammar structures or vocabulary. The game may be played at any time during the chapter.

Preparation Divide the class into two teams and announce a category. (for example, expressions to ask for help or request favors) (**¿Me podrías ayudar a...?, Hazme el favor de..., ¿Sería Ud. tan amable de...?**) Tell students that they may use the words or expressions in the category more than once.

Procedure The first player on Team A begins to tell a story. It can be on any topic, but the player must use the type of expression stipulated. Tell students it may take several sentences to work the phrase in. (**Un día un muchacho estaba hablando con un amigo. Dijo, "Por favor, ayúdame con el carro".**) The first player on Team B continues the story. (**"¿Yo?" dijo su amigo. "¿Serías tan amable de decirme qué quieres?"**) Play then passes to the second player of each team. If a player cannot use an expression, go quickly to the next player. Give one point for each expression used.

La lista más larga

This game adds fun to any vocabulary review. It is especially helpful with words of a specific category, such as food.

Preparation Decide which groups of words you would like to review. You might choose five or six categories.

Procedure Divide students into groups of four or five. Ask them to write as many words as possible in a particular category. (foods, colors, irregular past participles) Set a short time period—not more than one minute per category. Give 10 points to the group with the longest list of correct words. Give other groups one point for each correct word on their list that is not on the longest list.

COMMUNITY LINK

Invite native Spanish speakers from other classes or from the community to the *degustación.* This will enhance conversational opportunities for the class.

Storytelling

Mini-cuento

This story accompanies Teaching Transparency 4-2. The mini-cuento can be told and retold in different formats, acted out, written as dictation, and read aloud to give students additional opportunities to practice all four skills. The following story recounts what food was prepared for a special birthday.

La fiesta del abuelo Luis

Ayer fue el cumpleaños del abuelo Luis. Todos los parientes y amigos de la familia le prepararon un plato especial para su fiesta. Su cuñada María fue a la carnicería y pidió carne de cerdo. Ella le preparó chuletas con ensalada mixta. Su hermana Chelo fue a la lechería para comprar crema y leche. Ella le hizo dulce de lechosa. Su amigo Carlos fue a la panadería porque le preparó arepas. Su prima Lisa fue con su hijo Jorge a la pastelería. Ella no tuvo tiempo de preparar un postre. La dependiente le recomendó comprar la torta de chocolate. Su sobrino Paco no sabe cocinar. Él fue a la frutería y compró melocotones, plátanos y piñas. Llevó ensalada de frutas. Rafael, el hermano de Luis, fue a la pescadería para comprar pargo. Él le cocinó un delicioso huachinango que es el plato favorito del abuelo Luis.

¡Al abuelo Luis le encantó toda la comida deliciosa!

Traditions

Festivales

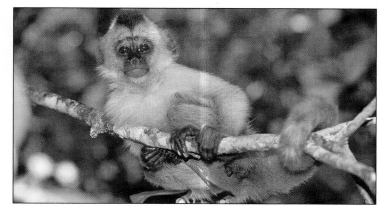

December 28, known as **los Santos inocentes,** is a celebration that has evolved into a day of playing tricks on others. The **Locos** or **Mamarrachos** dress in ragged clothing and cover their faces with masks or paint so as not to be recognized. In some areas, this day is celebrated as the **Fiesta del mono.**

There is a comic dance led by someone dressed as a monkey, and everyone joins in. Other celebrations on this date include **el gobierno de las mujeres,** when women dress as men and take over the duties of government and heads of households while the men occupy themselves with the care of the children and the home. Discuss with your students what celebrations in the United States are similar to the **Santos inocentes.** What holidays involve animals?

Receta

Flat breads are the mainstay of Latin American diets, and in Venezuela the two most popular are **arepas** *and* **cachapas,** *both made from corn.* **Arepas,** *like Mexican tortillas, are made with corn flour and are formed by hand. They are thicker, however, and contain cheese.* **Cachapas** *are made with fresh or canned corn and milk, and are cooked more like a pancake. They are served hot, sometimes topped with feta or Munster cheese.*

CACHAPAS

para 8 personas

3 tazas de maíz tierno (se puede usar de lata pero hay que escurrir bien el agua)

1 cucharadita de sal

1 taza de leche

1 cucharada de azúcar

1 huevo

6 cucharadas de harina

mantequilla para freír

Combine todos los ingredientes menos la mantequilla en una licuadora y licúelos. La mezcla debe quedar espesa. Eche tres cucharadas de la mezcla en una sartén untada con mantequilla, y cocine la masa a fuego mediano hasta que se formen burbujas encima. Dele la vuelta y cocínela por el otro lado. Cada vez que cocine más cachapas unte la sartén con mantequilla. Sirva las cachapas calientes. Hace aproximadamente dieciséis.

Capítulo 4: Alrededor de la mesa
Technology

Video Program

Videocassette 2, Videocassette 5 (captioned version)
See Video Guide, pages 23–28.

Dramatic episode • ¡Qué sabroso!

Javier and Zoraida are in the kitchen, where their father is preparing **paella.** Javier tells them about Mexican **mole,** a spicy sauce made with chocolate. Sergio shows up with photographs from Mexico. Zoraida teases Javier about Alejandra, but when she sees the picture of Carlos, she ignores them completely.

¡Adelante! • Platos favoritos

Venezuelans talk about their favorite foods, various traditional holiday dishes, and what they eat to stay healthy, as well as where they like to go to buy food and the tradition of the **sobremesa.**

¿Cuál es tu plato favorito?

People from Spanish-speaking countries talk about their favorite foods.

Videoclip

• **Aceite S y S®:** advertisement about a couple stranded in the middle of the ocean with only a bottle of cooking oil.

Interactive CD-ROM Tutor

The **Interactive CD-ROM Tutor** contains videos, interactive games, and activities that provide students an opportunity to practice and review the material covered in Chapter 4.

Activity	Activity Type	Pupil's Edition Page
1. Así se dice	¿Cuál es?	p. 101
2. Vocabulario	Imagen y sonido ¡Exploremos! ¡Identifiquemos!	p. 102
3. Así se dice	Patas arriba	p. 103
4. Gramática	¿Qué falta?	p. 103
5. Vocabulario	¡Super memoria!	p. 109
6. Gramática	¡Presta el oído!	p. 110
Panorama cultural	¿Cuál es tu plato favorito? ¡A escoger!	p. 111
¡A hablar!	*Guided recording*	pp. 120–121
¡A escribir!	*Guided writing*	pp. 120–121

Teacher Management System
Logging In

Logging in to the *¡Ven conmigo!* TMS is easy. Upon launching the program, simply type "admin" in the password area of the log-in screen and press RETURN. Log on to **www.hrw.com/CDROMTUTOR** for a detailed explanation of the Teacher Management System.

To preview all resources available for this chapter, use the **One-Stop Planner CD-ROM**, Disc 1.

Internet Connection

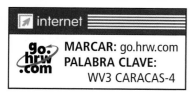

MARCAR: go.hrw.com
PALABRA CLAVE:
WV3 CARACAS-4

*Have students explore the **go.hrw.com** Web site for many online resources covering all chapters. All Chapter 4 resources are available under the keyword **WV3 CARACAS-4**. Interactive games help students practice the material and provide them with immediate feedback. You will also find a printable worksheet that provides Internet activities that lead to a comprehensive online research project.*

Juegos interactivos

You can use the interactive activities in this chapter

- to practice grammar, vocabulary, and chapter functions
- as homework
- as an assessment option
- as a self-test
- to prepare for the Chapter Test

Actividades Internet

Students search the Web for recipes from Venezuela. They find foods that sound interesting and then describe the dish, its ingredients, and where to buy those ingredients.

- To prepare students for the **Hoja de actividades,** review the **¡Adelante!** interviews. You might also ask if they know of any Venezuelan foods already.
- After they have finished the activity sheet, have students post their favorite Venezuelan recipe on a Web site. Suggest they make a dish to share with the class. Tell them to look for substitutes if they cannot find all the Venezuelan ingredients.

Proyecto

Have students choose one or two favorite meals. Ask them to describe the dishes and post the recipes on a personal Web site. They should list the ingredients and cooking instructions and explain where to buy the ingredients. Have students choose one of their classmates' recipes to try to prepare at home.

STANDARDS: 1.2, 1.3, 3.2, 5.1, 5.2

CAPÍTULO 4   TECHNOLOGY   95F

Capítulo 4: Alrededor de la mesa
Textbook Listening Activities Scripts

Primer paso

6 p. 101

1. Esto tiene sabor a grasa y le falta sal. ¿No podemos comer una ensalada o algo así? Tenemos lechuga y tomates. En realidad no me gusta el pollo frito.

2. Mamá, quiero que nos prepares un pastel mañana para mi cumpleaños. Sabe riquísimo tu pastel de chocolate. No hay nada en este mundo como tus pasteles.

3. La ensalada mixta que nos preparó Martín fue muy buena. Estuvo deliciosa, ¿no? Los vegetales estaban muy frescos. ¿Sabes dónde los compró?

4. ¡Guácala! No me prepares pescado, por favor. No es mi plato favorito. No me gusta para nada el pescado. No sé por qué. ¿Te gusta a ti?

5. El flan se hace con huevos y azúcar. No es difícil de preparar. Si quieres, te muestro cómo se prepara. ¿Quieres hacerlo esta noche?

Answers to Activity 6
1. una queja   3. un cumplido   5. un comentario neutro
2. un cumplido   4. una queja

11 p. 103

1. Lo siento, señora, pero, ¿está bien si le traigo la tarea mañana por la mañana? Estaba muy ocupada ayer y se me olvidó hacer la tarea. O si quiere, se la puedo llevar a su casa esta noche...

2. Ay, ¡qué frustración! ¿Ahora qué voy a hacer? Se me rompieron los anteojos y no puedo ver. ¿Cómo voy a ver lo que escribe en la pizarra el profesor?

3. Mamá se va a enojar conmigo. Se me perdió Julián en el almacén. ¿Dónde estará? Voy a llamar al almacén a ver si lo han visto. ¡Pobre Julián!

4. ¡No lo creo! Se me quedó el boleto en casa y ahora tengo que ir a buscarlo. Y no tengo tiempo de volver a casa por mi boleto. Voy a llamar a mi hermana. Tal vez ella me lo pueda traer.

5. ¡Ay, ay, ay! Mi esposa va a enojarse. Se me cayeron los platos, y son los platos que le dio su abuela. ¿Por qué dejaron allí los niños sus juguetes?

Answers to Activity 11
1. Beatriz   3. ningún dibujo   5. Pablo
2. Diana   4. Felipe

16 p. 107

1. Hay muchos platos que me gustan pero lo que me gusta más es la comida italiana. No soy italiana pero me gustaría visitar Italia algún día.

2. Mis padres, mis hermanas y yo casi nunca estamos en casa a la hora de comer. Todos trabajamos y por eso no tenemos mucho tiempo de estar juntos.

3. Conozco varios lugares donde puedo comprar frutas y vegetales. Hay muchos lugares donde se pueden comprar frutas y vegetales muy frescos en mi ciudad.

4. A mí me parece que los venezolanos comemos un poco de todo. Mucha gente ha venido a Venezuela de otros países. Por eso hay una gran variedad de comidas aquí.

5. Voy a preparar algo especial esta noche y no tengo todo lo que necesito en casa. Por eso hay varias cosas que necesito del mercado. ¿Puedes traérmelas?

6. Mi familia y yo hablamos de lo que pasa en nuestras vidas después de comer. Podemos hablar de cualquier cosa cuando estamos juntos. Me gusta discutir las cosas con ellos; somos muy unidos y nos llevamos bien.

Answers to Activity 16
1. Gisela
2. Gisela
3. Yamilé
4. Gisela
5. la mamá de Guillermo
6. Guillermo

The following scripts are for the listening activities found in the *Pupil's Edition*. For Student Response Forms, see *Listening Activities*, pages 27–29. To provide students with additional listening practice, see *Listening Activities*, pages 31–33.

One-Stop Planner CD-ROM

To preview all resources available for this chapter, use the **One-Stop Planner CD-ROM**, Disc 1.

Segundo paso

18 p. 108

1. — Disculpe usted, señor. ¿Podría usted decirme dónde queda el Palacio Nacional? Soy turista y no conozco muy bien la ciudad.
   — Sí. Está a cinco kilómetros de aquí, en la calle Santiago. Puede tomar un taxi o el autobús.

2. — ¿Me podría traer un café, por favor? Y hágame el favor de traerme un poco de leche también.
   — Sí, señor, con mucho gusto. Se lo traigo en seguida.

3. — Quiero el bistec a la parrilla. Y de postre, por favor tráigame un helado de chocolate.
   — Lo siento, señora, no tenemos helado esta noche pero tenemos pastel de chocolate y flan. ¿Qué se le ofrece, señora?

4. — Hágame el favor de darme una mesa cerca de la ventana, señor. Me gusta ver todo lo que pasa afuera en la calle.
   — Sí, señora. Por aquí, por favor. Tenemos la mesa perfecta para usted, cerca de una ventana grande.

5. — Perdone usted, señorita. Estoy de visita aquí en esta ciudad. ¿Sería tan amable de decirme dónde hay un buen restaurante?
   — Sí, señor. Vaya usted al Restaurante El Increíble. Es el mejor de la ciudad. Algunos de los platos son un poco extraños pero cocinan unas cosas exquisitas allí.

Answers to Activity 18

1. un transeúnte	3. el dependiente	5. un transeúnte
2. el cliente	4. el dependiente	

22 p. 110

1. ¿Dónde le puedo comprar un pastel a mi mamá? Hoy es su cumpleaños y quiero darle una fiesta de sorpresa.

2. ¿Quieres que te traiga un poco de carne de la carnicería? Necesitas más carne si quieres hacer pabellón criollo, y la carnicería está cerca.

3. ¿Dónde vas a comprarme los camarones? Los necesito para la paella que voy a preparar el domingo antes de la fiesta.

4. ¿Serías tan amable de traerme leche de la lechería? Quiero hacer flan pero no puedo si no tengo leche. La lechería está cerca, en la Calle Campos.

Answers to Activity 22

1. b   2. a   3. b   4. a

Repaso

1 p. 120

1. Coman los mejores mariscos de Caracas. Vendemos las mejores ostras y almejas de la ciudad. Estamos abiertos desde las once de la mañana hasta las diez de la noche.

2. ¿Qué desea usted? ¿Un buen bistec? ¿Chorizos ricos o chuletas de cerdo? No espere un momento más para visitar nuestra tienda. Tenemos esto y mucho más para usted y su familia.

3. La comida natural que ustedes buscan está aquí, señores y señoras. Melocotones, patillas, piñas... llenos de las vitaminas que necesitan para una dieta saludable... Cómprenlos aquí.

4. Señoras y señores, ¿se les ha olvidado algo? ¿El cumpleaños de su esposo o de su hija? ¿El aniversario de bodas de su mejor amigo? No se preocupen. Estamos listos para ayudarles con lo que necesiten para cualquier ocasión.

Answers to Repaso Activity 1

1. Corresponde.
2. Corresponde.
3. Corresponde.
4. No corresponde, porque no hay una tienda de regalos en el dibujo.

Capítulo 4: Alrededor de la mesa
Suggested Lesson Plans 50-Minute Schedule

Day 1

CHAPTER OPENER 5 min.
- Focusing on Outcomes, ATE, p. 97
- Present Culture Note, Background Information, Thinking Critically or Geography Link, ATE, pp. 96–97.

DE ANTEMANO 40 min.
- Presenting **De antemano** and Preteaching Vocabulary, ATE, p. 98
- Present Language Notes and Culture Note, ATE, p. 99.
- Do the Thinking Critically Activity, ATE, p. 99.
- Activities 1–5 and Comprehension Check, ATE, p. 100

Wrap-Up 5 min.
- Do the Additional Practice for Activity 5, ATE, p. 100.

Homework Options
Cuaderno de actividades, p. 37, Activities 1–2

Day 2

PRIMER PASO
Quick Review 5 min.
- Check homework.
- Bell Work, ATE, p. 101

Así se dice, p. 101 25 min.
- Presenting **Así se dice**, ATE, p. 101
- Review **¿Te acuerdas?,** p. 101.
- **Más práctica gramatical,** p. 116, Activity 1
- Do Activity 6 with the Audio CD, p. 101.
- Do Activities 7–8, p. 101.

Vocabulario, p. 102 15 min.
- Presenting **Vocabulario**, ATE, p. 102
- Present **También se puede decir...,** p. 102.

Wrap-Up 5 min.
- Do the Visual Learners Suggestion, ATE, p. 101.

Homework Options
Cuaderno de actividades, pp. 38–39, Activities 3–5
Cuaderno de gramática, pp. 28–30, Activities 1–5

Day 3

PRIMER PASO
Quick Review 10 min.
- Check homework.

Vocabulario, p. 102 15 min.
- Do the Auditory Learners Suggestion, ATE, p. 102.
- Have students do Activity 9 in pairs and Activity 10 in groups, p. 102.

Así se dice/Gramática, p. 103 20 min.
- Presenting **Así se dice** and **Gramática,** ATE, p. 103
- Present **A lo nuestro,** p. 103.
- Present the Language Note, ATE, p. 103.

Wrap-Up 5 min.
- Do the Thinking Critically Activity, ATE, p. 103.

Homework Options
Cuaderno de actividades, pp. 40–41, Activities 6–8
Cuaderno de gramática, pp. 30–32, Activities 6–10

Day 4

PRIMER PASO
Quick Review 10 min.
- Check homework.
- Review se + indirect object pronouns.

Gramática, p. 103 30 min.
- Do Activity 11 with the Audio CD, p. 103.
- Do Activity 12, p. 104.
- Review **¿Te acuerdas?,** then do Activity 13, p. 104.
- Read the **Tira cómica,** p. 104, then do Pair Work, ATE, p. 104.
- Read and discuss the **Nota cultural,** p. 104.

Wrap-Up 10 min.
- Follow Suggestion 3 for Teaching Transparency 4-1.
- Discuss the content and format of Quiz 4-1.

Homework Options
Study for Quiz 4-1.

Day 5

PRIMER PASO
Quick Review 5 min.
- Review the content of **Primer paso.**

ENCUENTRO CULTURAL 20 min.
- Presenting **Encuentro cultural,** p. 105
- Follow the Teaching Suggestions, ATE, p. 105.

Quiz 20 min.
- Administer Quiz 4-1A, 4-1B, or a combination of the two.

Wrap-Up 5 min.
- Do the **Mini-cuento** for Teaching Transparency 4-1.

Homework Options
Cuaderno de actividades, p. 41, Activity 9

Day 6

PRIMER PASO
Quick Review 5 min.
- Check homework.
- Bell Work, ATE, p. 108

¡ADELANTE! 20 min.
- Presenting **¡Adelante!** and Preteaching Vocabulary, ATE, p. 106
- Present the Culture Note, ATE, p. 107.
- Do Activities 14–17, pp. 106–107.

SEGUNDO PASO
Así se dice, p. 108 20 min.
- Presenting **Así se dice,** ATE, p. 108
- Do Activity 18 with the Audio CD, p. 108.
- Present Language Notes, ATE, p. 108.

Wrap-Up 5 min.
- Do Challenge Activity, ATE, p. 107.

Homework Options
Cuaderno de actividades, p. 42, Activities 10–11

One-Stop Planner CD-ROM

For alternative lesson plans by chapter section, to create your own customized plans, or to preview all resources available for this chapter, use the **One-Stop Planner CD-ROM,** Disc 1.

For additional homework suggestions, see activities accompanied by this symbol throughout the chapter.

Day 7

SEGUNDO PASO
Quick Review 5 min.
- Check homework.
- Follow Suggestion 2 for Teaching Transparency 4-2.

Así se dice/Nota gramatical, p. 108 25 min.
- Present the **Nota gramatical,** p. 108.
- **Más práctica gramatical,** p. 118, Activity 6
- Do Activity 19, p. 108.
- Have students do Activity 20 in pairs, p. 108.
- Read and discuss the **Nota cultural,** p. 108.

Vocabulario, p. 109 15 min.
- Presenting **Vocabulario,** ATE, p. 109
- Present **También se puede decir...,** p. 109.
- Do the Tactile Learners Activity, ATE, p. 109.

Wrap-Up 5 min.
- Name the places mentioned in **Vocabulario,** p. 109 then have students name something they might buy at each place.

Homework Options
Cuaderno de actividades, pp. 43–44, 46, Activities 12–14, 18
Cuaderno de gramática, pp. 33–34, Activities 11–14

Day 8

SEGUNDO PASO
Quick Review 10 min.
- Check homework.
- Do Vocabulary Practice Activities 1–2 for Transparency 4-2.

Vocabulario, p. 109 10 min.
- Have students do Activity 21 in pairs, p. 109.
- Read and discuss the **Nota cultural,** p. 109.

Gramática, p. 110 25 min.
- Presenting **Gramática,** ATE, p. 110
- Present the Teacher Note, ATE, p. 110.
- Do Activity 22 with the Audio CD, p. 110.
- **Más práctica gramatical,** p. 119, Activities 8–9

Wrap-Up 5 min.
- Have students answer questions using double object pronouns.

Homework Options
Cuaderno de actividades, pp. 44–45, Activities 15–17
Cuaderno de gramática, pp. 35–36, Activities 15–18

Day 9

SEGUNDO PASO
Quick Review 5 min.
- Check homework.

Gramática, p. 110 15 min.
- Have students do Activity 23 in pairs, p. 110.
- Have students do Activity 24, then peer-edit their work p. 110.

PANORAMA CULTURAL 15 min.
- Presenting **Panorama cultural,** ATE, p. 111
- Present the Language Note, ATE, p. 111.

Así se dice/Vocabulario/Gramática, pp. 108–110 10 min.
- Do Communicative Activity 4-2B, p. 16, in Activities for Communication.

Wrap-Up 5 min.
- Discuss the content and format of Quiz 4-2.

Homework Options
Study for Quiz 4-2.
Cuaderno de actividades, p. 46, Activity 19

Day 10

SEGUNDO PASO
Quick Review 5 min.
- Check homework for completion.
- Review the content of **Segundo paso.**

Quiz 20 min.
- Administer Quiz 4-2A, 4-2B, or a combination of the two.

VAMOS A LEER 20 min.
- Present Background Information and Culture Note, ATE, p. 112.
- Read **Estrategia** and do Activity A, p. 112.
- Read **¿Te acuerdas?** and do Activity B, pp. 112–113.
- Read **¿Te acuerdas?** and do Activity C, p. 113.

Wrap-Up 5 min.
- Do the Thinking Critically Activity, ATE, p. 113.

Homework Options
Assign **Vamos a leer** Activities D–E, pp. 113–114.

Day 11

VAMOS A LEER
Quick Review 10 min.
- Check and discuss homework.

VAMOS A LEER, 15 min.
- Have students do Activity F in pairs, p. 114.
- Do Activity G with the class, p. 114.

REPASO 20 min.
- Do Activity 1 with the Audio CD, p. 120.
- Have students do Activities 2 and 5 in pairs, pp. 120–121.
- Have students do Activity 3 in groups, p. 120.

Wrap-Up 5 min.
- Discuss **Vamos a escribir,** p. 115, and present Additional Vocabulary, ATE, p. 115.

Homework Options
Assign **Vamos a escribir,** p. 115.
Cuaderno de actividades, pp. 47–48, Activities 20–24
A ver si puedo..., p. 122

Day 12

REPASO
Quick Review 5 min.
- Check or collect homework.

Chapter Review 40 min.
- Review Chapter 4. Choose from **Más práctica gramatical,** Grammar Tutor for Students of Spanish, Activities for Communication, Listening Activities, Interactive CD-ROM Tutor, or **Juegos interactivos.**

Wrap-Up 5 min.
- Discuss the format of the Chapter 4 Test.

Homework Options
Study for the Chapter 4 Test.

Assessment

Quick Review 5 min.
- Answer any last-minute questions.

Test, Chapter 4 45 min.
- Administer Chapter 4 Test. Select from Testing Program, Alternative Assessment Guide, Test Generator, or Standardized Assessment Tutor.

Capítulo 4: Alrededor de la mesa
Suggested Lesson Plans 90-Minute Block Schedule

Block 1

CHAPTER OPENER 5 min.
- Focusing on Outcomes, ATE, p. 97
- Present Culture Note, Background Information, Thinking Critically, or Geography Link, ATE, pp. 96–97.

DE ANTEMANO 40 min.
- Presenting **De antemano** and Preteaching Vocabulary, ATE, p. 98
- Present Language Notes and Culture Note, ATE, p. 99.
- Do the Thinking Critically Activity, ATE, p. 99.
- Activities 1–5 and Comprehension Check, ATE, p. 100

Así se dice, p. 101 25 min.
- Presenting **Así se dice**, ATE, p. 101
- Review **¿Te acuerdas?**, p. 101.
- **Más práctica gramatical**, p. 116, Activity 1
- Do Activity 6 with the Audio CD, p. 101.
- Do Activities 7–8, p. 101.

Vocabulario, p. 102 15 min.
- Presenting **Vocabulario**, ATE, p. 102
- Present **También se puede decir...**, p. 102.

Wrap-Up 5 min.
- Do the Visual Learners Suggestion, ATE, p. 101.

Homework Options
Cuaderno de actividades, pp. 37–39, Activities 1–5
Cuaderno de gramática, pp. 28–30, Activities 1–5

Block 2

PRIMER PASO
Quick Review 10 min.
- Check homework.

Vocabulario, p. 102 20 min.
- Do the Auditory Learners Suggestion, ATE, p. 102.
- Have students do Activity 9 in pairs and Activity 10 in groups, p. 102.

Así se dice/Gramática, p. 103 50 min.
- Presenting **Así se dice** and **Gramática**, ATE, p. 103
- Present **A lo nuestro**, p. 103.
- Present the Language Note, ATE, p. 103.
- Do Activity 11 with the Audio CD, p. 103.
- Do Activity 12, p. 104.
- Review **¿Te acuerdas?**, then do Activity 13, p. 104.
- Read the **Tira cómica**, p. 104, then do Pair Work, ATE, p. 104.
- Read and discuss the **Nota cultural**, p. 104.

Wrap-Up 10 min.
- Follow Suggestion 3 for Teaching Transparency 4-1.
- Discuss the content and format of Quiz 4-1.

Homework Options
Study for Quiz 4-1.
Cuaderno de actividades, pp. 40–41, Activities 6–9
Cuaderno de gramática, pp. 30–32, Activities 6–10

Block 3

PRIMER PASO
Quick Review 10 min.
- Check homework.

ENCUENTRO CULTURAL 20 min.
- Presenting **Encuentro cultural**, ATE, p. 105
- Follow the Teaching Suggestions, ATE, p. 105.

Así se dice/Vocabulario/Gramática, pp. 101–104 10 min.
- Review the content of **Primer paso**.
- Do the **Mini-cuento** for Teaching Transparency 4-1.

Quiz 20 min.
- Administer Quiz 4-1A, 4-1B, or a combination of the two.

¡ADELANTE! 25 min.
- Presenting **¡Adelante!** and Preteaching Vocabulary, ATE, p. 106
- Present the Culture Note, ATE, p. 107.
- Do Activities 14–17, pp. 106–107.

Wrap-Up 5 min.
- Ask students what their favorite dishes are.

Homework Options
Cuaderno de actividades, p. 42, Activities 10–11

One-Stop Planner CD-ROM

For alternative lesson plans by chapter section, to create your own customized plans, or to preview all resources available for this chapter, use the **One-Stop Planner CD-ROM,** Disc 1.

 For additional homework suggestions, see activities accompanied by this symbol throughout the chapter.

Block 4

SEGUNDO PASO
Quick Review 5 min.
- Check homework.
- Bell Work, ATE, p. 108

Así se dice/Nota gramatical, p. 108 45 min.
- Presenting **Así se dice, Nota gramatical** ATE, p. 108
- Do Activity 18 with the Audio CD, p. 108.
- **Más práctica gramatical,** p. 118, Activity 6
- Do Activity 19, p. 108.
- Have students do Activity 20 in pairs, p. 108.
- Read and discuss the **Nota cultural,** p. 108.

Vocabulario, p. 109 35 min.
- Presenting **Vocabulario,** ATE, p. 109
- Present **También se puede decir...,** p. 109.
- Do the Tactile Learners Activity, ATE, p. 109.
- Have students do Activity 21 in pairs, p. 109.
- Read and discuss the **Nota cultural,** p. 109.
- Follow Suggestion 4 for Teaching Transparency 4-2.

Wrap-Up 5 min.
- Follow Suggestion 2 for Teaching Transparency 4-2.

Homework Options
Cuaderno de actividades, pp. 43–46, Activities 12–14, 16–18
Cuaderno de gramática, pp. 33–34, Activities 11–14

Block 5

SEGUNDO PASO
Quick Review 10 min.
- Check homework.

Gramática, p. 110 40 min.
- Presenting **Gramática,** ATE, p. 110
- Present the Teacher Note, ATE, p. 110.
- Do Activity 22 with the Audio CD, p. 110.
- **Más práctica gramatical,** p. 119, Activities 8–9
- Have students do Activity 23 in pairs, p. 110.
- Have students do Activity 24, then peer-edit their work, p. 110.

PANORAMA CULTURAL 15 min.
- Presenting **Panorama cultural,** ATE, p. 111
- Present the Language Note, ATE, p. 111.

VAMOS A LEER 20 min.
- Present Background Information and Culture Note, ATE, p. 112.
- Read **Estrategia** and do Activity A, p. 112.
- Read **¿Te acuerdas?** and do Activity B, pp. 112–113.
- Read **¿Te acuerdas?** and do Activity C, p. 113.

Wrap-Up 5 min.
- Do the Thinking Critically Activity, ATE, p. 113.
- Discuss the content and format of Quiz 4-2.

Homework Options
Study for Quiz 4-2.
Cuaderno de actividades, pp. 44, 46, Activities 15, 19
Cuaderno de gramática, pp. 35–36, Activities 15–18

Block 6

SEGUNDO PASO
Quick Review 10 min.
- Check homework.
- Review the content of **Segundo paso.**

Quiz 20 min.
- Administer Quiz 4-2A, 4-2B, or a combination of the two.

VAMOS A LEER 35 min.
- Do Activities D–E, pp. 113–114.
- Have students do Activity F in pairs, p. 114.
- Do Activity G with the class, p. 114.

REPASO 20 min.
- Do Activity 1 with the Audio CD, p. 120.
- Have students do Activities 2 and 5 in pairs, pp. 120–121.
- Have students do Activity 3 in groups, p. 120.

Wrap-Up 5 min.
- Discuss **Vamos a escribir,** p. 115, and Additional Vocabulary, ATE, p. 115.
- Discuss the content and format of the Chapter 4 Test.

Homework Options
Study for the Chapter 4 Test.
Vamos a escribir, p. 115
Cuaderno de actividades, pp. 47–48, Activities 20–24
A ver si puedo..., p. 122

Block 7

REPASO
Quick Review 5 min.
- Check homework and collect **Vamos a escribir,** p. 115.

Chapter Review 40 min.
- Review Chapter 4. Choose from **Más práctica gramatical,** Grammar Tutor for Students of Spanish, Activities for Communication, Listening Activities, Interactive CD-ROM Tutor, or **Juegos interactivos.**

Test, Chapter 4 45 min.
- Administer Chapter 4 Test. Select from Testing Program, Alternative Assessment Guide, Test Generator, or Standardized Assessment Tutor.

CAPÍTULO 4

One-Stop Planner CD-ROM

For resource information, see the **One-Stop Planner,** Disc 1.

Pacing Tips
Talking about unintentional events in Spanish may confuse some nonnative speakers. As you work through the **Primer paso,** you might want to add extra time to allow students to thoroughly practice the new material. For lesson plans and timing suggestions, see pages 95I–95L.

Meeting the Standards
Communication
- Talking about how food tastes, p. 101
- Talking about unintentional events, p. 103
- Asking for help and requesting favors, p. 108

Cultures
- Culture Note, p. 96
- Nota cultural, p. 104
- Encuentro cultural, p. 105
- Culture Note, p. 107
- Language Notes, p. 108
- Panorama cultural, p. 111
- Culture Note, p. 112

Connections
- Geography Link, p. 97
- History Link, p. 113

Comparisons
- Language Note, p. 103

Communities
- Career Path, p. 105
- Native Speakers, p. 109

Cultures and Communities

Culture Note
Caracas has a great number of **panaderías,** which serve coffee and pastries in addition to selling bread and cakes. Some **panaderías** serve sandwiches, ham and cheese croissants, and other snack or light lunch foods. **Fuentes de soda,** neighborhood coffee shops, are also popular and are found on almost every block in some parts of the city.

Background Information
If, in the future, students travel to South America as part of their careers, it might well be to Caracas. An estimated 20,000 Americans currently reside in Caracas, many of them associated with the oil industry.

CAPÍTULO

4

Alrededor de la mesa

Objectives

In this chapter you will learn to

Primer paso

- talk about how food tastes
- talk about unintentional events

Segundo paso

- ask for help and request favors

 internet

 MARCAR: go.hrw.com
PALABRA CLAVE:
WV3 CARACAS-4

◀ ¡Se nos olvidó preguntarle al mesero dónde queda el museo de arte!

CAPÍTULO 4

Photo Flash!
Caracas has several first-rate museums. The **Museo de Arte Contemporáneo** has paintings by some of the best European and Venezuelan painters. The **Museo Bolivariano** houses the documents, weapons, and belongings of Simón Bolívar. The **Museo de Arte Colonial** is a colonial house where the Marqués del Toro once lived.

Focusing on Outcomes
Encourage students to think about different situations in which they would use the chapter learner outcomes. Which ones do they think would be most useful if they were spending time abroad and why?

Connections and Comparisons

Thinking Critically
Synthesizing Ask students to name some of the reasons why people in different countries eat different foods. (Different foods are grown in different locales. Trade influences which imported foods are available.) Where would you expect to find the greatest variety of foods? (In cities, where people from many backgrounds create a demand for varied foods.)

Geography Link
Ask students to find out how geography and climate affect or determine the regional diet. Do the landscape and weather heavily influence local agriculture? Have students list typical dishes and staples and explain what environmental factors contribute to the prevalence of these foods. Students might compare their findings with information regarding a Spanish-speaking country.

Teaching Resources
pp. 98–100

PRINT
▸ Lesson Planner, p. 18
▸ Video Guide, pp. 23–24, 26
▸ Cuaderno de actividades, p. 37

MEDIA
▸ One-Stop Planner
▸ Video Program
   Contigo en la distancia
   Videocassette 2, 01:10–05:08
   Videocassette 5 (captioned version), 17:32–21:30
▸ Audio Compact Discs, CD 4, Trs. 1–3

Presenting
De antemano

Have students read and answer the question in **Estrategia para comprender.** Then have students work in pairs to make two lists: one of phrases used to talk about unintentional events and another of expressions used to describe how food tastes. Play the Audio CD and have students listen for the phrases they listed and circle the ones that they hear. Then present the Preteaching Vocabulary.

DE ANTEMANO ▪ *El anillo*

Cuaderno de actividades, p. 37, Acts. 1–2

CD 4
Trs. 1–3

Estrategia para comprender
¿Qué pasa en un restaurante? Pues, pedimos la comida, comemos y pagamos, naturalmente. Pero un restaurante puede ser el escenario de pequeños dramas humanos. Lee lo que le pasó a Fernando un día en el restaurante donde trabaja.

Manuel: ¿Qué tal, hombre? ¿Cómo anda lo del compromiso?
Fernando: Todavía no le he hecho la pregunta. Pero mira. Hoy le compré el anillo. Me costó un ojo de la cara. Voy a dárselo esta noche después del trabajo.
Manuel: ¡Buena suerte! ¡Que te vaya bien!

Fernando: ¡Caramba!
Manuel: ¿Qué te pasó?
Fernando: ¡El anillo! ¡Se me cayó y no lo puedo encontrar! ¡Ayúdame!

El jefe: ¡Basta ya! ¡Hay clientes que esperan!
Fernando: Hombre, ¿qué hago?
Manuel: Vete al comedor. El anillo a lo mejor está debajo del horno. Lo buscaremos después. No hay remedio.

Fernando: Eh, buenas noches, señora. ¿Qué desea Ud.?
Señora: ¿Me puede traer el menú, por favor?
Fernando: Perdone Ud., se me olvidó traérselo. En seguida vuelvo.

Preteaching Vocabulary

Identifying Keywords
First ask students to guess the context of **De antemano.** (a mishap in a restaurant) Then have them use the pictures to identify words or phrases that give them information about the action in each scene. Students may identify such phrases as: **Hoy le compré el anillo.; ¡Se me cayó y no lo** puedo encontrar!; Lo buscaremos después.; **Tráigame uno de todos los platos principales, por favor.; Oiga, ¿me hace el favor de traerme otro flanecito?; ¿Desde cuándo cocinan flan con anillos?; ¿Es posible pagar con este anillo?**

Fernando: ¿Qué le puedo traer? ¿Una ensalada mixta? ¿El puerco asado? ¿El arroz con frijoles? El pollo aquí es exquisito también.

Señora: Tráigame uno de todos los platos principales, por favor. Y de postre, un pastel de chocolate, el flan y helado de vainilla.

Fernando: Este… perdone, ¿van a llegar unos amigos suyos, señora?

Señora: No, estoy sola esta noche.

Señora: ¡Qué riquísimo sabor! ¡Qué arroz más sabroso! ¡Qué carne más deliciosa! ¡Sabe muy rico el flan!

Mesero: ¡Qué buen apetito tiene la señora! ¿Dónde pondrá tal cantidad de comida?

Fernando: ¡Ay, se me cayeron los platos!

Señora: Hay que tener más cuidado, joven. Oiga, ¿me hace el favor de traerme otro flanecito?

Señora: ¡Qué cosa más rara! ¿Desde cuándo cocinan flan con anillos?

Señora: ¿Puede traerme la cuenta, por favor?

Fernando: Sí, señora, se la traigo ahora mismo.

Señora: ¡Ay! ¡Se me perdió el dinero! ¡Qué vergüenza! Pero tengo una idea. ¿Es posible pagar con este anillo? Valdrá aun más que esta cena maravillosa.

Using the Captioned Video

As an alternative, you might want to show the captioned version of *Contigo en la distancia: ¡Qué sabroso!* on Videocassette 5. Some students may benefit from seeing the written words as they listen to the target language and watch the gestures and actions in context. This visual reinforcement of vocabulary and functions will facilitate students' comprehension and help reduce their anxiety before they are formally introduced to the new language in the chapter.

CAPÍTULO 4

Thinking Critically
Analyzing Ask students why this episode works so well as a mini-drama. (It has sympathetic characters, plenty of action, and suspense.)

Language Notes
- Point out to students that the expression **¡Que te vaya bien!** is commonly used to convey a wish for good luck. (The subjunctive mood to express hopes and wishes is presented in Chapter 5.)
- An **anillo de compromiso** is an engagement ring, while an **anillo de boda** is a wedding ring.

Culture Note
In Spanish-speaking countries, the engagement ring and wedding ring are commonly worn on the "ring finger," or **dedo anular,** of the right hand.

Contigo en la distancia
You may choose to show students Episode 4: *¡Qué sabroso!* now or wait until later in the chapter. In the video, Javier and Zoraida are in the kitchen where their father is preparing **paella.** Javier tells them about Mexican **mole,** a spicy sauce made with chocolate. Sergio then shows up with photographs from Mexico. Zoraida teases Javier about Alejandra, but when she sees the picture of Carlos, she ignores them completely. Before students view the video have them review chapter functions and vocabulary.

Answers

1 1. Compró un anillo de compromiso. Piensa dárselo a su novia esta noche después del trabajo.
2. Según Manuel el anillo está debajo del horno.
3. La cliente de Fernando es una señora delgada, mayor y elegante.
4. Se le olvida darle el menú.
5. La señora pide uno de todos los platos principales: el puerco asado, el arroz con frijoles y el pollo. De postre pide un pastel de chocolate, el flan y un helado.
6. Ellos piensan que van a llegar unos amigos a cenar con ella. También piensan que ella tiene buen apetito y se preguntan dónde pondrá ella tanta comida.
7. La señora no tiene dinero para pagar la cuenta y pide pagarla con el anillo de Fernando. *Answers will vary.*

2 1. no se sabe
2. falso; El anillo cayó en el flan.
3. cierto
4. falso; Va a cenar sola.
5. no se sabe
6. falso; Al mesero se le perdió el anillo.
7. falso; La señora encontró el anillo.
8. no se sabe

3 *Possible answers:*
1. Tráigame uno de todos los platos... ¿Me hace el favor de traerme...?
2. ¡Qué riquísimo sabor! ¡Qué arroz más sabroso!
3. ¡Ay, se me cayeron los platos! Se me olvidó traérselo.

4 e, a, c, b, d

7 *Sample answer:*
¿Sopa de crema de maní? ¡Guácala! Tiene sabor a grasa.

These activities check for comprehension only. Students should not yet be expected to produce language modeled in **De antemano**.

1 **¿Comprendes?** See answers below.

1. ¿Qué compró Fernando? ¿Por qué lo compró?
2. Según Manuel, ¿dónde está el anillo?
3. ¿Cómo es la cliente de Fernando?
4. ¿Qué se le olvida a Fernando darle a la señora?
5. ¿Qué platos pide la señora?
6. ¿Qué piensan los meseros de la cena de la señora?
7. ¿Qué problema tiene la señora al final? ¿Qué crees que Fernando va a hacer?

2 **¿Se sabe?** See answers below.

Responde a cada oración con **cierto, falso** o **no se sabe.** Corrige las oraciones falsas.

1. Manuel está casado.
2. El anillo cayó debajo del horno.
3. Al jefe de meseros no le importa el problema de Fernando. Dice que todos tienen que trabajar.
4. La señora va a cenar con unos amigos esta noche.
5. A la señora le gusta la paella.
6. A la señora se le perdió el anillo.
7. La señora comió el anillo sin darse cuenta.
8. Fernando va a pagar la cena de la señora.

3 **¿Qué palabras se usan?** See answers below.

Encuentra por lo menos dos expresiones por cada pregunta.

1. ¿Qué expresiones usa la señora para pedir comida en el restaurante?
2. ¿Qué expresiones usa ella para describir la comida?
3. ¿Cuáles son las expresiones que se usan para hablar de cosas que ocurrieron inesperadamente *(unexpectedly)?* (Por ejemplo: Se me cayó la sopa.)

4 **En orden** See answers below.

Pon las siguientes frases en orden cronológico.

a. El jefe de meseros se enoja con Fernando.
b. La señora pide muchos platos.
c. A Fernando se le olvida traer el menú.
d. La señora ofrece pagar con el anillo.
e. Fernando enseña el anillo a su amigo.

5 **Ahora te toca a ti**

 ¿Te ha pasado algo como lo que le pasó a Fernando? Dile a tu compañero(a) lo que te pasó. ¿Cómo te sentiste?

Comprehension Check

Additional Practice

2 If students write their answers individually, have them check them with a partner. They are to refer back to the story if they have different answers. Ask students to explain their answers to the class in Spanish.

Slower Pace

3 If students have difficulty with this activity, write the answers on the board and ask them to match the answers with the questions.

Additional Practice

5 After students have done this activity with a partner, ask for volunteers to tell their stories to the class.

Objectives Talking about how food tastes; talking about unintentional events

WV3 CARACAS-4

Así se dice

Talking about how food tastes

Si un plato no te gusta, puedes decir:

Le falta sal/sabor/no sé qué.
It doesn't have enough . . .

Tiene sabor a ajo. *It tastes like garlic.*

Lleva mucha grasa. *It has too much fat.*

Está echado a perder. *It's spoiled (ruined).*

Me cae gordo. *It disagrees with me.*

¡Guácala! ¡Qué asco!*
Yuck! How disgusting!

Si te gusta la comida, puedes decir:

¡Qué bueno/sabroso!

Sabe riquísimo.

Está en su punto.
It's just right.

Cuaderno de actividades,
p. 38, Act. 3

¿Te acuerdas?

The **-ísimo(a)** ending intensifies the meaning of an adjective or adverb. With adjectives, the ending must agree:

Las papas son **riquísimas** y las puedes preparar **rapidísimo**.

Cuaderno de gramática,
p. 28, Acts. 1–2

Más práctica gramatical,
p. 116, Act. 1

6 **¡Qué sabroso!** Script and answers on p. 95G.

Escuchemos Escucha las oraciones e indica si cada una es un **cumplido** (compliment), una **queja** o un **comentario neutro**.

CD 4 Tr. 4

7 **Y eso, ¿con qué se come?** See sample answers below.

Escribamos Imagina que te sirven platos poco usuales. Usa expresiones de **Así se dice** para describir el sabor. Luego expresa tu opinión de los platos servidos en la cafetería esta semana.

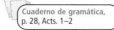

sopa de crema de maní
bistec con salsa de piña

atún con uvas
¿...?

helado de zanahoria
sándwich de papaya

8 **¡Ni en pintura!**

Leamos/Escribamos Lee la tira cómica. De niño(a), ¿qué comida no te gustaba? Usa las frases de **Así se dice** para escribir otro diálogo entre Calvin y sus padres acerca de esa comida.

© Watterson. Dist. by Universal Press Syndicate. Reprinted with permission. All rights reserved.

*These expressions can be used among friends but are not suitable in a formal situation.

Communication for All Students

Additional Practice

7 Emphasize to students that **¡Guácala!** and **¡Qué asco!** would never be used in formal situations or to comment on a host's cooking. Have students make a list of situations in which these negative reactions would and would not be appropriate.

Visual Learners

8 Have students create a comic strip about **Ricitos de Oro y los tres osos** (Goldilocks and the Three Bears) in which **Ricitos de Oro** tries different foods in the bears' kitchen and reacts with phrases from **Así se dice**.

Teaching Resources
pp. 101–104

PRINT
▸ Lesson Planner, p. 18
▸ Listening Activities, pp. 27, 31–32
▸ Activities for Communication, pp. 13–14, 60, 62, 95–96
▸ Cuaderno de gramática, pp. 28–32
▸ Grammar Tutor for Students of Spanish, Chapter 4
▸ Cuaderno de actividades, pp. 38–41
▸ Cuaderno para hispanohablantes, pp. 16–20
▸ Testing Program, pp. 67–70
▸ Alternative Assessment Guide, p. 33
▸ Student Make-Up Assignments, Chapter 4

MEDIA
▸ One-Stop Planner
▸ Audio Compact Discs, CD 4, Trs. 4–5, 23–25, 19
▸ Teaching Transparencies 4-1; **Más práctica gramatical** Answers; Cuaderno de gramática Answers
▸ Interactive CD-ROM Tutor, Disc 1

Bell Work

On the board, write:
Escribe cinco oraciones sobre lo que has hecho esta semana, usando el presente perfecto, y cinco oraciones, usando el futuro, sobre lo que harás mañana.

Presenting
Así se dice

Bring in a basket of fruit and vegetables, real or plastic. As you pretend to taste each piece, model phrases to indicate that you do or do not like it. Use facial expressions to convey your reaction.

Teaching Resources
pp. 101–104

PRINT
▶ Lesson Planner, p. 18
▶ Listening Activities, pp. 27, 31–33
▶ Activities for Communication, pp. 13–14, 60, 62, 95–96
▶ Cuaderno de gramática, pp. 28–32
▶ Grammar Tutor for Students of Spanish, Chapter 4
▶ Cuaderno de actividades, pp. 38–41
▶ Cuaderno para hispanohablantes, pp. 16–20
▶ Testing Program, pp. 67–70
▶ Alternative Assessment Guide, p. 33
▶ Student Make-Up Assignments, Chapter 4

MEDIA
▶ One-Stop Planner
▶ Audio Compact Discs, CD 4, Trs. 4–5, 23–25, 19
▶ Teaching Transparencies 4-1; **Más práctica gramatical** Answers; Cuaderno de gramática Answers
▶ Interactive CD-ROM Tutor, Disc 1

Presenting
Vocabulario

Write the days of the week on the board. Tell students you are planning a menu for dinner each evening. Then begin putting meals together, modeling phrases as you write. (**El lunes. ¿Qué carne voy a preparar? ¿Chorizo? No, no quiero chorizo el lunes. Prefiero...**) After you finish, erase the foods and ask the class to help you put together a new menu for the week.

Vocabulario

Ensaladas
ensalada mixta
ensalada de
  aguacate

Pescados
pargo   *red snapper*
bacalao   *cod*
trucha   *trout*

Legumbres
caraotas

Frutas
patilla
  watermelon
melocotones
  peaches
piña

Carnes
bistec a la parrilla
puerco asado   *roast pork*
chorizo   *sausage*
ternera   *veal*
chuletas de cerdo
pollo frito

Mariscos
almejas   *clams*
ostras   *oysters*

Postres
torta de chocolate
quesillo   *custard*

Cuaderno de gramática, pp. 29–30, Acts. 3–5

Cuaderno de actividades, pp. 38–39, Acts. 4–5

Más práctica gramatical, p. 116, Act. 2

9 **¿Dónde quieres comer?**

Leamos/Hablemos Lee los anuncios de los restaurantes y contesta las preguntas. Luego, reúnete con un(a) compañero(a) y escoge adónde quieren ir a comer.

1. ¿Qué restaurante ofrece la posibilidad de comer sin salir de casa? El Palacio Chino
2. A tu amigo(a) no le gusta comer carne. ¿Dónde vas a cenar con este(a) amigo(a)? Restaurante Frutos de la Tierra
3. ¿Cuál va a estar abierto a las tres de la tarde el domingo? Restaurante Frutos de la Tierra y Restaurante Las Olas
4. Quieres comer un bistec a la parrilla. ¿Qué restaurante te ofrece esta comida? El Pozo
5. El marisco favorito de tu amiga son los camarones. ¿Qué restaurante le recomiendas? Restaurante Las Olas

También se puede decir...

En algunos países
los frijoles negros
los duraznos
la sandía
el pastel
el puerco/el cerdo

En Venezuela
las caraotas
los melocotones
la patilla
la torta
el cochino

En México, se dice **huachinango** por **pargo**.

Restaurante Frutos de la Tierra
• Comida macrobiótica •
• Comida vegetariana •
Sólo usamos los ingredientes más naturales
Abierto todos los días de **12 am a 11 pm**
Calle Sotomayor con Robledo
Urb. La Feria
Teléfono 73.38.45

El Palacio Chino
Abierto de lunes a sábado de **12 a.m.** a **10 p.m.** *Servicio rápido a domicilios*
Teléfono: 367.9831
Urb. El Rosal

El Pozo
Carnes a la parrilla • Comida internacional
Avenida Campos, Urb. El Rosal
Edificio Rodríguez Peña
Teléfonos: 33-29-48 o 33-29-49

Restaurante Las Olas
Pescado y mariscos
Abierto domingos,
11 a.m. a 12 p.m.
Avenida Universidad
Cruce con Los Pinos
Teléfono 359.9631

10 **Escribamos/Hablemos** Júntate con tres o cuatro compañeros(as). Primero, preparen varios menús—uno para bajar de peso, otro para aumentar de peso y otro más para vegetarianos. Luego, en turnos, hagan el papel del mesero y los clientes. Los clientes deben pedir la comida, pedir la cuenta y comentar sobre la comida.

¿Se te ha olvidado?
ordering a meal
Ver la página R5

Communication for All Students

Auditory Learners
Have students think of a dish typical of a particular cuisine. Each student lists the ingredients, without identifying the food by name, and the class is to guess the name of the dish. The correct guesser then says whether or not she or he likes the type of food described. For visual learners, students can show pictures of different foods and have the class guess which picture he or she is describing.

Kinesthetic/Auditory Learners
10 Have a small group of students role-play a typical restaurant situation. Choose one or two students to introduce a situation that interrupts the group's normal interaction. How does the group respond? Have the group react to the interruption.

STANDARDS: 1.1, 1.2, 5.1, 5.2

Así se dice

Talking about unintentional events

Para hablar de eventos inesperados, puedes decir:

Cuaderno de actividades, pp. 40–41, Acts. 6–8

Se le rompió el vaso.   *He (She) broke the glass.*

Se me perdieron las llaves.   *I lost the keys.*

Se me acabó la comida.   *I ran out of food.*

El contestador **se nos descompuso.**
The answering machine broke.

¿Se te olvidaron los boletos?
Did you forget the tickets?

Se nos cayeron los libros.
We dropped the books.

¿Se les quedó el almuerzo en casa?
Did you (pl.) leave your lunch at home?

Gramática

Se + indirect object pronoun

Use se + indirect object pronoun + verb to talk about unintentional events.

1. The indirect object pronoun depends on whom the event happened to.
   Se les quedó el pan en casa.   *They left the bread at home.*

2. Use the plural of the verb if the item involved is plural.
   Se me perdieron las **fotos.**   *I lost the pictures.*

3. A clarifying phrase with **a** may be added to further identify the indirect object pronoun.
   A Teresa se **le** rompió el vaso.

Más práctica gramatical, p. 117, Acts. 3–5

Cuaderno de gramática, pp. 30–32, Acts. 6–10

---

11 **¡Qué desastre!** Script and answers on p. 95G.

CD 4
Tr. 5

Escuchemos Vas a escuchar cinco frases. Después de escuchar cada frase, decide a qué dibujo corresponde. ¡Ojo! Una frase no corresponde a ningún dibujo.

Pablo

Beatriz

Diana

Felipe

A lo nuestro

Spanish has many expressions using **se** plus an indirect object pronoun. Some of these can be used when the speaker wants to be more polite, or to soften what he or she is saying.

Se me pasó por alto.
It slipped my mind.

Se me hace un poco absurdo.
It seems a little absurd to me.

Se le nota que está enojada.
You can tell that she's angry.

Still others express unintentional events.

Se le hizo tarde.   *It got late on him.*

Se nos fue el tren.
The train went off and left us.

Presenting
Así se dice

With hand puppets, create a dialogue using the phrases in **Así se dice.** (First puppet: **¡Vámonos! Tengo prisa.** Second puppet: **¡Espérate un momento, por favor! Se me perdieron las llaves del auto. Las estoy buscando.**) Then hand the puppets to two students and have them create a new dialogue using different phrases from **Así se dice.**

Gramática

Se + **indirect object pronoun** This suggestion requires advance preparation. Cut a transparency into five strips and on them write the following: (1) **a mí, a ti, a Ud., a él, a ella, a nosotros, a nosotras, a Uds., a ellos, a ellas,** (2) **se,** (3) the indirect object pronouns, (4) the verb stem of ten verbs used with unintentional events, (5) some appropriate nouns **(el libro, las fotos, la computadora).** Order the strips on the projector to show students that the form of the verb always agrees in number with the item involved in the inadvertent action rather than with the indirect object pronoun. Next, create sentences that are complete except for the indirect object pronoun and the verb ending. **(A mí se _____ olvid__ los boletos.)** Ask students to complete the sentences.

Connections and Comparisons

Thinking Critically
Analyzing Ask students to note the difference in assigning responsibility in the expressions "I lost the keys" and **Se me perdieron las llaves.** *(The keys got lost on me.)* Ask students if they consider one statement a more accurate description of an unexpected event than the other. why? (Answers will vary.)

Language Note
Explain to students that many food items in different countries have different names, which often stem from indigenous languages. (Quechua in the Andes, Nahuatl in Mexico, Taíno in Puerto Rico) Have students find other Spanish words for *banana* **(guineo, plátano, cambur),** *beans* **(caraotas, frijoles, habichuelas, porotos, alubias),** and *corn* **(maíz, elote, choclo).**

Teaching Resources
pp. 101–104

PRINT

▶ Lesson Planner, p. 18
▶ Listening Activities, pp. 27, 31–32
▶ Activities for Communication, pp. 13–14, 60, 62, 95–96
▶ Cuaderno de gramática, pp. 28–32
▶ Grammar Tutor for Students of Spanish, Chapter 4
▶ Cuaderno de actividades, pp. 38–41
▶ Cuaderno para hispanohablantes, pp. 16–20
▶ Testing Program, pp. 67–70
▶ Alternative Assessment Guide, p. 33
▶ Student Make-Up Assignments, Chapter 4

MEDIA

▶ One-Stop Planner
▶ Audio Compact Discs, CD 4, Trs. 4–5, 23–25, 19
▶ Teaching Transparencies 4-1; **Más práctica gramatical** Answers; Cuaderno de gramática Answers
▶ Interactive CD-ROM Tutor, Disc 1

Assess

▶ Testing Program, pp. 67–70
  Quiz 4-1A, Quiz 4-1B
  Audio CD 4, Tr. 19
▶ Student Make-Up Assignments, Chapter 4, Alternative Quiz
▶ Alternative Assessment Guide, p. 33

Answers

12 *Answers will vary.*

13
1. La botella de jugo se me rompió.
2. La torta se me cayó.
3. La sal se me acabó.
4. *Answers may vary.*
5. *Answers may vary.*
6. *Answers may vary.*

---

12 Gramática en contexto

Escribamos Escribe un párrafo y explica por qué llegaron tarde los invitados a la fiesta de Natalia. Usa la información de cada lista.

MODELO	**Guillermo quería venir pero no pudo.**
	Se le acabó la gasolina. Answers will vary.

Guillermo	acabar la gasolina
Ángeles y yo	olvidar comprar un regalo
Yo	romper los discos compactos
Tú	perder las llaves del carro
Andrés y Gabriela	romper el reloj
Nosotros	caer un árbol encima del carro

13 Gramática en contexto Possible answers below.

Leamos/Escribamos Les has preparado una cena a tus amigos. Usa las ideas que siguen para explicar por qué algunos platos no saben muy bien y qué les falta a otros platos. Luego, inventa tus propias razones para explicar las tres últimas ideas.

1. la botella de jugo / romperse
2. la torta / caerse
3. la sal / acabarse
4. la ensalada sólo tiene lechuga
5. hay mucho puerco asado pero pocas papas
6. el plato de frutas sólo lleva melocotones

Nota cultural

En Venezuela y otros países hispanohablantes, muchas familias tienen la costumbre de quedarse sentadas para la **sobremesa**. Es un tiempo para tomar un café y hablar de temas de todo tipo. Se habla de problemas personales y profesionales, la política, los deportes y otros asuntos. La costumbre de la sobremesa se observa en los restaurantes también. ¿Y tú? ¿Cuánto tiempo te quedas sentado(a) a la mesa después de comer?

Communication for All Students

Pair Work

12 Have pairs of students come up with three situations and corresponding explanations. **(Guillermo quería venir pero no pudo. Se le acabó la gasolina.)** Have a student from one pair read his or her first situation. Then ask a student from another pair to read his or her first explanation in response. Students will be amused by the nonsensical and illogical outcomes.

Slower Pace

13 Have students work in pairs. Before beginning the activity, have the class brainstorm various explanations for situations 4–6. Write these on the board or on a transparency.

STANDARDS: 1.3, 2.1, 3.2, 4.2

Encuentro cultural

Personal que presta servicios

Si vas a un país extranjero, vas a conocer a muchas personas que prestan diferentes tipos de servicio. ¿Cómo te diriges a esas personas?

Emergencias Médicas	
Ambulancia	621
Hospital central	45-23-12
Maternidad Santa Lucía	33-21-48
Cruz Roja	25-25-25
BOMBEROS	112
POLICIA	123
TRANSITO	101
OTROS SERVICIOS	
Servicio de información	48-93-77
Quejas y reclamos	48-27-36

Para discutir...

1. Sabes qué hacer si tienes un problema, si te sientes mal o si se te descompone el carro? Imagínate que estás de visita en algún país de habla hispana. ¿Cómo encuentras el servicio necesario, y cómo pides ayuda?

2. Con un(a) compañero(a), escribe una lista de expresiones de cortesía para pedir ayuda. También imaginen cómo van a llamarle la atención a una persona desconocida.

Vamos a comprenderlo

Los servicios de emergencia son casi siempre iguales en todos los países. Generalmente, el personal médico está vestido de blanco, y los policías de azul. Siempre es buena idea consultar una guía telefónica para una lista de números de emergencia.

Para hablar con una persona que presta servicios hay que usar siempre el pronombre formal, **usted**. También es importante decir **por favor** siempre. Cuando se trata realmente de una emergencia, puedes gritar, **¡Auxilio!** o **¡Socorro!** En situaciones menos urgentes, puedes llamar la atención de alguien al decir **Oiga usted, Con permiso** o **Discúlpeme, por favor.**

Cultures and Communities

Teaching Resources
pp. 106–107

PRINT 📖
▶ Lesson Planner, p. 19
▶ Video Guide, pp. 23–25, 27
▶ Cuaderno de actividades, p. 42

MEDIA 💿 📼 🖥️
▶ One-Stop Planner
▶ Video Program
   Contigo en la distancia
   Videocassette 2, 01:10–05:08
   Videocassette 5 (captioned version), 17:32–21:30
   ¡Adelante!
   Videocassette 2, 05:09–09:06
▶ Audio Compact Discs, CD 4, Trs. 6–11

Presenting ¡Adelante!

Have students answer the questions in the introduction and discuss their answers. Play the video once while students look at the photos and read the text. Have students identify foods that were named that they consider healthful and others they consider unhealthful. Next, present the Preteaching Vocabulary.

 ¡Adelante!
Venezuelans talk about their favorite dishes, where they go to buy food, and the tradition of the **sobremesa**.

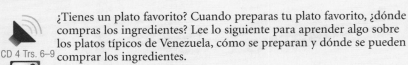
¡Adelante! · *Platos favoritos*

Cuaderno de actividades, p. 42, Acts. 10–11

CD 4 Trs. 6–9

¿Tienes un plato favorito? Cuando preparas tu plato favorito, ¿dónde compras los ingredientes? Lee lo siguiente para aprender algo sobre los platos típicos de Venezuela, cómo se preparan y dónde se pueden comprar los ingredientes.

Gisela Gil

P: ¿Cuál es su plato favorito?
R: Espagueti.
P: ¿Qué come para mantener la salud?
R: Eh, nada en especial, como muy mal, sándwich, como cualquier basura.
P: ¿Qué comida considera Ud. saludable?
R: Bueno, ensaladas, por supuesto, carnes sin grasas.
P: ¿Y no saludable?
R: Pues, hamburguesas, perros calientes, refrescos.
P: ¿Y qué comidas hay aquí en Venezuela… para Navidad o Semana Santa?
R: Bueno, en Semana Santa se come pescado; razones religiosas hacen que mucha gente evite comer carnes rojas, o carne de pollo

y en, pues, en Navidad, hallaca, pan de jamón…
P: ¿Y hay un plato típico de Venezuela?
R: Yo creo que ya Venezuela no tiene platos típicos, como dije, es una mezcla de muchos países, de muchas inmigraciones, de mucha gente. Entonces, hay… platos típicos ya también es la pasta, plato típico ya también es la hamburguesa, plato típico también es un sándwich. Hay… no se puede hablar de un plato típico en Venezuela, ¿no? Es una mezcla de todo.
P: ¿En su familia se hace la sobremesa?
R: No, tenemos todos horarios diferentes de comer. Entonces, no, pocas veces nos encontramos para comer.

Yamilé Anthony

P: ¿Adónde va Ud. para comprar frutas y vegetales…?
R: Bueno, por aquí en la zona existe lo que sacan directamente del campo, ¿okay? La producción propia ya, sin necesidad de tener que pasar por lo que implica el mercado, ¿no? Entonces es allí donde vamos y compramos los vegetales.
P: ¿Y para comprar… la comida en lata?

R: Se va a un automercado.
P: ¿Y ya también hay como … mercados al aire libre?
R: Sí, los hay pero son mercados más que todo a nivel de cosas naturales que son las frutas, los vegetales y las verduras, lo que llamamos papas, zanahorias, remolachas y otras.

These activities check for comprehension only. Students should not yet be expected to produce language modeled in **¡Adelante!**

14 **¿Comprendes?** See answers below.
Contesta las preguntas en español.

1. ¿Qué comidas se comen en los días festivos en Venezuela?
2. ¿Dónde compra Yamilé comida en lata?
3. ¿Dónde compra Yamilé las frutas y los vegetales?
4. ¿Por qué dice Gisela que no hay plato típico de Venezuela?
5. ¿Quiénes hacen la sobremesa después de una comida?
6. ¿Adónde irá Guillermo por la torta de cumpleaños?
7. ¿Qué necesita traer Guillermo para su mamá?

Preteaching Vocabulary

Recognizing Cognates

¡Adelante! contains several words that students will be able to recognize as cognates. Have students find these words and then guess what Gisela, Yamilé, and Guillermo are saying. Ask students to estimate the percentage of cognates in the selection. Do students feel more confident about the reading after identifying the cognates? Encourage students to think about how cognates help them understand unfamiliar words and phrases.

STANDARDS: 1.2, 2.2, 3.1, 3.2

Guillermo Enrique

P: ¿Cuál es su plato favorito?

R: **Bueno, el pabellón me gusta mucho.**

P: ¿Qué es el pabellón?

R: **Es un plato de arroz, caraota, carne tajada…**

P: ¿Qué comida come Ud. para mantener la salud?

R: **Bueno, en la mañana siempre tomo leche, así, eh, pan también y…**

P: ¿Qué comida se come aquí en Venezuela para ciertas fiestas…?

R: **En Navidad, la hallaca, eh, bueno y…**

P: ¿Qué es la hallaca?

R: **Es un… plato típico de las Navidades que es masa y con carne, varias cosas.**

P: ¿En su familia se hace la sobremesa…?

R: **Bueno sí, de vez en cuando.**

P: ¿Y de qué hablan?

R: **De los problemas que uno tenga, los asuntos de la casa, cosas así, personales.**

Querido Guillermo,

Por favor ayúdame con la comida de esta noche. El pabellón es el plato favorito de tu papá y quiero hacérselo esta noche para su cumpleaños. ¿Podrías hacerme el favor de traerme unas cosas? Cómprame dos kg de caraotas y unos plátanos en el mercado. Pedí carne de res en la carnicería… ¿puedes recogérmela? También ordené un pastel en la panadería… hazme el favor de pagarlo y traérmelo a casa. Vas a necesitar dinero… te lo dejé en la cocina, al lado del teléfono.

Un abrazo,
Mamá

Pabellón criollo

Carne mechada

Ingredientes:

1 kg carne, falda de res
2 cebollas grandes
aceite
onoto
una pizca de comino
3 dientes de ajo
ají dulce

2 tomates grandes y maduros
sal y pimienta al gusto

Sirva con:

caraotas negras
arroz
plátanos fritos

---

15 **¿Qué palabras se usan?**

En la nota que escribe la mamá de Guillermo, busca dos palabras que ella usa para decirle a Guillermo qué quiere que él haga, y las tres expresiones que usa para pedirle un favor.
See sample answers below

16 **¿Quién lo diría?** Script and answers on p. 83G.

Escucha cada frase e indica quién la diría, **¿Gisela, Yamilé, Guillermo o la mamá de Guillermo?**
CD 4 Tr. 11

17 **Es tu turno** Answers will vary.

Usa las mismas preguntas de la entrevista de Gisela para entrevistar a tu compañero(a). Luego cambien de papel.

Comprehension Check

Building on Previous Skills

15 Have students write Guillermo's response to his mother's note. Guillermo answers that he cannot do the things that his mother asks, gives explanations, and suggests alternatives. Guillermo closes by saying that he will be more reliable the next time.

Challenge

16 Have students compare what Gisela and Guillermo eat. Who eats more healthfully? Ask students to compare their own eating habits with those of the interviewees.

Culture Note

Guillermo mentions that **hallacas** are a special dish at Christmas. **Hallacas** were originally made by Venezuelan Indians. They are usually made of cornmeal **(masa),** filled with beef or sometimes pork or chicken, mixed with onion, pepper, raisins, and chickpeas, and wrapped in banana leaves before being steamed.

Contigo en la distancia

As an alternative or in addition to **¡Adelante!,** you may wish to show Episode 4 of *Contigo en la distancia.* For suggestions and activities, see the *Video Guide.*

Answers

14 1. En Semana Santa se come pescado y en Navidad se come el pan de jamón y las hallacas.
2. Va a un automercado.
3. Los compra en los mercados al aire libre.
4. Venezuela no tiene un plato típico porque la comida es una mezcla de la comida de muchos países.
5. Guillermo y su familia hacen la sobremesa.
6. Irá a la panadería.
7. Necesita traerle caraotas, plátanos del mercado, carne de res y el pastel.

15 …traerme…, Cómprame…, ¿Podrías hacerme el favor de…?, ¿Puedes recogérmela?, Hazme el favor de…

Segundo paso

Objective Asking for help and requesting favors

WV3 CARACAS-4

Teaching Resources
pp. 108–110

PRINT
▶ Lesson Planner, p. 19
▶ Listening Activities, pp. 28–29, 32–33
▶ Activities for Communication, pp. 15–16, 61–62, 95–96
▶ Cuaderno de gramática, pp. 33–36
▶ Grammar Tutor for Students of Spanish, Chapter 4
▶ Cuaderno de actividades, pp. 43–46
▶ Cuaderno para hispanohablantes, pp. 16–20
▶ Testing Program, pp. 71–74
▶ Alternative Assessment Guide, p. 33
▶ Student Make-Up Assignments, Chapter 4

MEDIA
▶ One-Stop Planner
▶ Audio Compact Discs, CD 4, Trs. 12–13, 26–28, 20
▶ Teaching Transparencies 4-2; **Más práctica gramatical** Answers; Cuaderno de gramática Answers
▶ Interactive CD-ROM Tutor, Disc 1

Bell Work

On the board or on a transparency, write: **Usando los verbos** *perder, olvidar, romper* **u otros, escribe cinco oraciones para explicar eventos inesperados.**

Presenting
Así se dice, Nota gramatical

Walk around the classroom with a load of books and ask different students to help you. After modeling the phrases, have students act out scenarios in which they ask each other for help.

Así se dice

Asking for help and requesting favors

Para pedir un favor, puedes decir:

Por favor, ayúdame con los platos.

Papá necesita las servilletas. **¿Se las llevas?**

Hazme/Hágame el favor de comprarme los ingredientes para las hallacas.

¿Podrías pasar por la panadería por abuelito, Chuy?

Necesito esa bolsa para estas flores. **¿Sería Ud. tan amable de dármela?**

 Cuaderno de actividades, pp. 43, 45, Acts. 13, 17

Nota gramatical

Por can mean *by, in exchange for, for the benefit of,* or *in favor of:*

¿Podrías pasar **por** la panadería **por** abuelito?

It is also used in many idiomatic expressions like **por favor, por cierto** and **por ahora**.

Para often implies *intended for* or *for the purpose of:*

Necesito esa bolsa **para** estas flores.

 Cuaderno de gramática, p. 33, Acts. 11–12

Más práctica gramatical, p. 118, Act. 6

Cuaderno de actividades, p. 46, Act. 18

18 **¿Qué se le ofrece?** Script and answers on p. 95H.

Escuchemos Indica si el hombre en cada conversación que escuchas es **el cliente, el dependiente,** o **un transeúnte** *(passerby)*.

CD 4 Tr. 12

19 **Gramática en contexto** Answers will vary.

Escribamos Imagina que te dio alguien un robot para tu cumpleaños. Dile al robot que te haga 10 cosas. Dile también para qué. Tienes que ser muy cortés.

MODELO ─**Limpie mi cuarto para la fiesta, por favor.**

20 **Organícenlo** Answers will vary.

Escribamos/Hablemos A ti y a tu compañero(a) les toca organizar la cena para el Club de Español. Primero preparen un plan de todo lo que tienen que hacer. Luego, imagínense que les están pidiendo ayuda a ocho compañeros con los preparativos de la cena. Usen las expresiones de **Así se dice.**

Nota cultural

La gran variedad cultural del pueblo venezolano se refleja en los platos típicos. Se nota la influencia de italianos, portugueses, alemanes, franceses y chinos. En algunos lugares, como en el Amazonas, uno puede comer bachacos fritos *(fried ants)* y pirañas. Pero la comida más típica es la arepa, un pan aplanado y redondo hecho de maíz. Se rellena con carne, huevos, queso y otros ingredientes. ¿Hay una comida típica de tu ciudad o región?

Cultures and Communities

Language Notes

• Have students look at the photo. Caracas has numerous **areperas,** small restaurants specializing in **arepas.** A variety of fillings is offered, and patrons can also order **batidos** (fruit shakes) or **jugo natural** (unprocessed juice). **Arepas** are so common in Venezuela that **ganar la arepa** means to earn one's bread and butter.

• Ice cream is also called **nieve**. A **barquillo**, or **cono de nieve**, is an ice-cream cone. A **raspa** is a snow cone. A **paleta de agua** is flavored ice (generally made from fruit juice extract and water) on a stick. When milk is substituted for water, it is called a **paleta de leche**. **Paletas** can also be made from nut and root extracts.

Vocabulario

Si necesitas comprar comida para una fiesta, puedes pasar por...

 la carnicería

 la lechería

 la pastelería

 la bodega

 la frutería

 la panadería

Si necesitas reparar el carro o un aparato, puedes pasar por...

 la pescadería

 la heladería

 el taller

 la ferretería

 la tienda de refacciones

Más práctica gramatical, p. 118, Act. 7

Cuaderno de gramática, p. 34, Acts. 13–14   Cuaderno de actividades, pp. 43, 45, Acts. 12, 14, 16

21 ¿Adónde voy?

Leamos/Hablemos Tu compañero(a) te va a preguntar adónde debe ir para encontrar lo siguiente. Basa tus sugerencias en el **Vocabulario** y en la página amarilla de abajo.

> **También se puede decir...**
> En México puedes decir **nevería** en vez de **heladería**.

MODELO
—Necesito una torta para la fiesta de cumpleaños. ¿Me podrías sugerir un buen lugar para comprar una?
—Sí, cómo no. Ve a comprarla a la Panadería y Pastelería La Yaya.

1. crema para un quesillo
2. pescado
3. vidrio para una ventana
4. bistec
5. cosas para el carro
6. un buen mecánico
7. galletas
8. unas naranjas y manzanas
9. helado

Nota cultural

En Venezuela, se come mucho pan de jamón en fiestas en los lugares de trabajo. También se comen los famosos churros españoles, tubos de masa fritos y salpicados de azúcar. Igualmente populares son los dulces, por ejemplo, el bienmesabe o el dulce de lechosa (papaya). En época de Navidad, la comida preferida es la hallaca—una masa de maíz rellena con carne sazonada, aceitunas, tomates y verduras, todo envuelto en hojas de plátano. ¿Tiene tu familia un plato tradicional que se come en una fiesta?

Bodega La Milagrosa
Calle 162 con Avenida 39 .... 51.2420
Carnicería Valles
Avenida Socorro, Edificio Elisa 33.1370
Charcutería Rosaura
Avenida Universidad, Edificio Brisas 83.3915
Ferretería El Martillo de Oro
Calle 158 con Avenida 38 .... 55.9328
Frutería Romualda
Avenida Nueva Granada a Anauco 96.3664
Heladería La Glacial
Curamiche a Viento 44.3165
Lechería El Polo Norte
Centro Comercial Este, Avenida Aldo 24.1905
Panadería y Pastelería La Yaya
Avenida Bosque, Esquina Av. Nieves 59.6327
Pescadería Monte Bello
Calle 161 con Avenida 39 .... 51.3738
Refacciones Chatarra
Carretera Norte 17000 .... 59.1725
Taller Auto-Médico
Avenida Industrial con Carretera 15 .... 59.8460

Communication for All Students

Tactile Learners

Prepare a closed box with a flap in the side large enough to allow a hand to reach in. Fill the box with objects such as plastic food items, tools, and small car parts. Have a student choose an item without looking, and attempt to identify it by touch. He or she is to guess where the item can be purchased. (a wrench; **la ferretería**)

Native Speakers

Ask students about a favorite dish from their cultural background. Does their family have a special recipe for it? How long has the recipe been in the family? Can the ingredients be found locally? Students may choose to share the recipe or samples with the class.

> ### Presenting
> #### Vocabulario
> Use the names of the shops in the **Vocabulario** in sentences as students follow in their books. Begin by associating them with an appropriate food. (**Para comprar una torta de chocolate voy a una pastelería.**) After this, ask students where they would buy some of the foods listed on page 102. (**¿Dónde se compran los melocotones?**)

Speaking Assessment

21 Before students begin Activity 21, review the criteria listed in the following rubric. After the class completes the activity, have each pair of students work with another to mention four places where they go to buy things. Have them evaluate the other pair's performance, using the rubric.

Speaking Rubric	Points			
	4	3	2	1
Content (Complete–Incomplete)				
Comprehension (Total–Little)				
Comprehensibility (Comprehensible–Incomprehensible)				
Accuracy (Accurate–Seldom accurate)				
Fluency (Fluent–Not fluent)				

18–20: A   14–15: C   Under
16–17: B   12–13: D   12: F

Presenting
Gramática

Double object pronouns
On the board, write the letters I and D. Have students name the direct and indirect object pronoun forms and write them under the appropriate heading. (It may help some learners to remember sentence order by thinking of their "ID card"— indirect before direct.) Have students take dictation, skipping every other line on their paper. **(Compro los mangos en la frutería para mis hijos. Juanita busca pan en la panadería para su esposo. ¿Quieres comprar helado para Teresa y para mí en la heladería?)** Ask students to underline the direct objects and to circle the indirect objects.

Teacher Note
Remind students that in **se la trajo a ella, se** is the indirect object pronoun, while in **se me perdieron las fotos** (which they learned in **Primer paso**), the word **se** indicates an unintentional event.

Assess
▸ Testing Program, pp. 71–74
  Quiz 4-2A, Quiz 4-2B
  Audio CD 4, Tr. 20

▸ Student Make-Up Assignments, Chapter 4, Alternative Quiz

▸ Alternative Assessment Guide, p. 33

Answers
23 1. Sí, dásela... / No, no se la des...
  2. Sí, envíasela... / No, no se la envíes...
  3. Sí, prepárasela... / No, no se la prepares...
  4. Sí, cómpratelo... / No, no te lo compres...
  5. Sí, cuídaselos... / No, no se los cuides...

Gramática

Double object pronouns

1. When a direct and an indirect object pronoun are used together, the indirect always comes before the direct object.
   Quiero la ensalada. **¿Me la** trae ahora, por favor?

2. The verb and the two pronouns form an unbreakable unit. Negative words and adverbs must come before or after this unit.
   ¿La ensalada? La mesera **no me la trajo nunca.**

3. **Se** replaces **le** and **les** before the direct object pronouns **lo, la, los,** and **las.**

   Es que **se la** trajo **a ella**.

4. Pronouns are attached to infinitives and affirmative commands. An accent is sometimes placed over the stressed syllable.
   Présta**melo**, por favor.

   Pronouns come before the verb in negative commands.
   ¡Hombre, no **se lo** prestes!

Más práctica gramatical, p. 119, Acts. 8–10

Cuaderno de actividades, p. 44, Act. 15

Cuaderno de gramática, pp. 35–36, Acts. 15–18

22 **¿Qué recomiendas?**   Script and answers on p. 95H.

Escuchemos Escucha las preguntas e indica cuál de las recomendaciones es correcta.

CD 4
Tr. 13

1. a. Cómpramelo en la Panadería Adriana.
   b. Cómpraselo en la Panadería Adriana.

2. a. No, no me la traigas.
   b. No, no me los traigas.

3. a. Voy a comprártela en la Pescadería Neptuno.
   b. Voy a comprártelos en la Pescadería Neptuno.

4. a. Cómo no, te la traigo en seguida.
   b. Cómo no, te las traigo en seguida.

23 **Gramática en contexto**   See answers below.

Leamos/Escribamos Imagina que tienes un programa de radio que se llama *Nuestra comunidad*. Dales consejos a las personas que te llaman con las siguientes preguntas. Explícales tus razones.

MODELO   **¿Les sirvo galletas a los niños en el parque?**
    —**Sí, sírveselas porque...** o **No, no se las sirvas porque...**

1. Juan no entiende bien la tarea. ¿Le doy mi tarea?

2. Hace cinco años que no le hablo a mi amiga. ¿Le envío esta carta?

3. Es el cumpleaños de Ana. ¿Le preparo la cena?

4. Ayer gané la lotería. ¿Me compro el carro que vimos?

5. Quiero sacar una A en el próximo examen. ¿Le cuido los niños a mi maestra?

24  Del colegio al trabajo

Escribamos Imagina que trabajas para una agencia de publicidad. Tienes que mejorar el anuncio de los jugos de La Costeña. Debes usar un complemento directo e indirecto en tu anuncio.

Communication for All Students

Challenge
23 Have pairs of students come up with similar problems that would elicit double object pronouns with verbs such as **dar, regalar, mandar, decir,** and **contar.** Each pair trades their problems with another pair, which in turn prepares a response. Have volunteers present their exchanges to the class. Other students can then "call in" with comments and other advice.

Group Work
24 Have small groups of students create the new campaign for **La Costeña** with magazine ads and TV commercials. If possible, have students film their commercials to show to the class.

CD 4
Trs. 14–17

¿Cuál es tu plato favorito?

¿Tienes un plato favorito? Escucha mientras tres jóvenes hablan de sus platos favoritos.

Claudia
Caracas, Venezuela

"Este, arroz con pollo, guisado con papas... pescado, este... arepas. Arepas es... una comida de aquí que se hace con masa, ¿no? y son redonditas... y son muy sabrosas... Es como un pan y Ud. lo rellena con lo que quiera, con queso, con carne, con cazón—que es un pescado".
CD 4 Tr. 15

Raquel
Miami, Florida

"Los nacatamales... Tiene[n] masa, tiene[n] arroz y son como los tamales cubanos, no sé si Uds. los habrán probado, los tamales cubanos, y tiene chancho *(pork)* adentro. Nacatamal es un plato muy típico de Nicaragua".
CD 4 Tr. 16

Paulina
Quito, Ecuador

"Las frutas me gustan mucho, ensalada de frutas. Me gustan... sándwiches, me gustan mucho, hamburguesas. Como muchas frutas y verduras, sopas y carbohidratos, nada más. No como muchas golosinas, no me gustan mucho". CD 4 Tr. 17

Para pensar y hablar...

A. ¿Quién menciona platos extranjeros en su entrevista? ¿En qué países se originaron los platos mencionados? ¿A qué comida se parece la hallaca venezolana? De todas las comidas mencionadas, ¿cuántas has probado tú? Nómbralas.

B. ¿Cuál es tu plato favorito? ¿Tiene Estados Unidos un plato típico nacional?

> Cuaderno para hispanohablantes, p. 20

Teaching Resources
p. 111

PRINT
▶ Video Guide, pp. 23, 25, 28
▶ Cuaderno de actividades, p. 48
▶ Cuaderno para hispanohablantes, p. 20

MEDIA
▶ One-Stop Planner
▶ Video Program, Videocassette 2, 09:07–11:58
▶ Audio Compact Discs, CD 4, Trs. 14–17
▶ Interactive CD-ROM Tutor, Disc 1

Presenting
Panorama cultural

After students identify on the map where the interviewees are from, have them read the captions. Then show the video. Afterward, ask content questions to check comprehension. After students have done the **Para pensar y hablar...** section, you might poll the class to determine the most popular foods among your students. Then discuss which are healthful and why.

Preguntas

1. **¿Cuántas chicas mencionan platos que se preparan con carne?** (tres)
2. **¿A cuál de las muchachas le gustan las legumbres o las frutas?** (Paulina)
3. **¿Cuál de las chicas habla de los tamales?** (Raquel)
4. **¿Qué chica menciona el pescado?** (Claudia)
5. **¿Cuáles de las comidas mencionadas son tus favoritas también?** *(Answers will vary.)*

Cultures and Communities

Culture Note
The **arepa** can be filled with combinations of egg, cheese, and meat, and is often eaten on the go. **Arepas** are eaten at all meals as well. Ask students what an equivalent food might be in Mexico. (tortilla) In the United States? (bread) In Greece? (pita bread)

Language Note
Claudia speaks of **guisado**, typically a stew. One of the **arepa** fillings Claudia mentions is **cazón**, a kind of shark. Raquel speaks of the **nacatamales** from her home country of Nicaragua. This word is from Nahuatl. In Nahuatl, **nacatl** is *meat*. **Nacatamales** throughout Central America are tamales made with meat. **Golosinas** are *sweets*.

Cocina y cultura

Es difícil imaginar un mundo sin papas. Las papas eran totalmente desconocidas en Europa antes de 1492. Este artículo trata de la importancia de la papa en la cultura e historia de las Américas.

Estrategia para leer

Sometimes an author talks about past, present, and future within the same article. If the information is not arranged chronologically, how can you identify the time of each event? One way is to look for clues like **en 1954, hoy día,** or **el próximo año.** Another way is to pay attention to verb endings.

¡A comenzar!

A. Indica si los siguientes verbos están en el presente, el pretérito, el imperfecto o el futuro. Si no te acuerdas de las formas, consulta la sección que comienza en la página R34. See answers below.

1. adoran	5. constituía
2. descubrieron	6. disputaban
3. comenzó	7. constituyen
4. serán	8. destruyeron

¿Te acuerdas?

Skim to get the gist. Look at titles, pictures, and—if you have time—the first sentence of each paragraph.

B. Lee el texto brevemente para averiguar de qué trata el artículo.
See answers below.

Teaching Resources
pp. 112–114

PRINT
▸ Lesson Planner, p. 20
▸ Cuaderno de actividades, p. 47
▸ Cuaderno para hispanohablantes, pp. 16–19
▸ Reading Strategies and Skills Handbook, Chapter 4
▸ ¡Lee conmigo! 3, Chapter 4
▸ Standardized Assessment Tutor, Chapter 4

MEDIA
▸ One-Stop Planner

Prereading
Activity A

Making Predictions
A. Have students read the first paragraph of the selection. Ask them to think about the information that **los alimentos cultivados originalmente** and **aún constituyen** give them about the reading. What predictions can they make about the content of the selections? Then have them read the first sentence of each paragraph to see if their predictions are correct.

Answers
A 1. presente
2. pretérito
3. pretérito
4. futuro
5. imperfecto
6. imperfecto
7. presente
8. pretérito

Una Causa
Picante

Papas, tomates, maíz y maníes eran los alimentos cultivados originalmente, hace muchos siglos, por talentosos agricultores indígenas en las terrazas andinas y que aún constituyen el núcleo de la dieta peruana.

²El desarrollo de estos cuatro rubros, solamente, bien puede considerarse una de las contribuciones más significativas a la despensa mundial. Pero los agricultores incas también pueden reivindicar por lo menos parte del crédito por el desenvolvimiento de variedades de maíz, pimientos, calabazas, mandioca, batatas y pal-

tas. El resultado es que desde los días en que constituía el corazón del imperio incaico, el Perú posee las claves de una cocina refinada que se considera, a menudo, la mejor del continente.

³La nación quechua, conocida universalmente por el nombre de su jefe supremo, el Inca, elaboró una refinada ciencia agrícola en las laderas y terrazas de los Andes. Un complejo sistema de riego, acaso más pulido que el de origen romano, irrigaba mesetas y terrazas. Los agricultores cultivaban una infinita variedad de verduras, concentrándose principalmente en el maíz, las papas y los pimientos. Hoy día, inclusive, el país se ufana de poseer por lo menos treinta variedades de papas: amarillas, azules y púrpuras; pequeñas como guijarros o grandes como cocos; suaves y algodonosas, o densas y crujientes.

Los quechuas también descubrieron métodos únicos para conservar las papas. Para elaborar el chuño las esparcían sobre esteros para secarlas al sol y las retiraban al llegar la noche. El proceso consistía en extraer la humedad, de manera muy similar a la utilizada para secar las vainas de vainilla y madurar su sabor. A veces, para exprimir la humedad de los

Cultures and Communities

Background Information
The foods not only of Peru but of all the Americas have profoundly influenced world cooking. The Spanish introduced such American foods as tomatoes, corn, potatoes, peppers, peanuts, pumpkins, cacao beans, and vanilla to the rest of the world.

Culture Note
The Incan Empire, founded around 1200 A.D., was flourishing when Francisco Pizarro began his conquest in 1533. The Incas created a form of government in which the state owned everything but the houses. The Incas were skillful farmers. They terraced their hillsides, used fertilizers, and irrigated their crops.

tubérculos, las mujeres danzaban sobre ellos después de cosecharlos, a la manera tradicional italiana de pisar la uva para hacer vino. Luego de secar las papas hasta dejarlas negras y duras como rocas, las restauraban para hacerlas comestibles, empapándolas y tostándolas. Las papas secas se preparaban de la misma forma, pero se las cocinaba antes del proceso de secado.

La "causa" puede ser tan complicada como lo disponga la imaginación del cocinero o tan simple como el sobrante de un plato de carne y verduras al horno o "casserole". Ésta es una receta básica, lista para cualquier combinación con carne, pescado y verduras, fritas o guisadas.

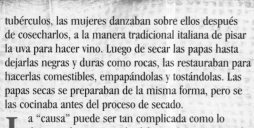

CAUSA

Seis porciones

8 papas medianas
1/2 taza de cebolla picada
1/2 cucharadita de pimiento rojo seco
6 cucharadas de jugo de limón
5 cucharadas de aceite de oliva
2 ajíes picantes frescos, sin semillas y cortados delgados
3/4 libras de queso fresco, Feta o Muenster, cortado en tajadas
Sal y pimienta
Hojas de lechuga
Aceitunas negras

Combine a su gusto las cebollas, el limón, los ajíes, la sal y la pimienta y déjelos aparte. Hierva las papas en agua salada, séquelas, pélelas y haga un puré, combinándolas luego con la mezcla inicial. Agregue el aceite y continúe mezclando. Añada los ajíes frescos y colóquela en un tazón para moldear el puré, viértalo en un plato de servir y rodee el puré con hojas de lechuga, aceitunas negras y tajadas de queso.

⁶En el antiguo Perú el maíz y las papas se disputaban la supremacía y hoy día continúan predominando en los menús y las chacras del país. El maíz que hoy se cultiva en el Perú es el más singular del mundo. Semillas rojas, anaranjadas, blancas, púrpuras y negras se presentan juntas o separadas en un arco iris de

---

1. A primera vista, ¿hay más verbos en el tiempo pasado, presente o futuro? ¿Qué te dice esto sobre la lectura?
2. ¿Cuál de las siguientes frases resume mejor el artículo?
   a. cómo preparar un plato que se llama **causa**
   b. la historia de la nación quechua: su política, arte, geografía y comida
   c. usos modernos e históricos de comidas en Perú

¿Te acuerdas?
When you encounter an unknown word, it's often best to keep reading rather than stop to look it up. The context allows you to guess the meaning.

C. Usando solamente el contexto, ¿puedes encontrar un lugar en el segundo párrafo para sustituir cada una de estas palabras?

cocina   desarrollo
nación   partes esenciales
con frecuencia   categoría
See answers below.

Al grano   See answers below.
D. Ahora miremos algunos detalles de cada párrafo, menos la receta.
   1. Según los párrafos 1 y 2, ¿qué importancia culinaria tenía el Perú?
   2. ¿Por qué están en el imperfecto los verbos **cultivaban** e **irrigaba** en el párrafo 3?
   3. Mira la primera frase del párrafo 4. ¿Cómo se expresa la misma frase en inglés?
   4. En el párrafo 4, ¿qué hacían las mujeres para extraer el agua de las papas?
   5. Según el párrafo 5, ¿qué ventajas tiene esta receta para la **causa?**

Reading
Activities B, C, and D

Using Context Clues
C. Have students work in pairs to locate the synonyms. They should discuss how they were able to determine the meanings of the words from context. After a short period of time, reunite the class and see if pairs found different ways to determine the words' meanings from context.

Answers
B 1. el pasado. El artículo trata del pasado.
   2. c.

C cocina = despensa
desarrollo = desenvolvimiento
nación = imperio
partes esenciales = las claves
con frecuencia = a menudo
categoría = variedad

D 1. Perú ha contribuido papas, tomates, maíz y maníes a la despensa mundial.
   2. La acción comienza en el pasado y sigue en el presente.
   3. The Quechua also discovered unique methods of preserving potatoes.
   4. Las mujeres danzaban sobre los tubérculos para extraer la humedad.
   5. Es una receta básica y simple.
   6. el clima y la altitud
   7. la llegada de Pizarro y la destrucción de la antigua civilización
   8. culturas indígenas, españolas y africanas

Connections and Comparisons

Thinking Critically
Analyzing Ask students to imagine that they are living in a region of the world with no electricity and no modern inventions. What kinds of food would they eat every day? How would they prepare it? How would they preserve it? *(Answers will vary.)*

History Link
Assign various groups or individuals to research Incan art, architecture, irrigation practices, cuisine, government, or other aspects of their life and culture. Have students report their findings to the class. You might assign this as an Internet activity.

Vamos a leer

CAPÍTULO 4

Teaching Resources
pp. 112–114

PRINT
▸ Lesson Planner, p. 20
▸ Cuaderno de actividades, p. 47
▸ Cuaderno para hispanohablantes, pp. 16–19
▸ Reading Strategies and Skills Handbook, Chapter 4
▸ ¡Lee conmigo! 3, Chapter 4
▸ Standardized Assessment Tutor, Chapter 4

MEDIA
▸ One-Stop Planner

Postreading
Activities E, F, and G

Determining the Main Idea
You may want to suggest that students use the strategy **La palabra principal** to find the main idea of the reading. They should write a brief paragraph explaining why their word is the most important, basing their arguments on evidence in the text. If this is too challenging, have students choose the most important word in each paragraph and then narrow their choices down to one word for the entire reading.

Answers
E 1. Combine las cebollas, el limón, los ajíes, la sal y la pimienta y déjelos aparte.
2. Hierva las papas en agua salada, séquelas, pélelas y haga un puré, combinándolas con la mezcla inicial.
3. Agregue el aceite y continúe mezclando.
4. Añada los ajíes frescos y colóquela en un tazón para moldear el puré.
5. Viértalo en un plato de servir y rodée el puré con hojas de lechuga, aceitunas y tajadas de queso.

F *Answers will vary.*

114 CIENTO CATORCE   VAMOS A LEER

---

6. ¿Qué determina el sabor de los ajíes, según el párrafo 7?

7. En el párrafo 8, ¿qué comentarios indican que los quechuas no dominan los Andes ahora?

8. Según el párrafo 8, ¿cuáles son las culturas que han contribuido a la cocina peruana moderna?
See answers below.

E. Ahora lee la receta y corrige las siguientes instrucciones para la **causa**.

1. Mezcle las cebollas, el limón, el queso y la pimienta, y déjelos aparte.

2. Hierva y seque las papas, y déjelas aparte.

3. Agregue cebolla y lechuga y continúe mezclando.

4. Añada los ajíes frescos y póngalos en un vaso para moldear el puré.

5. Viértalo en un plato de servir y rodee los ajíes y las papas de queso, aceite y aceitunas negras.

F. Trabaja con un(a) compañero(a). Resuman en dos o tres frases lo que dice el autor sobre cada uno de estos temas. Escriban las frases claves que comunican las ideas principales.

1. los cultivos más importantes de los quechuas

2. las distintas formas de preparar las papas en Perú

3. el maíz en relación a las papas

4. el uso del picante en América del Sur

5. la dieta peruana típica

G. What are the staples of the typical person's diet in the United States? What are the origins of these staples?

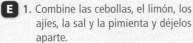
Cuaderno para hispanohablantes, pp. 16–19
Cuaderno de actividades, p. 47, Acts. 20–22

---

espigas multicolores. Tan variadas como los colores son las formas de los granos, que pueden llegar a ser tan grandes como uvas o fresas, duros y crocantes o suaves y brillantes.

El maíz y las papas serán productos del Perú, pero la gloria de la región la constituye el arco iris de ajíes que aquí se elaboró y se cultiva, siendo sus colores, tamaño y calidad de picante determinados por el clima y la altitud. Genéricamente se les conoce como ajíes, pero cuando los peruanos dicen ají se refieren al poderoso mirasol. En muchos platos los ajíes más picantes constituyen la base del sabor porque la comida peruana puede ser la más condimentada de América del Sur, aunque sin llegar a la fiereza de los platos más picantes de México o el Caribe.

[8]Aunque los quechuas dominaron los Andes con su sistema de caminos y viaductos y organizaron las aldeas remotas en un imperio disgregado, pocas son las constancias existentes que sirvan para enfrentar al esplendor culinario de los aztecas. A su llegada, Pizarro y sus hombres efectivamente destruyeron la antigua civilización, pero los quechuas que no fueron asesinados o diezmados por las enfermedades, siguieron cultivando la tierra. No trabajarían para los españoles y en algún momento comenzó la esclavización e importación de africanos para reemplazar a los reacios esclavos indígenas. La mezcla resultante de culturas indígena, española y africana creó la cocina peruana moderna.

Communication for All Students

Challenge
Ask interested students to prepare **causa**. Ask them to describe its preparation to the class in Spanish. If possible, have them bring some for the class to sample.

Group Work
Have groups of students pick one indigenous American food, such as corn, potatoes, tomatoes, peanuts, or peppers, and research how it was introduced to other parts of the world. They might also discuss its history, nutritional value, use in various dishes, or another aspect that appeals to them. Ask them to present their findings to the class.

STANDARDS: 1.2, 2.2, 3.1, 3.2, 4.2

Vamos a escribir

¿Alguna vez te has sentido intimidado(a) por una página en blanco, aun después de investigar tu tema y decidir cómo organizar la información? El escribir puede ser una tarea compleja, especialmente en un idioma extranjero. En esta actividad, aprenderás otra manera de hacer más fácil la tarea de escribir.

Tu receta favorita

Imagina que tu profesor(a) va a hacer una colección de las recetas favoritas de la clase de español. Escribe una receta sencilla para esta colección. Acuérdate que no sólo las comidas requieren recetas. Si prefieres, puedes escribir una receta para preparar el cemento, diferentes colores de pintura, el papel maché o un pegamento casero (*homemade glue*).

Estrategia para escribir

Making a writing plan Before writing, take a good look at your topic. Do you know all the vocabulary you'll need? If not, use a good bilingual dictionary or ask your teacher for assistance. Will your topic require you to use certain tenses frequently? If you're not sure you can use them correctly, consult your textbook or ask your teacher or other students for help.

A. Preparación

1. Decide qué receta quieres escribir. La receta debe ser interesante pero no muy complicada.

2. Considera bien la receta y prepara listas del vocabulario que vas a necesitar para los ingredientes y las instrucciones.

3. Puedes usar mandatos informales, infinitivos o construcciones con **se** para explicar cómo se hace la comida. ¿Conoces bien las formas? Repasa la información sobre los mandatos en esta lección antes de escribir o consulta la sección que comienza en la página R25. ¿Hay otras estructuras que vas a necesitar?

B. Redacción

1. Escribe la receta, poniendo en orden todos los pasos del proceso.

2. Si quieres, haz la comida en casa y saca una foto de cada paso para incluir con la receta.

3. Si usas palabras que otros(as) estudiantes no van a comprender, defínelas.

C. Evaluación

1. Dales la receta a tres o cuatro compañeros(as) de clase para leer. ¿La entienden? Si no, pregúntales por qué y haz los cambios necesarios.

2. ¿Escribiste bien las palabras y estructuras que usaste? Si no, busca las formas correctas.

3. ¿Se puede leer fácilmente tu receta? Si no, tal vez debes copiar la receta otra vez o escribirla a máquina.

Apply and Assess

Postwriting
Auditory Learners

Ask various students to read their recipes to the class without saying what they are. The class is to guess what the dish is.

Art Link

Compile the class recipes in a binder. You may want to make copies for each student. Invite students to design a cover for the class cookbook.

Native Speakers

Have native speakers role-play a TV cooking show in which they demonstrate their recipes. You may wish to videotape the cooking show.

Vamos a escribir

CAPÍTULO 4

Teaching Resources
p. 115

PRINT
▸ Lesson Planner, p. 20
▸ Cuaderno de actividades, pp. 145–156
▸ Cuaderno para hispanohablantes, p. 19
▸ Alternative Assessment Guide, p. 19
▸ Standardized Assessment Tutor, Chapter 4

MEDIA
▸ One-Stop Planner, Disc 1
▸ Test Generator, Chapter 4
▸ Interactive CD-ROM Tutor, Disc 1

Process Writing

Prewriting
Teaching Suggestions
• Bring in different kinds of recipes in Spanish for students to browse through for vocabulary and style.
• Review informal commands. (**Sara, escribe una receta sencilla. No escribas una receta complicada.**) Refer students to page R39 for additional review of commands.

Writing
Additional Vocabulary
añadir *to add*
asar *to roast*
calentar (ie) *to heat*
la cucharada *tablespoon*
la cucharadita *teaspoon*
dorar *to brown, to sauté*
freír (i) *to fry*
fuego lento *low heat*
hornear *to bake in the oven*
la lata *can*
media taza *one-half cup*
mezclar *to mix*
rellenar de *to fill, to stuff with*

For **Más práctica gramatical** Answer Transparencies, see the *Teaching Transparencies* binder.

Más práctica gramatical

internet

MARCAR: go.hrw.com
PALABRA CLAVE:
WV3 CARACAS-4

Primer paso   **Objectives** Talking about how food tastes; talking about unintentional events

1 Explica cómo está todo hoy en el restaurante La Fuente, usando la forma **-ísimo/a** de los adjetivos y siguiendo el modelo. **(p. 101)**

MODELO   **el flan/dulce**
        —El flan está dulcísimo.

1. las enchiladas/saladas
2. los frijoles/ricos
3. los mariscos/buenos
4. la sopa/mala
5. la salsa/sabrosa
6. nuestro mesero/cansado
7. los clientes/furiosos
8. los cocineros/ocupados

2 Lee lo que les gusta comer a todos. Después, explica lo que cada persona puede pedir de comer en un restaurante, según sus gustos. Usa estas palabras. **(p. 102)**

ostras	pargo	almejas
trucha	melocotones	
	caraotas	ensalada de aguacate
puerco asado	quesillo	patilla
	bacalao	
chorizo		chuletas
torta	ternera	

Al señor Molina le encantan los mariscos. Puede pedir ___1___ o/u ___2___.

A Leticia le gusta mucho la fruta. Puede pedir ___3___ o/u ___4___.

A mí me gusta el pescado. Puedo pedir ___5___, ___6___ o/u ___7___.

Ricardo prefiere comer legumbres. ¿Qué puede pedir? ___8___ o/u ___9___.

Y a Memito le encantan los postres. ¿Qué va a pedir? ___10___ o/u ___11___.

Beto y Alicia comen mucha carne. Pueden pedir ___12___, ___13___, ___14___ o/u ___15___.

Answers

1
1. Las enchiladas están saladísimas.
2. Los frijoles están riquísimos.
3. Los mariscos están buenísimos.
4. La sopa está malísima.
5. La salsa está sabrosísima.
6. Nuestro mesero está cansadísimo.
7. Los clientes están furiosísimos.
8. Los cocineros están ocupadísimos.

2 *Order of answers within each category may vary.*
1. almejas
2. ostras
3. patilla
4. melocotones
5. trucha
6. bacalao
7. pargo
8. Caraotas
9. ensalada de aguacate
10. Quesillo
11. torta
12. puerco asado
13. chorizo
14. ternera
15. chuletas

Grammar Resources for Chapter 4

The **Más práctica gramatical** activities are designed as supplemental activities for the grammatical concepts presented in the chapter. You might use them as additional practice, for review, or for assessment.

For more grammar presentation, review, and practice, refer to the following:
• Cuaderno de gramática
• Grammar Tutor for Students of Spanish

• Grammar Summary on pp. R25–R46
• Cuaderno de actividades
• Grammar and Vocabulary quizzes (Testing Program)
• Test Generator on the One-Stop Planner CD-ROM
• Interactive CD-ROM Tutor
• **Juegos interactivos** at <u>go.hrw.com</u>

3 La clase de español fue a un restaurante venezolano, y a muchos se les perdió algo. Explica qué se le perdió a quién, según la información en la tabla. **(p. 103)**

MODELO   **A la profesora se le perdió el libro de recetas venezolanas.**

LA PROFESORA	EL LIBRO DE RECETAS VENEZOLANAS
1. tú	¿qué?
2. el profesor	el mapa para llegar al restaurante
3. yo	la chaqueta
4. Rubén y Sara	el dinero
5. Enrique	nada
6. Marta y yo	las carteras
7. el mesero	la cuenta

4 La semana pasada el Club Internacional hizo una gran cena, pero todo salió mal. Explica qué les pasó a todos. Sigue el modelo. **(p. 103)**

MODELO   **Carolina/caer/los platos**
          —A Carolina se le cayeron los platos.

1. Héctor/quedar en casa/la música
2. Yo/quemar/los frijoles
3. Tú/olvidar/invitar al director
4. Elena y Samuel/romper/los vasos
5. Raquel/perder/el dinero para comprar refrescos
6. Natalia y yo/olvidar/hacer la ensalada
7. Nosotros/acabar/la comida
8. Esteban y Laura/romper/la cámara

5 El profesor Cuadra llevó a unos estudiantes a España. Completa su relato sobre sus primeros días allí. Usa el pronombre de objeto indirecto adecuado en el primer espacio, y usa la forma correcta del pretérito del verbo entre paréntesis en el segundo espacio. **(p. 103)**

¡Qué desastre fueron los primeros días! Primero a Tony se ___1___ (caer) la comida que le sirvieron en el avión. Luego a Allison se ___2___ (perder) las maletas en el aeropuerto. Cuando salimos del aeropuerto, a Mike se ___3___ (quedar) las gafas en el cuarto de baño. Al día siguiente cuando salimos a pasear, a Alex se ___4___ (romper) la cámara y a mí se ___5___ (descomponer) la bicicleta que alquilé. Por suerte, no se ___6___ (acabar) las ganas de quedarnos en España, porque ahora lo estamos pasando de maravilla.

Answers

3 1. ¿Qué se te perdió?
2. Al profesor se le perdió el mapa para llegar al restaurante.
3. A mí se me perdió la chaqueta.
4. A Rubén y a Sara se les perdió el dinero.
5. A Enrique no se le perdió nada.
6. A Marta y a mí se nos perdieron las carteras.
7. Al maestro se le perdió la cuenta.

4 1. A Héctor se le quedó en casa la música.
2. A mí se me quemaron los frijoles.
3. A ti se te olvidó invitar al director.
4. A Elena y a Samuel se les rompieron los vasos.
5. A Raquel se le perdió el dinero para comprar refrescos.
6. A Natalia y a mí se nos olvidó hacer la ensalada.
7. A nosotros se nos acabó la comida.
8. A Esteban y a Laura se les rompió la cámara.

5 1. le cayó
2. le perdieron
3. le quedaron
4. le rompió
5. me descompuso
6. nos acabaron

Communication for All Students

Visual Learners
Bring in pictures of foods clipped from magazines. Try to get foods that are listed in the **Vocabulario.** Show the pictures to different students and ask them to name the food and describe how it tastes.

Additional Practice
Ask students if they are going to do something (go to the movies, eat at a new restaurant, play basketball in the park). They should reply that they cannot and give an unexpected event as the reason. (**—Ismael, ¿vas al cine hoy? —No puedo porque se me olvidó el dinero.**)

Más práctica gramatical

CAPÍTULO 4

For **Más práctica gramatical** Answer Transparencies, see the *Teaching Transparencies* binder.

Más práctica gramatical

WV3 CARACAS-4

Segundo paso   **Objective** Asking for help and requesting favors

6 La señora Márquez llamó a casa y les dejó una lista de quehaceres y mandados a sus hijos. Completa su recado en el contestador con **por** o **para**. (p. 108)

Hola, hijos. Soy yo, mamá. Preparé la comida ——**1**—— ustedes y está en la mesa del comedor. Miguel, ——**2**—— favor, llama a la tía Luisa e invítala a cenar esta noche. Dile que papá pasará ——**3**—— ella a las siete. Chela, hijita, ve a la tienda ——**4**—— comprar leche y arroz. Y otra cosa… ¿también podrías ir al correo ——**5**—— papá ——**6**—— mandar esas cartas que están en la mesa? Después, pasen la aspiradora en la sala y saquen la basura ——**7**—— limpiar la casa un poco. Creo que es todo ——**8**—— ahora.

7 Hay muchas personas que están de compras hoy. Lee lo que dicen todos, y explica en qué tienda está cada uno. (p. 109)

MODELO **Necesito una batería para mi carro. ¿Cuánto vale?**
—**Está en la tienda de refacciones.**

la lechería   la heladería   la carnicería   el taller
la frutería   la pastelería
la pescadería   la tienda de refacciones   la bodega

1. ¿Me da cuatro chuletas y medio kilo de ternera, por favor?
2. Sí, dos litros de leche y un litro de crema.
3. ¿Qué lleva el pastel de la izquierda? ¿Es de limón o de vainilla?
4. ¿Qué más falta? A ver la lista… cereal, arroz, jugo, huevos… y galletas. Ya está.
5. Sí, deme dos kilos de plátanos. Y una piña bien madura, para comer hoy, por favor.
6. ¿Qué prefieres cenar esta noche? ¿camarones? ¿trucha? ¿pargo?
7. Mmm, qué rico. Y qué frío y cremoso. Aquí siempre pido una copa de chocolate con fresas. Las copas de piña también me gustan mucho.
8. No sé qué le pasa al carro. Por favor, ¿me lo revisa y me llama a casa esta tarde? Gracias.

Answers

6 1. para
2. por
3. por
4. para
5. por
6. para
7. para
8. por

7 1. Está en la carnicería.
2. Está en la lechería.
3. Está en la pastelería.
4. Está en la bodega.
5. Está en la frutería.
6. Está en la pescadería.
7. Está en la heladería.
8. Está en el taller.

Communication for All Students

Challenge

6 Have pairs of students create three sentences that require **por** and three that require **para,** leaving a blank where the preposition should be. Students then trade their sentences with another pair, which fills in the missing words. Ask volunteers to write their best sentences on the board for the class to complete.

Slower Pace

7 To review food stores and foods, ask the first student to name a store (**la frutería**). The second student is to name something you buy there, and then name another store (**piñas; la pastelería**). Students continue until all the names are reviewed.

8 Alberto's friends served all of his favorite foods at his surprise birthday party. Now Alberto's mom wants to know who made what dish for him. Write Alberto's answers to his mom's questions. Use double-object pronouns and follow the cues in parentheses. **(p. 110)**

MODELO   **¿Quién te hizo el flan? (Marcela)**
                 —Me lo hizo Marcela.

1. ¿Quién te preparó el arroz con pollo? (Alejandra)
2. ¿Quién te hizo el pastel? (Olivia)
3. ¿Quiénes te hicieron las empanadas? (Pedro y Catalina)
4. ¿Quién te preparó las galletas? (Juanito)
5. ¿Quién te hizo la ensalada de frutas? (Diego)
6. ¿Quién te preparó el gazpacho? (Martina)

9 Alberto got a lot of gifts at his party, and now you and another guest are trying to sort out who gave him each present. Answer the other guest's questions, using double-object pronouns and following the cues in parentheses. **(p. 110)**

MODELO   **¿Quién le regaló la novela? (Víctor)**
                 —Se la regaló Víctor.

1. ¿Quién le regaló la corbata? (Fátima)
2. ¿Quiénes le dieron los videos? (Pati y yo)
3. ¿Quién le regaló la planta? (José Luis)
4. ¿Quiénes le regalaron los dulces? (Inés y Javier)
5. ¿Quién le compró la camiseta? (Marcos)
6. ¿Quiénes le regalaron los discos compactos? (Ana y Nelson)

10 Completa las oraciones con la forma adecuada del pronombre de complemento indirecto. Escoge entre **le, les,** o **se. (p. 110)**

CLARA   Oye, Felipe. Se nos acabó la leche. ____1____ serví el último litro a los gatos.

FELIPE   ¿Qué tal el jugo? ¿ ____2____ lo serviste a los gatos también?

CLARA   No. ¡Qué tontería! Sólo ____3____ di la leche.

FELIPE   Muy bien. ¿Entonces me traes el jugo?

CLARA   Sí, pero ¿a quién ____4____ lo vas a dar?

FELIPE   Voy a dar ____5____ un poco al vecino.

CLARA   Pero, yo ____6____ di un litro de jugo a los vecinos ayer.

FELIPE   Parece que ya se ____7____ ha acabado.

Review and Assess

You may wish to assign the **Más práctica gramatical** activities as additional practice or homework after presenting material throughout the chapter. Assign Activity 1 after **¿Te acuerdas?** (p. 101), Activity 2 after **Vocabulario** (p. 102), Activities 3–5 after **Gramática** (p. 103), Activity 6 after **Nota gramatical** (p. 108), Activity 7 after

Vocabulario (p. 119), and Activities 8–10 after **Gramática** (p. 110). To prepare students for the **Paso** Quizzes and Chapter Test, have them do the **Más práctica gramatical** activities in the following order: complete Activities 1–4 before taking Quiz 4-1A or 4-1B and Activities 5–8 before taking Quiz 4-2A or 4-2B.

Answers

8 1. Me lo preparó Alejandra.
   2. Me lo hizo Olivia.
   3. Me las hicieron Pedro y Catalina.
   4. Me las preparó Juanito.
   5. Me la hizo Diego.
   6. Me lo preparó Martina.

9 1. Se la regaló Fátima.
   2. Se los dimos Pati y yo.
   3. Se la regaló José Luis.
   4. Se los regalaron Inés y Javier.
   5. Se la compró Marcos.
   6. Se los regalaron Ana y Nelson.

10 1. Les
   2. Se
   3. les
   4. se
   5. le
   6. les
   7. les

Repaso

internet

go.hrw.com
MARCAR: go.hrw.com
PALABRA CLAVE:
WV3 CARACAS-4

CAPÍTULO 4

The **Repaso** reviews all four skills and culture in preparation for the Chapter Test.

 1 Escucha cada anuncio e indica cuál o cuáles de ellos corresponde(n) al dibujo. Si el anuncio no corresponde, explica por qué. Script and answers on p. 95H.

CD 4
Tr. 18

Teaching Resources
pp. 120–121

PRINT 📖
▸ Lesson Planner, p. 21
▸ Listening Activities, p. 29
▸ Video Guide, pp. 23, 25, 28
▸ Grammar Tutor for Students of Spanish, Chapter 4
▸ Cuaderno para hispanohablantes, pp. 16–20
▸ Standardized Assessment Tutor, Chapter 4

MEDIA 💿
▸ One-Stop Planner
▸ Video Program, Videocassette 2, 11:59–12:46
▸ Audio Compact Discs, CD 4, Tr. 18
▸ Interactive CD-ROM Tutor, Disc 1

---

 2 Con un(a) compañero(a), dramatiza estas situaciones. Tu compañero(a) te preguntará si hiciste el deber. Tú explicarás por qué no lo pudiste hacer y le pedirás ayuda. Después intercambien papeles. See sample answers below.

MODELO —¿Ya compraste la torta para esta noche?
—¡Ay, se me olvidó pasar por la pastelería! ¿Puedes llevarme?
—Bueno, sí, pero vamos pronto.

1. preparar la comida
2. comprar las refacciones para el carro
3. hacer el proyecto para la clase de…
4. organizar tu cuarto
5. reparar la motocicleta
6. preparar un jugo

 3 Trabajen en grupos. Uno(a) de Uds. está enfermo(a) y no puede salir de casa. La persona enferma les pide ayuda a los compañeros, y éstos le explican si pueden ayudar o no. Continúen hasta determinar quién va a hacer cada uno de los deberes.

MODELO —¿Me podrías hacer un favor?
—Sí, claro, ¿qué necesitas?
—Mañana es miércoles y yo tengo que preparar la cena. ¿Sabes cocinar?
—Bueno, este…

ayudar a una amiga con el álgebra

recoger al hermanito del colegio

entregar la tarea

llevar el carro al taller

preparar la cena el miércoles

hacer las compras

Answers
2 *Sample answers:*

1. —¿Ya preparaste la comida?
—No, se me acabaron las papas. ¿Me haces el favor de ir al supermercado?
—Sí, cómo no.
2. —¿Ya compraste las refacciones?
—No, se me quedó en casa el dinero. ¿Podrías ayudarme hoy?
—Lo siento. No puedo porque…
3. —¿Hiciste el proyecto?
—No, se me perdieron las instrucciones. Hazme el favor de prestarme las tuyas.
—No hay problema.
4. —¿Ya organizaste tu cuarto?
—Iba a organizarlo pero se me olvidó. ¿Me podrías ayudar?
—No puedo porque…
5. —¿Ya reparaste la motocicleta?
—No, porque se me acabó el tiempo. Por favor, ayúdame a repararla mañana.
—Sí, llámame y te ayudo.
6. —¿Ya preparaste un jugo?
—No, porque se me acabaron las naranjas. ¿Serías tan amable de llevarme al supermercado?
—Sí, vamos.

Apply and Assess

Group Work
1 Divide students into groups of three to write their own commercial for a restaurant and to perform it for the class. You may want to videotape their performances.

Additional Practice
2 Have students make up additional questions and explanations and practice them with a partner.

Pair Work
3 Ask various pairs to perform their dialogues for the class.

4 Revisa las secciones culturales del capítulo y contesta estas preguntas. See answers below.

1. Nombra tres dulces que se comen en Venezuela y descríbelos.

2. En caso de comer con una familia venezolana, ¿qué crees que te servirían para Navidad? ¿Cuáles son los ingredientes de este plato?

3. Imagina que eres un(a) venezolano(a) que viene a Estados Unidos. ¿Cómo comparas la comida que encuentras aquí con las comidas típicas de tu país?

 5 Con un(a) compañero(a), imagina que están en una cafetería. Tu amigo(a) come cosas no muy saludables. Le aconsejas comer otras cosas, pero tu amigo(a) trata de convencerte de que no hay problema.

MODELO —**No comas ese postre. Tiene como mil calorías.**
—**¡Qué va! Me encantan los postres. Además voy a correr esta tarde.**

 6 Con un(a) compañero(a), imagina que son reseñistas *(reviewers)* de restaurantes. Visitaron el Restaurante Criollo y comieron un poco de todos los platos mencionados en el menú. Algunos de los platos estuvieron horribles y el servicio estuvo malísimo. Escriban sus comentarios acerca de cada plato y del servicio. Usen las frases de **Así se dice** en la página 103 para hablar de los problemas que encontraron. See sample answer below.

RESTAURANTE CRIOLLO

Sopa de mariscos	2020	Bs.
Ensalada mixta	1500	Bs.
Ensalada de aguacate con camarones	3050	Bs.
Arepa con queso blanco	790	Bs.
Bistec a la parrilla	4750	Bs.
Pabellón criollo	3250	Bs.
Espaguetis a la marinera	3100	Bs.
Quesillo	800	Bs.
Café	350	Bs.
Batido de patilla	700	Bs.

7 **S i t u a c i ó n**

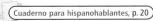

Trabajen en parejas. Escojan una de las siguientes situaciones y dramatícenla.

A. Un(a) amigo(a) quiere ir a un buen restaurante este fin de semana y le pide ayuda a otra persona, quien le da sugerencias y opiniones sobre la comida, el servicio y los precios.

B. Tú debías llevar a varios compañeros de clase al torneo regional de baloncesto, pero han pasado varias cosas inesperadas. Explícale a tu compañero(a) lo que te ha pasado y pídele ayuda.

C. Eres el anfitrión (la anfitriona) de un programa de cocina del Canal 5. Tu compañero(a) es tu invitado(a) del día. Presenten una breve escena en la que preparan una especialidad de Venezuela y comentan los resultados en distintas etapas de la preparación.

Cuaderno para hispanohablantes, p. 20

Apply and Assess

Additional Practice

4 Have students write five more statements about Venezuelan culture, and ask their partner comprehension questions about them. They can obtain information from the Location Opener on pages 62–65. Note that the Location Opener is not assessed on the Quizzes or Chapter Test.

Group Work

6 Have students form groups of three or four and write the worst thing about the restaurant. Encourage students to use words and phrases from **Vocabulario** on page 123. Then read some of the comments to the class.

📁 **Portfolio**

5 **Oral** You may want to have students include this activity in their oral Portfolios. For Portfolio suggestions, see Alternative Assessment Guide, p. 19.

Answers

4 1. dulce de lechoza, bienmesabe, churros españoles
2. hallacas (maíz, carne, aceitunas, tomates, verduras)
3. *Answers will vary.* La comida de Venezuela es de muchos países y así es la mayoría de la comida en los Estados Unidos.

6 *Sample answer:*
El Restaurante Criollo es más o menos bueno. Probé un poco de todos los platos del menú, y me gustaron algunos. Me gustó un poco la ensalada de aguacate con camarones pero tenía mucho sabor a ajo. Al bistec a la parrilla le faltaba sal. Pero, el pabellón criollo estuvo muy sabroso. El servicio estuvo bastante malo: al mesero se le olvidó traernos el menú y se le cayeron todos los postres. Me gustaría regresar de vez en cuando.

A ver si puedo...

CAPÍTULO 4

Teaching Resources
p. 122

PRINT
▶ Grammar Tutor for Students of Spanish, Chapter 4

MEDIA
▶ Interactive CD-ROM Tutor, Disc 1
▶ Online self-test

go.hrw.com
WV3 CARACAS-4

Answers

1 *Sample answers:*
1. Las empanadas están deliciosas.
2. La sopa de ostras sabe a grasa.
3. El pollo al limón lleva mucho ajo.
4. Las sardinas en ensalada, ¡guácala!
5. Las arepas saben riquísimas.
6. El café con leche está bueno.

2 *Possible answers:*
1. A la cocinera se le olvidó comprar azúcar. Puede ir al supermercado. "Se me olvidó comprar el azúcar".
2. Al mesero se le cayó la torta. Puede traer otra torta. "¡Ay! ¡Se me cayó la torta!"
3. Al hombre se le olvidaron los números. Puede ir a la ferretería. "¡Caramba! Se me olvidó".
4. Al chico se le descompuso el carro. Tiene que ir a la tienda de refacciones. "¿Dónde está una tienda de refacciones?"
5. A la chica se le perdieron las llaves. Puede usar otras llaves. "Se me perdieron las llaves".
6. Al hombre se le olvidó comprar comida para la cena. Pueden comer cereal. "Se me olvidó comprar comida".

3
1. Por favor, ayúdeme.
2. ¿Podría darme el pan, por favor?
3. Hágame el favor de traer el quesillo.
4. Por favor, ¿me pasa la sal?
5. ¿Puede poner el pastel en la mesa, por favor?
6. ¿Me podría cocinar la carne en la salsa?

Can you talk about how food tastes?
p. 101

1 Estás comiendo en el restaurante La Caraqueña en Caracas. Da tu opinión de cada cosa en la siguiente lista. *See sample answers below.*

1. empanadas
2. sopa de ostras
3. pollo al limón
4. sardinas en ensalada
5. arepas
6. café con leche

Can you talk about unintentional events?
p. 103

2 Para cada situación ilustrada, explica lo que pasó o no pasó, o lo que cada persona puede hacer y no hacer. También explica por qué. ¿Cómo explicaría cada persona la situación en sus propias palabras? *See answers below.*

1.

2.

3.

4.

5.

6.

Can you ask for help and request favors?
p. 108

3 Eres el chef de un restaurante y necesitas la ayuda de otros(as) cocineros(as). Expresa estos pedidos de una manera más cortés.

1. Ayúdeme.
2. Deme el pan.
3. Tráigame un quesillo.
4. Páseme la sal.
5. Ponga el pastel en la mesa.
6. Cocine la carne en la salsa.
See answers below.

Review and Assess

Group Work
Divide the class into groups of four students. Each group must decide on an activity or celebration (prom, wedding, birthday party), write an invitation, and plan the menu and entertainment. The group members must ask for help or favors to pull the event together. The group then talks about all the unexpected events that took place during the celebration, explaining the circumstances that caused each event.

Vocabulario

Primer paso

Talking about how food tastes

Está echado a perder.	It's spoiled (ruined).
Está en su punto.	It's just right.
¡Guácala! ¡Qué asco!	Yuck! How disgusting!
Le falta sal.	It lacks/needs/ doesn't have enough salt.
...sabor.	. . . flavor.
...no sé qué.	. . . something (I don't know what).
Lleva mucha grasa.	It has too much fat.
Me cae gordo.	It disagrees with me.
¡Qué bueno/ sabroso!	How good/tasty!
Sabe riquísimo.	It tastes delicious.
Tiene sabor a ajo.	It tastes like garlic.

Food

las almejas	clams
el bacalao	cod
el bistec a la parrilla	grilled steak
las caraotas	beans (Venezuela)
el chorizo	sausage
las chuletas de cerdo	pork chops
la ensalada mixta	tossed salad
...de aguacate	avocado salad
los mariscos	shellfish
el melocotón	peach
las ostras	oysters
el pargo	red snapper
la patilla	watermelon (Venezuela)
la piña	pineapple
el pollo frito	fried chicken
el puerco asado	roast pork
el quesillo	custard (Venezuela)

la sal	salt
la ternera	veal
la torta	cake
la trucha	trout

Talking about unintentional events

descomponer	to break down
Se le rompió...	He (She) broke . . .
Se les quedó...	They forgot/left . . .
Se me acabó/ acabaron...	I ran out of . . .
Se me perdió/ perdieron...	I lost . . .
Se nos cayó/ cayeron...	We dropped . . .
Se nos descompuso/ descompusieron...	. . . broke down on us.
¿Se te olvidó/ olvidaron...?	Did you forget . . .?

Segundo paso

Asking for help and requesting favors

Hágame/Hazme el favor de...	Do me the favor of . . .
¿Podrías...?	Could you . . .?
Por favor, ayúdame con...	Please help me with . . .
¿Se las llevas?	Will you take them to him (her)?
¿Sería(s) tan amable de dármela?	Would you be so kind as to give it to me?

Shops

la bodega	grocery store
la carnicería	butcher shop
la ferretería	hardware store
la frutería	fruit shop
la heladería	ice cream store
la lechería	dairy store
la panadería	bakery
la pastelería	pastry shop
la pescadería	fish market
el taller	shop; workshop
la tienda de refacciones	parts store

Review and Assess

♟ Game

VEINTE PREGUNTAS Students play this game with a partner. One writes the name of a food from the chapter vocabulary on a slip of paper but does not show it to the partner. The partner tries to guess the food with 20 questions or fewer. (¿Se cocina esta comida? ¿Es carne?) Then they exchange roles.

⟳ Circumlocution

Have students explain what each shop is without using its root word. For example, if the word is **lechería**, a student may not use the word **leche** to describe it. He or she might say **En esta tienda puedo comprar algo para tomar con galletas.** Other key phrases that the students may use are **Es un lugar donde...** and **En esta tienda se vende...**

CAPÍTULO 4

Teaching Suggestions

- Have students write a paragraph that is not over half a page long in which they use as many vocabulary words as possible.
- Briefly show food pictures cut from old magazines and have students call out the food in Spanish.
- Ask students to list as many foods as possible that can be bought at each of the stores in the **Vocabulario**.
- Write incomplete vocabulary words (f r _ _ _ r _ _) on the board and challenge students to identify them. (**frutería**)

Chapter 4 Assessment

▸ **Testing Program**
Chapter Test, pp. 75–80
 Audio Compact Discs, CD 4, Trs. 21–22
Speaking Test, p. 296

▸ **Alternative Assessment Guide**
Portfolio Assessment, p. 19
Performance Assessment, p. 33
CD-ROM Assessment, p. 47

▸ **Interactive CD-ROM Tutor, Disc 1**
 ¡A hablar!
¡A escribir!

▸ **Standardized Assessment Tutor**
Chapter 4

▸ **One-Stop Planner, Disc 1**
 Test Generator
Chapter 4

Teaching Resources
pp. 124–127

PRINT
▶ Lesson Planner, p. 22
▶ Video Guide, pp. 29–30

MEDIA
▶ One-Stop Planner
▶ Video Program,
  Videocassette 2, 12:59–14:45
▶ Interactive CD-ROM Tutor, Disc 2
▶ Map Transparency 3

 go.hrw.com
WV3 GUADALAJARA

 **Using the Almanac
and Map**

Terms in the Almanac

• **Clima:** Except for the rainy
season, which extends from July
to September, it is clear, dry, and
mild, with temperatures between
70° and 80°F (21° and 27°C)
year-round.

• **Economía:** Guadalajara's economy
is based on corn, livestock, and
production of textiles, shoes,
chemicals, building materials,
and soft drinks. Handicrafts are
also important.

• **Personajes famosos:** José
Clemente Orozco was one of
Mexico's famous muralists. Possibly
his best-known mural is *Man of
Fire* in the chapel of the **Hospicio
Cabañas** (shown on page 126).
María Izquierdo was the first
Mexican woman to exhibit her
works in the U.S. Considered one
of Mexico's greatest writers, Juan
Rulfo published only two works: a
collection of short stories, *El llano
en llamas;* and a novel, *Pedro
Páramo.* Luis Barragán designed
the **Jardines del Pedregal** and
the chapel for the **Capuchinas
Sacramentarius** in Tlalpan.

CAPÍTULOS 5 y 6

¡Ven conmigo a Guadalajara!

Jalisco

Población: 6.939.000

Área: 80.836 km²

Capital: Guadalajara (con aproximadamente 4.157.000 de habitantes)

Otras ciudades: Zapopan, Ciudad
Guzmán, Ocotlán, Puerto Vallarta,
Lagos de Moreno, Tepatitlán

Clima: Temperatura mínima promedio 10°C (50°F); temperatura
máxima promedio 25°C (78°F)

Economía: turismo; granos (maíz,
frijol y trigo); pesca; textiles;
industrias mineras, editoriales, de
computación y de bioquímica;
productos alimenticios, artesanías

Personajes famosos: José
Clemente Orozco (1883–1949),
muralista; Juan Rulfo
(1917–1986), escritor; María
Izquierdo (1902–1955), pintora; Luis
Barragán (1902–1988), arquitecto

Platos típicos: pozole, birria, chicharrones,
carnitas

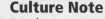 WV3 GUADALAJARA

La catedral de Guadalajara, con su
nave del siglo XVI y sus torres del
siglo XIX, es única en México. ▶

Cultures and Communities

Background Information

Guadalajara is the capital of the state of Jalisco in
west central Mexico. The city was founded in 1531
at Nochixtlán, about 60 miles north of its present
location, and was finally established at its present
site in 1542. Since 1940, Guadalajara has become
a major economic and industrial center for the
nation. It is now Mexico's second-largest city.

Culture Note

Pozole, a soup made with hominy,
chiles, and chicken or pork, is a typical
dish of Jalisco. **Birria** is barbecued beef, veal, kid,
or young pork that is served with a special sauce.
Chicharrones are pieces of fried pork skin.
Carnitas are grilled pieces of pork.

MAPQUEST.COM

go.hrw.com
HRW Atlas Interactivo Mundial

Have students use the interactive atlas at **go.hrw.com** to find out more about the geography of Mexico, and complete the Map Activities below.

Map Activities

Refer to the map of Mexico on page T75 (*Pupil's Edition* page xxv).

- Have students find Guadalajara and the state of Jalisco.
- Have students name the states that border Jalisco. (Nayarit, Zacatecas, Aguascalientes, Guanajuato, Michoacán)

CNN enEspañol.com

Have students check the **CNN en español** Web site for news on Mexico. The **CNN en español** site is also a good source of timely, high-interest readings for Spanish students.

Connections and Comparisons

Language Notes
- Guadalajara was named after the town of the same name in Spain. The name comes from the Arabic *wad-al-hidjara,* which means *river of stones.*
- A person from Guadalajara is called **guadala-jarense** or **guadalajareño(a).** People from Jalisco are called **jaliscienses,** but are nicknamed **tapatíos. Tapatío** is thought to come from the Nahuatl word *tlapatiotl,* which means *something valuable.*

History Link
La campanita del correo is located in one of the towers of the cathedral. The bell chimes for 15 minutes whenever the government receives good news about the country or the state of Jalisco.

Motivating Activity

If possible, play one of the following songs: **Jalisco** (Audio CD 6, Track 32), **Guadalajara, La bamba, Jarabe tapatío,** or **La cucaracha.** Ask students what they think of when they hear this kind of music. What do they think these songs are about?

Using the Photo Essay

❶ Influencia árabe en la arquitectura The **Plaza Tapatía** is a series of plazas near the **Teatro Degollado.** In this plaza, there is a monument commemorating Quetzalcóatl. (See the Culture Note on page 142 for information about Quetzalcóatl.)

❷ La cúpula del Instituto Cultural de Cabañas The **Hospicio Cabañas** used to be an orphanage but is now the **Instituto Cultural de Cabañas.** It has 22 patios where concerts, art exhibits, and ballet performances are held. Probably the most outstanding characteristic of the **Instituto** is the Orozco mural *Man of Fire* which decorates its cupola. When an observer stands below the painting, the man seems to be floating.

❸ La Plaza Tapatía Luis Barragán is known for minimalist building designs and breathtaking landscape settings that often incorporate fountains and pools. His frequent use of vibrant colors on the exteriors of his buildings evokes traditional Mexican village and ranch architecture. He was also inspired by Moorish gardens, with their fountains and walled enclosures.

Guadalajara

Después de México y Nuevo León, Jalisco es el tercer estado de México en importancia económica, con una base tanto industrial como agrícola. Su geografía es ideal porque tiene mar, parte de la Sierra Madre Occidental, lagos y bosques. De Jalisco provienen la charrería y la música de los mariachis, dos elementos folklóricos que forman uno de los símbolos que identifican a México como nación. Guadalajara es la capital del estado y la segunda ciudad más grande del país. Sus habitantes son conocidos como *tapatíos.*

✈ internet

MARCAR: go.hrw.com
PALABRA CLAVE:
WV3 GUADALAJARA

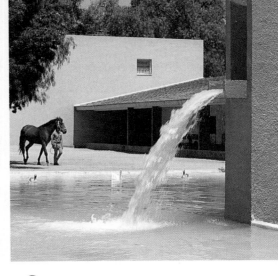

❶ Influencia árabe en la arquitectura
Este edificio fue diseñado por el famoso arquitecto tapatío Luis Barragán. Se nota la influencia árabe en el patio encerrado, con fuente y piscina. Los colores reflejan la herencia mexicana. Los arquitectos de Jalisco tienen fama internacional.

❷ La cúpula del Instituto Cultural de Cabañas
José Clemente Orozco pintó en 1939 los murales del Hospicio Cabañas, anteriormente un orfanato. Orozco fue uno de los más importantes representantes de la escuela muralista de México.

❸ La Plaza Tapatía
En esta plaza famosa se baila el típico jarabe tapatío y cantan los mariachis, quienes han exportado la música mexicana a todo el mundo.

Connections and Comparisons

Art Link

Have students research José Clemente Orozco and report their findings to the class. [He studied to be an agricultural engineer and an architect. He painted his first mural in 1922 and decorated such public buildings as the National Preparatory School (1922–1927), the House of Tiles (1925) in Mexico City, and the Industrial School in Orizaba (1926). In the U.S., he painted frescoes at the New School for Social Research in New York City (1930–1931), at Pomona College in California (1930), and at Dartmouth College in New Hampshire (1932). He returned to Mexico in 1934 and created major works such as *Man in His Four Aspects: The Worker, The Educator, The Creative Thinker, and The Rebel* (1936) at the University of Guadalajara, and *Man of Fire* (1936–1939).]

En los capítulos 5 y 6

vas a conocer las leyendas, la música y el arte de Guadalajara. La gente de esta región tiene un gran orgullo regional. Por eso son conocidos como *tapatíos,* una palabra indígena que quiere decir que valen tres veces más. ¡Aprenderás por qué son tan orgullosos los tapatíos!

4 El lago de Chalapa
Este lago natural, al sureste de Guadalajara, es el más grande de México. La variedad de peces blancos que habitan el lago sólo se encuentra ahí o en el Lago de Pátzcuaro, en Michoacán.

6 Un artesano de Tlaquepaque
Entre las artesanías de la región se destaca el vidrio soplado, artesanía que todavía se practica en el pequeño pueblo de Tlaquepaque, que ahora queda en las afueras de la capital.

5 Un exitoso grupo de *guacarock*
En todo el país la música rock ha aumentado en popularidad. El grupo Maná, de Guadalajara, ha alcanzado fama mundial. Los mexicanos le llaman *guacarock* al rock cantado en español por mexicanos (*guaca* de guacamole).

4 El lago de Chapala Lake Chapala is located about 32 miles southeast of Guadalajara, bordering Michoacán. At 53 miles (86 km) long and 16 miles (25 km) wide, it is the largest natural lake in Mexico. Chapala and Ajijic are resort villages around the lake that have large communities of retired U.S. and Canadian citizens. Ajijic is an artist colony where hand-loomed items and embroidery work are produced. One of the most famous residents of Ajijic was Tennessee Williams.

5 Un exitoso grupo de *guacarock* Although mariachi music originated in Jalisco, not all popular Guadalajaran groups are of this genre. **Maná** is a very popular pop group from Guadalajara. Their albums, among them **Sueños líquidos, Cuando los ángeles lloran,** and **¿Dónde jugarán los niños?,** have been hits throughout the Spanish-speaking world. **Maná** is famous for such songs as **"Rayando el sol"**, **"Falta amor"**, and **"Cómo dueles en los labios"**. Some songs, like **"¿Dónde jugarán los niños?"** and **"Chamán"**, reflect the group's keen interest in the environment; in fact, the group even sponsors an environmental organization, **Selva Negra**. If possible, play some of their music and have students compare this type of music to popular music in the United States. You may want to preview the song lyrics for age-appropriate content.

6 Un artesano de Tlaquepaque Tlaquepaque, which borders Guadalajara and is considered a suburb of the capital city, is famous for its handicrafts. Blown glass and ceramics—ranging from traditional to contemporary designs—are two of the most common crafts in this region.

Cultures and Communities

Culture Note
The **jarabe tapatío** is one of the most famous traditions of Mexico. In this folk dance, the costumes are almost as important as the dance itself. The **charro** wears a suit with a short wool jacket adorned with silver embroidery, fitted pants with silver buttons, and a large felt hat. The **china poblana** wears a full red silk skirt and an embroidered white blouse. You may want to have students research these costumes.

Music Link
Have students research several of the songs and dances of the state of Jalisco. **(La negra, La culebra, Camino real de Colima)** If possible, invite a dance teacher to give students a short lesson on the steps associated with each song.

Capítulo 5: Nuestras leyendas
Chapter Overview

FUNCTIONS	GRAMMAR	VOCABULARY	RE-ENTRY
Primer paso **pp. 133–136** • Expressing qualified agreement and disagreement, p. 133 • Reporting what others say and think, p. 135	• Impersonal **se**, p. 135	• Reporting about society, p. 136	• Verbs followed by an infinitive (**Capítulo 12**, I) • Expressions of agreement (**Capítulo 11**, II) • Expressions of opinion (**Capítulo 10**, I)

Segundo paso **pp. 140–143** • Talking about hopes and wishes, p. 141	• The subjunctive mood to express hopes and wishes, p. 142 • Subjunctive of **ir, estar, ser, dar**, p. 143	• Legends, p. 140	• Subjunctive (**Capítulo 12**, II) • Verbs followed by an infinitive (**Capítulos 7 and 12**, I) • Sequencing terms (**Capítulo 3**, I)

CULTURE

• **Nota cultural, Bartolomé de las Casas,** p. 132
• **A lo nuestro,** Emphatically negative expressions, p. 133
• **Nota cultural,** Aztec pictographs, p. 136

• **Panorama cultural, ¡Cuéntanos una leyenda!,** p. 137
• **Nota cultural,** The legend of Quetzalcóatl, p. 142

Capítulo 5: Nuestras leyendas
Chapter Resources

PRINT

Lesson Planning
One-Stop Planner

Lesson Planner with Substitute Teacher Lesson Plans, pp. 22–26, 69

Student Make-Up Assignments
- Make-Up Assignment Copying Masters, Chapter 5

Listening and Speaking
Listening Activities
- Student Response Forms for Listening Activities, pp. 35–37
- Additional Listening Activities 5-1 to 5-6, pp. 39–41
- Additional Listening Activities (song), p. 42
- Scripts and Answers, pp. 121–125

Video Guide
- Teaching Suggestions, pp. 32–33
- Activity Masters, pp. 34–36
- Scripts and Answers, pp. 95–97, 116

Activities for Communication
- Communicative Activities, pp. 17–20
- Realia and Teaching Suggestions, pp. 63–65
- Situation Cards, pp. 97–98

Reading and Writing
Reading Strategies and Skills Handbook, Chapter 5

¡Lee conmigo! 3, Chapter 5

Cuaderno de actividades, pp. 49–60

Grammar
Cuaderno de gramática, pp. 37–45

Grammar Tutor for Students of Spanish, Chapter 5

Assessment
Testing Program
- Grammar and Vocabulary Quizzes, **Paso** Quizzes, and Chapter Test, pp. 89–102
- Score Sheet, Scripts and Answers, pp. 103–109

Alternative Assessment Guide
- Portfolio Assessment, p. 20
- Performance Assessment, p. 34
- CD-ROM Assessment, p. 48

Student Make-Up Assignments
- Alternative Quizzes, Chapter 5

Standardized Assessment Tutor
- Reading, pp. 17–19
- Writing, p. 20
- Math, pp. 25–26

Native Speakers
Cuaderno para hispanohablantes, pp. 21–25

MEDIA

Online Activities
- Juegos interactivos
- Actividades Internet

Video Program
- Videocassette 2
- Videocassette 5 (captioned version)

Audio Compact Discs
- Textbook Listening Activities, CD 5, Tracks 1–15
- Additional Listening Activities, CD 5, Tracks 20–26
- Assessment Items, CD 5, Tracks 16–19

Interactive CD-ROM Tutor, Disc 2

Teaching Transparencies
- Situations 5-1 to 5-2
- **Más práctica gramatical** Answers
- **Cuaderno de gramática** Answers

One-Stop Planner CD-ROM

Use the **One-Stop Planner CD-ROM with Test Generator** to aid in lesson planning and pacing.

For each chapter, the **One-Stop Planner** includes:
- Editable lesson plans with direct links to teaching resources
- Printable worksheets from resource books
- Direct launches to the HRW Internet activities
- Video and audio segments
- Test Generator
- Clip Art for vocabulary items

Capítulo 5: Nuestras leyendas

Projects

Jarabe tapatío

In this project, students learn a portion of the jarabe tapatío, then teach their portion to other groups in the class. You may want to obtain a recording of the jarabe tapatío, performed by a mariachi band, or students may be able to perform this dance to "La bamba." Also, if possible, show students a video-taped performance of this dance before they attempt it.

MATERIALS

✂ **Students may need**
- Recorded music
- Videotaped performance
- Paper
- Markers

SUGGESTED SEQUENCE

1. Divide the class into dance pairs and assign one dance step of the **jarabe tapatío** to each pair of students.

2. Have students prepare an illustration that explains the action they are representing in their dance step.

3. In front of the class, have students describe their dance step with their illustration. Then have students perform the dance step they have learned.

4. After these first performances, combine pairs of students and have each pair teach the other pair their dance step.

DESCRIPTION OF DANCE STEPS

Throughout the dance, the **china poblana** takes her skirt with her fingertips and delicately fans it with each step she takes. The **charro** clasps his hands behind his back, pulls his hands up so that his elbows point straight out to the sides. He leans forward a bit, but keeps his head up looking at his partner.

Here are a few of the **jarabe tapatío** dance steps.

1. The first dance step evokes the image of two people strolling past each other and glancing at each other over the shoulder as they pass. At the beginning of the movement, the dancers face each other, ten to fifteen feet apart. Leading with the right foot, they pass each other on the left side, then take three steps toward each other, and three steps back. On the third step forward, they cross the right foot over the left, tapping the toe to the ground. On the third step back, they stomp the right heel on the ground. At the moment they pass, they glance at each other over the left shoulder.

2. The second dance step looks as though the dancers are chasing each other around a circle. The pair is facing one another. Leading with the right foot, the dancers take three quick small steps. The fourth step is actually a sideways kick, as though the dancers were kicking up dust.

3. This step suggests the image of the **charro** chasing the **china poblana** around a hat. The **charro** dances by hopping on one foot while dragging the other, and the **china poblana** dances with rapid, delicate, tiptoe steps. First, the **charro** chases the **china poblana** clockwise halfway around the hat, then counterclockwise, returning to where they began. They do the same thing again, this time going full circle around the hat. At this point, the **china poblana** scoops up the hat and puts it on. The couple dances one more time around the circle in the opposite direction. She then drops the hat into the center again, and he picks it up and puts it back on. The couple dances a final time around.

GRADING THE PROJECT

Suggested point distribution: (total = 100 points)

Appropriateness of Spanish vocabulary	20
Proper use of command forms	20
Clarity of instructions	20
Creativity of illustration	20
Performance of dance	20

Games

Tiritas

This game is good for reviewing syntax and grammar after Segundo paso. It should last about 15–20 minutes. It may be played by individuals or in small teams.

Preparation Write several sentences in large print on slips of paper. For each sentence, cut the strips one word at a time. You might want to add a few extra words to increase difficulty. Place each set of slips in an envelope.

Procedure Distribute two or three envelopes per group. When you say ¡Construyan!, students open one envelope and assemble the sentence. When a person or team completes a sentence, they call out ¡Construida! All players must stop. If the completed sentence is correct, that player or team gets a point.

Storytelling

Mini-cuento

*This story accompanies Teaching Transparency 5-2. The **mini-cuento** can be told and retold in different formats, acted out, written as dictation, and read aloud to give students additional opportunities to practice all four skills. The following story is about an old man telling children a Mexican legend.*

El abuelo les cuenta una leyenda antigua a los niños. Se dice que había un hombre que vino de algún lugar misterioso y que fue adorado por todos hasta convertirse en una deidad. Este hombre enseñó a los antiguos mexicanos la agricultura, el calendario y las artes. Este hombre era Quetzalcóatl, cuyo nombre significa "serpiente con plumas". Un día Quetzalcóatl se fue hacia el este en una balsa de serpientes y prometió que volvería. Él dijo que hombres rubios vendrían del mar a conquistar al imperio azteca. Cuando llegó Hernán Cortés, se creía que era Quetzalcóatl y los indígenas lo recibieron con regalos. Los guerreros indígenas al darse cuenta de que no era Quetzalcóatl lucharon contra los españoles pero fueron derrotados.

¡Oír leyendas es más interesante que ver la tele!

Traditions

La serenata

A very romantic tradition in Mexico, especially among young men and women, is the **serenata,** or serenade. When a young man falls in love, he goes with a group of mariachis to wake the young lady with romantic songs. Beneath the window or balcony of the girl's house, the mariachis play two or three songs. Have groups of students find a recording of a romantic song in Spanish to play in class and prepare a fill-in-the-blank sheet with missing lyrics for the other students to complete.

Receta

*Corn, the sacred plant of the Aztecs, has always been a staple of the Mexican diet. Sometimes the Aztecs ground corn into meal with a **molcajete** (a stone mortar and pestle), which required a great deal of work. Therefore, the Aztecs heated the kernels in a solution of lime until the hulls came off. When this mixture (**nixtamal**) was boiled in water, the kernels swelled up and became soft like spaghetti. This gruel or thick soup was called **pozole** and was one of the many indigenous methods of preparing corn. **Pozole,** also known as hominy, is traditionally made with pork. This recipe can be prepared with chicken, pork, or both.*

POZOLE

para 4–6 personas

1 libra de puerco (como para asar)

1 libra de pechugas de pollo

1/2 cucharadita de comino en polvo

1 cucharadita de orégano en polvo

1/2 taza de cebolla picada

2 cubitos de caldo de pollo

2 latas de *golden hominy,* sin agua

Ponga el puerco en una olla, y añada agua hasta cubrir el puerco. Cocine por una hora. Agregue las pechugas de pollo y cocine unos 30 minutos más, hasta que la carne esté blanda. Saque la carne de la olla, déjela enfriar, quitando cualquier grasa que tenga, y desmenúcela. Deje enfriar también el caldo, quitándole la grasa. Agregue agua hasta tener diez tazas de caldo. Añada los cubitos de caldo, las especias, la carne desmenuzada y la cebolla picada. Cuando vuelva a hervir, agregue el *golden hominy,* baje el fuego y cocine a fuego lento unos 15 ó 20 minutos. Sirva la sopa con tortillas de maíz frescas o con tostadas.

Capítulo 5: Nuestras leyendas
Technology

Video Program

Videocassette 2, Videocassette 5 (captioned version)
See Video Guide, pages 31–36.

Dramatic episode • El poder del amor

While floating among the beautiful gardens of Xochimilco, Alejandra and Irene listen to Irene's grandmother tell the legend of the volcanoes of Ixtaccíhuatl and Popocatépetl. According to this version of the famous Mexican legend, a beautiful Aztec princess falls in love with a warrior. When her father lies and tells her that the warrior was killed in battle, the princess dies, grief-stricken. The warrior then takes the princess's body to a valley and never leaves her side. The gods take pity and turn them into volcanoes, symbols of the enduring power of love.

¡Cuéntanos una leyenda!
People from Spanish-speaking countries tell legends from their regions.

Videoclips
- **Banco popular®**: advertisement for the computers of **Banco popular**
- **Una leyenda vallenata:** documentary about the encounter between the Tupe Indians of Colombia and the Spaniards

Interactive CD-ROM Tutor

The **Interactive CD-ROM Tutor** contains videos, interactive games, and activities that provide students an opportunity to practice and review the material covered in Chapter 5.

Activity	Activity Type	Pupil's Edition Page
1. Así se dice	¿Cuál es?	p. 133
2. Así se dice	¡Super memoria!	p. 135
3. Vocabulario	Imagen y sonido ¡Exploremos! ¡Identifiquemos!	p. 140
4. Así se dice	¡Atrévete!	p. 141
5. Gramática	¡A escoger!	p. 142
6. Gramática	¿Qué falta?	p. 143
Panorama cultural	¡Cuéntanos una leyenda! ¡A escoger!	p. 137
¡A hablar!	*Guided recording*	pp. 152–153
¡A escribir!	*Guided writing*	pp. 152–153

Teacher Management System
Logging In
Logging in to the *¡Ven conmigo!* TMS is easy. Upon launching the program, simply type "admin" in the password area of the log-in screen and press RETURN. Log on to **www.hrw.com/CDROMTUTOR** for a detailed explanation of the Teacher Management System.

Internet Connection

MARCAR: go.hrw.com
PALABRA CLAVE:
WV3 GUADALAJARA-5

*Have students explore the **go.hrw.com** Web site for many online resources covering all chapters. All Chapter 5 resources are available under the keyword **WV3 GUADALAJARA-5.** Interactive games help students practice the material and provide them with immediate feedback. You will also find a printable worksheet that provides Internet activities that lead to a comprehensive online research project.*

Juegos interactivos

You can use the interactive activities in this chapter

- to practice grammar, vocabulary, and chapter functions
- as homework
- as an assessment option
- as a self-test
- to prepare for the Chapter Test

Actividades Internet

Students answer questions about the Aztec, the Maya, and the Inca with online research. They also conduct additional research and record interesting facts about each culture using chapter functions for telling a story.

- To prepare for the **Hoja de actividades,** ask the class if anyone can differentiate between the Aztec, Maya, and Inca. With what region is each culture associated?
- After completing the activity sheet, have students ask the class about the cultures they researched, using the chapter functions.

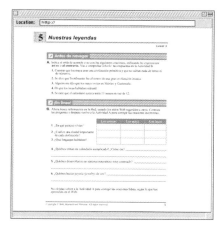

Proyecto

Divide the class into small groups. Assign each group one of the three civilizations from the **Hoja de actividades.** Ask each group to create a Web page about that culture. Encourage them to download free images and to record what Web sites they used for their research.

Textbook Listening Activities Scripts

 Primer paso

6   p. 133

1. —Es importantísimo hacer ejercicios todos los días.

   —Hombre, ¡qué va! Es suficiente hacerlos dos o tres veces por semana.

2. —Las playas de Cancún son las mejores del mundo.

   —Bueno, puede ser, pero yo prefiero las playas de la Florida.

3. —El baloncesto es el deporte más divertido.

   —¡Nada de eso! El voleibol es mucho más divertido.

4. —El invierno es la mejor estación del año, ¿no crees?

   —Depende de tu punto de vista. Si te gusta el frío, ¡sí!

5. —Las canciones de Juan Gabriel están muy de moda.

   —Desde luego. Son muy bonitas.

6. —La comida china es la más sabrosa.

   —Sí, pero hay que tener en cuenta que a algunas personas no les gustan las salsas chinas.

7. —El chocolate suizo sabe riquísimo. ¿A ti te gusta?

   —Por supuesto. Es mi favorito también.

Answers to Activity 6
1. para nada
2. más o menos
3. para nada
4. más o menos
5. totalmente
6. más o menos
7. totalmente

10   p. 135

1. La gente dice que hay unas ruinas misteriosas allá por la selva.

2. Supuestamente los indígenas americanos vinieron originalmente de Asia.

3. Según Pedro, la música caribeña tiene su origen en África.

4. Mi abuela siempre dice que el mundo era mejor hace treinta años.

5. Se cree que hay una mina de oro perdida por aquí.

6. Mi amiga Carla tiene unas ideas curiosas sobre los norteamericanos. Por ejemplo, ella cree que sólo comemos hamburguesas.

7. Dicen que los hombres son mejores en matemáticas que las mujeres. ¿Qué crees tú?

Answers to Activity 10
1. la gente
2. la gente
3. una persona específica
4. una persona específica
5. la gente
6. una persona específica
7. la gente

 Segundo paso

19   p. 140

Hace muchos años, en una tierra lejana, dos ejércitos se declararon la guerra. Los soldados valientes del ejército del rey Carlos lucharon con su príncipe Esteban al frente. Un día, en plena batalla, el ejército de Esteban tuvo que dejar de luchar. Unos soldados se dieron cuenta de que el mejor amigo de Esteban, un guerrero de nombre Leopoldo, lo había traicionado, dando al ejército enemigo los planes de batalla de Esteban. Esteban lloró cuando supo la traición de su amigo Leopoldo. Condenó la traición y lo mandó al exilio.

Esteban cambió su estrategia y salvó a sus soldados. Al vencer al ejército enemigo, las tropas de Esteban se regocijaron y celebraron su victoria, dando gracias a los dioses. El ejército derrotado acordó la paz y regresó a su tierra a lamentar su mala fortuna. Como ése era el día en que Esteban iba a casarse con su querida Alicia, todo el pueblo del rey Carlos celebró la boda en una casa muy suntuosa. Los soldados de Esteban nunca olvidaron a su valiente e inteligente héroe.

Answers to Activity 19
1. b
2. e
3. d
4. c
5. a

The following scripts are for the listening activities found in the *Pupil's Edition*. For Student Response Forms, see *Listening Activities*, pages 35–38. To provide students with additional listening practice, see *Listening Activities*, pages 39–41.

One-Stop Planner CD-ROM

To preview all resources available for this chapter, use the **One-Stop Planner CD-ROM**, Disc 2.

22 p. 141

Gregorio   Hola, Patricia. Te habla Gregorio desde Los Ángeles.

Patricia   ¿Desde Los Ángeles? Pero Gregorio, ¡ya deberías estar en Guadalajara!

Gregorio   Sí, ya lo sé, pero dile a tu tía Leonora que no voy a llegar a tiempo. Parece que van a posponer mi vuelo debido a la neblina.

Patricia   ¡Ay, Gregorio! Así vas a perder el viaje a Puerto Vallarta con nosotros.

Gregorio   Espero que no, pues ya sabes que ir a Puerto Vallarta es uno de los sueños de mi vida.

Patricia   Y yo tenía muchas esperanzas de enseñarte las maravillas de Jalisco.

Gregorio   Bueno, me las vas a enseñar, pero hoy no es posible. Voy a ver si puedo conseguir otro vuelo para mañana o para el fin de semana.

Patricia   Eso es, espero que sí. Voy a decirle a mamá que hable con la agencia de viajes. Ojalá se pueda cambiar la fecha de nuestras reservaciones.

Gregorio   Gracias, Patricia. Te hablo pronto.

Patricia   Sí, Gregorio, ¡qué lástima!, ¿eh?

Gregorio   Sí, pero, ¿qué quieres? Así es la vida. Bueno, chao, Patricia.

Patricia   Chao, Gregorio, y no te deprimas. Espero que todo se resuelva.

Answers to Activity 22
Gregorio: (2) Espero que no..., ...uno de los sueños de mi vida.
Patricia: (4) Y yo tenía muchas esperanzas de..., Espero que sí,
Ojalá se pueda cambiar..., Espero que todo se resuelva.

26 p. 143

Hijos, habla su mamá. Miren, su papá y yo no vamos a poder volver del trabajo hasta muy tarde hoy. Quiero que preparen el pollo que dejé en el refrigerador. Ofelia, hija, quiero que pases la aspiradora. Y Diego, tu papá quiere que laves la ropa. Luego quiero que laven los platos y que saquen la basura. Oigan, no quiero que pasen toda la noche viendo la tele, ¿eh? Y espero que hagan la tarea. Ojalá que podamos volver antes de las diez. Bueno, ¡pórtense bien! Un beso, ¡chao!

Answers to Activity 26
La madre quiere que preparen el pollo que les dejó, que laven los platos, que saquen la basura, que no pasen la noche viendo la tele, que hagan

la tarea, que Ofelia pase la aspiradora y que Diego lave la ropa.
Los niños prepararon el pollo, lavaron los platos, hicieron la tarea y no pasaron la noche viendo la tele. Ofelia pasó la aspiradora.
No sacaron la basura y Diego no lavó la ropa.

Repaso

1 p. 152

1. —Le gusta su nuevo trabajo, ¿no?
   —Así es, pero oí que tiene que estar sentada por mucho tiempo frente a la computadora. Luego dice que le duele mucho la espalda.
   —Bueno, espero que se sienta mejor.

2. —Es muy buen fotógrafo.
   —Sí, alguien me dijo que las fotos que sacó de unas flores en el parque estuvieron lindísimas.
   —Ojalá que pueda estudiar fotografía en la universidad.

3. —Ya no trabaja en el mismo lugar. Busca un nuevo empleo. ¿Sabes por qué?
   —Según los chismes siempre se le rompían los vasos y se le caían los platos.
   —¿En serio? Espero que encuentre otro trabajo. ¡Necesita el dinero!

4. —¿Son novios ellos?
   —Supuestamente no. Pero cada vez que se ven él hace algo tonto, como el otro día en el parque cuando se cayó.
   —Ojalá que salgan juntos. Tienen tanto en común.

5. —¿Quién es?
   —Dicen que es el nuevo estudiante. No conoce a nadie todavía. Según Ricardo, es un poco tímido.
   —Oí que alguien puso una nota en su espalda en la clase de álgebra.
   —¡Ay no! Espero que no sea cierto. No quiero que piense que todos somos así.

Answers to Repaso Activity 1
1. b; Espera que se sienta mejor.
2. ninguna foto; Espera que pueda estudiar fotografía en la universidad.
3. c; Espera que encuentre otro trabajo.
4. a; Espera que salgan juntos.
5. d; Espera que no sea cierto.

Capítulo 5: Nuestras leyendas
Suggested Lesson Plans *50-Minute Schedule*

Day 1

CHAPTER OPENER 5 min.
- Focusing on Outcomes, ATE, p. 129

DE ANTEMANO 40 min.
- Presenting **De antemano** and Preteaching Vocabulary, ATE, p. 130
- Present Language and Culture Notes, ATE, p. 131.
- Activities 1–5 and Comprehension Check, ATE, p. 132
- Read **Nota cultural**, p. 132. Present History Link, ATE, p. 132.

Wrap-Up 5 min.
- Have pairs of students orally summarize the story.

Homework Options
Cuaderno de actividades, p. 49, Activities 1–2

Day 2

PRIMER PASO
Quick Review 5 min.
- Check homework.
- Bell Work, ATE, p. 133

Así se dice, p. 133 40 min.
- Presenting **Así se dice**, ATE, p. 133
- Present **A lo nuestro**, p. 133.
- Do Activity 6 with the Audio CD, p. 133.
- Do Activities 7–8, pp. 133–134.
- Have students do Activity 9 in pairs, p. 134.
- Do Additional Practice, ATE, p. 134.

Wrap-Up 5 min.
- Do Vocabulary Practice Activities 1–2 for Teaching Transparency 5-1.

Homework Options
Cuaderno de actividades, pp. 50–51, Activities 3–4, 7
Cuaderno de gramática, p. 37, Activities 1–2

Day 3

PRIMER PASO
Quick Review 5 min.
- Check homework.
- Have students agree or disagree with statements you make.

Así se dice/Nota gramatical, p. 135 40 min.
- Presenting **Así se dice, Nota gramatical**, ATE, p. 135
- Present Additional Vocabulary, ATE, p. 135.
- Do Activity 10 with the Audio CD, p. 135.
- Do Activity 11, p. 135.
- Have students do Activity 12 in pairs, p. 136.
- Present **Vocabulario extra**, p. 136.
- Have students do Activity 13 in groups, p. 136.

Wrap-Up 5 min.
- Follow Suggestion 1 for Teaching Transparency 5-1.

Homework Options
Cuaderno de actividades, pp. 51–53, Activities 5–6, 8–11
Cuaderno de gramática, p. 38, Activities 3–4

Day 4

PRIMER PASO
Quick Review 10 min.
- Check homework.

Así se dice, p. 135 15 min.
- Read **Nota cultural**, p. 136.
- Have students do Activity 14 in groups, p. 136.

PANORAMA CULTURAL 15 min.
- Presenting **Panorama cultural**, ATE, p. 137

Wrap-Up 10 min.
- Do the **Mini-cuento** for Teaching Transparency 5-1.
- Discuss the content and format for Quiz 5-1.

Homework Options
Study for Quiz 5-1.

Day 5

PRIMER PASO
Quick Review 5 min.
- Review the content of **Primer paso**.

Quiz 20 min.
- Administer Quiz 5-1A, 5-1B, or a combination of the two.

¡ADELANTE! 20 min.
- Presenting **¡Adelante!** and Preteaching Vocabulary, ATE, p. 138
- Do Activities 15–18, pp. 138–139.

Wrap-Up 5 min.
- Do Thinking Critically and Additional Practice, ATE, p. 139.

Homework Options
Cuaderno de actividades, p. 54, Activities 12–13

Day 6

SEGUNDO PASO
Quick Review 5 min.
- Check homework.
- Bell Work, ATE, p. 140

Vocabulario, p. 140 40 min.
- Presenting **Vocabulario**, ATE, p. 140
- Do Activity 19 with the Audio CD, p. 140.
- Do Activity 20, p. 141.
- Have students do Activity 21, then peer-edit their work, p. 141.

Wrap-Up 5 min.
- Ask students to define or give examples of **Vocabulario** words and expressions, p. 140.

Homework Options
Cuaderno de actividades, p. 55, Activity 14
Cuaderno de gramática, p. 39, Activities 5–6

One-Stop Planner CD-ROM

For alternative lesson plans by chapter section, to create your own customized plans, or to preview all resources available for this chapter, use the **One-Stop Planner CD-ROM,** Disc 2.

For additional homework suggestions, see activities accompanied by this symbol throughout the chapter.

Day 7

SEGUNDO PASO

Quick Review 5 min.
- Check homework.
- **Más práctica gramatical,** p. 149, Activity 4

Así se dice, p. 141 20 min.
- Do Building on Previous Skills activity, ATE, p. 141.
- Presenting **Así se dice,** ATE, p. 141
- Present Language-to-Language, ATE, p. 141.
- Do Activity 22 with the Audio CD, p. 141.

Gramática, p. 142 20 min.
- Presenting **Gramática,** ATE, p. 142
- Do Activity 23, p. 142.
- **Más práctica gramatical,** p. 150, Activity 5

Wrap-Up 5 min.
- Do the Challenge activity as an oral exercise, ATE, p. 143.

Homework Options
Cuaderno de actividades, pp. 55–57, Activities 15–17, 19
Cuaderno de gramática, pp. 40–41, Activities 7–8

Day 8

SEGUNDO PASO

Quick Review 10 min.
- Check homework.

Gramática, p. 142 35 min.
- Review verbs + infinitives. Contrast with the subjunctive.
- Do Activities 9–10, pp. 41–42, in Cuaderno de gramática.
- Have students do Activity 24 in pairs, p. 142.
- Presenting **Nota gramatical,** ATE, p. 143
- Do Activity 25, p. 143.
- Do Activity 26 with the Audio CD, p. 143.

Wrap-Up 5 min.
- Have students finish your sentences with either the subjunctive or an infinitive.

Homework Options
Cuaderno de actividades, pp. 56–58, Activities 18, 20–22
Cuaderno de gramática, pp. 42–45, Activities 11–19

Day 9

SEGUNDO PASO

Quick Review 10 min.
- Check homework.

Gramática, p. 142 20 min.
- Read and discuss **Nota cultural,** p. 142.
- Have students do Activity 27, then peer-edit their work, p. 143.

VAMOS A LEER 15 min.
- Do Using Prior Knowledge, ATE, p. 144.
- Do Drawing Inferences, p. 144, then do Activity A, p. 144.

Wrap-Up 5 min.
- Discuss the content and format of Quiz 5-2.

Homework Options
Study for Quiz 5-2.

Day 10

SEGUNDO PASO

Quick Review 5 min.
- Review the content of **Segundo paso.**

Quiz 20 min.
- Administer Quiz 5-2A, 5-2B, or a combination of the two.

VAMOS A LEER 20 min.
- Read **Estrategia** and **¿Te acuerdas?,** p. 144, then review yesterday's discussion.
- Present Literature Link, ATE, p. 144.
- Do Activities B–C, p. 145.

Wrap-Up 5 min.
- Review lists from Activity C, p. 145.

Homework Options
Repaso Activity 3, p. 152
Cuaderno de actividades, pp. 59–60, Activities 23–27

Day 11

REPASO

Quick Review 5 min.
- Check and discuss the homework.

VAMOS A LEER 15 min.
- Have students do Activity D, p. 145.
- Do Activity E, p. 146.

REPASO 25 min.
- List concepts from Chapter 5.
- Do Activity 1 with the Audio CD, p. 152.
- Have students do Activities 2, 4, and 8 in pairs, pp. 152–153.
- Have students do Activity 5 in groups, p. 153.

Wrap-Up 5 min.
- Play **Todos los ejercicios,** ATE, p. 155.

Homework Options
Vamos a escribir, p. 147
Repaso Activities 6–7, p. 153

Day 12

REPASO

Quick Review 10 min.
- Check and/or collect homework.

Chapter Review 35 min.
- Review Chapter 5. Choose from **Más práctica gramatical,** Grammar Tutor for Students of Spanish, Activities for Communication, Listening Activities, Interactive CD-ROM Tutor, or **Juegos interactivos.**

Wrap-Up 5 min.
- Discuss the content of the Chapter 5 Test.

Homework Options
Study for the Chapter 5 Test.
A ver si puedo..., p. 154

Assessment

Quick Review 5 min.
- Check homework.

Test, Chapter 5 45 min.
- Administer Chapter 5 Test. Select from Testing Program, Alternative Assessment Guide, Test Generator, or Standardized Assessment Tutor.

Capítulo 5: Nuestras leyendas
Suggested Lesson Plans 90-Minute Block Schedule

Block 1

CHAPTER OPENER 5 min.
- Focusing on Outcomes, ATE, p. 129

DE ANTEMANO 40 min.
- Presenting **De antemano** and Preteaching Vocabulary, ATE, p. 130
- Present Language and Culture Notes, ATE, p. 131.
- Activities 1–5 and Comprehension Check, ATE, p. 132.
- Read **Nota cultural**, p. 132. Present History Link, ATE, p. 132.

Así se dice, p. 133 40 min.
- Presenting **Así se dice**, ATE, p. 133
- Present **A lo nuestro**, p. 133.
- Do Activity 6 with the Audio CD, p. 133.
- Do Activities 7–8, pp. 133–134.
- Have students do Activity 9 in pairs, p. 134.
- Do Additional Practice, ATE, p. 134.

Wrap-Up 5 min.
- Do Vocabulary Practice Activities 1–2 for Teaching Transparency 5-1.

Homework Options
Cuaderno de actividades, pp. 49–51, Activities 1–4, 7
Cuaderno de gramática, p. 37, Activities 1–2

Block 2

PRIMER PASO
Quick Review 10 min.
- Check homework.
- Have students agree or disagree with statements you make.

Así se dice/Nota gramatical, p. 135 55 min.
- Presenting **Así se dice, Nota gramatical,** ATE, p. 135
- Present Additional Vocabulary, ATE, p. 135.
- Do Activity 10 with the Audio CD, p. 135.
- Do Activity 11, p. 135.
- Have students do Activity 12 in pairs, p. 136.
- Present **Vocabulario extra**, p. 136.
- Have students do Activity 13 in groups, p. 136.
- Read **Nota cultural**, p. 136.
- Have students do Activity 14 in groups, p. 136.

PANORAMA CULTURAL 15 min.
- Presenting **Panorama cultural**, ATE, p. 137

Wrap-Up 10 min.
- Do the **Mini-cuento** for Teaching Transparency 5-1.
- Discuss the content and format for Quiz 5-1.

Homework Options
Study for Quiz 5-1.
Cuaderno de actividades, pp. 51–53, Activities 5–6, 8–11
Cuaderno de gramática, p. 38, Activities 3–4

Block 3

PRIMER PASO
Quick Review 10 min.
- Check homework.
- Review the content of **Primer paso.**

Quiz 20 min.
- Administer Quiz 5-1A, 5-1B, or a combination of the two.

¡ADELANTE! 25 min.
- Presenting **¡Adelante!** and Preteaching Vocabulary, ATE, p. 138
- Do Activities 15–18, pp. 138–139.
- Do Thinking Critically and Additional Practice, ATE, p. 139.

Vocabulario, p. 140 30 min.
- Presenting **Vocabulario,** ATE, p. 140
- Do Activity 19 with the Audio CD, p. 140.
- Do Activity 20, p. 141.

Wrap-Up 5 min.
- Ask students to define or give examples of **Vocabulario** words and expressions, p. 140.

Homework Options
Assign Activity 21, p. 141.
Cuaderno de actividades, pp. 54–55, Activities 12–14
Cuaderno de gramática, p. 39, Activities 5–6

One-Stop Planner CD-ROM

For alternative lesson plans by chapter section, to create your own customized plans, or to preview all resources available for this chapter, use the **One-Stop Planner CD-ROM**, Disc 2.

 For additional homework suggestions, see activities accompanied by this symbol throughout the chapter.

Block 4

SEGUNDO PASO
Quick Review 10 min.
- Check homework.
- **Más práctica gramatical**, p. 149, Activity 4

Así se dice, p. 141 20 min.
- Do Building on Previous Skills, ATE, p. 141.
- Presenting **Así se dice**, ATE, p. 141
- Present Language-to-Language, ATE, p. 141.
- Do Activity 22 with the Audio CD, p. 141.

Gramática, p. 142 55 min.
- Presenting **Gramática**, ATE, p. 142
- Do Activity 23, p. 142.
- **Más práctica gramatical**, p. 150, Activity 5
- Review verbs + infinitives.
- Do Activities 9–10, pp. 41–42, in Cuaderno de gramática.
- Have students do Activity 24 in pairs, p. 142.
- Presenting **Nota gramatical**, ATE, p. 143
- Cuaderno de gramática, pp. 43–44, Activities 12–13 and 15–16
- Do Activity 25, p. 143.

Wrap Up 5 min.
- Do Challenge as an oral exercise, ATE, p. 143.

Homework Options
Cuaderno de actividades, pp. 55–58, Activities 15–22
Cuaderno de gramática, pp. 40–45, Activities 7–8, 11, 14, 17–19

Block 5

SEGUNDO PASO
Quick Review 10 min.
- Check homework.

Gramática, p. 142 20 min.
- Do Activity 26 with the Audio CD, p. 143.
- Read and discuss **Nota cultural**, p. 142.
- Have students do Activity 27, then peer-edit, p. 143.

VAMOS A LEER 55 min.
- Read **Estrategia** and **¿Te acuerdas?,** p. 144.
- Do Activity A, p. 144.
- Do Drawing Inferences, ATE, p. 144.
- Do Activities B–D, p. 145.
- Read **Estrategia,** then do Activities E–F, p. 146.

Wrap-Up 5 min.
- Discuss the content and format of Quiz 5-2.

Homework Options
Study for Quiz 5-2.
Cuaderno de actividades, pp. 59–60, Activities 23–27

Block 6

SEGUNDO PASO
Quick Review 10 min.
- Check homework.
- Review the content of **Segundo paso.**

Quiz 20 min.
- Administer Quiz 5-2A, 5-2B, or a combination of the two.

REPASO 45 min.
- List concepts from Chapter 5.
- Do **Repaso** Activity 1 with the Audio CD, p. 152.
- Do **Repaso** Activities 3 and 6–7, pp. 152–153.
- Have students do **Repaso** Activities 2, 4, and 8 in pairs, pp. 152–153.
- Have students do **Repaso** Activity 5 in groups, p. 153.

VAMOS A ESCRIBIR 10 min.
- Read **Estrategia** and do Activity A, p. 147.

Wrap-Up 5 min.
- Discuss the content and format of the Chapter 5 Test.

Homework Options
Study for the Chapter 5 Test.
Assign **Vamos a escribir** Activities B–C, p. 147.
A ver si puedo..., p. 154

Block 7

REPASO
Quick Review 10 min.
- Check and/or collect homework.

Chapter Review 35 min.
- Review Chapter 5. Choose from **Más práctica gramatical,** Grammar Tutor for Students of Spanish, Activities for Communication, Listening Activities, Interactive CD-ROM Tutor, or **Juegos interactivos.**

Test, Chapter 5 45 min.
- Administer Chapter 5 Test. Select from Testing Program, Alternative Assessment Guide, Test Generator, or Standardized Assessment Tutor.

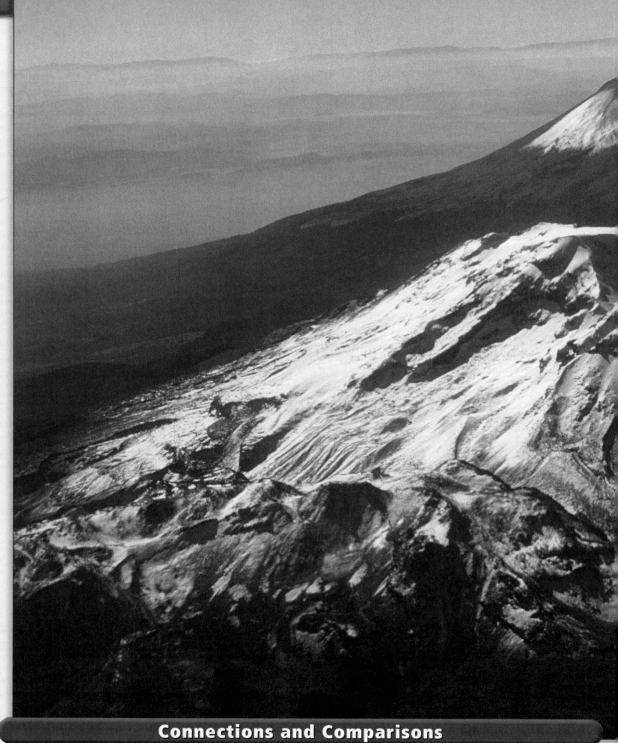

Chapter Opener

CAPÍTULO 5

One-Stop Planner CD-ROM

For resource information, see the **One-Stop Planner,** Disc 2.

Pacing Tips
In **Segundo paso,** students will begin working with the subjunctive in noun clauses. You might want to add extra time to allow students to thoroughly practice the new material. For additional pacing tips, see Suggested Lesson Plans, pp. 127I–127L.

Meeting the Standards

Communication
- Expressing qualified agreement and disagreement, p. 133
- Reporting what others say and think, p. 135
- Talking about hopes and wishes, p. 141

Cultures
- Culture Note, p. 131
- Language Note, p. 131
- Nota cultural, p. 132
- Nota cultural, p. 136
- Panorama cultural, p. 137
- Culture Note, p. 137
- Nota cultural, p. 142
- Culture Note, p. 142

Connections
- Geography Link, p. 128
- History Link, p. 132
- Language-to-Language, p. 141
- Literature Link, p. 144
- Language Notes, p. 145
- Literature Link, p. 153

Comparisons
- Multicultural Link, p. 128
- Multicultural Link, p. 137

Communities
- Career Path, p. 133

Connections and Comparisons

Multicultural Link
Cultures often share similar myths and legends. For example, the legend of Big Foot, a monster whose footprints are said to be seen in the forests of the western United States, has a counterpart in France (The Wolf of Gévaudan). Divide the class into groups. Have each group research legends of three different countries to find cultures that share a similar legend.

Geography Link
Have students report on the current status and most recent eruptions of other active volcanoes around the world. (St. Helens, Kilauea, Fujiyama, Krakatau, Etna, Vesuvius) If legends about a certain volcano exist, students can retell the stories in Spanish and illustrate them on poster board or in comic-book form to present to the class.

STANDARDS: 1.3, 3.1, 4.2

CAPÍTULO

5
Nuestras leyendas

Objectives

In this chapter you will learn to

Primer paso

- **express qualified agreement and disagreement**
- **report what others say and think**

Segundo paso

- **talk about hopes and wishes**

 internet

MARCAR: go.hrw.com
PALABRA CLAVE:
   WV3 GUADALAJARA-5

◄ **Cuentan que un guerrero y una princesa, Popo e Ixta, se enamoraron y se transformaron en estos dos volcanes.**

Photo Flash!

Mexico's second and third highest peaks, Popocatépetl, (17,930 ft) and Ixtaccíhuatl (17,160 ft) tower over the towns of Cholula and Puebla, and on clear days can be seen in Mexico City. Popocatépetl comes from the Nahuatl for "Smoking Mountain." "Popo" is one of Mexico's most active volcanoes. Ixtaccíhuatl means "Sleeping Woman," and from a distance the profile looks remarkably like that of a woman lying on her back. One of Mexico's best-known legends tells the story of the formation of these two volcanoes.

Focusing on Outcomes

Have students list words that express agreement and disagreement. Ask them what it means to qualify their opinions and to give examples of when they think they would want to do so.

Communication for All Students

Auditory Learners

To show students how a legend can be altered as it is passed on from one generation to another, play the game *Teléfono.* Whisper the following to a student: **Cuando se seca el pozo se sabe lo que vale el agua.** That student then whispers the message to another, who whispers it to the next person, and so on. The last person states the message out loud to the class. Now have students discuss which parts of the message remained true to the original, which parts changed, and why. Why would a legend change over time? (successive generations interpret inherited legends slightly differently; they may be influenced by any number of things, such as new knowledge about science, movement of cultures, or changes in the environment)

Teaching Resources
pp. 130–132

PRINT
▸ Lesson Planner, p. 23
▸ Video Guide, pp. 31–32, 34–35
▸ Cuaderno de actividades, p. 49

MEDIA
▸ One-Stop Planner
▸ Video Program
  Contigo en la distancia
  Videocassette 2, 14:46–21:08
  Videocassette 5 (captioned version), 21:34–27:57
▸ Audio Compact Discs, CD 5, Trs. 1–2

Presenting
De antemano

Have students read and answer the question in **Estrategia para comprender.** Play the Audio CD and have students read the captions of the story, focusing on known words. Then present the Preteaching Vocabulary.

DE ANTEMANO · *El virrey y el azteca*

CD 5
Trs. 1–2

Cuaderno de actividades, p. 49, Acts. 1–2

Estrategia para comprender

Los mitos y leyendas muchas veces simplifican o idealizan a los personajes y las situaciones. La siguiente leyenda interpreta las relaciones entre los españoles y los indios durante la época colonial. En ella, hay dos imágenes contrarias del español, un señor rico y malvado, y el virrey sabio y generoso. Del indio hay una sola imagen; es pobre, humilde y honrado. ¿Puedes expresar la moraleja de la leyenda?

La gente dice que una vez un señor azteca andaba por un camino cuando encontró un bolso lleno de oro. Como el señor era muy pobre, nunca había visto tanto oro...

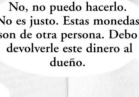
¡En mi vida he visto tanto oro!

¡Las cosas que podré comprar con este oro! ¡Qué alegría! Pero...

No, no puedo hacerlo. No es justo. Estas monedas son de otra persona. Debo devolverle este dinero al dueño.

¿Se le perdió a Ud. algo de valor, señor?

Sí. He perdido un bolso.

Aquí lo tiene, señor. Lo encontré en el camino.

¡Vaya ladrón malvado! ¡Me has robado dos monedas de oro!

¡En absoluto, señor!

¡Llamaré a los guardias y te llevarán a la cárcel!

¡Eso no es justo, señor! No robé nada del bolso. Se lo di igual como lo encontré.

Preteaching Vocabulary

Activating Prior Knowledge
Point out that the story in **De antemano** is an Aztec legend. The text contains several expressions that use the present perfect tense. Have students identify these phrases. Based on Spanish expressions students already know and what students know about legends in general, can they guess what these expressions mean? **¡En mi vida he visto tanto oro!; He perdido un bolso.; ¡Me has robado dos monedas de oro!; ...he venido en busca de justicia; El señor le ha dado el bolso.**

El pobre señor azteca estaba preocupado. Se dio cuenta que los guardias lo buscaban y no encontraba qué hacer. En aquel momento pensó en el virrey. Hasta cierto punto tenía miedo de este gran señor, pero se decía que el virrey era un hombre justo que ayudaba tanto a los pobres como a los ricos. Así que el señor azteca fue al palacio a verlo.

Culture Note
The son of a Spanish merchant, Bartolomé de las Casas dedicated himself to the study of Latin and came to the Americas in 1502. For most of his life he championed the cause of the **indios,** whose oppression he denounced as a sin. He wrote several accounts of the mistreatment of the natives, including his most famous book, *Brevísima relación de la destrucción de las Indias.*

Language Note
The **virrey,** or *viceroy,* was the highest-ranking representative of Spain's royal government in the Americas. Viceroys often attained impressive wealth and power surpassed only by that of the Spanish monarch.

Señor, perdone Ud., dicen que robé unas monedas de oro, pero no es así. Oí que Ud. es un hombre honrado y he venido en busca de justicia.

Durante un momento no se oyó nada en la gran sala del palacio. Luego el virrey le susurró algo al oído de su capitán. El capitán se fue y dentro de poco, volvió con el señor español.

¡Ese malvado me robó dos monedas de oro! Sólo había 26 en vez de 28 en el bolso cuando me lo devolvió.

 Contigo en la distancia
You may choose to show students Episode 5: *El poder del amor* now or wait until later in the chapter. In the video, Alejandra and Irene listen to Irene's grandmother tell the legend of the volcanoes Ixtaccíhuatl and Popocatépetl, in which a beautiful Aztec princess falls in love with a warrior. Her father lies and tells her that the warrior was killed in battle, and she dies, grief-stricken. The warrior takes the princess's body to a valley. The gods turn them into volcanoes, symbols of the enduring power of love. As students watch the episode they should write down expressions they hear and put them into the following categories: **acuerdo, desacuerdo, información,** and **esperanzas.**

El señor le ha dado el bolso. Por eso se ve claramente que es un hombre honrado. Entonces, claro está que éste no es el bolso que Ud. perdió. Su bolso tenía 28 monedas y éste sólo tiene 26. Como no podemos encontrar al dueño de este bolso, voy a darle el bolso al señor que lo encontró.

Digo que es suyo.

Gracias, señor.

Using the Captioned Video

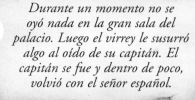 As an alternative, you might want to show the captioned version of *Contigo en la distancia: El poder del amor* on Videocassette 5. Some students may benefit from seeing the written words as they listen to the target language and watch the gestures and actions in context. This visual reinforcement of vocabulary and functions will facilitate students' comprehension and help reduce their anxiety before they are formally introduced to the new language in the chapter.

C A P Í T U L O 5

Kinesthetic Learners

1 Have student volunteers act out one of the statements. The class calls out what is happening. Ask students, **¿Qué pasó primero? ¿después?** Go through all the statements in this manner, and then have students call out the statements in order and have the volunteers act them out again.

History Link

Partly due to Las Casas' protests, in 1542 the **Nuevas Leyes** were promulgated to prevent abuses against indigenous people living on **encomiendas. Encomiendas** *(concessions, holdings)* were colonial estates granted to Spanish settlers in Latin America. Indians living on the estates were "commended" to the owner, or **encomendero,** who was to provide protection and religious and social services in exchange for the Indians' labor. The new laws were repealed in 1545, and the friar's critics called his writings the **Leyenda negra de España,** implying that his charges were untrue.

Answers

1 d, b, e, a, f, c

2 1. el virrey
2. Porque era un hombre justo.
3. un bolso de monedas de oro
4. Porque creyó que el bolso era del español y porque era un hombre honrado.
5. Se lo entregó al azteca.
6. *Answers will vary.*

3 Otras personas: La gente dice que una vez...; Dicen que robé...; Se decía que el Virrey...; Oí que Ud. es un hombre honrado...

4 el virrey: sabio, generoso, honrado
el español: rico, malvado
el azteca: pobre, humilde, honrado

These activities check for comprehension only. Students should not yet be expected to produce language modeled in **De antemano.**

1 **¿Qué pasó primero?** See answers below.

Pon las siguientes oraciones en el orden correcto.

a. El señor azteca fue a ver al virrey.
b. El señor español acusó al azteca de ser ladrón.
c. El virrey le dio el bolso al azteca.
d. El azteca encontró el bolso.
e. El azteca tenía miedo de ir a la cárcel.
f. El español se presentó ante el virrey.

2 **¿Entendiste?** See answers below.

1. ¿Cómo se le llamaba al representante del rey de España en las colonias americanas?
2. ¿Por qué merecía mucho respeto el virrey?
3. ¿Qué encontró el azteca?
4. ¿Por qué decidió el azteca devolver el bolso al español?
5. Por fin, ¿qué hizo el virrey con el dinero?
6. ¿Por qué tomó esa decisión el virrey? ¿Crees que fue justa la decisión?

3 **Expresiones útiles** See answers below.

En el cuento, hay cuatro expresiones que se usan para referirse a lo que dicen o lo que piensan otras personas. Búscalas y escríbelas en una lista.

4 **¿Cómo son?** See answers below.

 Mira la introducción y el cuento otra vez. Con un(a) compañero(a), haz una lista de las palabras que describen a cada uno de los personajes.

5 **Ahora te toca a ti** Answers will vary.

 ¿Alguna vez has encontrado algo que le pertenecía a otra persona? ¿Qué hiciste? Cuéntale a tu compañero(a) lo que pasó.

Nota cultural

Bartolomé de las Casas, un fraile dominicano que vino a las Américas en 1502, escribió una crítica de los conquistadores españoles en la que condena la explotación de los indígenas. Esto dio lugar a la "Leyenda negra", una representación a veces justa y a veces exagerada de la brutalidad y la avaricia de la conquista. La historia de los Estados Unidos también contiene temas muy controvertidos. Un ejemplo es el trato a las comunidades indígenas. ¿Conoces otros ejemplos?

Comprehension Check

Slower Pace

2 Have students answer these questions in groups. Once a group has written all possible answers, the members should ask each other to respond to the questions orally until everyone in the group is able to answer each question. Verify task completion by randomly picking a group member to answer a question.

Additional Practice

4 Have students work in pairs to do this activity. Have them discuss which descriptions they agree with. Can they think of any other adjectives?

Primer paso

Objectives Expressing qualified agreement and disagreement; reporting what others say and think

WV3 GUADALAJARA-5

Así se dice

Expressing qualified agreement and disagreement

Ya conoces algunas expresiones para expresar acuerdo:

Estoy de acuerdo.	**Así es.**
¡Claro que sí!	**¡Cómo no!**
Por supuesto.	**Desde luego.**
Eso es.	

Si crees que otra persona no tiene toda la razón, puedes decir:

Hasta cierto punto, sí, pero...
  Up to a point, yes, but . . .
Pero hay que tener en cuenta que...
  But you have to take into account that . . .
Depende de tu punto de vista.

¿Tú crees? No sé...
Es muy difícil de creer, pero es posible.
Bueno, puede ser, pero...
En efecto, parece ser así.

Más práctica gramatical, p. 148, Act. 1

Cuaderno de actividades, pp. 50–51, Acts. 3–4, 7

Si no estás de acuerdo para nada, puedes decir:

Al contrario.
¡Nada de eso! *Of course not!*
¡Qué tontería! *How silly!*

¡Claro que no!
¡Qué va!
¡Eso es muy difícil!
  That's very unlikely!

Cuaderno de gramática, p. 37 Acts. 1–2

---

6 ¿De veras? Script and answers on p. 127G.

Escuchemos Unos amigos están expresando sus opiniones sobre varias cosas. Escucha cada conversación e indica si no están de acuerdo **para nada** o si están de acuerdo **totalmente** o **más o menos.**

CD 5
Tr. 3

7 ¡Qué va! Answers will vary.

Leamos/Escribamos Las generalizaciones pueden ser peligrosas, aunque a veces dicen verdades. Responde a cada oración con una expresión de acuerdo total, acuerdo parcial o desacuerdo total.

MODELO
  —Las leyendas son para los niños.
  —Estoy de acuerdo. Pero hay que tener en cuenta que los adultos también las pueden disfrutar.

1. Las leyendas no tienen nada que ver con la realidad.
2. La leyenda del virrey y el azteca representa un retrato realista de la sociedad colonial.
3. Cuando hay contacto entre dos sociedades, una siempre domina a la otra.
4. Los diferentes grupos étnicos de hoy en día pueden aprender a vivir en paz y concordia.
5. La literatura puede enseñarnos algunas lecciones importantes sobre la vida.
6. En nuestros días, hay mucho menos discriminación racial y económica.
7. En nuestra época, la ciencia tiene las mismas funciones que tenían los mitos en las sociedades antiguas.

A lo nuestro

Some of the most emphatically negative expressions in Spanish don't use negative words at all! The negative meaning is understood. For example:

en absoluto *absolutely not*
en mi vida *never in my life*

Cultures and Communities

Career Path

Ask students what fields of study focus on groups of people—their legends, social structure, and so on. (anthropology, archaeology, sociology, political science, linguistics, folklore) Other fields can aid this work: mathematics, geology, geography, and physics. How can Spanish help anthropologists or archaeologists? (They can travel to sites in the Spanish-speaking world; they can gain access to research that has not been translated into English; they can communicate with local people.) Where might Spanish be most useful for doing this type of research? (Latin America, Spain, the southwestern United States)

Bell Work

Write on the board:
Acuerdo, Desacuerdo, Información, Esperanzas. Have students write three expressions that fit in each category.

Presenting
Así se dice

Present a statement and provide a qualified response. **(Dicen que el presidente tiene mucho poder. Estoy de acuerdo hasta cierto punto.)** Then present several more statements and have students agree or disagree with you. Have students work in small groups to express opinions and agreement or disagreement.

Teaching Resources
pp. 133–136

PRINT
▸ Lesson Planner, p. 23
▸ Listening Activities, pp. 35, 39–40
▸ Activities for Communication, pp. 17–18, 63, 65, 97–98
▸ Cuaderno de gramática, pp. 37–38
▸ Grammar Tutor for Students of Spanish, Chapter 5
▸ Cuaderno de actividades, pp. 50–53
▸ Cuaderno para hispanohablantes, pp. 21–25
▸ Testing Program, pp. 89–92
▸ Alternative Assessment Guide, p. 34
▸ Student Make-Up Assignments, Chapter 5

MEDIA
▸ One-Stop Planner
▸ Audio Compact Discs, CD 5, Trs. 3–4, 20–22, 16
▸ Teaching Transparencies 5-1; **Más práctica gramatical** Answers; Cuaderno de gramática Answers
▸ Interactive CD-ROM Tutor, Disc 2

Additional Practice

9 Have pairs of students work together to brainstorm additional topics of interest to them and express opinions on those topics. Then have them discuss their opinions with another pair of students.

---

8 **Del colegio al trabajo**

Leamos/Escribamos Trabajas de consejero(a) en una residencia de la universidad y tienes que revisar las solicitudes de los estudiantes que quieren vivir allí el año que viene. Lee los cuestionarios que completaron dos chicas —Marta y Rosalía— para determinar si son compatibles como compañeras de cuarto. Explica si son compatibles o no, y explica por qué.

¿Son compatibles Uds. como compañeros(as) de cuarto? ¡Tomen esta prueba para saberlo! Indiquen si están de acuerdo.

1. Es importante ser ordenado(a). Mi cuarto tiene que estar limpio y organizado.

   ¡Qué va! Confieso que soy un desastre.

2. Necesito silencio para concentrarme más en los estudios.

   No estoy de acuerdo para nada. Necesito el ruido para estudiar.

3. Es bueno tener amigos(as) de visita y ¡mejor si se quedan hasta muy tarde!

   Por supuesto. Pero siempre hay que tener en cuenta que, tal vez otra gente quiera estudiar.

4. Necesito hablar mucho por teléfono.

   De acuerdo. En mi familia somos ocho y hablamos a menudo.

5. Prefiero acostarme y levantarme tarde.

   ¡Desde luego! Me encanta levantarme tarde.

6. Para mí, las fiestas son más importantes que los estudios.

   ¡Nada de eso! Me gustan las fiestas pero quiero sacar buenas notas.

¿Son compatibles Uds. como compañeros(as) de cuarto? ¡Tomen esta prueba para saberlo! Indiquen si están de acuerdo.

1. Es importante ser ordenado(a). Mi cuarto tiene que estar limpio y organizado.

   Hasta cierto punto sí. No tolero la desorganización pero hay que ser flexible también.

2. Necesito silencio para concentrarme más en los estudios.

   ¡Desde luego! Me gusta el silencio.

3. Es bueno tener amigos(as) de visita y ¡mejor si se quedan hasta muy tarde!

   Claro que no. Me gusta la privacidad.

4. Necesito hablar mucho por teléfono.

   ¡Cómo no! Necesito llamar mucho a mi familia.

5. Prefiero acostarme y levantarme tarde.

   ¡Al contrario! Para mí, acostarme a las nueve es tarde.

6. Para mí, las fiestas son más importantes que los estudios.

   No es así. Yo estoy aquí para estudiar medicina.

9 **Personalmente...**

Leamos/Hablemos Expresa a tu compañero(a) tus opiniones de los temas que siguen. Explica tus opiniones. ¿Hasta qué punto estás de acuerdo con tu compañero(a)?

las leyendas
los carros de gasolina
los jóvenes
los cursos de...
los hombres
las mujeres

(no) debe(n)

manejar antes de cumplir los 18 años
hacer más de los quehaceres domésticos
ser obligatorios para graduarse
tomarse demasiado en serio
prohibirse por completo
quedarse en casa cuando los niños son chicos

Communication for All Students

Slower Pace

8 Have students number the survey questions on a piece of paper. Next, they read them aloud to a partner one item at a time, writing down whether each girl agrees, disagrees, or more or less agrees. Once finished, students should tally their columns to see if the girls are compatible.

Visual/Auditory Learners

9 Write the nouns in Activity 9 with other nouns on the board or a transparency. Then say a phrase in Spanish that corresponds to one of the nouns. (**...deben ser obligatorios para graduarse**) The first person to raise his or her hand comes to the board, circles the correct noun (**los cursos de ciencias**), and makes a sentence using the noun and the phrase.

Así se dice

Reporting what others say and think

Estas expresiones se usan cuando no se sabe quién dijo algo o cuando "todo el mundo" lo dice:

Alguien me dijo que cancelaron el concierto.

Se cree que los aztecas vinieron de Aztlán.

Oí que descubrieron un libro antiguo de fábulas.

Dicen que la gobernadora es un personaje muy popular.

Se dice que el pájaro choguí es la voz de un niño perdido.

Según la leyenda del Quetzal, **un hombre** *(man)* se transformó en pájaro.

Supuestamente el calendario azteca era más exacto que el moderno.

Cuentan que una mujer *(woman)* lloró hasta que se transformó en un río.

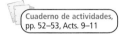
Cuaderno de actividades, pp. 52–53, Acts. 9–11

Nota gramatical

The impersonal construction **se** + verb often corresponds to sentences in English that use *people, they, you, we,* or *one . . .* It's usually used with the third person singular.

¿Cómo **se llega** al castillo?
How do you get to the castle?

¿Y cómo **se sabe** eso?
And how does one know that?

Cuaderno de gramática, p. 38, Acts. 3–4 → Más práctica gramatical, p. 149, Acts. 2–3

Cuaderno de actividades, p. 52, Act. 8

10 **¿Quién lo dice?** Script and answers on p. 127G.
Escuchemos Escucha estos comentarios e indica si lo dice **una persona específica** o **la gente**.
CD 5 Tr. 4

11 **Gramática en contexto** See answers below.
Leamos/Escribamos Lee el siguiente artículo, que trata de las figuras de Nazca. Encuentra dos usos de **se** como sujeto impersonal. Expresa las dos oraciones de otra manera sin el pronombre **se**. Luego encuentra dos oraciones en las que puedes sustituir **se** por el sujeto. Reemplaza los sujetos de estas oraciones con **se** como sujeto impersonal.

Las Figuras de Nazca

¿Qué te parece esta figura? Hay muchas figuras como ésta en el desierto de Nazca en el Perú. Algunas personas creen que estas figuras, que sólo se pueden ver desde un avión, parecen dibujos elaborados por seres del espacio. Se ha sugerido también que parecen pistas construidas en la antigüedad para el aterrizaje de vehículos del espacio. Otros piensan que fueron parte de un calendario que ayudaba a los indios a entender el movimiento de los cuerpos celestes. ¿Qué crees tú?

Communication for All Students

Slower Pace

11 Have students write all the verbs used with **se**. Point out that they have already learned that the **se** + third person singular form of a verb is a way to express an impersonal subject. Ask them why **se pueden** is in the plural form. (The subject of the verb is a plural noun: **figuras.**)

Additional Vocabulary

en cuanto a mí *as far as I'm concerned*
por otro lado *on the other hand*
se supone que *supposedly*

Primer paso

CAPÍTULO 5

Presenting
Así se dice,
Nota gramatical

Talk to the class as though you are retelling some great secrets that you think they would like to know. Use examples of well-known school figures, the local team, politicians, and popular music and TV personalities to model the boldface expressions in **Así se dice.** Next, on a transparency or the board, write similar sentences that the class suggests, making any needed corrections as you write them.

 Culture Note
The **pájaro choguí** is a legendary bird referred to in the popular South American folk song of the same name. It tells the tale of a boy who fell from a tree. As he died in his mother's arms, he was transformed into a **choguí** bird.

Answers
11 *Possible answers:*
1. Sólo se pueden ver desde un avión...; Sólo es posible verlas desde un avión.
2. Se ha sugerido también que parecen pistas...; Algunas personas han sugerido que parecen pistas...
3. Algunas personas creen que estas...; Se cree que estas...
4. Otros piensan que fueron...; Se piensa que fueron...

Primer paso

Culture Note
You might want to point out to your students that some Spanish speakers consider **martes trece** (Tuesday the thirteenth) to be a day of bad luck, not **viernes trece.** Teach the saying **Martes trece, ni te cases ni te embarques.**

Assess

▸ Testing Program, pp. 89–92
Quiz 5-1A, Quiz 5-1B
Audio CD 5, Tr. 16

▸ Student Make-Up Assignments, Chapter 5, Alternative Quiz

▸ Alternative Assessment Guide, p. 34

---

12 Dichos

Leamos/Hablemos Una parte importante del folklore son los dichos y refranes. Con un(a) compañero(a), encuentren los equivalentes de estos dichos en inglés. ¿Cuándo se usa cada dicho? Compartan sus ideas con la clase.

MODELO   No hay mal que por bien no venga.   *Every cloud has a silver lining.*

El árbol se conoce por su fruta.

Ojos que no ven, corazón que no siente.

Poco a poco se va lejos.

Antes que te cases, mira lo que haces.

Dime con quién andas y te diré quién eres.

13 He oído que...

Hablemos/Escribamos Imagina que un reportero ha llegado a investigar un acontecimiento legendario, por ejemplo un robo, que pasó hace muchos años en tu región. En grupos, escriban un diálogo en el cual diferentes personas cuenten su versión de la historia.

MODELO   —Se dice que el ladrón pudo entrar al banco al pasar por la pared.
—Eso es muy difícil de creer. Yo oí que fue el mismo director del banco...

Vocabulario extra

la cárcel	*jail*
el (la) guardia	*guard*
honrado(a)	*honorable*
la justicia	*justice*
el ladrón, la ladrona	*thief*
el (la) malvado(a)	*villain*
robar	*to steal*
sufrir	*to suffer*
la víctima	*victim*

14 Se dice que...

Hablemos Hay creencias que la gente usa para explicar cosas o explicar las coincidencias. Un ejemplo del inglés: se dice que cuando hay truenos es que Dios está moviendo los muebles. En un grupo, piensen en una creencia que conocen, o inventen una usando los temas que siguen.

1. la mala suerte
2. la enfermedad
3. el mal tiempo
4. el buen tiempo
5. el amor
6. la salud

Nota cultural

Los aztecas usaban una escritura pictográfica. Es decir, usaban dibujos para simbolizar ideas. Por ejemplo, la palabra Coatepec (nombre de un pueblo azteca) se escribía con el dibujo de una culebra y una loma. Las palabras para culebra y loma en náhuatl eran **coatl** y **tepetl**. Juntos, sonaban como Coatepec.

Communication for All Students

Slower Pace/Kinesthetic Learners

12 Have students work with a partner to define each **dicho.** Have them act out the sayings and see if the class can guess which one they are depicting.

Visual Learners/Challenge

12 Ask students to describe situations that illustrate each of these sayings. You might also ask students to illustrate each saying. Have students display their illustrations.

Native Speakers

Have students ask family members about **dichos** and **refranes** that they might know. Ask students to present and explain one or two sayings to the class. In which situations would it be appropriate to say each **dicho?**

¡Cuéntanos una leyenda!

CD 5 Trs. 5–7

Las siguientes personas nos contaron dos leyendas: "La carreta sin bueyes", de Costa Rica, y "La llorona", de Venezuela.

Libia
Caracas, Venezuela CD 5 Tr. 7

"Había una mujer en los llanos criollos, la cual tenía muchos hijos y un día, en una de las guerras de independencia, a su esposo lo querían... reclutar para que fuera a la guerra... La mujer y sus hijos huyeron hacia los montes y su esposo se quedó recogiendo el ganado... Llegaron los llaneros... y... arremetieron contra su familia y contra toda su persona, muriendo todos. La mujer quedó viva pero se trastornó de la cabeza, o sea se volvió loca. Esta mujer, cuenta la leyenda... vagaba de pueblo en pueblo gritando por sus hijos y su esposo que habían muerto".

criollos   *of the country, local; Venezuelan*
arremetieron contra   *attacked*

Para pensar y hablar...

A. Haz una lista de elementos que caracterizan las leyendas—por ejemplo, eventos fantásticos o ambiente misterioso... ¿Cuáles aparecen en estas dos leyendas? ¿Hay leyendas en inglés que tengan los mismos elementos?

B. En tu opinión, ¿para qué sirven las leyendas? Aunque no sean realistas, ¿hay algún sentido en que cuentan la verdad?

 Cuaderno para hispano-hablantes, pp. 24–25

Rafael Ángel
Alajuela, Costa Rica CD 5 Tr. 6

"Una carreta típica que tiene un sonido estrepitoso en las ruedas porque son de madera con un aro de metal. En este entonces, en la calle Ancha, que rodea a la ciudad, había un dicho... para [que] los niños... los ancianos y la gente... no trasnocharan. Le decían: 'Vaya, acuéstese y no pase por la calle Ancha porque ahí sale la carreta sin bueyes'... Se oía el ruido y se veía una carreta que no llevaba bueyes, el timón iba en el aire, y un boyero que iba con el chuzo y arreando la carreta pero sin cabeza. Entonces era una manera de asustar a la gente para que... se fuera a acostar temprano..."

aro   *hoop*
timón   *steering rod*
chuzo   *whip*
trasnochar   *to stay up late*
boyero   *ox driver*

PANORAMA CULTURAL

CAPÍTULO 5

Teaching Resources
p. 137

PRINT
▶ Video Guide, pp. 31–32, 35
▶ Cuaderno de actividades, p. 60
▶ Cuaderno para hispanohablantes, p. 24

MEDIA
▶ One-Stop Planner
▶ Video Program, Videocassette 2, 21:09–27:08
▶ Audio Compact Discs, CD 5, Trs. 5–7
▶ Interactive CD-ROM Tutor, Disc 2

Presenting
Panorama cultural

Play the audio or video recording once, stopping periodically to check comprehension. Then play it again and ask students what the two legends have in common. Have them answer the **Para pensar y hablar...** questions.

Preguntas

1. **Según Rafael Ángel, ¿por qué pasa por la Calle Ancha la carreta sin bueyes?** (Para que la gente no trasnoche.)

2. **¿En qué época de la historia de Venezuela tiene origen la leyenda de La Llorona?** (En la época de las guerras de independencia)

3. **En el cuento de Libia, ¿por qué se volvió loca la mujer?** (Porque los llaneros mataron a su familia.)

Cultures and Communities

Culture Note
Libia uses **criollo** to mean *Venezuelan,* but this word has other meanings as well. Historically, it refers to someone of Spanish descent born in the Americas. In some Latin American countries it is used to describe anything characteristic of that country, e.g., **música criolla, comidas criollas.**

Multicultural Link
Tell students that although this account of **La Llorona** comes from Venezuela, the legend comes from Spain (with roots in the ancient Greek myth of Medea). Versions of the woman who roams the night searching for her lost family are told in Mexico and in the United States by Mexican Americans. You might ask students to research the myth of Medea.

¡ADELANTE!

CAPÍTULO 5

Teaching Resources
pp. 138–139

PRINT
▸ Lesson Planner, p. 24
▸ Video Guide, pp. 31–32, 34
▸ Cuaderno de actividades, p. 54

MEDIA
▸ One-Stop Planner
▸ Video Program
  Contigo en la distancia
  Videocassette 2, 14:46–21:08
  Videocassette 5 (captioned version), 21:34–27:57
▸ Audio Compact Discs, CD 5, Trs. 8–11

Presenting ¡Adelante!

Play the Audio CD once, while students look at the drawings and read the text. Then play it a second time, stopping periodically to summarize the events as a class. Next, present the Preteaching Vocabulary and check for comprehension.

 Contigo en la distancia

As an alternative to ¡Adelante!, you may wish to show Episode 5 of **Contigo en la distancia**. For suggestions and activities, see the *Video Game*.

¡Adelante! ▪ *Los novios*

CD 5
Trs. 8–11

Hay tradiciones que explican por qué hay primavera, o por qué el coyote tiene negra la punta de su cola (dicen que robó el fuego para el ser humano y se quemó). La siguiente leyenda explica la formación de dos volcanes cerca de la capital de México.

Cuentan que hace muchos siglos en el Valle de Anáhuac habitaban los aztecas, conquistadores y guerreros famosos. Su emperador tenía una hija Ixtaccíhuatl cuya belleza era legendaria. Cuando la princesa llegó a edad para casarse, su padre le dijo:

—Espero que te cases con un príncipe azteca, hija mía.

La princesa trató de complacer a su padre y por largo tiempo buscó algún príncipe entre las familias nobles aztecas. Pero ninguno le llamó la atención.

Un día un príncipe chichimeca, Popocatépetl, llegó de visita a Tenochtitlán.

La princesa había salido en su litera y por casualidad se encontró con el príncipe en una calle estrecha. Cuando se vieron uno al otro ambos se enamoraron perdidamente.

Cuando llegó a su casa, Popocatépetl escribió una carta al emperador con una súplica franca y sencilla:

—Quiero casarme con su hija.

Desafortunadamente, el emperador se puso furioso e intentó que Ixtaccíhuatl se olvidara de su pretendiente.

These activities check for global comprehension only. Students should not yet be expected to produce language modeled in ¡Adelante!

15 **Ponlo en orden cronológico**

Después de leer la leyenda, pon estos acontecimientos en orden cronológico.

a. Ixtaccíhuatl muere de una enfermedad misteriosa. 5

b. Popocatépetl pide permiso para casarse con Ixtaccíhuatl. 2

c. Popocatépetl lleva a Ixtaccíhuatl a la cumbre de una montaña. 6

d. Los aztecas abandonan a los guerreros chichimecas. 3

e. La princesa busca un esposo entre los nobles aztecas. 1

f. El emperador anuncia que la princesa ha muerto. 4

16 **¿Cómo se expresan?** See answers below.

Encuentra ejemplos de lo siguiente en *Los novios*. Indica las expresiones que se usan.

1. Alguien reporta lo que dice la gente o un personaje en particular.

2. Alguien expresa un deseo o una esperanza.

Preteaching Vocabulary

Identifying Keywords
Have students look at the drawings and predict what will happen in this legend. Then have them identify words or phrases that give information about the action of the story. Students may identify such phrases as: **la princesa llegó a la edad para casarse; un príncipe chichimeca... llegó de visita a Tenochtitlán; Ixtaccíhuatl insistía en casarse con Popocatépetl; Popocatépetl... volvió a Tenochtitlán... y se reunió con Ixtaccíhuatl; la princesa se enfermó; en el momento de su muerte ocurrió un temblor... surgieron dos volcanes; desde entonces los dos volcanes vigilan sobre el Valle de Anáhuac.**

Cuaderno de actividades, p. 54, Acts. 12–13

Pero no tuvo éxito. Ixtaccíhuatl insistía en casarse con Popocatépetl. Vencido por fin, el emperador le escribió al príncipe diciéndole que estaba de acuerdo con el casamiento—pero sólo con una condición. El príncipe y su tribu tenían que apoyar al emperador en la guerra contra sus enemigos. En realidad el emperador quería que el príncipe muriera en la batalla. En el momento más feroz de la batalla, los aztecas abandonaron al príncipe y sus guerreros. Pero éstos lucharon con muchísimo valor y vencieron al enemigo. Mientras tanto, en Tenochtitlán, el emperador le dijo a la princesa que Popocatépetl estaba muerto. Luego mandó decir a Popocatépetl que la princesa había muerto de tristeza.

Popocatépetl no aceptó la mala noticia. Secretamente volvió a Tenochtitlán, donde entró en el palacio y se reunió con Ixtaccíhuatl.

Los dos se escaparon pero desde ese día el emperador se negó a verlos. Para él la princesa estaba muerta.

Los dos amantes huyeron a un lugar no muy lejos de la capital azteca y construyeron una casa humilde. Pasaron varios años y la princesa se enfermó. A pesar de los esfuerzos inagotables de Popocatépetl, ella se murió. En el momento de su muerte ocurrió un temblor, y en medio del cataclismo surgieron dos volcanes al otro lado del valle. Obedeciendo una voz que le llegaba de los cielos, Popocatépetl llevó a su amada a la cumbre de uno de los volcanes y la colocó en un lecho de flores que estaba preparado para ella. Y allí se quedó para vigilarla por siglos enteros.

Desde entonces los dos volcanes vigilan sobre el Valle de Anáhuac, donde está la Ciudad de México. La blanca nieve de Ixtaccíhuatl explica su nombre, que significa *blanca estrella*. Y la fumarola que sale de vez en cuando del cráter del Popo explica el nombre suyo, que significa *montaña humeante*.

 ¿A quién se refiere? See answers below.

¿A quién o a quiénes se refieren las siguientes descripciones?

1. Tienen que luchar con los aztecas en la guerra contra sus enemigos.
2. Tiene conflicto con un miembro de su familia.
3. Es declarado muerto falsamente.
4. Abandonan a sus aliados en medio de una lucha.
5. Simboliza la autoridad y la tradición.
6. Según la leyenda, se convirtieron en volcanes.

 Ahora te toca a ti

Con un(a) compañero(a), compara el cuento de *Los novios* con otros cuentos que ustedes conocen. ¿A qué cuento se parece más? ¿En qué son parecidos los dos cuentos?

Comprehension Check

Teaching Resources
pp. 140–143

PRINT
▶ Lesson Planner, p. 24
▶ Listening Activities, pp. 36–37, 40–41
▶ Activities for Communication, pp. 19–20, 64–65, 97–98
▶ Cuaderno de gramática, pp. 39–45
▶ Grammar Tutor for Students of Spanish, Chapter 5
▶ Cuaderno de actividades, pp. 55–58
▶ Cuaderno para hispanohablantes, pp. 21–25
▶ Testing Program, pp. 93–96
▶ Alternative Assessment Guide, p. 34
▶ Student Make-Up Assignments, Chapter 5

MEDIA
▶ One-Stop Planner
▶ Audio Compact Discs, CD 5, Trs. 12–14, 23–25, 17
▶ Teaching Transparencies 5-2; **Más práctica gramatical** Answers; Cuaderno de gramática Answers
▶ Interactive CD-ROM Tutor, Disc 2

Bell Work
Write the names of various historical or fictional characters on the board or a transparency. Have students write five things that are said about three of them. (**Se dice que Bill Gates es el hombre más rico del mundo.**)

Presenting
Vocabulario

Prepare descriptive examples from history or legends of each vocabulary item. (**dios: Es un ser muy poderoso como Thor o Zeus.**) As you present each example, have students identify the appropriate word or phrase.

Vocabulario

acordar (ue) la paz *to make peace*
celebrar la boda *to celebrate the wedding*
declarar la guerra *to declare war*
la derrota *defeat*
el dios *god*
la diosa *goddess*
el (la) guerrero(a) *warrior*
el héroe *hero*
la heroína *heroine*
lamentar *to mourn; to lament*
llorar *to cry*
luchar por *to struggle for; to fight for*

el (la) malvado(a) *villain*
quedar muerto(a) *to be left dead*
regocijarse *to rejoice*
el soldado, la mujer soldado *soldier*
los soldados valientes *brave soldiers*
traicionar *to betray*
vencer al ejército enemigo *to defeat the enemy army*
la victoria *victory*

Más práctica gramatical, p. 149, Act. 4

Cuaderno de actividades, p. 55, Act. 14
Cuaderno de gramática, p. 39, Acts. 5–6

19 **La historia nunca termina** Script and answers on page 127G.

Leamos/Escuchemos El **Vocabulario** representa un cuento tradicional para niños. Mira los dibujos mientras escuchas el cuento. Después combina los personajes con la mejor descripción de cada uno, según el cuento.

CD 5
Tr. 12

1. las tropas de Esteban
2. Esteban
3. Leopoldo
4. los dos ejércitos
5. el pueblo

a. celebró una boda
b. se regocijaron por su victoria
c. se declararon la guerra
d. traicionó a su amigo
e. lloró cuando supo que lo traicionaron

Communication for All Students

Visual Learners
Have students make vocabulary flash cards. Ask students to write each term in **Vocabulario** on the front of an index card. On the back of each card they can either illustrate or cut out images from magazines to represent the vocabulary term.

Slower Pace
19 Before students listen to the recording, have them think about which phrase from the second column would make the most sense with each character in the first column.

Visual Learners
21 Have students write their story in comic-book form with their own illustrations.

20 La leyenda

Escribamos Mira los dibujos del **Vocabulario** en la página 140. Escoge a dos personajes de cada dibujo. Para cada uno, escribe un título que diga lo que el personaje hace o quiere.

MODELO **El hombre de la capa roja toca el tambor. Quiere ser valiente.**

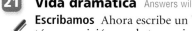 **21 Vida dramática** Answers will vary.

Escribamos Ahora escribe un breve cuento sobre un momento emocionante que viviste tú o que vivió uno de tus amigos. Puede ser un cuento real o imaginario. Trata de seguir un esquema como el siguiente.

Introducción: Dicen que la vida de todos los días no es muy interesante. ¡Qué tontería! Voy a contarles algo para demostrar que...

Antecedentes: Hace cinco años mi familia vivía en... Yo tenía ... años y...

Narración: Cuando el presidente declaró la guerra, mi hermana estaba en...

Conclusión: Ahora sé lo que significa ser valiente... ¡Y nunca me voy a olvidar del susto que todos sufrimos!

 Así se dice

Talking about hopes and wishes

Si quieres hablar de deseos y esperanzas, puedes decir:

Esperamos comprender la religión maya algún día.

Espero que la guerra **termine** pronto.

Ojalá que la lucha no **sea** muy larga.

El sueño de mi vida era conocer el valle del otro lado de la montaña.

Era una de mis grandes ambiciones.

Tenía muchas esperanzas de volver a la ciudad tapatía.

Los dioses **quieren que** los guerreros **acuerden** la paz.

CD-ROM DISC 2

Cuaderno de actividades, pp. 56, 58, Acts. 17, 21

  22 Cambio de planes Script and answers on p. 127H.

Escuchemos/Escribamos Gregorio le llama a Patricia por teléfono para decirle que tendrán que cambiar de planes. La primera vez que los escuchas, apunta cuántas veces cada uno de ellos expresa una esperanza. La segunda vez, apunta las expresiones de esperanza que usan.

CD 5 Tr. 13

Connections and Comparisons

Language-to-Language

Arabic, spoken by the Moors who occupied parts of Spain for nearly eight hundred years, has greatly influenced Spanish. **¡Ojalá!** (I hope so!) comes from the Arabic wa-sha' Allah (God willing). Many Spanish words from Arabic begin with **al-** (the Arabic word for the): **almohada** pillow, **alquilar** to rent, **algodón** cotton, and **alacrán** scorpion are

examples. Have students research **álgebra** (from Arabic al-jabr), a branch of mathematics that was brought to Europe by Islamic mathematicians. Ask students what the following words borrowed from Arabic suggest about the culture of the Moors and the breadth of their influence in Spain: **ajedrez, alguacil, albóndiga, azafrán, alfombra.**

Writing Assessment

21 Encourage students to use new vocabulary and functions from this and previous chapters. Challenge them to use the subjunctive during the assignment. You may wish to use the following rubric to assess student assignments.

Writing Rubric	Points			
	4	3	2	1
Content (Complete–Incomplete)				
Comprehensibility (Comprehensible–Incomprehensible)				
Accuracy (Accurate–Seldom accurate)				
Organization (Well organized–Poorly organized)				
Effort (Excellent–Minimal)				

18–20: A	14–15: C	Under
16–17: B	12–13: D	12: F

Building on Previous Skills

To review compound sentence structure, begin by saying a simple sentence. (**Quiero ir al zoológico.**) Then give a cue word (**cuando, porque**) and ask a student to add to the idea, keeping the sentence complete.

Presenting
Así se dice

Read the statements and ask comprehension questions: **¿Sabemos mucho o poco sobre la religión maya? Según esta persona, ¿debemos seguir luchando o debemos acordar la paz?** Ask students to use the phrases to state a hope or wish of their own.

Teaching Resources
pp. 140–143

PRINT

▸ Lesson Planner, p. 24
▸ Listening Activities, pp. 36–37, 40–41
▸ Activities for Communication, pp. 19–20, 64–65, 97–98
▸ Cuaderno de gramática, pp. 39–45
▸ Grammar Tutor for Students of Spanish, Chapter 5
▸ Cuaderno de actividades, pp. 55–58
▸ Cuaderno para hispanohablantes, pp. 21–25
▸ Testing Program, pp. 93–96
▸ Alternative Assessment Guide, p. 34
▸ Student Make-Up Assignments, Chapter 5

MEDIA

▸ One-Stop Planner
▸ Audio Compact Discs, CD 5, Trs. 12–14, 23–25, 17
▸ Teaching Transparencies 5-2; **Más práctica gramatical** Answers; Cuaderno de gramática Answers
▸ Interactive CD-ROM Tutor, Disc 2

Presenting
Gramática

The subjunctive mood to express hopes and wishes
Review formal commands. (**Lea mucho.**) Write subjunctive indicators in front of the commands. (**Espero que lea mucho.**)

Answers

23 1. Ojalá que Carlos traiga música.
2. Yolanda espera que Tomás no olvide su cámara.
3. Ella quiere sacar muchas fotos.
4. Ojalá que paseemos en velero.
5. Yo espero que Queta e Ignacio preparen barbacoa.

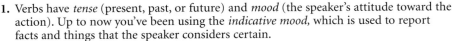
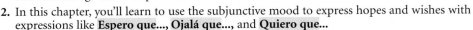

Gramática

The subjunctive mood to express hopes and wishes

1. Verbs have *tense* (present, past, or future) and *mood* (the speaker's attitude toward the action). Up to now you've been using the *indicative mood*, which is used to report facts and things that the speaker considers certain.

2. In this chapter, you'll learn to use the subjunctive mood to express hopes and wishes with expressions like **Espero que...**, **Ojalá que...**, and **Quiero que...**

3. When a sentence starts with these phrases and the subject of the sentence changes after **que**, the verb that follows **que** is in the subjunctive mood.

   Quiero que Juan me **ayude.**   *I want Juan to help me.*
   Espero que la guerra **termine** pronto.   *I hope that the war ends soon.*

4. To conjugate a regular verb in the subjunctive, start with the **yo** form of the verb in the present tense, take off the **-o**, and add the following endings. Most stem-changing verbs do not have the stem change in the **nosotros** and **vosotros** forms.

HABLAR	BEBER	VIVIR	DECIR	ACORDAR
hable	beba	viva	diga	acuerde
hables	bebas	vivas	digas	acuerdes
hable	beba	viva	diga	acuerde
hablemos	bebamos	vivamos	digamos	acordemos
habléis	bebáis	viváis	digáis	acordéis
hablen	beban	vivan	digan	acuerden

Más práctica gramatical, p. 150, Act. 5

Cuaderno de actividades, pp. 55–57, Acts. 15–16, 18–20

Cuaderno de gramática, pp. 40–41, Acts. 7–8

23 **Gramática en contexto** See answers below.

Leamos/Escribamos Nuria y sus amigos están planeando un día en la playa. Expresa sus deseos y esperanzas para la excursión con los elementos indicados.

1. Ojalá/Carlos/traer música
2. Yolanda/esperar/Tomás/no olvidar su cámara
3. Ella/querer/sacar muchas fotos
4. Ojalá/nosotros/pasear en velero
5. Yo/esperar/Queta e Ignacio/ preparar barbacoa

¿Se te ha olvidado?
verbs + infinitive
Ver páginas R34–R46

Cuaderno de gramática, pp. 41–42, Acts. 9–11

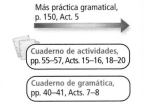

Nota cultural

En la antigua religión mexicana, Quetzalcóatl era el dios de la civilización y del aprendizaje. Se dice que Quetzalcóatl (su nombre quiere decir "serpiente con plumas") inventó el calendario y el libro. Según una leyenda, Quetzalcóatl partió un día hacia el este en una balsa de serpientes e iba a regresar algún día desde el este. Cuando llegó Hernán Cortés en 1519, se creía que él era Quetzalcóatl. ¿Cómo crees que esta creencia afectó la conquista?

24 **Gramática en contexto**

Hablemos Entrevista a un(a) compañero(a). Pregúntale qué desea para un mundo mejor y qué esperanzas tienen sus amigos y familiares.

MODELO   —¿Qué es lo que más quieres para tu futuro?
          —**Quiero que todos tengan la oportunidad de ser felices.**

Connections and Comparisons

Culture Note

Quetzalcóatl was an important deity in Mexico and Central America. Versions of the legend of the Feathered Serpent vary from tribe to tribe and throughout history. Originally, Quetzalcóatl was a vegetation god closely associated with Tlaloc, the rain god. In the 14th and 15th centuries, Quetzalcóatl was revered as the patron of the calendar and of books and as the protector of artisans. The Toltecs believed Quetzalcóatl resided in the heavens as the planet Venus. By the 16th and 17th centuries, he was worshipped as the god of learning, writing, and books.

Nota gramatical

Ir and **estar** are irregular in the subjunctive mood.

IR		ESTAR	
vaya	vayamos	esté	estemos
vayas	vayáis	estés	estéis
vaya	vayan	esté	estén

Cuaderno de gramática, p. 43, Acts. 12–14

Más práctica gramatical, p. 151, Act. 6

25 Gramática en contexto Answers will vary.

Escribamos Los estudiantes están planeando un viaje de fin de año. Escribe diez oraciones para explicar adónde esperan ir y qué esperan o quieren que pase.

MODELO   Ojalá que vayamos al lago este año.

26 Los quehaceres Script and answers on p. 127H.

CD 5
Tr. 14

Escuchemos/Escribamos Escucha el mensaje que dejó la mamá de Diego y Ofelia en el contestador. La primera vez que escuches el mensaje, haz una lista de las siete cosas que ella quiere que hagan. Luego escucha otra vez y mira el dibujo para ver si hicieron lo que ella les pidió.

MODELO   sacar la basura

Nota gramatical

Ser and **dar** are irregular in the subjunctive mood.

SER		DAR	
sea	seamos	dé	demos
seas	seáis	des	deis
sea	sean	dé	den

CD-ROM DISC 2

Cuaderno de gramática, pp. 44–45, Acts. 15–19

Más práctica gramatical, p. 151, Act. 7

27 Gramática en contexto Answers will vary.

Escribamos/Leamos En muchas leyendas existe el hada madrina. Imagina que tu hada madrina puede hacerte diez favores. Escríbele una carta para decirle lo que quieres para ti mismo(a), para tu familia y tus amigos, para tu ciudad y para el mundo. Luego cambia tu carta por la de un(a) compañero(a) y corrige su trabajo.

MODELO   Quiero que mi amigo sea presidente.

Communication for All Students

Slower Pace

26 Have students look at the picture and list in Spanish the things that need to be done. As they listen to the recording the first time, have them check off the items that the mother mentions. Next have students look at the picture again and write the chores that have already been done. As they listen to the recording again, they check off the rest of the requests.

Challenge

Have students pretend to be world leaders making a speech at the **Naciones Unidas.** Students are to describe five things that they hope or wish for. (**establecer la paz mundial, proteger el medio ambiente, eliminar el hambre infantil**) Once students have written their speeches, they can present them to the class.

Teaching Resources
pp. 144–146

PRINT
▸ Lesson Planner, p. 25
▸ Cuaderno de actividades, p. 59
▸ Cuaderno para hispanohablantes, pp. 21–23
▸ Reading Strategies and Skills Handbook, Chapter 5
▸ ¡Lee conmigo! 3, Chapter 5
▸ Standardized Assessment Tutor, Chapter 5

MEDIA
▸ One-Stop Planner

Prereading
Activity A

Using Prior Knowledge
Since students have already read a number of legends, they are familiar with the structure and features of legends in general. Have them list the features that they can expect to find in a legend. (**elementos de lo sobrenatural, un héroe, un malvado, un conflicto violento, un propósito definido**)

Drawing Inferences
A. After you have discussed Paul Bunyan or another legend, divide the board into three columns with the following headings: **Personajes, Acontecimientos/Conflictos, Propósito.** Have students list the characters in the legend, describe them, tell what happens, and reflect on the purpose of the legend.

Answers
A 1. *Answers will vary.*
2. *Answers may vary.*
3. *Answers will vary.*
4. *Answers will vary;* overcoming the odds in the Wild West

Vamos a leer

Un mito de Guatemala

Vas a leer una leyenda de los quiché, una tribu de Guatemala. Antes de leerla, piensa en otras leyendas americanas como la de Paul Bunyan.

Estrategia **para leer**
Before you read something, think about what its *genre* is. The genre tells what kind of text it is: a novel, a poem, a short story, or an essay. Then you will be able to predict and anticipate certain features of the text. For example, if you know you're reading a poem, you will remember that some words are figurative (not literal) and that some words may be out of their normal order so that the lines can rhyme.

¡A comenzar!

¿Te acuerdas?
Consider what you already know about a topic before you read in depth.

A. Júntate con dos o tres compañeros(as) y contesta estas preguntas sobre una leyenda como la de Paul Bunyan. See answers below.

1. ¿Qué recuerdas sobre Paul Bunyan o el héroe?
2. ¿Cuenta la historia el héroe mismo u otra persona?
3. ¿Aceptas la leyenda como verídica *(true)*? Explica.
4. ¿Crees que esta leyenda ayuda a explicar algunos aspectos de una cultura? ¿Cuáles?

Quetzal no muere nunca

Quetzal era un valiente muchacho, hijo del poderoso cacique de una tribu quiché. Era admirado y querido por todos. Esperaban de él grandes hazañas, pues, desde su nacimiento habían notado muchas señales de predestinación.

Cuando el joven llegó a la mayoría de edad, se reunió la tribu en un gran claro del bosque para celebrar la ocasión. Primero, los músicos tocaron los tambores, después las flautas y más tarde la

marimba. Entonces llegó el momento tan esperado cuando se daría a conocer el destino de Quetzal.

En medio de un silencio expectante, el adivino más anciano se levantó de su asiento bajo el árbol de color coral. Lentamente y con dignidad, arrojó a su alrededor los granos de coral. Los estudió por unos momentos, algo perplejo y lleno de admiración. Al fin anunció claro y firme:

—No has de morir nunca, Quetzal. Vivirás eternamente a través de generaciones de quichés.

Todas las personas reunidas se quedaron asombradas ante aquella profecía, y su entusiasmo por Quetzal aumentó.

Pero no toda la tribu lo amaba. A Chiruma, hermano del cacique, le molestaban los éxitos de Quetzal. Chiruma era casi tan joven como Quetzal y siempre había soñado con ser cacique. Pero ahora, ¿cómo podría él realizar su ambición? Era indudable que Quetzal, admirado por todos y considerado casi un dios, sería el jefe de la tribu al morir su padre.

Cultures and Communities

Literature Link
Paul Bunyan is the hero of a North American myth that celebrates the expanse of the American frontier. As a giant lumberjack, he is a symbol of strength and vitality. Along with his friends Babe the Blue Ox and Johnny Inkslinger, Bunyan is said to have carved out the western frontier, including Puget Sound, the Grand Canyon, and the Black Hills. He also has a legendary appetite; his camp stove is an acre wide, and men using bacon as skates glide over his pancake griddle to grease it. Paul Bunyan was first popularized in the 1910s. The myth has been kept alive in the stories and poems of Esther Shephard, James Stevens, Robert Frost, Carl Sandburg, and other American writers.

Poco después de la ceremonia en honor de Quetzal, él y los otros jóvenes de su edad participaron en una lucha contra un enemigo del sur. Chiruma aprovechó esta ocasión para mirar bien a Quetzal. Estaba perplejo al notar que las flechas que rodeaban al joven nunca lo herían. ¿Sería cierta la profecía? Pero no, ¡aquello era imposible! ¿Cómo iba a vivir Quetzal a través de generaciones?

De pronto, Chiruma tuvo una idea.

—Ya sé por qué la muerte respeta a Quetzal— pensó. Tiene algún amuleto poderoso que lo protege y yo voy a robárselo cuando esté durmiendo.

Esa misma noche, cuando Quetzal dormía profundamente sobre su estera, Chiruma se acercó a él con paso silencioso. Miró sobre su pecho. El amuleto no estaba allí. Iba ya a irse cuando vio a la cabeza de la estera una pluma de colibrí. Chiruma no dudó ni por un momento que aquello era lo que buscaba. Con todo cuidado sacó la brillante pluma mientras sonreía de felicidad.

Entonces recordó lo que había dicho el adivino cuando nació Quetzal: que el colibrí era el símbolo de la buena suerte del niño.

Pasó algún tiempo y murió el cacique. Inmediatamente los ancianos eligieron a Quetzal para ser el nuevo jefe. Chiruma, por supuesto, no dio ninguna seña de su enojo. Estaba seguro de que muy pronto el nuevo cacique, sin su amuleto poderoso, podría ser vencido.

Cierta tarde, Quetzal, el nuevo cacique, paseaba por el bosque, solitario, armado de su arco y sus flechas. De súbito un colibrí hermoso descendió de un árbol y sin miedo se posó sobre su hombro.

—Escúchame, Quetzal. Soy tu protector y vengo a prevenirte de que la muerte te persigue. Guárdate de cierto hombre.

Al grano

See answers below.

B. Lee el título y revisa el cuento para completar estas oraciones.

1. El personaje principal del cuento es ＿＿＿.

2. El personaje principal tiene una relación especial con un ＿＿＿ de Guatemala.

3. Alguien en este cuento (va a morir/no va a morir). Explica.

See possible answers below.

C. Ahora lee rápidamente el primer párrafo y los primeros renglones de los demás párrafos. Ten en cuenta también los dibujos y otros elementos visuales. Luego haz una lista de palabras descriptivas que se pueden aplicar al mito. Escoge de estos conceptos o usa tus propias ideas. Finalmente, compara tu lista con la de un(a) compañero(a). Al terminar el cuento, pueden volver a comparar sus ideas.

histórico   español
cómico   misterioso
dramático   moralista
trágico   de aventuras
indígena   realista

¿Te acuerdas?

Scan to find specific information. Locate characters, events, and facts by searching for key words.

See answers on p. 146.

D. Estudia las siguientes preguntas. Luego lee la leyenda otra vez y presta atención a estos detalles. Ahora contesta las preguntas.

1. ¿Qué pensaba de Quetzal la gente de la tribu? ¿Cómo lo sabes o cómo lo demostraban?

2. ¿Por qué hubo una celebración en el claro del bosque?

3. ¿Quién era Chiruma?

4. ¿Qué dijo el adivino sobre el destino de Quetzal? ¿Cómo sabía Chiruma que la profecía era cierta?

Making Predictions
B. After students have answered the questions, ask them to say how they arrived at their answers. Did they use the reading strategy? Why did they predict what they did? From what they have learned about myths and legends, do they think a legendary character will die?

Monitoring Reading
You might want to have students read the legend twice, once silently to themselves and a second time aloud in a group or with the class. Write the questions from Activity D on a transparency, then discuss the answers with the class and note the answers on the transparency.

Communication for All Students

Auditory Learners
Tell students that a modern proverb says, "Be careful what you wish for; you just might get it." What do students think this means? Have they ever had a dream come true and then wished it had not? Ask students to discuss this in small groups in Spanish.

Language Notes
- Tell students that **quetzal** comes from the Nahuatl word *quetzalli (precious feather)*.
- Point out that the expression **haber de** + infinitive is used much like the expressions **deber** + infinitive and **tener que** + infinitive: **¿De qué hombre he de guardarme?** *(Of which man must I be careful?)*

Answers

B 1. Quetzal, el hijo del cacique de una tribu quiché
2. pájaro
3. *Answers will vary.*

C *Possible answers:*
histórico, dramático, trágico, indígena, moralista

CAPÍTULO 5

Postreading
Activities E and F

Determining the Main Idea
E. Have students close their books and then ask them these questions: **¿Cuál es el propósito de esta leyenda? ¿Qué explica?** (el origen del pájaro quetzal) **¿Qué aspectos del carácter humano representan los personajes principales?** (Quetzal/la valentía, la virtud, la honestidad; el adivino/la sabiduría; Chiruma/la envidia)

Answers

D 1. Lo admiraba y lo quería. Se sabe por la celebración que le hicieron.
2. Había llegado a la mayoría de edad.
3. Chiruma era el hermano del cacique.
4. Dijo que Quetzal no había de morir nunca. Chiruma lo sabía porque las flechas de batalla nunca herían a Quetzal.
5. Chiruma le robó una pluma de colibrí porque creía que era un símbolo de la suerte del joven y sin ella Quetzal podría ser vencido.
6. Dijo que era su protector, pero le aconsejó guardarse de cierto hombre.
7. El quetzal está en el escudo nacional de armas y es el nombre de la moneda de Guatemala.

E un malvado que quiere algo que tiene el protagonista, la protección de la muerte, la muerte, la inmortalidad, un animal con poderes, un adivino; Answers will vary.

F *Possible answers:*
1. The purpose is to explain a natural phenomenon. It explains the origin of the quetzal bird.
2. The hummingbird feather signifies protection, luck, and Quetzal's invincibility. This feather is crucial to the story; once it is stolen, Quetzal can be killed.
3. Tradition, community, love of nature, respect for animals, respect for death, integrity

---

5. ¿Qué le robó Chiruma a Quetzal? ¿Por qué?
6. ¿Qué le dijo el colibrí a Quetzal?
7. ¿Qué cosas llevan el nombre de **quetzal**?

> #### Estrategia **para leer**
> When the theme of a reading is complex or abstract, one time through may not be enough to fully understand the concepts or the characters' motivations. Try closing the book and just thinking about what you've read. It can also be a good idea to read all or part of the story again, this time with a different point of view. You can ask yourself, why has the author told the story in just this way, and not another?

See possible answers below.

E. Con un(a) compañero(a), revisa la leyenda otra vez. ¿Qué acontecimientos encuentran que son comunes en las leyendas? ¿Por qué son comunes estos elementos?

F. Many legends explain the origins of a place or of a natural phenomenon or creature. Read the last three paragraphs again and answer these questions.
1. What is the purpose of the legend? What does it explain?
2. How does the legend use personification, or treating abstract things as living characters, to achieve its purpose?
3. What aspects of Guatemala's indigenous culture are represented by the main characters? You might mention such traits as honesty, cleverness . . .

> Cuaderno de actividades, pp. 59, Acts. 23–24

> Cuaderno para hispanohablantes, pp. 21–23

—¿De qué hombre he de guardarme, hermoso colibrí? —preguntó el joven.

Pero el pájaro no pronunció ni una palabra más. Después de mirar unos instantes a Quetzal, emprendió el vuelo y desapareció.

El joven, con una seña de incomprensión, continuó su camino. De pronto un agudo silbido llegó hasta él y

una flecha quedó clavada en su pecho. Cayó sobre la hierba verde y cerró los ojos dispuesto a morir.

Pero los dioses habían predicho su inmortalidad y Quetzal quedó convertido en un hermoso pájaro. Su cuerpo tomó el color verde de la hierba sobre la que había caído y su pecho conservó el color de la sangre. El sol dorado de la tarde puso en su larga cola una gran variedad de colores.

Por muchos siglos se ha considerado al quetzal como pájaro sagrado que hasta hoy día no se permite cazar. Guatemala ha honrado a este bello pájaro colocando su imagen en el

escudo nacional de armas. También la moneda de este país se llama el quetzal.

Así como lo predijo el adivino, y como lo quisieron los dioses, el joven y valiente cacique vive y vivirá para siempre en el país de los maya-quichés.

Communication for All Students

Group Work
Have groups of students research the many places the **quetzal** is depicted in Guatemalan culture today. Topics for research might include the currency, the coat of arms, and the national flag. Ask volunteers from each group to present the results of their research to the class.

Native Speakers
Have native speakers ask older friends or relatives about a myth or legend from a Spanish-speaking country that has not been discussed in class. They might draw some scenes from the story, then present it to the class.

STANDARDS: 1.2, 2.2, 3.1, 3.2

Vamos a escribir

Las leyendas y los mitos sirven para explicar acontecimientos misteriosos o para transmitir costumbres y cuentos con enseñanzas morales. Por ejemplo, la leyenda del Quetzal explica el origen de un pájaro hermoso nativo de Guatemala, y el cuento de George Washington y el cerezo muestra la importancia de decir la verdad. En esta actividad vas a elaborar y escribir tu propio mito.

Tu mito

Escribe un mito para explicar algo misterioso. Piensa en varias posibilidades... ¿Conoces algún lago, montaña, cueva, o valle misterioso? Puedes explicar su origen en un mito. ¿Por qué llueve y nieva? Estas cosas pueden explicarse en un mito también.

Estrategia para escribir

Using dialogue is a good way to make your writing more lively and vivid. When writing dialogue, consider who your characters are. What style would they use to express themselves? Are they old? young? sophisticated? shy? Would their tone be emotional or intellectual? Would they use bold action words? Match your characters' forms of expression to their personalities and backgrounds.

A. Preparación

1. Escribe una lista de temas posibles para tu mito y escoge uno.

2. Decide quiénes van a ser los personajes, y haz una lista de sus cualidades.

3. Prepara una lista de los eventos que van a ocurrir. ¿Cuáles son los conflictos dramáticos más importantes? Señálalos en tu lista de eventos con asteriscos (*).

B. Redacción

1. Escribe el primer párrafo. Este párrafo prepara a tu lector(a) para el resto de la acción. Comienza con detalles o con acciones que le llamen la atención.

2. Escribe otros párrafos para elaborar tu mito y describir los conflictos dramáticos. Usa palabras muy descriptivas para hablar de los personajes y sus acciones. Usa un poco de diálogo para dar vida a tu leyenda.

3. ¿Cómo se van a resolver los conflictos? Es decir, ¿cómo va a terminar tu mito?

4. Escribe una conclusión. Esta conclusión debe presentar el resultado del conflicto dramático. Debe estar claro que los resultados del conflicto son importantes hoy en día.

C. Evaluación

1. Lee cada párrafo de tu mito. Omite detalles no relacionados con la idea principal de cada párrafo.

2. ¿Son vívidos los personajes y los conflictos dramáticos? Quita palabras innecesarias y agrega otras más interesantes.

3. ¿Está clara la importancia de tu mito? Si es necesario, agrega unas frases que vinculen tu mito con el mundo de tu lector(a).

4. Lee el diálogo que escribiste y asegúrate que las identidades de los personajes estén claras para el lector.

Apply and Assess

Postwriting

Have each student use crayons or colored pencils while editing. Each color represents a different aspect that requires editing. For example: orange = spelling, green = grammar, purple = sentence fragment, blue = unnecessary or repetitive words, red = details to make the writing more vivid.

Discuss their work with them and have them write a second draft. If you have students peer-edit one another's work, you might have them consult the Peer Editing Rubric (found on page 8 of the *Alternative Assessment Guide)* for a proof-reader's checklist.

Teaching Resources
p. 147

MEDIA
▸ Lesson Planner, p. 25
▸ Cuaderno para hispanohablantes, p. 24
▸ Alternative Assessment Guide, p. 20
▸ Standardized Assessment Tutor, Chapter 5

MEDIA
▸ One-Stop Planner
  ⌁ Test Generator,
  ⌐ Chapter 5
▸ Interactive CD-ROM Tutor, Disc 2

Process Writing

Prewriting

- Have students decide if they want to write a myth that explains something, has a moral, or gives a warning. Students should brainstorm about the following things: **Explanation:** historical events, customs, natural phenomena; **Moral:** virtues, vices, proverbs and sayings; **Warning:** mysterious or unexplained occurrences. Have them choose one of their ideas to expand upon.

- Ask students to write the name of their central character in a circle on a piece of paper. Next, they draw circles near the edges of the paper representing other characters. Students write words around the circles that describe their characters and draw lines to connect the small circles to the center one. On each line, they state the relationship between the two characters.

Writing

Have students freewrite. They may write about the events in chronological or random order. After completing their free-writing, students arrange their writing chronologically, reread what they have written, then write an introduction and conclusion.

Más práctica gramatical

CAPÍTULO 5

For **Más práctica gramatical** Answer Transparencies, see the *Teaching Transparencies* binder.

Primer paso

Objectives Expressing qualified agreement and disagreement; reporting what others say and think

1 La clase de ciencias sociales tuvo un debate sobre la educación bilingüe. Completa las opiniones de todos. Usa cada palabra o frase sólo una vez. **(p. 133)**

nada	tontería	contrario
tú crees	tener en cuenta	
		de acuerdo
cierto punto	efecto	luego

MARTA   Sí, sí, así es. Estoy ——**1**—— con Miguel.

SAMUEL   Hasta ——**2**—— yo también, pero...

LUCILA   Pero hay que ——**3**—— lo que dice Ernesto, ¿no es así?

TOMÁS   Desde ——**4**——. Me parece que Ernesto tiene toda la razón.

REBECA   ¿——**5**——? No sé. Creo que Victoria tiene razón también.

GUILLE   Sí, en ——**6**——, creo que todos tienen opiniones válidas.

MIGUEL   No, creo que es al ——**7**——. Yo soy el único que tiene razón aquí.

TODOS   ¡Qué ——**8**——! ¡——**9**—— de eso!

Grammar Resources for Chapter 5

The **Más práctica gramatical** activities are designed as supplemental activities for the grammatical concepts presented in the chapter. You might use them as additional practice, for review, or for assessment.

For more grammar presentation, review, and practice, refer to the following:
• Cuaderno de gramática
• Grammar Tutor for Students of Spanish

• Grammar Summary on pp. R25–R46
• Cuaderno de actividades
• Grammar and Vocabulary quizzes (Testing Program)
• Test Generator on the One-Stop Planner CD-ROM
• Interactive CD-ROM Tutor
• **Juegos interactivos** at <u>go.hrw.com</u>

Answers

1 1. de acuerdo
2. cierto punto
3. tener en cuenta
4. luego
5. Tú crees
6. efecto
7. contrario
8. tontería
9. Nada

2 Las siguientes oraciones vienen de un cuento de hadas. Usa el **se** impersonal para expresarlas de otra manera. Sustituye la forma correcta de la construcción **se** + verbo por las frases subrayadas. **(p. 135)**

> **MODELO** Érase una vez una princesa.
> <u>Todos decían</u> que era muy lista.
> <u>Se decía</u> que era muy lista.

1. <u>La gente pensaba</u> que su padre, el rey, era bondadoso y generoso.
2. <u>Mucha gente creía</u> que había un hada madrina en el castillo.
3. <u>La gente hablaba</u> mucho de la linda princesa y los enanos.
4. <u>Muchos pensaban</u> que los enanos eran traviesos.
5. <u>Todos sabían</u> que la princesa estaba enamorada de un príncipe.
6. También <u>creían</u> que ella y el príncipe iban a casarse.
7. Pero <u>nadie sabía</u> que el rey tenía otro plan. Un día...

3 Marta va a pasar el verano en Chile y tiene muchas preguntas sobre las costumbres chilenas. Usa la información en inglés para escribir sus preguntas en español con **se**. **(p. 135)**

> **MODELO** when people eat lunch
> **¿Cuándo se almuerza?**

1. where people have a drink (tomarse un refresco)
2. what people do in their free time (en el tiempo libre)
3. whether people travel by train frequently (viajar por tren con frecuencia)
4. how often people visit their relatives (visitar a los parientes)
5. whether people leave a tip at restaurants (dejar propina en un restaurante)
6. whether they use air conditioning (usar el aire acondicionado)
7. how often they buy their food at an open-air market (comprar la comida en el mercado al aire libre)
8. what they eat in Chile (comer)

Segundo paso
Objective Talking about hopes and wishes

4 Indica la palabra o frase que sea lo contrario de las palabras de la primera columna. **(p. 140)**

1. regocijarse   **a.** ser honesto
2. traicionar   **b.** quedar muerto
3. empezar a luchar   **c.** lamentar
4. reírse   **d.** el amigo
5. la victoria   **e.** llorar
6. el héroe   **f.** la derrota
7. vivir   **g.** el malvado
8. el enemigo   **h.** acordar la paz

Communication for All Students

Challenge
2 Have students practice using the impersonal construction **se** + verb by creating and then translating English sentences into Spanish sentences using a third person singular subject (you, one, or people). For example: What can you do? **¿Qué se puede hacer?** How can one know? **¿Cómo se puede saber?**

Kinesthetic Learners
4 Have students work in pairs to dramatize the meanings of their vocabulary words. Each word is written on a slip of paper and placed in a stack in front of students. One student selects a word and acts it out while the partner tries to guess the word. If the partner guesses the correct term, he or she gets a point. If not, that term returns to the stack and another term is selected.

Answers
2
1. Se pensaba
2. Se creía
3. Se hablaba
4. Se pensaba
5. Se sabía
6. Se creía
7. no se sabía

3
1. ¿Dónde se toma un refresco?
2. ¿Qué se hace en el rato libre?
3. ¿Se viaja por tren con frecuencia?
4. ¿Con qué frecuencia se visita a los parientes?
5. ¿Se deja propina en un restaurante?
6. ¿Se usa el aire acondicionado?
7. ¿Con qué frecuencia se compra la comida en el mercado al aire libre?
8. ¿Qué se come en Chile?

4
1. c/e
2. a
3. h
4. e/c
5. f
6. g
7. b
8. d

For **Más práctica gramatical** Answer Transparencies, see the *Teaching Transparencies* binder.

Más práctica gramatical

WV3 GUADALAJARA-5

5 Leonor está leyendo un cuento de una princesa y un soldado guapo. ¿Qué quiere ella que pase en el cuento? Completa cada oración con la forma correcta del subjuntivo del verbo entre paréntesis. (**p. 142**)

MODELO   Leonor quiere que el malvado le _____ (decir) a la princesa dónde está el soldado guapo.
Leonor quiere que el malvado le <u>diga</u> a la princesa dónde está el soldado guapo.

1. Leonor quiere que la pobre princesa lo _____ (encontrar) pronto.
2. Ojalá que el soldado guapo no _____ (sufrir) mucho en la mazmorra.
3. Espera que sus enemigos no le _____ (hacer) daño al soldado.
4. También espera que el soldado _____ (poder) escribirle una carta secreta a la princesa.
5. Ojalá que la prima de la princesa le _____ (llevar) la carta secreta por la noche.
6. No quiere que la princesa _____ (llorar) ni que _____ (preocuparse).
7. También espera que los otros soldados no _____ (traicionar) al rey.
8. Ojalá que la guerra entre los dos ejércitos _____ (terminar) pronto.
9. Quiere que la princesa _____ (casarse) con el soldado guapo.
10. Espera que la reina _____ (hablar) con el rey sobre la boda.
11. Quiere que ellos _____ (celebrar) la boda pronto.
12. Ojalá que todos _____ (vivir) felices para siempre.
13. Espera que todo _____ (salir) bien, porque a Leonor no le gustan los cuentos tristes.

Answers
5 1. encuentre
2. sufra
3. hagan
4. pueda
5. lleve
6. llore, se preocupe
7. traicionen
8. termine
9. se case
10. hable
11. celebren
12. vivan
13. salga

Communication for All Students

Game
LA PATATA CALIENTE After you have presented the subjunctive mood, play this game. State an infinitive and a subject, then throw a foam ball to a student. The student conjugates the verb in the subjunctive and throws the ball back to you. Continue until students are comfortable with the new conjugations. Then put verbs into context. Say **Ojalá que Jaime...** The student catching the ball completes the phrase you began, **...me llame.** The next might answer **...venga a mi fiesta,** and so on.

6 Completa la conversación entre Blancanieves *(Snow White)* y uno de los enanos con las formas del subjuntivo de **estar** o **ir**. **(p. 143)**

ENANO   ¿Qué hacemos hoy? Narigón *(Sneezy)* quiere que todos nosotros ___1___ al lago para nadar. ¿Qué dices tú, Blancanieves?

BLANCANIEVES   Bien, pero nos va a visitar mi hada madrina, así que quiero que todos nosotros ___2___ en casa cuando llegue. Y también quiero que alguien ___3___ al pueblo para comprar galletas y helado.

ENANO   Bueno, voy yo, pero quiero que tú ___4___ también. No me gusta ir solo al pueblo.

BLANCANIEVES   Lo siento, pero no puedo. Dormilón *(Sleepy)* quiere que yo ___5___ con él al médico. Dice que no durmió bien anoche. Ojalá que ___6___ bien.

7 What does everyone want to receive as gifts this year? Explain what people want others to give them, using the correct subjunctive form of **dar** and following the model. Remember to include the correct object pronoun. **(p. 143)**

> **MODELO**   (yo)/mis padres/unos zapatos
> **Quiero que mis padres me den unos zapatos.**

1. Roberto/su novia/una foto grande
2. Carlota/sus padres/un perrito
3. mi hermano/yo/unos discos compactos
4. (yo)/tú/un videojuego
5. Yazmín y Elena/su abuela/flores y perfume
6. mamá/papá/un viaje a Puerto Rico
7. papá/nosotros/un reloj
8. ¿(tú)/tus padres/un carro?
9. Micaela/sus padres/un teléfono celular
10. ¿(tú)/yo/algo también?

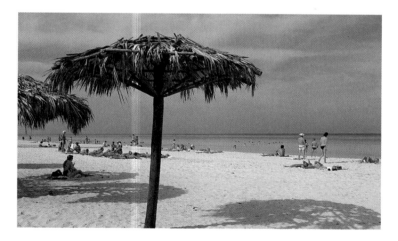

Review and Assess

You may wish to assign the **Más práctica gramatical** activities as additional practice or homework after presenting material throughout the chapter. Assign Activity 1 after **Así se dice** (p. 133), Activity 2 after **Así se dice** (p. 135), Activity 3 after **Nota gramatical** (p. 135), Activity 4 after **Vocabulario** (p. 140), Activity 5 after **Gramática** (p. 142), and Activities 6–7 after **Nota gramatical** (p. 143). To prepare students for the **Paso** Quizzes and Chapter Test, have them do the **Más práctica gramatical** activities in the following order: complete Activities 1–3 before taking Quiz 5-1A or 5-1B and Activities 4–7 before taking Quiz 5-2A or 5-2B.

Answers

6
1. vayamos
2. estemos
3. vaya
4. vayas
5. vaya
6. esté

7
1. Roberto quiere que su novia le dé una foto grande.
2. Carlota quiere que sus padres le den un perrito.
3. Mi hermano quiere que yo le dé unos discos compactos.
4. Quiero que me des un videojuego.
5. Yazmín y Elena quieren que su abuela les dé flores y perfume.
6. Mamá quiere que papá le dé un viaje a Puerto Rico.
7. Papá quiere que nosotros le demos un reloj.
8. ¿Quieres que tus padres te den un carro?
9. Micaela quiere que sus padres le den un teléfono celular.
10. ¿Quieres que yo te dé algo también?

Repaso

CAPÍTULO 5

The **Repaso** reviews all four skills and culture in preparation for the Chapter Test.

Teaching Resources
pp. 152–153

PRINT
▸ Lesson Planner, p. 26
▸ Listening Activities, p. 38
▸ Video Guide, pp. 31, 33, 36
▸ Grammar Tutor for Students of Spanish, Chapter 5
▸ Cuaderno para hispanohablantes, pp. 21–25
▸ Standardized Assessment Tutor, Chapter 5

MEDIA
▸ One-Stop Planner
▸ Video Program, Videocassette 2, 27:09–29:54
▸ Audio Compact Discs, CD 5, Tr. 15
▸ Interactive CD-ROM Tutor, Disc 2

Answers
2 *Sample answer:*
Quieren que no llueva. Esperan que la tormenta no dañe la casa. La familia espera que esté sano el bebé.

3 *Sample answer:*
Jacques, quiero que les des agua a mis plantas. También, espero que tengas tiempo para limpiar la casa. Espero que no trabajes demasiado: como tengo vacaciones, quiero que descanses también.

4 *Possible answers:*
1. Hay que ser fiel, leal, escuchar los problemas de otros y querer hacerlos felices.
2. Se tiene que hacer ejercicio y comer muchas verduras y poca grasa para gozar de buena salud.
3. Se dice que debes leer y estudiar mucho, aprender algo de ese trabajo y conocer a mucha gente.
4. Supuestamente, para ser feliz, hay que ser honrado(a), trabajar mucho, querer a tu familia y quererte a ti mismo.

Repaso

internet
MARCAR: go.hrw.com
PALABRA CLAVE:
WV3 GUADALAJARA-5

1 Escucha las siguientes conversaciones entre Marcela y Antonio e indica a qué foto corresponde cada conversación. Luego escucha otra vez e indica qué espera Marcela o Antonio. Hay una conversación que no corresponde a ninguna foto. Script and answers on p. 127H.

CD 5
Tr. 15

a.   b.   c.   d.

2 Mira los siguientes dibujos. Con un(a) compañero(a), expresa las esperanzas y deseos que tienen las personas en cada dibujo. See sample answers below.

3 Imagina que tienes un palacio y un mayordomo. Vas a ir de vacaciones y quieres que él haga algunas cosas para ti. Escríbele una nota con diez instrucciones sobre lo que quieres y esperas que haga o que no haga. See sample answers below.

4 ¿Qué dice la gente que hay que hacer para tener éxito en los siguientes asuntos? Escribe lo que se dice de cada asunto. Compara tu lista con la de un(a) compañero(a). See possible answers below.

1. ser buen(a) amigo(a)
2. gozar de buena salud
3. conseguir un buen trabajo
4. ser feliz en la vida

Apply and Assess

Challenge
2 Have students expand on this activity by creating a verbal description to accompany each picture. First, let students briefly study the picture. Then, have them take turns telling each other as much about the picture as they can.

Kinesthetic Learners
3 Have students work in pairs and act out the conversation between the head of the house and the butler. You might also have them use puppets or stuffed animals to present the dialogue.

---

5 Habla de los siguientes temas con un grupo de dos o tres compañeros(as). Usen expresiones de acuerdo total, acuerdo parcial o desacuerdo total.

1. Habrá astronautas en el planeta Marte para el año 2040.

2. Las mujeres son mejores en las artes que los hombres.

3. Una mujer será presidenta de los Estados Unidos dentro de 20 años.

4. Todos(as) deben estudiar por lo menos dos lenguas extranjeras en el colegio.

5. Algún día compraremos casi todo por Internet.

6 Basando tus respuestas en el artículo "Cada pueblo un desarrollo", nombra... See answers below.

1. algo que no tenían los incas pero los aztecas sí.

2. tres cosas que tenían en común los mayas, incas y aztecas.

3. una cosa que no inventó ninguna de las tres civilizaciones.

4. un concepto matemático clave que usaban los mayas.

5. un metal desconocido por las tres civilizaciones.

CADA PUEBLO UN DESARROLLO

A la llegada de los españoles, los pueblos americanos estaban en muy diferentes períodos de desarrollo. Algunos estaban prácticamente en la Edad de Piedra. Otros, como los mayas, incas y aztecas, habían alcanzado un alto grado de civilización. Sin embargo, su desarrollo era curiosamente irregular. Los mayas, que inventaron el más avanzado sistema de escritura de América, mejoraron el calendario y hasta calculaban con el cero, nunca pudieron constituir un estado. Los incas, que eran magníficos artesanos y tenían una compleja organización estatal, no inventaron ningún sistema de escritura. Los aztecas, que tenían escritura y grandes conocimientos astronómicos, eran inexpertos como navegantes. A pesar de ser excelentes constructores de caminos, ninguno de los tres pueblos inventó la rueda. Es más, estos expertos trabajadores del oro, la plata y el cobre desconocían el hierro.

7 Indica si las siguientes oraciones son **ciertas** o **falsas.** Si son falsas, corrígelas. See sample answer below.

1. La "Leyenda negra" habla de la crueldad de los indios hacia los españoles.

2. "La carreta sin bueyes" cuenta la historia de una mujer que perdió a sus hijos.

3. Cuando llegó Cristóbal Colón, los indios creyeron que era el dios Quetzalcóatl.

4. Los aztecas escribían con dibujos que expresaban sus ideas simbólicamente.

5. Según la leyenda, Quetzalcóatl inventó la rueda y el calendario.

8 ## Situación

Por casualidad, tú y un(a) amigo(a) van a tener que mudarse, y los dos van al mismo colegio nuevo. Uds. hablan de lo que dice la gente sobre el nuevo colegio y sobre sus maestros y estudiantes. Tu amigo(a) es algo pesimista sobre las posibilidades pero tú tratas de hacerle ver otro punto de vista. Expresa tus esperanzas positivas.

Cuaderno para hispanohablantes, p. 25

Literature Link

In most good stories, the hero or heroine faces some challenge or adversity. Ask students if they have a favorite book or story in which they identify with a character who is challenged and emerges heroic. Have students write a short description in Spanish about their favorite heroic character. You might also have them write why they admire the character and what heroic traits they see in themselves.

Portfolio

4 **Oral** Students may want to include this activity in their oral Portfolios. For Portfolio suggestions, see *Alternative Assessment Guide*, page 20.

Answers

6 1. un sistema de escritura

2. un alto grado de civilización; artesanías de oro, plata y cobre; caminos excelentes

3. la rueda

4. el cero

5. el hierro

7 1. falsa; La "Leyenda negra" cuenta la crueldad de la conquista y la explotación de los indígenas por los españoles.

2. falsa; "La Llorona" cuenta la historia de esa mujer. "La carreta sin bueyes" asusta a la gente para que no salga de la casa muy tarde.

3. falsa; Creían que Hernán Cortés era el dios Quetzalcóatl.

4. cierta

5. falsa; Se dice que Quetzalcóatl inventó el calendario y el libro.

Apply and Assess

Additional Practice

5 Have students form teams to debate each side of the issue expressed in these statements. This should not be an argument, but rather a means for students to develop their ideas into extended thoughts and opinions.

Thinking Critically

6 **Synthesizing** Have students write a two-sentence summary of the article. Ask them **¿Cuál es la idea principal del artículo? Explícala con dos frases.**

Slower Pace

7 Have students discuss these statements in pairs or groups of three.

A ver si puedo

CAPÍTULO 5

Teaching Resources
p. 154

PRINT 📖
▶ Grammar Tutor for Students of Spanish, Chapter 5

MEDIA 💿📼
▶ Interactive CD-ROM Tutor, Disc 2
▶ Online self-test

 go.hrw.com
WV3 GUADALAJARA-5

Teacher Note
This page is intended to help students prepare independently for the Chapter Test. It is a brief checklist of the major points covered in the chapter. The students should be reminded that this is only a checklist and does not necessarily include everything that will appear on the Chapter Test.

Answers

2 *Answer will vary. Students should use expressions such as:* Se cree que, Se dice, Supuestamente, *and* Oí que *in their responses.*

3 *Possible answers:*
El jugador quiere que su equipo gane el partido.
El papá quiere que la niña coma sus verduras, pero la niña no quiere comerlas.
La chica espera recibir un disco compacto.
La niñera espera que los padres lleguen pronto.

4 1. Espero ganar suficiente dinero para comprar una bicicleta.
2. Quiero que mis amigos y yo lo pasemos bien en los partidos de fútbol.
3. Espero que mi familia pueda ir a las montañas a esquiar.
4. Quiero que mis hermanos sean más simpáticos.
5. Espero que mis padres me den un carro para mi cumpleaños.

A ver si puedo...

WV3 GUADALAJARA-5

Can you express qualified agreement and disagreement?
p. 133

1 Piensa en los siguientes temas. Usa expresiones de acuerdo o desacuerdo, y explica tus opiniones.
1. Es buena idea eliminar el sistema de evaluación por notas.
2. Debería ser posible repetir un examen si uno no lo aprueba la primera vez.
3. Sería bueno tener clases doce meses al año.
4. Debería ser legal votar a la edad de 15 años.
5. Para el año 2020, todos usaremos carros solares.

Can you report what others say and think?
p. 135

2 ¿Qué dice la gente sobre los siguientes asuntos?
See note below.

los trabajos   los jóvenes
la falta de vivienda
las familias   la situación económica
la música   la contaminación del aire

Can you talk about hopes and wishes?
p. 141

3 Escribe oraciones sobre lo que quieren o esperan estas personas.
See possible answers below.

el jugador

la niña

la chica   **la niñera (babysitter)**

4 Es el Año Nuevo y José tiene muchas esperanzas y deseos. Escribe lo que desea y quiere José. See answers below.

| MODELO | mi novia/venir conmigo a la fiesta |
| | **Espero que mi novia venga conmigo a la fiesta.** |

1. yo/ganar suficiente dinero para comprar una bicicleta
2. mis amigos y yo/pasarlo bien en los partidos de fútbol
3. mi familia/poder ir a las montañas a esquiar
4. mis hermanos/ser más simpático
5. mis padres/darme un carro para mi cumpleaños

Review and Assess

Challenge
1 Divide the class into groups of four to debate one of the ideas from the activity. Two students will agree and two will disagree. Each side should come up with at least three statements in support of their opinion. Remind students that they must respond to what the opposing side says. Have groups volunteer to present their debate to the class.

Pair Work
2 Have pairs of students take each of the **asuntos** presented and write two or three sentences about what they hope or want regarding those issues. Ask volunteers to write one of their sentences on the board for the class to correct and discuss. Encourage the class to respond with opinion statements.

STANDARDS: 1.2

Primer paso

Expressing agreement

Así es.	That's right.
¡Claro que sí!	Of course!
¡Cómo no!	Of course!
Desde luego.	Of course.
Eso es.	That's right.
Estoy de acuerdo.	I agree.
Por supuesto.	Of course.

Expressing qualified agreement

Bueno, puede ser, pero...	Well, that may be, but . . .
Depende de tu punto de vista.	It depends on your point of view.
En efecto, parece ser así.	Actually, it seems to be that way.
Es muy difícil de creer, pero es posible.	That's very hard to believe, but it's possible.

Hasta cierto punto, sí, pero...	Up to a point, yes, but . . .
Pero hay que tener en cuenta que...	But you have to take into account that . . .
¿Tú crees? No sé.	Do you think so? I don't know.

Expressing disagreement

Al contrario.	On the contrary.
¡Claro que no!	Of course not!
¡Eso es muy difícil!	That's very unlikely!
¡Nada de eso!	Of course not!
¡Qué tontería!	How silly!
¡Qué va!	No way!

Reporting what others say and think

Alguien me dijo que...	Somebody told me that . . .
Cuentan que...	They say that . . .
Dicen que...	They say that . . .
el hombre	man
la mujer	woman
Oí que...	I heard that . . .
Se cree que...	It's believed that . . .
Se dice que...	They say that . . .
según	according to
supuestamente	supposedly

Segundo paso

Telling a legend

acordar(ue) la paz	to make peace
la boda	wedding
celebrar	to celebrate
declarar	to declare
la derrota	defeat
el dios	god
la diosa	goddess
el ejército	army
el (la) enemigo(a)	enemy
la guerra	war
el (la) guerrero(a)	warrior
el héroe	hero
la heroína	heroine
lamentar	to mourn; to lament

llorar	to cry
luchar por	to struggle for, to fight for
el (la) malvado(a)	villain
muerto(a)	dead
la mujer soldado	soldier (f.)
la paz	peace
quedar muerto(a)	to be left dead
regocijarse	to rejoice
el soldado	soldier
traicionar	to betray
valiente	brave
vencer	to defeat
la victoria	victory

Talking about hopes and wishes

la ambición	ambition
Era una de mis grandes ambiciones.	It was one of my great ambitions.
esperar + inf.	to hope to . . .
esperar que + subj.	to hope (that) . . .
ojalá que + subj.	hopefully . . .
querer que + subj.	to want . . . to . . .
el sueño de mi vida	my lifelong dream
Tenía muchas esperanzas de...	I had high hopes of . . .

Review and Assess

Game

TODOS LOS EJERCICIOS For each item in **A ver si puedo...**, assign a number and write it on a slip of paper to be drawn from a hat. The first player from each of two teams goes to the board. Pick a number and call out the task. Students write their responses on the board. The first one to write the correct response wins 10 points for his or her team. If the second student also responds correctly, he or she wins five points. If neither team has a perfect response, the teams discuss the response in a team huddle for one minute. The same students then go to the board to write the answer. The first one to finish correctly earns five points for his or her team. The team with the highest number of points when all the numbers have been drawn wins.

Visual/Kinesthetic Learners

Divide the class into two or three teams. Distribute flash cards with words and expressions that students will pantomime individually or in pairs. The rest of their team has three chances to guess what they are representing before the other team has a chance to guess and get a point.

Circumlocution

Have the class play **¿Cómo te diré?** (page 3C) to practice vocabulary from **Segundo paso.** As an alternative to using chapter vocabulary to define English words, you might have students define the target vocabulary in Spanish.

Chapter 5 Assessment

▶ **Testing Program**
Chapter Test, pp. 97–102
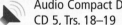 Audio Compact Discs, CD 5, Trs. 18–19
Speaking Test, p. 297

▶ **Alternative Assessment Guide**
Portfolio Assessment, p. 20
Performance Assessment, p. 34
CD-ROM Assessment, p. 48

▶ **Interactive CD-ROM Tutor, Disc 2**
 ¡A hablar!
¡A escribir!

▶ **Standardized Assessment Tutor**
Chapter 5

▶ **One-Stop Planner, Disc 2**
Test Generator
Chapter 5

Capítulo 6: El arte y la música
Chapter Overview

De antemano pp. 158–160	*Los murales de Orozco*

	FUNCTIONS	**GRAMMAR**	**VOCABULARY**	**RE-ENTRY**
Primer paso pp. 162–166	• Introducing and changing a topic of conversation, p. 162 • Expressing what needs to be done, p. 164 • Expressing an opinion, p. 165	• Gender of some nouns, p. 163 • Subjunctive after expressions of need, p. 164	• Art, p. 163 • Opinions, p. 165	• Infinitives vs. subjunctive **(Capítulo 5)** • Comparisons **(Capítulo 9, I)**

¡Adelante! pp. 168–169	*Una entrevista con Luis Miguel*

Segundo paso pp. 170–173	• Making suggestions and recommendations, p. 170 • Turning down an invitation, p. 172	• The subjunctive mood with recommendations, p. 170 • **nosotros** commands, p. 172	• The theater, p. 173	• Subjunctive of **ir, ser**, and **dar (Capítulo 5)** • **nosotros** commands **(Capítulo 11, II)** • Extending invitations **(Capítulo 7, I)**

Vamos a leer pp. 174–176	**Vida, pasión y muerte de Frida Kahlo**	**Reading Strategy:** Skimming to get the gist

Vamos a escribir p. 177	**Un acontecimiento importante**	**Writing Strategy:** Chronological ordering

Más práctica gramatical	**pp. 178–181** **Primer paso,** pp. 178–180	**Segundo paso,** pp. 180–181	

Review pp. 182–185	**Repaso,** pp. 182–183	**A ver si puedo...,** p. 184	**Vocabulario,** p. 185

CULTURE

• Mexican murals, pp. 156–159
• **Nota cultural,** Mexican mural movement of the 1920s and 1930s, p. 160
• **Panorama cultural, ¿Te consideras una persona artística?,** p. 161
• **A lo nuestro,** Expressing indifference, p. 165

• **Realia,** Botero, Varo, and Solar paintings, p. 166
• **Encuentro cultural, Los instrumentos musicales,** p. 167
• **Realia,** Cultural attractions of Guadalajara, p. 171
• **Realia, Eventos culturales,** p. 173

Capítulo 6: El arte y la música
Chapter Resources

Lesson Planning

One-Stop Planner

Lesson Planner with Substitute Teacher Lesson Plans, pp. 27–31, 70

Student Make-Up Assignments
- Make-Up Assignment Copying Masters, Chapter 6

Listening and Speaking

Listening Activities
- Student Response Forms for Listening Activities, pp. 43–45
- Additional Listening Activities 6-1 to 6-6, pp. 47–49
- Additional Listening Activities (song), p. 50
- Scripts and Answers, pp. 126–131

Video Guide
- Teaching Suggestions, pp. 38–39
- Activity Masters, pp. 40–42
- Scripts and Answers, pp. 97–99, 116–117

Activities for Communication
- Communicative Activities, pp. 21–24
- Realia and Teaching Suggestions, pp. 66–68
- Situation Cards, pp. 99–100

Reading and Writing

Reading Strategies and Skills Handbook, Chapter 6

¡Lee conmigo! 3, Chapter 6

Cuaderno de actividades, pp. 61–72

Grammar

Cuaderno de gramática, pp. 46–54

Grammar Tutor for Students of Spanish, Chapter 6

Assessment

Testing Program
- Grammar and Vocabulary Quizzes, **Paso** Quizzes, and Chapter Test, pp. 111–124
- Score Sheet, Scripts and Answers, pp. 125–131
- Midterm Exam, pp. 133–140
- Score Sheet, Scripts and Answers, pp. 141–146

Alternative Assessment Guide
- Portfolio Assessment, p. 21
- Performance Assessment, p. 35
- CD-ROM Assessment, p. 49

Student Make-Up Assignments
- Alternative Quizzes, Chapter 6

Standardized Assessment Tutor
- Reading, pp. 21–23
- Writing, p. 24
- Math, pp. 25–26

Native Speakers

Cuaderno para hispanohablantes, pp. 26–30

 Online Activities
- Juegos interactivos
- Actividades Internet

 Video Program
- Videocassette 2
- Videocassette 5 (captioned version)

 Audio Compact Discs
- Textbook Listening Activities, CD 6, Tracks 1–17
- Additional Listening Activities, CD 6, Tracks 26–32
- Assessment Items, CD 6, Tracks 18–25

 Interactive CD-ROM Tutor, Disc 2

 Teaching Transparencies
- Situations 6-1 to 6-2
- **Más práctica gramatical** Answers
- **Cuaderno de gramática** Answers

  One-Stop Planner CD-ROM

Use the **One-Stop Planner CD-ROM with Test Generator** to aid in lesson planning and pacing.

For each chapter, the **One-Stop Planner** includes:

- Editable lesson plans with direct links to teaching resources
- Printable worksheets from resource books
- Direct launches to the HRW Internet activities
- Video and audio segments
- Test Generator
- Clip Art for vocabulary items

Capítulo 6: El arte y la música

Projects

Los artistas

In this project, students select one of the artists mentioned in the chapter and obtain biographical information on him or her. Students then work in groups to create their own murals or paintings imitating the artist's style and depicting a historical event or period of their choice. You may want to give students at least one week to complete the project.

MATERIALS

✂ **Students may need**
- Poster board
- Colored markers

SUGGESTED SEQUENCE

1. Divide the class into groups of three to five.
2. Group members select an artist mentioned in the chapter that they would like to learn more about.
3. Group members research biographical information and any remarkable characteristics about the artist's work.
4. Students write a one-page biographical summary about the artist.
5. Groups decide what historical event they wish to depict and choose visual images to convey their message.
6. Students work in groups to create their mural.
7. Groups present an oral report about the artist and his or her art work. Each student in the group is responsible for a portion of the presentation.

GRADING THE PROJECT

Suggested point distribution (total = 100 points):
Biographical summary of artist's life	30
Use of Spanish in oral report	30
Originality of painting or mural	30
Neatness	10

Games

¿Quién soy?

In this game, students inquire about personal attributes, opinions, and facts. It is a good vocabulary review that can be used at any time during the chapter.

Preparation Prepare a game grid similar to a Bingo card, with enough squares to represent each member of the class. If there is an odd number of students, put a free space on the grid. Before beginning the game, ask students to write two things about themselves that are not common knowledge and that they are willing to share. (**Pienso que la música de... es fenomenal.**) Select one item per student and write it on the grid in Spanish. Make enough copies of the grid for each student to have one. Make an answer key by writing each student's name in the appropriate box.

Procedure Give each student a grid. Students circulate, asking each other questions in Spanish to find out the identity of the person described in each of the squares. When a student figures out which of his or her classmates has a particular attribute or opinion, he or she asks that person to initial the appropriate square on the grid. Students ask a follow-up question relating to the attribute or opinion and jot down the response next to the initials. (**¿Por qué te gusta tanto la música de...?**)

The first student to obtain initials in boxes forming a straight horizontal, vertical, or diagonal line wins the game. You may want to circulate and monitor the use of Spanish during the game.

COMMUNITY LINK

Have students contact local art museums to find out whether any works by the artists mentioned in this chapter are exhibited in your city or nearby.

Storytelling

Mini-cuento

This story accompanies Teaching Transparency 6-1. The **mini-cuento** *can be told and retold in different formats, acted out, written as dictation, and read aloud to give students additional opportunities to practice all four skills. The following story tells about the reactions of young people towards art.*

¿Qué piensan los jóvenes de las artes? Daniel admira mucho a los escultores que trabajan horas y horas para crear una sola escultura. Ricardo piensa que la música rock es de muy mal gusto y le cae gordo el cantante. Cuando Joselito era niño no soportaba la danza. Siempre se dormía cuando veía bailar a una bailarina. En la clase de Joaquín, el profesor Gavia es formidable y entretenido. El profesor dice que *don Quijote* es una obra maestra. Para Elena, la única cosa que es genial es pintar acuarelas. Ella piensa que la pintura es la más creativa de todas las artes.

Traditions

Costumbres

Long before the Spaniards came to the Americas, the Aztecs were cultivating a colorful red and green plant. They called it **cuetlaxochitl,** meaning "mortal flower that perishes and withers like all that is pure." The plant's red leaves were used to make a reddish-purple dye or were placed on a person's chest to stimulate circulation. The leaves were also crushed and applied to skin infections, and the white sap was made into a medicine to fight fevers. In the seventeenth century, Franciscan friars began using the colorful flowers at Christmas. But it was the first United States ambassador to Mexico, Joel Robert Poinsett, who not only gave the flower its modern name, poinsettia, but also introduced it to this country in 1825. Today, plant breeding has developed larger flowers in yellow, pink, and even mottled colors as well as the traditional red. Have

students research the development and commercialization of the varieties of poinsettias in North America and share their findings with the class.

Receta

One of the most popular dishes in Guadalajara is **chilaquiles,** *which can be red (tomato-based) or green (* **tomatillo-based).** **Chilaquiles** *are usually eaten for breakfast (some cooks add eggs and scramble them with the tortillas), or as a snack. It is not unusual to add leftover ingredients, such as chicken, to this dish.*

CHILAQUILES

para 4–6 personas

8 tortillas de maíz
aceite para freír

1 ó 2 chiles serranos o jalapeños (al gusto)

1 diente de ajo picado

2 tomates cocinados (se puede usar tomates de lata)

1/2 cucharadita de orégano

1/2 taza de agua

sal al gusto

1/2 taza de cebolla picada

1/2 taza de queso *Monterey Jack,* rallado

1/2 taza de crema ácida (agria)

Corte las tortillas en pedazos de 1" x 1". Licúe los tomates, el orégano, los chiles, el ajo picado y el agua en una licuadora. En una sartén grande, ponga una cucharada de aceite y añada la salsa de tomate, sazone con sal y cocine a fuego moderado, revolviendo de vez en cuando, por unos cinco minutos. Retírela del fuego, y manténgala caliente. En otra sartén, fría las tortillas a fuego un poco alto hasta que estén doradas. Escúrralas sobre toallas de papel. Cuando estén fritas todas las tortillas, saque el aceite de la sartén dejando sólo 1/2 taza. Ponga las tortillas y la cebolla en la sartén y cocine hasta que la cebolla esté transparente. Añada la salsa de tomate y cocine, dándole vueltas, por unos tres minutos. Sirva inmediatamente con el queso y la crema encima.

Capítulo 6: El arte y la música
Technology

Video Program

Videocassette 2, Videocassette 5 (captioned version)
See Video Guide, pages 37–42.

Dramatic episode • La obra maestra

Alejandra, Irene, and Carlos visit an art museum in Mexico City. They see various paintings, including **La ofrenda** by Mexican painter Saturnino Herrán, which reminds Alejandra of their trip to Xochimilco. As they leave the museum, Alejandra finds out that Carlos has been corresponding with Sergio and Javier via e-mail. She is angry at first that Carlos did not tell her he was in contact with their friends, but then Carlos offers to teach her how to use the Internet. They decide to meet the next day at the computer center.

¿Te consideras una persona artística?

People from different Spanish-speaking countries explain why they do or do not consider themselves artistic.

Videoclips

• **El Museo de Arte Moderno de Medellín:** commercial promoting **El Museo de Arte Moderno de Medellín** and its exposition of Colombian photographers

• **Fernando Botero:** documentary about Colombian artist Fernando Botero, with a description of his work, and a glimpse at the artist himself, as he explains the origin of his paintings and sculpture

Interactive CD-ROM Tutor

The **Interactive CD-ROM Tutor** contains videos, interactive games, and activities that provide students an opportunity to practice and review the material covered in Chapter 6.

Activity	Activity Type	Pupil's Edition Page
1. Así se dice	¡Presta el oído!	p. 162
2. Vocabulario	¡Super memoria!	p. 163
3. Gramática	¿Qué falta?	p. 164
4. Vocabulario	Imagen y sonido ¡Exploremos! ¡Identifiquemos!	p. 165
5. Así se dice	¿Cuál es?	p. 170
6. Gramática	¡A escoger!	p. 172
Panorama cultural	¿Te consideras una persona artística? ¡A escoger!	p. 161
¡A hablar!	*Guided recording*	pp. 182–183
¡A escribir!	*Guided writing*	pp. 182–183

Teacher Management System
Logging In

Logging in to the *¡Ven conmigo!* TMS is easy. Upon launching the program, simply type "admin" in the password area of the log-in screen and press RETURN. Log on to **www.hrw.com/CDROMTUTOR** for a detailed explanation of the Teacher Management System.

One-Stop Planner CD-ROM

To preview all resources available for this chapter, use the **One-Stop Planner CD-ROM,** Disc 2.

Internet Connection

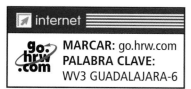

MARCAR: go.hrw.com
PALABRA CLAVE:
WV3 GUADALAJARA-6

*Have students explore the **go.hrw.com** Web site for many online resources covering all chapters. All Chapter 6 resources are available under the keyword **WV3 GUADALAJARA-6.** Interactive games help students practice the material and provide them with immediate feedback. You will also find a printable worksheet that provides Internet activities that lead to a comprehensive online research project.*

Juegos interactivos

You can use the interactive activities in this chapter

- to practice grammar, vocabulary, and chapter functions
- as homework
- as an assessment option
- as a self-test
- to prepare for the Chapter Test

Actividades Internet

Students research contemporary artists from Spanish-speaking countries. They write about the artists, their styles, artistic media, and materials.

- Have students prepare for the **Hoja de actividades** by reviewing the functions in **Primer paso.** You might also ask students about their artistic or musical preferences, especially any styles from Spanish-speaking countries.
- When students have finished the activity sheet, have them describe the work and the Web site on which they found it, and say what they like about it.

Proyecto

Ask students to choose one style of art or music they would like to learn more about. Have them find Web sites with information about that style. Suggest they download free images or music they find online, or bring in books or magazines. Ask students to share what they learn with the class or create a school-sponsored Web page devoted to what they have learned.

STANDARDS: 1.2, 1.3, 2.2, 3.1, 3.2, 5.1

CAPÍTULO 6 TECHNOLOGY 155F

Primer paso

6   **p. 162**

Answers to Activity 6
Cambian de tema cuatro veces.

— Oye, Pilar, ¿sabes algo sobre Remedios Varo?

— Sí, claro, es mi artista favorita. Pinta cuadros surrealistas bien padres.

— ¿Es mexicana?

— Nació en España pero hizo su carrera artística aquí en México.

— Hablando de España, ¿qué me cuentas de Joan Miró? ¿También era un pintor surrealista?

— No. Él era más bien un pintor abstracto. Salvador Dalí, ése sí era surrealista. ¿Has visto algo de Dalí?

— Sí, conozco algunos de sus cuadros. Pintó muchos relojes. Creo que los críticos describen su arte como fotografías de sueños.

— Ah, eso me recuerda. Tenemos que pintar algo que soñamos.

— Oye, cambiando de tema, ¿cuándo es el examen de matemáticas?

— ¡Híjole, se me había olvidado! ¡Es mañana!

8   **p. 163**

Answers to Activity 8
1. música   3. escultura
2. literatura   4. música

Conversación 1

— Joaquín, ven acá. Son las cuatro. Es la hora de ensayar tus lecciones de piano, ¿no?

— Pero papá, hoy hace buen tiempo. Iba a salir a jugar al fútbol un rato.

— Joaquín, el ejercicio es importante, pero ya sabes que si no tocas el piano todos los días no aprendes nada.

— Bueno, bueno, papá. De acuerdo.

Conversación 2

— Ay, Joaquín... ¡esta clase me tiene tan frustrada!

— ¿Por qué, Cristina? La clase es muy divertida.

— Para ti, sí. Pero para mí, no. No tengo talento y nada de lo que escribo me sale bien. Mis cuentos y poemas son horribles.

— Tranquila, Cristina. No es necesario tener mucho talento para sacar provecho de la clase. Sólo hay que leer las obras clásicas y crear tus propios cuentos.

Conversación 3

— Leí en el periódico esta mañana que la ciudad va a gastar cien mil dólares en una estatua para el Centro Infantil.

— ¿Y qué? Me parece muy bien.

— Pero hija, cien mil dólares es mucho dinero, ¿no crees? Con esa cantidad, se pueden arreglar escuelas o construir un parque nuevo...

— No, papi... no estoy de acuerdo. Me parece que hay que cultivar en los niños el interés por las artes. Es una parte importantísima de su educación. Además, la escultura es muy buena.

Conversación 4

— Oye, Joaquín, esta noche vamos a un concierto de la orquesta. ¿Nos quieres acompañar?

— Gracias, Alicia, pero... no. No sé nada de las sinfonías.

— Hombre, no seas tonto. ¿Eso qué importa? Sólo hay que escuchar... ¡y disfrutar!

— Quizás tengas razón.

Answers to Activity 10
1. Tere   4. Tere   7. Tere
2. ella misma   5. ella misma   8. ella misma
3. ella misma   6. Tere

10   **p. 164**

1. Es necesario que sepas quiénes tienen más talento para la danza.
2. Para conservar el medio ambiente es importante que recicle la basura.
3. Hace falta que utilice más colores en este cuadro.
4. Para mantener la salud es necesario que hagas ejercicios todos los días.
5. Es importante que aprenda acerca del arte antiguo antes de estudiar el arte contemporáneo.
6. Para tocar el piano como un maestro hace falta que practiques ocho horas diarias.
7. Es necesario que apoyes al grupo de teatro.
8. Para participar en la exhibición hace falta que pinte tres cuadros más.

12   **p. 165**

Answers to Activity 12
1. negativa   3. negativa   5. indiferencia
2. positiva   4. positiva   6. negativa

Comentario 1
El próximo mes tenemos que leer dos obras de Shakespeare. ¡Qué pesado! Francamente, las obras de Shakespeare no me interesan mucho, pero es importante leerlas.

Comentario 2
Me gusta ir a la casa de mi amigo Benito para escuchar música porque tiene una colección increíble de discos compactos. Anoche escuchamos unos discos de música de África, y me enseñó a bailar merengue. ¡Fue genial! Me encanta la música afrocaribeña.

Comentario 3
El año pasado, el director de nuestro colegio decidió poner una estatua en el patio. El único problema es que la estatua es horrible. Hay que verla... no sé si es hombre, pájaro, gorila, o qué. Para ser sincero, me parece la cosa más fea que jamás haya visto.

Comentario 4
Hace poco mi amiga Nuria empezó a tomar clases de pintura. En mi cumpleaños, me regaló un cuadro para mi habitación porque sabe que admiro mucho su arte. ¡Pinta muy bien!

Comentario 5
Anoche fui con mi amigo Javier a ver una nueva película de ciencia ficción. Era sobre varios planetas en guerra. Hubo unos efectos especiales buenos. No me pareció muy original ni interesante.

Comentario 6
A mi amiga Victoria le gusta la música y siempre va a muchos conciertos. Bueno... el otro día me invitó al estreno de un nuevo grupo musical. Se llaman "Los chimpancés locos". Para decir la verdad, los encontré insoportables.

18   **p. 168**

Answers to Activity 18
Claudia

Conversación 1

— Carlo Antonio es la estrella del momento. Su canción "Tú no sabes y yo tampoco" está en el primer lugar de las listas de popularidad en todo el país. Carlo Antonio, ¿cantar es tu razón de vivir?

— No, a mí me gusta más componer canciones. Cantar es una manera de ganarme la vida, pero yo soy más un compositor.

— Entonces, Carlo Antonio, ¿no has realizado tus sueños?

— No, la verdad no. Yo quiero hacer muchas cosas.

— ¿Haces ejercicio?

— Casi nunca.

— ¿Cómo describirías un día perfecto?

— Un día en el que pueda escribir canciones y compartir el día con mi familia y mis amigos.

— ¿Cómo es un día normal para ti?

— Igual que mi día perfecto.

Conversación 2

— Claudia es la reina de la música ranchera y acaba de presentar su nuevo disco, con el título "Las canciones de mi abuelo". Claudia, ¿cantar es tu razón de vivir?

The following scripts are for the Listening Activities found in the *Pupil's Edition*. For Student Response Forms, see *Listening Activites*, pages 43–45. To provide students with additional listening practice, see *Listening Activities*, pages 47–49.

One-Stop Planner CD-ROM

To preview all resources available for this chapter, use the **One-Stop Planner CD-ROM**, Disc 2.

— Por supuesto que sí. Cantar es lo más importante en mi vida.

— ¿Has realizado todos tus sueños?

— La mayoría de ellos, pero todavía sigo soñando. Quiero llevar la música ranchera a los más apartados rincones del mundo y también gozar de buena salud toda mi vida.

— ¿Haces ejercicio?

— Sí, me gusta muchísimo. Me encantan los deportes acuáticos. Pasear en velero es un deporte muy divertido.

— ¿Cómo es un día perfecto?

— Mira, lo único que pido es que sea un día en el que pueda dormir lo necesario. Por lo general, con tanta actividad, no puedo dormir lo suficiente.

— ¿Cómo es un día normal para ti?

— No hay días normales para mí, excepto cuando estoy de gira y tengo que viajar todo el tiempo. Lo único normal es que casi no duermo.

Segundo paso

21 p. 170

Answers to Activity 21
1. b 2. d 3. e 4. a 5. c

1. ¡Qué lata! No tenemos coche esta semana y queremos ir de compras antes de ir a Guadalajara. ¿Sabes a qué hora pasan los autobuses?

2. Vamos a vernos con nuestras amigas Ann y Judith en la ciudad, pero no sabemos dónde. ¿Tienen alguna idea?

3. Todo está listo para el viaje. El equipaje, los boletos de avión y los regalos. ¿Es todo?

4. La cantante Claudia y el Mariachi El Jarabe van a dar un concierto en el Teatro Regional. ¿Crees que alcancemos a comprar boletos en la taquilla?

5. Llevamos tres maletas grandes, dos maletas pequeñas y una caja. ¡Y eso que todavía no empacamos los regalos!

25 p. 172

Answers to Activity 25
1. No; Ya tiene planes.
2. No; Prefiere comer algo.
3. No; Va a hacer muchas cosas.
4. Sí.

Conversación 1

— Sara, a ti te gusta la música, ¿verdad?

— Sí, claro. ¿Por qué?

— Bueno, verás. Mi tío es músico en la orquesta municipal y me dio dos entradas para el concierto de Mozart este sábado. ¿Te gustaría ir?

— Ay, Humberto, gracias... pero el sábado ya tengo planes. Tal vez otra noche, ¿de acuerdo?

Conversación 2

— Éstas son las vacaciones más aburridas que he pasado en mi vida. No hay nada que hacer.

— Ay, Miguel, no te quejes. Para mí, estar descansando en casa viendo la tele son las mejores vacaciones. Oye, son casi las dos. Si quieres vamos al cine a la función de la tarde. Podemos ver el estreno de la película de Carlos Saura.

— No tengo ganas de ir. Estoy harto de ver películas. Mejor vamos a comer algo. Tengo hambre.

Conversación 3

— Oye, Laura, ¿ya tienes planes para esta noche?

— ¿Por qué lo preguntas?

— Bueno, hay una nueva comedia en el Teatro Carpa. ¿Por qué no vamos a verla?

— Pues... me gustaría ir al teatro, pero tengo muchas cosas que hacer. Mejor lo dejamos para otro día.

— Como tú digas.

Conversación 4

— Oye, Ricardo... ¿te acuerdas de la tarea de la clase de arte? Ir a un museo y escribir una composición sobre alguna obra de arte.

— Claro que me acuerdo, pero no tengo la menor idea de cómo la voy a hacer. No sé nada de arte y no me gustan los museos.

— Bueno, no te preocupes. Mi prima Rosa trabaja en el museo de arte, y ella dice que puede darnos una visita guiada al museo y explicarnos qué tienen allí.

— Regio. Sería bueno ir pronto, ¿no?

— Sí, sí. Vamos mañana por la tarde.

— Perfecto. Hasta luego.

Repaso

1 p. 182

Answers to Activity 1
La segunda versión corresponde a la ilustración.

Versión 1

— Hola, Shoji... ¿qué haces?

— Nada, pues. Estamos jugando un poco al fútbol para mantenernos en forma. ¿Quieres jugar un rato? Necesitamos un golista.

— Gracias, Shoji, pero ahora no puedo. Voy al concierto de la Orquesta Sinfónica.

— No sé cómo soportas la música clásica. A mí me cae muy gorda.

— Ja, ja. Mira, Shoji, te recomiendo que escuches un poco de música clásica antes de formar una opinión.

— No tengo ganas de perder el tiempo así. Oye, cambiando de tema, ¿qué has oído de Lupita?

— ¿Lupita Vicencio? ¿No sabías? Ya es toda una artista. Tiene una exposición en la Casa de la Cultura este fin de semana.

— Ahora, sí, eso es otra cosa. Si quieres vamos juntos.

— ¿A ver las pinturas?

— ¡Hombre!, a ver a Lupita. Eso sí que no sería mala idea.

Versión 2

— Hola, Ricardo, ¿cómo estás?

— Hola, Shoji.

— ¿Quieres jugar al fútbol con nosotros? Necesitamos un delantero.

— Claro que sí, Shoji. Tuve un día terrible. Tomé un taxi para ir al concierto de la sinfónica pero los boletos estaban agotados.

— ¿Te gusta la música clásica?

— La encuentro maravillosa. Admiro mucho a los compositores de música clásica. ¿A ti también te gustan, Shoji?

— No, para decir la verdad, no la soporto. A mí me gusta el rock. A propósito de rock, ¿conoces a Lupita?

— Sí, claro. ¿Qué me cuentas de ella?

— Pues ella está en un grupo de rock y tocan mañana en el teatro municipal.

— ¿De veras?

— Sí, ¿quieres ir? Yo ya tengo boletos.

— Pero a mí el rock me deja frío. No me gusta.

— Ni hablar, tú te lo pierdes.

Capítulo 6: El arte y la música
Suggested Lesson Plans 50-Minute Schedule

Day 1

CHAPTER OPENER 5 min.
- Focusing on Outcomes, ATE, p. 157
- Language Note, ATE, p. 156

DE ANTEMANO 40 min.
- Presenting **De antemano** and Preteaching Vocabulary, ATE, p. 158
- Present History Link, ATE, p. 159.
- Activities 1–5 and Comprehension Check, ATE, p. 160
- Read and discuss **Nota cultural,** p. 160.

Wrap-Up 5 min.
- Do the Thinking Critically activity, ATE, p. 159.

Homework Options
Cuaderno de actividades, p. 61, Activities 1–2

Day 2

PRIMER PASO
Quick Review 5 min.
- Check homework.
- Bell Work, ATE, p. 162

PANORAMA CULTURAL 10 min.
- Presenting **Panorama cultural,** ATE, p. 161

Así se dice, p. 162 15 min.
- Presenting **Así se dice,** ATE, p. 162
- Present **También se puede decir...,** p. 162.
- Do Activity 6 with the Audio CD, p. 162.
- Do Activity 7, p. 162.

Vocabulario, p. 163 15 min.
- Presenting **Vocabulario,** ATE, p. 163

Wrap-Up 5 min.
- Have students match definitions to vocabulary words.

Homework Options
Cuaderno de actividades, p. 62, Activity 3
Cuaderno de gramática, pp. 46–47, Activities 1–3

Day 3

PRIMER PASO
Quick Review 5 min.
- Check homework.
- Review **Así se dice** expressions, p. 162.

Vocabulario/Nota gramatical, p. 163 20 min.
- Do Activity 8 with the Audio CD, p. 163.
- Present Language-to-Language, ATE, p. 163.
- Have students do Activity 9, p. 163, in pairs.
- Present **Vocabulario extra,** p. 163.

Así se dice/Gramática, p. 164 20 min.
- Do the Reteaching activity, ATE, p. 165.
- Presenting **Así se dice** and **Gramática,** ATE, p. 164
- Do Activity 10 with the Audio CD, p. 164.
- Do Activity 11, p. 164.

Wrap-Up 5 min.
- Have students state what is necessary for tomorrow's class.

Homework Options
Cuaderno de gramática, pp. 47–49, Activities 4–8

Day 4

PRIMER PASO
Quick Review 5 min.
- Check homework.

Así se dice/Vocabulario, p. 165 40 min.
- Presenting **Así se dice** and **Vocabulario,** ATE, p. 165
- Present **A lo nuestro** and **También se puede decir...,** p. 165.
- Do Activity 12 with the Audio CD, p. 165.
- Present Culture Note, ATE, p. 165.
- Do Activity 13, p. 165.
- Have students do Activity 14, p. 166, in pairs.

Wrap-Up 5 min.
- Follow Suggestion 2 for Teaching Transparency 6-1.

Homework Options
Cuaderno de actividades, pp. 62–65, Activities 4–9
Cuaderno de gramática, p. 50, Activity 9

Day 5

PRIMER PASO
Quick Review 5 min.
- Check homework.

Vocabulario, p. 165 30 min.
- Present Culture Notes, ATE, p. 166.
- Review comparisons.
- Do Thinking Critically activity with the class, ATE, p. 166.
- Have students do Activity 15 in groups, p. 166.
- Have students do Activity 16, then peer-edit their work, p. 166.

ENCUENTRO CULTURAL 10 min.
- Presenting **Encuentro cultural,** ATE, p. 167

Wrap-Up 5 min.
- Review the content and format of Quiz 6-1.

Homework Options
Study for Quiz 6-1.
Cuaderno de gramática, p. 50, Activity 10

Day 6

PRIMER PASO
Quick Review 5 min.
- Check homework.
- Review the content of **Primer paso.**

Quiz 20 min.
- Administer Quiz 6-1A, 6-1B, or a combination of the two.

¡ADELANTE! 20 min.
- Presenting **¡Adelante!** and Preteaching Vocabulary, ATE, p. 168
- Present Culture Note, ATE, p. 169.
- Do Activities 17–20, pp. 168–169.

Wrap-Up 5 min.
- Have students share responses from Activity 20, p. 169.

Homework Options
Cuaderno de actividades, p. 66, Activities 10–11

One-Stop Planner CD-ROM

For alternative lesson plans by chapter section, to create your own customized plans, or to preview all resources available for this chapter, use the **One-Stop Planner CD-ROM,** Disc 2.

 For additional homework suggestions, see activities accompanied by this symbol throughout the chapter.

Day 7

SEGUNDO PASO

Quick Review 5 min.
- Check homework.
- Bell Work, ATE, p. 170

Así se dice/Gramática, p. 170 40 min.
- Presenting **Así se dice** and **Gramática,** ATE, p. 170
- Do Activity 21 with the Audio CD, p. 170.
- Do Activity 22, p. 170.
- Have students do Activity 23 in pairs, p. 171.
- Do Building on Previous Skills, ATE, p. 171, then have students do Activity 24 in groups, p. 171.

Wrap-Up 5 min.
- Do Additional Practice for Activity 23, ATE, p. 171.

Homework Options
Cuaderno de actividades, pp. 67, 69, Activities 12, 15
Cuaderno de gramática, pp. 51–53, Activities 11–14

Day 8

SEGUNDO PASO

Quick Review 5 min.
- Check homework.

Así se dice/Gramática p. 172 40 min.
- Presenting **Así se dice,** ATE, p. 172
- Do Activity 25 with the Audio CD, p. 172.
- Presenting **Gramática,** ATE, p. 172
- Present **Nota gramatical,** p. 172.
- Do Activity 26, p. 172.
- Present **Vocabulario extra,** p. 173.
- Have students do Activity 27 in pairs, p. 173.

Wrap-Up 5 min.
- Follow Suggestions 1–2 for Teaching Transparency 6-2.

Homework Options
Cuaderno de actividades, pp. 67–70, Activities 13–14, 16–17
Cuaderno de gramática, pp. 53–54, Activities 15–17

Day 9

SEGUNDO PASO

Quick Review 10 min.
- Check homework.

Así se dice/Gramática, p. 172 30 min.
- Have students do Activity 28, p. 173, then Group Work, ATE, p. 172.
- Have students do Activity 29, then peer-edit their work, p. 173.

Wrap-Up 10 min.
- Do the **Mini-cuento** for Teaching Transparency 6-2.
- Discuss the content and format of Quiz 6-2.

Homework Options
Study for Quiz 6-2.

Day 10

SEGUNDO PASO

Quick Review 5 min.
- Review the content of **Segundo paso.**

Quiz 20 min.
- Administer Quiz 6-2A, 6-2B, or a combination of the two.

VAMOS A LEER 20 min.
- Read **Estrategia** and **¿Te acuerdas?**, p. 174.
- Do Activities A–B, p. 174.

Wrap-Up 5 min.
- Present Culture Note, ATE, p. 174.

Homework Options
Have students list concepts and functions of the chapter.

Day 11

REPASO

Quick Review 5 min.
- Check and discuss homework.

VAMOS A LEER, 30 min.
- Have students do Activities C–E, p. 175, and Activities F–G in groups, p. 176.

REPASO 10 min.
- Do Activity 1 with the Audio CD, p. 182.
- Have students do Activities 2–3 in pairs, p. 182.

Wrap-Up 5 min.
- Read **Estrategia** and discuss **Vamos a escribir,** p. 177.

Homework Options
Vamos a escribir, p. 177
Repaso activities 4–6, pp. 182–183
Cuaderno de Actividades, pp. 71–72, Activities 18–19
A ver si puedo..., p. 184

Day 12

REPASO

Quick Review 10 min.
- Check and/or collect homework.
- Have students do Activity 7 in pairs, p. 183.

Chapter Review 35 min.
- Review Chapter 6. Choose from **Más práctica gramatical,** Grammar Tutor for Students of Spanish, Activities for Communication, Listening Activities, Interactive CD-ROM Tutor, or **Juegos interactivos.**

Wrap-Up 5 min.
- Discuss the content of the Chapter 6 Test.

Homework Options
Study for the Chapter 6 Test.

Assessment

Quick Review 5 min.
- Answer any last-minute questions.

Test, Chapter 6 45 min.
- Administer Chapter 6 Test. Select from Testing Program, Alternative Assessment Guide, Test Generator, or Standardized Assessment Tutor.

Capítulo 6: El arte y la música
Suggested Lesson Plans *90-Minute Block Schedule*

Block 1

CHAPTER OPENER 5 min.
- Focusing on Outcomes, ATE, p. 157
- Language Note, ATE, p. 156

DE ANTEMANO 40 min.
- Presenting **De antemano** and Preteaching Vocabulary, ATE, p. 158
- Present History Link, ATE, p. 159.
- Activities 1–5 and Comprehension Check, ATE, p. 160
- Read and discuss **Nota cultural**, p. 160.

PANORAMA CULTURAL 10 min.
- Presenting **Panorama cultural**, ATE, p. 161

Así se dice, p. 162 15 min.
- Presenting **Así se dice**, ATE, p. 162
- Present **También se puede decir...**, p. 162.
- Do Activity 6 with the Audio CD, p. 162.
- Do Activity 7, p. 162.

Vocabulario, p. 163 15 min.
- Presenting **Vocabulario**, ATE, p. 163

Wrap-Up 5 min.
- Have students match definitions to vocabulary words.

Homework Options
Cuaderno de actividades, pp. 61–62, Activities 1–3
Cuaderno de gramática, pp. 46–47, Activities 1–3

Block 2

PRIMER PASO
Quick Review 10 min.
- Check homework.
- Review **Así se dice** expressions, p. 162.

Vocabulario/Nota gramatical, p. 163 20 min.
- Do Activity 8 with Audio CD, p. 163.
- Present Language-to-Language, ATE, p. 163.
- Have students do Activity 9 in pairs, p. 163.
- Present **Vocabulario extra**, p. 163.

Así se dice/Gramática, p. 164 25 min.
- Do the Reteaching Activity, ATE, p. 165.
- Presenting **Así se dice** and **Gramática**, ATE, p. 164
- Do Activity 10 with the Audio CD, p. 164.
- Do Activity 11, p. 164.

Así se dice/Vocabulario, p. 165 30 min.
- Presenting **Así se dice** and **Vocabulario**, ATE, p. 165
- Present **A lo nuestro** and **También se puede decir...**, p. 165.
- Do Activity 12 with the Audio CD, p.165.
- Present Culture Note, ATE, p. 165.
- Do Activity 13, p. 165.

Wrap-Up 5 min.
- Follow Suggestion 2 for Teaching Transparency 6-1.

Homework Options
Cuaderno de actividades, pp. 62–65, Activities 4–9
Cuaderno de gramática, pp. 47–50, Activities 4–9

Block 3

PRIMER PASO
Quick Review 10 min.
- Check homework.

Vocabulario, p. 165 45 min.
- Have students do Activity 14 in pairs, p. 166.
- Present Culture Notes, ATE, p. 166.
- Review comparisons.
- Do Thinking Critically activity, ATE, p. 166.
- Have students do Activity 15 in groups, p. 166.
- Have students do Activity 16, then peer-edit their work, p. 166.

ENCUENTRO CULTURAL 10 min.
- Presenting **Encuentro cultural**, ATE, p. 167

¡ADELANTE! 20 min.
- Presenting **¡Adelante!** and Preteaching Vocabulary, ATE, p. 168
- Present Culture Note, ATE, p. 169.
- Do Activities 17–20, pp. 168–169.

Wrap-Up 5 min.
- Review the content and format of Quiz 6-1.

Homework Options
Study for Quiz 6-1.
Cuaderno de actividades, p. 66, Activities 10–11
Cuaderno de gramática, p. 50, Activity 10

One-Stop Planner CD-ROM

For alternative lesson plans by chapter section, to create your own customized plans, or to preview all resources available for this chapter, use the **One-Stop Planner CD-ROM**, Disc 2.

For additional homework suggestions, see activities accompanied by this symbol throughout the chapter.

Block 4

PRIMER PASO
Quick Review 10 min.
- Check homework.
- Review the content of **Primer paso**.

Quiz 20 min.
- Administer Quiz 6-1A, 6-1B, or a combination of the two.

SEGUNDO PASO
Así se dice/Gramática, p. 170 50 min.
- Presenting **Así se dice** and **Gramática,** ATE, p. 170
- Do Activity 21 with the Audio CD, p. 170.
- Do Activity 22, p. 170.
- Have students do Activity 23 in pairs, p. 171.
- Do Building on Previous Skills, ATE, p. 171.
- Have students do Activity 24 in groups, p. 171, then do Additional Practice for Activity 24, ATE, p. 171.

Wrap Up 10 min.
- Do Additional Practice for Activity 23, ATE, p. 171.

Homework Options
Cuaderno de actividades, pp. 67, 69, Activities 12, 15
Cuaderno de gramática, pp. 51–53, Activities 11–14

Block 5

SEGUNDO PASO
Quick Review 10 min.
- Check homework.
- Have students make recommendations to the class.

Así se dice/Gramática p. 172 70 min.
- Presenting **Así se dice,** ATE, p. 172
- Do Activity 25 with the Audio CD, p. 172.
- Presenting **Gramática,** ATE, p. 172
- Present **Nota gramatical,** p. 172.
- Do Activity 26, p. 172.
- Present **Vocabulario extra,** p. 173.
- Have students do Activity 27 in pairs, p. 173.
- Have students do Activity 28, p. 173, then the Group Work, ATE, p. 172.
- Have students do Activity 29, then peer-edit their work, p. 173.

Wrap-Up 10 min.
- Do the **Mini-cuento** for Teaching Transparency 6-2.
- Discuss the content and format of Quiz 6-2.

Homework Options
Study for Quiz 6-2.
Cuaderno de actividades, pp. 67–70, Activities 13–14, 16–17
Cuaderno de gramática, pp. 53–54, Activities 15–17

Block 6

SEGUNDO PASO
Quick Review 10 min.
- Check homework.
- Review the content of **Segundo paso**.

Quiz 20 min.
- Administer Quiz 6-2A, 6-2B, or a combination of the two.

VAMOS A LEER 45 min.
- Do Activities A–B, p. 174.
- Present Culture Note, ATE, p. 174.
- Do Activities C–H, pp. 175–176.

REPASO 10 min.
- Have students do Activities 1–3, p. 182.

Wrap-Up 5 min.
- Discuss the content and format of the Chapter 6 Test.

Homework Options
Study for the Chapter 6 Test.
Vamos a escribir, p. 177
A ver si puedo..., p. 184
Cuaderno de actividades, pp. 71–72, Activities 18–19

Block 7

REPASO
Quick Review 10 min.
- Check and/or collect homework.

Chapter Review 35 min.
- Review Chapter 6. Choose from **Más práctica gramatical**, Grammar Tutor for Students of Spanish, Activities for Communication, Listening Activities, Interactive CD-ROM Tutor, or **Juegos interactivos.**

Test, Chapter 6 45 min.
- Administer Chapter 6 Test. Select from Testing Program, Alternative Assessment Guide, Test Generator, or Standardized Assessment Tutor.

CAPÍTULO 6

One-Stop Planner CD-ROM

For resource information, see the **One-Stop Planner**, Disc 2.

Pacing Tips
Primer paso contains the bulk of the chapter vocabulary, in addition to a continuation of the uses of the subjunctive. You may want to allot extra time to present and practice this material. See Suggested Lesson Plans, pp. 155I–155L.

Meeting the Standards

Communication
- Introducing and changing a topic of conversation, p. 162
- Expressing what needs to be done, p. 164
- Expressing an opinion, p. 165
- Making suggestions and recommendations, p. 170
- Turning down an invitation, p. 172

Cultures
- Culture Note, p. 157
- Panorama cultural, p. 161
- Culture Note, p. 165
- Culture Notes, p. 166
- Culture Note, p. 169
- Culture Note, p. 174
- Culture Note, p. 182

Connections
- History Link, p. 159
- Art Link, p. 161
- Music Links, pp. 161, 167

Comparisons
- Language-to-Language, p. 163
- Multicultural Link, p. 167
- Language Notes, p. 173
- Language Note, p. 175
- Multicultural Link, p. 175

Communities
- Community Link, p. 170
- Career Path, p. 170

Connections and Comparisons

Language Note
The word **música** comes from the Greek *mousike* derived from *mousa* or muse, one of the nine mythological goddesses of the arts and sciences. Have students come up with a list of musical terms and instruments and find the Spanish equivalents. Music students might enjoy finding the similar words in French, German, or Italian. Ask students to speculate as to why there are so many cognates related to this topic. Then put the Spanish list on the board or on a transparency and have students talk about what instruments they play or would like to learn to play, and their favorite musicians and styles of music.

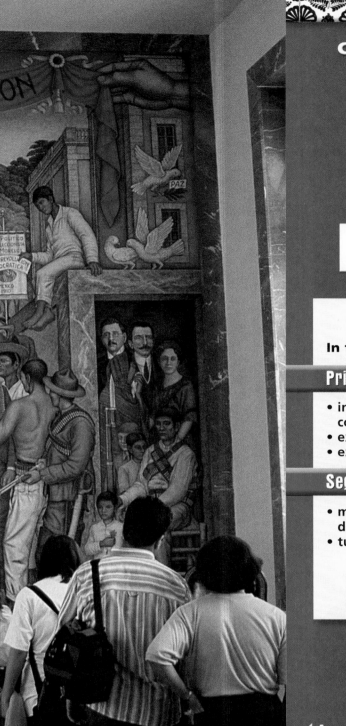

CAPÍTULO

6
El arte y la música

Objectives

In this chapter you will learn to

Primer paso

- introduce and change a topic of conversation
- express what needs to be done
- express an opinion

Segundo paso

- make suggestions and recommendations
- turn down an invitation

 internet

go.hrw.com
MARCAR: go.hrw.com
PALABRA CLAVE:
WV3 GUADALAJARA-6

◀ A propósito, ¿qué has leído del muralismo mexicano?

Chapter Opener

CAPÍTULO 6

Photo Flash!
The mural in the Chapter Opener photo is *Sufragio efectivo no reelección* (1968), and is located in the **Castillo de Chapultepec, Museo Nacional de Historia,** in Mexico City. It was painted by a well-known architect and muralist, Juan O'Gorman (1905–1982).

Focusing on Outcomes
Ask students to think of situations in which they would use the different chapter outcomes. What are some words or expressions they already know that they could use in these situations?

Chapter Sequence

Cultures and Communities

Culture Note
Murals are works of art that are painted on walls or ceilings. Some murals have been found among the ruins of Pompeii. The most influential examples date back to the Renaissance; famous among these works are Michelangelo's ceiling in the Sistine Chapel. Over time, muralism as an art form faded in importance. It was not until the 19th century that Mexican muralists revived the form. The impetus was to create artwork that was public property; thus, artists like Diego Rivera, José Clemente Orozco, and David Alfaro Siqueiros chose to paint on public buildings and walls, rather than creating paintings for private collections.

Cuaderno
de actividades,
p. 61, Acts. 1–2

Teaching Resources
pp. 158–160

PRINT
▸ Lesson Planner, p. 28
▸ Video Guide, pp. 37–38, 40
▸ Cuaderno de actividades, p. 61

MEDIA
▸ One-Stop Planner
▸ Video Program
  Contigo en la distancia
  Videocassette 2, 30:00–35:08
  Videocassette 5 (captioned
  version), 28:00–33:08
▸ Audio Compact Discs, CD 6,
  Trs. 1–2

Presenting
De antemano

Have students skim the dialogue
in **De antemano** and answer
the question in **Estrategia
para comprender.** Play the
Audio CD and have students
list expressions that state an
opinion or that change the conversation's topic. Then present
the Preteaching Vocabulary.

DE ANTEMANO · *Los murales de Orozco*

CD 6
Trs. 1–2

Estrategia para comprender
Lázaro, un muchacho cubano-americano que
vive ahora en México, tiene mucho interés
en el arte. Sus dos compañeros de clase,
Teresa y Luis, lo llevaron al Instituto Cultural
Cabañas en Guadalajara. Las paredes de este
gran edificio fueron pintadas por el famoso
muralista mexicano José Clemente Orozco.
¿Qué opinas de su arte?

LÁZARO ¡Qué sitio tan bonito! ¿Qué artista
pintó estos murales?

TERESA José Clemente Orozco, en 1939.
¿Has oído de él?

LÁZARO No. Bueno, sólo el nombre.

TERESA Pues él, Diego Rivera y David Alfaro
Siqueiros son los tres muralistas
más conocidos de México. Orozco
nació aquí, en Guadalajara. Me
encantan sus murales.

LÁZARO ¡Son espectaculares!

LUIS A mí, la verdad, me dejan frío. No
me gustan los colores oscuros y las
imágenes me parecen muy serias.

Preteaching Vocabulary

Guessing Words from Context
Have students brainstorm about types of words
and expressions they would use to describe a work
of art. How might they describe a painting? Point
out the following phrases from the text: **No me
gustan los colores oscuros y las imágenes me
parecen muy serias.; eso hace que la pintura**
**sea más dramática; Orozco pintó escenas de
la historia de México, y algunas fueron duras,
llenas de violencia.** Have students use context
and the pictures of the murals to determine the
meaning of these phrases.

STANDARDS: 1.2, 2.2, 3.1, 4.2

LÁZARO Pero, Luis, eso hace que la pintura sea más dramática.

TERESA Para apreciar su arte hace falta entender el mensaje. Orozco pintó escenas de la historia de México, y algunas fueron duras, llenas de violencia.

LUIS Eso es lo que no me gusta, pero es importante reconocer su valor histórico.

LÁZARO Sí, tal vez. En todo caso, me gusta Orozco. Espero estudiar más sobre el muralismo en la universidad.

TERESA A propósito de universidades, Orozco pintó murales en varias de ellas en los Estados Unidos.

LÁZARO ¿De veras?

TERESA Sí, hay uno muy interesante en Dartmouth College en New Hampshire, y otros en California y en Nueva York.

LUIS Oigan, cambiando de tema, ¿qué les parece si vamos a un concierto de música clásica esta noche?

LÁZARO Sí, ¡buena idea!

Using the Captioned Video

 As an alternative, you might want to show the captioned version of *Contigo en la distancia: La obra maestra* on Videocassette 5. Some students may benefit from seeing the written words as they listen to the target language and watch the gestures and actions in context. This visual reinforcement of vocabulary and functions will facilitate students' comprehension and help reduce their anxiety before they are formally introduced to the new language in the chapter.

DE ANTEMANO

CAPÍTULO 6

Thinking Critically

Analyzing Ask students to analyze their own reactions to art they have seen. Do they agree with Luis about the dark colors in Orozco's murals? Do they like abstract art? Do they appreciate Orozco's messages, even if they are angry or sad ones?

History Link

The great Mexican muralists often depict scenes from the Mexican Revolution (1910–1920). Have students research other historical events portrayed in art. (Picasso's *Guernica,* Spanish Civil War; DeWeldon's *Marine Corps Memorial,* World War II; Goya's *El 3 de mayo de 1808...,* the Napoleonic Wars)

Contigo en la distancia

You may choose to show students Episode 6: *La obra maestra* now or wait until later in the chapter. In the video, Alejandra, Irene, and Carlos visit an art museum in Mexico City. They see various paintings, including *La ofrenda* by Saturnino Herrán. As they leave the museum, Alejandra finds out that Carlos has been corresponding with Sergio and Javier via e-mail. She is angry that Carlos did not tell her he was in contact with their friends, but then Carlos offers to teach her how to use the Internet. Before students view the video, have them review chapter functions and vocabulary. As they watch the episode they should keep track of the number of times the characters change the topic of conversation, express an opinion, make suggestions, or turn down invitations.

CAPÍTULO 6

Kinesthetic Learners

1 Give students three index cards each. On one card they write the word **cierta** in large, clear letters, on the second card they write **falsa,** on the third they write **no se sabe.** As you read the statements from this activity aloud, have students respond by holding up the card that is the best response to the statement.

Visual Learners

5 Give students sheets of unlined paper and have them do a pencil sketch of the mural they would create. Have them use the back of their sketch sheet to write at least five sentences telling what they would put in their mural (people, events, and images) and which colors they would use.

Answers

1 1. falsa; son Orozco, Rivera y Siqueiros
2. cierta
3. no se sabe
4. falsa; está en Guadalajara
5. no se sabe
6. falsa; usaba colores oscuros
7. cierta

2 1. Orozco fue un famoso muralista mexicano.
2. Pintó escenas de la historia de México.
3. A ella le encanta.
4. Él dice que es espectacular.
5. No le gusta porque los colores son muy oscuros y las imágenes muy serias.

3 1. hace falta
2. ¿Has oído de él?
3. Oigan, cambiando de tema...
4. Me encantan los murales. ¡Son espectaculares!
5. A mí, la verdad, me dejan frío. Eso es lo que no me gusta.

These activities check for comprehension only. Students should not yet be expected to produce language modeled in **De antemano.**

1 **Cierto o falso?** See answers below.

Indica si cada oración que sigue es **cierta** o **falsa**, o si **no se sabe**. Si es falsa, corrígela.

1. Los tres grandes muralistas mexicanos son Orozco, Rivera y Kahlo.
2. Orozco era del estado de Jalisco.
3. Orozco vivió mucho tiempo en los Estados Unidos.
4. El Instituto Cultural Cabañas se encuentra en la Ciudad de México.
5. La vida de Orozco fue muy difícil.
6. Orozco usaba colores vivos como el amarillo y el verde.
7. Hay murales de Orozco en varias ciudades estadounidenses.

2 **¿Comprendiste?** See answers below.

1. ¿Quién es José Clemente Orozco?
2. ¿De qué temas tratan sus murales?
3. ¿Qué le parece el arte de Orozco a Teresa?
4. ¿Qué palabras usa Lázaro para describir el mural?
5. ¿A Luis le gusta Orozco? Explica tu respuesta.

3 **Busca las expresiones** See answers below.

Busca las expresiones en **De antemano** que se usan para...
1. expresar la necesidad o la obligación de hacer algo.
2. sugerir un tema de conversación.
3. cambiar el tema de conversación.
4. expresar opiniones positivas.
5. expresar opiniones negativas.

4 **Diversas opiniones** Answers will vary.

¿Qué opinas del arte de Orozco? Reúnete con un(a) compañero(a) y expresa tu opinión. Explica por qué te gusta o no te gusta su pintura.

5 **Ahora te toca a ti** Answers will vary.

Orozco representa la conquista y otros eventos históricos de México en sus murales. Imagina que vas a pintar un mural. ¿Quieres representar algún evento de tu comunidad o un evento de importancia nacional o internacional? ¿A cuáles personas quieres representar? ¿Por qué? ¿Qué colores e imágenes vas a usar?

Nota cultural

El muralismo mexicano de las décadas de 1920 y 1930 se dedicó a representar la historia del país y a rescatar el pasado indígena de la nación. El Secretario de Educación José Vasconcelos fue el primero en considerar que la pintura mural es un medio perfecto para enseñar al pueblo mexicano su historia nacional. Por eso encargó a varios pintores que representaran pasajes de la historia en edificios públicos y escuelas. El muralismo también fue parte del movimiento nacionalista de las artes del país, que incluyó la música, la literatura, el teatro y el cine.

Comprehension Check

Additional Practice

1 Have students work with a partner to change the statements in this activity to questions. Students should take turns asking and answering these questions. (—**¿Quiénes son los tres grandes muralistas mexicanos? —Orozco, Rivera y Siqueiros.**)

Challenge

4 Have students present a summary of their partner's responses to the class. Then have them expand on these responses by stating whether or not they agree with their partner.

CD 6
Trs. 3–6

¿Te consideras una persona artística?

Las artes son una manera de expresar nuestra individualidad. Estas personas son unos artistas muy activos. ¿Cómo usan ellos el arte para expresarse?

Teaching Resources
p. 161

PRINT
▸ Video Guide, pp. 37–39, 41
▸ Cuaderno de actividades, p. 72
▸ Cuaderno para hispanohablantes, pp. 29–30

MEDIA
▸ One-Stop Planner
▸ Video Program, Videocassette 2, 35:09–38:59
▸ Audio Compact Discs, CD 6, Trs. 3–6
▸ Interactive CD-ROM Tutor, Disc 2

Alfredo CD 6 Tr. 4
Caracas, Venezuela

"Bueno, me considero artista... porque desempeño lo que es la música... Mi instrumento es... trompeta... A mí me gusta la salsa... porque eso viene de herencia y de la familia... toda mi familia es salsera... me gusta mucho la música *latin jazz* y la salsa..."

David CD 6 Tr. 5
Ciudad de México, México

"Bueno, no soy artístico, pero me gusta, me gusta crear. O sea, no que me considere muy artístico pero sí toco el piano, me gusta ser culto. Mi músico favorito... pues yo creo que uno de los pianistas, Beethoven, Bach, pero música, pues el rock, cosas así".

Christian CD 6 Tr. 6
San Antonio, Texas

"Sí, me considero artístico por muchas razones. Me gusta escribir mucho, me gustan las artes dramáticas, leo muchas obras... Me gustan mucho, mucho Shakespeare, Edgar Allan Poe, me gustan los escritores americanos, Ambrose Bierce. Y también me encanta el bailar, tengo cuatro años de bailar ballet... Soy muy activo en el teatro".

Para pensar y hablar...

A. ¿Cuál es el arte que más practican estos jóvenes? ¿Cuáles son las artes que a ti te gustan? ¿Cuántas artes practica Christian?

B. En tu opinión, ¿por qué son importantes las artes? ¿Cómo nos ayudan las artes a expresarnos mejor? ¿Cuál es el papel de las artes en el desarrollo cultural de una persona? ¿Qué características comparten los mejores artistas?

Cuaderno para hispanohablantes, pp. 29–30

Presenting
Panorama cultural

Have students discuss the statement in the introductory paragraph. What kind of art would they like to try? (music, dance, painting, photography, drawing, pottery) Play the video and ask students which of the interviewees would be most interesting to talk to about art or music.

Preguntas

1. **¿Qué clase de música le gusta a Alfredo? ¿De dónde viene su preferencia?** (La salsa; viene de la familia, es su herencia)

2. **¿Por qué se considera artístico Christian?** (Escribe mucho, le gustan las artes dramáticas y lee muchas obras.)

3. **¿Cuál de los tres no se considera artístico? ¿Qué tipo de música le gusta?** (David; la música rock, pero también le gustan algunos músicos clásicos)

Connections and Comparisons

Art Link
Have students research and report on Latin American contributions to: painting (Alberto Gironella, Wilfredo Lam, Julio Le Parc); music (José Pablo Moncayo, Alberto Ginastera); literature (Jorge Luis Borges, Octavio Paz, Isabel Allende, Gabriel García Márquez, Pablo Neruda, Gabriela Mistral); dance (Alicia Alonso, Amalia Hernández); theater (Rodolfo Usigli, Griselda Gambaro); and architecture (Luis Barragán, Juan O'Gorman).

Music Link
Ask students to research salsa and Latin jazz. Who are the most famous musicians? What instruments are most commonly used? Where are these styles of music most popular? Have students listen to samples of the two styles and compare them.

Objectives Introducing and changing a topic of conversation; expressing what needs to be done; expressing an opinion

WV3 GUADALAJARA-6

Teaching Resources
pp. 162–166

PRINT
- Lesson Planner, p. 28
- Listening Activities, pp. 43–44, 47–48
- Activities for Communication, pp. 21–22, 66, 68, 99–100
- Cuaderno de gramática, pp. 46–50
- Grammar Tutor for Students of Spanish, Chapter 6
- Cuaderno de actividades, pp. 62–65
- Cuaderno para hispanohablantes, pp. 26–30
- Testing Program, pp. 111–114
- Alternative Assessment Guide, p. 35
- Student Make-Up Assignments, Chapter 6

MEDIA
- One-Stop Planner
- Audio Compact Discs, CD 6, Trs. 7–10, 26–28, 18
- Teaching Transparencies 6-1; **Más práctica gramatical** Answers; Cuaderno de gramática Answers
- Interactive CD-ROM Tutor, Disc 2

Bell Work
Have students write a short paragraph using the following words: **luchar, celebrar, la diosa, el gue-rrero, la victoria, acordar la paz.**

Presenting
Así se dice
Read aloud passages from **De antemano** that model changing the subject. Have students tap on their desks with each change of topic.

Answers
7 *Possible answers:*
1. recuerda
2. cambiando
3. Hablando
4. propósito
5. dices *or* cuentas

Así se dice

Introducing and changing a topic of conversation

Si quieres sugerir o cambiar de tema en una conversación, puedes decir:

¿Has leído algo de Pablo Picasso?

Eso me recuerda el concierto de anoche.
That reminds me of . . .

Eso me hace pensar en una pintura de Frida Kahlo.
That brings to mind . . .

Cambiando de tema, ¿qué me dices de la danza folklórica?
Changing subjects, what can you tell me about . . .?

Hablando del arte, **¿qué me cuentas de** los museos en Guadalajara?
Speaking of . . . what can you tell me about . . .?

A propósito, ¿qué has oído de la nueva novela de Isabel Allende?
By the way, what have you heard about . . .?

> Cuaderno de actividades, pp. 63–64, Act. 6

También se puede decir...
Otra forma de decir **A propósito** es **Por cierto.**

6 **De todo un poco** Script and answers on p. 155G.

Escuchemos Pilar y Jorge están hablando de los artistas Joan Miró, Salvador Dalí y Remedios Varo. Escucha la conversación e indica cuántas veces cambian de tema.
CD 6 Tr. 7

7 **En el periódico** See possible answers below.

Leamos Carolina y Alberto están conversando sobre unas noticias que se publicaron esta mañana en el periódico. Completa su conversación con palabras y expresiones adecuadas de **Así se dice.**

CAROLINA — Es increíble lo que sucedió en Suecia el jueves pasado. Unos ladrones robaron unas pinturas del Museo Nacional.

ALBERTO — Sí. Eso me ____1____ un robo que ocurrió en Madrid hace pocos años.

CAROLINA — Me acuerdo de ese robo. Por suerte pudieron recuperar casi todas las pinturas. Oye, ____2____ de tema, ¿has leído algo acerca de la contaminación?

ALBERTO — Sí, han dicho que el nivel de contaminación está bien alto hoy. ____3____ de la contaminación, el periódico dice que en 50 años habrá mucho menos contaminación porque los carros no usarán gasolina.

CAROLINA — A ____4____, ¿qué me ____5____ de los carros del último modelo?

ALBERTO — Son bien padres. Y yo aquí con mi bicicleta...

Communication for All Students

Visual Learners
Write the six **Así se dice** phrases on the board or on a transparency. Begin talking about an art exhibit, a book, or a concert you may have experienced recently and point out each phrase as you insert it into your speech to the class. Continue until you have used all six phrases.

Auditory Learners
9 Ask students to write the transitional phrases from **Así se dice** onto three by five index cards. Tell students to review their dialogue and underline any of the six phrases that they incorporated into it. Then, each pair of students reads its dialogue to the class. Ask their classmates to identify the transitional phrases as they hear them read by raising the corresponding card.

Vocabulario

la cantante

la escultura

el escultor

el músico

el bailarín

la bailarina

la artista

Más práctica gramatical,
p. 178, Act. 1

Cuaderno de activi-
dades, p. 62, Act. 3

Cuaderno de gramática,
pp. 46–47, Acts. 1–3

antiguo(a)   *old; ancient*
aprender a + inf.   *to learn (to do something)*
contemporáneo(a)   *contemporary*
la danza   *dance* (as an art form)

el dibujo   *drawing*
diseñar   *to design*
la estatua   *statue*
la exhibición   *exhibition*

intentar   *to try*
la orquesta   *orchestra*
patrocinar   *to sponsor*
la pintura   *painting*

Nota gramatical

Words that end in **-ista** can be masculine or feminine depending on the person they refer to: **el artista, la artista.** Likewise, the word **modelo** can be masculine or feminine: **el modelo, la modelo.** In these cases, the article indicates the gender of the person. Feminine words that begin with a stressed **a-** take **el** in the singular: **el arte, las artes.**

Cuaderno de gramática,
p. 47, Act. 4

Más práctica gramatical,
p. 179, Act. 2

Vocabulario extra

la acuarela   *watercolor*
la cerámica   *pottery*
la cinematografía   *art of filmmaking*
el diseño por computadora   *computer-assisted design*
el grabado   *engraving*
la serigrafía   *silkscreening*
el tallado en madera   *woodworking*
el tejido   *weaving, knitting*

8   **Bellas artes**   Script and answers on p. 155G.

 Escuchemos   Escucha varias conversaciones breves e indica si las personas están hablando de **música, danza, literatura, escultura** o **pintura.**
CD 6
Tr. 8

9   **Gramática en contexto**   Answers will vary.

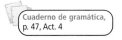 **Hablemos/Escribamos**   Estabas hablando con tu compañero(a) de clase sobre la escultura romana y terminaron hablando del nuevo bailarín cubano. Escribe el diálogo en que hablaron de todos estos temas. Usa expresiones de **Así se dice** y del **Vocabulario.**

1. la escultura romana   2. los cuerpos ideales   3. el ejercicio   4. el bailarín cubano

Connections and Comparisons

Language-to-Language

The changing role of women in Spanish-speaking countries is reflected in the usage of words such as **la presidenta.** It can still mean *the president's wife,* but now is used more often to mean *the president.* Have students look up **zapatero, carpintero,** and **herrero** in a recent dictionary. Do all these words have feminine counterparts? (All but **herrero** do.) If not, why not? (Blacksmiths are

no longer numerous, and most are men.) Remind students that English-speaking countries have undergone similar social changes and that, as in Spanish, such changes are also reflected in the terms used to specify a person's profession. Forms in which gender is expressed, such as waiter, waitress, and policeman exist alongside gender-neutral forms such as server and police officer.

Presenting
Vocabulario

Present the vocabulary by expressing what you would like to do to become more involved in the arts. (**Pienso aprender a dibujar mejor.**) Then tell students to imagine that they have just participated in a summer arts program sponsored by an art school. Have pairs of students ask each other about what they would like to do with what they have learned in the workshops. (**—¿Qué te gustaría hacer en el futuro? —Me gustaría diseñar trajes para la danza contemporánea.**)

Nota gramatical

Hold up photos of famous male and female artists or singers and ask students questions about them. (**En tu opinión, ¿es Picasso un artista único? Y Frida Kahlo, ¿es buena artista o no?**) List other words that follow this rule (**piloto, turista, pianista, soprano, cantante**) and have students work in pairs to make up and answer similar questions.

Teaching Suggestions

8
• Have students bring in prints, posters, or magazine pictures. Display the art to create a museum atmosphere. Have students role-play a trip to the museum. Roles can include: art critic, curator, guard, guide, and visitors.

• Have small groups of students draw up a floorplan for a center for the arts. Tell them to include spaces for dance studios, music practice rooms, photo developing labs, pottery studios, computer design labs, and so on. Have them label their floorplans with words from **Vocabulario extra.** Then have students present their floor plans to the class.

Teaching Resources
pp. 162–166

PRINT
▸ Lesson Planner, p. 28
▸ Listening Activities, pp. 43–44, 47–48
▸ Activities for Communication, pp. 21–22, 66, 68, 99–100
▸ Cuaderno de gramática, pp. 46–50
▸ Grammar Tutor for Students of Spanish, Chapter 6
▸ Cuaderno de actividades, pp. 62–65
▸ Cuaderno para hispanohablantes, pp. 26–30
▸ Testing Program, pp. 111–114
▸ Alternative Assessment Guide, p. 35
▸ Student Make-Up Assignments, Chapter 6

MEDIA
▸ One-Stop Planner
▸ Audio Compact Discs, CD 6, Trs. 7–10, 26–28, 18
▸ Teaching Transparencies 6-1; **Más práctica gramatical** Answers; Cuaderno de gramática Answers
▸ Interactive CD-ROM Tutor, Disc 2

Presenting
Así se dice, Gramática

Point out to students the use of the subjunctive with expressions like **es necesario que** and **es importante que.** Ask students to suggest a wall in the school that would be appropriate for a mural. They are to convince the principal that they should be allowed to undertake this project. Pronounce the new phrases and have the class explain how they will argue. Then play the role of the principal and have volunteers plead the case for the mural.

Así se dice

Expressing what needs to be done

Si es importante que alguien haga cierta cosa, puedes decir:

Hace falta que pintemos un nuevo mural.   *We need to paint . . .*
Es necesario que busquemos nuevos artistas.   *Its necessary that we look for . . .*
Para ser artista **es importante que reconozcas** tu talento.   *. . . it's important that you recognize . . .*

10   **Así lo veo yo** Script and answers on p. 155G.

Escuchemos Ana está hablando con su amiga Tere. Indica si Ana habla de lo que **ella misma** debe hacer o de lo que es necesario que haga **Tere.**

CD 6 Tr. 9

Gramática

Subjunctive after expressions of need

1. You learned in Chapter 5 that verbs are in the subjunctive mood when they come after expressions of hopes and wishes.

    Espero que la guerra **termine** pronto.

    Más práctica gramatical, p. 179, Act. 3

2. Verbs are also in the subjunctive mood when they come after expressions of the importance or need for someone to do something.

    Es necesario que practiquemos un deporte.

    Cuaderno de gramática, pp. 48–49, Acts. 5–8

3. Use the infinitive after these expressions if something needs to be done in general or by everyone.

    Es necesario practicar un deporte.

4. The subjunctive forms of verbs that end in **-car**, **-gar**, or **-zar** have the following spelling changes: c→qu (busque, busques…); g→gu (llegue, llegues…); z→c (empiece, empieces…).

11   **Gramática en contexto**

Hablemos/Escribamos El concierto es mañana, pero ¡el teatro no está listo! ¿Qué hay que hacer? Usa las expresiones de **Así se dice** y verbos como **organizar, poner, comprar,** y **limpiar.**

Communication for All Students

Slower Pace
11 Have students make a list of the problems they see on the stage before they begin the activity.

Challenge
13 Have students bring in, or report on, a work of art or an artist representative of their culture of origin. Ask them to use words from **Vocabulario** on page 165 in their presentations.

Native Speakers
Divide native speakers into groups of three or four. Assign a work of art from the chapter to each group. Pair up the groups to stage a debate, with one group defending the art and the second group criticizing it. You may want to have students present their debates to the class.

Así se dice

Expressing an opinion

Para discutir las cualidades de un(a) artista o una obra de arte, puedes decir:

> Cuaderno de gramática, pp. 64–65, Acts. 7–9

¿Qué opinas de Diego Rivera?	**Lo encuentro** impresionante. **Admiro mucho** su arte.
¿Qué te parece el cuadro?	**Para ser sincero(a), me parece que** le falta imaginación. **Me deja frío(a).** *It doesn't do anything for me.*
¿Qué piensas de la cantante?	**Para decir la verdad, me cae gordo.** **No la soporto.** *I can't stand her.*

12 ### Comentarios positivos y negativos

Escuchemos Vas a escuchar unos comentarios. Indica si cada comentario expresa una opinión **positiva, negativa** o de **indiferencia**.

CD 6
Tr. 10

Script and answers on p. 155H

A lo nuestro

Para describir algo que no provoca sentimientos ni positivos ni negativos, los hispanohablantes a veces dicen **No es ni fu ni fa.** Para expresar indiferencia a algo, puedes decir **Me es indiferente.**

Vocabulario

creativo(a)	*creative*	**original**	*original*
entretenido(a)	*entertaining*	**realista**	*realistic*
formidable	*tremendous*	**convencional**	*conventional*
genial	*great*	**de muy mal gusto**	*in very bad taste*
hermoso(a)	*beautiful*	**incomprensible**	*incomprehensible*
imaginativo(a)	*imaginative*	**insignificante**	*trivial*
magnífico(a)	*magnificent*	**insoportable**	*unbearable, intolerable*
maravilloso(a)	*marvelous*	**superficial**	*superficial*
una obra maestra	*masterpiece*	**pésimo(a)**	*awful*

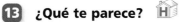

> Cuaderno de actividades, pp. 62–63, Acts. 4–5

> Cuaderno de gramática, p. 50, Act. 9

> Más práctica gramatical, p. 180, Act. 4

También se puede decir...

También se puede decir **tremendo** en vez de **magnífico: Rufino Tamayo me parece un artista tremendo.** Pero ¡hay que tener cuidado! **Un niño tremendo** es un niño muy mal educado *(ill-mannered).*

13 ### ¿Qué te parece? [H] Answers will vary.

Escribamos En una excursión reciente, varios amigos comentaron unas obras de arte que vieron. Responde a cada declaración con tu propia opinión de las obras indicadas.

1. Encuentro los murales de Orozco imaginativos pero nada entretenidos. (pp. 158, 159)

2. Me parece que los murales en los edificios públicos son superficiales e insignificantes. (p. 160)

3. Encuentro insoportables los murales en los cielos rasos *(ceilings)*. Aunque sean magníficos, es demasiado difícil verlos. (p. 158)

4. Déjame decirte que la violencia del mural con los caballos y soldados me parece de muy mal gusto. (p. 159)

Cultures and Communities

Culture Note

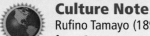

Rufino Tamayo (1899–1991), a Zapotec from Oaxaca, was one of many artists who attracted international attention to Mexican art. Tamayo's colorful work demonstrates pre-Colombian and Mexican folk influence. Fellow artists and the media in the 1920s disapproved of his political neutrality and harshly criticized Tamayo. He eventually left Mexico for New York, where he taught at the Dalton School and founded the Tamayo Workshop at the Art School of The Brooklyn Museum.

Language Note

Tremendo(a) is generally used to describe something terrible, dreadful, huge, or loud, such as **un crimen tremendo** or **un golpe tremendo.** Its more colloquial use means *marvelous* or *fantastic.*

Primer paso

CAPÍTULO 6

Culture Notes

• Fernando Botero (b. 1932) received some of his earliest art training in bullfighting school in Medellín, Colombia, where he used to sketch the animals and the arena. In 1951, he left Colombia to study in Europe for several years. By the mid 1950s, he had developed a unique style in which figures are rotund and inflated.

• Remedios Varo (1913–1963) was born in Spain, but moved to Mexico in 1942. She did not dedicate herself completely to painting until 1953. Her works, influenced by El Greco and Bosch, hint at her feelings about her struggle to make a place for herself in the art world.

• Xul Solar's (1887–1963) full name is Óscar Agustín Alejandro Schultz Solari. By birth an Argentine, he was of German and Italian descent. For more on Xul Solar, see page 189.

Assess

▶ Testing Program, pp. 111–114
Quiz 6-1A, Quiz 6-1B
Audio CD 6, Tr. 18

▶ Student Make-Up Assignments, Chapter 6, Alternative Quiz

▶ Alternative Assessment Guide, p. 35

---

14 **Mis cosas favoritas**   Answers will vary.

Escribamos/Hablemos   Cada persona tiene sus preferencias. Haz una lista de tus cosas favoritas, usando la lista siguiente, y explica por qué te gustan. Comparte tus opiniones con un(a) compañero(a).

MODELO   —Mi clase favorita es la de arte. La encuentro muy entretenida porque...
—Para ser sincero(a), la clase de arte me parece horrible. Prefiero la clase de inglés porque...

1. mi artista favorito(a)
2. mi músico(a) favorito(a)
3. mi programa de televisión favorito
4. mi película favorita
5. mi canción favorita
6. mi libro favorito

¿Se te ha olvidado?
comparisons
Ver la página R30

Cuaderno de gramática, p. 50, Act. 10

15 **Arte latinoamericano**   Answers will vary.

Hablemos   ¿Qué opinas de las siguientes obras de arte? Usa las expresiones de **Así se dice** para indicar tus opiniones. Después, pídele a unos(as) compañeros(as) sus opiniones. ¿Están de acuerdo?

National Holiday, Fernando Botero

Uno, Xul Solar

Armonía, Remedios Varo

16 **La exhibición**   Answers will vary.

Escribamos   Tu clase piensa ir a una exhibición de arte. En un párrafo, recomienda uno de los tres artistas representados en la Actividad 15. Explica claramente tu recomendación, dando tus opiniones del artista.

Communication for All Students

Group Work

14   Divide the class into groups of three. Have two students converse as called for in the direction lines. The third student listens to their conversation and then summarizes what the other two have said. Have students change roles with each numbered item.

Thinking Critically

15   **Comparing and Contrasting**   Have students look closely at the paintings and write a paragraph comparing two of them. How does each painting's style contribute to its mood? What significance might the colors, forms, details, and titles have? Use **Vocabulario** and **Así se dice** on page 165.

Los instrumentos musicales

En todo el continente americano existe una gran variedad de instrumentos y tipos de música que cambian según la región o el país. Mira las siguientes fotos. ¿Qué instrumentos reconoces?

la quena

el charango

el güiro

el banjo

Para discutir

A. ¿Cuál de estos instrumentos crees que sería el más fácil de tocar? ¿Cuál sería el más difícil? ¿Por qué?

B. ¿Qué instrumentos son típicos de Estados Unidos? ¿Son originarios de aquí? ¿Cómo reflejan la cultura local? (Puedes mencionar materiales, emociones que evocan, ritmos, tecnología...)

Vamos a comprenderlo

La quena, el charango y el güiro son tres instrumentos muy conocidos e importantes en las culturas de Latinoamérica. La **quena**, una flauta dulce de sonido melancólico que se sopla por arriba, es muy popular en la región andina. El **charango**, de origen andino, es un instrumento pequeño de cinco cuerdas que se toca como una guitarra. Su cuerpo está hecho a veces de la concha de un armadillo e incluye hasta las orejas. El **güiro**, hecho de calabaza hueca, es un instrumento de percusión del Caribe que se raspa con un palito de madera. Los antiguos instrumentos indígenas, la flauta y el tambor, se han combinado con una gran variedad de instrumentos europeos para crear el sonido de la música americana de nuestros días.

Presenting
Encuentro cultural

Have students read **Vamos a comprenderlo** aloud. Periodically interrupt the reading to ask students comprehension questions. (**¿Qué tipo de instrumento es el güiro? ¿Cómo se toca?**) Have students identify which of the instruments pictured is not discussed in the reading. (banjo) Then have students answer the questions from **Para discutir.**

Teacher Notes

• Explain to students that none of the instruments on this page are of European origin. The **quena, charango,** and **güiro** originated in the Americas, and the banjo may have originated in Africa or Asia.

• You may want to contact your school's music teacher to see if he or she can locate any of the instruments pictured on this page and perhaps give a demonstration of how they are played.

Connections and Comparisons

Music Link
Locate recordings of music characteristic of the following places, performed by the artists suggested: Andes (Toque Amaru); Caribbean (Rubén Blades or Tito Puente); Mexico (Mariachi Vargas); United States (Carlos Santana, Woody Guthrie, Stanley Brothers, Flaco Jiménez). Play this music for the class and have your students discuss their reactions to what they hear.

Multicultural Link
Have students research instruments from around the world. (*Di-tzi, erhu,* and *pipa,* China; *sitar* and *tambura,* India; *oud* and *qanun,* Arab nations of Middle East and North Africa; *sansa* or *mbira,* sub-Saharan Africa.) They might look for recordings using these instruments and bring the recordings to class. Sound clips may be available online.

 Contigo en la distancia

As an alternative to **¡Adelante!**, you may wish to show Episode 6 of **Contigo en la distancia**. For suggestions and activities, see the *Video Guide*.

¡Adelante! ▪ *Una entrevista con Luis Miguel*

Cuaderno de actividades, p. 66 Acts. 10–11

 CD 6 Trs. 11–13

¿Qué opinas de la música rock? ¿La escuchas mucho? Vas a leer una entrevista con Luis Miguel, un famoso cantante de rock mexicano. ¿Tienes algo en común con él? Imagina que alguien te invita a un concierto de Luis Miguel. ¿Te gustaría ir?

-1-
Siempre has dicho que eres afortunado por estar haciendo lo que más te gusta. ¿Cantar sigue siendo tu razón para vivir?
Sí, y todavía más porque mi compromiso es mayor, conmigo mismo y con mi gente, y cantar es uno de los placeres más grandes de mi vida, lo disfruto mucho, mucho.

-2-
¿Hay algún sueño que todavía no hayas realizado?
Los sueños que tuve de niño, la verdad, la gran mayoría ya los he cumplido, y sigo soñando y espero seguir cumpliéndolos y seguir teniéndolos. Generalmente son sueños profesionales, como de lograr cosas que todavía no he hecho, y los personales son: gozar de mucha salud el resto de mi vida.

-3-
¿Tienes alguna manía?
Híjole, yo creo que no tengo, excepto la del pelo, creo que no tengo otra. No sé si sea manía, pero me gusta dormir como vampiro, el cuarto muy, muy frío, helado y sin nada de luz, oscuro completamente.

Luis Miguel
I al II
Premier, Mexico, D.F.
18 al 22
Caesar's Palace, Las Vegas

These activities check for global comprehension only. Students should not yet be expected to produce language modeled in **¡Adelante!**

17 **¿Comprendes?** See answers on page 169.
1. ¿Qué piensa Luis Miguel de la música?
2. ¿Qué sueños profesionales tiene? ¿Cuáles son sus sueños personales?
3. ¿Qué manías tiene Luis Miguel?
4. ¿Cómo describe él un día normal? ¿un día perfecto?
5. ¿Qué tipo de deportes le gusta a él?

18 **Se parecen** Script and answers on p. 135H.

 CD 6 Tr. 14

Vuelve a revisar los hábitos y las opiniones de Luis Miguel. Luego escucha dos entrevistas más e indica cuál de los entrevistados se parece más a Luis Miguel—**Carlo Antonio** o **Claudia.**

Preteaching Vocabulary

Recognizing Cognates
¡Adelante! contains several words that students will be able to recognize as cognates. (**compromiso, profesionales, personales, resto, manía, vampiro, oscuro, completamente,** **acuáticos, ski, normal, perfecto, horas, cierto**) Have students find these words and determine what Luis Miguel is saying about rock music.

STANDARDS: 1.2

-4-
¿Haces ejercicio?
Si puedo, sí; me gusta mucho lo que hicimos hoy, por ejemplo, ir a la laguna, me gustan mucho los deportes acuáticos; cuando tengo oportunidad me voy a dar una vuelta, hacer ski, todo. Generalmente, así es mi vida normal.

¿Qué tal si vamos a un concierto de Luis Miguel este fin de semana? Sería buena idea ir al concierto del sábado porque todos nuestros amigos van a ir. Recomiendo que compremos las entradas hoy. Es mejor que tomemos un taxi al concierto también. Va a haber mucho tránsito.
Silvia

Gracias por invitarme pero el sábado no puedo. Tengo muchas cosas que hacer. Mejor vamos el domingo, ¿no?
Jorge

-5-
¿Cómo describirías un día perfecto para ti?
Es un día en que duermo 8 horas o más de 8 horas, pero mejor 8 horas exactas, en donde hay un sol maravilloso afuera y que estoy en un lugar tan bello como Acapulco o tan bello como México, el cual amo y adoro con toda mi alma, porque me ha dado todo.

-6-
Ahora, ¿cómo es un día normal en tu vida?
Pues un día normal en mi vida sería no dormir 8 horas... ¡no, no es cierto, no!... Sería ir al avión, volar a una ciudad distinta o un país distinto, y trabajar y desarrollar mi trabajo, y cantar y estar con la gente de esa ciudad, y cada día aprender algo más. Eso sería un día normal, porque todos los días aprendo algo.

19 **Encuentra las expresiones**

¿Qué dice...? See answers below.

1. Silvia para recomendar qué día ir al concierto
2. Silvia para recomendar el mejor día para comprar los boletos
3. Silvia para sugerir un tipo de transporte
4. Jorge cuando dice que el sábado no es buen día para él
5. Jorge para sugerir otro día mejor para ir al concierto

20 **Ahora te toca a ti**
Revisa las preguntas que le hicieron a Luis Miguel. ¿Crees que eres parecido(a) a él? ¿En qué te pareces a él? ¿Cómo eres diferente?

Comprehension Check

Objectives Making suggestions and recommendations; turning down an invitation

WV3 GUADALAJARA-6

Teaching Resources
pp. 170–173

PRINT
▸ Lesson Planner, p. 29
▸ Listening Activities, pp. 44, 48–49
▸ Activities for Communication, pp. 23–24, 67–68, 99–100
▸ Cuaderno de gramática, pp. 51–54
▸ Grammar Tutor for Students of Spanish, Chapter 6
▸ Cuaderno de actividades, pp. 67–70
▸ Cuaderno para hispanohablantes, pp. 26–30
▸ Testing Program, pp. 115–118
▸ Alternative Assessment Guide, p. 35
▸ Student Make-Up Assignments, Chapter 6

MEDIA
▸ One-Stop Planner
▸ Audio Compact Discs, CD 6, Trs. 15–16, 29–31, 19
▸ Teaching Transparencies 6-2; **Más práctica gramatical** Answers; Cuaderno de gramática Answers
▸ Interactive CD-ROM Tutor, Disc 2

Bell Work
Write the following on the board or on a transparency: **Escribe el nombre de un(a) artista contemporáneo(a). Haz una lista de tres preguntas para hacerle.**

Presenting
Así se dice, Gramática
Model these expressions by acting out both someone giving advice and a friend reluctant to take advice. Then have students take turns suggesting how to prepare for an upcoming exam.

Así se dice

Making suggestions and recommendations

Para hacer sugerencias y recomendaciones puedes usar las siguientes expresiones:

Te aconsejo que llegues temprano.

Sugiero que compres las entradas ahora.
I suggest that . . .

Es mejor que tomes un taxi.

No te conviene estacionarte aquí.
It's not advisable that you . . .

No te olvides de pedir un autógrafo.

¿Has pensado en comprar las entradas?

Sería buena/mala idea sacar fotos.

Le recomiendo a Juan que vaya a ver el Ballet Folklórico de Jalisco.

Cuaderno de actividades, pp. 67, 69–70, Acts. 12–13, 15–17   Cuaderno de gramática, p. 51, Act. 11

21 Planes para un viaje Script and answers on p. 155H.

CD 6
Tr. 15

Escuchemos/Leamos Escucha mientras Anya y Lenora hacen planes para un viaje a Guadalajara. Luego escoge la recomendación o sugerencia que mejor corresponda a cada situación que ellas presentan.

a. Sería buena idea reservar las entradas por teléfono antes de salir.

b. Les aconsejo que dejen las compras hasta la próxima semana.

c. No les conviene llevar tantas cosas.

d. Sugerimos que se reúnan en la Plaza de Armas.

e. No se olviden de traer los papeles.

Gramática

The subjunctive mood with recommendations

1. In Chapter 2 you learned to use the infinitive after expressions for making suggestions or recommendations. Instead of the infinitive, you can also use a phrase with **que** and a verb in the subjunctive mood:

   Te recomiendo que tomes las cosas con calma.

2. The subjunctive forms of **dar, estar, ir,** and **ser** are irregular. See page 143.

Más práctica gramatical, pp. 180–181, Acts. 5–6

Cuaderno de gramática, pp. 52–53, Acts. 12–14

22 Gramática en contexto Answers will vary.

Escribamos Este año tu comunidad quiere dar un concierto dedicado a la música internacional. ¿Qué sugerencias y recomendaciones tienen estas personas para el programa?

MODELO   Te recomiendo que des el concierto a las…

yo	(no) sugerir que	tú	dar el concierto a las…
Alicia	recomendar que	ellos	cantar después de…
tú	(no) olvidar que	Paco y Elsa	ser el/la solista
nosotros	aconsejar que	Alicia	invitar a…
las autoridades	(no) convenir que	nosotros	

Connections and Comparisons

Career Path
Have students brainstorm about careers related to the journalism industry. (reporter, writer, editor, publisher, photographer, columnist) Ask how the knowledge of a second language might be useful. (ability to communicate with people worldwide, increased customer base, improved relationships with international clients) How might students prepare for a career in journalism? Suggest that students interested in journalism research major Spanish-language newspapers online.

Community Link
22 Have students check the arts section in a newspaper from a big city to see what types of international music or arts programs are taking place in the near future. Have students report their findings to the class.

STANDARDS: 1.2, 1.3, 5.1

23 ¿Qué le recomiendan?

Leamos/Escribamos En parejas, imaginen que escriben una columna de consejos en un periódico. Primero lean la carta que Pablo Chi les envió por correo electrónico. Luego discutan los consejos que le quieren dar, y finalmente contesten su carta por escrito.

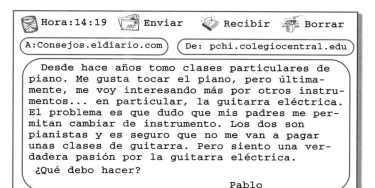

> 🗄 Hora:14:19 📨 Enviar 📩 Recibir 🗑 Borrar
>
> A:Consejos.eldiario.com   De: pchi.colegiocentral.edu
>
> Desde hace años tomo clases particulares de piano. Me gusta tocar el piano, pero última-mente, me voy interesando más por otros instru-mentos... en particular, la guitarra eléctrica. El problema es que dudo que mis padres me per-mitan cambiar de instrumento. Los dos son pianistas y es seguro que no me van a pagar unas clases de guitarra. Pero siento una ver-dadera pasión por la guitarra eléctrica.
> ¿Qué debo hacer?
>
> Pablo

24 Del colegio al trabajo

Leamos/Hablemos Trabaja con dos compañeros(as) de clase. Imaginen que dos de Uds. trabajan en la oficina de turismo en el centro de Guadalajara. La tercera persona es turista en Guadalajara. Quiere ver la ciudad pero sólo puede quedarse unas horas. Den consejos a la tercera persona sobre qué debe ver. Usen la información del folleto.

MODELO
—Me interesa mucho la historia de la ciudad.
—Pues, te recomiendo que veas el Instituto Cultural Cabañas. También te conviene…

¡Guadalajara!

Palacio del gobierno
El Palacio, que data del siglo XVIII, tiene murales del muralista moderno **José Clemente Orozco.**

Teatro Degollado
El teatro es un magní-fico ejemplo de la arquitectura neoclásica. Su fachada presenta esculturas.

Palacio Municipal
Tiene un maravilloso fresco pintado por **Gabriel Flores** de la fundación de Guadalajara en 1542.

Catedral metropolitana
Construida en el siglo XVI, sus torres son un símbolo de la ciudad.

Additional Practice
23 Ask students to write a problem on a slip of paper and place it in a hat or in a bag. Students take a slip of paper from the bag with-out looking at it. Have them write a recommendation for how to solve the problem. Then ask students to share the problems and solutions with the class.

Building on Previous Skills
24 **Giving Directions** Before students do this activity, you may want to review words that are necessary when giving directions. Have students brainstorm direction words such as **a la derecha, a la izquierda, derecho, detrás de, enfrente de, cerca de, lejos de, junto a.** You might also ask students to list some verbs that are useful when giving directions. (**doblar, continuar, seguir**)

Additional Practice
24 Tell students to imagine they have just returned from Guadalajara and have visited all the brochure's points of interest. Ask them to report on where they went and what they did. You may want to have them use the following words: **hermoso, magnífico, aburrido, cansado, contento, fantástico, gigantesco, horrible, turístico,** and **interesante.**

Teaching Resources
pp. 170–173

PRINT
▸ Lesson Planner, p. 29
▸ Listening Activities, pp. 44, 48–49
▸ Activities for Communication, pp. 23–24, 67–68, 99–100
▸ Cuaderno de gramática, pp. 51–54
▸ Grammar Tutor for Students of Spanish, Chapter 6
▸ Cuaderno de actividades, pp. 67–70
▸ Cuaderno para hispanohablantes, pp. 26–30
▸ Testing Program, pp. 115–118
▸ Alternative Assessment Guide, p. 35
▸ Student Make-Up Assignments, Chapter 6

MEDIA
▸ One-Stop Planner
▸ Audio Compact Discs, CD 6, Trs. 15–16, 29–31, 19
▸ Teaching Transparencies 6-2; **Más práctica gramatical** Answers; Cuaderno de gramática Answers
▸ Interactive CD-ROM Tutor, Disc 2

Presenting
Así se dice

Have students brainstorm a list of weekend activities. Using **Así se dice,** model extending an invitation and turning it down. Then call on pairs of students to make and turn down invitations.

Gramática, Nota Gramatical

Nosotros commands Hold up classroom props and model the nosotros commands. Then ask volunteers to hold up props and give commands to the class.

Así se dice

Turning down an invitation

Si no quieres aceptar una invitación, puedes explicarte o excusarte así:

Gracias por invitarme, pero no puedo.
Lo siento, pero ya tengo otros planes.
Tengo mucho que hacer. La próxima vez iré.
Hagámoslo mañana. Estoy tan cansado(a).

Hoy no. **¿Por qué no lo dejamos para** la próxima semana?
No tengo ganas de ir al ensayo. Mejor veamos una película.

Cuaderno de actividades, p. 68, Act. 14

25 **Invitaciones y excusas** Script and answers on p. 155H.

 Escuchemos/Hablemos Escucha las conversaciones entre Humberto y sus amigos e indica si los siguientes amigos aceptan sus invitaciones o no. Si no aceptan, indica qué van a hacer.

CD 6
Tr. 16

1. Sara   2. Miguel   3. Laura   4. Ricardo

Gramática

Nosotros commands

1. To say *Let's . . .* in Spanish, use either the **nosotros** form of the present subjunctive or **vamos a** + infinitive.

Veamos una película esta noche.
Comamos después en un restaurante.

Vamos a ver esa exhibición.
Vamos a comer algo.

2. Use the **nosotros** forms of the present subjunctive to say *Let's not . . .*

No compremos esas entradas.

No visitemos el museo.

3. **Vamos** can mean either *We're going* or *Let's go.* The context clarifies the meaning. The equivalent of *Let's not go* is **No vayamos.**

Vamos al Museo de Arte Moderno.

No vayamos al Museo de Historia.

Cuaderno de gramática, p. 53, Act. 15

26 **Gramática en contexto**

Escribamos No quieres hacer lo que tu amigo(a) te sugiere. Contesta sus preguntas por escrito en el negativo y con la información entre paréntesis.

MODELO
—¿Vamos de compras? (visitar la nueva galería)
—No, no vayamos de compras. Visitemos la nueva galería.

1. ¿Escuchamos este disco compacto? (ver una película)
2. ¿Acompañamos a Isabel y Tony al concierto? (ir solos)
3. ¿Tomamos una clase de escultura? (tomar una de dibujo)
4. ¿Ensayamos nuestro dueto? (ver la nueva obra de Leñero)
5. ¿Compramos dos entradas? (comprar cuatro)
6. ¿Vemos el estreno de la película nueva? (alquilar un video)
7. ¿Vamos a la función de la tarde? (ir a la de la noche)
8. ¿Hacemos la tarea para la clase de arte? (estudiar para el examen de música)

Nota gramatical

To form **nosotros** commands of most verbs, simply add **-mos** to the **Ud.** command form: **mire → miremos; ponga → pongamos.** See irregular forms on pages R43–R45.

Cuaderno de gramática, p. 54, Acts. 16–17

Más práctica gramatical, p. 181, Act. 7

Communication for All Students

Group Work

28 Assign students to groups of three. Using the information from the **cartelera**, Student One invites Student Two to an event. Student Two then turns down the invitation, but Student Three tries to convince Student Two to accept it. Encourage students to use the following words in their dialogues: **bonito, buena idea, cómico,**

deberías, disfrutar, divertido, encontrarse (con), estar cerca, estupendo, recomendar.

Challenge

Have students design tickets for different functions (the ballet, a movie, a rock concert). Place the tickets in a bowl and have each student draw one. Have pairs of students practice inviting and accepting or rejecting the invitation.

27 Por el amor a la cultura

Leamos/Hablemos Lee la siguiente cartelera que indica algunas actividades culturales de la ciudad de Guadalajara. Después, invita a un(a) compañero(a) a cuatro actividades. Tu compañero(a) debe dar una explicación y hacer otra sugerencia, según el modelo.

MODELO —Veamos la obra *Bodas de sangre*, ¿quieres?
—Gracias por invitarme, pero no puedo. Tengo muchas cosas que hacer. Vamos otro día.

Vocabulario extra

acompañar	*to accompany; to go with*
ensayar	*to rehearse*
el ensayo	*rehearsal*
la entrada	*ticket*
el estreno	*opening* (of a movie or play)
la función	*showing, performance*
la obra de teatro	*play* (theater)

Cartelera

exposiciones

Nuevas visiones del arte.
Exposición colectiva y concierto de rock.
Sábado 4 de junio a las 17:00 horas
Facultad de Arquitectura de la U. de G.

Gabriela de Castro y Virginia Rivas
Exposición de pintura.

Galería Valentín Gómez Farías.
Edificio Administrativo de la U. de G.

teatro

Lo que vio el mayordomo
De Joe Orton. Director: Enrique Martínez.
Viernes y sábados a las 20:30 horas.
Domingos a las 18:00 horas.
Casa de la Cultura de Zapopan.
Vicente Guerrero 233.

danza

**Ballet Folklórico de México
Amalia Hernández**
Sábado 4 a las 20:30 horas y domingo
5 de junio a las 18:00 horas.
Teatro Degollado. Teléfono 614-47-73.

música

Los Garigoles
Sábado 4 de junio a las 21:00 horas.
Centro Cultural Roxy.
Mezquitán 80.

Concierto Coro Quintano
Director invitado Harlam Snow.
Sábado 4 de junio a las 20:00 horas.
Cine Foro de la U. de G.
Vallarta y Enrique Díaz de León.

28 ¿Qué les pareció?

Hablemos Con dos compañeros(as), presenten un diálogo basado en lo siguiente. Imaginen que fueron a algunos de los eventos anunciados en la cartelera de la Actividad 27. O si prefieren, pueden pensar en eventos a los que realmente asistieron. Hablen de sus opiniones de los artistas y las funciones. Cambien de tema varias veces.

29 En mi cuaderno See sample answer below.

Escribamos Imagina que eres reseñista para el periódico. Escribe un artículo de un concierto al que asististe. Escribe tu opinión del concierto y de los músicos. Da tu recomendación al público acerca del concierto. ¿Qué recomiendas que hagan los artistas para mejorar?

Connections and Comparisons

Language Notes

- The word **estreno** comes from the verb **estrenar** meaning *to use for the first time*. The noun generally means *first time* or *debut*. Both forms are often used to talk about the opening or premiere of a show or movie but also to talk about wearing new clothes. (**¿Vas a estrenar el vestido rojo esta noche?**)

- The word **ensayo** can have a similar meaning to the word *essay*, but is generally used in a more literal sense to mean *rehearsal* or *trial*. (**Esta noche será el primer ensayo de la obra. Vamos a comenzar el ensayo de la máquina.**)

Segundo paso

CAPÍTULO 6

Speaking Assessment

28 Before students present Activity 28 to the class, have each group evaluate another. You may wish to have groups use the following rubric to assess each other's performance.

Speaking Rubric	Points			
	4	3	2	1
Content (Complete–Incomplete)				
Comprehension (Total–Little)				
Comprehensibility (Comprehensible–Incomprehensible)				
Accuracy (Accurate–Seldom accurate)				
Fluency (Fluent–Not fluent)				

18–20: A	14–15: C	Under 12: F
16–17: B	12–13: D	

Assess

▸ Testing Program, pp. 115–118
  Quiz 6-2A, Quiz 6-2B
  Audio CD 6, Tr. 19

▸ Student Make-Up Assignments, Chapter 6, Alternative Quiz

▸ Alternative Assessment Guide, p. 35

Answer
29 *Sample Answer*
Querido público,
El sábado, 20 de julio, por la noche asistí al primer concierto de Los Reyes de Rock en El Instituto Cultural de Cabañas en Guadalajara. ¡Qué original! En mi opinión, el concierto fue formidable y bastante entretenido. Me parece que los músicos fueron magníficos. Les recomiendo a ustedes que vayan al concierto el próximo sábado a las 20:00 horas. Sugiero que compren las entradas temprano. Y no se olviden de llegar temprano.

¡Hasta pronto!

CAPÍTULO 6

Teaching Resources
pp. 174–176

PRINT
▸ Lesson Planner, p. 30
▸ Cuaderno de actividades, p. 71
▸ Cuaderno para hispanohablantes, pp. 26–30
▸ Reading Strategies and Skills Handbook, Chapter 6
▸ ¡Lee conmigo! 3, Chapter 6
▸ Standardized Assessment Tutor, Chapter 6

MEDIA
▸ One-Stop Planner

Prereading
Activities A and B

Establishing a Purpose for Reading
Explain to students that establishing a reason or motive for reading increases their efficiency and their understanding of the text. They can establish a purpose by looking at the title and the illustrations, as well as skimming the text. They may want to use these strategies to formulate questions that they can answer during and after a more thorough reading.

Vida, pasión y arte

La pintora mexicana Frida Kahlo es famosa por sus autorretratos, en los que transforma su sufrimiento personal en obras de arte. Esta selección es parte de una biografía de Kahlo escrita por Martha Zamora.

¡A comenzar!

Estrategia para leer
As you know, it's a good idea to skim before reading in detail, in order to get a general idea of what each section or paragraph is about. This information allows you to guess the meaning of unfamiliar words more easily. You can get even more out of your skimming by jotting down your ideas. Then, after you've read more closely, check your notes to see how well you predicted the content of the selection.

A. Primero, toma dos o tres minutos dándole una ojeada al texto entero. Luego escribe todas las ideas que recuerdes. Guarda tus apuntes, porque las vas a usar después.

¿Te acuerdas?
Remember that in some situations, stopping to look up new words can actually get in the way of understanding the reading. Use intelligent guesswork whenever you can.

B. Compara lo que tienes escrito con uno(a) o dos compañeros(as) de clase. Noten las semejanzas y las diferencias entre sus ideas.

Vida, pasión y muerte de Frida Kahlo

1 **F**rida Kahlo nació el 6 de julio de 1907 en Coyoacán, México. La tercera hija de cuatro, fue desde siempre la más intensa, la más inteligente y conflictiva. Un exótico ejemplar que no podría adaptarse nunca a un ambiente plano.

2 Llegó a la escuela preparatoria en 1922. Un poco antes había regresado a México el pintor Diego Rivera. Ya un artista consagrado en Europa, principia aquí su labor como muralista que llegaría a transformarse en una gloria nacional, precisamente pintando el mural denominado *La creación* dentro de la escuela preparatoria a la que Frida acudía. Ella presencia el desarrollo del trabajo, coquetea y hace al maestro objeto de sus más peligrosas bromas, todo con tal de llamar su atención.

3 Sus estudios se interrumpen cuando, en 1925, un tranvía urbano comprime hasta hacerlo explotar al camión en que viajaba. Así, al iniciarse su vida, todos los planes se derrumbaron y da comienzo la larga historia clínica de la pintora.

4 **D**urante su recuperación, imposibilitada para moverse, su madre idea poner un dosel a su cama recubierto por un espejo en su parte inferior para que pudiera usar su propia imagen como modelo. Con pinceles de su padre, acuarelista aficionado, principia por hacer retratos de sus amigos y sus hermanas.

Cultures and Communities

Culture Note
Frida Kahlo was born in Coyoacán, Mexico, in 1907. She began painting while recovering from a trolley accident that had left her severely injured. Although her working life was fairly short, she produced over 200 paintings. Most of her paintings were self-portraits in which she presented images of her emotional and physical pain, as well as politcally charged depictions of her Mexican heritage. **Casa Azul,** her house in Coyoacán, was built by her father Guillermo Kahlo, a Hungarian-Jewish immigrant and professional photographer, before she was born. It now houses her collection of Mexican folk art.

5 Casi tres años después reen-
cuentra a Diego Rivera y acude a él
para obtener una opinión sobre su calidad artística. La relación progresa y se casan el
21 de agosto de 1929, él de 43 años y ella de 22,
marcando así el inicio de una convivencia amorosa
llena de profunda dependencia de ambos, hasta la
muerte de ella en 1954.

6   La pintura de Frida Kahlo nos va llevando de la
mano, simbólicamente, a lo largo de las experiencias
más importantes en su vida. Sus obsesiones, la muerte
de su madre, así como sus problemas físicos, el deseo
de regresar a su país, a su barrio, cuando viaja con
Diego Rivera durante cuatro años de estancia en San
Francisco, Detroit y Nueva York.

7   Hasta entonces era sólo su acompañante, su sombra y su camarada de protestas y simpatías políticas,
pero, en 1938, realiza su primera exposición individual en la galería artística de Julien Levy en Nueva
York. La seguridad que adquiere con su éxito se
derrumba al regreso cuando se ve obligada a
enfrentar un doloroso divorcio impuesto por Diego.

8   **D**e ésta, como de sus otras experiencias traumáti-
cas, llena su arte y plasma su pena por la separación en la que quizá sea su pintura más conocida,
Las dos Fridas, autorretrato doble en que presenta,
según ella, "a la Frida que Diego amó y a la que ya
no quiere".

Al grano

C. Ahora estás listo(a) para leer con
más cuidado. En cada párrafo,
sigue estos dos pasos:

   1. Lee el párrafo y trata de
   comprender la idea principal
   y los detalles.

   2. Apunta tus ideas e impresiones en una lista por aparte.

Después de terminar el texto entero,
compara tus nuevas ideas con las de
un(a) compañero(a) de la Actividad B.

¿Te acuerdas?

Use context to figure out meaning.
Rely on the words and sentences
around the unknown word. Remember
that only a few logical guesses will
make sense in context.

See answers below.

D. Ya que entiendes las ideas
principales de cada párrafo, trata
de adivinar los significados de
algunas palabras nuevas. Usa el
contexto para adivinar el significado de las siguientes palabras.

   1. consagrado (párrafo 2,
   oración 3)

   2. se derrumbaron (párrafo 3,
   oración 2)

   3. acude (párrafo 5, oración 1)

   4. estancia (párrafo 6, oración 2)

   5. compendia (párrafo 10,
   oración 1)

   6. quebranto (párrafo 12,
   oración 3)

   7. vagar (párrafo 14, oración 1)

E. El título de la biografía resume
la obra bajo tres temas: vida,
pasión y muerte. Trabaja con
un(a) compañero(a) y hablen
del significado de estos tres
temas. Revisen la obra párrafo
por párrafo. ¿De qué tema(s)
trata cada uno?

Reading
Activities C, D, and E

Summarizing
Have students make a list of
direct quotations in order to make
statements about the main facts.
Then have them use the quotations
to write a four- to five-sentence paragraph in Spanish, summing up the
narration.

Monitoring Reading
Have pairs of students take turns
reading the biography aloud. After
completing the reading, have them
tell you what they remember about
the passage. Write their answers on
the board or on a transparency.

Analyzing Chronological Order
On index cards, write a sentence
from each paragraph. Distribute
cards to all students and have them
position themselves in the order that
the sentences appear in the passage.

Connections and Comparisons

Multicultural Link
Frida Kahlo stood out as an artist in a society in which women did not have the same rights
as they do currently. Mexican women did not get
full suffrage until 1953. Have students identify the
date when women earned the right to vote in a
particular country. You might assign blocks of
countries to students. (North America, Europe,
South America, Far East, Africa)

Language Note
The word **camión** means *truck* in many countries,
but in Mexico, it is often used to mean *bus*. The
diminutive **camioneta** means *light truck* or
station wagon.

Answers

D 1. consagrado   *consecrated*
   2. se derrumbaron   *were shattered*
   3. acude   *she turns to*
   4. estancia   *stay*
   5. compendia   *summarizes*
   6. quebranto   *affliction*
   7. vagar   *to wander about*

E *Answers will vary.*

CAPÍTULO 6

Postreading
Activities F, G, and H

Evaluating Motivation and Credibility

F. You may want to explain to students that understanding a writer's motivation can help them evaluate the credibility of the text. Ask students to determine whether the author's intent is to inform, convince, or entertain. (Her primary motivation is to inform, although her admiration for the artist is evident.) Can the facts of the narrative be proven? (Most of the biographical facts can be confirmed with other sources.) Does the author present a particular point of view? (The favorable analysis of Kahlo's life and works could be debated by others.)

Drawing Inferences

G. Have students use the reading strategy **El texto dice... yo digo...** to answer the following question: **¿Se beneficia Kahlo de sus sufrimientos en alguna forma?** To complete the chart, students should indicate what the text says (**El texto dice...**), what they think (**Yo digo**), and what they have inferred (**Por lo tanto...**).

Answers
F *Sample answers:*
1. Escogió como tema a Frida Kahlo porque era muy creativa y original. Su vida inspira a la gente.
2. La admira mucho. Por eso dice que tiene talento y que también es muy fuerte, porque transforma su dolor en arte.
3. La autora quería enseñarnos un poco de la vida de una persona fascinante y extraordinaria. Frida Kahlo siempre tuvo muchos problemas físicos, y por eso vivió con mucho dolor durante años. Su pasión por Diego Rivera y su propio arte fueron las cosas más importantes para ella. Usó las experiencias más importantes de su vida para crear sus pinturas.

See sample answers below.

F. En grupos, comenten las siguientes preguntas y preparen una breve reseña de la lectura.
  1. ¿Por qué creen que la autora escogió la vida y arte de Frida Kahlo como tema?
  2. ¿Qué actitud muestra la autora hacia Kahlo? ¿Cómo influye esto en su biografía de la artista?
  3. ¿Qué creen que la autora quería lograr con su biografía de Kahlo?

G. Trabajando con el mismo grupo de la Actividad F, miren la foto y las pinturas que aparecen con la biografía. Consideren lo siguiente.
  1. ¿Qué les comunica la foto de la artista en la página 174? ¿Apoya las ideas de la biografía o les presenta alguna idea nueva?
  2. Comparen los autorretratos de la artista con la foto.
  3. Las piezas que ilustran el texto, como el pie y la pierna, se llaman milagros. ¿Qué representan en estas páginas?

H. Many an artist has drawn upon suffering in his or her life to produce art. Would you consider Frida a good example of a person who has succeeded despite personal hardships? Explain your opinion. Do you know of any other artists who have overcome difficult challenges?

Cuaderno de actividades, p. 71, Act. 18a

Cuaderno para hispanohablantes, pp. 28–29

9   Emplea el mecanismo de defensa que Sigmund Freud llamó capacidad de sublimación y transforma en arte su angustia, su dolor. Lo deja ahí para exorcizarlo, sacarlo de su vida y es por eso quizá que quienes la conocieron tienen como recuerdo una mujer siempre alegre, malhablada, impecablemente decorada, alhajada como una princesa llena de incisivo buen humor.

10   Durante el año que dura el divorcio escribe Frida en su diario un mensaje a Diego que compendia su amor: "Jamás olvidaré tu presencia en mi vida. Tú me acogiste destrozada y me devolviste entera".

Frida Kahlo, *Fulang-Chang and Me*, 1937, 25 1/4 x 19 1/8 x 1 3/4 inches, including frame. The Museum of Modern Art, New York. Mary Sklar Bequest.

11   La simbiosis que formaban les era indispensable así, un año después vuelven a casarse en San Francisco, California, para no separarse ya.

12   Un año antes de morir se organiza una exposición retroactiva de su pintura, la única individual que tuvo en vida en su país. Ella acude a la inauguración en ambulancia, postrada; en su camilla la llevan hasta su cama convertida en centro de la exhibición. Es notorio su quebranto físico, pero su espíritu aún conserva su vigor al declarar a un periodista: "No estoy enferma, estoy rota".

13   Entonces Frida, la indomable fuerza vital, se deja ir. Abandona la lucha y, días antes del veinticincoavo aniversario de bodas con Diego Rivera, muere en su casa de Coyoacán el 13 de julio durante la noche, a los 47 años de edad.

14   Cuatro años después, su casa es abierta al público como museo, para permitirnos vagar en sus jardines, visitar su recámara, su estudio y empaparnos del universo que ella creó para sí, del reflejo de esta mujer que parecía hecha de un concentrado de arco iris.

Communication for All Students

Native Speakers
Have native speakers research Spanish language texts to discover something about Frida Kahlo that was not presented in the biography. Ask them to present their findings to the class. You might want to have them use the Internet to do their research.

Challenge
Have students research a painting by Frida Kahlo that is not found on these pages and write a paragraph describing and critiquing the work. You may want to have students present their findings to the class. Provide a photograph of the painting if possible.

Vamos a escribir

Un grave accidente en 1925 afectó profundamente a Frida Kahlo. No se dejó vencer por su condición física y expresó en el arte sus frustraciones. Un acontecimiento positivo también puede cambiarle la vida a una persona. Por ejemplo, uno puede conocer a alguien que llegue a ser un(a) mentor(a) o un(a) íntimo(a) amigo(a).

¿Recuerdas un acontecimiento que te ha transformado la vida y a la vez ayudado a comprender mejor quién eres? ¿Cuál es la mejor forma de presentar tal acontecimiento para que otras personas lo comprendan y le saquen provecho? En esta actividad, vas a escribir sobre un acontecimiento importante de tu vida y vas a aprender cómo organizar tu historia.

Un acontecimiento importante

Describe un acontecimiento importante de tu vida en unas 15 o 20 frases. ¿Por qué lo consideras importante? ¿Cómo cambió tu vida? ¿Cuál es su importancia para otras personas?

> ### Estrategia **para escribir**
> **Chronological ordering** Putting events in chronological order means listing them in the order they occurred. This usually means starting with the first event and continuing to the last. You can also use reverse chronological order if it's more appropriate for the story you're telling.

A. Preparación

1. Examina tus recuerdos. ¿Qué acontecimientos te han transformado la vida? ¿Cuándo y dónde ocurrieron? ¿Quiénes estaban allí? ¿Qué tiempo hacía? Si quieres, mira fotos de tu niñez y habla de tus recuerdos con amigos y familiares.

2. Haz una lista de esos eventos y escoge uno que quieras compartir.

3. Organiza la información en orden cronológico.

B. Redacción

1. Escribe tu historia en el orden más adecuado. Si es necesario, usa palabras como **antes de, después de, luego...**

2. Usa palabras relacionadas con los sentidos. Habla de lo que viste, escuchaste, sentiste y oíste.

3. Incluye un poco de diálogo para hacer más interesante la historia.

C. Evaluación

1. ¿Olvidaste poner información importante? Si es necesario, agrega detalles. ¿Incluiste cosas no relacionadas con tu tema? Quita los detalles innecesarios.

2. ¿Es lógica la historia? Ponla en otro orden si no está clara.

3. ¿Es evidente por qué este acontecimiento es importante para ti y para otras personas? Tal vez sea necesario incluir más información o usar palabras más expresivas.

4. Muestra lo que escribiste a un(a) compañero(a) y ten en cuenta sus opiniones.

Teaching Resources
p. 177

PRINT
▶ Lesson Planner, p. 30
▶ Cuaderno para hispanohablantes, p. 29
▶ Alternative Assessment Guide, p. 21
▶ Standardized Assessment Tutor, Chapter 6

MEDIA
▶ One-Stop Planner, Disc 2
   Test Generator, Chapter 6
▶ Interactive CD-ROM Tutor, Disc 2

Process Writing

Prewriting

Ask students to write the answers to the following questions: **¿Quiénes son tres personas que te han influido profundamente? ¿Qué han hecho estas personas? ¿Por qué te han afectado tanto?**

Writing

Before students begin writing, have them brainstorm about what they want to include in their paragraphs. They should use this information to outline the events that will be included in their essays. Encourage students to use words such as **primero, segundo, después, finalmente, por fin,** as transitions from one event to another. Students may wish to write from the perspective of a celebrity or someone they admire.

Apply and Assess

Postwriting
Cooperative Learning

After students have finished writing, assign them to groups of three. Ask each group member to assess one of the following elements: choice of topic, clarity of expression, or vividness of language. You may want to have each student use a different color of ink. The students exchange and read each other's paper. Then have students comment on the paper based on the element they chose to assess. Have students exchange papers again. Each student edits the new paper. After the papers have been edited by each group member, students reclaim their own paper and make any necessary changes. You might have them consult the Peer Editing Rubric found on page 8 of the *Alternative Assessment Guide*.

Más práctica gramatical

MARCAR: go.hrw.com
PALABRA CLAVE:
WV3 GUADALAJARA-6

For **Más práctica gramatical**
Answer Transparencies, see the
Teaching Transparencies binder.

Primer paso

Objectives Introducing and changing a topic of conversation; expressing what needs to be done; expressing an opinion

1 Lee lo que hacen estas personas y después explica qué le gustaría hacer a cada uno. Usa estas expresiones. Usa cada expresión sólo una vez. (p. 163)

MODELO   Hace cuatro años que Liliana estudia el baile. ¡Le encanta bailar!
Le gustaría estudiar danza en la universidad.

> estudiar danza en la universidad
>
> patrocinar un festival de arte
>
> ver la exhibición de arte español en el museo
>
> ser miembro de una orquesta
>
> ser músico o cantante
>
> aprender a diseñar ropa
>
> conocer a un escultor famoso
>
> comprar un libro sobre la pintura mexicana

1. Enrique toca la flauta, el clarinete y el piano. Espera aprender a tocar el banjo este año.
2. Marcela lee todas las revistas de moda americanas y europeas. Siempre se entera de las últimas modas antes que sus amigos.
3. Hace años que Rafael estudia el arte. Sus pintores favoritos son Picasso y Goya.
4. Laura está loca por la música. Colecciona discos y también escribe canciones.
5. Teresa viajó a México el año pasado y vio unas obras de Orozco que le gustaron mucho. Ahora quiere saber más sobre los muralistas mexicanos.
6. Don Ramón tiene mucho dinero y una gran colección de arte. Siempre trata de ayudar a los artistas jóvenes.
7. ¡Felicia es muy creativa! Sabe hacer figuras muy bonitas de madera y de barro *(clay)*.

Answers

1 1. Le gustaría ser miembro de una orquesta.
2. Le gustaría aprender a diseñar ropa.
3. Le gustaría ver la exhibición de arte español en el museo.
4. Le gustaría ser músico o cantante.
5. Le gustaría comprar un libro sobre la pintura mexicana.
6. Le gustaría patrocinar un festival de arte.
7. Le gustaría conocer a un escultor famoso.

Grammar Resources for Chapter 6

The **Más práctica gramatical** activities are designed as supplemental activities for the grammatical concepts presented in the chapter. You might use them as additional practice, for review, or for assessment.

For more grammar presentation, review, and practice, refer to the following:
• Cuaderno de gramática
• Grammar Tutor for Students of Spanish

• Grammar Summary on pp. R25–R46
• Cuaderno de actividades
• Grammar and Vocabulary quizzes (Testing Program)
• Test Generator on the One-Stop Planner CD-ROM
• Interactive CD-ROM Tutor
• **Juegos interactivos** at go.hrw.com

2 Mañana Esther tiene un examen de vocabulario en la clase de español, y necesita tu ayuda. Completa la lista de palabras que debe aprender de memoria. Usa los artículos definidos correctos. Si la palabra puede ser masculina o feminina, escribe los dos artículos. **(p. 163)**

1. _____ cantante
2. _____ mano
3. _____ problema
4. _____ goma de borrar
5. _____ papel
6. _____ disfraz
7. _____ revista
8. _____ guía

9. _____ baile
10. _____ cartel
11. _____ agua
12. _____ foto
13. _____ cine
14. _____ exhibición
15. _____ modelo

3 Doña Serafina es una pianista famosa y es profesora de música también. Completa lo que dice sobre las clases de música con las formas correctas del subjuntivo de los verbos entre paréntesis. **(p. 164)**

Hace falta que nosotros los pianistas profesionales les ___1___ (explicar) a ustedes por qué es necesario estudiar piano. Claro, creo que también hace falta que el público nos ___2___ (pagar) más por las clases que damos. Es importante que los profesores ___3___ (buscar) sólo a los mejores estudiantes. Si eres estudiante, y si quieres aprender a tocar realmente bien, pues hace falta que ___4___ (comenzar) a estudiar música desde muy joven. Es necesario que los estudiantes ___5___ (tocar) varias horas todos los días y que ___6___ (llegar) a tiempo a sus clases. ¿Y después de la clase? Pues, es necesario que ustedes ___7___ (sacar) sus cuadernos de música y que ___8___ (empezar) a practicar inmediatamente.

Answers
2 1. el/la
2. la
3. el
4. la
5. el
6. el
7. la
8. el/la
9. el
10. el
11. el
12. la
13. el
14. la
15. el/la

3 1. expliquemos
2. pague
3. busquen
4. comiences
5. toquen
6. lleguen
7. saquen
8. empiecen

Communication for All Students

Additional Practice
2 Have students choose ten of the words in the activity and use each in an original sentence, including an adjective. Encourage students to practice the plural forms of the words as well. **(La foto que tomaste en Sevilla es muy buena. Los guías argentinos hablan español e italiano.)**

Pair Work
3 Have pairs of students write a brief paragraph similar to the one presented about why one should study Spanish and what must be done to succeed in a Spanish class. Pairs can exchange papers and edit each other's paragraphs.

CAPÍTULO 6

For **Más práctica gramatical** Answer Transparencies, see the *Teaching Transparencies* binder.

Más práctica gramatical

WV3 GUADALAJARA-6

4 Germán tiene unas opiniones muy fuertes del arte. Completa lo que dice con los comparativos en español. Usa las expresiones entre paréntesis y no te olvides de usar la forma correcta del adjetivo. (**p. 165**)

MODELO Para mí, la pintura es ‗‗‗‗‗ la escultura. (*less realistic than*)
Para mí, la pintura es **menos realista que** la escultura.

1. Las obras de Fernando Botero son ‗‗‗‗‗ las de Juan Gris, ¿no te parece? (*more original than*)
2. En mi opinión, los museos son ‗‗‗‗‗ los videojuegos. (*more entertaining than*)
3. Me parece que el arte de Salvador Dalí es ‗‗‗‗‗ el de Joan Miró. (*as incomprehensible as*)
4. La música popular latinoamericana es ‗‗‗‗‗ la música pop de Estados Unidos. (*less conventional than*)
5. Para mí, no hay nada ‗‗‗‗‗ las canciones de Celia Cruz. (*as marvelous as*)
6. ¿Crees que los edificios de Frank Lloyd Wright sean ‗‗‗‗‗ los de Antonio Gaudí? (*more creative than*)
7. Pienso que las esculturas de Julio González son ‗‗‗‗‗ las de Brancusi. (*less imaginative than*)

Segundo paso **Objectives** Making suggestions and recommendations; turning down an invitation

5 Nadie sabe qué hacer este fin de semana. ¿Qué sugerencias hacen todos? Escribe oraciones completas, usando la forma correcta del subjuntivo de **ir** y siguiendo el modelo. (**p. 170**)

MODELO el guía/Guille y Carlos/la galería
El guía les sugiere a Guille y a Carlos que vayan a la galería.

1. la profesora/sus estudiantes/el concierto
2. (yo)/tú/Museo Folklórico
3. nosotros/turistas/Teatro Municipal
4. los artistas/sus amigos/exhibición
5. Carmela/yo/su clase de arte
6. ¿(tú)/yo/festival de música?
7. (yo)/mi amigo/cine para ver la nueva película
8. todos/tú y yo/tienda de música para escuchar los nuevos discos compactos

Answers

4
1. más originales que
2. más entretenidos que
3. tan incomprensible como
4. menos convencional que
5. tan maravilloso como
6. más creativos que
7. menos imaginativas que

5
1. La profesora les sugiere a sus estudiantes que vayan al concierto.
2. Te sugiero que vayas al Museo Folklórico.
3. Les sugerimos a los turistas que vayan al Teatro Municipal.
4. Los artistas les sugieren a sus amigos que vayan a la exhibición.
5. Carmela me sugiere que vaya a su clase de arte.
6. ¿Me sugieres que vaya al festival de música?
7. Le sugiero a mi amigo que vaya al cine para ver la nueva película.
8. Todos nos sugieren que vayamos a la tienda de música para escuchar los nuevos discos compactos.

Communication for All Students

Auditory Learners

4 Organize students into pairs to share their opinions on Orozco's art work. Have students express their opinions by stating why they like or dislike the artwork using the expressions **más... que** or **menos... que.** Remind students to use the correct form of the adjectives.

Building on Previous Skills

5 Students may benefit from a review of the subjunctive forms of **ir** since these forms are irregular. To provide practice using the subjunctive mood, have students imagine they will create their own mural. Then ask them to write at least five sentences telling what elements they would put into a mural of their own. (people, events, images, and colors)

6 Los profesores de tu colegio quieren que todos los alumnos tengan profesiones artísticas. Escribe oraciones completas con sus recomendaciones, usando la forma correcta del subjuntivo de **ser.** Sigue el modelo. **(p. 170)**

> **MODELO**   **el profesor de música/yo/cantante**
> **El profesor de música me recomienda que sea cantante.**

1. la profesora de arte/Isabel/escultora
2. la profesora de arte/Diego y yo/pintores
3. el profesor de baile/Tania y Leo/bailarines
4. el profesor de música/tú/pianista
5. la profesora de literatura/yo/novelista
6. la profesora de arte/Elena y Marisa/artistas

7 La clase de español está en Madrid. ¿Qué actividades sugiere el grupo? Escribe las sugerencias usando mandatos en la forma de **nosotros. (p. 172)**

> **MODELO**   ¡═══ (Hacer) una excursión a Toledo!
> ¡**Hagamos** una excursión a Toledo!

1. ═══ (Sacar) fotos de la Plaza Mayor.
2. ¡═══ (Ver) la estatua de don Quijote en la Plaza de España!
3. ¡═══ (Ir) al Museo del Prado!
4. ═══ (Comprar) entradas para la visita al Palacio Real.
5. ═══ (Visitar) el Museo de Arte Contemporáneo.
6. ═══ (Pasear) por el Parque del Retiro.
7. ¡═══ (Asistir) a una obra de teatro!
8. ¡═══ (Salir) a escuchar un concierto de guitarra!

Answers

6 1. La profesora de arte le recomienda (a Isabel) que sea escultora.
2. La profesora de arte nos recomienda que seamos pintores.
3. El profesor de baile les recomienda (a Tania y Leo) que sean bailarines.
4. El profesor de música te recomienda que seas pianista.
5. La profesora de literatura me recomienda que sea novelista.
6. La profesora de arte les recomienda (a Elena y Marisa) que sean artistas.

7 1. Saquemos
2. Veamos
3. Vayamos
4. Compremos
5. Visitemos
6. Paseemos
7. Asistamos
8. Salgamos

Review and Assess

You may wish to assign the **Más práctica gramatical** activities as additional practice or homework after presenting material throughout the chapter. Assign Activity 1 after **Vocabulario** (p. 163), Activity 2 after **Nota gramatical** (p. 163), Activity 3 after **Así se dice** and **Gramática** (p. 164), Activity 4 after **Vocabulario** (p. 165), Activities 5 and 6 after **Así se dice** and **Gramática** (p. 170), and Activity 7 after **Gramática** (p. 172). To prepare students for the **Paso** Quizzes and Chapter Test, have them do the **Más práctica gramatical** activities in the following order: complete Activities 1–4 before taking Quiz 6-1A or 6-1B; Activities 5–7 before taking Quiz 6-2A or 6-2B.

Repaso

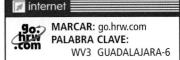

MARCAR: go.hrw.com
PALABRA CLAVE:
WV3 GUADALAJARA-6

CAPÍTULO 6

The **Repaso** reviews and integrates all four skills and culture in preparation for the Chapter Test.

Teaching Resources
pp. 182–183

PRINT
▸ Lesson Planner, p. 31
▸ Listening Activities, p. 45
▸ Video Guide, pp. 37, 39, 42
▸ Grammar Tutor for Students of Spanish, Chapter 6
▸ Cuaderno para hispanohablantes, pp. 26–30
▸ Standardized Assessment Tutor, Chapter 6

MEDIA
▸ One-Stop Planner
▸ Video Program, Videocassette 2, 39:00–41:33
▸ Audio Compact Discs, CD 6, Tr. 17
▸ Interactive CD-ROM Tutor, Disc 2

Culture Note
The students in the photo are participating in a mural project directed by Jorge Somarriba and sponsored by the Latin American Youth Center. The center serves youths in the Washington, D.C. community by offering such services as transitional living skills, literacy programs, health and social services, and employment training. If your students have Internet access, have them research the center and its projects.

1 Escucha dos versiones de una tarde en la vida de Ricardo. Indica cuál de las versiones corresponde a la tarde representada por los dibujos. Script and answers on p. 155H.

CD 6
Tr. 17

2 Con un(a) compañero(a), habla de los temas indicados. Usa una expresión adecuada para introducir cada tema. Tu compañero(a) responde con una opinión del tema y luego él o ella cambia el tema cortésmente.

ESTUDIANTE 1	ESTUDIANTE 2
un actor o una actriz famosa	la última película que viste
un concierto al que te encantaría asistir	un chisme de un(a) cantante
un(a) artista famoso(a)	tu programa favorito de televisión

3 Este fin de semana tienes muchos planes. Invita a un(a) compañero(a) a cuatro actividades. Tu compañero(a) debe responder con una explicación o con una opinión positiva de la actividad que mencionaste. Sigue el modelo.

MODELO —Vamos a esa nueva discoteca el viernes, ¿qué te parece?
—Gracias por invitarme pero no puedo. Tengo muchas cosas que hacer...

4 Este año, el club de español tiene la oportunidad de pintar un mural en el pasillo del colegio. Con dos compañeros(as), habla de tus ideas para un mural. Usen las siguientes expresiones. Deben expresar por lo menos una opinión y hacer dos sugerencias sobre qué necesitan hacer.

Es importante que...

Es necesario que...

Recomiendo que...

Conviene + inf.

Sería buena/mala idea + inf.

Hace falta que...

Apply and Assess

Slower Pace
1 Before playing the audio recording, have students list what they see happening in each of the drawings.

Additional Practice
4 After discussing their ideas for a mural with their partners, have students write their suggestions in paragraph form.

Challenge
5 Divide the class into small groups. Have each group choose a famous singer or musical group and form a "fan club." As officers of the fan club, each group designs a presentation promoting the artists. The presentation should include a brochure, a speech, and, if possible, a sample of the music.

STANDARDS: 1.1, 1.2, 2.1, 3.1

5 Lee el artículo sobre el éxito reciente del grupo Maná. Luego escribe una conversación entre un miembro del grupo y un(a) reportero(a) de una revista de música. El (la) reportero(a) le pregunta sobre las actividades del grupo, sus nuevas canciones y los lugares que ha visitado este año. El cantante le da la información y sus opiniones sobre cada cosa.

MANÁ

Después de años y años en que los solistas dominaron por completo el mercado, este año los grupos se convirtieron en una fuerte amenaza para su supremacía, y de entre todos ellos, sin duda fue Maná el grupo que más éxitos tuvo durante el año. "Cómo te deseo", "Vivir sin aire" y "Oye mi amor" se escucharon fuertemente en la radio y provocaron que cualquier lugar donde se presentara el grupo, estuviera a reventar. En una época dominada por las multitudinarias presentaciones de artistas internacionales, Maná tuvo el orgullo de llenar durante dos noches el Palacio de los Deportes. Fueron muchos años de lucha los de estos jóvenes tapatíos. Por eso su éxito es sólo una justa recompensa.

6 Contesta cada pregunta con información cultural de este capítulo. See answers below.

1. ¿Qué es el Instituto Cultural Cabañas?
2. ¿Quién fue el muralista más famoso de Jalisco?
3. ¿Qué pintaba Frida Kahlo?
4. ¿Para qué sirven los murales?
5. ¿Cuál es un instrumento popular en la región andina?
6. ¿Qué instrumento se puede hacer de la concha de un armadillo?

7

Situación

A. Para tu cumpleaños, tu abuela te mandó 30 dólares... ¡pero ahora hay un problema! Tus padres quieren que acompañes a tu abuelita a un concierto de violín, pero tú prefieres usar el dinero para ir a un concierto de rock. Con dos compañeros(as), haz los papeles de padre, madre e hijo(a). Deben expresar sus opiniones de las dos actividades mencionadas. También deben explicar qué hay que hacer para resolver el conflicto.

B. Estás hablando con un miembro de un grupo de danza y teatro sobre la posibilidad de implementar un programa de artes en tu comunidad. Durante la conversación, ustedes cambian de tema varias veces y hablan de sus opiniones de diferentes artes y artistas. Tu amigo(a) te invita a ver la próxima función de su grupo en México pero tú explicas por qué no puedes ir.

Cuaderno para hispanohablantes, p. 30

Apply and Assess

Group Work

6 Tell students to pretend they are taking a survey to see how much teenagers know about Latin American culture. Have them write a cultural quiz using the questions given and four questions of their own. After all groups have prepared their quizzes, they exchange them with other groups and take each other's quizzes. When all groups have taken the quizzes, students report the results to the class.

Repaso

CAPÍTULO 6

Teaching Suggestion

5 You may want to ask students the following comprehension questions about the piece of realia: **¿Maná es un grupo de deportistas, de músicos o de bailarines?** (de músicos) **¿La música de Maná es vieja o contemporánea?** (contemporánea) **¿De dónde es este grupo?** (Jalisco) **¿Qué les parece la música de Maná a sus fanáticos?** (que es formidable, maravillosa...) **¿Y a los que no les gusta su música?** (que es de muy mal gusto, insoportable, pésima...)

Portfolio

5 **Written** You might have students include this activity in their written Portfolios. For Portfolio suggestions, see *Alternative Assessment Guide,* page 21.

Answers

6 1. Es un lugar que tiene murales pintados por José Clemente Orozco.
2. José Clemente Orozco
3. Pintaba autorretratos, eventos de su vida y a su familia.
4. Los murales mexicanos representan la historia del país y rescatan el pasado indígena de la nación.
5. la quena
6. el charango

Teacher Note
This page is intended to help students prepare independently for the Chapter Test. It is a brief checklist of the major points covered in the chapter. The students should be reminded that this is only a checklist and does not necessarily include everything that will appear on the Chapter Test.

Answers

2 *Sample answers:*
1. Es necesario que los estudiantes asistan a clase todos los días.
2. Es importante que tomes buenos apuntes.
3. Hace falta que leamos el libro de texto y otros libros de arte.
4. Es necesario que Uds. vean programas sobre el arte en la televisión.
5. Es importante que Mari visite muchos museos.

4 *Sample answers:*
1. Sugerimos que hagamos una limpieza general.
2. Es mejor que pongan basureros en los pasillos.
3. Sería buena idea colgar obras de los estudiantes en la cafetería.
4. ¿Has pensado en pintar un mural en las paredes del gimnasio?
5. *Answers will vary.*

A ver si puedo...

Can you introduce and change a topic of conversation? p. 162

1 Escribe un minidiálogo en que una persona sugiere un tema de conversación y la otra persona cambia el tema. Answers will vary.

MODELO
—¿Sabes algo de la música de Emanuel?
—Sí, es genial. A propósito, ¿vas al concierto mañana?

1. el arte de Frida Kahlo; los murales de Orozco
2. el Ballet Folklórico; el baile de la escuela
3. la música clásica; las sinfonías de Silvestre Revueltas
4. el examen de la clase de arte; el proyecto final

Can you express what needs to be done? p. 164

2 Usa varias expresiones para indicar que es necesario hacer las siguientes cosas para sacar notas excelentes en la clase de arte moderno. See sample answers below.
1. los estudiantes / asistir a clase todos los días
2. tú / tomar buenos apuntes
3. nosotros / leer el libro de texto y otros libros de arte
4. Uds. / ver programas sobre el arte en la televisión
5. Mari / visitar muchos museos

Can you express an opinion? p. 165

3 Escribe minidiálogos en que una persona pide una opinión sobre las siguientes cosas y la otra persona responde. Answers will vary.

MODELO
—¿Qué te parece el arte moderno?
—Para decir la verdad, no lo soporto.

1. la arquitectura mexicana
2. las pinturas de Frida Kahlo
3. la Mona Lisa
4. los instrumentos musicales de Latinoamérica
5. los murales de Diego Rivera

Can you make suggestions and recommendations? p. 170

4 El director de tu escuela quiere que el Consejo Estudiantil haga sugerencias para embellecer el campus. ¿Qué recomiendan Uds.? See sample answers below.
1. hacer una limpieza general
2. poner basureros en...
3. colgar obras de los estudiantes en...
4. pintar un mural en las paredes de...
5. ¿?

Can you turn down an invitation? p. 172

5 Responde a cada invitación y explica por qué no puedes aceptarla. Answers will vary.
1. Voy a una exhibición de pinturas de Xul Solar. ¿Me acompañas?
2. El concierto de Luis Miguel es este fin de semana. ¿Quieres ir?
3. Hay un programa sobre Frida Kahlo esta noche. ¿Te gustaría verlo?
4. El Ballet Folklórico de México viene la semana próxima. ¿Qué te parece si vamos juntos(as)?

Review and Assess

Additional Practice
2 Have students work in pairs and ask each other about their artistic skills and interests. Once these are known, each partner should express the importance of developing additional skills or interests. **(Es formidable que sepas tocar la guitarra eléctrica, pero es importante que aprendas a dibujar o pintar también.)**

Group Work
4 Have students work in groups of three or four and come up with recommendations for end-of-year programs and/or school parties. Students can respond to each other's ideas and should ultimately come up with a set of recommendations that all group members agree upon. Have a spokesperson report to the class. **(Sugerimos que..., Nos parece buena idea que...)**

Primer paso

Introducing and changing a topic of conversation

A propósito...	By the way . . .
Cambiando de tema, ¿qué me dices de...?	Changing subjects, what can you tell me about . . .?
Eso me hace pensar en...	That brings to mind . . .
Eso me recuerda...	That reminds me of . . .
Hablando de...	Speaking of . . .
¿Has leído algo de...?	Have you read anything about . . .?
¿Qué has oído de...?	What have you heard about . . .?
¿Qué me cuentas de...?	What can you tell me about . . .?

The arts

antiguo(a)	old; ancient
aprender a + inf.	to learn (to do something)
el (la) artista	artist
el bailarín/la bailarina	dancer
el (la) cantante	singer
contemporáneo(a)	contemporary
la danza	dance (as an art form)
el dibujo	drawing
diseñar	to design

el (la) escultor(a)	sculptor
la escultura	sculpture
la estatua	statue
la exhibición	exhibition
intentar	to try
el (la) músico(a)	musician
la orquesta	orchestra
patrocinar	to sponsor
la pintura	painting

Expressing what needs to be done

Es importante que reconozcas...	It's important that you recognize . . .
Es necesario que busquemos...	It's necessary that we look for . . .
Hace falta que pintemos...	We need to paint . . .

Expressing an opinion

Admiro mucho...	I admire very much . . .
Lo (La) encuentro...	I find it . . .
Me cae gordo.	I hate it.
Me deja frío(a).	It doesn't do anything for me.
Me parece que...	It seems to me that . . .

No lo (la) soporto.	I can't stand it (him/her).
Para decir la verdad...	To tell the truth . . .
Para ser sincero(a)...	To be honest . . .
¿Qué opinas (piensas) de...?	What do you think of . . .?
¿Qué te parece...?	How do you feel about . . .?

Describing

creativo(a)	creative
de muy mal gusto	in very bad taste
entretenido(a)	entertaining
formidable	tremendous
genial	great
hermoso(a)	beautiful
imaginativo(a)	imaginative
incomprensible	incomprehensible
insignificante	trivial
insoportable	unbearable, intolerable
magnífico	magnificent
una obra maestra	masterpiece
pésimo(a)	awful
realista	realistic

Segundo paso

Making suggestions and recommendations

Es mejor que...	It's better for . . . to . . .
¿Has pensado en...?	Have you thought of . . .?
No te conviene...	It's not advisable that you . . .
No te olvides de...	Don't forget to . . .
Sería buena/mala idea...	It would be a good/ bad idea to . . .
Sugiero que...	I suggest that . . .
Te aconsejo que...	I advise you to . . .

Le recomiendo a Juan que...	I recommend that Juan . . .

Turning down an invitation

Gracias por invitarme, pero no puedo.	Thanks for inviting me, but I can't.
Hagámoslo mañana.	Let's do it tomorrow.

Lo siento, pero ya tengo otros planes.	I'm sorry, but I already have other plans.
No tengo ganas de + inf.	I don't feel like . . .
¿Por qué no lo dejamos para...?	Why don't we leave it for (another time)?
Tengo mucho que hacer. La próxima vez iré.	I have a lot to do. Next time I'll go.

Review and Assess

Circumlocution

This is a version of the game Twenty Questions. Bring to class pictures of familiar works of art, familiar musical instruments, or both. *(Mona Lisa, Las dos Fridas, piano clarinete)* Have students form two teams. Team A gets one of the pictures. Then, using words from the art vocabulary and other words they know, students from Team B try to find out (in Spanish) what is in the photo. Set a time limit, and insist that only Spanish be spoken until the name or identity of the piece is discovered. Discourage students from asking questions about specific items too soon (e.g., ¿**Es una guitarra?**). At the end of the specified time period, if the guessing team has not succeeded, the other team scores a point and takes a turn at guessing.

Teaching Suggestions

- Write each student's name on a small slip of paper. Then assign a number to each vocabulary word. Place the students' names in one bag or a hat, and the numbers in a second one. Select a name and a number, and have students use the word that was selected in a sentence.
- Challenge students to use the vocabulary words to see who can create the longest logical sentence.

Chapter 6 Assessment

▸ **Testing Program**
Chapter Test, pp. 119–124
 Audio Compact Discs, CD 6, Trs. 20–21

Speaking Test, p. 297

Midterm Exam, pp. 133–140
Score Sheet, pp. 141–143
Listening Scripts, pp. 144–145
Answers, p. 146
 Audio Compact Discs, CD 6, Trs. 22–25

▸ **Alternative Assessment Guide**
Portfolio Assessment, p. 21
Performance Assessment, p. 35
CD-ROM Assessment, p. 49

▸ **Interactive CD-ROM Tutor, Disc 2**
¡A hablar!
¡A escribir!

▸ **Standardized Assessment Tutor**
Chapter 6

▸ **One-Stop Planner, Disc 2**
Test Generator
Chapter 6

Teaching Resources
pp. 186–189

PRINT
▸ Lesson Planner, p. 32
▸ Video Guide, pp. 43–44

MEDIA
▸ One-Stop Planner
▸ Video Program,
  Videocassette 3, 01:12–03:01
▸ Interactive CD-ROM Tutor, Disc 2
▸ Map Transparency 4

 go.hrw.com
WV3 BUENOS AIRES

Using the Almanac and Map

Terms in the Almanac
- **Argentina:** The name *Argentina* comes from the Latin word *argentum,* meaning *silver.* Early Spanish explorers found silver there.
- **Población:** About 90% of all Argentines live in urban areas and 10% in rural areas. The ethnic composition is approximately 85% European, and 15% mestizo (a mixture of Native American and white), Amerindian, or "other."
- **Área:** At 2,360 miles long and 880 miles wide, Argentina is the eighth largest country in the world.
- **Productos agrícolas:** The **Pampas,** fertile plains, make Argentina a leading producer of wheat and beef.
- **Platos típicos: Asado** and **carbonada criolla** are barbecued meat; **alfajores** are snack cakes; **chimichurri** is a sauce; **empanadas** are turnovers; **mate** is a kind of tea; **parrillada** is grilled meat; **pucheros** are stews.

¡Ven conmigo a Buenos Aires!

Argentina

Población: 39.301.755. Buenos Aires: 3.061.858 (zona metropolitana: 9.679.791)

Área: 2.780.400 km², cuatro veces más grande que Texas

Ciudades principales: Buenos Aires, Córdoba, Rosario, Mendoza, La Plata, Tucumán, Mar del Plata

Productos agrícolas: maíz, algodón, uvas, leche, sorgo, trigo, soja, carne de res

Industrias: productos químicos, vehículos, textiles, petróleo, pesca

Personajes famosos: Gabriela Sabatini (n. 1970), tenista; Jorge Luis Borges (1899–1986), escritor; Alberto Ginastera (1916–1983), compositor; José de San Martín (1778–1850), militar y político

Platos típicos: asado, empanadas con chimichurri, carbonada criolla, parrillada, alfajores, pucheros, mate (una bebida)

go.hrw.com
WV3 BUENOS AIRES

Ésta es la Avenida 9 de Julio en Buenos Aires, una de las calles más anchas del mundo. ▶

Cultures and Communities

Background Information
Argentina is the second-largest country in South America in both area and population. Only Brazil is larger. The capital, Buenos Aires, is also the nation's economic and cultural center. It is often called the "Paris of South America" because of its wide boulevards, large parks, and ornate buildings in baroque, roccoco, and neoclassical styles. The main street is Avenida 9 de Julio, named for the date in 1816 on which Argentina's independence from Spain was declared. Inspired by the Champs Élysées in Paris, it is one of the widest streets in the world, measuring 460 feet from sidewalk to sidewalk. In the center of the street is an obelisk built in 1936 to commemorate the 400th anniversary of the founding of Buenos Aires.

MAPQUEST.COM

go.hrw.com

HRW Atlas Interactivo Mundial

Have students use the interactive atlas at **go.hrw.com** to find out more about the geography of Argentina, and complete the Map Activities below.

Map Activities
- Ask students to identify the countries that border Argentina. (Bolivia, Brazil, Chile, Paraguay, Uruguay)
- Have students locate the Río de la Plata. Point out that Buenos Aires lies around this funnel-shaped bay.

CNN enEspañol.com

Have students check the **CNN en español** Web site for news on Argentina. The **CNN en español** site is also a good source of timely, high-interest readings for Spanish students.

ciento ochenta y siete **187**

Connections and Comparisons

Language Note
Lunfardo is spoken by the working class in Buenos Aires. It is a hybrid of languages, and may have originated as street slang. The word **lunfardo** originally meant **ladrón** *(thief)*. **Lunfardo** words may be heard in tango lyrics, and some have become part of Argentine Spanish. Some examples are **cana** (police, prison), **minga** (no, nothing) and **menega** (money).

History Link
Divide students into groups of four and have them research a person who has been an important figure in Argentina's history. (Juan de Garay, Pedro de Mendoza, Juan de Solís, Domingo F. Sarmiento, Juan Manuel de Rosas, Juan Perón, Eva Perón, Raúl Alfonsín)

Motivating Activity

Ask students what they know about the tango. Explain that it is an expressive form of music and dance that probably began as an Argentine dance called the **milonga**, with elements of the Cuban **habanero**. The tango involves alternating long, slow steps with short, quick ones and incorporating elaborate poses. You may want to play some tango music for your students.

Using the Photo Essay

1 La Calle Florida Calle Florida, one of many pedestrian-only zones of the city, is the principal shopping district of Buenos Aires. The thick crowds of people enjoy the folk musicians and street performers or stop and listen to political debates that start up all along the avenue.

2 El Congreso Nacional The Congress building houses the Argentine Senate on the south side and the House of Representatives on the north. In front of the building is the Plaza de los dos Congresos. The plaza honors two "congresses": the 1813 assembly that abolished slavery and the 1816 Congress of Tucumán that declared Argentina's independence.

3 El tango The tango reached its height of popularity in the era before World War II. Although it was at first considered socially unacceptable, it later became widely regarded as elegant and graceful. Carlos Gardel, the first international star singer of tango, helped it gain wide appeal. You may want to mention that tango has become very popular as a ballroom dance throughout the world. In Europe and in the United States, it is often part of dance competitions.

Argentina

El segundo país de Latinoamérica en tamaño, Argentina es una tierra de gran diversidad geográfica, con montañas nevadas, bosques espesos, llanos inmensos y hermosas playas blancas. Su población es única en la América Latina por la proporción de inmigrantes de origen italiano, alemán y de otras culturas no hispanohablantes. El centro cultural del país es Buenos Aires, la capital. Es una ciudad cosmopolita que se considera el París de las Américas.

internet

MARCAR: go.hrw.com
PALABRA CLAVE:
WV3 BUENOS AIRES

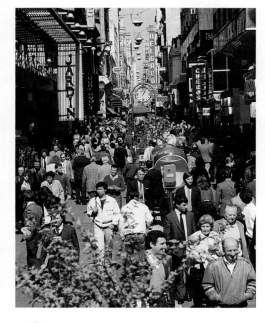

1 La Calle Florida
No importa cuál sea la época del año ni cómo esté el tiempo, los porteños siempre están en las calles, que están llenas de cafés y muchos otros comercios.

2 El Congreso Nacional
En este edificio se reúne el Congreso Argentino.

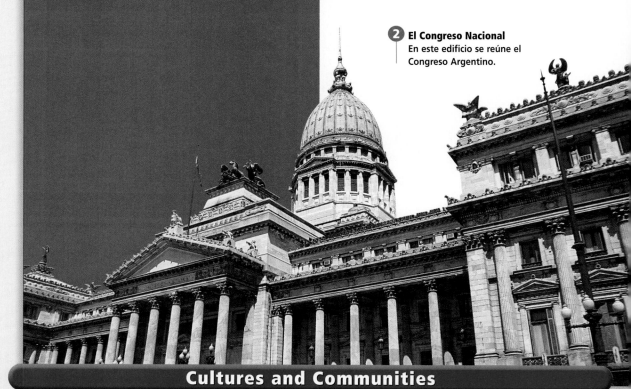

Cultures and Communities

Culture Notes
• José de San Martín was an Argentine general and a leader of the independence movement against Spain. He realized that the independence of the Río de la Plata provinces would never be secure as long as the Spanish still controlled Lima. San Martín and the Chilean patriot Bernardo O'Higgins led an army over a pass in the Andes mountains nearly 15,000 feet high and defeated the Spanish troops in the battle of Chacabuco near Santiago, Chile, on February 12, 1817. He also led an army to Peru and liberated that country in 1821.

• Xul Solar was born Óscar Agustín Alejandro Schulz Solari in San Fernando, Argentina, in 1887. After studying architecture, he traveled to Europe, where he was influenced by such artists as Emilio Pettoruti and Paul Klee.

3 El tango
De Argentina se ha exportado a todo el mundo el tango. Este baile fue en un tiempo censurado y ahora es el símbolo argentino por excelencia.

5 Un símbolo de la independencia argentina
Los parques de Buenos Aires, llenos de estatuas y monumentos históricos, son una de sus atracciones más bellas. Ésta es una estatua de José de San Martín, quien liberó Argentina, Chile y Perú del dominio español.

En los capítulos 7 y 8

vas a aprender un poco de Argentina. Aunque Argentina es todavía la tierra del gaucho tradicional que trabaja en las pampas, es también un país modernísimo con rascacielos y tecnología avanzada. Vas a conocer la vida de la capital y paisajes que incluyen selvas tropicales y las zonas heladas de la Tierra del Fuego.

4 El pato, deporte argentino
Los residentes de Buenos Aires, los porteños, gozan de muchas actividades de recreo, como el pato (arriba) y el polo. Los jugadores de polo tienen ligas bien establecidas y los jugadores llegan a ser famosos.

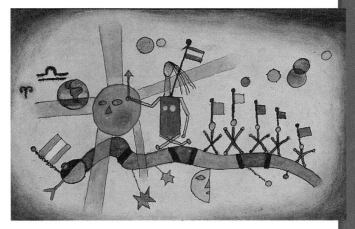

6 Horóscopo, Xul Solar
Uno de los pintores porteños más famosos es Xul Solar. Muchas de sus obras están en el museo de arte que lleva su nombre.

4 El pato, deporte argentino
Polo has become one of the most popular sports in the country. It was introduced to Argentina in the mid-nineteenth century by the British. The British also built much of Argentina's infrastructure, including the rail system. The Anglo-Argentine community has maintained its own ethnic identity. The English-language newspaper *The Buenos Aires Herald* is published daily.

5 Un símbolo de la independencia argentina In Latin American countries, streets are often named for important dates in the country's history and also for famous people. In Quito, Avenida 24 de Mayo is named for Ecuadorean Independence Day and in Buenos Aires, the Avenida 9 de Julio for Argentine Independence Day. Most cities in Argentina have landmarks named in honor of José de San Martín, known as the father of Argentine independence.

6 *Horóscopo,* Xul Solar Xul Solar (1887–1963) was one of Argentina's most prominent painters and an example of its sophistication in the arts. Solar's talents were not limited to painting; he also invented new languages, which he called *neocreol, neocriollo,* and *panlengua.* He attempted to give them visual form in his art during the late 1950s. Three of his paintings, for example, embody the phrase *Lu kene ten lu base nel nergie, sin nergie, lu kene no e kan.* (Knowledge has its base in energy, without energy knowledge is not possible.)

Connections and Comparisons

Literature Link
Jorge Luis Borges was an essayist, poet, and short story writer who brought worldwide attention to Argentine literature with such works as *Fervor de Buenos Aires, poemas* (1923), *Historia universal de la infamia* (1935), *Ficciones* (1938–1944), and *Otras inquisiciones* (1937–1952). In 1961, he and Samuel Beckett shared the prestigious Formentor Prize. You may want to have students read a selection and discuss it.

Multicultural Link
Divide the class into groups of four or five to research the culture and history of one Argentine ethnic group. (Italian, Spanish, English, Jewish, Welsh, Quechua, German, Guaraní, Syrian, Diaguita)

Capítulo 7: Dime con quién andas
Chapter Overview

	FUNCTIONS	GRAMMAR	VOCABULARY	RE-ENTRY
Primer paso pp. 195–199	• Expressing happiness and unhappiness, p. 195 • Comforting someone, p. 199	• The subjunctive with expressions of feelings, p. 196 • Reflexive verbs for reciprocal actions, p. 197 • The present perfect subjunctive, p. 198	• Friendship and love, p. 197	• The use of the infinitive vs. the subjunctive (**Capítulo 5**) • Irregular subjunctive (**Capítulo 5**) • Past participles (**Capítulo 3**)

Segundo paso pp. 203–206	• Making an apology, p. 203 • Describing an ideal relationship, p. 205	• The subjunctive with the unknown or nonexistent, p. 205	• Problems and solutions, p. 203	• Affirmative and negative words (**Capítulo 5, I**) • Subjunctive forms (**Capítulo 5**)

CULTURE

• **Nota cultural,** Latin American use of **vos,** p. 194
• **Nota cultural, Confiterías,** p. 197
• **A lo nuestro,** Responses to proverbs, p. 199
• **Encuentro cultural, La Organización de Estados Americanos,** p. 202

• **Nota cultural,** Movies in Argentina, p. 204
• **Nota cultural,** Sports in Argentina, p. 206
• **Panorama cultural, ¿Has tenido algún conflicto con un(a) amigo(a)?,** p. 207

Capítulo 7: Dime con quién andas
Chapter Resources

PRINT

Lesson Planning

One-Stop Planner

Lesson Planner with Substitute Teacher Lesson Plans, pp. 32–36, 71

Student Make-Up Assignments
- Make-Up Assignment Copying Masters, Chapter 7

Listening and Speaking

Listening Activities
- Student Response Forms for Listening Activities, pp. 51–53
- Additional Listening Activities 7-1 to 7-6, pp. 55–57
- Additional Listening Activities (poem), p. 58
- Scripts and Answers, pp. 132–136

Video Guide
- Teaching Suggestions, pp. 46–47
- Activity Masters, pp. 48–50
- Scripts and Answers, pp. 99–101, 117

Activities for Communication
- Communicative Activities, pp. 25–28
- Realia and Teaching Suggestions, pp. 69–71
- Situation Cards, pp. 101–102

Reading and Writing

Reading Strategies and Skills Handbook, Chapter 7

¡Lee conmigo! 3, Chapter 7

Cuaderno de actividades, pp. 73–84

Grammar

Cuaderno de gramática, pp. 55–63

Grammar Tutor for Students of Spanish, Chapter 7

Assessment

Testing Program
- Grammar and Vocabulary Quizzes, **Paso** Quizzes, and Chapter Test, pp. 147–160
- Score Sheet, Scripts and Answers, pp. 161–167

Alternative Assessment Guide
- Portfolio Assessment, p. 22
- Performance Assessment, p. 36
- CD-ROM Assessment, p. 50

Student Make-Up Assignments
- Alternative Quizzes, Chapter 7

Standardized Assessment Tutor
- Reading, pp. 27–29
- Writing, p. 30
- Math, pp. 51–52

Native Speakers

Cuaderno para hispanohablantes, pp. 31–35

MEDIA

Online Activities
- Juegos interactivos
- Actividades Internet

Video Program
- Videocassette 3
- Videocassette 5 (captioned version)

Audio Compact Discs
- Textbook Listening Activities, CD 7, Tracks 1–21
- Additional Listening Activities, CD 7, Tracks 26–32
- Assessment Items, CD 7, Tracks 22–25

Interactive CD-ROM Tutor, Disc 2

Teaching Transparencies
- Situations 7-1 to 7-2
- **Más práctica gramatical** Answers
- **Cuaderno de gramática** Answers

One-Stop Planner CD-ROM

Use the **One-Stop Planner CD-ROM with Test Generator** to aid in lesson planning and pacing.

For each chapter, the **One-Stop Planner** includes:

- Editable lesson plans with direct links to teaching resources
- Printable worksheets from resource books
- Direct launches to the HRW Internet activities
- Video and audio segments
- Test Generator
- Clip Art for vocabulary items

Capítulo 7: Dime con quién andas

Projects

Tarjetas

In this project, students create greeting cards in Spanish addressing some of the topics in the chapter (expressing happiness, comforting someone, making an apology). As the students work, it may be appropriate to have check points to evaluate grammar, vocabulary, etc. You may want to allow three to five days for students to complete this project.

MATERIALS

✂ **Students may need:**
- Construction paper
- Glue or tape
- Glitter, ribbon, etc.
- Magazine pictures
- Colored markers, paint, or crayons

SUGGESTED SEQUENCE

1. Students design four greeting cards and sketch them on sheets of paper. Monitor their work and answer any questions they may have about the project.

2. Students write their messages. Make sure they include expressions and vocabulary from this chapter.

3. Have students trade cards with another student for peer-editing. Partners check cards for spelling, grammar, and punctuation.

4. Individuals complete their cards with their own artwork or with pictures clipped from magazines and then display them.

GRADING THE PROJECT

Suggested point distribution: (25 points per card; total 100 points):

Correct grammar 10
Creativity of card 5
Neatness 5
Vocabulary 5

Games

Juego de dados

In this game, students work in pairs to practice the forms of the present perfect subjunctive.

Preparation Arrange students in pairs with desks facing each other. Give a pair of differently colored dice to each pair of students. (e.g., one red and one white) Before class, prepare several transparencies similar to the one below, suggesting subjects and verbs as follows:

PRESENT PERFECT SUBJUNCTIVE	
Es imposible que...	
Rojo	Blanco
1. yo	1. comprar
2. nosotros	2. hablar
3. ellos	3. vivir
4. tú	4. comer
5. él	5. dar
6. usted	6. hacer

Procedure Students take turns rolling the dice on their desks. The number on the red die indicates the subject they will use to complete the sentence beginning **Es imposible que...** and the number on the white die indicates the verb for the second half of the sentence. (e.g, **rojo-4** and **blanco-3 = tú hayas vivido.** The student should then complete or embellish the sentence; he or she might say, for example, **Es imposible que tú hayas vivido en la luna.**) The partner checks the answer and then takes his or her turn. You may want to change transparencies every few minutes.

COMMUNITY LINK

If there is a Hispanic neighborhood or community nearby, you may want to have students go to a store and look at greeting cards in Spanish. Have them compare and contrast them to greeting cards in English. How are the cards the same? How are they different? What events are celebrated?

Storytelling

Mini-cuento

This story accompanies Teaching Transparency 7-1. The ***mini-cuento*** *can be told and retold in different formats, acted out, written as dictation, and read aloud to give students additional opportunities to practice all four skills. The following story recounts how two old friends reminisce about their lifetime of friendship.*

Dolores y Victoria se han apoyado toda la vida. La amistad entre las dos ha durado más de 60 años. Se han reunido hoy para celebrar el cumpleaños de Dolores. Desde que se conocieron cuando eran niñas siempre han querido compartir los momentos importantes de sus vidas. Se graduaron juntas del Colegio Simón Bolívar. Hubo muchos momentos felices: cuando hacían excursiones, cuando nacieron sus nietos y cuando visitaron París. Ahora se encuentran contentas y juntas.

Traditions

Los gauchos

Gauchos are the most famous cultural symbols of Argentina, personifying pride, courage, honor, and a love of liberty. The word **gaucho** comes from the Quechua word for "orphan," and in the eighteenth century, the first **gauchos** were **mestizos. Gauchos** live out of doors, sleeping on their **recados,** which are both saddle and bedding. The **gauchos'** diet consists mainly of beef and **mate,** the traditional tea-like drink of Argentina. The **gaucho** can be characterized as a **rastreador,** interpreting imprints left by horses; a **boleador,** who hunts on horseback with **bolas** (three stones covered with leather, attached by long leather cords); or a **gato moro,** running from justice. Have students compare and contrast the customs and cultural significance of **gauchos** and cowboys and present the findings to the class.

Receta

Argentinos *eat more beef per capita than the people of any other country in the world. A very popular cut of beef in Argentina is a rolled, stuffed flank steak, called* ***matambre,*** *which means "hunger killer." This dish can be served hot, as a main course, or cold, as an appetizer.*

MATAMBRE

para 8 personas

1 *flank steak* grande, cortado en una rebanada larga y delgada

1/2 taza de vinagre de vino

1 cucharadita de ajo, picado

1/2 cucharadita de tomillo *(thyme)*

1 cucharadita de sal

1/2 cucharadita de semillas de pimiento rojo

1 manojo de espinaca, bien lavado y sin tallos

2 zanahorias, en juliana fina

2 huevos duros, cortados en 4 tiras

1 cebolla mediana, cortada en rodajas finas

2 cucharadas de perejil, picado

2 cucharadas de aceite

2–3 tazas de caldo de res

Ponga la carne en un recipiente. Aparte, mezcle el vinagre, el ajo y el tomillo y viértalo todo sobre la carne. Deje remojar por 1 hora. Luego espolvoree la carne con la sal y las semillas de pimiento rojo, y cúbrala con las espinacas. Coloque las zanahorias y los huevos en tiras y cubra todo con el perejil y la cebolla. Con cuidado comience a enrollar la carne como un brazo de gitano *(jellyroll)*. Puede reforzarlo con palillos y atarlo todo con hilo. Caliente el aceite en una olla y dore el matambre por todos lados. Agregue el caldo de res, cubra la olla y póngala en el horno a 375°F por 1 1/2 a 2 horas.

Capítulo 7: Dime con quién andas
Technology

Video Program

Videocassette 3, Videocassette 5 (captioned version)
See Video Guide, pages 45–50.

Dramatic episode • ¡Mira, tienes una carta!

Alejandra arrives at the computer center, eager to use the computer to communicate with Sergio. She is annoyed at Carlos for arriving late; however, as soon as Carlos accesses her school's Web site, she gets excited about learning more. She has a message in her mailbox, but Carlos cannot open it without a password. Alejandra calls the assistant, Lola, who is able to open the e-mail. A secret admirer has signed the message. Alejandra assumes right away that it is Sergio and is ecstatic. As for Carlos, he is awestruck by Lola's beauty.

¿Has tenido algún conflicto con un(a) amigo(a)?

People from various Spanish-speaking countries talk about conflicts they have had with friends.

Videoclips

- **Mensajes cívicos:** three public service messages promoting good civic behavior in Antioquia, a region of Colombia
- **No muera la cumbia:** music video about **cumbia,** a form of music and dance popular in Colombia

Interactive CD-ROM Tutor

The **Interactive CD-ROM Tutor** contains videos, interactive games, and activities that provide students an opportunity to practice and review the material covered in Chapter 7.

Activity	Activity Type	Pupil's Edition Page
1. Así se dice	¡Super memoria!	p. 195
2. Gramática	¿Qué falta?	p. 196
3. Gramática	¡Presta el oído!	p. 198
4. Vocabulario	Imagen y sonido ¡Exploremos! ¡Identifiquemos!	p. 203
5. Así se dice	¿Cuál es?	p. 205
6. Gramática	¡A escoger!	p. 205
Panorama cultural	¿Has tenido algún conflicto con un(a) amigo(a)? ¡A escoger!	p. 207
¡A hablar!	*Guided recording*	pp. 216–217
¡A escribir!	*Guided writing*	pp. 216–217

Teacher Management System
Logging In

Logging in to the *¡Ven conmigo!* TMS is easy. Upon launching the program, simply type "admin" in the password area of the log-in screen and press RETURN. Log on to **www.hrw.com/CDROMTUTOR** for a detailed explanation of the Teacher Management System.

One-Stop Planner CD-ROM

To preview all resources available for this chapter, use the **One-Stop Planner CD-ROM**, Disc 2.

Internet Connection

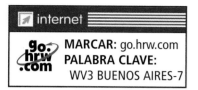

internet

MARCAR: go.hrw.com
PALABRA CLAVE:
WV3 BUENOS AIRES-7

Have students explore the **go.hrw.com** *Web site for many online resources covering all chapters. All Chapter 7 resources are available under the keyword* **WV3 BUENOS AIRES-7**. *Interactive games help students practice the material and provide them with immediate feedback. You will also find a printable worksheet that provides Internet activities that lead to a comprehensive online research project.*

Juegos interactivos

You can use the interactive activities in this chapter

- to practice grammar, vocabulary, and chapter functions
- as homework
- as an assessment option
- as a self-test
- to prepare for the Chapter Test

Actividades Internet

Students look for songs and their lyrics online. They find songs with different themes and messages and write about emotions they feel when listening to the songs.

- To prepare students for the **Hoja de actividades,** have them review the phrases on page 195 for expressing happiness and unhappiness.
- After students have completed the activity sheet, have them write what songs and lyrics remind them of friends and family members, and why.

Proyecto

Ask students to choose a genre of music from a Spanish-speaking region they would like to learn about. For example: Andalusian flamenco, Andean woodwind music, Mexican **campesino** songs, Latin jazz in Miami, Caribbean **son,** or New York salsa. Ask them to post what they learn, including free downloadable images, lyrics, or song clips on a school-sponsored Web site. Remind them to always give credit to the songwriter or musician.

Textbook Listening Activities Scripts

Primer paso

6 p. 195

1. —¡Estoy en la gloria! ¡No lo puedo creer!
   —¿Por qué? ¿Qué pasó?
   —¡Mis papás me compraron un coche en mi cumpleaños! ¿Quieres verlo?
2. —Me alegro de que nos casemos. No puedo esperar el día de la boda.
   —Yo también. Estoy muy contenta.
3. —¿Qué tal, Concha? ¿Estás bien?
   —Me siento frustrada. Trabajo mucho pero la profesora siempre me pone siete en los exámenes de química. ¿Qué me aconsejas hacer?
4. —¡Laura! ¡Mi prima favorita! ¡Me alegro de que estés aquí!
   —¡Gusto de verte, Enrique! Y tú, ¿cómo estás?
5. —¿Recibiste muchas cartas?
   —Sí, una carta de mi primo y otra de un amigo de la Argentina.
   —Estoy desilusionado... nadie me escribe.

Answers to Activity 6
1. b   4. a
2. d   5. c
3. none

11 p. 197

1. ¡Estoy contentísimo! ¡Tuve un malentendido con mi mejor amigo! Ya no nos hablamos.
2. Estoy dolida porque mi hermana ha dejado de hablarme. Era mi mejor amiga. Ahora ¿con quién voy a hablar?
3. ¡Estoy en la gloria! ¡Mi novio y yo vamos a reconciliarnos! No nos vimos durante dos semanas pero ahora estamos más contentos que nunca.
4. Estoy de buenas porque hay rumores sobre mí en la escuela. Me encanta cuando la gente cuenta mentiras sobre mí. Mis mejores amigos lo hacen.
5. Estoy desilusionado porque mi mejor amigo está chismeando sobre mí. Lo consideraba un buen amigo pero ahora veo que no lo es.

Answers to Activity 11
1. ilógica   3. lógica   5. lógica
2. lógica   4. ilógica

13 p. 198

1. Los abuelos no están seguros si van a visitarnos la semana que viene. Espero que vengan. Hace mucho que no los veo.
2. Hace mucho tiempo que Carlos y Reinita no se hablan. Dejaron de hablarse hace un mes. Ojalá que hayan hecho las paces porque quiero invitarlos a la fiesta.
3. Me duele mucho que mis amigos me hayan dejado plantado en el cine. ¿Por qué no pudieron llamarme?
4. El profesor está muy orgulloso de que todos hayamos salido bien en el examen de final de curso.
5. María y José han tenido un malentendido. Esperamos que pronto resuelvan el problema. Son muy buenos amigos y no quiero que se peleen.
6. Mis padres y yo estamos muy decepcionados de que mis hermanos ya no se hablen.

Answers to Activity 13
1. c   4. b
2. d   5. c
3. b   6. a

18 p. 200

1. El tiempo resolverá todo. Espera mucho tiempo antes de discutir el problema. Debes esperar por lo menos dos meses, especialmente si es tu amiga la que tiene la culpa.
2. Si hiciste algo malo, sé adulto y admítelo. Esto te ayudará a hacer las paces con tu amigo.
3. Cálmate bien antes de hablar con tu amiga. Si todavía estás enojada, puedes ofenderla aún más.
4. Toma la mayor parte de la discusión con tus opiniones. No tomes tiempo para escuchar lo que dice tu amigo; lo que él quiere decirte no importa para nada.
5. Si tu amigo viene para discutir el problema, no hables con él. ¿Para qué discutirlo si tú sabes que tienes razón?

Answers to Activity 18
1. no   4. no
2. sí   5. no
3. sí

The following scripts are for the listening activities found in the *Pupil's Edition*. For Student Response Forms, see *Listening Activities*, pages 51–53. To provide students with additional listening practice, see *Listening Activities*, pages 55–58.

One-Stop Planner CD-ROM

To preview all resources available for this chapter, use the **One-Stop Planner CD-ROM**, Disc 2.

Segundo paso

23 p. 203

1. —Estoy muy triste porque mi gatito murió ayer.
   —Mi más sentido pésame. ¿Qué puedo hacer por ti?
2. —Me dijiste una mentira. Somos amigas. ¿Por qué me tratas así?
   —Perdóname, Chely. No lo haré más, te lo prometo.
3. —No me interrumpas cuando estoy hablando. Tú sabes que eso me ofende, Rafael.
   —Discúlpame, no lo volveré a hacer. ¿Qué decías?
4. —¡Rompiste mis anteojos! ¡Ahora no puedo ver y tengo que jugar al tenis esta tarde!
   —Lo hice sin querer, Ana. Lo siento mucho.
5. —Mis padres me han dicho que no puedo salir de casa por un mes entero porque el profesor de historia me puso "cuatro" en el examen.
   —No te preocupes. No hay mal que por cien años dure. Vas a tener más tiempo de estudiar, y todavía podemos hablar por teléfono.

Answers to Activity 23
1. consuelo
2. disculpa
3. disculpa
4. disculpa
5. consuelo

28 p. 206

1. Buscamos a la profesora de idiomas que habla alemán. Dicen que es la mejor profesora de la escuela. ¿Sabes dónde está?
2. Queremos amigos y amigas que sean amables. Preferimos personas que sean honestas y que tengan una personalidad buena.
3. Tengo un primo que vive en tu ciudad. Es alto, moreno y muy guapo y se llama Rafael. ¿Lo conoces?
4. Necesito un amigo que tenga una casa en Hawai porque quiero ir a Hawai este verano y no tengo dinero para un hotel.
5. Busco un novio que venga de Marte. Es importante que sea simpático también.

Answers to Activity 28
1. sí
2. no
3. sí
4. no
5. no

Repaso

1 p. 216

1. Mi perrito Chachi murió anoche. De veras lo consideraba un buen amigo.
2. ¡Mis padres acaban de darme un carro nuevo! No me lo puedo creer. ¿Quieres verlo?
3. ¿Se te perdieron las llaves de mi coche? No te voy a prestar nada más; siempre lo pierdes todo.
4. Lo siento mucho, pero no puedo ir al cine contigo esta noche. Tengo un examen en mi clase de ciencias naturales y tengo que estudiar.
5. No puedo ir a tu fiesta; estoy enfermo y voy a quedarme en casa para dormir. Lo siento mucho.

Answers to Repaso Activity 1
Answers will vary; correct expressions will fall under the following categories:
1. consuelo
2. felicidad
3. desilusión
4. desilusión
5. desilusión or consuelo

Capítulo 7: Dime con quién andas
Suggested Lesson Plans 50-Minute Schedule

Day 1

CHAPTER OPENER 5 min.
- Focusing on Outcomes, ATE, p. 191
- Read the Language and Culture Notes, ATE, p. 191.

DE ANTEMANO 40 min.
- Presenting **De antemano** and Preteaching Vocabulary, ATE, p. 192
- Activities 1–5 and Comprehension Check, ATE, p. 194
- Read **Nota cultural**, p. 194.
- Present Language Note, ATE, p. 194.

Wrap-Up 5 min.
- Ask students to describe the perfect friend.

Homework Options
Cuaderno de actividades, p. 73, Activities 1–2

Day 2

PRIMER PASO
Quick Review 5 min.
- Check homework.
- Bell Work, ATE, p. 195

Así se dice, p. 195 25 min.
- Presenting **Así se dice**, ATE, p. 195
- Do Activity 6 with the Audio CD, p. 195.
- Do Activity 7, p. 195.

Gramática, p. 196 15 min.
- Presenting **Gramática**, ATE, p. 196
- Do Activity 8, p. 196.

Wrap-Up 5 min.
- Do the Auditory and Visual Learners Activities, ATE, p. 196.

Homework Options
Cuaderno de actividades, pp. 75–76, Activities 5–6
Cuaderno de gramática, pp. 55–56, Activities 1–2, 4

Day 3

PRIMER PASO
Quick Review 5 min.
- Check homework.
- Follow the Vocabulary Practice Suggestion for Teaching Transparency 7-1.

Gramática, p. 196 15 min.
- Have students do Activity 9 in pairs, p. 196.
- Review **¿Te acuerdas?**, p. 196.
- Do Activity 3, p. 56, in Cuaderno de gramática.
- Do Activity 10, p. 197.

Vocabulario/Nota gramatical, p. 197 25 min.
- Presenting **Vocabulario** and **Nota gramatical**, ATE, p. 197
- Do Activity 11 with the Audio CD, p. 197.
- Do Activity 12, p. 198.
- Read and discuss **Nota cultural**, p. 197.
- Present Culture Note, ATE, p. 197.

Wrap-Up 5 min.
- Follow Teaching Suggestion 4 for Teaching Transparency 7-1.

Homework Options
Cuaderno de actividades, pp. 74, 76, Activities 3–4, 7–8
Cuaderno de gramática, pp. 56–58, Activities 5–9

Day 4

PRIMER PASO
Quick Review 5 min.
- Check homework.

Gramática, p. 198 25 min.
- Presenting **Gramática**, ATE, p. 198
- Do Activity 13 with the Audio CD, p. 198.
- Do Slower Pace or Challenge Activity, ATE, p. 198.
- Have students do Activity 14 in pairs, p. 199.

Así se dice, p. 199 15 min.
- Presenting **Así se dice**, ATE, p. 199
- Present **A lo nuestro**, p. 199.
- Do Activity 15, p. 199.

Wrap-Up 5 min.
- Do Additional Practice for Activity 14, ATE, p. 199.

Homework Options
Cuaderno de actividades, p. 77, Activities 9–10
Cuaderno de gramática, pp. 58–59, Activities 10–12

Day 5

PRIMER PASO
Quick Review 5 min.
- Check homework.
- Review **Así se dice** expressions, p. 199.

Así se dice, p. 199 20 min.
- Have students do Activity 16 in groups, p. 199.
- Have students do Activity 17, then peer-edit, p. 199.

¡ADELANTE! 20 min.
- Presenting **¡Adelante!** and Preteaching Vocabulary, ATE, p. 200
- Do Activities 18–22, pp. 200–201.

Wrap-Up 5 min.
- Do the Auditory Learners Activity, ATE, p. 201.
- Discuss the content and format of Quiz 7-1.

Homework Options
Study for Quiz 7-1.
Cuaderno de actividades, p. 78, Activities 11–12

Day 6

PRIMER PASO
Quick Review 10 min.
- Check homework.
- Review the content of **Primer paso.**

Quiz 20 min.
- Administer Quiz 7-1A, 7-1B, or a combination of the two.

SEGUNDO PASO
Así se dice/Vocabulario, p. 203 15 min.
- Presenting **Así se dice** and **Vocabulario**, ATE, p. 203

Wrap-Up 5 min.
- Have students make apologies for different situations.

Homework Options
Cuaderno de actividades, p. 79, Activities 13–14
Cuaderno de gramática, p. 60, Activities 13–14

One-Stop Planner CD-ROM

For alternative lesson plans by chapter section, to create your own customized plans, or to preview all resources available for this chapter, use the **One-Stop Planner CD-ROM**, Disc 2.

 For additional homework suggestions, see activities accompanied by this symbol throughout the chapter.

Day 7

SEGUNDO PASO

Quick Review 5 min.
- Check homework.

Así se dice/Vocabulario, p. 203 30 min.
- Do Activity 23 with the Audio CD, p. 203.
- Do Activities 24–25, p. 204.
- Have students do Activity 26 in pairs, p. 204.
- Read and discuss **Nota cultural,** p. 204.
- Do the Native Speakers or Kinesthetic/Visual Learners Activities, ATE, p. 204.

ENCUENTRO CULTURAL 10 min.
- Presenting **Encuentro cultural,** ATE, p. 202
- Present Culture Note and Background Information, ATE, p. 202.

Wrap-Up 5 min.
- Follow Vocabulary Practice Suggestion 2 for Teaching Transparency 7-2.

Homework Options
Cuaderno de actividades, pp. 80–81, Activities 15–16

Day 8

SEGUNDO PASO

Quick Review 5 min.
- Check homework.
- Follow Teaching Suggestion 3 for Teaching Transparency 7-2.

Así se dice/Gramática, p. 205 40 min.
- Presenting **Así se dice** and **Gramática,** ATE, p. 205
- Present Language-to-Language, ATE, p. 205.
- Do Activity 27, p. 205.
- Do Activity 28 with the Audio CD, p. 206.
- Have students do Activity 29 in pairs, p. 206.
- Do Activity 30, p. 206.

Wrap-Up 5 min.
- Have students state something they want, need, or are looking for.

Homework Options
Cuaderno de actividades, pp. 81–82, Activities 17–20
Cuaderno de gramática, pp. 61–63, Activities 15–20

Day 9

SEGUNDO PASO

Quick Review 10 min.
- Check homework.

Gramática, p. 205 25 min.
- Have students do Activity 31 in groups, p. 206.
- Have students do Activity 32, then peer-edit their work, p. 206.
- Read **Nota cultural,** p. 206.
- Present Culture Note, ATE, p. 206.

PANORAMA CULTURAL 10 min.
- Presenting **Panorama cultural,** ATE, p. 207

Wrap-Up 5 min.
- Discuss the content and format of Quiz 7-2.

Homework Options
Study for Quiz 7-2.

Day 10

SEGUNDO PASO

Quick Review 5 min.
- Review the content of **Segundo paso.**

Quiz 20 min.
- Administer Quiz 7-2A, 7-2B, or a combination of the two.

VAMOS A LEER 20 min.
- Do Activity A, p. 208.
- Read **¿Te acuerdas?,** p. 208, then have students do Activity B in pairs, p. 209.

Wrap-Up 5 min.
- Present Literature Link, ATE, p. 208.
- Present Language and Culture Notes, ATE, p. 210.

Homework Options
Repaso Activities 5–6, pp. 216–217
Cuaderno de actividades, pp. 83–84, Activities 21–25

Day 11

REPASO

Quick Review 10 min.
- Check and discuss homework.

VAMOS A LEER 20 min.
- Do Activities C–E, pp. 209–210.

REPASO 15 min.
- List the concepts studied in Chapter 7.
- Do Activity 1 with the Audio CD, p. 216.
- Have students do Activities 3 and 7 in pairs, pp. 216–217.

Wrap-Up 5 min.
- Play **Carreras,** ATE, p. 219.

Homework Options
Vamos a escribir, p. 211
Repaso Activities 2 and 4, p. 216
A ver si puedo..., p. 218

Day 12

REPASO

Quick Review 10 min.
- Check and/or collect homework.
- Do Activity 8 in pairs, p. 217.

Chapter Review 35 min.
- Review Chapter 7. Choose from **Más práctica gramatical,** Grammar Tutor for Students of Spanish, Activities for Communication, Listening Activities, Interactive CD-ROM Tutor, or **Juegos interactivos.**

Wrap-Up 5 min.
- Discuss the format of the Chapter 7 Test.

Homework Options
Study for the Chapter 7 Test.

Assessment

Quick Review 5 min.
- Answer any last-minute questions.

Test, Chapter 7 45 min.
- Administer Chapter 7 Test. Select from Testing Program, Alternative Assessment Guide, Test Generator, or Standardized Assessment Tutor.

Capítulo 7: Dime con quién andas
Suggested Lesson Plans *90-Minute Block Schedule*

Block 1

CHAPTER OPENER 5 min.
- Focusing on Outcomes, ATE, p. 191
- Read Language and Culture Notes, ATE, p. 191.

DE ANTEMANO 40 min.
- Presenting **De antemano** and Preteaching Vocabulary, ATE, p. 192
- Activities 1–5 and Comprehension Check, ATE, p. 194
- Read **Nota cultural**, p. 194.
- Present Language Note, ATE, p. 194.

PRIMER PASO
Así se dice, p. 195 25 min.
- Presenting **Así se dice**, ATE, p. 195
- Do Activity 6 with the Audio CD, p. 195.
- Do Activity 7, p. 195.

Gramática, p. 196 15 min.
- Presenting **Gramática**, ATE, p. 196
- Do Activity 8, p. 196.

Wrap-Up 5 min.
- Do the Auditory and Visual Learners activities, ATE, p. 196.

Homework Options
Cuaderno de actividades, pp. 73–76, Activities 1–2, 5–6
Cuaderno de gramática, pp. 55–56, Activities 1–2, 4

Block 2

PRIMER PASO
Quick Review 10 min.
- Check homework.
- Follow the Vocabulary Practice Suggestion for Teaching Transparency 7-1.

Gramática, p. 196 15 min.
- Have students do Activity 9 in pairs, p. 196.
- Review **¿Te acuerdas?**, p. 196.
- Do Activity 3, p. 56, in Cuaderno de gramática.
- Do Activity 10, p. 197.

Vocabulario/Nota gramatical, p. 197 30 min.
- Presenting **Vocabulario** and **Nota gramatical**, ATE, p. 197
- Do Activity 11 with the Audio CD, p. 197.
- Do Activity 12, p. 198.
- Read and discuss **Nota cultural**, p. 197.
- Present Culture Note, ATE, p. 197.

Gramática, p. 198 25 min.
- Presenting **Gramática**, ATE, p. 198
- Do Activity 13 with the Audio CD, p. 198.
- Do Slower Pace or Challenge activity, ATE, p. 198.
- Have students do Activity 14 in pairs, p. 199.

Wrap-Up 10 min.
- Follow Teaching Suggestion 4 for Teaching Transparency 7-1.
- Do the Additional Practice for Activity 14, ATE, p. 199.

Homework Options
Cuaderno de actividades, pp. 74, 76–77, Activities 3–4, 7–9
Cuaderno de gramática, pp. 56–59, Activities 5–12

Block 3

PRIMER PASO
Quick Review 10 min.
- Check homework.

Así se dice, p. 199 35 min.
- Presenting **Así se dice**, ATE, p. 199
- Present **A lo nuestro**, p. 199.
- Do Activity 15, p. 199.
- Have students do Activity 16 in groups, p. 199.
- Have students do Activity 17, then peer-edit, p. 199.

¡ADELANTE! 25 min.
- Presenting **¡Adelante!** and Preteaching Vocabulary, ATE, p. 200
- Do Activities 18–22, pp. 200–201.

ENCUENTRO CULTURAL 10 min.
- Presenting **Encuentro cultural**, ATE, p. 202
- Present Culture Note and Background Information, ATE, p. 202.

Wrap-Up 10 min.
- Have students suggest solutions for various problems.
- Discuss the content and format of Quiz 7-1.

Homework Options
Study for Quiz 7-1.
Cuaderno de actividades, pp. 77–78, Activities 10–12

One-Stop Planner CD-ROM

For alternative lesson plans by chapter section, to create your own customized plans, or to preview all resources available for this chapter, use the **One-Stop Planner CD-ROM**, Disc 2.

For additional homework suggestions, see activities accompanied by this symbol throughout the chapter.

Block 4

PRIMER PASO
Quick Review 10 min.
- Check homework.
- Review the content of **Primer paso**.

Quiz 20 min.
- Administer Quiz 7-1A, 7-1B, or a combination of the two.

SEGUNDO PASO
Así se dice/Vocabulario, p. 203 50 min.
- Presenting **Así se dice** and **Vocabulario**, ATE, p. 203
- Present **También se puede decir,** p. 203.
- Do Activity 23 with the Audio CD, p. 203.
- Do Activities 24–25, p. 204.
- Have students do Activity 26 in pairs, p. 204.
- Read and discuss **Nota cultural,** p. 204.

Wrap-Up 10 min.
- Have students make apologies in different situations.
- Follow Vocabulary Practice Suggestion 2 for Teaching Transparency 7-2.

Homework Options
Cuaderno de actividades, pp. 79–81, Activities 13–16
Cuaderno de gramática, p. 60, Activities 13–14

Block 5

SEGUNDO PASO
Quick Review 10 min.
- Check homework.
- Follow Teaching Suggestion 3 for Teaching Transparency 7-2.

Así se dice/Gramática, p. 205 60 min.
- Presenting **Así se dice** and **Gramática**, ATE, p. 205
- Present Language-to-Language, ATE, p. 205.
- Do Activity 27, p. 205.
- Do Activity 28 with the Audio CD, p. 206.
- Have students do Activity 29 in pairs, p. 206.
- Do Activity 30, p. 206.
- Have students do Activity 31 in groups, p. 206.
- Have students do Activity 32, then peer-edit, p. 206.
- Read **Nota cultural,** p. 206.
- Present Culture Note, ATE, p. 206.

PANORAMA CULTURAL 15 min.
- Presenting **Panorama cultural,** ATE, p. 207

Wrap-Up 5 min.
- Discuss the content and format of Quiz 7-2.

Homework Options
Study for Quiz 7-2.
Cuaderno de actividades, pp. 81–82, Activities 17–20
Cuaderno de gramática, pp. 61–63, Activities 15–20

Block 6

SEGUNDO PASO
Quick Review 10 min.
- Check homework.
- Review the content of **Segundo paso**.

Quiz 20 min.
- Administer Quiz 7-2A, 7-2B, or a combination of the two.

VAMOS A LEER 40 min.
- Do Activity A, p. 208.
- Present Literature Link, ATE, p. 208.
- Read **¿Te acuerdas?,** p. 208, then have students do Activity B, in pairs, p. 209.
- Do Activities C–F, pp. 209–210.

REPASO 15 min.
- List the concepts studied in Chapter 7.
- Do Activity 1 with the Audio CD, p. 216.
- Have students do Activities 3 and 7 in pairs, pp. 216–217.

Wrap-Up 5 min.
- Discuss the content and format of the Chapter 7 Test.

Homework Options
Study for the Chapter 7 Test.
Assign **Vamos a escribir,** p. 211.
Assign **Repaso** Activities 4–6, pp. 216–217.
A ver si puedo..., p. 218

Block 7

REPASO
Quick Review 10 min.
- Check and/or collect homework.
- Do Activity 8 in pairs, p. 217.

Chapter Review 35 min.
- Review Chapter 7. Choose from **Más práctica gramatical,** Grammar Tutor for Students of Spanish, Activities for Communication, Listening Activities, Interactive CD-ROM Tutor, or **Juegos interactivos.**

Test, Chapter 7 45 min.
- Administer Chapter 7 Test. Select from Testing Program, Alternative Assessment Guide, Test Generator, or Standardized Assessment Tutor.

CAPÍTULO 7

One-Stop Planner CD-ROM

For resource information, see the **One-Stop Planner,** Disc 2.

Pacing Tips

Primer paso contains the bulk of the chapter vocabulary and an introduction to the subjunctive. You may want to allot extra time for student practice using activities that require students to identify the subjunctive form and then apply it in a similar context. For instance, combine the Calvin and Hobbes comic strip (p.198) and Activity 13 (p.198). For lesson plans and timing suggestions, see pages 189I–189L.

Meeting the Standards

Communication
- Expressing happiness and unhappiness, p. 195
- Comforting someone, p. 199
- Making an apology, p. 203
- Describing an ideal relationship, p. 205

Cultures
- Background Information, p. 186
- Culture Notes, pp. 188, 191, 202, 206
- Language Notes, pp. 191, 194, 195
- Nota cultural, pp. 197, 204

Connections
- History Link, p. 187
- Literature Links, pp. 189, 193

Comparisons
- Multicultural Links, pp. 189, 190
- Nota cultural, pp. 194, 206
- Language-to-Language, p. 205
- Panorama cultural, p. 207

Communities
- Career Path, p. 202

Connections and Comparisons

Multicultural Link

The majority of people who live in Buenos Aires are of European descent. In the second half of the 19th century, European immigrants settled in Argentina in large numbers. Today, people of Italian descent make up the largest ethnic group in Buenos Aires. Have students research immigration to the United States and compare it with immigration to Argentina. What ethnic groups came to the two countries? When and why did they come? Where did they settle? What are each country's attitudes toward ethnic diversity?

CAPÍTULO

7

Dime con quién andas

Objectives

In this chapter you will learn to

Primer paso

- **express happiness and unhappiness**
- **comfort someone**

Segundo paso

- **make an apology**
- **describe an ideal relationship**

 internet

 go. hrw .com

MARCAR: go.hrw.com
PALABRA CLAVE:
WV3 BUENOS AIRES-7

◀ **Estamos en la gloria porque hemos ganado el campeonato. Siempre podemos contar con nuestros compañeros.**

CAPÍTULO 7

Photo Flash!
In Latin America, soccer plays a central role in many young people's lives. Winning is important, but just being a part of the sport is a source of great satisfaction and national pride.

Focusing on Outcomes
In this chapter, students will acquire the language shared in close relationships and be able to communicate their feelings. By the end of the chapter, students will be able to express emotions of happiness, unhappiness, consolation, and apology.

Cultures and Communities

Language Notes
- Spanish is the official language of Argentina, but it is not the only common language in Buenos Aires. Since there is such a large population of Anglo-Argentines, English is common. The city has a dozen community newspapers published in languages other than Spanish.
- Several languages are spoken by the Argentine

indigenous people: Guaraní, Quechua, Aymara, and Tehuelche, to name a few.

 Culture Note
People who live in Buenos Aires are known as **porteños.** That is because Buenos Aires is the main port in Argentina and a major world port. It is on the Río de la Plata estuary, where the river meets the Atlantic Ocean.

Teaching Resources
pp. 192–194

PRINT
▸ Lesson Planner, p. 33
▸ Video Guide, pp. 45–46, 48
▸ Cuaderno de actividades, p. 73

MEDIA
▸ One-Stop Planner
▸ Video Program
  Contigo en la distancia
  Videocassette 3, 03:02–09:03
  Videocassette 5 (captioned
  version), 33:12–39:14
▸ Audio Compact Discs, CD 7,
  Trs. 1–7

Presenting
De antemano

Have students identify phrases that describe friendship. Then play the Audio CD and have students listen for the phrases they listed. Next, present the Preteaching Vocabulary.

DE ANTEMANO · *Las amistades*

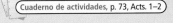
Cuaderno de actividades, p. 73, Acts. 1–2

CD 7
Trs. 1–7

Estrategia para comprender
El escritor escocés Robert Louis Stevenson dijo que "un amigo es el mejor regalo que nos hacemos a nosotros mismos". Un(a) amigo(a) puede traernos mucha felicidad y puede enseñarnos mucho. Para conservar una buena amistad, hay varias cosas que debes tener en cuenta:

Aprovecha los medios de comunicación. Deja mensajes amables y graciosos en las contestadoras de tus amigos y amigas. También el sistema de FAX te permite decir a los amigos y amigas que no ves con frecuencia que estás pensando en ellos.

Escribe a tus amigos y amigas siempre que puedas. No necesitan ser largas cartas. Pero si no puedes ver a tus amigos y amigas con la frecuencia que quisieras, mantén viva la relación enviándoles de vez en cuando notitas, tarjetas o simples pensamientos que se te ocurran.

Señala ciertos momentos en tu agenda para tus amigos y amigas. Pueden ser quince para una llamada telefónica, media tarde para tomar un refresco, o una mañana en un club o gimnasio para hacer ejercicio juntos.

Mantente objetivo(a). Tendemos a pensar primero en cómo las decisiones de nuestros amigos y amigas afectarán nuestra propia vida. Pero éstos son momentos en que nuestros amigos y amigas necesitan apoyo, no juicios críticos. A veces ésa es la mejor ayuda que puedes ofrecerles.

" Chely, habla Miguel. Estoy tan contento, no te lo vas a creer. ¡El profe me puso 10 en el examen de biología! ¡Estoy en la gloria! ¡Llámame! "

Preteaching Vocabulary

Identifying Keywords
First ask students to guess the context of **De antemano.** (preserving friendships) Then have them scan the notes to find specific suggestions about how to be a good friend. Students may identify such phrases as: **Deja mensajes amables y graciosos en las contestadoras...; Señala ciertos momentos en tu agenda...; Mantente objectivo(a).; Escribe a tus amigos y amigas...;** **Conmemora días especiales.; Ten una agenda con los cumpleaños y fechas importantes...; Hazles saber que los recuerdas...; Escucha con paciencia...; Ofrécele tu consejo...** Then have students look at the notes. Which of these suggestions do the note writers seem to be following?

"Tu amistad es para mí un tesoro."

MARZO

19
Cumpleaños-
Elena

20
Aniversario-
abuelos

Conmemora días especiales. Ten una agenda con los cumpleaños y fechas importantes de tus mejores amigos y amigas. Hazles saber que los recuerdas con una llamada telefónica, un arreglo de flores, una tarjeta postal, un telegrama o un pequeño regalo gracioso.

Cuando un(a) amigo(a) esté en crisis, de cualquier tipo, está dispuesto(a) a ayudar. Escucha con paciencia, ante todo. Ofrécele tu consejo... si te lo pide. Ofrécele tu ayuda... si la necesita. Pero bríndale siempre tu presencia y tu tiempo.

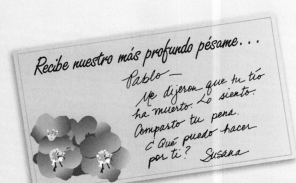

Recibe nuestro más profundo pésame...

Pablo—
Me dijeron que tu tío ha muerto. Lo siento. Comparto tu pena. ¿Qué puedo hacer por ti? Susana

REMY—
ME SIENTO FRUSTRADO CON CARLOTA. PENSABA QUE ERA BUENA AMIGA... PERO TUVO UNA FIESTA Y NO ME INVITÓ. ESTOY DOLIDO Y NO QUIERO HABLAR CON ELLA.
TOÑO

DE ANTEMANO

CAPÍTULO 7

Auditory Learners
You may want to use the phone message or one of the paragraphs as a dictation. Play the recording through once, then play it again in smaller portions and have students write it. Then play the whole passage a third time for students to correct their work.

Literature Link
Born in 1850, Robert Louis Stevenson wrote several novels and short stories that have been translated into many languages: *Treasure Island* (*La isla del tesoro*), 1881; *The Strange Case of Dr. Jekyll and Mr. Hyde* (*El extraño caso del doctor Jekyll y de Mr. Hyde*), 1886; and *Kidnapped* (*Secuestrado*), 1886. Perhaps the best known of Stevenson's translators was the Argentine writer Jorge Luis Borges.

Visual Learners
Have students write emotion words on index cards. (**triste, alegre, preocupado**) Then have them draw or paste pictures clipped from magazines reflecting the emotion on the card. Read aloud several sentences from **De antemano** and have students hold up one of the cards describing how they would feel in that situation.

 Contigo en la distancia
You may choose to continue with **Episodio 7:** *¡Mira, tienes una carta!* Alejandra arrives at the computer center. As soon as Carlos accesses her school's Web site, she becomes excited to learn more. She has a message in her mailbox, but Carlos cannot open it without a password. Alejandra calls the assistant, Lola, who is able to open the e-mail.

CAPÍTULO 7

Additional Practice

1 Have students explain their answers by citing the appropriate phrase or sentence from **De antemano.**

Language Note

In Argentina, Uruguay, Paraguay, Central America, and the Mexican state of Chiapas, **vos** is used to replace **tú.** This practice is called **voseo.** There is regional variation in the conjugation of **vos** forms. In Argentina the present tense forms of **tomar, tener,** and **vivir** are **tomás, tenés,** and **vivís;** the present subjunctive, **tomés, tengás, vivás;** the imperative, **tomá, tené, viví;** and the preterite, **tomaste, tuviste, viviste.**

Answers

1 1. falsa; Miguel sacó una nota muy buena.
2. falsa; La nota "10" es muy buena.
3. falsa; Toño se siente frustrado porque Carlota no lo invitó a su fiesta.
4. cierta
5. falsa; Susana le manda una tarjeta de pésame a Pablo.

3 *Possible answers:*
1. Escríbeles cartas o tarjetas para mantenerte en contacto.
2. Respeta las decisiones de tus amigos y acuérdate que se pueden ver durante las vacaciones.
3. Escribe en el calendario las fechas importantes y nunca te olvidarás de ellas.
4. Debes estar siempre dispuesto a oír y darles apoyo a tus amigos.

These activities check for comprehension only. Students should not yet be expected to produce language modeled in **De antemano.**

1 **¿Cierto o falso?** See answers below.

Indica si cada oración es **cierta** o **falsa.** Si es falsa, corrígela.
1. Miguel está feliz porque Chely sacó una nota muy buena.
2. La nota "10" es muy mala para Miguel.
3. Remy está triste porque Toño no le escribe.
4. Toño le escribe a Remy porque está triste.
5. Susana le manda una tarjeta a Pablo para su cumpleaños.

2 **¿Qué palabras usan?**

¿Qué expresiones usa...?

1. Miguel para decir que está feliz Estoy tan contento, estoy en la gloria.
2. Toño para decir que no le gusta lo que le hizo Carlota Estoy dolido.
3. Susana para hacer a su amigo sentirse mejor Lo siento, comparto tu pena.

3 **Consejos para amigos** See possible answers below.

¿Qué consejos les das a las siguientes personas?
1. Jaime no tiene mucho tiempo para hablar con sus amigos.
2. Rosa está triste porque su mejor amiga quiere estudiar en otra ciudad.
3. Natalia siempre se olvida de los cumpleaños de sus amigos.
4. Los papás de un amigo de Hernán se divorciaron y su amigo está triste.

4 **Diálogos** Answers will vary.

 Con un(a) compañero(a), prepara un diálogo en el que Remy le dice a Carlota que Toño está triste y por qué. Luego Remy le da unos consejos a Carlota sobre cómo ser una mejor amiga.

5 **Ahora te toca a ti**

 Escribe en un párrafo lo que consideras importante en tus amistades y algunas cosas que haces para mantenerlas. Usa frases como **Es necesario que mis amigos(as)...** y **Quiero que mis compañeros(as)...**

Nota cultural

Los argentinos y muchos otros latinoamericanos usan **vos** en lugar de **tú.** Las formas del verbo que se usan con **vos** son diferentes también. Por ejemplo, "¿Vos hablás español?" significa "¿Hablas tú español?" y "Decime la verdad" significa "Dime la verdad". ¿Qué significan las oraciones siguientes? "Vos bebés mate, ¿no?" "¿Vos escribís muchas cartas?" "Sentate aquí, por favor."

Comprehension Check

Group Work

3 Ask pairs or groups of students to write a short dialogue to fit a situation. Have each group act out one of the situations.

Challenge

4 You may want to have students choose between this situation and one of the following for their dialogues: **Chely llama a Miguel** para contestar su recado; una "conversación" entre dos personas que dejan recado tras recado en los contestadores; una llamada telefónica a una amiga que no has visto desde hace mucho tiempo.

Challenge

5 Ask students to write a short public service announcement about friendships.

Así se dice

Expressing happiness and unhappiness

CD-ROM DISC 2

Cuando estás feliz, puedes decir:

Estoy contento(a).
Estoy de buen humor.
  I'm in a good mood.
Estoy encantado(a) que puedas venir.
  I'm delighted that . . .
¡Estoy en la gloria!
  I'm in heaven!
Estoy orgulloso(a) de mi hija
  . . . proud of . . .
Me alegro que tu tío esté mejor.
Me encanta que haya venido mi prima.
  I'm delighted that . . .

Cuando las cosas van mal, puedes decir:

Estoy decepcionado(a)/desilusionado(a).
  I'm disappointed.
Temo que mi amigo se enoje conmigo.
  I'm afraid my friend will be angry with me.
Estoy dolido(a).
  I'm hurt.
Me dan ganas de llorar.
  It makes me feel like crying.
Me duele mucho que Emilia no me hable.
  It really hurts me that . . .
Me frustra que mis amigos no me hayan llamado.
Me siento frustrado(a).

Cuaderno de actividades, p. 75, Act. 5

6 **¡Qué alegría!** Script and answers on p. 189G.

CD 7
Tr. 8

Escuchemos Escucha los siguientes diálogos e indica qué foto corresponde a cada diálogo. Hay un diálogo que no corresponde a ninguna foto.

a.   b.   c.   d.

7 **¿Estás contento(a)?**

Leamos/Hablemos ¿Cómo te sientes si...?

1. un(a) amigo(a) no te saluda antes de las clases   estoy dolido(a)
2. un(a) buen(a) amigo(a) de otra ciudad viene a visitarte hoy   estoy contento(a)
3. tu novio(a) te invita a cenar pero no viene al restaurante   estoy desilusionado(a)
4. haces las paces con alguien después de un conflicto   estoy de buen humor
5. el (la) director(a) anuncia que eres el (la) mejor estudiante del año en tu colegio   estoy en la gloria

Cultures and Communities

Language Notes

• In addition to **dolido(a)** to express feeling hurt, one can say **ofendido(a),** especially to refer to hurt feelings.

• Another way to say you are disappointed is **me siento defraudado(a). Sufrir un desengaño amoroso** is *to be disappointed in love.*

• There are various words in Spanish for angry, including **enfadado(a), enfurecido(a),** and **rabioso(a).** The latter two words have a stronger emotional impact, meaning *really furious.*

Teaching Resources
pp. 195–199

PRINT
▶ Lesson Planner, p. 33
▶ Listening Activities, pp. 51–52, 55–56
▶ Activities for Communication, pp. 25–26, 69, 71, 101–102
▶ Cuaderno de gramática, pp. 55–59
▶ Grammar Tutor for Students of Spanish, Chapter 7
▶ Cuaderno de actividades, pp. 74–77
▶ Cuaderno para hispanohablantes, pp. 31–35
▶ Testing Program, pp. 147–150
▶ Alternative Assessment Guide, p. 36
▶ Student Make-Up Assignments, Chapter 7

MEDIA
▶ One-Stop Planner
▶ Audio Compact Discs, CD 7, Trs. 8–10, 26–28, 22
▶ Teaching Transparencies 7-1; **Más práctica gramatical** Answers; Cuaderno de gramática Answers
▶ Interactive CD-ROM Tutor, Disc 2

Bell Work
Write: **¿Qué cosas te hacen sentir feliz? ¿triste? ¿orgulloso(a)?** Ask volunteers to compile answers on the board under the headings **Feliz, Triste,** and **Orgulloso.**

Presenting
Así se dice
Before class, write on a transparency a letter to an advice columnist in which you use as many expressions as possible from **Así se dice.** Use other new expressions in a reply. Read the two letters to students.

Teaching Resources
pp. 195–199

PRINT 📖
▶ Lesson Planner, p. 33
▶ Listening Activities, pp. 51–52, 55–56
▶ Activities for Communication, pp. 25–26, 69, 71, 101–102
▶ Cuaderno de gramática, pp. 55–59
▶ Grammar Tutor for Students of Spanish, Chapter 7
▶ Cuaderno de actividades, pp. 74–77
▶ Cuaderno para hispanohablantes, pp. 31–35
▶ Testing Program, pp. 147–150
▶ Alternative Assessment Guide, p. 36
▶ Student Make-Up Assignments, Chapter 7

MEDIA
▶ One-Stop Planner
▶ Audio Compact Discs, CD 7, Trs. 8–10, 26–28, 22
▶ Teaching Transparencies 7-1; **Más práctica gramatical** Answers; Cuaderno de gramática Answers
▶ Interactive CD-ROM Tutor, Disc 2

Presenting
Gramática

Subjunctive with expressions of feelings

Write expressions of feelings on the board. **(Me alegro...)** Complete them with both the infinitive and subjunctive. **(Me alegro de estar aquí contigo. Me alegro que estés aquí conmigo.)**

Sample answers:
8 1. Me alegro mucho que mi padre cocine la cena.
2. Me duele mucho que mi novia me deje por otro.
3. Me frustra mucho que no vivamos en una casa bonita.

Gramática

The subjunctive with expressions of feelings

1. Spanish speakers use the subjunctive after verbs and expressions that convey feelings, such as **alegrarse que, sentir que, temer que, ojalá que,** and **es triste que.**

   Me alegro que mis amigos **puedan** estar unos días aquí.
   Tememos que María **se enferme**.
   ¡Ojalá que Ricardo no **llegue** tarde!

2. A change of subject after a verb that conveys feelings is shown by **que.** If there isn't a change of subject, the infinitive is normally used.

   Siento **que tengas** que trabajar hoy.
   Me alegro de **pasar** unos días aquí.
   Es triste **estar** solo en días especiales.

   Cuaderno de actividades, pp. 75–76, Act. 6
   Más práctica gramatical, pp. 212–213, Acts. 1–2
   Cuaderno de gramática, p. 55, Acts. 1–2

8 **Gramática en contexto** See sample answers below.

Escribamos Usa las expresiones para desarrollar una oración. Combina una frase que expresa sentimiento con una frase que describe la situación.

irregular subjunctive
¿Se te ha olvidado?
Ver la página R38

MODELO
> tú / tener una entrada para el concierto
> Me alegro muchísimo que tengas una entrada para el concierto.

1. Me alegro — mi padre / cocinar la cena
2. Me duele — mi novia / dejarme por otro
3. Me frustra — nosotros / vivir en una casa bonita
4. Me encanta — Rafaela / vivir sola
5. Estoy orgulloso(a) — los amigos de Rómulo / no hablarle
6. Estoy contento(a) — tú / pensar estudiar con nosotros
7. Temo — llover durante la boda de Mariana
8. Espero — yo / estar aquí para la boda

Cuaderno de gramática, p. 56, Acts. 4–5

9 **Gramática en contexto** See sample answers below.

Leamos/Hablemos Trabaja con un(a) compañero(a). Respondan a cada situación que sigue, expresando un sentimiento o una esperanza.

MODELO
> —Nuestros primos nos visitarán por un mes.
> —Me alegro que vengan porque les interesa hacer de todo.
> —Temo que no se diviertan.

1. Hay una fiesta en casa de Juan, pero sus fiestas son aburridas.
2. Ustedes están solos(as) en casa durante una tormenta.
3. Rosa no se sentía bien ayer cuando ustedes la llamaron.
4. Ustedes le entregaron sus exámenes finales al profesor.
5. Ustedes están jugando en las finales de baloncesto.

¿Te acuerdas?

If there is no change of subject after a verb conveying feelings, the infinitive is used, as in **Me encanta patinar en línea** and **¿Te duele no poder hablar con ella?**

Cuaderno de gramática, p. 56, Act. 3

Communication for All Students

Auditory Learners

8 Write predictions on strips of paper and put them into a hat or a bag. **(Hoy vas a sacar una "A" en un examen.)** Have each student select one and read it aloud. Have other students respond appropriately using an expression of feeling.

Visual Learners

8 Have students draw a horizontal and a vertical line to divide a large piece of paper into four boxes. The students then draw four different situations and write how they feel in each. For example, a student draws a picture of a sunny day and writes **Me siento feliz que haga sol.**

10 Una mamá preocupada

Leamos/Escribamos Lee la carta de Blanca. Luego lee las oraciones e indica si son **ciertas** o **falsas.** Si son falsas, corrígelas.

1. A Blanca le encanta que Nilda vaya a muchas fiestas.
2. Está contenta que sus hijos tengan buenos amigos.
3. Le preocupa a Blanca que Beto maneje tan rápido.
4. Se alegra que sus hijos no cuenten con ella para todo.
5. Le frustra tener hijos como Beto y Caty.

See answers below.

Vivi,

Siento molestarte pero sé que te puedo hablar de esto porque eres mi hermana. Tú sabes que tengo mucha suerte en tener buenos hijos. Pero andan con unos amigos... Nilda, una amiga de mi hija Caty — es muy alegre, pero no sé... parece que toda su vida es una fiesta. Y Marcos, el amigo de mi hijo Beto, siempre maneja rápido y además saca malas notas. Me gusta que mis hijos sean independientes pero temo que tengan problemas. ¿Debo decirles a mis hijos que no me gustan sus amigos? ¿Qué crees tú? Contéstame pronto. Un abrazo.

Blanca

Vocabulario

la amistad	*friendship*
apoyar	*to support*
chismear	*to gossip*
confiar en	*to trust*
contar (ue) con	*to count or depend on*
dejar de hablarse	*to stop speaking to each other*
dejar plantado(a) a alguien	*to stand someone up*
El problema está resuelto.	*The problem is solved.*
pelearse	*to have a fight*
reconciliarse	*to make up, to reconcile*
resolver (ue) un problema	*to solve a problem*
el rumor	*rumor*
tener un malentendido	
	to have a misunderstanding

¡Qué carro más bonito!

hacerle un cumplido a alguien
to compliment someone

 Cuaderno de gramática, p. 57, Acts. 6–8   Cuaderno de actividades, p. 74 Acts. 3–4, 7

Nota gramatical

In Spanish, plural reflexive verb forms can be used to express the idea of *each other.*

Josué y Carlota no **se hablan.**
Josué and Carlota aren't speaking (to each other).
María y yo siempre **nos apoyamos.**
María and I always support each other.

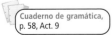 Cuaderno de gramática, p. 58, Act. 9

Más práctica gramatical, p. 213, Act. 3 →

Cuaderno de actividades, p. 76, Act. 8

11 Escucha bien Scripts and answers on p. 189G.

Escuchemos Escucha las frases e indica si cada frase que oyes es **lógica** o **ilógica.**

CD 7 Tr. 9

Nota cultural

Los cafés, que se llaman **confiterías,** tienen mucha importancia en las vidas de los residentes de Buenos Aires. Muchas veces la gente se reúne en una confitería para hablar o para tomar té o café antes de ir al cine o a la ópera. Otras personas van para pensar o estar solas. Algunas confiterías son centros de actividad intelectual, con discusiones diarias sobre la política y la literatura. ¿Son tan importantes los cafés en Estados Unidos?

Cultures and Communities

Language Note

Students may also know other verbs that express reciprocity such as **casarse, comprometerse, divorciarse, amarse, quererse, conocerse, verse,** and **ayudarse.**

Culture Note

Many **confiterías** are housed in old buildings (the oldest in Buenos Aires was established in 1858), while others are located in cellars. Most of them serve coffee, tea, soft drinks, sandwiches, salads, and pastries like the **media luna,** which resembles a croissant. Some **confiterías** have live entertainment in the evenings ranging from jazz to cabaret to concerts.

STANDARDS: 1.2, 2.1, 3.2, 4.1, 4.2

Teaching Resources
pp. 195–199

PRINT
▸ Lesson Planner, p. 33
▸ Listening Activities, pp. 51–52, 55–56
▸ Activities for Communication, pp. 25–26, 69, 71, 101–102
▸ Cuaderno de gramática, pp. 55–59
▸ Grammar Tutor for Students of Spanish, Chapter 7
▸ Cuaderno de actividades, pp. 74–77
▸ Cuaderno para hispanohablantes, pp. 31–35
▸ Testing Program, pp. 147–150
▸ Alternative Assessment Guide, p. 36
▸ Student Make-Up Assignments, Chapter 7

MEDIA
▸ One-Stop Planner
▸ Audio Compact Discs, CD 7, Trs. 8–10, 26–28, 22
▸ Teaching Transparencies 7-1; **Más práctica gramatical** Answers; Cuaderno de gramática Answers
▸ Interactive CD-ROM Tutor, Disc 2

Presenting
Gramática

The present perfect subjunctive First, have each student prepare a sentence using the preterite. Then begin your presentation by making statements with expressions of happiness or unhappiness followed by the present perfect subjunctive. Next, have a student read his or her prepared sentence aloud. Respond with the present perfect subjunctive.

---

12 **Gramática en contexto** Answers will vary. See sample answers below.

Leamos/Hablemos Indica cómo te sientes cuando...

1. un amigo chismoso inicia un rumor sobre ti
2. comienzas una nueva amistad
3. un(a) amigo(a) te hace un cumplido
4. descubres que no puedes confiar en un(a) amigo(a)
5. dos de tus mejores amigos(as) dejan de hablarse
6. descubres que no puedes contar con un(a) amigo(a)
7. te reconcilias con un(a) amigo(a)

Gramática

The present perfect subjunctive

1. The present perfect subjunctive is formed with the subjunctive of **haber** and a past participle.

haya comprado	hayamos comprado
hayas comprado	hayáis comprado
haya comprado	hayan comprado

2. Use the present perfect subjunctive to express an emotion about or hope that something has already happened.

   Juan **ha recibido** mi carta.   *Juan has gotten my letter.*
   Me alegro que Juan **haya recibido** mi carta.
     I'm glad Juan has gotten my letter.
   No **han resuelto** el problema todavía.
     They haven't solved the problem yet.
   Espero que lo **hayan resuelto.**
     I hope they've solved it.

Cuaderno de actividades, p. 77 Act. 9

Más práctica gramatical, p. 214, Act. 4

Cuaderno de gramática, pp. 58–59, Acts. 10–12

13 **La emoción y la esperanza** Script and answers on p.189G.

Escuchemos For each statement you hear, indicate whether the speaker is:

CD 7
Tr. 10

a. expressing emotion about a current situation
b. expressing emotion about something that has already happened
c. hoping that something will happen
d. hoping that something has already happened

¿Se te ha olvidado?
past participles
Ver las páginas R34–R35

¡GUAU! NO PUEDO CREER QUE HAYAMOS ENCONTRADO UN CRÁNEO DE DINOSAURIO EN NUESTRA PRIMERA EXCAVACIÓN.

¡ADEMÁS ESTÁ INTACTO! ¡QUÉ DESCUBRIMIENTO!

TAL VEZ EL RESTO DEL ESQUELETO ESTÉ CERCA.

¡SÍ! ¡SI LOGRAMOS ENCONTRARLO TODO SEREMOS MUNDIALMENTE FAMOSOS!

CON EL DINERO QUE NOS DEN, NOS COMPRAREMOS UN PORSCHE.

¿CÓMO ME VERÍA EN LA PORTADA DE "NATIONAL GEOGRAPHIC"?

Communication for All Students

Slower Pace

13 Before students do the activity, have them work in pairs to make one list of expressions for expressing happiness or unhappiness and another list of expressions for hoping. Then have them write a sentence for each of the categories a–d in Activity 13. Stress the difference between the present and present perfect subjunctive in these four sentences.

Challenge

Have students read the Calvin and Hobbes cartoon, identifying the present perfect subjunctive and the simple present subjunctive forms and give a reason why Calvin and Hobbes use the subjunctive in each case. Ask them the following comprehension questions: **¿Por qué están tan emocionados Calvin y Hobbes? ¿Qué espera Calvin que pase? ¿Y Hobbes?**

14 Gramática en contexto

Hablemos Con un(a) compañero(a), habla sobre seis cosas buenas que han ocurrido en los últimos tres meses. Deben comenzar cada oración con una expresión como **me alegro que** o **me encanta que.**

MODELO Me encanta que mis primos hayan venido a visitarme.

Así se dice

Comforting someone

Si alguien necesita consuelo, puedes usar estas expresiones:

Cuaderno de actividades, p. 77, Act. 10

¡Ánimo!   *Cheer up!*
Comparto tu pena.   *I share your grief.*
Esto pasará pronto.   *This will soon pass.*
Lo siento mucho.
Mi más sentido pésame.
My most heartfelt condolences.

No hay mal que cien años dure.
It won't last forever.
No hay mal que por bien no venga.
Every cloud has a silver lining.
No te preocupes.
¿Qué puedo hacer por ti?
What can I do for you?
Tranquilo(a).   *Calm down.*

15 ¿Respuestas lógicas?

Leamos/Escribamos Lee los diálogos e indica si las respuestas son lógicas o ilógicas para dar consuelo. Si son ilógicas, sugiere una respuesta más apropiada.

1. BECKY: El horario de mi trabajo me tiene loca. ¿Trabajar los fines de semana? ¡No lo aguanto más!
   ELENA: Me alegro que tengas ese horario.
2. ARTURO: No me lo puedo creer. Anoche me dijo mi novia que quiere romper conmigo.
   IRMA: No te preocupes. No hay mal que por bien no venga.
3. KAREEM: ¡Qué locura! Tengo que cuidar a mi hermana menor.
   BERNARDO: Me gusta que tengas tanta responsabilidad.
4. LUCITA: Nadie me ha invitado al baile y soy muy tímida.
   EDSON: ¡Ánimo! Voy con Rafael y Susana. Ven con nosotros.

A lo nuestro

Sometimes proverbs like **no hay mal que cien años dure** can provoke an interesting response. A person might respond, **¡Ni persona que lo aguante!,** meaning *It may not last forever, but neither will I!*

1. ilógica
2. lógica
3. ilógica
4. lógica

16 Los altibajos de la vida

Escribamos/Hablemos Con unos(as) compañeros(as), escribe una lista de cinco o seis acontecimientos imaginarios. Tres deben ser positivos y tres negativos. Luego den su lista a otro grupo. Ese grupo responderá de forma adecuada a cada acontecimiento.

17 No pude hacer la tarea porque...

Escribamos Escribe un diálogo entre un profesor y varios estudiantes que vienen a explicarle que no pudieron hacer la tarea a causa de las cosas malas que les han ocurrido. El profesor responde a todos con expresiones adecuadas de consuelo (¡aunque de todas maneras tienen que hacer la tarea!).

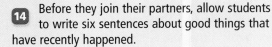

Slower Pace

14 Before they join their partners, allow students to write six sentences about good things that have recently happened.

Group Work

16 Divide the class into small groups to create a skit. One student is the emcee of a TV talk show and the others are celebrities who discuss the best and worst things that happened to them last year.

Additional Practice

14 Have students discuss things that have caused them unhappiness in the last three months. They should begin each sentence with **Me duele mucho que...** or **Me frustra que...,** and so on.

Presenting
Así se dice

Bring in appropriate magazine pictures. Hold them up one at a time while modeling the expressions in **Así se dice.** (Picture of someone with a headache: **Esto pasará pronto.** or **¿Qué puedo hacer por ti?**) Then ask students to react with an appropriate expression as you hold up pictures.

Auditory Learners

15 Have pairs of students create and perform similar minidialogues. The rest of the class listens and decides if the dialogues are logical or illogical.

Assess

▶ Testing Program, pp. 147–150
Quiz 7-1A, Quiz 7-1B
Audio CD 7, Tr. 22

▶ Student Make-Up Assignments, Chapter 7, Alternative Quiz

▶ Alternative Assessment Guide, p. 36

Answers

12 *Sample answers:*
1. Estoy de mal humor y decepcionado(a).
2. Estoy contento(a).
3. Estoy orgulloso(a) de mí mismo(a).
4. Me frustra que no pueda confiar en mi amigo(a).
5. Me duele mucho que ellos no se hablen.
6. Estoy desilusionado(a).
7. Estoy contento(a).

Cuaderno de actividades,
p. 78, Acts. 11–12

CAPÍTULO 7

Teaching Resources
pp. 200–201

PRINT
▶ Lesson Planner, p. 34
▶ Video Guide, pp. 45–46, 48
▶ Cuaderno de actividades, p. 78

MEDIA
▶ One-Stop Planner
▶ Video Program
   Contigo en la distancia
   Videocassette 3, 03:02–09:03
   Videocassette 5 (captioned version), 33:12–39:14
▶ Audio Compact Discs, CD 7, Trs. 11–14

Presenting
¡Adelante!

Play the Audio CD once while students look at the photos and read the text. Have students work in pairs to list the reasons for the conflicts and then to list advice for how to solve each conflict. Next, present the Preteaching Vocabulary. Replay the Audio CD and have students raise their hands each time they hear a cognate.

 ### Contigo en la distancia

As an alternative or in addition to **¡Adelante!,** you may wish to show Episode 7 of **Contigo en la distancia.** For suggestions and activities, see the *Video Guide.*

¡Adelante! ▪ *Los conflictos personales*

CD 7
Trs. 11–13

No hay nada que sea más frustrante que un conflicto entre amigos o novios. ¿Cómo puedes hacer las paces con alguien después?

1 No dejes que pasen muchos días porque se irán acentuando los rencores. Alguien tiene siempre que dar el primer paso.

2 Cuando le pides hablar, no dramatices ni exageres. Asegúrate de estar muy calmado(a). Si te enojas podrías empeorar la situación.

Ana,
   Te dije que te iba a llamar anoche pero se me olvidó por completo. Lo hice sin querer, te lo juro. Estaba estudiando para mi clase de álgebra. Rafael estaba conmigo, pregúntale a él. Perdóname, Ana— no lo haré más.

Víctor

3 No te hagas el (la) ofendido(a) o víctima. Escucha lo que la otra persona tenga que decir al respecto.

These activities check for comprehension only. Students should not yet be expected to produce language modeled in ¡Adelante!

18 **Lo que debes hacer es...** Script and answers on p. 165G.

Marta le da consejos a su amigo Rafael, que tiene un conflicto personal con otro amigo. Escucha cada consejo e indica si es bueno o no según la información de **¡Adelante!**

CD 7 Tr. 14

19 ¿Cómo se expresa?
Indica qué expresiones usa Víctor para disculparse.
1. Lo siento muchísimo.
2. Lo hice sin querer.
3. No lo haré más.
4. Perdóname.
5. Discúlpame.
6. No lo volveré a hacer.

20 Un conflicto entre amigos   Answers will vary.
Contesta las preguntas con un(a) compañero(a).
1. ¿Qué puede pasar si cometes un error y no lo admites a tu amigo(a)?
2. ¿Por qué no debes esperar mucho tiempo para discutir un problema?
3. ¿Por qué debes estar tranquilo(a) cuando hablas de un problema?
4. ¿Qué debes hacer si tu amigo(a) viene a disculparse?

Preteaching Vocabulary

Recognizing Cognates

¡Adelante! contains several words that students will be able to recognize as cognates. Have students find these words and decide which might be involved in describing conflicts. Then have students identify those cognates that might be used to resolve a conflict. (**pasen, acentuando, exageres, situación, Perdóname, ofendido, víctima, respeto, fatal, imposible, generosidad**)

4 No reconocer la falta puede ser fatal. Si tuviste la culpa acéptala y discúlpate.

Víctor,

La verdad es que sí estaba enojada, pero muchísimas gracias por tu cartita. No sabes cuánto te lo agradezco. No necesito hablar con Rafael, confío en ti completamente. Sé que puedo contar contigo para decirme la verdad.

Ana

5 Si la otra persona da el primer paso, no cometas la imperdonable falta de ser imposible. Facilítale las cosas y agradécele su generosidad.

6 ¿Qué significa una gotita de enojo al lado de una inmensa amistad o un gran amor? Vamos, no seas terco(a), da un paso al frente y ¡saca tu bandera blanca!

21 **En orden de importancia**   Answers will vary.

Escribe estas sugerencias en orden de importancia. Luego, con un(a) compañero(a), explica por qué las pusiste en ese orden. Si quieren, pueden discutir sus ideas con la clase.

1. No esperes mucho tiempo antes de discutir un conflicto.
2. No te enojes cuando discutes un conflicto.
3. Escucha lo que la otra persona tiene que decir.
4. Si cometes un error, admítelo.
5. Recuerda que la amistad es más importante que un poco de enojo.

22 **Ahora te toca a ti**

¿Cuáles de las sugerencias para resolver conflictos has usado? ¿Tuviste buen resultado? ¿Cuáles de las sugerencias son las más fáciles? ¿las más difíciles? ¿Por qué?

Language Note

A synonym for **rencores** (*grudges*) is **resentimientos**. Synonyms for **terco** (*stubborn*) are **intransigente** and **testarudo**. In Ecuador, **terco** means *cold, indifferent*.

Auditory Learners

22 Volunteers read the following dialogues, or others you create, while the rest of the class guesses the corresponding picture.

—Te lo agradezco. Son tan bonitas.
—¿Me perdonas, entonces?
—Por supuesto, mi vida.
(couple with flowers)

—No hice nada.
—¿Nada? Dejaste mi mochila en la lluvia y mi almuerzo se mojó. ¿Por qué la dejaste afuera?
—¡Yo no sabía que no la llevaste contigo!
—¡Caramba! ¡Qué tonto!
(couple standing back to back)

Native Speakers

22 Ask students to discuss advice columns they may have read in teen magazines. Have they read about problems similar to the conflict between Ana and Víctor? Are the suggestions in the columns similar or different? If magazines are available, ask students to bring them in and share them with the class.

Comprehension Check

Kinesthetic Learners

21 Write the sentences on cards made from colored construction paper. Put pieces of tape on the backs of the cards so students can rearrange the sentences during the discussion.

Thinking Critically

Synthesizing Ask pairs of students to write letters asking for advice. Then redistribute the letters to other pairs to answer. You may have students read their answers aloud, send a written response to the original writer, or post the letters and responses for the whole class to read. Problems could be real or fictitious, but should be realistic enough to elicit answers similar to the suggestions in ¡**Adelante!**

Encuentro cultural

CAPÍTULO 7

Motivating Activity
Ask students to discuss the following: **A veces hay conflictos entre un país y otro. ¿Cuáles son algunas razones por este tipo de problema? ¿Qué clases de problemas se presentan entre naciones?**

Presenting
Encuentro cultural
Have volunteers read the first paragraph aloud, changing readers with each sentence. Then invite students to answer the question in **Para discutir** as a class. Continue with volunteers reading the **Vamos a comprenderlo** section aloud. Ask students to try to identify the 35 countries that belong to the OAS.

Career Path
Have students think of careers related to international relations and diplomacy. (work in an embassy, the OAS, the United Nations) How would a second language be helpful in these careers? (ability to communicate as a bilingual delegate, to be an ambassador to a Spanish-speaking country, to translate documents, to be an interpreter)

Background Information
The Organization of American States (OAS) was established in 1948. It seeks to provide for collective self-defense, regional cooperation, and the peaceful settlement of controversies.

The OAS publishes a magazine that is quite useful in the classroom, *Américas.* It is available in either Spanish or English text for a small subscription fee. The address is Américas, P.O. Box 3000 Denville, NJ 07834-3000.The phone number is 1–800–222–5405. Students might look for the OAS Web site.

La Organización de Estados Americanos

La Organización de Estados Americanos (OEA) es una asociación de 35 países de las Américas, incluyendo Estados Unidos y Canadá. El centro de operaciones está en Washington, D.C. El movimiento panamericano entre los países latinoamericanos comenzó al principio del siglo XIX. En 1826, el general venezolano Simón Bolívar realizó su sueño de unir las nuevas repúblicas de Latinoamérica cuando convocó la primera conferencia panamericana.

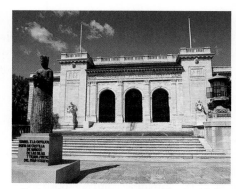

Centro de operaciones en Washington, D.C.

Simón Bolívar

Para discutir

¿Para qué crees que existe la Organización de Estados Americanos? ¿Qué puede hacer una organización como ésta? ¿Hay otras organizaciones parecidas a la OEA en el mundo, en Estados Unidos o en tu comunidad?

Vamos a comprenderlo

La Organización de Estados Americanos sirve para fomentar la cooperación económica y la justicia social, y para resolver los problemas políticos de una forma pacífica. Las organizaciones de este tipo pueden prevenir las guerras y los conflictos internacionales antes de que comiencen. Otras organizaciones parecidas son las Naciones Unidas, la Corte Mundial y las legislaturas de cada país y de cada estado.

Cultures and Communities

Culture Note

Simón Bolívar (1783–1830) led the revolt against Spanish rule in Nueva Granada (renamed Gran Colombia in 1819, encompassing Venezuela, Colombia, Panama, and Ecuador), Peru, and Upper Peru (Bolivia). *La carta de Jamaica,* written from exile in 1814, outlined his vision of a united Central and South America. He proposed constitutional republics with a hereditary upper house, an elected lower house, and a president chosen for life. Have your students research Bolívar's vision of a united America. They should write a short composition answering the following question: **¿Se realizó la visión de Bolívar en la creación de la Organización de Estados Americanos?**

Así se dice

Making an apology

Si necesitas pedirle perdón a un(a) amigo(a), puedes decir:

Discúlpame.	*Forgive me.*
Lo hice sin querer.	*I didn't mean to do it.*
Lo siento mucho, es que no sabía.	*I'm very sorry; I didn't know.*
No lo haré más.	*I won't do it anymore.*
No lo volveré a hacer.	*I won't do it again.*
Perdóname.	*Forgive me.*

23 **¿Cómo contestas?** Script and answers on p. 189H.

Escuchemos Escucha cada diálogo e indica si oyes una **disculpa** o una expresión de **consuelo**.

CD 7 Tr. 15

Vocabulario

Problemas y soluciones

admitir/cometer un error
  to admit/make a mistake
comprarle un regalo
  to buy someone a gift
darle un abrazo
  to give someone a hug
darse tiempo para pensar
  to give oneself time to think
discutir el problema
  to discuss the problem
insultar   *to insult*
mentir (ie, i)   *to lie*
no guardar los secretos
  not to keep secrets
respetar sus sentimientos
  to respect someone's feelings
romper con   *to break up with someone*
ser desleal   *to be disloyal*
ser infiel   *to be unfaithful*
tener celos de   *to be jealous of*

echarle la culpa a otro(a)
to blame someone else

Más práctica gramatical, p. 214, Act. 5

Cuaderno de actividades, pp. 79–80, Acts. 13–16

Cuaderno de gramática, p. 60, Acts. 13–14

También se puede decir...
Puedes usar **cortar con** por **romper con**.

Segundo paso

CAPÍTULO 7

Teaching Resources
pp. 203–206

PRINT
▶ Lesson Planner, p. 34
▶ Listening Activities, pp. 52–53, 56–57
▶ Activities for Communication, pp. 27–28, 70–71, 101–102
▶ Cuaderno de gramática, pp. 60–63
▶ Grammar Tutor for Students of Spanish, Chapter 7
▶ Cuaderno de actividades, pp. 79–82
▶ Cuaderno para hispanohablantes, pp. 31–35
▶ Testing Program, pp. 151–154
▶ Alternative Assessment Guide, p. 36
▶ Student Make-Up Assignments, Chapter 7

MEDIA
▶ One-Stop Planner
▶ Audio Compact Discs, CD 7, Trs. 15–16, 29–31, 23
▶ Teaching Transparencies 7-2; **Más práctica gramatical** Answers; Cuaderno de gramática Answers
▶ Interactive CD-ROM Tutor, Disc 2

Bell Work
Write: **Escribe oraciones que comiencen con: Me alegro que... Siento que... Me frustra que... Me duele mucho que... Estoy orgulloso(a) que...**

Presenting
Así se dice
Read students a short note of apology that you have composed and have students identify the expressions you used.

Vocabulario
Relate a story about a conflict that ended a relationship with a friend. Use as much of the new vocabulary as possible.

Communication for All Students

Pair Work
Ask the class to come up with reasons or situations in which each of the apologies might be used. (forgetting to help someone with a homework assignment, canceling plans to go to the movies) Then have students work in pairs to write a note of apology for one of these situations and explain the reasons.

Native Speakers
Have students, as a class or in small groups, create a list of the top ten reasons that one might feel hurt or betrayed by someone else. Ask students how easily they forgive others and can apologize for their own mistakes.

Teaching Resources
pp. 203–206

PRINT
▶ Lesson Planner, p. 34
▶ Listening Activities, pp. 52–53, 56–57
▶ Activities for Communication, pp. 27–28, 70–71, 101–102
▶ Cuaderno de gramática, pp. 60–63
▶ Grammar Tutor for Students of Spanish, Chapter 7
▶ Cuaderno de actividades, pp. 79–82
▶ Cuaderno para hispanohablantes, pp. 31–35
▶ Testing Program, pp. 151–154
▶ Alternative Assessment Guide, p. 36
▶ Student Make-Up Assignments, Chapter 7

MEDIA
▶ One-Stop Planner
▶ Audio Compact Discs, CD 7, Trs. 15–16, 29–31, 23
▶ Teaching Transparencies 7-2; **Más práctica gramatical** Answers; Cuaderno de gramática Answers
▶ Interactive CD-ROM Tutor, Disc 2

Additional Practice

24 Ask students to write three more items like the ones in this activity. Have students exchange papers with a partner and complete his or her sentences.

Pair Work

26 Have students change partners. They tell their new partner what happened to them in the skit. **(Mi mejor amigo(a) me pidió perdón por no guardar mi secreto. Dijo a todo el mundo que...)**

Answers
25 1. tiene celos de
2. mentía
3. rompió
4. cometió

---

24 **Problemas y soluciones**

Leamos/Escribamos Completa las oraciones con las palabras más adecuadas.

1. Si un amigo necesita tiempo para pensar a solas, debes (admitir tu error, respetar sus sentimientos).
2. Si ya tienes novio(a) y sales con otra persona, (tienes celos, eres infiel).
3. Sabes que cometiste un error. Debes (echarle la culpa a otro, admitir tu error).
4. Tienes una amiga que nunca guarda tus secretos. Han discutido el problema pero no cambia nada. Tal vez debes (darle un abrazo, romper con esa persona).
5. Has insultado a tu hermanito. Debes disculparte y (darle un abrazo, mentir).

25 **Problemas sentimentales** See answers below.

Leamos/Hablemos Lee el artículo. Luego completa las siguientes oraciones con la forma más apropiada de una expresión del **Vocabulario.**

1. La novia de Roberto ════ las otras chicas con quienes Roberto coqueteaba.
2. Cuando su novia le preguntaba a Roberto dónde estaba, él le ════.
3. Al descubrir que su novio era infiel, ════ con él.
4. Roberto ════ un error y no lo quiso (wouldn't) admitir.

 Un novio infiel

"**C**uando conocí a Roberto me enamoré de él como una loca. El era encantador. Es más, era demasiado encantador. Me volvía loca verlo coquetear con otras chicas, pero juraba que sólo tenía ojos para mí. Varios fines de semana se me desaparecía y no había forma humana de localizarlo. Cuando le reclamaba, casi siempre me salía con que había estado ayudando a algún amigo a arreglar el auto, a mudarse, a resolver no sé qué problemas, etc. Una tarde pensé sorprender a mi novio del alma en su casa…y la sorprendida fui yo. Allí estaba en la sala, estudiando con otra muchacha. Así que corté con él ahí mismo.**"**

26 **Del colegio al trabajo**

Escribamos Tu compañero y tú son guionistas para una telenovela muy popular. Tienen que preparar el episodio final en que el(la) malvado(a) le pide perdón al protagonista. Escriban un minidrama de dos o tres páginas.

¿Se te ha olvidado?
present perfect subjunctive
Ver la página 198

Nota cultural

El cine es tan popular como la televisión entre la gente de la capital argentina. Buenos Aires tiene alrededor de 80 cines que dan películas de Argentina, Estados Unidos y Europa. Es interesante ver una película en el Instituto de Realización Cinematográfica Argentina. Allí casi todos se sientan en el piso para ver la película, y después hay discusiones sobre su contenido social y político. Algunas películas argentinas son famosas en los Estados Unidos. Una de ellas, *La historia oficial,* ganó un *Academy Award* en 1986. ¿Tus amigos y tú discuten las películas que ven?

Communication for All Students

Native Speakers

26 Ask native speakers if they have seen a **telenovela.** How are these shows different from American soap operas? You may also have students ask their grandparents what the differences are between the **telenovelas** they used to watch and the ones they watch now. Then have them summarize their findings for the class.

Kinesthetic/Visual Learners

Have students work in groups of three to write and act out a skit about two friends resolving a problem. On two sheets of paper, they also write two pieces of advice for the "friends in conflict," such as **Admite tu error.** One person holds up the cards at key moments so that the class and the two acting in the skit can see them. The two students acting respond to the cards in their dialogue.

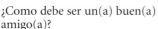

Así se dice

Describing an ideal relationship

Si quieres hablar de unas relaciones ideales, puedes decir:

¿Como debe ser un(a) buen(a) amigo(a)?	Debe ser alguien **que me apoye** y **que respete** mis sentimientos.
	...que no tenga celos de mis otros(as) amigos(as).
¿Qué buscas en **un(a) novio(a)?** *. . . a boyfriend/girlfriend?*	Busco a alguien **a quien le gusten** los deportes y **que sepa** algo de la música.
	...que nunca me mienta, que siempre me diga la verdad.
	No aguanto a nadie que sea descortés. *I can't stand anyone who's rude.*

Cuaderno de actividades, pp. 81–82, Acts. 17, 19

Cuaderno de gramática, p. 61, Acts. 15–16

27 **Unos novios ideales** Answers will vary.

Leamos/Escribamos Lee estas descripciones. Para cada una escribe una oración que explique lo que la persona busca en un(a) novio(a).

MODELO
> Sara es una gran aficionada a Bach; también toca el violín en la orquesta.
> Sara busca un novio que sepa algo de la música clásica.

1. Marcos es muy atlético. Pasa mucho tiempo practicando el fútbol norteamericano.
2. A Simón le encantan los animales. Tiene un perro, dos gatos y un loro.
3. Sara no aguanta a nadie que sea descortés.
4. En su tiempo libre Edgardo pinta, dibuja y hace esculturas.
5. Marisol pasa mucho tiempo navegando por Internet.

Gramática

The subjunctive with the unknown or nonexistent

1. When describing a person or thing that is unknown or indefinite, the subjunctive follows **que.** The personal **a** is omitted before nouns but not before **alguien.**
   Busco un novio que **sea** simpático. Busco a alguien que me **apoye.**
2. When using negative words like **nada, nadie,** or **ninguno(a)** before a **que** clause, use the subjunctive. The personal **a** always precedes **nadie** when it's a direct object.
   No hay nada que **podamos** hacer. No conozco a nadie que **viva** allí.

   Más práctica gramatical, p. 215, Acts. 6–7

3. The present subjunctive of **saber** is irregular:

sepa	sepamos
sepas	sepáis
sepa	sepan

See pages R40–R41 for information about stem-changing verbs in the subjunctive.

Cuaderno de actividades, p. 81, Act. 18

Cuaderno de gramática, pp. 62–63, Acts. 17–20

Connections and Comparisons

Math Link
Have groups of students create a survey asking the respondents to rate in order of importance ten qualities they would look for in an ideal relationship. Each group member can interview five people. The group can then compile the data in order to calculate the percentages of the top three responses. Have each group present their findings to the class.

Language-to-Language
Where Spanish constructions call for the subjunctive with the unknown or nonexistent, English sometimes makes use of helping, or *modal*, verbs: **Buscamos a alguien que trabaje los sábados.** *We're looking for someone who will work Saturdays.* Ask your students if they can think of other subjunctive constructions which may be rendered in English using helping verbs.

Writing Assessment

32 You may wish to assess the writing assignment using the following rubric.

Writing Rubric	Points			
	4	3	2	1
Content (Complete–Incomplete)				
Comprehensibility (Comprehensible–Incomprehensible)				
Accuracy (Accurate–Seldom accurate)				
Organization (Well organized–Poorly organized)				
Effort (Excellent–Minimal)				

18–20: A	14–15: C	Under
16–17: B	12–13: D	12: F

Assess

▶ Testing Program, pp. 151–154
  Quiz 7-2A, Quiz 7-2B
  Audio CD 7, Tr. 23

▶ Student Make-Up Assignments, Chapter 7, Alternative Quiz

▶ Alternative Assessment Guide, p. 36

Answers

29 *Possible answers:*
1. No tenemos amigos que nos respeten.
2. No hay restaurantes que sirvan buena comida.
3. No hay emisoras de radio que toquen buena música.
4. No tenemos conocidos que nos llamen.
5. No hay cine que dé buenas películas.

30 *Possible answers:*
Leticia quiere un carro que sea rápido y bonito. Mario quiere una casa que tenga muchas ventanas y una piscina.

---

28 **Gramática en contexto** Script and answers on p. 189H.

 Escuchemos Escucha lo que dice cada persona. Si habla de alguien que existe con certeza, escribe **sí.** Escribe **no** si habla de alguien que **no** existe o si no se sabe si existe o no.
CD 7 Tr. 16

¿Se te ha olvidado?
subjunctive forms
Ver la página R38

29 **Gramática en contexto** See possible answers below.

 Leamos/Hablemos Imagina que tú y un(a) compañero(a) se sienten muy pesimistas sobre su ciudad y sus vidas. Contradigan las siguientes oraciones para expresar lo que piensan.

> **MODELO**   Hay buenos cafés donde podemos conversar.
> Al contrario, no hay buenos restaurantes donde podamos conversar.

1. Tenemos amigos que nos respetan.
2. Hay restaurantes que sirven buena comida.
3. Hay emisoras de radio que tocan buena música.
4. Tenemos conocidos(as) que nos llaman.
5. Hay un cine que da buenas películas.

30 **Sueños y ambiciones** See possible answers below.

Escribamos Mira los dibujos e indica qué buscan, necesitan o quieren estas personas.

Leticia

Mario

31 **Mi amigo(a) ideal**

 Hablemos/Escribamos Con unos(as) compañeros(as), hablen de sus relaciones ideales. Hagan una lista de lo que buscan en sus amigos (¡y lo que no aguantan!).

32 **En mi cuaderno**

 Escribamos Escribes obras de teatro para el centro de bellas artes en tu ciudad. Escribe un pequeño drama en tres actos en que una persona deja plantada a otra. La persona ofendida llama a la otra persona para expresar su desilusión. Luego la otra persona le pide perdón. La persona ofendida acepta la disculpa. Usa expresiones de **Así se dice** en la página 203.

Nota cultural

Los argentinos, como los estadounidenses, son muy aficionados a los deportes. El fútbol es el deporte más popular. Hay mucha competencia entre los equipos de los barrios de las ciudades grandes. El tenis es muy popular en parte debido a jugadores como Guillermo Vilas y Gabriela Sabatini. Hay mucho interés en los deportes ecuestres también. ¿Participan tú y tus amigos(as) en equipos o ligas locales?

Cultures and Communities

Language Note

32 The following are idiomatic expressions that students may want to use in their drama.

Te doy toda la razón.   *You're absolutely right.*
¡Haberlo dicho antes!   *Why didn't you say so?*
¡Metí la pata!   *I put my foot in my mouth!*
Te fuiste con otro(a).   *You left me for another.*

Culture Note

Buenos Aires has about ten major-league soccer teams, each owned by a different social-athletic club. Each club also owns a huge stadium. Games can draw up to 120,000 fans. Fans are often very enthusiastic at games, especially the World Cup, which Argentina won in 1978 and 1986.

CD 7
Trs. 17–20

¿Has tenido algún conflicto con un(a) amigo(a)?

Una amistad es difícil de romper. ¿Son parecidos a los tuyos los conflictos que describen estas jóvenes?

Vanesa
Coronado,
Costa Rica CD 7 Tr. 18

"Sí, tuve uno y fue con mi mejor amiga... Yo estaba enamorada de un muchacho y ella lo sabía, éramos muy amigas, y ella se fue con el muchacho, sabiéndolo. Pero luego hablamos y la verdad [es que] muchas veces supo ser una amiga... preferí la amistad de ella. Un error lo comete cualquiera".

Angeline
Ponce,
Puerto Rico CD 7 Tr. 19

"Me gustaba este muchacho y... [a] mi supuestamente amiga... le gustaba a ella también. Y yo le dije a ella que nuestra amistad valía mucho para un muchacho que no valía la pena y nosotros lo dejamos ir así".

María José
Buenos Aires,
Argentina CD 7 Tr. 20

"Sí, tuve una amiga hace..., hasta marzo era mi mejor amiga, y nos separamos porque ella se puso de novia y se separó de mí. Y estoy intentando resolverlo todavía porque... no me quiere escuchar".

Para pensar y hablar...

A. Dos de las entrevistadas tuvieron problemas similares. ¿Quiénes son? ¿Has tenido conflictos parecidos a los de las entrevistadas? ¿Cómo los solucionaste?

B. En tu opinión, ¿qué es un(a) buen(a) amigo(a)? ¿Cuáles son unas características que buscas en un(a) amigo(a)? ¿Por qué es importante la amistad? ¿Cómo resuelves conflictos con tus amigos?

Cuaderno para hispanohablantes, p. 35

Teaching Resources
p. 207

PRINT
▶ Video Guide, pp. 45–47, 49
▶ Cuaderno de actividades, p. 84
▶ Cuaderno para hispanohablantes, p. 35

MEDIA
▶ One-Stop Planner
▶ Video Program, Videocassette 3, 09:04–12:22
▶ Audio Compact Discs, CD 7, Trs. 17–20
▶ Interactive CD-ROM Tutor, Disc 2

Presenting
Panorama cultural

Have students watch the video or listen to the audio recording. Discuss the questions in **Para pensar y hablar...** Play the video again and have students answer **Preguntas.**

Preguntas

1. **¿Por qué se separaron María José y su amiga? ¿Por qué no pueden resolver su conflicto?** (La amiga se puso de novia y se separó de ella.)

2. **¿Por qué tienen un conflicto Angeline y su amiga? ¿Lo resolvieron?** (Les gustaba a las dos el mismo muchacho; sí, el muchacho no valía la pena)

3. **¿Qué pasó entre Vanesa y su amiga?** (Estaban enamoradas del mismo muchacho.)

4. **¿Qué tienen en común las tres muchachas? ¿Cómo puede uno evitar esta clase de problemas?** (Se pelearon con sus amigas por el amor; *Answers will vary.*)

Connections and Comparisons

Language Note

Argentine Spanish has a combination of characteristics that set it apart from other dialects of the language. The nation's Italian heritage is reflected in the intonation of words and phrases, as well as in borrowed words. Another characteristic is the strengthening of the fricative /y/ to /zh/, the sound in "leisure." For example, the word **calle** is pronounced /kazhe/. For information on the use of **vos,** see page 194. Have students listen for these characteristics as they listen to María José's response.

Vamos a leer

CAPÍTULO 7

Teaching Resources
pp. 208–210

PRINT
▶ Lesson Planner, p. 35
▶ Cuaderno de actividades, p. 83
▶ Cuaderno para hispanohablantes, pp. 31–34
▶ Reading Strategies and Skills Handbook, Chapter 7
▶ ¡Lee conmigo! 3, Chapter 7
▶ Standardized Assessment Tutor, Chapter 7

MEDIA
▶ One-Stop Planner

Prereading
Activity A

Determining Writer's Purpose
Explain to students that it is the writer's intent to influence their thinking in some way. By previewing the text, students should be able to formulate some initial predictions. Is the purpose of the text to inform, to tell a story, to stir a particular emotion, or to persuade the reader?

Using Prior Knowledge
Ask students what they know about dowries. (A dowry is money or property given by a bride's family to the groom or his family at marriage.) Point out that in other cultures, the groom and his family present gifts of money or property to the prospective bride and her family.

A Answers
Answers will vary.
El propósito principal del cuento es entretener al lector. También explica el origen de una expresión que, según el escritor, antes se usaba en Lima. No tiene una moraleja, pero comenta sobre los valores de la sociedad. Puede ser un cuento de verdad. El escritor dice que lo es, pero es improbable porque es un poco exagerado.

Un conflicto entre familias

Este cuento, escrito por el peruano Ricardo Palma, se llama una *tradición*. Las tradiciones son cuentos satíricos de la época colonial de América Latina.

Estrategia para leer
Every time you read, you draw conclusions by "reading between the lines." This is called making inferences. If you read "The boy cried and said he was going to run away," you probably infer that he's sad and having some family problems. Making inferences is a valuable tool you can use when reading.

¡A comenzar! See answers below.
A. Lee el título, los dos primeros párrafos y el último párrafo del texto. ¿Cuál es el propósito del cuento? ¿Explica el origen de algo? ¿Contiene una moraleja? ¿Qué opinas? ¿Es "La camisa de Margarita" un cuento de verdad o de ficción?

Al grano

¿Te acuerdas?
Think about how an article or story is organized as you read. Making a chart or outline can help you see the organization.

La Camisa de Margarita

Es posible que algunos dé mis lectores les hayan oído decir a las viejas de Lima, cuando quieren ponderar un precio alto:

—Que si esto es más caro que la camisa de Margarita Pareja.

Margarita Pareja era (por los años de 1765) la hija más mimada de don Raimundo Pareja, caballero de Santiago, y colector general de Callao. La muchacha era tan bella que cautivaba al mismo diablo. Tenía ojos negros como dos torpedos cargados con dinamita que hacían explosión en el alma de los galanes limeños.

Llegó por entonces de España un arrogante mancebo, don Luis Alcázar. Tenía en Lima un rico tío solterón que era más orgulloso que los hijos de un rey. Por supuesto que, mientras llegaba la ocasión de heredar al tío, vivía don Luis muy pobre.

En la procesión de Santa Rosa conoció Alcázar a la linda Margarita. La muchacha le llenó el ojo y le flechó el corazón. Le echó flores, y aunque ella no le contestó ni sí ni no, dio a entender con sonrisitas que el galán era muy de su gusto. La verdad es que se enamoraron hasta la raíz del pelo.

Como los amantes olvidan que existe la aritmética, creyó don Luis que su presente pobreza no sería obstáculo, y fue al padre de Margarita

---

Connections and Comparisons

Literature Link
Point out to students that Ricardo Palma (1833–1919) was a Peruvian writer famous for his short stories, plays, history, poetry, nonfiction, and **tradiciones.** You may want to explain that **tradiciones** are collections of stories, folktales, and anecdotes from and about the colonial period.

Many are about **criollos** (Peruvians of Spanish descent) and **peninsulares** (those born in Spain), and provide a humorous and often satirical social commentary. You may want to have students work in groups to read another of these **tradiciones** and report on it to the class.

y le pidió la mano de su hija.

A don Raimundo no le cayó bien la petición, y cortésmente despidió al postulante, diciéndole que Margarita era muy niña para casarse. Pero ésta no era la verdadera razón. Era que don Raimundo no quería ser suegro de un pobretón; y así se lo dijo a sus amigos. Cuando llegó el chisme a don Honorato, el tío de don Luis, se puso rabioso y dijo:

—¿Cómo? Muchos harían cualquier cosa para

emparentar con el muchacho. ¡Qué insolencia!

Margarita, pues, era muy nerviosa, lloró, se arrancó el pelo, y tuvo convulsiones. —O de Luis o de Dios— gritaba cuando los nervios se le sublevaban.

Don Raimundo, alarmado, llamó a médicos y curanderos y todos declararon que la cosa era muy seria. O casarla con el hombre de su gusto, o encerrarla en el cajón de palma y corona. Tal fue el "ultimátum" médico.

Don Raimundo (¡al fin padre!), se encaminó como loco a casa de don Honorato, y le dijo:

—Vengo a que consienta usted en que mañana mismo se case su sobrino con Margarita, porque si no, la muchacha se nos va a morir. —No puede ser— contestó sin interés el tío. Mi sobrino es un pobretón y lo que usted debe buscar para su hija es un hombre que sea rico.

El diálogo fue violento. Mientras más rogaba don Raimundo, más se enojaba don Honorato. Iba a retirarse don Raimundo cuando apareció don Luis y dijo:

B. Una lectura siempre tiene algún tipo de organización. Este cuento tiene una organización cronológica. Puedes dividirlo en más o menos nueve partes cronológicas. Con un(a) compañero(a), lee el texto y pon las nueve secciones en orden del uno al nueve.

3 **a.** Margarita y Luis se conocen y se enamoran.

4 **b.** Petición por la mano de Margarita y la reacción de su padre.

1 **c.** Descripción general de Margarita.

5 **d.** La reacción furiosa de don Honorato.

8 **e.** La promesa de don Raimundo.

6 **f.** La enfermedad de Margarita.

7 **g.** La discusión entre don Raimundo y don Honorato.

9 **h.** La descripción de la camisa de Margarita.

2 **i.** Descripción general de Luis.

C. Ahora sabes mucho del cuento de Margarita. Algunas de las cosas que sabes están en el texto, y otras son inferencias que hiciste. Lee las siguientes oraciones e indica **a, b** o **c** para cada una.

a. claramente expresado en el texto

b. inferido del texto

c. ni expresado ni inferido

c **1.** Luis no era de Lima originalmente.

a **2.** Luis le preguntó al padre de Margarita si podía casarse con ella.

b **3.** Un amigo de don Raimundo no podía guardar un secreto.

c **4.** La madre de Margarita estaba enferma también.

b **5.** Don Raimundo estaba preocupado por la vida de su hija.

Reading
Activities B, C, and D

Using Text Structures
B. Ask students to determine whether the author uses one of the following text structures: chronological order, comparison and contrast, or cause and effect. Point out that writers often use more than one text structure, but generally have a predominant pattern. (The predominant pattern is chronological order, although comparison and contrast is a secondary text structure.)

Drawing Inferences
C. For points that were clearly expressed or inferred, have students cite the passage or passages that support their answer.

Communication for all Students

Tactile/Visual Learners
B. Write descriptions of the nine sections (a–i) on index cards. Have students arrange the cards in the correct order without using their books. You may want to laminate the cards for future use.

Kinesthetic Learners
Have students pantomime the story as you or a native speaker read it aloud.

Challenge
Have students write a three- to four-paragraph story in Spanish about the origin of a popular English expression.

Thinking Critically
Analyzing Have students discuss the characters of the two men. Why do they think Honorato does not want Raimundo's money?

CAPÍTULO 7

Postreading
Activities E and F

Determining the Main Idea
Have students use the reading strategy **Vuelve a escribir el texto** to reformulate the story into a play. This approach encourages students to think critically about the text without overwhelming them. They will determine the main idea of the story in the process of reformulating the text. You may want to have the class use one of the scripts to stage the play for a Level 1 or Level 2 Spanish class. Encourage them to use props and costumes in the dramatic enactment.

Comparing and Contrasting
Have students compare this story with Shakespeare's *Romeo and Juliet*. You may want to have students list the similarities and differences. (Both stories are about lovers whose families oppose their marriage. In the case of don Luis and Margarita, they do not marry secretly nor do they kill themselves.)

Language Note
The expression **encajes de Flandes** refers to Belgian lace. Bobbin lace *(encaje de bolillos)* originated in Flanders, Belgium, in the early 16th century. Bruges, Belgium, and Almagro, in La Mancha, Spain, are among the few places in the world where lace is still made by hand.

a **6.** Don Raimundo y don Honorato se pelearon.

a **7.** Don Honorato y Luis dijeron que renunciarían a la dote.

c **8.** Había un nuevo sacerdote en la misa.

a **9.** Después de darle la camisa, don Raimundo no le dio nada más a Margarita.

D. En español, escribe dos frases que describen a cada persona del cuento. ¡No menciones el nombre de la persona! Luego lee tus descripciones a un(a) compañero(a). Tu compañero(a) va a adivinar quiénes son.

E. Con un(a) compañero(a), prepara un minidrama con base en una de las siguientes ideas.

1. Margarita le cuenta a un(a) amigo(a) de su amor por don Luis y su frustración con su papá.

2. Luis habla con un(a) amigo(a) sobre su amor por Margarita y sobre su plan de casarse.

3. El padre de Margarita habla con un(a) costurero(a) para darle instrucciones para la camisa.

F. Do you think people under the age of 21 need their parents' permission to marry? What can happen if a family doesn't approve of the marriage? What do you think of the custom of the dowry?

Cuaderno para hispanohablantes, pp. 31–34

Cuaderno de actividades, p. 83, Acts. 21–22

—Pero, tío, no es de cristianos que matemos a quien no tiene la culpa.

—¿Tú estás satisfecho?

—De todo corazón, tío y señor.

—Pues bien, muchacho, pero con una condición, y es ésta: don Raimundo me tiene que jurar que no regalará un centavo a su hija ni le dejará nada de herencia.

Aquí empezó de nuevo el argumento.

—Pero, hombre —arguyó don Raimundo—, mi hija tiene veinte mil duros de dote.

—Renunciamos a la dote. La niña vendrá a casa de su marido nada más con la ropa que lleva puesta.

—Permítame usted entonces darle los muebles y el ajuar de novia.

—Ni un alfiler. Si no está de acuerdo, que se muera la chica.

—Sea usted razonable, don Honorato. Mi hija necesita llevar por lo menos una camisa para reemplazar la puesta.

—Bien. Consiento en que le regale la camisa de novia, y nada más.

Al día siguiente don Raimundo y don Honorato se dirigieron muy temprano a la iglesia de San Francisco para oír misa, y, según lo pactado, dijo el padre de Margarita:

—Juro no dar a mi hija más que la camisa de novia.

Y don Raimundo Pareja cumplió al pie de la letra su juramento, porque ni en la vida ni en la muerte dio después a su hija cosa que valiera un centavo.

Los encajes de Flandes que adornaban la camisa de la novia costaron dos mil setecientos duros. El cordoncillo que ajustaba el cuello era una cadenita de brillantes, valorizada en treinta mil monedas de plata.

Los recién casados hicieron creer al tío que la camisa valía muy poco porque don Honorato era tan obstinado que, al saber la verdad, habría forzado al sobrino a divorciarse.

Por esto fue muy merecida la fama de la camisa nupcial de Margarita Pareja.

Cultures and Communities

Culture Note
The procession of Santa Rosa at which Margarita and Luis meet celebrates the festival of Santa Rosa de Lima (1586–1617). It is held each year on August 30 in honor of the patron saint of Lima. Santa Rosa de Lima was the first person born in the Western Hemisphere to be canonized by the Roman Catholic Church (in 1671). A member of the Dominican religious order, she ran an infirmary for the elderly and for poor children in the garden of her home.

There are few canonized Americans, and Peru is home to two of them. San Martín de Porres (1579–1639) was canonized in 1962. He is the Peruvian national patron of social justice. Also of the Dominican order, San Martín de Porres is famous for nursing the sick and educating the poor.

Vamos a escribir

¿Qué conflictos has tenido con otras personas? ¿Cómo resolvieron los conflictos? ¿Cuál se presta mejor para escribir una historia? En esta actividad vas a escribir sobre uno de esos conflictos y vas a aprender a captar la atención del lector desde un principio.

¡Qué lío!

Escribe una composición de tres o cuatro párrafos sobre un conflicto interesante que has tenido con otra(s) persona(s) y cómo lo resolvieron.

Estrategia para escribir

Snappy introductions An interesting introduction will get your reader involved in your story immediately. One good way to begin is to ask a question to pique his or her curiosity. Another way to hook your reader is to start with an interesting or funny fact or incident related to your story.

A. Preparación

1. Haz una lista de conflictos que has tenido. Luego escoge el conflicto que te parezca más importante, interesante o cómico. Considera las posibilidades que están a la derecha.

   el teléfono   conciertos   fiestas
   rumores
   novios(as)   mentiras   clases

2. Haz otra lista de las cosas esenciales que ocurrieron en el conflicto.

3. Habla con otras personas que estaban allí para recordar detalles interesantes. Luego ponlos en tu lista.

B. Redacción

1. Escribe una buena introducción usando la **Estrategia para escribir.**

2. Consulta tu lista de cosas que ocurrieron y escribe en párrafos lo que pasó. Usa palabras como **primero, luego, antes (de)** y **después (de).**

3. Escribe una conclusión en que explicas por qué este incidente fue tan importante, qué aprendiste o por qué no lo olvidarás nunca.

C. Evaluación

1. Pídeles a unos(as) amigos(as) que lean tu introducción. Si dicen que no les llama la atención, cámbiala usando una pregunta más interesante o detalles más vívidos.

2. Lee los párrafos con cuidado. ¿Tiene sentido cada párrafo? Si no, agrega u omite detalles.

3. ¿Está organizada lógicamente la historia? Si no, cambia el orden de la historia para que sea más lógico.

Vamos a escribir

CAPÍTULO 7

Teaching Resources
p. 211

PRINT
▸ Lesson Planner, p. 35
▸ Cuaderno para hispanohablantes, p. 34
▸ Alternative Assessment, p. 22
▸ Standardized Assessment Tutor, Chapter 7

MEDIA
▸ One-Stop Planner, Disc 2
  Test Generator, Chapter 7
▸ Interactive CD-ROM Tutor, Disc 2

Process Writing

Additional Practice
A. After students choose their topic and list supporting details, have them organize their notes in outline format. Suggest that they outline their introduction only after they finalize the body of their composition.

Prewriting/Writing

Teaching Suggestion
Remind students to use double or triple spacing, or to skip lines if writing longhand, to allow enough room for readers' comments and peer-editing of rough drafts.

Visual Learners
Suggest that students sketch any important setting they are trying to describe. The visual reinforcement may remind them of details that make their story more authentic and interesting.

Apply and Assess

Postwriting
Group Work
When they have completed their first draft, have students peer-evaluate introductions in groups of four. Have group members read each introduction one by one, critique them for interest level, point out strengths, and suggest improvements.

Pair Work
Have students pair up to peer-edit compositions. Remind them that they should focus on content and organization, as well as on details such as spelling and grammar. Partners should point out both strengths and weaknesses and make specific suggestions to help the writer improve the text.

For **Más práctica gramatical** Answer Transparencies, see the *Teaching Transparencies* binder.

Más práctica gramatical

CD-ROM DISC 2

internet

MARCAR: go.hrw.com
PALABRA CLAVE:
WV3 BUENOS AIRES-7

Primer paso **Objectives** Expressing happiness and unhappiness; comforting someone

1 Julia y Clara son amigas. Completa las cartas que se escribieron la semana pasada sobre la fiesta de Clara. Usa las formas correctas del subjuntivo de los verbos entre paréntesis. **(p. 196)**

Querida Clara,

Lo siento, pero no puedo ir a tu fiesta. Tengo gripe, y el doctor me recomienda que ___1___ (descansar) en casa unos días más. No es nada serio, y no quiero que tú ___2___ (preocuparse). Claro, mis padres están muy preocupados. ¡Me frustra que ellos no me ___3___ (dejar) llamar a mis amigas! Temo que nosotras no ___4___ (poder) ir al parque de atracciones el sábado próximo tampoco. Ojalá que yo ___5___ (sentirme) mejor antes de nuestro partido de voleibol.

Hasta luego,

Julia

Answers

1
1. descanse
2. te preocupes
3. dejen
4. podamos
5. me sienta
6. estés
7. te sientas
8. vayas
9. vengan
10. traiga

2
1. Me alegro que Lourdes pueda asistir.
2. Me frustra que nosotros no tengamos la dirección de Andrés.
3. Tememos que unos invitados no reciban las invitaciones.
4. ¡Ojalá que haga buen tiempo!
5. Sentimos que unos compañeros vivan demasiado lejos.
6. ¿Temes que Micaela se olvide de venir?
7. Espero que todos se diviertan mucho.
8. Me alegro que (tú) quieras ayudar con la comida.
9. ¡Ojalá que nadie se enferme ese día!
10. Nos duele que Sandra no tenga interés en la reunión.
11. A Marisa le frustra que no haya más tiempo para organizar todo.
12. Siento que sea imposible tener la reunión en la playa.

Hola Julia,

¡Qué triste que tú ___6___ (estar) enferma! Espero que ___7___ (sentirse) mejor pronto. Siento que no ___8___ (ir) a venir a la fiesta, pero lo entiendo. Temo que Álvaro y Paula no ___9___ (venir) tampoco. Oye, ¿necesitas algo del colegio? ¿Quieres que yo te ___10___ (traer) tus libros y la tarea?

Cuídate,

Clara

Grammar Resources for Chapter 7

The **Más práctica gramatical** activities are designed as supplemental activities for the grammatical concepts presented in the chapter. You might use them as additional practice, for review, or for assessment.

For more grammar presentation, review, and practice, refer to the following:
• Cuaderno de gramática
• Grammar Tutor for Students of Spanish

• Grammar Summary on pp. R25–R46
• Cuaderno de actividades
• Grammar and Vocabulary quizzes (Testing Program)
• Test Generator on the One-Stop Planner CD-ROM
• Interactive CD-ROM Tutor
• **Juegos interactivos** at <u>go.hrw.com</u>

2 Unos amigos están planeando una reunión de compañeros de la escuela primaria. Forma oraciones completas para expresar lo que dicen todos sobre los planes. Usa la forma correcta del subjuntivo y sigue el modelo. (p. 196)

MODELO   **Ojalá/Imelda/acordarse de comprar las invitaciones**
                   Ojalá que Imelda se acuerde de comprar las invitaciones.

1. Me alegro/Lourdes/poder asistir
2. Me frustra/nosotros/no tener la dirección de Andrés
3. Tememos/unos invitados/no recibir las invitaciones
4. ¡Ojalá/hacer buen tiempo!
5. Sentimos/unos compañeros/vivir demasiado lejos
6. ¿Temes/Micaela/olvidarse de venir?
7. Espero/todos/divertirse mucho
8. Me alegro/tú/querer ayudar con la comida
9. ¡Ojalá/nadie/enfermarse ese día!
10. Nos duele/Sandra/no tener interés en la reunión
11. A Marisa le frustra/no haber más tiempo para organizar todo
12. Siento/ser imposible tener la reunión en la playa

3 Tomás filled out a magazine questionnaire about best friends. Read his responses. Then write a sentence explaining how often he and his best friend do the activities listed. Use the information in the questionnaire and follow the model. (p. 197)

MODELO   **Tomás y su mejor amigo nunca se escriben.**

	NUNCA	A VECES	SIEMPRE
escribirse	✔		
1. llamarse por teléfono			✔
2. verse en el colegio			✔
3. verse después de clases		✔	
4. ayudarse con la tarea		✔	
5. contarse sus problemas			✔
6. comprarse regalos		✔	
7. hacerse cumplidos	✔		

Communication for All Students

Challenge
Have students write an e-mail message to a good friend telling about one of the following situations: **tu primo(a) viene de visita por una semana pero no le gusta ninguna de las actividades que tú haces; la banda de ustedes está en las finales de una competencia; acabas de ver una película muy mala.** Students should use at least two expressions that require the subjunctive.

Pair Work
1 Ask pairs of students to choose one of the following situations and write a paragraph telling how they feel about it. They are to use at least two reciprocal constructions. **un compañero de clase te cuenta un rumor negativo sobre tu mejor amigo; tienes un malentendido con tus padres u otro pariente; tu novio(a) te deja plantado(a) el sábado.**

Answers
3 1. Tomás y su mejor amigo siempre se llaman por teléfono.
   2. Siempre se ven en el colegio.
   3. A veces se ven después de clases.
   4. A veces se ayudan con la tarea.
   5. Siempre se cuentan sus problemas.
   6. A veces se compran regalos.
   7. Nunca se hacen cumplidos.

For **Más práctica gramatical**
Answer Transparencies, see the
Teaching Transparencies binder.

Más práctica gramatical

CD-ROM
DISC 2

go.
hrw
.com
WV3 BUENOS AIRES-7

4 Abelardo y Manolo están hablando sobre los problemas que han tenido Manolo y otros amigos. Forma oraciones completas para expresar lo que dice Abelardo. Usa el perfecto *(present perfect)* del subjuntivo y sigue el modelo. **(p. 198)**

> **MODELO**   Temo/Rogelio y Victoria/pelearse
> **Temo que Rogelio y Victoria se hayan peleado.**

1. Le duele mucho/Victoria/no aceptar tu invitación
2. No le gusta para nada/ella/salir con otro chico
3. A Victoria le frustra/Rogelio/no confiar en ella
4. Y a Rogelio le molesta/yo/no decirle qué estaba pasando
5. Tampoco le gusta/Victoria/no querer decirle la verdad
6. A Victoria le duele/tú y Rogelio/no llamarla anoche
7. Es triste/ustedes/tener un malentendido
8. Ojalá/ustedes/empezar a resolver el problema ya

Segundo paso

Objectives Making an apology; describing an ideal relationship

5 La señorita Herrera trabaja como consejera en tu colegio. Completa los consejos que les da a los estudiantes. Usa cada verbo sólo una vez. **(p. 203)**

darle	guardar		admitir	romper	comprarle
		discutir	tiene		
mentir	insultar	darte		respetar	echarle

1. Si no tienes razón, es mejor ═══════ tu error.
2. Les recomiendo a todos que traten siempre de ═══════ los sentimientos de los demás.
3. Si una persona no sabe ═══════ tus secretos, es mejor que no le digas nada.
4. Antes de ═══════ con tu novio o novia para siempre, debes ═══════ tiempo para pensar.
5. Cuando has cometido un error, no deberías ═══════ la culpa a otra persona.
6. Cuando un amigo te hace una pregunta sincera, nunca le deberías ═══════. Dile la verdad siempre.
7. Si tu novio o novia ═══════ celos, trata de ═══════ el problema con él o ella.
8. Para reconciliarte con un amigo, deberías ═══════ un regalo y ═══════ un fuerte abrazo.
9. Nunca es bueno ═══════ a la gente. Los insultos no resuelven nada.

Answers

4 1. Le duele mucho que Victoria no haya aceptado tu invitación.
2. No le gusta para nada que ella haya salido con otro chico.
3. A Victoria le frustra que Rogelio no haya confiado en ella.
4. Y a Rogelio le molesta que yo no le haya dicho qué estaba pasando.
5. Tampoco le gusta que Victoria no haya querido decirle la verdad.
6. A Victoria le duele que tú y Rogelio no la hayan llamado anoche.
7. Es triste que ustedes hayan tenido un malentendido.
8. Ojalá que ustedes hayan resuelto el problema ya.

5 1. admitir
2. respetar
3. guardar
4. romper, darte
5. echarle
6. mentir
7. tiene, discutir
8. comprarle, darle
9. insultar

Communication for All Students

Challenge

4 Ask a student to express in the past tense some pleasant or unpleasant experience that he or she had. (**Lo pasé muy bien en tu fiesta. Nadie me llamó por mi cumpleaños.**) Another student responds with an appropriate reaction using the subjunctive. (**Me alegro que lo hayas pasado bien. Me duele mucho que nadie te haya llamado.**)

Pair Work

5 Have pairs of students write a letter to an advice column describing a relationship problem. Students should use as much of the new vocabulary as possible. Pairs can then trade letters and write the columnist's response, using vocabulary and reactions and recommendations with the subjunctive.

6 You work for a pen-pal organization, and today you are trying to match up potential pen pals. Does your computer database have people with these characteristics? Remember that when describing a person who is unknown or nonexistent with a **que** clause, you need to use the subjunctive. **(p. 205)**

MODELO   **hacer el esquí acuático (sí)**
Hay muchas personas que hacen el esquí acuático.
hacer la escalada deportiva (no)
No hay nadie que haga la escalada deportiva.

1. coleccionar estampillas (sí)
2. coleccionar monedas (no)
3. tocar el piano (sí)
4. tocar la guitarra eléctrica (no)
5. saber inglés (sí)
6. saber japonés (no)
7. ser vegetarianas (sí)
8. cocinar en un restaurante vegetariano (no)
9. jugar al voleibol (sí)
10. jugar al jai alai (no)

7 The following people have posted classified and personal ads in their local newspaper. Write a sentence that reflects what they are looking for, following the **Modelo**. **(p. 205)**

MODELO   **el Sr. y la Sra. Fuentes/alguien/llevarse bien con los niños**
Buscan a alguien que se lleve bien con los niños.

1. Manolo/alguien/saber alemán
2. Luisa/un joven simpático/saber bailar el tango
3. Carlos/una chica/nunca estar a dieta
4. los músicos/dos personas/tocar el saxofón y la batería
5. nosotros/alguien/tener un buen sentido del humor
6. el jefe de la empresa/alguien/trabajar a tiempo completo
7. Carmen/alguien/saber montar a caballo
8. Miguel/alguien/saber bucear
9. tú/un(a) amigo(a) ideal/ser bilingüe

Review and Assess

You may wish to assign the **Más práctica gramatical** activities as additional practice or homework after presenting material throughout the chapter. Assign Activities 1 and 2 after **Así se dice** (p. 195), Activity 3 after **Nota gramatical** (p. 197), Activity 4 after **Gramática** (p. 198), Activity 5 after **Vocabulario** (p. 203), and Activity 6 after **Así se dice** and **Gramática** (p. 205). To prepare students for the **Paso** Quizzes and Chapter Test, have them do the **Más práctica gramatical** activities in the following order: complete Activities 1–4 before taking Quizzes 7-1A or 7-1B; Activities 5–6 before taking Quizzes 7-2A or 7-2B.

Answers

6 1. Hay muchas personas que coleccionan estampillas.
2. No hay nadie que coleccione monedas.
3. Hay muchas personas que tocan el piano.
4. No hay nadie que toque la guitarra eléctrica.
5. Hay muchas personas que saben inglés.
6. No hay nadie que sepa japonés.
7. Hay muchas personas que son vegetarianos.
8. No hay nadie que cocine en un restaurante vegetariano.
9. Hay muchas personas que juegan al voleibol.
10. No hay nadie que juegue al jai alai.

7 1. Busca a alguien que sepa alemán.
2. Busca un joven simpático que sepa bailar el tango.
3. Busca una chica que nunca esté a dieta.
4. Buscan a dos personas que toquen el saxofón y la batería.
5. Buscamos a alguien que tenga un buen sentido del humor.
6. Busca a alguien que trabaje a tiempo completo.
7. Busca a alguien que sepa montar a caballo.
8. Busca a alguien que sepa bucear.
9. Buscas a un(a) amigo(a) ideal que sea bilingüe.

MARCAR: go.hrw.com
PALABRA CLAVE:
    WV3 BUENOS AIRES-7

CAPÍTULO 7

The **Repaso** reviews all four skills and culture in preparation for the Chapter Test.

Teaching Resources
pp. 216–217

PRINT 📖
▸ Lesson Planner, p. 36
▸ Listening Activities, p. 53
▸ Video Guide, pp. 45, 47, 50
▸ Grammar Tutor for Students of Spanish, Chapter 7
▸ Cuaderno para hispanohablantes, pp. 31–35
▸ Standardized Assessment Tutor, Chapter 7

MEDIA
▸ One-Stop Planner
▸ Video Program, Videocassette 3, 12:23–17:27
▸ Audio Compact Discs, CD 7, Tr. 21
▸ Interactive CD-ROM Tutor, Disc 2

📁 Portfolio

⑤ **Written** You might have students include this activity in their written Portfolios. For Portfolio suggestions, see *Alternative Assessment Guide*, page 22.

① Escucha lo que dice cada persona y responde con una expresión apropiada de felicidad, desilusión, consuelo o disculpa. Script and answers on p. 189H.
CD 7 Tr. 21

② Completa las oraciones con información cultural de este capítulo. See answers below.

1. Gabriela Sabatini es famosa porque...
2. A los porteños les gusta ir a las confiterías para...
3. En lugar de **tú**, los argentinos usan el pronombre...
4. La Organización de Estados Americanos sirve para...
5. Es interesante ver una película en el Instituto de Realización Cinematográfica Argentina porque...

③ Imagina que estás buscando un(a) amigo(a) ideal por correspondencia. Discute el tema con tu compañero(a). Usen frases como **¿Qué buscas...?, Busco a alguien que...** o **No aguanto a nadie que...**

④ Con tres o cuatro compañeros(as), diseña unas tarjetas para...

1. expresar felicidad
2. dar consuelo
3. pedir perdón

Luego compartan sus tarjetas con la clase.

Eres mi amiga ahora y para siempre...

Gracias por todo.
Nunca lo olvidaré.
Alonso

No te preocupes... esto pasará pronto.

⑤ Imagina que un(a) amigo(a) rico(a) te dio 10.000 dólares para tu cumpleaños. Escríbele una carta para expresar tu felicidad.

Answers
② 1. jugaba al tenis a nivel internacional.
2. tomar café y hablar un poco.
3. **vos.**
4. fomentar la cooperación económica y la justicia social, y para resolver los problemas de una forma pacífica.
5. todos se sientan en el piso y luego discuten la película.

Apply and Assess

Slower Pace

① Before conducting this activity, give students two minutes to write as many of the new expressions from the chapter as they can remember without using the book. Have them list the expressions in categories such as **los sentimientos, los amigos,** or **problemas y soluciones.** Then have them check their list against the **Así**
se dice sections in this chapter. You may want to allow students to refer to this list as they listen to the audio recording.

Additional Practice

③ Have students write a newspaper ad specifying the qualities they want their prospective pen pal to have.

STANDARDS: 1.1, 1.2, 1.3, 5.1

6 Usa las expresiones de **Así de dice** y otras expresiones de emoción para indicar cómo te sientes en cada situación. See sample answers below.

MODELO   **Un(a) amigo(a) te dice que su perro ha muerto.**
          —Siento que haya muerto. Sé que lo querías mucho.

1. Un amigo te dice que el equipo de tu escuela ha perdido el campeonato de baloncesto.

2. Una amiga te dice que el equipo de tu escuela ha ganado el campeonato de debate.

3. Un amigo te dice que te ha comprado entradas para el concierto de tu grupo favorito.

4. Una amiga te dice que su novio ha roto con ella.

5. Tu hermano mayor te dice que ha recibido una beca de 5.000,00 dólares.

7 Con un(a) compañero(a), lee la carta que escribió Héctor Antonio a una revista. Luego prepara una conversación en la que Héctor Antonio habla con su amigo para expresar su desilusión. Su amigo le pide perdón y los dos amigos resuelven el problema.

> "Queridos amigos y amigas: Tengo problemas con un amigo mío. Lo consideraba un buen amigo mío pero ahora no sé. Anda ahora con unas personas que no me gustan mucho. Ya no me llama tanto como antes y casi nunca nos hablamos. Antes íbamos a bailar con otros amigos y amigas del colegio e íbamos también al cine, pero ahora casi nunca nos vemos. ¿Qué me aconsejan Uds.?"
>
> ~ Héctor Antonio Varema

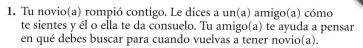

8 **S i t u a c i ó n**

1. Tu novio(a) rompió contigo. Le dices a un(a) amigo(a) cómo te sientes y él o ella te da consuelo. Tu amigo(a) te ayuda a pensar en qué debes buscar para cuando vuelvas a tener novio(a).

2. Tú tienes un problema con tu amigo(a) por unos rumores que escuchó de ti. Discute el problema con tu amigo(a) y busca la solución al problema. Tú y tu amigo(a) se disculpan y se reconcilian.

Cuaderno para hispanohablantes, p. 35

Apply and Assess

Group Work

6 Assign students to groups of four. Have each group write a dialogue for one of the situations and present its dialogue to the class.

Pair Work

6 Have students create two or three additional situations. Then ask them to read their situations to the class to elicit reactions.

Additional Practice

7 Have students write a response to the letter. Encourage them to use at least three subjunctive expressions in their writing.

Answers
6 *Sample answers:*
1. No lo puedo creer. Lo siento mucho y estoy muy triste.
2. Estoy en la gloria.
3. Estoy encantado(a) que me haya comprado las entradas.
4. No hay mal que por bien no venga.
5. Estoy bien contento(a).

A ver si puedo

CAPÍTULO 7

Teaching Resources
p. 218

PRINT
▸ Grammar Tutor for Students of Spanish, Chapter 7

MEDIA
▸ Interactive CD-ROM Tutor, Disc 2
▸ Online self-test

go.hrw.com
WV3 BUENOS AIRES-7

Answers

1 *Sample answers:*
1. Me alegro mucho.
2. Me alegro que quieran dármelo.
3. Estoy muy contento(a).
4. Estoy contento(a).
5. Estoy en la gloria.

2 *Sample answers:*
1. Esto pasará pronto.
2. No te preocupes. Vamos a encontrarlo.
3. ¡Ánimo! No hay mal que cien años dure.
4. Tranquilo(a). ¿Qué puedo hacer por ti?
5. Lo siento mucho. Te aconsejo hablar con el profesor después de clase.
6. No hay mal que por bien no venga. Tal vez puedes visitarla allí.

3 *Possible answers:*
1. Mamá, lo siento mucho. Lo hice sin querer.
2. Hijo, perdóname. Usé tu carro sin tu permiso.

4 *Answers will vary. Possible answers:*
1. Busca a alguien que sea paciente.
2. Busca a alguien que sea buena estudiante.
3. No aguanta a nadie que se quede frente a la tele.
4. Eduardo busca a alguien que sepa algo de la música.

A ver si puedo...

WV3 BUENOS AIRES-7

Can you express happiness and unhappiness? p. 195

1 ¿Cómo te sientes si...? *See sample answers below.*
1. tu profesor(a) dice que está orgulloso(a) de ti
2. tus padres te dicen que van a darte un televisor
3. alguien te dice que tú eres su amigo(a) favorito(a)
4. un(a) amigo(a) gana entradas para el cine y quiere compartirlas contigo
5. tus abuelos te regalan un viaje a Europa

Can you comfort someone? p. 199

2 Responde a lo que dicen las siguientes personas. ¿Qué les dices para darles consuelo? *See sample answers below.*
1. Tu mejor amigo(a): No puedo mirar la tele por un mes.
2. Una niña de cinco años: ¡Se me perdió mi juguete!
3. Tu hermano(a): Nadie quiere salir conmigo.
4. Un(a) amigo(a): ¡Mira el carro! Mi padre no me dio permiso para usarlo, pero lo hice, ¡y tuve un accidente! Ahora no me deja salir.
5. Otro(a) estudiante: No me gusta la clase de historia... ¡me pongo tan nervioso(a) cuando el profesor me hace una pregunta!
6. Una compañera de clase: Estoy muy triste. Mi mejor amiga va a mudarse a otra ciudad.

Can you make an apology? p. 203

3 Hay una persona en cada dibujo que necesita disculparse. Escribe una disculpa apropiada para cada persona. *See possible answers below.*

Can you describe an ideal relationship? p. 205

4 Estas personas buscan amigos ideales que sean como ellos. Para cada persona escribe si busca a alguien o si no aguanta a nadie que tenga la característica entre parentesis. *See possible answers below.*
1. Marcos está loco por coleccionar estampillas. (ser paciente)
2. Toña pasa mucho tiempo leyendo los libros de texto. (ser buen(a) estudiante)
3. A Carla le gusta mucho salir al parque. Nunca ve televisión. (quedarse frente a la tele)
4. Eduardo toca muchos instrumentos musicales. (saber de música)

Review and Assess

Pair Work
1 Have pairs of students choose one of the situations listed in the activity and create a brief dialogue to present to the class. Students should include as much of the new vocabulary and as many uses of the subjunctive as possible.

Challenge
4 Have students write two or three sentences further describing ideal friends for each of the four people in the activity without mentioning the names. Ask volunteers to read one of their sentences aloud so the class can guess which person is being discussed. **(Esta persona busca a alguien que tenga muchos discos compactos. —Eduardo)**

STANDARDS: 1.2

Primer paso

Expressing happiness

Estoy contento(a).	I'm happy.
Estoy de buen humor.	I'm in a good mood.
¡Estoy en la gloria!	I'm in heaven!
Estoy encantado(a) que...	I'm delighted that . . .
Estoy orgulloso(a) de...	I'm proud of . . .
Me alegro que...	I'm glad that . . .
Me encanta que...	I'm delighted that . . .

Expressing unhappiness

Estoy decepcionado(a).	I'm disappointed.
Estoy desilusionado(a).	I'm disappointed.
Estoy dolido(a).	I'm hurt.
Me dan ganas de llorar.	It makes me feel like crying.
Me duele mucho que...	It really hurts me that . . .
Me frustra que...	It frustrates me that . . .

Me siento frustrado(a).	I'm frustrated.
Temo que...	I'm afraid that . . .

Friendship

la amistad	friendship
apoyar	to support
chismear	to gossip
confiar en	to trust
contar (ue) con	to count or depend on
dejar de hablarse	to stop speaking to each other
dejar plantado(a) a alguien	to stand someone up
El problema está resuelto.	The problem is solved.
hacerle un cumplido a alguien	to compliment someone
pelearse	to have a fight
reconciliarse	to make up, to reconcile

resolver (ue) un problema	to solve a problem
el rumor	rumor
tener un malentendido	to have a misunderstanding

Comforting someone

¡Ánimo!	Cheer up!
Comparto tu pena.	I share your grief.
Esto pasará pronto.	This will soon pass.
Lo siento mucho.	I'm very sorry.
Mi más sentido pésame.	My most heartfelt condolences.
No hay mal que cien años dure.	It won't last forever.
No hay mal que por bien no venga.	Every cloud has a silver lining.
No te preocupes.	Don't worry.
¿Qué puedo hacer por ti?	What can I do for you?
Tranquilo(a).	Calm down.

Segundo paso

Making an apology

Discúlpame.	Forgive me.
Lo hice sin querer.	I didn't mean to do it.
Lo siento mucho, es que no sabía.	I'm very sorry; I didn't know.
No lo haré más.	I won't do it anymore.
No lo volveré a hacer.	I won't do it again.
Perdóname.	Forgive me.

Problems and solutions

admitir/cometer un error	to admit/make a mistake
comprarle un regalo	to buy someone a gift
darle un abrazo	to give someone a hug

darse tiempo para pensar	to give oneself time to think
discutir el problema	to discuss the problem
echarle la culpa a otro(a)	to blame someone else
insultar	to insult
mentir (ie, i)	to lie
no guardar los secretos	not to keep secrets
respetar sus sentimientos	to respect someone's feelings
romper con	to break up with someone
ser desleal	to be disloyal
ser infiel	to be unfaithful
tener celos de	to be jealous of

Describing an ideal relationship

Busco a alguien...	I look for someone . . .
a quien le guste(n)...	who likes . . .
que me apoye...	who'll support me.
que no tenga celos de...	who won't be jealous of . . .
que nunca me mienta.	who'll never lie to me.
que respete...	who'll respect . . .
que sepa...	who knows . . .
que siempre me diga...	who'll always tell me . . .
No aguanto a nadie que sea descortés.	I can't stand anyone who's rude.
el (la) novio(a)	boyfriend/girlfriend

Review and Assess

Game

CARRERAS Prepare several sentences using the vocabulary from this chapter. **(Estoy en la _____ que mi mejor amiga me visite.** or **No hay mal que cien años _____.)** Divide the class into two teams. On the board or a transparency, write the sentences with the vocabulary words from the chapter omitted. Have one member from each team race to be the first to fill in the blank with the correct word. The student who writes the correct response first earns a point for the team. Two new players go to the board after each sentence. For a less active version, have teammates race to write the word at their desk and be the first to hold it up for you to see.

CAPÍTULO 7

Kinesthetic Learners

Ask a student to pantomime an emotion from **Vocabulario**. The student who guesses the emotion is the next to pantomime.

Circumlocution

Have pairs of students make slips of paper with the vocabulary for talking about friendship **(Primer paso)** and problems and solutions **(Segundo paso)**. A student then draws one of the slips of paper and describes the activity to his or her partner without using the original phrase. The partner must guess the phrase: **Es decirle a alguien que has hecho algo malo. (¿Es admitir tu error?)**

Chapter 7 Assessment

▶ **Testing Program**
Chapter Test, pp. 155–160
 Audio Compact Discs, CD 7, Trs. 24–25
Speaking Test, p. 298

▶ **Alternative Assessment Guide**
Portfolio Assessment, p. 22
Performance Assessment, p. 36
CD-ROM Assessment, p. 50

▶ **Interactive CD-ROM Tutor, Disc 2**
 ¡A hablar!
¡A escribir!

▶ **Standardized Assessment Tutor**
Chapter 7

▶ **One-Stop Planner, Disc 2**
 Test Generator
Chapter 7

Capítulo 8: Los medios de comunicación
Chapter Overview

De antemano pp. 222–224	*La radio y la televisión*

	FUNCTIONS	**GRAMMAR**	**VOCABULARY**	**RE-ENTRY**
Primer paso pp. 225–228	• Expressing doubt and disbelief, p. 225 • Expressing certainty, p. 227	• Subjunctive after expressions of doubt and disbelief, p. 225 • **por** in fixed expressions, p. 227	• The television, p. 226 • To know and not to know, p. 228	• **por** and **para** (**Capítulo 4**) • Uses of **se** (**Capítulos 4, 5**)

¡Adelante! pp. 230–231	*Los medios de comunicación*

Segundo paso pp. 232–235	• Expressing possibility and impossibility, p. 232 • Expressing surprise, p. 234	• Subjunctive after impersonal expressions, p. 232	• The newspaper, p. 233	• Expressions of opinion (**Capítulo 3**)

Vamos a leer pp. 236–238	**Signos de puntuación**	**Reading Strategy:** Summarizing important ideas

Vamos a escribir p. 239	**El concierto**	**Writing Strategy:** Connecting words

Más práctica gramatical	**pp. 240–243** **Primer paso,** pp. 240–241	**Segundo paso,** pp. 242–243

Review pp. 244–247	**Repaso,** pp. 244–245	**A ver si puedo…,** p. 246	**Vocabulario,** p. 247

CULTURE

• **Nota cultural,** Radios in Latin America, p. 224

• **Nota cultural,** Internet in Argentina, p. 227

• **A lo nuestro,** Sayings to express difficulties, p. 228

• **Panorama cultural, ¿Cómo te afectan los anuncios comerciales?,** p. 229

• **Nota cultural,** Newsstands in Buenos Aires, p. 235

Capítulo 8: Los medios de comunicación
Chapter Resources

PRINT

Lesson Planning

One-Stop Planner

Lesson Planner with Substitute Teacher Lesson Plans, pp. 37–41, 72

Student Make-Up Assignments
- Make-Up Assignment Copying Masters, Chapter 8

Listening and Speaking

Listening Activities
- Student Response Forms for Listening Activities, pp. 59–61
- Additional Listening Activities 8-1 to 8-6, pp. 63–65
- Additional Listening Activities (poem), p. 66
- Scripts and Answers, pp. 137–141

Video Guide
- Teaching Suggestions, pp. 52–53
- Activity Masters, pp. 54–57
- Scripts and Answers, pp. 101–103, 118

Activities for Communication
- Communicative Activities, pp. 29–32
- Realia and Teaching Suggestions, pp. 72–74
- Situation Cards, pp. 103–104

Reading and Writing

Reading Strategies and Skills Handbook, Chapter 8

¡Lee conmigo! 3, Chapter 8

Cuaderno de actividades, pp. 85–96

Grammar

Cuaderno de gramática, pp. 64–69

Grammar Tutor for Students of Spanish, Chapter 8

Assessment

Testing Program
- Grammar and Vocabulary Quizzes, **Paso** Quizzes, and Chapter Test, pp. 169–182
- Score Sheet, Scripts and Answers, pp. 183–189

Alternative Assessment Guide
- Portfolio Assessment, p. 23
- Performance Assessment, p. 37
- CD-ROM Assessment, p. 51

Student Make-Up Assignments
- Alternative Quizzes, Chapter 8

Standardized Assessment Tutor
- Reading, pp. 31–33
- Writing, p. 34
- Math, pp. 51–52

Native Speakers

Cuaderno para hispanohablantes, pp. 36–40

MEDIA

Online Activities
- Juegos interactivos
- Actividades Internet

Video Program
- Videocassette 3
- Videocassette 5 (captioned version)

Audio Compact Discs
- Textbook Listening Activities, CD 8, Tracks 1–19
- Additional Listening Activities, CD 8, Tracks 24–30
- Assessment Items, CD 8, Tracks 20–23

Interactive CD-ROM Tutor, Disc 2

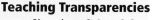
Teaching Transparencies
- Situations 8-1 to 8-2
- **Más práctica gramatical** Answers
- **Cuaderno de gramática** Answers

One-Stop Planner CD-ROM

Use the **One-Stop Planner CD-ROM with Test Generator** to aid in lesson planning and pacing.

For each chapter, the **One-Stop Planner** includes:
- Editable lesson plans with direct links to teaching resources
- Printable worksheets from resource books
- Direct launches to the HRW Internet activities
- Video and audio segments
- Test Generator
- Clip Art for vocabulary items

Capítulo 8: Los medios de comunicación

Projects

El periódico estudiantil

In this project, the class writes its own newspaper. The students work cooperatively as a class and alone on individual articles. Allow part of several class periods and some time outside of class to complete the project.

SITUATION

Tell students to imagine that they work for their town's newspaper and that it is their responsibility to keep the public informed.

> **MATERIALS**
>
> ✂ **Students may need**
> - Plain white paper
> - Audio tape recorder and cassette(s)
> - Markers
> - Computer
> - Scissors
> - Glue
> - White poster board

SUGGESTED SEQUENCE

1. Begin by taking suggestions for the newspaper's name and then have students vote for their final choice.
2. Assign students to different sections of the newspaper.
3. Students turn in their first drafts for your comments. They then work on their individual assignments until the "deadline," two or three days later.
4. When all articles are ready to go to press, students assemble the paper as a class. They should cut, arrange, and paste the articles to the poster board. Any blank areas can be filled in with illustrations or designs.
5. Copy the paper and distribute it.
6. You might suggest that students produce an audio edition of the paper for the visually-impaired.

GRADING THE PROJECT

Suggested point distribution: (total = 100 points)

Language use	40
Originality	30
Participation	20
Appearance	10

Games

Categorías

This game will help students remember the chapter vocabulary and expressions.

Preparation Have the following categories written on the board or on a transparency: **La certeza, Radio y televisión, Posibilidad e imposibilidad, El periódico.**

Procedure Divide the class into two groups and have all students stand up. Begin by asking the first student from Team A to name a Spanish word or phrase that belongs to one of these categories.

Alternate teams and write the words as students name them. A student who cannot think of a new word or makes a mistake must sit down. The team with the most students still standing at the end of a predetermined time period wins.

Fuera de lugar

With this game, students are able to review vocabulary and parts of speech.

Procedure Give an index card to each student and ask students to write four words or phrases on the card. Three words should belong to a group based on meaning or part of speech; one should not belong. (nouns: **el artículo, la primera plana, la calle, anunciar**) Collect the cards and shuffle them.

Divide the class into two teams and give each person on both teams a card. The first person on Team A asks the first person on Team B **¿Qué palabra está fuera de lugar?** and then reads the four words on his or her card. If the person on Team B answers correctly, he or she scores a point. Teams alternate asking the questions until all cards have been read. The team with the most points wins.

> **COMMUNITY LINK**
>
> You may want to ask a local bookstore or newspaper stand to display copies of the students' paper for their customers. Your students get a chance to present the product of their efforts to the public, and the bookstore or stand owner gets to show his or her support of education.

Storytelling

Mini-cuento

This story accompanies Teaching Transparency 8-2. The **mini-cuento** *can be told and retold in different formats, acted out, written as dictation, and read aloud to give students additional opportunities to practice all four skills. The following story recounts how a group of students designs the layout of their school newspaper.*

Todo el mundo piensa que el periódico de nuestro colegio es increíble. Somos muchos los que trabajamos en este equipo para presentar un periódico cada semana. Aquí estamos en una junta. Como editor, tengo que escuchar todos los puntos de vista. Juan defiende un artículo que los demás queremos quitar de la primera plana. Leeming espera con paciencia para ofrecer su opinión mientras Susana explica su punto de vista sobre el asunto. Pedro está tomando apuntes porque le parece interesante lo que discuten Juan y Susana o puede ser que está acabando de escribir su artículo para la sección de editoriales.

Traditions

El tango

The origins of the tango are as complicated as its dance steps. Music historians believe that it is derived from the music of African slaves and a combination of indigenous rhythms and early Spanish colonial music. The tango emerged in the mid-nineteenth century in the poorer neighborhoods of Buenos Aires; its moods and rhythms seem to reflect the character of the city's people, called **porteños.** The music's most characteristic sound comes from the **bandoneón,** an accordion-like instrument with buttons instead of keys. The dance itself is improvised: the man chooses the steps and timing, depending on the music, the partner, and the space. The woman, in turn, adds her own embellishments. Since this is done with a complex series of body signals, the tango is sometimes called a "conversation without words." Have students listen to tango music and describe the emotional tone. (nostalgic, sad, passionate) With what other style of music would students compare the tango's feel and themes? (Some might see a parallel with country music or blues, which reflect the concerns of common people.)

Receta

The **pampas** *is the chief agricultural and cattle ranching area of Argentina. The ranches, called* **estancias,** *maintain the traditional life of the* **gauchos,** *or cowboys. Gauchos were the originators of the famous Argentine* **parrillada,** *but it was the influence of the Italian immigrants that gave the* **parrillada** *its distinctive sauce,* **chimichurri.** *It is very similar to the Italian* **salsa verde,** *but substitutes cilantro for the capers.*

CHIMICHURRI

para 4 personas

1/2 taza de aceite de oliva

1/2 taza de vinagre de vino

2 cucharadas de perejil, picado

1 cucharada de hojas frescas de orégano, picadas

1 cucharada de cilantro, picado

1 cucharadita de ajo, picado fino

jugo de un limón (o limón verde)

1/2 cucharadita de pimienta, recién molida

1 cucharadita de sal

Combine todos los ingredientes en un recipiente. Se puede usar la mezcla inmediatamente, pero sabe mejor después de 24 horas. Si no se usa en seguida, guarde en la refrigeradora, bien tapada, unos 2 días. Remuévalo bien antes de servir. Se puede emplearlo como un remojo para carnes o pescados antes de cocinar a la parrilla, o más tradicionalmente como una salsa.

Capítulo 8: Los medios de comunicación
Technology

Video Program

Videocassette 3, Videocassette 5 (captioned version)
See Video Guide, pages 51–57.

Dramatic episode • Al mundo le hace falta más romance

Outside their home in Seville, Javier and Zoraida share a newspaper. Javier plans to attend college in Mexico and work part time to save money. When Sergio arrives, Javier tells him he has already sent his application to the UNAM College of Communications. Javier, confident about his academic future, is unsure about his future with Alejandra.

¿Cómo te afectan los anuncios comerciales?

People from various Spanish-speaking countries talk about whether or not they are influenced by commercials.

De antemano • La radio y la televisión

People talk about their television viewing habits. One man talks about his job at a radio station.

¡Adelante! • Los medios de comunicación

Two teenagers say that they read the newspaper daily. They also talk about magazines.

 Videoclips

• **Radio Boliviariana**: advertisement for a classical music station

• **TVE**: public service message encouraging people not to watch too much television

Interactive CD-ROM Tutor

The **Interactive CD-ROM Tutor** contains videos, interactive games, and activities that provide students an opportunity to practice and review the material covered in Chapter 8.

Activity	Activity Type	Pupil's Edition Page
1. Así se dice	Imagen y sonido ¡Exploremos! ¡Identifiquemos!	p. 225
2. Vocabulario	¿Qué falta?	p. 226
3. Así se dice	¡Presta el oído!	p. 227
4. Así se dice	¡Atrévete!	p. 232
5. Gramática	¿Cuál es?	p. 232
6. Vocabulario	¡Super memoria!	p. 233
Panorama cultural	¿Cómo te afectan los anuncios comerciales? ¡A escoger!	p. 229
¡A hablar!	*Guided recording*	pp. 244–245
¡A escribir!	*Guided writing*	pp. 244–245

Teacher Management System
Logging In

Logging in to the *¡Ven conmigo!* TMS is easy. Upon launching the program, simply type "admin" in the password area of the log-in screen and press RETURN. Log on to **www.hrw.com/CDROMTUTOR** for a detailed explanation of the Teacher Management System.

One-Stop Planner CD-ROM

To preview all resources available for this chapter, use the **One-Stop Planner CD-ROM,** Disc 2.

Internet Connection

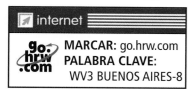

MARCAR: go.hrw.com
PALABRA CLAVE:
WV3 BUENOS AIRES-8

*Have students explore the **go.hrw.com** Web site for many online resources covering all chapters. All Chapter 8 resources are available under the keyword **WV3 BUENOS AIRES-8.** Interactive games help students practice the material and provide them with immediate feedback. You will also find a printable worksheet that provides Internet activities that lead to a comprehensive online research project.*

Juegos interactivos

You can use the interactive activities in this chapter

- to practice grammar, vocabulary, and chapter functions
- as homework
- as an assessment option
- as a self-test
- to prepare for the Chapter Test

Actividades Internet

Students reflect on their knowledge of current events and research some news articles of interest online. They analyze the typical news formula: who, what, where, when, how, and why.

- In preparation for the **Hoja de actividades,** have students review **Panorama cultural** and answer the question: **¿Cómo te afectan los comerciales?**
- After students have completed the activity sheet, ask them to review the headlines from section B. What question(s) (who, what, when, and so on) does each of the article's headlines answer? Ask students what a good headline should communicate and why.

Proyecto

Have students choose one major controversial current event. Ask them to download two articles in Spanish about the event, preferably from news sources in different countries. First ask students to underline the article's answers to "who, what, where, when, how, and why." Then have them pick out differences in writing style or facts covered in the different news stories.

Primer paso

6 p. 225

1. Leí un artículo en una revista acerca de los juegos violentos de los niños de hoy, comparados con los de hace un siglo. Creo que la violencia en la televisión tiene una influencia mala sobre los niños. Debemos enseñarles a los niños el valor de los juegos no violentos.

2. No hay duda de que hay demasiada violencia en la televisión. Por eso, los padres deben evitar que los niños vean mucha televisión, en particular cuando los programas son violentos.

3. No puedo creer que la violencia afecte tanto a los niños. Los niños de hoy son muy independientes. Yo no creo que los niños sean violentos sólo porque los programas de la televisión son violentos.

4. Es increíble que los niños puedan ver programas tan violentos en la tele. Parece mentira que se sientan tan atraídos por programas en que haya guerras y muertes todo el tiempo.

5. No estoy segura que haya tanta violencia en la tele. Dudo que haya mucha violencia en la televisión. Creo que hay más violencia en el hogar o en las ciudades. Los niños son violentos por otras razones, no por la televisión.

Answers to Activity 6
1. Juana   3. Clarice   5. Clarice
2. Juana   4. Juana

11 p. 226

1. Es la persona que presenta sus opiniones sobre las noticias.

2. Es el programa en que se presentan las noticias del día.

3. Es la persona que busca las noticias y escribe los reportajes.

4. Es la persona que presenta las noticias en un noticiero.

5. Es un reportaje que, con base en una investigación, presenta información sobre un solo tema.

Answers to Activity 11
1. el (la) comentarista   3. el (la) reportero(a)   5. el documental
2. el noticiero   4. el (la) locutor(a)

Segundo paso

23 p. 232

1. Es probable que mucha gente compre el periódico este año.

2. Es imposible que incluyamos artículos en otras lenguas.

3. Es posible que tengamos reporteros en otras partes del mundo.

4. Es fácil que todo en el periódico esté en blanco y negro.

Answers to Activity 23
1. c
2. a
3. d
4. b

The following scripts are for the listening activities found in the *Pupil's Edition.* For Student Response Forms, see *Listening Activities,* pages 59–61. To provide students with additional listening practice, see *Listening Activities,* pages 63–66.

One-Stop Planner CD-ROM

To preview all resources available for this chapter, use the **One-Stop Planner CD-ROM**, Disc 2.

26 p. 234

1. El próximo sábado va a ser un día importante para la familia Rodríguez de Castro de Navacerrada. Es probable que lleguen unos visitantes muy importantes. Según la información que recibieron unos periodistas del Diario 16, la familia real se quedará en el chalet de los Rodríguez durante el fin de semana. Es dudoso que el Rey esquíe con su familia durante su estancia por culpa del accidente que tuvo el mes pasado.

2. Es posible que la estrella argentina busque otro equipo con quien jugar en el campo internacional después de su participación sobresaliente con su equipo nacional en la Copa Mundial. Su apodo de Batigol nos recuerda que este jugador lleva el récord tanto de su equipo nacional como del equipo italiano con el cual ha jugado.

3. Es cierto que es una de las cantantes más famosas de Cuba y es evidente que sigue siendo tan popular hoy en día como hace veinte años. Hay que verla en su próximo concierto para entender que en la música, no hay edad.

4. Este otoño esta supermodelo estadounidense de origen cubano va a ser la nueva estrella de Milán y París. Es fácil que muchos de ustedes la reconozcan como "Vee Jay" de MTV; sin embargo ahora va a modelar la ropa de los mejores diseñadores de Europa.

Answers to Activity 26
1. el rey Juan Carlos
2. Gabriel Batistuta
3. Celia Cruz
4. Daisy Fuentes

Repaso

4 p. 245

1. La Bolsa hoy mantuvo su valor por primera vez en dos semanas. Los accionistas, cuando lo supieron, reaccionaron de una manera muy aliviada. Pero los analistas dicen que es posible que esta calma en la Bolsa sea breve. El valor del nuevo peso mexicano contra el dólar está estable pero eso puede cambiar. Aunque por ahora descansan cómodos, no niegan que la situación es delicada.

2. La nueva película de Carlota Fuentes no es nada menos que una obra maestra. El estreno anoche en el Teatro Municipal atrajo a muchos que querían felicitar a la jovencita directora de 27 años. Es posible que sea la película más grande del año tanto entre los cinematógrafos como en la taquilla.

3. Hoy más de cincuenta personas quedaron muertas después de la llegada de huracán Zoraida a la costa del sur. Con vientos de más de doscientos cincuenta kilómetros por hora, es fácil que esta tormenta sea la más poderosa que hayamos visto este siglo.

4. Hoy se oficiará una misa para el alma de Juan Carlos Vicente, quien ha muerto hace tres días, el sábado 14 de septiembre. Que en paz descanse. Pueden ofrecer el pésame a la familia: su padre, esposa e hijos.

5. Es imposible lo que está pasando en nuestra ciudad. El tráfico va empeorando cada día y el gobierno municipal no hace nada. Puede ser que no vea los problemas desde las sillas cómodas de sus oficinas, pero no cabe la menor duda que los hay. Todo el mundo sabe que si no hacemos nada para mejorar el tráfico, tendremos peores problemas en el futuro.

6. El nuevo vestuario del verano todavía no ha salido y todo el mundo está ansioso para hacer sus predicciones. Posiblemente los vestidos largos estén de moda para las mujeres este año pero ¿quién sabe? Es posible que los diseñadores salgan con estilos totalmente distintos a los del pasado.

Answers to Repaso Activity 4
1. c
2. a
3. e
4. f
5. b
6. d

Capítulo 8: Los medios de comunicación
Suggested Lesson Plans *50-Minute Schedule*

Day 1

CHAPTER OPENER 5 min.
- Focusing on Outcomes, ATE, p. 221
- Discuss Community Link, ATE, p. 221.

DE ANTEMANO 40 min.
- Presenting **De antemano** and Preteaching Vocabulary, ATE, p. 222
- Activities 1–5 and Comprehension Check, ATE, p. 224
- Read and discuss **Nota cultural**, p. 224.

Wrap-Up 5 min.
- Do the Thinking Critically activity, ATE, p. 223.

Homework Options
Cuaderno de actividades, p. 85, Activities 1–2

Day 2

PRIMER PASO
Quick Review 5 min.
- Check homework.
- Bell Work, ATE, p. 225

Así se dice/Nota gramatical, p. 225 40 min.
- Presenting **Así se dice** and **Nota gramatical**, ATE, p. 225
- Do Activity 6 with the Audio CD, p. 225.
- Do Activity 7, p. 225.
- Have students do Activity 8 in pairs, p. 225.
- Do Activity 9, p. 226.
- Have students do Activity 10 in groups, p. 226.

Wrap-Up 5 min.
- Follow the Slower Pace suggestion, ATE, p. 225.

Homework Options
Cuaderno de actividades, p. 86, Activity 4
Cuaderno de gramática, pp. 64–65, Activities 1–3

Day 3

PRIMER PASO
Quick Review 5 min.
- Check homework.
- Have students express doubt about your statements.

Vocabulario, p. 226 40 min.
- Presenting **Vocabulario**, ATE, p. 226
- Do Activity 11 with the Audio CD, p. 226.
- Do Activity 12, p. 227.
- Have students do Activity 13 in groups, p. 227.
- Read and discuss **Nota cultural**, p. 227.

Wrap-Up 5 min.
- Follow Vocabulary Practice Suggestions 1–2 for Teaching Transparency 8-1.

Homework Options
Cuaderno de actividades, pp. 86–87, Activities 3, 5–6
Cuaderno de gramática, p. 65, Activities 4–5

Day 4

PRIMER PASO
Quick Review 5 min.
- Check homework.

Así se dice, p. 227 40 min.
- Presenting **Así se dice**, ATE, p. 227
- Present **Nota gramatical**, p. 227, then do Building on Previous Skills, ATE, p. 227.
- Do Activity 14, p. 227.
- Do the Reteaching activity, ATE, p. 227.
- Have students do Activity 15 in pairs, p. 228.
- Do Activity 16, p. 228.

Wrap-Up 5 min.
- Have students finish sentences with an expression of certainty or doubt.

Homework Options
Cuaderno de actividades, pp. 88–89, Activities 8–9
Cuaderno de gramática, p. 66, Activity 6

Day 5

PRIMER PASO
Quick Review 5 min.
- Check homework.
- Follow Suggestion 1 for Teaching Transparency 8-1.

Vocabulario, p. 228 25 min.
- Presenting **Vocabulario**, ATE, p. 228
- Present **A lo nuestro**, p. 228.
- Review the uses of **se.**
- Have students do Activity 17 in pairs, p. 228.
- Have students do Activity 18 in groups, p. 228.

PANORAMA CULTURAL 10 min.
- Presenting **Panorama cultural**, ATE, p. 229

Wrap-Up 10 min.
- Do the Thinking Critically activity, ATE, p. 229.
- Discuss the content and format of Quiz 8-1.

Homework Options
Study for Quiz 8-1.
Cuaderno de actividades, p. 88, Activity 7
Cuaderno de gramática, p. 67, Activities 8–9

Day 6

PRIMER PASO
Quick Review 5 min.
- Check homework.
- Review the content of **Primer paso.**

Quiz 20 min.
- Administer Quiz 8-1A, 8-1B, or a combination of the two.

¡ADELANTE! 20 min.
- Presenting **¡Adelante!** and Preteaching Vocabulary, ATE, p. 230
- Do Activities 19–22, pp. 230–231.

Wrap-Up 5 min.
- Follow the Visual Learners suggestion, ATE, p. 231.

Homework Options
Cuaderno de actividades, p. 90, Activities 10–11

One-Stop Planner CD-ROM

For alternative lesson plans by chapter section, to create your own customized plans, or to preview all resources available for this chapter, use the **One-Stop Planner CD-ROM,** Disc 2.

For additional homework suggestions, see activities accompanied by this symbol throughout the chapter.

Day 7

SEGUNDO PASO
Quick Review 5 min.
- Check homework.
- Bell Work, ATE, p. 232

Así se dice/Gramática, p. 232 30 min.
- Presenting **Así se dice,** ATE, p. 232
- Do Activity 23 with the Audio CD, p. 232.
- Do Activity 24, p. 233.
- **Más práctica gramatical,** p. 242, Activity 5

Vocabulario, p. 233 10 min.
- Presenting **Vocabulario,** ATE, p. 233

Wrap-Up 5 min.
- Follow Suggestion 2 for Teaching Transparency 8-2.

Homework Options
Cuaderno de actividades, pp. 91–92, Activities 12–14
Cuaderno de gramática, pp. 68–69, Activities 10–12

Day 8

SEGUNDO PASO
Quick Review 10 min.
- Check homework.
- Follow Vocabulary Practice Suggestion 2 for Teaching Transparency 8-2.

Vocabulario, p. 233 25 min.
- Do Activity 25, p. 233.
- Do Activity 26 with the Audio CD, p. 234.
- Have students do Activity 27 in groups, p. 234.

Así se dice, p. 234 10 min.
- Presenting **Así se dice,** ATE, p. 234
- Do Activity 28, p. 234.

Wrap-Up 5 min.
- Have students react to headlines and categorize them.

Homework Options
Cuaderno de actividades, pp. 92–94, Activities 15–18
Cuaderno de gramática, p. 69, Activities 13–14

Day 9

SEGUNDO PASO
Quick Review 5 min.
- Check homework.

Así se dice, p. 234 40 min.
- Read and discuss the **Nota cultural,** p. 235.
- Have students do Activities 29–30, p. 235.
- Have students do Activity 31 in groups, p. 235.
- Have students do Activity 32, then peer-edit their work, p. 235.

Wrap-Up 5 min.
- Discuss the content and format of Quiz 8-2.

Homework Options
Study for Quiz 8-2.

Day 10

SEGUNDO PASO
Quick Review 5 min.
- Review the content of **Segundo paso.**

Quiz 20 min.
- Administer Quiz 8-2A, 8-2B, or a combination of the two.

VAMOS A LEER 20 min.
- Do Activities A–B, p. 236.
- Have students do Activities C–D in groups, pp. 236–237.

Wrap-Up 5 min.
- Present Language-to-Language, ATE, p. 238.
- Do Activity E, p. 237.

Homework Options
Repaso Activities 1–2, p. 244
Cuaderno de actividades, pp. 95–96, Activities 19–22

Day 11

VAMOS A LEER
Quick Review 5 min.
- Check and discuss the homework.

VAMOS A LEER 15 min.
- Discuss Activity F, p. 237.
- Have students do Activities I–J in groups, p. 238.

REPASO 25 min.
- List the concepts from Chapter 8.
- Do Activity 4 with the Audio CD, p. 245.
- Have students do Activities 3 and 5 in pairs, pp. 244–245.
- Have students do Activities 6–7 in groups, p. 245.

Wrap-Up 5 min.
- Play **¿Cómo te diré?,** ATE, p. 247.

Homework Options
Vamos a escribir, p. 239

Day 12

REPASO
Quick Review 5 min.
- Check and/or collect homework.

Chapter Review 40 min.
- Review Chapter 8. Choose from **Más práctica gramatical,** Grammar Tutor for Students of Spanish, Activities for Communication, Listening Activities, Interactive CD-ROM Tutor, or **Juegos interactivos.**

Wrap-Up 5 min.
- Discuss the content and format of the Chapter 8 Test.

Homework Options
Study for the Chapter 8 Test.

Assessment

Quick Review 5 min.
- Check homework.

Test, Chapter 8 45 min.
- Administer Chapter 8 Test. Select from Testing Program, Alternative Assessment Guide, Test Generator, or Standardized Assessment Tutor.

Capítulo 8: Los medios de comunicación
Suggested Lesson Plans 90-Minute Block Schedule

Block 1

CHAPTER OPENER 5 min.
- Focusing on Outcomes, ATE, p. 221
- Discuss Community Link, ATE, p. 221.

DE ANTEMANO 40 min.
- Presenting **De antemano** and Preteaching Vocabulary, ATE, p. 222
- Activities 1–5 and Comprehension Check, ATE, p. 224
- Read and discuss **Nota cultural**, p. 224.

Así se dice/Nota gramatical, p. 225 40 min.
- Presenting **Así se dice** and **Nota gramatical,** ATE, p. 225
- Do Activity 6 with the Audio CD, p. 225.
- Do Activity 7, p. 225.
- Have students do Activity 8 in pairs, p. 225.
- Do Activity 9, p. 226.
- Have students do Activity 10 in groups, p. 226.

Wrap-Up 5 min.
- Discuss Visual/Kinesthetic Learners Activity, ATE, p. 226.

Homework Options
Cuaderno de actividades, pp. 85–86, Activities 1–2, 4
Cuaderno de gramática, pp. 64–65, Activities 1–3

Block 2

PRIMER PASO
Quick Review 5 min.
- Check homework.

Vocabulario, p. 226 40 min.
- Presenting **Vocabulario,** ATE, p. 226
- Do Activity 11 with the Audio CD, p. 226.
- Do Activity 12, p. 227.
- Have students do Activity 13 in groups, p. 227.
- Read and discuss **Nota cultural**, p. 227.

Así se dice, p. 227 40 min.
- Presenting **Así se dice,** ATE, p. 227
- Present **Nota gramatical,** p. 227, then do Building on Previous Skills, ATE, p. 227.
- Do Activity 14, p. 227.
- Do the Reteaching activity, ATE, p. 227.
- Have students do Activity 15 in pairs, p. 228.
- Do Activity 16, p. 228.

Wrap-Up 5 min.
- Follow Vocabulary Practice Suggestions 1–2 for Teaching Transparency 8-1.

Homework Options
Cuaderno de actividades, pp. 86–89, Activities 3, 5–6, 8–9
Cuaderno de gramática, pp. 65–66, Activities 4–6

Block 3

PRIMER PASO
Quick Review 10 min.
- Check homework.
- Follow Suggestion 1 for Teaching Transparency 8-1.

Vocabulario, p. 228 25 min.
- Presenting **Vocabulario,** ATE, p. 228
- Present **A lo nuestro,** p. 228.
- Review the uses of **se.**
- Have students do Activity 17 in pairs, p. 228.
- Have students do Activity 18 in groups, p. 228.

PANORAMA CULTURAL 10 min.
- Presenting **Panorama cultural,** ATE, p. 229

¡ADELANTE! 20 min.
- Presenting **¡Adelante!** and Preteaching Vocabulary, ATE, p. 230
- Do Activities 19–22, pp. 230–231.

Así se dice/Gramática, p. 232 15 min.
- Presenting **Así se dice,** ATE, p. 232

Wrap-Up 10 min.
- Have students react to statements using expressions and vocabulary from **Primer paso.**
- Discuss the content and format of Quiz 8-1.

Homework Options
Study for Quiz 8-1.
Cuaderno de actividades, pp. 88, 90–91, Activities 7, 10–13
Cuaderno de gramática, pp. 66–67, Activities 7–9

 **One-Stop** Planner CD-ROM

For alternative lesson plans by chapter section, to create your own customized plans, or to preview all resources available for this chapter, use the **One-Stop Planner CD-ROM,** Disc 2.

 For additional homework suggestions, see activities accompanied by this symbol throughout the chapter.

Block 4

PRIMER PASO
Quick Review 10 min.
- Check homework.
- Review the content of **Primer paso.**

Quiz 20 min.
- Administer Quiz 8-1A, 8-1B, or a combination of the two.

Así se dice/Gramática, p. 232 20 min.
- Review **Así se dice** and **Gramática,** p. 232.
- Do Activity 23 with the Audio CD, p. 232.
- Do Activity 24, p. 233.
- **Más práctica gramatical,** p. 242, Activity 5

Vocabulario, p. 233 35 min.
- Presenting **Vocabulario,** ATE, p. 233
- Do Activity 25, p. 233.
- Do Activity 26 with the Audio CD, p. 234.
- Have students do Activity 27 in groups, p. 234.

Wrap-Up 5 min.
- Follow Vocabulary Practice Suggestion 3 and Suggestion 2 for Teaching Transparency 8-2.

Homework Options
Cuaderno de actividades, pp. 92–93, Activities 14–16
Cuaderno de gramática, pp. 68–69, Activities 10–14

Block 5

SEGUNDO PASO
Quick Review 5 min.
- Check homework.

Así se dice, p. 234 45 min.
- Presenting **Así se dice,** ATE, p. 234
- Do Activity 28, p. 234.
- Cuaderno de actividades, p. 94, Activity 17
- Read and discuss **Nota cultural,** p. 235.
- Have students do Activities 29–30, p. 235.
- Have students do Activity 31 in groups, p. 235.
- Have students do Activity 32, then peer-edit their work, p. 235.

VAMOS A LEER 30 min.
- Do Activities A–B, p. 236.
- Have students do Activities C–D in groups, pp. 236–237.
- Present Language-to-Language, ATE, p. 238.
- Do Activity E, p. 237.

Wrap-Up 10 min.
- Follow the second suggestion for Monitoring Reading, ATE, p. 237.
- Discuss the content and format of Quiz 8-2.

Homework Options
Study for Quiz 8-2.
Vamos a leer activities F–H, pp. 237–238
Cuaderno de actividades, pp. 95–96, Activities 19–22

Block 6

SEGUNDO PASO
Quick Review 10 min.
- Check homework for completion.
- Review the content of **Segundo paso.**

Quiz 20 min.
- Administer Quiz 8-2A, 8-2B, or a combination of the two.

VAMOS A LEER 20 min.
- Discuss Activity F, p. 237.
- Have students do Activities I–J in groups, p. 238.

REPASO 35 min.
- List the concepts from Chapter 8.
- Do Activities 1–2, p. 244.
- Do Activity 4 with the Audio CD, p. 245.
- Have students do Activities 3 and 5 in pairs, pp. 244–245.
- Have students do Activities 6–7 in groups, p. 245.

Wrap-Up 5 min.
- Discuss the content and format of the Chapter 8 Test.

Homework Options
Study for the Chapter 8 Test.
Vamos a escribir, p. 239
A ver si puedo..., p. 246

Block 7

REPASO
Quick Review 5 min.
- Check and/or collect homework.

Chapter Review 40 min.
- Review Chapter 8. Choose from **Más práctica gramatical,** Grammar Tutor for Students of Spanish, Activities for Communication, Listening Activities, Interactive CD-ROM Tutor, or **Juegos interactivos.**

Test, Chapter 8 45 min.
- Administer Chapter 8 Test. Select from Testing Program, Alternative Assessment Guide, Test Generator, or Standardized Assessment Tutor.

Chapter Opener

CAPÍTULO 8

  One-Stop Planner CD-ROM

For resource information, see the **One-Stop Planner,** Disc 2.

Pacing Tips

Primer paso contains the bulk of the chapter vocabulary, in addition to a continuation of the uses of the subjunctive. You may want to allot extra time to allow for role-play and group work where students can create and perform dialogues. These exercises may help students better understand the subtleties of the subjunctive. See Suggested Lesson Plans, pp. 219I–219L.

Meeting the Standards

Communication
- Expressing doubt and disbelief, p. 225
- Expressing certainty, p. 227
- Expressing possibility and impossibility, p. 232
- Expressing surprise, p. 234

Cultures
- Nota cultural, p. 227
- Panorama cultural, p. 229
- Nota cultural, p. 235

Connections
- Reteaching, p. 227
- Thinking Critically, p. 229
- Visual/Tactile Learners, p. 231

Comparisons
- Multicultural Link, p. 220
- Nota cultural, p. 224
- A lo nuestro, p. 228
- Language Note, p. 229
- Multicultural Link, p. 236
- Language-to-Language, p. 238

Communities
- Community Links, pp. 221, 235
- Family Link, p. 227
- Career Path, p. 228

Connections and Comparisons

Multicultural Link

Divide the class into pairs or groups and assign each group a Spanish-speaking country. Have students read newspapers or news magazines from their countries. (They may find sources in the library or consult online periodicals.) Have all groups read articles written during a specific time period, then ask each group to name several stories that were reported in their countries during that time. Can students explain why some stories may have received more coverage in one country than in another, or why a story may only have been reported in one country or region?

CAPÍTULO

8
Los medios de comunicación

Objectives

In this chapter you will learn to

Primer paso

- express doubt and disbelief
- express certainty

Segundo paso

- express possibility and impossibility
- express surprise

 internet

go.hrw.com

MARCAR: go.hrw.com
PALABRA CLAVE:
WV3 BUENOS AIRES-8

◄ No cabe duda que la Torre Entel de Santiago de Chile es magnífica de noche.

Cultures and Communities

Community Link

Ask students to name the various media that are part of their lives. Which media do students use most? Ask them what their favorite television programs, radio stations, and Web sites are and why. How much time do students spend watching television, listening to the radio, and surfing the Internet every day? Have the class poll students and teachers and compile and discuss the results of the survey. Is the class representative of the school as a whole? Do teachers and students have the same media-related habits?

Chapter Opener

CAPÍTULO 8

Photo Flash!

In the following chapter, students will be introduced to information about mass media. Ask students if they can identify what kind of structure is in the photograph. **La Torre Entel** was built in 1974 in Santiago, Chile. It is a contemporary symbol of the power of telecommunications.

Focusing on Outcomes

Remind students that one benefit of being bilingual is that they are able to increase their cultural awareness by accessing information from the mass media in other communities. Mass communication such as radio, television, film, or print media make it possible for messages to reach millions of people. Students will learn to raise questions, offer solutions, and express their opinions.

Chapter Sequence

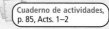
Cuaderno de actividades, p. 85, Acts. 1–2

Teaching Resources
pp. 222–224

PRINT
▶ Lesson Planner, p. 38
▶ Video Guide, pp. 51–52, 54–55
▶ Cuaderno de actividades, p. 85

MEDIA
▶ One-Stop Planner
▶ Video Program
  Contigo en la distancia
  Videocassette 3, 17:43–22:14
  Videocassette 5 (captioned version), 39:20–43:51
  De antemano
  Videocassette 3, 22:15–24:52
▶ Audio Compact Discs, CD 8, Trs. 1–5

CD 8 Trs. 1–5

Estrategia para comprender
La televisión afecta la vida de muchas personas. Y mucha gente pasa horas escuchando la radio. Otras personas tienen empleos relacionados con estos medios de comunicación. Lee lo que dicen estos estudiantes. ¿Qué tienes en común con ellos? ¿De qué maneras son diferentes?

¡ENCUENTRA TU TESORO!

Alejandro

P: ¿Te gusta ver la televisión?

R: Televisión prácticamente no veo porque no tengo tiempo para dedicarle a la televisión, pero de vez en cuando me gusta sentarme un rato a mirar televisión.

P: Y cuando sí miras, ¿qué tipo de programa te gusta ver?

R: Generalmente películas ... series.

P: ¿Qué tipo de programa no te gusta?

R: ¿Qué tipo de programa? Los concursos, eh, ... todo ese tipo de programas de concursos o programas que duran a lo mejor muchísimas horas y que tienen demasiados temas o cosas, programas musicales, eso no.

Juan

P: ¿Cómo se llama Ud. y de dónde es?

R: Bueno, mi nombre es Juan Andrés Hernández García, nacionalidad venezolana y mi profesión en la actualidad, bueno, tengo dos: acá en el Hotel Continental eh... la... funciono como mesero, y aparte soy locutor también y desempeño las funciones en un programa especial en Radio Bonita, emisora 1520 AM. . . . Allí yo tengo un programa dominical, el cual lo realizo con una proyección de enfoque mundial, sobre costumbres, tradiciones, culturas de varios países, y el cual llevo a cabo en Radio Bonita, una emisora de Guatire.

Presenting
De antemano

Have students answer the questions in **Estrategia para comprender.** Then have students watch **La radio y la televisión** and decide whether Alejandro, Juan, and Mariel like the same television programs. Present the Preteaching Vocabulary. Have students read **De antemano,** making note of expressions that support their answer.

De antemano
La radio y la televisión
People talk about their television-viewing habits. One man talks about his job at a radio station.

Preteaching Vocabulary

Guessing Words from Context
Ask students what types of expressions they would use to describe their favorite television shows and radio programs. Have students identify expressions in **De antemano** that describe these types of shows. Then point out the following phrases: **Televisión prácticamente no veo porque no tengo tiempo...; ...soy locutor... desempeño las funciones en un programa** especial en Radio Bonita, emisora 1520 AM; ...tengo un programa dominical... sobre costumbres, tradiciones, culturas de varios países... Have students use context to determine the phrases' meanings. What do students think these phrases say about the characters' personalities?

DELGADO: ¿Podría decirme qué pasó aquí?

POLICIA: Este... a las ocho de la mañana entraron un hombre y una mujer en el banco. Sacaron pistolas y amenazaron a los empleados del banco con la muerte si no les entregaban 100.000 dólares en seguida.

DELGADO: ¿Podrá reconocerlos alguno de los empleados?

POLICIA: No creo que los reconozca nadie pues llevaban máscaras.

DELGADO: ¿Ha encontrado la policía a los ladrones?

POLICIA: Dudamos que estén todavía en la ciudad. Estamos seguros de que había cómplices que los esperaban en un carro para escaparse. No sabemos dónde están pero se han ido de la ciudad sin duda alguna.

DELGADO: Parece mentira que hayan podido robar el banco tan fácilmente.

POLICIA: Y es increíble que se hayan escapado tan rápidamente, pero los vamos a encontrar y meter a la cárcel. No cabe la menor duda.

JUEVES

Radio 1000 AM

12:00

OIGA DOCTOR
Consulte sin previa cita a médicos de gran prestigio
CONDUCE: MARÍA DE LA LUZ TORRES - CANO NEWTON

13:00

LA CIUDAD
2ª emisión
CONDUCE: MAYTÉ NORIEGA
Noticias nacionales e internacionales

14:00

LA MISCELÁNEA DEL ÁNGEL
Genio y figura...
CONDUCE: GERMÁN DEHESA

15:00

DEL TINGO AL TANGO
Comentarios y chismes del mundo del espectáculo
CONDUCEN: RONNA FLETCHER Y AGUSTÍN ROMO ORTEGA

P: ¿Le gusta ver televisión?

R: Sí, me gusta ver televisión.

P: ¿Qué programas ve?

R: Veo novelas.

P: ¿Algo más?

R: Informativo y algún programa de entretenimiento.

P: ¿Qué tipo de programa no le gusta?

R: De política.

P: ¿Por qué?

R: Porque a mí no me gusta la política.

P: ¿A Ud. le influencian mucho los anuncios publicitarios?

R: No, no, no le presto atención. Me es indiferente.

Mariel

Using the Captioned Video

 As an alternative, you might want to show the captioned version of *Contigo en la distancia: Al mundo le hace falta más romance* on Videocassette 5. Some students may benefit from seeing the written words as they listen to the target language and watch the gestures and actions in context. This visual reinforcement of vocabulary and functions will facilitate students' comprehension and help reduce their anxiety before they are formally introduced to the new language in the chapter.

Thinking Critically
Comparing and Contrasting/ Drawing Inferences Have students define as many different types of television programs as they can. Obtain a day's listings for an English- and a Spanish-language television or radio station and have the students compare the types of shows on each. Ask students what they can infer from the similarities and differences that they find.

Contigo en la distancia

You may choose to show students Episode 8: *Al mundo le hace falta más romance* now or wait until later in the chapter. In the video, Javier and Zoraida are in Seville sharing a newspaper. Javier plans to attend college in Mexico and work part time. When Sergio arrives, Javier tells him he has sent in his college application. Javier is worried because Alejandra has not written in a long time. Sergio calls him a romantic and urges him to call her, or write a letter. Javier, sure of his academic future, is unsure about his future with Alejandra.

DE ANTEMANO

CAPÍTULO 8

Additional Practice

1 Have students point out the information in the text that indicates whether the statements are true or false.

Slower Pace

3 Give students the comprehension questions before the interviews. Have them look up any unfamiliar vocabulary.

Answers

1 1. No se sabe.
2. falsa; El programa de Juan es sobre las costumbres.
3. falsa; La señorita Delgado es reportera y está investigando el robo para el Canal 3.
4. cierta
5. cierta
6. falsa; A Mariel no le gustan los programas de política.

2 Duda: no creo que, dudamos que, es increíble que, parece mentira que
Certeza: estamos seguros, sin duda alguna, no cabe la menor duda

3 1. Le gustan las películas y series; no le gustan los programas de concursos, los programas demasiado largos, ni los programas musicales; *Answers will vary.*
2. las costumbres, tradiciones, culturas mundiales; *Answers will vary.*
3. Llevaban máscaras. Había cómplices que los esperaban en un carro para escaparse; *Answers will vary.*
4. médicos de gran prestigio; *Answers will vary.*
5. Le son indiferentes.

4 1. c 4. a
2. b 5. d
3. d

7 1. sea 4. hagan
2. tenga 5. diga
3. gaste 6. quieras

These activities check for comprehension only. Students should not yet be expected to produce language modeled in **De antemano**.

1 **¿Tú crees que sea verdad?** See answers below.

Indica si cada frase es **cierta** o **falsa** o si **no se sabe**. Si es falsa, corrígela.

1. A Alejandro no le gustan los programas de deportes.
2. Juan tiene un programa especial en la emisora Radio Bonita sobre la música rock.
3. El señor Delgado está investigando el robo para la policía.
4. El agente de policía está seguro que van a encontrar a los ladrones.
5. Radio 1000 AM presenta información sobre el país y el mundo.
6. A Mariel le encantan los programas políticos.

2 **Busca las expresiones** See answers below.

¿Qué expresiones se usan para expresar duda? ¿Cuáles se usan para expresar certeza? Haz una lista de estas expresiones.

3 **¿Comprendiste?** See answers below.

Contesta estas preguntas con un(a) compañero(a).

1. ¿Qué tipo de programas le gusta y no le gusta a Alejandro? ¿Por qué?
2. ¿Cuál es el enfoque del programa de Juan? ¿Escuchas programas de este tipo?
3. ¿Por qué no podrán reconocer a los ladrones los empleados del banco? ¿Cómo se escaparon del banco tan fácilmente?
4. ¿A quiénes puedes consultar si llamas a Radio 1000 AM a las 12? ¿Llamas tú a programas de este tipo?
5. ¿Qué opina Mariel de los anuncios publicitarios?

4 **¿Qué significa?** See answers below.

Lee las frases de la primera columna. Usa el contexto para escoger la frase de la segunda columna que mejor define la(s) palabra(s) en negrilla. Usarás una definición dos veces.

1. Soy **locutor** de un programa especial en Radio Bonita.
2. Radio Bonita es una **emisora** de Guatire.
3. **Es increíble** que se hayan escapado los ladrones.
4. ¿A Ud. le influencian los **anuncios** publicitarios?
5. **Dudamos** que estén todavía en la ciudad.

a. lo que dicen para vender algo
b. estación de radio
c. una persona que habla por la radio
d. es difícil de creer

5 **Ahora te toca a ti** Answers will vary.

Imagina que tú y dos o tres compañeros(as) son miembros de un comité que está planeando la programación para los viernes. Sugieran programas para la noche entre las ocho y las once y expliquen por qué cada programa es el más apropiado para cada hora.

Nota cultural

Es probable que la gente de América Latina dependa más de la radio que los estadounidenses. Hay más radios que televisores en América Latina, y muchas personas cuentan con la radio para escuchar las noticias, música, programas deportivos y novelas. ¿Es muy importante en tu vida la radio? ¿Qué tipo de programas prefieres escuchar?

¡TELEVIVA!
Canal 4
¡Tu emisora favorita!

Viernes	
8 PM	Novela: "Esperanza sueña"
9 PM	Documental: "Los volcanes"
10 PM	Noticias locales e internacionales
11 PM	Película: "Mi perro Frufrú"

Comprehension Check

Native Speakers

2 Have native speakers work with a partner to come up with ways to express doubt and certainty other than those used in **De antemano**. Can they substitute the expressions they came up with for those in **De antemano**?

Circumlocution

Have pairs of students choose additional radio and television vocabulary in **De antemano** and **Nota cultural** to continue Activity 4. **(noticias, documental, película, novela, música, programa deportivo, serie, comentario)** One partner should give a definition in Spanish without using the word, while the other tries to guess what it is.

Así se dice

Expressing doubt and disbelief

Si quieres indicar que no crees algo, puedes decir:

Dudo que comience el noticiero antes de las once.

Parece mentira que haya corresponsales allí durante la guerra.

No estoy seguro(a) que el comentarista tenga razón.

Cuaderno de actividades, p. 86, Act. 4

CD-ROM DISC 2

No creo que tengan buenos programas en ese canal.

No puedo creer que los anuncios sean tan largos.

Es increíble que Internet tenga tanta información.

Nota gramatical

Spanish uses the subjunctive after expressions of doubt and disbelief:

No creo que nuestro periódico **sea** muy bueno.

Dudo que haya tiempo para ver la tele.

Haya is the subjunctive of **hay**.

Cuaderno de gramática, pp. 64–65, Acts. 1–3
Más práctica gramatical, p. 240, Act. 1

6 ¿Juana o Clarice? Script and answers on p. 219G.
CD 8 Tr. 6
Escuchemos Juana piensa que hay demasiada violencia en la televisión. Clarice cree que el problema de la violencia es exagerado. Escucha cada frase e indica si la dijo Juana o Clarice.

7 Gramática en contexto See answers below.
Leamos/Escribamos Toni está leyendo noticias sensacionalistas en el periódico. Completa sus pensamientos con la forma correcta de uno de los verbos.

querer gastar hacer decir ser tener

1. Dudo que la senadora Rodríguez ===== billonaria.
2. No puedo creer que ella ===== veinticinco carros.
3. Es increíble que la senadora ===== un millón de dólares cada día.
4. Parece mentira que la senadora y sus amigos ===== un viaje a Europa cada mes.
5. No estoy seguro que este periódico ===== la verdad en sus artículos.
6. No creo que tú ===== comprar este periódico. ¡Es malísimo!

8 Gramática en contexto
Leamos/Hablemos Con un(a) compañero(a), combina elementos de las dos columnas para expresar por lo menos cinco opiniones sobre la programación violenta y su efecto en los niños. Luego indica si estás de acuerdo con estas opiniones y por qué.

No creo que	haber tantos programas violentos
Dudo que	los padres no ver los programas con sus hijos
Parece mentira que	nosotros tener programas apropiados para los niños
Es increíble que	los padres no quejarse más de la violencia
No puedo creer que	los niños poder ver tanta violencia sin malos efectos
No estoy seguro(a) que	el Congreso permitir tanta violencia en la tele

Communication for All Students

Pair Work
7 Have pairs of students write three headlines for a sensationalistic newspaper. Ask volunteers to write their best one on the board. The class will then respond with doubt and disbelief. (**¡Una familia tiene pirañas en su piscina! —No creo que la familia tenga pirañas en su piscina.**) The pair who wrote the headline can then try to convince the class that it is true.

Slower Pace
8 Remind students that they already know the subjunctive forms of **haber** from Chapter 7. Form one sentence as a class, asking for volunteers to choose a beginning and ending, to identify the subject, and to give the subjunctive form. Then have students form the remaining sentences individually before sharing opinions with a partner.

Teaching Resources
pp. 225–228

PRINT
- Lesson Planner, p. 38
- Listening Activities, pp. 59, 63–64
- Activities for Communication, pp. 29–30, 72, 74, 103–104
- Cuaderno de gramática, pp. 64–67
- Grammar Tutor for Students of Spanish, Chapter 8
- Cuaderno de actividades, pp. 86–89
- Cuaderno para hispanohablantes, pp. 36–40
- Testing Program, pp. 169–172
- Alternative Assessment Guide, p. 37
- Student Make-Up Assignments, Chapter 8

MEDIA
- One-Stop Planner
- Audio Compact Discs, CD 8, Trs. 6–7, 24–26, 20
- Teaching Transparencies 8-1; **Más práctica gramatical** Answers; Cuaderno de gramática Answers
- Interactive CD-ROM Tutor, Disc 2

Bell Work
Write the following on a transparency: **Necesito un trabajo que..., Quiero un carro que..., No conozco a nadie que...** Students write original conclusions for each.

Presenting
Así se dice, Nota gramatical
Complete boldfaced **Así se dice** expressions in original ways to model the subjunctive. Make untrue statements and then ask students to express doubt as to the truth of these statements.

Primer paso

CAPÍTULO 8

Teaching Resources
pp. 225–228

PRINT
▶ Lesson Planner, p. 38
▶ Listening Activities, pp. 59, 63–64
▶ Activities for Communication, pp. 29–30, 72, 74, 103–104
▶ Cuaderno de gramática, pp. 64–67
▶ Grammar Tutor for Students of Spanish, Chapter 8
▶ Cuaderno de actividades, pp. 86–89
▶ Cuaderno para hispanohablantes, pp. 36–40
▶ Testing Program, pp. 169–172
▶ Alternative Assessment Guide, p. 37
▶ Student Make-Up Assignments, Chapter 8

MEDIA
▶ One-Stop Planner
▶ Audio Compact Discs, CD 8, Trs. 6–7, 24–26, 20
▶ Teaching Transparencies 8-1; **Más práctica gramatical** Answers; Cuaderno de gramática Answers
▶ Interactive CD-ROM Tutor, Disc 2

Presenting
Vocabulario

Use the new words in sentences describing local television. **(Elena Gómez es la locutora del noticiero del Canal 13.)** Then ask students questions and have them use the new words in their answers. (—¿Cuál es tu programa favorito? —Mi programa favorito es...)

Answers
9 *Sample answer:*
1. Según lo que leí en el artículo, no puedo creer que la televisión les haga daño a los niños.

9 **Lo dudo** Answers will vary. See sample answer below.

Leamos/Escribamos Lee el artículo. Si no crees que las oraciones que siguen sean ciertas según lo que leíste, responde con expresiones de duda. Si crees que son ciertas, responde con **Es cierto.**

> ### Claves para ver mejor la televisión
>
> El doctor Brandom Centerwall de la Escuela de Salud Pública de Seattle ha afirmado que "ver la televisión a menudo no debería ser dañino si los niños aprenden a interpretar lo que ven". Según él, restringir el acceso a ciertos programas es una solución eficaz pero pasajera. Lo más importante es enseñar al televidente desde pequeño a controlar la televisión. Esto significa explicar a los niños cómo funciona la tecnología audiovisual, quién diseña los programas, cómo se miden las audiencias, y qué significa cada pieza del lenguaje televisivo".
>
> Precisamente por eso hemos hecho este artículo. Porque, en contra de lo que muchos opinan, ver la televisión no tiene por qué ser malo. Sólo hay que saber hacerlo.

1. Ver la televisión les hace daño a los niños.
2. Los niños deben tener acceso a todos los programas de televisión.
3. Los niños ya saben interpretar lo que ven en la televisión.
4. Debemos enseñarles a los niños a interpretar lo que ven en la televisión.
5. El autor cree que ver la televisión es malo.

10 **No puedo creer que...**

Escribamos/Hablemos Con dos o tres compañeros(as), escribe una lista de cinco oraciones absurdas o difíciles de creer. Luego den sus frases a otro grupo. Ese grupo debe expresar dudas sobre lo que Uds. han escrito.

MODELO —¡Vamos a salir en la televisión hoy!
—No podemos creer que Uds. salgan en la tele hoy.

Vocabulario

anunciar   *to announce*
el anuncio   *commercial*
la cadena   *(broadcast) network*
el canal   *channel*

el (la) comentarista   *commentator*
el documental   *documentary*
la emisora   *radio station*
en línea   *online*
el (la) locutor(a)   *announcer, anchorperson*
el noticiero   *news program*
por cable   *on cable*
la prensa   *press*
el programa   *program*
el reportaje   *report*
el (la) reportero(a)   *reporter*
el sitio Web   *Web site*

Más práctica gramatical, p. 240, Act. 2

Cuaderno de actividades, pp. 86–87, Acts. 3, 5

Cuaderno de gramática, p. 65, Acts. 4–5

11 **En la tele** Script and answers on p. 219G.

Escuchemos Vas a escuchar cinco oraciones. Indica qué palabra del **Vocabulario** va mejor con cada frase que escuchas.

CD 8 Tr. 7

Communication for All Students

Visual/Kinesthetic Learners
Have students make flashcards for the new vocabulary by drawing or pasting a representation of the word on one side and writing the vocabulary item on the other.

Auditory Learners
11 Replay the recording of the sentences one at a time as a dictation activity.

Slower Pace
12 Before beginning the activity, have students brainstorm problems with the Internet. (verifying accuracy, determining what is fact and what is opinion, slow speed, and unstable sites) Make a list of ideas on the board or on a transparency.

STANDARDS: 1.2, 3.1

12 Un debate

Escribamos Imagina que dos políticos están debatiendo los problemas de Internet. Cuando una persona da su opinión, la otra persona indica que no está de acuerdo y da su propia opinión. Escribe por lo menos 10 oraciones.

MODELO
> SENADORA GARCÍA:
> **Creo que debemos controlar y limitar lo que sale en Internet.**
>
> SENADOR FREIRE:
> **Dudo que la variedad de ideas tenga tan mala influencia.**

 13 ¿Qué piensan Uds.?

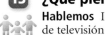 **Hablemos** Imagina que tú y dos compañeros(as) son los invitados(as) en un programa de televisión para hablar de los problemas de la televisión. El anfitrión/la anfitriona *(host)* hace preguntas un poco ridículas. El grupo debe responder con expresiones de **Así se dice.**

MODELO
> —Hay demasiados programas para personas de su edad, ¿no les parece?
> —No creemos que haya demasiados programas para nosotros(as).

Nota cultural

Argentina, como país inmenso al extremo del continente, se ha aplicado al uso de Internet. Este medio de comunicación sirve para unir a los argentinos con culturas, información y costumbres de otras regiones. Un estudiante en la Patagonia puede comunicarse por e-mail con alguien en Tucumán, leer un periódico de Buenos Aires, investigar la ecología de Costa Rica, comprar un diccionario ruso, todo por medio de Internet. ¿Qué cambios sociales crees que esto produce? ¿Qué cambios ha producido Internet en tu comunidad?

Así se dice

Expressing certainty

Si quieres expresar certeza, puedes decir:

> Cuaderno de actividades, pp. 88–89, Acts. 8–9
> Cuaderno de gramática, p. 66, Act. 6
> CD-ROM DISC 2

Es cierto que hubo un documental anoche.
Estoy seguro(a) que el programa empieza a las siete.
Estoy convencido(a) que el noticiero de las diez es el mejor.
Sin duda alguna.   *Without a doubt.*
No cabe la menor duda.   *There is absolutely no doubt.*
Claro que todos recibimos tu anuncio por correo electrónico.
Todo el mundo sabe que hay periódicos en línea de muchas ciudades.
Es evidente que hay muchos anuncios durante los programas.

Es obvio que la emisora presenta una programación variada.   *It's obvious that . . .*
Por cierto.   *Certainly.*
Por supuesto.   *Of course.*

Nota gramatical

The preposition **por** is used in many fixed expressions, like **por cierto** and **por supuesto.** For an explanation of the uses of **por** and **para**, see page R32.

> Más práctica gramatical, p. 241, Act. 3

 14 Gramática en contexto   *See possible answers below.*

Leamos/Escribamos Usa expresiones de **Así se dice** para afirmar que las siguientes oraciones son ciertas. Si no estás de acuerdo, cambia la oración para poder usar una expresión de duda.

1. Tenemos programas que estimulan a los jóvenes intelectualmente.
2. La televisión e Internet son útiles en la educación.
3. Los jóvenes pasan suficiente tiempo con los estudios.
4. Los jóvenes pasan demasiado tiempo viendo la tele y navegando por la Red.

Connections and Comparisons

Family Link

Have students ask their parents and grandparents about the media and means of communication that were most widely used when they were the students' age. Students should ask them what advantages or disadvantages they see in the modern media as opposed to the media of their youth.

How did their parents' and grandparents' lives change when a new medium or means of communication came along? (television, fax, cellular telephone, Internet) Have students report their findings to the class.

Reteaching

Future Review the future tense by saying what will happen in the near future at school. **(Este viernes habrá un baile en el gimnasio. El sábado muchos estudiantes asistirán al partido.)** Then have students make predictions about five news events in the coming week. **(Pete Sampras dejará de jugar al tenis como profesional. El presidente hará un viaje a Europa.)**

Presenting
Así se dice, Nota gramatical

Read the expressions of certainty aloud to the class. Where appropriate, complete the boldfaced expressions in original ways. **(Es cierto que estamos en la clase de español. Es obvio que Uds. son muy listos.)** Then ask the students to do the same.

Building on Previous Skills

You may want to prepare an overhead transparency with sentences similar to the following: **Este programa no es _____ los niños. _____ favor, no cambies de canal. Puse la televisión _____ ver el noticiero.** Have students decide whether to use **por** or **para** for each sentence. Review with students the reasons for choosing **por** or **para** in each case.

Answers

14 *Possible answers:*
1. Es cierto que tenemos programas que estimulan a los jóvenes intelectualmente.
2. Dudo que la televisión e Internet sean útiles en la educación.
3. No creo que los estudiantes pasen suficiente tiempo con los estudios.
4. Es obvio que los jóvenes pasan demasiado tiempo viendo la tele y navegando por la Red.

Presenting
Vocabulario

Role-play both sides of a dialogue in which one person uses the vocabulary to respond to the statements and queries of the other. (**—Tenemos una prueba mañana en la clase de inglés. —¡Ya lo sé! —¿Qué debemos estudiar? —No tengo la menor idea.**) Then make similar statements and queries to the students and have them incorporate the vocabulary in their responses.

Teaching Suggestion

17 After completing the activity, have students repeat it using their own categories. Instruct them to ask each other what they know about a given subject.

Assess

▸ Testing Program, pp. 169–172
Quiz 8-1A, Quiz 8-1B
Audio CD 8, Tr. 20

▸ Student Make-Up Assignments, Chapter 8, Alternative Quiz

▸ Alternative Assessment Guide, p. 37

15 **Gramática en contexto**   Answers will vary.

Hablemos Imagina que estás entrevistando a tu invitado(a) para el programa **El futuro de la comunicación**. Usa estas preguntas. Tu invitado(a) debe contestar con expresiones de duda o certeza usando las frases entre paréntesis u otras ideas que tenga.

1. ¿Cómo será el periódico en unos diez años? (periódico en papel/periódico en línea)
2. Todos tendrán cable dentro de cinco años, ¿no crees? (antena parabólica/cable)
3. ¿Crees que cada familia tendrá su propio sitio Web en quince años? (en línea/Red)
4. En tu opinión, ¿cómo se usará la Red en el futuro? (noticieros/en línea)

16 **¡Entrevista exclusiva!**

Escribamos Imagina que eres reportero(a) para un noticiero sobre estrellas del cine y de la televisión. Escribe un diálogo breve en que el agente de una estrella responda a tus preguntas con expresiones de certeza o de duda.

MODELO   —La señorita Rulfo va a hacer una película este año, ¿no?
—Sí, es cierto que va a hacer una película en dos meses.

Vocabulario

¡Ya lo sé!	*I know!*
estar al tanto de	*to be up to date on*
estar bien informado(a)sobre	*to be well informed about*
Que yo sepa...	*As far as I know . . .*
no saber ni jota de	*to know absolutely nothing about*
no tener la menor idea	*not to have the slightest idea*
Me suena a chino.	*It's Greek to me.*
¿Qué sé yo?	*How should I know?*

A lo nuestro

Different cultures have different ways of saying that something is hard for them to understand. English uses the expression "It's Greek to me." Spanish uses **Me suena a chino** (*It sounds like Chinese to me*), while German speakers say **Das kommt mir spanisch vor** (*That's Spanish to me*).

Cuaderno de actividades, p. 88, Act. 7   Cuaderno de gramática, p. 66, Act. 7

Más práctica gramatical, p. 241, Act. 4

17 **Un programa de concurso**   See sample answers below.

Hablemos Imagina que un(a) compañero(a) quiere participar en el programa **¡Encuentra tu fortuna!** y que tú entrevistas a cada participante acerca de los temas del programa. Pregúntale a tu compañero(a) qué sabe sobre estos temas, y él o ella responderá con vocabulario de este **paso**.

1. las comidas de Estados Unidos
2. los idiomas que se hablan en Estados Unidos
3. los automóviles
4. los programas en la tele los viernes
5. las clases que dan en las escuelas secundarias

¿Se te ha olvidado?
uses of se
Ver la página R27

Cuaderno de gramática, p. 67, Acts. 8–9

18 **¿Quién sabe?**

Escribamos/Hablemos Con dos o tres compañeros, escribe cinco preguntas. Luego, otro grupo tiene que contestarlas, usando las expresiones de este **paso** cuando sea posible.

MODELO   —¿Hay vida en el planeta Marte?
—¿Quién sabe? Que nosotros sepamos, no hay vida allí.

Cultures and Communities

Career Path

On the board or on a transparency, list fields related to communications. (advertising, journalism, radio, television, film, and speech communication sciences) Ask students to think about careers in each of these fields. (advertising graphic designer, foreign correspondent, disc jockey, broadcast journalist, film director, script writer, speech pathologist) How might Spanish be useful in these careers? (establish relationships with Spanish-speaking clients or contacts, reach a broader audience, access information published in Spanish) Discuss the role technology plays in these careers.

Answers

17 *Sample answers:*
1. Que yo sepa son buenas.
2. Estoy bien informado(a) sobre los idiomas que se hablan en los Estados Unidos.
3. No sé ni jota de los automóviles.
4. ¿Qué sé yo? No miro la tele.
5. Estoy al tanto de eso.

CD 8
Trs. 8–11

¿Cómo te afectan los anuncios comerciales?

Muchas empresas gastan millones de dólares al año en campañas publicitarias para promover sus productos. Escucha las respuestas de estas personas hispanohablantes acerca de la influencia de los anuncios comerciales.

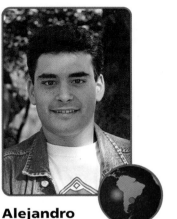

Alejandro
Buenos Aires, Argentina CD 8 Tr. 9

"No. Creo que no. En algunos casos... pueda influir o me pueda llegar un mensaje pero [para que] me hagan tomar distintas decisiones... creo que ya esa parte de la elección es mía y no depende de la televisión o de un anuncio".

Ricardo
Ciudad de México, México CD 8 Tr. 10

"No, no me influencian mucho los anuncios publicitarios... Los anuncios que están muy bien hechos, me interesan por cómo están hechos, pero la información en general no me influencia".

Vivian
Miami, Florida CD 8 Tr. 11

"Sí, me influyen mucho. Bueno, me informan, me hacen pensar en una manera, me dicen qué está pasando e influyen en mis pensamientos sobre ese tópico".

Para pensar y hablar...

A. Dos entrevistados coinciden en que los anuncios comerciales no afectan sus decisiones. Sólo uno de ellos dice que le dan otros puntos de vista y otro dice que le atrae el modo en que los comerciales están hechos. ¿Quiénes son?

B. ¿Para qué sirven los anuncios comerciales? ¿Son distintos los comerciales que promueven productos de los anuncios que apoyan causas sociales? ¿De qué manera son distintos? ¿Están planeados los anuncios comerciales para un público de hombres y mujeres? ¿Para un público de todas las edades? Incluye detalles que apoyen tus respuestas.

Cuaderno para hispanohablantes, pp. 39–40

Teaching Resources
p. 229

PRINT
▸ Video Guide, pp. 51, 53, 57
▸ Cuaderno de actividades, p. 96
▸ Cuaderno para hispanohablantes, p. 39

MEDIA
▸ One-Stop Planner
▸ Video Program, Videocassette 3, 26:05–28:51
▸ Audio Compact Discs, CD 8, Trs. 8–11
▸ Interactive CD-ROM Tutor, Disc 2

Presenting
Panorama cultural

Have students read the questions in **Para pensar y hablar...** before you play the video. After each interview, ask students to summarize what the interviewee said. Play the video again and have students answer the **Preguntas**.

Preguntas

1. ¿Escoge Alejandro los productos que compra por lo que dicen los anuncios? (no)
2. ¿Qué le puede llegar a Alejandro por medio de un anuncio? (un mensaje)
3. ¿Qué tipo de anuncio le interesa a Ricardo? (los que están muy bien hechos)
4. ¿Por qué le interesan? (por cómo están hechos)
5. ¿Influyen los anuncios en los pensamientos de Vivian? (sí)

Connections and Comparisons

Thinking Critically
Analyzing Ask students to pay attention to ads in the media and to determine the strategies used to get consumers to buy goods or services. (featuring glamorous people, comedy, celebrity endorsements, exotic settings) Ask students which strategies they find most and least effective, and why. They should choose an ad and discuss its strengths or faults with the class.

Language Note
Ricardo and Vivian use synonymous verbs meaning *to influence,* **influenciar** and **influir**. **Influir** is generally preferred. **Influenciar** can only be used relating to people; **influir** can be applied to people or things. (**Se piensa que la contaminación del aire influye en los cambios de clima.**)

Cuaderno de actividades, p. 90 Acts. 10–11

Teaching Resources
pp. 230–231

PRINT
▶ Lesson Planner, p. 39
▶ Video Guide, pp. 51, 53, 56
▶ Cuaderno de actividades, p. 90

MEDIA
▶ One-Stop Planner
▶ Video Program
Contigo en la distancia
Videocassette 3, 17:43–22:14
Videocassette 5 (captioned version), 39:20–43:51
¡Adelante!
Videocassette 3, 24:53–26:04
▶ Audio Compact Discs, CD 8, Trs. 12–16

Presenting
¡Adelante!

Have students skim the articles and interviews. Then play the video **Los medios de comunicación.** Ask students to name the media that Jorge and Ramiro prefer. Then present the Preteaching Vocabulary and check for understanding.

¡Adelante!
Los medios de comunicación In the video, two more interviews are presented with Spanish speakers about their newspaper- and magazine-reading habits.

¡Adelante! ▪ *Los medios de comunicación*

CD 8 Trs. 12–16

Los periódicos y las revistas son importantes medios de comunicación. ¿Lees el periódico o una revista con frecuencia?

P: **¿Lees el periódico todos los días y qué partes te gustan más?**

R: **Este... partes políticas, informativa, informe general y deportes.**

P: **¿Lees todos los días?**

R: **Todos los días, trato aunque sea...**

P: **¿Lees también revistas?**

R: **Eh... sí, no muchas pero leo bastante.**

P: **¿Cuáles?**

R: **Este, *Caras*, *Gente*, eh... *Gráfico*, este... y no, ninguna más.**

Jorge

Los chicos periodistas

Son inquietos y recuriosos. No se cansan de preguntar y a la hora de mirar no se les escapa nada. Estos chicos se preparan y hacen temblar a los más experimentados profesionales.

Trabajan muy fuerte durante todo el año en los talleres de Periodismo y Medios de Comunicación que tiene cada escuela de la Municipalidad de Buenos Aires. Analizan la información de los medios y editan sus propias revistas. Y después se juntan para "comunicarse". Así es, más de 400 chicos, de tercero a séptimo grado, una vez por año se reúnen para intercambiar experiencias.

Asisten "todos juntos" a talleres en los que elaboran una encuesta, llenando formularios y preguntando—grabador en mano—sobre distintos temas; aprendiendo a armar la primera plana de un diario o a hacer su propio periódico con nombre y todo; otros se dedican a producir un programa de radio con efectos especiales o a grabar en video a los compañeros que trabajan; y nunca faltan los que le ponen el toque gracioso al encuentro, fabricando las páginas de humor. Y todas estas actividades son dirigidas por profesionales de verdad que confían a los chicos todos los secretos de la comunicación.

These activities check for comprehension only. Students should not yet be expected to produce language modeled in ¡Adelante!

19 **¿Comprendiste?** See answers below.

1. ¿Cuándo lee Jorge el periódico?
2. ¿Qué secciones del periódico prefiere Jorge?
3. ¿Qué sección del periódico lee Ramiro para saber el resultado de un partido?
4. ¿En qué grados están los chicos que están estudiando periodismo en Buenos Aires?
5. ¿Quiénes enseñan las clases de periodismo?

6. Según el artículo en la página 231, ¿cómo ayudará a los estudiantes tener más horas de clase?

20 **Busca las expresiones** See sample answers below.

¿Qué palabras o frases se usan para...?
1. expresar la posibilidad y la imposibilidad
2. hablar de las partes del periódico

Preteaching Vocabulary

Activating Prior Knowledge

Point out that in **¡Adelante!**, Jorge and Ramiro are talking about means of communication, especially newspapers and magazines. Based on Spanish expressions students already know, can they guess what Jorge means when he says **"Este... partes políticas, informativa, informe general y deportes."**? Would the accompanying magazine article be something that Jorge would like? What does Eduardo mean when he says **"No, lo leo todo, todo."**? What expression indicates that he might turn to a particular section first? (**... si quiero saber el resultado de unos partidos, miro la parte de deportes...**)

Comentario:
Se necesitan más horas de clase

Creemos que los estudiantes de nuestro país necesitan más horas de clase para competir con estudiantes de otros países. Si nuestros estudiantes no aprenden lo suficiente, es posible que tengan graves desventajas en el mundo comercial. Es imposible que nuestros estudiantes obtengan buenos empleos si continuamos con el programa de hoy. Puede ser que las horas adicionales de clase constituyan un problema para algunos estudiantes que trabajan, pero es probable que a la larga las horas adicionales ayuden a los estudiantes a encontrar buenos trabajos más tarde. Tal vez sea mejor introducir este plan experimentalmente en algunas ciudades. Esperamos que se pongan en contacto con sus representantes lo más pronto posible para discutir este problema.

P: **¿Lees el periódico todos los días?**

R: **Sí, leo el periódico todos los días.**

P: **¿Qué partes te gustan más?**

R: **No, lo leo todo, todo.**

P: **¿No tienes una sección preferida?**

R: **No, a veces depende; si quiero saber el resultado de unos partidos, miro la parte de deportes, pero normalmente leo todo.**

P: **¿Lees revistas también?**

R: **A veces también leo revistas.**

Ramiro

21 Para discutir

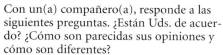

Con un(a) compañero(a), responde a las siguientes preguntas. ¿Están Uds. de acuerdo? ¿Cómo son parecidas sus opiniones y cómo son diferentes?

1. ¿Lees el periódico todos los días? ¿Por qué lees el periódico?

2. ¿Qué parte del periódico lees primero? ¿la primera plana? ¿los editoriales? ¿la sección de deportes? ¿la sección de noticias locales o internacionales? ¿Por qué?

3. ¿Lees muchas revistas? ¿Lees revistas en línea? ¿Qué revistas lees? ¿Por qué?

4. ¿Cuáles son las ventajas de tener clases de periodismo para los jóvenes? ¿Hay clases parecidas en tu colegio o ciudad?

5. ¿Es buena idea tener más horas de clase cada día? ¿Por qué sí o por qué no?

22 Ahora te toca a ti

Además de las revistas y el periódico, ¿qué medios de comunicación usas regularmente? ¿Qué ventaja o desventaja tiene cada uno?

Comprehension Check

Visual Learners
Hold up different sections from a magazine or newspaper. Ask students to identify each section and to comment on it according to their own likes and dislikes, beliefs, or feelings.

Visual/Tactile Learners
Have all students bring in a favorite magazine. (You may want to preview the magazines for appropriate content.) Divide the class into small groups. Each group is to take one page from each student's magazine and recreate it in Spanish. Together, the class will create one magazine that represents the collective set of interests.

Thinking Critically
Synthesizing Explain that *synthesize* comes from a Greek verb meaning *to put together*. Have students read the editorial on page 231 and decide if they agree or disagree with it. Then group students according to their reactions. Have groups either write an editorial agreeing with the first one, or a counterpoint arguing against extending the school year. Students should first list reasons for or against extending the school year, and then as a group synthesize their ideas into one coherent editorial.

 Contigo en la distancia

As an alternative or in addition to **¡Adelante!,** you may wish to show Episode 8 of *Contigo en la distancia.* For suggestions and activities, see the *Video Guide.*

Answers

19 1. todos los días
2. partes políticas, informativa, deportes e informe general
3. la sección de los deportes
4. tercero a séptimo grado
5. periodistas profesionales
6. Ayudará a los estudiantes a encontrar buenos trabajos más tarde.

20 *Sample answers:*
1. Puede ser que..., es probable que..., Tal vez..., es posible que... Es imposible que...
2. los deportes, partes políticas, informativa, informe general

Teaching Resources
pp. 232–235

PRINT
▸ Lesson Planner, p. 39
▸ Listening Activities, pp. 60, 64–65
▸ Activities for Communication, pp. 31–32, 73–74, 103–104
▸ Cuaderno de gramática, pp. 68–69
▸ Grammar Tutor for Students of Spanish, Chapter 8
▸ Cuaderno de actividades, pp. 91–94
▸ Cuaderno para hispanohablantes, pp. 36–40
▸ Testing Program, pp. 173–176
▸ Alternative Assessment Guide, p. 37
▸ Student Make-Up Assignments, Chapter 8

MEDIA
▸ One-Stop Planner
▸ Audio Compact Discs, CD 8, Trs. 17–18, 27–29, 21
▸ Teaching Transparencies 8-2; **Más práctica gramatical** Answers; Cuaderno de gramática Answers
▸ Interactive CD-ROM Tutor, Disc 2

Bell Work
Write the following phrases on the board for students to complete in writing: **Estoy seguro(a) que…, Es evidente que…, No creo que…, Es increíble que…**

Presenting
Así se dice
Have students make statements which you can contradict using the given expressions.
Gramática
The subjunctive after impersonal expressions
Read the explanations and examples aloud. Then give some original examples.

Así se dice

Expressing possibility and impossibility

Si quieres indicar que algo es posible o imposible, puedes decir:

Es posible que la cadena cancele mi programa favorito.

Posiblemente podamos grabar el documental en videocasete.

Puede ser que comience tarde el noticiero.

Quizás / Tal vez / A lo mejor haya información sobre eso en el periódico.

Es fácil que el artículo de Juan salga en una revista en línea.
It's likely that . . .

Es difícil que el DVD elimine completamente el videocasete.
It's unlikely that . . .

Es probable que mi hermano lea sólo la sección deportiva.

Es imposible que Andrés estudie mientras su hermana escucha la radio.

Cuaderno de actividades, p. 91, Act. 13

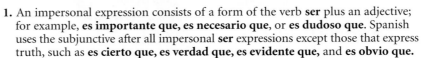

Gramática

The subjunctive after impersonal expressions

1. An impersonal expression consists of a form of the verb **ser** plus an adjective; for example, **es importante que, es necesario que,** or **es dudoso que.** Spanish uses the subjunctive after all impersonal **ser** expressions except those that express truth, such as **es cierto que, es verdad que, es evidente que,** and **es obvio que.**

   Es dudoso que la carta **llegue** pronto. *(subjunctive)*
   Es cierto que tenemos un buen periódico. *(indicative)*

2. When expressions like **es cierto que** are made negative, the subjunctive follows **que** because they then imply doubt.

   No es cierto que Alberto **sea** periodista para esa revista.

3. When expressions like **es dudoso que** are made negative, the indicative follows **que** because they no longer indicate doubt.

   No es dudoso que mucha gente **lee** sólo las tiras cómicas.

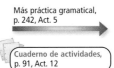

Más práctica gramatical, p. 242, Act. 5

Cuaderno de actividades, p. 91, Act. 12

Cuaderno de gramática, pp. 68–69, Acts. 10–12

---

23 **Una revista internacional**   Script and answers on p. 219G

Escuchemos Indica qué frase expresa lo contrario de cada frase que escuchas.

CD 8
Tr. 17

a. Es probable que haya artículos en otras lenguas.
b. Puede ser que usemos fotografías a colores.
c. Es difícil que vendamos muchos periódicos este año.
d. Es dudoso que tengamos corresponsales en otros países.

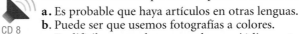

Communication for All Students

Pair Work
On the board or on a transparency, write several sentences beginning with affirmative impersonal expressions. (**Es verdad que la gramática es interesante. Es cierto que leen mucho. Es evidente que estudian.**) Have pairs of students work together to change the sentences to the negative. (**No es verdad que la gramática sea interesante. No es cierto que lean mucho.**

No es evidente que estudien.) Ask students to explain or elaborate on the negative statements.

Slower Pace
23 Have students write at least two sentences that express the opposite of each statement before listening to the recording. After students have listened to the recording, have them compare the statements they wrote with the ones they heard.

---

24 Gramática en contexto See answers below.

Leamos/Escribamos Lee el artículo e indica si cada oración es **cierta** o **falsa**. Si es falsa, usa expresiones de **Así se dice** y **Gramática** para corregirla. Basa tus respuestas en el texto.

1. Es probable que la televisión no se relacione con la vida real.
2. Tal vez aumente la televisión nuestra experiencia del mundo.
3. Es posible que no haya relación entre nuestros sentimientos y lo que vemos en la tele.
4. Quizás a Pilar Aguilar no le guste la televisión.

La tele recrea situaciones idénticas a las de la vida real

En los programas televisados, según Pilar Aguilar, se vierten algunas de nuestras pasiones, miedos y deseos que reprimimos en la vida real. Además, las imágenes de televisión enriquecen nuestra experiencia y nuestra percepción limitada del mundo. Para colmo, el truco del medio audiovisual es que recrea situaciones que se parecen como una gota de agua a la realidad que nos rodea, pero que pertenecen a realidades muy lejanas.

Presenting Vocabulario

Bring in a local newspaper and samples of Spanish-language newspapers. Use the local newspaper as a prop to demonstrate the new words. Then divide the class into small groups and give each group pages of the Spanish-language newspapers. Ask them to find the various sections of the newspaper and to write the titles of the sections they find. Ask for volunteers to write the titles on the board. Then have students scan the drawing on this page. Do the titles they find correspond to any of these sections? Check comprehension by asking questions. (—¿**Quién lee la sección deportiva y por qué? —La muchacha la lee porque le gusta jugar al tenis y le interesan los resultados de Wimbledon.**)

Vocabulario

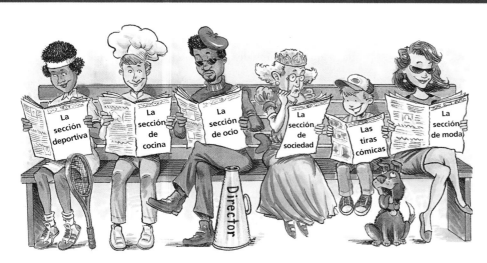

los anuncios clasificados *classified ads*	**la primera plana** *front page*
el artículo *article*	**la sección financiera** *financial section*
los editoriales *editorials*	**los titulares** *headlines*
los obituarios *obituaries*	
el (la) periodista *journalist*	

Cuaderno de actividades, pp. 92–93, Acts. 14–16   Cuaderno de gramática, p. 69, Acts. 13–14   Más práctica gramatical, p. 243, Acts. 6–7

25 Los titulares See answers below.

Hablemos ¿En qué sección del periódico puedes leer algo sobre las siguientes cosas?

1. la inflación
2. la ropa en París
3. las películas
4. la comida
5. el fútbol
6. fiestas de gente famosa
7. opiniones de los periodistas
8. Calvin y Hobbes®
9. las noticias más importantes

Connections and Comparisons

Thinking Critically

Analyzing Have students work in groups and research online newspapers from several different Spanish-speaking countries. Do students find any unexpected section heads? What cultural or social information might be inferred by a such a head? (For example, *El Universal* in Venezuela has a section called **Petróleo**.) Do any newspapers have different names for a particular section? (**Obituarios** may be called **Necrológicos**.) If a newspaper has no international or political stories, what inferences can students draw about the focus of the periodical? Students might also study the use of the subjunctive in headlines or advertisements.

Answers

24
1. falsa; Es probable que la televisión se relacione con la vida real.
2. cierta
3. falsa; Es probable que la televisión y los sentimientos tengan relación.
4. falsa; Es fácil que le guste la televisión a Pilar Aguilar.

25
1. la sección financiera
2. la sección de moda
3. la sección de ocio
4. la sección de cocina
5. la sección deportiva
6. la sección de sociedad
7. los editoriales
8. las tiras cómicas
9. la primera plana

Teaching Resources
pp. 232–235

PRINT 📖
▸ Lesson Planner, p. 39
▸ Listening Activities, pp. 60, 64–65
▸ Activities for Communication, pp. 31–32, 73–74, 103–104
▸ Cuaderno de gramática, pp. 68–69
▸ Grammar Tutor for Students of Spanish, Chapter 8
▸ Cuaderno de actividades, pp. 91–94
▸ Cuaderno para hispanohablantes, pp. 36–40
▸ Testing Program, pp. 173–176
▸ Alternative Assessment Guide, p. 37
▸ Student Make-Up Assignments, Chapter 8

MEDIA 💿
▸ One-Stop Planner
▸ Audio Compact Discs, CD 8, Trs. 17–18, 27–29, 21
▸ Teaching Transparencies 8-2; **Más práctica gramatical** Answers; Cuaderno de gramática Answers
▸ Interactive CD-ROM Tutor, Disc 2

Presenting
Así se dice

Act out both sides of a dialogue in which one person says outrageous things and the other responds with one of the new expressions. Make similar incredible statements to the students and have them respond with one of the new expressions.
(—Descubrieron que la Luna es de queso. —¡No me lo puedo creer!)

---

26 **Fama y fortuna** Script and answers on p. 219H.

CD 8
Tr. 18

Escuchemos Escucha las siguientes noticias e indica a qué personaje famoso se refiere cada una.

Gabriel Batistuta   Celia Cruz   el rey Juan Carlos   Daisy Fuentes

27 **El periódico escolar**

Hablemos Imagina que trabajas para el periódico de tu colegio. En grupos de cuatro, decidan cuáles van a ser los temas de esta semana. Cada persona debe escoger dos secciones del periódico y mencionar varias ideas para los artículos.

> **MODELO**   sección deportiva
> —Es probable que el equipo de tenis participe en las finales.

Así se dice

Expressing surprise

Si quieres expresar sorpresa, puedes decir:

Cuaderno de actividades, pp. 93–94, Acts. 17–18

¡No puede ser!   ¡Qué sorpresa!   No me lo esperaba.
It caught me by surprise.

¡No me digas!   No me lo puedo creer.   ¡No es posible!

28 **¡No me digas!** Answers will vary.

Leamos/Hablemos Lee los siguientes titulares de la primera plana de un periódico que compraste en el supermercado. Luego expresa sorpresa de una manera diferente para cada titular.

> ¡Presidente de Estados Unidos es del planeta Júpiter!

> ¡Niño de 7 años levanta coche para salvar a su padre!

> ¡¡Serpiente gigante come ciudad entera!!

> ¡Estados Unidos vende Texas a la Argentina!

Communication for All Students

Auditory Learners
26 You might want to select one of the news items in this activity to use as a dictation. Stop the audio recording after each sentence and ask students to write the news related in that sentence.

Kinesthetic Learners
Write the words representing the sections of the newspaper on one set of index cards. **(la sección de cocina, la sección deportiva)** Write imaginary headlines on a second set. **(Una cena de maravilla, Equipo Santander ganó otra vez)** Distribute the cards and instruct students to find the person who has the headline that best matches their section. Ask partners to stand together until the activity is finished.

29 Historia completa

Escribamos Escoge dos de los titulares en la Actividad 28 y escribe un artículo corto para cada uno. Usa algunas de las siguientes expresiones.

es difícil que

no lo esperaba

quizás

tal vez

no puede ser

es imposible que

no puedo creer que

Nota cultural

En Estados Unidos se encuentran revistas y periódicos en muchas tiendas. Pero en la Argentina y otros países latinoamericanos, se venden periódicos y revistas en pequeños puestos que se llaman kioscos. En Buenos Aires los kioscos son más que pequeños puestos: son verdaderas tiendas en miniatura, muy bien arregladas y con anuncios luminosos. En los kioscos, los porteños pueden comprar de todo, desde dulces hasta champú. Por lo general, un buen kiosco está abierto 24 horas al día. ¿Hay algo similar en tu ciudad?

30 Eso no lo puedo creer

Leamos/Hablemos Con un(a) compañero(a), lee los artículos que Uds. escribieron en la Actividad 29. Después de leer los artículos, cada estudiante debe responder con las expresiones de **Así se dice** de este **Paso**.

31

Del colegio al trabajo

Hablemos/Escribamos Eres director(a) del periódico de tu escuela y necesitas escribir un artículo sobre uno de los temas de abajo. Entrevista a dos o tres compañeros(as) de clase y apunta sus opiniones sobre el tema. Incluye sus comentarios en el artículo.

Es posible que sea necesario, pero para mí, nos dan demasiada tarea en el colegio. La tarea no debe ser obligatoria.

Nosotros ganamos dinero para el colegio. Creo que las escuelas deben pagarles a los atletas.

No entiendo por qué no puedo estudiar sólo ciencias. Sé que quiero ser químico. Tal vez podamos aprender mejor con un plan de estudios más especializado.

32 En mi cuaderno

Escribamos ¿Cuáles son las últimas noticias de tu colegio? Imagina que te toca a ti escribir el artículo de la primera plana para el periódico escolar. Escoge un tema de interés para tu colegio y escribe el artículo. Incluye expresiones de certeza y otras de posibilidad e imposibilidad.

CAPÍTULO 8

Teaching Resources
pp. 236–238

PRINT
- Lesson Planner, p. 40
- Cuaderno de actividades, p. 95
- Cuaderno para hispanohablantes, pp. 36–38
- Reading Strategies and Skills Handbook, Chapter 8
- ¡Lee conmigo! 3, Chapter 8
- Standardized Assessment Tutor, Chapter 8

MEDIA
- One-Stop Planner

Prereading
Activities A and B

Reading Drama
Ask students in what kind of literature they have seen lists of characters, scene descriptions, and instructions. (plays) Discuss why such elements are necessary. (to help the reader visualize the setting and the action in the story)

Making Predictions
A. Have students brainstorm possible themes for the reading. Tell them to base their predictions on the art and the information from the first two sections.

Answers
A La sección de "Personajes" es una lista de los actores que se necesitan. "Escena" describe dónde tiene lugar la historia. Está incluida esta información porque es una obra de teatro.

B *Answers will vary.*

Signos de puntuación

Vas a leer un fragmento de una obra de teatro escrita por M. Toledo y Benito. Un hombre, el señor Álvarez, se ha muerto y en esta obra se lee su testamento *(will)*. Como verás, los diferentes personajes tienen muy diferentes interpretaciones del testamento.

Estrategia **para leer**
Summarizing ideas is an easy way to help you concentrate on what you are reading. Simply stop and write down a short summary after each important idea you read. If you have any questions about what you are reading, jot them down also. As you continue reading, the answers will probably become clear.

See answers below.

¡A comenzar!
A. Revisa las secciones de **Personajes** y **Escena**. ¿De qué se tratan? ¿Por qué está incluida esta información en la obra?

B. Busca las instrucciones para los actores que se encuentran dentro de varias secciones de diálogo. Resume las acciones que los actores toman durante la obra.

Al grano
C. Trabaja con unos(as) compañeros(as). Lean la obra en voz alta y con buena pronunciación. El testamento se repite seis veces. Resuman el contenido de cada versión en una oración.

D. ¿Entendiste todos los detalles? Trata de contestar todas estas preguntas sin mirar el texto. Si no sabes una respuesta, búscala en la lectura.
See possible answers below.

Signos de puntuación

I. Personajes

El juez	El mendigo
El maestro	El hermano
El sastre	El sobrino

Escena (Una sala. Los personajes están sentados delante de una mesa. Habrá una pizarra colocada frente al público.)

* * * * * * * * * * *

El juez: Y ya, señores, para que todos aprecien las diversas interpretaciones del testamento que dejó nuestro buen amigo el señor Álvarez, vamos a copiar en esa pizarra la forma en que lo dejó. *(al maestro)* Hágame el favor de copiarlo usted, señor maestro, que sabe usar la tiza con más soltura que cualquiera de nosotros...

El maestro: Permítame el original, señor juez.

El juez: *(dándoselo)* Sírvase.

Connections and Comparisons

Multicultural Link
In Venezuela, where inheritance is determined according to the Napoleonic Code, the laws are very specific about the ways an estate can be divided. By law, if a married man with children dies, his wife receives half his estate, while the other half goes to his children in proportional amounts. Wills are not as widely used as they are in the United States because they cannot contradict the division of the estate according to law.

The national laws of many Latin American countries follow the Napoleonic Code, borrowed from the French. The United States judicial system, on the other hand, follows British common law. In the United States, individuals may leave a will which specifies who inherits how much of the estate.

El hermano:	(mientras el maestro copia en la pizarra el testamento que dice: "Dejo mis bienes a mi sobrino no a mi hermano tampoco jamás se pagará la cuenta del sastre nunca de ningún modo para los mendigos todo lo dicho es mi deseo yo Federico Álvarez".) Señor juez, como hermano, quisiera hacer la primera interpretación.
El juez:	Puede hacerla, señor.

El hermano:	(Puntúa el testamento y lo lee en la siguiente forma:) "¿Dejo mis bienes a mi sobrino? No: a mi hermano. Tampoco jamás se pagará la cuenta del sastre. Nunca, de ningún modo para los mendigos. Todo lo dicho es mi deseo. Yo, Federico Álvarez".
El sobrino:	Está equivocado, completamente equivocado, señor juez. La verdadera intención de mi tío fue otra, como les puedo demostrar. (Puntúa el testamento y lee.) "Dejo mis bienes a mi sobrino, no a mi hermano. Tampoco jamás se pagará la cuenta del sastre. Nunca de ningún modo para los mendigos. Todo lo dicho es mi deseo. Yo, Federico Álvarez".

II.

El sastre:	Y ahora, señor juez, me toca a mí demostrar la intención del señor Álvarez. (Puntúa el testamento y lo lee.) "¿Dejo mis bienes a mi sobrino? No. ¿A mi hermano? Tampoco, jamás.

¿Te acuerdas?

If you know specific details you want to find, you can scan the text quickly, looking only for those details.

1. ¿Quién escribe el testamento durante el drama?

2. ¿Dónde lo escribe?

3. ¿Por qué quiere dinero el sastre?

4. ¿Quién toma la decisión final sobre el testamento?

5. ¿Quién pone los signos de puntuación en la versión del testamento que el juez acepta?

6. Al final, ¿quién va a recibir los bienes (possessions) y el dinero del señor Álvarez?

E. Con unos(as) compañeros(as), copia la primera versión del testamento (la ambigua) en una hoja de papel. Escojan uno de los posibles herederos (el sobrino, el hermano, el sastre, los mendigos o el juez) y escriban los signos de puntuación adecuados sin consultar el libro de texto. Luego, den el testamento a otro grupo. El otro grupo tiene que adivinar quién recibirá los bienes del señor Álvarez.

F. En tu opinión, ¿cuál fue la meta del autor al escribir esta historia? ¿Qué defectos humanos está tratando de señalar? ¿Tiene la historia algún mensaje moral? ¿Cuál es?

G. Con un(a) compañero(a), escribe otro fin para la obra en el cual el juez escoge a la persona que debe recibir los bienes del señor Álvarez y explica por qué.

Vamos a leer

CAPÍTULO 8

Reading
Activities C, D, and E

Monitoring Reading

- Read the various versions of the will aloud and represent the punctuation with your voice inflection and facial expressions.

- Write the identities of the various potential heirs on separate pieces of paper, put them into a container, and have each student draw one. Then have the students read aloud the version of the will endorsed by their heir, using their voice to reflect the punctuation in the text. The rest of the class should try to guess which version of the will they are reading.

Communication for All Students

Challenge
Tell students to imagine that they are attorneys helping a wealthy client to prepare an incontestable will. The client has one million dollars to leave. Have the class work together to create the characters of the wealthy client and his or her heirs. Then put students into groups of three or four and ask them to write a will. After the wills are completed, have the groups exchange them. Assign each group a different heir and have them examine the will they received in the exchange. They should give their opinion as to the will's validity. (**Este testamento no es válido. No puedo creer que la señora no me haya dejado nada.**) They should then try to interpret it to their heir's best advantage.

Answers

D 1. el maestro
2. en una pizarra
3. El señor Álvarez le debía dinero.
4. el juez
5. el maestro
6. el Estado

CAPÍTULO 8

Postreading
Activities F–J

Summarizing
Have students use the strategy **Vuelve a escribir el texto** to rewrite the drama as a short magazine or newspaper article. You may want to have them work in pairs or groups.

Appreciating a Writer's Craft
Have students discuss why the author chose this particular literary genre. What is the impact of rewriting the story as an article? How would the story be altered in another genre such as a short story? (The immediacy and directness of hearing the story through each character's own voice is lost.)

Determining the Main Idea
Engage students in a discussion about the point the author is making about language and language usage. (Language needs to be used precisely in order to unambiguously communicate information.) How effectively did the author communicate this idea? By what means was it communicated? (By using a humorous narrative the author shows the chaos that results from the lack of precise language.)

H. Imagina que un milagro ha ocurrido — el señor Álvarez no ha muerto en realidad y entra en la corte. Cuando descubre lo que dijeron los herederos, se pone furioso. Inventa una conversación en que el señor Álvarez habla con cada uno de los herederos.

I. Reúnete con unos(as) compañeros(as). Cada persona del grupo toma el punto de vista de uno de los personajes de la historia y explica por qué él o ella debe heredar los bienes del señor Álvarez. Las otras personas explican por qué no debe ser así.

J. Discuss these questions with two or three of your classmates and compare your opinions with those of the rest of your class.

1. Do you agree with the judge's decision? Why or why not?
2. Do you believe a similar situation could occur in real life? Explain your opinions.
3. Is it important to leave a will? Why or why not?
4. What are some ways to make sure that a will is clearly understood and carried out?
5. What form do you think wills will take in the future? In 50 years, will there still be documents written on paper? If a will were left on audiotape or videotape, could the message be as confusing as it is in this play? Explain your answers.

Cuaderno para hispanohablantes, pp.36–38

Cuaderno de actividades, p. 95, Acts. 19–20

Se pagará la cuenta del sastre. Nunca de ningún modo para los mendigos. Todo lo dicho es mi deseo. Yo, Federico Álvarez".

El mendigo: Permítame, señor juez, puntuar el testamento como lo habría querido el señor Álvarez. (*Puntúa el testamento y lo lee.*) "¿Dejo mis bienes a mi sobrino? No. ¿A mi hermano? Tampoco jamás. ¿Se pagará la cuenta del sastre? Nunca, de ningún modo. Para los mendigos todo. Lo dicho es mi deseo. Yo, Federico Álvarez". Esto y nada más es lo que quiso mandar el señor Álvarez, téngalo por seguro.

El maestro: Yo no lo creo. El señor Álvarez habría querido que yo puntuara el testamento para él. (*Lo hace y lee este testamento en esta forma.*) "¿Dejo mis bienes a mi sobrino? No. ¿A mi hermano? Tampoco. Jamás se pagará la cuenta del sastre. Nunca, de ningún modo para los mendigos. Todo lo dicho es mi deseo. Yo, Federico Álvarez".

El sastre: En esa forma el señor Álvarez no habría dejado herederos.

El juez: Así es, en efecto, y, visto y considerando que esta última interpretación es correcta, declaro terminado el juicio, incautándome de esta herencia en nombre del Estado.

Connections and Comparisons

Language-to-Language
Students have seen some of the differences in Spanish and English punctuation. For example, Spanish uses inverted question and exclamation marks to show the reader what intonation to use when reading a sentence aloud. Although comma usage is similar in both languages, Spanish never puts a comma before **y** in a series: **pan, tortillas y galletas.** Nor are commas used in numbers; instead, periods are used: **4.346.210.** (In Mexico, commas are used.) Where speech is being quoted, students may have seen «...» as well as "..." In sustained dialogue, however, they are more likely to have seen the **raya,** or dash. Point out that punctuation (except for question and exclamation marks) at the end of a sentence is most often placed outside a dash or quotation mark.

Vamos a escribir

La obra de teatro **Signos de puntuación** muestra la importancia de usar la puntuación para organizar las ideas de una manera clara y lógica. En esta actividad, vas a escribir un reportaje sobre un concierto para una revista de música y vas a aprender otra manera de hacer fluir lo que escribes de una manera lógica y organizada.

El concierto

Imagina que trabajas para la revista **Megamúsica 17**. Escribe un reportaje de cuatro o cinco párrafos sobre un gran concierto en tu ciudad patrocinado por la organización **Juventud Contra la Droga**. Describe todas las cosas importantes que viste y oíste en el concierto.

Estrategia para escribir

Connecting words Have you ever read a paragraph or composition that seemed more like a collection of unrelated sentences than a unified whole? Connecting words help solve that problem by joining thoughts together in a logical, unified way. For example, the words **primero, luego, antes (de), después (de),** and **por fin** help you describe a chain of events in a way that your reader can easily understand.

A. Preparación

1. Imagina que llegas antes del comienzo del concierto. ¿Dónde es el concierto? ¿Quiénes están allí? ¿Qué ves y oyes? Haz una lista de todas tus impresiones. Si quieres, puedes hacer diagramas para vincular ideas relacionadas.

2. El concierto comienza. ¿Qué hora es? ¿Qué ves y qué oyes ahora? ¿Quiénes son los músicos? ¿Cómo son? ¿Qué tipo de canciones tocan? Añade estas impresiones a tu lista.

3. El concierto termina. ¿Qué tal estuvo? ¿Qué ves y oyes? ¿Cómo se siente la gente al salir del concierto?

B. Redacción

1. Escribe una introducción en la que menciones qué grupo tocó y dónde.

2. Escribe dos o tres párrafos para dar detalles de lo que pasó en el concierto. Menciona las cosas más importantes de la lista que preparaste, y usa palabras adecuadas para vincular tus ideas.

3. Escribe una buena conclusión. Incluye lo que pensó la gente del concierto y tus opiniones globales. ¿Les gustó el concierto? ¿Habrá otros conciertos del mismo grupo?

C. Evaluación

1. Lee tus párrafos. ¿Están bien organizados? Si no, cambia el orden de los elementos. ¿Usaste palabras apropiadas para vincular tus ideas?

2. Pídeles a dos o tres compañeros(as) que lean tu reportaje. ¿Les parece lógico? Agrega otros detalles e impresiones si son necesarios.

3. ¿Escribiste bien todas las palabras? Consulta un diccionario bilingüe, o a tus compañeros(as) o a tu profesor(a). ¿Usaste correctamente las formas verbales? Consulta tu libro de texto y habla con tu profesor(a) si necesitas ayuda.

Apply and Assess

Postwriting
Group Work

After the written assignment is complete, ask the students to break into groups of two or three. Have them read their paragraphs aloud and give one another constructive feedback. All students are responsible for jotting down notes from the feedback given to them, whether they agree with it or not. Ask students to listen for creative descriptions. Have each group identify two or three of the best descriptive sentences to share with the whole class.

Teaching Resources
p. 239

PRINT
▶ Lesson Planner, p. 40
▶ Cuaderno para hispanohablantes, p. 39
▶ Alternative Assessment Guide, p. 23
▶ Standardized Assessment Tutor, Chapter 8

MEDIA
▶ One-Stop Planner, Disc 2
▶ Test Generator, Chapter 8
▶ Interactive CD-ROM Tutor, Disc 2

Process Writing

Prewriting
Motivating Activity
Ask students if they have ever attended a live music concert or seen a video of one. Have them give their impressions of the experience.

Slower Pace
Some students may need further help with the guided writing assignment. As a class, students can develop an outline for their paper. With your help, students can come up with topic sentences for each paragraph. Have students fill in the outline with basic ideas. After you check the outlines, have them begin writing.

Writing
Teaching Suggestion
Encourage students to use complex sentence structure and literary devices such as similes and metaphors to add interest to their writing. Discuss why the first sentence is more interesting than the second. **Asistimos al concierto en el auditorio de la ciudad, un antiguo edificio que parece una enorme caverna. Asistimos al concierto en un auditorio grande.**

Más práctica gramatical

CAPÍTULO 8

For **Más práctica gramatical** Answer Transparencies, see the *Teaching Transparencies* binder.

Más práctica gramatical

Primer paso

Objectives Expressing doubt and disbelief; expressing certainty

1 La señora Dávila ve el noticiero todas las noches, pero nunca cree lo que dicen los locutores. Ahora está viendo un reportaje sobre un robo en el Museo de Arte. Forma oraciones completas para expresar lo que dice la señora. (**p. 225**)

> **MODELO** **Dudo/el ladrón/quedarse en la ciudad por mucho tiempo**
> **Dudo que el ladrón se quede en la ciudad por mucho tiempo.**

1. Dudo/la policía/encontrar al ladrón del Museo de Arte
2. Parece mentira/el museo/no tener mejor sistema de seguridad
3. Es increíble/ellos/no entender cómo entró al museo
4. No puedo creer/el director del museo/no saber más sobre el robo
5. No creo/la pintura/ser ninguna obra maestra
6. Dudo/alguien/querer comprar la pintura robada
7. Parece mentira/una obra tan fea/costar tanto
8. Es increíble/los artistas famosos/pintar cuadros tan horribles

2 Carlota está estudiando para un examen en su clase de periodismo y tiene una lista de palabras para memorizar. Escribe la palabra que corresponde a cada definición. (**p. 226**)

el noticiero	el documental	los reporteros
los comentaristas	los locutores	
la emisora	la prensa	

1. tipo de programa en el que típicamente se habla de la política, la historia, las ciencias o la cultura
2. las personas que escriben artículos para un periódico o una revista
3. Estas personas nos explican sus opiniones de las noticias. Pueden trabajar para un periódico o la televisión.
4. los periódicos y las revistas
5. el programa que presenta información todos los días sobre la política, el tiempo, los deportes, etcétera
6. Estas personas son como reporteros, pero nos cuentan las noticias en la televisión o por la radio.
7. el lugar donde se hacen los programas de música o de noticias que la gente escucha en la radio

Answers

1
1. Dudo que la policía encuentre al ladrón del Museo de Arte.
2. Parece mentira que el museo no tenga mejor sistema de seguridad.
3. Es increíble que ellos no entiendan cómo entró al museo.
4. No puedo creer que el director del museo no sepa más sobre el robo.
5. No creo que la pintura sea ninguna obra maestra.
6. Dudo que alguien quiera comprar la pintura robada.
7. Parece mentira que una obra tan fea cueste tanto.
8. Es increíble que los artistas famosos pinten cuadros tan horribles.

2
1. el documental
2. los reporteros
3. los comentaristas
4. la prensa
5. el noticiero
6. los locutores
7. la emisora

Grammar Resources for Chapter 8

The **Más práctica gramatical** activities are designed as supplemental activities for the grammatical concepts presented in the chapter. You might use them as additional practice, for review, or for assessment.

For more grammar presentation, review, and practice, refer to the following:
• Cuaderno de gramática
• Grammar Tutor for Students of Spanish

• Grammar Summary on pp. R25–R46
• Cuaderno de actividades
• Grammar and Vocabulary quizzes (Testing Program)
• Test Generator on the One-Stop Planner CD-ROM
• Interactive CD-ROM Tutor
• **Juegos interactivos** at <u>go.hrw.com</u>

3 Susana Carrilla trabaja como reportera. Usando **por** o **para**, completa lo que dice su amigo Leo de ella. (**p. 227**)

Susana Carrilla es reportera ___1___ el periódico de nuestra ciudad. ___2___ mí, es una reportera excelente. Sus artículos siempre me parecen muy interesantes. ___3___ ejemplo, el artículo sobre los problemas con el sistema de metro fue escrito por ella. Ella estudió periodismo ___4___ cuatro años en la universidad. ___5___ supuesto, le encanta su trabajo, aunque siempre está muy ocupada. Llega a su oficina muy temprano ___6___ la mañana. Todos los días tiene que hablar con mucha gente y hacer muchas llamadas ___7___ saber qué está pasando. De vez en cuando, ella pasa ___8___ el banco donde trabajo y nosotros salimos a almorzar. A veces, ___9___ terminar un artículo a tiempo, ella se queda trabajando hasta muy tarde. Ella tiene que terminar su próximo artículo ___10___ este jueves. ___11___ eso, no tiene tiempo ___12___ almorzar conmigo hoy.

4 Ramón y Elsa necesitan preparar un reportaje para la clase de ciencias sociales. Completa lo que dicen con las expresiones que faltan. (**p. 228**)

al tanto de	ya lo sé
estar bien informados	que yo sepa
tengo la menor idea	sabemos ni jota

RAMÓN   Elsa, acuérdate que tenemos que hacer nuestro reportaje el próximo martes.

ELSA   Sí, ___1___. Pero todavía no sabemos de qué vamos a hablar. ¿Qué ideas tienes tú?

RAMÓN   Francamente, no ___2___. ¿Qué tal si hablamos sobre el medio ambiente?

ELSA   Pero, Ramón... Tú y yo no ___3___ del medio ambiente. Para hacer un reportaje, creo que debemos ___4___, ¿no te parece?

RAMÓN   De acuerdo. Entonces, ¿por qué no hablamos con mi prima? Ella trabaja en la emisora KVVG y siempre está ___5___ todo lo que pasa en la ciudad. Tal vez ella pueda darnos algunas ideas.

ELSA   Me parece una idea excelente. ___6___, seremos los únicos de la clase que van a hablar con alguien de la prensa. Hablemos con ella esta noche.

Communication for All Students

Pair Work

3 Have pairs of students write ten fill-in-the-blank sentences using **por** and **para**. Pairs then trade their papers and fill in the missing prepositions. Ask volunteers to read a sentence aloud for the class to complete orally.

Challenge

4 Have students write a sentence describing a situation that would elicit the use of each of the phrases in the box. (**Mi hermano nunca ha estudiado la física. —Pues, no sabe ni jota de esa materia.**) Ask volunteers to read their situation aloud so the class can respond using the phrases.

Answers

3
1. para
2. Para
3. Por
4. por
5. Por
6. por
7. para
8. por
9. para
10. para
11. Por
12. para

4
1. ya lo sé
2. tengo ni idea
3. sabemos ni jota
4. estar bien informados
5. al tanto de
6. Que yo sepa

For **Más práctica gramatical** Answer Transparencies, see the *Teaching Transparencies* binder.

Más práctica gramatical

CD-ROM DISC 2   WV3 BUENOS AIRES-8

Segundo paso   Objectives Expressing possiblity and impossibility; expressing surprise

5 Are these predictions likely to come true by the time your class has its ten-year high school reunion? Express whether each prediction is certain, possible, or doubtful based on the responses in the chart. Remember that you need to use the subjunctive after expressions of doubt or possibility. **(p. 232)**

MODELO   **Es cierto que habrá una computadora para cada estudiante.**

PREDICCIÓN	CIERTO	POSIBLE	DUDOSO
Habrá una computadora para cada estudiante.	✔		
1. Pondrán una pizzería en la cafetería.			✔
2. El colegio tendrá su propia emisora de música rock.		✔	
3. El equipo de voleibol jugará en los Juegos Olímpicos.		✔	
4. Habrá clases durante todo el año.	✔		
5. Construirán una piscina grande detrás del colegio.			✔
6. Comprarán videojuegos y discos compactos para la biblioteca.		✔	
7. Los estudiantes llegarán al colegio en carros eléctricos.		✔	
8. Unos estudiantes serán artistas o músicos famosos.	✔		

Answers

5 1. Es dudoso que pongan una pizzería en la cafetería.
2. Es posible que el colegio tenga su propia radioemisora de música rock.
3. Es posible que el equipo de voleibol juegue en los Juegos Olímpicos.
4. Es cierto que habrá clases durante todo el año.
5. Es dudoso que construyan una piscina grande detrás del colegio.
6. Es posible que compren videojuegos y discos compactos para la biblioteca.
7. Es posible que los estudiantes lleguen al colegio en carros eléctricos.
8. Es cierto que unos estudiantes serán artistas o músicos famosos.

Communication for All Students

Additional Practice

5 Have students respond to the activity, changing the predictions from **cierto** to **posible** or **dudoso,** and vice-versa. Then ask students to express and explain their own opinions about the statements.

Challenge

Have students develop their own tabloid news headlines using fictitious names. They can draw pictures to accompany some of their outrageous stories or use computer graphics for illustration. Require that students use expressions of surprise. You may want to display students' work around the room.

6 Indica qué sección del periódico están leyendo todos los miembros de la familia Fuentes en este momento, según las descripciones. **(p. 233)**

a. la sección de sociedad
b. las tiras cómicas
c. los editoriales
d. la sección de cocina
e. los anuncios clasificados

f. la primera plana
g. la sección de moda
h. la sección deportiva
i. la sección de ocio
j. la sección financiera

1. Roberto piensa comprar un carro usado.
2. La señora Fuentes quiere saber la opinión del comentarista sobre las elecciones.
3. La tía Ofelia quiere saber todo acerca de la boda de la hija de su amiga.
4. El señor Fuentes tiene mucha prisa, y sólo quiere leer los titulares más importantes.

5. Margarita quiere saber quién ganó el partido de baloncesto.
6. Arturo quiere saber a qué hora es el concierto este sábado.
7. A abuelita le parece excelente la receta de sopa de pollo.
8. Alejandra se está riendo de las travesuras de los personajes.

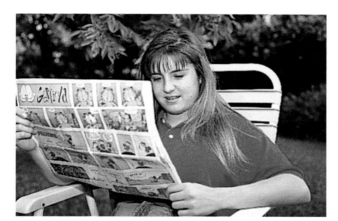

7 Ahora, completa las oraciones con la forma correcta del verbo e indica a qué sección del periódico se refiere cada oración. **(pp. 232, 233)**

1. Es importante que usted ＿＿＿ (guardar) los ingredientes en la nevera.
2. Es verdad que esos personajes ＿＿＿ (ser) muy graciosos.
3. Es dudoso que la hija del Sr. Ramos ＿＿＿ (casarse) con nuestro alcalde.
4. Es evidente que mi equipo favorito no ＿＿＿ (ir) a ganar el campeonato.
5. Es necesario que la inflación no ＿＿＿ (aumentar).
6. No es cierto que los cines ＿＿＿ (ir) a pasar la película esta noche.
7. ¡Es imposible que esos trajes de baño ＿＿＿ (ser) de seda! El periodista se ha equivocado.
8. Es obvio que muchas personas ＿＿＿ (querer) vender sus coches.

Review and Assess

You may wish to assign the **Más práctica gramatical** activities as additional practice or homework after presenting material throughout the chapter. Assign Activity 1 after **Así se dice** and **Nota gramatical** (p. 225), Activity 2 after **Vocabulario** (p. 226), Activity 3 after **Nota gramatical** (p. 227), Activity 4 after **Vocabulario** (p. 228), Activity 5 after **Así**

se dice and **Gramática** (p. 232), and Activity 6 after **Vocabulario** (p. 233). To prepare students for the **Paso** Quizzes and Chapter Test, have them do the **Más práctica gramatical** activities in the following order: complete Activities 1–4 before taking Quiz 8-1A or 8-1B; Activities 5–6 before taking Quiz 8-2A or 8-2B.

Answers

6 1. e
2. c
3. a
4. f
5. h
6. i
7. d
8. b

7 1. guarde; la sección de cocina
2. son; las tiras cómicas
3. se case; la sección de sociedad
4. va; la sección deportiva
5. aumente; la sección financiera
6. vayan; la sección de ocio
7. sean; la sección de moda
8. quieren; los anuncios clasificados

Repaso

CAPÍTULO 8

The **Repaso** reviews all four skills and culture in preparation for the Chapter Test.

Teaching Resources
pp. 244–245

PRINT
▸ Lesson Planner, p. 41
▸ Listening Activities, p. 61
▸ Video Guide, pp. 51, 53, 57
▸ Grammar Tutor for Students of Spanish, Chapter 8
▸ Cuaderno para hispanohablantes, pp. 36–40
▸ Standardized Assessment Tutor, Chapter 8

MEDIA
▸ One-Stop Planner
▸ Video Program, Videocassette 3, 28:52–30:40
▸ Audio Compact Discs, CD 8, Tr. 19
▸ Interactive CD-ROM Tutor, Disc 2

Additional Practice

1 As an extension, have pairs of students work together to create new captions for the cartoon, using expressions they have learned in this chapter. Have them each take the role of a character and read their captions for the class.

Answers
1 *Sample answers:*
1. No creo que sea buena idea cocinar las palomitas sin la tapa.
2. Claro que hay muchas palomitas en el piso.
3. No es probable que les guste encontrar palomitas en el piso.
4. Es probable que cocinen más.
5. Es cierto que Calvin cree que cocinar palomitas sin la tapa es mejor que hacer explotar una papa en el microondas.

1 Lee la tira cómica de Calvin y Hobbes® y responde a las siguientes oraciones con las expresiones de certeza, duda y sorpresa que aprendiste en este capítulo. See sample answers below.

MODELO **Calvin quiere cocinar las palomitas *(popcorn)* sin la tapa *(lid)*.**
—No puedo creer que quiera cocinarlas sin la tapa.

1. Es buena idea cocinar las palomitas sin la tapa.
2. Hay muchas palomitas en el piso.
3. A los padres de Calvin les encanta encontrar palomitas en el piso.
4. Van a cocinar más palomitas de maíz.
5. Según Calvin, cocinar palomitas de maíz sin la tapa es mejor que hacer explotar una papa en el horno de microondas.

2 Imagina que tu escuela ha instalado una nueva red de computadoras que te permite comunicarte electrónicamente con otros estudiantes de tu colegio. Escribe un mensaje para enviar a un(a) amigo(a) en el que expresas tus opiniones del sistema. Usa todas las expresiones de **Así se dice** que puedas.

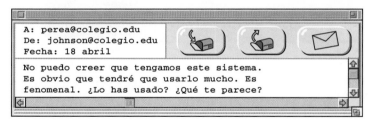

A: perea@colegio.edu
De: johnson@colegio.edu
Fecha: 18 abril

No puedo creer que tengamos este sistema. Es obvio que tendré que usarlo mucho. Es fenomenal. ¿Lo has usado? ¿Qué te parece?

3 Imagina que tú y un(a) compañero(a) están en la televisión reseñando *(reviewing)* una película que han visto. Usa expresiones de **Así se dice** para responder a lo que dice tu compañero(a) sobre los actores, el argumento, los personajes y las situaciones.

MODELO —Creo que la actriz principal va a ganar muchos premios de la Academia de Cinematografía.
—No es probable que gane ningún premio; es más fácil que el actor principal lo gane.

Apply and Assess

Cooperative Learning
Give small groups of two to three students a situation. In each situation, one student portrays a talk show host who is interviewing one or two guests. The identity of the guests will differ in each situation. (a famous sports figure, cartoonist, newspaper reporter) The students should be given time to brainstorm about the vocabulary needed for each situation. They can role-play the situations in front of the class while their classmates evaluate them, or you may want to use this as an oral exam that you evaluate.

STANDARDS: 1.1, 1.2, 1.3, 5.1

4 ¿Qué parte del periódico estás escuchando? Para cada selección que oyes, indica de qué sección del periódico viene. Script and answers on p. 219H.

CD 8
Tr. 19

a. la sección de ocio

b. los editoriales

c. la sección financiera

d. la sección de moda

e. la primera plana

f. los obituarios

5 Menciona por lo menos cinco noticias sobre tu ciudad a un(a) compañero(a). Tu compañero(a) debe responder a cada noticia con expresiones de **Así se dice.**

MODELO   —No van a abrir la piscina municipal este verano.
              —¡No me digas! No puedo creer que no abran la piscina.

6 Con dos o tres compañeros(as), contesta las preguntas con información cultural de este capítulo. See answers below.

1. Los estadounidenses cuentan mucho con la televisión para informarse. ¿Con qué cuentan muchos latinoamericanos?

2. ¿Para qué usan Internet los estudiantes argentinos?

3. ¿Dónde se pueden comprar revistas y periódicos en Latinoamérica?

4. ¿Qué horario tienen los buenos kioscos en Argentina?

5. ¿Qué se puede comprar en un kiosco argentino, además de periódicos y revistas? ¿Hay algo parecido a los kioscos en Estados Unidos? Expliquen sus respuestas.

7 ## Situación

Con unos(as) compañeros(as), diseña parte de un noticiero de televisión, de radio o de Internet. Cada grupo en tu clase tendrá que hacer una presentación de cinco minutos sobre uno de los siguientes temas. Usen, cuando sea posible, las expresiones de **Así se dice** de este capítulo.

1. noticias locales e internacionales

2. comentario político

3. el clima / el tiempo

4. los deportes

5. las artes / las diversiones

6. reportajes de interés general

Cuaderno para hispanohablantes, p. 40

Repaso

CAPÍTULO 8

 Portfolio

5 **Oral** You may want to suggest to students that they record their answers as a part of their oral Portfolio. For Portfolio suggestions, see *Alternative Assessment Guide,* page 23.

Apply and Assess

Additional Practice

6 Have the students do a similar activity focusing on what they know about Argentina. Divide the students into groups and have them develop questions for the other groups. Challenge them to write questions that the others may not be able to answer, but remind them that the information needs to come from the chapter, their class notes, or any guest speakers they might have heard. You set the limit for the number of questions to be developed, and the time allotted for writing the questions and answers. Questions can be written one day, copied, and then used for a warm-up activity the next day. The student-developed questions and answers might also be used later to review before the exam.

Answers

6 1. la radio
2. Como nosotros, los argentinos usan Internet para comunicarse, divertirse, leer, investigar e informarse.
3. en kioscos
4. Un buen kiosco está abierto las 24 horas al día.
5. todo, desde dulces hasta champú; *Answers will vary.*

A ver si puedo

CAPÍTULO 8

Teaching Resources
p. 246

PRINT
▸ Grammar Tutor for Students of Spanish, Chapter 8

MEDIA
▸ Interactive CD-ROM Tutor, Disc 2
▸ Online self-test

go.hrw.com
WV3 BUENOS AIRES-8

Teacher Note
This page is intended to help students prepare independently for the Chapter Test. It is only a checklist and does not necessarily include everything that will appear on the Chapter Test.

Answers
1 *Possible answers:*
1. Estoy seguro que quiere comprar algo.
2. Dudo que tenga dinero.
3. Claro que Valerie lee una revista.
4. Parece mentira que Valerie esté sufriendo de mucho estrés.
5. Es imposible que Kwang haya perdido el campeonato.
6. Por cierto, Kwang está en la gloria.

2 *Possible answers:*
1. Sin duda alguna.
2. Por supuesto.
3. No cabe la menor duda.
4. Es obvio que se pueden comprar en un kiosco.
5. Todo el mundo sabe esto.

3 *Possible answers:*
1. Es posible que llueva mañana.
2. Es probable que haga buen tiempo mañana.
3. Puede ser que haya niebla mañana.
4. Quizás quiera ir a la playa mañana.

4 *Answers will vary. Possible answers:*
1. ¡No es posible!
2. No me lo esperaba.
3. ¡No me lo puedo creer!
4. ¡No puede ser!
5. ¡No me digas!

A ver si puedo...

WV3 BUENOS AIRES-8

Can you express doubt and disbelief? p. 225

1 Mira los dibujos y contesta las preguntas con expresiones de duda o de certeza. See possible answers below.

Sr. Gonsalves   **Valerie**   **Kwang**

1. ¿Quiere comprar algo el señor Gonsalves?
2. ¿Tiene suficiente dinero el señor Gonsalves para comprar un periódico?
3. ¿Lee una revista Valerie?
4. ¿Está sufriendo de mucho estrés Valerie?
5. ¿Ha perdido Kwang el campeonato de tenis?
6. ¿Está en la gloria Kwang?

Can you express certainty? p. 227

2 Responde a cada oración con una expresión de certeza. See possible answers below.
1. Hay muchas emisoras en los Estados Unidos.
2. Leemos los periódicos para saber qué pasa en el mundo.
3. Escuchamos a los comentaristas para saber qué piensan.
4. Se pueden comprar periódicos y revistas en un kiosco.
5. Los periodistas expresan sus opiniones en los comentarios.

Can you express possibility and impossibility? p. 232

3 ¿Qué tiempo va a hacer mañana? Contesta las preguntas con expresiones de posibilidad o imposibilidad. See possible answers below.
1. ¿Va a llover mañana?
2. ¿Va a hacer buen tiempo?
3. ¿Habrá mucha niebla?
4. ¿Querrás ir a la playa mañana?

Can you express surprise? p. 234

4 Estás mirando la televisión y ves y oyes las siguientes cosas. Responde a cada acontecimiento con una expresión de sorpresa. See possible answers below.
1. Un perro está cantando Beethoven.
2. Una señora gana una casa nueva.
3. Una chica de quince años es graduada en la universidad.
4. Un carro deportivo cuesta 120.000 dólares.
5. El jabón nuevo se puede usar para lavarse la ropa y el pelo.

Review and Assess

Native Speakers
1 Have groups of students create background stories for each of the pictures, describing the people and what led up to the situations depicted. Students should include as many expressions using the subjunctive as possible. Ask volunteers to share their stories with the class.

Pair Work
4 Have pairs of students write five other amusing or incredible statements in the present tense. Volunteers can read their statements to which the class responds with surprise, doubt, or disbelief.

STANDARDS: 1.2

Primer paso

Expressing doubt and disbelief

Dudo que...	I doubt that . . .
Es increíble que...	It's unbelievable that . . .
No creo que...	I don't believe that . . .
No estoy seguro(a) que...	I'm not sure that . . .
No puedo creer que...	I can't believe that . . .
Parece mentira que...	It's hard to believe that . . .

Media

anunciar	to announce
el anuncio	commercial
la cadena	(broadcast) network
el canal	channel
el (la) comentarista	commentator
el documental	documentary
la emisora	station
en línea	online

el (la) locutor(a)	announcer, anchorperson
el noticiero	news program
por cable	on cable
la prensa	press
el programa	program
el reportaje	report
el (la) reportero(a)	reporter
el sitio Web	Web site

Expressing certainty

Claro que...	Of course . . .
Es cierto que...	It's true that . . .
Es evidente que...	It's evident that . . .
Es obvio que...	It's obvious that . . .
Estoy convencido(a) que...	I'm convinced that . . .
Estoy seguro(a) que...	I'm certain that . . .
No cabe la menor duda.	There is absolutely no doubt.
Por cierto.	Certainly.

Por supuesto.	Of course.
Sin duda alguna.	Without a doubt.
Todo el mundo sabe que...	Everyone knows that . . .

Talking about what you know

estar al tanto de	to be up to date on
estar bien informado(a) sobre	to be well-informed about
Me suena a chino.	It's Greek to me.
no saber ni jota de	to know absolutely nothing about
no tener la menor idea	not to have the slightest idea
¿Qué sé yo?	How should I know?
Que yo sepa...	As far as I know . . .
¡Ya lo sé!	I know!

Segundo paso

Expressing possibility and impossibility

A lo mejor...	Perhaps . . .
Es difícil que...	It's unlikely that . . .
Es fácil que...	It's likely that . . .
Es imposible que...	It's impossible that . . .
Es posible que...	It's possible that . . .
Es probable que...	It's probable that . . .
Posiblemente...	Possibly . . .
Puede ser que...	It's possible that . . .
Quizás...	Maybe . . .
Tal vez...	Maybe . . .

Newspaper

los anuncios clasificados	classified ads
el artículo	article

los editoriales	editorials
los obituarios	obituaries
el (la) periodista	journalist
la primera plana	front page
la sección de cocina	food/cooking section
la sección de moda	fashion section
la sección de ocio	entertainment section
la sección de sociedad	society section
la sección deportiva	sports section
la sección financiera	financial section
las tiras cómicas	comics

los titulares	headlines

Expressing surprise

No es posible.	It's not possible.
¡No me digas!	You don't say!
No me lo esperaba.	It caught me by surprise.
No me lo puedo creer.	I can't believe it.
¡No puede ser!	It can't be!
¡Qué sorpresa!	What a surprise!

Review and Assess

Circumlocution

To review media vocabulary, have students play ¿CÓMO TE DIRÉ? Write the following questions and statements on the board for students to use: **¿Cómo se llama la cosa que...?,** **Es lo que..., ¿Cómo se llama la persona que...?, Es la persona que..., y ¿Cuál es la sección que...?** See page 3C for the complete rules and procedures.

Teaching Suggestions

- Bring in examples of the vocabulary items and ask students to give the word in Spanish.
- Ask students to work with a partner. Each partner picks five to ten vocabulary items from this page and writes them down. Students then take turns asking each other questions using the words from their lists. Only one word can be used per question.

Challenge

Ask students to complete all of the open-ended phrases on this page in an original way.

Chapter 8 Assessment

▸ **Testing Program**
Chapter Test, pp. 177–182
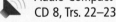 Audio Compact Discs, CD 8, Trs. 22–23
Speaking Test, p. 298

▸ **Alternative Assessment Guide**
Portfolio Assessment, p. 23
Performance Assessment, p. 37
CD-ROM Assessment, p. 51

▸ **Interactive CD-ROM Tutor, Disc 2**
 ¡A hablar!
¡A escribir!

▸ **Standardized Assessment Tutor**
Chapter 8

▸ **One-Stop Planner, Disc 2**
Test Generator
Chapter 8

Teaching Resources
pp. 248–251

PRINT
▶ Lesson Planner, p. 42
▶ Video Guide, pp. 58–59

MEDIA
▶ One-Stop Planner
▶ Video Program,
   Videocassette 3, 30:52–32:43
▶ Interactive CD-ROM Tutor, Disc 3
▶ Map Transparency 5

 go.hrw.com
WV3 NEW YORK

 **Using the Almanac
and Map**

Terms in the Almanac

• **Población:** Brooklyn is the most heavily populated borough. Queens has the second-largest population in the state. Manhattan is the oldest of the boroughs. The Bronx is chiefly a residential area. Staten Island is the smallest borough.

• **Economía:** New York is the home of Wall Street, a name that is now synonymous with the New York and American Stock Exchanges. New York hosts over 24,000 companies specializing in such business services as banking, finance, advertising, management and consulting, public relations, and commercial research computer services.

• **Comunicaciones:** New York is home to more publishing and broadcasting company headquarters than any other city in the United States. Three general newspapers are published daily here: *The Daily News, The New York Post,* and *The New York Times.* There are several Spanish-language newspapers, including ***El Diario, Noticias del Mundo, La prensa,*** and ***El vocero.***

CAPÍTULOS 9 y 10

¡Ven conmigo a Nueva York!

Nueva York

Población: 8.008.278, en cinco distritos: Manhattan, Bronx, Queens, Brooklyn y Staten Island

Población de habla hispana: 2.160.554

Área: 780 km²

Economía: servicios financieros, servicios publicitarios, cultura y arte, teatro, turismo, moda, medios de comunicación

Hispanos famosos: Tito Puente (1923–2000), músico y compositor; Martina Arroyo (n. 1937), cantante de ópera; Jimmy Smits (n. 1955), actor; Irene Cara (n. 1959), cantante y actriz; Bobby Bonilla (n. 1963), jugador de béisbol

Platos hispanos típicos: arroz con plátanos fritos; lechón asado; ropa vieja; arroz con habichuelas

go.hrw.com
WV3 NEW YORK   VIDEO   CD-ROM DISC 3

La silueta de Nueva York, con sus rascacielos grandes, es impresionante. ▶

Connections and Comparisons

History Link

Have students research the history of New York City and report their findings to the class. (established as a permanent settlement in Manhattan in 1625 by Dutch immigrants, who called it *Nieuw Amsterdam;* in 1664 the British took control of New Amsterdam and renamed it New York, after the Duke of York; from 1784 to 1796 it was the capital of New York state; from 1789 to 1790 it was the first capital of the United States under the Constitution; in 1898, having outgrown Manhattan, the city merged with Brooklyn, Queens, the Bronx, and Staten Island)

MAPQUEST.COM

go.hrw.com

HRW Atlas Interactivo Mundial

Have students use the interactive atlas at **go.hrw.com** to find out more about the geography of New York and complete the Map Activities below.

Map Activities

- Have students identify the states bordering New York state. (Connecticut, Massachusetts, New Jersey, Pennsylvania, Vermont)
- Have students identify the bodies of water surrounding New York state. (Lake Ontario, Lake Erie, Atlantic Ocean)
- Ask students to find the Hudson River. Into what large body of water does it flow? (Atlantic Ocean)

CNN enEspañol.com

Have students check the **CNN en español** Web site for news on New York. The **CNN en español** site is also a good source of timely, high-interest readings for Spanish students.

Cultures and Communities

Background Information
New York City has been the largest city in the United States since 1790. It is divided into five boroughs: Manhattan, Brooklyn, Queens, the Bronx, and Staten Island.

 ### Culture Note
There are many Caribbean restaurants in New York that serve such dishes as **arroz con plátanos** *(rice with plantains)*, **lechón asado** *(roast suckling pig)*, **ropa vieja** *(beef strips with seasonings)*, and **arroz con habichuelas** *(rice and beans)*.

Location Opener

CHAPTERS 9, 10

Using the Photo Essay

1 Símbolo que conmemora la libertad *Liberty Enlightening the World,* more commonly referred to as the Statue of Liberty, towers over the entrance to New York harbor. Each year, millions of people visit the 225-ton, 151-foot monument that symbolizes freedom and opportunity. Liberty was sculpted by the French sculptor Frédéric-Auguste Bartholdi, and the framework was designed by Alexandre-Gustave Eiffel. The statue was unveiled in 1886 by President Grover Cleveland. It was a gift from the French people to celebrate America's Centennial.

2 Lugar donde los hispanos expresan su arte El Museo del Barrio in East Harlem houses pre-Columbian artifacts and displays contemporary painting and sculpture. The museum also hosts lunchtime concerts, film series, lectures, and performances by a resident theater group, **Teatro Cuatro.**

3 Símbolo de la unión de las naciones The United Nations Charter was signed in April 1945 by representatives of 50 countries. A year later, the General Assembly and Security Council decided to locate the permanent UN headquarters in the United States. In 1952, the first meetings were held. Today over 5,155 employees and civil servants from member nations work together at the United Nations.

Nueva York

Nueva York es una ciudad enorme, la más grande de Estados Unidos, y una de las más grandes del mundo. Es un gran centro financiero, cultural y de negocios. Los hispanos, sobre todo los puertorriqueños, cubanos y dominicanos, forman aproximadamente la cuarta parte de la población. El español es el segundo idioma más hablado aquí. Nueva York atrae a gente creativa del mundo entero. Por ejemplo, el escritor español Federico García Lorca y el poeta cubano José Martí vivieron aquí; también el compositor mexicano Carlos Chávez y el músico panameño Rubén Blades. Más que ninguna otra ciudad estadounidense, Nueva York pertenece al mundo.

internet

go.hrw.com

MARCAR: go.hrw.com
PALABRA CLAVE:
WV3 NEW YORK

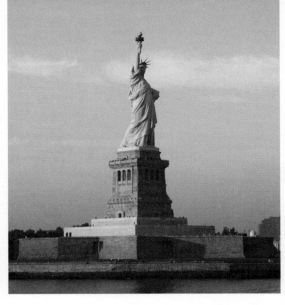

1 Símbolo que conmemora la libertad
Para muchos inmigrantes, la primera vista que tuvieron de Estados Unidos fue la de la Estatua de la Libertad. Aunque muchos llegan ahora al aeropuerto, la estatua todavía domina la vista al puerto y simboliza la puerta a una vida nueva.

2 Lugar donde los hispanos expresan su arte
No muy lejos del Parque Central está el Museo del Barrio, que comenzó como una sala de clase. Hoy día este museo de Harlem se dedica a la cultura hispana, sobre todo a la puertorriqueña.

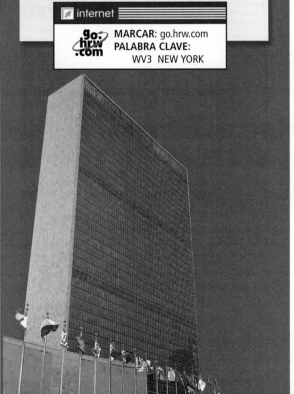

3 Símbolo de la unión de las naciones
La construcción del edificio de Las Naciones Unidas se terminó en 1963. Esta organización de 185 países existe para fomentar la paz y el bienestar en el mundo. Javier Pérez de Cuéllar, de Perú, fue Secretario-General durante diez años, de 1982 a 1992.

Connections and Comparisons

Multicultural Link
Ask students to research a New York immigrant ethnic group. Then have them write a journal entry in Spanish from an immigrant's point of view. Have them explain why they came to the city; say where they live and work; and give their impressions of the city.

Literature Link
Have students read Emma Lazarus' poem "The New Colossus," which was engraved on the pedestal of the Statue of Liberty in 1903.

4 Reserva de la vida animal salvaje Como muchas ciudades grandes, Nueva York también tiene un zoológico. El del Bronx es el más grande del país, con especies de todos los continentes.

En los capítulos 9 y 10, conocerás Nueva York, el hogar de más de dos millones de hispanos. Conocerás también a varios neoyorquinos, y es posible que descubras que son semejantes a ti. Verás algunas de las muchas atracciones de esta variada metrópolis, que es una capital del mundo.

5 El pulmón de Nueva York El Parque Central es una isla verde con lagos y plantas en medio de Manhattan. Ocupa 840 acres a lo largo de 50 cuadras. Más de 14 millones de personas gozan de las canchas de tenis, los lugares para montar a caballo, los jardines y el zoológico que hay en el parque.

7 Siglo de expresión artística El Museo Metropolitano de Arte es uno de los más famosos del mundo. Uno puede pasar muchas horas, hasta días enteros, recorriendo todas sus salas.

6 Gran diversidad étnica y cultural Nueva York es una ciudad de inmigrantes. Además de hispanos, hay mucha gente de China, Italia, Irlanda, Rusia y otros países. Los barrios italianos y chinos son famosos por sus restaurantes, sus festivales y por sus tiendas y mercados.

4 Reserva de la vida animal salvaje The Bronx Zoo, officially the International Wildlife Conservation Park, is the largest zoo in the United States. Here over 4,000 animals of more than 700 species live in landscaped areas simulating their natural habitats. Animals are separated from spectators by artificial rivers or ravines instead of cages. The Bronx Zoo is known for its collection of rare and endangered animals from all seven continents.

5 El pulmón de Nueva York Central Park, a great rectangle of greenery in the heart of Manhattan, has been one of the city's primary sources of recreation for over 100 years. This 840-acre plot was originally suggested in 1850 by William Cullen Bryant, who foresaw the need for a recreational area in this fast-growing city. Today, more than 14 million people visit the park each year.

6 Gran diversidad étnica y cultural The multiethnicity of New York City is evident in the calendar of festivals and events for a typical year. In January, Chinatown celebrates the Chinese New Year. In February, lectures on and exhibitions of African American culture and history take place. In March, parades celebrating Greek Independence Day and Saint Patrick's Day fill the streets. Other celebrations include: Japanese Cherry Blossom Festival, Ukrainian Festival, Feast of St. Anthony of Padua, and Puerto Rican Day Parade.

7 Siglo de expresión artística The Metropolitan Museum of Art, founded in 1870, is the largest art museum in the United States. Approximately four million visitors a year view its two-million-piece collection that represents nearly every culture of the last 5,000 years.

Cultures and Communities

Career Path

The United Nations employs many translators and interpreters in New York and elsewhere. As a translator for the UN, one might translate documents from Spanish into English for a delegate from the United States. An interpreter might simultaneously interpret the speech of a Spanish-speaking delegate into English. Translating and interpreting are also useful skills for international business. Ask students when a company doing business abroad would need a translator or interpreter. (translator: for manuals, legal documents, and agreements; interpreter for court proceedings, meetings, and seminars)

Capítulo 9: Las apariencias engañan
Chapter Overview

De antemano pp. 254–256	*A veces las apariencias engañan*

	FUNCTIONS	**GRAMMAR**	**VOCABULARY**	**RE-ENTRY**
Primer paso pp. 257–260	• Talking about emotional reactions, p. 257 • Expressing disagreement, p. 259	• Use of preterite for emotional reactions, p. 258 • The subjunctive with disagreement and denial, p. 259	• Describing personalities, p. 260	• Reflexive verbs **(Capítulo 7, I)** • The subjunctive with expressions of feeling **(Capítulo 7)** • The subjunctive with impersonal expressions **(Capítulo 8)**

¡Adelante! pp. 262–263	*Me gustaría viajar a...*

Segundo paso pp. 264–267	• Expressing an assumption, p. 264 • Making hypothetical statements, p. 264	• The conditional, p. 265	• Discrimination, p. 266	• Irregular stems in the future **(Capítulo 3)** • The preterite **(Capítulo 5, II)** • Expressions of opinion **(Capítulo 3)**

Vamos a leer pp. 268–270	**Escena neoyorquina** and **Biografía de José Martí**	**Reading Strategy:** Recognizing literary devices

Vamos a escribir p. 271	**¿Cuál es tu opinión?**	**Writing Strategy:** Finding good details

Más práctica gramatical	**pp. 272–275** **Primer paso,** pp. 272–274	**Segundo paso,** pp. 274–275

Review pp. 276–279	**Repaso,** pp. 276–277	**A ver si puedo...,** p. 278	**Vocabulario,** p. 279

CULTURE

• **Nota cultural,** Hispanics in New York City, p. 260

• **A lo nuestro,** Comic ways to say someone is presumptuous, p. 260

• **Panorama cultural, ¿Qué piensas de la gente de los Estados Unidos?,** p. 261

• **Nota cultural,** Spanish-language media in New York, p. 264

Capítulo 9: Las apariencias engañan
Chapter Resources

PRINT

Lesson Planning

One-Stop Planner

Lesson Planner with Substitute Teacher Lesson Plans, pp. 42–46, 73

Student Make-Up Assignments
- Make-Up Assignment Copying Masters, Chapter 9

Listening and Speaking

Listening Activities
- Student Response Forms for Listening Activities, pp. 67–69
- Additional Listening Activities 9-1 to 9-6, pp. 71–73
- Additional Listening Activities (poem), p. 74
- Scripts and Answers, pp. 142–146

Video Guide
- Teaching Suggestions, pp. 61–62
- Activity Masters, pp. 63–65
- Scripts and Answers, pp. 104–106, 118

Activities for Communication
- Communicative Activities, pp. 33–36
- Realia and Teaching Suggestions, pp. 75–77
- Situation Cards, pp. 105–106

Reading and Writing

Reading Strategies and Skills Handbook, Chapter 9

¡Lee conmigo! 3, Chapter 9

Cuaderno de actividades, pp. 97–108

Grammar

Cuaderno de gramática, pp. 70–77

Grammar Tutor for Students of Spanish, Chapter 9

Assessment

Testing Program
- Grammar and Vocabulary Quizzes, **Paso** Quizzes, and Chapter Test, pp. 191–204
- Score Sheet, Scripts and Answers, pp. 205–211

Alternative Assessment Guide
- Portfolio Assessment, p. 24
- Performance Assessment, p. 38
- CD-ROM Assessment, p. 52

Student Make-Up Assignments
- Alternative Quizzes, Chapter 9

Standardized Assessment Tutor
- Reading, pp. 35–37
- Writing, p. 38
- Math, pp. 51–52

Native Speakers

Cuaderno para hispanohablantes, pp. 41–45

MEDIA

 Online Activities
- Juegos interactivos
- Actividades Internet

 Video Program
- Videocassette 3
- Videocassette 5 (captioned version)

 Audio Compact Discs
- Textbook Listening Activities, CD 9, Tracks 1–20
- Additional Listening Activities, CD 9, Tracks 25–31
- Assessment Items, CD 9, Tracks 21–24

 Interactive CD-ROM Tutor, Disc 3

Teaching Transparencies
- Situations 9-1 to 9-2
- **Más práctica gramatical** Answers
- **Cuaderno de gramática** Answers

  One-Stop Planner CD-ROM

Use the **One-Stop Planner CD-ROM with Test Generator** to aid in lesson planning and pacing.

For each chapter, the **One-Stop Planner** includes:
- Editable lesson plans with direct links to teaching resources
- Printable worksheets from resource books
- Direct launches to the HRW Internet activities
- Video and audio segments
- Test Generator
- Clip Art for vocabulary items

Capítulo 9: Las apariencias engañan

Projects

Una encuesta

In this activity students create and carry out a survey examining the issue of stereotypes. Part of two days and some time outside of class should be allotted for the completion of this project. Stereotypes are, of course, a sensitive topic. You may wish to limit topics or to modify some procedures suggested here, depending on circumstances in your classroom. You may also wish to check with parents before sending students into the community to do research or to conduct interviews.

Students' questionnaires should include the following:

• Five questions exploring attitudes about stereotypes

• Space for comments

• Space for those surveyed to add optional demographic information about themselves (age, race, and gender)

MATERIALS
✄ **Students may need**
• Lined paper suitable for photocopying
• Access to a copy machine

SUGGESTED SEQUENCE

1. Tell the students they are going to conduct a survey examining people's attitudes about stereotypes.

2. Assign groups of four students to work on each survey.

3. The students should think of five yes-or-no questions or questions that require quantifiable responses. (How often do you feel stereotyped by people? 1–Often, 2–Sometimes, 3–Seldom, 4–Never) The questions should be written in English and Spanish.

4. Each student in the group should interview five people in the community. The questions should include at least one about Spanish speakers.

5. The students should then meet to discuss their results with other group members.

6. Have each group prepare a chart detailing its survey and discussing its results. You might set aside some class time for groups to talk about what they learned.

GRADING THE PROJECT

Suggested point distribution: (total = 100 points)
Survey questions..30
Use of Spanish 40
Compilation of results 30

Games

El crucigrama

This game helps students practice chapter vocabulary and concentrate on idea organization. It may be played at any time during the chapter.

Preparation Students will need at least two sheets of graph paper each.

Procedure Have each student create a crossword puzzle for a classmate to solve. They should fit about twenty vocabulary words or phrases into the grid going across and down. The words should be numbered and a clue in both English and Spanish should be given for each word. Definitions, equivalent words, fill-in-the-blank sentences, or other clues can be used. Have each student create the final puzzle on another sheet of graph paper with just the numbers, blank squares, and clues. The games are then exchanged and solved by other students.

Todo es posible

*This game provides practice with the imperfect subjunctive and conditional tenses and exercises the students' imaginations. It should be played after **Segundo paso**.*

Preparation Prepare a set of hypothetical questions to ask during this game. Turn two desks to face each other at the front of the room. Have a bell or buzzer on each one.

Procedure Divide the class into two teams and have one player from each team sit in the desks facing each other. Ask a hypothetical question of the contestants. The first player to ring the bell has the opportunity to give a logical answer in the conditional.

Two points are awarded for a correct answer on the first try. If the answer is incomplete or grammatically incorrect, the opposing team's contestant may answer it for one point.

COMMUNITY LINK

Ask students to contact the local chamber of commerce, a local newspaper, or a polling service. Have them ask if any surveys on race or ethnic relations have been conducted recently in their community. If there have been, have students gather that information and share it with the class.

Storytelling

Mini-cuento

This story accompanies Teaching Transparency 9-2. The ***mini-cuento*** *can be told and retold in different formats, acted out, written as a dictation, and read aloud to give students additional opportunities to practice all four skills. The following story recounts two friends thinking about things they would like to do.*

Marco y Gloria viven en Nueva York y son muy buenos amigos. Cada noche se imaginan las cosas que les gustaría hacer en el futuro. Si Marco pudiera, a él le gustaría jugar al basquetbol en un equipo profesional de la NBA. Además con el dinero que ganara se compraría un automóvil magnífico. Pero en realidad sus planes para el futuro son trabajar como profesor de literatura en la Universidad de Harvard. Gloria siempre ha pensado que si ella pudiera, sería una cantante muy popular. Además a ella le gustaría viajar a Egipto y ver las pirámides. Sin embargo, Gloria sabe que sería mejor estudiar medicina y trabajar en un hospital ayudando a las personas.

Si tú pudieras hacer cualquier tipo de trabajo, ¿qué harías?

Traditions

Salsa en Nueva York

This New York-Afro-Caribbean style of music is distinguished by its pronounced rhythmic character. New York salsa music reflects rhythms of Africa which, in the 1700s, found their way to Cuba via slave ships. There, and especially in Puerto Rico, these rhythms blended with Spanish music and American jazz. The music developed further as musicians brought it to New York City in the 1950s and 1960s. The word "salsa" was coined by New York's Fania Record Company. When Fidel Castro came to power in Cuba, Puerto Rico and New York became the primary sources of contemporary salsa music. New York City celebrates its Annual Salsa Festival in Madison Square Garden, and boasts of hundreds of salsa clubs. Have students research dances with African or Caribbean roots. How are they different or similar to salsa?

Receta

Puerto Ricans are the largest of several Spanish-speaking ethnic groups in New York City. They make up a substantial percentage of the city's population, roughly 1 million, and two-thirds of all the Puerto Rican population of the United States. Some Puerto Ricans even refer to themselves as ***Nuyoricans.*** *Like so many other immigrants, they brought their foods to New York City, among which are melt-in-your-mouth* ***merengues.***

MERENGUES

para hacer 50 merengues

4 claras de huevo (huevos medianos)

1/16 cucharadita de sal

1/2 cucharadita de crémor tártaro

1 1/2 tazas de azúcar

1/2 cucharadita de cáscara de limón, rallada

bandejas para hornear galletas, forradas con papel encerado *(wax paper)*

Caliente el horno a 200°. Bata las claras con batidora eléctrica en un plato hondo hasta que se formen picos. Añada la sal y el crémor tártaro. Continúe batiendo unos minutos más. Añada el azúcar poco a poco y siga batiendo por dos minutos. Agregue la rallada y bata dos minutos más, hasta que las claras queden a punto de nieve. Deposite por cucharadas el merengue en las bandejas para hornear galletas. Deje un espacio entre las cucharadas de merengue. Hornée de 30 a 35 minutos. Quítelos del papel y deje que se enfríen. Se pueden guardar en un recipiente bien sellado.

Capítulo 9: Las apariencias engañan
Technology

Video Program

Videocassette 3, Videocassette 5 (captioned version)
See Video Guide, pages 60–65.

Dramatic episode • En casa del tío Guadalupe

Alejandra and Irene are in Cuernavaca. Alejandra is convinced her secret admirer is Sergio, but Irene starts to suspect the admirer is really Javier. Guadalupe takes them to the Borda Gardens where they meet Carlos. All four start to talk about stereotypes and how they are really exaggerations.

¡Adelante! • Me gustaría viajar a...

Spanish-speaking people talk about where they would like to travel and about their impressions of the United States.

¿Qué piensas de la gente de los Estados Unidos?

People in Spanish-speaking countries explain what they think people in the United States are like.

 Videoclip

• **Alcaldía de Medellín:** public service message promoting the importance of people getting along

Interactive CD-ROM Tutor

The **Interactive CD-ROM Tutor** contains videos, interactive games, and activities that provide students an opportunity to practice and review the material covered in Chapter 9.

Activity	Activity Type	Pupil's Edition Page
1. Así se dice	Imagen y sonido ¡Exploremos! ¡Identifiquemos!	p. 257
2. Gramática	¿Cuál es?	p. 258
3. Gramática	¿Qué falta?	p. 259
4. Vocabulario	¡Super memoria!	p. 260
5. Gramática	¡A escoger!	p. 265
6. Vocabulario	¡Presta el oído!	p. 266
Panorama cultural	¿Qué piensas de la gente de los EEUU? ¡A escoger!	p. 261
¡A hablar!	*Guided recording*	pp. 276–277
¡A escribir!	*Guided writing*	pp. 276–277

Teacher Management System
Logging In

Logging in to the *¡Ven conmigo!* TMS is easy. Upon launching the program, simply type "admin" in the password area of the log-in screen and press RETURN. Log on to **www.hrw.com/CDROMTUTOR** for a detailed explanation of the Teacher Management System.

To preview all resources available for this chapter, use the **One-Stop Planner CD-ROM**, Disc 3.

Internet Connection

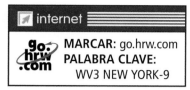

MARCAR: go.hrw.com
PALABRA CLAVE:
WV3 NEW YORK-9

*Have students explore the **go.hrw.com** Web site for many online resources covering all chapters. All Chapter 9 resources are available under the keyword **WV3 NEW YORK-9**. Interactive games help students practice the material and provide them with immediate feedback. You will also find a printable worksheet that provides Internet activities that lead to a comprehensive online research project.*

Juegos interactivos

You can use the interactive activities in this chapter
- to practice grammar, vocabulary, and chapter functions
- as homework
- as an assessment option
- as a self-test
- to prepare for the Chapter Test

Actividades Internet

Students explore their preconceived notions about various Latino groups in the United States, and then research the facts online.

- To prepare students for the **Hoja de actividades,** have them review the grammar from **Primer paso.** Also ask them to consider people's answers in **Panorama cultural.** Do they have similar notions about other cultures?
- After students have completed the **Hoja de actividades,** have them compare their answers for section B. Are there conflicting results?

Proyecto

Have students choose one of the Latino groups they research in the **Hoja de actividades**. Ask them to learn more online about this group, specifically about typical reasons for immigration. Then ask students to find out about a non-Latino ethnic population that had similar immigration circumstances earlier in American history. Remind students that the ancestors of most Europeans and Asians, as well as Latin Americans, were immigrants to this country.

Primer paso

9 p. 258

1. Felipe me dijo que mi novio salió con otra chica. Cuando supe que Felipe me mintió, estuve muy decepcionada. Casi me puse a llorar.

2. Me sentía muy presionado cuando llegué a la clase de matemáticas porque no estudié para el examen.

3. Cuando mi hijo menor supo que les di permiso para salir a sus hermanos, se sintió muy frustrado por ser el más pequeño.

4. Cuando supe que Manuel estaba enfermo y no podía ir al baile de fin de curso, estuve desilusionado. Él es mi mejor amigo y nunca me quejo de él.

5. Mis amigos y yo nos sentíamos muy frustrados cuando fuimos a hablar al profesor. No entendíamos la materia para nada.

6. Mi abuelo estaba enojado cuando le pregunté si quería enseñarme a manejar. Por eso me dijo que no. Le volveré a preguntar mañana.

Answers to Activity 9
1. una reacción
2. ya se sentía
3. una reacción
4. una reacción
5. ya se sentían
6. ya se sentía

12 p. 259

ALFREDO   Buenas tardes, Estelina, y gracias por estar con nosotros esta tarde.

ESTELINA   Muy buenas, Alfredo. Encantada de estar en tu programa.

ALFREDO   Dime, Estelina, tu nueva película se estrena este viernes, ¿no?

ESTELINA   Sí, y quiero que todos los que están escuchando vayan a verla. Está muy buena. También sale en la película el actor Enrique Rico. Es una película muy romántica.

ALFREDO   ¿No crees que a muchas personas ya no les gustan tanto las películas románticas?

ESTELINA   No, no es verdad que ya no les gusten. Al contrario, les fascinan las películas románticas, sobre todo si yo salgo en la película.

ALFREDO   ¿Es verdad que cantas en la película?

ESTELINA   Así es. Se trata de una película musical.

ALFREDO   Hablando de romance, según los chismes estás muy enamorada de Enrique Rico.

ESTELINA   Ay, Enrique es un encanto pero no es cierto que esté enamorada de él. Somos amigos nada más.

ALFREDO   Parece que te va muy bien en tu carrera. Ganas millones de dólares y tienes tres carros.

ESTELINA   Bueno, Alfredo, sí, estoy ganando mucho, pero en realidad no tengo tres carros; tengo cuatro.

Answers to Activity 12
1. cierta
2. falsa; A muchas personas les fascinan las películas románticas.
3. cierta
4. falsa; Son amigos nada más.
5. cierta
6. falsa; Tiene cuatro carros.

One-Stop Planner CD-ROM

To preview all resources available for this chapter, use the **One-Stop Planner CD-ROM**, Disc 3.

Segundo paso

22 p. 264

REPORTERO   Buenos días, señor. ¿Usted adónde viaja?

SEÑOR   Voy con mi esposa a Nueva York. Vamos a visitar a nuestra hija y a su familia por dos semanas.

REPORTERO   ¿Han estado ustedes en los Estados Unidos antes?

SEÑOR   Yo sí, hace treinta años. Mi esposa no.

REPORTERO   Señora, ¿cómo cree usted que son los estadounidenses?

SEÑORA   Bueno, este... supongo que muy simpáticos, ¿no?

REPORTERO   ¿Cómo se imaginan que es Nueva York actualmente?

SEÑORA   Es una ciudad enorme, por supuesto. Me imagino que la vida allá es mucho más agitada.

REPORTERO   Además de visitar a su hija, ¿qué piensan hacer?

SEÑORA   Nos gustaría ir de compras, aunque tengo entendido que las cosas allá son un poco más caras.

SEÑOR   Y también queremos ir a los museos. Me acuerdo que son fantásticos.

REPORTERO   ¿Les gustaría agregar algo más?

SEÑORA   Hemos visto en el mapa de la ciudad un parque que se llama "Parque Central". Es muy grande. Supongo que es un buen lugar para llevar a los nietos porque tiene unos lagos pequeños que deben ser muy lindos.

REPORTERO   Bueno, les deseo un buen viaje. Gracias y que lo pasen bien en Nueva York.

Answers to Activity 22

1. lo suponen	3. lo suponen	5. lo saben	7. lo suponen
2. lo saben	4. lo suponen	6. lo saben	

25 p. 265

REYNALDO   ¿Todo está listo para la fiesta?

ADELA   Bueno, casi, casi. Ya limpié la casa, y preparé un pastel y una ensalada de fruta. Compré el regalo también. Gracias a Adolfo, tenemos la música. Trajo su colección de discos compactos. Sin él, ¡creo que nunca bailaríamos!

REYNALDO   ¿Necesitas algo más?

ADELA   Sí, los refrescos. Los compraría si tuviera tiempo.

REYNALDO   No te preocupes. Ya fui al supermercado esta mañana a comprarlos. Bueno, parece que estamos bien. Todos dijeron que llegarían a las ocho. Para entonces tenemos tiempo de hacer algo. ¿Quieres jugar al tenis un rato?

ADELA   No, gracias. Jugaría contigo, ¡pero estoy cansadísima!

Answers to Activity 25

1. lo hizo	4. lo hizo	7. lo hizo
2. lo hizo	5. lo haría	8. lo haría
3. lo hizo	6. lo hizo	9. lo haría

Repaso

1 p. 276

1. Tengo tres hijos: Jorge, Pedrito y Ana. Los tres son muy lindos pero también muy traviesos. Los quiero mucho pero me enojo con ellos cuando se portan mal.

2. Disfruto mucho vivir sola en casa, pero me encanta estar con mis nietos. Tengo ocho nietos, dos hombrecitos y seis mujercitas. Desafortunadamente no vienen a visitar con frecuencia porque viven muy lejos. Me alegro mucho cuando me escriben unas cartas para decirme cómo están y qué pasa en sus vidas.

3. Me encantan los animales. Tengo dos gatitos que adoro: Jaimito y Trilbi. Jaimito es amigable, travieso y perezoso. Trilbi es tímida, callada y muy egoísta. Me río mucho al verlos jugar.

4. ¡Qué día tan bonito! Se siente el calor del sol. Me alegro cuando tengo tiempo de hacer ejercicio. En el invierno no hay muchos días como éste en los que pueda salir a caminar o correr un rato.

5. Ay, es casi la medianoche y no voy a terminar de estudiar para el examen de mañana. Me siento tan presionado cuando no estoy lo suficientemente preparado para un examen. No me voy a dormir hasta que termine de estudiar el último capítulo.

Answers to Repaso Activity 1

1. ningún dibujo	4. a
2. d	5. c
3. b	

Capítulo 9: Las apariencias engañan
Suggested Lesson Plans *50-Minute Schedule*

Day 1

CHAPTER OPENER 5 min.
- Focusing on Outcomes, ATE, p. 253
- Present Thinking Critically, ATE, p. 252.

DE ANTEMANO 40 min.
- Presenting **De antemano** and Preteaching Vocabulary, ATE, p. 254
- Do Activities 1–5, p. 256, and Comprehension Check, ATE, p. 256.

Wrap-Up 5 min.
- Have volunteers share responses from Activity 5, p. 256.

Homework Options
Cuaderno de actividades, p. 97, Activities 1–2

Day 2

PRIMER PASO
Quick Review 5 min.
- Check homework.
- Bell Work, ATE, p. 257

Así se dice, p. 257 30 min.
- Presenting **Así se dice**, ATE, p. 257
- Do Activity 6, p. 257.
- Have students do Activity 7 in pairs and Activity 8 in groups, pp. 257–258.

Gramática, p. 258 10 min.
- Presenting **Gramática**, ATE, p. 258
- Present the Slower Pace suggestion, ATE, p. 258.

Wrap-Up 5 min.
- Do the TPR activity, ATE, p. 257.

Homework Options
Cuaderno de actividades, pp. 98–99, Activities 3–5
Cuaderno de gramática, pp. 70–72, Activities 1–5

Day 3

PRIMER PASO
Quick Review 10 min.
- Check homework.
- Review irregular preterite verb forms.

Gramática, p. 258 15 min.
- Do Activity 9 with the Audio CD, p. 258.
- Do Activity 10, p. 258.
- Have students do Activity 11 in pairs, p. 259.

Así se dice/Gramática, p. 259 20 min.
- Presenting **Así se dice** and **Gramática**, ATE, p. 259
- Do Activity 12 with the Audio CD, p. 259.
- Have students do Activity 13 in pairs, p. 259.

Wrap-Up 5 min.
- Do the Pair Work, ATE, p. 259.

Homework Options
Cuaderno de actividades, pp. 99–100, Activities 6–7
Cuaderno de gramática, pp. 72–73, Activities 6–9

Day 4

PRIMER PASO
Quick Review 5 min.
- Check homework.

Vocabulario, p. 260 40 min.
- Presenting **Vocabulario**, ATE, p. 260
- Present **También se puede decir...** and **A lo nuestro**, p. 260.
- Have students do Activity 14 in pairs and Activity 15 in groups, p. 260.
- Have students do Activity 16, then peer-edit, p. 260.
- Read and discuss the **Nota cultural**, p. 260.

Wrap-Up 5 min.
- Do the TPR activity, ATE, p. 260.

Homework Options
Cuaderno de actividades, pp. 100–101, Activities 8–10
Cuaderno de gramática, p. 74, Activities 10–11

Day 5

PRIMER PASO
Quick Review 10 min.
- Check homework.
- Do Suggestion 1 for Teaching Transparency 9-1.

PANORAMA CULTURAL 10 min.
- Presenting **Panorama cultural**, ATE, p. 261

¡ADELANTE! 20 min.
- Presenting **¡Adelante!** and Preteaching Vocabulary, ATE, p. 262
- Activities 17–21, p. 263

Wrap-Up 10 min.
- Do the Thinking Critically Activity, ATE, p. 263.
- Discuss the content and format of Quiz 9-1.

Homework Options
Study for Quiz 9-1.
Cuaderno de actividades, p. 102, Activities 11–12

Day 6

PRIMER PASO
Quick Review 5 min.
- Check homework.
- Review the content of **Primer paso**.

Quiz 20 min.
- Administer Quiz 9-1A, 9-1B, or a combination of the two.

SEGUNDO PASO
Así se dice, p. 264 20 min.
- Presenting **Así se dice**, ATE, p. 264
- Do Activity 22 with the Audio CD, p. 264.
- Read and discuss the **Nota cultural**, p. 264.
- Have students do Activity 23 in pairs, p. 264.

Wrap-Up 5 min.
- Do the Group Work Activity, ATE, p. 264.

Homework Options
Cuaderno de actividades, p. 103, Activity 13

One-Stop Planner CD-ROM

For alternative lesson plans by chapter section, to create your own customized plans, or to preview all resources available for this chapter, use the **One-Stop Planner CD-ROM**, Disc 3.

For additional homework suggestions, see activities accompanied by this symbol throughout the chapter.

Day 7

SEGUNDO PASO
Quick Review 5 min.
- Check homework.
- Do Suggestion 2 for Teaching Transparency 9-2.

Así se dice/Gramática, pp. 264–265 40 min.
- Presenting **Así se dice** and **Gramática,** ATE, p. 265
- Do Building on Previous Skills, ATE, p. 265.
- Present Language-to-Language, ATE, p. 265.
- Have students do Activity 24 in groups, p. 265.
- Do Activity 25 with the Audio CD, p. 265.

Wrap-Up 5 min.
- Follow Suggestion 5 for Teaching Transparency 9-2.

Homework Options
Cuaderno de actividades, pp. 103–104, Activities 14–16
Cuaderno de gramática, pp. 75–76, Activities 12–15

Day 8

SEGUNDO PASO
Quick Review 5 min.
- Check homework.

Gramática, p. 265 20 min.
- Do Activities 26–27, p. 266.
- Present the Background Information, ATE, p. 266.
- Have students do Activity 28 in groups, p. 266.

Vocabulario, p. 266 20 min.
- Presenting **Vocabulario,** ATE, p. 266
- Do Activity 29, p. 267.
- Have students do Activity 30 in pairs, p. 267.

Wrap-Up 5 min.
- Discuss the content and format of Quiz 9-2.

Homework Options
Study for Quiz 9-2.
Cuaderno de actividades, pp. 105–106, Activities 17–20
Cuaderno de gramática, p. 77, Activities 16–17

Day 9

SEGUNDO PASO
Quick Review 10 min.
- Check homework.
- Review the content of **Segundo paso.**

Vocabulario, p. 266 10 min.
- Do Activity 31 with the class, p. 267.

Quiz 20 min.
- Administer Quiz 9-2A, 9-2B, or a combination of the two.

VAMOS A LEER 5 min.
- Read **Estrategia,** p. 268, then do Prereading Activities, ATE, p. 268.

Wrap-Up 5 min.
- Present the Language Note and follow Reading suggestions, ATE, p. 269.

Homework Options
Vamos a leer Activities A–C, pp. 268–269

Day 10

VAMOS A LEER
Quick Review 10 min.
- Discuss homework.

VAMOS A LEER, p. 268 35 min.
- Have students do Activity D in pairs, p. 269.
- Do Activity E, p. 270.
- Have students do Activity F in groups and Activity G in pairs, p. 270.

Wrap-Up 5 min.
- Have students share ideas from Activity G with the class, p. 270.

Homework Options
Vamos a escribir, p. 271
Cuaderno de actividades, pp. 107–108, Activities 21–26

Day 11

REPASO
Quick Review 5 min.
- Check and/or collect homework.
- Have students list Chapter 9 concepts and functions.

Repaso, pp. 276–277 40 min.
- Do Activity 1 with the Audio CD, p. 276.
- Have students do Activity 2 in pairs, p. 276.
- Do Activity 3, p. 276, then present the Culture Note, ATE, p. 277.
- Do Activities 4–6, p. 277.
- Have students do Activity 7 in groups, p. 277.

Wrap-Up 5 min.
- Play **Expresiones misteriosas,** ATE, p. 279.

Homework Options
A ver si puedo..., p. 278

Day 12

REPASO
Quick Review 5 min.
- Check homework.

Chapter Review 40 min.
- Review Chapter 9. Choose from **Más práctica gramatical,** Grammar Tutor for Students of Spanish, Activities for Communication, Listening Activities, Interactive CD-ROM Tutor, or **Juegos interactivos.**

Wrap-Up 5 min.
- Discuss the content of the Chapter 9 Test.

Homework Options
Study for the Chapter 9 Test.

Assessment

Quick Review 5 min.
- Answer any questions students may have.

Test, Chapter 9 45 min.
- Administer Chapter 9 Test. Select from Testing Program, Alternative Assessment Guide, Test Generator, or Standardized Assessment Tutor.

Capítulo 9: Las apariencias engañan
Suggested Lesson Plans *90-Minute Block Schedule*

Block 1

CHAPTER OPENER 5 min.
- Focusing on Outcomes, ATE, p. 253
- Present Thinking Critically, ATE, p. 252.

DE ANTEMANO 40 min.
- Presenting **De antemano** and Preteaching Vocabulary, ATE, p. 254
- Do Activities 1–5 and Comprehension Check, ATE, p. 256.

PRIMER PASO
Así se dice, p. 257 30 min.
- Presenting **Así se dice,** ATE, p. 257
- Do Activity 6, p. 257.
- Have students do Activity 7 in pairs and Activity 8 in groups, pp. 257–258.

Gramática, p. 258 10 min.
- Presenting **Gramática,** ATE, p. 258
- Present the Slower Pace suggestion, ATE, p. 258.

Wrap-Up 5 min.
- Do the TPR Activity, ATE, p. 257.

Homework Options
Cuaderno de actividades, pp. 97–99, Activities 1–5
Cuaderno de gramática, pp. 70–72, Activities 1–5

Block 2

PRIMER PASO
Quick Review 10 min.
- Check homework.
- Review irregular preterite verb forms.

Gramática, p. 258 15 min.
- Do Activity 9 with the Audio CD, p. 258.
- Do Activity 10, p. 258.
- Have students do Activity 11 in pairs, p. 259.

Así se dice/Gramática, p. 259 20 min.
- Presenting **Así se dice** and **Gramática,** ATE, p. 259
- Do Activity 12 with the Audio CD, p. 259.
- Have students do Activity 13 in pairs, p. 259.

Vocabulario, p. 260 40 min.
- Presenting **Vocabulario,** ATE, p. 260
- Present **También se puede decir...** and **A lo nuestro,** p. 260.
- Have students do Activity 14 in pairs and Activity 15 in groups, p. 260.
- Have students do Activity 16, then peer-edit, p. 260.
- Read and discuss the **Nota cultural,** p. 260.

Wrap-Up 5 min.
- Discuss the content and format of Quiz 9-1.

Homework Options
Study for Quiz 9-1.
Cuaderno de actividades, pp. 99–101, Activities 6–10
Cuaderno de gramática, pp. 72–74, Activities 6–11

Block 3

PRIMER PASO
Quick Review 10 min.
- Check homework.

PANORAMA CULTURAL 10 min.
- Presenting **Panorama cultural,** ATE, p. 261

Así se dice/Gramática/Vocabulario, pp. 257–260 10 min.
- Do the TPR activity, ATE, p. 260.
- Follow Suggestions 1 and 4 for Teaching Transparency 9-1.

Quiz 20 min.
- Administer Quiz 9-1A, 9-1B, or a combination of the two.

¡ADELANTE! 20 min.
- Presenting **¡Adelante!** and Preteaching Vocabulary, ATE, p. 262
- Do Activities 17–21, p. 263.

SEGUNDO PASO
Así se dice, p. 264 15 min.
- Presenting **Así se dice,** ATE, p. 264
- Do Activity 22 with the Audio CD, p. 264.
- Read and discuss the **Nota cultural,** p. 264.

Wrap-Up 5 min.
- Do the Group Work Activity, ATE, p. 264.

Homework Options
Cuaderno de actividades, pp. 102–103, Activities 11–13

One-Stop Planner CD-ROM

For alternative lesson plans by chapter section, to create your own customized plans, or to preview all resources available for this chapter, use the **One-Stop Planner CD-ROM,** Disc 3.

 For additional homework suggestions, see activities accompanied by this symbol throughout the chapter.

Block 4

SEGUNDO PASO

Quick Review 10 min.
- Check homework.
- Do Suggestion 2 for Teaching Transparency 9-2.

Así se dice, p. 264 5 min.
- Have students do Activity 23 in pairs, p. 264.

Así se dice/Gramática, pp. 264–265 60 min.
- Presenting **Así se dice** and **Gramática,** ATE, p. 265
- Do Building on Previous Skills, ATE, p. 265.
- Present Language-to-Language, ATE, p. 265.
- Have students do Activity 24 in groups, p. 265.
- Do Activity 25 with the Audio CD, p. 265.
- Do Activities 26–27, p. 266.
- Present Background Information, ATE, p. 266.
- Have students do Activity 28 in groups, p. 266.

Vocabulario, p. 266 10 min.
- Presenting **Vocabulario,** ATE, p. 266

Wrap-Up 5 min.
- Follow Vocabulary Practice Suggestions 1–2 for Teaching Transparency 9-2.

Homework Options
Cuaderno de actividades, pp. 103–105, Activities 14–18
Cuaderno de gramática, pp. 75–77, Activities 12–17

Block 5

SEGUNDO PASO

Quick Review 10 min.
- Check homework.

Vocabulario, p. 266 20 min.
- Do Activity 29, p. 267.
- Have students do Activity 30 in pairs, p. 267.
- Have students do Activity 31, then share with the class, p. 267.

VAMOS A LEER 50 min.
- Read **Estrategia,** p. 268, then do Prereading Activities, ATE, p. 268.
- Do Activities A–B, pp. 268–269.
- Present the Language Note and follow Reading suggestions, ATE, p. 269.
- Have students do Activity C, then Activity D in pairs, p. 269.
- Do Activity E, p. 270.
- Have students do Activity F in groups, p. 270.

Wrap-Up 10 min.
- Do Activity G with the class, p. 270.
- Discuss the content and format of Quiz 9-2.

Homework Options
Study for Quiz 9-2.
Cuaderno de actividades, pp. 106–108, Activities 19–26

Block 6

SEGUNDO PASO

Quick Review 10 min.
- Check homework.
- Review the content of **Segundo paso.**

Quiz 20 min.
- Administer Quiz 9-2A, 9-2B, or a combination of the two.

REPASO 40 min.
- Do Activity 1 with the Audio CD, p. 276.
- Have students do Activity 2 in pairs, p. 276.
- Do Activity 3, p. 276, then present the Culture Note, ATE, p. 277.
- Do Activities 4–6, p. 277.
- Have students do Activity 7 in groups, p. 277.

VAMOS A ESCRIBIR 10 min.
- Read the **Estrategia** and discuss the assignment, p. 271.
- Have students begin Activity A, p. 271.

Wrap-Up 10 min.
- Review the information in the Teacher Notes, ATE, p. 271.
- Discuss the content and format of the Chapter 9 Test.

Homework Options
Study for the Chapter 9 Test.
Assign **Vamos a escribir,** p. 271.
A ver si puedo..., p. 278

Block 7

REPASO

Quick Review 5 min.
- Check and/or collect homework.

Chapter Review 40 min.
- Review Chapter 9. Choose from **Más práctica gramatical,** Grammar Tutor for Students of Spanish, Activities for Communication, Listening Activities, Interactive CD-ROM Tutor, or **Juegos interactivos.**

Test, Chapter 9 45 min.
- Administer Chapter 9 Test. Select from Testing Program, Alternative Assessment Guide, Test Generator, or Standardized Assessment Tutor.

Chapter Opener

CAPÍTULO 9

 One-Stop Planner CD-ROM

For resource information, see the **One-Stop Planner,** Disc 3.

Pacing Tips
The content of this chapter relates to expressing emotions, and reacting to different situations. The use of emotional language lends itself to interactive activities. As you introduce the grammar and vocabulary, you may want to consider incorporating the Pair Work activities on pp. 259 and 264. See Suggested Lesson Plans, pp. 251I–251L.

Meeting the Standards
Communication
- Talking about emotional reactions, p. 257
- Expressing disagreement, p. 259
- Expressing an assumption, p. 264
- Making hypothetical statements, p. 264

Cultures
- Background Information, p. 266
- Background Information, p. 268

Connections
- Language Notes, pp. 253, 260, 269
- Social Studies Link, p. 261
- History Link, p. 270

Comparisons
- Panorama cultural, p. 261
- Multicultural Link, p. 261
- Language-to-Language, p. 265

Communities
- Language Notes, p. 260

Connections and Comparisons

Thinking Critically
Analyzing Ask students the following questions: **¿Qué es un estereotipo?** (It's an assumption about someone or something that is made without finding out if it is really true. Often it is a generalization about a group of people.) **¿Son positivos o negativos los estereotipos?** (They can be either.) **¿Cuáles son unos ejemplos de estereotipos positivos y negativos?** (Negative: Anybody who does not work is lazy. Positive: Anybody who reads a lot is brilliant.) **¿Por qué hay estereotipos? ¿Cómo sabemos si lo que creemos es un estereotipo?**

C A P Í T U L O

9

Las apariencias engañan

Objectives

In this chapter you will learn to

Primer paso

- talk about emotional reactions
- express disagreement

Segundo paso

- express an assumption
- make hypothetical statements

🖥 internet

go. hrw .com

MARCAR: go.hrw.com
PALABRA CLAVE:
WV3 NEW YORK-9

◀ **¡Qué felices estuvimos cuando volvimos a vernos!**

Photo Flash!

Teens in New York frequently attend schools that are culturally diverse. Students often find that stereotypes create false impressions. Share these expressions with the class: **"Caras vemos, corazones no sabemos."**; **"No todos los que tienen libros son lectores."**

Focusing on Outcomes

In this chapter, students will learn to discuss their emotional reactions to different situations. They will be able to agree or disagree with stereotypes, express assumptions, and discuss hypothetical situations.

Cultures and Communities

Language Notes

- The word **engañar** comes from the Latin word *ingannare,* meaning *to make fun of.* Ask students to think about how **engañar** (meaning *to fool)* relates to making fun of someone.

- The prefix **estereo-** comes from the Greek *stereós* and means *solid, robust,* or *cubic.* **Estereotipo** and **estereotipar** are formed with *typos,* meaning *impression, trace,* or *mold.* How do students explain the connection between the two elements?

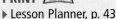
CAPÍTULO 9

PRINT
▶ Lesson Planner, p. 43
▶ Video Guide, pp. 60–61, 63
▶ Cuaderno de actividades, p. 97

MEDIA
▶ One-Stop Planner
▶ Video Program,
  Contigo en la distancia
  Videocassette 3, 32:22–39:12
  Videocassette 5 (captioned version), 43:55–50:45
▶ Audio Compact Discs, CD 9, Trs. 1–7

Presenting
De antemano

Have students read and answer the question in **Estrategia para comprender**. Review any unfamiliar vocabulary before playing the audio recording. Play the Audio CD and have students read along, focusing on known words. Next, present the Preteaching Vocabulary.

DE ANTEMANO · *A veces las apariencias engañan*

CD 9
Trs. 1–7

Cuaderno de actividades, p. 97, Acts. 1–2

Estrategia para comprender

Todos formamos parte de un grupo pero al mismo tiempo somos todos únicos y originales. A veces, por falta de información, una persona juzga mal a otra y ve sólo un estereotipo y no una persona. Vas a leer sobre las experiencias personales de seis estudiantes de la Sra. Nancy Stevens, profesora de español de Milford High School en Cincinnati, Ohio. ¿Te identificas con uno(a) de ellos?

Una impresión errónea

Me gustaría creer que tengo una mente abierta. Por eso, cuando estoy equivocado, me gusta reconocerlo.

El año pasado, en una clase de inglés, yo estaba sentado cerca de un estudiante con una reputación de "malo". Era bastante descortés, hablaba en clase todo el tiempo y su actitud era como su reputación: mala. No hacía nada de tarea y les contaba muchos chistes horribles a los otros estudiantes. Pensaba que iba a pasar un año malo a causa de ese chico.

Un día, tuve que trabajar con él en un proyecto. Empezamos a hablar y nos caímos muy bien. Aprendí que a él le gusta escribir cuentos y poemas, que puede cantar muy bien y que tenemos mucho en común. Tenía una impresión equivocada de él; en realidad es muy inteligente y creativo. Hoy, es mi mejor amigo.

Brian Reynolds

Las asiáticas

Karen Kim

Soy coreana. Muchas personas piensan que las mujeres asiáticas somos tímidas. Me frustro cuando la gente me coloca en esta categoría porque no soy así. Soy mi propia persona y tomo mis propias decisiones. También tengo sentimientos y una personalidad con muchas facetas diferentes. Mis características son tan variadas que no se pueden colocar debajo de ningún rótulo. Tampoco es verdad que seamos calladas. Conozco a muchas chicas asiáticas que se animan y hablan en voz alta cuando tienen emociones fuertes.

Otra cosa que no es verdad es la idea de que todos los asiáticos sean expertos en ciencias y matemáticas. No me gustan estas materias y me siento presionada cuando algunos profesores de ciencias o matemáticas esperan demasiado de mí.

Así, los estereotipos raciales sólo resultan en malas interpretaciones.

La gente callada

Me enfado cuando la gente observa a una persona tímida y ve un esnob. Sólo porque una persona sea callada y no se comunica con palabras, otros creen que él o ella es egoísta. El aura del callado parece como un aire de presumido al resto del mundo. Sin embargo, las personas calladas son muy amigables y no hablan simplemente porque no quieren expresarse o porque no desean oír las opiniones que llegan a sus oídos.

Este estereotipo tiene mucha significación para mí. A veces soy tímida y no hablo. Pero cuando no me comunico con palabras, no pienso en mí misma sino en las noticias y en los problemas del mundo. ¡Creo que se debe respetar la timidez del otro!

Tracy Shanks

Preteaching Vocabulary

Activating Prior Knowledge

Point out that **De antemano** is about appearances and how they can be misleading. Based on Spanish expressions students already know and what students know about stereotypes, what do they think Sra. Stevens's students mean when they make the following statements? **Tenía una impresión equivocada de él...; Así, los estereotipos raciales sólo resultan en malas interpretaciones.; Creo que se debe respetar la timidez de otro.; ...un estereotipo que me irrita mucho es la idea que los jugadores de fútbol americano somos tontos y torpes.; Espero que la gente haga un esfuerzo por aprender de las culturas diferentes.**

Miembro de la banda

Me llamo Emily Seitz y soy miembro de la banda de mi colegio. Me enojo cuando la gente se refiere a mí como una nerd de banda. Los del equipo de fútbol americano dicen que los miembros de la banda somos inútiles. ¡Al contrario! Trabajamos tanto como ellos. Cada año pasamos más de cien horas en el campamento de la banda. Como los jugadores de fútbol, practicamos cinco días a la semana. Y nunca estamos en casa los sábados porque tenemos competencias que duran todo el día.

Pasamos muchos años aprendiendo a tocar un instrumento musical. Es muy difícil tocar perfectamente el instrumento y marchar al mismo tiempo. Nos divertimos mucho y estamos muy orgullosos de lo que hacemos. Sólo queremos una cosa: que los otros equipos de la escuela nos respeten.

Emily Seitz

El jugador de fútbol americano

Yo juego al fútbol americano y un estereotipo que me irrita mucho es la idea de que los jugadores de fútbol americano somos tontos y torpes. Además de esto, creo que los otros estudiantes nos ven como muy arrogantes. La idea es absurda y me río un poco cuando me dicen "atleta bobo" porque es probable que nosotros saquemos notas mejores que los demás. Es difícil encontrar tiempo para todas las actividades y responsabilidades cuando uno entrena para un deporte, y los que no juegan no entienden la presión que existe sobre los atletas. ¡Nosotros trabajamos mucho! Sin embargo, los viernes por la noche, durante los partidos, los estudiantes nos animan porque representamos a la escuela. Ellos no recuerdan sus comentarios pero nosotros sí.

Brad Spier

Los italiano-americanos

En el mundo de hoy hay estereotipos en todas partes. ¿Por qué tienen que existir? Por lo general, es simplemente porque el grupo, la religión o la cultura es diferente del suyo.

En mi vida, no he sido víctima de los prejuicios. Pero mi familia, especialmente mis abuelos, ha sido prejuzgada por otros. Mi familia es italiana, de Sicilia. Cuando mi abuelo trató de obtener un trabajo hace muchos años, fue muy difícil porque había muchos prejuicios contra los italianos. Nuestro apellido fue cambiado a causa de esta discriminación.

Cada grupo étnico tiene su propio estereotipo. Soy italiana pero tengo los ojos azules, la piel blanca y el pelo rubio. Nadie pensaría que soy italiana, pero sí soy italiana y tengo orgullo de mi familia, nuestras tradiciones y nuestra cultura.

Espero que la gente haga un esfuerzo por aprender de las culturas diferentes en vez de prejuzgarlas. Este mundo tiene culturas con tesoros para compartir con otros. El mundo sería un lugar aburrido si cada persona fuera igual a todas las demás.

Jill Cardinal

Using the Captioned Video

As an alternative, you might want to show the captioned version of *Contigo en la distancia: En casa del tío Guadalupe* on Videocassette 5. Some students may benefit from seeing the written words as they listen to the target language and watch the gestures and actions in context. This visual reinforcement of vocabulary and functions will facilitate students' comprehension and help reduce their anxiety before they are formally introduced to the new language in the chapter.

Native Speakers

Ask students to discuss the stereotypes that people from other countries hold about the United States. Have them discuss how these stereotypes might have begun or might be perpetuated. (newspapers and magazines, movies and television, U.S. travelers, advertisements) Students might share their ideas with the class or write a short paragraph.

Thinking Critically

Analyzing Ask students to indicate whether these statements are (a) assumptions or (c) clearly stated in the reading.

Brad saca buenas notas. (a)

El estereotipo que los jugadores de fútbol americano son tontos le molesta mucho a Brad. (c)

A Karen no le gustan las ciencias ni las matemáticas. (c)

Tracy no es un esnob. (a)

Emily se enoja cuando sus compañeros de escuela le llama una nerd de banda. (c)

Jill nunca ha sido víctima de los prejuicios. (c)

Brian lo pasó bien en la clase de inglés este año. (a)

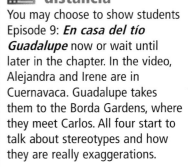

Contigo en la distancia

You may choose to show students Episode 9: *En casa del tío Guadalupe* now or wait until later in the chapter. In the video, Alejandra and Irene are in Cuernavaca. Guadalupe takes them to the Borda Gardens, where they meet Carlos. All four start to talk about stereotypes and how they are really exaggerations.

Auditory Learners

Read aloud the **De antemano** essay "**El jugador de fútbol americano**" as a dictation. Give students a copy of the reading with blanks they must fill in. Examples of words for students to listen for are **estereotipo, saquemos, difícil,** and **comentarios**.

These activities check for comprehension only. Students should not yet be expected to produce language modeled in **De antemano**.

1 **¿Los reconoces?** See answers below.

¿A quién se refiere cada una de las siguientes descripciones?

1. Aunque la gente piense que esta persona no es muy lista, saca buenas notas.
2. Quiere que todos sepan que es una persona independiente y que tiene sus propias ideas.
3. Dice que la gente introvertida no es necesariamente arrogante.
4. Le caía muy mal un compañero de clase hasta que un día realmente lo conoció.
5. Desea que todo el mundo conozca a personas de otras culturas para eliminar prejuicios.
6. Esta persona se siente muy orgullosa del trabajo y del esfuerzo de sus compañeros.

2 **¿Cierto o falso?** See answers below.

Indica si cada frase es **cierta**, **falsa** o si **no se sabe**. Si es falsa, corrígela.

1. Emily practica muchas horas con la banda.
2. Según Tracy, las personas tímidas sólo piensan en sí mismas.
3. Brian se dio cuenta de que el otro estudiante no tenía ningún pasatiempo.
4. Jill dice que no ha sido víctima de prejuicios.
5. Karen piensa estudiar química en la universidad.
6. Brad tiene un promedio perfecto.
7. Según Brian, la primera impresión que tuvo del otro estudiante fue bastante negativa.

3 **¿Quién lo diría?** See answers below.

Lee cada descripción. Según lo que los estudiantes escribieron, ¿quién diría lo siguiente?

1. Me considero muy trabajador(a).
2. Soy una persona seria; prefiero oír las noticias que los chismes.
3. Quiero que la gente me vea como verdaderamente soy.
4. Las primeras impresiones no representan necesariamente a la persona.
5. Me siento herido(a) por lo que dicen mis compañeros y no me olvido de lo que dicen.

4 **Busca las expresiones** See answers below.

1. ¿Qué expresiones usan estas personas para decir cómo se sienten en las siguientes situaciones?
   a. Emily, cuando los estudiantes la llaman una *nerd*
   b. Karen, cuando la gente la coloca en cierta categoría; cuando sus profesores esperan mucho de ella
   c. Brad, cuando la gente lo llama "atleta bobo"
   d. Tracy, cuando la gente piensa que los callados son presumidos
2. ¿Qué expresiones usan estas personas para negar lo que dice o piensa la gente?
   a. Emily, cuando algunos dicen que los miembros de la banda son inútiles
   b. Karen, cuando piensan que las asiáticas son calladas; cuando dicen que los asiáticos son expertos en las ciencias y matemáticas

5 **Ahora te toca a ti**

¿Te identificas con alguno de los estudiantes en **De antemano**? ¿Cuál? ¿Por qué? ¿Conoces a gente parecida a los estudiantes de **De antemano**? Escribe tus respuestas.

Answers

1
1. Brad	3. Tracy	5. Jill
2. Karen	4. Brian	6. Emily

2
1. cierta
2. falsa; La gente callada es amigable y no habla porque no quiere expresarse.
3. falsa; Brian aprendió que era un chico creativo que escribía poemas y cuentos y que cantaba.
4. cierta
5. falsa; No le gustan ni las ciencias ni las matemáticas.
6. no se sabe
7. cierta

3
1. Emily *or* Brad
2. Tracy
3. Jill, Brad, Karen, *or* Tracy
4. Brian
5. Brad

4
1. a. me enojo; b. me frustro, me siento presionada; c. me río un poco; d. me enfado
2. a. al contrario; b. no soy así, no es verdad

5 *Answers will vary.*

Comprehension Check

Slower Pace

To help students understand the reading, first have them work individually or in pairs to find the answers to Activity 2. Have students scan each passage to get the information they need. Then, once they have reviewed the passages and are more familiar with their content, have them answer the questions in Activity 1.

Challenge

3 Tell students that some statements in Activity 3 apply to more than one of the teenagers. Have them find more than one logical match for statements 1, 3, and 4. Ask them to support each of their answers with information from the passages.

Así se dice

Talking about emotional reactions

Si alguien te pregunta:

¿Cómo te sentiste cuando **supiste** *(you found out)* que sacaste buena nota?

¿Cómo se sintió Juan cuando conoció a su prima?

¿Te quejaste cuando tus compañeros **se burlaron de** *(made fun of)* ti?

¿Cómo se sintieron tus amigos cuando se dieron cuenta del error?

¿Cómo **reaccionaron** *(did they react)* cuando les contaste el chiste?

Para contestar, puedes decir:

Estuve muy contenta cuando lo supe.
I was very happy when I found out.
Se alegró mucho.
He was very happy.
No, pero **me frustré y me enojé (me enfadé).**
Quise llorar.
*. . . I got frustrated and I got angry.
I wanted . . .*
Se pusieron rojos *(They blushed)* de verdad.
Se sintieron **presionados por** *(pressured to)* corregirlo.
Claro que **se rieron** *(they laughed).*

(Cuaderno de actividades, pp. 98, 101 Acts. 3, 9) (Cuaderno de gramática, p. 70, Acts. 1–2)

6 **Un semestre excepcional**

Leamos/Escribamos Completa esta entrevista con una expresión de **Así se dice**.

TERESA Me va bien en la escuela. Saqué una A en mi clase de cálculo.

MANOLO No me digas. ¿Cómo ======= cuando supiste de la nota? te sentiste/reaccionaste

TERESA Pues, claro que ======= muy contenta. Me puse a bailar, pero también he tenido algunas decepciones. Por ejemplo me frustré cuando ======= que la Universidad Nacional no me aceptó. ======= llorar. estuve, supe, Quise

MANOLO Ay, lo siento mucho. Pero vas a ir a la Universidad Técnica, ¿no?

TERESA Así es. ======= mucho cuando lo supe. me alegré

7 **¿Cómo te sentiste?** See possible answers below.

Hablemos Imagina que eres una de las personas del dibujo. Describe lo que pasó ayer. Luego, cuéntale a tu compañero(a) cómo te sentiste cuando pasó lo que ves en el dibujo.

Communication for All Students

(TPR) Write phrases describing emotional reactions on index cards (Examples: **se puso muy nervioso(a), se enfadó, se frustró, se alegró**) and distribute to students. Call on students to act out the reaction on their cards, then ask classmates to describe the reaction they just saw using the expressions from **Así se dice**.

Native Speakers
Have students think about alternate expressions they might commonly use for situations similar to those modeled in **Así se dice**. (Se ruborizaron de la vergüenza. Se avergonzaron. Soltaron tremenda carcajada. Se echaron a reír.)

Teaching Resources
pp. 257–260

PRINT
▶ Lesson Planner, p. 43
▶ Listening Activities, pp. 67, 71–72
▶ Activities for Communication, pp. 33–34, 75, 77, 105–106
▶ Cuaderno de gramática, pp. 70–74
▶ Grammar Tutor for Students of Spanish, Chapter 9
▶ Cuaderno de actividades, pp. 98–101
▶ Cuaderno para hispanohablantes, pp. 41–45
▶ Testing Program, pp. 191–194
▶ Alternative Assessment Guide, p. 38
▶ Student Make-Up Assignments, Chapter 9

MEDIA
▶ One-Stop Planner
▶ Audio Compact Discs, CD 9, Trs. 8–9, 25–27, 21
▶ Teaching Transparencies 9-1, **Más práctica gramatical** Answers; Cuaderno de gramática Answers
▶ Interactive CD-ROM Tutor, Disc 3

Bell Work
On the board, write: **Escribe tres frases que usas para decir que estás seguro(a) de algo y tres frases para expresar duda.**

Presenting
Así se dice

Model several short conversations between two friends. One asks the other how he or she felt in a given situation.

Answers
7 *Possible answers:*
Me caí. Me puse rojo cuando la chica se rió de mí. La señora se enfadó porque la chica se burlaba de mí. El señor se rió cuando encontró dinero.

Teaching Resources
pp. 257–260

PRINT
▶ Lesson Planner, p. 43
▶ Listening Activities, pp. 67, 71–72
▶ Activities for Communication, pp. 33–34, 75, 77, 105–106
▶ Cuaderno de gramática, pp. 70–74
▶ Grammar Tutor for Students of Spanish, Chapter 9
▶ Cuaderno de actividades, pp. 98–101
▶ Cuaderno para hispanohablantes, pp. 41–45
▶ Testing Program, pp. 191–194
▶ Alternative Assessment Guide, p. 38
▶ Student Make-Up Assignments, Chapter 9

MEDIA
▶ One-Stop Planner
▶ Audio Compact Discs, CD 9, Trs. 8–9, 25–27, 21
▶ Teaching Transparencies 9-1; **Más práctica gramatical** Answers; Cuaderno de gramática Answers
▶ Interactive CD-ROM Tutor, Disc 3

Presenting
Gramática

More on preterite versus imperfect Model sentences using the preterite for emotional reactions. Remind students that the imperfect conveys the existing state in the past while the preterite conveys the change of state.

Answers
 10 1. nos pusimos 5. me puse
2. se rieron 6. quise
3. nos enojamos 7. supieron
4. me quejé 8. estuvieron

---

8 Por qué reaccionaron así?

 Escribamos Estás con tus amigos en la reunión de la Clase de 1999. Completa las siguientes oraciones para explicar lo que causó las reacciones de cada persona.

1. Quisimos llorar cuando…
2. Alicia se sintió presionada cuando…
3. Mis amigos y yo nos reímos cuando…
4. Me alegré cuando…
5. Recuerdo que te enojaste cuando…
6. Tito e Inés se pusieron rojos cuando…

Gramática

More on preterite versus imperfect

1. You've used the imperfect tense of verbs like **estar** and **sentirse** to say how people were already feeling at the moment something happened:

   Juan **se sentía** mal cuando le dieron el examen.

2. Use the preterite to say how someone reacted to an event or to a piece of news:

   Juan **se sintió** mal cuando le dieron el examen. (The feeling resulted from the event.)

3. The verbs **estar** and **ponerse** (to become) are irregular in the preterite:

estuve	estuvimos	me puse	nos pusimos
estuviste	estuvisteis	te pusiste	os pusisteis
estuvo	estuvieron	se puso	se pusieron

Más práctica gramatical, pp. 272–273, Acts. 1–4

4. The verb **saber** is irregular in the preterite and often means *found out*. The verb **querer** in the preterite means *wanted* when it refers to a reaction. It can sometimes mean *tried*.

supe	supimos	quise	quisimos
supiste	supisteis	quisiste	quisisteis
supo	supieron	quiso	quisieron

Cuaderno de actividades, pp. 98–99 Acts. 4–5

Cuaderno de gramática, pp. 71–72, Acts. 3–5

9 Gramática en contexto Script and answers on p. 251G.

Escuchemos Decide si cada oración que escuchas trata de cómo **ya se sentía** la persona cuando pasó el evento o si habla de **una reacción** causada por el evento.
CD 9 Tr. 8

10 Gramática en contexto   See answers below.

 Leamos/Escribamos Completa la carta que Vicente le escribió al supermercado Santa Isabel para quejarse de una experiencia que tuvo.

> Estimados señores:
>
> Quiero contarles una experiencia que tuve en su negocio. Mi esposa y yo estábamos mirando algunas cosas cuando de repente se nos cayeron unos paquetes y se rompieron. Claro que ____1____ (ponerse) rojos los dos. Pero imagínense la vergüenza que nos dio cuando unos empleados de la tienda ____2____ (reírse) de nosotros. Bueno, tal vez ellos lo encontraron cómico, pero nosotros no. Así que nosotros ____3____ (enojarse). Eso no fue nada profesional. Entonces fui a buscar al gerente y ____4____ (quejarse) con él, pero él no hizo nada. Yo ____5____ (ponerse) tan furioso que ____6____ (querer) gritar. Espero que ustedes se den cuenta de lo grave de la situación. Se lo conté a mis amigos y cuando lo ____7____ (saber), ellos no ____8____ (estar) nada contentos. Decidieron dejar de comprar en Santa Isabel también.

Communication for All Students

Game

CHARADES Divide the class into groups of four. Each group member is to mime a different expression from **Así se dice** on page 257. The other groups try to guess the expression, and the first to do so gets one point. The group with the highest score wins.

Slower Pace

Some students may have difficulty with the preterite forms of **reírse**. Point out that it is an **-ir** stem-changing verb like **pedir,** and as such is very predictable. However, due to the nature of its stem (**re-**), many of its forms require accent marks in order to prevent the stem and endings from forming a diphthong. Hence **me río, te ríes, nos reímos, te reíste,** and so on.

11 Cuando eso pasó...

Hablemos Piensa en un evento importante, cómico o emocionante que pasó este año o el año pasado. Primero, descríbele a un(a) compañero(a) lo que pasó. Luego dile cómo te sentiste tú cuando pasó y también cómo reaccionaron tus amigos o tu familia.

MODELO —La semana pasada mis amigos me hicieron una travesura.
—¿Qué pasó?
—Bueno, ellos se rieron, pero yo me enojé.

Así se dice

Expressing disagreement

Si quieres negar lo que dice o piensa la gente puedes decir:

Niego haberme burlado de los callados.
No es cierto que los miembros de la banda no trabajen. **¡Al contrario!**
No es verdad que los atletas estudien menos.
No estoy de acuerdo en que toda la gente italiana sea baja con pelo negro.

 12 Entrevista con Estelina Script and answers on p. 251G.

Escuchemos/Escribamos La actriz Estelina Estrella habla por la radio en una entrevista. Escucha la conversación y luego indica si las siguientes oraciones son **ciertas** o **falsas**. Si son falsas, corrígelas.

CD 9
Tr. 9

1. El estreno de su nueva película será el viernes.
2. Las películas románticas no son populares.
3. Cantará en su próxima película.
4. Está enamorada de Enrique Rico.
5. Gana millones de dólares.
6. Tiene tres carros.

Gramática

The subjunctive with disagreement and denial

1. Expressions of disagreement and denial are followed by the subjunctive.

   No es verdad que los hombres **manejen** mejor que las mujeres.
   Juan niega que los atletas **sean** todos bobos.

2. However, **es verdad que, es cierto que**, and **no niego que** are followed by the indicative since they don't deny the truth of something but rather affirm it.

   Es cierto que **cantan** bien.   No niego que **tienen** talento.

Más práctica gramatical, p. 274, Act. 5

Cuaderno de actividades, p. 99, Act. 6

Cuaderno de gramática, pp. 72–73, Acts. 6–9

 13 Gramática en contexto See possible answers below.

Hablemos Ignacio piensa que la vida es mejor hoy en día; su abuelo piensa que era mejor hace 50 años. Con un(a) compañero(a), toma el papel de Ignacio o del abuelo. ¿Cuál sería su opinión de las siguientes oraciones?

1. los actores son peores
2. los estudiantes estudian menos
3. la gente tiene buenos modales
4. los carros no funcionan bien
5. la gente se viste con ropa elegante
6. los políticos dicen la verdad
7. los niños no respetan a los mayores
8. los jóvenes gastan menos dinero

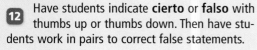 **Communication for All Students**

Slower Pace

12 Have students indicate **cierto** or **falso** with thumbs up or thumbs down. Then have students work in pairs to correct false statements.

Pair Work

13 Have pairs create a dialogue for a phone conversation. One partner expresses an opinion on some subject—school, a TV program, friends. The other disagrees.

Thinking Critically

Analyzing Remind students of the difference between fact and opinion. Ask them to clip or download a news article and scan it for facts and opinions. Have them categorize the ideas in the article as **opiniones** or **hechos**.

Presenting

Así se dice
Gramática

The subjunctive wih disagreement and denial
On the board or on a transparency, use the phrases in **Así se dice** and **Gramática** to write a letter to the editor expressing your disagreement with an idea concerning a current event. (**No estoy de acuerdo de que los estudiantes tengan que llevar uniformes. ¡Al contrario!**) Point out the use of the subjunctive. Then have students look at **Gramática**. Focus on the use of the subjunctive to deny something and the indicative to affirm it. When the letter is finished, have each student read one sentence aloud and use the new expressions to agree or disagree politely with your statements.

Answers
13 *Possible answers:*
1. I: No es cierto que los actores sean...
   A: Es cierto que son...
2. I: No es verdad que los estudiantes estudien...
   A: Es verdad que estudian...
3. I: Niego que la gente tenga...
   A: No niego que tiene...
4. I: No estoy de acuerdo que los carros no funcionen...
   A: Estoy de acuerdo que no funcionan...
5. I: No niego que la gente se viste...
   A: Niego que la gente se vista...
6. I: Es cierto que los políticos dicen...
   A: No es cierto que los políticos digan...
7. I: No estoy de acuerdo que los niños no respeten...
   A: Estoy de acuerdo que no respetan...
8. I: Es verdad que los jóvenes gastan...
   A: No es verdad que gasten...

Presenting
Vocabulario

Show the class pictures of people or animals, accompanying each with a short description using the new vocabulary. Use all the new adjectives in **Vocabulario**. Then, using a mixture of new and old pictures, ask students to use the vocabulary to describe what they see. Ask students to include as many adjectives as they logically can in each of their descriptions. (Example: **Ese perro es travieso. También es un poco bobo.**)

 **TPR** Call out each vocabulary word and have students mime or make a face to illustrate the word. For example, for **perezoso(a)**, students might yawn or stretch.

Assess

▶ Testing Program, pp. 191–194
Quiz 9-1A, Quiz 9-1B
Audio CD 9, Tr. 21

▶ Student Make-Up Assignments, Chapter 9, Alternative Quiz

▶ Alternative Assessment Guide, p. 38

Answers

14 *Possible answers:*

a. La chica es muy egoísta. El chico necesita la silla. Me frustro y me enojo cuando una persona no ayuda a alguien que lo necesita.

b. Él está enfermo pero la chica es amable y simpática. Me alegro cuando alguien como esta chica ayuda a los demás.

c. El chico que está guardando los libros es serio. Los otros dos son chismosos. Me enfado cuando la gente cuenta chismes.

d. La chica es muy traviesa. Me río con la gente que tiene buen sentido del humor.

Vocabulario

amigable *friendly*
arrogante *arrogant*
bobo(a) *silly, dumb*
callado(a) *quiet*
chismoso(a) *gossipy*
descortés *rude*
egoísta *selfish*

melancólico(a) *gloomy*
perezoso(a) *lazy*
presumido(a) *conceited*
seco(a) *cold, curt*
tímido(a) *shy*
torpe *slow, dull, clumsy*
travieso(a) *mischievous*

Cuaderno de actividades, p. 100, Act. 8

Cuaderno de gramática, p. 74, Acts. 10–11

14 **Las personalidades** See possible answers below.

Hablemos ¿Cómo son las personas en los dibujos? ¿Cómo te sientes cuando la gente se porta así? ¿Por qué? Júntate con un(a) compañero(a) para comparar sus opiniones.

También se puede decir…

También se dice **creído(a)** por **presumido(a)**. Se dice **cohibido(a)** por **tímido(a)**.

a.   b.

c.   d.

15 **Sólo es un estereotipo**

Leamos/Hablemos En grupos de tres o cuatro, indiquen si están de acuerdo con los siguientes estereotipos. Usen expresiones como **(no) es cierto que** y **(no) es verdad que**. Expliquen sus respuestas.

1. Los niños son más amigables que los mayores.
2. Los gatos son más bobos que los perros.
3. Las personas de las ciudades grandes son descorteses.
4. Las mujeres son más chismosas que los hombres.
5. La gente rica es presumida.
6. Los actores son arrogantes.
7. Los artistas son melancólicos.
8. Los profesores son secos.

16 **Una impresión falsa**

Escribamos ¿Alguna vez tuviste una impresión equivocada de alguien? ¿Cómo supiste que no tenías una impresión correcta de esa persona? ¿Alguna vez tuvo otra persona una impresión falsa de ti? ¿Cómo te sentiste?

 **A lo nuestro**

Una forma cómica de decir que alguien es presumido es **Se cree la mamá de Tarzán** o **Se cree el rey de Roma**.

Nota cultural

Los hispanos forman uno de los grupos minoritarios más grandes de la ciudad de Nueva York, con más de dos millones de personas de ascendencia hispana. Vienen de varios lugares del mundo hispano, sobre todo de la República Dominicana, Puerto Rico, Perú, Colombia y Ecuador. Con la excepción de Puerto Rico, hay más puertorriqueños en Nueva York que en cualquier otra parte del mundo. ¿Hay una comunidad hispana donde vives tú?

Cultures and Communities

Language Notes

• **Bobo(a)** comes from the Latin word *balbus* meaning *stuttering*. Have students think about what the equivalent word is in English. What stereotype do these words communicate?

• **Chismoso(a)** is a form of the word **chisme**, meaning "a rumor that is false or not proven." The origin of this word is uncertain.

• **Torpe** comes from a Latin word meaning *ugly* or *deformed*. **Torpeza**, meaning *clumsiness* or *awkwardness*, is used in the expression **cometer una torpeza**, *to make a blunder*.

• The verb form of **presumido(a)** can be very useful. **Presume de valiente.** (*He thinks he's brave.*) **Presume demasiado de su inteligencia.** (*He overestimates his intelligence.*)

CD 9 Trs.
10–13

¿Qué piensas de la gente de los Estados Unidos?

En muchos casos, las únicas impresiones que tenemos de la gente de otros países, regiones o culturas dependen de lo que oímos o de las imágenes que nos presentan los medios de comunicación. Escucha las opiniones que tienen estos jóvenes hispanohablantes acerca de la gente de los Estados Unidos.

Jenny
Los Teques, Venezuela

"Me los imagino... no muy parecidos a los venezolanos... tal vez viven en mejores condiciones que nosotros. Estudian y a la vez trabajan, tengo entendido... No sé, unos jóvenes muy activos". CD 9 Tr. 11

Juan René
Quito, Ecuador

"Me las imagino personas muy amigables y gente fácil de tratar".
CD 9 Tr. 12

Nayeli
San Diego, California

"[Me los imaginaba] mejor vestidos... que vivían mejor, o sea que había menos pobreza que en México. Sí la hay pero no hay mucha diferencia".
CD 9 Tr. 13

Para pensar y hablar...

A. ¿Qué respuesta crees que es la más cercana a la realidad? ¿Por qué? ¿Crees que algunas de las respuestas estereotipan a los estadounidenses? ¿Cuál o cuáles? Explica tus respuestas.

B. ¿Cómo defines tú la palabra "estereotipo"? En tu opinión, ¿por qué existen los estereotipos? ¿Cómo se pueden cambiar o evitar?

Cuaderno para hispanohablantes, p. 45

Teaching Resources
p. 261

PRINT
▸ Video Guide, pp. 60, 62, 65
▸ Cuaderno de actividades, p. 108
▸ Cuaderno para hispanohablantes, p. 45

MEDIA
▸ One-Stop Planner
▸ Video Program, Videocassette 3, 41:43–44:17
▸ Audio Compact Discs, CD 9, Trs. 10–13
▸ Interactive CD-ROM Tutor, Disc 3

Presenting
Panorama cultural

Play the interviews on the audio or video recording one at a time. Check for comprehension after each. Have students answer the **Para pensar y hablar...** questions. Then play the recording again and have students answer the **Preguntas**.

Preguntas

1. ¿Qué quiere expresar Juan René cuando dice que la gente es "fácil de tratar"? *(easy to get along with)*

2. ¿Estás de acuerdo con la descripción que da Jenny? *(Answers will vary.)*

3. ¿Por qué crees que dice Nayeli que "no hay mucha diferencia" entre la gente de los Estados Unidos y la gente de México? *(Answers will vary.)*

Connections and Comparisons

Multicultural Link
Have students bring in an article about a Spanish-speaking country from a newspaper or magazine. Ask each student to give a brief synopsis of the article they read and to say how he or she felt about the country after reading the article. Do students feel that most media reports are accurate, or are they sometimes misleading? Do they see any stereotyping? Have them explain.

Social Studies Link
Have students work in small groups to answer the following questions: Why do we stereotype others? What kinds of groups within a society are most often stereotyped? What can one person do to change his or her stereotyped views of others?

Teaching Resources
pp. 262–263

PRINT
▸ Lesson Planner, p. 44
▸ Video Guide, pp. 60–64
▸ Cuaderno de actividades, p. 102

MEDIA
▸ One-Stop Planner
▸ Video Program
  Contigo en la distancia
  Videocassette 3, 32:22–39:12
  Videocassette 5 (captioned version), 43:55–50:45
  ¡Adelante!
  Videocassette 3, 39:13–41:42
▸ Audio Compact Discs, CD 9, Trs. 14–17

Presenting
¡Adelante!

Have students identify adjectives in the interviews that might be stereotypical. Then have students watch the video for **¡Adelante!** and identify the opinions that the teens interviewed have about the United States. Next, present the Preteaching Vocabulary. Then have students read **¡Adelante!**, making note of expressions that support their answer.

 ¡Adelante!
Me gustaría viajar a...
Three Spanish speakers give their impressions of certain stereotypes and talk about places they would like to visit.

¡Adelante! · *Me gustaría viajar a...*

Cuaderno de actividades, p. 102 Acts. 11–12

CD 9 Trs. 14–17

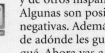

Todos estereotipamos a veces, incluso los hispanohablantes. Tienen sus impresiones de los Estados Unidos y de otros hispanohablantes. Algunas son positivas, otras son negativas. Además, tienen sus ideas de adónde les gustaría viajar y por qué. Ahora vas a leer las opiniones de tres jóvenes del mundo hispano. ¿Crees que tienen razón?

Taís

Sevilla

P: ¿Adónde te gustaría viajar a ti?

R: A Estados Unidos.

P: ¿Por qué? Explícame.

R: No sé, porque se ve divertido, y quiero ir para conocer gente.

P: ¿Cómo te imaginas a los jóvenes de Estados Unidos?

R: Me imagino a los jóvenes de Estados Unidos como a los jóvenes de España.

P: Y las ciudades, ¿cómo te las imaginas?

R: Eh... grandes y nuevas.

P: ¿De dónde has sacado tus ideas de los Estados Unidos?

R: He conocido gente de los Estados Unidos que me ha hablado acerca de sus diferentes países y principalmente a través de la televisión.

P: ¿Qué estereotipos tiene la gente de otros países sobre la gente de España?

R: Yo creo que principalmente creen que somos perezosos.

P: ¿Y es verdad?

R: No.

P: ¿Cuáles estereotipos te parecen más dañosos?

R: Eh... que seamos perezosos, o que nos cueste trabajar o...

P: ¿Alguna vez alguien te ha tratado según cierto estereotipo?

R: Sí, por... precisamente por ser de Bilbao, um... hubo un tiempo en que la gente, eh... tenía miedo y nos llamaba terroristas. Lo que pasa es que eso también es falta de información.

P: ¿Les dijiste algo sobre eso?

R: Por supuesto.

P: ¿Qué dijiste?

R: Que era más la información que les daban a través de la televisión que la realidad.

P: ¿Cómo se pueden combatir las actitudes difundidas por los estereotipos?

R: Principalmente yendo a los lugares, conociendo a la gente, y conociendo la forma de vida de la gente del lugar.

Bilbao

Christina

Lindia

San José

P: Si pudiera vivir en cualquier país del mundo por un año, ¿adónde iría?

R: Um... a los Estados Unidos.

P: ¿Por qué?

R: Porque me gusta.

P: ¿Qué es lo que te gusta de Estados Unidos?

R: Pues... que hay muchas razas, o sea, muchas clases de idiomas, así, se juntan muchas culturas.

Preteaching Vocabulary

Identifying Keywords
Have students skim the interviews and summarize main points. Then have them identify words or phrases that give information about teens' impressions of the United States and other Spanish speakers. Students may identify such phrases as: **...se ve divertido, y quiero ir para conocer gente.; Me imagino a los jóvenes de Estados Unidos como a los jóvenes de España.; Yo creo que principalmente creen que somos perezosos.; ...que hay muchas razas, o sea, muchas clases de idiomas, así, se juntan muchas culturas.**

STANDARDS: 1.2, 3.2

These activities check for comprehension only. Students should not yet be expected to produce language modeled in ¡Adelante!

17 ¿Quiénes son? See answers below.

¿Quién es la persona indicada por cada descripción?

1. Le gustaría viajar a Estados Unidos porque allí viven juntas varias culturas.
2. Esta persona quiere conocer a gente estadounidense.
3. Piensa que la televisión influye en las actitudes.
4. Cree que los estereotipos se combaten viajando a los lugares y conociendo a la gente.

18 ¿Se sabe? See answers below.

Indica si cada frase es **cierta, falsa** o si **no se sabe.** Si es falsa, corrígela.

1. Cristina es de Madrid pero ha vivido en Bilbao.
2. Según Taís, Estados Unidos es divertido.
3. Lidia dice que no hay muchas razas en Estados Unidos.
4. Cristina cree que hay más información sobre terrorismo en la televisión del que realmente ocurre.
5. Según Lidia, en Estados Unidos se hablan muchos idiomas.
6. Cristina cree que las ciudades estadounidenses son viejas.

19 ¿Comprendiste? See answers below.

1. ¿Cómo ha aprendido Cristina lo que sabe de la gente de Estados Unidos?
2. Según Cristina, ¿qué problema hay en la información que la gente tiene de otros países?
3. ¿Qué estereotipo de la gente de España le ha causado problemas a Cristina? ¿Y qué estereotipo de la gente de Bilbao?
4. ¿Cómo se imagina Lidia Estados Unidos?
5. Según Cristina, ¿cómo se pueden combatir los estereotipos?

20 Completa las oraciones See answers below.

Completa las siguientes oraciones con las expresiones correctas de **¡Adelante!**

1. _____ a los jóvenes de Estados Unidos como a los jóvenes de España.
2. ¿Adónde _____ viajar?
3. Si _____ vivir en cualquier país del mundo por un año, ¿adónde _____ ?

| te gustaría | pudieras |
| me imagino | irías |

21 Ahora te toca a ti

¿Te identificas con alguna de las estudiantes de **¡Adelante!**? ¿Con cuál? ¿Por qué? ¿En qué país te gustaría vivir durante un año? ¿Por qué? ¿Te han afectado alguna vez los estereotipos? ¿Qué pasó? ¿Cómo te sentiste?

 Contigo en la distancia

As an alternative or in addition to **¡Adelante!,** you may wish to show Episode 9 of *Contigo en la distancia.* For suggestions and activities, see the *Video Guide.*

¡ADELANTE!

CAPÍTULO 9

Answers

17 1. Lidia 3. Cristina
2. Taís 4. Cristina

18 1. falsa; Es de Bilbao.
2. cierta
3. falsa; Dice que hay muchas razas, clases de idiomas y culturas.
4. cierta
5. cierta
6. falsa; Cree que las ciudades de los Estados Unidos son grandes y nuevas.

19 1. Por la televisión y hablando con gente de los Estados Unidos.
2. La gente cree lo que ve en la televisión y a veces no es la realidad.
3. Se cree que los españoles son perezosos y que los habitantes de Bilbao son terroristas.
4. Cree que en los Estados Unidos hay muchas razas y culturas juntas.
5. Viajando a los lugares y conociendo a la gente se combaten los estereotipos.

20 1. Me imagino
2. te gustaría
3. pudieras, irías

Comprehension Check

Thinking Critically

Comparing and Contrasting Have students make a list of characteristics that all people have. On another list, have them make a list of some traits that not all people share. The first list **(Lo que todos tenemos en común)** might have **todos hablamos idiomas, todos queremos vivir en paz.** The other list **(Algunas de nuestras diferencias)** might have **no todos hablan los mismos idiomas, no todos están de acuerdo en cómo acordar la paz.** They should do this using as much Spanish as possible.

Objectives Expressing an assumption; making hypothetical statements

WV3 NEW YORK-9

Teaching Resources
pp. 264–267

PRINT
▶ Lesson Planner, p. 44
▶ Listening Activities, pp. 68, 72–73
▶ Activities for Communication, pp. 35–36, 76–77, 105–106
▶ Cuaderno de gramática, pp. 75–77
▶ Grammar Tutor for Students of Spanish, Chapter 9
▶ Cuaderno de actividades, pp. 103–106
▶ Cuaderno para hispanohablantes, pp. 41–45
▶ Testing Program, pp. 195–198
▶ Alternative Assessment Guide, p. 38
▶ Student Make-Up Assignments, Chapter 9

MEDIA
▶ One-Stop Planner
▶ Audio Compact Discs, CD 9, Trs. 18–19, 28–30, 22
▶ Teaching Transparencies 9-2; **Más práctica gramatical** Answers; Cuaderno de gramática Answers
▶ Interactive CD-ROM Tutor, Disc 3

Bell Work
On the board or on a transparency write the following: **Haz oraciones completas con las siguientes expresiones: Me alegré mucho cuando..., Me enfadé cuando..., Me sentí... cuando..., No es verdad que...**

Presenting
Así se dice
As you read the sentences aloud to the class, ask students if the indicative or the subjunctive is used with these expressions. Then ask various students questions to elicit replies using the expressions.

Así se dice

Expressing an assumption

Si no sabes algo pero quieres decir lo que supones, puedes decir:

> **Me imagino que** los jóvenes estadounidenses son como los jóvenes españoles.
> **Supongo que** la gente saca sus ideas de otras culturas a través de la tele.
> **Tengo entendido que** hay muchas culturas distintas en Estados Unidos.
> **Tengo la impresión de que** la gente es muy abierta en Puerto Rico.

Cuaderno de actividades, p. 103, Act. 13

22 Impresiones de Nueva York   Script and answers on p. 251H.

CD 9
Tr. 18

Escuchemos/Escribamos Un reportero está entrevistando a una pareja de la República Dominicana en el aeropuerto antes de que salgan para Nueva York. Escucha la entrevista y luego, para cada oración que sigue, indica si **lo saben** o si **lo suponen.**

1. Los estadounidenses son simpáticos.
2. Nueva York es una ciudad muy grande.
3. La vida en Nueva York es agitada.
4. Todo es más caro en Nueva York.
5. Los museos son buenísimos.
6. El Parque Central es grande.
7. El Parque Central es un buen lugar para niños.

23 Tengo entendido que...

Hablemos ¿Qué impresiones tienes de las siguientes cosas? Con un(a) compañero(a), habla de lo que supones sobre cada tema. Usa expresiones de **Así se dice.**

1. la comida española
2. el clima de Buenos Aires en enero
3. los murales mexicanos
4. la música del Caribe
5. los teléfonos celulares en Venezuela

Nota cultural

Nueva York es un centro importante de los medios de comunicación en español. Además de los sitios en Internet, el hispanohablante puede encontrar varios periódicos, revistas y emisoras de televisión y radio en su idioma. Los periódicos de mayor distribución en español son **El Diario** y **Hoy**. También hay estudios de grabación para la música latina. ¿Tienes un sitio favorito en la red que sea en español?

Así se dice

Making hypothetical statements

Si quieres hablar de algo que no es pero que podría ser, puedes preguntar:

> **Si pudieras** vivir en cualquier país del mundo por un año, **¿adónde irías?**
> *If you could . . . where would you go?*

> **Si fueras** rico(a), **¿qué harías?**
> *If you were . . . what would you do?*

Se puede contestar:

> **Si pudiera, viviría** en el Caribe.
> *If I could, I would live . . .*

> **Si tuviera** cien dólares, **compraría** muchos regalos.
> *If I had . . . , I would buy . . .*

Cuaderno de actividades, p. 106, Act. 20

Communication for All Students

Group Work
Have students work in small groups to make a guest list for a party. Group members discuss whether different guests will come and what they should bring. (**Tengo entendido que Susana trabaja los fines de semana. Supongo que Mike puede llevar los refrescos.**)

Auditory Learners
To practice the conditional, play the song from Chapter 3, **"Por un beso de tu boca",** and have students sing along. To use the song as a dictation, retype the lyrics with blanks for the conditional. Have students fill in the blanks as they listen.

STANDARDS: 1.1, 1.2, 2.2, 3.2, 4.2, 5.1

24 **¿Te conoces de verdad?**

Leamos/Hablemos Si tuvieras más tiempo o dinero, ¿qué harías? Completa esta prueba y luego compara tus resultados con los de dos compañeros(as).

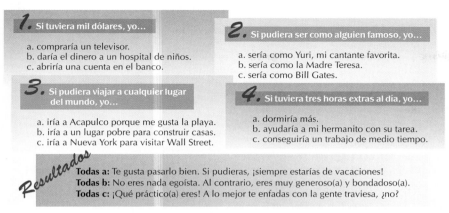

1. Si tuviera mil dólares, yo...

a. compraría un televisor.
b. daría el dinero a un hospital de niños.
c. abriría una cuenta en el banco.

2. Si pudiera ser como alguien famoso, yo...

a. sería como Yuri, mi cantante favorita.
b. sería como la Madre Teresa.
c. sería como Bill Gates.

3. Si pudiera viajar a cualquier lugar del mundo, yo...

a. iría a Acapulco porque me gusta la playa.
b. iría a un lugar pobre para construir casas.
c. iría a Nueva York para visitar Wall Street.

4. Si tuviera tres horas extras al día, yo...

a. dormiría más.
b. ayudaría a mi hermanito con su tarea.
c. conseguiría un trabajo de medio tiempo.

Resultados

Todas a: Te gusta pasarlo bien. Si pudieras, ¡siempre estarías de vacaciones!
Todas b: No eres nada egoísta. Al contrario, eres muy generoso(a) y bondadoso(a).
Todas c: ¡Qué práctico(a) eres! A lo mejor te enfadas con la gente traviesa, ¿no?

Gramática

The conditional

1. The conditional is used to express what *would* happen if . . ., as opposed to what usually does happen.

Yo **iría** a la fiesta.   *I would go to the party.*
¿Qué **harías** entonces?   *What would you do then?*

2. The regular conditional consists of the future stem plus one set of endings for all verbs. The infinitive serves as the future stem for most verbs.

Ayudar	Leer	Preferir
ayudaría	leería	preferiría
ayudarías	leerías	preferirías
ayudaría	leería	preferiría
ayudaríamos	leeríamos	preferiríamos
ayudaríais	leeríais	preferiríais
ayudarían	leerían	preferirían

3. The conditional of **poder** is also used to soften a request.

¿Podrías hacerme un favor?   *Could you do me a favor?*

Más práctica gramatical, pp. 274–275, Acts. 6–7

Cuaderno de actividades, pp. 103–106, Acts. 14–16, 18–20

Cuaderno de gramática, pp. 75–76, Acts. 12–15

¿Te acuerdas?

The same verbs that have irregular stems in the future have irregular stems in the conditional.

caber: **cabr-**	poder: **podr-**
decir: **dir-**	salir: **saldr-**
hacer: **har-**	poner: **pondr-**
haber: **habr-**	venir: **vendr-**
querer: **querr-**	tener: **tendr-**
saber: **sabr-**	valer: **valdr-**

25 **Gramática en contexto**   Script and answers on p. 251H.

Escuchemos/Hablemos Vas a escuchar a Adela y Reynaldo hablar de una fiesta. Para cada verbo que sigue, indica si alguien ya **lo hizo** o si **lo haría.**

CD 9
Tr. 19

1. limpiar la casa
2. preparar comida
3. comprar un regalo
4. traer la música
5. bailar
6. comprar los refrescos
7. ir al supermercado
8. llegar a las ocho
9. jugar al tenis

Connections and Comparisons

Presenting
Así se dice,
Gramática

The conditional When you model the hypothetical statements in **Así se dice** at the bottom of page 264, point out that the conditional is used in the result clause and the imperfect subjunctive in the **si** clause. Then have students look at the **Gramática**. Point out that irregular conditional stems are the same as irregular future stems. (**tendré/tendría, podré/podría**) Start out by asking students questions. (**Si pudieras ir a cualquier restaurante, ¿adónde irías?**) The student might answer **Si pudiera, iría a un restaurante puertorriqueño.** Then have students ask each other questions similar to the examples in **Así se dice.**

Building on Previous Skills
Have students take turns asking favors of each other using the conditional for politeness. The partner should give a response, saying why he or she can or cannot oblige. (**—Por favor, ¿me podrías limpiar el carro? —Hoy no, lo siento. Tengo que ir al médico.**)

Language-to-Language

Beginning students may be confused by hypothetical statements in Spanish, and by the relationship between the two parts of these statements. Point out that English has an identical structure and give some examples: *I wouldn't do that if I were you; I'd help you if I could.* Ask students for other examples and write responses on the board. Have students identify the "if" parts and the "would" parts of each statement, then have them read **Así se dice,** on page 264, again. Ask them to explain how the Spanish questions and answers there correspond to the English pattern you have just reviewed. Tell students they will learn more about making hypothetical statements in Chapters 11 and 12.

Teaching Resources
pp. 264–267

PRINT 📖
▸ Lesson Planner, p. 44
▸ Listening Activities, pp. 68, 72–73
▸ Activities for Communication, pp. 35–36, 76–77, 105–106
▸ Cuaderno de gramática, pp. 75–77
▸ Grammar Tutor for Students of Spanish, Chapter 9
▸ Cuaderno de actividades, pp. 103–106
▸ Cuaderno para hispanohablantes, pp. 41–45
▸ Testing Program, pp. 195–198
▸ Alternative Assessment Guide, p. 38
▸ Student Make-Up Assignments, Chapter 9

MEDIA 💿📹📼
▸ One-Stop Planner
▸ Audio Compact Discs, CD 9, Trs. 18–19, 28–30, 22
▸ Teaching Transparencies 9-2; **Más práctica gramatical** Answers; Cuaderno de gramática Answers
▸ Interactive CD-ROM Tutor, Disc 3

Presenting
Vocabulario

Address your class in Spanish, asking students how to avoid stereotypes. **(La base de la discriminación es la ignorancia...)** Try to use several of the new vocabulary words. Then write a topic sentence for a paragraph on the board. **(¿Cómo podemos evitar los estereotipos?)** Ask each student to add a sentence in which he or she uses a vocabulary word that hasn't already been used.

---

26 **Gramática en contexto** See answers below.

Leamos/Escribamos Hui Chun, el presidente del Club Internacional de su colegio, está haciendo planes para una fiesta internacional. Completa las oraciones con el condicional del verbo entre parentesis.

Si yo tuviera la oportunidad, yo ══ (organizar) una fiesta internacional para todo el colegio. Tranh ══ (preparar) comida vietnamita como la que prepara su mamá. Soledad y Mateo ══ (tocar) la guitarra y ══ (cantar) música típica de Colombia. Kumiko ══ (traer) instrumentos típicos de Japón. Misha y Dimitri ══ (bailar) bailes folklóricos de Rusia. Nabil y Amira ══ (llevar) ropa tradicional de Marruecos. Nosotros ══ (enseñarles) a los otros estudiantes un poco de la cultura de nuestros países.

27 **Gramática en contexto** See sample answer below.

Escribamos Escribe dos oraciones para explicar lo que supones que harías de vacaciones en cada lugar.

MODELO   Me imagino que iría al lago...

a.   b.   c.   d.

28 ### Un viaje a Nueva York

Escribamos/Hablemos Imagina que vas a viajar a Nueva York con tres compañeros(as). Sólo tienen dos días para conocer la ciudad. Hagan un itinerario del viaje. Pueden incluir los siguientes lugares. Usen verbos como **comprar, comer, cruzar, ver, visitar, subir, escuchar** y **patinar.**

1. el Parque Central
2. Broadway
3. el edificio Empire State
4. la Quinta Avenida
5. el Centro Rockefeller
6. el Museo de Historia Natural
7. la Pequeña Italia
8. el puente de Brooklyn
9. la Estatua de la Libertad
10. el Teatro Metropolitano de la Ópera
11. Greenwich Village
12. Harlem

Vocabulario

la actitud hacia	*attitude toward*	**la ignorancia**	*ignorance*
apreciar	*to appreciate*	**juzgar**	*to judge*
combatir	*to combat*	**la minoría**	*minority*
contra	*against*	**respetar**	*to respect*
darse cuenta de	*to realize*	**el prejuicio**	*prejudice*
la discriminación	*discrimination*	**el respeto hacia**	*respect for*
el estereotipo	*stereotype*	**tratar**	*to treat*
estereotipar	*to stereotype*		
la falta (de)	*lack (of)*		

CD-ROM DISC **3**

Más práctica gramatical, p. 275, Act. 8

(Cuaderno de actividades, p. 105, Act. 17) (Cuaderno de gramática, p. 77 , Acts. 16–17)

Cultures and Communities

Background Information

28 Central Park is about 50 blocks long and several avenues wide. Broadway is a famous street that begins in lower Manhattan and runs the entire length of the island. The Empire State Building was the tallest building in the world from 1931 to 1971. A quarter of a million people work in Rockefeller Center's 21 office buildings daily. The American Museum of Natural History houses thousands of exhibits. Little Italy is famous for its restaurants and festivals. The Brooklyn Bridge connects Manhattan to Brooklyn. Greenwich Village has been home to writers Louisa May Alcott, Mark Twain, Edith Wharton, and e. e. cummings, as well as artists Jackson Pollack and Edward Hopper. Harlem is now an important ethnic neighborhood for African Americans and Puerto Ricans.

29 En mi opinión Answers will vary.

Escribamos Completa las siguientes oraciones con el **Vocabulario** de la página 266.

1. Para mí es importante apreciar...
2. Me enojo cuando hay discriminación contra...
3. Creo que debemos combatir...
4. Quiero que la gente me trate...
5. Antes pensaba que... pero un día me di cuenta de que...
6. En este mundo hay una falta de...

30 Del colegio al trabajo Answers will vary.

 Leamos/Hablemos Eres columnista y consejero de una revista para jóvenes. Lee las cartas de dos estudiantes que enfrentan algunos estereotipos de parte de sus compañeros de clase. Dales consejos sobre lo que tú harías en el lugar de cada uno.

> Acabo de llegar del Ecuador y estoy asistiendo a un colegio en que soy el único hispano. ¡Me siento como una minoría de uno! Me enojo cuando oigo las ideas absurdas que tienen algunos estudiantes sobre mi país. Me preguntan si en el Ecuador tenemos teléfonos, si hay casas o si es jungla. Los estudiantes no son malos, me tratan muy bien; simplemente es una falta de información. Quiero que aprecien mi cultura. ¿Cómo combatirías la ignorancia?
>
> Un ecuatoriano mal entendido

> Soy buena estudiante. El problema es que mis compañeros de clase se burlan de mí porque piensan que me la paso estudiando y que soy aburrida. ¡No es cierto que sea aburrida! Al contrario, tengo muchos pasatiempos. Me encanta la fotografía y tengo una colección de fotos de gente famosa que he conocido. Nadie la ha visto. También me gusta la música y me gusta conversar, aunque soy un poco callada en clase. ¿Qué harías tú?
>
> Callada pero interesante

31 En mi cuaderno

 Leamos/Escribamos Lee la tira cómica de Susi, la amiga de Calvin. ¿Qué no te gusta del mundo en que vives? Si tuvieras una varita mágica (*magic wand*), ¿qué harías? ¿Qué cosas del mundo cambiarías? ¿Estás de acuerdo con las maneras en que otros han tratado de resolver estos problemas?

© Watterson. Dist. by Universal Press Syndicate. Reprinted with permission. All rights reserved.

Communication for All Students

Native Speakers
Ask students to search the Internet for Latino music, art, dance, literary, or theater events in New York City. Have them share their findings with the class and discuss which event(s) interest(s) them.

Visual Learners
Ask students to create cluster diagrams. Have them choose a word from the **Vocabulario** on page 266 as the subject of the cluster and circle it. **(la discriminación)** Around the subject, students write related words. **(el prejuicio, la ignorancia)** They should circle these words and draw lines to connect them to the subject or with each other. They may use additional words from **Vocabulario** on page 260 to make new connections.

Segundo paso

CAPÍTULO 9

Writing Assessment
31 Encourage use of varied vocabulary and grammar from this and previous chapters. Answer any questions, but explain that simple errors are expected and that risk-taking is rewarded in the grading system. You may wish to assess the writing assignment using the following rubric.

Writing Rubric	Points			
	4	3	2	1
Content (Complete– Incomplete)				
Comprehensibility (Comprehensible– Incomprehensible)				
Accuracy (Accurate– Seldom accurate)				
Organization (Well organized– Poorly organized)				
Effort (Excellent–Minimal)				

18–20: A   14–15: C   Under
16–17: B   12–13: D   12: F

Assess
▶ Testing Program, pp. 195–198
Quiz 9-2A, Quiz 9-2B
Audio CD 9, Tr. 22

▶ Student Make-Up Assignments, Chapter 9, Alternative Quiz

▶ Alternative Assessment Guide, p. 38

Answers
26 organizaría, prepararía, tocarían, cantarían, traería, bailarían, llevarían, les enseñaríamos

27 *Sample answer:*
Supongo que iríamos de vacaciones al campo. Nos vestiríamos con ropa de invierno. Me imagino que esquiaríamos todo el tiempo.

Vamos a leer

CAPÍTULO 9

Teaching Resources
pp. 268–270

PRINT
- Lesson Planner, p. 45
- Cuaderno de actividades, p. 107
- Cuaderno para hispanohablantes, pp. 41–44
- Reading Strategies and Skills Handbook, Chapter 9
- ¡Lee conmigo! 3, Chapter 9
- Standardized Assessment Tutor, Chapter 9

MEDIA
- One-Stop Planner

Prereading
Activities A and B

Using Prior Knowledge
- Ask students what they know about New York City in the late 1800s. (city of immigrants; undergoing urbanization; trains and the Brooklyn Bridge were symbols of industrialization and urbanization) List relevant facts on the board.
- Review the literary devices *simile, metaphor,* and *personification.* Ask students to give examples of each. Review words in Spanish that are used in similes. (**igual que, como, parece**) You might ask students to find these in the selection.

Answers
A *Possible answers:*
1. Significa que la lectura describe algo en particular de Nueva York.
2. Trata del puente de Brooklyn.
3. un ensayo
4. el puente, los carros, el tranvía, la gente, el río, la calle, los edificios, el tren, los botes

Vamos a leer

Nueva York

Vas a leer una descripción de una escena en la ciudad de Nueva York en un momento particular. Después hay una biografía de José Martí, que habla de la importancia mítica que tenía Nueva York para este autor cubano a fines del siglo XIX.

Estrategia para leer
When you read literature, it's important to recognize literary devices. Writers use these to offer an original view of the world or the human experience. Two of these devices are the *simile* and *personification.* A simile is a figure of speech that compares two basically unlike things: "the child clung to his mother like a stamp". Personification gives human characteristics to animals or things, as in "the wind sang me to sleep". Recognizing these devices will help you understand nonliteral meaning in a reading.

¡A comenzar!
A. Sigue los siguientes pasos para ayudarte a leer y entender esta obra. See possible answers below.
1. Pensando solamente en el título, ¿qué puedes decir de la lectura?
2. Ojea la lectura. ¿De qué crees que trata?
3. Según tu ojeada de la lectura y el título, ¿qué crees que vas a leer: un cuento con un argumento y personajes o un ensayo?
4. Las fotos te dan claves para adivinar de qué trata la obra. Prepara una lista de los elementos que ves en las fotos.

Escena neoyorquina
JOSÉ MARTÍ

Es mañana de otoño, clara y alegre. El sol amable calienta y conforta. Agólpase la gente a la puerta del tranvía del puente de Brooklyn: que ya corre el tranvía y toda la ciudad quiere ir por él.

Suben a saltos la escalera de granito y repletan de masa humana los andenes. ¡Parece como que se ha entrado en casa de gigantes y que se ve ir y venir por todas partes a la dueña de la casa!

Bajo el amplio techado se canta este poema. La dama es una linda locomotora en traje negro. Avanza, recibe, saluda, lleva a su asiento al huésped, corre a buscar otro, déjalo en nuevo sitio, adelántase a saludar a aquel que llega. No pasa de los dinteles de la puerta. Gira: torna: entrega: va a diestra y a siniestra: no reposa un instante. Dan deseos, al verla venir, campaneando alegremente, de ir a darle la mano. Como que se la ve tan avisada y diligente, tan útil y animosa, tan pizpireta y gentil, se siente amistad humana por la linda locomotora. Viendo a tantas cabecillas menudas de hombres asomados al borde del ancho salón donde la dama colosal deja y toma carros y revolotea, como rabelaisiana mariposa, entre rieles, andenes y casillas — dijérase que los tiempos se han trocado y que los liliputienses han venido a hacer visita a Gulliver.

Los carros que atraviesan el puente de Brooklyn vienen de New York, traídos por la cuerda movible que entre los rieles se desliza velozmente por sobre ruedas de hierro, y, desde las seis de la mañana hasta la una de la madrugada del día siguiente, jamás para. Pero donde empieza la colosal estación, el carro suelta la cuerda que ha venido arrastrándolo, y se detiene. La locomotora, que va y viene como ardilla de hierro, parte a buscarlo. Como que mueve al andar su campana sonora,

The Granger Collection, New York

Connections and Comparisons

Background Information
Some of the metaphors in **Escena neoyorquina** will be clearer if students understand that the train described by Martí is not the kind with a locomotive at the front and cars behind. The Brooklyn Bridge train in the essay is a line of cable cars. The line of cars hitches onto a moving cable under the track and is then pulled across the bridge to the other side. The **locomotora** is an engine that stays in the station and arranges the cars, linking and unlinking them. This is why it is easy to see the engine as a busy hostess, receiving guests (cars) and sending them on their way.

268 DOSCIENTOS SESENTA Y OCHO   VAMOS A LEER   STANDARDS: 1.2, 2.2, 3.1, 3.2

parece que habla. Llega al carro, lo unce a su zaga; arranca con él, estación adentro, hasta el vecino chucho; llévalo, ya sobre otros rieles, con gran son de campana vocinglera, hasta la salida de la estación, donde abordan el carro, ganosos de contar el nuevo viaje, centenares de pasajeros. Y allá va la coqueta de la casa en busca de otro carro, que del lado contiguo deja su carga de transeúntes neoyorquinos.

Abre el carro los grifos complicados que salen de debajo de su pavimento; muerde con ellos la cuerda rodante, y ésta lo arrebata a paso de tren, por entre ambas calzadas de carruajes del puente, por junto a millares de curiosos, que en el camino central de a pie miran absortos; por sobre las casas altas y vastos talleres, que como enormes juguetes se ven allá en lo hondo; arrastra la cuerda al carro por sobre el armazón del ferrocarril elevado, que parece fábrica de niños; por sobre los largos muelles, que parecen siempre abiertas fauces; por sobre los topes de los mástiles; por sobre el río turbio y solemne, que corre abajo, como por cauce abierto en un abismo; por entre las entrañas solitarias del puente magnífico, gran trenzado de hierro, bosque extenso de barras y puntales, suspendido en longitud de media legua, de borde a borde de las aguas. ¡Y el vapor, que parece botecillo! ¡Y el botecillo, que parece mosca! ¡Y el silencio, cual si entrase en celestial espacio! ¡Y la palabra humana, palpitante en los hilos numerosos de enredados telégrafos, serpeando, recodeando, hendiendo la acerada y colgante maleza, que sustenta por encima del agua vencida sus carros volantes!

Y cuando se sale al fin al nivel de las calzadas del puente, del lado de New York, no se siente que se llega, sino que se desciende.

Y se cierran involuntariamente los ojos, como si no quisiera dejarse de ver la maravilla.

B. Ojea la biografía de Martí. Busca información sobre la relación del autor con Nueva York. También busca información que ubique (places) a la lectura con respecto al tiempo. ¿Cuándo crees que el autor escribió la obra? See answers below.

Al grano

C. Lee **Escena neoyorquina.** Mientras lees busca los símiles en el texto. Recuerda que un símil es una comparación entre dos cosas con palabras como "igual que", "como", "más que" o "parecido". Ahora decide qué cosas compara el autor en los siguientes símiles. Busca las palabras claves en el diccionario si no las sabes. See answers below.

MODELO **los largos <u>muelles</u>, que parecen siempre abiertas <u>fauces</u>**
muelles— *piers*;
fauces— *mouths*

1. la locomotora, que va y viene como ardilla de hierro
2. el botecillo que parece mosca
3. el vapor que parece botecillo
4. sobre las casas altas y vastos talleres, que como enormes juguetes se ven allá en lo hondo

D. Trabaja con un(a) compañero(a) para interpretar el significado de cada símil en la Actividad C. Usen el contexto de las frases para explicar la imagen que el autor quiere proyectar. También pueden mirar las fotos para ver si hay algunas imágenes parecidas al símil. See answers below.

MODELO **La locomotora, que va y viene como ardilla de hierro.** *The locomotive runs back and forth looking for people like a squirrel looks for food.*

Reading
Activities C, D, and E

Monitoring Comprehension
- Some sentences in **Escena neoyorquina** are quite long. Advise students to figure out the main sentence pattern (noun-verb, noun-verb-noun, and so on) before breaking down smaller sentence parts.
- Have students locate cognates. Encourage them to guess the meaning of words as they read. For example, **velozmente** looks like *velocity.* Since **-mente** is used with adverbs in Spanish **(especialmente, inmediatamente),** students can guess that the word means *swiftly.*
- Remind students that modifiers add to basic meaning. Lead the class through the first paragraph of the story, listing modifiers on the board. **(clara, alegre, amable)** Encourage students to focus on nouns and verbs to get the gist of the sentence.

Answers

B Nueva York tenía una gran atracción para Martí. Le fascinaba la ciudad. Escribió la obra en las últimas décadas del siglo XIX.

C 1. locomotive; squirrel
2. small boat; fly
3. steam boat; small boat
4. houses, workshops; toys

D 2. The small boat looks like a fly because the bridge is so high.
3. The steam boat looks like a small boat because of the distance.
4. The houses and workshops look like toys in the distance.

Communication for All Students

Language Note
Point out to students that this reading has some features that they will probably see only in literature. For example, sometimes object or reflexive pronouns are attached to a conjugated verb: **agólpase, déjalo.** Give students the equivalent verb phrases: **se agolpa, lo deja.**

Visual Learners
Go over the first sentence of the fifth paragraph together with the class. Have a volunteer sketch the scene on the board. (the train crossing the bridge, loaded with passengers; the view from high above the city)

CAPÍTULO 9

Postreading
Activities F and G

Comparing and Contrasting

Remind students of metaphors Martí uses to describe the Brooklyn Bridge. (a braid of iron; a forest of posts and supports) Ask students why Martí compares the train cars and station locomotive to humans whereas he compares the bridge to trees. (The train is moving and noisy; the bridge is silent and awe-inspiring)

Appreciating a Writer's Craft

Lead a discussion with the class about the literary elements of this piece. How do the literary elements tie in with the writer's purpose? (Martí's intent is to describe a scene and communicate how the scene stirs his emotions. In order to accomplish this he uses a great deal of detail and figurative language to paint a literary picture and convey the intensity of his feelings.)

Answers

E *Sample answers:*
1. la locomotora; Es linda, vestida de traje negro; Se siente así porque es tan trabajadora y tan alegre.
2. Encuentra la locomotora parecida a una dama. Por eso el sonido de la campana le parece el hablar de la locomotora.
3. Los muelles tienen la forma de una boca abierta. La cara sería grande e impresionante.

F *Possible answers:*
En una foto del siglo XXI habría gente, carros, botes, edificios, un tren, tráfico y aviones. Lo que no ha cambiado comparado con el siglo XIX son los botes, la gente y el tren. Las cosas diferentes son los aviones, los carros y el tráfico. También hay más gente y edificios más altos.

E. Martí da características humanas a las cosas. Ésta es una técnica literaria que se llama personificación. Vuelve a leer **Escena neoyorquina** para contestar las preguntas. See sample answers below.

1. ¿Qué máquina describe como una "dama" *(lady)*? ¿Cómo es la dama? Martí escribe que "se siente amistad humana" por esta cosa. ¿Por qué se siente así?

2. Martí escribe "como que mueve al andar su campana *(bell)* sonora, parece que habla". ¿A qué crees que se refiere?

3. ¿Por qué dice el autor que "los largos muelles *(piers)*, que parecen siempre abiertas fauces *(mouths)*"? Si los muelles son las bocas, ¿será la ciudad la cara? ¿Qué tipo de cara tendrá la ciudad para el autor?

F. Con un grupo imagina que un autor está describiendo la misma escena de Nueva York hoy en día. ¿Qué creen que ha cambiado desde el tiempo en que Martí escribió la lectura? ¿Qué cosas habría en una foto del siglo XXI del puente de Brooklyn? ¿Qué cosas son parecidas a lo que ves en las fotos del siglo XIX? ¿Qué cosas son diferentes? Usen la lectura, las fotos y sus conocimientos.   See possible answers below.

G. What do you think José Martí's feelings are about New York and the Brooklyn Bridge? Discuss with a partner how the literary devices he uses give you clues about his relationship to his subject. Also discuss clues in Martí's biography that help explain his use of similes and personification.
Answers will vary.

Cuaderno para hispanohablantes, pp. 41– 44

Cuaderno de actividades, p. 107, Acts. 21–23

José Martí

(1853–1895), el autor de "Escena neoyorquina", no sólo fue un periodista, ensayista y poeta de talento, sino también un patriota valiente que defendió la causa de la liberación cubana. A lo largo de su vida utilizó su don de la palabra para proclamar insistentemente que la humanidad era capaz de algo más que

The Granger Collection, New York

brutalidad y represión. Murió combatiendo por la libertad.

Hijo de españoles, José Martí nació en La Habana, Cuba. Durante su adolescencia, se dedicó a escribir y editar periódicos que proponían la independencia para Cuba. En aquellos días, Cuba era una colonia española. En 1869 sus actividades llamaron la atención de las autoridades y fue detenido y condenado a trabajos forzados en las canteras de San Lázaro, en La Habana. Como testimonio de esta experiencia escribió *El presidio político de Cuba* (1871), obra en la que proponía una reforma política. Conmutada su condena por el exilio en España, Martí consiguió licenciarse en derecho y filosofía por las universidades de Zaragoza y Madrid. Realizó numerosos viajes por toda Latinoamérica y residió en México, Guatemala y Venezuela, donde escribió constantemente poesía y ensayos. En 1879 regresó a La Habana, donde su fuerte oposición al gobierno lo llevó nuevamente al exilio en España.

De España se trasladó primero a Francia y luego a Nueva York, donde el editor Charles A. Dana le pidió que escribiera para el *New York Sun*. Nueva York ejercía sobre Martí una atracción especial. La gran ciudad le fascinaba y horrorizaba a la vez.

Martí escribió tres celebrados libros de poemas y una novela, además de dedicarse con pasión a la causa de la libertad cubana. Organizó y encabezó la rebelión de 1895, para la cual regresó a Cuba y perdió la vida combatiendo en ella. Se consideraba ciudadano de las Américas y es recordado como un magnífico escritor y como hombre dispuesto a morir por sus ideales.

Connections and Comparisons

History Link

Work began on the Brooklyn Bridge in 1869 and was finished in 1883. Its construction involved many innovations: steel was used for cable wire, and the main suspension towers were built, at great cost in terms of workers' lives, using techniques that had never been tried before. Students may want to investigate the relationship of "caisson disease" ("the bends") to the building of the Brooklyn Bridge. (Workers went into tunnels, or caissons, underwater to sink supports for the towers; returning too quickly to surface level brought about the illness.) The bridge has a main span (distance between suspension towers) of 1,595 feet that connects Brooklyn to Manhattan. It supports automobile traffic and a wooden boardwalk for pedestrians and bicyclists.

Vamos a escribir

Los estereotipos culturales nos influyen en la manera en que percibimos lo que vemos y oímos. Nos limitan la habilidad de apreciar a los individuos de diferentes razas y con diferentes estilos de vida. ¿Qué efectos tienen los estereotipos culturales? En esta actividad, escribirás un artículo para un periódico sobre los estereotipos culturales y aprenderás una manera fácil de escoger qué detalles incluir.

¿Cuál es tu opinión?

Imagina que eres escritor(a) para el periódico de tu escuela. Escribe una composición de cuatro o cinco párrafos sobre los efectos de los estereotipos en tu escuela o ciudad y lo que se puede hacer para mejorar la situación.

Estrategia para escribir

Finding good details Things you write don't make sense unless they include appropriate details. Interesting details add color and life to what you write and give it more substance. A good way to choose the right details to include is to ask these questions: Who? What? Where? Why? When? How?

A. Preparación

1. Haz preguntas para encontrar buenos detalles y escribe las respuestas en una lista. Puedes hacerles preguntas a tus amigos(as) también. Algunas preguntas buenas son **¿Quiénes** sufren de los estereotipos?, ¿De **qué** estereotipos sufren?, **¿Cómo** sufren? y **¿Qué** podemos hacer para mejorar la situación?

2. Mira las respuestas y escoge los mejores detalles. Si necesitas más información, haz más preguntas.

3. Organiza los detalles en un orden lógico para presentarlos en tu composición.

B. Redacción

1. Escribe una buena introducción. Puedes hacer una pregunta para llamar la atención de tu lector(a), o puedes mencionar algo interesante relacionado con el tema de los estereotipos.

2. Escribe tres o cuatro párrafos para hablar de los estereotipos, quiénes los tienen que soportar, cómo sufren estas personas, etc. Incluye detalles relevantes e interesantes de tu lista.

3. En tu conclusión, describe cómo se puede mejorar la situación.

C. Evaluación

1. Lee bien tu composición. ¿Contiene toda la información necesaria? ¿Contiene detalles interesantes? Si no, añade más detalles.

2. Muestra tu composición a dos o tres compañeros(as) y pídeles su opinión. Considera sus opiniones y haz los cambios necesarios.

3. ¿Usaste buena puntuación? Consulta a tus compañeros(as) o a tu profesor(a) si necesitas ayuda.

4. ¿Escribiste bien todas las palabras? ¿Usaste bien todas las formas verbales? Si necesitas ayuda, consulta las páginas R34–R46 o mira un diccionario bilingüe. También puedes hablar con tus compañeros(as) o con tu profesor(a).

Apply and Assess

Postwriting
Pair Work

Have pairs of students peer-edit each other's essays. In addition to focusing on spelling and grammar, ask students to summarize the main idea communicated by the writer. Remind them the main idea is the most important message that the writer wants the reader to remember.

Ask students to determine whether the details explain or illustrate the main idea. If the peer-editor is unable to state the main idea after consultation with the teacher, or if the main idea is not well supported, suggestions should be offered to help the writer improve the clarity and organization of the text. Should the details be better organized to present a more coherent message? Are more details needed?

Teaching Resources
p. 271

PRINT
▶ Lesson Planner, p. 45
▶ Cuaderno para hispanohablantes, p. 44
▶ Alternative Assessment Guide, p. 24
▶ Standardized Assessment Tutor, Chapter 9

MEDIA
▶ One-Stop Planner, Disc 3
✦ Test Generator, Chapter 9
▶ Interactive CD-ROM Tutor, Disc 3

Process Writing

Prewriting
Teacher Note

Tell students that they may write about an imaginary situation in their school or city if they do not feel comfortable writing about a real one.

Writing
Teacher Notes

• Encourage students to define their topic in the first paragraph. **(Hay muchos estereotipos en nuestra escuela. ¿Te sorprende? Pues considera la situación...)** Each succeeding paragraph can be devoted to explaining one major facet of the situation.

• Make sure students have a topic sentence in each paragraph so they can build around it when they begin adding details.

• Tell students that one way to include details is to describe a situation in which stereotyping has occurred. Another way is to describe a person who has experienced discrimination because of stereotyping. Their writing could be based on either situation or both.

Más práctica gramatical

CAPÍTULO 9

For **Más práctica gramatical** Answer Transparencies, see the *Teaching Transparencies* binder.

Más práctica gramatical

internet

MARCAR: go.hrw.com
PALABRA CLAVE:
WV3 NEW YORK-9

Primer paso   **Objectives** Talking about emotional reactions; expressing disagreement

1 Ya termina el año escolar. Usa el pretérito de los verbos entre paréntesis para explicar cómo reaccionaron todos durante la semana de los exámenes finales. **(p. 257)**

1. Micaela ═══════ (alegrarse) porque las clases ya terminaron.
2. Yo ═══════ (querer) llorar cuando me despedí de los profesores.
3. Yo ═══════ (frustrarse) porque no tuve suficiente tiempo para estudiar.
4. Isa, tú ═══════ (quejarse) antes del examen de computación, pero luego sacaste una nota excelente.
5. Alejandro y yo ═══════ (enfadarse) porque los profesores nos hicieron preguntas muy difíciles.
6. Todos nosotros ═══════ (sentirse) cansadísimos después del examen de inglés.
7. ¡Qué antipáticos son Federico y Araceli! Ellos ═══════ (burlarse) y ═══════ (reírse) de los compañeros que no salieron bien en los exámenes.
8. Marta y Fede son muy tímidos. Cuando la profesora les hizo una pregunta en clase, ═══════ (ponerse) rojos y no pudieron contestar.

2 ¡Qué sorpresa! La profesora de matemáticas tuvo trillizos. Explica cuándo supieron todos la noticia y cómo reaccionaron. Usa el pretérito de los verbos entre paréntesis. **(p. 258)**

1. Pues, yo ═══════ (saber) las noticias el viernes. Claro que yo ═══════ (ponerse) muy feliz.
2. La directora lo ═══════ (saber) el jueves. Ella ═══════ (estar) muy contenta.
3. Los padres de la profesora ═══════ (saber) las noticias el miércoles. Ellos ═══════ (estar) contentísimos.
4. Tina, ¿cuándo lo ═══════ (saber) tú? Seguro que ═══════ (ponerse) feliz también.
5. ¿Y esposo de la profesora? Pues, él lo ═══════ (saber) inmediatamente. ¡Y él ═══════ (estar) más contento que nadie!
6. El viernes también Regina y yo ═══════ (saber) que la profesora y sus tres hijos estaban todos muy bien. Nosotros ═══════ (estar) muy contentos.

Answers

1
1. se alegró
2. quise
3. me frustré
4. te quejaste
5. nos enfadamos
6. nos sentimos
7. se burlaron, se rieron
8. se pusieron

2
1. supe, me puse
2. supo, estuvo
3. supieron, estuvieron
4. supiste, te pusiste
5. supo, estuvo
6. supimos, estuvimos

Grammar Resources for Chapter 9

The **Más práctica gramatical** activities are designed as supplemental activities for the grammatical concepts presented in the chapter. You might use them as additional practice, for review, or for assessment.

For more grammar presentation, review, and practice, refer to the following:
• Cuaderno de gramática
• Grammar Tutor for Students of Spanish

• Grammar Summary on pp. R25–R46
• Cuaderno de actividades
• Grammar and Vocabulary quizzes (Testing Program)
• Test Generator on the One-Stop Planner CD-ROM
• Interactive CD-ROM Tutor
• **Juegos interactivos** at <u>go.hrw.com</u>

3 ¡Qué emoción durante la ceremonia de graduación! Completa cada oración con el pretérito si trata de una reacción momentánea. Complétala con el imperfecto si trata de una situación ya en curso o una habitual. **(p. 258)**

1. Yo ya ═════ (estar) muy nervioso cuando llegué al coliseo.
2. Cuando a Yoli y a Mari les entregaron el diploma ═════ (ponerse) tan emocionadas que ═════ (querer) llorar.
3. El director del colegio contó un chiste muy gracioso y todos ═════ (reírse).
4. Mientras todos esperábamos recibir nuestros diplomas, ═════ (estar) muy nerviosos.
5. Durante su discurso de despedida, Leticia ═════ (ponerse) nerviosa. Pero todos lo esperaban porque en años pasados Leticia siempre ═════ (ponerse) nerviosa frente al público.
6. Nadie ═════ (saber) que había una fiesta de sorpresa después de la ceremonia, pero cuando lo ═════ (saber), todos ═════ (alegrarse).

4 Completa el cuento de Mario con la forma correcta del pretérito o del imperfecto según el contexto. **(p. 258)**

Mi hermano y yo __1__ (estar) muy tristes cuando __2__ (saber) que teníamos que cambiar de escuela. Me acuerdo que nosotros no __3__ (querer) cambiar porque ya __4__ (tener) muchos amigos. Así que cuando comenzó el año en la nueva escuela, __5__ (estar) un poco nerviosos. Al principio, no __6__ (saber) qué hacer ni adónde ir porque no __7__ (conocer) bien el lugar.

Pero todo cambió cuando conocí a Victoria, que __8__ (estar) en mi clase de biología. Un día me caí delante de la clase durante mi presentación oral y todos __9__ (reírse). Yo __10__ (ponerse) tan rojo que __11__ (querer) llorar. Pero Victoria se levantó y me ayudó. Después de la clase, comenzamos a hablar un poco. Ella me __12__ (caer) muy bien y ahora es mi mejor amiga.

Answers

3 1. estaba
2. se pusieron, quisieron/querían
3. se rieron
4. estábamos
5. se puso, se ponía
6. sabía, supieron, se alegraron

4 1. estábamos
2. supimos
3. queríamos
4. teníamos
5. estábamos
6. sabíamos
7. conocíamos
8. estaba
9. se rieron
10. me puse
11. quise/quería
12. cayó

Communication for All Students

Additional Practice

2 Have students write a brief paragraph that describes a big surprise that they received. Students should explain how and when they found out about the surprise **(saber),** how they initially reacted **(ponerse)** and felt **(estar, sentirse).** What did they do after receiving the surprise?

Visual/Kinesthetic Learners

3 Write adjectives that describe emotional and physical states on slips of paper. [**feliz, triste, deprimido(a), cansado(a), contento(a), nervioso(a), preocupado(a)**] Ask a student to mime an adjective in front of the class. The class guesses by saying **Se sintió feliz.** Ask another student to invent a reason for the reaction. **(Se sintió feliz porque sacó una buena nota.)**

Más práctica gramatical

CAPÍTULO 9

For **Más práctica gramatical** Answer Transparencies, see the *Teaching Transparencies* binder.

Answers

5
1. son
2. sacan
3. hagan
4. saca
5. contesta
6. haya
7. sigue
8. sepa
9. dé
10. sea
11. espera
12. aprendemos
13. va
14. tienen
15. seamos
16. tengamos

6
1. Yo viviría en otro país.
2. Felipe sería atleta profesional.
3. Sergio y Julia asistirían a una universidad grande.
4. Tú comprarías un carro italiano.
5. Mi hermano y yo trabajaríamos como locutores de televisión.
6. Papá iría de vacaciones a Hawai.
7. Nelson saldría con su actriz favorita.

Más práctica gramatical

WV3 NEW YORK-9

5 Tomás y Fátima siempre tienen opiniones opuestas. Completa lo que dicen con el indicativo o subjuntivo de los verbos entre paréntesis. Recuerda que el subjuntivo se usa para indicar duda o para negar algo. **(p. 259)**

TOMÁS   Para mí, es cierto que los atletas ___1___ (ser) menos inteligentes y ___2___ (sacar) las peores notas. Y dudo que los profesores les ___3___ (hacer) tantas preguntas como a los demás.

FÁTIMA   ¡Qué va! Víctor es atleta y creo que ___4___ (sacar) las mejores notas de la clase de química. Y estoy segura que él ___5___ (contestar) más preguntas que tú.

TOMÁS   No creo que ___6___ (haber) mucha discriminación en este colegio. ¿Tú qué dices?

FÁTIMA   No estoy de acuerdo. Pienso que la discriminación ___7___ (seguir) siendo un problema aquí y en todas partes. Además, no creo que nadie aquí ___8___ (saber) resolver el problema.

TOMÁS   ¿Qué opinas del nuevo profesor? No me parece que nos ___9___ (dar) mucha tarea ni que ___10___ (ser) muy exigente con nosotros.

FÁTIMA   ¡Al contrario! Sé que él ___11___ (esperar) mucho de sus estudiantes, y estoy segura que nosotros ___12___ (aprender) mucho con él.

TOMÁS   ¿Conoces a la nueva estudiante? Pienso que te ___13___ (ir) a caer muy bien. Me parece que tú y ella ___14___ (tener) mucho en común.

FÁTIMA   Pues, ya la conocí, y dudo que ella y yo ___15___ (ser) muy amigas. ¡No creo que nosotras ___16___ (tener) nada en común!

Segundo paso

Objectives Expressing an assumption; making hypothetical statements

6 ¿Qué harían todos si pudieran realizar sus sueños? Usa el condicional. **(p. 265)**
1. (yo)/vivir en otro país
2. Felipe/ser atleta profesional
3. Sergio y Julia/asistir a una universidad grande
4. (tú)/comprar un carro italiano
5. mi hermano y yo/trabajar como locutores de televisión
6. papá/ir de vacaciones a Hawai
7. Nelson/salir con su actriz favorita

Communication for All Students

Auditory Learners

4 Prepare a list of ten to fifteen sentences like the ones in the activity. Some of your sentences should use the subjunctive and indicative incorrectly. **(No creo que mis amigos son perezosos. Es verdad que muchos estudiantes estudien en la biblioteca.)** Read a sentence aloud and ask students to clap if they hear the subjunctive after the **que** and to snap their fingers if they hear the indicative. Then ask students if the tense was used correctly. If not, call on a student to restate the sentence with the appropriate tense.

Additional Practice

5 Write a letter seeking advice about several problems and display it on the overhead. Then have the class come up with replies using the conditional and past subjunctive.

7 Este año Laura se presenta como candidata para el Concejo Estudiantil (*Student Council*). Ahora está hablando con Elena de sus planes. Completa lo que dice Laura con el condicional de los verbos entre paréntesis. **(p. 265)**

Imagínate, Elena... Si yo fuera presidenta del colegio, __1__ (hacer) muchas cosas. ¿__2__ (Querer) tú ser la vice-presidenta? Así tú me __3__ (ayudar) con todos los cambios que hay que hacer. Por ejemplo, nosotras __4__ (poner) computadoras en la cafetería. Entonces los estudiantes __5__ (poder) hacer la tarea o enviar cartas electrónicas durante el almuerzo. Claro, primero __6__ (ser) necesario comprar las computadoras. Y yo __7__ (tener) que hablar con la directora, pero creo que ella __8__ (decir) que es una idea excelente.

8 Sofía escribió una composición sobre la discriminación que sufre la gente mayor de edad (*senior citizens*). Completa su composición con las palabras que faltan. Usa cada palabra sólo una vez. **(p. 266)**

> tratar   se burlan   respeto
> aprecio   actitud   falta
> me di cuenta de   estereotipo
> prejuicios   ignorancia   discriminación

Creo que existe una fuerte __1__ negativa hacia las personas mayores. En este país me parece que ellos son víctimas de la __2__. Por ejemplo, existe un __3__ que los viejos ya no pueden hacer nada. Hay muchas personas que cuentan chistes de los viejos y que __4__ de ellos. Me parece que hay una __5__ de contacto entre los mayores de edad y los otros miembros de la sociedad. En realidad, nosotros los jóvenes no sabemos __6__ a los mayores de edad. El año pasado, pasé todo el verano con mi abuela. Después de unas semanas, yo __7__ que era una mujer fuerte y valiente. Ahora la __8__ y __9__ mucho más. Creo que la solución al problema de los __10__ contra los viejos es pasar más tiempo con ellos.

Answers

7
1. haría
2. Querrías
3. ayudarías
4. pondríamos
5. podrían
6. sería
7. tendría
8. diría

8
1. actitud
2. discriminación/ignorancia
3. estereotipo
4. se burlan
5. falta
6. tratar
7. me di cuenta de
8. aprecio/respeto
9. respeto/aprecio
10. prejuicios

Review and Assess

You may wish to assign the **Más práctica gramatical** activities as additional practice or homework after presenting material throughout the chapter. Assign Activity 1 after **Así se dice** (p. 257), Activities 2 and 3 after **Gramática** (p. 258), Activity 4 after **Así se dice** and **Gramática** (p. 259), Activities 5 and 6 after **Gramática** (p. 265), and Activity 7 after **Vocabulario** (p. 266). To prepare students for the **Paso** Quizzes and Chapter Test, have them do the **Más práctica gramatical** activities in the following order: complete Activities 1–5 before taking Quiz 9-1A or 9-1B; Activities 6–7 before taking Quiz 9-2A or 9-2B.

CAPÍTULO 9

The **Repaso** reviews all four skills and culture in preparation for the Chapter Test.

Teaching Resources
pp. 276–277

PRINT
▸ Lesson Planner, p. 46
▸ Listening Activities, p. 69
▸ Video Guide, pp. 60, 62, 65
▸ Grammar Tutor for Students of Spanish, Chapter 9
▸ Cuaderno para hispanohablantes, pp. 41–45
▸ Standardized Assessment Tutor, Chapter 9

MEDIA
▸ One-Stop Planner
▸ Video Program, Videocassette 3, 44:39–45:17
▸ Audio Compact Discs, CD 9, Tr. 20
▸ Interactive CD-ROM Tutor, Disc 3

Additional Practice

1 Have students draw a picture for the one description that isn't illustrated in the *Pupil's Edition.*

internet

MARCAR: go.hrw.com
PALABRA CLAVE:
WV3 NEW YORK-9

1 Mira los dibujos. Luego escucha lo que dice cada persona e indica qué dibujo corresponde a cada persona. Hay una oración que no corresponde a ningún dibujo.

Script and answers on p. 251H.

CD 9 Tr. 20

a.

b.

c.

d.

2 En una hoja de papel, escribe tres opiniones un poco polémicas. Dale tu hoja de papel a un(a) compañero(a), que usará las expresiones de **Así se dice** para negar lo que escribiste.

MODELO
—**Los hombres siempre son arrogantes.**
—**No estoy de acuerdo que todos los hombres sean arrogantes. Algunos son callados y tímidos.**

3 Indica si las siguientes frases son **ciertas** o **falsas**. Si son falsas, corrígelas.

1. Hay más de dos millones de hispanos en Nueva York.
2. Los hispanos forman un grupo minoritario bastante pequeño en Nueva York.
3. La mayoría de los hispanos en Nueva York vienen de Centroamérica.
4. Nueva York es un núcleo importante para la prensa y la televisión en español.
5. Los dos periódicos en español que se conocen mejor son **El Sol** y **El Heraldo.**
6. Hay colombianos y dominicanos en Nueva York.
7. Todavía no hay emisoras de radio en español en Nueva York. See answers below.

Answers

3 1. cierta
2. falsa; Los hispanos forman un grupo minoritario bastante grande.
3. falsa; La mayoría de los hispanos en Nueva York vienen de Puerto Rico, la República Dominicana, Perú, Colombia y Ecuador.
4. cierta
5. falsa; Los dos periódicos en español son *El Diario* y *Hoy.*
6. cierta
7. falsa; Hay muchas emisoras de radio en español en Nueva York.

Apply and Assess

Challenge

2 If your class setting is conducive to this type of exercise, you might want to have the students write their own opinions anonymously in Spanish on pieces of paper. Collect the papers. Redistribute those that are appropriate to individuals or groups for discussion. You might choose only one or two of the student opinions and use them to do Activity 2 as a class.

Slower Pace

3 Have students work in pairs or groups of three to do this activity. As a follow-up, you might have them write three additional true-or-false statements about New York and exchange them with another group.

4 Escribe un párrafo para dar las impresiones que tienes o lo que supones sobre uno de los siguientes temas.

1. las costumbres de los indígenas yanomami del Amazonas

2. lo que dirían los animales, si pudieran hablar, de los seres humanos

3. la comida en las colonias de Estados Unidos en 1700

5 Les preguntaron a tres jóvenes cuáles son los tres deseos que pedirían si tuvieran una lámpara maravillosa *(magic lamp)*. ¿Cómo contestarías tú esa pregunta?

Si tuvieras una lámpara maravillosa, ¿qué pedirías?

ANTHONY: Pediría más tiempo para tocar la guitarra, una buena nota en el examen de francés y un viaje por el mundo.

AKUA: Estaría feliz con buena salud, dinero y amor. ¿Qué más se puede pedir?

MEGAN: Me encantaría poder despertarme tarde todos los días, comprarme un avión y ser piloto.

6 Usa las expresiones de **Así se dice** en la página 257 para describir cómo reaccionaron las personas en las siguientes situaciones. ¿Cómo se sintieron?

1. La señora Bermúdez vio a un chico burlándose de su hija Nancy.

2. Manuel oyó un chiste muy cómico.

3. Ayer cancelaron las clases para los estudiantes.

4. A Elena se le rompieron los zapatos.

5. Los abuelos de Sandra y Manuel llegaron de visita.

7

Situación

Con unos(as) compañeros(as), imagina que ustedes son políticos(as) invitados(as) a un programa de televisión en el cual se discuten temas polémicos. Cada persona supone algo. Las otras personas responden y niegan lo que dijo esa persona.

Cuaderno para hispanohablantes, p. 45

Apply and Assess

Additional Practice

5 After students have answered the question, you might ask them to embellish their answers. Ask them: **¿Por qué harías eso? ¿Qué harías si tuvieras todo lo que querías? ¿Adónde irías a lograr tus sueños?**

Pair Work

6 Have students work in pairs. Students will take turns describing things that happened to someone. The partners will respond by stating how the person felt or reacted.

Portfolio

6 **Oral** Suggest to students that they include this activity in their oral Portfolios. For Portfolio suggestions, see *Alternative Assessment Guide,* page 24.

Culture Note

Nearly a million Puerto Ricans live in New York City today. Puerto Ricans are citizens of the United States by birth and have been elected as state senators, assembly members, and U.S. representatives from various states.

Teacher Note

This page is intended to help students prepare for the Chapter Test. It is a brief checklist of the major points covered in the chapter. The students should be reminded that it is only a checklist and does not necessarily include everything that will appear on the Chapter Test.

Answers
Sample answers:

1
1. Martín y Laura se enfadaron cuando la gente se burló de sus amigos.
2. Fernanda se sintió presionada cuando sus profesores le dieron mucha tarea.
3. Cristóbal y yo nos enfadamos porque la gente habló muy alto en el cine.
4. Tú te reíste cuando viste tu programa favorito de cómicos.
5. Tus amigos se frustraron cuando no supieron la respuesta en clase.
6. Gabriela se alegró cuando recibió flores en su cumpleaños.

3 *Answers will vary. In their answers, students should include:*
Supongo que..., Tengo entendido que..., Tengo la impresión de que..., Me imagino que...

A ver si puedo...

1 ¿Cómo se sintieron estas personas en las siguientes situaciones? Escribe oraciones completas. See sample answers below.
1. Martín y Laura/la gente se burló de sus amigos
2. Fernanda/sus profesores le dieron mucha tarea
3. Cristóbal y yo/ la gente habló muy alto en el cine
4. tú/viste tu programa favorito de cómicos
5. tus amigos/no supieron la respuesta en clase
6. Gabriela/recibió flores en su cumpleaños

Can you talk about emotional reactions? p. 257

2 Ana y Simón tienen opiniones muy diferentes sobre sus compañeros. Para cada descripción que sigue, indica cómo piensan Ana y Simón. Answers will vary.

MODELO **Elisa y Paco practican el piano todos los días.**
ANA **Es verdad que practican todos los días.**
SIMÓN **No es cierto que practiquen todos los días.**

1. Juan Carlos aprecia el arte y la música indígena.
2. Bárbara tiene una actitud muy positiva.
3. Gregorio nunca juzga a nadie.
4. Luis y Raquel son los únicos que nos comprenden.
5. Tatiana quiere combatir la discriminación.
6. Alejandro siempre ayuda a otros estudiantes con la tarea.

Can you express disagreement? p. 259

3 Usa expresiones de **Así se dice** para expresar tus ideas sobre los siguientes temas. See sample answers below.
1. la vida estudiantil en el año 2050
2. las clases en las universidades
3. la discriminación racial en el año 2075
4. el clima del Polo Norte en contraste con el clima de Nueva York

Can you express an assumption? p. 264

4 Crea oraciones con las siguientes frases. ¿Harías las siguientes cosas si tuvieras... o si pudieras...? Answers will vary.

MODELO **ir de compras**
—Iría de compras si tuviera tiempo.
1. patinar en el parque
2. jugar al tenis
3. nadar en la piscina
4. montar a caballo
5. preparar una tortilla española
6. estudiar para el examen
7. pasear en velero
8. escuchar música

Can you make hypothetical statements? p. 264

Review and Assess

Group Work

2 Ask students to write five to eight statements that express something believable or incredible. (**Mis tíos tienen doce hijos. Mi hermana entiende el francés.**) In groups of three, one student reads one of his or her sentences to which the other two students respond. The second student plays the role of the skeptic who doubts everything. (**No es verdad que tus tíos tengan doce hijos.**) The third student will believe anything. (**Yo creo que tus tíos tienen doce hijos.**) Students rotate roles.

Pair Work

4 Have pairs of students talk about what they would do if they went to New York City. What sites would they visit? Where and what would they eat? Ask volunteers to share their itinerary.

Primer paso

Talking about emotional reactions

estuve contento(a)...	I was happy . . .
me enfadé	I got angry
me enojé	I got angry
me frustré	I got frustrated
presionados(as) por...	pressured to . . .
Quise...	I wanted (tried)
reaccionaron	they reacted
Se alegró mucho.	He (She) was very happy.
se burlaron de	they made fun of
Se pusieron rojos.	They blushed.
se rieron	they laughed
supe	I knew (found out)
supiste	you knew (found out)

Expressing disagreement

¡Al contrario!	On the contrary!
Niego haberme burlado de...	I deny having made fun of . . .
No es cierto que...	It's not true that . . .
No es verdad que...	It's not true that . . .
No estoy de acuerdo en que...	I don't agree that . . .

Adjectives that describe people

amigable	friendly
arrogante	arrogant
bobo(a)	silly, dumb
callado(a)	quiet
chismoso(a)	gossipy
descortés	rude
egoísta	selfish

melancólico(a)	gloomy
perezoso(a)	lazy
presumido(a)	conceited
seco(a)	cold, curt
tímido(a)	shy
torpe	slow, dull, clumsy
travieso(a)	mischievous

Segundo paso

Expressing an assumption

Me imagino que...	I imagine that . . .
Supongo que...	I suppose that . . .
Tengo entendido que...	I understand that . . .
Tengo la impresión de que...	I'm under the impression that . . .

Making hypothetical statements

Si fueras... ¿qué harías?	If you were . . . what would you do?
Si pudiera... viviría...	If I could . . . I would live . . .

Si pudieras... ¿adónde irías?	If you could . . . where would you go?
Si tuviera... compraría...	If I had . . . I would buy . . .

Talking about stereotypes

la actitud hacia	attitude toward
apreciar	to appreciate
combatir	to combat
contra	against
darse cuenta de	to realize
la discriminación	discrimination

estereotipar	to stereotype
el estereotipo	stereotype
la falta (de)	lack (of)
la ignorancia	ignorance
juzgar	to judge
la minoría	minority
el prejuicio	prejudice
respetar	to respect
el respeto hacia	respect for
tratar	to treat

CAPÍTULO 9

Circumlocution

¿CÓMO SOY? Divide the class into groups of five. Each student writes an adjective on a slip of paper but shows it to no one. Each student describes himself or herself in terms of, but without saying, the adjective he or she wrote on the paper. For example, a group member writes **callado(a)**. The student then tells others **No me gusta hablar mucho. Es mejor escuchar lo que dicen los otros.** The other group members try to guess the adjective. Students are to keep track of how many guesses are required to identify each word. The students whose word requires the fewest guesses wins.

Chapter 9 Assessment

▶ **Testing Program**
Chapter Test, pp. 199–204
 Audio Compact Discs, CD 9, Trs. 23–24

Speaking Test, p. 299

▶ **Alternative Assessment Guide**
Portfolio Assessment, p. 24
Performance Assessment, p. 38
CD-ROM Assessment, p. 52

▶ **Interactive CD-ROM Tutor, Disc 3**
¡A hablar!
¡A escribir!

▶ **Standardized Assessment Tutor**
Chapter 9

▶ **One-Stop Planner, Disc 3**
Test Generator
Chapter 9

Review and Assess

Game

EXPRESIONES MISTERIOSAS Select a vocabulary expression, a play on words, a familiar sentence, or a grammatical phrase. On the board, draw as many short lines as there are letters in the word or expression, leaving a blank space between words. Have students take turns in teams or individually, asking if the word contains various letters.

(**¿Hay una c?**) Fill in each correct letter guessed over the appropriate underline. Allow students to continue their turn until they guess a letter that is not used. The student or team that guesses the word or expression gets one point. The person or team with the most points wins.

Capítulo 10: La riqueza cultural
Chapter Overview

De antemano pp. 282–284	**¿Qué significa ser hispano?**

	FUNCTIONS	**GRAMMAR**	**VOCABULARY**	**RE-ENTRY**
Primer paso pp. 285–289	• Talking about accomplishments, p. 285 • Talking about future plans, p. 288	• Subjunctive after certain conjunctions, p. 289	• Successes, p. 286 • Your roots, p. 287	• Present perfect tense (Capítulo 3) • Forms of the subjunctive (Capítulo 6)

¡Adelante! pp. 290–291	**La herencia cultural**

Segundo paso pp. 293–296	• Expressing cause and effect, p. 293 • Expressing intention and purpose, p. 295	• Infinitives after prepositions, p. 293 • Subjunctive with **para que**, p. 296	• How to realize your goals, p. 294	• Reflexive pronouns (Capítulo 3, II) • Preterite and imperfect (Capítulo 10, II)

Vamos a leer pp. 298–300	**Gringa/Chicana** and **Yo soy Joaquín**	**Reading Strategy:** Paraphrasing to help understand content
Vamos a escribir p. 301	**La diversidad cultural**	**Writing Strategy:** Combining sentences for better flow

Más práctica gramatical	**pp. 302–305** **Primer paso,** pp. 302–303	**Segundo paso,** pp. 304–305.
Review pp. 306–309	**Repaso,** pp. 306–307	**A ver si puedo...,** p. 308 **Vocabulario,** p. 309

CULTURE

- **Realia,** Article about Gloria Estefan, p. 285
- **Nota cultural,** New York City's El Barrio, p. 288
- **Panorama cultural, ¿Cómo te defines?,** p. 292
- **Nota cultural, La Sociedad Hispánica de América,** p. 296
- **Encuentro cultural, El Ballet Hispánico de Nueva York,** p. 297

Capítulo 10: La riqueza cultural
Chapter Resources

Lesson Planning

One-Stop Planner

Lesson Planner with Substitute Teacher Lesson Plans, pp. 47–51, 74

Student Make-Up Assignments
• Make-Up Assignment Copying Masters, Chapter 10

Listening and Speaking

Listening Activities
• Student Response Forms for Listening Activities, pp. 75–77
• Additional Listening Activities 10-1 to 10-6, pp. 79–81
• Additional Listening Activities (poem), p. 82
• Scripts and Answers, pp. 147–151

Video Guide
• Teaching Suggestions, pp. 67–68
• Activity Masters, pp. 69–71
• Scripts and Answers, pp. 106–109, 119

Activities for Communication
• Communicative Activities, pp. 37–40
• Realia and Teaching Suggestions, pp. 78–80
• Situation Cards, pp. 107–108

Reading and Writing

Reading Strategies and Skills Handbook, Chapter 10
¡Lee conmigo! 3, Chapter 10
Cuaderno de actividades, pp. 109–120

Grammar

Cuaderno de gramática, pp. 78–86
Grammar Tutor for Students of Spanish, Chapter 10

Assessment

Testing Program
• Grammar and Vocabulary Quizzes, **Paso** Quizzes, and Chapter Test, pp. 213–226
• Score Sheet, Scripts and Answers, pp. 227–233

Alternative Assessment Guide
• Portfolio Assessment, p. 25
• Performance Assessment, p. 39
• CD-ROM Assessment, p. 53

Student Make-Up Assignments
• Alternative Quizzes, Chapter 10

Standardized Assessment Tutor
• Reading, pp. 39–41
• Writing, p. 42
• Math, pp. 51–52

Native Speakers

Cuaderno para hispanohablantes, pp. 46–50

Online Activities
• Juegos interactivos
• Actividades Internet

Video Program
• Videocassette 4
• Videocassette 5 (captioned version)

Audio Compact Discs
• Textbook Listening Activities, CD 10, Tracks 1–18
• Additional Listening Activities, CD 10, Tracks 23–29
• Assessment Items, CD 10, Tracks 19–22

Interactive CD-ROM Tutor, Disc 3

Teaching Transparencies
• Situations 10-1 to 10-2
• **Más práctica gramatical** Answers
• **Cuaderno de gramática** Answers

One-Stop Planner CD-ROM

Use the **One-Stop Planner CD-ROM with Test Generator** to aid in lesson planning and pacing.

For each chapter, the **One-Stop Planner** includes:

• Editable lesson plans with direct links to teaching resources
• Printable worksheets from resource books
• Direct launches to the HRW Internet activities
• Video and audio segments
• Test Generator
• Clip Art for vocabulary items

Capítulo 10: La riqueza cultural

Projects

La feria del empleo

In this project, students explore the careers they would like to pursue by preparing a presentation and display for a job fair. This is an individual project, although students with similar aspirations might coordinate their research efforts.

SITUATION

Tell students to imagine that they work for an expanding company that has come to the job fair to recruit new employees. They will need to emphasize the reasons why careers in their particular field are interesting and rewarding.

MATERIALS

✂ **Students may need**
- Paper
- Glue
- Poster board
- Magazines
- Scissors
- Markers
- Pens
- Pencils

SUGGESTED SEQUENCE

1. Students choose a career or field that interests them.
2. They gather as much information as possible about their career or field on the Internet, in the library, or from their guidance counselor.
3. Students write a report in which they explain the nature of the work, why that career or field interests them, and the goals they would pursue through their work.
4. They clip appropriate pictures from magazines or create their own artwork to assemble an appealing visual presentation that will entice their classmates to pursue a career in that field.
5. Students post their displays and make their oral presentations to the class.

GRADING THE PROJECT

Suggested point distribution: (total = 100 points)
Language use 40
Oral presentation 30
Originality 20
Appearance 10

Games

Parejas

*In this game, students review the functions and grammar from both **Pasos** in this chapter, but it can be modified for use with other chapters as well.*

Preparation Ask each student to write one sentence based on **Así se dice** and **Gramática** in Chapter 10. Make enough copies so that each team of four or five students will have a complete set. Cut the sentences into strips and then cut the strips in half. Place each set of sentences into a separate envelope.

Procedure Divide the students into teams. Give each team a set of sentences. Teams take turns drawing and reading a sentence fragment aloud. The listening teams race to complete the sentence logically. The first team to do so earns a point. There may be more than one logical completion to a given fragment. The team with the most points at the end of the game wins.

Frijoles saltarines

This game provides a review of reflexive verbs.

Procedure Read sentences containing either a reflexive or a nonreflexive verb. (**La clase se levanta. Salí de la casa.**) You may want to include commands. (**Vámonos. Estudien.**) If students hear a reflexive verb, they should stand; otherwise, they should remain seated. A student who stands or remains seated inappropriately is out. The last student remaining in the game wins.

COMMUNITY LINK

You may want to have students interview people who work in their chosen field to help them better understand what careers in that field are like. Have students report what they learned from the interviews to the class.

Storytelling

Mini-cuento

This story accompanies Teaching Transparency 10-1. The mini-cuento can be told and retold in different formats, acted out, written as a dictation, and read aloud to give students additional opportunities to practice all four skills. The following story recounts how students see their futures and how they will reach their professional goals.

Roberto y su amiga Matilde pusieron todo su esfuerzo en alcanzar el éxito. Hoy ellos, como muchos otros hispanos, reciben un premio porque han triunfado en los campos del periodismo y del arte. El éxito de Roberto y Matilde se debe a que fueron muy buenos estudiantes y por ser bilingües. Ellos también tuvieron excelentes maestros. Desde joven Matilde pensaba que su destino era trabajar como artista y graduarse de la universidad. Roberto quería ser reportero y comprarse el auto de sus sueños. El consejo que Roberto y Matilde le dan a la gente es que el éxito es el resultado de mucho trabajo y que es necesario que todos logren superar obstáculos.

Traditions

Celebraciones

Celebrating a girl's fifteenth birthday is a very important tradition among Puerto Ricans, Mexicans, Cubans, and other Latin Americans. In New York City, where Puerto Ricans make up a substantial percentage of the population (in addition to other Hispanic groups), the tradition continues. The **quinceañera** tradition celebrates a young girl's coming of age and is an elaborate celebration, almost resembling a wedding. It can involve invitations, caterers, limousines, choreographers, and beautiful gowns.

The **quinceañera** wears a long, white (or pastel pink) dress with gloves and a tiara. She chooses fourteen girls (**las damas**), and fourteen boys (**los chambelanes**) to escort her. The **damas** dress in identical long dresses, while the **chambelanes** wear tuxedos. At the party, the **quinceañera** dances the first dance with her father. Sometimes, the **damas** and **chambelanes** perform choreographed dances that they have rehearsed for weeks. Then everyone joins in the dancing and a traditional meal. In a culture that values family and tradition, the **quinceañera** represents the best of both. Do young girls or boys have coming-of-age parties in the United States? Have students research similar customs from other cultures and countries and report to the class.

Receta

*When Columbus arrived in Puerto Rico, the native **taínos** were already using yucca, peppers, and corn, which are still very much a part of the Puerto Rican diet today. With the Spaniards came new ingredients, such as olives, garlic, cilantro, and of course, cheese. **Sorullitos** are a delicious blend of old-world and new-world ingredients. **Sorullitos** can be served as appetizers or with meat or fish.*

SORULLITOS

para hacer 18 sorullitos

1 1/2 tazas de agua

1/2 cucharadita de sal

1 taza de harina de maíz amarillo

1 taza de queso *Edam, Gouda* o *Cheddar*

aceite vegetal para freír

Hierva el agua con sal. Agregue la harina de maíz, poco a poco, y revuélvala hasta que la mezcla quede espesa y lisa. Retírela del fuego y añada el queso. Mézclelo bien y déjelo enfriar. Tome un poco de la masa fría y forme palitos de tres pulgadas de largo y aproximadamente una pulgada de diámetro. Fríalos en aceite hasta que estén dorados y déjelos escurrir sobre toallas de papel.

Video Program

Videocassette 4, Videocassette 5 (captioned version)
See Video Guide, pages 66–71.

 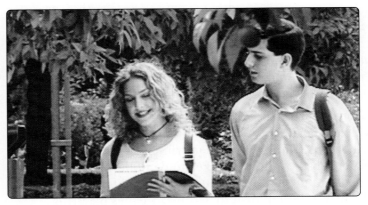

Dramatic episode • Cuando sea mayor...

As the end of the school year approaches, Javier starts to feel nervous about his upcoming trip to Mexico. He expresses pride in being Andalusian and confesses that it will be difficult to leave Seville for such a long time. He doesn't lose his sense of humor, however, and he plays along with Zoraida as she says sarcastically that she hopes to be just like him when she grows up. He also begins to suspect that Alejandra likes Sergio and not him.

¿Cómo te defines?

People from Spanish-speaking countries talk about their cultural identity, including how they define themselves and what they are proud of.

Videoclips

• **AKO Fandango:** music video about **son,** a form of music popular in Spanish-speaking Caribbean countries

• **Los árabes en España:** documentary about the Arab cultural presence in Spain and in other Spanish-speaking countries

Interactive CD-ROM Tutor

The **Interactive CD-ROM Tutor** contains videos, interactive games, and activities that provide students an opportunity to practice and review the material covered in Chapter 10.

Activity	Activity Type	Pupil's Edition Page
1. Vocabulario	Patas arriba	p. 287
2. Así se dice	¿Cuál es?	pp. 288–289
3. Gramática	¡Atrévete!	p. 289
4. Vocabulario	¡A escoger!	p. 294
5. Así se dice	Imagen y sonido ¡Exploremos! ¡Identifiquemos!	p. 295
6. Gramática de repaso	¿Qué falta?	p. 296
Panorama cultural	¿Cómo te defines? ¡A escoger!	p. 292
¡A hablar!	*Guided recording*	pp. 306–307
¡A escribir!	*Guided writing*	pp. 306–307

Teacher Management System
Logging In

Logging in to the *¡Ven conmigo!* TMS is easy. Upon launching the program, simply type "admin" in the password area of the log-in screen and press RETURN. Log on to **www.hrw.com/CDROMTUTOR** for a detailed explanation of the Teacher Management System.

One-Stop Planner CD-ROM

To preview all resources available for this chapter, use the **One-Stop Planner CD-ROM,** Disc 3.

Internet Connection

MARCAR: go.hrw.com
PALABRA CLAVE:
WV3 NEW YORK-10

*Have students explore the **go.hrw.com** Web site for many online resources covering all chapters. All Chapter 10 resources are available under the keyword **WV3 NEW YORK-10.** Interactive games help students practice the material and provide them with immediate feedback. You will also find a printable worksheet that provides Internet activities that lead to a comprehensive online research project.*

Juegos interactivos

You can use the interactive activities in this chapter

- to practice grammar, vocabulary, and chapter functions
- as homework
- as an assessment option
- as a self-test
- to prepare for the Chapter Test

Actividades Internet

Students learn about famous Hispanic people and write a short biography about one person.

- In preparation for the **Hoja de actividades,** ask students to name a few famous Hispanics. Then ask them to think harder about people who are equally, important, if not more so, but who are less well known. Whom do they find more interesting? Why?

- After they have completed the activity sheet, have students post the biography and any free images of the famous person, articles, or other relevant information and links to a personal Web page.

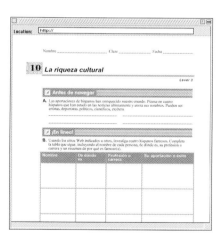

Proyecto

The use of the Internet is a great way to learn about people, but it can be unreliable and inaccurate. Have the class compile a list of Web sites they have found useful, accurate, and reliable. Have them write a short description about each site and explain why it is good. When the list is complete, post it to a school Web site as a resource for other Spanish students.

Primer paso

6 p. 285

Teacher Note
You may want to play the audio recording several times and have students conduct this activity as a dictation. Then have students change the illogical sentences to logical ones.

1. — Adela pasa casi todo el día tocando el violín, ¿no?
— Es cierto. Si sigue practicando mucho, nunca va a alcanzar el éxito.

2. — ¡Lorenzo aprendió a hablar el italiano en seis meses! ¿Cómo lo hizo?
— Verás, puso todo su esfuerzo en aprenderlo. No hacía nada más que eso.

3. — Carolina va a enseñar una clase de escalar montañas. ¿Sabe mucho de alpinismo?
— Por supuesto. El año pasado logró escalar la montaña más alta de Sudamérica.

4. — El pobre Miguel no ganó ningún premio en la carrera de bicicleta.
— Tienes razón. Estamos muy orgullosos de él.

5. — Dice Juan que cantó en la fiesta de Guadalupe y que a todos les gustó mucho.
— Sí, fue un éxito total. Ojalá que cante otra vez.

6. — Cuando llegó Estrella a los Estados Unidos no sabía inglés y no tenía trabajo, pero ahora es profesora de historia en la universidad.
— ¡Qué lástima! No ha tenido mucho éxito.

Answers to Activity 6
1. ilógica; Sample answer: Es cierto. Si sigue practicando mucho, sí va a alcanzar el éxito.
2. lógica
3. lógica
4. ilógica; Sample answer: Tienes razón. Estamos muy tristes por él.
5. lógica
6. ilógica; Sample answer: ¡Qué bueno! Ha tenido mucho éxito.

11 p. 287

ADRIANA Muchos padres hispanos recién llegados a Estados Unidos no saben hablar inglés. Para ellos es mucho más difícil encajar en la sociedad estadounidense. Normalmente sus hijos aprenden inglés y se adaptan a las costumbres de aquí antes que los padres. Por eso es importante que los padres aprendan inglés pero sin olvidar el español. Así se asimilan pero sin olvidar sus raíces al mismo tiempo.

JOSÉ LUIS Yo creo que deben estar orgullosos de sus raíces. Es importante asimilarse a otra cultura sin perder su propio modo de ser. Como hispanos, pueden hacer una gran aportación no sólo a la comunidad hispana sino a la comunidad en general. Pero todo empieza con la familia; ésas son sus raíces. Hay que respetar primero a sus padres, y ellos les ayudarán a alcanzar el éxito.

Answers to Activity 11
1. los dos   3. Adriana   5. Adriana
2. José Luis   4. José Luis

One-Stop Planner CD-ROM

To preview all resources available for this chapter, use the **One-Stop Planner CD-ROM**, Disc 3.

Segundo paso

20 p. 293

1. José Luis era el chico más inteligente en el colegio. Siempre sacó buenas notas, pero no va a poder asistir a la universidad nacional. No sé por qué.

2. ¿Te acuerdas de Marilú? Ella habla perfectamente seis lenguas: español, francés, alemán, italiano, inglés y árabe. Ella dice que su facilidad con los idiomas se debe a sus profesores de lengua. Siempre dije que la universidad tiene los mejores profesores de idiomas.

3. Miguel no tiene nada de ritmo ni sabe absolutamente nada de música. ¡Imagina mi sorpresa cuando vi su nombre entre los miembros de la sinfónica! ¿Miguel Sánchez tocando el violín en la sinfónica? No era él. Era otra persona que tenía el mismo nombre.

4. Marco habla perfectamente el español. No lo habla como extranjero y puede conversar con cualquier persona que hable español. Marco dice que por el hecho de haber vivido cinco años en México habla muy bien el español. Y yo sí se lo creo.

5. Me encontré a Kira el viernes en un restaurante. Ahora ella es la directora de un banco muy importante del país. Le pregunté a qué se debía su éxito. Ella dijo que sus años de estudio resultaron en un buen trabajo. Y se lo merece.

6. Andrés López sorprendió a todos en la universidad. Podía leer libros en alemán de un día para otro y además escribía alemán perfectamente. Lo que nadie sabía era que Andrés es de Alemania, así que sabe muy bien el alemán.

Answers to Activity 20
1. no   3. no   5. sí
2. sí   4. sí   6. sí

26 p. 295

1. Es un maestro en las canchas de tenis. Juega tenis cuatro horas diarias todos los días, pero es muy desorganizado. Tenía la intención de jugar un poco más hoy, pero se le ha perdido su raqueta.

2. Andar de compras es su deporte favorito: el lunes, unos zapatos nuevos; el martes, unos pantalones; el miércoles, un juguete para sus sobrinos. No se detiene. Hoy fue al almacén con la intención de comprarse una maleta nueva.

3. Desde que era niña le gustaba copiar los dibujos de las tiras cómicas. Ahí estaba días enteros dibujando. Y siempre dibujaba con la idea de regalar el dibujo a un amigo o familiar. Hoy hizo un dibujo para dárselo a su padre.

4. Le encantan los animales. Con el tiempo, se hizo veterinaria y ahora es dueña de una granja. ¡Tiene un gran corazón y adora a su abuela! Compró un pájaro bellísimo con la idea de dárselo a su abuela como regalo.

Answers to Activity 26
1. b   3. d
2. c   4. a

Repaso

1 p. 306

1. Nunca ha querido comprar un despertador nuevo. El que tiene es muy viejo y por lo tanto no funciona muy bien. Esta mañana su despertador no funcionó, así que se despertó tarde y perdió el autobús para ir al trabajo. Por poco y lo despiden.

2. Logró superar muchos obstáculos en la vida, pero al final alcanzó el éxito en el maratón. Está agradecido con el entrenador porque siempre lo apoyó. Puso mucho esfuerzo en ganar la carrera y al fin ganó el premio.

3. Se siente orgulloso de pertenecer al equipo de la escuela y entrena todos los días. Le fascina el reto de superarse. Por eso, estoy seguro que cuando sea mayor, va a jugar con un equipo profesional como segunda base.

4. Se siente orgullosa de haber alcanzado el éxito en los deportes. Su aportación al éxito del programa deportivo de la escuela es muy importante. Después de graduarse de la escuela va a jugar en un equipo de la universidad.

5. Le fascina hablar con la gente. Su modo de ser es muy abierto, extrovertido. Sabe español muy bien y como hay muchos jugadores hispanos no hay nadie que le pueda negar una entrevista. Hoy fue al partido con la intención de entrevistar a los jugadores.

Answers to Repaso Activity 1
1. b
2. no corresponde
3. c
4. a
5. d

Capítulo 10: La riqueza cultural
Suggested Lesson Plans *50-Minute Schedule*

Day 1

CHAPTER OPENER 5 min.
- Focusing on Outcomes, ATE, p. 281
- Discuss History Link, ATE, p. 280.

DE ANTEMANO 40 min.
- Presenting **De antemano** and Preteaching Vocabulary, ATE, p. 282
- Present the Culture Note, ATE, p. 283.
- Activities 1–5, p. 284, and Comprehension Check, ATE, p. 284

Wrap-Up 5 min.
- Have students share responses from Activity 5, p. 284.

Homework Options
Cuaderno de actividades, p. 109, Activities 1–2

Day 2

PRIMER PASO
Quick Review 5 min.
- Check homework.
- Bell Work, ATE, p. 285

Así se dice, p. 285 20 min.
- Presenting **Así se dice**, ATE, p. 285
- Do Activity 6 with the Audio CD, p. 285.
- Do Activity 7, p. 285.

Vocabulario, p. 286 20 min.
- Presenting **Vocabulario**, ATE, p. 286
- Present **También se puede decir...**, p. 286.
- Follow the suggestion in Challenge, ATE, p. 286, then do Activity 8, p. 286.
- Have students do Activity 9 in pairs, p. 286.

Wrap-Up 5 min.
- Have students guess whose accomplishments you describe.

Homework Options
Cuaderno de actividades, p. 110, Activities 3–5
Cuaderno de gramática, pp. 78–79, Activities 1–3

Day 3

PRIMER PASO
Quick Review 5 min.
- Check homework.

Vocabulario, p. 287 35 min.
- Presenting **Vocabulario**, ATE, p. 287
- Do Activity 10, p. 287.
- Do Activity 11 with the Audio CD, p. 287.
- Have students do Activity 12 in groups, p. 287.
- Read the **Nota cultural**, p. 288. Then present the Culture Note, ATE, p. 288.

Wrap-Up 10 min.
- Follow Vocabulary Practice Suggestions 2 and 4 for Teaching Transparency 10-1.

Homework Options
Cuaderno de actividades, pp. 111–112, Activities 6, 9
Cuaderno de gramática, pp. 79–80, Activities 4–5

Day 4

PRIMER PASO
Quick Review 5 min.
- Check homework.

Así se dice, p. 288 15 min.
- Presenting **Así se dice**, ATE, p. 288
- Do Activity 13, p. 288.

Gramática, p. 289 25 min.
- Presenting **Gramática**, ATE, p. 289
- **Más práctica gramatical,** p. 303, Activity 2
- Have students do Activity 14 in pairs, p. 289.
- Do Activity 15, p. 289.

Wrap-Up 5 min.
- Discuss the content and format of Quiz 10-1.

Homework Options
Study for Quiz 10-1.
Cuaderno de actividades, pp. 111–113, Activities 7–8, 10–11
Cuaderno de gramática, pp. 80–81, Activities 6–9

Day 5

PRIMER PASO
Quick Review 10 min.
- Check homework.
- Review the content of **Primer paso**.

Quiz 20 min.
- Administer Quiz 10-1A, 10-1B, or a combination of the two.

¡ADELANTE! 15 min.
- Presenting **¡Adelante!** and Preteaching Vocabulary, ATE, p. 290
- Activities 16–18, pp. 290–291, and Comprehension Check, ATE, p. 291
- Present the Culture Note, ATE, p. 291.

Wrap-Up 5 min.
- Do the Additional Practice with the class, ATE, p. 291.

Homework Options
Activity 19, p. 291
Cuaderno de actividades, p. 114, Activities 12–14

Day 6

SEGUNDO PASO
Quick Review 5 min.
- Check homework.
- Bell Work, ATE, p. 293

PANORAMA CULTURAL 10 min.
- Presenting **Panorama cultural**, ATE, p. 292
- Present the Language Notes, ATE, p. 292.

Así se dice, p. 293 30 min.
- Presenting **Así se dice/Nota gramatical,** p. 293
- Do Activity 20 with the Audio CD, p. 293.
- Do Activity 21, p. 293.
- Have students do Activity 22 in pairs, p. 294.

Wrap-Up 5 min.
- Do Pair Work, ATE, p. 293.

Homework Options
Cuaderno de actividades, pp. 115–116, Activities 15–16
Cuaderno de gramática, pp. 82–83, Activities 10–12

One-Stop Planner CD-ROM

For alternative lesson plans by chapter section, to create your own customized plans, or to preview all resources available for this chapter, use the **One-Stop Planner CD-ROM**, Disc 3.

 For additional homework suggestions, see activities accompanied by this symbol throughout the chapter.

Day 7

SEGUNDO PASO
Quick Review 10 min.
- Check homework.
- Follow Suggestion 2 for Teaching Transparency 10-2.

Vocabulario, p. 294 35 min.
- Presenting **Vocabulario**, ATE, p. 294
- Do Slower Pace or Group Work, ATE, p. 294.
- Review **¿Te acuerdas?**, p. 294.
- Have students do Activity 23 in pairs, p. 294.
- Do Activity 24, p. 294.
- Have students do Activity 25 in pairs, p. 295.

Wrap-Up 5 min.
- Follow Vocabulary Practice Suggestion 1 for Teaching Transparency 10-2.

Homework Options
Cuaderno de actividades, p. 117, Activities 17–18
Cuaderno de gramática, pp. 83–85, Activities 13–17

Day 8

SEGUNDO PASO
Quick Review 5 min.
- Check homework.

Así se dice, p. 295 25 min.
- Presenting **Así se dice**, ATE, p. 295
- Do Activity 26 with the Audio CD, p. 295.
- Do Activity 27, p. 295.
- Have students do Activity 28 in pairs, p. 295.

Gramática de repaso, p. 296 15 min.
- Presenting **Gramática de repaso**, ATE, p. 296
- Do Activity 29, p. 296.
- Read the **Nota cultural**, p. 296.
- Do Activity 30, p. 296.

Wrap-Up 5 min.
- Discuss the content and format of Quiz 10-2.

Homework Options
Study for Quiz 10-2.
Cuaderno de actividades, p. 118, Activities 19–20
Cuaderno de gramática, pp. 85–86, Activities 18–20

Day 9

SEGUNDO PASO
Quick Review 5 min.
- Check homework.

Gramática de repaso, p. 296 10 min.
- Have students do Activity 31, then peer-edit their work, p. 296.

ENCUENTRO CULTURAL 10 min.
- Presenting **Encuentro cultural**, ATE, p. 297
- Present the Culture Note, ATE, p. 297.

Quiz 20 min.
- Administer Quiz 10-2A, 10-2B, or a combination of the two.

Wrap-Up 5 min.
- Read and discuss the **Vamos a escribir** assignment, p. 301.

Homework Options
Vamos a escribir, p. 301

Day 10

VAMOS A LEER
Quick Review 5 min.
- Collect homework.

VAMOS A LEER, p. 298 40 min.
- Read the **Estrategia** and **¿Te acuerdas?**, p. 298.
- Do Activities A–B, pp. 298–299.
- Follow the Prereading suggestions, ATE, p. 298.
- Do Activities C–D, pp. 299–300.
- Follow the Reading suggestions, ATE, p. 299.
- Do Activities E–G, p. 300.

Wrap-Up 5 min.
- Do the Visual Learners Activity, ATE, p. 300.

Homework Options
Cuaderno de actividades, pp. 119–120, Activities 21–25

Day 11

REPASO
Quick Review 5 min.
- Check homework.

REPASO, p. 306 40 min.
- Do Activity 1 with the Audio CD, p. 306.
- Have students do Activities 2 and 6 in pairs, pp. 306–307.
- Do Activities 3–4 and 7, pp. 306–307.
- Have students do Activity 5, then peer-edit their work, p. 307.
- Have students do Activity 8 in pairs, p. 307.

Wrap-Up 5 min.
- Follow the Teaching Suggestion for **Vocabulario**, ATE, p. 309.

Homework Options
A ver si puedo..., p. 308

Day 12

REPASO
Quick Review 5 min.
- Check homework.

Chapter Review 40 min.
- Review Chapter 10. Choose from **Más práctica gramatical**, Grammar Tutor for Students of Spanish, Activities for Communication, Listening Activities, Interactive CD-ROM Tutor, or **Juegos interactivos**.

Wrap-Up 5 min.
- Discuss the content of the Chapter 10 Test.

Homework Options
Study for the Chapter 10 Test.

Assessment

Quick Review 5 min.
- Answer any questions students may have.

Test, Chapter 10 45 min.
- Administer Chapter 10 Test. Select from Testing Program, Alternative Assessment Guide, Test Generator, or Standardized Assessment Tutor.

Capítulo 10: La riqueza cultural
Suggested Lesson Plans 90-*Minute Block Schedule*

Block 1

CHAPTER OPENER 5 min.
- Focusing on Outcomes, ATE, p. 281
- Discuss History Link, ATE, p. 280.

DE ANTEMANO 40 min.
- Presenting **De antemano** and Preteaching Vocabulary, ATE, p. 282
- Present the Culture Note, ATE, p. 283.
- Activities 1–5, p. 284, and Comprehension Check, ATE, p. 284

PRIMER PASO
Así se dice, p. 285 20 min.
- Presenting **Así se dice**, ATE, p. 285
- Do Activity 6 with the Audio CD, p. 285.
- Do Activity 7, p. 285.

Vocabulario, p. 286 20 min.
- Presenting **Vocabulario**, ATE, p. 286
- Present **También se puede decir...**, p. 286.
- Follow the suggestion in Challenge, ATE, p. 286, then do Activity 8, p. 286.
- Have students do Activity 9 in pairs, p. 286.

Wrap-Up 5 min.
- Have students guess the person whose accomplishments you describe.

Homework Options
Cuaderno de actividades, pp. 109–110, Activities 1–5
Cuaderno de gramática, pp. 78–79, Activities 1–3

Block 2

PRIMER PASO
Quick Review 10 min.
- Check homework.

Vocabulario, p. 287 35 min.
- Presenting **Vocabulario**, ATE, p. 287
- Do Activity 10, p. 287.
- Do Activity 11 with the Audio CD, p. 287.
- Have students do Activity 12 in groups, p. 287.
- Read the **Nota cultural**, p. 288. Then present the Culture Note, ATE, p. 288.

Así se dice, p. 288 15 min.
- Presenting **Así se dice**, ATE, p. 288
- Do Activity 13, p. 288.

Gramática, p. 289 25 min.
- Presenting **Gramática**, ATE, p. 289
- **Más práctica gramatical**, p. 303, Activity 2
- Have students do Activity 14 in pairs, p. 289.
- Do Activity 15, p. 289.

Wrap-Up 5 min.
- Discuss the content and format of Quiz 10-1.

Homework Options
Study for Quiz 10-1.
Cuaderno de actividades, pp. 111–113, Activities 6–11
Cuaderno de gramática, pp. 79–81, Activities 4–9

Block 3

PRIMER PASO
Quick Review 10 min.
- Check homework.

Así se dice/Vocabulario/Gramática, pp. 285–289 15 min.
- Review the content of **Primer paso.**
- Follow Suggestions 3–4 for Teaching Transparency 10-1.

Quiz 20 min.
- Administer Quiz 10-1A, 10-1B, or a combination of the two.

PANORAMA CULTURAL 10 min.
- Presenting **Panorama cultural**, ATE, p. 292.
- Present the Language Notes, ATE, p. 292.

¡ADELANTE! 25 min.
- Presenting **¡Adelante!** and Preteaching Vocabulary, ATE, p. 290
- Activities 16–19, pp. 290–291, and Comprehension Check, ATE, p. 291
- Present the Culture Note, ATE, p. 291.

Wrap-Up 10 min.
- Do the Additional Practice with the class, ATE, p. 291.

Homework Options
Cuaderno de actividades, p. 114, Activities 12–14
Thinking Critically activity, ATE, p. 291

One-Stop Planner CD-ROM

For alternative lesson plans by chapter section, to create your own customized plans, or to preview all resources available for this chapter, use the **One-Stop Planner CD-ROM**, Disc 3.

 For additional homework suggestions, see activities accompanied by this symbol throughout the chapter.

Block 4

SEGUNDO PASO

Quick Review 5 min.
- Check homework.
- Bell Work, ATE, p. 293

Así se dice/Nota gramatical, p. 293 30 min.
- Presenting **Así se dice,** p. 293
- Do Activity 20 with the Audio CD, p. 293.
- Do Activity 21, p. 293.
- Have students do Activity 22 in pairs, p. 294.

Vocabulario, p. 294 35 min.
- Presenting **Vocabulario,** ATE, p. 294
- Review **¿Te acuerdas?,** p. 294.
- Have students do Activity 23 in pairs, p. 294.
- Do Activity 24, p. 294.
- Have students do Activity 25 in pairs, p. 295.

Así se dice, p. 295 15 min.
- Presenting **Así se dice,** ATE, p. 295
- Do Activity 26 with the Audio CD, p. 295.
- Do Activity 27, p. 295.

Wrap-Up 5 min.
- Follow Suggestion 2 for Teaching Transparency 10-2.

Homework Options
Cuaderno de actividades, pp. 115–117, Activities 15–18
Cuaderno de gramática, pp. 82–85, Activities 10–17

Block 5

SEGUNDO PASO

Quick Review 10 min.
- Check homework.

Así se dice, p. 295 10 min.
- Review **Así se dice** expressions, p. 295.
- Have students do Activity 28 in pairs, p. 295.

Gramática de repaso, p. 296 25 min.
- Presenting **Gramática de repaso,** ATE, p. 296
- Do Activity 29, p. 296.
- Read the **Nota cultural,** p. 296.
- Do Activity 30, p. 296.
- Have students do Activity 31, then peer-edit their work, p. 296.

ENCUENTRO CULTURAL 10 min.
- Presenting **Encuentro cultural,** ATE, p. 297
- Present the Culture Note, ATE, p. 297.

VAMOS A LEER 30 min.
- Read the **Estrategia** and **¿Te acuerdas?,** p. 298.
- Do Activities A–B, pp. 298–299.
- Do Activities C–D, pp. 299–300.

Wrap-Up 5 min.
- Follow the Reading suggestions, ATE, p. 299.
- Discuss the content and format of Quiz 10-2.

Homework Options
Study for Quiz 10-2.
Cuaderno de actividades, p. 118, Activities 19–20
Cuaderno de gramática, pp. 85–86, Activities 18–20

Block 6

SEGUNDO PASO

Quick Review 10 min.
- Check homework.
- Review the content and format of **Segundo paso.**

Quiz 20 min.
- Administer Quiz 10-2A, 10-2B, or a combination of the two.

VAMOS A LEER 20 min.
- Do Activities E–G, p. 300.

REPASO 35 min.
- Do Activity 1 with the Audio CD, p. 306.
- Have students do Activities 2, 6, and 8 in pairs, pp. 306–307.
- Do Activities 3–5 and 7, pp. 306–307.

Wrap-Up 5 min.
- Discuss the content and format of the Chapter 10 Test.

Homework Options
Study for the Chapter 10 Test.
Vamos a escribir, p. 301
A ver si puedo..., p. 308
Cuaderno de actividades, pp. 119–120, Activities 21–25

Block 7

REPASO

Quick Review 10 min.
- Check and/or collect homework.

Chapter Review 35 min.
- Review Chapter 10. Choose from **Más práctica gramatical,** Grammar Tutor for Students of Spanish, Activities for Communication, Listening Activities, Interactive CD-ROM Tutor, or **Juegos interactivos.**

Test, Chapter 10 45 min.
- Administer Chapter 10 Test. Select from Testing Program, Alternative Assessment Guide, Test Generator, or Standardized Assessment Tutor.

CAPÍTULO 10

One-Stop Planner CD-ROM

For resource information, see the **One-Stop Planner**, Disc 3.

Pacing Tips

Primer paso contains the majority of this chapter's vocabulary. This section also introduces new uses of the subjunctive. Encourage students to share their experiences or perceptions of cultural diversity. For additional pacing tips, see Suggested Lesson Plans, pp. 279I–279L.

Meeting the Standards

Communication
- Talking about accomplishments, p. 285
- Talking about future plans, p. 288
- Language Notes, pp. 292, 298

Cultures
- Culture Notes, pp. 281, 283, 288, 291, 297, 298
- Multicultural Link, p. 286
- Background Information, p. 288
- Panorama cultural, p. 292
- Nota cultural, p. 296
- Encuentro cultural, p. 297

Connections
- History Link, pp. 280, 291
- Native Speakers, p. 287
- Native Speakers, p. 299

Comparisons
- Multicultural Link, p. 297
- Comparing and Contrasting, p. 299

Communities
- Multicultural Link, p. 286
- Nota cultural, p. 288
- Community Link, p. 297
- Additional Practice, p. 307

Connections and Comparisons

History Link

Tell students that immigrants have been an important part of New York City for generations. Between 1892 and 1954, over 12 million people immigrated to the United States through Ellis Island in New York Harbor. Approximately 30 percent of the city's current residents were born in another country. Ellis Island became a national historic site in 1965. After closing in the 1980s for restoration, the island reopened in 1990 as the Ellis Island Immigration Museum. Have students research how their families arrived in the U.S. Ask volunteers to report what they learn to the class, using as much Spanish as possible.

Objectives

In this chapter you will learn to

Primer paso

- talk about accomplishments
- talk about future plans

Segundo paso

- express cause and effect
- express intention and purpose

 internet

go.hrw.com

MARCAR: go.hrw.com
PALABRA CLAVE:
WV3 NEW YORK-10

◀ **Los dominicanos de Nueva York se sienten muy orgullosos de su herencia cultural.**

Chapter Opener

CAPÍTULO 10

Photo Flash!
The young adults in this photograph are celebrating their close ties to the Dominican Republic by participating in this parade in downtown New York City. It is a source of pride to continually learn about their cultural heritage and celebrate it.

Focusing on Outcomes
Ask students to think of situations in which they would use the different chapter outcomes. What are some words or expressions they already know that they could use in these situations?

Cultures and Communities

Culture Note
Tell students that New York City is one of the most ethnically and culturally diverse cities in the world. The public schools offer bilingual instruction in seven foreign languages and additional classes in eight others. Depending on the neighborhood you are in, there will likely be advertisements and traffic signs in Spanish, Chinese, Hebrew, Italian, Greek, or Russian. There are several non-English newspapers and magazines in circulation in New York, and over 200 internationally-based banks. Ask students to research one cultural community of New York City, taking into account its language, cuisine, and artistic and political influence. They should report to the class in Spanish the information they learn.

Teaching Resources
pp. 282–284

PRINT
▶ Lesson Planner, p. 48
▶ Video Guide, pp. 66–67, 69
▶ Cuaderno de actividades, p. 109

MEDIA
▶ One-Stop Planner
▶ Video Program
  Contigo en la distancia
  Videocassette 4, 01:10–05:29
  Videocassette 5 (captioned version), 50:49–55:08
▶ Audio Compact Discs, CD 10, Trs. 1–6

Presenting
De antemano

Have students skim the responses to the interview questions in **De antemano** and discuss the definition of the word **hispano** as it is presented in **Estrategia para comprender**. Play the Audio CD and have students list expressions used to talk about accomplishments. Next, present the Preteaching Vocabulary.

DE ANTEMANO • ¿Qué significa ser hispano?

Cuaderno de actividades, p. 109, Acts. 1–2

CD 10
Trs. 1–6

Estrategia para comprender
La palabra *hispano* en los Estados Unidos se refiere a gente de muchos países y diversos grupos étnicos, pero también significa mucho más. Antes de comenzar, piensa en lo que has aprendido de los hispanohablantes en tus estudios del español. Luego lee cómo explicaron la palabra *hispano* varios estudiantes de la Sra. Dora Villani del colegio John F. Kennedy en Nueva York.

Todos somos diferentes y tenemos diferentes opiniones sobre lo que significa ser hispano. Queremos saber lo que tú piensas y qué planes tienes para el futuro.

1. ¿Qué significa ser hispano para ti?
2. En tu opinión, ¿cómo te ve la gente de origen no hispano?
3. Si acabas de venir a los Estados Unidos, ¿has tenido que adaptarte o asimilarte a la cultura norteamericana? ¿Cómo?
4. ¿Has compartido tu cultura con la gente no hispana?
5. ¿De qué estás orgulloso(a)?
6. ¿Qué quieres lograr antes de graduarte de la escuela secundaria?
7. ¿Qué quieres hacer cuando seas mayor? ¿Por qué?

" Los hispanos tenemos una gran cultura. "

Teany Hidalgo

Me llamo Teany Hidalgo. Tengo dieciséis años y soy de la República Dominicana. Yo estoy muy orgullosa de ser hispana porque los hispanos tenemos una gran cultura. Somos un grupo étnico que tiene costumbres muy variadas y gentes de diferentes países. Quienes vivimos en los Estados Unidos hemos aprendido a superarnos y a tener buenas profesiones. Mi objetivo es llegar a ser ingeniera de computación, y con la ayuda de mi familia sé que lo voy a alcanzar. Mi intención es cambiar todos los estereotipos que la gente tiene de los hispanos para que todos podamos tener un futuro feliz.

Mi nombre es Jessica Jiménez y nací en el Bronx. Estoy en el equipo de esgrima. Gané un trofeo el año pasado. Yo he vivido en Puerto Rico y es muy distinto a vivir aquí en los Estados Unidos. Aquí hay algunas personas que discriminan a otras

" Me siento orgullosa de ser hispana. "

Jessica Jiménez

Preteaching Vocabulary

Recognizing Cognates

De antemano contains several words that students will be able to recognize as cognates. (**diferente, futuro, cultura, étnico, discriminan, asimilar, compromiso, adaptarnos, oportunidad**)

Have students find these and determine what each student is saying about what it means to him or her to be Hispanic.

por el hecho de tener padres hispanos. Yo me siento orgullosa de ser hispana porque, además del inglés, sé hablar muy bien el español. Cuando sea mayor, quiero ser médica para ayudar a otras personas, especialmente a los hispanos que no saben expresarse en inglés.

❝Ser hispano aquí es para mí un desafío a ser mejor.❞
Paul Bravo

Me llamo Paul Bravo. Soy colombiano y vivo en el Bronx, Nueva York. Me interesa mucho el arte. Quiero llegar a ser arquitecto cuando sea mayor. Me siento parte de una colectividad que, sin perder su modo de ser, trata de asimilar la cultura estadounidense. Ser hispano aquí esta para mí un desafío a ser mejor, porque tengo que asimilar dos culturas. También es un compromiso porque tengo que llegar a ser igual o mejor que otros hipanos que han triunfado en todos los ámbitos de esta sociedad. Me siento muy orgulloso de ser hispano.

Me llamo Mayra Rivera y soy puertorriqueña. Tengo catorce años. Para mí, ser hispana en los Estados Unidos es un orgullo y a la vez un reto. Es un orgullo porque puedo expresarme en dos idiomas y compartir mis costumbres y tradiciones con mis amigos no hispanos. Es un reto porque es una nueva sociedad, con diferentes costumbres a las cuales debemos adaptarnos, y un nuevo idioma que tenemos que aprender. Si no dominamos el idioma, las oportunidades de

❝Ser hispana en los Estados Unidos es un orgullo.❞
Mayra Rivera

triunfar en este país son pocas. Cuando uno no sabe el idioma la discriminación es mayor. Yo he puesto todo mi esfuerzo en aprender inglés y adaptarme. Pienso que todos los hispanos debemos sentirnos orgullosos de nuestra historia y no olvidar nunca nuestras raíces y costumbres.

Mi nombre es Ruth Cruz y soy nicaragüense. Ahora vivo en la ciudad de Nueva York. Tengo dieciséis años. Para mí, ser hispana es un orgullo. Este país me ha abierto las puertas para seguir adelante. Desde que vine a este país he estudiado mucho para así un día poder realizar mis metas. Aquí he podido conocer las diferentes culturas que existen y al mismo tiempo compartir la mía. Es muy importante tratar de superarnos en este país para que todos puedan tener en alto el nombre de los hispanos. Todos debemos hacer un esfuerzo,

❝Este país me ha abierto las puertas para seguir adelante.❞
Ruth Cruz

especialmente la juventud. Nosotros tenemos la mayor oportunidad ya que estamos estudiando. Lo tenemos que lograr para nuestro futuro. Estoy segura que poco a poco lo lograremos.

DE ANTEMANO

CAPÍTULO 10

Tactile/Visual Learners
As students listen to **De antemano**, display the map transparency of each speaker's country of origin. Then give students a copy of the transparency master for Map 2 (**Europa y las Américas**) and have students outline the country each speaker is from and write his or her name by that country.

Culture Note
The word **latino** is often used instead of **hispano** or *Hispanic*. In his book *Latinos: A Biography of the People,* Earl Shorris states that **latino** is preferred in Chicago and California, while **hispano** or *Hispanic* are the preferred terms in the Southwest. In New York, **latino, hispano,** and *Hispanic* are all used.

 ### Contigo en la distancia
You may choose to show students Episode 10: *Cuando sea mayor...* now or wait until later in the chapter. In the video, the end of the school year approaches and Javier starts to feel nervous about his trip to Mexico. He expresses pride in being Andalusian and confesses that it will be difficult to leave Seville for such a long time. He does not lose his sense of humor, however, and he plays along with Zoraida as she says sarcastically that she hopes to be just like him when she grows up. He also begins to suspect that Alejandra likes Sergio and not him.

Native Speakers

4 Have native speakers work in pairs to brainstorm as many alternative expressions as possible.

Teaching Suggestion

5 Have students write about family traditions, cultural traditions, or the pride they take in the language(s) they speak. Ask volunteers to share this information with the class.

Answers

1
1. Jessica
2. Teany
3. Mayra, Ruth
4. Ruth
5. Paul
6. Mayra
7. Paul

2 *Possible answers:*
1. Ruth
2. Teany
3. Paul
4. Jessica
5. Teany
6. Mayra, Ruth
7. Paul
8. Teany
9. Mayra, Paul
10. Jessica

3 *Possible answers:*
1. Para ellos ser hispano es un reto, un desafío y algo de lo cual uno debe sentirse orgulloso.
2. Sí, dicen que uno puede asimilarse pero debe conservar la identidad hispana.
3. Dicen que se debe ser bilingüe para que muchas puertas se abran y se pueda triunfar.

4 *Possible answers:*
estoy muy orgullosa, tenemos una gran cultura, mi intención es, me siento orgullosa, cuando sea mayor, me interesa mucho el arte, me siento parte de una colectividad, es un orgullo y a la vez un reto, yo he puesto todo mi esfuerzo, es muy importante tratar de superarnos, estoy segura de que poco a poco lo lograremos

7
1. Gloria ha logrado ser una artista "crossover" (triunfar en el mercado hispano y anglo).
2. Ha superado la pobreza, el exilio, el no hablar inglés, la muerte de su papá y un accidente en que se rompió la espalda.
3. Los superó con la disciplina y el esfuerzo.
4. La comunidad hispana se siente orgullosa de ella.

These activities check for comprehension only. Students should not yet be expected to produce language modeled in De antemano.

1 **¿A quién se refiere?** See answers below.

Indica a quién se refiere cada frase.

1. Quiere ser médico(a) porque quiere ayudar a los hispanos que no saben hablar el inglés.
2. Cuando sea mayor, va a cambiar todos los estereotipos que la gente tiene de los hispanos.
3. Quieren compartir su cultura con sus amigos no hispanos.
4. Según ella, la juventud tiene la mayor oportunidad de mejorarse.
5. Le gusta mucho el arte y quiere llegar a ser arquitecto(a).
6. Dice que el hispano no debe olvidar nunca sus costumbres cuando llegue a Estados Unidos.
7. Piensa que tiene que ser igual o mejor que los otros hispanos.

2 **¿Quién lo diría?** See possible answers below.

Indica quién diría las siguientes oraciones.

Mayra   **Paul**   **Teany**   **Jessica**   **Ruth**

1. Este país me ha dado muchas oportunidades para triunfar.
2. La cultura hispana es muy rica y tiene mucha diversidad.
3. Ser hispano me inspira a ser mejor.
4. Es una ventaja ser bilingüe; sé hablar muy bien el inglés y el español.
5. Para mí, los estudios y el trabajo son importantísimos para que siga adelante.
6. Me gusta compartir mis costumbres con gente no hispana.
7. Los hispanos asimilan la cultura de Estados Unidos pero sin perder su identidad.
8. No quiero que la gente estereotipe a los hispanos y espero cambiar esas actitudes.
9. Es importante adaptarse a la cultura.
10. Quiero ayudar a los hispanos que no son bilingües.

3 **¿Entendiste?** See answers below.

Contesta las preguntas según la información de las entrevistas.

1. ¿Qué opinan estos jóvenes del hecho de ser hispanos?
2. ¿Quieren conservar sus tradiciones estos jóvenes? ¿Por qué?
3. ¿Qué opinan ellos sobre el inglés? ¿Qué opinan sobre ser bilingües?

4 **¿Cómo lo dicen?** See answers below.

Busca las expresiones que usan estos jóvenes hispanohablantes para expresar su orgullo, sus opiniones, sus valores y sus esperanzas para el futuro.

5 **Ahora te toca a ti**

Prepara una lista de las cosas que te hacen sentir orgulloso(a) de tu propio grupo étnico, cultural o lingüístico.

Comprehension Check

Tactile Learners

1 Have students create collector's cards (like baseball cards) for each individual in **De antemano.** On separate index cards or larger pieces of cardboard, have students write each character's name or sketch his or her picture. On the reverse side of the cards, ask them to write the person's age, country of origin, a physical description, and two sentences about him or her.

Challenge

2 When students have finished making the cards from the previous activity, collect and shuffle all the cards. Call on a student to pick a card. He or she then identifies the person on the card and makes a statement that he or she thinks that character would say. The class is to say **cierto** or **falso,** according to what they have learned in **De antemano.**

Así se dice

Talking about accomplishments

Si quieres hablar de las cosas de las que estás orgulloso(a), puedes decir:

Yo **puse todo mi esfuerzo** en aprender el inglés.
. . . *I put a lot of effort into* . . .

Toshiro **domina el francés**. . . . *speaks French very well.*

Edmundo **se siente orgulloso de haber** ganado el premio.
. . . *feels proud of having* . . .

Alicia **logró superar muchos obstáculos** en su vida.
. . . *succeeded in overcoming many obstacles* . . .

Alcancé éxito en mi papel de Romeo. . . . *achieved success in* . . .

Birgitte **tuvo mucho éxito** este año; ganó todas las competencias de música.

Muchos hispanos **han triunfado** en los campos de ciencia y medicina.
. . . *have succeeded* . . .

> Cuaderno de actividades, pp. 110, 112 Acts. 3, 9

6 **Eso no es lógico** Script and answers on p. 279G.

Escuchemos/Escribamos Escucha las siguientes conversaciones e indica si las respuestas son **lógicas** o **ilógicas**. Luego escucha otra vez y cambia las respuestas ilógicas para que sean lógicas.

CD 10 Tr. 7

7 **El camino al éxito** See answers below.

Leamos/Escribamos Lee el siguiente artículo sobre Gloria Estefan, la cantante cubanoamericana. Después contesta las preguntas.

1. ¿Qué ha logrado Gloria Estefan?
2. ¿Qué obstáculos ha superado ella?
3. ¿Cómo los superó?
4. ¿Qué piensan de Gloria los hispanos?

Gloria Estefan

SUPERANDO OBSTÁCULOS, ALCANZANDO ÉXITO

Gloria Estefan ha alcanzado éxito en su profesión y ha logrado algo no muy común para los cantantes hispanos: ser artista "crossover". Es decir, tiene éxitos en el mercado anglo e hispano. Sin embargo, el camino hacia el éxito no ha sido fácil para esta cubanoamericana. Ha superado muchos obstáculos. Salió de Cuba con sus papás cuando era muy joven. Llegaron a Miami sin mucho dinero y sin hablar el inglés. Su papá murió cuando ella tenía 16 años. En el año 1990 se rompió la espalda en un terrible accidente de autobús. Los que pensaban que Gloria nunca volvería a caminar no la conocían. Es una mujer de mucha disciplina y puso todo su esfuerzo en recuperarse del accidente. La comunidad hispana se siente orgullosa de tener a Gloria como miembro de la familia.

Communication for All Students

Slower Pace

6 You may want to play the audio recording several times and have students write this activity as a dictation. Then have students change the illogical statements to logical ones.

Challenge

7 After students have read the article about Gloria Estefan and have answered the four questions, ask them to write a brief paragraph about another famous person using the four questions in this exercise as a guideline.

Primer paso

CAPÍTULO 10

Teaching Resources
pp. 285–289

PRINT
- Lesson Planner, p. 48
- Listening Activities, pp. 75, 79–80
- Activities for Communication, pp. 37–38, 78, 80, 107–108
- Cuaderno de gramática, pp. 78–81
- Grammar Tutor for Students of Spanish, Chapter 10
- Cuaderno de actividades, pp. 110–113
- Cuaderno para hispanohablantes, pp. 46–50
- Testing Program, pp. 213–216
- Alternative Assessment Guide, p. 39
- Student Make-Up Assignments, Chapter 10

MEDIA
- One-Stop Planner
- Audio Compact Discs, CD 10, Trs. 7–8, 23–25, 19
- Teaching Transparencies 10-1; **Más práctica gramatical** Answers; Cuaderno de gramática Answers
- Interactive CD-ROM Tutor, Disc 3

 Bell Work

On the board or on a transparency, write: **Escribe varios ejemplos de la influencia hispana en los Estados Unidos.**

Presenting
Así se dice

Use the expressions in original sentences in which you talk about the accomplishments of famous or successful people. As you describe someone's accomplishments, see whether students can name different people who fit the description.

Teaching Resources
pp. 285–289

PRINT
▸ Lesson Planner, p. 48
▸ Listening Activities, pp. 75, 79–80
▸ Activities for Communication, pp. 37–38, 78, 80, 107–108
▸ Cuaderno de gramática, pp. 78–81
▸ Grammar Tutor for Students of Spanish, Chapter 10
▸ Cuaderno de actividades, pp. 110–113
▸ Cuaderno para hispanohablantes, pp. 46–50
▸ Testing Program, pp. 213–216
▸ Alternative Assessment Guide, p. 39
▸ Student Make-Up Assignments, Chapter 10

MEDIA
▸ One-Stop Planner
▸ Audio Compact Discs, CD 10, Trs. 7–8, 23–25, 19
▸ Teaching Transparencies 10-1; **Más práctica gramatical** Answers; Cuaderno de gramática Answers
▸ Interactive CD-ROM Tutor, Disc 3

Presenting
Vocabulario

Use the new expressions and words to paraphrase the story of Gloria Estefan. You may want to write the new vocabulary items on the board before telling the story, or as you use them. You may choose to tell a similar story about another famous person.

Answers
8 1. c.; Estados Unidos (Nancy López)
2. a.; Cuba (Andy García)
3. f.; España (Salvador Dalí)
4. b.; Venezuela (Ómar Vizquel)
5. e.; España (Plácido Domingo)
6. d.; México (Giselle Fernández)

alcanzar *to achieve, to attain*
aportar *to contribute*
la aportación *contribution*
el esfuerzo *effort*
estar agradecido(a) por *to be grateful for*
el éxito *success, hit song*
el orgullo *pride*
el reto *challenge*
sentirse (ie, i) orgulloso(a) de *to feel proud of*

superar *to overcome*
superarse *to better oneself*
tener éxito *to succeed*

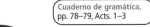
Más práctica gramatical, p. 302, Act. 1

Cuaderno de actividades, p. 110, Acts. 4–5

Cuaderno de gramática, pp. 78–79, Acts. 1–3

También se puede decir…
Se puede decir **el aporte** por **la aportación**. También se dice **triunfar** por **tener éxito** y **desafío** por **reto**.

8 **La aportación hispana** See answers below.
Leamos/Hablemos La aportación de los hispanos al mundo de la literatura, arte, cine y deportes es muy grande. Indica qué persona corresponde a las siguientes descripciones. ¿Sabes también de qué países son?

1. Nancy López

2. Andy García

3. Salvador Dalí

4. Omar Vizquel

5. Plácido Domingo

6. Giselle Fernández

a. Ha alcanzado mucho éxito en varias películas de Hollywood.

b. Se siente orgulloso(a) de haber ganado el premio del Guante de Oro.

c. Ha aportado mucho al campo deportivo así como a su familia.

d. Ha tenido mucho éxito como reportero(a).

e. Ha puesto mucho esfuerzo en superarse en el campo de la ópera.

f. Sus pinturas son el orgullo de su país.

9 **Sus éxitos**

Hablemos Con un(a) compañero(a), habla de las aportaciones que ustedes han hecho a sus familias, a su escuela o a su comunidad. ¿Qué obstáculos han superado para alcanzar el éxito? ¿De qué están más orgullosos(as) en sus vidas? Si quieren, pueden imaginar que su conversación tiene lugar 10 años en el futuro.

Communication for All Students

 Multicultural Link
Ask students to interview a person they know who has experience assimilating into a new culture. This may be someone who has adapted to life in the United States or it can be someone who has lived abroad. Tell them to ask the person about his or her challenges, impressions, and achievements. Although it may be necessary for students to conduct these interviews in English, they should describe the interviews and what they learned from the person in Spanish.

Challenge
8 Ask students: **Además de las aportaciones mencionadas aquí, ¿saben de otras aportaciones hispanas de la literatura, el arte, el cine y los deportes? ¿Saben de qué países son las personas mencionadas?**

Vocabulario

asimilarse *to assimilate*
el compromiso *commitment, obligation*
la costumbre *custom*
criarse *to grow up; to be raised*
encajar *to fit in*

mantener *to preserve, to keep*
el modo de ser *nature, disposition*
las raíces *roots*

| Cuaderno de actividades, p. 111, Act. 6 | Cuaderno de gramática, pp. 79–80, Acts. 4–5 | Más práctica gramatical, p. 302, Act. 1 |

10 **¿Qué palabra es mejor?** H   See answers below.

Leamos/Escribamos Completa las oraciones con la forma correcta de la mejor palabra del **Vocabulario.**

1. **Responsabilidad** y **obligación** son sinónimos de ———.
2. El proceso de hacerse parte de otra cultura se llama ———.
3. El carácter y las costumbres de una persona definen su ———.
4. Muchos cubanoamericanos nacieron en Cuba y ——— allí también.
5. El término "las ———" se refiere al origen de una persona y su familia.
6. ——— quiere decir una tradición o algo que se ha hecho por muchas generaciones.

11 **Consejos para padres y jóvenes hispanos**   Script and answers on p. 279G.

CD 10
Tr. 8

Escuchemos/Hablemos Escucha los consejos que Adriana y José Luis dan a padres y jóvenes hispanos. Luego indica quién diría cada frase: **Adriana, José Luis** o **los dos.**

1. Es necesario que nos asimilemos sin olvidar quiénes somos.
2. Los hispanos pueden aportar mucho a este país.
3. Los padres hispanos deben hacer el esfuerzo de aprender el inglés.
4. Es importante respetar el compromiso que uno tiene con su familia.
5. Es más fácil para los hijos encajar en la sociedad estadounidense.

12 **Costumbres y raíces**

Escribamos/Hablemos Contesta las siguientes preguntas con dos compañeros(as). Comparen y expliquen sus respuestas.

1. ¿Creen Uds. que los ciudadanos nuevos en nuestro país se asimilan fácilmente?
2. ¿Creen Uds. que es posible encajar en una nueva cultura y no olvidar sus raíces al mismo tiempo? ¿Cómo demuestran su orgullo los distintos grupos étnicos aquí en Estados Unidos?
3. ¿Siguen viviendo Uds. ahora en el mismo lugar en que se criaron? ¿Qué dificultades tiene alguien al mudarse *(upon moving)* a un lugar nuevo?
4. ¿Qué costumbres mantienen sus familias? ¿Cuál es el origen de esas costumbres? ¿Creen que es importante mantener las costumbres?

Connections and Comparisons

Multicultural Link

The boy in the photo is reading from the Torah (the first five books of the Old Testament). Jews have long been a presence in the Spanish-speaking world. In the Middle Ages, they played a vital role in the cultural flowering of both Moorish and Christian Spain. In 1492, King Ferdinand and Queen Isabella expelled all Jews from Spain who would not convert to Catholicism. These Jews, who called themselves *Sephardim,* from the Hebrew name for Spain, settled in various Mediterranean lands, where they continued to speak Ladino, a form of medieval Spanish. Although a great many *Sephardim* moved to Israel after its founding in 1948, many live in Latin America. You might have students research the history of Sephardic Jews and their language.

Answers
10 1. compromiso
2. asimilarse
3. modo de ser
4. se criaron
5. raíces
6. La costumbre

Teaching Resources
pp. 285–289

PRINT
▸ Lesson Planner, p. 48
▸ Listening Activities, pp. 75, 79–80
▸ Activities for Communication, pp. 37–38, 78, 80, 107–108
▸ Cuaderno de gramática, pp. 78–81
▸ Grammar Tutor for Students of Spanish, Chapter 10
▸ Cuaderno de actividades, pp. 110–113
▸ Cuaderno para hispanohablantes, pp. 46–50
▸ Testing Program, pp. 213–216
▸ Alternative Assessment Guide, p. 39
▸ Student Make-Up Assignments, Chapter 10

MEDIA
▸ One-Stop Planner
▸ Audio Compact Discs, CD 10, Trs. 7–8, 23–25, 19
▸ Teaching Transparencies 10-1; **Más práctica gramatical** Answers; Cuaderno de gramática Answers
▸ Interactive CD-ROM Tutor, Disc 3

Presenting
Así se dice

Use these expressions in original sentences in which you talk about a few of your own aspirations. Then elicit the first part of the statements with questions and have students complete them. You might want to give one question orally for the whole class to think about for a few minutes. Then ask students to raise their hand when they have an idea.

Nota cultural

Hay una fuerte influencia puertorriqueña en Nueva York. Esta influencia se ve especialmente en el Barrio, una sección de East Harlem. El Barrio es famoso por sus deliciosas comidas, su música "salsa", sus cines y sus publicaciones en español. Una de las atracciones del Barrio es el Museo del Barrio, dedicado a las culturas de Latinoamérica y de Puerto Rico. Tiene una colección fascinante de objetos precolombinos y frecuentemente hay exhibiciones sobre la pintura, escultura y video latinoamericanos. ¿Qué influencias hispanas ves en tu comunidad?

Así se dice

Talking about future plans

Si quieres hablar de tus planes para el futuro, puedes decir:

Me gustaría ser doctora **cuando sea mayor** para ayudar a otras personas.

Cuando cumpla los 18 años, voy a registrarme para votar.

Ofelia quiere trabajar **antes de que empiecen las clases** en la universidad.

Antes de terminar el colegio quiero conseguir una beca *(scholarship)*.

Después de graduarnos vamos a tener una fiesta muy grande.

Cuaderno de actividades, pp. 111, 113, Acts. 7, 11

13 **Tus planes y tu modo de ser**   Answers will vary.

Leamos Toma esta pequeña prueba para saber qué vínculo hay entre tus planes y tu modo de ser. Selecciona las respuestas que sean más parecidas a tus planes.

1. Cuando sea mayor yo
   a. seré un(a) guía para safaris.
   b. trabajaré en Wall Street.
   c. escribiré un libro de poesía

2. Antes de que cumpla los 40 años me gustaría
   a. viajar al Polo Sur.
   b. formar mi propia compañía internacional de finanzas.
   c. aprender a tocar la guitarra eléctrica.

3. Cuando tenga suficiente dinero pienso
   a. comprarme un barco y navegar alrededor del mundo.
   b. invertirlo en telecomunicaciones.
   c. construir un nuevo museo de arte.

4. Después de graduarme en el colegio
   a. voy a ir a Egipto para escalar las pirámides.
   b. voy a tomar clases de administración de empresas.
   c. voy a tomar clases de escultura.

Resultados: Tus respuestas a las preguntas de la prueba indican algo sobre tu modo de ser. Vamos **a** ver qué dicen sobre tu personalidad las respuestas que escogiste. Si escogiste **a** la mayoría de las veces, tu tendencia natural es de ser una persona aventurera. Si escogiste **b**, eres empresario(a) por instinto. Si preferiste **c**, lo normal para ti es ser creativo(a) y artístico(a).

Cultures and Communities

Culture Note
Tell students that in this photo of the **Museo del Barrio** they can see several **vejigante** masks. These masks are worn during Puerto Rico's festivals, mainly by young people who dress in costume. These colorfully decorated masks were originally made of coconuts or other gourds. Today, many of them are made of papier mâché.

Background Information
More African Americans live in New York than in any other state in the United States. Almost a third of the three million Puerto Ricans and people of Puerto Rican descent living in the contiguous 48 states live in New York City. That's more than twice as many as live in San Juan, the largest city in Puerto Rico.

The subjunctive after certain conjunctions

1. These conjunctions always take the subjunctive:

a menos (de) que *unless*
antes de que *before*
con tal (de) que *provided*

en caso de que *in case*
para que *so, in order that*

2. The subjunctive follows some conjunctions when they refer to a future action.

Cuando vayas a Madrid, tienes que conocer los museos. *When you go . . .*
En cuanto llegues a casa llámame. *As soon as you get home . . .*

3. Here are some other conjunctions that take the subjunctive when they refer to the future. They often introduce a new subject.

después de que *after*
hasta que *until*

tan pronto como *as soon as*

Más práctica gramatical,
p. 303, Acts. 2–3

Cuaderno de
actividades,
p. 112, Act. 8

Cuaderno de
gramática,
pp. 80–81, Acts. 6–9

4. Use the indicative if the action happens regularly or already happened.

Cuando vamos a Chicago, siempre vamos a los museos.
En cuanto salimos, empezó a llover.

 14 **Gramática en contexto**   See possible answers below.

Leamos/Hablemos Leonora va a tener una entrevista para un trabajo. Con un(a) compañero(a), dale consejos usando la siguiente información. Cambien los verbos si es necesario.

1. Cuando (tener) una entrevista,...
2. Antes de (ir),...
3. Tan pronto como (llegar),...
4. Cuando (hablar) con la jefa,...
5. Después de que Uds. (terminar) la entrevista,...

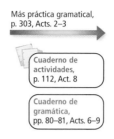

ponte ropa profesional

sé cortés

ve a la oficina de la jefa

agradécele su tiempo

debes seguir estos consejos

 15 **Gramática en contexto**   See possible answers below.

Escribamos Los siguientes jóvenes están pensando en lo que les gustaría hacer cuando sean mayores. Escribe unas frases que indiquen lo que quiere hacer cada persona según el dibujo. Usa las frases **Cuando sea mayor..., Antes de cumplir...** y **Después de que...**

el (la) carpintero(a)

el (la) médico(a)

el (la) programador(a)

a.

b.

c.

d.

Communication for All Students

Auditory Learners

15 Divide the class into groups and ask students to interview each other: **Cuando cumplas los 25 años, ¿qué tipo de trabajo vas a tener? ¿Vas a casarte? ¿Dónde quieres vivir?** After the interviews, ask someone from each group to describe a group member without revealing his or her name. Other groups guess who is being described.

Tactile Learners

Write ten sentences using the conjunctions and make photocopies so that groups of four each have all the sentences. Cut the sentences into strips, then cut the strips in half, after the conjunctions. Mix the strips in envelopes and give an envelope to each group. Ask the groups to put the sentences back together. Remind students that the sentences must use the indicative or subjunctive correctly.

Presenting
Gramática

The subjunctive after certain conjunctions
Review the structure of the subjunctive. Then write these incomplete sentences on the board or on a transparency.

1. **Cuando... visitaré a mis parientes en la República Dominicana.**
2. **No puedo graduarme hasta que... con la clase de español.**
3. **Después de que mi hermano... mi familia se irá a otra ciudad.**
4. **Con tal de que... puedo terminar el proyecto.**
Ask students to fill in the missing verb or grammatical expression.

Assess
▸ Testing Program, pp. 213–216
 Quiz 10-1A, Quiz 10-1B
 Audio CD 10, Tr. 19

▸ Student Make-Up Assignments, Chapter 10, Alternative Quiz

▸ Alternative Assessment Guide, p. 39

Answers
14 *Possible answers:*
  1. tengas... debes seguir estos consejos.
  2. ir... ponte ropa profesional.
  3. llegues... ve a la oficina de la jefa.
  4. hables... sé cortés.
  5. terminen... agradécele su tiempo.

15 *Possible answers:*
  a. Antes de cumplir los cuarenta años quiero ser profesor.
  b. Cuando sea mayor quisiera ser médica.
  c. Después de que termine la escuela voy a ser carpintera.
  d. Cuando sea mayor me gustaría ser programador de computadoras, y antes de que cumpla los sesenta y cinco quiero ser violinista.

Teaching Resources
pp. 290–291

PRINT
▶ Lesson Planner, p. 49
▶ Video Guide, pp. 66–67, 69
▶ Cuaderno de actividades, p. 114

MEDIA
▶ One-Stop Planner
▶ Video Program,
  Contigo en la distancia
  Videocassette 4, 01:10–05:29
  Videocassette 5 (captioned version), 50:49–55:08
▶ Audio Compact Discs, CD 10, Trs. 9–11

Presenting
¡Adelante!

Play the Audio CD once while students read along. You may want to stop the recording periodically to check for comprehension. Then have students work in pairs to create two lists: one of positive statements from Joaquín's letter and a second of negative statements. Next, present the Preteaching Vocabulary.

 Contigo en la distancia

As an alternative to **¡Adelante!** you may wish to show Episode 10 of **Contigo en la distancia.** For suggestions and activities, see the *Video Guide.*

¡Adelante! ▪ *La herencia cultural*

 CD 10 Trs. 9–11 Lee lo que escribió Joaquín Veracruz sobre su herencia cultural. Sus palabras reflejan el orgullo que tiene por ser quién es. ¿Cómo describirías tu herencia cultural?

Cuaderno de actividades, p. 114, Acts. 12–14

Cartas
AL EDITOR

Estimado editor:

Me llamo Joaquín Veracruz y soy de Río Piedras, Puerto Rico. Desde hace cinco años vivo en Brooklyn, Nueva York. Me encanta su revista y la leo todos los meses. Quería escribirles para contarles un poco sobre mi experiencia aquí en Nueva York.

Por lo general, ha sido una experiencia muy buena y he conocido a gente maravillosa. Pero por el hecho de venir de Puerto Rico, hay algunas personas que opinan que no soy estadounidense. Me oyen hablar español y por consiguiente deciden, sin conocer los hechos, que soy inmigrante ilegal o que no tengo derecho a vivir aquí. Sin saber nada de mí, llegan a la conclusión de que soy inferior o incapaz de contribuir a la sociedad.

En mi opinión, en la mayoría de los casos esta actitud proviene de la ignorancia, no de la maldad. Por eso, la mejor forma de cambiar la opinión de esta gente es educarla, mostrarle que nosotros los hispanos tenemos mucho que ofrecer. Soy bilingüe; por lo tanto mis oportunidades para la comunicación se duplican.

Me esfuerzo en mis estudios por salir adelante. Respeto las diferentes culturas y costumbres de este país y creo que enriquecen a todo el mundo.

Es importante sentirse orgulloso del propio origen. Quiero pedirles a mis hermanos y hermanas hispanos que sigan luchando para que todo el mundo se dé cuenta de nuestras contribuciones. Les pido paciencia y amor para los que todavía no ven la realidad. La mejor manera de cambiar a una persona es hacerse su amigo.

Atentamente,
Joaquín Veracruz

NUESTRO TIEMPO   3

These activities check for comprehension only. Students should not yet be expected tp produce language modeled in **¡Adelante!**

16 **¿Comprendiste?** See answers on p. 291.
Completa las frases con información de **¡Adelante!**

1. Joaquín quería escribir una carta a la revista porque...
2. Algunas personas creen que Joaquín no es estadounidense porque...
3. Hay gente que cree erróneamente que Joaquín es un inmigrante ilegal porque...
4. En el nuevo programa del presidente, algunos estudiantes tendrán oportunidades de...
5. El grupo Juntos Avanzamos ha publicado una lista de sus objetivos porque quiere que...

17 **Encuentra las expresiones con *por***
¿Qué expresión usa Joaquín para hablar de la ventaja de ser bilingüe? ¿Qué dice para expresar la reacción de algunas personas cuando lo oyen hablar español?
See answers on p. 291.

Preteaching Vocabulary

Guessing Words from Context
Point out to students that **¡Adelante!** discusses discrimination. Have students brainstorm about types of expressions they would use regarding the causes of discrimination. How might students describe the effects of discrimination? What might they propose as solutions? Point out the following phrases: **Me oyen hablar español y deciden...**; que soy inmigrante ilegal...; En mi opinión, en la mayoría de los casos esta actitud proviene de la ignorancia, no de la maldad.; Quiero pedirles a mis hermanos y hermanas hispanos que sigan luchando para que todo el mundo se dé cuenta de nuestras contribuciones.

El presidente: reunión con grupo Juntos Avanzamos

(NUEVA YORK) Hoy se reúne el presidente con el grupo Juntos Avanzamos, cuyas ambiciones incluyen leyes contra la discriminación y programas para combatir los estereotipos culturales. Este año el grupo ha publicado una lista de sus objetivos con la idea de difundirlos a nivel nacional. Se cree que el presidente viene a la reunión con la intención de anunciar su apoyo para esos objetivos y para dar a conocer un nuevo programa nacional para combatir los estereotipos. Se reporta que el programa incluye oportunidades para que jóvenes de distintos grupos étnicos y culturales de todas partes del país puedan conocerse y discutir la discriminación y los estereotipos.

18 ¿Cuál es tu opinión?

Contesta las preguntas con un(a) compañero(a). Comparen sus respuestas y expliquen las diferencias de opinión que tengan.

1. ¿Está abierto este país a personas de muchas culturas diferentes? Explica tu opinión.

2. ¿Cuál es la mejor manera de lograr mayor tolerancia hacia otras culturas?

3. ¿Cuáles son las ventajas de conocer más de una cultura?

4. ¿Es importante que los diferentes grupos étnicos y culturales mantengan su identidad cultural? ¿Por qué sí o por qué no?

5. ¿Te sientes seguro(a) de tu identidad cultural? ¿De dónde viene esa seguridad?

19 Ahora te toca a ti

Escribe una composición de unas quince oraciones describiendo una experiencia con la intolerancia. Puede ser tu propia experiencia o una que observaste. Explica lo que pasó y cómo se sintieron los que tuvieron la experiencia y los que la observaron.

Comprehension Check

Challenge

Ask students to write a response to Joaquín's letter, as if they were the editor of the magazine to which he has written.

Additional Practice

19 After reading the newspaper article, ask pairs of students to write at least two objectives that might be proposed by **Juntos Avanzamos** to fight intolerance. Ask each pair to share its objectives with the rest of the class. You may wish to record a list of common objectives on a transparency or on the board.

CAPÍTULO 10

Teaching Resources
p. 292

PRINT
▸ Video Guide, pp. 66–68, 70
▸ Cuaderno de actividades, p. 120
▸ Cuaderno para hispanohablantes, pp. 49–50

MEDIA
▸ One-Stop Planner
▸ Video Program, Videocassette 4, 05:30–10:45
▸ Audio Compact Discs, CD 10, Trs. 12–15
▸ Interactive CD-ROM Tutor, Disc 3

Presenting
Panorama cultural

Play the audio or video recording. As students listen to each interview, have them make a list of the words that the speakers use to describe themselves. After discussing the interviews, have students answer the **Para pensar y hablar...** questions and the **Preguntas.**

Preguntas

1. **¿Por qué se considera Sally chicana?** (Nació en los Estados Unidos y sus padres en México.)

2. **¿Estás de acuerdo con Sergio en pensar que "Hispano y latinoamericano... es lo mismo"? ¿Por qué?** *(Answers will vary.)*

3. **Según Sally, ¿cuál es el resultado de la discriminación contra los latinos?** (menos oportunidades)

4. **Según Ivette, ¿qué tipo de gente son los hispanohablantes?** (gente con su propia mente y capaz de hacer cualquier cosa)

¿Cómo te defines?

CD 10
Trs. 12–15

Estos estudiantes hispanos nos dijeron cómo se definen y por qué se definen así.

Sally CD 10 Tr. 13
San Diego, California

"Yo me considero chicana porque soy nacida aquí y mis padres son de México y latino lo considero... son todas las personas mexicanas, de Cuba, de Argentina, de todo... En veces sí hay [discriminación]... En veces nos ponen abajo, nos dan menos oportunidades a nosotros que somos chicanos o latinos... Lo que deberían de hacer es tratarnos a todos igual, porque no somos diferentes, somos igual[es]".

Sergio CD 10 Tr. 14
Miami, Florida

"Hispano y latinoamericano también. Es lo mismo, son sinónimos... Les brindamos [a Estados Unidos] nuestra ética de trabajo, nuestros valores culturales y familiares, nuestra unión familiar, nuestras creencias en Dios y en la democracia, y también tenemos... muy amplio espíritu de superación".

Ivette CD 10 Tr. 15
Ponce, Puerto Rico

"Soy puertorriqueña, soy latina, soy americana... Puertorriqueña, pues, el centro de mi corazón; latina, mi piel; americana, mi mente... Yo creo que pese a la opinión que tienen muchas personas, los hispanohablantes somos personas que tenemos nuestra propia mente, somos muy capaces para hacer cualquier cosa que queramos".

Para pensar y hablar...

A. ¿Cómo se siente Ivette en su corazón? Según Sally, ¿cuál es la diferencia entre chicano y latino? Según Sergio, ¿cuál es la diferencia entre hispano y latinoamericano? ¿Qué aportación han hecho los latinos a Estados Unidos, según Sergio?

B. ¿Por qué crees que les importa a estos estudiantes definir quiénes son? Escoge tres palabras para definirte a ti mismo(a).

Cultures and Communities

Language Notes

• Point out that Sally uses the expression **nos ponen abajo** to say *they put us down* instead of a standard expression such as **nos menosprecian.** Explain that bilingual speakers of any two languages sometimes translate expressions word for word from one language to another. Such expressions can be puzzling to monolingual speakers of either language.

• Ask students if they can guess the meaning of the prepositional phrase **Pese a** *(despite, in spite of)* as used by Ivette in the phrase **pese a la opinión que tienen muchas personas.**

Objectives Expressing cause and effect; expressing intention and purpose

WV3 NEW YORK-10

Así se dice

Expressing cause and effect

Si quieres hablar de la relación entre causa y consecuencia, puedes decir:

> Cuaderno de actividades, pp. 115–116, Acts. 15–16

Mis éxitos en natación **se deben a** mis excelentes entrenadores.
> . . . *are due to* . . .

Soy bilingüe; **por lo tanto**, tengo muchas oportunidades en el trabajo.
> . . . *therefore* . . .

Por tener padres hispanos, me siento orgullosa de la cultura hispana.
Because I have . . .

No estudié, **así que** salí con malas notas.
> . . . *so* . . .

Las leyes han cambiado **de tal forma que** hay menos discriminación.
> . . . *in such a way that* . . .

Sé español y portugués; **en consecuencia**, puedo viajar fácilmente en América Latina.

Discutimos el problema; **por consiguiente**, hay más tolerancia.
> . . . *consequently* . . .

Las acciones de los líderes **resultaron en** leyes contra la discriminación.

Nota gramatical

Verbs are not conjugated after a preposition. Infinitives are used instead, and no new subject is introduced.

> Marisa consiguió varias becas **por ser** buena estudiante.

> Rubén llamó a sus padres **antes de salir.**

> Cuaderno de gramática, pp. 82–83, Acts. 10–12

> Más práctica gramatical, p. 304, Act. 4

 20 **Por lo tanto...** Script and answers on p. 279H.

Escuchemos/Hablemos Escucha las siguientes frases. Indica si cada frase expresa una relación entre causa y efecto o no.

CD 10 Tr. 16

21 **Gramática en contexto** Answers will vary.

Leamos/Escribamos ¿Cuáles son las consecuencias de estas acciones o hechos? Lee cada frase y combínala con una de estas expresiones. Luego añade una conclusión propia.

> MODELO   **Ángel trabaja para una compañía internacional.**
> —Él necesita hablar con gente de otros lugares, así que estudia idiomas.

1. Tomás ha trabajado en la compañía por 35 años.
2. Alberto es un genio en matemáticas.
3. María Carlota se crió en Buenos Aires.
4. Mi hermano quiere comprar un carro.
5. Eva y Dalia empezaron a practicar la natación desde muy jóvenes.
6. He estudiado español.

por lo tanto   así que

de tal forma que   en consecuencia

por consiguiente   resultar en

Teaching Resources
pp. 293–296

PRINT
▶ Lesson Planner, p. 49
▶ Listening Activities, pp. 76, 80–81
▶ Activities for Communication, pp. 39–40, 79–80, 107–108
▶ Cuaderno de gramática, pp. 82–86
▶ Grammar Tutor for Students of Spanish, Chapter 10
▶ Cuaderno de actividades, pp. 115–118
▶ Cuaderno para hispanohablantes, pp. 46–50
▶ Testing Program, pp. 217–220
▶ Alternative Assessment Guide, p. 39
▶ Student Make-Up Assignments, Chapter 10

MEDIA
▶ One-Stop Planner
▶ Audio Compact Discs, CD 10, Trs. 16–17, 26–28, 20
▶ Teaching Transparencies 10-2; **Más práctica gramatical** Answers; Cuaderno de gramática Answers
▶ Interactive CD-ROM Tutor, Disc 3

Bell Work
On the board or on a transparency, write: **Escribe cinco planes que tienes para el futuro. Puedes referirte a tu vida personal o al porvenir del mundo.**

Presenting
Así se dice,
Nota gramatical

Have students bring in magazine pictures of people they admire. Use a few to create sentences that use expressions from **Así se dice**. Return pictures to students and have them write similar sentences to accompany the pictures they brought.

Communication for All Students

Challenge
20 After students identify which items on the audio recording express a cause-and-effect relationship, play the recording again. Ask students to identify the specific cause and effect expressed. Pause after each item to allow students to take notes.

Pair Work
Ask each student to share with a partner the effect of at least two of his or her actions this past week. (**Anoche no llegué a casa a tiempo; en consecuencia tengo que quedarme en casa esta semana. Estudié mucho para el examen de álgebra, así que saqué una buena nota.**)

Teaching Resources
pp. 293–296

PRINT 📖
▶ Lesson Planner, p. 49
▶ Listening Activities, pp. 76, 80–81
▶ Activities for Communication, pp. 39–40, 79–80, 107–108
▶ Cuaderno de gramática, pp. 82–86
▶ Grammar Tutor for Students of Spanish, Chapter 10
▶ Cuaderno de actividades, pp. 115–118
▶ Cuaderno para hispanohablantes, pp. 46–50
▶ Testing Program, pp. 217–220
▶ Alternative Assessment Guide, p. 39
▶ Student Make-Up Assignments, Chapter 10

MEDIA 💿📹
▶ One-Stop Planner
▶ Audio Compact Discs, CD 10, Trs. 16–17, 26–28, 20
▶ Teaching Transparencies 10-2; **Más práctica gramatical** Answers; Cuaderno de gramática Answers
▶ Interactive CD-ROM Tutor, Disc 3

Presenting
Vocabulario

To present the words in context, ask students questions such as:
¿Cuál es una de tus metas? ¿Qué esperas lograr antes de graduarte? Después de graduarte, ¿a qué aspiras? ¿En qué materias quieres enfocarte?

Answers
23 *Possible answers:*
1. meta *or* aspiración
2. enfocarnos en
3. aspiran a *or* sueñan con
4. tomar la iniciativa
5. llevar a cabo *or* realizar

---

 22 Causas y efectos

 Escribamos Mira los dibujos. Luego, con un(a) compañero(a), escribe una frase para describir la causa y el efecto que ves en cada dibujo.

Vocabulario

la aspiración *aspiration, ambition*	**el objetivo** *objective*
aspirar a *to aspire to*	**realizar (un sueño)** *to fulfill (a dream)*
enfocarse en *to focus on*	**soñar (ue) con** + inf. *to dream of (doing something)*
esforzarse (ue) por *to make an effort to*	**tomar la iniciativa** *to take the initiative*
lograr *to achieve; to manage to*	
llevar a cabo *to carry out*	
la meta *goal*	

CD-ROM DISC 3

Cuaderno de actividades, p. 117, Acts. 17–18 | Cuaderno de gramática, p. 83, Acts. 13–14 | Más práctica gramatical, p. 304, Act. 5

See possible answers below.

 23 Las metas del grupo folklórico

Escribamos/Hablemos El grupo Amigos de la República Dominicana está anunciando sus metas para este año. Completa cada frase con una expresión del **Vocabulario**. Luego escribe cinco oraciones similares e intercámbialas con un(a) compañero(a). Traten de adivinar las palabras que se necesitan para completar las oraciones del (de la) compañero(a).

1. Nuestra ════ es fomentar el aprecio del arte dominicano en Nueva York.
2. Este año vamos a ════ el arte que mejor refleja el espíritu y el alma de los dominicanos.
3. Tendremos un programa de clases especiales para jóvenes dominicanos que ════ aprender sobre la música tradicional de la República Dominicana.
4. Nuestro comité tiene que ════ en esta área porque ninguna otra organización está trabajando en ella.
5. Vamos a hacer todo lo posible para ════ nuestros planes.

¿Te acuerdas?

The reflexive pronoun you use varies according to the subject of the sentence.

Debes enfoca**rte** más en tus objetivos.
Nos esforzamos por lograr nuestras metas.

Cuaderno de gramática, pp. 84–85, Acts. 15–17

24 Por el bien de todos

Escribamos Enumera ocho metas en las que tu comunidad debe enfocarse dentro de los próximos diez años. Completa las oraciones usando las frases de **Así se dice**.

MODELO construir un estadio de béisbol
—Queremos enfocarnos en los deportes; por lo tanto, nuestra meta es construir un estadio de béisbol.

Communication for All Students

Slower Pace
24 You may wish to have the class brainstorm the goals as you make a list on the board or on a transparency. Then have students work in pairs to write the sentences. They may exchange papers with another pair to peer-edit.

Group Work
Divide the class into groups of three or four. Explain to them that each group is planning to start a club or organization. Ask them to give their club or organization a name and to write at least three goals they hope to accomplish. When they have completed their work, ask that a spokesperson from each group share the information with the remainder of the class.

25 **Propongamos una solución**

 Escribamos/Hablemos Con un(a) compañero(a), enumera los cinco problemas más graves que afectan tu ciudad. Luego escojan uno de los problemas y escriban una composición de 15 oraciones. Expliquen la causa del problema y sus consecuencias. Mencionen los objetivos que tienen para resolver el problema y cómo pueden lograrlos.

Así se dice

Expressing intention and purpose

Si quieres hablar de tus intenciones y objetivos, puedes decir:

Cuaderno de actividades, p. 118, Act. 19

Pienso aprender un poco de la música hispana.
Tengo la intención de viajar a Puerto Rico.
Escribieron la carta **con la intención de** persuadirnos a visitarlos.

Fuimos allí **con la idea de** comprar libros sobre los hispanos famosos.
Pablo quiere ir a Chile **para** conocer a su gente.
Vamos a eliminar los estereotipos **para que** haya menos discriminación.

 26 **¿Quién es?** Script and answers on p. 279H.

CD 10
Tr. 17

Escuchemos Mira los siguientes dibujos. Luego escucha cada descripción e indica a qué persona en los dibujos se refiere.

a.　　　　b.　　　　c.　　　　d.

27 **No pudo porque...** See possible answers below.

Leamos/Escribamos Usa las expresiones de **Así se dice** para explicar por qué cada persona no pudo hacer las siguientes cosas.

MODELO　　Mario / ir al Museo Guggenheim
　　　　　Mario tenía la intención de ir al Museo Guggenheim pero tuvo que trabajar.

1. Claudia / ir al desfile del Día de la Raza
2. Ignacio / conocer la Sociedad Hispánica de América
3. Kristin / asistir a un concierto en el Radio City Music Hall
4. Chen / escuchar una ópera en Carnegie Hall
5. Alishia / ir de compras a la Quinta Avenida

 28 **¡Qué generosidad!**

 Hablemos Tú y un(a) compañero(a) tienen 20.000 dólares para fomentar una conciencia cultural en su ciudad. Hablen de lo que deben hacer con el dinero y expliquen los objetivos.

MODELO　　**Debemos dar 5.000 dólares a la escuela para que pueda comprar libros.**

Communication for All Students

Challenge

Have students write sentences saying what they would like for parents, siblings, or friends to do, and why. Students should use **para** or **para que** in their sentences. (**Quiero que mis padres me compren un carro para que pueda salir con mis amigos. Quiero que mi amigo me llame para invitarme a su fiesta.**)

Native Speakers

28 Ask students to imagine that they are preparing a cultural exhibit for a local museum. The exhibit is to be about the culture of their country of origin. What things would they choose to include in such an exhibit? How will their choices help others understand and appreciate their culture?

Presenting
Así se dice

Use the new expressions to make statements to the class, illustrating your sentences with magazine pictures. Next place three pictures so that students can see them. Make a statement about one of them and have students point to the correct picture.

Speaking Assessment

28 You may wish to evaluate students' dialogues by using the following rubric.

Speaking Rubric	Points			
	4	3	2	1
Content (Complete– Incomplete)				
Comprehension (Total–Little)				
Comprehensibility (Comprehensible– Incomprehensible)				
Accuracy (Accurate– Seldom accurate)				
Fluency (Fluent–Not fluent)				

18–20: A　　14–15: C　　Under
16–17: B　　12–13: D　　12: F

Answers
27 *Possible answers:*
1. Claudia tenía la intención de ir al desfile pero tuvo que ir al hospital.
2. Ignacio iba a visitar la Sociedad Hispánica de América pero tuvo que estudiar.
3. Kristin pensaba asistir a un concierto pero no tenía suficiente dinero.
4. Chen fue a Nueva York con la idea de escuchar una ópera pero no pudo porque no tenía una entrada.
5. Alishia tenía la intención de ir de compras a la Quinta Avenida pero no pudo porque no trajo dinero.

Gramática de repaso

The subjunctive with *para que*

The conjunction **para que** introduces a new subject and is always followed by the subjunctive. Any verbs that go after **para**, however, are left in the infinitive. No new subject is introduced.

Más práctica gramatical, p. 305, Act. 6

Les escribo a mis representantes **para que sepan** mis opiniones.
Llamé a la senadora **para discutir** los programas multiculturales.

Cuaderno de gramática, pp. 85–86, Acts. 18–20

29 **Gramática en contexto**   See answers below.

Leamos/Escribamos Completa cada frase con **para** o con **para que**.

1. Mis padres emigraron de América Latina. Estoy ahorrando dinero _____ viajar allá algún día.
2. Mis abuelos no hablan inglés. Yo les hablo en español _____ me entiendan.
3. Debemos enfocarnos en los detalles de la situación _____ comprenderla.
4. Tendré que estudiar muchos años _____ realizar mi sueño de ser médico.
5. Una persona anónima ha dado 1.000 dólares al programa _____ compre obras de arte para la Sociedad Hispánica de América.

Nota cultural

La Sociedad Hispánica de América, fundada en 1904 por Archer M. Huntington, se encuentra en la calle Broadway en un edificio impresionante de estilo renacentista *(Renaissance)* español. Tiene una colección exquisita de arte español y portugués, incluso pinturas de Velázquez, El Greco y Goya.

30  Del colegio al trabajo

Leamos/Escribamos Trabajas para una agencia de empleos que ayuda a estudiantes a encontrar trabajos de verano en el extranjero. Necesitas obtener información sobre sus metas o planes para el futuro. Completa las oraciones de algunos de los candidatos.

MODELO Pienso tomar clases de español…
Pienso tomar clases de español para poder trabajar en Perú.

1. Tengo la intención de viajar a España…
2. Deseo superarme con la idea de…
3. Quiero aprender bien el español…
4. Pienso tomar clases de arte mexicano…
5. Tengo la intención de estudiar comercio internacional…
6. Quiero aprender literatura inglesa…

SUGERENCIA

One way to make the task of writing easier is to make sure you know most of the words you will need to use. With a classmate, make a list of the words you will probably need to complete your task. Then look up the words you don't know in the dictionary. Always look up the Spanish word in the dictionary to be sure it fits the context.

31 **En mi cuaderno**

Escribamos Imagina que estás pidiendo una beca para asistir a tu universidad favorita. Escribe una carta a la universidad para contarle cuáles son tus planes para el futuro. Menciona también tus logros más notables, y explica cómo te ayudará la beca a realizar tus sueños.

Cultures and Communities

Culture Notes
• Born Domenikos Theotokopoulos, El Greco (1541 or 1542–1614) was so named because of his Greek origins. El Greco was supported mostly by commissions from the Church; his paintings therefore often express religious themes.

• Diego Velázquez (1599–1660), as court painter for Felipe IV, painted the royal family, as well as subjects portraying daily life and mythological themes. Velázquez is considered one of the world's greatest artists.

• Francisco de Goya (1746–1828) served as court painter for Carlos IV. Goya's early works are representative of baroque and rococo styles; his later works are thought to anticipate modern art.

El Ballet Hispánico de Nueva York

Fundado en 1970 por la venezolana Tina Ramírez, el Ballet Hispánico de Nueva York ofrece toda una variedad de bailes y música al público por medio de funciones en Estados Unidos, Latinoamérica y Europa y por medio de su escuela de baile en Nueva York. ¿Qué elementos culturales ves en estas fotos? ¿Crees que estos elementos expresan algo típico o universal de la cultura hispana?

Para discutir

¿Qué se expresa en un baile? ¿Cómo se puede usar el baile para expresar los sentimientos? ¿Cómo se puede usar para expresar el orgullo nacional o étnico y los sentimientos de un pueblo? Explica tus respuestas. ¿Qué tipos de baile hay en Estados Unidos? ¿Qué revelan esos bailes acerca de la gente de este país?

Vamos a comprenderlo

El Ballet Hispánico de Nueva York combina ritmos y música del mundo hispano con elementos de la danza moderna para explorar temas de la historia y de la actualidad hispanas. Un bailarín, por ejemplo, demostró cómo un problema puede afectar todos los aspectos de la vida de una persona al bailar los pasos tradicionales del flamenco mientras balanceaba en la cabeza un cuenco (bowl) de agua. La escuela de baile del Ballet Hispánico tiene más de 900 estudiantes, el 70 por ciento de ellos hispanos, que aprenden el baile hispano y también ballet de instructores e instructoras profesionales. Muchos de los graduados de la escuela de baile hacen carreras en la danza, el teatro, el cine y la televisión.

Presenting
Encuentro cultural
Ask students to look carefully at the images of the dancers on this page. As you ask the **Para discutir** questions, have students refer to the pictures to help them answer. You might want to bring in a picture book or a video of dancing or a tape of Latin American music. Have students look at the pictures and listen to the music. How do the sounds and movements make them feel? Do they think they could express themselves through dance? Then read **Vamos a comprenderlo** as a class. Stop periodically to ask comprehension questions.

Culture Note
Tell students that Tina Ramírez is a tireless advocate of the arts in New York City. In addition to being the founder and artistic director of the **Ballet Hispánico de Nueva York,** she has served as a panelist or advisor for the National Endowment for the Arts, the New York State Council on the Arts, and the New York City Department of Cultural Affairs. She has been honored by several groups throughout the city and the state of New York for her work in ballet and the arts. You may wish to have students conduct an Internet search for information on the Ballet Hispánico.

Connections and Comparisons

Community Link
Have students research their city or town's involvement in the arts. Does the town have a public theater? Is there funding for local artists and dancers? Does the city subsidize new companies or promote innovation among the arts community? Ask students to report to the class in Spanish what they learn.

Multicultural Link
Show a video of **Ballet Hispánico de Nueva York.** Ballet Hispánico's performances are a mixture of modern dance, classical ballet, and Latin American dance influences. Its educational outreach program, **Primeros pasos,** visits schools nationwide. Ask students how this dance company celebrates and seeks to educate people about Hispanic heritage.

Teaching Resources
pp. 298–300

PRINT
▸ Lesson Planner, p. 50
▸ Cuaderno de actividades, p. 119
▸ Cuaderno para hispanohablantes, pp. 46–48
▸ Reading Strategies and Skills Handbook, Chapter 10
▸ ¡Lee conmigo! 3, Chapter 10
▸ Standardized Assessment Tutor, Chapter 10

MEDIA
▸ One-Stop Planner

Prereading
Activities A and B

Establishing a Purpose for Reading
Ask students: **¿De qué tratan los dos poemas? ¿Puedes adivinar el tema al leer solamente los títulos?** (They are about personal identity and self-definition.) Then ask students to formulate a question they hope to have answered by the poems.

Drawing on Your Experience
A. Ask students to tell you what the words **gringa** and **chicana** mean to them. Do they imply culturally specific characteristics? Do they imply a certain history or family line? Do the students consider either one derogatory? Ask them to think about slang or informal words they would use to describe themselves.

Answers
🅐 *Possible answers:*
1. La palabra "gringo(a)" normalmente se refiere a la gente y a la cultura angloamericanas.
2. "Chicana" se refiere a una mexicana nacida en los Estados Unidos.
3. *Sample answer:* La línea diagonal indica separación de dos partes, personalidades o tradiciones de una persona.

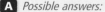

Vamos a leer

Dos poemas

Vas a leer dos selecciones de poesía. La primera, por Maia Chávez Dean (n. 1964), se llama "Gringa/Chicana"; la otra es un extracto de "Yo soy Joaquín", por Rodolfo "Corky" Gonzales (n. 1928). Maia Chávez Dean se crió en Nueva York, Nuevo México y Colorado e hizo sus estudios en el idioma y la cultura hispanos. Gonzales es hijo de obreros migratorios chicanos. Ahora es periodista y autor dedicado al movimiento chicano.

Estrategia para leer
Paraphrasing is an easy way to help you understand the content of a text, especially when you encounter unfamiliar vocabulary. You paraphrase when you put a text's ideas into your own words. While summarizing involves only the main ideas, paraphrasing involves putting all or almost all of the text's ideas in your own words. You can paraphrase even if you do not understand every word of the text.

See possible answers below

¡A comenzar!
A. Responde a las siguientes preguntas sobre "Gringa/Chicana".
1. ¿Qué quiere decir "gringa"?
2. ¿Qué quiere decir "chicana"?
3. ¿Qué implica la línea diagonal entre "Gringa" y "Chicana"?

¿Te acuerdas?
Make predictions about a text. Before you read, try to anticipate what's in the text by the way it's written and by whatever you know about the text already.

Gringa/Chicana
por Maia Chávez Dean

I
El sol brilla
caliente sobre el polvo negro
caliente sobre la tierra amarilla
caliente sobre las caras morenas
piel morena
calle de la ciudad
y el polvo negro en mis pies
en mis zapatos
y el calor sale del pavimento
a través del desierto
a través de las piedras
—pirámides
muy lejos
grandes templos de los dioses
subiendo
subiendo
y el cielo ancho y amarillo
color de la tierra
color de la sequía
y el polvo negro de la ciudad
en mis pies blancos—
cabello claro—
¡Güera!
sí,
aunque me dijeron allí donde nací
que era morena
niña morena
ojos latinos
chicana
bella

II
Sí pero eso fue en los Estados Unidos de América
"Home of the brave"
Los Estados Unidos
unidos
un gran magnífico "crisol"
unidos
"All for one and one for all"
herencia
raíces—

Cultures and Communities

Language Notes
• Point out the usage of English words and phrases in "Gringa/Chicana." Do native speakers find this use of language authentic?

• **Güero(a)** is an adjective meaning *blond* or *fair.*

• **Crisol,** in its figurative use, means *melting pot.* A related word is **fundido,** from the verb **fundir** *(to melt, to merge,* or *to blend).*

Culture Note
In the 1960s, young Mexican American college students organized the Chicano movement which emphasized pride in Mexican culture and heritage. Such pride was reflected in Mexican American political parties that sprang up around the country, notably **La Raza Unida.**

¿Pero no es esto mi herencia?
¿Aquí bajo el cielo amarillo?
cielo de sequía
tierra morena,
¿caras morenas?
y ¡Güera! ¡Güera!
piel blanca
cabello claro
¡No! —digo— ¡No!
soy una de ustedes
¡Mira!
Cómo mis pies caminan en el polvo negro.
¡Mira!
"my soul"
¡Mi alma! — grito.
Pero de pronto la lengua se me vuelve extraña
y no puedo hablar en su idioma
Lo sé
pero no puedo hablar
Lo siento
pero no puedo hablar
y todo está perdido en el gran crisol.

III
Perdido
todo fundido
y mezclado con las lágrimas
los lamentos nostálgicos
lamentos, lágrimas
palabras habladas en voces dulces desde una tierra
    extranjera
una lengua extranjera
una canción extranjera
Lloro
Llorando
lágrimas por la tierra amarilla
por el polvo negro
por el hogar que nunca conocí
¿Qué es lo que soy?
chicana—gringa
media chicana, si tal caso.
Yo
Con mis manos contra la tierra
con las lágrimas cayendo
llenas
tan llenas de amor
¡Güera!—pero soy
¡Chicana!—pero soy
¡Gringa!—pero soy
¡Nada!—ay, no, pero ¡SOY!
Mis manos cogen la tierra morena,
y soy.

See possible answers below.

B. Responde a las siguientes preguntas del poema "Yo soy Joaquín" en la página 300.

1. Dado que "Yo soy Joaquín" es un poema, ¿qué predicciones puedes hacer acerca de la forma del texto?

2. Lee la última línea del poema junto con el título. ¿Qué puedes decir del poema basado en esta información?

3. Ahora compara este poema con "Gringa/Chicana". ¿Qué diferencias hay en la estructura de los dos poemas?

Al grano See answers below

C. Lee las tres partes de "Gringa/Chicana" rápidamente y escoge la frase que mejor resume *(sums up)* cada parte.

1. Parte I
   a. En los desiertos de México hace calor y hay mucho polvo debido al sol.
   b. Bajo el sol, una chica piensa en la cultura y naturaleza mexicana, y en su verdadera identidad.

2. Parte II
   a. La chica vive en Estados Unidos. Va perdiendo su idioma y busca su identidad racial y cultural.
   b. La chica no habla inglés y sigue confiada en su identidad mexicana.

3. Parte III
   a. La chica echa de menos a México y nada puede hacerla dejar de llorar.
   b. La chica está llorando a causa de su confusión de identidad, pero al final decide que tiene una identidad como persona única.

Vamos a leer

CAPÍTULO 10

Reading
Activities C and D

Appreciating a Writer's Craft
Read the first four lines of the poem. Ask students which words are repeated. **(caliente sobre...)** Ask students what the repetition suggests. (that it's very hot) Describe how *anaphora,* or the repetition of words, is used to give the poem rhythm and to stress important ideas. Have students list the other repeated words.

Comparing and Contrasting
Have students look for three places in the poem where **chicano** and Anglo culture are contrasted. What words are used in these contrasts? What are Joaquín's views on each culture? Why is living between two cultures a struggle? What answer does Joaquín find to that struggle?

Answers
B *Possible answers:*
1. Probablemente va a ser corto, con palabras expresivas.
2. El poema trata de la identidad, especialmente la identidad racial.
3. El poema "Gringa/Chicana" está escrito en tres partes. No está escrito en oraciones completas. "Yo soy Joaquín" tiene una sola parte y está escrito en oraciones largas y cortas. Las líneas tienen diferentes formas.

C 1. b
2. a
3. b

Postreading
Activities E, F, and G

Drawing Inferences
Ask students to consider the last two lines of each of the poems. What images or ideas are conveyed by these lines? (both convey permanence of history and of nature) What attitudes or feelings are the authors expressing with these lines? (They are expressing confidence and security in themselves and in the world around them.) What significance does the imagery of **la tierra morena** and **el círculo de vida** hold for students? Why do they think **SOY** and **MI RAZA** are in capital letters? Have students brainstorm about these lines and discuss the poems' conclusions.

Connecting Literature to Current Events
F. Invite someone from your community who has immigrated to the United States to speak to the class about his or her experiences. What aspects of the person's native country does he or she miss most? Would it be possible to incorporate those things into his or her life in the United States? Have students discuss the process of adapting to a new culture.

Answers
D *Possible answers:*
1. un mexicano que vive en los Estados Unidos, un chicano que guarda las costumbres de la cultura mexicana
2. en el suroeste del país
3. los éxitos económicos, la lucha de supervivencia cultural, de haberse asimilado sin olvidar sus raíces, la unidad familiar
4. el racismo, la confusión de identidad

¿Te acuerdas?
Use your background knowledge. Think about what you already know about a topic before you read in depth.

See possible answers below.

D. "Yo soy Joaquín" trata de un chico que experimenta confusión entre la cultura chicana y la norteamericana. Con dos compañeros(as), habla de lo que sabes sobre el fenómeno de ser méxicoamericano. Pueden usar estas preguntas como guía.
1. ¿Qué quiere decir "méxicoamericano"?
2. ¿Dónde viven la mayoría de los méxicoamericanos en Estados Unidos?
3. ¿De qué aspectos de la cultura mexicana estaría orgulloso(a) un(a) méxicoamericano(a)?
4. ¿Qué problemas experimentan algunos méxicoamericanos?

E. Escribe una paráfrasis de "Yo soy Joaquín" o de "Gringa/Chicana" con un(a) compañero(a) de clase. Escríbanla en forma de un párrafo, no un poema. Recuerden que no necesitan entender cada palabra para hacer una buena paráfrasis.

F. Conversa con un(a) compañero(a), imaginando que uno(a) de Uds. es Joaquín y la otra persona es un(a) reportero(a) que escribe sobre los problemas de los inmigrantes.

G. Which of the two selections is your favorite? Why? Do you sympathize more with one character than the other?

Cuaderno para hispanohablantes, pp. 46–48
Cuaderno de actividades, p. 119, Acts. 21–23

YO SOY JOAQUÍN
por Rodolfo "Corky" Gonzales

Yo soy Joaquín,
perdido en un mundo de confusión,
enganchado en el remolino de una
        sociedad gringa,
confundido por las reglas,
despreciado por las actitudes,
sofocado por manipulaciones,
y destrozado por la sociedad moderna.
Mis padres
        perdieron la batalla económica
y conquistaron
        la lucha de supervivencia cultural.
Y ¡ahora!
        yo tengo que escojer
                en medio
        de la paradoja de
triunfo del espíritu,
a despecho de hambre física,
                o
        existir en la empuñada
de la neurosis social americana,
esterilización del alma
        y un estómago repleto.
Sí,
vine de muy lejos a ninguna parte,
desinclinadamente arrastrado por ese
        gigante, monstruoso, técnico, e
        industrial llamado
                Progreso
y éxito angloamericano...
Yo mismo me miro.
 Observo a mis hermanos.
  Lloro lágrimas de desgracia.
   Siembro semillas de odio.
Me retiro a la seguridad dentro del
círculo de vida-
                MI RAZA.

Communication for All Students

Slower Pace
E. To help students deal with unfamiliar vocabulary, have them list words that look like English words. For example, from the first eight lines they might list **confusión, sofocado, manipulaciones,** and **sociedad.**

Visual Learners
Have students make a cluster diagram for each section of the poem to help them understand its structure and meaning. The first diagram (on the first eight lines of the poem) might have **Joaquín** in the center, with surrounding circles containing descriptive phrases such as **perdido en...,** **enganchado en...,** and so on.

Vamos a escribir

Todos somos parte de un mosaico cultural rico y variado. Nuestra singularidad e individualidad cultural se expresan de muchas maneras, incluyendo las tradiciones que mantenemos a través de las generaciones, la manera en que vestimos, el lenguaje que hablamos y los alimentos que comemos. ¿Se te ocurren otras maneras de expresar la diversidad cultural? En esta actividad, vas a describir algunas de las diversidades culturales que conoces y aprenderás a mejorar tu estilo de escritura mediante la combinación de oraciones.

La diversidad cultural

Escribe una composición de cinco o seis párrafos sobre una persona o grupo que represente la diversidad cultural de tu comunidad o área.

Estrategia para escribir

Combining sentences Your paragraphs may lose their impact if they are made up only of short, choppy sentences. One way to improve the flow of your paragraphs is to combine sentences with **y, o,** or **pero.** For example, **"Mi abuelo prefiere comidas tradicionales pero lleva ropa muy moderna,"** is more interesting than **"Mi abuelo prefiere comidas tradicionales. Lleva ropa muy moderna."** Likewise, **"Svetlana habla y escribe sólo en ruso,"** sounds better than **"Svetlana habla sólo en ruso. Svetlana escribe sólo en ruso."**

A. Preparación

1. Piensa en la diversidad cultural que existe en tu comunidad o área. Haz una lista de personas o grupos interesantes.

2. Escoge la persona o grupo más interesante de tu lista. Haz preguntas para encontrar más detalles. Si puedes, habla con esa persona o con alguien que pertenezca al grupo.

3. Busca fotos que demuestren la individualidad de la persona o grupo que describes. Si quieres, puedes sacar las fotos tú mismo(a).

4. Organiza tu información en orden lógico.

B. Redacción

1. Escribe una buena introducción con un hecho interesante sobre la persona o grupo o con una pregunta.

2. Escribe dos o tres párrafos sobre los detalles interesantes que encontraste. Usa palabras y frases descriptivas y coloridas. Incluye las fotos como ejemplos.

3. En tu conclusión, da tu opinión sobre la importancia de la diversidad cultural y menciona alguna cosa especial que aprendiste mientras trabajabas en este proyecto.

C. Evaluación

1. ¿Contiene cada párrafo sólo una idea principal? Si un párrafo contiene más de una idea, sepáralas y colócalas en párrafos distintos. Si quieres, pídele ayuda a un(a) compañero(a).

2. Si hay muchas frases cortas y abruptas, busca maneras de combinarlas con **y, o, pero.**

3. ¿Está organizada lógicamente tu composición? Si no, pon los párrafos o los detalles en un orden más lógico.

4. Dales tu composición a unos(as) compañeros(as) para que busquen errores. Considera sus sugerencias e incorpora las mejores.

Apply and Assess

Postwriting
Auditory Learners

Ask students to read their composition or poem aloud to a partner so he or she can hear what they have written. They may find that they want to make changes to improve the flow of the paragraphs or words.

Group Work

Ask small groups of students to choose two sentences from each composition. The group should work together to develop suggestions for the writer about how to make the sentences more complex and interesting by adding descriptors or using contrast.

Teaching Resources
p. 301

PRINT
▶ Lesson Planner, p. 50
▶ Cuaderno para hispanohablantes, p. 49
▶ Alternative Assessment Guide, p. 25
▶ Standardized Assessment Tutor, Chapter 10

MEDIA
▶ One-Stop Planner, Disc 3
  Test Generator, Chapter 10
▶ Interactive CD-ROM Tutor, Disc 3

Process Writing
Prewriting
Slower Pace

Have students create a list of descriptive words, phrases, and actions that come to mind when they think about culture and diversity. You might create cluster diagrams on the board in which you write a word that a student says and then have other students say words that are related to that one. Draw lines connecting words that are related.

Visual Learners

Have students draw images that represent diversity for them, or they may choose to clip such images from magazines. They might use their drawings or magazine clippings as a starting point for their compositions.

Writing
Challenge

You might have students write a poem for their writing assignment. They might begin by writing ideas about cultural diversity. Then they would use those ideas to write a free-verse poem. Finally, have them read the poem aloud or to them-selves and make changes to improve the flow and rhythm.

For **Más práctica gramatical** Answer Transparencies, see the *Teaching Transparencies* binder.

Más práctica gramatical

CD-ROM DISC 3

internet

MARCAR: go.hrw.com
PALABRA CLAVE:
WV3 NEW YORK-10

Primer paso   Objectives Talking about accomplishments; talking about future plans

1   Completa la descripción que escribió Ernesto de sus abuelos. Cada palabra se usará sólo una vez. (pp. 286–287)

superarse	las costumbres	se asimilaron	agradecidos	me crié
superado	raíces	éxito	aportación	esfuerzos	retos	orgulloso

Mis abuelos se llaman Raimundo y Margarita Dávalos. Estoy muy ___1___ de ellos. ¿Por qué? Primero, porque ellos han ___2___ muchos obstáculos en la vida y han tenido ___3___. Mis abuelos se fueron de México y llegaron a este país en 1948. Al principio, enfrentaron muchos ___4___: el idioma, la cultura, el trabajo, todo. Fueron unos años difíciles para ellos pero sus ___5___ tuvieron buen resultado. Aprecio a mis abuelos porque ellos ___6___ a su cultura nueva, pero también mantuvieron ___7___ de su cultura mexicana. Nunca se han olvidado de sus ___8___. Yo soy estadounidense y ___9___ aquí, pero me considero mexicano también. Respeto a mis abuelos porque nunca han dejado de tratar de ___10___. Siguen trabajando y haciendo una gran ___11___ a nuestra comunidad. Todos estamos muy ___12___ por la ayuda y el ejemplo que nos han dado.

Answers

1
1. orgulloso
2. superado
3. éxito
4. retos
5. esfuerzos
6. se asimilaron
7. las costumbres
8. raíces
9. me crié
10. superarse
11. aportación
12. agradecidos

Grammar Resources for Chapter 10

The **Más práctica gramatical** activities are designed as supplemental activities for the grammatical concepts presented in the chapter. You might use them as additional practice, for review, or for assessment.

For more grammar presentation, review, and practice, refer to the following:
- Cuaderno de gramática
- Grammar Tutor for Students of Spanish

- Grammar Summary on pp. R25–R46
- Cuaderno de actividades
- Grammar and Vocabulary quizzes (Testing Program)
- Test Generator on the One-Stop Planner CD-ROM
- **Juegos interactivos** at <u>go.hrw.com</u>

2 Every year Señora Garza organizes a summer exchange program in Ecuador. Read the sentences from a conversation with one of her students. If the sentence refers to a habitual action, write (H) and complete the sentence with the present indicative form of the verb. If the sentence refers to a future action, write (F) and choose the present subjunctive form of the verb. **(p. 289)**

1. Cuando (llegas/llegues) a Quito, vas a tener mucho que aprender rápidamente.
2. Al principio siempre es difícil cuando (eres/seas) estudiante de intercambio.
3. Sí, profesora. Tan pronto como (aprendemos/aprendamos) palabras nuevas en clase, trato de estudiarlas todos los días.
4. Y pienso hablar sólo en español tan pronto como (salimos/salgamos).
5. Típicamente, después de que los estudiantes de intercambio (conocen/conozcan) al director, hay una pequeña fiesta.
6. Nunca sé cuántos estudiantes van hasta que todos (presentan/presenten) sus exámenes finales.
7. Y no sabremos qué clases vas a tomar hasta que (empieza/empiece) el semestre.
8. Después del viaje, siempre me siento cansada y generalmente me gusta descansar en cuanto (me bajo/me baje) del avión.
9. ¿Podré llamar a mis padres en cuanto (encontramos/encontremos) el hotel?

3 Celia y Laura quieren visitar a un amigo enfermo. Completa su conversación con la forma correcta de los verbos entre paréntesis. Recuerda que siempre hay que usar el subjuntivo después de las expresiones **a menos (de) que, antes (de) que, con tal (de) que, en caso (de) que** y **para que. (p. 289)**

CELIA　Laura, ya sabes que Diego ___1___ (estar) enfermo. ¿Quieres ir a verlo esta tarde?

LAURA　Sí, me encantaría ir, a menos de que mamá ___2___ (necesitar) mi ayuda en casa. ¿A qué hora pensabas ir?

CELIA　A las cinco. Antes de que nosotras ___3___ (ir), quiero pasar por la florería. Comprémosle unas flores para que el pobre ___4___ (sentirse) mejor, ¿no te parece?

LAURA　Bueno... no sé. Creo que nosotras ___5___ (deber) comprarle unas revistas también, en caso de que no le ___6___ (gustar) las flores.

CELIA　Muy bien, le compramos flores y unas revistas. Voy a llamar a Diego esta mañana, y con tal de que él ___7___ (tener) ganas de vernos, vamos.

LAURA　Está bien. Entonces yo te ___8___ (llamar) a las cuatro. Y en caso de que mamá no me ___9___ (dejar) ir esta tarde, podemos ir mañana. Otra cosa... ¿Debemos llevarle unos libros para que ___10___ (poder) estudiar un poco en casa?

CELIA　Sí, buena idea.

Answers

2
1. F, llegues
2. H, eres
3. H, aprendemos
4. F, salgamos
5. F, conozcan
6. F, presenten
7. F, empiece
8. H, me bajo
9. F, encontremos

3
1. está
2. necesite
3. vayamos
4. se sienta
5. debemos
6. gusten
7. tenga
8. llamo
9. deje
10. pueda

Communication for All Students

Additional Practice

2 On the board or on a transparency, write the first half of ten sentences using the conjunctions with a variety of tenses. **(No vamos a empezar el examen hasta que..., Me acosté anoche tan pronto como...)** Have students complete each sentence with a verb in the appropriate tense. Then ask volunteers to restate the entire sentence in a different tense. **(No empezamos el examen hasta que llegó David.)**

Pair Work

3 Have pairs of students write and present to the class their own dialogue about two people making plans to do something later. Students should use all of the conjunctions and/or prepositions at least once.

For **Más práctica gramatical** Answer Transparencies, see the *Teaching Transparencies* binder.

Segundo paso Objectives Expressing cause and effect; expressing intention and purpose

4 Todos están pensando en el verano. Completa los planes de cada uno con las palabras que faltan. Si no se necesita una palabra, escribe X. (**pp. 293–294**)

por		con		a
	que		de	

1. Voy a aprender ———— patinar en línea.
2. Me parece que tengo ———— buscar un trabajo.
3. Este verano, sueño ———— visitar a mi amiga en California.
4. Pienso ———— bajar de peso. Tengo la intención ———— hacer ejercicio todos los días.
5. Voy a dejar ———— ver tanta televisión.
6. Mamá me dijo que este verano necesitaba ———— ayudar más en casa. No me voy a quejar ———— tener muchos quehaceres.
7. Tengo ganas ————tomar unas clases de tenis.
8. Me gustaría ———— hacer un viaje a las Montañas Rocosas con mi familia.

5 Lee las definiciones y escoge la palabra que corresponde a cada una. (**p. 294**)

1. un plan o sueño para el futuro
   a. la aspiración   **b.** la aspiradora
2. realizar algo
   a. lugar   **b.** lograr
3. el objetivo
   a. el martes   **b.** la meta
4. concentrarse en o dedicarse a algo
   a. enfocarse   **b.** enamorarse
5. trabajar mucho
   a. esforzarse   **b.** encajar
6. querer o esperar hacer algo
   a. aportar   **b.** aspirar
7. trabajar en algo hasta realizarlo
   a. llevar a cabo   **b.** llegar a tiempo
8. intentar con muchas ganas
   a. esforzarse   **b.** esperar

Answers

4 1. a
2. que
3. con
4. X, de
5. de
6. X, por
7. de
8. X

5 1. a
2. b
3. b
4. a
5. a
6. b
7. a
8. a

Communication for All Students

Additional Practice

4 Have groups of students write the first half of ten sentences with verbs that do and do not require a preposition. (**Anoche soñé..., Los estudiantes siempre necesitan...**) Then have groups exchange papers to write endings for each of the phrases with prepositions as necessary and logical verbs. Ask volunteers from each group to read one of their sentences to the class.

Native Speakers

5 After identifying the correct answers, students can use all of the targeted vocabulary to describe long-term goals and specify what they must do to achieve these goals. As an option, have students write a graduation speech that includes advice to younger students.

6 Teresa está en Nueva York por primera vez, y su amiga Débora le hace
sugerencias para la visita. Completa las sugerencias con **para** o **para que. (p. 296)**

1. Quiero que vayamos al Parque Central ======= veas lo lindo que es. Muchas veces
   voy allí ======= correr o leer.
2. Y mientras estemos allí, pasemos por el zoológico ======= ver todos los animales
   que tienen.
3. Esta tarde, llamemos a la taquilla ======= saber si todavía quedan entradas para
   alguna obra de teatro.
4. Luego te voy a llevar a mi restaurante favorito del Barrio Chino ======= pruebes
   unos platos realmente ricos.
5. Paseemos por la Quinta Avenida ======= puedas comprar unos regalos.
6. Hay que llamar al museo ======= preguntar a qué hora abren.
7. ¿Te gustaría ir al Museo del Barrio ======= ver la exposición de arte puertorriqueño?
8. Y tenemos que subirnos al último piso del edificio Empire State ======= saques
   unas fotos de toda la ciudad.
9. Y las excursiones a la Isla Ellis y a la Estatua de la Libertad son muy interesantes.
   Hay que ir en lancha ======= llegar allí.
10. ¿Te gustaría subir a la Estatua de la Libertad ======= ver toda la bahía?
11. No olvides usar zapatos cómodos ======= los pies no te duelan.

Review and Assess

You may wish to assign the **Más práctica gramatical** activities as additional practice or homework after presenting material throughout the chapter. Assign Activity 1 after **Vocabulario** (pp. 286, 287), Activities 2 and 3 after **Gramática** (p. 289), Activity 4 after **Nota gramatical** (p. 293) and **Vocabulario** (p. 294), Activity 5 after **Vocabulario** (p. 294), and Activity 6 after **Gramática de repaso** (p. 296). To prepare students for the **Paso** Quizzes and Chapter Test, have them do the **Más práctica gramatical** activities in the following order: complete Activities 1–3 before taking Quiz 10-1A or 10-1B; Activities 4–6 before taking Quiz 10-2A or 10-2B.

Answers
6 1. para que, para
2. para
3. para
4. para que
5. para que
6. para
7. para
8. para que
9. para
10. para
11. para que

Repaso

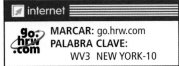
internet

MARCAR: go.hrw.com
PALABRA CLAVE:
WV3 NEW YORK-10

CAPÍTULO 10

The **Repaso** reviews all four skills and culture in preparation for the Chapter Test.

Teaching Resources
pp. 306–307

PRINT
▸ Lesson Planner, p. 51
▸ Listening Activities, p. 77
▸ Video Guide, pp. 66, 68, 71
▸ Grammar Tutor for Students of Spanish, Chapter 10
▸ Cuaderno para hispanohablantes, pp. 46–50
▸ Standardized Assessment Tutor, Chapter 10

MEDIA
▸ One-Stop Planner
▸ Video Program, Videocassette 4, 10:46–18:09
▸ Audio Compact Discs, CD 10, Tr. 18
▸ Interactive CD-ROM Tutor, Disc 3

Pair Work

2 Ask each pair to use its report to create a dialogue between the team captain and the coach. Have each pair present its dialogue to the class.

Teacher Note

3 Remind students that they may make up experiences for this activity.

Answers

4 1. Es importante por el estilo renacentista español y por su colección de arte español y portugués.
2. Hay mucha influencia puertorriqueña en East Harlem en la sección que se llama El Barrio.
3. Es famoso por su comida, la música "salsa", el cine, sus publicaciones en español y su museo.
4. El museo tiene exhibiciones de objetos precolombinos, pintura, escultura y videos latinoamericanos.

---

1 Escucha las siguientes oraciones e indica cuál corresponde a cada dibujo. Hay una oración que no corresponde a ningún dibujo. Script and answers on p. 279H.

CD 10
Tr. 18

a.

b.

c.

d.

2 Imagina que eres el capitán o la capitana de un equipo deportivo. Con un(a) compañero(a), escribe un reportaje de ocho oraciones de los planes y metas del equipo para el año que viene. Explica cómo piensan lograr estas metas.

MODELO **Nuestro equipo aspira a ganar todos sus juegos el año que viene. Para mejorar, vamos a poner todo nuestro esfuerzo en...**

3 Haz una lista de tres cosas que te hayan salido bien en la vida y otras tres que te hayan salido mal. Pueden ser cosas importantes o pequeñas frustraciones. Pueden estar relacionadas con el deporte o con la vida familiar o social. Escribe cuál fue la causa y su efecto en tu vida.

MODELO **He aumentado de peso estos últimos meses; por lo tanto, tengo que hacer ejercicio.**

4 Contesta estas preguntas con información cultural de este capítulo. See answers below.
1. ¿Por qué es notable el edificio en que se encuentra la Sociedad Hispánica de América?
2. ¿En qué parte de Nueva York se siente especialmente la influencia de Puerto Rico?
3. ¿Cuáles son algunas de las atracciones de El Barrio?
4. ¿Qué tipos de exhibiciones tiene El Museo del Barrio?

Apply and Assess

Challenge

1 After the students have listened to the audio recording and decided which statement corresponds to each drawing, ask them to make up additional sentences that would go with each of the drawings.

Additional Practice

4 Have students work in pairs to write a short dialogue between a reporter and the director of the New York City Chamber of Commerce. The reporter asks questions about New York City and the director answers. Remind students to refer to the cultural information in the chapter.

5 Escribe en un párrafo los logros de los que estás orgulloso(a). Usa expresiones como las siguientes.

Puse todo mi esfuerzo en...   Alcancé éxito en...
Me siento orgulloso(a) de...   He triunfado en...
Logré superar...

6 Con un(a) compañero(a), usa expresiones de **Así se dice** para hablar de sus planes para el futuro. Consideren estas posibilidades antes de escribir:

los pasatiempos   la familia   el trabajo
la casa   los carros
la educación   las amistades   los viajes

See possible answers below.

7 Lee la carta y completa las frases con palabras o frases apropiadas.

1. Laura sabía hablar francés muy bien, ▭▭▭ Constancia la invitó a acompañarla como intérprete.

2. Las dos muchachas fueron al museo del Louvre ▭▭▭ ver la Mona Lisa y otras obras de arte.

3. No tenían suficiente dinero para cenar en el restaurante elegante; ▭▭▭, fueron a un lugar más barato.

4. Fueron a la Torre Eiffel y al Palacio de Versalles ▭▭▭ sacar fotografías.

5. El año que viene, Constancia ▭▭▭ ir a Dinamarca.

> *Querida Felicia,*
> *¡Mi viaje a Francia estuvo estupendo! Sabías que Laura me acompañó, ¿no? Fue mi intérprete porque yo no sé ni jota de francés. Fuimos al museo del Louvre a ver la Mona Lisa y otras obras de arte. Íbamos a cenar en un restaurante elegante pero los precios eran muy altos, así que decidimos cenar en un restaurante más barato. Fuimos también a la Torre Eiffel y al Palacio de Versalles a sacar fotos. El año que viene, quiero ir a Dinamarca. ¡Ojalá que puedas acompañarme! Un abrazo,*
> *Constancia*

8 **Situación**

Trabajen en parejas e imaginen que uno(a) de ustedes es un(a) nuevo(a) ciudadano(a) de Estados Unidos. Esta persona habla de las experiencias buenas y malas que ha tenido desde que llegó a este país. Las otras dos personas quieren saber más de su vida y su herencia cultural y le hacen algunas preguntas. También le ofrecen ayuda para que se acostumbre a su nueva situación.

Apply and Assess

Kinesthetic Learners

6 Ask students to act out their future goals and have the other students in the class guess what the goals are by using the vocabulary and expressions from the **Así se dice** sections of this chapter.

Additional Practice

8 Tell students to imagine that they are new citizens of the United States. Ask each student to write a letter to a relative or a friend in his or her native country about good and bad experiences he or she has had since coming to this country.

Repaso

CAPÍTULO 10

Portfolio

5 **Written** You might suggest that students include their paragraphs in their written Portfolios. For Portfolio suggestions, see *Alternative Assessment Guide*, page 25.

Teaching Suggestion

5 Ask students to share their paragraphs with a partner. Have they listed any of the same items? You might also encourage a class discussion about the similarities and differences among the classmates' accomplishments.

Answers

7 *Possible answers:*
1. así que
2. para
3. por lo tanto
4. con la intención de
5. piensa

Teaching Resources
p. 308

PRINT
▶ Grammar Tutor for Students of Spanish, Chapter 10

MEDIA
▶ Interactive CD-ROM Tutor, Disc 3
▶ Online self-test

go.hrw.com
WV3 NEW YORK-10

Answers

1 *Possible answers:*
1. Elías se siente orgulloso de su trabajo en el proyecto de ciencias.
2. Sabina y su hermana dominan el griego.
3. Cecilia se siente orgullosa de haber sacado buenas notas.
4. Fue difícil pero al fin Bao y Tranh lograron encajar en su nueva cultura.
5. Gerardo ha triunfado en su negocio.

2
1. Antes de empezar un proyecto, deben enfocarse en la meta.
2. Después de que alcances tus objetivos, tus padres van a sentirse orgullosos de ti.
3. El problema se resolverá cuando alguien tome la iniciativa.
4. Antes de poder superar los retos, debemos esforzarnos.
5. Cuando domine el alemán entenderé mejor la cultura alemana.

3 *Possible answers:*
1. se deben
2. Por
3. en consecuencia
4. resultaron en
5. por consiguiente

4 *Possible answers:*
1. El chico lee con la intención de aprender más acerca de la historia de su familia. Hace esto para entender mejor su cultura.
2. Una muchacha se entrena para ganar la carrera de atletismo.
3. Dolores y Antonio practican para aprender a cocinar comida italiana.
4. La chica que está corriendo afuera piensa terminar la carrera.

A ver si puedo...

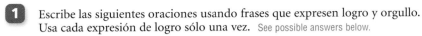

Can you talk about accomplishments?
p. 285

1 Escribe las siguientes oraciones usando frases que expresen logro y orgullo. Usa cada expresión de logro sólo una vez. See possible answers below.
1. Elías trabajó mucho en su proyecto de ciencias.
2. Sabina y su hermana hablan perfectamente el griego.
3. Cecilia se siente muy bien porque sacó muy buenas notas.
4. Fue difícil al principio pero al fin Bao y Tranh pudieron asimilarse.
5. Le fue muy bien a Gerardo en su negocio.

Can you talk about future plans?
p. 288

2 Usa la siguiente información para escribir oraciones completas. See answers below.
1. Antes de / empezar un proyecto / (Uds.) deber enfocarse
2. Después de que / (tú) alcanzar tus objetivos / tus padres sentirse orgulloso(a)
3. El problema resolverse / cuando / alguien tomar la iniciativa
4. Antes de / poder superar los retos / (nosotros) deber esforzarse
5. Cuando / (yo) dominar el alemán / entender mejor la cultura alemana

Can you express cause and effect?
p. 293

3 En estas frases, Roberto explica un poco sobre la historia de su ciudad. Completa cada frase con la expresión más apropiada. See possible answers below.
1. Los nombres indígenas de las calles ＝＝＝ a la influencia de la gente indígena que habitaba esta área hace 200 años.
2. ＝＝＝ la influencia indígena, hay mucho arte indio en esta región.
3. Muchos franceses poblaron esta región en 1800; ＝＝＝, mucha gente todavía habla un tipo de francés.
4. Las horribles batallas ＝＝＝ muchas tragedias.
5. Hay mucha gente hispana aquí; ＝＝＝ hay muchos hispanohablantes.

Can you express intention and purpose?
p. 295

4 ¿Cómo expresaría sus intenciones cada persona en el dibujo? See possible answers below

Review and Assess

Auditory Learners
Give the following dictation to students, leaving out the expressions in parentheses. Then have students complete the sentences with an appropriate expression of intent and purpose. **He estado trabajando más horas (para) ahorrar dinero. Me he esforzado tanto (con la intención de/con la idea de) hacer un viaje a Nueva York después de graduarme. Necesito dinero (para) el vuelo pero también (para que) pueda conocer los variados restaurantes que sirven comida latinoamericana. También (pienso/tengo la intención de) ir al Museo del Barrio.**

Vocabulario

Primer paso

Talking about accomplishments

Alcancé éxito en...	*I achieved success in . . .*	el esfuerzo	*effort*	encajar	*to fit in*
Domina el francés.	*He (She) speaks French very well.*	estar agradecido(a) por	*to be grateful for*	mantener	*to preserve, to keep*
Han triunfado...	*They have succeeded . . .*	el éxito	*success; hit song*	el modo de ser	*nature, disposition*
Logró superar muchos obstáculos...	*She (He) succeeded in overcoming many obstacles . . .*	el orgullo	*pride*	las raíces	*roots*
		el reto	*challenge*	**Talking about future plans**	
Puse todo mi esfuerzo en...	*I put a lot of effort into . . .*	sentirse (ie,i) orgulloso(a) de	*to feel proud of*	Antes de que empiecen las clases	*Before classes begin . . .*
Se siente orgulloso(a) de haber...	*He (She) feels proud of having . . .*	superar	*to overcome*	Antes de terminar...	*Before finishing . . .*
		superarse	*to better oneself*	Cuando cumpla los 18 años...	*When I turn 18 . . .*
Tuvo mucho éxito...	*He (She) was very successful . . .*	tener éxito	*to succeed*	Cuando sea mayor...	*When I'm older . . .*
El éxito		**Las raíces**		Después de graduarnos...	*After we graduate . . .*
alcanzar	*to achieve, to attain*	asimilarse	*to assimilate*		
aportar	*to contribute*	el compromiso	*commitment, obligation*		
la aportación	*contribution*	la costumbre	*custom*		
		criarse	*to grow up; to be raised*		

Segundo paso

Expressing cause and effect

				Expressing intention and purpose	
así que...	*so . . .*	enfocarse en	*to focus on*	con la intención de...	*with the intention of . . .*
de tal forma que...	*in such a way that . . .*	esforzarse (ue) por	*to make an effort to*	para	*in order to*
en consecuencia...	*therefore . . .*	lograr	*to achieve; to manage to*	para que	*so that*
por lo tanto...	*therefore . . .*			Pienso...	*I intend to . . .*
por consiguiente...	*consequently . . .*	llevar a cabo	*to carry out*	Tengo la intención de...	*I intend to . . .*
por tener...	*because I have . . .*	la meta	*goal*		
resultaron en...	*resulted in . . .*	el objetivo	*objective*		
se deben a...	*are due to . . .*	realizar (un sueño)	*to fulfill (a dream)*		
Las metas		soñar (ue) con + inf.	*to dream of (doing something)*		
la aspiración	*aspiration, ambition*	tomar la iniciativa	*to take the initiative*		
aspirar a	*to aspire to*	con la idea de...	*in order to . . .*		

Review and Assess

Game

AEIOU On the board write **1–A, 2–E, 3–I, 4–O, 5–U, 6–A escoger.** Divide the class into two teams. Have the first player from Team A come up and roll a die. If he rolls a 1, he must say a vocabulary word that has an A in it. (If he rolls a 2, he must say an E-word, and so on.) If he is successful, the Team A gets a point, and play continues with a player from Team B. If the first player is not successful, a player from Team B gets to say a word with that letter in it. No word may be repeated, so you might ask a player to write the words on the board as they are used. The team with more points wins.

Teaching Resources
pp. 310–313

PRINT
▸ Lesson Planner, p. 52
▸ Video Guide, pp. 72–73

MEDIA
▸ One-Stop Planner
▸ Video Program,
  Videocassette 4, 18:21–20:22
▸ Interactive CD-ROM Tutor, Disc 3
▸ Map Transparency 2

 go.hrw.com
WV3 COSTA RICA

 Using the Almanac and Map

Terms in the Almanac
- **Clima:** Like most tropical countries, Costa Rica has just two seasons, rainy and dry. Temperatures vary according to altitude.
- **Productos agrícolas:** Until the 19th century, Costa Rica's economy was based on subsistence agriculture. Today, coffee, bananas, beef, and sugar are produced for mass consumption and exportation.
- **Platos típicos: Gallo pinto** is a mixture of rice and black beans traditionally served for breakfast with sour cream or eggs. **Tamales** consist of chicken or pork wrapped in cornmeal, then steamed in banana leaves. **Ceviche** is fish marinated with lemon, onion, garlic, and sweet red peppers. **Picadillo de arracache** is a kind of casserole consisting of meat and vegetables. **Cajeta** is a heavy milk fudge similar to caramel. **Gallina de palo** is iguana, and **sopa negra** is black bean soup.

CAPÍTULOS 11 y 12

¡Ven conmigo a Costa Rica!

Población: 3.674.200 (San José: 893.000)

Área: 51.100 km²; un poco más pequeño que West Virginia

Clima: temperatura promedio 26°–28°C (79°–82°F) anual

Ciudades principales: San José, Alajuela, Cartago, Limón, Puntarenas

Productos agrícolas: bananos, café, azúcar, arroz, maíz, ganado

Industrias: comestibles, turismo, ropa, materiales de construcción

Personajes famosos: Óscar Arias Sánchez (n. 1941), presidente de Costa Rica (1986–1990) y ganador del Premio Nobel de la Paz en 1987; Claudia Poll (n. 1972), medallista olímpica; Franklin Chang-Díaz (n. 1950), astronauta del vehículo espacial Columbia

Platos típicos: gallo pinto, tamales, ceviche, picadillo de arracache, cajeta, gallina de palo, sopa negra

go.hrw.com
WV3 COSTA RICA   VIDEO   CD-ROM DISC 3

Costa Rica se ha dedicado a conservar sus selvas tropicales, que tienen muchas especies de pájaros y otros animales. ▸

Cultures and Communities

Background Information
Costa Rica has tropical rain forests, smoking volcanoes, and sandy beaches. More than 1,400 types of orchids, 850 species of birds, 35,000 species of insects, and over 200 species of mammals can be found there. Costa Rica is famous for its protection of its flora and fauna. In response to deforestation, in the 1960s the Costa Rican government created a system of national parks to save the remaining tropical forests. Roughly 27 percent of the country's land is protected, 11 percent of it by the national park system.

Language Note
Most Costa Ricans call themselves **ticos.** The nickname comes from their substitution of the diminutive suffix **-ico** for the more common **-ito.** (In Costa Rica **momentito** becomes **momentico.**)

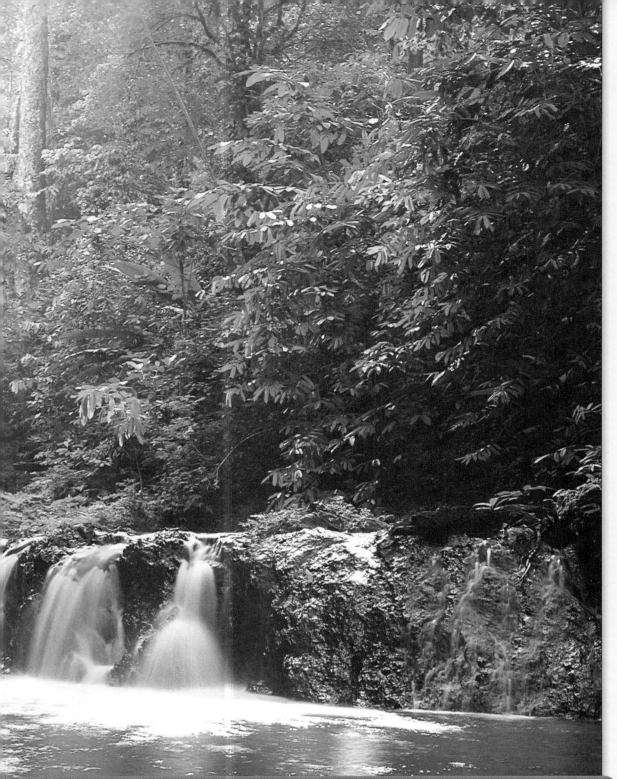

MAPQUEST.COM

**HRW
Atlas Interactivo
Mundial**

Have students use the interactive atlas at **go.hrw.com** to find out more about the geography of Costa Rica, and complete the Map Activities below.

Map Activities

- Ask students to identify the two Central American countries bordering Costa Rica (Nicaragua and Panama) and the two bodies of water on either side of it (Pacific Ocean and Caribbean Sea).

- Have students research the national park system of Costa Rica. Then provide each student with a copy of the transparency master of *Map Transparency 11-4* and have them plot federally protected areas on their maps.

CNNenEspañol.com

Have students check the **CNN en español** Web site for news on Costa Rica. The **CNN en español** site is also a good source of timely, high-interest readings for Spanish students.

Connections and Comparisons

History Link

Costa Rica is one of the Central American countries that in the past were referred to pejoratively as "banana republics" because of their economic reliance on bananas grown for export. Have students research the economic and political ramifications of the relationship between the nations of Central America and foreign fruit companies.

Science Link

Ask students to research the Costa Rican rain forest. Have them find out how much Costa Rican territory is covered by tropical rain forest. What species of flora and fauna are unique to Costa Rica? What are some products that students use on a weekly basis that come from the rain forest? What medicines are derived from rain-forest plants?

Motivating Activity

Costa Rica is known for having a remarkably free and stable political climate. Ask students to list conditions that characterize a stable democracy.

Using the Photo Essay

① El centro de la capital San José, at an elevation of 3,800 feet, is set in the wide and fertile Valle Central. The people who live here are called **josefinos**. San José is the economic and political center of Costa Rica. Many tourist attractions are within a three-hour drive of the capital.

② Uno de los volcanes activos de Costa Rica El Arenal is currently the most active volcano in the country and one of the most active in the world. El Arenal was dormant until July of 1968, when an earthquake triggered a massive eruption. The volcano has been in an almost constant state of eruption ever since. Volcanic ash is the source of the very fertile soil of the Meseta Central.

③ Más de mil especies de mariposas Costa Rica is home to the malachite *(Siproeta stelenes)* shown here. Costa Ricans have set up classes and international networks to protect the delicate insects.

④ Diversidad étnica y cultural Most Costa Ricans are of European descent. Roughly three percent of the population is of African descent, while two percent is of East Asian origin. In the Caribbean province of Limón, a third of the inhabitants trace their ancestry to West Indians of African descent who came to Costa Rica in the late nineteenth century to build railways and work on banana plantations. Only a small number of indigenous people remain in Costa Rica. There are 22 reservations throughout the country for eight different indigenous groups.

Costa Rica

En realidad, Costa Rica tiene dos costas ricas: la costa del mar Caribe y la costa del océano Pacífico. Las dos costas están separadas por apenas 125 kms (75 millas) en la banda más estrecha del país. Aunque es pequeño, Costa Rica es un país variado con montañas y selvas. Hay también una meseta central donde se encuentra la zona de mayor población y agricultura. Situado como un puente entre los dos continentes americanos, Costa Rica es considerada una de las regiones climáticas más diversas, lo cual hace del país un destino preferido de los científicos y turistas.

internet

go.hrw.com **MARCAR:** go.hrw.com
PALABRA CLAVE:
WV3 COSTA RICA

① El centro de la capital
San José, la capital de Costa Rica, goza de un clima primaveral durante todo el año. Alrededor del 30 por ciento de la población del país vive en esta ciudad, que ofrece museos, parques y muchos eventos culturales.

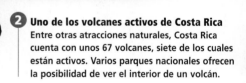

② Uno de los volcanes activos de Costa Rica
Entre otras atracciones naturales, Costa Rica cuenta con unos 67 volcanes, siete de los cuales están activos. Varios parques nacionales ofrecen la posibilidad de ver el interior de un volcán.

③ Más de mil especies de mariposas
Muchas especies de mariposas viven en Costa Rica. Los meses de junio y julio son los mejores para verlas.

Connections and Comparisons

Social Studies Link

Costa Rica has one of the highest per capita gross domestic products, the most equitable distribution of wealth, and the highest rates of school attendance and literacy in Central America. (Even before it abolished its army in 1949, Costa Ricans were proud to boast that they had more teachers than soldiers.) All of these factors have contributed to the peace, stability, and relatively high standard of living that Costa Ricans have enjoyed for decades. Divide students into five groups and assign each group one of the following countries: Guatemala, El Salvador, Honduras, Nicaragua, and Panama. Have each group research the political history of its country and identify the type of government.

En los capítulos 11 y 12, vas a conocer Costa Rica. Conocerás a algunos costarricenses y verás un poco del magnífico paisaje por el cual este país es conocido por todo el mundo. Aprenderás un poco de la historia de Costa Rica y el carácter de la nación, y verás por qué Costa Rica es considerada una joya cuyo valor natural y cultural es inestimable.

4 Diversidad étnica y cultural
Los costarricenses, o "ticos", representan una gran mezcla de culturas y costumbres. Muchos de los habitantes de la costa del Atlántico son de ascendencia africana y hablan inglés además del español. Hay también muchos costarricenses de ascendencia alemana y china.

5 La flor nacional de Costa Rica Costa Rica is home to 1,400 species of orchids. The most famous orchid is the *Cattleya skinneri,* which blooms in March. It is the national flower of Costa Rica and is known as the **guaria morada.**

6 Las famosas carretas costarricenses Brightly colored wooden oxcarts were a common form of transportation in the country-side a few decades ago. Although they are now used only in small towns, they have become a form of folk art and a symbol of traditional Costa Rican life. Most are made in the small town of Sarchí.

7 Un "dinosaurio" pequeño The *Iguana iguana,* or green iguana, has long been a Central American delicacy. Although once widespread in Central American rainforests, their numbers have diminished because of hunting and destruction of habitat. In an effort to strengthen their population and preserve their rainforest habitat, a German biologist named Dr. Dagmar Werner hit upon the idea of raising iguanas commercially. Popularly known as "Iguana Mama", she has encouraged farmers to raise iguanas in captivity, and then release them into the forests. Raising iguanas commercially yields as much meat per acre as cattle ranching.

5 La flor nacional de Costa Rica
Costa Rica tiene una abundancia de especies de plantas. Una de las plantas más famosas del país es la orquídea, que crece principalmente en las selvas tropicales.

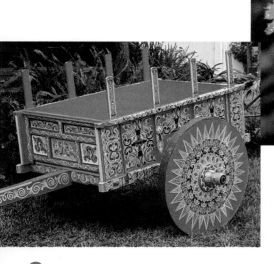

6 Las famosas carretas costarricenses
Alrededor de 1910, según cuenta una leyenda, se le ocurrió a un campesino pintar su carreta. Las carretas, que se usaban para transportar café y otros productos agrícolas, todavía se usan en los pueblos pequeños.

7 Un "dinosaurio" pequeño
Uno de los reptiles más famosos del país es la iguana. Algunos costarricenses usan la iguana como comida en un plato que se llama "gallina de palo".

Teacher Note
There are many interesting Web sites on Costa Rica's natural wonders. Have students check the Web site of the **Jardín Botánico Lankester,** at the **Universidad de Costa Rica,** for information and photos of Costa Rican orchids and other plants.

Cultures and Communities

Culture Note
In 1856, William Walker, an American citizen acting on his own behalf, invaded Costa Rica with an army of mercenaries. At an **hacienda** called La Casona in the northern province of Guanacaste, a volunteer army of 9,000 Costa Ricans defeated Walker's forces and pursued them as they retreated. Eventually, Walker was surrounded in a wooden fortress in Nicaragua.

On April 11, 1856, Juan Santamaría, the volunteer army's drummer, gave his life in order to set fire to the fortress and drive Walker out. Today, Juan Santamaría is a national hero. The international airport in San José is named for him, and there is a statue honoring him in the city's Parque Nacional. La Casona, site of the Costa Rican victory, is now part of Santa Rosa National Park.

Capítulo 11: El mundo en que vivimos
Chapter Overview

De antemano pp. 316–318	*El proyecto de Néstor*

	FUNCTIONS	**GRAMMAR**	**VOCABULARY**	**RE-ENTRY**
Primer paso pp. 319–322	• Pointing out problems and their consequences, p. 319 • Talking about how you would solve a problem, p. 321	• **se** + verb constructions, p. 319	• Social problems, p. 319	• Uses of **se** as an impersonal object (**Capítulo 4, Capítulo 5**) • The conditional (**Capítulo 9**)

¡Adelante! pp. 324–325	*Algunas soluciones*

Segundo paso pp. 326–329	• Talking about hypothetical situations, p. 326	• The past subjunctive in contrary-to-fact **si** clauses, p. 327	• Talking about hypothetical situations, p. 326	• The subjunctive (**Capítulos 5, 6, 7, 8**) • The preterite (**Capítulo 12, I**)

Vamos a leer pp. 330–332	**Las abejas de bronce**	**Reading Strategy:** Guessing words through context

Vamos a escribir p. 333	**Un fax**	**Writing Strategy:** Using note cards

Más práctica gramatical	**pp. 334–337** **Primer paso,** pp. 334–335	**Segundo paso,** pp. 336–337

Review pp. 338–341	**Repaso,** pp. 338–339	**A ver si puedo...,** p. 340	**Vocabulario,** p. 341

CULTURE

• **Nota cultural,** Costa Rica's democracy, p. 318
• **Panorama cultural, ¿Cuál es el mayor problema ambiental de tu comunidad?,** p. 323

• **Nota cultural,** Ecological conservation in Costa Rica, p. 328

Capítulo 11: El mundo en que vivimos
Chapter Resources

Lesson Planning

One-Stop Planner

Lesson Planner with Substitute Teacher Lesson Plans, pp. 52–56, 75

Student Make-Up Assignments
- Make-Up Assignment Copying Masters, Chapter 11

Listening and Speaking

Listening Activities
- Student Response Forms for Listening Activities, pp. 83–85
- Additional Listening Activities 11-1 to 11-6, pp. 87–89
- Additional Listening Activities (poem), p. 90
- Scripts and Answers, pp. 152–156

Video Guide
- Teaching Suggestions, pp. 75–76
- Activity Masters, pp. 77–79
- Scripts and Answers, pp. 109–111, 119–120

Activities for Communication
- Communicative Activities, pp. 41–44
- Realia and Teaching Suggestions, pp. 81–83
- Situation Cards, pp. 109–110

Reading and Writing

Reading Strategies and Skills Handbook, Chapter 11

¡Lee conmigo! 3, Chapter 11

Cuaderno de actividades, pp. 121–132

Grammar

Cuaderno de gramática, pp. 87–94

Grammar Tutor for Students of Spanish, Chapter 11

Assessment

Testing Program
- Grammar and Vocabulary Quizzes, **Paso** Quizzes, and Chapter Test, pp. 235–248
- Score Sheet, Scripts and Answers, pp. 249–255

Alternative Assessment Guide
- Portfolio Assessment, p. 26
- Performance Assessment, p. 40
- CD-ROM Assessment, p. 54

Student Make-Up Assignments
- Alternative Quizzes, Chapter 11

Standardized Assessment Tutor
- Reading, pp. 43–45
- Writing, p. 46
- Math, pp. 51–52

Native Speakers

Cuaderno para hispanohablantes, pp. 51–55

 Online Activities
- Juegos interactivos
- Actividades Internet

 Video Program
- Videocassette 4
- Videocassette 5 (captioned version)

 Audio Compact Discs
- Textbook Listening Activities, CD 11, Tracks 1–19
- Additional Listening Activities, CD 11, Tracks 24–30
- Assessment Items, CD 11, Tracks 20–23

 Interactive CD-ROM Tutor, Disc 3

 Teaching Transparencies
- Situations 11-1 to 11-2
- **Mas práctica gramatical** Answers
- **Cuaderno de gramática** Answers

 One-Stop Planner CD-ROM

Use the **One-Stop Planner CD-ROM with Test Generator** to aid in lesson planning and pacing.
For each chapter, the **One-Stop Planner** includes:
- Editable lesson plans with direct links to teaching resources
- Printable worksheets from resource books
- Direct launches to the HRW Internet activities
- Video and audio segments
- Test Generator
- Clip Art for vocabulary items

Capítulo 11: El mundo en que vivimos

Projects

En la ciudad de . . .

In this project, students work in groups of three or four to research a city and write a short newscast reporting on the challenges that the city faces. You may want to allow a week for groups to collect information on the city they choose.

MATERIALS

✂ **Students may need**
- Paper
- Dictionary
- Poster board
- Markers
- Videotaping equipment

SUGGESTED SEQUENCE

1. Divide the class into groups of three to four students and assign them a city to research. Allow them library time to research the addresses of and write letters to the Chamber of Commerce or the Tourist Bureau of their chosen city. Have students also collect as much information from the Internet as possible.

2. After students have gathered their information, they may begin preparing their written newscast. They should be encouraged to report on the city's current events, cultural information, recent problems and solutions, and outlook for the near future.

3. Students prepare several broadcast screen inserts (icons or pictures that appear behind the shoulder of the newscaster as he or she is introducing the upcoming story). Encourage students to be creative in their representations and to choose an image that depicts the main idea of their reports.

4. Students present their news broadcasts to the class. You may want to record groups' projects on videocassette.

GRADING THE PROJECT

Suggested point distribution: (total = 100 points)

Use of Spanish	30
Vocabulary	30
Creativity of visuals	20
Presentation	20

Games

¿Cierto o falso?

This game helps students review the impersonal se and the vocabulary from this chapter and previous chapters. It may be played among several students or between two teams.

Preparation Have students write true or false statements using the impersonal **se** on ten index cards. (**Se prohibe leer en la escuela. Se juega al tenis en la cancha de tenis.**)

Procedure Small teams or several individuals take turns showing the index cards to other students and reading the sentences aloud. The first team or student to correctly respond **cierto** or **falso** earns a point. The team or student with the most points at the end of the game wins.

Variation Have students write compound sentences with the conditional and past subjunctive.

La carrera

In this game, students practice the past subjunctive and si clauses by using art as prompts.

Preparation Have *Teaching Transparencies 11-1* and *11-2* ready.

Procedure Divide the class into two teams. Display a transparency and have one student from each team write a corresponding sentence. For example, if *Transparency 11-2* is displayed, have each student write a sentence on the board about what he or she would do in one of the three daydreams shown. The first student to write a correct sentence with the subjunctive wins a point for his or her team. Then another person from each team has a turn. The team with the most points wins.

COMMUNITY LINK

You may want to invite a language arts or a business teacher to instruct students on the correct way to write a form letter requesting information. You should also limit the number of letters going to any one agency.

STANDARDS: 1.3, 3.1, 5.1

Storytelling

Mini-cuento

This story accompanies Teaching Transparency 11-1. The ***mini-cuento*** *can be told and retold in different formats, acted out, written as dictation, and read aloud to give students additional opportunities to practice all four skills. The following tells about various people attending a city meeting to solve social problems.*

Villalimpia siempre fue una ciudad muy limpia y sin problemas sociales. Pero la ciudad ha crecido y ahora hay muchos problemas de contaminación, salud pública y pobreza. La comunidad se ha reunido para hablar y ha decidido actuar. Linda, la directora del programa para el medio ambiente, dice que si no actúan ya la situación va a empeorarse. Ella propone muchas cosas: limpiar los ríos, aumentar el reciclaje e incluir a los jóvenes en programas de educación. También se habló de crear campañas de salud y de crear más hospitales para los pobres. Linda dice que intentará iniciar un programa de ayuda para las familias pobres de la ciudad.

¿Cuál es el mayor problema ambiental o social de tu comunidad?

Traditions

Volcanes y ecoturismo

Costa Rica, with one-third of its land devoted to national parks, has been at the forefront of ecotourism in Central America and the world. This tiny country has over 200 identified volcanic formations. Only a few, however, are active today. The most famous volcanoes in Costa Rica are **Arenal,** a picture-perfect cone, and one of the most active volcanoes in the world; **Poás,** with a mile-wide crater and, at 1000 feet deep, an acid lake and a lava dome; and **Irazú,** with four craters. **Irazú** is the largest (200 square miles) and the highest (11,260 feet) volcano. Have students research the answers to these questions: Where does the word "volcano" come from? What is the ring of fire?

Receta

Chancletas *are stuffed* ***chayotes,*** *and* ***chayotes*** *are a Latin American vegetable with a very mild taste. They look like pears.* ***Chancletas*** *means "slippers" and might refer to the appearance of a cut and cooked* ***chayote.*** ***Chayotes*** *can be peeled, boiled, diced, and sauteed with butter; but the tastiest way of eating them is stuffed. You may substitute yellow squash or zucchini for* ***chayotes.***

CHANCLETAS

para 5 personas

3 chayotes, cortados por la mitad a lo largo

2 cucharaditas de sal y agua para hervir

1 taza de cebolla, picada

1 diente de ajo, picado

2 1/2 tazas de pan molido italiano *(Italian breadcrumbs)*

pimienta negra y sal al gusto

2 huevos, ligeramente batidos

3 cucharadas de queso parmesano, rallado

mantequilla

Hierva los chayotes en agua con sal por 20 minutos. Escurra el agua y deje que se enfríen. Con mucho cuidado, para no romper la cáscara, quite la semilla y limpie bien alrededor. Con una cuchara saque la carne del chayote, dejando media pulgada alrededor de la cáscara. Guarde la cáscara. Corte la carne en pedazos. En una sartén grande, sofría *(sautee)* la cebolla y el ajo en un poco de mantequilla. Agregue 2 tazas de pan molido, el queso, la pimienta y los huevos. Mezcle todo y rellene las cáscaras. Mezcle la media taza restante de pan molido con el queso parmesano y espolvoréelo encima de los chayotes. Póngalos en el horno, a 450°, por unos 15 a 20 minutos hasta que estén calientes y dorados.

Video Program

Videocassette 4, Videocassette 5 (captioned version)
See Video Guide, pages 74–79.

Dramatic episode • Si yo fuera presidenta

Irene and Alejandra are working on a video project for school. They interview people on the street, including Carlos, and ask their opinions about Mexico City's problems. Carlos talks about crime and how he would like to convince today's youth to have hope for the future. The girls review the finished video that night, and Irene tells Alejandra that if Irene were president, she would appoint Alejandra ambassador to Spain. That reminds Alejandra of Sergio, and she wonders why he has not revealed his identity yet.

¿Cuál es el mayor problema ambiental de tu comunidad?

Spanish-speaking people talk about environmental problems in their areas and around the world.

Videoclips

- **Comfama** and **Cámara de Comercio de Medellín y Teleantioquia:** public service messages about protecting water resources, avoiding noisy environments, and protecting trees for the sake of air quality

- **El cóndor:** documentary about the South American condor, its habitat, and the people who study it

Interactive CD-ROM Tutor

The **Interactive CD-ROM Tutor** contains videos, interactive games, and activities that provide students an opportunity to practice and review the material covered in Chapter 11.

Activity	Activity Type	Pupil's Edition Page
1. Así se dice	¡Atrévete!	p. 319
2. Vocabulario	¡Presta el oído!	p. 319
3. Así se dice	Imagen y sonido ¡Exploremos! ¡Identifiquemos!	p. 321
4. Así se dice	Patas arriba	p. 326
5. Gramática	¿Qué falta?	p. 327
6. Gramática	¡A escoger!	p. 327
Panorama cultural	¿Cuál es el mayor problema ambiental de tu comunidad? ¡A escoger!	p. 323
¡A hablar!	*Guided recording*	pp. 338–339
¡A escribir!	*Guided writing*	pp. 338–339

Teacher Management System
Logging In

Logging in to the *¡Ven conmigo!* TMS is easy. Upon launching the program, simply type "admin" in the password area of the log-in screen and press RETURN. Log on to **www.hrw.com/CDROMTUTOR** for a detailed explanation of the Teacher Management System.

One-Stop Planner CD-ROM

To preview all resources available for this chapter, use the **One-Stop Planner CD-ROM**, Disc 3.

Internet Connection

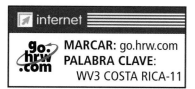

MARCAR: go.hrw.com
PALABRA CLAVE:
WV3 COSTA RICA-11

*Have students explore the **go.hrw.com** Web site for many online resources covering all chapters. All Chapter 11 resources are available under the keyword **WV3 COSTA RICA-11**. Interactive games help students practice the material and provide them with immediate feedback. You will also find a printable worksheet that provides Internet activities that lead to a comprehensive online research project.*

Juegos interactivos

You can use the interactive activities in this chapter

- to practice grammar, vocabulary, and chapter functions
- as homework
- as an assessment option
- as a self-test
- to prepare for the Chapter Test

Actividades Internet

Students research social problems in other cities. They study one problem in depth, and write the consequences of taking no action to solve the problem. They then prepare a letter to their mayor about a similar problem in their own city.

- As preparation for the **Hoja de actividades,** have students review the functions in **Primer paso.** Also have them watch the interviews in **Panorama cultural.**

- After students complete the activity sheet, have them discuss problems in other cites that are also issues in their city. Are the possible solutions and the consequences of doing nothing similar?

Proyecto

Have students work in small groups to build a Web site about the local issue they learned about in the **Hoja de actividades.** Ask each student in the group to contribute at least one link or article about the problem. The group should come to a consensus about the best way to solve the problem and should post this opinion on their site as well.

De antemano

2   p. 318

1. La gente que ha participado en los programas preventivos ha superado su adicción a las drogas.

2. Es mejor que los jóvenes vean películas con temas e imágenes positivos.

3. Me alegro cuando veo plantas y árboles en las carreteras. Se ve mucho más bonito que papeles desechados.

4. Me alegro cuando veo a la gente cooperar con otros y ayudar a los demás—sobre todo a los niños.

5. Los problemas económicos nos afectan a todos. ¡Hoy en día los precios están muy altos!

6. Lo que vemos y leemos nos afecta mucho; por eso hay que proteger a los niños de la violencia en la tele.

Answers to Activity 2

1. b	3. a	5. c
2. e	4. d	6. e

Primer paso

6   p. 319

1. Muy buenos días desde nuestros estudios centrales en San José. Les habla Jorge Gonsalves con las últimas noticias. Según el gobierno municipal, la contaminación del aire en la ciudad ha aumentado a causa de los gases que emiten los carros. Recomendamos que no manejen sus carros si no es necesario.

2. Se dice que menos jóvenes usan drogas este año que el año pasado. El gobierno cree que esto se está relacionado con la campaña contra las drogas en las escuelas.

3. Muchas personas se han fijado en que los precios de la gasolina no han aumentado durante los últimos dos meses. El gobierno dice que esto se debe a una reducción en la tasa de inflación.

4. Esta mañana dijo el Director de los Parques Nacionales que los ríos de varios parques están contaminados. No se sabe por qué. El Director declaró, "Si no hacemos nada, tendremos que cerrar varios parques por dos o tres años."

5. Algunas entrevistas con personas en la calle han revelado que la gente está frustrada con el alto nivel de crimen que ven en nuestra ciudad. Una señora dijo, "Estoy harta de tener miedo en mi propia casa."

6. Una estadística nueva: según la doctora María Luisa Vargas Smith, psicóloga de la Universidad de Costa Rica, ha habido cinco por ciento menos crímenes violentos este año. La doctora cree que esto se debe a mejoras en la economía nacional.

Answers to Activity 6

1. mala	3. buena	5. mala
2. buena	4. mala	6. buena

11   p. 321

Queridos compatriotas. Estoy aquí frente a ustedes porque los problemas de nuestro estado necesitan de soluciones inmediatas y claras. La situación ha empeorado durante los tres últimos años y si no hacemos nada, lo lamentaremos en el futuro.

1. Uno, empezaría por hacer públicas todas las actividades del gobierno. El gobierno debe ser responsable de sus acciones ante los ciudadanos. No habrá secretos en la actividad gubernamental. Nadie está por encima de la ley.

2. Dos, me dedicaría a obtener los mejores profesores y materiales para las escuelas. Todos sabemos que el futuro del estado está en la educación. Mi gobierno fomentará una mejor educación para nuestros hijos.

3. Tres, nuestro estado necesita lugares apropiados para la gente que viene a disfrutar de nuestros paisajes. Me he fijado en la mala situación en la que están los parques públicos y las áreas de recreo. Por eso, los mejoraría.

4. Cuatro, intentaría reformar el sistema de justicia. La seguridad de los ciudadanos es importante. La delincuencia y el homicidio han aumentado mucho.

5. Cinco, mi gobierno buscará soluciones acerca de los trabajos. La creación de trabajos ha bajado en los últimos años. Por eso, la solución que planteo es la creación de una organización para ayudar a la gente a encontrar trabajo.

Answers to Activity 11

1. b	3. e	5. a
2. d	4. c	

One-Stop Planner CD-ROM

To preview all resources available for this chapter, use the **One-Stop Planner CD-ROM,** Disc 3.

Segundo paso

21 p. 326

1. — Dice que le gustaría ayudar a la gente.

— Hay gente sin empleo y otros que no tienen dónde vivir que estarían muy agradecidos por su esfuerzo.

— Qué bueno sería si realizara su sueño y ganara la elección, ¿no?

2. — Dice que el secreto de entender y ayudar a la gente es escucharle.

— Sí, dice que si pudiera, estudiaría sicología. Le gusta fijarse en el modo de ser de cada persona.

— Sería maravilloso si asistiera a la universidad este año.

3. — Sus éxitos se deben a sus padres. Tuvieron que superar muchos retos pero al fin triunfaron.

— Y ahora dice que quiere aportar algo a los demás. Da becas a estudiantes sin muchos recursos que quieren asistir a la universidad.

— Es una persona muy generosa con su dinero. Sería maravilloso si muchos estudiantes pudieran asistir a la universidad con su ayuda.

4. — Siempre está pensando en hacer investigaciones.

— Él siempre dice que sería bonito si no hubiera más enfermedades en el mundo.

— Si sigue trabajando no hay duda que lo logrará.

Answers to Activity 21
1. b
2. ningún dibujo
3. c
4. a

Repaso

1 p. 338

NARRATOR Señoras y señores, la señora Cecilia Reyes contestará nuestra primera pregunta y el señor Juan Luis Benavides tendrá tres minutos para responder. Señora Reyes, ¿cuál es el problema más grave que nos afecta hoy día y cómo lo resolvería?

CECILIA Sin duda el mayor problema que nos afecta a todos es la alta criminalidad que encontramos no sólo en las grandes ciudades, sino también en el campo. Me he fijado en el hecho de que cuando hay mucho desempleo, hay más crimen. Me dedicaría a bajar el desempleo y empezaría por crear miles de empleos construyendo centros de recreo para nuestros hijos. Si no realizamos un programa de educación fuera de las escuelas que les dé a nuestros jóvenes una alternativa al crimen, nunca vamos a reducir la delincuencia en nuestro país.

NARRATOR Señor Benavides, usted tiene tres minutos para responder.

JUAN LUIS Aunque yo también creo que la criminalidad es un problema actual, no diría que es el más grave. Nuestro sistema de justicia es sin duda el mejor del mundo. Lo que nos falta es construir más prisiones de alta seguridad. Los programas de educación por lo general no ayudan nada. La única manera de educar a los criminales es ponerlos en la prisión. Habrá que crear más empleo pero yo propongo que construyamos más cárceles. Si no actuamos ahora, los criminales van a tener más oportunidades en nuestro país que la gente trabajadora.

Answers to Activity 1
1. D   4. B
2. B   5. R
3. R

Capítulo 11: El mundo en que vivimos
Suggested Lesson Plans 50-Minute Schedule

Day 1

CHAPTER OPENER 5 min.
- Focusing on Outcomes, ATE, p. 315
- Discuss Language Note, ATE, p. 315.

DE ANTEMANO 40 min.
- Presenting **De antemano** and Preteaching Vocabulary, ATE, p. 316
- Activities 1–5, p. 318, and Comprehension Check, ATE, p. 318
- Present and discuss the **Nota cultural**, p. 318.

Wrap-Up 5 min.
- Do the Thinking Critically activity, ATE, p. 317.

Homework Options
Cuaderno de actividades, p. 121, Activities 1–2

Day 2

PRIMER PASO
Quick Review 5 min.
- Check homework.
- Bell Work, ATE, p. 319

Así se dice/Vocabulario, p. 319 40 min.
- Presenting **Así se dice** and **Vocabulario**, ATE, p. 319
- Present **También se puede decir...**, p. 319.
- Review **¿Te acuerdas?**, p. 319.
- Do Activity 6 with the Audio CD, p. 319.
- Do Activity 7, p. 320.
- Have students do Activity 8 in pairs, p. 320.

Wrap-Up 5 min.
- Have students rank the country's problems and their consequences.

Homework Options
Cuaderno de actividades, p. 122, Activity 4
Cuaderno de gramática, pp. 87–89, Activities 1–6

Day 3

PRIMER PASO
Quick Review 10 min.
- Check homework.
- Do Vocabulary Practice activities 2–3 for Teaching Transparency 11-1.

Así se dice/Vocabulario, p. 319 20 min.
- Have students do Activity 9 in pairs, p. 320.
- Present **Vocabulario extra**, p. 320.
- Do the Thinking Critically Activity, ATE, p. 320.
- Have students do Activity 10 in groups, p. 320.

Así se dice, p. 321 15 min.
- Presenting **Así se dice**, ATE, p. 321
- Review the conditional tense.
- Do Activity 11 with the Audio CD, p. 321.

Wrap-Up 5 min.
- Do the Challenge activity, ATE, p. 321.

Homework Options
Cuaderno de actividades, pp. 122–124, Activities 3, 5–7
Cuaderno de gramática, p. 90, Activities 7–8

Day 4

PRIMER PASO
Quick Review 10 min.
- Check homework.
- Review **Así se dice** expressions, p. 321.

Así se dice, p. 321 35 min.
- Have students do Activity 12 in groups, p. 321.
- Have students do Activity 13 in pairs, p. 322.
- Have students do Activity 14 in groups, p. 322.
- Do Activity 15, p. 322.

Wrap-Up 5 min.
- Do the Thinking Critically activity, ATE, p. 321.

Homework Options
Cuaderno de actividades, pp. 124–125, Activities 8–11

Day 5

PRIMER PASO
Quick Review 5 min.
- Check homework.

Así se dice, p. 321 10 min.
- Have students do Activity 16, then peer-edit their work, p. 322.

PANORAMA CULTURAL 10 min.
- Presenting **Panorama cultural**, ATE, p. 323

¡ADELANTE! 20 min.
- Presenting **¡Adelante!** and Preteaching Vocabulary, ATE, p. 324
- Activities 17–20, pp. 324–325

Wrap-Up 5 min.
- Do the Thinking Critically activity, ATE, p. 325.
- Discuss the content and format of Quiz 11-1.

Homework Options
Study for Quiz 11-1.
Cuaderno de actividades, p. 126, Activities 12–14

Day 6

PRIMER PASO
Quick Review 10 min.
- Check homework.
- Review the content of **Primer paso**.

Quiz 20 min.
- Administer Quiz 11-1A, 11-1B, or a combination of the two.

SEGUNDO PASO
Así se dice, p. 326 15 min.
- Presenting **Así se dice**, ATE, p. 326
- Do Activity 21 with the Audio CD, p. 326.
- Do Activity 22, p. 326.

Wrap-Up 5 min.
- Do Vocabulary Practice Activity 1 for Teaching Transparency 11-2.

Homework Options
Cuaderno de actividades, p. 127, Activity 15
Cuaderno de gramática, p. 91, Activities 9–10

One-Stop Planner CD-ROM

For alternative lesson plans by chapter section, to create your own customized plans, or to preview all resources available for this chapter, use the **One-Stop Planner CD-ROM,** Disc 3.

 For additional homework suggestions, see activities accompanied by this symbol throughout the chapter.

Day 7

SEGUNDO PASO
Quick Review 5 min.
- Check homework.

Gramática, p. 327 40 min.
- Review preterite conjugations.
- Presenting **Gramática**, ATE, p. 327
- Do Activities 23–26, pp. 327–328.
- Read and discuss the **Nota cultural**, p. 328.
- Present the Culture Notes, ATE, p. 328.
- Have students do Activity 27 in pairs, p. 328.

Wrap-Up 5 min.
- Follow Suggestion 3 for Teaching Transparency 11-2.

Homework Options
Cuaderno de actividades, pp. 127–129, Activities 16–19
Cuaderno de gramática, pp. 92–93, Activities 11–14

Day 8

SEGUNDO PASO
Quick Review 5 min.
- Check homework.

Gramática, p. 327 40 min.
- Do Activity 28, p. 329.
- Have students do Activity 29 in pairs and Activity 30 in groups, p. 329.
- Have students do Activity 31, then peer-edit their work, p. 329.

Wrap-Up 5 min.
- Discuss the content and format of Quiz 11-2.

Homework Options
Study for Quiz 11-2.
Cuaderno de actividades, p. 130, Activities 20–21
Cuaderno de gramática, p. 94, Activities 15–16

Day 9

SEGUNDO PASO
Quick Review 10 min.
- Check homework.
- Review the content of **Segundo paso.**

Quiz 20 min.
- Administer Quiz 11-2A, 11-2B, or a combination of the two.

VAMOS A LEER 15 min.
- Read the **Estrategia**, p. 330.
- Follow the Slower Pace suggestion, ATE, p. 330.

Wrap-Up 5 min.
- Do Activity A, pp. 330–331.

Homework Options
Vamos a leer Activity B, p. 331
Have students do **Vamos a escribir** Activity A, p. 333.

Day 10

VAMOS A LEER
Quick Review 5 min.
- Check homework.

VAMOS A LEER 25 min.
- Have students do Activity D in groups, p. 332.
- Do Activity E, p. 332.

VAMOS A ESCRIBIR 15 min.
- Have students begin Activity B, p. 333.

Wrap-Up 5 min.
- Discuss the concepts from Chapter 11 to be used in student faxes.

Homework Options
Finish **Vamos a escribir** Activity B, p. 333.
Cuaderno de actividades, pp. 131–132, Activities 22–27

Day 11

REPASO
Quick Review 10 min.
- Check homework.
- Have students do **Vamos a escribir** Activity C, p. 333.

REPASO 35 min.
- Do Activity 1 with the Audio CD, p. 338.
- Have students do Activities 2, 7, and 8 in pairs, pp. 338–339.
- Have students do Activity 3 in groups, p. 338.

Wrap-Up 5 min.
- Have students list the main concepts from Chapter 11.

Homework Options
Have students write **Vamos a escribir** final draft, p. 333.
Repaso Activities 4–6, pp. 338–339
A ver si puedo..., p. 340

Day 12

REPASO
Quick Review 5 min.
- Check and collect homework.

Chapter Review 40 min.
- Review Chapter 11. Choose from **Más práctica gramatical,** Grammar Tutor for Students of Spanish, Activities for Communication, Listening Activities, Interactive CD-ROM Tutor, or **Juegos interactivos.**

Wrap-Up 5 min.
- Review content and format of Chapter 11 Test.

Homework Options
Study for Chapter 11 Test.

Assessment

Quick Review 5 min.
- Answer any last-minute questions.

Test, Chapter 11 45 min.
- Administer Chapter 11 Test. Select from Testing Program, Alternative Assessment Guide, Test Generator, or Standardized Assessment Tutor.

Capítulo 11: El mundo en que vivimos
Suggested Lesson Plans *90-Minute Block Schedule*

Block 1

CHAPTER OPENER 5 min.
- Focusing on Outcomes, ATE, p. 315
- Discuss Language Note, ATE, p. 315.

DE ANTEMANO 40 min.
- Presenting **De antemano** and Preteaching Vocabulary, ATE, p. 316
- Activities 1–5, p. 318, and Comprehension Check, ATE, p. 318
- Present and discuss the **Nota cultural**, p. 318.

PRIMER PASO
Así se dice/Vocabulario, p. 319 40 min.
- Presenting **Así se dice** and **Vocabulario,** ATE, p. 319
- Present **También se puede decir...,** p. 319.
- Review **¿Te acuerdas?,** p. 319.
- Do Activity 6 with the Audio CD, p. 319.
- Do Activity 7, p. 320.
- Have students do Activity 8 in pairs, p. 320.

Wrap-Up 5 min.
- Have students rank the country's problems and their consequences.

Homework Options
Cuaderno de actividades, pp. 121–122, Activities 1–2, 4
Cuaderno de gramática, pp. 87–89, Activities 1–6

Block 2

PRIMER PASO
Quick Review 10 min.
- Check homework.

Así se dice/Vocabuario, p. 319 20 min.
- Have students do Activity 9 in pairs, p. 320.
- Present **Vocabulario extra**, p. 320.
- Do the Thinking Critically activity, ATE, p. 320.
- Have students do Activity 10 in groups, p. 320.

Así se dice, p. 321 50 min.
- Presenting **Así se dice**, ATE, p. 321
- Review the conditional tense.
- Do Activity 11 with the Audio CD, p. 321.
- Have students do Activity 12 in groups, p. 321.
- Have students do Activity 13 in pairs, p. 322.
- Have students do Activity 14 in groups, p. 322.
- Do Activity 15, p. 322.

Wrap-Up 10 min.
- Follow Suggestions 1–2 for Teaching Transparency 11-1.
- Do the Thinking Critically activity, ATE, p. 321.

Homework Options
Cuaderno de actividades, pp. 122–125, Activities 3, 5–11
Cuaderno de gramática, p. 90, Activities 7–8

Block 3

PRIMER PASO
Quick Review 10 min.
- Check homework.

Así se dice, p. 321 15 min.
- Have students do Activity 16, then peer-edit their work, p. 322.

PANORAMA CULTURAL 10 min.
- Presenting **Panorama cultural**, ATE, p. 323

¡ADELANTE! 25 min.
- Presenting **¡Adelante!** and Preteaching Vocabulary, ATE, p. 324
- Activities 17–20, pp. 324–325
- Do the Thinking Critically activity, ATE, p. 325.

SEGUNDO PASO
Así se dice, p. 326 20 min.
- Presenting **Así se dice**, ATE, p. 326
- Do Activity 21 with the Audio CD, p. 326.
- Do Activity 22, p. 326.

Wrap-Up 10 min.
- Do the **Mini-cuento** for Teaching Transparency 11-1.
- Discuss the content and format of Quiz 11-1.

Homework Options
Study for Quiz 11-1.
Cuaderno de actividades, pp. 126–127, Activities 12–15
Cuaderno de gramática, p. 91, Activities 9–10

 **One-Stop** Planner CD-ROM

For alternative lesson plans by chapter section, to create your own customized plans, or to preview all resources available for this chapter, use the **One-Stop Planner CD-ROM,** Disc 3.

 For additional homework suggestions, see activities accompanied by this symbol throughout the chapter.

Block 4

PRIMER PASO
Quick Review 10 min.
- Check homework.
- Review content of **Primer paso.**

Quiz 20 min.
- Administer Quiz 11-1A, 11-1B, or a combination of the two.

SEGUNDO PASO
Gramática, p. 327 50 min.
- Review preterite conjugations.
- Presenting **Gramática,** ATE, p. 327
- Do Activities 23–26, pp. 327–328.
- Read and discuss the **Nota cultural,** p. 328.
- Present the Culture Notes, ATE, p. 328.
- Have students do Activity 27 in pairs, p. 328.
- Do Activity 28, p. 329.

Wrap-Up 10 min.
- Follow Suggestions 1–3 for Teaching Transparency 11-2.

Homework Options
Cuaderno de actividades, pp. 127–130, Activities 16–21
Cuaderno de gramática, pp. 92–94, Activities 11–16

Block 5

SEGUNDO PASO
Quick Review 10 min.
- Check homework.

Gramática, p. 329 35 min.
- Have students do Activity 29 in pairs and Activity 30 in groups, p. 329.
- Have students do Activity 31, then peer-edit their work, p. 329.

VAMOS A LEER 40 min.
- Read the **Estrategia,** p. 330.
- Follow the Slower Pace suggestion, ATE, p. 330.

Wrap-Up 5 min.
- Do Activity A, pp. 330–331.
- Discuss the content and format of Quiz 11-2.

Homework Options
Study for Quiz 11-2.
Vamos a escribir Activities A–B, p. 333
Repaso Activities 4–6, pp. 338–339

Block 6

SEGUNDO PASO
Quick Review 5 min.
- Check homework.
- Review the content of **Segundo paso.**

Quiz 20 min.
- Administer Quiz 11-2A, 11-2B, or a combination of the two.

VAMOS A LEER 20 min.
- Have students do Activity D in groups, p. 332.
- Do Activity E, p. 332.

VAMOS A ESCRIBIR 10 min.
- Have students do Activity C, p. 333.

REPASO 30 min.
- Do Activity 1 with the Audio CD, p. 338.
- Have students do Activities 2, 7, and 8 in pairs, pp. 338–339.
- Have students do Activity 3 in groups, p. 338.

Wrap-Up 5 min.
- Discuss the content and format of the Chapter 11 Test.

Homework Options
Study for the Chapter 11 Test.
Write the final draft for **Vamos a escribir,** p. 333.
Cuaderno de actividades, pp. 131–132, Activities 22–27
A ver si puedo…, p. 340

Block 7

REPASO
Quick Review 10 min.
- Check and collect homework.

Chapter Review 35 min.
- Review Chapter 11. Choose from **Más práctica gramatical,** Grammar Tutor for Students of Spanish, Activities for Communication, Listening Activities, Interactive CD-ROM Tutor, or **Juegos interactivos.**

Test, Chapter 11 45 min.
- Administer Chapter 11 Test. Select from Testing Program, Alternative Assessment Guide, Test Generator, or Standardized Assessment Tutor.

Chapter Opener

One-Stop Planner CD-ROM

For resource information, see the **One-Stop Planner,** Disc 3.

Pacing Tips
The content of this chapter relates to pointing out problems, consequences, and possible solutions. Most of the new vocabulary is concentrated in **Primer paso;** however, **Segundo paso** introduces new and challenging grammar rules. As such, allot about the same time for both **Pasos,** but be sure to incorporate interactive activities that allow students adequate practice with the use of the past subjunctive. Try including Additional Practice (p. 327) and Slower Pace (p. 327). For more tips on pacing, see Suggested Lesson Plans, pp. 313I–313L.

Meeting the Standards

Communication
- Pointing out problems and their consequences, p. 319
- Talking about how you would solve a problem, p. 321
- Talking about hypothetical situations, p. 326

Cultures
- Nota cultural, p. 318
- Nota cultural, p. 328
- Culture Notes, p. 328

Connections
- Recognizing cognates, p. 316
- Visual Learners, p. 329
- Literature Link, p. 332

Comparisons
- Panorama cultural, p. 323
- Language Note, p. 315
- Multicultural Links, pp. 323, 332

Communities
- Family Links, pp. 320, 332
- Career Path, p. 323

Cultures and Communities

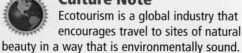

Culture Note
Ecotourism is a global industry that encourages travel to sites of natural beauty in a way that is environmentally sound. Tourism has many different consequences on the environment. Traveling responsibly not only has the potential to reduce the negative effects that tourism has on the Earth's fragile environment, it attempts to help conserve natural resources while also supporting indigenous cultures. One of the most popular habitats to visit today is a tropical rain forest. Whether you are visiting the Amazon Rain Forest of South America, or the Congo in Central Africa you will be entering a unique and fragile habitat. Ecotourism is about being a responsible traveler, learning about the unique nature of the habitats you visit, and a desire overall to preserve the natural resources of our planet.

C A P Í T U L O

11
El mundo en que vivimos

Objectives

In this chapter you will learn to

Primer paso

- point out problems and their consequences
- talk about how you would solve a problem

Segundo paso

- talk about hypothetical situations

 internet

 MARCAR: go.hrw.com
PALABRA CLAVE:
  WV3 COSTA RICA-11

◄ **Si pudieras, ¿cómo cambiarías el mundo?**

C A P Í T U L O   11

Photo Flash!
From this point of view, the Earth appears to be peaceful and clean. Unfortunately, in addition to many peaceful and clean environments, we would also find many embattled and polluted ones. You may want to ask your students if they can name any environmental issues that are of concern in your community.

Focusing on Outcomes
In this chapter students will be introduced to vocabulary and grammar that will allow them to communicate past and present problems, their consequences, and some solutions, as well as expectations for the future. Students will have the opportunity to develop the language skills necessary for discussing possible, foreseeable, and hypothetical situations.

Cultures and Communities

Language Note
Many of the Spanish words for plants and animals native to the Americas are borrowed from indigenous languages. In their explorations, Spaniards came into contact with many kinds of flora and fauna unknown to Europeans. Since they had no names for these in Spanish, they adopted the indigenous names. **Jaguar** and **tapir,** for example, come from Guaraní, spoken in parts of Paraguay, Brazil, and Argentina. **Caimán, manatí,** and **iguana** were borrowed from Taino and other Caribbean languages. **Quetzal** is from the Nahuatl word *quetzalli.* Many of these loanwords have since come into English as well, and for the same reasons. Ask students if they can find other examples of Spanish borrowings from indigenous American languages.

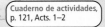
Cuaderno de actividades,
p. 121, Acts. 1–2

DE ANTEMANO ▪ *El proyecto de Néstor*

CD 11
Trs. 1–6

Estrategia para comprender

Néstor tiene que hacer un proyecto para su clase de ciencias sociales. La primera parte de su proyecto trata de los problemas de la sociedad moderna. Néstor ha buscado material para su proyecto en varios periódicos y revistas. Lee los artículos, las cartas al editor y los titulares que ha escogido. Si tú fueras Néstor, ¿escogerías materiales similares o diferentes? ¿Por qué?

Carreteras hechas un desastre

Catalina Márquez de los Ríos

Los alumnos del Colegio Los Altos celebraron el Día del Árbol con la siembra de 25 árboles.

Estoy harta de la basura que se ve a los lados de los caminos de nuestro hermoso país. Viajo mucho por las carreteras y me pongo triste al ver botellas plásticas y de vidrio y papeles desechados por todas partes. Si yo fuera policía, yo aplicaría una multa de cincuenta mil colones. Prestaría más atención a este delito.

Es mejor prevenir este problema y educar a la gente a usar basureros e implementar programas de limpieza de las carreteras. ¡Sembremos flores, no basura!

Gran desafío para próximo gobierno
▪ Delincuencia y criminalidad aumentan 8 por ciento cada año

La policía:
En guerra contra la droga

"Si no realizamos programas contra la droga, lo lamentaremos después", dijo ayer el jefe de policía de esta ciudad. Indicó que el desempleo y la falta de apoyo social hacen difíciles las campañas preventivas contra las drogas. Dijo también: "Los programas que se han implementado en otras partes han tenido mucho éxito. Si fuera posible, haría obligatoria la asistencia a por lo menos un programa contra las drogas cada año."

Preteaching Vocabulary

Recognizing Cognates

De antemano contains several words that students will be able to recognize as cognates. Review common Spanish prefixes and suffixes with students, such as **pre-, pro-, pos-, des-, con-, sub-, -dad, -ción, -sión** and **-cia.** Then have students identify as many of these words as possible from the passages.

(**problemas, asistencia, delincuencia, violencia, asociación, cooperación, inflación, televisión, criminalidad, personalidad,** and **sensibilidad**)

¿Se frenará la inflación?

El Gobierno confesó que por el momento no tiene plan para luchar contra la inflación, que durante varios años no ha bajado del 15 por ciento. Dijo ayer la Secretaria de Comercio: "Si no hacemos nada para combatir la inflación, hará gran daño a la economía. Si pudiera imponer controles de precio, lo haría en seguida".

SE NECESITAN TUTORES

Para enseñar a niños en primaria cuatro horas los fines de semana. Todas las materias. Estudiantes de escuela secundaria que quieren enseñar, llamar al Instituto Gabriela Mistral. Tel. 31-4000

ASOCIACIÓN CONTRA LA VIOLENCIA

La Asociación Contra la Violencia suplica a todos los ciudadanos costarricenses que se den cuenta del gran peligro a que se enfrenta la juventud de hoy. Nos referimos a los programas de televisión, las películas y videocintas que presentan imágenes y temas cargados de violencia.

Nos preocupa muchísimo el efecto que esta violencia tiene sobre nuestros hijos. Tarde o temprano se va a manifestar en sus personalidades y modos de ser. No decimos que todos se vayan a convertir en ladrones o asesinos; el efecto es mucho más sutil. Poco a poco van a perder la sensibilidad y no les será motivo de alarma el oír de un asesinato en su barrio, pues ya habrán visto miles de asesinatos en la tele.

Queremos elevar nuestra voz e invitar a todos los costarricenses a luchar contra este mal. Queremos películas, videos y programas de televisión que promuevan el amor al vecino, la cooperación y una actitud positiva frente al mundo de hoy.

Using the Captioned Video

 As an alternative, you might want to show the captioned version of *Contigo en la distancia: Si yo fuera presidenta* on Videocassette 5. Some students may benefit from seeing the written words as they listen to the target language and watch the gestures and actions in context. This visual reinforcement of vocabulary and functions will facilitate students' comprehension and help reduce their anxiety before they are formally introduced to the new language in the chapter.

Auditory/Visual Learners

If possible, ask students to watch or listen to a Spanish-language news broadcast. Have them choose a story about a Spanish-speaking country. They should report on what the story is about and where it takes place. (It should describe a current event in a country other than the United States.)

Thinking Critically

Comparing and Contrasting Ask students if they think that Néstor's project would look different if he were a student in the United States. (**¿Son distintos los problemas sociales de los Estados Unidos de los que tiene Costa Rica? ¿Crees que los estudiantes norteamericanos se preocupan más por los problemas ambientales que los estudiantes en Costa Rica? ¿Por qué?**)

Contigo en la distancia

You may choose to continue with **Episodio 11:** *Si yo fuera presidenta.* In this episode, Irene and Alejandra are working on a video project for school. They interview people on the street, including Carlos, and ask their opinions about Mexico City's problems. Carlos talks about crime and how he would like to convince today's youth to have hope for the future. The girls review the finished video that night, and Irene tells Alejandra that if Irene were president, she would appoint Alejandra ambassador to Spain. That reminds Alejandra of Sergio, and she wonders why he hasn't revealed his identity yet.

DE ANTEMANO

CAPÍTULO 11

Teaching Suggestions

1 Have students skim selections for key words. Pair students and have them use recognizable vocabulary and context to summarize the sections' meanings.

2 As students listen, encourage them to take notes. Stop the recording after each statement to allow students time to think.

Answers

1
1. la basura que se ve a los lados de las carreteras
2. para enseñarles a los niños de primaria todas las materias
3. La Asociación Contra la Violencia se preocupa por el efecto de la violencia en los programas de televisión, las películas y las videocintas.
4. El gobierno confesó que por el momento no tiene un plan para luchar contra la inflación.
5. El desempleo y la falta de apoyo social hacen difíciles estas campañas.

3
1. Viajo mucho por las carreteras y me pongo triste al ver botellas plásticas y de vidrio y papeles desechados por todas partes.
2. Yo aplicaría una multa de 50.000 colones.
3. Si no realizamos programas contra la droga, lamentaremos después.
4. Haría obligatoria la asistencia a por lo menos un programa contra las drogas cada año.
5. Dice que hará gran daño a la economía.
6. Si pudiera imponer controles de precio, lo haría en seguida.

These activities check for comprehension only. Students should not yet be expected to produce language modeled in **De antemano**.

1 **¿Comprendiste?** See answers below.

Responde en español a las siguientes preguntas.
1. ¿Qué problema señala Catalina Márquez de los Ríos?
2. ¿Para qué se necesitan tutores en el Instituto Gabriela Mistral?
3. Según la Asociación Contra la Violencia, ¿qué representa una gran amenaza para los niños?
4. ¿Qué piensa hacer el gobierno para combatir la inflación?
5. ¿Qué dificultades han tenido las campañas preventivas contra las drogas?

2 **Lo leí en el periódico** Script and answers on p. 313G.

CD 11
Tr. 7

Escucha seis comentarios e indica a cuál de los siguientes artículos, cartas o anuncios se refiere cada uno. Hay uno que se usa más de una vez.
a. Carreteras hechas un desastre
b. La policía: En guerra contra la droga
c. ¿Se frenará la inflación?
d. Se necesitan tutores
e. Asociación Contra la Violencia

3 **¿Qué dicen?** See answers below.
1. ¿Qué dice Catalina Márquez de los Ríos para indicar que hay un problema con la contaminación?
2. ¿Qué dice ella para sugerir una solución legal al problema de la contaminación?
3. ¿Cómo indica el jefe de policía que es importante enfrentarse con el problema de la droga?
4. ¿Qué dice el jefe de policía para sugerir una solución?
5. ¿Cómo indica la Secretaria de Comercio que la inflación es un problema grave?
6. ¿Qué dice la Secretaria para indicar su solución preferida?

4 **Problemas de aquí y allí**

Con un(a) compañero(a), lee otra vez todos los materiales que Néstor ha acumulado. Discutan qué problemas son parecidos a los problemas de tu comunidad y cuáles les parecen diferentes.

5 **Ahora te toca a ti**

Pon los problemas mencionados en **De antemano** en orden de importancia. Empieza por el más grave (número uno). Luego escribe las soluciones sugeridas en los artículos a los problemas. Al lado de cada solución escribe **F** (fácil) o **D** (difícil), según tu opinión de la dificultad de implementar esa solución.

Nota cultural

Costa Rica es famosa por su larga tradición de democracia, paz y progresismo. En 1890 se llevaron a cabo elecciones democráticas, las primeras en todo Centroamérica. Costa Rica abolió su ejército en 1949 y una pequeña Guardia Nacional tomó su lugar. Desde 1949, la violencia política es casi desconocida. La asistencia a la escuela es obligatoria, y casi el 93 por ciento de los costarricenses saben leer y escribir. ¿Crees que son similares Costa Rica y Estados Unidos en estos aspectos?

Comprehension Check

Tactile Learners

4 Ask students to bring a disposable object that they normally throw away. (soda can, magazine, plastic container, pen, food wrapper) Using the trash as a source of ideas, students discuss problems such as: recycling, littering, plastics and petroleum, corporate and civic responsibility.

Native Speakers

5 As a vocabulary-building activity, ask native speakers to read the articles from **De antemano** again and list unknown words and phrases. After they have looked up the words, have students associate each new word or phrase with a synonym or related word they already know. For example: **aumentan–suben; realizamos–hacemos; se han implementado–han hecho.**

318 TRESCIENTOS DIECIOCHO DE ANTEMANO

STANDARDS: 1.1, 1.2, 2.1, 3.1, 3.2, 4.2, 5.1

Primer paso

Objectives Pointing out problems and their consequences; talking about how you would solve a problem

go.hrw.com
WV3 COSTA RICA-11

Así se dice

Pointing out problems and their consequences

Para señalar un problema o hablar de sus consecuencias, puedes decir:

Me he fijado en la contaminación del río.   *I've noticed . . .*
Se dice que el hambre afecta a miles de personas cada día.
Según el gobierno, la criminalidad está aumentando.
Si no actuamos ahora, la situación **va a empeorarse.**   *If we don't act now . . .*
Si no hacemos nada por el medio ambiente, **temo que el deterioro continúe.**
         . . . I'm afraid the deterioration will continue.
Si no realizamos campañas preventivas contra las drogas, **lo lamentaremos** en
   el futuro.   *If we don't carry out . . . we'll regret it . . .*

Cuaderno de actividades, pp. 122–123, Acts. 3, 5

6   Buenas noticias   Script and answers on p. 313G.

Escuchemos/Escribamos Escucha el siguiente noticiero de radio. Si oyes una buena noticia, escribe **buena**. Si no, escribe **mala**.

CD 11 Tr. 8

Vocabulario

CD-ROM
DISC **3**

Más práctica gramatical, p. 335, Act. 2

Cuaderno de gramática, pp. 87–88, Acts. 1–3

Cuaderno de actividades, pp. 122, 125, Acts. 4, 9

aumentar *to increase*	**el homicidio**
bajar *to decrease*	*homicide*
cometer *to commit*	**implementar**
el crimen *major crime*	*to implement*
la criminalidad *crime rate*	**el ladrón** *thief*
la delincuencia *crime*	**la ladrona** *thief*
el delito *minor crime*	**promover (ue)**
el desempleo *unemployment*	*to promote*
la drogadicción	**el robo**
drug addiction	*robbery*
la enfermedad *disease*	**la sensibilidad**
el hambre (f.) *hunger*	*sensitivity*

¿Te acuerdas?

The Spanish construction **se** + verb corresponds to impersonal subjects in English, such as *people, they, you, we, one.*

Se dice que la inflación está peor.
People say inflation is worse.

This construction also can be translated using the English passive voice.

Se rompieron muchas ventanas durante el terremoto.
Many windows were broken during the earthquake.

Cuaderno de gramática, pp. 88–89, Acts. 4–6

Más práctica gramatical, pp. 334–335, Acts. 1, 3

También se puede decir...

Se puede decir **asesinato** por **homicidio**. En España se dice **paro forzoso** por **desempleo**.

Communication for All Students

Slower Pace
To review and reteach the use of the impersonal **se,** state some true and false school rules in Spanish. (**No se come en las salas de clase.**) Have students say whether or not the statements are actual rules. If students do not believe a rule is real, they must change it to what they think the rule actually is. Then have students add other behaviors that are either permitted or not allowed.

Auditory/Visual Learners
You may want to use the *Video Program* to model some expressions from **Así se dice** and **Vocabulario:** Videocassette 4, *Contigo en la distancia,* Episode 11.

Teaching Resources
pp. 319–322

PRINT
▶ Lesson Planner, p. 53
▶ Listening Activities, pp. 83–84, 87–88
▶ Activities for Communication, pp. 41–42, 81, 83, 109–110
▶ Cuaderno de gramática, pp. 87–90
▶ Grammar Tutor for Students of Spanish, Chapter 11
▶ Cuaderno de actividades, pp. 122–125
▶ Cuaderno para hispanohablantes, pp. 51–55
▶ Testing Program, pp. 235–238
▶ Alternative Assessment Guide, p. 40
▶ Student Make-Up Assignments, Chapter 11

MEDIA
▶ One-Stop Planner
▶ Audio Compact Discs, CD 11, Trs. 8–9, 24–26, 20
▶ Teaching Transparencies 11-1; **Más práctica gramatical** Answers; Cuaderno de gramática Answers
▶ Interactive CD-ROM Tutor, Disc 3

Bell Work
On the board or on a transparency, write the following: **Escribe cinco planes para tu futuro y el modo de lograrlos.**

Presenting
Así se dice, Vocabulario

Write a paragraph on the board or on a transparency, substituting a blank space for words and phrases presented in **Vocabulario** or **Así se dice.** Read the paragraph aloud while students guess what words or expressions to put in the blanks.

Teaching Resources
pp. 319–322

PRINT 📖
▸ Lesson Planner, p. 53
▸ Listening Activities, pp. 83–84, 87–88
▸ Activities for Communication, pp. 41–42, 81, 83, 109–110
▸ Cuaderno de gramática, pp. 87–90
▸ Grammar Tutor for Students of Spanish, Chapter 11
▸ Cuaderno de actividades, pp. 122–125
▸ Cuaderno para hispanohablantes, pp. 51–55
▸ Testing Program, pp. 235–238
▸ Alternative Assessment Guide, p. 40
▸ Student Make-Up Assignments, Chapter 11

MEDIA 💿📹
▸ One-Stop Planner
▸ Audio Compact Discs, CD 11, Trs. 8–9, 24–26, 20
▸ Teaching Transparencies 11-1; **Más práctica gramatical** Answers; Cuaderno de gramática Answers
▸ Interactive CD-ROM Tutor, Disc 3

Answers

8 *Possible answers:*
1. Si no actuamos ahora lo lamentaremos más tarde.
2. Según el gobierno hay mucho desempleo.
3. Se dice que la criminalidad ha aumentado.
4. Este año me he fijado en el aumento de la delincuencia en el colegio.
5. Se dice que hay mucha gente sin suficiente comida.

9 *Possible answers:*
1. Ha aumentado el número de pintadas en las paredes.
2. Se dice que la violencia en la televisión promueve la criminalidad.
3. La inflación ha aumentado y ahora los aparatos electrónicos son más caros que antes.

---

7 **¿Qué palabra es mejor?**

Leamos/Escribamos Completa cada oración con la palabra más apropiada del **Vocabulario** de la página 319. Luego escribe algunas oraciones incompletas y pídele a un(a) compañero(a) que las complete con palabras apropiadas del **Vocabulario**.

1. La gente que depende de las drogas sufre de ========. drogadicción
2. Cuando no hay suficiente trabajo para todos, se dice que la tasa *(rate)* de ======== está muy alta. desempleo
3. El acto de matar *(killing)* a alguien se llama ========. homicidio
4. Se dice que el problema de las drogas en las escuelas ======== la criminalidad. aumenta
5. El homicidio es un ========. crimen

8 **Me he fijado en...** See possible answers below.

Hablemos Trabaja con un(a) compañero(a). Usa frases de **Así se dice** para expresar las siguientes ideas en otras palabras.

> **MODELO** Veo mucha drogadicción en esta ciudad.
> —Me he fijado en el problema de la drogadicción en esta ciudad.

1. Hay que llevar a cabo el programa ahora o nos va a pesar.
2. El gobierno dice que hay mucha gente sin trabajo.
3. La gente dice que el número de crímenes ha aumentado.
4. He notado un aumento en la delincuencia en el colegio este año.
5. Parece que mucha gente no tiene suficiente comida.

9 **¿Cuáles son los problemas?** See possible answers below.

Hablemos Con un(a) compañero(a), mira el siguiente dibujo. Indiquen los problemas en el dibujo y sus posibles consecuencias.

10 **Hablando de nuestra generación**

Escribamos/Hablemos Con dos o tres compañeros(as), escribe una lista de los ocho problemas más graves que afectan a los jóvenes de tu edad. Escriban la lista en orden de importancia y discutan por qué es importante cada cosa en su lista.

Vocabulario extra

la corrupción	*corruption*
la falta de oportunidades	*lack of opportunities*
la guerra	*war*
la violencia	*violence*

Connections and Comparisons

Thinking Critically

9 **Analyzing** Ask students to list the problems and their consequences in order of importance. They should also be ready to tell why they arranged them as they did.

Language Note

9 *Graffiti* comes from the Greek word *graphikos* meaning "referring to writing or drawing." Ask students to think of words that use the same root. (**autógrafo, fotografía**)

Family Link

10 Have students conduct interviews with older relatives or neighbors to compare and contrast problems of today's generation to the problems of previous generations.

Así se dice

Talking about how you would solve a problem

Si quieres hablar de lo que harías para mejorar el mundo, puedes decir:

Me dedicaría a construir hospitales para los pobres. *I would devote myself to . . .*
Propongo mejores sistemas de transporte público. *I propose . . .*
Habrá que crear más trabajos. *It will be necessary to . . .*
Intentaría iniciar un programa de limpieza de las calles. *I would try to . . .*
Yo empezaría por mejorar el sistema de salud pública.
La solución que planteo es aumentar el reciclaje. *The solution I propose is . . .*

> Cuaderno de actividades, pp. 122–123, Acts. 3, 6

11 Soluciones Script and answers on p. 313G.

 CD 11 Tr. 9

Escuchemos Escucha las soluciones que propone un candidato para los problemas de su estado. Empareja cada solución con el problema más apropiado de la lista.

a. el desempleo
b. la corrupción en el gobierno
c. la criminalidad
d. los problemas de los colegios
e. la falta de turismo
f. el costo del tratamiento médico

¿Se te ha olvidado?
the conditional
Ver la página 265

> Cuaderno de gramática, p. 90, Acts. 7–8

12 Lo que planteo See possible answers below.

Hablemos Imagina que tú y tus compañeros han decidido resolver algunos de los problemas de la juventud en su comunidad. Piensan desarrollar un centro de recreo. Ya han encontrado el lugar para el centro. ¿Qué problemas de los jóvenes pueden solucionar con el centro? Miren la foto del lugar y decidan con qué empezarían a crear el centro. ¿Qué ideas plantean para el centro?

MODELO
—Yo empezaría por...
—Habrá que comprar...

STANDARDS: 1.2, 1.3

Communication for All Students

Challenge

11 After listening to the solutions proposed, have students choose a problem from the list and think of one more solution. Or ask them to name one problem affecting their community and to propose a solution. Encourage students to use words and phrases from **Vocabulario** on page 319 and from **Así se dice** on page 321.

Visual Learners

12 Have groups of students draw the community center represented in this activity as it would be after improvements have been made. Ask them to label what they would do to make it a better place. Display the drawings around the class and have students vote on the most-improved center.

Presenting
Así se dice

Start by making a statement about a problem at school and how to solve it. (**La comida de la cafetería no es muy saludable. Me dedicaría a mejorar la comida de la cafetería.**) Ask students to formulate two or three sentences and put them on the board. When they have done this, conduct a survey to see how many agree and disagree with the statements. If students disagree with a statement, ask them to suggest an alternative. You may want to have students make a poster of ways the class could make the school better.

Thinking Critically

Analyzing In pairs or in groups of three, have students discuss the problems they feel they have the power to control. (clutter in the classroom, difficulty seeing or hearing because of their location, carrying books from class to class) How might they improve these situations?

Answers
12 *Answers will vary. Possible answer:*
Me he fijado que los jóvenes no tienen nada que hacer por la tarde. Habrá que comprar muebles y juegos y organizar programas deportivos después del colegio.

Según la policía, se ha empeorado mucho el problema de las drogas entre los jóvenes. Yo empezaría por iniciar un programa para los jóvenes y sus padres en el centro donde se podría hablar del problema.

Writing Assessment

16 Encourage use of varied vocabulary and grammar from this and previous chapters. Challenge students to write as dramatically as possible in order to help incorporate the vocabulary from this chapter. Answer any questions, but explain that simple errors are expected and that risk-taking is rewarded in the grading system. You may wish to assess the writing assignment using the following rubric.

Writing Rubric	Points			
	4	3	2	1
Content (Complete–Incomplete)				
Comprehensibility (Comprehensible–Incomprehensible)				
Accuracy (Accurate–Seldom accurate)				
Organization (Well organized–Poorly organized)				
Effort (Excellent–Minimal)				

18–20: A	14–15: C	Under
16–17: B	12–13: D	12: F

Assess

▸ Testing Program, pp. 235–238
Quiz 11-1A, Quiz 11-1B
Audio CD 11, Tr. 20

▸ Student Make-Up Assignments, Chapter 11, Alternative Quiz

▸ Alternative Assessment Guide, p. 40

Answers

15 1. falsa; Los caminos son pequeños y están en malas condiciones.
2. cierta
3. cierta
4. falsa; Las playas están que da pena verlas.
5. falsa; Quiere gozar de los beneficios económicos del turismo.

---

13 **¿Qué harías tú?** Answers will vary.

 Leamos/Hablemos Con un(a) compañero(a), discute los siguientes problemas y las mejores maneras de resolverlos.

MODELO
La banda no tiene suficiente dinero para comprar uniformes.
—Lo que yo propongo es vender dulces hasta que tengan suficiente dinero.
—La solución que planteo es compartir el dinero de los programas atléticos.

1. Hay demasiados estudiantes en cada clase.
2. No hay bastantes libros en la biblioteca.
3. No hay igualdad entre los programas atléticos de las muchachas y los de los muchachos.
4. Se necesita un mayor interés en las actividades de la escuela por parte de los estudiantes y sus padres.
5. Los estudiantes quieren más variedad de comida en la cafetería.
6. El club de español quiere hacer un viaje a México.

14 **La campaña** Answers will vary.

 Leamos/Hablemos Imagina que tú y tres compañeros(as) trabajan en una campaña política. Respondan a las siguientes preguntas de un reportero sobre lo que haría su partido.

MODELO
—¿Qué harían con las fábricas que contaminan?
—Lo que nosotros proponemos es iniciar un programa de limpieza de las fábricas.

1. Todavía hay muchas enfermedades que no tienen cura. ¿Tienen un plan para combatir eso?
2. ¿Qué harían para eliminar el desempleo en este estado?
3. ¿Qué van a hacer para ayudar a las personas que no tienen casa?
4. ¿Tienen planes para traer equipos profesionales de deportes a este estado?
5. ¿Qué van a hacer para mejorar el sistema de educación?
6. ¿Qué harían para disminuir el ruido en las ciudades?
7. ¿Qué proponen para las personas que sufren de enfermedades incurables?
See answers below.

15 **Una carta en el periódico** See answers below.

 Leamos/Escribamos Lee la carta que el señor Fonseca escribió a un periódico costarricense. Luego indica si las siguientes oraciones son **ciertas** o **falsas**. Si son falsas, corrígelas.

1. Hay varios buenos caminos hacia la ciudad.
2. Casi nadie sabe que existe la ciudad.
3. Hay pocos restaurantes de buena calidad.
4. Las playas son hermosísimas y están limpias.
5. Él no quiere que mucha gente conozca la ciudad.

16 **Un plan de acción** Answers will vary.

 Escribamos Imagina que eres miembro del Comité Municipal para el Fomento del Turismo. Escribe un plan de dos o tres párrafos para resolver los problemas que mencionó el señor Fonseca.

> Estimado señor:
> Me parece que nuestra ciudad no aprovecha el turismo. Lo que es peor, nadie se da cuenta de que existe nuestra ciudad.
> No es fácil llegar aquí porque los caminos son pequeños y están en malas condiciones. Tampoco hay restaurantes buenos. Y las playas están que da pena verlas. Si no hacemos nada, tendremos pocos visitantes y no gozaremos de los beneficios económicos del turismo.
>
> -Alberto Fonseca Vargas

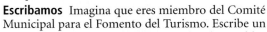
Communication for All Students

Slower Pace

16 Have students list in their own words the problems that Señor Fonseca mentions in his letter.

Visual/Tactile Learners

16 Have students design a model or blueprint addressing solutions for the problems that Señor Fonseca names. Then write a description of what the design accomplishes and what problems it eliminates.

¿Cuál es el mayor problema ambiental de tu comunidad?

CD 11
Trs. 10–13

Estos jóvenes están muy conscientes de cuáles son los problemas ambientales de sus comunidades. Escucha atentamente sus respuestas. ¿Tienes ideas parecidas?

Julio CD 11 Tr. 11
San Diego, California

"El drenaje que va a caer a las playas. Y el problema es que cuando uno quiere ir a bañar a la playa, no se puede, y cuando quiere ir a pescar no se puede o están contaminados los pescados".

Alan CD 11 Tr. 12
San José, Costa Rica

"En mi comunidad, el mayor problema ambiental es la bota de basura, ¿no? la basura que se produce en las casas... ahora, no se está recogiendo y esto produce contaminación".

Mónica
Ciudad de México, México CD 11 Tr. 13

"El mayor problema ambiental en el D.F. es definitivamente la contaminación. La contaminación viene de los coches o cualquier medio de transporte; bueno, a excepción del metro, claro".

Para pensar y hablar...

A. ¿Cuáles de los problemas ambientales de arriba se encuentran sólo en los grandes centros urbanos y cuáles en un sitio cerca del mar? ¿Cuáles de los problemas ambientales mencionados por los entrevistados existen en tu comunidad?

B. ¿Por qué es importante proteger el medio ambiente? ¿Cómo podemos protegerlo mejor? ¿Qué puedes hacer tú para mejorar la situación? ¿Crees que hay un conflicto entre la protección del medio ambiente y los intereses del sector industrial? Explica.

Cuaderno para hispanohablantes, pp. 54–55

Connections and Comparisons

Multicultural Link

Ask students to choose another country and to research one of its environmental problems. Have them look at the impact the problem has on the people and the land. They should also find out what is being done to solve the problem. Have students report their findings to the class.

Career Path

In many scientific careers, it is useful to know Spanish to conduct research. In fields such as botany, pharmacology, environmental biology, and oceanography, scientists study plants, animals, and marine life in Central and South America. Have students locate scientific Web sites that are sponsored by academic or research institutions in Spanish-speaking countries.

CAPÍTULO 11

Teaching Resources
p. 323

PRINT
▸ Video Guide, pp. 74–76, 78
▸ Cuaderno de actividades, p. 132
▸ Cuaderno para hispanohablantes, pp. 54–55

MEDIA
▸ One-Stop Planner
▸ Video Program, Videocassette 4, 25:35–28:36
▸ Audio Compact Discs, CD 11, Trs. 10–13
▸ Interactive CD-ROM Tutor, Disc 3

Presenting
Panorama cultural

Play the interviews on the audio or video recording. Have students answer the **Para pensar y hablar...** and the **Preguntas.** Then ask students for their suggestions on how to solve the problems mentioned here.

Preguntas

1. **Según Mónica, ¿de dónde viene la contaminación del aire en el D.F.?** (los coches o cualquier medio de transporte)

2. **Según Alan, ¿por qué está produciendo contaminación la basura en su ciudad?** (porque no se está recogiendo)

3. **Según Julio, ¿cuál es el problema en San Diego, California?** (el drenaje) **¿Qué no puede hacer la gente?** (irse a bañar a la playa e ir a pescar)

Teaching Resources
pp. 324–325

PRINT
▸ Lesson Planner, p. 54
▸ Video Guide, pp. 74–75, 77
▸ Cuaderno de actividades, p. 126
▸ Cuaderno para hispanohablantes, pp. 54–55

MEDIA
▸ One-Stop Planner
▸ Video Program
   Contigo en la distancia
   Videocassette 4, 20:23–25:34
   Videocassette 5 (captioned version), 55:13–1:00:25
▸ Audio Compact Discs, CD 11, Trs. 14–17

Presenting

¡Adelante!

Play the audio recording once without stopping it. Then play it again and stop it periodically. Ask students to write any solution they hear. Their list should include: **...si no contamináramos los lagos; ...limpiar las carreteras; Los niños aprenden a defenderse contra las drogas; ...si recicláramos nuestros papeles y periódicos.**

 Contigo en la distancia

As an alternative to **¡Adelante!**, you may wish to show Episode 11 of *Contigo en la distancia.* For suggestions and activities, see the *Video Guide.*

¡Adelante! • *Algunas soluciones*

 Cuaderno de actividades, p. 126, Acts. 12–14

CD 11
Trs. 14–17

Néstor ha trabajado mucho en su proyecto. La segunda parte trata de maneras de solucionar varios problemas de este mundo. Lee los recortes que Néstor ha preparado.

El mundo sería tan bonito si recicláramos nuestros papeles y periódicos.

¡Juntos lo lograremos!

Campaña ecológica
El Club Amigos Pro Tierra les invita a todos los interesados a participar en una campaña para limpiar las carreteras. Reunión organizadora: viernes 9 de mayo, 20:00 h., Edificio Buganvilla

These activities check for comprehension only. Students should not yet be expected to produce language modeled in ¡Adelante!

17 **¿Comprendiste?** See answers below.
1. ¿De qué trata la segunda parte del proyecto de Néstor?
2. ¿Dónde se reunirá el Club Amigos Pro Tierra?
3. ¿Qué programas han tenido efectos beneficiosos en la lucha contra las drogas?
4. ¿Quién es Omar Ruiz Díaz?
5. ¿Cuál es la meta de Omar?
6. ¿Qué quiere promover en las ciudades?

18 **¿Sí o no?** See answers on p. 325.
Escribe **sí** o **no** para indicar si las siguientes frases están de acuerdo o no con las ideas expresadas en **¡Adelante!** Si contestas **no,** explica por qué.
1. Es inútil tratar de solucionar los problemas del país.
2. Se puede participar en las campañas para limpiar las carreteras.
3. Los programas educativos no tienen ningún efecto en la lucha contra las drogas.
4. Es imposible usar la basura como un recurso.
5. Si más gente montara en bicicleta en vez de viajar en automóviles, habría menos contaminación.
6. Los municipios deben crear más vías para bicicletas.

Preteaching Vocabulary

Activating Prior Knowledge
Point out that Néstor is describing environmental and social problems and solutions. Based on expressions students already know and on what they know about the environment, can they guess what the phrase **¡Juntos lo lograremos!** means? What are the two related activities? (recycling and keeping lakes clean) What is a **campaña ecológica?** (environmental campaign) Who would participate?

(todos los interesados en una campaña para limpiar las carreteras) What does it mean to **defenderse contra las drogas?** (to defend oneself against drugs) How are students accomplishing this? (educational programs and support systems) What is a **caballito de hierro?** (an iron horse or a bicycle) What environmental or social problems does this address? (**la agitada vida de la ciudad, la contaminación atmosférica y el ruido**)

Los niños aprenden a defenderse contra las drogas

Poco a poco, la educación les está ganando a las drogas. Muchos colegios han desarrollado programas educativos y sistemas de apoyo para sus estudiantes. Todos soñamos con un mundo en que las drogas nunca tengan la oportunidad de hacer daño a los jóvenes. Según las nuevas investigaciones del gobierno, estos programas han tenido un efecto beneficioso.

El mundo sería tan bonito si no contamináramos los lagos.

¡Juntos lo lograremos!

Pedaleando por la vida

Tres bicicletas y 17.000 kilómetros a cuestas hacen de Omar Ruiz Díaz un experto de los pedales, pues ha recorrido buena parte del continente americano en su caballito de hierro.

En estos días, Omar se encuentra entre nosotros para iniciar la tercera etapa de su plan de viaje. Éste culminará en Alaska en algún momento, pero el tiempo no es lo importante.

Este singular visitante es enfático al destacar que para él sí importa ayudar a que la gente tome conciencia de las virtudes de la bicicleta contra la agitada vida de la ciudad, la contaminación atmosférica y el ruido.

Como parte de su llamado por llevar una vida más sana, en los distintos lugares por donde ha pasado, Omar resalta la importancia de que las municipalidades

creen vías para bicicleta a fin de promover este medio de transporte en las ciudades.

Recalcó que esta idea ha demostrado tener excelentes resultados en otras partes, como la ciudad de Curitiba, Brasil, pues reduce los congestionamientos de tránsito y agiliza el movimiento de los habitantes de manera saludable.

Andrés Formoso

19 **Un bello porvenir** See answers below.

Para que sea bonito el mundo, ¿qué hay que hacer? Usa los carteles que Néstor ha preparado para contestar.

20 **Ahora te toca a ti** Answers will vary.

¿Qué opinas de las siguientes ideas? ¿Estás de acuerdo con ellas? Explica por qué.
1. En veinte años se habrá eliminado el problema de la drogadicción.
2. Muy pronto habrá más bicicletas que automóviles.
3. En un futuro cercano, el mar estará tan contaminado que nadie querrá nadar en él.
4. En diez años, habrá más tráfico pero menos contaminación, ya que los vehículos utilizarán un combustible especial.
5. Vemos tantos problemas del mundo en la televisión que ya no nos parecen importantes.

Comprehension Check

Challenge
Ask students to look at Néstor's articles on pages 316–317. What solutions would they suggest for those problems? Have them write articles offering solutions like those presented in **¡Adelante!**

Slower Pace
17 Ask students to take notes and answer these questions using their notes.

Thinking Critically
20 **Comparing and Contrasting** Ask students what they do to protect the environment. Have them brainstorm additional things they could do. (use cloth bags instead of paper ones to bring their lunch to school, walk to school, recycle cans)

Answers
17 1. Se trata de maneras de solucionar varios problemas del mundo.
2. Se reunirá en el edificio Buganvilla.
3. Han desarrollado programas educativos y sistemas de apoyo que han tenido efectos beneficiosos.
4. Es un ciclista que ha recorrido 17.000 km.
5. La meta de Omar es llevar una vida más sana.
6. Quiere que las municipalidades creen más vías para andar en bicicleta.

18 1. No; el mundo sería más bonito si tratáramos de solucionar los problemas.
2. Sí
3. No; poco a poco, la educación les está ganando a las drogas.
4. No; se puede hacer muchas cosas de lo que hemos reciclado.
5. Sí
6. Sí

19 *Sample answers:*
Hay que reciclar nuestros papeles y periódicos.
Hay que proteger los lagos de la contaminación.

Teaching Resources
pp. 326–329

PRINT
- Lesson Planner, p. 54
- Listening Activities, pp. 84, 88–89
- Activities for Communication, pp. 43–44, 82–83, 109–110
- Cuaderno de gramática, pp. 91–94
- Grammar Tutor for Students of Spanish, Chapter 11
- Cuaderno de actividades, pp. 127–130
- Cuaderno para hispanohablantes, pp. 51–55
- Testing Program, pp. 239–242
- Alternative Assessment Guide, p. 40
- Student Make-Up Assignments, Chapter 11

MEDIA
- One-Stop Planner
- Audio Compact Discs, CD 11, Trs. 18, 27–29, 21
- Teaching Transparencies 11-2; **Más práctica gramatical** Answers; Cuaderno de gramática Answers
- Interactive CD-ROM Tutor, Disc 3

Bell Work
Write the following on the board or on a transparency: **¿Qué harías si tuvieras un millón de dólares?**

Presenting
Así se dice
Using pictures clipped from magazines, use these expressions to talk about a dream you have. **(Qué bonito sería si no hubiera tanta contaminación del aire en Los Ángeles. Si yo viviera allá, sólo usaría transporte público.)**

Segundo paso

Objective Talking about hypothetical situations

WV3 COSTA RICA-11

Así se dice

Talking about hypothetical situations

Si quieres hablar de situaciones hipotéticas, puedes decir:

Qué bonito sería **si hubiera paz** en el mundo.
. . . if there were peace . . .

¿Qué harías para proteger el medio ambiente **si tuvieras** tu propia compañía?
. . . if you had . . .

Sería maravilloso **si se encontrara una cura** para el cáncer.
. . . if a cure were found . . .

Si yo fuera presidente(a), hablaría más con la juventud de nuestro país.
If I were . . .

Si yo viviera en una ciudad grande, sólo usaría transporte público.
If I lived . . .

Si tú pudieras cambiar el mundo en un instante, ¿qué cambiarías?
If you could . . .

> Cuaderno de actividades, pp. 127, 130, Acts. 15, 20

> Cuaderno de gramática, p. 91, Acts. 9–10

21 **¡Qué bonito sería!** Script and answers on p. 313H.

CD 11
Tr. 18

Escuchemos/Hablemos Escucha cada conversación e indica de quién hablan las personas. Hay una conversación que no corresponde a ningún dibujo.

a.

b.

c.

22 **¿Qué pasaría si...?**

Leamos/Escribamos Completa las oraciones de forma lógica usando las frases de la segunda columna.

1. Qué bonito sería… c
2. Si hablara con el presidente… e
3. Qué difícil sería… a
4. Si fuera gobernador(a) de este estado… b or d
5. Si tuviera tiempo… d or b

a. si en todo el mundo no hubiera compasión.
b. iniciaría programas de música para niños.
c. si no hubiera enfermedades.
d. ayudaría a la gente pobre.
e. le diría que se preocupe más por la educación.

Communication for All Students

Challenge
21 After students have identified the conversation that does not correspond to any of the illustrations, replay that conversation. Have students illustrate it or give students the alternative of describing the drawing in words rather than actually illustrating it.

Kinesthetic Learners
22 Write the clauses from this activity separately on large cards. Give one card to each student. Have the students stand at the front of the room and hold up their cards. Call on members of the class to match two people who hold the two halves of a phrase and to read the resulting sentence. Continue until all the phrases have been paired.

The past subjunctive in contrary-to-fact *si* clauses

1. It's easy to form the past subjunctive if you remember the third person plural (**ellos/ellas**) form of the preterite. Simply remove the **-on** and add the appropriate endings, as shown below. Note that the **nosotros** form always has an accent.

TRABAJAR (trabajar**on**)	HACER (hicier**on**)	SER/IR (fuer**on**)
trabajar**a**	hicier**a**	fuer**a**
trabajar**as**	hicier**as**	fuer**as**
trabajar**a**	hicier**a**	fuer**a**
trabajár**amos**	hiciér**amos**	fuér**amos**
trabajar**ais**	hicier**ais**	fuer**ais**
trabajar**an**	hicier**an**	fuer**an**

¿Se te ha olvidado?

the preterite

Ver la página R36

Cuaderno de gramática, pp. 92–93, Acts. 11–13

2. Spanish uses the past subjunctive after **si** *(if)* to express situations that are contrary to fact or unlikely to happen. The conditional usually follows in the next clause.

> **Si yo fuera tú, no haría eso.**   *If I were you, I wouldn't do that.*
> **Si tuviéramos tiempo, iríamos.**   *If we had time, we would go.*

3. However, when a situation is considered likely to happen, use the indicative instead.

> **Si tenemos tiempo, iremos.**   *If we have the time, we'll go.*
> **Ven si puedes.**   *Come if you can.*

Cuaderno de actividades, pp. 127–128, Acts. 16–18   *Cuaderno de gramática, pp. 93–94, Acts. 14–16*   Más práctica gramatical, pp. 336–337, Acts. 4–6

23 ### Gramática en contexto

Leamos/Escribamos Completa las siguientes oraciones con la palabra correcta. Hay un verbo que no se usa.

pudieras	habláramos	fueran	hiciera	tuviera	vinieran

1. Si yo ＿＿＿ dinero, lo usaría para promover las artes. tuviera
2. Si ＿＿＿ conocer a cualquier persona en el mundo, ¿a quién conocerías? pudieras
3. Miguel y Sara dicen que no trabajarían si ＿＿＿ ricos. fueran
4. Si no ＿＿＿ frío, podríamos ir a la piscina. hiciera
5. Viajaríamos a Bélgica si ＿＿＿ mejor el francés. habláramos

24 ### Gramática en contexto   See answers below.

Leamos/Escribamos Cambia cada frase para formar una oración que exprese una hipótesis.

MODELO   **Si tengo dinero, voy a donarlo a la campaña contra el cáncer.**
       —Si tuviera dinero, lo donaría a la campaña contra el cáncer.

1. Si hacemos de la basura un recurso, podemos eliminar mucha contaminación.
2. Si la gente utiliza menos pesticidas, el aire estará más limpio.
3. Nuestros hijos sufrirán las consecuencias si no protegemos el medio ambiente.
4. Si ellos saben algo de la ecología, no contaminarán los mares, lagos y ríos.
5. Puedes hacer mucho para proteger el medio ambiente si tienes recursos.

Communication for All Students

Slower Pace

24 Before students convert the sentences, have them first identify which verbs will change to past subjunctive. Ask students to write the third-person plural preterite forms of those verbs, and then have them write the corresponding past subjunctive form of the verb. Example: **hacemos— hicieron—hiciéramos.**

Native Speakers

Have students generate a list of four topics relating to current events. Suggest that the topics relate to politics, the environment, education, or criminal justice. Have students develop a hypothetical statement about each. Give an example such as **Si hubiera menos contaminación del agua, habría más peces en el río.** Ask students to share their statements with the class.

Presenting
Gramática

The past subjunctive in contrary-to-fact *si* clauses

Point out that contrary-to-fact sentences with **si...** are similar to *If . . . then . . .* statements. These statements speculate about what would happen if a certain event took place or a certain condition existed. In contrary-to-fact statements, the past subjunctive is always used in the **si** clause and the conditional is used to express the possible outcome. Write sample contrary-to-fact Spanish sentences on the board, and ask students for English equivalents. When students seem comfortable with the structure, ask volunteers to complete a sentence: **Si yo tuviera más tiempo/Si yo fuera rico(a)/Si yo tuviera un carro...**

Additional Practice

23 Poll students about what they would do in these hypothetical situations.

Answers
24
1. Si hiciéramos de la basura un recurso, podríamos eliminar mucha contaminación.
2. Si la gente utilizara menos pesticidas, el aire estaría más limpio.
3. Nuestros hijos sufrirían las consecuencias si no protegiéramos el medio ambiente.
4. Si ellos supieran algo de la ecología, no contaminarían los mares, lagos y ríos.
5. Podrías hacer mucho para proteger el medio ambiente si tuvieras recursos.

Teaching Suggestion

25 You may wish to display *Teaching Transparency 11-2* to have students practice talking about hypothetical situations.

Pair Work

25 Pair students and assign each pair one of the pictures in the activity. Students should write a narrative for the picture, in either the first person or the third person. The groups with common picture assignments should then get together and compare and contrast what they wrote about the picture. Students may read their narratives to the class.

Visual Learners

26 Ask students to create a cluster diagram for each of the words in the boxes. Then, using the adjoining verb list and the clusters, they can develop a complete paragraph for each combination.

Native Speakers

27 Ask native speakers to write out Activity 27 rather than doing it orally.

25 **Sueños** See possible answers below.

Leamos/Hablemos ¿Qué están pensando las siguientes personas? Usa las expresiones de **Así se dice** de la página 326.

a.

b.

c.

d.

26 **¿Qué cambiarías?** Answers will vary.

Escribamos ¿Cómo quieres cambiar el mundo? Combina las siguientes palabras e ideas para formar seis oraciones que expliquen lo que harías.

MODELO   eliminar/el hambre
—Si yo pudiera, eliminaría el hambre en nuestra ciudad.

1. promover
2. reducir
3. aumentar
4. desarrollar
5. descubrir
6. luchar por
7. iniciar

la educación   los parques
la paz   una cura para el cáncer
la guerra   la pobreza
el hambre   la violencia

Nota cultural

Costa Rica es un tesoro ecológico. Su sistema de parques nacionales, que protege muchas especies de animales, plantas e insectos, ocupa más del 11 por ciento del territorio nacional. Debido al espíritu conservador del país, muchas organizaciones ecológicas van allí para hacer sus investigaciones. ¿Está interesada tu comunidad en la conservación?

27 **Una entrevista**

Leamos/Hablemos Usa estas preguntas para entrevistar a tu compañero(a). Después cuéntale a la clase lo que haría tu compañero(a) en estas circunstancias.

1. Si pudieras ser otra persona, ¿quién te gustaría ser? ¿Por qué?
2. Si tuvieras una máquina para viajar a través del tiempo, ¿a qué época irías? ¿Por qué?
3. Si fueras a una isla desierta, ¿qué llevarías contigo? ¿Por qué?
4. Si pudieras conocer a la persona más inteligente del mundo, ¿qué le preguntarías?
5. Si pudieras viajar a cualquier parte del mundo, ¿adónde irías? ¿Por qué?
6. Si tuvieras la oportunidad de cenar con cualquier persona, ¿a quién escogerías? ¿Por qué?

Answers

25 *Possible answers:*
a. Qué bonito sería si yo tuviera una motocicleta.
b. Sería maravilloso si todos limpiáramos el río.
c. Si yo fuera rica, iría a España.
d. Si pudiera practicar más, ganaría el trofeo.

Cultures and Communities

Culture Notes

• Tell students that Costa Rica is home to 10 percent of the world's species of birds. Over 850 of the species known to humans live in Costa Rica for at least part of the year. Many of the earth's endangered bird species make their home in Costa Rica, including the elusive, shimmering quetzal and the brilliantly-colored scarlet macaw (**guacamaya roja**). You might bring in a book about tropical birds to share with students.

• Since 1970, Costa Rica has protected more of its land in the form of national parks than has any other nation. Over a quarter of a million people visit Costa Rica's parks every year, and even these protected areas are showing signs of damage. Ask students what they think can be done to preserve national parks.

28  **Del colegio al trabajo**

Escribamos Trabajas para una compañía que hace estudios sociales sobre personas de habla hispana. Tú has creado un cuestionario para saber cómo mejorar los problemas de la ciudad. Con dos compañeros completa las respuestas de los entrevistados para presentárselas a tu supervisor(a).

MODELO Si tuviera dinero, …
Si tuviera dinero, regalaría una parte para programas de reciclaje.

1. Si pudiera mejorar la situación de mi ciudad,…
2. Si hubiera más transporte público,…
3. Si fuera el alcalde,…
4. Si fuera el director de mi colegio,…
5. Si hubiera mucha contaminación,…
6. Si aumentara la violencia,…
7. Si tuviera más tiempo,...

SUGERENCIA

It will be easier to decide what to write about if you brainstorm. Brainstorming means writing down all the ideas that come to mind without being critical of them. After you've listed all your ideas, write about the ones that appeal to you most.

29 **Por un buen porvenir**

Hablemos/Escribamos Se dice que "querer es poder". ¿Estás de acuerdo con este dicho? Con un(a) compañero(a), escribe un plan de dos o tres párrafos para explicar qué harían para mejorar el mundo.

30 **El foro público**

Hablemos Trabaja con tres compañeros(as) para presentar a la clase sus ideas de la Actividad 29. Escojan una o dos ideas para la presentación. Si quieren, pueden debatir las ideas con otro grupo de compañeros(as). Tomen en cuenta lo siguiente:

1. la importancia del problema
2. la lógica de la solución
3. las consecuencias de no resolver el problema
4. el beneficio del plan a la comunidad total

31 **En mi cuaderno**

Escribamos ¿Cuáles son los sueños de tu vida? Haz una lista de estos sueños. Luego escribe tres o cuatro párrafos sobre tus sueños y cómo esperas realizarlos. Menciona los problemas u obstáculos que complican la realización de tus sueños. No te olvides de mencionar también las consecuencias de no superar esos obstáculos. Sugiere algunas maneras de resolver estos problemas. Incluye también unas hipótesis; por ejemplo, "Si yo tuviera tiempo y dinero, podría…" Considera los siguientes aspectos de tu vida antes de comenzar.

recreo   trabajo
casa   familia   educación
dinero   amigos(as)
viajes   amor

Mis sueños
1. *Una casa en el campo*
2. *Quiero ser cantante*
3. *Vacaciones en otros países*
4. *Quiero escribir una novela*
5. *Quiero aprender a jugar al tenis*

Segundo paso

CAPÍTULO 11

Assess
▸ Testing Program, pp. 239–242
Quiz 11-2A, Quiz 11-2B
Audio CD 11, Tr. 21

▸ Student Make-Up Assignments, Chapter 11, Alternative Quiz

▸ Alternative Assessment Guide, p. 40

Communication for All Students

Slower Pace

28 Create two decks of cards (about business card size). One deck has verb clauses with the past subjunctive (**si yo pudiera, si tuviera, si fuera**) and another deck has the thing, action, or quality (**talento** or **mi propio carro**). Have students work in pairs to choose a card from each deck and formulate logical sentences using the elements from each card.

Visual Learners

29 Ask students to imagine a machine, a city plan, an ecology program, or a communications system and to design an advertising campaign to promote its usefulness for making the world a better place.

Teaching Resources
pp. 330–332

PRINT

▶ Lesson Planner, p. 55
▶ Cuaderno de actividades, p. 131
▶ Cuaderno para hispanohablantes, pp. 51–54
▶ Reading Strategies and Skills Handbook, Chapter 11
▶ ¡Lee conmigo! 3, Chapter 11
▶ Standardized Assessment Tutor, Chapter 11

MEDIA

▶ One-Stop Planner

Prereading
Activity A

Drawing on Your Experience
Ask students what stories they remember from their childhood and what messages the stories conveyed. Have them recall different fables and morals from children's stories.

Slower Pace
Provide students with a list of new or challenging vocabulary words and their English equivalents.

Additional Practice
Ask students if they recognize any words as cognates of English words and have them point out any they recognize as familiar Spanish words.

Answers

A 1. el Zorro y las Abejas
2. el Zorro; *(Possible answer:)* Los zorros son inteligentes, pero no son honestos. No se puede confiar mucho en los zorros.

Vamos a leer

Una fábula de la tecnología

Vas a leer una fábula titulada "Las abejas de bronce", por el argentino Marco Denevi. Una fábula es un cuento ficticio que trata de enseñar algo. ¿Conoces las fábulas de Esopo *(Aesop)*? ¿Conoces otras fábulas? ¿Cuáles?

Estrategia **para leer**
Don't forget the strategy of guessing words through context. If you understand the context, sometimes there will be only one sensible guess as to the meaning of the word. Using context also helps you guess a word's "approximate" meaning, when you just can't pin down its exact meaning.

¡A comenzar!
En las fábulas casi siempre hay animales que hablan. En "Las abejas de bronce" los personajes son:

el Petirrojo — *Robin*
las Abejas — *Bees*
las Arañas — *Spiders*
los Pájaros — *Birds*
el Oso — *Bear*
el Cuervo — *Crow*
el Zorro — *Fox*
el Ruiseñor — *Nightingale*
la Gansa — *Goose*

¿Te acuerdas?
If you know of specific details you want to find, you can scan the text quickly, looking only for those details.

A. Revisa la fábula y contesta las preguntas de arriba para prepararte antes de leer.

Las abejas de bronce

Desde el principio del tiempo el Zorro vivió de la venta de la miel. Nadie tenía la maña del Zorro para tratar a las Abejas y hacerles rendir al máximo. Esto por un lado. Por otro lado el Zorro sabía entenderse con el Oso, gran consumidor de miel y, por lo mismo, su mejor cliente. No resultaba fácil llevarse bien con el Oso. El Oso era un sujeto un poco brutal, un poco salvaje.

El Zorro sabía manejar a las Abejas y sabía manejar al Oso. Pero, ¿a quién no sabía manejar ese zorro del Zorro?

Hasta que un día se inventaron las Abejas artificiales.

Sí. Insectos de bronce, dirigidos electrónicamente, a control remoto, podían hacer el mismo trabajo que las Abejas vivas. Pero con enormes ventajas. No se fatigaban, no se perdían, no quedaban atrapadas en las redes de las Arañas,

no eran devoradas por los Pájaros, resultaban infinitamente superiores a las Abejas vivas.

El Zorro en seguida vio el negocio y no dudó. Mató todos sus enjambres, demolió las colmenas de cera, compró mil Abejas de bronce, mandó instalar el tablero de control, y una mañana los animales presenciaron, atónitos, cómo las Abejas de bronce atravesaban por primera vez el espacio.

Los insectos de bronce volaban a velocidades nunca vistas, sorbían rápidamente el néctar, regresaban a la colmena, y a los pocos instantes destilaban la miel, una miel pura, dorada, incontaminada, aséptica; y ya estaban en condiciones de recomenzar. Y así las veinticuatro horas del día. El Zorro no cabía en sí de contento.

La primera vez que el Oso probó la nueva miel puso los ojos en blanco, hizo chasquear la lengua y, no atreviéndose a opinar, le preguntó a su mujer:

"Vaya, ¿qué te parece?"

Cultures and Communities

Background Information
Marco Denevi (1922–1998) was born in Sáenz Peña, Argentina. At the age of 33, Denevi, who had been educated as a lawyer and was working at a bank, won a literary contest and great public acclaim with his novel, *Rosaura a las diez.* In 1968, he quit his job in order to write full-time. Denevi died in Buenos Aires in 1998.

STANDARDS: 1.2, 2.2, 3.1, 3.2

"No sé", dijo ella. "Le siento gusto a metal".

Pero sus hijos protestaron a coro: "Papá, mamá, qué disparate. Si se ve a la legua que esta miel es muy superior. ¿Cómo pueden preferir aquella otra, elaborada por unos bichos tan sucios? En cambio ésta es más limpia, más higiénica, más moderna y, en una palabra, más miel".

Y, con todo esto, las ganancias del Zorro crecían como un incendio en el bosque. Tuvo que tomar a su servicio un ayudante y eligió al Cuervo, sobre todo porque le aseguró que <u>aborrecía</u> la miel. Las mil Abejas fueron pronto cinco mil; las cinco, diez mil. El Zorro se sonreía y <u>se frotaba</u> las manos.

Y cuando ya el Zorro paladeaba su prosperidad, comenzaron a aparecer los inconvenientes.

La serie de desastres quedó inaugurada con el episodio de las rosas artificiales. Una tarde, al vaciar una colmena, el Zorro descubrió entre la miel rubia unos goterones grises, de un color nauseabundo y sabor acre. Tuvo que tirar toda la miel restante, que había quedado contaminada. Pronto supo el origen de aquellos goterones repugnantes. Había sucedido que las Abejas de bronce, desprovistas de instintos, confundieron un ramo de rosas artificiales de propiedad de la Gansa con rosas naturales, y les sorbieron la cera pintada de que estaban hechas y las dejaron convertidas en un guiñapo. El Zorro no solamente debió de sufrir la pérdida de la miel, sino indemnizar a la Gansa por daños y perjuicios.

"Malas Abejas", vociferaba mentalmente. "Las otras jamás habrían caído en semejante error. Tenían un instinto infalible. Pero quién piensa en las otras. En fin, nada es perfecto en este mundo".

Al cabo de unos días observó que los insectos tardaban cada vez más tiempo en regresar a las colmenas.

"¿Por qué tardan tanto?", decía el Zorro.

"Patrón", dijo el Cuervo. "Yo conozco un Pájaro que, si se le unta la mano, se ocuparía del caso".

1. ¿Cuáles son los animales más importantes de la fábula? (Son los dos que se mencionan más en el cuento.) See answers below.

2. Según los dibujos, ¿qué animal es el protagonista de la fábula? ¿Qué cualidades asociamos con este animal en nuestros mitos, cuentos y leyendas?

Al grano See answers below.

B. En esta actividad vas a demostrar que entiendes el argumento básico del cuento. Primero lee las oraciones que siguen. Después comienza a leer el cuento. Luego pon las oraciones en orden cronológico. Cuando encuentres lo que pasó primero, escribe "1". Continúa con 2, 3, etc., hasta que termines el cuento y la actividad.

 a. Los hijos del Oso insisten en que la nueva miel es mejor.

 b. Se inventan las Abejas artificiales.

 c. El Oso amenaza al Zorro.

 d. Las Abejas vuelan al extranjero.

 e. El Zorro contrata al Cuervo.

 f. El Zorro cierra su negocio.

 g. El Zorro se lleva bien con las Abejas y el Oso.

 h. Las Abejas comienzan a regresar a sus colmenas muy tarde.

 i. El Zorro inicia el negocio de las Abejas artificiales.

 j. Los colores del Petirrojo palidecen.

C. Usa el contexto para adivinar el significado de estas palabras, que están subrayadas en el texto.

 1. enjambres
 2. chasquear
 3. aborrecía
 4. se frotaba
 5. acre
 6. desprovistas
 7. comarca
 8. mueca

Reading
Activities B, C, and D

Monitoring Comprehension
- In addition to having them use contextual clues, have students identify key words. You might have them list key words as they read. By focusing on key words and skimming over connectors and added descriptions, students may be able to better comprehend the main idea.
- Remind students that, while they may not know the exact word, they can guess its meaning from the context of the reading.

Making Predictions
B. Ask students to order the sentences after first skimming the text, using guesswork and logic to predict sequence. Then have them read the text to see if their predictions about sentence order were correct.

Determining the Main Idea
Knowing that the story is a fable, have students predict the moral. If they have difficulty, have them tell as much as they can in English about each illustration.

Answers

B 1. g
   2. b
   3. i
   4. a
   5. e
   6. h
   7. d
   8. j
   9. c
   10. f

C 1. swarm
   2. to click or snap
   3. hated, abhorred
   4. rubbed
   5. sour, bitter, acrid
   6. lacking
   7. area, region
   8. face, expression

Communication for All Students

Visual Learners
- Have students draw illustrations of the components of the text listed A–J. Then have them order the pictures as well as the text captions.
- Read excerpts from the story aloud and have students match the quotations with the illustrations.

Challenge
Have partners write true/false statements and an answer key. Then collect their papers and read the statements aloud to the class. You might make this activity a game, with players from two teams competing to respond to the statements.

CAPÍTULO 11

Postreading
Activity E

Comparing and Contrasting

Ask students to compare and contrast this story to another that they have read or to a movie they have seen. How are the two similar or different?

Appreciating a Writer's Craft

You may want to remind students that they already know the writer's purpose. As a fable, this piece is intended to highlight a moral lesson. Ask them to point out the major literary device Denevi uses to communicate his message. (Through personification, the author creates the characterization of the animals. They are all imbued with human characteristics and feelings.) Remind students that this literary device is common to all fables.

D. Todas las fábulas tienen una moraleja. En un grupo de tres o cuatro personas, discutan el propósito y la técnica de esta fábula. Usen las preguntas de abajo como punto de partida para su discusión. Si pueden, hablen en español sobre las preguntas. Si prefieren prepararse un poco, pueden escribir sus respuestas primero y luego discutirlas con su grupo.

  1. Las Abejas artificiales simbolizan un fenómeno de la vida moderna. ¿Cuál es?

  2. ¿Cuál es la moraleja del cuento?

  3. ¿Por qué se usan animales en las fábulas en vez de personas?

  4. El autor habría podido *(could have)* expresar su opinión muy claramente en un ensayo. ¿Por qué crees que prefirió usar una fábula?

  5. ¿Es válida para el mundo de hoy la preocupación del autor por el progreso?

E. ¿Crees que las cosas nuevas y modernas siempre son mejores que las cosas viejas y conocidas? ¿Por qué? ¿Puedes enumerar algunos adelantos que mejoraron las cosas? ¿Y otros adelantos que las empeoraron?

Cuaderno para hispanohablantes, pp. 51–54

Cuaderno de actividades, p. 131, Acts. 22–24

"¿Y quién es ese Pájaro?"

"Un servidor".

El Zorro optó por aceptar. Pues cualquier recurso era preferible a quedarse con los brazos cruzados, contemplando la progresiva e implacable disminución de las ganancias.

El Cuervo regresó muy tarde, jadeando como si hubiera vuelto volando desde la China. —Patrón—dijo—, no sé cómo decírselo. Pero las Abejas tardan, y tardarán cada vez más, porque no hay flores en la comarca y deben ir al extranjero.

"¿Cómo que no hay flores en la comarca? ¿Qué tontería es ésa?"

"Lo que oye, Patrón. Parece ser que las flores, después que las Abejas les han sorbido el néctar, se debilitan y se mueren".

"¡Se mueren! ¿Y por qué se mueren?"

"No resisten la trompa de metal de las Abejas. Y no termina ahí la cosa. La planta, después que las Abejas le mataron sus flores, se niega a florecer nuevamente. Consecuencia: en toda la comarca no hay más flores".

Se dice que ese día ocurrieron extraños acontecimientos. El Ruiseñor quedó afónico y los colores del Petirrojo palidecieron. Se dice que los ríos dejaron de correr, y las fuentes de cantar.

El Zorro se desesperó. Sus negocios se desmoronaron. Debió despedir al Cuervo, cerrar la tienda, perder la clientela.

El único que no se resignaba era el Oso.

"Zorro", vociferaba, "o me consigues miel o te levanto la tapa de los sesos".

Finalmente, una noche el Zorro desconectó los cables, destruyó el tablero de control, enterró en un pozo las Abejas de bronce, y huyó con rumbo desconocido.

Cuando iba a cruzar la frontera escuchó a sus espaldas unas risitas y unas vocecitas de vieja que lo llamaban.

"¡Zorro! ¡Zorro!"

Eran las Arañas, que a la luz de la luna tejían sus telas prehistóricas. El Zorro les hizo una <u>mueca</u> obscena y se alejó a grandes pasos. Desde entonces nadie volvió a verlo jamás.

Connections and Comparisons

Multicultural Link

Have students interview someone from another culture to find out if that person knows of fables similar to this one. You might encourage students to invite this person to class to share the fable. As an alternative, students may paraphrase it in Spanish and recount it to the class.

Family Link

As an outside assignment, have students ask an older relative or neighbor about something that was better in the past than it is now.

Literature Link

Have groups list other morals for stories. (Don't put all your eggs in one basket. The grass is always greener on the other side of the fence.)

Vamos a escribir

¿Cómo es vivir en tu comunidad? ¿Cómo es la calidad del medio ambiente en tu área? ¿Cuál es la condición del agua y del aire? ¿Hay seguridad en las calles? ¿Existen actividades recreativas para jóvenes de tu edad? ¿Qué piensas que se puede hacer para mejorar tu comunidad? En esta actividad, vas a escribir un fax a un funcionario público sobre uno o algunos de los problemas de tu comunidad. Aprenderás una manera para formular y organizar los detalles que vas acumulando sobre el tema.

Un fax

Escríbele un fax de cinco o seis párrafos a un funcionario público. Puede ser el (la) presidente(a), el (la) gobernador(a), un(a) senador(a) o un(a) representante. Descríbele las condiciones de tu comunidad. Menciona los problemas especiales y sus causas, y recomienda soluciones a estos problemas.

Estrategia para escribir

Using note cards Keeping track of details written on lists can sometimes be a challenge. Note cards are a way to solve this problem. On each 4" x 6" card or piece of paper, write in your own words the information you found and where. You can store the cards in a filing box until you begin writing. At that point, take them out and rearrange them until they present the information in the most logical order. Then use that order as the structure for your writing.

A. Preparación

1. Discute las condiciones de tu comunidad con tus amigos(as) y con tu familia. ¿Hay problemas especiales? ¿Cuáles son? Puede ser una calle con mucha basura o un parque sin flores y árboles, etc. ¿Qué causa estos problemas? ¿Qué se puede hacer para resolver-los? Anota esta información en fichas *(note cards)* y apunta qué dijo cada persona.

2. Busca más información en periódicos y revistas. Anota en fichas los detalles que descubras.

3. Pon las fichas en orden lógico y sigue este orden para escribir tu fax.

B. Redacción

1. Comienza tu fax con **Estimado(a) Sr(a). Presidente(a)** u otro título apropiado.

2. Escribe un párrafo breve que explique por qué le estás escribiendo este fax.

3. Escribe dos o tres párrafos sobre los problemas de tu comunidad. Sigue el orden de tus fichas. Si descubres que el orden no es lógico, cámbialo.

4. Escribe en una conclusión tus impresiones generales de los problemas y tus sugerencias para resolverlos.

5. Termina el fax con **Cordialmente** y tu firma *(signature)*.

C. Evaluación

1. Pídeles a varios(as) compañeros(as) que lean tu fax para buscar áreas que necesiten más detalles. Busca la información que necesitas e incorpórala.

2. ¿Omitiste algún detalle o idea que quisieras mencionar? Inclúyelo en el lugar lógico.

3. ¿Está bien organizado tu fax? Si no, cambia el orden de las ideas que presentas.

Teaching Resources
p. 333

PRINT
▶ Lesson Planner, p. 55
▶ Cuaderno para hispanohablantes, p. 54
▶ Alternative Assessment Guide, p. 26
▶ Standardized Assessment Tutor, Chapter 11

MEDIA
▶ One-Stop Planner, Disc 3
▶ Test Generator, Chapter 11
▶ Interactive CD-ROM Tutor, Disc 3

Teacher Note
You might do this activity over several days to allow students to interview family members or people in the community in order to get the input needed to do this writing project.

Process Writing

Prewriting
Motivating Activity
Ask students if they have ever written a letter to a public official. Have them list problems they would like to discuss with their elected representatives.

Writing
Slower Pace
Review correct usage of titles that students may need: **alcalde/alcaldesa, senador/senadora, diputado/diputada o representante, miembro del consejo municipal,** and **super-intendente de escuelas.** Remind students to use formal language in their correspondence.

Apply and Assess

Postwriting
Pair Work
Have partners exchange their note cards and the writing assignment to determine how well they were able to shape their initial thoughts and information into a narrative. One student can read the details on each note card while his or her partner checks them off in the fax.

Cooperative Learning
Have students form groups of four to peer-edit their papers. One person checks for spelling and accents, a second checks for transitions used, a third checks for the proper use of the past subjunctive and the conditional, and a fourth checks for new expressions from this chapter.

Más práctica gramatical

CAPÍTULO 11

For **Más práctica gramatical**
Answer Transparencies, see the
Teaching Transparencies binder.

Más práctica gramatical

internet

MARCAR: go.hrw.com
PALABRA CLAVE:
WV3 COSTA RICA-11

Primer paso   **Objectives** Pointing out problems and their consequences; talking about how you would solve a problem

1 La clase de ciencias sociales hizo una lista de las medidas *(actions)* que se tomaron y que se van a tomar en la ciudad para resolver unos problemas ambientales. Escribe las frases de nuevo, usando el **se** impersonal. (**p. 319**)

> **MODELO**   Antes <u>todos pensaban</u> que la contaminación no era muy grave.
> Antes <u>se pensaba</u> que la contaminación no era muy grave.

1. Luego, en la universidad <u>hicieron</u> un estudio de los niveles de contaminación.
2. <u>Descubrieron</u> que hubo *(there was)* un aumento muy grande en el nivel de smog.
3. Por eso, en el ayuntamiento <u>decidieron</u> no construir la carretera nueva.
4. En cambio, <u>establecieron</u> una zona peatonal en el centro.
5. <u>Algunos hablaban</u> de implementar un sistema de transporte público mejor y más eficiente.
6. También <u>trataron</u> de reducir el nivel de contaminación del río.
7. Por ejemplo, <u>destruyeron</u> la vieja fábrica cerca del río y <u>construyeron</u> un parque.
8. <u>Han logrado</u> realizar otras medidas también.
9. Por ejemplo, este verano <u>van a sembrar</u> un árbol en la plaza central.
10. La próxima semana, <u>discutirán</u> el plan para el nuevo centro de reciclaje.

Answers

1 1. se hizo
2. Se descubrió
3. se decidió
4. se estableció
5. Se hablaba
6. se trató
7. se destruyó, se construyó
8. Se ha logrado
9. se va a sembrar
10. se discutirá

Grammar Resources for Chapter 11

The **Más práctica gramatical** activities are designed as supplemental activities for the grammatical concepts presented in the chapter. You might use them as additional practice, for review, or for assessment.

For more grammar presentation, review, and practice, refer to the following:
• Cuaderno de gramática
• Grammar Tutor for Students of Spanish

• Grammar Summary on pp. R25–R46
• Cuaderno de actividades
• Grammar and Vocabulary quizzes (Testing Program)
• Test Generator on the One-Stop Planner CD-ROM
• Interactive CD-ROM Tutor
• **Juegos interactivos** at <u>go.hrw.com</u>

2 Indica qué palabra se asocia con las frases siguientes. (p. 319)

> los ladrones el hambre el desempleo
> aumentar
> el homicidio implementar la enfermedad

1. lo contrario de la salud
2. una falta de comida suficiente
3. empezar algo o tomar la iniciativa
4. el que queda muerto de una manera violenta es víctima de este crimen
5. los que roban
6. subir o hacerse más grande
7. la falta de trabajo para todos

3 Escuchas las noticias de un programa de radio en español. Vuelve a escribir cada frase para cada una de las oraciones usando el **se** impersonal. (p. 319)

> **MODELO** **La gente dice que se frenará la inflación.**
> **—Se dice que se frenará la inflación.**

1. La gente dice que el crimen ha aumentado.
2. La gente ha hecho mucho para reducir la delincuencia.
3. Hoy en día, muchas personas promueven campañas contra las drogas.
4. Muchos grupos ecologistas han implementado programas de reciclaje.
5. Los doctores saben que ahora hay más enfermedades.
6. La gente cree que la situación va a empeorarse.

Answers

2 1. la enfermedad
2. el hambre
3. implementar
4. el homicidio
5. los ladrones
6. aumentar
7. el desempleo

3 1. Se dice que el crimen ha aumentado.
2. Se ha hecho mucho para reducir la delincuencia.
3. Hoy en día, se promueven campañas contra las drogas.
4. Se han implementado programas de reciclaje.
5. Se sabe que ahora hay más enfermedades.
6. Se cree que la situación va a empeorarse.

Communication for All Students

Visual/Kinesthetic Learners

2 Have students write each word or phrase from the word bank onto a single index card. On the reverse side of each card, have students write a definition and draw an illustration. Instruct students to lay the cards across their desks with the drawings facing up. Then, while they are working on Activity 2, they can refer to the cards in order to make word associations.

Additional Practice

3 Remind students that although **se** is usually used with the third person singular, it may also be used with the plural. Have students write the verb used with **se** in each item and mark the subject of each verb. Then ask students to complete the activity by writing the new sentences.

For **Más práctica gramatical** Answer Transparencies, see the *Teaching Transparencies* binder.

Más práctica gramatical

CD-ROM DISC 3   WV3 COSTA RICA-11

Segundo paso   Objectives Talking about hypothetical situations

4 Completa las oraciones con el pretérito y con el pasado del subjuntivo del verbo entre paréntesis. Recuerda que las formas del imperfecto del subjuntivo se basan en el pretérito. **(p. 327)**

MODELO   El año pasado Jorge y sus padres ══════ a Costa Rica. Si tú ══════ a Centroamérica, ¿adónde irías? (ir)
—**El año pasado Jorge y sus padres fueron a Costa Rica. Si tú fueras a Centroamérica, ¿adónde irías?**

1. Thomas Edison y Alexander Bell ══════ unos aparatos importantísimos. Si tú ══════ algo, ¿qué sería? (inventar)
2. Simón Bolívar y Benito Juárez ══════ presidentes y líderes revolucionarios. ¿Qué harías si tú ══════ presidente? (ser)
3. Miguel de Cervantes y William Shakespeare ══════ unas obras maestras. Si tú ══════ una novela o una obra de teatro, ¿de qué se trataría? (escribir)
4. Gabriela Mistral, Octavio Paz y Gabriel García Márquez ══════ el Premio Nobel de Literatura. Si tú ══════ un premio igual, ¿cómo te sentirías? (ganar)
5. Los astronautas Neil Armstrong, Buzz Aldrin y Michael Collins ══════ a la luna en 1969. ¿Te asustarías si ══════ a otra galaxia? (viajar)
6. Los artistas mexicanos Diego Rivera, David Alfonso Siqueiros y José Clemente Orozco ══════ unos murales mundialmente conocidos. Si tú ══════ un mural, ¿en dónde te gustaría hacerlo? (pintar)
7. Hernán Cortés y los soldados españoles ══════ al Valle de México en 1519. Si tú ══════ a un mundo nuevo, ¿qué te gustaría hacer allí? (llegar)

Communication for All Students

Pair Work
Organize students into pairs. Ask each student to prepare a list of five things they would do if they suddenly had no financial limits. Tell them to include a list of goals they would set and places they would visit. Next, have students peer-edit each other's work. Finally, have each student share their list with the class.

Game
CATEGORÍAS Give each team of four to five students the same category. **(la violencia, la paz, las drogas)** Give them time to create as many realistic sentences as possible saying what they would do to solve the problem. Share the sentences with the class. The team with the most possible sentences per category wins.

Answers
4 1. inventaron, inventaras
2. fueron, fueras
3. escribieron, escribieras
4. ganaron, ganaras
5. viajaron, viajaras
6. pintaron, pintaras
7. llegaron, llegaras

5 Todos los de tu clase tienen aspiraciones distintas. Explica qué haría cada uno si pudiera. Usa las formas correctas del pasado del subjuntivo y del condicional. (p. 327)

> MODELO   **Si Pablo** _____ **(tener) más dinero,** _____ **(viajar) a Chile.**
> —**Si Pablo tuviera más dinero, viajaría a Chile.**

1. Si Fátima _____ (poder) estudiar música, _____ (ser) una cantante famosa.
2. Si Belén _____ (ser) presidenta, _____ (luchar) contra la discriminación.
3. Si Jorge y Tina _____ (tener) la oportunidad, _____ (conocer) al presidente.
4. Si Marisa _____ (poder) inventar cualquier cosa, _____ (inventar) un videojuego estupendo.
5. Si mis hermanos y yo _____ (vivir) en una casa más grande, no _____ (pelearse) tanto.
6. Si tú _____ (ser) explorador, ¿_____ (ir) al Polo Norte?
7. Si Lucila y Julia _____ (vivir) en el campo, no _____ (estar) aburridas.
8. Si Daniel _____ (conocer) a su actriz favorita, _____ (invitarla) a salir.

6 Iván likes to hypothesize about how his life could be different. Read each situation, and then restate it with a contrary-to-fact clause. Use the conditional and past subjunctive of the verbs in parentheses. (p. 327)

> MODELO   **Me gustaría aprender a hacer tabla de vela, pero las clases son muy caras.**
> **(yo/tomar unas clases/no ser caras)**
> —**Tomaría unas clases de tabla de vela si las clases no fueran tan caras.**

1. Sería bueno tener un trabajo pero ahora con mis clases estoy muy ocupado.
   (yo/buscar un trabajo/no estar ocupado)
2. Necesito ayudar más en casa pero los profesores me dan mucha tarea.
   (yo/ayudar/ellos/no dar tanta tarea)
3. Me gustaría bajar de peso pero ¡hacer ejercicio es tan aburrido!
   (yo/estar en plena forma/los ejercicios/no ser aburridos)
4. Debería estudiar más en la clase de química pero no me interesa.
   (yo/sacar mejores notas/gustarme la materia)
5. Algún día quiero viajar a Miami a visitar a mis amigos, pero el viaje es muy caro.
   (yo/hacer un viaje/no costar tanto)
6. Me gustaría invitar a Maribel a salir, pero me siento nervioso cuando estoy con ella.
   (yo/hablarle/no sentirme nervioso)
7. Debería ser más paciente con mi hermana menor, pero ¡es tan pesada a veces!
   (nosotros/llevarnos bien/ella/no ser pesada)

Answers

5
1. pudiera, sería
2. fuera, lucharía
3. tuvieran, conocerían
4. pudiera, inventaría
5. viviéramos, nos pelearíamos
6. fueras, irías
7. vivieran, estarían
8. conociera, la invitaría

Answers will vary. Possible answers:

6
1. Buscaría un trabajo si no estuviera tan ocupado.
2. Ayudaría más en casa si no me dieran tanta tarea.
3. Estaría en plena forma si hacer ejercicio no fuera tan aburrido.
4. Sacaría mejores notas en la clase de química si me gustara la materia.
5. Haría un viaje a Miami y visitaría a mis amigos si no costara tanto.
6. Le hablaría con Maribel si no me sintiera nervioso.
7. Nos llevaríamos mejor con mi hermana menor si ella no fuera tan pesada.

Review and Assess

You may wish to assign the **Más práctica gramatical** activities as additional practice or homework after presenting material throughout the chapter. Assign Activities 1 and 3 after **¿Te acuerdas?** (p. 319), Activity 2 after **Vocabulario** (p. 319), and Activities 4–6 after **Gramática** (p. 327).

To prepare students for the **Paso** Quizzes and Chapter Test, have them do the **Más práctica gramatical** activities in the following order: complete Activities 1–3 before taking Quiz 11-1A or 11-1B, and Activities 4–6 before taking Quiz 11-2A or 11-2B.

Repaso

CAPÍTULO 11

The **Repaso** reviews all four skills and culture in preparation for the Chapter Test.

Teaching Resources
pp. 338–339

PRINT
▸ Lesson Planner, p. 56
▸ Listening Activities, p. 85
▸ Video Guide, pp. 74, 76, 79
▸ Grammar Tutor for Students of Spanish, Chapter 11
▸ Cuaderno para hispanohablantes, pp. 51–55
▸ Standardized Assessment Tutor, Chapter 11

MEDIA
▸ One-Stop Planner
▸ Video Program, Videocassette 4, 28:37–32:32
▸ Audio Compact Discs, CD 11, Tr. 19
▸ Interactive CD-ROM Tutor, Disc 3

Portfolio

2 **Oral** Suggest to students that they record their responses for this activity in their oral Portfolio. For Portfolio suggestions, see *Alternative Assessment Guide,* page 26.

Repaso

MARCAR: go.hrw.com
PALABRA CLAVE:
WV3 COSTA RICA-11

1 Escucha el siguiente debate entre dos candidatos, Juan Luis Benavides y Cecilia Reyes. Luego lee las siguientes frases y escribe **B** si representan opiniones de Benavides, **R** si representan opiniones de Reyes o **D** si son opiniones de los dos. Script and answers on p. 273H.

CD 11
Tr. 19

1. El problema de la criminalidad en nuestro país es de muchísima importancia.
2. Yo voy a enfocarme más en crear leyes más fuertes contra el crimen.
3. Yo propongo que usemos más dinero en los programas para informar a los jóvenes sobre las drogas.
4. La sensibilidad hacia los criminales es una pérdida de dinero y de tiempo.
5. La criminalidad de nuestro país es el resultado de una falta de programas que ofrezcan alternativas a la delincuencia.

2 Con un(a) compañero(a), indica una alternativa positiva para cada una de las siguientes malas ideas. See possible answers below.

MODELO   **Tiremos los periódicos a la calle.**
—**Sería mejor si los tiráramos al basurero.**
—**Si pudiéramos reciclarlos, eliminaríamos mucha contaminación.**

1. Compremos carros grandes.
2. Todos debemos ir al trabajo todos los días en nuestros propios carros.
3. No prestemos atención al problema de la drogadicción.
4. Talemos todos los árboles.
5. No combatamos la delincuencia.
6. Usemos muchos productos que no se pueden reciclar.

3 Con unos(as) compañeros(as), considera los siguientes problemas. Escojan tres de los problemas, indiquen sus consecuencias y hablen de cómo los resolverían. Answers will vary.

1. la extinción de plantas y animales
2. las personas viejas que viven solas
3. los jóvenes que no terminan la secundaria
4. la gente que no tiene casa
5. la destrucción de edificios y barrios históricos
6. las personas que no saben leer ni escribir

4 Contesta estas preguntas con la información cultural de las secciones culturales de este capítulo. See answers below.

1. ¿Cuándo adoptó Costa Rica un sistema democrático de gobierno?
2. ¿Qué porcentaje de los habitantes de Costa Rica saben leer y escribir?
3. ¿Quién tomó el lugar del ejército de Costa Rica?
4. ¿Qué porcentaje del territorio nacional de Costa Rica está dedicado a parques nacionales?
5. ¿Por qué vienen muchas organizaciones ecológicas a Costa Rica para hacer sus investigaciones?

Apply and Assess

Visual/Auditory Learners
1 Ask students to draw or describe the facial expressions they would expect to see on each candidate for each opinion represented.

Challenge
2 Ask students to say each sentence and then to rephrase it as a question. (**Compremos carros grandes. ¿Por qué no compramos carros grandes?**) Another student responds with an alternative and then rephrases it as a question for the first student to answer.

Visual/Tactile Learners
3 Have students create a collage, drawing, or vivid description of the chosen problem. Then have them label it with ways of resolving the problem.

5 Lee el siguiente artículo sobre las selvas tropicales. Luego identifica los problemas, beneficios y soluciones que menciona el artículo. See possible answers below.

¿Podremos salvar las selvas tropicales?

Hoy en día se destruyen grandes secciones de las selvas tropicales. Parte del problema es que en muchas regiones, grandes empresas entran a talar los árboles por la madera. También existe el petróleo y otros recursos naturales. Al extraer estos recursos, se destruye la selva. De las selvas recibimos gran parte del oxígeno del mundo. Y cada año descubrimos plantas medicinales en la selva. Otro beneficio de la selva tropical es que produce gran cantidad de agua. Además de agua, la selva tropical produce otros elementos que afectan el clima de otras partes del mundo. Si destruyéramos estos elementos, cambiaríamos la atmósfera. Debemos comprar menos productos y animales que vienen de la selva. Tenemos que convencer a los gobiernos que tienen que limitar la destrucción de las selvas. También sería una buena idea iniciar una campaña de publicidad para crear conciencia de los beneficios medicinales y ambientales de la selva.

6 Escribe una carta al director o a la directora de tu escuela para convencerlo(la) de iniciar un programa de reciclaje. Menciona los problemas que el reciclaje podría aliviar, las consecuencias de no hacer nada y los beneficios del programa.

7 Imagina que tú y un(a) compañero(a) son miembros del club "Protejamos Nuestros Parques". Hablen sobre los problemas de los parques en este país y sobre lo que se puede hacer para protegerlos. Mencionen también las consecuencias de no resolver los problemas.

8
Situación

Imagina que tú y unos(as) compañeros(as) son miembros del Comité Nacional Contra la Drogadicción. Discutan el problema del abuso de las drogas. Mencionen los problemas que ven, las soluciones que proponen y qué harían para resolver el problema si tuvieran fondos y recursos suficientes.

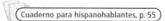
Cuaderno para hispanohablantes, p. 55

Apply and Assess

Group Work

5 Have students work in small groups. One person reads the article aloud. The other group members stop the reader to ask questions or offer opinions or comments at any point in the reading. Students identify the problem, benefits, and solutions together as a group.

Additional Practice

8 Have students design a poster, button, or brochure for the slogan **Contra la drogadicción.** Encourage students to create a catchy slogan for their designs. (**Ayudemos a todos a vencer la drogadicción.**) You may want to contact your local police department to see if it has D.A.R.E. materials available in Spanish.

Teaching Suggestion

7 After students are finished with their pair work, engage the class in a debate about how to protect national parks. You might ask native speakers to help moderate these discussions.

Answers

2 *Sample answers:*
1. Sería mejor si pudiéramos manejar carros pequeños. Si pudiéramos eliminar los carros grandes, no habría tanta contaminación.
2. Sería maravilloso si todos compartiéramos los carros para manejar al trabajo. Si pudiéramos compartir carros, habría menos tráfico.
3. Sería mejor si prestáramos atención al problema de la drogadicción. Si hiciéramos programas contra las drogas, los jóvenes tendrían un mejor porvenir.
4. Si protegiéramos los árboles, habría mejor calidad del aire. Sería bueno sembrar más arboles.
5. Si intentáramos combatir la delincuencia, la vida sería mejor en nuestra ciudad. Si los chicos tuvieran actividades positivas, no habría tanta delincuencia.
6. Sería bueno usar productos reciclables. No habría tanta basura si recicláramos más.

4
1. en 1890
2. 93%
3. la Guardia Nacional
4. el 11% del territorio
5. por su espíritu conservacionista

5 *Possible answers:*
Los problemas: Las grandes empresas cortan los árboles y también destruyen la selva al extraer el petróleo y otros recursos naturales.
Los beneficios de la selva: Produce gran cantidad de agua, gran parte del oxígeno del mundo y muchas plantas medicinales.
Las soluciones: Hay que iniciar una campaña de publicidad y convencer a los gobiernos que limiten la destrucción. Debemos comprar menos productos que vienen de la selva.

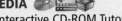
Teacher Note

This page is intended to help students prepare for the Chapter Test. It is a brief checklist of the major points covered in the chapter. The students should be reminded that it is only a checklist and does not necessarily include everything that will appear on the Chapter Test.

Answers

1 *Possible answers:*
1. Si los turistas botan basura, pronto nuestras playas estarán contaminadas.
2. Si los jóvenes no cuidan sus uniformes, van a verse mal en los conciertos.

3 *Possible answers:*
1. Si los carros no contaminaran el ambiente, el aire estaría más limpio.
2. Si hubiera leyes más fuertes, habría menos violencia.
3. Si yo ganara un millón de dólares, podría ayudar a los pobres.
4. Si la gente viera menos violencia en la tele, no se cometerían tantos crímenes.

A ver si puedo...

Can you point out problems and their consequences? p. 319

1 Mira los siguientes dibujos y usa expresiones de **Así se dice** para señalar problemas y consecuencias. See possible answers below.

Si los turistas botan basura...

Si los jóvenes no cuidan sus uniformes...

Can you talk about how you would solve a problem? p. 321

2 Indica cómo resolverías los siguientes problemas. Answers will vary.

1. La cafetería de tu escuela sirve la misma comida todas las semanas.
2. Quieres hacer más ejercicio pero no puedes porque tienes que trabajar.
3. Tu clase de español desea viajar a España pero no tiene suficiente dinero.
4. Alguien de tu ciudad quiere destruir una hermosa casa histórica para construir una fábrica. Tú crees que la casa debe ser conservada.

See possible answers below.

Can you talk about hypothetical situations? p. 326

3 Usa esta información para escribir frases sobre situaciones hipotéticas.

Situación hipotética	**Consecuencia**
los carros / no contaminar el aire	el aire / estar limpio
haber leyes más fuertes	haber menos violencia
yo / ganar un millón de dólares	ayudar a los pobres
la gente / ver menos violencia en la tele	cometer menos crímenes

Review and Assess

Additional Practice

2 Have students talk about how they would solve the problems shown in the illustrations for Activity 1.

Challenge

3 After students complete the sentences with hypothetical statements, have them go back and point out the problems and the consequences that make these solutions necessary. For **los carros/no contaminar el aire** and **el aire/estar limpio**, students might say **Si los carros siguen contaminando el aire, pronto no vamos a poder respirar bien.**

Primer paso

Pointing out problems and their consequences

Lo lamentaremos.	We'll regret it.
Me he fijado en...	I've noticed . . .
Se dice que...	They say that . . .
Según el gobierno,...	According to the government, . . .
Si no actuamos ahora...	If we don't act now . . .
Si no hacemos nada por...	If we don't do anything about . . .
Si no realizamos...	If we don't carry out . . .
Temo que el deterioro continúe.	I'm afraid the deterioration will continue.
Va a empeorarse.	It's going to get worse.

Problemas sociales

aumentar	to grow
bajar	to decrease
cometer	to commit
el crimen	major crime
la criminalidad	crime rate
la delincuencia	crime
el delito	minor crime
el desempleo	unemployment
la drogadicción	drug addiction
la enfermedad	disease
el hambre (f.)	hunger
el homicidio	homicide
implementar	to implement
el ladrón, la ladrona	thief
promover (ue)	to promote

el robo	robbery
la sensibilidad	sensitivity

Talking about how you would solve a problem

Habrá que...	It will be necessary to . . .
iniciar	to initiate
Intentaría...	I would try to . . .
La solución que planteo es...	The solution I propose is . . .
Me dedicaría a...	I would devote myself to . . .
Propongo...	I propose . . .
Yo empezaría por...	I would start by . . .

Segundo paso

Talking about hypothetical situations

Si hubiera paz...	If there were peace . . .
Si se encontrara una cura...	If a cure were found . . .

Si tuvieras...	If you had . . .
Si tú pudieras...	If you could . . .
Si yo fuera...	If I were . . .
Si yo viviera...	If I lived . . .

Circumlocution

For review, have students play ¿CÓMO TE DIRÉ? For game rules and procedures, see page 3C. Have them use the vocabulary listed under **Problemas sociales.** For example, **la enfermedad: Es lo contrario de la salud; el hambre: Es lo que sientes cuando necesitas comer.**

Chapter 11 Assessment

▸ **Testing Program**
Chapter Test, pp. 243–248
Audio Compact Discs, CD 11, Trs. 22–23
Speaking Test, p. 300

▸ **Alternative Assessment Guide**
Portfolio Assessment, p. 26
Performance Assessment, p. 40
CD-ROM Assessment, p. 54

▸ **Interactive CD-ROM Tutor, Disc 3**

¡A hablar!
¡A escribir!

▸ **Standardized Assessment Tutor**
Chapter 11

▸ **One-Stop Planner, Disc 3**

Test Generator
Chapter 11

Review and Assess

Game

COSTA RICA After students have completed the **Repaso,** have them write two or three either/or questions about Costa Rica. **(En Costa Rica, ¿hay una larga tradición democrática o comunista?)** Have them do extra research to write additional questions. Then collect the questions and form three teams. Have one member from each team read one of the team's questions. The first player from one of the other two teams to answer the question correctly wins a point for his or her team. Continue until all of the questions have been asked or until one team has earned ten points.

Capítulo 12: Mis planes para el futuro
Chapter Overview

Review Chapter

De antemano pp. 344–346	*¿Cuáles son tus planes?*			

	FUNCTIONS	**GRAMMAR**	**VOCABULARY**	**RE-ENTRY**
Primer paso pp. 347–350	• Talking about former jobs and goals, p. 347 • Talking about future career plans, p. 349	• Review: Preterite and imperfect, p. 348	• Careers and vocations, p. 347	• Chapter 12 is a global review of Chapters 1–11.

¡Adelante! pp. 352–353	*Cuando buscas un trabajo*			

Segundo paso pp. 354–358	• Giving advice about job interviews, p. 354	• Review: Subjunctive with recommendations, p. 354 • Review: Subjunctive with the unknown or nonexistent, p. 355 • Review: Conditional and past subjunctive, p. 357	• The business world, p. 356	• Chapter 12 is a global review of Chapters 1–11.

Vamos a leer pp. 360–362	**El árbol de oro**	**Reading Strategy:** Utilizing multiple reading strategies

Vamos a escribir p. 363	**En el año 3000**	**Writing Strategy:** Good conclusions

Más práctica gramatical	**pp. 364–367** **Primer paso,** pp. 364–366	**Segundo paso,** pp. 366–367

Review pp. 368–371	**Repaso,** pp. 368–369	**A ver si puedo...,** p. 370	**Vocabulario,** p. 371

CULTURE

• **Nota cultural, El ecoturismo,** p. 346
• **Nota cultural, La licenciatura,** p. 350
• **Panorama cultural, ¿Qué planes tienes para el futuro?,** p. 351

• **Encuentro cultural, La formalidad,** p. 359

Capítulo 12: Mis planes para el futuro
Chapter Resources

Lesson Planning
One-Stop Planner
Lesson Planner with Substitute Teacher Lesson Plans, pp. 57–61, 76
Student Make-up Assignments
- Make-Up Assignment Copying Masters, Chapter 12

Listening and Speaking
Listening Activities
- Student Response Forms for Listening Activities, pp. 91–93
- Additional Listening Activities 12-1 to 12-6, pp. 95–97
- Additional Listening Activities (poem), p. 98
- Scripts and Answers, pp. 157–161

Video Guide
- Teaching Suggestions, pp. 81–82
- Activity Masters, pp. 83–85
- Scripts and Answers, pp. 111–113, 120

Activities for Communication
- Communicative Activities, pp. 45–48
- Realia and Teaching Suggestions, pp. 84–86
- Situation Cards, pp. 111–112

Reading and Writing
Reading Strategies and Skills Handbook, Chapter 12
¡Lee conmigo! 3, Chapter 12
Cuaderno de actividades, pp. 133–144

Grammar
Cuaderno de gramática, pp. 95–104
Grammar Tutor for Students of Spanish, Chapter 12

Assessment
Testing Program
- Grammar and Vocabulary Quizzes, **Paso** Quizzes, and Chapter Test, pp. 257–270
- Score Sheet, Scripts and Answers, pp. 271–277
- Final Exam, pp. 279–286
- Score Sheet, Scripts and Answers, pp. 287–292

Alternative Assessment Guide
- Portfolio Assessment, p. 27
- Performance Assessment, p. 41
- CD-ROM Assessment, p. 55

Student Make-Up Assignments
- Alternative Quizzes, Chapter 12

Standardized Assessment Tutor
- Reading, pp. 47–49
- Writing, p. 50
- Math, pp. 51–52

Native Speakers
Cuaderno para hispanohablantes, pp. 56–60

 Online Activities
- Juegos interactivos
- Actividades Internet

 Video Program
- Videocassette 4
- Videocassette 5 (captioned version)

 Audio Compact Discs
- Textbook Listening Activities, CD 12, Tracks 1–18
- Additional Listening Activities, CD 12, Tracks 27–33
- Assessment Items, CD 12, Tracks 19–26

 Interactive CD-ROM Tutor, Disc 3

Teaching Transparencies
- Situations 12-1 to 12-2
- **Más práctica gramatical** Answers
- **Cuaderno de gramática** Answers

  One-Stop Planner CD-ROM

Use the **One-Stop Planner CD-ROM with Test Generator** to aid in lesson planning and pacing.
For each chapter, the **One-Stop Planner** includes:
- Editable lesson plans with direct links to teaching resources
- Printable worksheets from resource books
- Direct launches to the HRW Internet activities
- Video and audio segments
- Test Generator
- Clip Art for vocabulary items

Capítulo 12: Mis planes para el futuro *Review Chapter*

Projects

La entrevista

In this project, the class role-plays both sides of a job inter-view to practice talking about former jobs and future plans and goals.

MATERIALS
✂ **Students may need**
- Plain white paper
- Business attire
- Computer
- Office furniture

SUGGESTED SEQUENCE

1. Have students write a description in Spanish of the busi-ness or organization they would like to run later in life.

2. They then describe the type of entry-level position they would expect to take in that business to enable them eventually to reach the top.

3. Pair up students and have them exchange descriptions with their partners. Students read their partner's descriptions and think about what the head of such a business would look for in a candidate for that entry-level position. They then create a job application which will elicit that information from an applicant.

4. Partners exchange job applications, fill them out, and return them to their partner.

5. Schedule a day for interviews. On that day, students come to class dressed as they would for a job interview.

6. In turns, students play the role of the head of the business or organization described by their partner and interview him or her for the entry-level position, using the job application for reference.

7. Students hand in their job descriptions and applications for grading.

8. You might videotape the interviews and then show them to the class so that students can critique each other's performance and offer suggestions.

GRADING THE PROJECT
Suggested point distribution: (total = 100 points)
Written work...35
Oral presentation...............................35
Originality...20
Appearance 10

Games

En mi familia hay...

This game provides a review of vocabulary from this chapter. It may be played at any time.

Procedure Students sit in a circle. The first student to play says **En mi familia hay...** and completes the sentence with an item from the **Vocabulario. (un médico)** The student to his or her left repeats what he or she said and adds another item. (**En mi familia hay un médico y una contadora.**)

Play continues with each student repeating everything said previously and adding a new element. Any student who for-gets anything said previously, who says it in the wrong order, or who cannot add a new word is out. The player who stays in the game longest wins.

La búsqueda

This game is a review of the subjunctive for describing the indefinite and unknown. It should be played after Segundo paso.

Procedure Divide students into groups of four. Tell a group to find someone who fits one of the situations in the list below. (**Busca a alguien que lleve chancletas.**) The students have a minute to walk around the room asking questions in Spanish. The group with the most matches wins.

Busca a alguien que...
lleve chancletas
haya saltado en paracaídas
haya explorado la selva
use bloqueador en el verano
tenga un traje de baño verde
haya bajado un río en canoa
toque la guitarra eléctrica

COMMUNITY LINK
You might invite students' family members and profes-sionals to come to class to discuss strategies that will help students succeed in job interviews. Have students paraphrase the advice in Spanish.

Storytelling

Mini-cuento

*This story accompanies Teaching Transparency 12-1. The **mini-cuento** can be told and retold in different formats, acted out, written, and read aloud as a dictation to give students additional opportunities to practice all four skills. The following story tells about a journalist interviewing famous people who turn their hobbies into a job.*

La famosa periodista Crispina anuncia el tema de su programa de televisión: "Las personas que convirtieron sus pasatiempos en trabajos que aman". Cuando tenía ocho años, Bill Puertas jugaba a los videojuegos. Hace diez años creó la famosa "Compañía Manzana" que diseña videojuegos y ha tenido mucho éxito. Cuando Lisa tenía cuatro años jugaba con bloques de plástico. Hace tres años se graduó de ingeniera civil. Ahora tiene su propio negocio de construcción de casas y edificios. De niño, a Jorge le gustaba sacar fotografías. Ahora es fotógrafo profesional y escribe para una revista famosa. También a Crispina cuando era niña le gustaba entrevistar a las personas pero en especial a su perra Mina.

¿Cuáles son tus planes para el futuro?

Traditions

Carretas

Costa Rica's most famous handmade craft began modestly and for practical reasons in the nineteenth century. **Carretas** (oxcarts) were the only means of transporting hand-picked coffee beans from the countryside over the mountains to the coast. At times, they also were the only form of transportation for people. They became somewhat of a status symbol in the early part of the twentieth century, and thus began the tradition of decorating the **carretas.** Eventually each region developed its own design and one could identify where the driver came from by the distinctive decorative style. Now **carretas** have become the symbol of Costa Rican rural life. Today in a town named Sarchí they are still manufactured using time-tested methods. Have students trace the development of carts and wagons as people traveled west in the United States.

Receta

*This dish is, without a doubt, the national dish of Costa Rica. Literally translated, it means "spotted rooster." **Gallo pinto** is usually served for breakfast with tortillas, hard cheese, and scrambled or fried eggs. If shredded raw cabbage and tomato salad, meat or fish, and **plátanos fritos** are added, it becomes **casado** (married) and is served for lunch or dinner.*

GALLO PINTO

para 2 personas

4 cucharadas de aceite

2 tazas de arroz cocido

1 lata (15 a 19 onzas) de frijoles negros o rojos, sin líquido

1 cebolla mediana, picada

1 diente de ajo, picado

unas ramitas de cilantro, picado

1 pimiento verde, picado

salsa *Worcestershire* al gusto

salsa picante al gusto

Caliente el aceite en una sartén a fuego mediano. Agregue la cebolla, el pimiento verde y el ajo, y cocine hasta que la cebolla esté transparente (unos 10 minutos). Añada el arroz, los frijoles y el cilantro; revuelva todo y cocine por 5 minutos. Sazone con la salsa *Worcestershire* y la salsa picante. Sírvalo con un huevo frito encima, acompañado de tortillas y queso.

Technology

Video Program

Videocassette 4, Videocassette 5 (captioned version)
See Video Guide, pages 80–85.

Dramatic episode • El tiempo vuela, ¿no?

The school year is coming to an end. Zoraida doesn't know what she wants to study and feels sad at the thought of seeing everyone leave. Javier is going to Mexico and her friend Macarena plans to study fashion in Paris. Sergio is off to Madrid that night for a job interview. Javier finally reveals himself as Alejandra's secret admirer, and he wonders how she will react. Overjoyed, she decides to call him.

De antemano • ¿Cuáles son tus planes?

In the interviews about their career plans, Jennifer says she hopes to become a psychologist, while Eliéser hopes to become an agricultural engineer. Alan discusses the steps he had to take to become a lifeguard at a city pool, and Caryn recalls some childhood experiences that helped prepare her for a career in drama.

¿Qué planes tienes para el futuro?

Spanish-speaking people talk about the professions they would like to pursue.

Videoclip

- **El PAE 3:** public service message explaining what is being done for educational planning and development in Costa Rica

Interactive CD-ROM Tutor

The **Interactive CD-ROM Tutor** contains videos, interactive games, and activities that provide students an opportunity to practice and review the material covered in Chapter 12.

Activity	Activity Type	Pupil's Edition Page
1. Vocabulario	¡Super memoria!	p. 347
2. Gramática	¡A escoger!	p. 348
3. Así se dice	Imagen y sonido ¡Exploremos! ¡Identifiquemos!	p. 349
4. Así se dice *and* Gramática	¡Atrévete!	p. 354
5. Gramática	¿Qué falta?	p. 355
6. Vocabulario	¡Presta el oído!	p. 356
Panorama cultural	¿Qué planes tienes para el futuro? ¡A escoger!	p. 351
¡A hablar!	*Guided recording*	pp. 368–369
¡A escribir!	*Guided writing*	pp. 368–369

Teacher Management System

Logging In

Logging in to the *¡Ven conmigo!* TMS is easy. Upon launching the program, simply type "admin" in the password area of the log-in screen and press RETURN. Log on to **www.hrw.com/CDROMTUTOR** for a detailed explanation of the Teacher Management System.

Internet Connection

*Have students explore the **go.hrw.com** Web site for many online resources covering all chapters. All Chapter 12 resources are available under the keyword **WV3 COSTA RICA-12**. Interactive games help students practice the material and provide them with immediate feedback. You will also find a printable worksheet that provides Internet activities that lead to a comprehensive online research project.*

Juegos interactivos

You can use the interactive activities in this chapter

- to practice grammar, vocabulary, and chapter functions
- as homework
- as an assessment option
- as a self-test
- to prepare for the Chapter Test

Actividades Internet

Students describe a job opening at an imaginary company. They then search online for résumés for possible job candidates who have the proper qualifications for the job.

- To prepare students for the **Hoja de actividades,** have students review **Vocabulario** on page 347 and **Así se dice** on page 349.
- After completing the activity sheet, have students write what they liked about each job candidate they recommended.

Proyecto

Ask students to look for a job on the Spanish-language Web sites of at least three companies. Encourage them to think critically about the skills and qualifications that are common to each job listing (for example: **honrado, trabajador, que le gusten los retos**). Have students write a short report on what these common qualifications are and share them with the class.

Primer paso

7   p. 347

KERRI   Hola. Me llamo Kerri. Cuando era niña soñaba con ser maestra. Me interesaba mucho lo que hacían mis profesores y profesoras. Hace cinco años me gradué de la universidad y enseñé por un año. El año pasado decidí cambiar de carrera y tomé un trabajo como vendedora de carros usados. ¿Quieres comprar un carro?

RENATO   Y yo me llamo Renato. Pienso que una persona debería tener varias carreras durante su vida. El año pasado comencé un trabajo nuevo. Antes trabajé como consejero en un colegio, pero ahora trabajo en un banco.

PAOLA   Yo me llamo Paola. Hace diez años sólo pensaba en ser médica. Hasta asistí a la Escuela de Medicina por tres años. Decidí tomar unas clases de arquitectura y hace dos años encontré un buen trabajo como arquitecta en San José.

DOUGLAS   Hola, soy Douglas. De niño, siempre me encantaba trabajar y ganar mi propio dinero. A los siete años, vendía limonadas en mi calle y cuando tenía quince años comencé a trabajar en el supermercado. El año pasado encontré un trabajo en una tienda de computadoras y me gustó mucho.

Answers to Activity 7
1. falsa; A Kerri le encanta su trabajo de vendedora de carros.
2. cierta
3. falsa; Renato ha trabajado como consejero y como banquero.
4. cierta
5. falsa; Paola ahora trabaja felizmente como arquitecta.
6. falsa; Douglas trabajó de niño vendiendo limonada y a los quince años empezó a trabajar en el supermercado.

12   p. 349

1. Yo soy Mario. Creo que hay gran necesidad de personas que quieran dedicarse a encontrar curas para enfermedades como el cáncer. Cuando tenía diez años, quería ser médico, y el año que viene pienso asistir a la Facultad de Medicina.

2. Me llamo Juana. Me gusta hablar y creo que tengo buena personalidad y buena presencia. Me gustaría trabajar en algo que me ofrezca muchas oportunidades de hablar con la gente. Voy a buscar un trabajo en ventas.

3. Soy Miguel. De niño, me encantaba mirar los partidos de baloncesto en la tele. Sólo pensaba en hacer ejercicio y jugar al baloncesto. El año pasado, una universidad me dio una beca para jugar.

4. Hola. Me llamo Claudia. Quiero llegar a ser una artista famosa. Me encantaría pintar y vender mis cuadros por todo el mundo. Estoy tomando clases de arte en mi colegio, y quiero trabajar algún día con un artista profesional y aprender más.

5. Soy Teresa y tengo 18 años. No sé exactamente qué carrera quiero seguir, pero me interesaría estudiar una carrera relacionada con las ciencias. Estoy muy preocupada por el medio ambiente y estoy segura que trabajaré en algo relacionado con su conservación.

Answers to Activity 12
1. A   2. F   3. P   4. F   5. F

Segundo paso

22   p. 354

1. ¿Quieres un consejo? Mira, cuando vayas a la entrevista, es importante que te vistas con cuidado y elegancia. Te recomiendo que uses colores serios, como negro, gris, azul o café. Lo ideal es tener mucho cuidado en el vestir. ¿Me entiendes?

2. Te puedo recomendar muchas cosas, pero hay algo que estoy segura que molesta mucho a la gente que te entrevista. Es mejor que no comas dulces ni mastiques chicle. ¿Te puedes imaginar una persona bien vestida masticando chicle? Eso no lo debes hacer, ¿entendido?

3. ¿Quieres que te dé un buen consejo? Te aconsejo que no hables mucho de tu experiencia. La persona que te entrevista no quiere escuchar una lista de todas tus experiencias profesionales.

4. Te aconsejo que te quedes en silencio. Lo ideal es no hacerle preguntas al entrevistador, sobre todo sobre los sueldos y beneficios. Ellos quieren saber que tú no estás interesada en el dinero.

5. El mejor consejo que puedo darte es el siguiente. Lleva tu currículum vitae y dos cartas de recomendación. La persona que te haga la entrevista va a leerlos con mucha atención.

6. No debes preocuparte mucho por la entrevista. No importa tu apariencia porque debemos aceptar a las personas tal como son. No olvides que lo importante es ser auténtico.

One-Stop Planner CD-ROM

To preview all resources available for this chapter, use the **One-Stop Planner CD-ROM**, Disc 3.

7. A los entrevistadores no les gusta la gente muy callada. Prepara unas preguntas para el entrevistador. Debes mostrar interés en todos los aspectos del trabajo.

8. A los entrevistadores les gusta la gente que habla bien. Te recomiendo que te expreses bien. Si tú te expresas bien, eso demuestra que puedes pensar bien. Y eso es muy importante en el trabajo que tú buscas.

Answers to Activity 22

1. lógico	3. ¡Qué va!	5. lógico	7. lógico
2. lógico	4. ¡Qué va!	6. ¡Qué va!	8. lógico

 p. 355

1. Mira, el trabajo que ofrecemos es importante para nosotros. Necesitamos una persona que sea lista y creativa. Buscamos una persona que sea independiente y segura de sí misma.

2. Los logros en la escuela son importantes para ellos. Prefieren estudiantes que saquen buenas notas. Buscan personas que sean o hayan sido excelentes estudiantes.

3. Acabo de conversar con María. Ella prefiere trabajar con la chica que tiene experiencia en ventas. María no quiere perder mucho tiempo enseñándole a alguien cómo vender.

4. Ayer tomamos nuestra decisión acerca de la persona que queremos que trabaje aquí. Vamos a escoger una persona que tenga buenas referencias. De modo que tengo que hacer muchas llamadas telefónicas hoy.

5. Hablé con el jefe de ventas de la Tienda La Moda Parisina. La tienda quiere a la vendedora que es bilingüe. Dicen que muchos de sus clientes hablan francés y ella sería la persona ideal.

6. Buenas tardes. Busco a Roberto, un señor que sabe reparar computadoras. ¿Lo ha visto por aquí?

7. Hoy por la mañana hablé con la contadora Martínez acerca del nuevo puesto. No queremos trabajar con alguien que siempre llegue tarde. Eso sería un problema para todo el grupo ya que hay que entregar el trabajo a tiempo todos los días.

Answers to Activity 25

1. no específico	3. específico	5. específico	7. no específico
2. no específico	4. no específico	6. específico	

Repaso

1 **p. 368**

Cuando era niña, mi gran ambición era ser arqueóloga. Cuando tenía diez años, quería más que nada ir a Egipto a ver las pirámides y las ruinas. A los doce años mi familia y yo fuimos a Egipto. Me divertí tanto que decidí ahí mismo que sí iba a ser arqueóloga. Hace cinco años, oí de un programa especial de verano para estudiantes que quieren aprender más sobre las culturas antiguas. Fui con otros estudiantes de mi edad a Honduras, donde exploramos varios templos y edificios construidos por los mayas. El año pasado, me gradué de la universidad con mi doctorado en arqueología y quiero seguir explorando las ruinas mayas en Honduras.

Answers to Repaso Activity 1

1. falsa; Josefina se graduó con un doctorado en arqueología.
2. cierta
3. falsa; Oyó hablar de un programa de verano en Honduras.
4. no se sabe
5. cierta

Capítulo 12: Mis planes para el futuro

Review Chapter

Suggested Lesson Plans *50-Minute Schedule*

Day 1

CHAPTER OPENER 5 min.
- Focusing on Outcomes, ATE, p. 343
- Background Information, Thinking Critically, and Culture Note, ATE, pp. 342–343

DE ANTEMANO 40 min.
- Presenting **De antemano** and Preteaching Vocabulary, ATE, p. 344
- Do Thinking Critically, ATE, p. 345.
- Activities 1–5, p. 346, and Comprehension Check, ATE, p. 346
- Present and discuss the **Nota cultural,** p. 346.

Wrap-Up 5 min.
- Present the Language Note, ATE, p. 345.

Homework Options
Cuaderno de actividades, p. 133, Activities 1–2

Day 2

PRIMER PASO
Quick Review 5 min.
- Check homework.
- Bell Work, ATE, p. 347

Vocabulario/Así se dice, p. 347 40 min.
- Presenting **Vocabulario** and **Así se dice,** ATE, p. 347
- Present the Additional Vocabulary, ATE, p. 347.
- Do Activity 6, p. 347.
- Do Activity 7 with the Audio CD, p. 347.
- Do Activity 8 in pairs, p. 348.

Wrap-Up 5 min.
- Have students name the profession you act out.

Homework Options
Cuaderno de actividades, p. 134, Activities 3–4
Cuaderno de gramática, p. 95, Activities 1–2

Day 3

PRIMER PASO
Quick Review 10 min.
- Check homework.
- Follow Vocabulary Practice Suggestions 1 and 3 for Teaching Transparency 12-1.

Gramática de repaso, p. 348 35 min.
- Presenting **Gramática de repaso,** ATE, p. 348
- Do Activities 9–10, pp. 348–349.
- Have students do Activity 11, then peer-edit their work, p. 349.

Wrap-Up 5 min.
- Follow Suggestion 2 for Teaching Transparency 12-1.

Homework Options
Cuaderno de actividades, pp. 135–136, Activities 5–6
Cuaderno de gramática, pp. 96–98, Activities 3–7

Day 4

PRIMER PASO
Quick Review 10 min.
- Check homework.

Así se dice, p. 349 35 min.
- Presenting **Así se dice,** ATE, p. 349
- Review **¿Te acuerdas?,** p. 349.
- Do Activity 12 with the Audio CD, p. 349.
- Review the future tense.
- Have students do Activity 13 in pairs, p. 350.
- Do Activity 14, p. 350.

Wrap-Up 5 min.
- Have students indicate if your statements are about the past, present, or future.

Homework Options
Cuaderno de actividades, p. 137, Activities 7–8
Cuaderno de gramática, pp. 98–99, Activities 8–11

Day 5

PRIMER PASO
Quick Review 10 min.
- Check homework.

Así se dice, p. 349 25 min.
- Have students do Activity 15, then peer-edit, p. 350.
- Have students do Activity 16 in groups, p. 350.
- Read and discuss the **Nota cultural,** p. 350.
- Present the Culture Note, ATE, p. 350.

PANORAMA CULTURAL 10 min.
- Presenting **Panorama cultural,** ATE, p. 351

Wrap-Up 5 min.
- Discuss the content and format of Quiz 12-1.

Homework Options
Study for Quiz 12-1.

Day 6

PRIMER PASO
Quick Review 5 min.
- Review the content of **Primer paso.**

Quiz 20 min.
- Administer Quiz 12-1A, 12-1B, or a combination of the two.

¡ADELANTE! 20 min.
- Presenting **¡Adelante!** and Preteaching Vocabulary, ATE, p. 352
- Activities 17–20, p. 353, and Comprehension Check, ATE, p. 353

Wrap-Up 5 min.
- Do the Thinking Critically Activity, ATE, p. 353.

Homework Options
Activity 21, p. 353
Cuaderno de actividades, p. 138, Activities 9–11

One-Stop Planner CD-ROM

For alternative lesson plans by chapter sections, to create your own customized plans, or to preview all resources available for this chapter, use the **One-Stop Planner CD-ROM**, Disc 3.

For additional homework suggestions, see activities accompanied by this symbol throughout the chapter.

Day 7

SEGUNDO PASO

Quick Review 5 min.
- Check homework.

Así se dice/Gramática de repaso, p. 354
40 min.
- Presenting **Así se dice** and **Gramática de repaso**, ATE, p. 354
- Do Activity 22 with the Audio CD, p. 354.
- Do Activity 23, p. 354.
- Have students do Activity 24 in pairs, p. 355.

Wrap-Up 5 min.
- Do the Slower Pace Activity, ATE, p. 354.

Homework Options
Cuaderno de actividades, p. 139, Activities 12–13
Cuaderno de gramática, pp. 100–101, Activities 12–13

Day 8

SEGUNDO PASO

Quick Review 5 min.
- Check homework.
- Have students give advice about job interviews.

Gramática de repaso, p. 355 15 min.
- Presenting **Gramática de repaso**, ATE, p. 355
- Review **¿Te acuerdas?**, p. 355.
- Present Language-to-Language, ATE, p. 355.
- Do Activity 25 with the Audio CD, p. 355.

Vocabulario, p. 356 25 min.
- Presenting **Vocabulario**, ATE, p. 356
- Present **También se puede decir...**, p. 356.
- Do Activity 26, p. 356.
- Have students do Activity 27 in pairs, p. 356.

Wrap-Up 5 min.
- Do the Visual/Auditory Learners Activity, ATE, p. 356.

Homework Options
Cuaderno de actividades, p. 140, Activities 14–16
Cuaderno de gramática, pp. 101–103, Activities 14–18

Day 9

SEGUNDO PASO

Quick Review 5 min.
- Check homework.

Vocabulario, p. 356 15 min.
- Have students do Activity 28 in pairs and Activity 29 in groups, pp. 356–357.

Gramática de repaso, p. 357 25 min.
- Presenting **Gramática de repaso**, ATE, p. 357
- Do Activities 30–31, pp. 357–358.
- Have students do Activity 32 in pairs, p. 358.

Wrap-Up 5 min.
- Follow Suggestions 1–2 for Teaching Transparency 12-2.

Homework Options
Activity 33, p. 358
Cuaderno de actividades, pp. 141–142, Activities 17–22
Cuaderno de gramática, pp. 103–104, Activities 19–21

Day 10

SEGUNDO PASO

Quick Review 10 min.
- Check homework.

ENCUENTRO CULTURAL 10 min.
- Presenting **Encuentro cultural**, ATE, p. 359

VAMOS A LEER 25 min.
- Do Activities A–B, p. 360.
- Have students do Activity C in pairs, p. 361.

Wrap-Up 5 min.
- Present the Culture Note, ATE, p. 361.
- Discuss the content and format for Quiz 12-2.

Homework Options
Study for Quiz 12-2.
Vamos a leer Activities D–F, pp. 361–362

Day 11

SEGUNDO PASO

Quick Review 5 min.
- Review the content of **Segundo paso**.

Quiz 20 min.
- Administer Quiz 12-2A, 12-2B, or a combination of the two.

VAMOS A LEER 20 min.
- Discuss homework.
- Have students do Activity G in pairs, p. 362.
- Do Activity H, p. 362.

Wrap-Up 5 min.
- Have students list the main concepts of Chapter 12.
- Discuss **Vamos a escribir**, p. 363.

Homework Options
Vamos a escribir, p. 363
Cuaderno de actividades, pp. 143–144, Activities 23–27
Repaso Activities 2 and 4–7, pp. 368–369
A ver si puedo..., p. 370

Day 12

REPASO

Quick Review 10 min.
- Check and/or collect homework.

Chapter Review 35 min.
- Review Chapter 12. Choose from **Más práctica gramatical**, Grammar Tutor for Students of Spanish, Activities for Communication, Listening Activities, Interactive CD-ROM Tutor, or **Juegos interactivos**.

Wrap-Up 5 min.
- Review content and format of Chapter 12 Test.

Homework Options
Study for Chapter 12 Test.

Assessment

Quick Review 5 min
- Answer any last-minute questions.

Test, Chapter 12 45 min.
- Administer Chapter 12 Test. Select from Testing Program, Alternative Assessment Guide, Test Generator, or Standardized Assessment Tutor.

Capítulo 12: Mis planes para el futuro

Review Chapter

Suggested Lesson Plans   90-Minute Block Schedule

Block 1

CHAPTER OPENER 5 min.
- Focusing on Outcomes, ATE, p. 343
- Background Information, Thinking Critically, and Culture Note, ATE, pp. 342–343

DE ANTEMANO 40 min.
- Presenting **De antemano** and Preteaching Vocabulary, ATE, p. 344
- Do Thinking Critically, ATE, p. 345.
- Activities 1–5, p. 346, and Comprehension Check, ATE, p. 346
- Present and discuss the **Nota cultural,** p. 346.

PRIMER PASO
Vocabulario/Así se dice, p. 347 40 min.
- Presenting **Vocabulario** and **Así se dice,** ATE, p. 347
- Present the Additional Vocabulary, ATE, p. 347.
- Do Activity 6, p. 347.
- Do Activity 7 with the Audio CD, p. 347.
- Do Activity 8 in pairs, p. 348.

Wrap-Up 5 min.
- Have students name the profession you act out.

Homework Options
Cuaderno de actividades, pp. 133–134, Activities 1–4
Cuaderno de gramática, p. 95, Activities 1–2

Block 2

PRIMER PASO
Quick Review 10 min.
- Check homework.
- Follow Vocabulary Practice Suggestions 1 and 3 for Teaching Transparency 12-1.

Gramática de repaso, p. 348 35 min.
- Presenting **Gramática de repaso,** ATE, p. 348
- Do Activities 9–10, pp. 348–349.
- Have students do Activity 11, then peer-edit their work, p. 349.

Así se dice, p. 349 35 min.
- Presenting **Así se dice,** ATE, p. 349
- Review **¿Te acuerdas?,** p. 349.
- Do Activity 12 with the Audio CD, p. 349.
- Review the future tense.
- Have students do Activity 13 in pairs, p. 350.
- Do Activity 14, p. 350.

Wrap-Up 10 min.
- Follow Suggestions 1–3 for Teaching Transparency 12-1.

Homework Options
Cuaderno de actividades, pp. 135–137, Activities 5–8
Cuaderno de gramática, pp. 96–99, Activities 3–11

Block 3

PRIMER PASO
Quick Review 10 min.
- Check homework.

Así se dice, p. 349 25 min.
- Have students do Activity 15, then peer-edit their work, p. 350.
- Have students do Activity 16 in groups, p. 350.
- Read and discuss **Nota cultural,** p. 350.
- Present the Culture Note, ATE, p. 350.

PANORAMA CULTURAL 10 min.
- Presenting **Panorama cultural,** ATE, p. 351

¡ADELANTE! 25 min.
- Presenting **¡Adelante!** and Preteaching Vocabulary, ATE, p. 352
- Activities 17–21, p. 353, and Comprehension Check, ATE, p. 353

Así se dice/Gramática de repaso, p. 354 15 min.
- Presenting **Así se dice** and **Gramática de repaso,** ATE, p. 354

Wrap-Up 5 min.
- Discuss the content and format of Quiz 12-1.

Homework Options
Study for Quiz 12-1.
Cuaderno de actividades, pp. 138–139, Activities 9–13

341K   SUGGESTED LESSON PLANS • 90-MINUTE SCHEDULE   CAPÍTULO 12

One-Stop Planner CD-ROM

For alternative lesson plans by chapter sections, to create your own customized plans, or to preview all resources available for this chapter, use the **One-Stop Planner CD-ROM**, Disc 3.

For additional homework suggestions, see activities accompanied by this symbol throughout the chapter.

Block 4

PRIMER PASO
Quick Review 10 min.
- Check homework.
- Review the content of **Primer paso**.

Quiz 20 min.
- Administer Quiz 12-1A, 12-1B, or a combination of the two.

SEGUNDO PASO
Así se dice/Gramática de repaso, p. 354
20 min.
- Presenting **Así se dice** and **Gramática de repaso,** p. 354
- Do Activity 22 with the Audio CD, p. 354.
- Do Activity 23, p. 354.
- Have students do Activity 24 in pairs, p. 355.

Gramática de repaso, p. 355 20 min.
- Presenting **Gramática de repaso,** ATE, p. 355
- Review **¿Te acuerdas?,** p. 355.
- Present Language-to-Language, ATE, p. 355.
- Do Activity 25 with the Audio CD, p. 355.

Vocabulario, p. 356 15 min.
- Presenting **Vocabulario,** ATE, p. 356
- Present **También se puede decir…,** p. 356.
- Do Activity 26, p. 356.

Wrap-Up 5 min.
- Do Visual/Auditory Learners Activity, ATE, p. 356.

Homework Options
Cuaderno de actividades, p. 140, Activities 14–16
Cuaderno de gramática, pp. 100–103, Activities 12–18

Block 5

SEGUNDO PASO
Quick Review 10 min.
- Check homework.

Vocabulario, p. 356 25 min.
- Have students do Activities 27–28 in pairs, p. 356.
- Have students do Activity 29 in groups, p. 357.

Gramática de repaso, p. 357 40 min.
- Presenting **Gramática de repaso,** ATE, p. 357
- Do Activities 30–31, pp. 357–358.
- Have students do Activity 32 in pairs, p. 358.
- Have students do Activity 33, then peer-edit, p. 358.

ENCUENTRO CULTURAL 10 min.
- Presenting **Encuentro cultural,** ATE, p. 359

Wrap-Up 5 min.
- Discuss the content and format for Quiz 12-2.

Homework Options
Study for Quiz 12-2.
Cuaderno de actividades, pp. 141–142, Activities 17–22
Cuaderno de gramática, pp. 103–104, Activities 19–21

Block 6

SEGUNDO PASO
Quick Review 10 min.
- Check homework.
- Review the content of **Segundo paso**.

Quiz 20 min.
- Administer Quiz 12-2A, 12-2B, or a combination of the two.

VAMOS A LEER 55 min.
- Do Activities A–D, pp. 360–361.
- Do Activities E–H, p. 362.

Wrap-Up 5 min.
- Discuss the content and format of Chapter 12 Test.

Homework Options
Study for Chapter 12 Test.
Vamos a escribir, p. 363
Cuaderno de actividades, pp. 143–144, Activities 23–27
A ver si puedo…, p. 370

Block 7

REPASO
Quick Review 10 min.
- Check and/or collect homework.

Chapter Review 35 min.
- Review Chapter 12. Choose from **Más práctica gramatical,** Grammar Tutor for Students of Spanish, Activities for Communication, Listening Activities, Interactive CD-ROM Tutor, or **Juegos interactivos.**

Test, Chapter 12 45 min.
- Administer Chapter 12 Test. Select from Testing Program, Alternative Assessment Guide, Test Generator, or Standardized Assessment Tutor.

CAPÍTULO 12

One-Stop Planner CD-ROM

For resource information, see the **One-Stop Planner**, Disc 3.

Pacing Tips
This chapter introduces new vocabulary and reviews numerous grammar points covered in previous chapters. You may wish to spend an equal amount of time introducing the new vocabulary in both **Pasos** in order to incorporate communicative activities such as: Pair Work (p. 347), Teaching Suggestions (p. 349), Additional Practice (p. 350), Pair Work (p. 354), Visual/Auditory Learners (p. 356), and Native Speakers (p. 356). For more tips on pacing, see Suggested Lesson Plans, pp. 341I–341L.

Meeting the Standards

Communication
• Talking about former jobs and goals, p. 347
• Talking about future career plans, p. 349
• Giving advice about job interviews, p. 354

Cultures
• Background Information, p. 342
• Thinking Critically, p. 343
• Nota cultural, p. 346
• Culture Notes, pp. 343, 350, 361

Connections
• Thinking Critically, p. 345
• Literature Link, p. 362

Comparisons
• Nota cultural, p. 350
• Panorama cultural, p. 351
• Language-to-Language, p. 355
• Encuentro cultural, p. 359
• Culture Note, p. 359

Communities
• Community Link, p. 346

Connections and Comparisons

Background Information
The University of Costa Rica in San José is the country's oldest university. Some 35,000 students attend UCR every year. In addition to the public universities, Costa Rica has several private institutions that offer a wide variety of degrees.

Thinking Critically
Drawing Inferences Ask students to imagine they are high school students in Costa Rica. They are about to graduate and either enter the work force or attend a university. Given what they have learned about Costa Rica, what field would they choose to pursue?

CAPÍTULO

12
Mis planes para el futuro

Objectives

In this chapter you will learn to

Primer paso

- talk about former jobs and goals
- talk about future career plans

Segundo paso

- give advice about job interviews

📶 internet

go.hrw.com

MARCAR: go.hrw.com
PALABRA CLAVE:
WV3 COSTA RICA-12

◀ **Cuando éramos niños, queríamos llegar a ser médicos.**

CAPÍTULO 12

Photo Flash!
For most people, planning for their future includes getting an education. For many, getting an education means going to college or even further to graduate school, law school, or medical school. The individuals in this image decided that their future plans involved practicing medicine. Each of them set out to meet the first set of major milestones: applying to, getting accepted to, and finishing medical school. Ask students to discuss their plans for the future.

Focusing on Outcomes
In this chapter students will acquire vocabulary that will enable them to discuss past experiences, current goals, and strategies for the future that will help them get the job they hope for.

Cultures and Communities

Thinking Critically
Analyzing Tell students that Costa Rica has one of the highest literacy rates among the countries of Central America; over 90% of the people can read and write. Primary education is free and compulsory. The government spends 25% of its national budget on education. Ask students what effects they think such a high literacy rate might have on Costa Rican society.

Culture Note
In addition to having the highest Spanish-language literacy rate of any Latin American country, Costa Rica also has a high percentage of citizens who speak some English. This is due in part to the national commitment to education and in part to the large population of Jamaicans and their descendants who live in Costa Rica.

Presenting
De antemano

Play the video while students read along. Have students write interview questions that they would ask Jennifer and Eliéser. Present the Preteaching Vocabulary. Have students answer the questions in **Estrategia para comprender**.

De antemano
Young people from Costa Rica talk about their future plans.

DE ANTEMANO ▪ *¿Cuáles son tus planes?*

Cuaderno de actividades, p. 133, Acts. 1–2

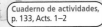

CD 12 Trs. 1–5

Estrategia para comprender
¿Qué planes tienes para tu vida después de graduarte en el colegio? ¿Sabes qué carrera te interesa? ¿Son similares tus planes a los de Jennifer y Eliéser?

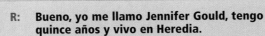

R: Bueno, yo me llamo Jennifer Gould, tengo quince años y vivo en Heredia.

P: ¿Qué planes tiene Ud. para su futuro?

R: Bueno, me gustaría llegar a ser sicóloga, me gustaría llegar a ser una muy buena modelo y terminar mis estudios.

P: ¿Qué trabajo le gustaría tener?

R: Me gustaría ser sicóloga.

P: ¿Qué le importa más, ganar mucho dinero o tener un trabajo que le guste?

R: Tener un trabajo que me guste porque me diver–tiría en mi trabajo.

P: ¿Cómo se imagina su vida en diez años? ¿Qué hará?

R: ¡Ay! Me gustaría cumplir todo lo que deseo, casarme con mi novio y ser muy feliz.

P: ¿Y sus padres tienen planes distintos para Ud.?

R: No, yo creo que ellos me apoyan en lo que yo deseo.

Jennifer

66 **Hace dos años tomé un curso para aprender a ser salvavidas. No crean que era sólo agua, sol y playa. Tuve que entrenarme duro para aprobar el examen de aptitud física. El curso me ayudó a conseguir el trabajo de salvavidas de la ciudad el año pasado.** 99

Alan

Preteaching Vocabulary

Identifying Keywords
First ask students to guess the context of **De antemano.** (plans for the future) Then have them scan the interviews to identify people's plans. Students may identify such phrases as: **me gustaría llegar a ser psicóloga; me gustaría llegar a ser una muy buena modelo y terminar mis estudios; Me gustaría cumplir todo lo que deseo, casarme con mi novio y ser muy feliz;** **pienso estudiar... para tener... una carrera; me gustaría ingeniería agrónoma.** Then have students look at Alan's and Caryn's responses. What were their plans? **(aprender a ser salvavidas; ser actriz)** Did they accomplish them or are they still in the process of acquiring more skills? (Alan accomplished his, and Caryn is still interested in learning more.)

P: ¿Qué planes tiene Ud. para el futuro?

R: Pues... pienso estudiar para ser... pues para tener...una carrera.

P: ¿Cuál carrera?

R: Me gustaría ingeniería agrónoma.

P: ¿Qué le importa más, ganar mucho dinero o tener un trabajo que le guste?

R: Pues, lo importante es que me guste bastante, ¿no?

Eliéser

Centro Universitario Calderón

LIC. EN DERECHO
LIC. EN CONTABILIDAD
LIC. EN SICOLOGÍA
LIC. EN ARQUITECTURA
LIC. EN INGENIERÍA MECÁNICA

LIC. EN INFORMÁTICA
LIC. EN FARMACOLOGÍA
LIC. EN ADMINISTRACIÓN HOTELERA
LIC. EN DISEÑO GRÁFICO

El Centro Universitario Calderón significa:
¡Educación para el futuro!

"De niña quería ser actriz. A los ocho años hice un papel en una obra de teatro en mi ciudad. Hace dos años estudié en el Taller Cultural distintas técnicas para expresar emociones como la tristeza, la alegría y el dolor. Me interesaría saber más sobre las artes dramáticas. "

Caryn

Using the Captioned Video

As an alternative to reading the conversations in the book, you might want to show the captioned version of *Contigo en la distancia: El tiempo vuela, ¿no?...* on Videocassette 5. Some students may benefit from seeing the written words as they listen to the target language and watch the gestures and actions in context. This visual reinforcement of vocabulary and functions will facilitate students' comprehension and help reduce their anxiety before they are formally introduced to the new language in the chapter.

Language Note
Lic. is the abbreviation for **licenciado(a),** which refers to college graduates. **Lic. en derecho** is a law graduate. **Licenciatura** is the Spanish word for *degree.*

Thinking Critically
Analyzing Bring in the classified ads from a Spanish-language newspaper or print them from an online publication. Have students clip ads and group them by field. Have them count the number of jobs in each field and sequence the qualifications desired according to the frequency with which they are mentioned.

Contigo en la distancia

You may choose to continue with **Episodio 12:** *El tiempo vuela, ¿no?...* The school year is coming to an end. Zoraida still doesn't know what she wants to study and already feels sad at the thought of seeing everyone leave. Not only is Javier going to Mexico, but her friend Macarena plans to study fashion in Paris. Moreover, Sergio says that he is off to Madrid that night for a job interview. Javier has finally written Alejandra a letter in which he reveals himself as her secret admirer, and he wonders how she will react. Alejandra, who has fallen in love with the author of the letters, accepts the idea that her admirer is Javier. Overjoyed, she decides to call him.

Teaching Suggestion
Before they listen to **De antemano**, have students make a list of things they plan to do after graduation. As students listen to the audio recording, they should place a check beside their plans if they are similar to what the speaker says.

Community Link
Nota cultural Have students contact a local travel agency or search the Internet for more information on ecotourism. What other countries offer these types of tours? What special qualifications would be needed to work for an international ecotourism agency?

Answers

1 1. falsa; Jennifer quiere ser psicóloga.
2. falsa; Jennifer quiere casarse con su novio.
3. falsa; Eliéser estudia para ser ingeniero agrónomo.
4. cierta
5. cierta
6. falsa; Caryn estudió en el Taller Cultural.

2 1. Caryn y Jennifer
2. Eliéser y Jennifer
3. Alan
4. Caryn
5. Jennifer
6. Jennifer y Eliéser

3 1. me gustaría llegar a ser...; Me gustaría ser...
2. pienso estudiar para...; Me gustaría...
3. De niña, quería ser...
4. Me interesaría saber más...
5. Hace dos años...

6 1. trabajadora social
2. farmacéutico
3. contador
4. vendedor
5. periodista
6. diseñador *or* arquitecto
7. ingeniera

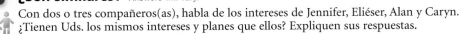
These activities check for comprehension only. Students should not yet be expected to produce language modeled in **De antemano**.

1 **¿Cierto o falso?** See answers below.
Indica si cada oración es **cierta** o **falsa**. Si es falsa, corrígela.
1. Jennifer quiere ser profesora.
2. Jennifer no quiere casarse.
3. Eliéser estudió para ser salvavidas.
4. Es probable que Jennifer vaya a asistir a la universidad.
5. Alan tuvo que trabajar muy duro para prepararse para su trabajo.
6. Caryn estudió en el Centro Universitario Calderón.

2 **¿Quién es?** See answers below.
Indica a quién o a quiénes se refieren estas frases.
1. Le interesan mucho las emociones humanas.
2. Quiere estudiar para una carrera que le guste mucho.
3. Su trabajo era vigilar a *(watch over)* la gente que nadaba.
4. Las artes dramáticas eran uno de sus intereses.
5. Sus padres no interfieren en sus planes para el futuro.
6. Le importa más gozar de su trabajo que ganar mucho dinero.

3 **Busca las expresiones** See answers below.
1. ¿Qué dice Jennifer para indicar qué carrera le interesa?
2. ¿Qué dice Eliéser para hablar de sus planes para el futuro?
3. ¿Qué dice Caryn para hablar de la ambición que tenía cuando era niña?
4. ¿Cómo expresa Caryn su deseo de estudiar más las artes dramáticas?
5. ¿Qué dice Alan para indicar cuándo aprendió a ser salvavidas?

4 **¿Son similares?** Answers will vary.
 Con dos o tres compañeros(as), habla de los intereses de Jennifer, Eliéser, Alan y Caryn. ¿Tienen Uds. los mismos intereses y planes que ellos? Expliquen sus respuestas.

5 **Ahora te toca a ti**
Imagina que una estudiante habla sobre sus planes para el futuro con un consejero en el colegio. Escribe un diálogo en que el consejero le pregunta qué clases y pasatiempos le gustan y la estudiante contesta.

Nota cultural

El ecoturismo—viajes de aventura a lugares naturales—trata de proteger el medio ambiente mientras desarrolla un aprecio de la conservación. Es de gran beneficio a la economía de zonas rurales. El ecoturismo es muy popular en Costa Rica. Algunas compañías han construido senderos *(trails)* y otras estructuras que protegen especies frágiles y limitan la erosión. Otros promueven la idea de "ver y no tocar", lo cual protege plantas y animales. ¿Hay atracciones para ecoturistas en la parte de Estados Unidos donde tú vives?

Cuaderno de actividades, p. 144, Act. 24

Comprehension Check

Auditory Learners
1 Read the sentences aloud and have students respond **cierta** by pointing their thumbs up and **falsa** by pointing them down.

Slower Pace
2 Before conducting this activity, have students read **De antemano** and put each interviewee's name on a sheet of paper. Instruct them to leave sufficient space after the name to write information about each person. Then ask them to list information about each person below the name. Allow students to refer to their papers during the activity.

Kinesthetic Learners
5 Have students role-play the dialogues. Encourage them to use props and costumes.

Vocabulario

el (la) **abogado(a)**	*lawyer*	el (la) **médico(a)**	*doctor*
el (la) **arquitecto(a)**	*architect*	el (la) **periodista**	*journalist*
el (la) **banquero(a)**	*banker*	el (la) **policía**	*police officer*
el (la) **carpintero(a)**	*carpenter*	el (la) **diseñador(a)**	*designer*
el (la) **científico(a)**	*scientist*	el (la) **programador(a)** de computadoras	*computer programmer*
el (la) **comerciante**	*businessman (-woman)*		
el (la) **contador(a)**	*accountant*	el (la) **sicólogo(a)**	*psychologist*
el (la) **enfermero(a)**	*nurse*	el (la) **trabajador(a) social**	*social worker*
el (la) **escritor(a)**	*writer*	el (la) **vendedor(a)**	*salesman (-woman)*
el (la) **farmacéutico(a)**	*pharmacist*		
el (la) **ingeniero(a)**	*engineer*		
el (la) **mecánico(a)**	*mechanic*		

Cuaderno de actividades, p. 134, Acts. 3–4

Más práctica gramatical, p. 364, Act. 1

Cuaderno de gramática, p. 95, Acts. 1–2

6 **¿Qué profesión es?** See answers below.

Leamos/Escribamos Completa las frases con palabras apropiadas del **Vocabulario**.

1. Mireya trabaja en una agencia que ayuda a los pobres. Mireya es ▭▭▭.
2. Fernando distribuye medicinas y llena recetas. Fernando es ▭▭▭.
3. Necesito un ▭▭▭ que me ayude a calcular cuánto debo de impuestos.
4. Héctor es ▭▭▭ de carros usados.
5. A Marisol le encanta ser ▭▭▭. Entrevista a muchos políticos para *El Heraldo*.
6. A Rubén siempre le ha gustado dibujar; por eso trabaja como ▭▭▭ en Nueva York.
7. Como es ▭▭▭, Paula va a trabajar con el estado para construir nuevas carreteras.

Así se dice

Talking about former jobs and goals

Si quieres hablar de un trabajo o una ambición que tenías antes, puedes decir:

Hace diez años, trabajé en una tienda de computadoras.

Cuando tenía cinco años, quería ser banquera.

El año pasado, trabajé de programador de computadoras.

Cuando era joven, quería ser bombero *(firefighter)*.

De niña, vendía periódicos.
As a child, . . .

Cuaderno de actividades, p. 135, Act. 5

7 **¿Cuándo fue?** Script and answers on p. 341G.

CD 12
Tr. 6

Escuchemos/Escribamos Escucha lo que dicen Paola, Douglas, Kerri y Renato. Luego indica si las siguientes frases son **ciertas** o **falsas**. Si son falsas, corrígelas.

1. Actualmente, a Kerri le encanta su trabajo de diseñadora.
2. Después de graduarse, Kerri trabajó de profesora.
3. Renato siempre ha trabajado de banquero.
4. De niña, Paola pensaba hacerse médica.
5. Ahora, Paola trabaja felizmente de abogada.
6. Su trabajo de vendedor de computadoras fue el primero para Douglas.

Communication for All Students

Pair Work

Have pairs of students work together to write sentences about each profession. Ask each pair to choose its best two or three sentences to share with the class.

Additional Vocabulary

You may want to present the following words:
terapeuta físico(a) *physical therapist*
consejero(a) *counselor, advisor*
paramédico(a) *paramedic*
el piloto, la mujer piloto *pilot*
veterinario(a) *veterinarian*
arqueólogo(a) *archaeologist*
fotógrafo(a) *photographer*

STANDARDS: 1.2

Teaching Resources
pp. 347–350

PRINT
- Lesson Planner, p. 58
- Listening Activities, pp. 91, 95–96
- Activities for Communication, pp. 45–46, 84, 86, 111–112
- Cuaderno de gramática, pp. 95–99
- Grammar Tutor for Students of Spanish, Chapter 12
- Cuaderno de actividades, pp. 134–137
- Cuaderno para hispanohablantes, pp. 56–60
- Testing Program, pp. 257–260
- Alternative Assessment Guide, p. 41
- Student Make-Up Assignments, Chapter 12

MEDIA
- One-Stop Planner
- Audio Compact Discs, CD 12, Trs. 6–7, 27–29, 19
- Teaching Transparencies 12-1; **Más práctica gramatical** Answers; Cuaderno de gramática Answers
- Interactive CD-ROM Tutor, Disc 3

Bell Work
On the board or on a transparency, write the following: **Si yo viajara a Costa Rica... Si tuviera mil dólares...** Have students complete the sentences.

Presenting
Vocabulario, Así se dice

Describe the professions: **Esta persona estudia las personalidades y las acciones de la gente. [psicológo(a)]** Have students identify the careers described. Then make sentences about careers using phrases from **Así se dice.**

Teaching Resources
pp. 347–350

PRINT
▶ Lesson Planner, p. 58
▶ Listening Activities, pp. 91, 95–96
▶ Activities for Communication, pp. 45–46, 84, 86, 111–112
▶ Cuaderno de gramática, pp. 95–99
▶ Grammar Tutor for Students of Spanish, Chapter 12
▶ Cuaderno de actividades, pp. 134–137
▶ Cuaderno para hispanohablantes, pp. 56–60
▶ Testing Program, pp. 257–260
▶ Alternative Assessment Guide, p. 41
▶ Student Make-Up Assignments, Chapter 12

MEDIA
▶ One-Stop Planner
▶ Audio Compact Discs, CD 12, Trs. 6–7, 27–29, 19
▶ Teaching Transparencies 12-1; **Más práctica gramatical** Answers; Cuaderno de gramática Answers
▶ Interactive CD-ROM Tutor, Disc 3

Presenting

Gramática de repaso
Preterite and imperfect
Before presenting the **Gramática de repaso,** on three large index cards write the words **información descriptiva, acción en progreso,** and **evento concluido.** Prepare at least ten sentences using the preterite or imperfect. As you say each sentence, hold up the appropriate card(s). **(Eran las seis de la tarde cuando mi amigo me llamó:** hold up card one and card three.) After some examples, pass the cards to your students to read and display the correct cards.

---

8 **En el pasado...** Answers will vary.

 Hablemos/Escribamos Usa estas preguntas para entrevistar a un(a) compañero(a). Luego, presenta a la clase un resumen de lo que dijo tu compañero(a).

1. De niño(a), ¿qué soñabas?
2. Cuando eras joven, ¿qué querías ser?
3. ¿Has trabajado en el verano? ¿Dónde?
4. ¿Dónde trabajaste el año pasado?
5. ¿Qué metas tienes ahora? ¿Son las mismas metas que tenías cuando eras niño(a)?

Gramática de repaso

Preterite and imperfect

1. As you know, Spanish uses the preterite and the imperfect to talk about the past. Here is a review of their uses.

Use the preterite:

• to report completed past actions viewed as a whole.
  Trabajé de mesero el año pasado.
  Estudié un año en París.
  La película estuvo buena.
  Conocí (met) **a su tío ayer.**
• to report one-time emotional reactions in the past.
  Estuve muy triste cuando oí las noticias.
  Quise llorar cuando se burlaron de mí.
• to report instantaneous realizations in the past.
  Cuando lo vi, supe (knew, found out) **la verdad.**

Use the imperfect:

• to describe habitual, ongoing past actions.
  Eva trabajaba mucho de joven.
  No salía a menudo.
• to refer to mental or physical states in the past.
  Susana era alta y bonita.
• to tell time in the past.
  Eran las diez y cuarto.
• to give someone's age in the past.
  Tenía doce años en esta foto.
• to give background information to an event.
  Estaba nublado cuando ocurrió el accidente.

2. When the preterite and imperfect occur in the same sentence, the imperfect describes the background (what was going on) and the preterite points out completed actions within that setting.

Había mucha gente cuando llegué.
  There were a lot of people when I arrived.

Hacía mal tiempo; por eso fuimos a casa.
  The weather was bad; that's why we went home.

Cuaderno de actividades, p. 136, Act. 6

Más práctica gramatical, pp. 364–365, Acts. 2–4

Cuaderno de gramática, pp. 96–98, Acts. 3–7

9 **Gramática en contexto** See answers below.

Leamos/Escribamos Para describir la vida de Miguel, completa las oraciones con la forma adecuada del verbo.

1. Cuando (**a.** tuvo, **b.** tenía) cinco años, (**a.** empezó, **b.** empezaba) a asistir a la escuela.
2. De niño (**a.** fue, **b.** era) alto y atlético y (**a.** quería, **b.** quiso) ser tenista profesional.
3. Cuando (**a.** conoció, **b.** conocía) a un tenista profesional, (**a.** supo, **b.** sabía) que no quería seguir esa carrera.
4. El año pasado (**a.** se graduaba, **b.** se graduó) del colegio y quería estudiar para una carrera de matemáticas.
5. Hace diez meses Miguel (**a.** comenzó, **b.** comenzaba) sus estudios en la universidad.
6. Cuando lo (**a.** aceptaron, **b.** aceptaban) en la universidad, (**a.** estuvo, **b.** estaba) muy contento.

Communication for All Students

Group Work
Have students work in groups of four to write a short fictional article about a career day held at school last week. Students use the imperfect to describe the scene and the preterite to narrate the events. Each student should contribute at least two sentences to the article. Ask groups to share their articles with the class.

Slower Pace
9 As students complete the sentences, have them refer to the summary of preterite and imperfect usage in the **Gramática de repaso** box. Call on students to give their answers. Students should explain why they chose preterite or imperfect based on the information in the grammar summary.

⑩ Gramática en contexto

Escribamos Completa cada frase con el pretérito o el imperfecto de los verbos entre paréntesis.

1. Cuando yo ═══ (ser) niña, ═══ (querer) ser bombera.
2. Pero una vez me ═══ (decir) mi abuelo que las niñas no deben ser bomberas.
3. Después se me ═══ (ocurrir) hacer una carrera de ciencias.
4. Otra vez, mi abuelo ═══ (pedirme) estudiar una carrera menos difícil para una chica.
5. Cuando ═══ (tener) 18 años, ═══ (comenzar) a estudiar farmacología en la universidad, y a los 23 años, por fin ═══ (llegar) a ser farmacéutica. Ahora estoy segura de que la mejor carrera para mí es el trabajo que más me guste. See answers below.

SUGERENCIA

Sometimes it may seem hard to remember how to use verb tenses in Spanish, especially the preterite and the imperfect. To make learning them easier:
1. Pay close attention to how the tenses are used in sample sentences in the textbook and in sentences your teacher gives you.
2. Find examples of the tenses in reading passages, magazines, or books. Identify how the tenses are used in each example. Then check the accuracy of your conclusions with your teacher.
3. Use the tenses to say or write sentences of your own. Then check them with your teacher.

⑪ ¿Qué aspiraciones tenías?

Escribamos Escribe una breve descripción de ti mismo(a). Incluye información sobre cuándo y dónde naciste, qué sueños tenías cuando eras niño(a) y qué aspiraciones tenías a los trece años. Incluye cosas interesantes que ocurrieron durante tu niñez y cómo reaccionaste a cada una.

Así se dice

Talking about future career plans

Si quieres hablar de tus planes para el futuro, puedes decir:

Me gustaría/Me encantaría ser un cantante famoso.
Buscaré un trabajo en las ciencias.
Voy a ser contadora.
Quiero ser trabajador social.

Pienso trabajar en una farmacia.
Me interesaría estudiar para profesora.
  I'd be interested in studying to be a . . .
Quiero llegar a ser médica.
  I want to become . . .

CD-ROM DISC 3

¿Te acuerdas?

As you know, there's more than one way to talk about the future in Spanish. You can use the **ir a** + infinitive form: **Voy a trabajar este verano.** You can also use the future tense: **Irene se graduará en mayo.**

Más práctica gramatical, p. 366, Act. 5

Cuaderno de gramática, pp. 98–99, Acts. 8–11

⑫ ¿Pasado o futuro? Script and answers on p. 341G.

Escuchemos/Escribamos Escucha lo que dice cada persona. Si habla de trabajos o planes que tenía en el pasado, escribe **P.** Si habla de sus planes para el futuro, escribe **F.** Si habla de ambas cosas, escribe **A.**

CD 12
Tr. 7

Additional Practice

15 Have students write a classified ad seeking a position in their ideal career. Ask them to include their qualifications. **(Busco un trabajo de asistente de arquitecto. He trabajado por dos años en una oficina...)**

Assess

▶ Testing Program, pp. 257–260
  Quiz 12-1A, Quiz 12-1B
  Audio CD 12, Tr. 19

▶ Student Make-Up Assignments,
  Chapter 12, Alternative Quiz

▶ Alternative Assessment Guide,
  p. 41

13 Answers
Possible answers:
1. Me gustaría ser trabajador(a) social este verano en Cuba.
2. Sí, me gustaría tomar una clase de ciencias.
3. Quiero ser maestra porque quiero ayudar a los niños.
4. Quiero ser rica pero no famosa. No quiero que todo el mundo sepa todos los eventos de mi vida.
5. En diez años viviré en Nueva York. Dentro de 20 años estaré viajando. Dentro de 30 años viviré en una casa en los Alpes suizos.

---

13 **¿Qué te gustaría hacer?** See possible answers below.

Hablemos Usa las siguientes preguntas para entrevistar a un(a) compañero(a). ¿Están de acuerdo Uds. en todas sus respuestas?

1. ¿Te gustaría trabajar este verano? ¿Dónde?
2. ¿Te interesaría tomar clases en la universidad? Si decides asistir a una universidad, ¿qué clases vas a tomar?
3. ¿Qué carrera piensas seguir? ¿Por qué?
4. ¿Quieres llegar a ser rico(a) o famoso(a) algún día? Explica tu respuesta.
5. ¿Dónde vivirás en 10 años? ¿en 20? ¿en 30? Explica tus respuestas.

14 Tus planes para el futuro

Leamos/Escribamos Lee estos anuncios de personas que están buscando empleo. Luego escribe una frase que indique los planes de cada persona en los anuncios.

> Estudiante, recién graduado de universidad, busca trabajo como contador. Buenas referencias. Llamar a Emilio Juárez, 379-54-69

> 5 años experiencia en computadoras. Técnico y programador. Solicito trabajo en compañía internacional. Buena presentación. Javier Mondragón Real. 949-77-83.

> Artista, 20 años de experiencia. Pintura y dibujo. Solicito trabajo como profesora de arte. Horas flexibles. Llame a Alfonsina James, 323-67-94

> CONSEJERA. Títulos en sicología y sociología. Deseo trabajo en programas para jóvenes. Jenny Benavides. 775-12-35.

> INGENIERA QUIMICA. Título universitario. Buenos antecedentes. Desea mudarse a esta ciudad. Llamar al 525-33-34.

15 **Mi carrera ideal**

Escribamos Prepara una descripción de tu carrera ideal. Incluye las características personales que requiere la carrera, lo que tendrás que hacer para seguir esa carrera y por qué te consideras perfecto(a) para ella.

16 **Sueños y planes**

Hablemos Júntate con unos(as) compañeros(as). Hablen de los sueños que tenían cuando eran niños(as). Luego comparen esos sueños con los planes que tienen ahora para el futuro. ¿Tienen las mismas ambiciones que antes? ¿Creen que sus planes van a cambiar otra vez en el futuro? Expliquen sus respuestas.

Nota cultural

En la mayoría de los países latinoamericanos, el primer título que se puede obtener de la universidad, generalmente después de cinco años de estudio, es la **licenciatura**. En contraste con el *bachelor's degree* en Estados Unidos, la **licenciatura** requiere un examen sobre todo lo que se ha estudiado. En muchos casos, hay que escribir una tesis también. ¿Se dan exámenes de este tipo en tu estado?

Cuaderno de actividades, p. 144, Act. 26

Cultures and Communities

Culture Note

High-school students in Mexico who plan to go on to a university attend three years of **preparatoria**, known as **prepa**, after the **secundaria**. There are public and private **preparatorias**, and students must pass rigorous exams to enter and graduate. A degree from a **preparatoria** is called a **bachillerato**. Students in Mexico do not refer to themselves as freshmen, sophomores, and so on, but instead say that they are in the **primer**, **segundo**, or **tercer año**. In the third year, **preparatoria** students are required to choose their subject area for university study. Students not planning to enter a university may do vocational or technical training during their high-school years at an **escuela vocacional**.

 CD 12
Trs. 8–11

 CD-ROM
DISC 3

¿Qué planes tienes para el futuro?

Las metas son importantes en la vida, pero llegar a ser una persona famosa no es siempre sinónimo a una vida feliz. Escucha los planes futuros de los siguientes jóvenes.

Bárbara
Sevilla, España

"Me gustaría... ser sicóloga a lo mejor, algo que tenga que ver con la gente, con relacionarme con mucha gente y poder ayudar a quien sea y ganar dinero".
CD 12 Tr. 9

Adelina
Los Teques, Venezuela

"Mi futuro sería graduarme en informática y trabajar... [en] una empresa, un banco".
CD 12 Tr. 10

Gabriel
Quito, Ecuador

"Me gustaría ser cirujano plástico... porque me gusta mucho todo lo que tiene que ver con la cirugía plástica".
CD 12 Tr. 11

Para pensar y hablar...

A. ¿Qué profesión va a estudiar cada uno de los entrevistados? ¿Por qué le gustaría a Bárbara estudiar sicología? ¿A quién le gustaría trabajar en un banco? ¿Estás interesado(a) en las mismas carreras que estos jóvenes? ¿Qué carreras te interesan más a ti?

B. En tu opinión, ¿es importante planear tu carrera ahora mismo? ¿Por qué? ¿Qué puedes hacer ahora para ayudar a planear tu carrera? ¿Qué recursos puedes usar que te ayuden con tus planes?

Cuaderno para hispanohablantes, p. 60

Teaching Resources
p. 351

PRINT
▸ Video Guide, pp. 80, 82, 85
▸ Cuaderno de actividades, p. 144
▸ Cuaderno para hispanohablantes, p. 60

MEDIA
▸ One-Stop Planner
▸ Video Program, Videocassette 4, 40:04–42:48
▸ Audio Compact Discs, CD 12, Trs. 8–11
▸ Interactive CD-ROM Tutor, Disc 3

Presenting
Panorama cultural

Have students watch the video. Stop the recording after each interview and ask students to summarize what the person said. When all interviews have been shown, have students answer the **Para pensar y hablar...** questions. Then show the video again and have students answer the **Preguntas.**

Preguntas

1. **¿A Bárbara qué le gustaría ser?** (psicóloga) **¿Por qué?** (Le gusta relacionarse con mucha gente y quisiera poder ayudar a quien sea.)

2. **¿Qué quiere hacer Adelina?** (Quiere graduarse en informática y trabajar para una empresa como un banco.)

3. **¿Por qué quiere Gabriel estudiar cirujía plástica?** (A él le gusta todo lo que tiene que ver con la cirujía plástica.)

Connections and Comparisons

Thinking Critically
Drawing Inferences Ask students to think about how a person's environment shapes his or her hopes and dreams for the future. Is a person who grows up in a rural village in Costa Rica likely to aspire to be a symphony conductor? why or why not? Can it be inferred that someone growing up in Venezuela is more likely to want to be a petroleum engineer than someone in Switzerland?

why? Do they think that it can be inferred that someone from rural Minnesota is more likely to want to be a dairy farmer than someone from Los Angeles? Ask students if they have considered a career that they know little about. If so, what inspired them to think about that profession? Have students ever considered a career for which there are no opportunities in the area where they live? If so, what does this mean to them?

Presenting
¡Adelante!

Have students answer the questions preceding the ads. Then present the Preteaching Vocabulary and check for comprehension. Play the Audio CD, pausing after each paragraph. Have students write a short summary of each. Ask volunteers to share their summaries with the class.

 Contigo en la distancia

As an alternative to **¡Adelante!**, you may wish to show Episode 12 of **Contigo en la distancia**. For suggestions and activities, see the *Video Guide.*

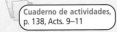
Cuaderno de actividades, p. 138, Acts. 9–11

¡Adelante! ▪ *Cuando buscas un trabajo*

CD 12
Trs. 12–15

¿Piensas trabajar algún día? ¿Qué tipo de empleo te gustaría tener? Si tuvieras una entrevista mañana, ¿qué harías para prepararte? Este artículo te puede ayudar.

ESCUELA DE IDIOMAS
NECESITA
PROFESORES DE ESPAÑOL

que tengan experiencia en la enseñanza del español como lengua extranjera.
Enviar currículum al Apdo. 498, Alajuela

Prestigiosa
EMPRESA
requiere
VENDEDOR(A)

Requisitos:
✔ Dominio del inglés
✔ Buena presentación
✔ Experiencia en ventas
✔ Excelentes relaciones públicas
✔ Dinámico(a)

Se ofrece:
✔ Buen salario
✔ Agradable ambiente de trabajo
✔ Oportunidad de desarrollo profesional

Interesados favor llamar al teléfono 24-8776

Estrategias para triunfar
Prepárate para tu primera entrevista de trabajo:

● **Imagen:** como ya sabes, la primera impresión es fundamental. Cuida hasta el más mínimo detalle… tus uñas, tu cabello, tu ropa. Lo ideal es ir limpio(a), bien arreglado(a) y mantener una elegancia sobria.

● Lleva tu currículum vitae actualizado. Adjunta copias de tus certificados de estudios, calificaciones y cartas de referencias de trabajos anteriores. Lleva todo bien presentado en una carpeta organizada. No olvides que esto hablará por ti.

● Es importante que seas espontáneo(a) y comunicativo(a) con la persona que te entreviste. No respondas con monosílabos. Debes ser explícito(a) con tus respuestas, pero procura no salirte del tema.

● Averigua todos los pormenores del empleo: horario, sueldo, etc. Pregunta sobre los beneficios que ofrece la empresa: vacaciones, seguro médico, etc.

Preteaching Vocabulary

Guessing Words from Context

Ask students what types of expressions they would use regarding job interviews. Have students identify these types of expressions in **¡Adelante!** Then point out the following phrases: **Cuida hasta el más mínimo detalle… tus uñas, tu cabello, tu ropa; Lleva todo bien presentado en una** carpeta organizada; Es importante que seas espontáneo(a) y comunicativo(a)…; Averigua todos los pormenores del empleo: horario, sueldo, etc. What are the steps one should take to prepare for an interview? Do students think this is adequate preparation? What else might one do?

17 **¿Se sabe?** See answers below.

Indica si las siguientes oraciones son **ciertas, falsas** o si **no se sabe,** según la información del artículo. Si son falsas, corrígelas.

1. Para conseguir un trabajo, no importa cómo estés vestido(a).
2. Durante una entrevista, no tienes que hacer preguntas, sólo contestar las que te hacen.
3. Debes llevar tu currículum vitae actualizado en una forma organizada.
4. Debes escribirle una carta de agradecimiento al jefe o a la jefa después de tu entrevista.
5. Hay que llevar copias de certificados de estudios, calificaciones y cartas de referencia.
6. Antes de la entrevista, es preferible no saber mucho acerca del empleo.

18 **¿Comprendes?** See answers below.

Usa la información de **¡Adelante!** para contestar las siguientes preguntas.

1. Según lo que leíste, ¿qué es fundamental antes de una entrevista de trabajo?
2. ¿Qué se debe llevar en una carpeta?
3. ¿Cómo se debe responder a las preguntas que le hacen a uno(a) en una entrevista?
4. ¿Qué tipo de preguntas debes hacer durante tu entrevista de trabajo?
5. Compara los dos anuncios de trabajo en **¡Adelante!** ¿Cómo son parecidos? ¿En qué son diferentes?

19 **¿Cuál es el (la) mejor?** See possible answers below.

Los siguientes jóvenes están solicitando el trabajo de vendedor(a) que aparece en la página 352. Con un(a) compañero(a), lee las descripciones y luego indica cuál es la persona indicada para el trabajo. Expliquen por qué las otras personas no son apropiadas.

1. Silvia se vistió para la entrevista con mucho cuidado. Planchó la ropa y se arregló el pelo. Piensa ir a la entrevista después de su clase de inglés de primer semestre.
2. Guillermo siempre se ve muy bien arreglado. Quiere trabajar como vendedor porque domina el inglés y siempre ha querido trabajar en ventas.
3. Aunque mucha gente piensa que Víctor es bastante antipático, él cree que es perfecto para un trabajo de ventas. Habla inglés y tiene experiencia en ventas.
4. Verónica vivió cinco años en Inglaterra donde trabajó en una tienda. Es atractiva y se lleva bien con la gente. Tiene todo ya listo en su carpeta para la entrevista.
5. Alfredo ha enseñado inglés en clases particulares y le encanta tratar con el público. Tan pronto como se ponga sus zapatos de tenis y una camiseta, va a ir a la entrevista.

20 **Busca las expresiones** See answers below.

Busca en el artículo una sugerencia que trate de la apariencia, otra sobre cómo organizarse para la entrevista y una más que hable de la comunicación.

21 **Ahora te toca a ti**

Si tuvieras una entrevista para un trabajo mañana, ¿tendrías listo tu currículum vitae? Prepara un currículum breve que contenga la siguiente información: trabajos que has tenido (dónde, cuándo, por cuánto tiempo, etc.), tus calificaciones y cualquier experiencia que tengas.

Comprehension Check

Challenge
Have pairs of students choose one of the two employment ads, and then decide on advice to give an applicant regarding **su imagen, el currículum, la manera de comunicarse y los pormenores del empleo.** Students might wish to refer to the article for ideas. When they have finished, have them share their advice with another pair.

Slower Pace
21 Prepare a form with blanks for students to fill in. Headings might include **Nombre, Puesto que busco, Educación, Experiencia, Honores,** and **Pasatiempos.**

Thinking Critically

Comparing and Contrasting
19 Ask students to assign a numerical value to various personal traits and score each job applicant based on these traits. The applicant with the highest score should be the best person for the job. Have students explain their point system.

Answers

17 1. falsa; Debes cuidar las uñas, el cabello y la ropa.
2. falsa; Debes averiguar los pormenores del empleo y preguntar sobre los beneficios ofrecidos.
3. cierta
4. no se sabe
5. cierta
6. no se sabe

18 1. Antes de una entrevista, es importante cuidar hasta el más mínimo detalle.
2. En una carpeta, debes llevar un currículum vitae actualizado, copias de los certificados de estudios, calificaciones y cartas de referencia de trabajos anteriores.
3. Debes ser explícito con las respuestas sin salir del tema.
4. Debes averiguar los pormenores del empleo, como el horario, sueldo, etc.
5. *Answers will vary.*

19 *Possible answer:*
Me parece que es Verónica porque tiene los requisitos que pide el anuncio: habla inglés, tiene experiencia en ventas y se lleva bien con la gente. Silvia no domina el inglés, Guillermo no tiene experiencia en ventas, Víctor no tiene buenas relaciones públicas y Alfredo no tiene buena presentación.

20 *Possible answers:*
Cuida hasta el más mínimo detalle; lo ideal es ir limpio; lleva todo bien presentado; es importante que seas espontáneo; debes ser explícito; averigua todos los pormenores

Segundo paso

Objectives Giving advice about job interviews

Teaching Resources
pp. 354–358

PRINT
- Lesson Planner, p. 59
- Listening Activities, pp. 92, 96–97
- Activities for Communication, pp. 47–48, 85–86, 111–112
- Cuaderno de gramática, pp. 100–104
- Grammar Tutor for Students of Spanish, Chapter 12
- Cuaderno de actividades, pp. 139–142
- Cuaderno para hispanohablantes, pp. 56–60
- Testing Program, pp. 261–264
- Alternative Assessment Guide, p. 41
- Student Make-Up Assignments, Chapter 12

MEDIA
- One-Stop Planner
- Audio Compact Discs, CD 12, Trs. 16–17, 30–32, 20
- Teaching Transparencies 12-2; **Más práctica gramatical** Answers; Cuaderno de gramática Answers
- Interactive CD-ROM Tutor, Disc 3

 Bell Work
Write: **Haz una lista de por lo menos diez empleos en que trabajan personas que conoces.**

Presenting
Así se dice, Gramática de repaso

The subjunctive with recommendations Role-play both sides of a dialogue between an employment counselor and a client. (—**Lo ideal es prepararte. —¿Es importante que yo aprenda de memoria lo que voy a decir?**) Have pairs of students create a dialogue between one friend preparing for an interview and another giving advice.

Así se dice

Giving advice about job interviews
Si quieres dar consejos o recomendar algo, puedes decir:

Para conseguir un buen trabajo, **debes** vestirte bien.

Te recomiendo que llegues temprano a la entrevista.

Te aconsejo que no mastiques chicle.
(. . . *you not to chew gum.*)

Lo ideal es preparar unas preguntas.

No olvides que las apariencias cuentan en las entrevistas.

Es importante que seas sincero y espontáneo.

Cuaderno de actividades, p. 139, Acts. 12–13

22 Buenos consejos Script and answers on p. 341G.

Escuchemos/Escribamos Escucha los siguientes consejos. Si te parece un buen consejo para una persona que va a entrevistarse, escribe **lógico**. Si no es un buen consejo, escribe **¡Qué va!**

CD 12, Tr. 16

Gramática de repaso

The subjunctive with recommendations

1. Spanish uses the subjunctive to imply commands after verbs and expressions such as **aconsejar que, recomendar que**, and **es importante que.**

   Es importante que tengas paciencia.   **Te aconsejo que estudies más.**
   Les recomiendo que no vuelvan tarde.

   Más práctica gramatical, p. 366, Act. 6

2. Spanish also uses the subjunctive after verbs or expressions that convey hope or desire that someone do something.

   Ojalá que Uds. vengan a la reunión.   **¿Quieres que yo te ayude?**

   Cuaderno de gramática, pp. 100–101, Acts. 12–13

23 Gramática en contexto See possible answers below.

Leamos/Escribamos Completa cada recomendación para una entrevista con una de las siguientes expresiones.

1. Al entrar en la oficina es importante que...
2. Si no sabes dónde queda la oficina, te recomiendo que...
3. Si el (la) entrevistador(a) te pregunta algo de tus empleos anteriores, es importante que...
4. Por si te piden referencias, te aconsejo que...
5. Las apariencias importan mucho. Te recomiendo que...
6. Siempre buscan entusiasmo en un(a) empleado(a). Es necesario que...

arreglarte lo mejor posible   salir de casa temprano   tener teléfonos y direcciones de referencias

llevar dos o tres cartas de referencia   mostrar confianza   darle la mano al (a la) entrevistador(a)

Communication for All Students

Pair Work
24 Ask each pair of students to choose one of the drawings on which to base a dialogue. One student is to be an interviewer and the other, an interviewee. Ask pairs to present their work to the class.

Slower Pace
24 Ask students to sequence the stages of a job interview. (entrance, introduction, presentation of résumé, asking and answering questions, exit, follow-up) Students should make their suggestions according to this sequence.

24 Te damos un consejo

Escribamos Los jóvenes en las siguientes fotos están solicitando un empleo pero necesitan ayuda. Con un(a) compañero(a), escribe algunas oraciones con consejos y estrategias para mejorar sus posibilidades de triunfar en la entrevista. Answers will vary.

a.

b.

c.

d.

Gramática de repaso

The subjunctive with the unknown or nonexistent

1. Spanish uses the subjunctive after phrases with negative words like **nada que, nadie que,** or **ninguno(a) que**, to imply nonexistence.

> No hay **nadie que diga** eso.
> No conozco a **ningún estudiante que se adapte** mejor que él.

2. Spanish also uses the subjunctive to describe people or things that aren't specified or known to exist. Remember that no personal **a** is used when there isn't a definite or specific person.

> Busco un abogado que **sepa** hablar español.
> Necesitamos algo que **cueste** menos.

3. When there's a specific person or thing in mind, however, use the indicative.

> Busco al abogado que **habla** español.
> Tenemos algo aquí que **cuesta** menos.

Cuaderno de actividades, pp. 140–141, Acts. 15, 17

Más práctica gramatical, p. 367, Act. 7

Cuaderno de gramática, pp. 101–102, Acts. 14–16

25 Gramática en contexto Script and answers on p. 341H.

Escuchemos/Hablemos Escucha las siguientes oraciones e indica si la persona habla de alguien **específico** o **no específico**.

CD 12
Tr. 17

¿Te acuerdas?

Alguien and **nadie** take personal **a** when used as direct objects.

> ¿Conoces **a alguien** que pueda ayudarme?
> No, no conozco **a nadie**.

Connections and Comparisons

Thinking Critically

Analyzing Engage students in a discussion about the appropriate clothing for various kinds of interviews. What factors might influence the attire? Have students think about what one might wear to an interview for a fast-food job, for a job in a bank, for a job as a gardener, or for a corporate public relations position.

Language-to-Language

Where Spanish calls for the subjunctive in sentences with the unknown or nonexistent, English often makes use of infinitival phrases: **Buscamos a alguien que trabaje los sábados.** *We're looking for someone to work Saturdays.* Ask your students if they can think of other subjunctive constructions that can be rendered in English using infinitival phrases.

Teaching Resources
pp. 354–358

PRINT
▶ Lesson Planner, p. 59
▶ Listening Activities, pp. 92, 96–97
▶ Activities for Communication, pp. 47–48, 85–86, 111–112
▶ Cuaderno de gramática, pp. 100–104
▶ Grammar Tutor for Students of Spanish, Chapter 12
▶ Cuaderno de actividades, pp. 139–142
▶ Cuaderno para hispanohablantes, pp. 55–60
▶ Testing Program, pp. 261–264
▶ Alternative Assessment Guide, p. 41
▶ Student Make-Up Assignments, Chapter 12

MEDIA
▶ One-Stop Planner
▶ Audio Compact Discs, CD 12, Trs. 16–17, 30–32, 20
▶ Teaching Transparencies 12-2; **Más práctica gramatical** Answers; Cuaderno de gramática Answers
▶ Interactive CD-ROM Tutor, Disc 3

Presenting
Vocabulario

Present the vocabulary by reviewing the steps one must take when looking for a job. **(Necesito actualizar mi currículum vitae. Debo escribir una carta que tenga información más específica...)** Then have students complete Activity 26.

Answers
26 1. puestos
2. solicitar; el salario
3. currículum; actualizar
4. el (la) jefe(a); medio tiempo
5. empresa; empleados

Vocabulario

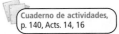

actualizar *to update*	**el puesto (de trabajo)** *position, job*
el ambiente de trabajo *workplace environment*	**los requisitos** *requirements*
los beneficios *benefits*	**el salario** *salary*
el currículum (vitae) *résumé*	**el seguro** *insurance*
el (la) empleado(a) *employee*	**solicitar** *to apply for; to request*
la empresa *business, company*	**la solicitud** *application*
el (la) gerente *manager*	**tiempo completo** *full time*
el horario *work hours, schedule*	
el jefe, la jefa *boss*	
medio tiempo *part time, half time*	

> Cuaderno de actividades, p. 140, Acts. 14, 16

> Cuaderno de gramática, pp. 102–103, Acts. 17–18

26 **El mundo del empleo** See answers below.
Leamos/Escribamos Completa cada oración con la palabra más apropiada del **Vocabulario**, incluyendo el artículo cuando sea necesario. Usa la forma correcta de los verbos.

> **También se puede decir...**
> Se puede decir **sueldo** por **salario**. También se dice **trabajador(a)** por **empleado(a)**.

1. Con la nueva fábrica se espera que abran cinco ▦▦▦ de trabajo.
2. Antonio no va a ▦▦▦ el nuevo empleo con la compañía de computadoras. Dice que ▦▦▦ que ofrecen es muy bajo.
3. Tengo todo listo para la entrevista menos mi ▦▦▦. Lo tengo que ▦▦▦ con toda la información sobre mi último trabajo.
4. Voy a hablar con ▦▦▦ para ver si puedo trabajar ▦▦▦, preferiblemente de la una hasta las seis de la tarde.
5. La familia de Hernán tiene una ▦▦▦ muy grande. Tienen por lo menos 140 ▦▦▦ que trabajan para ellos.

27 **Del colegio al trabajo**

 Escribamos Imagina que tú y un(a) compañero(a) escriben y diseñan anuncios de trabajo para compañías. Escriban un anuncio para cada puesto que sigue. Mencionen los requisitos (experiencia, etc.), beneficios y otra información sobre el trabajo.

1. farmacéutico(a); Farmacia González
2. programador(a) de computadoras; Compañía Nacional de Tecnología
3. trabajador(a) social; Agencia del Bienestar *(Welfare)* Público
4. ingeniero(a) civil; Ministerio de Obras Públicas
5. guía turística; Caribetours

> INSTITUTO HUMBOLDT
> Necesita sicólogo(a) bilingüe. Queremos a alguien que tenga mínimo cinco años de experiencia. Se ofrece buen salario y ambiente de trabajo. Presentar currículum y dos cartas de recomendación. **Llamar al 32-90-85.**

28 **Las entrevistas**

 Hablemos Trabaja con tu compañero(a). Usen los anuncios que escribieron en Actividad 27. Tú decides qué puesto quieres solicitar. Tu compañero(a) te entrevista para el puesto, explicando los requisitos y el horario de trabajo. Tú respondes diciendo por qué serías buen empleado(a) y preguntando sobre el salario y los beneficios. Luego entrevista a tu compañero(a).

Communication for All Students

Visual/Auditory Learners

26 Display *Teaching Transparency 12-2* and divide the class into pairs. Ask each pair of students to take turns describing the characters in the transparency and the careers they are imagining. They should use as many words from the **Vocabulario** as they can in their descriptions.

Native Speakers

28 Ask native speakers to do an Internet search for three specific job advertisements or companies that seek bilingual employees. Suggest that they search through Hispanic online newspapers and magazines first. Have students make a printout of their findings and turn it in.

29 Quiero un trabajo que...

Hablemos ¿Cuál es tu trabajo ideal? Entrevista a tres o cuatro compañeros para ver si tienen ideas similares sobre qué es un trabajo perfecto. Usen frases como **Quiero un trabajo que...**, **Busco un empleo que…**, **Prefiero un(a) jefe(a) que...**, etc. ¿Tienen ideas en común?

Gramática de repaso

The conditional and the past subjunctive

1. To talk about hypothetical situations, you use the conditional and **si** with the past subjunctive.

   Si pudiera conseguir una beca, estudiaría en España.
   Empezaríamos nuestra empresa si tuviéramos suficiente dinero.

2. The conditional is used to express what would happen or what someone would do. Like the future, the conditional consists of the future stem plus one set of endings for all verbs. The future stem is usually the infinitive of the verb.

HABLAR	CORRER	PEDIR
hablaría	correría	pediría
hablarías	correrías	pedirías
hablaría	correría	pediría
hablaríamos	correríamos	pediríamos
hablaríais	correríais	pediríais
hablarían	correrían	pedirían

¿Se te ha olvidado?
irregular future stems
Ver la página 265

3. To form the past subjunctive, start with the **ellos/ellas** form of the preterite. Remove the **-on** and add the following endings:

HABER (hubier**on**)	VENDER (vendier**on**)	SER/IR (fuer**on**)
hubiera	vendiera	fuera
hubieras	vendieras	fueras
hubiera	vendiera	fuera
hubiéramos	vendiéramos	fuéramos
hubierais	vendierais	fuerais
hubier**an**	vendier**an**	fuer**an**

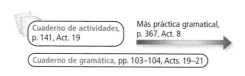
Cuaderno de actividades, p. 141, Act. 19
Más práctica gramatical, p. 367, Act. 8
Cuaderno de gramática, pp. 103–104, Acts. 19–21

30 Gramática en contexto See possible answers below.

Escribamos Escribe oraciones completas con la siguiente información.

MODELO A la jefa no (gustarle) / si los empleados (llegar) tarde al trabajo
—A la jefa no le gustaría si los empleados llegaran tarde al trabajo.

1. Si Eduardo (ser) bilingüe / (poder) trabajar con las aerolíneas
2. Nosotros (aceptar) los puestos / si la compañía (ofrecer) mejores beneficios
3. (Gustarme) el horario / si yo (poder) trabajar medio tiempo
4. Ellos (comprar) un carro / si sus jefes les (aumentar) el salario
5. Si el ambiente de trabajo (ser) más cómodo / yo no (buscar) otro puesto
6. Si tú (actualizar) tu currículum / (tener) más oportunidades de entrevistarte con compañías
7. Hisoka (solicitar) ese puesto / si no (haber) tantos requisitos
8. Si Rosa (saber) más sobre el puesto / te (decirlo)

Communication for All Students

Auditory Learners
You may want to play the song **La Adelita,** Audio CD 4, Track 29. It contains several instances of the conditional and **si** with the past subjunctive. The printed lyrics are on page 34 of Listening Activities.

Challenge
Ask students what famous person they would like to meet if they had the opportunity. Have them describe the meeting. Would they like to have lunch with the person? work with or play a sport with him or her? What would they talk about?

Additional Practice

29 Have students compare their ideal jobs to a job they have now, or to a job someone they know currently has: **El trabajo que tengo ahora es de martes a jueves por la tarde y los sábados por la mañana. Busco un trabajo que sea de lunes a jueves por la noche.**

Presenting
Gramática de repaso

The conditional and the past subjunctive Present the conditional with the past subjunctive by telling students what you would do if you suddenly found yourself free to do as you wished for a year. **(Si yo pudiera, viajaría a muchos lugares exóticos y escribiría guías turísticas.)** Ask students to give as many different responses as possible to the question **Si fueras millonario(a), ¿qué harías?**

Answers
30 1. Si Eduardo fuera bilingüe, podría trabajar con las aerolíneas.
2. Nosotros aceptaríamos los puestos si la compañía ofreciera mejores beneficios.
3. Me gustaría el horario si yo pudiera trabajar medio tiempo.
4. Ellos comprarían un carro si sus jefes les aumentaran el salario.
5. Si el ambiente de trabajo fuera más cómodo, yo no buscaría otro puesto.
6. Si tú actualizaras tu currículum, tendrías más oportunidades de entrevistarte con compañías.
7. Hisoka solicitaría ese puesto si no hubiera tantos requisitos.
8. Si Rosa supiera más sobre el puesto, te lo diría.

Writing Assessment

33 Encourage use of varied vocabulary and grammar from this and previous chapters. Challenge students to write as descriptively as possible. Answer any questions, but explain that simple errors are expected and that risk-taking is rewarded in the grading system. You may wish to assess the writing assignment using the following rubric.

Writing Rubric	Points			
	4	3	2	1
Content (Complete–Incomplete)				
Comprehensibility (Comprehensible–Incomprehensible)				
Accuracy (Accurate–Seldom accurate)				
Organization (Well organized–Poorly organized)				
Effort (Excellent–Minimal)				

18–20: A 14–15: C Under
16–17: B 12–13: D 12: F

Assess

▶ Testing Program, pp. 261–264
Quiz 12-2A, Quiz 12-2B
Audio CD 12, Tr. 20

▶ Student Make-Up Assignments, Chapter 12, Alternative Quiz

▶ Alternative Assessment Guide, p. 41

---

31 **Después de la graduación** Answers will vary.

Leamos/Hablemos Los siguientes jóvenes hablan de lo que harían después de graduarse. Lee lo que dicen y luego indica con qué persona tienes más en común y explica por qué. ¿Conoces a alguien que tenga los mismos planes e ideas que alguno de ellos?

"Si pudiera trabajar en cualquier campo sería en medicina. Es un campo que siempre me ha gustado. Me interesa hacer investigación".

Alfonso

Lourdes

"Me gusta todo lo que tiene que ver con los negocios. Si pudiera, tendría mi propia empresa. Así tendría la libertad de trabajar en casa también. Después de graduarme estudiaré administración de empresas".

"Mis papás quieren que estudie ingeniería, pero eso no me interesa para nada. Si fuera ingeniera no sería feliz. A mí me interesa más la sicología. Quiero trabajar con niños".

Ana Lucía

"Iré a la capital para estudiar música clásica. Si hubiera un buen instituto de música en mi ciudad me quedaría aquí para estudiar".

Daniel

32 **Si fuera profesora...**

Escribamos/Hablemos ¿Qué harías si fueras arquitecto(a)? ¿Cómo serías si fueras profesor(a)? ¿Serías estricto(a) con tus estudiantes? Di qué harías o cómo serías si te dedicaras a las siguientes profesiones. Luego compara tus respuestas con las de un(a) compañero(a).

MODELO Si fuera arquitecta, construiría casas grandes y bonitas de dos pisos.

1. arquitecto(a)
2. profesor(a)
3. trabajador(a) social
4. sicólogo(a)
5. médico(a)
6. abogado(a)

¿Se te ha olvidado?
past subjunctive
Ver la página 327

33 **En mi cuaderno**

Escribamos Imagina que trabajas para la compañía **Imágenes, S.A.**, que ayuda a la gente a mejorar su presentación en las entrevistas. Escribe un intercambio de correo electrónico con una persona que se presenta muy mal en las entrevistas y te explica el problema y te pide consejos. Tú le respondes con recomendaciones para mejorar su presentación y para ser el tipo de empleado(a) que están buscando.

Connections and Comparisons

Social Studies Link

Review with students what they know about labor laws in the United States. Do students know what the minimum wage is? How is it established? Discuss Social Security taxes and Workers' Compensation Insurance. What is their purpose? Ask students what they know about child labor laws in the United States. Do students think such laws are reasonable? You may want to make sure that students understand the historical context within which the laws were established. Then ask students to work in small groups and research the employment/labor laws of a Spanish-speaking country. Have them report their findings to the class.

Encuentro cultural

La formalidad

Estas fotos son de una oficina en una empresa.
Hay una cosa que no se debe hacer y dos cosas
que no se deben decir. ¿Puedes encontrarlas?

¡Hola, Sra. Díaz! ¿Qué tal? ¿Cómo está tu familia?

Para discutir

1. ¿Cómo está sentada la mujer en la primera foto? ¿Te sentarías así si tuvieras un trabajo en una oficina?
2. ¿Hablarías así con tu jefe(a)? ¿Cómo saludarías a tu jefe(a)? ¿Cómo saludas a tus profesores(as)?

Vamos a comprenderlo

El hispanohablante tiende a ser más formal en su forma de hablar y sentarse. En la primera foto, la mujer tiene sus pies encima del escritorio y la mano detrás de la cabeza, lo cual se considera demasiado informal para una oficina. Sólo en las situaciones muy informales se pueden poner los pies encima de un escritorio o una mesa. En la segunda foto, el hombre es demasiado informal en su forma de hablar con la jefa también. No se debe tratar a la jefa (o al jefe) de **tú.** Tampoco se deben hacer preguntas personales (como preguntar por la familia) a menos que la persona sea un(a) amigo(a) o alguien que se conoce bien.

Teaching Resources
pp. 360–362

PRINT 📖
- Lesson Planner, p. 60
- Cuaderno de actividades, p. 143
- Cuaderno para hispanohablantes, pp. 56–59
- Reading Strategies and Skills Handbook, Chapter 12
- ¡Lee conmigo! 3, Chapter 12
- Standardized Assessment Tutor, Chapter 12

MEDIA 💿📱
- One-Stop Planner

Prereading
Activities A and B

Making Predictions
Ask students to use the information they garnered from skimming to forecast what happens in the story. Do they anticipate that the narrator will be the main character in the development of the plot? why or why not? A discussion of their predictions may lead to some questions that students want to answer during their thorough reading of the narrative.

Answers

A *Possible answer:*
La introducción: los dos primeros párrafos en los cuales se presentan los personajes
La parte principal: todo entre los dos primeros párrafos y los dos últimos párrafos, en que se explora la fantasía del árbol de oro
La conclusión: los dos últimos párrafos en que se resuelve el cuento

B Los personajes: la señorita Leocadia, profesora; Mateo Heredia, compañero de clase; Ivo Márquez, compañero de clase; La narradora es una niña.
Los personajes con diálogos: la narradora, Ivo, Mateo

Fantasía y realidad

En este cuento, la escritora española Ana María Matute combina el realismo con la fantasía para describir algo de su niñez. Se ven dos mundos en contraste: el mundo realista de la narradora y el mundo de la imaginación de un niño.

Estrategia para leer
Utilize multiple reading strategies. Throughout this book you have learned about a number of strategies. Some are for the prereading stage, such as skimming and activating background knowledge. Others help you during your reading, both on a global level, such as summarizing and outlining, and on a specific level, such as guessing word meanings and scanning.

¡A comenzar! See answers below.

¿Te acuerdas?
As you know, it's a good idea to skim before reading in detail, in order to get a general idea of what each section or paragraph is about.

A. Revisa el cuento. Identifica la introducción, la parte principal del cuento y la conclusión.

B. Vuelve a revisar el cuento. Identifica a todos los personajes. ¿Quién es el (la) narrador(a) del cuento? ¿Quiénes son los personajes que tienen diálogos?

El árbol de oro

Asistí durante un otoño a la escuela de la señorita Leocadia, en la aldea, porque mi salud no andaba bien y el abuelo retrasó mi vuelta a la ciudad. Como era el tiempo frío y estaban los suelos embarrados y no se veía rastro de muchachos, me aburría dentro de la casa, y pedí al abuelo asistir a la escuela. El abuelo consintió, y acudí a aquella casita alargada y blanca de cal, a las afueras del pueblo.

La señorita Leocadia era alta y gruesa y tenía el carácter más bien áspero. Las clases en la escuela, con la lluvia rebotando en el tejado y los cristales, tenían su atractivo. Recuerdo especialmente a un muchacho de unos diez años, hijo de un aparcero muy pobre, llamado Ivo. Era un muchacho delgado, de ojos azules, que bizqueaba ligeramente al hablar. Todos los muchachos y muchachas de la escuela admiraban y envidiaban un poco a Ivo, por el don que poseía de atraer la atención sobre sí, en todo momento. No es que fuera ni inteligente ni gracioso, y, sin embargo, había algo en él, en su voz quizás, en las cosas que conseguía cautivar a quien le escuchase. También la señorita Leocadia se dejaba prender de aquella red de plata que Ivo tendía a cuantos atendían sus enrevesadas conversaciones, y —yo creo que muchas veces contra su voluntad—la señorita Leocadia le confiaba a Ivo tareas deseadas por todos, o distinciones que merecían alumnos más estudiosos y aplicados.

Quizá lo que más se envidiaba de Ivo era la posesión de la codiciada llave de la torrecita. Ésta era, en efecto, una pequeña torre situada en un ángulo de la escuela, en cuyo interior se guardaban los libros de lectura. Allí entraba Ivo a buscarlos, y allí volvía a dejarlos, al terminar la clase.

Ivo estaba muy orgulloso de esta distinción, y por nada del mundo la hubiera cedido. Un día, Mateo Heredia, el más aplicado y estudioso de la escuela, pidió encargarse de

---

Communication for All Students

Slower Pace
Familiarize students with the story's structure by having them skim the reading, looking at verb tenses. Ask the following questions: What verb tense is used most often in the first two paragraphs and why? (the imperfect; to set the stage, to narrate the introduction) How do the verb tenses change in the third paragraph, and why do you think that happens? (There is a switch from imperfect to preterite to show a transition from the introduction to the main part of the story's action.) Remind students that the lines beginning with dashes represent dialogue. Why do students think there is a wide variety of tenses used in the dialogue sections? (The narrator is reproducing or retelling the conversations that took place at the time of the story.)

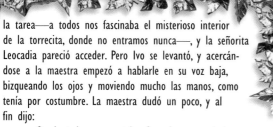

la tarea—a todos nos fascinaba el misterioso interior de la torrecita, donde no entramos nunca—, y la señorita Leocadia pareció acceder. Pero Ivo se levantó, y acercándose a la maestra empezó a hablarle en su voz baja, bizqueando los ojos y moviendo mucho las manos, como tenía por costumbre. La maestra dudó un poco, y al fin dijo:

—Quede todo como estaba. Que siga encargándose Ivo de la torrecita.

A la salida de la escuela le pregunté:

—¿Qué le has dicho a la maestra?

Ivo me miró de través y vi relampaguear sus ojos azules.

—Le hablé del árbol de oro.

Sentí una gran curiosidad.

—¿Qué árbol?

—Si no se lo cuentas a nadie...

—Te lo juro, que a nadie se lo diré.

Entonces Ivo me explicó:

—Veo un árbol de oro. Un árbol completamente de oro: ramas, tronco, hojas... ¿sabes? Las hojas no se caen nunca. En verano, en invierno, siempre. Resplandece mucho; tanto, que tengo que cerrar los ojos para que no me duelan.

—¡Qué embustero eres!—dije, aunque con algo de zozobra. Ivo me miró con desprecio.

—No te lo creas —contestó—. Me es completamente igual que te lo creas o no... ¡Nadie entrará nunca en la torrecita, y a nadie dejaré ver mi árbol de oro! ¡Es mío! La señorita Leocadia lo sabe, y no se atreve a darle la llave a Mateo Heredia, ni a nadie... ¡Mientras yo viva, nadie podrá entrar allí y ver mi árbol!

Lo dijo de tal forma que no pude evitar preguntarle:

—¿Y cómo lo ves... ?

—Ah, no es fácil —dijo, con aire misterioso—. Cualquiera no podría verlo. Yo sé la rendija exacta. Una que hay corriendo el cajón de la derecha: me agacho y me paso horas y horas... ¡Cómo brilla el árbol! Fíjate que si algún pájaro se le pone encima también se vuelve de oro. Eso me digo yo: si me subiera a una rama, ¿me volvería acaso de oro también?

No supe qué decirle, pero, desde aquel momento, mi deseo de ver el árbol creció de tal forma que me

---

Al grano   See sample answers below.

¿Te acuerdas?

Predicting what will happen in a story is a helpful strategy. To make predictions while you read, pause after each main idea to think about what you have just read and what might happen.

C. Lee la introducción. Después, imagínate lo que va a pasar en la parte principal. Después de leer la parte principal, imagina cómo será la conclusión. Luego reúnete con un(a) compañero(a) para comparar lo que se ha imaginado cada uno.

¿Te acuerdas?

Summarize main points. After you come across an important idea, summarize that information briefly.

D. Ahora lee el texto otra vez, pero con mucho cuidado. Trata de entenderlo bien. Después de terminar cada sección, escribe un resumen de la sección. El resumen debe ser de una o dos oraciones en español. Será útil saber el significado de las siguientes palabras:

> **aldea** *village*
> **aparcero** *sharecropper*
> **bizquear** *to squint*
> **embustero** *liar*
> **rendija** *crack*
> **hucha** *piggy bank*
> **estafar** *to swindle*

¿Te acuerdas?

Scan to find specific information. Locate specific information quickly by searching for key words.

Vamos a leer

CAPÍTULO 12

Reading
Activities C, D, E, and F

Summarizing

D. Suggest that students jot down a sentence or two after reading the introduction, a few sentences for the main part of the story, and one or two about the conclusion. Then have them go back and decide if they can tighten up their summaries. Remind them that summaries restate only the main events and principal ideas of the text in a few words. If some students have difficulty with this task, you may want to allow them to paraphrase instead of summarizing.

Answers

C *Possible answers:*
Predicción después de la introducción: Se sabe que hay alguna razón por la cual a Ivo le dan tantas distinciones. Él tiene o sabe algo especial.
Predicción después de la parte principal: La narradora ya no cree en el árbol de oro y se va a olvidar de él.

D *Possible answers:*
La introducción: La narradora asiste a una escuela mientras visita a su abuelo. Conoce a Ivo, el favorito de la maestra.
La parte principal: Ivo tiene la llave de la torrecita y le dice a la maestra del árbol de oro. Dice que nadie va a poder entrar en la torre y ver el árbol mientras él esté vivo. La narradora consigue la llave cuando Ivo se enferma y trata de ver el árbol de oro. No ve nada y decide olvidarse de todo.
La conclusión: La narradora regresa a la aldea y ve una cruz con el nombre de Ivo al lado de un árbol que parece ser de oro.

Cultures and Communities

Culture Note

Ana María Matute (b. 1926) was born in Barcelona, Spain. The Spanish Civil War broke out when she was ten years old and this had a profound impact on her life as well as her work. **"El árbol de oro"** is from *Historias de la Artámila,* a collection of stories that evoke childhood recollections. As a child, Matute attended a small village school similar to the one described in **"El árbol de oro"**. Her literary language is generally simple and direct, but poetic. The majority of her work has been translated into English and other languages. She has written and won awards for such works as *Los hijos muertos, Primera memoria,* and *Los soldados lloran de noche.*

Vamos a leer

CAPÍTULO 12

Postreading
Activities G and H

Drawing Inferences

H. As a class, read the first question in Activity H and allow students a few minutes to think about their responses. Write **embustero** and **imaginación fantástica** on the board or on a transparency, then ask students to explain which trait describes Ivo and why. Students should justify their answers based on the story: **Creo que Ivo es un embustero porque las otras personas no ven el árbol. Me parece a mí que Ivo tiene una imaginación fantástica porque su intención no es engañar, sino compartir lo que siente, aunque sea increíble.** Note students' answers on the board. After the discussion, ask students to reread the last two paragraphs of the story. How does their opinion of Ivo affect their interpretation of the ending?

Answers

E 1. Estaba visitando a su abuelo cuando se enfermó y decidió ir a la escuela para no aburrirse.

2. Ivo era un niño delgado, de ojos azules. Había algo en él o en su voz que le llamaba la atención a la gente.

3. La maestra le daba a Ivo tareas que los otros estudiantes querían y merecían. También tenía posesión de la llave de la torrecita.

4. Ivo veía un árbol de oro que resplandecía tanto que le dolían los ojos al verlo.

5. Vio la tierra seca alargándose hacia el cielo.

F don *special gift*
relampaguear *to flash like lightning*
resplandece *gleams, glows, shines, glitters*

G *Answers will vary.*

H *Answers will vary.*

See answers below.

E. Vuelve a leer el texto para contestar estas preguntas específicas.

1. ¿Por qué asistió la narradora a la escuela de la señorita Leocadia?

2. ¿Cómo era Ivo? ¿Qué cualidad especial tenía?

3. ¿Por qué envidiaban (*envied*) los muchachos a Ivo?

4. ¿Qué veía Ivo por la rendija?

5. ¿Qué vio la narradora por la rendija?

¿Te acuerdas?

Use context to figure out meaning. Rely on the words and sentences around the unknown word.

F. Adivina el significado de estas palabras, con la ayuda del contexto.

1. don
2. relampaguear
3. resplandece

G. El cuento pone en contraste el mundo de la realidad y el de la fantasía. Con un(a) compañero(a), indica qué palabras y frases usa la narradora para describir a las personas, la naturaleza, etc. Indiquen qué palabras y frases usa Ivo para describir el árbol. ¿Cuál es la diferencia?

H. ¿Crees que Ivo era un embustero o que simplemente tenía una imaginación fantástica? ¿Alguna vez lo que soñaste se hizo realidad? ¿Crees que es importante tener imaginación? ¿Por qué sí o por qué no?

Cuaderno para hispanohablantes, pp. 56–59

Cuaderno de actividades, p. 143, Acts. 23–24

---

desasosegaba. Todos los días, al acabar la clase de lectura, Ivo se acercaba al cajón de la maestra, sacaba la llave y se dirigía a la torrecita. Cuando volvía, le preguntaba:

—¿Lo has visto?

—Sí —me contestaba. Y, a veces, explicaba alguna novedad:

—Le han salido unas flores raras. Mira: así de grandes, como mi mano lo menos, y con los pétalos alargados.

Ocurrió entonces algo que secretamente yo deseaba; me avergonzaba sentirlo, pero así era: Ivo enfermó, y la señorita Leocadia encargó a otro la llave de la torrecita. Primeramente, la disfrutó Mateo Heredia. Yo espié su regreso, el primer día, y le dije:

—¿Has visto un árbol de oro?

—¿Qué andas graznando? —me contestó de malos modos, porque no era simpático, y menos conmigo. Unos días después, me dijo:

—Si me das algo a cambio, te dejo un ratito la llave y vas durante el recreo. Nadie te verá...

Vacié mi hucha, y, por fin, conseguí la codiciada llave. Mis manos temblaban de emoción cuando entré en el cuartito de la torre. Allí estaba el cajón. Lo aparté y vi brillar la rendija en la oscuridad. Me agaché y miré.

Cuando la luz dejó de cegarme, mi ojo derecho sólo descubrió una cosa: la seca tierra de la llanura alargándose hacia el cielo. Nada más. Tuve una gran decepción y la seguridad de que me habían estafado.

Olvidé la llave y el árbol de oro. Antes de que llegaran las nieves regresé a la ciudad.

Dos veranos más tarde volví a las montañas. Un día, pasando por el cementerio—era ya tarde y se anunciaba la noche en el cielo: el sol, como una bola roja, caía a lo lejos— vi algo extraño. De la tierra pedregosa, entre las cruces caídas, nacía un árbol grande y hermoso, con las hojas anchas de oro: encendido y brillante todo él, cegador. Algo me vino a la memoria, como un sueño, y pensé: "Es un árbol de oro". Busqué al pie del árbol, y no tardé en dar con una crucecilla de hierro negro, mohosa por la lluvia. Mientras la enderezaba, leí IVO MÁRQUEZ, DE DIEZ AÑOS DE EDAD.

Y no daba tristeza alguna, sino, tal vez, una extraña y muy grande alegría.

Connections and Comparisons

Literature Link

Have students generate a list of titles of works of fantasy and then discuss any themes that become apparent from the titles. Then engage students in a discussion of the elements that make these works fantastic. What distinguishes fantasy from other forms of fiction? Do students characterize

"El árbol de oro" as a work of fantasy? why or why not? Then have students consider whether fantasy or other imaginative works are for children and young adults exclusively or if they have appeal across generations.

STANDARDS: 1.2, 2.2, 3.1

Vamos a escribir

En "El árbol de oro" leíste sobre un niño que tuvo una visión del futuro. Su visión llegó a ser real a pesar de las dudas de los demás. ¿Tienes alguna idea clara sobre lo que nos depara el futuro? En esta actividad vas a escribir tus ideas sobre el futuro y aprenderás algunas maneras de escribir buenas conclusiones.

En el año 3000

¿Cómo será el mundo en el año 3000? ¿Será similar o distinto al mundo de hoy? ¿En qué aspectos será distinto y en cuáles será similar? Si vivieras en el mundo del año 3000, ¿qué querrías cambiar? En una composición de tres o cuatro párrafos, describe tu visión del mundo en el año 3000.

Estrategia para escribir

Good conclusions It's always a good idea to end what you write with a good conclusion that draws your main ideas together. For example, your conclusion can review ideas you introduced earlier and give a few sentences that tie them together. Your conclusion can also summarize your main idea in other words, or it can close with an interesting comment that leaves your reader wanting to know more about your topic.

A. Preparación

1. Antes de escribir, piensa en las cosas que podrían ser afectadas por el paso del tiempo. Considera estas categorías y agrega otras si es necesario.

| el transporte | las ciencias | la medicina | la tecnología |

| las casas | la comida | el medio ambiente | el recreo | la geografía |

2. Haz una lista de las cosas que podrían cambiar en cada categoría mencionada.

3. Organiza la información en orden lógico. Si quieres, usa fichas para organizarla.

B. Redacción

1. Comienza tu composición con una introducción que llame la atención de tu lector(a). Puede ser una pregunta o una idea interesante sobre el futuro.

2. Luego escribe unos párrafos sobre cómo van a ser las cosas en el año 3000. Describe las cosas que serán similares y las que serán distintas al mundo de hoy. Si hay cosas que te gustaría cambiar, menciónalas y explica por qué las quieres cambiar.

3. Incluye detalles interesantes. Por ejemplo, si mencionas que la gente viajará en platillos voladores, explica cómo funcionarán, a qué velocidad volarán, etc.

4. Escribe una buena conclusión que resuma tus ideas.

C. Evaluación

1. ¿Pusiste la información en orden lógico? Si no, organízala en un orden más apropiado.

2. Pídeles a unos(as) compañeros(as) que lean tu composición. ¿Qué opinan de tu introducción y de tu conclusión? Ten en cuenta sus comentarios e incorpóralos si es necesario.

3. Después de leer varias veces tu composición, ¿qué te parecen los detalles que incluiste? Si hay algunos que no te parecen interesantes o útiles, puedes cambiarlos u omitirlos.

Apply and Assess

Postwriting
Additional Practice

Have peer-editors evaluate how well the summary draws together the main ideas of the composition. Do the supporting details relate to the main ideas?

Comparing and Contrasting

Point out that people have always imagined what the future might be like. You may want to compare past predictions with current reality. (Compare life in the late twentieth century to the world portrayed in Orwell's novel *1984;* compare the world of the Kubrick/Clarke film *2001: A Space Odyssey* to the contemporary United States.)

Teaching Resources
p. 363

PRINT 📖
▸ Lesson Planner, p. 60
▸ Cuaderno para hispanohablantes, p. 59
▸ Alternative Assessment Guide, p. 27
▸ Standardized Assessment Tutor, Chapter 12

MEDIA 📀📼
▸ One-Stop Planner
  Test Generator, Chapter 12
▸ Interactive CD-ROM Tutor, Disc 3

Process Writing

Prewriting
Motivating Activity

Describe the world as it was in the year 1000. (Vikings occupying Great Britain, Iceland, and Greenland and visiting North America; much of Spain occupied by Moslems from North Africa; consolidation of the Sung Dynasty in China; rise of Pueblo culture in North America; decline of Mayas, rise of Toltecs in Central America) Have students list ways in which the world has changed. Then ask them to describe how the world might change in the next millennium.

Writing
Slower Pace

B. Have students write the categories they used in Part A on a sheet of paper. Tell them to organize the categories using cluster diagrams or a chart. Then, under or next to each category, have them list the ways in which they foresee those things changing or staying the same; they should also include changes they would like to see. After they have some ideas to go with each category, students can use their diagrams or charts to organize their outlines and to begin writing.

Más práctica gramatical

CAPÍTULO 12

For **Más práctica gramatical** Answer Transparencies, see the *Teaching Transparencies* binder.

Más práctica gramatical

MARCAR: go.hrw.com
PALABRA CLAVE:
WV3 COSTA RICA-12

Primer paso

Objectives Talking about former jobs and goals; talking about future career plans

1 De cada grupo de profesiones y oficios, indica la palabra que lógicamente no se asocia con las otras dos. **(p. 347)**

MODELO	contador(a)	sicólogo(a)	banquero(a)
1.	científico(a)	farmacéutico(a)	vendedor(a)
2.	periodista	carpintero(a)	arquitecto(a)
3.	enfermero(a)	escritor(a)	médico(a)
4.	escritor(a)	periodista	programador(a) de computadoras
5.	muralista	trabajador(a) social	escultor(a)
6.	mecánico(a)	policía	abogado(a)
7.	profesor(a)	vendedor(a)	comerciante

2 Read the interviews with Alan and Caryn at the bottom of pages 344–345. Based on what you read, do the sentences below probably refer to Alan or Caryn? Which of the uses on page 348 explains why the preterite or imperfect is called for in each sentence? **(p. 348)**

1. Le gustó tanto su curso que <u>quiso</u> ser salvavidas.
2. <u>Tuvo</u> un examen importante hace dos años.
3. Me imagino que <u>iba</u> al cine mucho de joven.
4. <u>Tuvo</u> que ponerse en forma para conseguir el trabajo que quería.
5. Cuando <u>tenía</u> ocho años actuó en una obra de teatro.
6. Hace dos años <u>hizo</u> un curso en el Taller Cultural.
7. El año pasado le <u>dieron</u> un puesto y ahora trabaja para la ciudad.

Answers

1
1. vendedor(a)
2. periodista
3. escritor(a)
4. programador(a) de computadoras
5. trabajador(a) social
6. mecánico(a)
7. profesor(a)

2
1. Alan; to describe an ongoing past action
2. Alan; to report a completed past action
3. Caryn; to describe a habitual past action
4. Alan; to report a completed past action
5. Caryn; to describe age in the past
6. Caryn; to report a completed past action
7. Alan; to report a completed past action

Grammar Resources for Chapter 12

The **Más práctica gramatical** activities are designed as supplemental activities for the grammatical concepts presented in the chapter. You might use them as additional practice, for review, or for assessment.

For more grammar presentation, review, and practice, refer to the following:

• Cuaderno de gramática
• Grammar Tutor for Students of Spanish

• Grammar Summary on pp. R25–R46
• Cuaderno de actividades
• Grammar and Vocabulary quizzes (Testing Program)
• Test Generator on the One-Stop Planner CD-ROM
• Interactive CD-ROM Tutor
• **Juegos interactivos** at <u>go.hrw.com</u>

3 Aitana le está haciendo una entrevista a Patricia Forment, una comerciante famosa y dueña *(owner)* de su propia empresa internacional. Completa estas preguntas y respuestas de la entrevista con el pretérito o el imperfecto. **(p. 348)**

1. Señora Forment, ¿cómo (supo/sabía) usted que quería hacerse comerciante?
2. Pues, cuando (fui/era) niña, mi abuelo y mi papá (trabajaron/trabajaban) en un banco.
3. Ellos (ayudaron/ayudaban) a las empresas a establecerse.
4. De niña, yo (fui/iba) a esas empresas con ellos, y (pensé/pensaba) que sería interesante tener mi propia empresa.
5. Así que cuando (fui/iba) a la universidad, (estudié/estudiaba) muchas materias: contabilidad, derecho, diseño, arte, idiomas...
6. Recuerdo que en aquel entonces (estuve/estaba) ocupadísima y (tuve/tenía) que estudiar mucho.
7. Cuando (encontré/encontraba) mi primer puesto en un banco internacional, (estuve/estaba) muy contenta.
8. El puesto (fue/era) interesante, pero a veces (me sentí/me sentía) frustrada porque (quise/quería) trabajar para mí misma.
9. Así que hace diez años, (abrí/abría) mi primera tienda.

4 Jorge now works in Hollywood as a veterinarian and pet consultant to the stars, but he wasn't always so famous. Complete his explanation of how he got started in his career with the preterite or imperfect of the verbs in parentheses. **(p. 348)**

Recuerdo muy bien mi primer trabajo. Cuando yo __1__ (tener) 14 años, __2__ (empezar) a trabajar como paseaperros para los vecinos. En aquel entonces, mi familia y yo __3__ (vivir) en un edificio de apartamentos, y muchas de las familias __4__ (tener) perros. Todos los días, de mañana y de tarde, los perros y yo __5__ (ir) al parque a pasear. Los perros siempre __6__ (ponerse) muy felices al verme y casi siempre yo lo __7__ (pasar) bien con mis clientes de cuatro patas. Pero una vez yo __8__ (tener) un problema grave. Un día, yo __9__ (estar) en el parque con cinco perros cuando de repente, uno de ellos __10__ (ver) una gata. En seguida, el perro __11__ (salir) corriendo, y todos los demás perros lo __12__ (seguir). La pobre gata __13__ (asustarse) tanto que __14__ (querer) subirse a un árbol muy grande. Luego, yo __15__ (tratar) de bajar a la gata, pero al final __16__ (tener) que llamar a los bomberos. La dueña de la gata __17__ (ponerse) furiosa conmigo y con los perros. ¡Qué horrible! Los perros y yo no __18__ (volver) a ese parque durante mucho tiempo.

Answers

3
1. supo
2. era, trabajaban
3. ayudaban
4. iba, pensaba
5. fui, estudié
6. estaba, tenía
7. encontré, estuve
8. era, me sentía, quería
9. abrí

4
1. tenía
2. empecé
3. vivíamos
4. tenían
5. íbamos
6. se ponían
7. pasaba
8. tuve
9. estaba
10. vio
11. salió
12. siguieron
13. se asustó
14. quiso
15. traté
16. tuve
17. se puso
18. volvimos

Más práctica gramatical

CAPÍTULO 12

For **Más práctica gramatical**
Answer Transparencies, see the
Teaching Transparencies binder.

Más práctica gramatical

WV3 COSTA RICA-12

5 Lee lo que todos van a hacer este verano. Cambia las expresiones con **ir a** + infinitivo al tiempo futuro. (**p. 349**)

> **MODELO**   Efraín <u>va a buscar</u> un trabajo en el banco.
> Efraín **buscará** un trabajo en el banco.

1. En agosto, mi hermano y yo <u>vamos a hacer</u> un viaje en bicicleta por Vermont y Nueva York.
2. Creo que mi primo Esteban <u>va a venir</u> con nosotros.
3. Me parece que <u>vamos a salir</u> la segunda semana de agosto.
4. Esteban <u>va a tener</u> que volver a casa después de una semana.
5. Pero mi hermano y yo <u>vamos a ir</u> tres semanas enteras.
6. Todos <u>vamos a necesitar</u> dinero para poder hacer el viaje.
7. <u>Voy a trabajar</u> de mesera. <u>Voy a poner</u> todo mi salario y mis propinas en el banco.
8. Si trabajo mucho, <u>voy a poder</u> pagar el viaje sin tener que pedirles dinero a mis padres.
9. No sé qué <u>van a hacer</u> Esteban y mi hermano. Supongo que <u>van a encontrar</u> trabajo pronto.
10. ¿Y qué planes tienes para el verano? ¿<u>Te vas a quedar</u> en casa o <u>vas a viajar</u> a alguna parte?

Segundo paso   Objectives Giving advice about job interviews

6 Juan Luis quiere encontrar un trabajo. Su hermana mayor tiene unos consejos para él. Completa lo que Blanca le dice a Juan Luis con el subjuntivo de los verbos entre paréntesis. (**p. 354**)

Juan Luis, te recomiendo que ___**1**___ (empezar/tú) a buscar un trabajo pronto.
Conviene que primero ___**2**___ (hacer/tú) una lista de los trabajos que te interesen.
Después, sugiero que ___**3**___ (pedir/tú) una cita con la consejera de tu colegio, y
que luego ustedes dos ___**4**___ (preparar) un currículum. Luego, sugiero que tú y yo
___**5**___ (leer) tu currículum juntos y que ___**6**___ (hablar) de las posibilidades que
hay. Si quieres, te puedo buscar un puesto en el banco donde trabajo, pero es necesario
que ___**7**___ (tener/tú) paciencia. Mi jefa es una persona muy seca y callada. Si te dan
una entrevista con ella, sugiero que ___**8**___ (tratar/tú) de contestar sus preguntas de
la forma más breve posible. ¡Y no le gusta esperar! Su secretario siempre nos dice que
___**9**___ (llegar) con mucha anticipación a las citas. Y otra cosa: te recomiendo que
___**10**___ (comprar) una corbata y una chaqueta nuevas. Hay que vestirse bien para las
entrevistas.

Answers

5
1. haremos
2. vendrá
3. saldremos
4. tendrá
5. iremos
6. necesitaremos
7. Trabajaré, Pondré
8. podré
9. harán, encontrarán
10. Te quedarás, viajarás

6
1. empieces
2. hagas
3. pidas
4. preparen
5. leamos
6. hablemos
7. tengas
8. trates
9. lleguemos
10. compres

Communication for All Students

Additional Practice

6 Have the class sit in a circle. One student makes a recommendation about job interviews. A second repeats the recommendation and adds a new one, and so forth around the circle. If someone cannot remember the order or content of previous recommendations, or cannot add a new one, he or she moves out of the circle. Continue until only one or two students are left.

Building on Previous Skills

7 Have students rewrite each of their answers for Activity 7, but substituting **Hay muchas personas…** and **No hay nadie…** with phrases referring to specific or unknown people. (**Tengo unos amigos…; Escogimos a la persona…; No conozco a ninguna persona…; Buscamos a alguien…**)

7 You work in the personnel department of a large company. Right now several departments are looking for employees with different skills. Explain if there are or are not people in your applicant pool with the following qualifications. Remember that the subjunctive is used in the **que** clause to describe someone or something unknown or nonexistent. (**p. 355**)

MODELO   **querer trabajar de noche (sí)**
          Hay muchas personas que quieren trabajar de noche.
          querer trabajar los fines de semana (no)
          No hay nadie que quiera trabajar los fines de semana.

1. tener computadora en casa (sí)
2. tener 10 años de experiencia trabajando con computadoras (no)
3. ser ingeniero(a) (no)
4. ser contador(a) (sí)
5. saber algo de diseño (sí)
6. saber algo de carpintería (no)
7. hablar portugués y japonés (no)
8. hablar inglés y español (sí)
9. haber trabajado como técnico(a) (no)
10. haber trabajado como periodista (sí)

8 Completa las frases de las aspiraciones de todos. Lee las frases con cuidado para decidir si debes usar el imperfecto del subjuntivo o el condicional. (**p. 357**)

MODELO   **Si Andrea ═══ (ser) arquitecta, ═══ (diseñar) casas para los pobres.**
          Si Andrea fuera arquitecta, diseñaría casas para los pobres.

1. Si yo ═══ (poder) ser comerciante, creo que me ═══ (gustar) mucho.
2. ¿Uds. ═══ (viajar) mucho si ═══ (tener) su propia empresa?
3. Si Miguel ═══ (estudiar) medicina en la universidad, él ═══ (poder) ser un científico famoso algún día.
4. Él ═══ (descubrir) curas para muchas enfermedades si ═══ (trabajar) en un laboratorio.
5. ¿Raquel ═══ (dedicarse) a las artes si eso ═══ (ser) posible?
6. Pero si ella les ═══ (decir) a sus padres que quiere ser artista, ellos ═══ (estar) muy enfadados con ella.
7. Martín, creo que tú ═══ (ser) un maestro excelente si ═══ (enfocarse) más en los estudios.
8. Si tú ═══ (hacerse) maestro, ¿═══ (abrir) tu propia escuela?
9. Creo que si tú y yo no ═══ (hacer) un gran esfuerzo, no ═══ (lograr) graduarnos en la universidad en tres años.
10. Y si nosotros no ═══ (tener) que pagar un año más de clases en la universidad, entonces ═══ (poder) usar el dinero para otras cosas.

Answers

7
1. Hay varias personas que tienen computadora en casa.
2. No hay nadie que tenga 10 años de experiencia trabajando con computadoras.
3. No hay nadie que sea ingeniero(a).
4. Hay varias personas que son contadores.
5. Hay varias personas que saben algo de diseño.
6. No hay nadie que sepa algo de carpintería.
7. No hay nadie que hable portugués y japonés.
8. Hay varias personas que hablan inglés y español.
9. No hay nadie que haya trabajado como técnico(a).
10. Hay varias personas que han trabajado como periodista.

8
1. pudiera, gustaría
2. viajarían, tuvieran
3. estudiara, podría
4. descubriría, trabajara
5. se dedicaría, fuera
6. dijera, estarían
7. serías, te enfocaras
8. te hicieras, abrirías
9. hiciéramos, lograríamos
10. tuviéramos, podríamos

Review and Assess

You may wish to assign the **Más práctica gramatical** activities as additional practice or homework after presenting material throughout the chapter. Assign Activity 1 after **Vocabulario** (p. 347); Activities 2–4 after **Gramática de repaso** (p. 348); Activity 5 after **¿Te acuerdas?** (p. 349); Activity 6 after **Gramática de repaso** (p. 354);

Activity 7 after **Gramática de repaso** (p. 355); and Activity 8 after **Gramática de repaso** (p. 357). To prepare students for the **Paso** Quizzes and Chapter Test have them do the **Más práctica gramatical** activities in the following order: complete Activities 1–5 before taking Quiz 12-1A or 12-1B; and Activities 6–8 before taking Quiz 12-2A or 12-2B.

Repaso

CAPÍTULO 12

The **Repaso** reviews all four skills and culture in preparation for the Chapter Test.

Teaching Resources
pp. 368–369

PRINT
▸ Lesson Planner, p. 61
▸ Listening Activities, p. 93
▸ Video Guide, pp. 80, 82, 85
▸ Grammar Tutor for Students of Spanish, Chapter 12
▸ Cuaderno para hispanohablantes, pp. 56–60
▸ Standardized Assessment Tutor, Chapter 12

MEDIA
▸ One-Stop Planner
▸ Video Program, Videocassette 4, 42:49–43:54
▸ Audio Compact Discs, CD 12, Tr. 18
▸ Interactive CD-ROM Tutor, Disc 3

Repaso

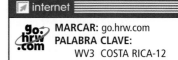

MARCAR: go.hrw.com
PALABRA CLAVE:
WV3 COSTA RICA-12

1 Escucha mientras habla Josefina de los sueños que tenía de ser arqueóloga. Luego lee las siguientes frases e indica si cada frase es **cierta, falsa** o si **no se sabe.** Si la frase es falsa, corrígela.   Script and answers on p. 297H.

CD 12
Tr. 18

1. Josefina se graduó con un doctorado en computación.

2. De niña, Josefina fue a Egipto con su familia.

3. Oyó hablar de un programa de verano en Egipto.

4. A los veinte años fue a Argentina a ver unas ruinas.

5. Cuando era niña, le gustaban mucho las ruinas antiguas.

2 Tu consejero te recomienda que escribas un párrafo sobre tus planes para el futuro. Escribe por lo menos cinco frases sobre lo que harás y lo que te gustaría hacer dentro de los próximos cinco años.

3 Júntate con tres compañeros(as) y lean los planes para el futuro que prepararon en la Actividad 2. Dales a los compañeros algunos consejos y recomendaciones sobre cómo pueden realizar sus metas.

4 See answers below.
Contesta las preguntas con información cultural de este capítulo.

1. ¿Cuál es el primer título que se puede obtener en una universidad latinoamericana?

2. ¿Cuál es la diferencia entre la licenciatura y el *bachelor's degree*?

3. ¿Qué es el ecoturismo?

4. ¿Qué esfuerzos han hecho las compañías turísticas para conservar el medio ambiente en Costa Rica?

5. ¿Cuál es el efecto del ecoturismo sobre la economía rural?

5 Termina las siguientes oraciones de una manera original para dar consejos sobre las entrevistas de empleo.

1. El día de la entrevista, es importante que...

2. Al llegar a la entrevista, debes...

3. Es importante que...

4. Durante la entrevista, te aconsejo que...

5. Al preparar las cosas que vas a llevar a la entrevista, te recomiendo que...

6. Al terminar la entrevista, es importante...

Answers
4 1. Se obtiene la licenciatura.
2. Para la licenciatura se toma un examen después de cinco años de estudios.
3. Las compañías de turismo se dedican a conservar el ambiente.
4. Han construido senderos para evitar la erosión del terreno y promueven la idea de "ver y no tocar".
5. Es de gran beneficio a la economía de zonas rurales.

Apply and Assess

Auditory Learners

2 Have students read the paragraphs they have written to a partner. Ask the partners to provide any suggestions that might improve the paragraph. Remind students to be constructive in their feedback.

Additional Practice

Have students work in pairs and ask each to tell what he or she wanted to be at age five, age ten, and what he or she wants to be now. After students have had the opportunity to talk with their partners, ask each pair to join another pair and share the information about their partners.

See answers below.

6 Lee los siguientes anuncios e indica qué puesto debe solicitar cada persona mencionada abajo.

Se Requieren 2
Diseñadores de Videojuegos
Requisitos: Licenciado en computación, 2 años de experiencia diseñando programas, creatividad. Ofrecemos: Beneficios de salud, 3 semanas de vacaciones, salario competitivo.
AQUI EN JUEGOS SANTANDER
TRABAJAR ES JUGAR
Solicite una cita al 352-8790

TALLER SAN ESTEBAN
NECESITA MECÁNICOS
Mínimo 2 años de experiencia. Especialista en coches japoneses. Entusiasmo y dedicación. Vehículo propio (preferible).
BENEFICIOS Y SALARIO
COMPETITIVO
Solicite una cita al teléfono: 352-1913

BURGER REINA
necesita
GENTE TRABAJADORA
Si tiene la motivación pero no tiene experiencia
NO SE DESESPERE
Gane un buen salario mientras gana experiencia.
HORAS FLEXIBLES • MEDIO TIEMPO O TIEMPO
COMPLETO. LLAME AL 352-9975

---

1. Ana se graduó de computación en la Universidad de Quito.

2. Hace tres años que Roberto trabaja con su padre. Sabe arreglar todo tipo de carros.

3. Laura es una persona muy creativa y muy entusiasta. Le encanta jugar a los videojuegos y salir con sus amigos pero nunca tiene dinero. Necesita un trabajo pero no tiene experiencia ni título.

4. Antonio busca un puesto con buenos beneficios y vacaciones. Estudió computación y es buen diseñador.

7 Escoge uno de los anuncios y escribe una carta para acompañar tu currículum. Escribe por lo menos tres párrafos para explicar por qué eres la mejor persona para el trabajo y por qué quieres trabajar allí.

8

Situación

Con un(a) compañero(a), escoge uno de los anuncios de arriba. Dramaticen una entrevista entre tú y el (la) gerente para solicitar el puesto que escogiste. Luego presenten la entrevista a la clase.

Cuaderno para hispanohablantes, p. 60

Apply and Assess

Visual Learners
Ask students to bring in pictures of themselves or others at various ages. Ask them also to clip magazine pictures representing various professions and activities. Have a student choose one age photo and one job or activity photo and say something about former jobs and goals relevant to those pictures. **(Cuando tenía doce años, Ramón quería trabajar en una tienda de comestibles.)**

Kinesthetic Learners
Ask one student at a time to stand up and mime his or her future plans. Call on someone from the class to say what the person's future plans are.

A ver si puedo

Teaching Resources
p. 370

PRINT
▶ Grammar Tutor for Students of Spanish, Chapter 12

MEDIA
▶ Interactive CD-ROM Tutor, Disc 3
▶ Online self-test

 go.hrw.com
WV3 COSTA RICA-12

Teacher Note
This page is intended to help students prepare for the Chapter Test. It is a brief checklist of the major points covered in the chapter. The students should be reminded that it is only a checklist and does not necessarily include everything that will appear on the Chapter Test.

Answers
1 *Possible answers:*
1. De niño, Juan Pablo llevaba los periódicos a las casas de los clientes.
2. Cuando tenía 15 años, trabajaba en la cocina de un restaurante.
3. En el año 2015, él estudió computación. Estudiaba mucho en la biblioteca.
4. Cuatro años después, consiguió su primer empleo en una compañía de computadoras.

3 *Sample answers:*
1. Scott, para conseguir empleo debes vestirte bien en un traje formal.
2. Jim, debes escuchar atentamente al entrevistador y hacerle algunas preguntas.
3. Raquel, debes llevar contigo una carpeta con todos tus papeles bien organizados.
4. Lily, para conseguir un empleo debes mostrar interés y hacer algunas preguntas.
5. Rosalinda, debes pedirles cartas de referencia a tus profesores.

A ver si puedo...

Can you talk about former jobs and goals? p. 347

See possible answers below.

1 Imagina que es el año 2025. Juan Pablo está pensando en su juventud y los trabajos que tenía. Mira los siguientes dibujos y describe lo que pasa en cada dibujo. Usa expresiones de **Así se dice** para indicar cuándo ocurre cada cosa.

niñez

edad: 15 años

2015

2019

Can you talk about future career plans? p. 349

2 Indica los planes de cada persona para el futuro. Usa diferentes expresiones para cada persona. *Possible answers:*
1. Mónica: sicóloga Mónica estudiará para sicóloga.
2. Rosana: escritora para una revista Rosana piensa ser escritora para una revista.
3. Robert: arquitecto Robert va a ser arquitecto.
4. Víctor Alejandro: banquero A Víctor Alejandro le gustaría ser banquero.
5. Justina: diseñadora Justina quiere llegar a ser diseñadora.

Can you give advice about job interviews? p. 354

3 Dales consejos a las siguientes personas para que tengan éxito en sus entrevistas de trabajo. See sample answer below.
1. Scott no sabe qué ropa debe llevar para su entrevista.
2. Jim quiere causar buena impresión en su entrevista, pero a veces habla demasiado.
3. Raquel siempre parece estar mal preparada porque llega a las entrevistas sin su currículum.
4. Lily es buena gente y es trabajadora pero apenas habla durante una entrevista.
5. Rosalinda quiere un buen empleo pero no tiene cartas de referencia.

Review and Assess
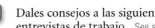

Cooperative Learning
1 Have students work in small groups. Give each group an illustration of a person carrying out a particular career. Have each group develop a story about the former jobs the person had, what his or her goals were, and how he or she got to practice the career shown in the illustration. Ask each group to select a spokesperson to report the story to the class.

Additional Practice
2 Have students conduct a survey about future career plans by interviewing ten juniors or seniors who study Spanish. Students should also ask about the interviewees' plans to use Spanish in their future careers. Ask students to report their findings in writing using a variety of expressions.

STANDARDS: 1.2

Primer paso

Professions

el (la) abogado(a)	lawyer	el (la) periodista	journalist	
el (la) arquitecto(a)	architect	el (la) policía	police officer	
el (la) banquero(a)	banker	el (la)	computer	
el (la) carpintero(a)	carpenter	programador(a)	programmer	
el (la) científico(a)	scientist	de computadoras		
el (la) comerciante	businessman	el (la) sicólogo(a)	psychologist	
	(-woman)	el (la) trabajador(a)	social worker	
el (la) contador(a)	accountant	social		
el (la) diseñador(a)	designer	el (la) vendedor(a)	salesman (-woman)	
el (la) enfermero(a)	nurse			
el (la) escritor(a)	writer			

Talking about former jobs and goals

el (la) farmacéutico(a)	pharmacist	Cuando era joven,...	When I was young, ...
el (la) ingeniero(a)	engineer	Cuando tenía cinco años,....	When I was five, ..
el (la) mecánico(a)	mechanic		
el (la) médico(a)	doctor	De niño(a),...	As a child, ...

El año pasado,...	Last year, . . .
Hace diez años,...	Ten years ago, . . .

Talking about future career plans

Buscaré...	I'll look for . . .
Me encantaría ser...	I'd love to be . . .
Me gustaría ser...	I'd like to be . . .
Me interesaría estudiar para...	I'd be interested in studying to be a . . .
Pienso trabajar en...	I intend to work in . . .
Quiero llegar a ser...	I want to become . . .
Quiero ser...	I want to be . . .
Voy a ser...	I'm going to be . . .

Segundo paso

Giving advice about job interviews

Debes...	You should . . .
Es importante que...	It's important that . . .
Lo ideal es...	The best thing is . . .
No olvides que...	Don't forget that . . .
Te aconsejo que...	I advise you to . . .
Te recomiendo que...	I recommend that you . . .

Work

actualizar	to update
el ambiente de trabajo	workplace environment

los beneficios	benefits
el currículum (vitae)	résumé
el (la) empleado(a)	employee
la empresa	business, company
el (la) gerente	manager
el horario	work hours, schedule
la jefa	boss
el jefe	boss
medio tiempo	part time, half time
el puesto (de trabajo)	position, job

los requisitos	requirements
el salario	salary
el seguro	insurance
solicitar	to apply for; to request
la solicitud	application
tiempo completo	full time

Review and Assess

Game
ADIVINANZA Write each of the nouns in **Vocabulario** on a small sheet of paper and put the papers in a hat or container. Divide the class into two teams. The first player on Team One draws a word and gives a definition in Spanish without using the word itself. If his or her teammates can guess the word, Team One receives a point. Team Two then takes a turn. The team with the most points at the end of play wins.

C A P Í T U L O   1 2

Teaching Suggestion
Ask the students to create a story (**un cuento loco**) by using the vocabulary words in original sentences. Ask the first student to use a vocabulary word or expression in an original sentence. Another student adds an original sentence using another vocabulary word. Continue with the rest of the class until all the words have been used. As a word or expression is used, write it on the board so that none is used more than once.

 Circumlocution
Write the name of a profession and ask one student to come forward so that you can secretly reveal the profession to him or her. The class must try to guess what his or her profession is by asking **sí** or **no** questions. The student who correctly guesses the profession is the next to come forward.

Chapter 12 Assessment

▸ **Testing Program**
Chapter Test, pp. 265–270
 Audio Compact Discs, CD 12, Trs. 21–22

Speaking Test, p. 300

Final Exam, pp. 279–286
Score Sheet, pp. 287–289
Audio Compact Discs, CD 12, Trs. 23–26

▸ **Alternative Assessment Guide**
Portfolio Assessment, p. 27
Performance Assessment, p. 41
CD-ROM Assessment, p. 55

▸ **Interactive CD-ROM Tutor, Disc 3**
 ¡A hablar!
¡A escribir!

▸ **Standardized Assessment Tutor**
Chapter 12

▸ **One-Stop Planner, Disc 3**
Test Generator
Chapter 12

Reference Section

Summary of Functions

Functions are probably best defined as the ways in which you use a language for particular purposes. When you find yourself in specific situations, such as in a restaurant, in a grocery store, or at a school, you will want to communicate with those around you. In order to do that, you have to "function" in Spanish: you place an order, make a purchase, or talk about your class schedule.

Such functions form the core of this book. They are easily identified by the boxes in each chapter that are labeled **Así se dice**. These functional phrases are the building blocks you need to become a speaker of Spanish. All the other features in the chapter—the grammar, the vocabulary, even the culture notes—are there to support the functions you are learning.

Here is a list of the functions and the Spanish expressions you'll need in order to communicate in a wide range of situations. Following each function is a Roman numeral I, II, or III to indicate Levels 1, 2, or 3, along with the chapter and page where it was introduced.

Socializing

Saying hello
I, Ch. 1, p. 21

Buenos días.	Buenas noches.
Buenas tardes.	Hola.

Saying goodbye
I, Ch. 1, p. 21

Adiós.	Hasta luego.
Bueno, tengo clase.	Hasta mañana.
Chao.	Tengo que irme.

Introducing people and responding to an introduction
I, Ch. 1, p. 22

Me llamo...	Se llama...
Soy...	¡Mucho gusto!
¿Cómo te llamas?	Encantado(a).
Éste es mi amigo...	Igualmente.
Ésta es mi amiga...	

Introducing yourself and others
II, Ch. 1, p. 9

Éste es...	Soy...
Ésta es...	Tengo... años.
Me llamo...	Tiene... años.
Se llama...	

Introducing and changing a topic of conversation
III, Ch. 6, p. 162

¿Has leído algo de...?
Eso me recuerda...
Eso me hace pensar en...
Cambiando de tema, ¿qué me dices de...?
Hablando de..., ¿qué me cuentas de...?
A propósito, ¿qué has oído de...?

Asking how someone is and saying how you are
I, Ch. 1, p. 24

¿Cómo estás?	Estupendo.
¿Y tú?	Excelente.
¿Qué tal?	Regular.
Estoy (bastante) bien, gracias.	Más o menos.
	(Muy) mal.
Yo también.	¡Horrible!

Talking on the telephone
I, Ch. 7, p. 207

Aló.	La línea está ocupada.
Diga.	¿Puedo dejar un recado?
¿Quién habla?	Un momento...
¿Está..., por favor?	Llamo más tarde.
¿De parte de quién?	

Extending and accepting invitations
I, Ch. 7, p. 208

¿Te gustaría...?	¿Quieres...?
Sí, me gustaría...	Te invito.
Nos gustan...	¡Claro que sí!

Making plans
I, Ch. 7, p. 212

¿Qué piensas hacer hoy?	Pienso...
	¿Piensas...?

II, Ch. 4, p. 111

Pienso...	Sí, me encantaría.
De acuerdo.	Mejor...
Paso por ti...	Muy bien. Entonces
Si quieres...	quedamos en vernos...

Talking about getting ready
I, Ch. 7, p. 214

¿Estás listo(a)?	No, todavía necesito...
No, porque necesito...	

Turning down an invitation and explaining why
I, Ch. 7, p. 217

¡Qué lástima!	Tengo una cita.
Ya tengo planes.	Tengo que...
Tal vez otro día.	Me gustaría, pero no puedo.
Lo siento, pero no.	Estoy cansado(a) y un poco enfermo(a).
Estoy ocupado(a).	

Turning down an invitation
III, Ch. 6, p. 172

Gracias por invitarme, pero no puedo.
Lo siento, pero ya tengo otros planes.
Tengo muchas cosas que hacer.
Hagámoslo mañana.
La próxima vez iré.
¿Por qué no lo dejamos para...?
No tengo ganas de...

Giving an explanation
II, Ch. 5, p. 143

Bueno, es que...
Iba a... pero no pude.
No me dieron permiso.

Saying why you couldn't do something
II, Ch. 8, p. 230

Quería... pero no pude. Tenía que...
Esperaba... pero no pude.
Pensaba...

Bargaining in a market
II, Ch. 9, p. 269

¿Qué precio tiene...?
¿Cuánto vale...?
¿Me puede rebajar el precio?
¿En cuánto lo deja?
Se lo regalo por 15 dólares pero es mi última oferta.
Aquí no se puede regatear; tenemos precios fijos.
A Ud. se lo doy por 20 dólares.

EXCHANGING INFORMATION

Asking and saying how old someone is
I, Ch. 1, p. 27

¿Cuántos años tienes?	¿Cuántos años tiene?
Tengo... años.	Tiene... años.

Asking where someone is from and saying where you're from
I, Ch. 1, p. 28

¿De dónde eres?	¿De dónde es...?
Soy de...	Es de...

Talking about what you want and need
I, Ch. 2, p. 52

¿Qué quieres?	¿Necesitas...?
Quiero...	Necesito...
Quiere...	Necesita...
¿Qué necesitas?	Ya tengo...
¿Qué necesita?	

Expressing what needs to be done
III, Ch. 6, p. 164

Hace falta que pintemos...	Es importante que reconozcas...
Es necesario que busquemos...	

Talking about accomplishments
III, Ch. 10, p. 285

Puse todo mi esfuerzo en...
Él domina el francés.
...se siente orgulloso(a) de haber...
...logró superar muchos obstáculos...
...tuvo mucho éxito...
Alcancé éxito en...
Ellas han triunfado en...

Describing the contents of your room
I, Ch. 2, p. 57

¿Qué hay en tu cuarto?
(No) tengo... en mi cuarto.
¿Qué hay en el cuarto de...?
Hay... en su cuarto.
¿Tienes...?
¿Qué tiene... en su cuarto?
Tiene... en su cuarto.

Talking about what you need and want to do
I, Ch. 2, p. 60

¿Qué necesitas hacer?	¿Qué quieres hacer?
Necesito...	Quiero hacer...
¿Qué necesita hacer...?	¿Qué quiere hacer...?
Necesita...	No sé, pero no quiero...
	Quiere...

Talking about classes and sequencing events
I, Ch. 3, p. 84

¿Qué clases tienes este semestre?	Primero tengo..., después... y luego...
Tengo...	¿Y cuándo tienes un día libre?
¿Qué clases tienes hoy?	Mañana, por fin...

Telling time
I, Ch. 3, p. 85

¿Qué hora es?	Son las... y cuarto.
Es la una.	Son las... y media.
Es la una y cuarto.	¿Ya son las...?

Es la una y media.   Es tarde.
Son las...

Telling at what time something happens
I, Ch. 3, p. 88

¿A qué hora es...?   ¡Es ahora!
(Es) a las... de la   Es a las... en punto.
  tarde.

Talking about being late or in a hurry
I, Ch. 3, p. 90

Estoy atrasado(a).   Tengo prisa.
Está atrasado(a).   ¡Date prisa!

Describing people and things
I, Ch. 3, p. 92

¿Cómo es...?   ¿Cómo son...?
Es...   Son...
No es...   No son...

I, Ch. 6, p. 178

¿Cómo es...?   ¿De qué color es...?
Tiene...   ¿De qué color son...?

II, Ch. 1, p. 10

Mido...   Tengo ojos de color...
Mide...   Tiene pelo...

Describing yourself and others
III, Ch. 1, p. 17

Tiene bigote y barba, y es calvo.
Es pelirrojo(a) y tiene el pelo rizado.
Es de estatura mediana y lleva gafas.
Es serio(a) pero es muy buena gente.
Es pesado(a).
Es un(a) tío(a) estupendo(a).
¡No hay quien lo (la) aguante!
Es muy abierto(a) y tiene un buen sentido del
  humor.

Talking about what you and others do during free time
I, Ch. 4, p. 114

¿Qué haces después de clases?
Antes de regresar a casa...
En el tiempo libre...
¡Descanso!
Toco la guitarra.
Jugamos al...

I, Ch. 4, p. 123

¿Adónde vas?   ¿Adónde va...?
Voy a...   Va a/al/a la...

II, Ch. 1, p. 15

¿Qué haces los fines de semana?
¿Adónde van?
¿A qué hora salen?

Telling where people and things are
I, Ch. 4, p. 118

¿Dónde estás?   ¿No está en...?
Estoy en...   No, no está aquí. Está en...

Discussing how often you do things
I, Ch. 5, p. 145

¿Con qué   ¿Todavía...?
  frecuencia...?   Durante la semana...
Todos los días...   A veces...
Siempre...   Muchas veces...
Nunca...   Sólo cuando...

Talking about your daily routine
I, Ch. 5, p. 151

¿Qué haces típicamente durante el día?
¿Qué hace... por la mañana?
¿Qué hacen... por la tarde?
¿Qué hacen... por la noche?

II, Ch. 3, p. 73

¿Cómo es un día típico?
¿Cuánto tiempo gastas en...?
¿...todos los días?
Por lo general,...
Normalmente, gasto mucho tiempo en...
Sí, siempre.
A veces.
Nunca.

Giving today's date
I, Ch. 5, p. 154

¿Cuál es la fecha?   Hoy es el primero de...
Qué fecha es hoy?   Hoy es el... de...
El cuatro de este
  mes hay...

Talking about the weather
I, Ch. 5, p. 156

¿Qué tiempo hace?
Hace buen tiempo.
Hace muy mal tiempo hoy.

Describing a family
I, Ch. 6, p. 174

¿Cuántas personas hay en tu familia?
Somos cinco.
Hay... en mi familia.
¿Cómo es tu familia?
Somos muy unidos.
Tenemos...

Discussing things a family does together
I, Ch. 6, p. 180

¿Qué hacen Uds. los fines de semana?
¿Hacen Uds. algo durante el verano?

Talking about meals and food
I, Ch. 8, p. 235

¿Qué tomas para el desayuno?
¿Qué tomas para el almuerzo?
A veces tomo...
No me gusta... para nada.
Tengo sed. ¿Qué hay para tomar?
¿Qué prefieres?

Ordering dinner in a restaurant
I, Ch. 8, p. 246

¿Qué vas a pedir?   ¿Qué le puedo traer?
Voy a pedir...   Yo quisiera...

II, Ch. 6, p. 172

¿Ya sabe(n) qué va(n) a pedir?
Recomiendo la especialidad de la casa.
¿Qué le(s) traigo de tomar?
¿Qué desea(n) de postre?
¿Se le(s) ofrece algo más?
No. ¿Qué me recomienda?
Está bien, pero no está muy picante, ¿verdad?
Para mí,...
Por favor, me trae...
No, gracias, sólo la cuenta.

Asking for and paying the bill in a restaurant
I, Ch. 8, p. 246

¿Nos puede traer la cuenta?
La cuenta, por favor.
¿Desean algo más?
¿Cuánto es?
¿Está incluida la propina?
No, no está incluida. Es aparte.

Discussing gift suggestions
I, Ch. 9, p. 269

¿Qué piensas regalarle a...?
Le voy a dar...
¿Para quién es el regalo?
El regalo es para...
¿Qué tipo de regalo buscas?
Busco...

Asking for and giving directions
I, Ch. 9, p. 271

Perdón, ¿dónde está...?
Está a... cuadras de aquí.
¿Me puede decir dónde queda...?
Queda al lado de...

II, Ch. 9, p. 258

Disculpe, ¿vamos bien para...?
No, van mal. Hay que seguir derecho hasta...
   No se puede perder.
Perdón, ¿dónde queda...?
Queda a la izquierda, junto al...

¿Cómo se va...?
Tome esta calle hasta llegar al... y doble a la
   derecha. Allí se encuentra...

Making comparisons
I, Ch. 9, p. 277

¿Cuál es más barato?
El... cuesta menos.
El... es más caro.
¿Son los... tan caros como el...?
Son del mismo precio.

II, Ch. 4, p. 107

más... que...   ...mejor que...
menos... que...   ...menor que...
...mayor que...   ...peor que...

Asking about prices and paying for something
I, Ch. 9, p. 280

¿Cuánto cuesta...?   ¿Cuánto cuestan...?
Cuesta...   Cuestan...

Talking about what you are doing right now
I, Ch. 10, p. 298

¿Qué estás haciendo?
Estoy colgando las decoraciones.
Él está limpiando la sala.
¿Todos están decorando la casa?
Sí, estamos decorando la casa.

Talking about past events
I, Ch. 10, p. 307

¿Qué hiciste anoche?
Bailé y hablé con...
¿Qué hizo... ayer?
¿Lo pasaron bien la semana pasada?
Sí, lo pasamos bien.

Saying what you did
I, Ch. 11, p. 340

¿Qué hiciste anoche?
Jugué...
¿Ganaste?
Jugó...

Talking about what has happened
III, Ch. 3, p. 72

Caracas ha cambiado...
Mucha gente ha venido...
La contaminación del aire ha empeorado...

Talking about where you went and when
I, Ch. 11, p. 342

¿Adónde fuiste anteayer?
¿Adónde fuiste anteanoche?
Anoche fui...

Talking about what you do and like to do every day
I, Ch. 12, p. 361

¿Qué haces todos los días?
Primero...
Después...
Y luego...

¿Con qué frecuencia...?
¿Qué te gusta hacer después de clases?
Me gusta...

Making future plans
I, Ch. 12, p. 362

¿Adónde piensas viajar algún día?
¿Quieres viajar a...?
No, pero espero hacer un viaje a...
¿Qué vas a hacer este verano?

Talking about future career plans
III, Ch. 12, p. 349

Me gustaría ser...
Buscaré...
Voy a ser...
Quiero ser...
Pienso trabajar en...

Me interesaría estudiar para...
Quiero llegar a ser...
Me encantaría ser...

Talking about future events
III, Ch. 3, p. 78

El futuro va a ser...
Va a haber...
Todo va a estar...
Mañana recogemos...
La comunicación entre países mejorará...
Más gente va a usar...
Todo el mundo hablará...

Talking about future plans
III, Ch. 10, p. 288

Cuando sea mayor...
Cuando cumpla los 18 años...
Antes de que empiecen las clases...
Antes de terminar...
Después de graduarnos...

Saying where you went and what you did on vacation
I, Ch. 12, p. 371

¿Adónde viajaste el verano pasado?
No fui a ningún lugar.
¿Adónde fueron durante las vacaciones?
Fuimos a...
¿Qué hiciste cuando fuiste a...?

Saying if something has already been done
II, Ch. 2, p. 42

¿Ya...?
Sí, ya...

No, todavía no.

Describing your city or town
II, Ch. 2, p. 49

Mi ciudad es...
Está lejos del océano.
En el centro, hay...

Está cerca de las montañas.
En el invierno, hace...

Talking about responsibilities
II, Ch. 3, p. 77

¿A quién le toca?
Le toca a...

Me toca a mí.
Te toca a ti.

III, Ch. 3, p. 81

Hay que...
Nos toca a nosotros...
Tanto los jóvenes como... deben...
Es nuestra responsabilidad...
Estamos obligados a...
Es nuestro deber...

Talking about hobbies and pastimes
II, Ch. 3, p. 81

En tus ratos libres, ¿qué te gusta hacer?
¿Cuál es tu pasatiempo favorito?
Estoy loco(a) por...
Me interesan...

Saying how long something has been going on
II, Ch. 3, p. 82

¿Cuánto tiempo hace que...?
Hace... que...
Empecé...

Talking about things and people you know
II, Ch. 4, p. 106

¿Conoces a...?
¿Conoces...?

No, no los conozco.

Talking about staying fit and healthy
II, Ch. 5, p. 134

¿Qué haces para estar en plena forma?
¿Duermes lo suficiente?
Es preciso...
Sigo una dieta sana y balanceada.
Dormí por ocho horas.
Sí, ya lo sé. También es importante...

Talking about taking care of yourself
III, Ch. 2, p. 44

Le echo mucha sal a la comida.
Hago ejercicio (aeróbico)...
Me quedo frente a la tele.
Duermo lo suficiente.
Estoy a dieta.
Me peso...
Comparto mis problemas...
Me siento muy solo(a).

Tengo buenos hábitos de alimentación.
Como comida sana.
Para no broncearme, me pongo crema protectora.
Me mantengo en forma.

Asking for and giving information
II, Ch. 6, p. 164
¿Sabe Ud...?
¿Me podría decir...?
¿Sabes...?
Disculpe,...
Sí, claro.
Por supuesto.
No estoy seguro(a). Lo puedes averiguar...
Lo siento, pero no tengo ni idea.

Asking for information
III, Ch. 1, p. 16

¿Quién...?	¿Qué...?
¿Por qué...?	¿Cuándo...?
¿De dónde...?	¿Dónde...?
¿Cuántos...?	¿Cómo?

Expressing cause and effect
III, Ch. 10, p. 293
Mis éxitos se deben a...
Soy bilingüe; por lo tanto...
Por tener padres hispanos...
No estudié, así que...
Las leyes han cambiado de tal forma que...
Sé español y portugués; en consecuencia...
Discutimos el problema; por consiguiente...
Las acciones de los líderes resultaron en...

Expressing intention and purpose
III, Ch. 10, p. 295
Pienso...
Tengo la intención de...
Escribieron la carta con la intención de...
Fuimos allí con la idea de...
Quiere visitar Chile para...
Vamos a eliminar los estereotipos para que...

Relating a series of events
II, Ch. 6, p. 168

Para empezar...	Después...
Primero...	Luego...
A continuación...	Por último...

Using conversational fillers
III, Ch. 3, p. 75

Bueno...	A ver...
Este...	Pues...
La verdad es que...	Eh...

Talking about what you used to do
II, Ch. 7, p. 196
Cuando era niño(a),...
De niño(a),...
De pequeño(a),...
De chiquito(a),...
Cuando era joven,...
Cuando tenía trece años,...

Talking about former jobs and goals
III, Ch. 12, p. 347
Hace diez años, trabajé...
Cuando tenía cinco años, quería ser...
El año pasado, trabajé...
Cuando era joven, quería...
De niño(a), vendía...

Describing what people and things were like
II, Ch. 7, p. 202
¿Cómo era... en aquel entonces?
¿Cómo era... en aquellos tiempos?
En aquella época... era...
En mis tiempos era...

Using comparisons to describe people
II, Ch. 7, p. 206
Tan bueno(a) como un ángel.
Tan feliz como una lombriz.
Tan noble como un perro.
Tan fuerte como un toro.
Tan aburrido(a) como un pato.
Dormía tan bien como un lirón.

Describing a past event
II, Ch. 8, p. 225

¿Qué tal lo pasaste?	Lo pasé de maravilla.
	De película.
¿Qué tal estuvieron...?	Aburridísimo(a).
¿Cómo estuvo...?	Más o menos bien.
¿Cómo te fue?	

Talking about unintentional events
III, Ch. 4, p. 103

Se me perdieron...	¿Se te olvidaron...?
Se me acabó...	Se nos cayeron...
Se nos descompuso...	Se me rompió...
	Se les quedó...

Reporting what someone said
II, Ch. 8, p. 235

¿Qué dijo?	Dijo que...
¿Qué te dijeron?	Me dijeron que...

Talking about how clothes look and fit
II, Ch. 9, p. 265
¿Cómo te queda...?
¿Cómo me veo...?

Me queda un poco estrecho(a).
Te ves guapísimo(a). ...está muy de moda.
De verdad, no hace juego con...

Setting the scene for a story
II, Ch. 10, p. 289

Estaba soleado en el valle.
Eran... (with time)
...jugaban... cantaban... estaba enfermo(a).
Se sentía muy mal.
Érase una vez...
Hace mucho tiempo...
Se cuenta que...

Continuing and ending a story
II, Ch. 10, p. 295

En seguida...	Por eso...
De repente...	Al final...
Fue cuando...	Así que...
Entonces...	En fin...

Talking about the latest news
II, Ch. 10, p. 299

Oye, ¿has oído hablar de...?	No, dime.
	¡Qué va!
Fíjate, leí que...	No, cuéntamelo todo.
¿Te enteraste de...?	

Describing a problem
II, Ch. 11, p. 322

Hay demasiado ruido.
Es uno de los problemas más graves.
Lo malo es que...
Cada vez hay más... y menos...
El sistema no funciona.
¿No podemos hacer nada para mejorar la situación?
Estoy preocupado(a) por...

Pointing out problems and their consequences
III, Ch. 11, p. 319

Me he fijado en...
Se dice que...
Según el gobierno...
Si no actuamos ahora..., va a empeorarse.
Si no hacemos nada por..., temo que el deterioro continúe.
Si no realizamos campañas preventivas, lo lamentaremos.

Talking about how you would solve a problem
III, Ch. 11, p. 321

Me dedicaría a...	Intentaría iniciar...
Propongo...	Yo empezaría por...
Habrá que...	La solución que planteo es...

Exchanging the latest news
II, Ch. 12, p. 351

¿Sabes si...?	¿Sigues trabajando tanto?
¿Qué noticias tienes de...?	¿Ya sabías que...?
	No lo vas a creer, pero...

Talking about where you went and what you did
II, Ch. 12, p. 352

¿Adónde fuiste el verano pasado?	Fui a la costa.
	No hice nada.
¿Qué hiciste?	Me hice amigo(a) de...

Telling when something happened
II, Ch. 12, p. 353

El viernes...	Dos días después...
Al día siguiente...	Una semana entera...
El día anterior...	

Describing places
II, Ch. 12, p. 358

Quedé muy impresionado(a) con...
Me pareció lindísimo(a)...
Está rodeado(a) de colinas.
El clima es muy seco y hace bastante calor.

Saying when you're going to do something
II, Ch. 12, p. 360

(La semana/El mes) que viene...	Algún día...
	Dentro de...
Para fines de...	Cuando vuelva a...
Pronto...	Inmediatamente.

EXPRESSING ATTITUDES AND OPINIONS

Talking about likes and dislikes
I, Ch. 1, p. 32

¿Qué te gusta?	Me gusta (más)...
¿Te gusta...?	No me gusta...

I, Ch. 3, p. 95

¿Te gustan...?	Sí, a ella le gustan mucho.
Sí, me gustan.	¿Por qué?
¿Cuál es...?	Porque...
¿A ella le gustan...?	

II, Ch. 1, p. 21

Me fascina...
Sí, me encantan.
No me gustan para nada.
Me chocan...

Expressing interest, indifference, and displeasure
III, Ch. 1, p. 9

Estoy loco(a) por...	Me da lo mismo.
Me la paso...	No me importa.

Soy un(a) gran
   aficionado(a) a...
Soy un(a)
   fanático(a) de...
Me da igual.

Como quieras.
¡Qué paliza!
Estoy harto(a) de...
Me parece un rollo.
No me interesa para nada.

Talking about what you like to do
I, Ch. 4, p. 113

¿Qué te gusta hacer?
Me gusta...
¿A él le gusta...?
No, no le gusta..., pero le gusta...
¿A quién le gusta...?
A mí me gusta...
Por eso me gustan...

Talking about what you and your friends like to do together
I, Ch. 5, p. 148

¿Qué les gusta
   hacer?
Nos gusta...

¿Les gusta... juntos?
Especialmente durante las
   vacaciones...

Discussing problems and giving advice
I, Ch. 6, p. 184

Tengo un
   problema.
Dice que... pero
   no es cierto.

¿Qué debo hacer?
Debes... menos.
Debes... más.

II, Ch. 4, p. 101

Deberías...
Hay que...

Debes...
Es importante...

Asking for and giving advice
III, Ch. 2, p. 37

¿Qué me aconsejas hacer?
Te aconsejo...
¿Qué me recomiendas hacer?
Te recomiendo...
¿Puedes darme algún consejo?
Deberías...
¿Qué debo hacer?
No debes...

Giving advice about job interviews
III, Ch. 12, p. 354

Debes...
Te recomiendo
   que...
Te aconsejo que...

Lo ideal es...
No olvides que...
Es importante que...

Commenting on food
I, Ch. 8, p. 240

¿Cómo está...?
Está...

¿Cómo están...?
Están...

Talking about how food tastes
III, Ch. 4, p. 101

Le falta sal/sabor/no sé que.
Tiene sabor a...
Lleva mucho(a)...
Está echado(a) a perder.
Me cae gordo.
¡Guácala!
¡Qué asco!
¡Qué bueno(a)/sabroso(a)!
Sabe riquísimo.
Está en su punto.

Commenting on clothes
I, Ch. 9, p. 274

¿Qué ropa vas a llevar?
¡Lo de siempre!
¿No tienes algo más formal?
Prefiero llevar ropa cómoda.

Expressing preferences
I, Ch. 9, p. 279

¿Cuál de estos... prefieres?
Prefiero el azul.
¿Qué camisa te gusta más? ¿La verde
   o la amarilla?
La verde. Además, te queda muy bien.

Asking for and giving an opinion
I, Ch. 10, p. 300

¿Crees que...?
Creo que sí.
¿Qué te parece si...?

Me parece bien.
Perfecto.
Buena idea.

II, Ch. 4, p. 100

¿Qué te parece...?
¿Te parece que...?
¿Crees que...?
¿En tu opinión...?

Me parece...
Sí, me parece que...
No, yo creo que...
Sí, para mí...

Expressing an opinion
III, Ch. 6, p. 165

¿Qué opinas de...?
Lo encuentro...
Admiro mucho su arte.
¿Qué te parece...?
Para ser sincero(a), me parece que...
Me deja frío(a).
¿Qué piensas de...?
Para decir la verdad, me cae gordo.
No lo (la) soporto.

Expressing an assumption
III, Ch. 9, p. 264

Me imagino que...
Supongo que...

Tengo entendido que...
Tengo la impresión de
   que...

Making hypothetical statements
III, Ch. 9, p. 264

Si pudieras..., ¿adónde irías?
Si pudiera, viviría en...
Si fueras..., ¿qué harías?
Si tuviera..., compraría...

Talking about hypothetical situations
III, Ch. 11, p. 326

Qué bonito sería, si hubiera paz...
¿Qué harías..., si tuvieras...?
Sería maravilloso si se encontrara una
   cura para...
Si fuera..., hablaría...
Si yo viviera..., sólo usaría...
Si tú pudieras..., ¿qué cambiarías?

Expressing and supporting a point of view
III, Ch. 3, p. 74

...ten en cuenta que...
Me imagino que...
Lo que noto es que...
Me parece que...
Se me hace que...
Lo que es importante es...
Creo que vale la pena...
Es cierto que..., pero por otro lado...

Talking about hopes and wishes
III, Ch. 5, p. 141

Esperamos...	Era una de mis grandes
Espero que...	ambiciones.
Ojalá que...	Tenía muchas esperanzas
El sueño de mi	de...
vida...	Los dioses quieren que...

Expressing doubt and disbelief
III, Ch. 8, p. 225

Dudo que...
Parece mentira que...
No estoy seguro(a) que...
No creo que...
No puedo creer que...
Es increíble que...

Expressing certainty
III, Ch. 8, p. 227

Es cierto que...
Estoy seguro(a) que...
Estoy convencido(a) que...
Sin duda alguna.
No cabe la menor duda.
Por cierto.
Por supuesto.
Claro que...
Todo el mundo sabe que...

Es evidente que...
Es obvio que...

Talking about possibility and impossibility
III, Ch. 8, p. 232

Es posible que...	Es fácil que...
Posiblemente...	Es difícil que...
Puede ser que...	Es probable que...
Quizás/Tal vez/	Es imposible que...
A lo mejor...	

Reporting what others say and think
III, Ch. 5, p. 135

Alguien me dijo	Se cree que...
que...	Oí que...
Cuentan que	Según (la leyenda),
una mujer...	un hombre...
Dicen que...	Supuestamente...
Se dice que...	

Discussing what you would like to do on vacation
I, Ch. 12, p. 367

¿Qué te gustaría hacer este verano?
A mí me gustaría...
¿Adónde te gustaría ir este verano?
¿Qué tienes ganas de hacer?
Tengo ganas de...

Saying what you used to like and dislike
II, Ch. 7, p. 198

¿Odiabas...?	Lo encontraba genial.
¿Te molestaba...?	Me fastidiaba.
¿Te parecía	No, me fascinaba.
pesado...?	No, me caía mal.
¿Te caía bien...?	

Reacting to news
II, Ch. 10, p. 300

¡No me digas!	Bueno, no me extraña.
¿De veras?	Lo dudo.
¡No lo puedo creer!	No puede ser.
¿Tú crees?	Y eso, ¿qué?
¡N'hombre!	

Expressing surprise
III, Ch. 8, p. 234

¡No puede ser!	No me lo puedo creer.
¡No me digas!	No me lo esperaba.
¡Qué sorpresa!	¡No es posible!

Expressing agreement and disagreement
II, Ch. 11, p. 329

Así es la cosa.	Lo siento, pero no es así.
¡Claro que sí!	Me parece que no tienes
¡Eso es!	razón.
Estoy de acuerdo.	Mira...
Hasta cierto punto...	No estoy de acuerdo.

Sin duda (alguna).
Sí, tienes razón.
¡Al contrario!

No lo creo.
No me parece.
¡Te equivocas!

Expressing disagreement
III, Ch. 9, p. 259

Niego haberme
  burlado...
No es cierto que...
No es verdad que...

No estoy de acuerdo
  en que...

Expressing qualified agreement and disagreement
III, Ch. 5, p. 133

Estoy de acuerdo.
¡Claro que sí!
Por supuesto.
Eso es.
Así es.
¡Cómo no!
Desde luego.
Hasta cierto
  punto, sí, pero...
Pero hay que tener
  en cuenta que...
Depende de tu
  punto de vista.

¿Tú crees? No sé...
Es muy difícil de creer,
  pero es posible.
Bueno, puede ser, pero...
En efecto, parece ser así.
Al contrario.
¡Nada de eso!
¡Qué tontería!
¡Claro que no!
¡Qué va!
¡Eso es muy difícil!

Describing an ideal relationship
III, Ch. 7, p. 205

¿Qué es un buen amigo?
Debe ser alguien que...
¿Qué buscas en un(a) novio(a)?
Busco a alguien a quien le...
Busco a alguien que...
No aguanto a nadie que sea descortés.

EXPRESSING FEELINGS

Making suggestions and expressing feelings
I, Ch. 11, p. 331

¿Qué tal si...?
Gracias, pero no quiero.
En realidad no tengo ganas.
¿Qué tienes? ¿Te sientes mal?
No me siento bien.
Estoy un poco cansado(a), nada más.
Entonces, ¿por qué no...?

II, Ch. 2, p. 41

¿Por qué no...?
¿Qué tal si...?

Buena idea.
Me gustaría, pero tengo
  que...

Talking about moods and physical condition
I, Ch. 11, p. 334

¿Cómo estás?
Estoy...

Tengo gripe.
¿Qué le pasa a...?

¿Cómo te sientes?

Está preocupado(a) por
  algo.

Talking about how you're feeling
II, Ch. 2, p. 40

¿Cómo estás?
Estoy contento(a).

¿Cómo te sientes?
Me siento enfermo(a).

Talking about emotional reactions
III, Ch. 9, p. 257

¿Cómo te sentiste cuando...?
Estuve muy contento(a).
Quise...
¿Cómo se sintió cuando...?
Se alegró.
¿Se quejaron cuando...?
No, pero nos enojamos (frustramos/enfadamos).
¿Cómo se sintieron cuando...?
Se pusieron...
¿Cómo reaccionaron cuando...?
Se rieron.

Expressing happiness and unhappiness
III, Ch. 7, p. 195

Estoy contento(a).
¡Estoy en la gloria!
Estoy de buen
  humor.
Me alegro que...
Me encanta que...
Estoy encantado(a)
  que...
Estoy orgulloso(a)
  de...

Estoy decepcionado(a).
Estoy desilusionado(a).
Me siento frustrado(a).
Me frustra que...
Me dan ganas de llorar.
Estoy dolido(a).
Me duele mucho que...
Temo que...

Complaining
II, Ch. 3, p. 78

¡No es justo!
¡Ay, qué pesado!
¡Siempre me toca
  a mí!

Estoy harto(a) de...
Yo ya lo hice mil veces.

Making an apology
III, Ch. 7, p. 203

Perdóname.
Discúlpame.
Lo siento mucho,
  es que no sabía.

No lo volveré a hacer.
No lo haré más.
Lo hice sin querer.

Saying how you feel about people
II, Ch. 12, p. 356

Me cae muy bien.
Me cayó mal.

Es muy buena gente.
Me llevo muy bien con él.

Comforting someone
III, Ch. 7, p. 199

Tranquilo(a).
No te preocupes.

No hay mal que por bien
  no venga.

Lo siento mucho.
¡Ánimo!
¿Qué puedo hacer
    por ti?
Esto pasará pronto.

Mi más sentido pésame.
Comparto tu pena.
No hay mal que cien años
    dure.

PERSUADING

Making polite requests
I, Ch. 8, p. 244

Camarero(a), ¿nos puede traer..., por favor?
¿Me puede traer..., por favor?

Asking for and offering help
I, Ch. 10, p. 302

¿Me haces el
    favor de...?
Claro que sí.
¿Me ayudas a...?
Cómo no.
¿Me traes...?
¡Con mucho gusto!

Un momentito.
¿Me pasas...?
Lo siento, pero en este
    momento estoy
    ocupado(a).
Perdóname, pero...

II, Ch. 2, p. 46

¿Quieres ayudarme?
¿Puedes ayudarme a...?
Ayúdame, por favor.
¿Puedo ayudar?
¿Te ayudo a...?
¿Qué quieres que haga?

Asking for help and requesting favors
III, Ch. 4, p. 108

Por favor, ayúdame con...
¿Se las (los) llevas?
Hazme/Hágame el favor de...
¿Podrías pasar por la panadería por...?
¿Sería Ud. tan amable de dármela?

Telling a friend what to do
I, Ch. 10, p. 304

Prepara... y limpia..., ¿quieres?
De acuerdo.
Por favor, decora... y llama...
Está bien.

II, Ch. 5, p. 138

Ponte en forma.
Deja de fumar.
Ten cuidado.

No seas flojo(a).
No fumes más.
No añadas sal.

Making suggestions and recommendations
III, Ch. 6, p. 170

Te aconsejo que...
Sugiero que...
Es mejor que...
No te conviene...

No te olvides de...
¿Has pensado en...?
Sería buena/mala idea...
Le recomiendo a... que...

Asking for help in a store
II, Ch. 9, p. 264

¿Con permiso, me puede atender, por favor?
Uso el número 38...
Usa talla...
¿Me la puedo probar?
¿En qué le puedo servir?
No nos quedan.
La tenemos en...
Los probadores...

Talking about consequences
II, Ch. 11, p. 328

Por lo tanto es urgente...
Por eso...
Por consiguiente...
Si no dejamos de desperdiciar los recursos,
    podemos enfrentar una crisis.

Talking about obligations and solutions
II, Ch. 11, p. 332

Es importante conservar energía...
Es necesario cambiar nuestro estilo de vida.
Todos deberíamos...
Hay que...
No hay que desesperarse.
Podemos resolver...
¡A todos nos toca hacer algo!

This list includes additional vocabulary that you may want to use to personalize activities. If you can't find words you need here, try the Spanish-English and English-Spanish vocabulary sections beginning on page R47.

Colores *(Colors)*

amarillo(a)	*yellow*
anaranjado(a)	*orange*
azul	*blue*
blanco(a)	*white*
gris	*gray*
morado(a)	*purple*
negro(a)	*black*
pardo(a)	*brown*
rojo(a)	*red*
rosado(a)	*pink*
verde	*green*

En la Escuela *(At School)*

el almuerzo	*lunch*
el arte	*art*
el bolígrafo	*ballpoint pen*
la calculadora	*calculator*
la carpeta	*folder*
las ciencias	*science*
las ciencias sociales	*social sciences*
el colegio	*high school*
la computación	*computer science*

el cuaderno	*notebook*
el descanso	*recess, break*
un día libre	*a free day*
el diccionario	*dictionary*
el(la) director(a)	*principal*
la educación física	*physical education*
el escritorio	*desk*
la escuela primaria	*primary school*
el español	*Spanish*
el francés	*French*
la geografía	*geography*
la goma de borrar	*eraser*
el inglés	*English*
la lámpara	*lamp*
el lápiz	*pencil*
la librería	*bookstore*

el libro	*book*
las matemáticas	*mathematics*
la materia	*subject*
la mochila	*book bag, backpack*
el papel	*paper*
la preparatoria	*high school*
la regla	*ruler*
el semestre	*semester*
la tarea	*homework*

Números *(Numbers)*

cero	*zero*
uno	*one*
dos	*two*
tres	*three*
cuatro	*four*
cinco	*five*
seis	*six*
siete	*seven*
ocho	*eight*
nueve	*nine*
diez	*ten*
once	*eleven*
doce	*twelve*
trece	*thirteen*
catorce	*fourteen*
quince	*fifteen*
dieciséis	*sixteen*
diecisiete	*seventeen*
dieciocho	*eighteen*
diecinueve	*nineteen*
veinte	*twenty*
veintiuno	*twenty-one*
veintidós	*twenty-two*
treinta	*thirty*
treinta y uno	*thirty-one*
treinta y dos	*thirty-two*
cuarenta	*forty*
cincuenta	*fifty*
sesenta	*sixty*
setenta	*seventy*
ochenta	*eighty*
noventa	*ninety*
cien	*one hundred*

ciento uno	*one hundred and one*
ciento dos	*one hundred and two*
doscientos	*two hundred*
trescientos	*three hundred*
cuatrocientos	*four hundred*
quinientos	*five hundred*
seiscientos	*six hundred*
setecientos	*seven hundred*
ochocientos	*eight hundred*
novecientos	*nine hundred*
mil	*one thousand*

El Calendario *(Calendar)*

los días de la semana	*days of the week*
el lunes	*Monday*
el martes	*Tuesday*
el miércoles	*Wednesday*
el jueves	*Thursday*
el viernes	*Friday*
el sábado	*Saturday*
el domingo	*Sunday*
los meses	*months*
enero	*January*
febrero	*February*
marzo	*March*
abril	*April*
mayo	*May*
junio	*June*
julio	*July*
agosto	*August*
septiembre	*September*
octubre	*October*
noviembre	*November*
diciembre	*December*

las estaciones	*seasons*
el invierno	*winter*
el otoño	*fall*
la primavera	*spring*
el verano	*summer*

La Hora *(Telling Time)*

Es la una.	*It's one o'clock.*
¿Qué hora es?	*What time is it?*
Son las dos.	*It's two o'clock.*
¿Ya son las…?	*Is it already …?*
…y cuarto	*quarter past (the hour)*
…y media	*half past (the hour)*
…menos cuarto	*quarter to (the hour)*

Familia *(Family)*

la abuela	*grandmother*
el abuelo	*grandfather*
los abuelos	*grandparents*
el gato	*cat*
la hermana	*sister*
el hermano	*brother*
los hermanos	*brothers and sisters*
la hija	*daughter*
el hijo	*son*
los hijos	*children*
la madrastra	*stepmother*
la madre	*mother*
la media hermana	*half-sister*
el medio hermano	*half-brother*
el padrastro	*stepfather*
el padre	*father*
los padres	*parents*
el perro	*dog*
la prima, el primo	*cousin*
la tía, el tío	*aunt, uncle*

Descripciones *(Descriptions)*

cariñoso(a)	*affectionate*
de color café	*brown*
¿De qué color es(son)…?	*What color is(are)…?*
delgado(a)	*thin*
listo(a)	*smart*

mayor	*older*
menor	*younger*
los ojos	*eyes*
pelirrojo(a)	*redheaded*
moreno(a)	*dark-haired, dark-skinned*
rubio(a)	*blond*
el pelo	*hair*
un poco gordo(a)	*a little overweight*
Se ve joven.	*He(She) looks young.*
Tiene canas.	*He(She) has gray hair.*
viejo(a)	*old*
feo(a)	*ugly*
grande	*big*
guapo(a)	*good-looking*
inteligente	*intelligent*
interesante	*interesting*
malo(a)	*bad*
pequeño(a)	*small*
simpático(a)	*nice*
antipático(a)	*disagreeable*

Deportes y Pasatiempos
(Sports and Pastimes)

acampar	*to camp*
asistir a una clase de ejercicios aeróbicos	*to attend an aerobics class*
bajar el río en canoa	*to go canoeing*
el baloncesto	*basketball*
el béisbol	*baseball*
bucear	*to scuba dive*
correr	*to run*
escalar montañas	*to go mountain climbing*
escuchar música	*to listen to music*
esquiar	*to ski*
explorar	*to explore*
el fútbol	*soccer*
el fútbol norteamericano	*football*
hablar por teléfono	*to talk on the phone*
hacer ejercicio	*to exercise*

mirar la televisión	*to watch television*
nadar	*to swim*
patinar	*to skate*
pescar	*to fish*
pintar	*to paint*
saltar en paracaídas	*to go skydiving*
el tenis	*tennis*
el videojuego	*videogame*
el voleibol	*volleyball*

Ropa *(Clothing)*

los bluejeans	*bluejeans*
la blusa	*blouse*
las botas	*boots*
la bufanda	*scarf*
los calcetines	*socks*
la camisa	*shirt*
la camiseta	*T-shirt*
el cinturón	*belt*
las chancletas	*sandals, slippers*
la chaqueta	*jacket*
la corbata	*necktie*
la falda	*skirt*
los pantalones	*pants*
los pantalones cortos	*shorts*
las sandalias	*sandals*
el suéter	*sweater*
el traje	*suit*
el traje de baño	*bathing suit*
el vestido	*dress*
las zapatillas de tenis	*tennis shoes* (Spain)
el zapato	*shoe*

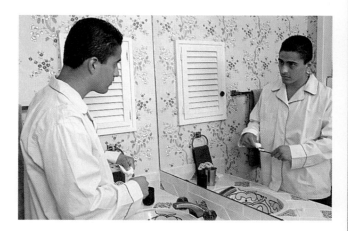

Rutina Diaria *(Daily Routine)*

afeitarse	*to shave*
ducharse	*to take a shower*
lavarse	*to wash oneself*
lavarse los dientes	*to brush your teeth*

maquillarse	*to put on makeup*
peinarse	*to comb your hair*

En la Ciudad *(Places Around Town)*

la biblioteca	*library*
el centro	*downtown*
el centro comercial	*shopping mall*
el cine	*movie theater*
el correo	*post office*
el museo	*museum*
el parque de atracciones	*amusement park*
el teatro	*theater*
el zoológico	*zoo*

Comida *(Food)*

el agua mineral	*mineral water*
el aguacate	*avocado*
el almuerzo	*lunch*

el atún	*tuna*
el batido	*milkshake*
la bebida	*beverage*
el bistec	*steak*
el café con leche	*coffee with milk*
los camarones	*shrimp*
la carne de res	*beef*
la cebolla	*onion*
el cereal	*cereal*
el chocolate	*chocolate*
la comida mexicana/ italiana/china	*Mexican/Italian/Chinese food*
la crema de maní	*peanut butter*
los dulces	*candy*
la ensalada	*salad*
el flan	*custard*
los frijoles	*beans*
la fruta	*fruit*
la galleta	*cookie*
los huevos	*eggs*
el jamón	*ham*
el jugo de naranja	*orange juice*
la leche	*milk*
la lechuga	*lettuce*
las legumbres	*vegetables*
la limonada	*lemonade*
el maíz	*corn*
el mango	*mango*
la manzana	*apple*
el pan dulce	*sweet rolls*
el pan tostado	*toast*
la papa	*potato*
las papas fritas	*French fries*
la papaya	*papaya*
las papitas	*potato chips*
el pastel	*cake*
el perro caliente	*hot dog*
el pescado	*fish*
la piña	*pineapple*
la pizza	*pizza*
el plátano	*banana*
el pollo	*chicken*
el queso	*cheese*
el refresco	*soft drink*
el sándwich	*sandwich*
la sopa	*soup*
el tocino	*bacon*
el tomate	*tomato*
la toronja	*grapefruit*
las uvas	*grapes*
las verduras	*vegetables*
la zanahoria	*carrot*

This list includes additional vocabulary that you may want to use to personalize activities. If you can't find words you need here, try the Spanish-English and English-Spanish vocabulary sections beginning on page R47.

Artes

la acuarela	*watercolor*
el bronce	*bronze*
la cerámica	*pottery*
el (la) coreógrafo(a)	*choreographer*
el coro	*choir*
el cuadro	*painting*
el decorado	*stage scenery*
el dibujo al pastel	*pastel drawing*
el (la) director(a) (de la orquesta)	*(orchestra) conductor*
el ensayo	*rehearsal*
el escenario	*stage*
el instrumento de cobre	*brass instrument*
el instrumento de cuerda	*string instrument*
el instrumento electrónico	*electronic instrument*
el instrumento de percusión	*percussion instrument*
el instrumento de viento	*wind instrument*
el mármol	*marble*
el pincel	*paintbrush*
la pintura al óleo	*oil painting*

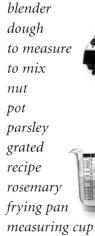

Cocina

la albahaca	*basil*
asar	*to roast*
la batidora	*mixer*
batir	*to beat*
la canela	*cinnamon*
congelar	*to freeze*
correoso(a)	*chewy*
crudo(a)	*raw*
crujiente	*crunchy*
la cucharada	*tablespoon*
la cucharadita	*teaspoon*
dorar	*to brown*
la especia	*spice*
freír (i, i)	*to fry*
la harina	*flour*
hervir (ie, i) a fuego lento	*to simmer*
la licuadora	*blender*
la masa	*dough*
medir (i, i)	*to measure*
mezclar	*to mix*
la nuez	*nut*
la olla	*pot*
el perejil	*parsley*
rayado(a)	*grated*
la receta	*recipe*
el romero	*rosemary*
la sartén	*frying pan*
la taza de medir	*measuring cup*
el trozo	*piece*
verter (ie)	*to pour*

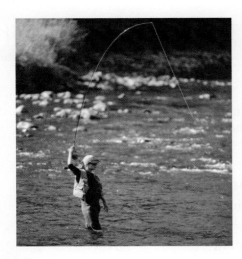

el maratón	marathon
el palo	golf club
la pelota	ball
la plataforma, la tabla	diving board
la raqueta	racket
rebotar	to bounce
la red	net
servir, sacar la pelota	to serve the ball
zambullirse	to dive

Deportes

el (la) árbitro	umpire, referee
el (la) arquero(a)	goalie
el bate	bat
el (la) bateador(a)	batter
el (la) boxeador(a)	boxer
boxear	to box
el cesto	basket
disparar el balón (al gol, ...)	to shoot the ball (at the goal, . . .)
el (la) entrenador(a)	coach, trainer
el hoyo	(golf) hole
ir de cacería	to go hunting
ir de pesca	to go fishing
ir en balsa en aguas blancas	white water rafting
el jonrón	homerun
el kayac	kayak
la liga	league
la lucha libre	wrestling
el (la) luchador(a)	wrestler

Descripciones

apestoso(a)	smelly
asombroso(a)	surprising
áspero(a)	rough
breve	brief
chato(a)	flat
claro(a)	light
cuadrado(a)	square
decaído(a)	weak, discouraged
dorado(a)	golden
gruñón(ona)	grouchy, grumpy
lento(a)	slow
liso(a)	smooth
llorón(ona)	whining
manso(a)	tame
oloroso(a)	fragrant
oscuro(a)	dark
redondo(a)	round
reluciente	shining
ruidoso(a)	noisy
salvaje	wild
veloz	fast

La Ecología

la capa de ozono	*ozone layer*
los combustibles fósiles	*fossil fuels*
consumir	*to consume*
la desforestación	*deforestation*
deforestar	*to deforest*
el (la) ecólogo(a)	*ecologist*
el efecto invernadero	*greenhouse effect*
la erosión	*erosion*
extinto(a)	*extinct*
los fertilizantes orgánicos (químicos)	*organic (chemical) fertilizers*
industrializado(a)	*industrialized*
el insecticida	*insecticide*
malgastar los recursos naturales	*to waste natural resources*
los productos orgánicos	*organic produce*
la superpoblación	*overpopulation*

Empleos

el (la) agente de viajes	*travel agent*
el (la) agricultor(a)	*farmer*
el (la) albañil	*mason; bricklayer*
el (la) aprendiz	*apprentice*
el (la) camionero(a)	*truck driver*
el (la) chofer	*driver*
el (la) constructor(a)	*construction worker, builder*

la costurera	*seamstress*
el (la) electricista	*electrician*
el (la) entrenador(a)	*coach, trainer*
el (la) físico(a)	*physicist*
el (la) fisioterapeuta	*physical therapist*
el (la) intérprete	*interpreter*
el (la) investigador(a)	*researcher*
el (la) modista	*dressmaker, designer*
el (la) plomero(a)	*plumber*
el (la) repostero(a)	*baker*
el sastre, la sastra	*tailor*
el (la) técnico(a)	*technician*
el (la) traductor(a)	*translator*
el (la) veterinario(a)	*veterinarian*

En La Ciudad

la acera	*sidewalk*
el aeropuerto	*airport*
las afueras	*the outskirts*
el anuncio luminoso de neón	*neon sign*
el barrio	*neighborhood*

el callejón	alley
la cartelera	billboard
la caseta de baño	public bathroom
la comisaría de policía	police station
el farol	street light
la zona industrial	industrial zone
la urbanización	development neighborhood (Mexico)
el zócalo	main square (Mexico)

Enlaces

a causa de (que)	due to
a consecuencia de	as a consequence of
a fin de cuentas	after all
a pesar de que	in spite of
aunque	although
de ninguna manera	in no way
en breve (pocas palabras)	in a few words
en primer lugar	in the first place
en todo caso	in any case
mientras (que)	while
no obstante	nonetheless
(no) tiene que ver con	it does (not) have to do with
para resumir	to summarize
por adelantado	in advance
por un lado... por otro	on one hand . . . on the other

Eventos Importantes

el bautizo	baptism
el bar mitzvah	bar mitzvah
el bas mitzvah	bat mitzvah
la confirmación	confirmation

el embarazo	pregnancy
el entierro	burial
los funerales	funeral
la graduación	graduation
el matrimonio	marriage
la muerte	death
el nacimiento	birth
el noviazgo	engagement
la primera comunión	first communion
la reunión familiar	family reunion
el velorio	wake

Expresiones de Cortesía

(Nombre), a sus órdenes.	(Name), at your service.
(Nombre), para servirle.	(Name), at your service.
(Nombre), servidor(a).	(Name), your humble servant.
Con el permiso de Ud...	May I . . .
De nada.	You're welcome.
Gracias por todo.	Thanks for everything.
Me gustaría...	I would like to . . .
¿Me podría...?	Could (Would) you . . .?
Mil gracias.	Many thanks.
Muchísimas gracias.	Thank you so much.
No hay de qué.	You're welcome. Don't mention it.
Por favor...	Please . . .
¿Sería Ud. tan amable de...?	Would you be so kind as to . . .?

Si no es molestia...	*If it isn't a bother . . .*
Tenga Ud. la bondad de...	*If you would be so kind as to . . .*

Geografía

el arroyo	*stream*
la bahía	*bay*
la cima de la montaña	*top of a mountain*
la cueva	*cave*
el hemisferio	*hemisphere*
la laguna	*lagoon*
la meseta	*plateau*
la orilla	*bank*
el pantano	*swamp, marsh*
la península	*peninsula*
la vega	*fertile plain*

El Hogar

el abrelatas	*can opener*
la alfombra	*rug, carpet*
el armario con cajones	*chest of drawers*
el ascensor	*elevator*
las cortinas	*curtains*
el desván	*attic*
el domicilio	*home*
el espejo	*mirror*
el fregadero	*kitchen sink*

el gabinete	*cabinet*
el garaje	*garage*
el hogar	*home*
la lavadora	*washing machine*
el lavaplatos	*dishwasher*
la mecedora	*rocking chair*
la secadora	*(clothes) dryer*
el sofá	*couch*
el sótano	*basement*

Leyendas

el calabozo	*dungeon*
el castillo	*castle*
convertirse (ie, i) en (animal)	*to turn into (an animal)*
el dragón	*dragon*
envenenar	*to poison*
el (la) gigante	*giant*
el hada madrina	*fairy godmother*
hechizar	*to cast a spell*
la magia	*magic*
el (la) pobre	*poor person, pauper*
el reino	*kingdom*
rescatar	*to rescue*
secuestrar	*to kidnap*
el veneno	*poison*

Las Fuerzas Armadas

el (la) almirante	*admiral*
la batalla	*battle*
el capitán, la capitana	*captain*
el (la) coronel(a)	*colonel*
la fuerza aérea	*air force*

las fuerzas armadas	armed forces
el (la) general(a)	general
la marina	navy
el (la) oficial	officer
el (la) recluta	enlisted man (woman)
reclutar	to draft, to recruit

Política y Economía

el alcalde, la alcaldesa	mayor
las cámaras	the houses (of congress)
el (la) capitalista	capitalist
el (la) comunista	communist
el congreso	congress
el (la) derechista	rightist, right-wing
el (la) dictador(a)	dictator
en vías de desarrollo	developing
la inflación	inflation
el (la) izquierdista	leftist, left-wing
el liderazgo	leadership
el mercado libre	free market
los ministerios	ministries
los partidos políticos	political parties
la política exterior	foreign policy
la regulación	regulation
las relaciones internacionales	international relations
el sector privado	private sector
el sector público	public sector
el senado	senate
el sistema bicameral	bicameral system (of legislature)
el sistema parlamentario	parliamentary system
el (la) socialista	socialist

| el subdesarrollo | underdevelopment |
| la tasa | rate |

Quehaceres

arrancar las hierbas	to pull the weeds
atornillar	to screw in
el clavo	nail
colgar (ue) un cuadro	to hang a picture
el destornillador	screwdriver
la escoba	broom
el gancho	hook, clothes pin, hanger
martillar	to hammer
el martillo	hammer
la pala	shovel
podar los árboles	to prune the trees
recoger con el rastrillo	to rake
regar (ie) con la manguera	to water with the hose
el tendero	clothesline

Sociedad

los derechos civiles	civil rights
el (la) desamparado(a)	homeless person
la huelga	strike
la igualdad	equality
la inmigración	immigration
la liberación femenina	women's liberation

la libertad	*freedom*
la manifestación	*march; protest*
los obreros migratorios	*migrant workers*
la pobreza	*poverty*
el racismo	*racism*
el (la) refugiado(a)	*refugee*
la riqueza	*wealth*
el SIDA	*AIDS*
tener derecho a	*to have the right to*

Tecnología

el archivo	*file*
arrastrar y soltar (ue)	*to drag and drop*
los audífonos	*headphones*
bajar archivos	*to download files*
las bocinas	*speakers*
la búsqueda	*search*
el canal de chat	*chat room*
charlar	*to chat*
la computadora portátil	*laptop computer*

la conexión de banda ancha	*broad band connection*
la contraseña, el código	*password*
la copia de respaldo	*backup*
el correo de voz	*voice mail*
el DVD	*DVD*
el diskette	*floppy disk, diskette*
el doble pulso	*double click*
las gráficas	*graphics*
la guía	*prompt*
el ícono	*icon*
el indicador, el puntero	*pointer, cursor*
el menú de cortina	*pull-down menu*
la página inicial	*homepage*
el procesamiento de textos	*word processing*
pulsar	*to click*
el ratón	*mouse*
la realidad virtual	*virtual reality*
la tecla de aceptación	*return key, enter key*
la tecla de borrar	*delete key*
la tecla de mayúsculas	*shift key*
la ventana	*window*
el vínculo	*link*

la computadora, el ordenador

la unidad de CD-ROM

el CD-ROM

el teclado

el ratón

Grammar Summary

Grammar Summary

NOUNS AND ARTICLES

GENDER OF NOUNS

In Spanish, nouns (words that name a person, place, or thing) are grouped into two classes or genders: masculine and feminine. All nouns, both persons and objects, fall into one of these groups. Most nouns that end in **-o** are masculine and most that end in **-a**, **-ción**, **-tad**, and **-dad** are feminine.

Masculine Nouns		Feminine Nouns	
libro	bolígrafo	universidad	mesa
cuaderno	vestido	situación	libertad

Some nouns ending in -**o** are feminine:

la mano
la modelo

Some nouns ending in -**a** are masculine:

el clima   **el mapa**
el día   **el planeta**

Nouns ending in -**e** or -**ista**, such as **estudiante** and **artista**, can either be masculine or feminine:

el (la) estudiante
el (la) artista

Some words ending in the same consonant may have a different gender:

el disfraz
la nariz

Feminine nouns that begin with a stressed **a**- or **ha**- take the definite article **el** in the singular:

el agua
el hambre

FORMATION OF PLURAL NOUNS

Add -**s** to nouns that end in a vowel.		Add -**es** to nouns that end in a consonant.		With nouns that end in -**z**, the -**z** changes to a -**c**.	
SINGULAR	**PLURAL**	**SINGULAR**	**PLURAL**	**SINGULAR**	**PLURAL**
libro	libros	profesor	profesores	vez	veces
casa	casas	papel	papeles	lápiz	lápices

DEFINITE ARTICLES

There are words that signal the class of the noun. One of these is the *definite article*. In English there is one definite article: *the*. In Spanish, there are four: **el, la, los, las.**

SUMMARY OF DEFINITE ARTICLES

	Masculine	Feminine
Singular	**el** gato	**la** gata
Plural	**los** gatos	**las** gatas

CONTRACTIONS

a + el	⟶	**al**
de + el	⟶	**del**

INDEFINITE ARTICLES

Another group of words used with nouns is the indefinite article: **un, una** *(a or an),* and **unos, unas** *(some).*

SUMMARY OF INDEFINITE ARTICLES

	Masculine	**Feminine**
Singular	**un** gato	**una** gata
Plural	**unos** gatos	**unas** gatas

PRONOUNS

Subject Pronouns	Direct Object Pronouns	Indirect Object Pronouns	Reflexive Pronouns	Objects of Prepositions
yo	me	me	me	mí
tú	te	te	te	ti
él, ella, Ud.	lo, la	le (se)	se	él, ella, Ud.
nosotros, nosotras	nos	nos	nos	nosotros, nosotras
vosotros, vosotras	os	os	os	vosotros, vosotras
ellos, ellas, Uds.	los, las	les (se)	se	ellos, ellas, Uds.

Double object pronouns

When used together, the indirect object pronoun always comes before the direct object pronoun.

¿Me la puedes traer?

Se replaces **le** and **les** before the direct object pronouns **lo, la, los,** and **las.**

Se lo di al director.

Reflexives

Reflexive pronouns indicate that the subject both performs and receives the action of the verb.

Carlos se levantó temprano.

Reflexive pronouns are used with some verbs to indicate inner processes or emotional reactions:

Amanda se enojó cuando oyó las noticias.

The reflexive pronouns **nos, os,** and **se** can be used to express reciprocal actions:

Él y su abuelo se abrazaron.

Uses of se

Se can be combined with an indirect object pronoun and a verb to express an unintentional event:

Se me olvidó el libro.

Se can also be used to express an indefinite subject:

Se habla español.

Se can also be used to express the passive voice:

Se construyeron muchas casas.

Lo que

The neuter relative pronoun **lo que** can be translated as *what, whatever,* or *which*.

Eso es lo que dijo Susana.

ADJECTIVES

Adjectives are words that describe nouns. The adjective must agree in gender (masculine or feminine) and number (singular or plural) with the noun it modifies. Adjectives that end in **-e** or a consonant only agree in number. Descriptive adjectives are usually placed after the noun they modify.

ADJECTIVE AGREEMENT

Adjectives ending...		Masculine	Feminine
with an **-o(a)**	Singular	el gato simpático	la gata simpática
	Plural	los gatos simpáticos	las gatas simpáticas
with an **-e**	Singular	el amigo inteligente	la amiga inteligente
	Plural	los amigos inteligentes	las amigas inteligentes
with a consonant	Singular	el traje azul	la blusa azul
	Plural	los trajes azules	las blusas azules

DEMONSTRATIVE ADJECTIVES

Demonstrative adjectives are used to point things out with their relationship to the speaker. They correspond to the English demonstrative adjectives *this, that, these,* and *those*.

	Masculine	Feminine
Singular	**este** chico	**esta** chica
Plural	**estos** chicos	**estas** chicas

	Masculine	Feminine
Singular	**ese** chico	**esa** chica
Plural	**esos** chicos	**esas** chicas

	Masculine	Feminine
Singular	**aquel** chico	**aquella** chica
Plural	**aquellos** chicos	**aquellas** chicas

POSSESSIVE ADJECTIVES

Possessive adjectives tell you *whose* object or person is being referred to (*my* car, *his* book, *her* mother).

Singular		Plural	
Masculine	**Feminine**	**Masculine**	**Feminine**
mi libro	**mi** casa	**mis** libros	**mis** casas
tu libro	**tu** casa	**tus** libros	**tus** casas
su libro	**su** casa	**sus** libros	**sus** casas
nuestro libro	**nuestra** casa	**nuestros** libros	**nuestras** casas
vuestro libro	**vuestra** casa	**vuestros** libros	**vuestras** casas

Note: Possession can also be expressed with the preposition **de: Es la casa** de **Fernando** instead of **Es su casa.**

STRESSED POSSESSIVE ADJECTIVES

Stressed possessive adjectives are used for emphasis and always follow the noun they modify: **Ellos son amigos míos.** Stressed possessive adjectives may be used as pronouns by using the definite article and the adjective and simply dropping the noun: **Los zapatos tuyos son más caros que los míos.**

Singular		Plural	
Masculine	**Feminine**	**Masculine**	**Feminine**
mío	mía	míos	mías
tuyo	tuya	tuyos	tuyas
suyo	suya	suyos	suyas
nuestro	nuestra	nuestros	nuestras
vuestro	vuestra	vuestros	vuestras
suyo	suya	suyos	suyas

AFFIRMATIVE AND NEGATIVE EXPRESSIONS

Affirmative			Negative		
sí	algún, alguno(a)	también	no	ningún, ninguno(a)	tampoco
algo	algunos, algunas	o...o	nada	ningunos, ningunas	ni...ni
alguien	siempre	ya	nadie	nunca	todavía no

INTERROGATIVE WORDS

¿Adónde?	¿Cuánto(a)?	¿Por qué?
¿Cómo?	¿Cuántos(as)?	¿Qué?
¿Cuál(es)?	¿De dónde?	¿Quién(es)?
¿Cuándo?	¿Dónde?	

COMPARATIVES

Comparatives are used to compare people or things. With comparisons of inequality, the same structure is used with adjectives, adverbs, or nouns. With comparisons of equality, **tan** is used with adjectives and adverbs, and **tanto/a/os/as** with nouns.

COMPARATIVE OF INEQUALITY

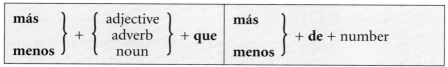

COMPARATIVE OF EQUALITY

tan + adjective or adverb + **como**
tanto/a/os/as + noun + **como**

SUPERLATIVES

To single out something as *the most* or *the least*, use **el/la/los/las** + (noun) + **más/menos** + adjective (+ **de**): **Es la película más divertida del año.**

**IRREGULAR FORMS OF
COMPARATIVES AND SUPERLATIVES**

Adjectives	Regular	Irregular
bueno(a)		mejor
malo(a)		peor
grande	más grande	mayor
viejo(a)	más viejo(a)	
pequeño(a)	más pequeño(a)	
joven	más joven	menor

The suffix **-ísimo** added to the stem of the adjective is another form of the superlative in Spanish: **grande: grandísimo, guapa: guapísima.**

ADVERBS

Adverbs modify the action of a verb. They can be formed by adding **-mente** to the feminine singular form of adjectives. This is the equivalent of adding *-ly* to an adjective in English.

Adjectives ending with an **-o** change **o** to **a** and add **-mente**: **claro→claramente**
Adjectives ending with an **-a,** an **-e,** or with a consonant, just add **-mente:**   **general: generalmente** **horrible: horriblemente** **feliz: felizmente**

PREPOSITIONS

Prepositions define relationships in space and time between two or more elements in a sentence. These are common prepositions in Spanish:

a	*to*	**detrás**	*behind*
al lado	*next to*	**en**	*in, on*
arriba	*over, above*	**encima**	*over, on top of*
con	*with*	**hacia**	*toward*
de	*of, from*	**hasta**	*until*
debajo	*under*	**para**	*for, in order to*
delante	*before*	**por**	*for, by*
desde (que)	*from, since*	**sin**	*without*

A number of Spanish verbs require a preposition:

abusar de	*to abuse*	**contrar con**	*to count on*
acabar de	*to have just finished*	**dejar de**	*to stop*
acordarse de	*to remember*	**depender de**	*to depend on*
aprender a	*to learn to*	**fijarse en**	*to notice*
asistir a	*to attend*	**insistir en**	*to insist on*
ayudar a	*to help*	**pasar por**	*to go by*
casarse con	*to get married to*	**pensar en**	*to think of*
comenzar a	*to begin to*	**soñar con**	*to dream of*

POR VS. PARA

Even though the English preposition *for* translates into Spanish as both **por** and **para**, they cannot be used interchangeably:

PARA	POR
Expresses purpose: **Estudio para aprender.**	Expresses "through" or "by": **Caminamos por el parque.**
Indicates a recipient: **El regalo es para papá.**	Expresses mode of transportation: **Carlos fue por autobús.**
Indicates destination: **Salieron para Perú.**	Indicates a period of time: **Estudié por tres horas.**
Indicates employment: **Trabajo para el señor López.**	Expresses "in exchange for": **Pagué $20.000 por mi carro.**
Indicates a deadline: **Completen la tarea para mañana.**	Expresses "per": **La gasolina cuesta $1,45 por galón.**
Indicates a person's opinion: **Para mí, esa novela es exelente.**	Indicates the agent of an action: **Fue construido por los romanos.**

USE OF *E* INSTEAD OF *Y*, *U* INSTEAD OF *O*

> Use **e** instead of **y** before words beginning with **i-** or **hi-**:
> guapo **e** inteligente
> madres **e** hijas
> This rule does not apply to words beginning with **hie-**:
> agua y hielo

> Use **u** instead of **o** before words beginning with **o-** or **ho-**:
> camarones **u** ostras
> mujer **u** hombre

ORDINAL NUMBERS

Ordinal numbers are used to express ordered sequences. They agree in number and gender with the noun they modify. The ordinal numbers **primero** and **tercero,** just like **bueno,** drop the final **o** before a singular masculine noun.

1st	**primero(a)**
2nd	**segundo(a)**
3rd	**tercero(a)**
4th	**cuarto(a)**
5th	**quinto(a)**
6th	**sexto(a)**
7th	**séptimo(a)**
8th	**octavo(a)**
9th	**noveno(a)**
10th	**décimo(a)**

EXPRESSIONS WITH *TENER*

tener... años	*to be . . . years old*	**tener (mucha) prisa**	*to be in a (big) hurry*
tener (mucho) calor	*to be (very) hot*	**tener que**	*to have to*
tener ganas de	*to feel like*	**tener (la) razón**	*to be right*
tener (mucho) frío	*to be (very) cold*	**tener (mucha) sed**	*to be (very) thirsty*
tener (mucha) hambre	*to be (very) hungry*	**tener (mucho) sueño**	*to be (very) sleepy*
tener (mucho) miedo	*to be (very) afraid*	**tener (mucha) suerte**	*to be (very) lucky*

EXPRESSIONS OF TIME

To ask how long someone has been doing something, use
¿Cuánto tiempo hace que + present tense?

To say how long someone has been doing something, use
Hace + quantity of time + **que** + present tense.
  Hace **seis meses** que **vivo** en Los Ángeles.
You can also use present tense + **desde hace** + quantity
of time.
  Vivo en Los Ángeles **desde hace seis meses**.

WEATHER EXPRESSIONS

Hace muy buen tiempo.	*The weather is very nice.*
Hace (mucho) calor.	*It's (very) hot.*
Hace fresco.	*It's cool.*
Hace (mucho) frío.	*It's (very) cold.*
Hace (muy) mal tiempo.	*The weather is (very)bad.*
Hace (mucho) sol.	*It's (very) sunny.*
Hace (mucho) viento.	*It's (very) windy.*
But:	
Está lloviendo (mucho).	*It's raining (a lot).*
Hay (mucha) neblina.	*It's (very) foggy.*
Está nevando.	*It's snowing.*
Está nublado.	*It's overcast.*

VERBS

Verbs are the basic elements of a sentence. They tell us about the subject, the attitude of the speaker, the type of action, and when the action took place. Much of this information is found in the verb ending. For example, **llegarás** tells us that the subject is *you* (singular, familiar), that the action is *to arrive*, and that the speaker is referring to an action that will take place in the future.

PERSON, NUMBER, TENSE, AND MOOD

Spanish assigns an ending to each verb according to person, number, tense, and mood.

There are three PERSONS: first, second, and third. For each person, there are two NUMBERS: singular and plural.

Singular	Plural
yo tú usted, él, ella	nosotros/as vosotros/as ustedes, ellos, ellas

There are three basic TENSES:

past
present
future

Moods express the attitude of a speaker toward an action. The speaker may report (indicative); request, express doubt, disbelief, or denial (subjunctive); or give an order (imperative). The three MOODS are called:

indicative
subjunctive
imperative

There are other forms of the verbs that do not reflect the subject or the attitude of the speaker. One of the forms is the infinitive. Dictionaries list verbs as infinitives, which end in **-ar, -er**, or **-ir**. The other two forms, present and past participles, often appear in dictionaries as well.

Infinitive		Present Participle		Past Participle	
hablar comer vivir	*to speak* *to eat* *to live*	hablando comiendo viviendo	*speaking* *eating* *living*	hablado comido vivido	*spoken* *eaten* *lived*

Some verbs have irregular past participles:

abrir	**abierto**		morir	**muerto**
decir	**dicho**		poner	**puesto**
describir	**descrito**		resolver	**resuelto**
descubrir	**descubierto**		romper	**roto**
escribir	**escrito**		satisfacer	**satisfecho**
freír	**frito**		ver	**visto**
hacer	**hecho**		volver	**vuelto**

REGULAR VERBS

All verbs have a tense and mood, and agree with the person or thing which is the subject. We call this "conjugation." To conjugate a regular verb, drop the (-**ar**, -**er**, -**ir**) and add the endings in the following charts.

INDICATIVE MOOD

Present

The present tense is used for action taking place now or in general.

-ar	-er	-ir
habl**o**	com**o**	viv**o**
habl**as**	com**es**	viv**es**
habl**a**	com**e**	viv**e**
habl**amos**	com**emos**	viv**imos**
habl**áis**	com**éis**	viv**ís**
habl**an**	com**en**	viv**en**

Present Progressive

If you want to emphasize that the action is in progress, use the present progressive. To do this, use the auxiliary verb **estar** (**estoy, estás, está, estamos, estáis, están**) with the present participle of the main verb: **hablando, comiendo, viviendo.**

Present Perfect

If the action has been completed, but still affects the present, use the present perfect. Form the present perfect by using the auxiliary form **haber** (**he, has, ha, hemos, habéis, han**) with the past participle of the main verb: **hablado, comido, vivido**.

Imperfect

The imperfect is used for ongoing or habitual actions in the past. It also describes the way things were, what used to happen or was going on, and mental and physical states in the past including age, clock time, and the way people felt in general. The verbs **ir, ser,** and **ver** are irregular in the imperfect.

-ar	-er	-ir
hablaba	comía	vivía
hablabas	comías	vivías
hablaba	comía	vivía
hablábamos	comíamos	vivíamos
hablabais	comíais	vivíais
hablaban	comían	vivían

IR	SER	VER
iba	era	veía
ibas	eras	veías
iba	era	veía
íbamos	éramos	veíamos
íbais	érais	veíais
iban	eran	veían

Preterite

The preterite is used for actions that were completed in the past and to describe past actions viewed as a completed whole. It also describes how a person reacted emotionally to a particular event.

-ar	-er	-ir
hablé	comí	viví
hablaste	comiste	viviste
habló	comió	vivió
hablamos	comimos	vivimos
hablasteis	comisteis	vivisteis
hablaron	comieron	vivieron

The preterite also gives special meaning to certain verbs:

conocer	Lo **conocí** ayer. *I met him yesterday.*
saber	Lo **supe** ayer. *I found out about it yesterday.*

querer	**Quiso** llamar. *He tried to call.*
no querer	**No quise** hacerlo. *I refused to do it.*

The following verbs are irregular in the preterite:

estar	estuv-	
poder	pud-	
poner	pus-	-e, -iste, -o
querer	quis-	-imos, -isteis
saber	sup-	-ieron
tener	tuv-	
venir	vin-	

decir	dij-	-e, -iste, -o
traer	traj-	-imos, -isteis
		-eron

Dar, hacer, ser, and **ir** are also irregular in the preterite

DAR	HACER	SER/IR
di	hice	fui
diste	hiciste	fuiste
dio	hizo	fue
dimos	hicimos	fuimos
disteis	hicisteis	fuisteis
dieron	hicieron	fueron

Future

The future tense is used to describe what will take place. It can also be used to indicate probability about the present. It is formed by adding the following endings to the future stem of the verb. The infinitive serves as the future stem for most verbs.

REGULAR		
-ar	**-er**	**-ir**
hablar**é**	comer**é**	vivir**é**
hablar**ás**	comer**ás**	vivir**ás**
hablar**á**	comer**á**	vivir**á**
hablar**emos**	comer**emos**	vivir**emos**
hablar**éis**	comer**éis**	vivir**éis**
hablar**án**	comer**án**	vivir**án**

Some verbs have irregular stems in the future tense:

caber	**cabr-**	
haber	**habr-**	
poder	**podr-**	
querer	**querr-**	
saber	**sabr-**	**-é, -ás, -á**
poner	**pondr-**	**-emos, -éis,**
salir	**saldr-**	**-án**
tener	**tendr-**	
valer	**valdr-**	
venir	**vendr-**	
decir	**dir-**	
hacer	**har-**	

The future can also be expressed with **ir a** + infinitive: **Voy a hablar con mi jefa.**

Conditional

The conditional expresses what would happen under certain circumstances. It is also used after if-clauses and to express probability about the past. The verbs that have irregular stems in the future tense have the same stems in the conditional.

-ar	**-er**	**-ir**
hablar**ía**	comer**ía**	vivir**ía**
hablar**ías**	comer**ías**	vivir**ías**
hablar**ía**	comer**ía**	vivir**ía**
hablar**íamos**	comer**íamos**	vivir**íamos**
hablar**íais**	comer**íais**	vivir**íais**
hablar**ían**	comer**ían**	vivir**ían**

SUBJUNCTIVE MOOD

Present Subjunctive

The subjunctive is required in all dependent clauses in which the verb of the main clause indicates request, intention, wish, or preference. Typical verbs of this type are: **querer, desear, prohibir, sugerir, preferir,** and **aconsejar**: **Mamá quiere que yo compre pan.**

The subjunctive is also used with expressions of emotion, such as **espero que** *(I hope that),* **¡ojalá!** *(hopefully),* **siento que** *(I'm sorry that),* **me alegro que** *(I'm happy that),* **es triste que** *(it's sad that),* and **me sorprende que** *(it surprises me that):*

> **¡Ojalá que lleguemos a tiempo!**

You must use the subjunctive if the verb in the main clause expresses doubt, disbelief, uncertainty, disagreement, or denial:

> **Dudo que podamos salir temprano.**

The subjunctive can be used to refer to something or someone whose existence is indefinite or that doesn't exist.

> **Busco una casa que tenga tres cuartos.**
> **No hay nadie aquí que conozca Italia.**

The subjunctive is used after all impersonal expressions that do NOT express certainty or truth:

> **Es importante que estudies otro idioma.**
>   but:
> **Es verdad que ese restaurante es malo.**

The subjunctive must be used after certain conjunctions such as: **antes (de) que** *(before),* **para que** *(so that, in order that),* **a fin de que** *(so that, in order that),* **a menos que** *(unless),* **con tal (de) que** *(provided that),* **en caso (de) que** *(in case),* and **sin que** *(without);*

> **Siempre entra sin que yo lo vea.**

The conjunctions **cuando, después de que, en cuanto, hasta que,** and **tan pronto como** require the subjunctive when they refer to actions that have not yet taken place:

> **No comeremos hasta que llegue Felipe.**

When there is not a change of subject, the infinitive is often used:

> **Espero graduarme en cuatro años.**

-ar	-er	-ir
hable	coma	viva
hables	comas	vivas
hable	coma	viva
hablemos	comamos	vivamos
habléis	comáis	viváis
hablen	coman	vivan

The following verbs are irregular in the subjunctive:

> **dar: dé, des, dé, demos, deis, den**
> **estar: esté, estés, esté, estemos, estéis, estén**
> **haber: haya, hayas, haya, hayamos, hayáis, hayan**
> **ir: vaya, vayas, vaya, vayamos, vayáis, vayan**
> **saber: sepa, sepas, sepa, sepamos, sepáis, sepan**
> **ser: sea, seas, sea, seamos, seáis, sean**

Present Perfect Subjunctive

The present perfect subjunctive is formed with the present subjunctive of **haber** (**haya, hayas, haya, hayamos, hayáis, hayan**) and a past participle. It is used like the present perfect indicative but only after verbs and expressions that require the subjunctive:

Me alegro de que hayas venido.

Past Subjunctive

The past subjunctive is formed by removing **-on** from the **ellos/ellas/Uds.** form of the preterite and adding the following endings:

-ar	-er	-ir
hablara	pudiera	durmiera
hablaras	pudieras	durmieras
hablara	pudiera	durmiera
hablaramos	pudiéramos	durmiéramos
hablarais	pudierais	durmierais
hablaran	pudieran	durmieran

The past subjunctive is used in the contrary to fact if-clauses:

Si pudiera, iría.

IMPERATIVE MOOD

The imperative is used to get people to do things. Its forms are sometimes called *commands:*

	-ar	-er	-ir
tú	habla (no hables)	come (no comas)	vive (no vivas)
Ud.	hable (no hable)	coma (no coma)	viva (no viva)
nosotros	hablemos (no hablemos)	comamos (no comamos)	vivamos (no vivamos)
vosotros	hablad (no habléis)	comed (no comáis)	vivid (no viváis)
Uds.	hablen (no hablen)	coman (no coman)	vivan (no vivan)

Several verbs have irregular **tú** imperative forms:

decir	**di**	**(no digas)**
hacer	**haz**	**(no hagas)**
ir	**ve**	**(no vayas)**
poner	**pon**	**(no pongas)**

salir	**sal**	**(no salgas)**
ser	**sé**	**(no seas)**
tener	**ten**	**(no tengas)**
venir	**ven**	**(no vengas)**

Negative **tú** and **vosotros(as)** commands are formed with the present subjunctive:

No compres ese carro. **No salgáis sin abrigo.**

Affirmative **nosotros(as)** commands can also be formed using **vamos a** + infinitive:

¡Vamos a jugar!

Pronouns are always connected to affirmative commands. When attaching pronouns to an affirmative command, regular rules of accentuation may call for written accents over the stressed syllable. Pronouns always come right before the verb in negative commands.

¡Tráemelo! **No me lo traigas.**

STEM-CHANGING VERBS

Stem-changing verbs have a spelling change in the stem.

THE -AR AND -ER STEM-CHANGING VERBS

Some verbs ending in -ar and -er change from e to ie and o to ue. These changes occur in all persons except the **nosotros** and **vosotros** forms.

Infinitive	Present Indicative	Imperative	Present Subjunctive
querer (ie) *(to want)*	quiero quieres quiere queremos queréis quieren	quiere (no quieras) quiera (no quiera) queramos (no queramos) quered (no queráis) quieran (no quieran)	quiera quieras quiera queramos queráis quieran
pensar (ie) *(to think)*	pienso piensas piensa pensamos pensáis piensan	piensa (no pienses) piense (no piense) pensemos (no pensemos) pensad (no penséis) piensen (no piensen)	piense pienses piense pensemos penséis piensen
probar (ue) *(to try)*	pruebo pruebas prueba probamos probáis prueban	prueba (no pruebes) pruebe (no pruebe) probemos (no probemos) probad (no probéis) prueben (no prueben)	pruebe pruebes pruebe probemos probéis prueben
volver (ue) *(to return)*	vuelvo vuelves vuelve volvemos volvéis vuelven	vuelve (no vuelvas) vuelva (no vuelva) volvamos (no volvamos) volved (no volváis) vuelvan (no vuelvan)	vuelva vuelvas vuelva volvamos volváis vuelvan

Verbs that follow the same pattern:

acordar(se)	**despertarse**	**poder**
acostarse	**doler**	**preferir**
almorzar	**empezar**	**querer**
comenzar	**llover**	**sentar**
costar	**pensar**	**soñar**

THE -IR STEM-CHANGING VERBS

Stem-changing verbs ending in -ir may change from e to ie, from e to i, or from o to ue or u.

e→ie, e→i

o→ue, o→u

Such verbs also undergo a stem change in the preterite for the third persons singular and plural. The same stem change occurs in the -ndo form. For example: **pedir→pidió, pidieron, pidiendo; dormir→durmió, durmieron, durmiendo.**

Infinitive	Indicative		Imperative	Subjunctive
	Present	**Preterite**		**Present**
sentir (ie) *(to feel)* **-ndo** FORM sintiendo	siento sientes siente sentimos sentís sienten	sentí sentiste sintió sentimos sentisteis sintieron	siente (no sientas) sienta (no sienta) sintamos (no sintamos) sentid (no sintáis) sientan (no sientan)	sienta sientas sienta sintamos sintáis sientan
dormir (ue) *(to sleep)* **-ndo** FORM durmiendo	duermo duermes duerme dormimos dormís duermen	dormí dormiste durmió dormimos dormisteis durmieron	duerme (no duermas) duerma (no duerma) durmamos (no durmamos) dormid (no durmáis) duerman (no duerman)	duerma duermas duerma durmamos durmáis duerman

Verbs that follow this pattern:
mentir, morir
e→i
The verbs in this category are irregular in the same tenses as those of the first type. The only difference is that they only have one change: **e→i**.

Infinitive	Indicative		Imperative	Subjunctive
	Present	**Preterite**		**Present**
pedir (i) *(to ask for, request)* **-ndo** FORM pidiendo	pido pides pide pedimos pedís piden	pedí pediste pidió pedimos pedisteis pidieron	pide (no pidas) pida (no pida) pidamos (no pidamos) pedid (no pidáis) pidan (no pidan)	pida pidas pida pidamos pidáis pidan

Verbs that follow this pattern:
seguir, servir, vestir, repetir, reír

VERBS WITH SPELLING CHANGES

Some verbs have a change in the spelling in some tenses in order to maintain the sound of the final consonant of the stem. The most common ones are those with the consonants **g** and **c**. Remember that **g** and **c** have a soft sound in front of **e** or **i**, but a hard sound in front of **a, o,** or **u**. In order to maintain the soft sound in front of **a, o,** or **u**, the letters **g** and **c** change to **j** and **z**, respectively. In order to maintain the hard sound of **g** or **c** in front of **e** and **i, u** is added to the **g** (**gu**) and the **c** changes to **qu**. The following verbs appear in the textbook.

1. Verbs ending in -**gar** change from **g** to **gu** before **e** in the first person of the preterite, in all persons of the present subjunctive, and in some persons of the imperative. Some verbs that follow the same pattern are **entregar, llegar,** and **jugar.**

   pagar *to pay*
   Preterite: pa**gu**é, pagaste, pagó, etc.
   Pres. Subj.: pa**gu**e, pa**gu**es, pa**gu**e, pa**gu**emos, pa**gu**éis, pa**gu**en
   Imperative: paga (no pa**gu**es), pa**gu**e, pa**gu**emos, pagad (no pa**gu**éis), pa**gu**en

2. Verbs ending in **-ger** or **-gir** change from **g** to **j** before **o** and **a** in the first person of the present indicative, in all the persons of the present subjunctive, and in some persons of the imperative. Some verbs that follow the same pattern: **recoger, escoger, elegir.**

   proteger   *to protect*
   Pres. Ind.: prote**j**o, proteges, protege, etc.
   Pres. Subj.: prote**j**a, prote**j**as, prote**j**a, prote**j**amos, prote**j**áis, prote**j**an
   Imperative: protege (no prote**j**as), prote**j**a, prote**j**amos, proteged (no prote**j**áis), prote**j**an

3. Verbs ending in **-guir** change from **gu** to **g** before **o** and **a** in the first person of the present indicative, in all persons of the present subjunctive, and in some persons of the imperative.

   seguir   *to follow*
   Pres. Ind.: si**g**o, sigues, sigue, etc.
   Pres. Subj.: si**g**a, si**g**as, si**g**a, si**g**amos, si**g**áis, si**g**an
   Imperative: sigue (no si**g**as), si**g**a, si**g**amos, seguid (no si**g**áis), si**g**an

4. Verbs ending in **-car** change from **c** to **qu** before **e** in the first person of the preterite, in all persons of the present subjunctive, and in some persons in the imperative. Some verbs that follow the same pattern: **buscar, practicar, sacar, tocar.**

   explicar   *to explain*
   Preterite: expli**qu**é, explicaste, explicó, etc.
   Pres. Subj.: expli**qu**e, expli**qu**es, expli**qu**e, expli**qu**emos, expli**qu**éis, expli**qu**en
   Imperative: explica (no expli**qu**es), expli**qu**e, expli**qu**emos, explicad (no expli**qu**éis),
      expli**qu**en

5. Verbs that end in **-cer** or **-cir** and are preceded by a consonant change from **c** to **zc** before **o** and **a**. This change occurs in the first person of the present indicative and in all persons of the present subjunctive. Some verbs that follow the same pattern: **parecer, pertenecer, producir.**

   conocer   *to know, be acquainted with*
   Pres. Ind.: cono**zc**o, conoces, conoce, etc.
   Pres. Subj.: cono**zc**a, cono**zc**as, cono**zc**a, cono**zc**amos, cono**zc**áis, cono**zc**an

6. Verbs ending in **-zar** change from **z** to **c** before **e** in the first person of the preterite and in all persons of the present subjunctive. Verbs that follow the same pattern: **almorzar, empezar.**

   comenzar   *to start*
   Preterite: comen**c**é, comenzaste, comenzó, etc.
   Pres. Subj.: comien**c**e, comien**c**es, comien**c**e, comen**c**emos, comen**c**éis, comien**c**en

7. Verbs ending in **-aer** or **-eer** change from the unstressed **i** to **y** between vowels in the preterite third persons singular and plural, in all persons of the past subjunctive, and in the **-ndo** form. Note the accent marks over **i** in the **tú, nosotros** and **vosotros** forms in the preterite. Other verbs that follow the same pattern are **leer** and **caer.**

   creer   *to believe*
   Preterite: creí, creíste, cre**y**ó, creímos, creísteis, cre**y**eron
   Past Subj.: cre**y**era, cre**y**eras, cre**y**era, cre**y**éramos, cre**y**erais, cre**y**eran
   -ndo form: cre**y**endo
   Past Part.: creído

8. Verbs ending in **-uir** (except **-guir** and **-quir**) change from the unstressed **i** to **y** between vowels.

   construir   *to build*
   Pres. Part.: constru**y**endo
   Pres. Ind.: constru**y**o, constru**y**es, constru**y**e, construimos, construís, constru**y**en
   Preterite: construí, construiste, constru**y**ó, construimos, construisteis, constru**y**eron
   Pres. Subj.: constru**y**a, constru**y**as, constru**y**a, constru**y**amos, constru**y**ais, constru**y**an
   Past. Subj.: constru**y**era, constru**y**eras, constru**y**era, constru**y**éramos, constru**y**erais, constru**y**eran
   Imperative: constru**y**e (no constru**y**as), constru**y**a, constru**y**amos, construid
      (no constru**y**áis), constru**y**an

9. Some verbs stems ending in **i-** or **u-** change to **í** or **ú** respectively in the present indicative and present subjunctive in all persons except **nosotros** and **vosotros**. Some verbs that follow this pattern are **actuar, confiar, graduarse,** and **continuar.**

> **enviar** *to send*
> Pres. Ind.: **envío, envías, envía, enviamos, enviáis, envían**
> Pres. Subj.: **envíe, envíes, envíe, enviemos, enviéis, envíen**

IRREGULAR VERBS

These tenses are irregular in some tenses. Only those tenses included in this book are shown.

abrir *to open*
> Past. Part.: abierto

dar *to give*
> Pres. Ind.: doy, das, da, damos, dais, dan
> Preterite: di, diste, dio, dimos, disteis, dieron
> Imperative: da (no des), dé, demos, dad (no deis), den
> Pres. Subj.: dé, des, dé, demos, deis, den
> Past Subj.: diera, dieras, diera, diéramos, dierais, dieran

decir *to say, tell*
> Pres. Ind.: digo, dices, dice, decimos, decís, dicen
> Preterite: dije, dijiste, dijo, dijimos, dijisteis, dijeron
> Future: diré, dirás, dirá, diremos, diréis, dirán
> Conditional: diría, dirías, diría, diríamos, diríais, dirían
> Imperative: di (no digas), diga, digamos, decid (no digáis), digan
> Pres. Subj.: diga, digas, diga, digamos, digáis, digan
> Past Subj.: dijera, dijeras, dijera, dijéramos, dijerais, dijeran
> Past Part.: dicho
> **-ndo** Form: diciendo

escribir *to write*
> Past Part.: escrito

estar *to be*
> Pres. Ind.: estoy, estás, está, estamos, estáis, están
> Preterite: estuve, estuviste, estuvo, estuvimos, estuvisteis, estuvieron
> Imperative: está (no estés), esté, estemos, estad (no estéis), estén
> Pres. Subj.: esté, estés, esté, estemos, estéis, estén
> Past Subj.: estuviera, estuvieras, estuviera, estuviéramos, estuvierais, estuvieran

haber *to have*
> Pres. Ind.: he, has, ha, hemos, habéis, han
> Preterite: hube, hubiste, hubo, hubimos, hubisteis, hubieron
> Future: habré, habrás, habrá, habremos, habréis, habrán
> Conditional: habría, habrías, habría, habríamos, habríais, habrían
> Pres. Subj.: haya, hayas, haya, hayamos, hayáis, hayan
> Past Subj.: hubiera, hubieras, hubiera, hubiéramos, hubierais, hubieran

hacer *to do, make*
> Pres. Ind.: hago, haces, hace, hacemos, hacéis, hacen
> Preterite: hice, hiciste, hizo, hicimos, hicisteis, hicieron
> Future: haré, harás, hará, haremos, haréis, harán
> Conditional: haría, harías, haría, haríamos, haríais, harían
> Imperative: haz (no hagas), haga, hagamos, haced (no hagáis), hagan
> Pres. Subj.: haga, hagas, haga, hagamos, hagáis, hagan
> Past Part.: hecho

ir *to go*
  Pres. Ind.: voy, vas, va, vamos, vais, van
  Imp. Ind.: iba, ibas, iba, íbamos, ibais, iban
  Preterite: fui, fuiste, fue, fuimos, fuisteis, fueron
  Imperative: ve (no vayas), vaya, vamos, id (no vayáis), vayan
  Pres. Subj.: vaya, vayas, vaya, vayamos, vayáis, vayan
  Past Subj.: fuera, fueras, fuera, fuéramos, fuerais, fueran
  -**ndo** Form: yendo

mantener *to maintain, to keep*
  (See **tener** for pattern to follow.)

poder *to be able to, can*
  Pres. Ind.: puedo, puedes, puede, podemos, podéis, pueden
  Preterite: pude, pudiste, pudo, pudimos, pudisteis, pudieron
  Future: podré, podrás, podrá, podremos, podréis, podrán
  Conditional: podría, podrías, podría, podríamos, podríais, podrían
  Pres. Subj.: pueda, puedas, pueda, podamos, podáis, puedan
  Past Subj.: pudiera, pudieras, pudiera, pudiéramos, pudierais, pudieran

poner *to place, put*
  Pres. Ind.: pongo, pones, pone, ponemos, ponéis, ponen
  Preterite: puse, pusiste, puso, pusimos, pusisteis, pusieron
  Future: pondré, pondrás, pondrá, pondremos, pondréis, pondrán
  Conditional: pondría, pondrías, pondría, pondríamos, pondríais, pondrían
  Imperative: pon (no pongas), ponga, pongamos, poned (no pongáis), pongan
  Pres. Subj.: ponga, pongas, ponga, pongamos, pongáis, pongan
  Past Part.: puesto

romper(se) *to break*
  Past Part.: roto

saber *to know*
  Pres. Ind.: sé, sabes, sabe, sabemos, sabéis, saben
  Preterite: supe, supiste, supo, supimos, supisteis, supieron
  Future: sabré, sabrás, sabrá, sabremos, sabréis, sabrán
  Conditional: sabría, sabrías, sabría, sabríamos, sabríais, sabrían
  Imperative: sabe (no sepas), sepa, sepamos, sabed (no sepáis), sepan
  Pres. Subj.: sepa, sepas, sepa, sepamos, sepáis, sepan
  Past Subj.: supiera, supieras, supiera, supiéramos, supierais, supieran

salir *to leave, go out*
  Pres. Ind.: salgo, sales, sale, salimos, salís, salen
  Future: saldré, saldrás, saldrá, saldremos, saldréis, saldrán
  Conditional: saldría, saldrías, saldría, saldríamos, saldríais, saldrían
  Imperative: sal (no salgas), salga, salgamos, salid (no salgáis), salgan
  Pres. Subj.: salga, salgas, salga, salgamos, salgáis, salgan

ser *to be*
  Pres. Ind.: soy, eres, es, somos, sois, son
  Imp. Ind.: era, eras, era, éramos, erais, eran
  Preterite: fui, fuiste, fue, fuimos, fuisteis, fueron
  Imperative: sé (no seas), sea, seamos, sed (no seáis), sean
  Pres. Subj.: sea, seas, sea, seamos, seáis, sean
  Past Subj.: fuera, fueras, fuera, fuéramos, fuerais, fueran

tener *to have*
 Pres. Ind.: tengo, tienes, tiene, tenemos, tenéis, tienen
 Preterite: tuve, tuviste, tuvo, tuvimos, tuvisteis, tuvieron
 Future: tendré, tendrás, tendrá, tendremos, tendréis, tendrán
 Conditional: tendría, tendrías, tendría, tendríamos, tendríais, tendrían
 Imperative: ten (no tengas), tenga, tengamos, tened (no tengáis), tengan
 Pres. Subj.: tenga, tengas, tenga, tengamos, tengáis, tengan
 Past Subj.: tuviera, tuvieras, tuviera, tuviéramos, tuvierais, tuvieran

traer *to bring*
 Pres. Ind.: traigo, traes, trae, traemos, traéis, traen
 Preterite: traje, trajiste, trajo, trajimos, trajisteis, trajeron
 Imperative: trae (no traigas), traiga, traigamos, traed (no traigáis), traigan
 Pres. Subj.: traiga, traigas, traiga, traigamos, traigáis, traigan
 Past Subj.: trajera, trajeras, trajera, trajéramos, trajerais, trajeran
 Past Part.: traído
 -**ndo** Form: trayendo

valer *to be worth*
 Pres. Ind.: valgo, vales, vale, valemos, valéis, valen
 Future: valdré, valdrás, valdrá, valdremos, valdréis, valdrán
 Conditional: valdría, valdrías, valdría, valdríamos, valdríais, valdrían
 Pres. Subj.: valga, valgas, valga, valgamos, valgáis, valgan

venir *to come*
 Pres. Ind.: vengo, vienes, viene, venimos, venís, vienen
 Preterite: vine, viniste, vino, vinimos, vinisteis, vinieron
 Future: vendré, vendrás, vendrá, vendremos, vendréis, vendrán
 Conditional: vendría, vendrías, vendría, vendríamos, vendríais, vendrían
 Imperative: ven (no vengas), venga, vengamos, venid (no vengáis), vengan
 Pres. Subj.: venga, vengas, venga, vengamos, vengáis, vengan
 Past Subj.: viniera, vinieras, viniera, viniéramos, vinierais, vinieran
 -**ndo** Form: viniendo

ver *to see*
 Pres. Ind.: veo, ves, ve, vemos, veis, ven
 Imp. Ind.: veía, veías, veía, veíamos, veíais, veían
 Preterite: vi, viste, vio, vimos, visteis, vieron
 Imperative: ve (no veas), vea, veamos, ved (no veáis), vean
 Pres. Subj.: vea, veas, vea, veamos, veáis, vean
 Past Subj.: viera, vieras, viera, viéramos, vierais, vieran
 Past Part.: visto

GUSTAR AND VERBS LIKE IT

Gustar, encantar, fascinar, chocar, interesar, and **faltar** are used to talk about things you like, love, dislike, are interested in, or lack. The verb endings for **gustar** and verbs like it always agree with what is liked or disliked. The indirect object pronouns always precede the verb forms.

If one thing is liked:	If more than one thing is liked:
me te le nos os les } gusta	me te le nos os les } gustan

SABER AND CONOCER

For the English verb *to know*, there are two verbs in Spanish, **saber** and **conocer**.

Saber means *to know* something or *to know how to* do something.
¿Sabes que mañana no hay clase? *Do you know that there is no school tomorrow?*
¿Sabes chino? *Do you know Chinese?*
¿Sabes patinar? *Do you know how to skate?*

Conocer means *to be acquainted with* somebody or something:
¿Conoces a Alicia? *Do you know Alicia?*
¿Conoces Madrid? *Do you know Madrid?*
Conocer is followed by the personal **a** when it takes a person as an object.

THE VERBS SER AND ESTAR

Both **ser** and **estar** mean *to be*, but they differ in their uses.

Use **ser:**
1. with nouns to identify and define the subject
   La mejor estudiante de la clase es Katia.
2. with **de** to indicate place of origin, ownership, or what something is made of
   Carmen es de Venezuela.
   Este libro es de mi abuela.
   La blusa es de algodón.
3. to give characteristics, such as physical and personality traits, nationality, religion, and profession
   Mi tío es profesor. Es simpático e inteligente.
4. to express the time, date, season and location of an event
   Hoy es sábado y la fiesta es a las ocho.
5. with the past participle to form the passive voice
   El libro fue escrito por Octavio Paz.

Use **estar:**
1. to indicate location or position of the subject
   Lima está en Perú.
2. to describe a condition that is subject to change
   Maricarmen está enfadada.
3. with the present participle (-**ndo** form) to describe an action in progress
   Marion está escribiendo un poema.
4. to convey the idea of *to look, to feel, to seem, to taste*
   Tu hermano está muy guapo hoy.
   La sopa está sabrosa.
5. with the past participle to refer to a condition which is the result of a previous action
   La cama está tendida. La tendió Carlos.

Spanish-English Vocabulary

This vocabulary includes almost all words in the textbook, both active (for production) and passive (for recognition only). Active words and phrases are practiced in the chapter and are listed on the **Vocabulario** page at the end of each chapter. You are expected to know and be able to use active vocabulary. An entry in **boldface** type indicates that the word or phrase is active.

All other words are for recognition only. These are found in **De antemano**, in the **Pasos**, in realia (authentic Spanish-language documents), in **Panorama cultural, Encuentro cultural, Vamos a leer**, and in the Location Openers (travelogue sections). The meanings of these words and phrases can usually be understood from the context or may be looked up in this vocabulary. Many words have more than one definition; the definitions given here correspond to the way the words are used in the book.

Nouns are listed with definite article and plural form, when applicable. The numbers after each entry refer to Level 1, Level 2, or Level 3 and the chapter where the word or phrase first appears or where it becomes an active vocabulary word.

Although the **Real Academia** has deleted the letters **ch** and **ll** from the alphabet, many dictionaries still have separate entries for these letters. This end-of-book vocabulary follows the new rules, with **ch** and **ll** in the same sequence as in English.

Stem changes are indicated in parentheses after the verb: **poder (ue)**.

a *to, at, in order to*, I; a cargo *in charge*, 1; a causa de *because of, due to*, 7; a condición de que *on condition that*, 3; **a continuación** *next*, II; a la larga *in the long run*, 8; **a la vez** *at the same time*, III3; a lo largo *along*, 9; a lo lejos *in the distance*, 12; **A lo mejor...** *Perhaps...*, III8; **a menos (de) que** *unless*, III10; a menudo *often*, 4; a nivel (nacional) *at the (national) level*, 10; a pesar de *in spite of*, 5; **A propósito...** *By the way...*, III6; **...a quien le guste(n)...,** *...who likes...*, III7; a solas *alone*, 7; a través *through, throughout*, 5; **A ver...** *Let's see...*, III3
abajo *down*, 10
las abdominales *sit-ups*, II
la abeja *bee*, 11
abierto(a) (past participle of **abrir**) *opened, open*, III1
el abismo *abyss*, 9
el abogado, la abogada *lawyer*, III12
abolir *to abolish*, 11
abordar *to board*, 9
aborrecer (zc) to abhor, 11
el abrazo *hug*, III7; **darle un abrazo** *to give someone a hug*, III7
abril (m.) *April*, I

abrir *to open*, I
abrumado(a) *overwhelmed*, 2
absorto(a) *engrossed*, 9
absurdo(a) *absurd*, 8
la abuela *grandmother*, I
el abuelo *grandfather*, I
los abuelos *grandparents*, I
la abundancia *abundance*, 11
aburrido(a) (with **ser**) *boring*, I; (with **estar**) *bored, boring*, II
el aburrimiento *boredom*, 7
acabar *to finish*, 1; acabar de *to have just*, 10
acabarse *to run out of*, III4; **Se me acabó (acabaron)...** *I ran out of...*, III4
acampar *to camp*, I
acceder *to agree*, 3
el acceso *access*, 3
el accidente *accident*, 6
la acción *action*, 10
el aceite *oil*, 2
la aceituna *olive*, 1
acentuar *to increase*, 7
acerado(a) *steely*, 9
acerca de *concerning*, 4
el acero *steel*
acoger *to take in; to welcome*, 6
acompañar (a) *to go with*, II
aconsejar *to advise*, III2; **Te aconsejo** + inf. *I advise you to...*, III2; **Te aconsejo que...** *I recommend that you...*, III6
el acontecimiento *happening, event*, 5
acordar (ue) la paz *to make peace*,

III5; **Los dioses quieren que los guerreros acuerden la paz.** *The gods want the warriors to make peace.*, III5
acordarse (ue) de *to remember*, II
acostarse (ue) *to go to bed*, II
acostumbrado(a) *used to*, 1
acostumbrarse *to get used to*, 10
acre *acrid*, 11
la actitud *attitude*, III9
la actividad *activity*, 3
los actores *actors*, 5
la actriz (pl. las actrices) *actress*, 8
la actualidad *present time*, 8
actualizar *to update*, III12
actuar *to act*, III11; **Si no actuamos ahora...** *If we don't act now...*, III11
la acuarela *watercolor*, 6
el acuarelista, la acuarelista *water-color painter*, 6
el acuario *aquarium*, I
acudir *to go*, 6
el acuerdo *agreement*; **De acuerdo.** *Agreed.*, I; *All right.*, II
acumulado(a) *accumulated*, 11
acusar *to accuse*, 5
adaptarse *to adapt, to adjust*, III3
adecuado(a) *appropriate*, 3
los adelantos *advances*, III3
además *besides*, I
adentro *inside*, 4
el adhesivo *sticker*, III1; **coleccionar adhesivos** *to collect stickers*, III1
Adiós. *Goodbye.*, I

adivinar *to guess*, 1

el adivino, la adivina *fortune teller*, 5

adjuntar *to attach*, 12

la administración de empresas *business administration*, 10

la administración hotelera *hotel administration*, 12

admirar *to admire*, 5; **Admiro mucho...** *I admire ... very much*, III6

admitir un error *to admit a mistake*, III7

¿adónde? *to where?*, I

adorar *to adore*, 4

adquirir (ie) *to acquire*, 6

la aerolínea *airline*, 12

el aeropuerto *airport*

afectar *to affect*, 3

afeitarse *to shave*, I

aficionado(a) *enthusiastic*, 6

el aficionado, la aficionada *fan*, III1; **Soy un(a) gran aficionado(a) a...** *I'm a big fan of ...*, III1

afirmar *to affirm*, 8

afónico(a) *silent*, 11

afortunado(a) *fortunate*, 6

agacharse *to bend down, to duck*, 12

la agencia de publicidad *ad agency*, 4

agilizar *to make active or quick, to facilitate*, 3

agitado(a) *upset, agitated*, 7

agobiado(a) *worn out, overwhelmed*, III2

agolparse *to crowd in*, 9

agosto (m.) *August*, I

agotado(a) *exhausted*, III2

el agotamiento *exhaustion*, 2

agradable *pleasant*

agradecer (zc) *to be grateful for*, 7

agradecido(a) *grateful*, III10

agregar *to add*, 2

agrícola (m./f.) *agricultural*

los agricultores *farmers*, 4

el agua (f.) *water*, I

el aguacate *avocado*, III4; **la ensalada de aguacate** *avocado salad*, III4

el aguacero *downpour*, II

aguantar *to bear, to put up with, to stand*, III7; **No aguanto a nadie que sea descortés.** *I can't stand anyone who's rude.*, III7; **No hay quien lo (la) aguante.** *Nobody can stand him (her).*, III1

agudo(a) *sharp*, 5

el águila (f.) *eagle*, II

el agujero *hole*, 7

ahora *now*, I

ahorrar *to save (money)*, 2

el aire *air*; **el aire acondicionado** *air conditioning*, II; **el aire libre** *open air*, II; **el aire puro** *fresh air*, II

el ají (dulce) *sweet pepper*, 4

el ají (picante) *hot pepper*, 4

el ajo *garlic*, III4; **Tiene sabor a ajo.** *It tastes like garlic.*, III4

el ajuar *trousseau*, 7

ajustar *to adjust, to fit*

al (a + el) *to the*, I; al + inf. *upon (doing)*, 1; **Al contrario.** *On the contrary.*, III5; **Al final...** *Finally ...*, II; al gusto *to taste*, 4; **al lado de** *next to*, I; *alongside*, II; al respecto *on the matter*, 7; **al ... siguiente** *on the next (day, year, ...)*, II

alargado(a) *elongated*, 12

alargar *to lengthen*, 2

el **albergue juvenil** *youth hostel*, II

el alcalde, la alcaldesa *mayor*, 1

alcanzar *to achieve, to attain*, III10; **Alcancé éxito en...** *I achieved success in ...*, III10; no les alcanza para vivir *they don't have enough to live on*, 3

la aldea *village*, 4

alegrarse *to be glad*, III7; **Me alegro que...** *I'm glad that ...*, III7; **Se alegró mucho.** *He (She) was very happy.*, III9

alegre *happy*, 3

la alegría *happiness*, 2

alejarse *to distance oneself*, 11

el alemán *German (language)*, 7

Alemania (f.) *Germany*, I

los alfajores *snack consisting of two or three cookies layered with chocolate or caramel and covered with chocolate*

el alfiler *pin*, 7

algo *something, anything*, I

el algodón *cotton*, I

algodonoso(a) *downy*, 4

alguien *somebody*, III5; **Alguien me dijo que...** *Somebody told me that ...*, III5; **Bueno, debe ser alguien...** *Well, it's someone ...*, III7; **Busco a alguien...** *I look for someone ...*, III7

algún día *someday*, II

alhajado(a) *decked with jewels*, 6

el aliado, la aliada *ally*, 5

la **alimentación** *nutrition*, III2; **tener buenos hábitos de alimentación** *to have good eating habits*, III2

alimentarse bien (mal) *to eat well (poorly)*, III2

el alimento *nourishment, food*, 10

aliviar el estrés *to relieve stress*, III2

allá *there*, I

el alma *soul*, 6

el almacén (pl. **los almacenes**) *department store*, I

las **almejas** *clams*, III4

almorzar (ue) *to eat lunch*, I

el **almuerzo** *lunch*, I

Aló. *Hello. (telephone greeting)*, I

el alpinismo *mountain climbing*, 1

alquilar *to rent*, 4

alrededor *around*, 10; los alrededores *surroundings*, 5

los altibajos *ups and downs*, 7

alto(a) *tall*, III1

la altura *height*

el aluminio *aluminum*, II

amable *nice, kind*, III4; **¿Serías tan amable de dármela?** *Would you be so kind as to give it to me?*, III4

el amado, la amada *loved one*, 5

el amante, la amante *lover*, 5

amar *to love*, 1

amarillo(a) *yellow*, I

amazónico(a) *relating to the Amazon region*

ambarino(a) *relating to amber*, 1

la **ambición** (pl. **las ambiciones**) *ambition*, III5; **Era una de mis grandes ambiciones.** *It was one of my great ambitions.*, III5

ambiental *environmental*, 11

el ambiente *environment*, 5; **el ambiente de trabajo** *workplace environment*, III12

ambiguo(a) *ambiguous*, 8

el **ámbito de...** *the field of ...*, 10

ambos(as) *both*, 6

la ambulancia *ambulance*, 4

la amenaza *threat*, 6

amenazar *to threaten*, 8

amigable *friendly*, III9

el amigo, la amiga *friend*, I; **hacerse amigo(a) de** *to make friends with*, II

la amistad *friendship*, III7

el amor *love*, 10

amplio(a) *broad*, 9

el amuleto *amulet*, 5

el ananás *pineapple*, 4

anaranjado(a) *orange*, I

ancho(a) *loose (clothes)*, II

anciano(a) *old*, 5

los ancianos *elderly people*, 5

andar *to go, to walk, to move*, 2; andar (bien) *to be going (well)*, 12; andar con *to hang around with*, 7

el andén (pl. **los andenes**) *platform*, II

el andinismo *mountain climbing*, 1

andino(a) *Andean, relating to the Andes mountains*

anduvo (pret. of andar) *he (she/it) went*, 1

el anfitrión, la anfitriona *host, hostess*, 4

el ángel *angel*; **tan bueno(a) como un ángel** *(as good as) a saint*, II

la anguila *eel*, 1

el ángulo *angle*, 12

la angustia *anguish*, 6

el anillo *ring*, 4

animar *to liven up*, 9

¡Ánimo! *Cheer up!*, III7

animoso(a) *brave, determined*, 9

anoche *last night*, I

anónimo(a) *anonymous*, 10

anotar *to write down*, 2

ansioso(a) *anxious*, III2

anteanoche *the night before last*, I

anteayer *the day before yesterday*, I

los antecedentes *background*, 12

la antena parabólica *satellite dish*, III3

los anteojos *glasses*, 1

anterior *previous, before*, II; **el día anterior** *the day before*, II

antes de *before,* I; **Antes de terminar...** *Before finishing . . .,* III10
Antes que empiecen las clases... *Before classes begin . . .,* III10
anticuado(a) *out-of-date,* 3
antiguo(a) *old, ancient,* III6
antipático(a) *disagreeable,* I
antipatiquísimo(a) *not at all nice,* 2
la antropología *anthropology,* I
el anuario *yearbook,* 3
anunciar *to announce,* III8
el **anuncio** *commercial, advertisement,* III8; **los anuncios clasificados** *classified ads,* III8
añadir *to add,* II
el **año** *year,* I; **el Año Nuevo** *New Year's Day,* I; **tener... años** *to be . . . years old,* I
el **aparato eléctrico** *electrical appliance,* III3
aparecer (zc) *to appear,* 3
el aparcero, la aparcera *sharecropper,* 12
la apariencia *physical appearance,* 2; las apariencias *appearances,* 9
aparte *separate,* I
el apellido *last name,* 9
apenas *scarcely, barely,* 1
la apertura *opening,* 3
el apetito *appetite,* 4
aplacar *to pacify,* 2
aplanado(a) *flattened,* 4
aplazar *to put off,* 2
aplicado(a) *studious,* II
la aportación *contribution,* III10
aportar *to contribute,* III10
el aporte *contribution,* 10
el apóstol *apostle*
apoyar *to support,* III7; **que me apoye** *that supports me,* III7
el apoyo *support,* 2
apreciar *to appreciate,* III9
el aprecio *appreciation,* 10
aprender a + inf. *to learn (to do something),* III6
aprender de memoria *to memorize,* II
el aprendizaje *learning,* 5
aprobar (ue) *to pass (an exam),* II
apropiado(a) *appropriate,* 1
aprovechar *to take advantage of, to use,* 1
aproximadamente *approximately,* 3
la aptitud física *physical fitness,* 12
apuntar *to make a note of, to write down,* II
los **apuntes** *notes;* **tomar apuntes** *to take notes,* II
el apuro *difficult situation,* trouble, 4
aquel *that;* **en aquel entonces** *at that point in time,* II
aquí *here,* I
árabe *Arabic*
la araña *spider,* 11
el árbol *tree,* II
el arco *bow,* 5
el arco iris *rainbow,* 4

la ardilla *squirrel,* 9
la arepa *flattened, round bread made of fried or baked cornmeal*
el **arete** *earring,* I
argentino(a) *Argentine,* II
el argumento *plot,* 8
armar *to arm,* 5
el **armario** *closet,* I
el armazón *framework,* 9
el aro *hoop,* 5
el arqueólogo, la arqueóloga *archeologist,* 3
el **arquitecto, la arquitecta** *architect,* III12
la arquitectura *architecture,* 12
arrancar *to tear off,* 3
arrastrar *to drag,* 9
arrear *to urge on,* 5
arrebatar *to wrench,* 9
arreglar *to fix,* 3
arreglarse bien *to dress well,* 12
el arreglo de flores *flower arrangement,* 7
arremetieron contra *attacked,* 5
arriba *above,* 6
arrepentir (ie, i) *to regret,* 11
arrogante *arrogant,* III9
arrojar *to throw down,* 5
el **arroz** *rice,* I
el **arte** (m./f.) (pl. las artes) *art,* I; las artes dramáticas *drama,* 6; **las artes marciales** *martial arts,* II
la artesanía *crafts*
el artesano, la artesana *craftsman,* 5
el **artículo** *article,* III8
el **artista, la artista** *artist,* III6
artístico(a) *artistic,* II
el asado *roast*
asado(a) *roast,* III4; **el puerco asado** *roast pork,* III4
la ascendencia *ancestry,* 9
la ascensión *ascension,* 1
asco: **¡Qué asco!** *How disgusting!,* III4
asegurar *to ensure, to reassure,* 5
aséptico(a) *clean,* 11
asesinar *to murder, to assassinate,* 4
el asesinato *murder, assassination,* 11
el asesino, la asesina *murderer, assassin,* 11
así *so, thus, here's how,* II; **Así es.** *That's right.,* III5; **así que** *so,* III10
asiático(a) *Asian,* 9
el asiento *seat,* 5
asimilarse *to assimilate,* III10
asistir a *to attend,* I
asomarse *to lean out,* 9
asombrar *to amaze,* 9
áspero(a) *rough, rude,* 12
la aspiración (pl. **las aspiraciones**) *aspiration, ambition,* III10
la aspiradora *vacuum cleaner,* I; **pasar la aspiradora** *to vacuum,* I
aspirar a *to aspire to,* III10
asqueroso(a) *disgusting,* 2
el asunto *subject, matter,* 4
asustarse *to be frightened,* II
atar *to tie,* 3

atender (ie) *to help, to be of help, to assist,* II
Atentamente *Yours truly,* 10; *attentively,* 11
el aterrizaje *landing,* 5
el atleta, la atleta *athlete,* 8
el atletismo *track and field,* II
la atmósfera *atmosphere,* 11
atmosférico(a) *atmospheric,* 11
atónito(a) *astonished,* 11
la atracción (pl. las atracciones) *attraction,* 10
atraer *to attract,* 8
atrapado(a) *trapped, entrapped,* 3
atrasado(a) *late,* I
atravesar (ie) *to go through, to cross,* 9
atreverse *to dare,* 11
el **atún** *tuna,* I
la audiencia *audience,* 8
aumentar *to grow,* III11; *to increase,* 12; **aumentar de peso** *to put on weight,* II
aunque *although,* 12
el **autobús** (pl. los autobuses) *bus,* I
el automercado *supermarket,* 4
el automóvil *automobile,* 3
la autopista *freeway, highway,* III3
el autor, la autora *author,* 3
las autoridades *authorities,* 6
el autorretrato *self-portrait,* 6
¡Auxilio! *Help!,* 4
el avance *advance,* 3
avanzado(a) *advanced,* 3
avanzar *to move forward, to advance,* 3
la avaricia *greed,* 5
el ave (f.) *bird,* II
la avenida *avenue*
aventurero(a) *adventurous,* II
avergonzarse (üe) *to be embarrassed,* 12
averiguar *to find out,* II
la aversión *dislike,* 1
el avión (pl. los aviones) *airplane,* 11
avisado(a) *wise,* 9
¡Ay! *Oh!,* II
ayer *yesterday,* I
el ayudante, la ayudante *helper,* 11
ayudar *to help,* I; **ayudar a** + inf. *to help (do something),* I; **¿Me podrías ayudar a...?** *Could you help me (to) . . .?,* III4; **Por favor, ayúdame con...** *Please help me with . . .,* III4
el **ayuntamiento** *town hall,* III3
el **azúcar** *sugar,* I
azul *blue,* I

baboso(a) *runny,* 3
el bacalao *cod,* III4
el bachaco *big ant,* 4

la bahía *bay*
bailar *to dance*, I
el **bailarín, la bailarina** *dancer*, III6
el **baile** *dance*, I
bajar *to decrease*, III11; **bajar de peso** *to lose weight*, II; **bajar el río en canoa** *to go canoeing*, I; **bajar por** *to go down (a street or road)*, II; **bajarse del autobús** *to get off the bus*, II
bajo(a) *short, low*, I
balanceado(a) *balanced*, II
balancear *to balance*, 10
el balcón *balcony*, 1
la **ballena** *whale*, II
el **baloncesto** *basketball*, I
la balsa *float, raft*, 5
el **banco** *bank*, II
la **banda** *band*, II
la bandera *flag*, 7
el **banquero, la banquera** *banker*, III12
bañarse *to take a bath*, II; *to go swimming*, 1
barato(a) *cheap*, I; **en barata** *on sale*, II
la **barba** *beard*, III1
el barco *boat*
la barra *pole*, 9
barrer *to sweep*, II
el barril *barrel*, 3
el barrio *neighborhood*, 2
el barro *clay*, 6
basarse *to base*, 4
bastante *enough, pretty, quite*, I
bastar *to be enough*, 2; me basta *it's enough for me*, 2
la **basura** *garbage, trash*, II
el **basurero** *trash can*, III3
la batalla *battle*, 5
la batata *sweet potato*, 4
la **batería** *drum set*, III1
la batida *milkshake* (Puerto Rico)
el **batido** *milkshake*, I
beber *to drink*, I
la **bebida** *beverage*, I
la beca *scholarship*, 7
el **béisbol** *baseball*, I
la belleza *beauty*
bello(a) *beautiful*, 6
los **beneficios** *benefits*, III12
beneficioso(a) *beneficial*, 11
el beso *kiss*, 2
la **biblioteca** *library*, I
el bicho *insect*, 11
la **bicicleta** *bike*, I; **montar en bicicleta** *to ride a bike*, I
bien *well, good, all right, O.K.*, I; bien hecho(a) *well made*, 8
los bienes *possessions*, 8
el **bienestar** *well-being*, II
el **bigote** *moustache*, III1
bilingüe *bilingual*, 10
el billonario, la billonaria *billionaire*, 8
la bioquímica *biochemistry*
Birmania *Burma (Myanmar)*, 1

la birria *pork stew with red chile sauce*
el **bistec** *steak*, I; **el bistec a la parrilla** *grilled steak*, III4
bizquear *to squint*, 12
blanco(a) *white*, I
blindado(a) *iron-clad, armored*, 1
el **bloqueador** *sunscreen*, I
los bloques *row housing*, 3
los **bluejeans** *bluejeans*, I
la **blusa** *blouse*, I
bobo(a) *silly, dumb*, III9
la **boca** *mouth*, I
la **boda** *wedding*, III5; **celebrar la boda** *to celebrate the wedding*, III5
la **bodega** *grocery store*, III4
la bola *ball*, 12
el **boleto** *ticket*, I
el **bolígrafo** *ballpoint pen*, I
boliviano(a) *Bolivian*, II
la bolsa *bag*, 4
el bolsillo *pocket*, 3
el bolso *purse, moneybag*, 5
el bombero, la bombera *firefighter*, 4
bondadoso(a) *kind*, II
bonito(a) *pretty, nice*, I
el borde *edge*, 9
el **bosque** *forest*, I
la bota *throwing* (colloquial), 11
botánico(a) *botanical*, II
botar *to throw out*, III3
las **botas** *boots*, I
el botecillo *small boat*, 9
la botella *bottle*, 11
el boyero, la boyera *ox driver*, 5
el **brazo** *arm*, I
breve *brief*, 4
brillar *to shine*, 12
brindar *to offer*, 7
la broma *joke, prank*, 6
el bronce *bronze*, 11
broncearse *to suntan*, III2
brutal *rough*, 11
la brutalidad *brutality*, 5
bucear *to go scuba diving*, III1
el **buceo** *scuba diving*, III1
buen consejo *good advice*, 2
el **buen humor** *good mood*, III7; **Estoy de buen humor.** *I'm in a good mood.*, III7
buena gente *nice (person, people)*, III1
bueno(a) *good*, I
Bueno... *Well...*, III3; **Bueno, puede ser, pero...** *Well, that may be, but...*, III5
el buey *ox*, 5
la **bufanda** *scarf*, I
el buitre *vulture*, 5
la bujía *spark plug*, 4
burlarse de *to make fun of*, III9; **Niego haberme burlado de...** *I deny having made fun of...*, III9; **se burlaron de** *they made fun of*, III9
buscar *to look for*, I; **Buscaré...** *I'll look for...*, III12; Busco a

alguien... *I look for someone...*, III7; **Es necesario que busquemos...** *It's necessary for us to look for...*, III6
la **búsqueda** *search*, 2

el caballero *gentleman*, 7
el **caballo** *horse*, I; **montar a caballo** *to ride a horse*, I
la cabecilla *head*, 9
el cabello *hair*, 2
caber: **No cabe la menor duda.** *There's absolutely no doubt.*, III8; no cabía en sí *couldn't contain himself (herself)*, 11
la **cabeza** *head*, I
el **cable** *cable*, III8; **por cable** *on cable*, III8
la cachapa *fresh-corn pancake*
el cacique *Indian chief*, 5
cada *each, every*, I; **cada vez hay más... y menos...** *there are more and more... and less and less...*, II
la **cadena** *(broadcast) network*, III8; *chain*, 7
caer bien (mal): Me (Te,...) cae bien (mal) *I (You,...) really like (don't like) someone*, II
caerse *to fall down*, II; **Se nos cayó (cayeron)...** *We dropped...*, III4
el **café** *coffee*, I; **de color café** *brown*, I
la **cafetería** *cafeteria*, I
la **caja** *cash register*, II
el **cajero, la cajera** *cashier*, II
la cajeta *caramelized milk*
el cajón *drawer*, 12; el cajón de palma y corona *casket*, 7
la cal *lime*, 12
la calabaza *pumpkin*, 4
los calamares *squid*, 1; los calamares en su tinta *squid cooked in its ink*, 1
el **calambre** *cramp*, II
los **calcetines** *socks*, I
la calcomanía *sticker*, 1
la **calculadora** *calculator*, I
calcular *to calculate*, 3
el caldo gallego *soup made with greens, potatoes, sausage, pork, and beef*
la **calefacción** *heat*, II
el calendario *calendar*, 5
calentar (ie) *to heat*, 9
la **calidad** *quality*, 4; l**a calidad del aire** *air quality*, III3
caliente *hot*, I
la calificación *grade* (on an assignment), 2
callado(a) *quiet*, III9
la calle *street*
la calma: **tomar las cosas con calma** *to take things calmly*, III2
la caloría *calorie*, 4

calvo(a) *bald,* II
la **calzada** *roadway,* 9; las calzadas *footings, foundation,* 9
la **cama** *bed,* I
la **cámara** *camera,* I
el **camarada,** la camarada *comrade,* 6
la **camarera** *waitress,* I
el **camarero** *waiter,* I
los **camarones** *shrimp,* I
cambiar *to change,* II; **Cambiando de tema, ¿qué me dices de...?** *Changing subjects, what can you tell me about . . .?,* III6; **ha cambiado mucho** *has changed a lot,* III3
la **camilla** *stretcher,* 6
caminar *to walk,* I; **caminar con el perro** *to walk the dog,* I
la **caminata** *hike, stroll, walk,* I
el **camino** *path, road,* 3
el **camión** *bus (Mexico),* 6
la **camisa** *shirt,* I
la **camiseta** *T-shirt,* I
el **campamento** *camp,* 9
la **campana** *bell,* 9
campanear *to ring bells,* 9
la **campaña** *campaign,* 11; la campaña **publicitaria** *advertising campaign,* 8
el **campeonato** *championship,* 7
el **campesino,** la campesina *peasant,* 11
el **campo** *country,* I; *field,* 10; el campo **deportivo** *playing field,* 10
el **canal** *channel,* III8
las **canas** *gray hair,* I
cancelar *to cancel,* 8
la **cancha de (fútbol, tenis)** *(soccer) field, (tennis) court,* I
la **canción** (pl. las canciones) *song,* 8
la **canoa** *canoe,* I
canoso(a) *white-haired,* II
cansado(a) *tired,* I
cansarse *to get tired,* II
el **cantante,** la cantante *singer,* III6
cantar *to sing,* I
la **cantera** *quarry,* 9
la **cantidad** *quantity,* 4
la **caña de azúcar** *sugarcane*
la **capa** *cape,* 5; **la capa de ozono** *ozone layer,* II
la **capacidad** *ability,* 6
capaz (pl. capaces) *capable,* 9
el **capitán,** la capitana *captain,* 10
la **cápsula de información** *time capsule,* 3
captar *to capture,* 7
la **cara** *face,* 10
el **carácter** *character,* 10
¡Caramba! *My goodness!,* 4
las **caraotas** *beans* (Venezuela), III4
el **caraqueño,** la caraqueña *resident of Caracas*
el **carbohidrato** *carbohydrate,* 4
la **carbonada criolla** *barbecued meat*
la **carcajada** *loud laughter,* 2
la **cárcel** *jail,* 5
cardinal *cardinal* (adj.), 1
la **carga** *load,* 9

cargado(a) *heavy, loaded,* 3
caribeño(a) *Caribbean* (adj.)
el **cariño** *affection,* II; **con cariño** *affectionately,* II
cariñoso(a) *affectionate,* I
la **carne** *meat,* I; **la carne de res** *beef,* I
la **carnicería** *butcher shop,* III4
las **carnitas** *fried or roast pork bits*
caro(a) *expensive,* I
la **carpeta** *folder,* I
el **carpintero,** la carpintera *carpenter,* III12
la **carrera** *race,* 10; *career,* 10
la **carreta** *cart,* 5
la **carretera** *road,* 11
el **carro** *car,* I; **los carros chocone**s *bumper cars,* II; **el carro eléctrico** *electric car,* III3
la **carroza** *(parade) float,* II
el **carruaje** *carriage,* 9
la **carta** *letter,* I; **la carta electrónica** *e-mail,* III3; **enviar una carta electrónica** *to send an e-mail,* III3
las **cartas** *(playing) cards,* II
el **cartel** *poster,* I
la **cartera** *wallet,* I
la **casa** *house, home,* I; **en casa** *at home,* II
el **casamiento** *marriage,* 5
casarse *to get married,* II
casero(a) *homemade,* 4
casi *almost,* I; **casi siempre** *almost always,* I
la **casilla** *ticket office,* 9
el **caso** *instance,* 5; **en caso de que** *in case,* III10; **hacer caso** *to pay attention,* 2
el **castillo** *castle,* 5
casualidad: por casualidad *by coincidence,* 5
el **cataclismo** *major disaster, cataclysm,* 2
el **catalán** *Catalan (language of Catalonia),* 2
la **catarata** *waterfall*
catedral *cathedral*
catorce *fourteen,* I
el **cauce** *bed (of a river),* 9
el **caudillo** *leader, chief*
la **causa** *cause,* 8
causar el estrés *to cause stress,* III2
cauteloso(a) *cautious,* 2
cautivar *to captivate,* 7
cazar *to hunt,* 5
el **cazón** *shark,* 4
la **cebolla** *onion,* I
ceder *to give up, to yield,* 3
cegador(a) *blinding,* 12
celebrar *to celebrate,* III5; **celebrar la boda** *to celebrate the wedding,* III5
celestial *heavenly,* 9
los **celos: que no tenga celos** *who won't be jealous,* III7; **tener celos de** *to be jealous of,* III7
céltico(a) *Celtic*
el **cementerio** *cemetery,* 12

el **cemento** *cement,* 4
la **cena** *dinner,* I
cenar *to eat dinner,* I
la **ceniza** *ash,* 3
censurado(a) *censored*
el **centavo** *cent,* 7
centenares *hundreds,* 9
el **centollo** *crab,* 1
el **centro** *downtown,* II
el **centro comercial** *shopping mall,* I
cepillarse *to brush (one's hair, teeth, etc.),* II
el **cepillo de dientes** *toothbrush,* II
la **cera** *wax,* 11
la **cerámica** *pottery,* 6
cerca de *near,* I; *close to,* II
el **cerdo** *pork, pig,* III4; **las chuletas de cerdo** *pork chops,* III4
el **cereal** *cereal,* I
el **cerebro** *brain,* 2
la **ceremonia de graduación** *graduation ceremony,* 9
el **cerezo** *cherry tree,* 5
cero *zero,* I
cerrar (ie) *to close,* 1
la **certeza** *certainty,* 7
el **césped** *the grass,* I
el **ceviche** *fish or shellfish marinated in lemon and spices*
la **chacra** *farm (Andean countries),* 4
el **champú** *shampoo,* II
el **chancho** *pork (Andean countries),* 4
las **chancletas** *sandals, slippers,* I
Chao. *'Bye.,* I
la **chaqueta** *jacket,* I
el **charango** *Andean stringed instrument,* 6
la **charcutería** *store that sells prepared meats,* 4
la **charla** *talk, conversation,* 4
la **charrería** *rodeo-like horseback riding*
chasquear *to snap, to click,* 11
chévere *terrific (Venezuela),* 3
la **chica** *girl,* I
el **chicano,** la chicana *Mexican that has emigrated to the United States,* 10
el **chicharrón** *fried pork rind*
el **chicle** *chewing gum,* 12
chico(a) *small,* 5
el **chico** *boy,* I
chileno(a) *Chilean,* II
el **chimichurri** *pesto-like sauce served with meat*
China (f.) *China,* I
el **chino** *Chinese (language);* **Me suena a chino.** *It's Greek to me.,* III8
chino(a) *Chinese,* I
el **chiquito,** la chiquita *small child,* II
el **chisme** *gossip,* II
chismear *to gossip,* III7
chismoso(a) *gossipy,* III9
el **chismoso,** la chismosa *gossip (person),* II
el **chiste** *joke,* II
chocar: Me (Te,...) choca(n)... *I (You, . . .) dislike strongly,* II
chocones: los carros chocones

bumper cars, II
el chocolate *chocolate,* I
el chorizo *sausage,* III4
el chucho *electric switch,* 9
las chuletas de cerdo *pork chops,* III4
el chuño *potato starch,* 4
los churros *sugar-coated fritters,* 4
el chuzo *whip,* 5
el ciclismo *cycling,* III1; **practicar ciclismo** *to practice cycling,* III1
el cielo *sky,* 1; el cielo raso *ceiling,* 6
cien, ciento *one hundred,* I; **por ciento** *percent,* II
la ciencia ficción *science fiction,* II
las ciencias *science,* I; **las ciencias sociales** *social studies,* I
el científico, la científica *scientist,* III12
cierto(a) *sure, certain, true,* I; *specific,* 5; **Por cierto.** *Certainly.,* III8
cinco *five,* I
cincuenta *fifty,* I
el cine *movie theater,* I
la cinematografía *filmmaking,* 6
cinético(a) *kinetic, pertaining to motion*
el cinturón *belt,* I
el circo *circus,* I
el círculo *circle,* 10
la cirugía *surgery,* 12
el cirujano, la cirujana *surgeon,* 12
la cita *date, appointment,* I
la ciudad *city,* II
el ciudadano, la ciudadana *citizen,* 9
la claridad *clarity,* 2
el clarinete *clarinet,* III1
el claro *clearing,* 5
claro(a) *light (color),* 10
Claro que... *Of course . . .,* III8; **¡Claro que no!** *Of course not!,* III5; **¡Claro que sí!** *Of course!,* III5
la clase *class, classroom;* **la clase de ejercicios aeróbicos** *aerobics class,* I; la clase particular *individual instruction,* 6
clásico(a) *classical,* I
clavado(a) *nailed,* 5
las claves *clues,* 4
el cliente, la cliente *customer,* II
la clientela *customers,* 11
el clima *climate,* II; el clima templado *temperate or moderate climate*
el cobrador, la cobradora *bill collector,* 3
el cobre *copper,* 5
el coche *car,* 2
el cochino *pork, pig,* 4
la cocina *kitchen,* I; *stove* (Venezuela), 3; *cooking,* III8; **la sección de cocina** *food (cooking) section,* III8
cocinar *to cook,* III3; **cocinar en el horno de microondas** *to cook in the microwave oven,* III3
el cocinero, la cocinera *cook,* 4
el cocodrilo *crocodile,* II
codiciado(a) *much desired,* 12

codicioso(a) *greedy,* 2
el codo *elbow,* II
coger *to take,* 10
cohibido(a) *shy, inhibited,* 9
coincidir *to coincide,* 8
la cola *tail, line,* II; **hacer cola** *to stand in line,* II
coleccionar *to collect,* II; **coleccionar adhesivos** *to collect stickers,* III1; **coleccionar sellos** *to collect stamps,* III1
la colectividad *community,* 10
colectivo(a) *collective,* 6
el colegio *high school,* I
colgante *hanging,* 9
colgar (ue) *to hang,* I
el colibrí *hummingbird,* 5
el coliseo *coliseum,* 9
el collar *necklace,* I
la colmena *beehive,* 11
el colmo *high point,* 8; para colmo *to top things off,* 8
colocar *to place,* 4
colombiano(a) *Colombian,* II
el colón *Costa Rican monetary unit,* 11
el color *color,* I; **el color café** *brown,* I
los colores vivos *bright colors,* 6
colorido(a) *colorful,* 10
colosal *fantastic,* 9
la comarca *area, region,* 11
combatir *to combat,* III9
el combustible *fuel,* II
el comedor *dining room,* II
comentario *comment,* 4
el comentarista, la comentarista *commentator,* III8
comenzar (ie) *to start, to begin,* II
comer *to eat,* I; **comer comida sana** *to eat healthy food,* III2
el comerciante, la comerciante *businessman, businesswoman,* III12
el comercio *commerce, shop,* 9
cometer *to commit,* III11; **cometer un error** *to make a mistake,* III7
cómico(a) *funny,* I
la comida *food, meal, lunch* (Mexico), I
el comino *cumin (spice),* 4
el comité *committee,* 10
como *like, as,* I; **¡Cómo no!** *Of course!,* III5; **Como quieras.** *Whatever (you want).,* III1
¿Cómo? *How?,* III1; *What?,* I
cómodo(a) *comfortable,* I
el compañero, la compañera *friend, pal, classmate,* I
la compañía *company,* 11
la comparación (pl. las comparaciones) *comparison,* 3
compartir *to share,* II; **compartir con alguien** *to share with someone,* III2; **Comparto tu pena.** *I share your grief.,* III7
compatible *compatible,* 5
compendiar *to summarize,* 6
la competencia *competition,* II
complacer (zc) *to please,* 5
el complejo *complex,* 4

complejo(a) *complex,* 4
completar *to complete,* 4
completo(a) *complete,* III12; **tiempo completo** *full time,* III12
complicado(a) *complicated,* 9
el cómplice, la cómplice *accomplice,* 8
componer *to put together*
la composición (pl. las composiciones) *composition, essay,* 3
el compositor, la compositora *composer*
comprar *to buy,* I; **comprarle un regalo** *to buy someone a gift,* III7
comprender *to understand, to comprehend,* 9
comprimir *to compress,* 6
comprometido(a) *committed,* 3
el compromiso *commitment, obligation,* III10; *engagement,* 4
compuesto(a) *made up of*
la computación *computer science,* I
la computadora *computer,* III3
comunicativo(a) *communicative,* 12
común: tener(ie) en común *to have in common,* 1
con *with,* I; **con la idea de...** *in order to . . .,* III10; **con la intención de...** *with the intention of . . .,* III10; **con sí mismo(a)** *with himself (herself),* 2; **con tal (de) que** *provided that,* III10; **conmigo** *with me,* I; **contigo** *with you,* I
el concentrado *concentrate,* 6
el concesionario, la concesionaria *owner or operator of a concession,* 3
la concha *shell,* 6
la conciencia cultural *cultural awareness,* 10
el concierto *concert,* I
la concordia *harmony,* 5
el concurso *contest, game show,* 1
la condena *sentence,* 9
condenar *to condemn,* 5
la condición física *physical condition,* 6
condimentado(a) *seasoned,* 4
el cóndor *condor,* II
el conductor, la conductora *driver,* II
confesar (ie) *to confess,* 5
la confianza *trust, confidence,* 3
confiar en *to trust,* III7
la confitería *confectionery, coffee shop* (Argentina), 7
conflictivo(a) *conflicting,* 6
el conflicto *conflict,* 7
el congelador *freezer,* 3
el congestionamiento *overcrowding,* 11
conmemorar *to commemorate,* 7
conmutar *to commute* (a sentence), 9
conocer (zc) *to know (a person), to meet (for the first time), to be familiar with (something),* I
el conocido, la conocida *acquaintance,* 7
el conocimiento *knowledge, familiarity,* 5
la conquista *conquest,* 5
el conquistador, la conquistadora

conqueror, 5
consagrar *to consecrate, to dedicate one's life*, 1
consecuencia: **en consecuencia** *therefore*, III10
conseguir (i, i) *to get*, 2
el consejero, la consejera *counselor, advisor*, 2
el consejo *advice*, 2
consentido(a) *spoiled (person)*, II
consentir (ie, i) *to consent*, 7
conservador(a) *conservationist*, 11
conservar *to conserve*, II
consiguiente: **por consiguiente** *consequently*, III10
consolar (ue) *to offer comfort*, 7
la constancia *evidence*, 4
constituir *to set up, to make up, to constitute*, 3
el constructor, la constructora *builder*, 5
construir *to build*, II
el consuelo *comfort*, 7
el consumidor, la consumidora *consumer*, 11
la contabilidad *accounting*, 12
el contador, la contadora *accountant*, III12
la contaminación *pollution*, II
contar (ue) *to count, to tell*, II; **contar con** *to count on*, III7; **Cuentan que...** *They say that . . .*, III5; **¿Qué me cuentas de...?** *What can you tell me about . . . ?*, III6
contemplar *to view, to contemplate*, 2
contemporáneo(a) *contemporary*, III6
el contenido *content*, 7
contento(a) *happy*, II
el contestador *answering machine*, III3
la contestadora *answering machine*, 3
contestar *to answer*, 7
contiguo(a) *adjoining*, 9
el continente *continent*, 4
continuar *to go on, to continue*, III11; **Temo que el deterioro continúe.** *I'm afraid the deterioration will continue.*, III11
contra *against*, III9
contradecir (i) *to contradict*, 7
contrario(a) *opposite*, 5; **de lo contrario** *otherwise*, 3
el contraste *contrast*
la contribución (pl. las contribuciones) *contribution*, 4
contribuir *to contribute*, III2
el control remoto *remote control*, 11
controvertido(a) *controversial*, 5
convencer *to convince*, 4
convencido(a): Estoy convencido(a) que... *I'm convinced that . . .*, III8
convencional *conventional*, III6
convendrás *you will arrange*, 3
convenir (ie) *to be convenient*, III6; **No te conviene...** *It's not advisable that you . . .*, III6
la conversación (pl. las conversaciones)

conversation, 1
conversador(a) *talkative*, II
convertirse (ie, i) en *to turn into*, 2
la convivencia *living together*, 6
convocar *to call together*, 7
la convulsión (pl. las convulsiones) *convulsion*, 7
copiar *to copy*, II
la coqueta *flirt*, 9
coquetear *to flirt*, 6
el corazón (pl. los corazones) *heart*, 4
la corbata *tie*, I
el cordoncillo *small cord*, 7
coreano(a) *Korean*, 9
el coro *choir, chorus*, 6
la corrección (pl. las correcciones) *correction*, 2
correcto(a) *correct*, 4
corregir (i, i) *to correct*, 1
el correo *post office*, I; **el correo electrónico** *e-mail*, II
correr *to run*, I
el corresponsal *correspondent*, 8
la corriente *current*
corriente: **el agua (f.) corriente** *running water*, II
la corrupción *corruption*, 11
cortar *to cut*, I; cortar con *to break up with someone*, 7
la corte *court*, 7
cortés *polite, courteous*, 4
la cortesía *courtesy, respect*, 4
cortésmente *politely*, 7
la cosa *thing*, I; **tomar las cosas con calma** *to take things calmly*, III2
cosechar *to harvest*, 4
cosmopolita *cosmopolitan*
la costa *coast*, II
costar (ue) *to cost*, I; **¿Cuánto cuesta(n)?** *How much does it (do they) cost?*, I; cuesta un ojo de la cara *costs an arm and a leg*, 4
costarricense (m./f.) *Costa Rican*, II
la costumbre *custom*, III10
la costurera *seamstress*, 7
el costurero *tailor*, 7
cotidiano(a) *daily*, 1
el cráneo *skull*, 7
el cráter *crater*, 5
crear *to create*, 3; crear conciencia *to create awareness*, 4
creativo(a) *creative*, III6
crecer (zc) *to grow*, III3
el crecimiento *growth*, 9
el crédito *credit*, 3
la creencia *belief*, 5
creer *to believe, to think*, I; **Creo que vale la pena...** *I think it's worth it . . .*, III3; **Es muy difícil de creer, pero es posible.** *That's very hard to believe, but it's possible.*, III5; **se cree que** *it is believed that*, III5
creído(a) *conceited*, 9
la crema *cream*, 4; **la crema de maní** *peanut butter*, I
criarse *to grow up, to be raised*, III10
el crimen *crime*, III11

la **criminalidad** *crime rate*, III11
la **crisis** *crisis*, II
el crisol *melting pot*, 10
los cristales *windows*, 12
la **crítica** *critique*, 5
criticar *to criticize*, 1
crocante *crunchy*, 4
cronológico(a) *chronological*, 4
el cruce *intersection, crossroad*, II
la crucecilla *cross*, 12
el crucigrama *crossword puzzle*, 2
crujiente *crunchy*, 4
cruzar (en...) *to cross (at . . .)*, II
el cuaderno *notebook*, I
la cuadra *city block*, I
cuadrado(a) *squared (measurement)*, 1
el cuadro *square*; **de cuadros** *plaid*, I
¿Cuál? *Which? What?*, I
la cualidad *quality*, 12
cualquiera *anybody*, 12
cuando *when*, I; **Cuando cumpla los 18 años...** *When I turn 18 . . .*, III10; **Cuando era joven...** *When I was young . . .*, III12; **Cuando sea mayor** *When I'm older . . .*, III10; **Cuando tenía cinco años...** *When I was five . . .*, III12
¿Cuándo? *When?*, III1
cuanto: **en cuanto** *as soon as*, III10
¿Cuánto(a)? *How much?*, III1
¿Cuántos(as)? *How many?*, III1
cuarenta *forty*, I
el cuarto *room*, I; **el cuarto de baño** *bathroom*, II
cuarto: **... menos cuarto** *quarter to . . .*, I; **... y cuarto** *quarter past . . .*, I
cuatro *four*, I
cuatrocientos(as) *four hundred*, I
cubano(a) *Cuban*, II
la cuchara *spoon*, I
la cucharada *tablespoon*, 4
la cucharadita *teaspoon*, 4
el cuchillo *knife*, I
el cuello *neck*, I
el cuenco *earthenware bowl*, 10
la cuenta *check*, II; *bill*, I; la cuenta (de banco) *(bank) account*, 9
el cuento *story, tale*, II; **el cuento de hadas** *fairy tale*, II
la cuerda *rope, string*, II; **saltar a la cuerda** *to jump rope*, II
el cuero *leather*, I
el cuerpo *body*, I; el cuerpo *celestial heavenly body*, 5
el cuervo *crow*, 11
la cuesta *hill*, 11
el cuestionario *questionaire*, 11
la cueva *cave*, 5
el cuidado *care*, 3; **Ten cuidado.** *Be careful.*, II
cuidar *to take care of*, I
cuidarse el peso *to watch one's weight*, III2
la culebra *snake*, 5
culinario(a) *having to do with cooking*, 4

culminar *to culminate*, 11

la culpa *fault*, III7; **echarle la culpa a otro(a)** *to blame someone else*, III7

cultivar *to cultivate, to grow*, 4

culto(a) *cultured*, 6

la cumbre *peak*, 5

el cumplido *compliment*, III7; **hacerle un cumplido a alguien** *to compliment someone*, III7

cumplir *to accomplish, to carry out*, 3; *to turn (a specific age)*; **Cuando cumpla los 18 años...** *When I turn 18...*, III10

la cúpula *dome, cupola*

el curandero, la curandera *healer*, 7

el currículum (vitae) *résumé*, III12

el curso *course*, 1

cuyo(a) *whose, of which*, 1

la dama *lady*, 9

la danza *dance (as an art form)*, III6

danzar *to dance*, 4

el daño *damage, harm*, 8; **hacerse daño** *to hurt oneself*, II

dañoso(a) *damaging, harmful*, 8

dar *to give*, I; dar la mano *to shake hands*, 12; dar películas *to show movies*, 7 **dar una caminata** *to go hiking*, I; **darle un abrazo** *to give someone a hug*, III7; **Me da igual.** *It's all the same to me.*, III1; **Me da lo mismo.** *It's all the same to me.*, III1; **Me dan ganas de llorar.** *It makes me feel like crying.*, III7; **¿Serías tan amable de dármela?** *Would you be so kind as to give it to me?*, III4

darse: darse cuenta (de) *to realize*, III9; **darse tiempo para pensar** *to give oneself time to think*, III7

datar *to date*, 6

de *of, from, made of, in, as*, I; **¿de dónde?** *from where?*, III1; **de estatura mediana** *of medium height*, III1; de (malos) modos *in a (bad) way*, 12; **de muy mal gusto** *in very bad taste*, III6; de ningún modo *no way*, 8; **De niño(a),...** *As a child...*, III12; **de repente** *all of a sudden*, II; **de tal forma que...** *in such a way that...*, III10

debajo de *under, beneath*, I

debatir *to debate*, 3

deber *should, ought to*, I; **Deben...** *They should...*, III3; **Deberías +** inf. *You should...*, III2; **Debes...** *You should...*, III12; **¿Qué debo hacer?** *What should I do?*, III2; **se deben a** *are due to*, III10

el deber *duty*, III3; **Es nuestro deber...** *It's our duty...*, III3

la debilidad *weakness*, 2

debilitar *to weaken*, 11

la década *decade*, 3

la decepción *disappointment*, 12

decepcionado(a) *disappointed*, III7; **Estoy decepcionado(a).** *I'm disappointed.*, III7

decidir *to decide*, 4

decir *to say, to tell*, I; **Alguien me dijo que...** *Somebody told me that...*, III5; **Cambiando de tema, ¿qué me dices de...?** *Changing subjects, what can you tell me about...?*, III6; **Dicen que...** *They say that...*, III5; **¡No me digas!** *You don't say!*, III8; **Para decir la verdad...** *To tell the truth...*, III6; **...que siempre me diga...** *...who always tells me...*, III7; **Se dice que** *They say that*, III5

declarar *to declare*, III5

las decoraciones (sing. **la decoración**) *decorations*, I

decorar *to decorate*, I

dedicar *to dedicate*, II

dedicarse *to devote oneself*, III11; **Me dedicaría a...** *I would devote myself to...*, III11

el dedo *finger, toe*, I

el defecto humano *human failing*, 8

defender (ie) *to defend*, 11

definir *to define*, 4

dejar *to leave (behind), to let go*, II; **dejar plantado(a) a alguien** *to stand someone up*, III7; **¿En cuánto lo deja?** *How much will you let it go for?*, II; **¿Por qué no lo dejamos para...?** *Why don't we leave it for (another time)?*, III6

dejar de + inf. *to stop (doing something)*, II; **dejar de hablarse** *to stop speaking to each other*, III7

del (de + el) *of the, from the*, I

delante de *in front of*, II

deletrear *to spell*, 3

el delfín (pl. **los delfines**) *dolphin*, II

delgado(a) *thin*, I

delicioso(a) *delicious*, I

la delincuencia *crime*, III11

el delito *minor crime*, III11

demasiado(a) *too much*, I

la democracia *democracy*, 10

demoler (ue) *to demolish*, 11

demostrar (ue) *to show, to demonstrate*, 2

denominar *to name*, 6

denso(a) *dense*, 4

dentro de... *within (a day, month,...)*, II

deparar *to present*, 12

depender *to depend*, III5; **Depende de tu punto de vista.** *It depends on your point of view.*, III5

el dependiente, la dependiente *store clerk*, II

los deportes *sports*, I

deportivo(a) *sports (adj.)*, III8; **la sección deportiva** *sports section*, III8

deprimido(a) *depressed, sad*, II

el derecho *right, law (field of study)*, 9

derecho *straight*, II

derecho(a) *right*; **a la derecha** *to the right*, II

derivar *to derive, to descend*

la derrota *defeat*, III5

derrumbar *to knock down*, 6

el desacuerdo *disagreement*, 5

desafiar *to defy, to challenge*, 1

el desafío *challenge*, 10

desafortunadamente *unfortunately*, 5

desaparecer (zc) *disappear*, 5

desarrollar *to develop*, III3

el desarrollo *development*, 4

desasosegar (ie) *to make uneasy*, 12

el desastre *disaster*, 4

desayunar *to eat breakfast*, I

el desayuno *breakfast*, I

descansar *to rest*, I

el descanso *recess, break*, I

descender (ie) *to descend*, 9

descomponerse *to break down*, III4; **Se nos descompuso (descompusieron)...** *...broke down on us.*, III4

desconectar *to disconnect*, 11

desconocer *to be unfamiliar with*, 1

desconocido(a) *unknown, unfamiliar*, 11

descontrolado(a) *out of control*, 2

descortés *rude*, III8; **No aguanto a nadie que sea descortés.** *I can't stand anyone who's rude.*, III7

describir *to describe*, 6

descubierto(a) (past participle of **descubrir**) *discovered*, 3

el descubrimiento *discovery*, 7

descubrir *to discover*, III3

el descuento *discount*, II

descuidar *to neglect*, 2

desde *since*, 3; **Desde luego.** *Of course.*, III5

desear *to wish*, 12; *to desire*, 12; *to want (formal)*; **¿Desean algo más?** *Would you like anything else?*, I

desechable *disposable*, 3

desechado(a) *thrown out*, 11

desempeñar *to carry out*, 6

el desempleo *unemployment*, III11

el desenvolvimiento *development*, 4

el deseo *wish, desire*, 5

desesperarse *to lose hope*, II

desfilar *to march, to parade*, II

el desfile *parade*, II

la desgracia *misfortune*, 10

el desierto *desert*, 5

la desilusión *disappointment*, 7

desilusionado(a) *disappointed*, III7; **Estoy desilusionado(a).** *I'm disappointed.*, III7

desilusionar *to destroy an illusion*
desinclinadamente *unwillingly*, 10
desleal *disloyal*, III7
el desliz (pl. los deslices) *slip, slide*, 1
deslizar *to slide*, 9
desmoronar *to crumble*, 11
el despecho *despair*, 10
despedirse (i, i) de *to say goodbye to*, II
despejado(a) *clear*, II
la despensa *pantry*, 4
desperdiciar *to waste*, II
el desperdicio *waste*, II
el despertador *alarm clock*, II
despertarse (ie) *to wake up*, II
despreciado(a) *belittled*, 10
el desprecio *contempt*, 12
desprovisto(a) *lacking*, 11
después (de) *after*, I; *afterward*, II; **Después de graduarnos...** *After we graduate . . .*, III10; **después de que** *after* (conj.), III10
destacar *to point out*, 11
destilar *to distill*, 11
el destino *destiny, destination*, 5
destrozado(a) *destroyed*, 6
destrozar *to destroy*, 10
la destrucción *destruction*, II
destruir *to destroy*, III3
desvelarse *to stay up late*, 2
la desventaja *disadvantage*, III3
el detalle *detail*, 1
detener (ie) *to stop*, 9
el deterioro *deterioration*, III11; **Temo que el deterioro continúe** *I'm afraid the deterioration will continue*, III11
detrás de *behind*, II
el deudor, la deudora *debtor*, 3
devolver (ue) *to give back*, 5
el día *day*, I; **el Día de Acción de Gracias** *Thanksgiving Day*, I; **el Día de la Independencia** *Independence Day*, I; **el Día de la Raza** *Columbus Day*, 10; **el Día de las Madres** *Mother's Day*, I; **el Día de los Enamorados** *Valentine's Day*, I; **el Día del Padre** *Father's Day*, I; **hoy (en) día** *nowadays*, III3
el diablo *devil*, 7
diario(a) *daily*, III3; **la vida diaria** *daily life*, III3
dibujar *to draw*, I
el dibujo *drawing*, III6
el diccionario *dictionary*, I
Dicen que... *They say that . . .*, III5
el dicho *saying, proverb*, 5
dicho *(past participle of* **decir***) said*, III3
diciembre (m.) *December*, I
diecinueve *nineteen*, I
dieciocho *eighteen*, I
dieciséis *sixteen*, I
diecisiete *seventeen*, I
el diente *tooth*, I; **los dientes** *teeth*, I
diestra: a diestra y a siniestra *right and left*, 9

la dieta *diet*, II
diez *ten*, I
diezmar *to decimate*, 4
difícil *difficult, unlikely*, I; **Es difícil que** *It's unlikely that*, III8; **Es muy difícil de creer, pero es posible.** *That's very hard to believe, but it's possible.*, III5
la dificultad *difficulty*, 10
difundir *to spread, to broadcast*, 9
Diga. *Hello.* (telephone greeting), I
diligente diligent, speedy, 9
la dinamita *dynamite*, 7
el dinero *money*, I
el dinosaurio *dinosaur*, 11
el dintel *threshold*, 9
el dios *god*, III5; **Los dioses quieren que los guerreros acuerden la paz.** *The gods want the warriors to make peace.*, III5
la diosa *goddess*, III5
el diploma *diploma*, 9
dirigir *to direct*, 8
la disciplina *discipline*, 10
el disco compacto *compact disc*, I
la discriminación *discrimination*, III9
disculpar *to excuse, to forgive*, III7; **Discúlpame.** (informal) *Forgive me.*, III7; **Disculpe.** (formal) *Excuse me.*, II
el discurso *speech*, 3; **el discurso de despedida** *farewell speech*, 9
discutir el problema *to discuss the problem*, III7
el diseñador, la diseñadora *designer*, III12
diseñar *to design*, III6
el diseño *design*; **el diseño gráfico** *graphic design*, 12; **el diseño por computadora** *computer-assisted design*, 6
el disfraz (pl. los disfraces) *costume*, II
disfrutar *to enjoy*, II
disgregar *to disintegrate*, 4
la disminución *reduction*, 11
disminuir *to lessen*, 2
el disparate *foolish act*, 11
disponer *to arrange*, 4
dispuesto(a) *ready, willing*, 5
disputar *to dispute*, 4
distinto(a) *different*, 6
el distrito *district*
la diversidad *diversity*, 10
diverso(a) *varied*, 6
divertido(a) *fun, amusing*, I
divertirse (ie, i) *to have fun*, II
divorciarse *to get divorced*, 7
divulgación *publication*, 3
doblar *to turn*, II
el doble *double*, 3
doce *twelve*, I
el documental *documentary*, III8
el dólar *dollar*, I
doler (ue) *to hurt, to ache*, I; **Estoy dolido(a).** *I'm hurt.*, III7; **Me duele mucho que...** *It really hurts*

me that . . ., III7
el dolor *pain*, 12
doloroso(a) *painful*, 6
doméstico(a) *household* (adj.), I; **los quehaceres domésticos** *household chores*, I
el domicilio *home*, 4
dominar *to dominate*, 4; **Domina el francés.** *He (She) speaks French very well.*, III10
el domingo *Sunday*, I
dominical *Sunday* (adj.), 8
dominicano(a) *Dominican* (from the Dominican Republic), II
el dominio *mastery*, 12; *domination, control*
el don *gift, talent*, 9
donar *to donate*, 11
donde *where*, I
¿Dónde? *Where?*, III1
dorado(a) *golden*, 5
dormir (ue, u) *to sleep*, II; **dormir lo suficiente** *to get enough sleep*, III2
dormirse (ue, u) *to fall asleep*, III2
dos *two*, I; **dos por uno** *two for one*, II
doscientos(as) *two hundred*, I
el dosel *canopy, curtain*, 6
la dote *dowry*, 7
dramatizar *to act out, to dramatize*, 4
el drenaje *drainage*, 11
la droga *drug*, 11
la drogadicción *drug addiction*, III11
ducharse *to take a shower*, III2
la duda *doubt*, II; **No cabe la menor duda.** *There's absolutely no doubt.*, III8; **Sin duda (alguna).** *Without a doubt.*, II
dudar *to doubt*, II; **Dudo que...** *I doubt that . . .*, III8
el dueño, la dueña *owner*, 5
el dueto *duet*, 6
dulce *sweet*, I
la dulcería *candy store*, I
los dulces *candy*, I
duplicar *to double*, 10
durante *during*, I
durar *to last*, 1
el durazno *peach*, 4
el duro *five-peseta coin*, 7
duro(a) *hard*, 1; *difficult*, 6
el DVD *DVD (Digital Versatile Disc)*, 3

e *and* (before words beginning with **i** or **hi**), II
el e-mail *e-mail*, II
echado(a): **Está echado(a) a perder.** *It's spoiled (ruined).*, III4
echar *to throw, to toss*, II; **echar (a alguien) de menos** *to miss*

(*someone*), II; **echarle flores** *to compliment someone*, 7; **echarle la culpa a otro(a)** *to blame someone else*, III7; echar la siesta *to take a nap*, 2; **echarle mucha sal a la comida** *to put a lot of salt on food*, III2

el ecólogo, la ecóloga *ecologist*, 3

ecuatoriano(a) *Ecuadorean*, II

ecuestre *equestrian*, 1

la edad *age*, 2

el edificio *building*, II

la editorial *publisher*

los editoriales *editorials*, III8

la educación *education*, I

educar *to educate*, 3

el efecto *effect*, II; **los efectos especiales** *special effects*, II; **En efecto, parece ser así.** *Actually, it seems to be that way.*, III5

eficaz (pl. eficaces) *effective*, 8

Egipto (m.) *Egypt*, I

egoísta *selfish*, III9

Eh... *Uh . . .*, III3

el ejemplar *example*, 6

ejercer *to exert*, 9

el ejercicio *exercise*, I

el ejército *army*, III5

el (article) *the*, I; **el . . .** *on the (date)*, I; **El año pasado...** *Last year . . .*, III12

el/la ... que viene *next (year, week, . . .)*, II

él (pron.) *he, him* (after preposition), I

elaborar *to produce, to manufacture*, 4

la elección *choice*, 8

la electricidad *electricity*, II

electrónicamente *electronically*

elegante *elegant*, II

elegir (i, i) *to elect, to select*, 3

elevar *to raise*, 11

eliminar *to eliminate*, 10

ella *she; her* (after preposition), I

ellas *they; them* (after preposition), I

ellos *they; them* (after preposition), I

embargo: sin embargo *nevertheless*, 5

embarrado(a) *muddy*, 12

embellecer (zc) *to beautify*, 6

el embustero, la embustera *liar*, 12

emigrar *to emigrate*, 10

la emisora *radio or TV station*, III8

emitir *to emit, to send out*, 3

la emoción *emotion*, 9

emocionado(a) *excited*, II

emocionante *moving, exciting*, 9

empacado(a) *packaged*, II

la empanada *turnover filled with meat, fish, cheese, or fruit*, 1

empapar *to soak, to drench*, 4

emparejar *to match*, 11

emparentarse (ie) *to become related by marriage*, 4

empeorar *to get worse*, III3; **ha empeorado bastante** *has gotten quite a bit worse*, III3; **La situación va a empeorarse.** *The situation will get worse.*, III11

el emperador, la emperadora *emperor, empress*, 5

empezar(ie) *to begin*, I; **Antes que empiecen las clases...** *Before classes begin . . .*, III10; **Yo empezaría por** *I'd start by*, III11

el empleado, la empleada *employee*, III12

el empleo *job*, II

emprender *to start*, 5

la empresa *business, company*, III12

el empresario, la empresaria *entrepreneur*, 10

la empuñada *hold, grip*, 10

en *in, on, at*, I; en absoluto *absolutely not*, 5; en caso *in case*, 4; en común *in common*, 1; **en consecuencia** *therefore*, III10; en contra *against*, 8; **en cuanto** *as soon as*, III10; **En efecto, parece ser así**. *Actually, it seems to be that way.*, III5; **en fin** *in short*, II; **en línea** *online*, III8; en mi vida *never in my life*, 5; **en seguida** *right away, immediately*, III3; en su lugar *in his (her) place*, 9; en vez *instead of*, 5; en voz alta *out loud*, 5

enamoradizo(a) *amorous*, 2

enamorarse de *to fall in love with*, II

el enano, la enana *dwarf*, II

encabezar *to lead*, 9

encajar *to fit in*, III10

el encaje *lace*, 7

encaminarse *to set out*, 7

Encantado(a). *Delighted to meet you.*, I

encantador(a) *enchanting*, 7

encantar *to delight*, III7; **Estoy encantado(a) que...** *I'm delighted that . . .*, III7; **Me (Te,...) encanta(n)...** *I (You, . . .) love . . .*, II; **Me encanta que...** *I'm delighted that . . .*, III7; **Me encantaría ser...** *I'd love to be . . .*, III12

encargar *to put in charge of*, 6

encargarse de *to take charge of*, 3

encender (ie) *to turn on, to light*, 3

encendido(a) *lit*, 12

encerrar(ie) *to enclose, to shut in*, 2

encima de *on top of*, I

encontrar (ue) *to find*, I; **Si se encontrara una cura...** *If a cure were found . . .*, III11

encontrarse (ue) *to be located*, II; **encontrarse (con)** *to meet up (with)*, II

la encuesta *survey, poll*, 8

enderezar *to straighten*, 12

el enemigo, la enemiga *enemy*, III5

la energía *energy*, II; la energía geotérmica *geothermal energy*, 3; **la energía nuclear** *nuclear energy*, III3; **la energía solar** *solar energy*, III3

enero (m.) *January*, I

enfadado(a) *angry*, II

enfadarse *to get angry*, III9; **me enfadé** *I got angry*, III9

enfático(a) *emphatic*, 11

enfermarse *to become ill*, II

la enfermedad *disease*, III11

el enfermero, la enfermera *nurse*, III12

enfermo(a) *sick*, I

enfocarse en *to focus on*, III10

el enfoque *focus*, 8

enfrentar *to face*, II; *to confront*, 4

engañar *to fool*, 9

enganchar *to hang up*, 10

engreído(a) *conceited, arrogant*, 2

el enjambre *swarm*, 11

los enlaces *connections, links*, 1

enojado(a) *angry*, I

enojarse *to get angry*, III9; **me enojé** *I got angry*, III9

enorme *enormous*, 2

enredado(a) *tangled*, 9

enrevesado(a) *complicated*, 12

enriquecer (zc) *to enrich*, 8

la ensalada *salad*, I; **la ensalada de aguacate** *avocado salad*, III4; **la ensalada mixta** *tossed salad*, III4

ensayar *to rehearse*, 6

el ensayista, la ensayista *essayist*, 9

el ensayo *essay*, 9; *rehearsal*, 6

la enseñanza *teaching*, 1

enseñar *to show, to teach*, 6

entender (ie) *to understand*, 2; **Tengo entendido que...** *I understand that . . .*, III9

enterarse (de) *to find out (about)*, II

entero(a) *whole, entire*, II

enterrar (ie) *to bury*, 3

entonces *then*, II; **en aquel entonces** *back then*, II; **Entonces...** *So, then . . .*, II

la entrada *ticket*, 6

las entrañas *bowels*, 9

entrar *to enter, to go in*, 9

entregar *to hand in*, II

el entrenador, la entrenadora *trainer*, 1

el entrenamiento *training*, 1

entrenarse *to train*, II

entretenido(a) *entertaining*, III6

el entrevistado, la entrevistada *interviewee*, 11

entrevistar *to interview*, 1

entusiasta *enthusiastic*, II

enumerar *to number, to list*, 10

enviar *to send, to mail*, III3; **enviar una carta electrónica** *to send an e-mail*, III3

envidiar *to envy*, 12

envolverse (ue) en *to get wrapped up in*, 2

la época: **en aquella época** *in those days*, II

equilibrado(a) *balanced*, 2

el equipo *team*, 2

la equitación *horseback riding*, III1

el equivalente *equivalent*, 5

equivocado(a) *mistaken, wrong*, 8

equivocarse *to be wrong*, II

Era una de mis grandes ambiciones. *It was one of my great ambitions.*, III5

Érase una vez… *Once upon a time . . .*, II

erróneamente *incorrectly*, 10

erróneo(a) *incorrect*, 9

el error *mistake*, III7; **admitir un error** *to admit a mistake*, III7; **cometer un error** *to make a mistake*, III7

es *he (she/it) is*, I; **Es cierto que…** *It's true that . . .*, III3; **Es difícil que…** *It's unlikely that . . .*, III8; **Es evidente que…** *It's evident that . . .*, III8; **Es fácil que…** *It's likely that . . .*, III8; **Es importante que** + *subj. It's important that . . .*, III6; **Es imposible que…** *It's impossible that . . .*, III8; **Es increíble que…** *It's unbelievable that . . .*, III8; **Es mejor que…** *It's better for . . . to . . .*, III6; **Es muy difícil de creer, pero es posible.** *That's very hard to believe, but it's possible.*, III5; **Es necesario que** + subj. *It's necessary for . . . to . . .*, III6; **Es nuestra responsabilidad…** *It's our responsibility . . .*, III3; **Es nuestro deber…** *It's our duty . . .*, III3; **Es obvio que…** *It's obvious that . . .*, III8; **Es posible que…** *It's possible that . . .*, III8; **Es probable que…** *It's probable that . . .*, III8; **es que** *it's just that*, II

esa, ese *that* (adj.), I

esas, esos *those* (adj.), I

la escalada deportiva *rock climbing*, III1

escalar *to climb*, I; **escalar montañas** *to go mountain climbing*, III1

la escalera *stairs*, 9

escapar *to escape*, 3

el escaparate *show window, display case*, II

la escena *scene*, 8

el escenario *stage*, 4

escoger *to choose*, 3

escojer *see* escoger

la esclavización *enslavement*, 4

el esclavo *slave*, 4

escribamos *let's write*, 1

escribir *to write*, I

escrito (past participle of **escribir**) *written*, III3

el escritor, la escritora *writer*, III12

el escritorio *desk*, I

la escritura *writing*, 1

la escritura pictográfica *pictographs*, 5

escuchar *to listen*, I; **escuchar música** *to listen to music*, III1

escuchemos *let's listen*, 1

el escudo nacional de armas *national shield*, 5

la escuela preparatoria *high school*, 6

la escuela secundaria *high school*, 11

el escultor, la escultora *sculptor*, III6

la escultura *sculpture*, III6

ese, esa *that* (adj.), I

esforzarse (ue) por *to make an effort to*, III10

el esfuerzo *effort*, III10; **Puse todo mi** esfuerzo en… *I put a lot of effort into . . .*, III10

la esgrima *fencing*, 10

esmerar *to take great pains*, 2

el esnob *snob*, 9

eso, ésos *that, those* (pron.), I; **Eso es.** *That's right.*, III5; **¡Eso es muy difícil!** *That's very unlikely!*, III5; **Eso me hace pensar en…** *That brings to mind . . .*, III6; **Eso me recuerda…** *That reminds me of . . .*, III6; **Y eso, ¿qué?** *So what?*, II

el espacio *space*, 3

los espaguetis *spaghetti*, 4

la espalda *back*, I

el español *Spanish (language)*, I

español(a) *Spanish* (nationality), II

esparcir *to spread*, 4

especial *special*, II

la especialidad *specialty*, II

especialmente *especially*, I

las especies *species*, II

espectacular(m./f.) *spectacular*

el espejo *mirror*, II

los espejuelos *glasses*, 1

la esperanza *hope*, III5; **Tenía muchas esperanzas de…** *I had high hopes of . . .*, III5

esperar *to wait, to expect*, 8; **esperar** + inf. *to hope to . . .*, III5; **esperar que** + subj. *to hope (that) . . .*, III5; **Espero que la guerra termine pronto.** *I hope the war ends soon.*, III5; **No me lo esperaba.** *It caught me by surprise.*, III8

espiar *to spy*, 12

la espiga *ear (of a plant)*, 4

el espíritu *spirit*, 2

el esplendor *splendor*, 4

espontáneo(a) *spontaneous*, 12

la esposa *wife*, I

el esposo *husband*, I

el esqueleto *skeleton*, 7

el esquema *outline*, 2

el esquí acuático *water skiing*, III1; **hacer el esquí acuático** *to go water skiing*, III1

esquiar *to ski*, I

la esquina *corner*, II

los esquís *skis*, I

esta, este *this* (adj.), I

ésta, éste *this* (pron.), I

establecer (zc) *to set up, to establish*, III3; **establecer una zona peatonal** *to set up a pedestrian zone*, III3

la estación (pl. **las estaciones**) *season (of the year)*, I

la estación (pl. **las estaciones**) **de tren** *train station*, II

el estacionamiento *parking (area)*, II

el estadio *stadium*, I

el estado *state*

estadounidense *from the United States*, II

estafar *to swindle*, 12

estallar *to burst, to explode*, 1

Estamos obligados a… *We're obligated to . . .*, III3

la estampilla *stamp*, II

la estancia *stay*, 6

estar *to be*, I; **Está echado a perder.** *It's spoiled (ruined).*, III4; **Está en su punto.** *It's just right.*, III4; **estar a dieta** *to be on a diet*, III2; **estar agradecido(a) por** *to be grateful for*, III10; **estar al tanto de…** *to be up to date on . . .*, III8; **estar bien informado(a) sobre…** *to be well informed about . . .*, III8; estar hecho(a) *polvo to be worn out*, 2; **estar rendido(a)** *to be worn out*, III2; **Estoy contento(a).** *I'm happy.*, III7; **Estoy convencido(a) que…** *I'm convinced that . . .*, III8; **Estoy de acuerdo.** *I agree.*, III5; **Estoy de buen humor.** *I'm in a good mood.*, III7; **Estoy decepcionado(a).** *I'm disappointed.*, III7; **Estoy desilusionado(a).** *I'm disappointed.*, III7; **Estoy dolido(a).** *I'm hurt.*, III7; **¡Estoy en la gloria!** *I'm in heaven!*, III7; **Estoy encantado(a) que…** *I'm delighted that . . .*, III7; **Estoy harto(a) de…** *I'm fed up with . . .*, III1; **Estoy loco(a) por…** *I'm crazy about . . .*, III1; **Estoy orgulloso(a) de…** *I'm proud of . . .*, III7; **Estoy seguro(a) que…** *I'm certain that . . .*, III8; **Estuve muy contento(a).** *I was very happy.*, III9

estas, estos *these* (adj.), I

éstas, éstos *these* (pron.), I

estatal *state* (adj.), 5

la estatua *statue*, III6

la estatura *height*, III1; **de estatura mediana** *of medium height*, III1

el este *east*, II

Este… *Umm . . .*, III3

este, esta *this* (adj.), I

éste, ésta *this* (pron.), I

la estera *mat*, 5

estereotipar *to stereotype*, III9

el estereotipo *stereotype*, III9

el estero *mat*, 4

el estilista, la estilista *stylist*, 2

el estilo *style*, II; **el estilo de vida** *lifestyle*, II

estirarse *to stretch*, I

esto *this* (pron.), I; **Esto pasará pronto.** *This will soon pass.*, III7

el estómago *stomach*, I

estos *these* (adj.), I
éstos *these* (pron.), I
estrecho(a) *tight-fitting*, II; *narrow*, 5
la estrella *star*, II; **la estrella de cine** *movie star*, II
el estreno *premiere*, II
estrepitoso(a) *noisy, deafening*, 5
el estrés *stress*, III2; **aliviar el estrés** *to relieve stress*, III2; **causar el estrés** *to cause stress*, III2
estricto(a) *strict*, I
la estructura *structure*, 4
el estudiante, la estudiante *student*, 4
estudiar *to study*, I; **Me interesaría estudiar para...** *I'd be interested in studying to be a . . .*, III12
la estufa *stove*, II
Estupendo(a). *Great., Marvelous.*, I
estúpido(a) *stupid*, 9
estuve (pret. of **estar**) *I was*, III9
la etapa *phase, stage*, 4
eternamente *eternally*, 5
la ética *ethic*, 10
la etiqueta *price tag*, II
étnico(a) *ethnic*, 10
europeo(a) *European*, 8
el euskera *Basque (language)*, 2
el evento *event*, I
evitar *to avoid*, II
exacto(a) *exact*, 5
la exageración *exaggeration*, 3
exagerado(a) *exaggerated*, 5
exagerar *to exaggerate*, 7
el examen (pl. **los exámenes**) *exam*, I
la excavación (pl. las excavaciones) *(archeological) dig*, 7
Excelente. *Great., Excellent.*, I
el exceso *excess, too much*, 2
exclusivo(a) *exclusive*, 3
la excursión (pl. **las excursiones**) *outing*, 1
la exhibición (pl. **las exhibiciones**) *exhibition*, III6
exigente *demanding*, II
el exilio *exile*, 9
el éxito *success*, III10; **tener éxito** *to succeed*, III10
exitoso(a) *successful*
exorcizar *to exorcise*, 6
experimentado(a) *experienced*, 8
experimentar *to experience*, 10
explicar *to explain*, 5
explícito(a) *explicit*, 12
explorar *to explore*, I
la explotación *exploitation*, 3
explotar *to explode*, 6
exportar *to export*
la exposición (pl. las exposiciones) *exhibit*, 6
expresar *to express*, 1
exprimir *to squeeze*, 4
exquisito(a) *exquisite*, 4
extenuante *exhausting*, 2
el extracto *excerpt*, 10
extraer *to extract*, 4
el extranjero *foreigner*, 4;

abroad, 11
extranjero(a) *foreign*, 3
extrañar: **Bueno, no me extraña.** *Well, I'm not surprised.*, II
extraño(a) *strange*, 10
extrovertido(a) *extroverted, outgoing*, 2

la fábrica *factory*, III3
fabricar *to manufacture, to make*, 3
la fábula *fable*, 5
la faceta *side*, 9
la fachada *façade*, 2
fácil *easy*, I; **es fácil que...** *it's likely that . . .*, III8; **fácil de tratar** *easy to get along with*, 9
facilitar *to make easy*, 3
la facultad de (arquitectura,...) *college of (architecture, . . .)*, 6
la falda *skirt*, I; la falda de res *skirt steak*, 4
la falta *lack*, III9; *mistake*, 7 **hace falta que busquemos** *we need to look for*, III6
faltar *to need, to lack*, III4; **Le falta no sé qué.** *It needs something (I don't know what).*, III4; **Le falta sabor.** *It doesn't have enough flavor.*, III4; **Le falta sal.** *It needs (lacks/doesn't have enough) salt.*, III4
la fama *fame*, 7
la familia *family*, I
los familiares *family members*, 6
famoso(a) *famous*, 6
el fanático, la fanática *fan*, III1; **Soy un(a) fanático(a) de...** *I'm a big fan of . . .*, III1
la fantasía *fantasy*, 12
el farmacéutico, la farmacéutica *pharmacist*, III12
la farmacia *pharmacy*, II
la farmacología *pharmacology*, 12
el faro *lighthouse*
fascinante *fascinating*, 10
fascinar: A mí me (A ti te) fascina(n)... *I (You) love . . .*, II
fastidiar *to annoy*, II
fatigar *to tire*, 11
las fauces *mouth*, 9
el favor *favor*, 5; a favor de *on behalf of*, 1; **Hágame (Hazme) el favor de...** *Do me the favor of . . .*, III4; **por favor** *please*, I
favorito(a) *favorite*, I
el fax *fax, fax machine*, III3
febrero (m.) *February*, I
la fecha *date* (on a calendar), I; **¿Cuál es la fecha?** *What is today's date?*, I
la felicidad *happiness*, 7

feliz (pl. **felices**) *happy*, II
fenomenal *great*, III1
feo(a) *ugly*, I
feroz (pl. feroces) *fierce*, 5
la ferretería *hardware store*, III4
el festival *festival*, II
festivo(a) *festive*, I; **el día festivo** *holiday*, I
la fibra óptica *fiber optic*, 3
la ficha *notecard*, 11
ficticio(a) *fictitious*, 11
la fiebre *fever*, I
la fiereza *fierceness*, 4
la fiesta *party*, I; **la fiesta de aniversario** *anniversary party*, I; **la fiesta de cumpleaños** *birthday party*, I; **la fiesta de graduación** *graduation party*, I; **la fiesta de sorpresa** *surprise party*, I
la figura *shape, form*, 5
fijarse *to notice, take notice*, II; **¡Fíjate!** *Imagine!*, II; **Me he fijado en...** *I've noticed . . .*, III11
fijo(a) *fixed*, II
el fin *end*, II; **el fin de semana** *weekend*, I; **en fin** *in short*, II; **para fines de** *by the end of*, II; **por fin** *at last*, I
financiero(a) *financial*, III8; **la sección financiera** *financial section*, III8
las finanzas *finance*, 10
la finca *farm, ranch*, 2
el fiordo *fjord*
la firma *signature*, 11
físico(a) *physical*, I
el fisicoculturismo *body building*, 2
el flan *custard*, I
la flauta *flute*, III1
la flecha *arrow*, 5
flechar *to shoot with an arrow*, 7
flojo(a) *lazy*, II
florecer (zc) *to flower*, 11
la florería *flower shop*, I
las flores *flowers*, I
fluir *to flow*, 3
el folleto *brochure*, 6
fomentar *to encourage, to promote*, 7
los fondos *funds*, 11
la forma *shape, form, way*, II
formal *formal*, I
formidable *tremendous*, III6
formular *to formulate*, 11
el formulario *form*, 8
fortalecer (zc) *to strengthen*, 2
forzado(a) *forced*, 3
la fotocopiadora (a colores) *(color) photocopier*, III3
la fotografía *photography*, III1
el fraile *monk*, 5
francamente *frankly*, 2
el francés *French (language)*, I
Francia (f.) *France*, I
la frecuencia: **con frecuencia** *often*, I; **¿Con qué frecuencia?** *How often?*, I
frenar *to brake*, 11

frenético(a) *frantic*, 3
frente a *in the face of*, 11
la fresa *strawberry*, I
los frijoles *beans*, I
frío(a) *cold*, I; **Me deja frío(a).** *It doesn't do anything for me.*, III6
frito (past participle of **freír**) *fried*, III4; **el pollo frito** *fried chicken*, III4
la frontera *frontier*, 11
fronterizo(a) *border (adj.)*, 1
frotar *to rub*, 11
la frustración *frustration*, 6
frustrado(a) *frustrated*, 1
frustrante *frustrating*, 7
frustrarse *to be frustrated*, III7; **Me frustra que...** *It frustrates me that...*, III7; **me frustré** *I got angry*, III9
la fruta *fruit*, I
la frutería *fruit shop*, III4
Fue cuando... *It was when...*, II
el fuego *fire*, 5
la fuente *source, fountain*, 8
fuera *outside*, III3; **Mucha gente ha venido de fuera.** *Many people have come from outside.*, III3
fuera (past subjunctive of **ser**): **Si fueras rico(a)...** *If you were rich...*, III9; **Si yo fuera presidente(a)...** *If I were president...*, III11
fuerte *strong, heavy*, I
la fuerza vital *vital force*, 6
fumar *to smoke*, II
la fumarola *hole in volcano from which gases emerge*, 5
la función (pl. las funciones) *performance*, 3
el funcionario público *public official*, 11
las funciones *duties*, 8
la fundación (pl. las fundaciones) *foundation*, 6
fundar *to found*, 10
fundir *to merge*, 10
la furia *rage*, 2
furioso(a) *furious*, 8
la fusión nuclear *nuclear fusion*, 3
el fútbol *soccer*, I; **el fútbol norteamericano** *football*, I

las gafas *glasses*, III1
la gaita *bagpipe*
el galán (pl. los galanes) *suitor*, 7
la galaxia *galaxy*, II
el gallego *Galician (language)*, 2
gallego(a) *Galician*
la galleta *cookie*, I
la gallina de palo *iguana meat*
el gallo pinto *rice and black beans*

la gana: **Me dan ganas de llorar.** *It makes me feel like crying.*, III7; **tener ganas de** + inf. *to feel like (doing something)*, I
el ganado *cattle*, 5
el ganador, la ganadora *winner*, 11
las ganancias *earnings*, 11
ganar *to win, to earn*, I; *to gain*, 3
la ganga *bargain*, I
ganoso(a) *wanting*, 9
la gansa *goose*, 11
la garantía *guarantee*, 3
garantizado(a) *guaranteed*, 3
la garganta *throat*, I
el gas natural *natural gas*, 3
la gasolina *gasoline*, II; la gasolina sin plomo *unleaded gasoline*, 3
la gasolinera *gas station*, II
gastar *to spend, to waste*, II
el gato, la gata *cat*, I
la generación (pl. las generaciones) *generation*, 10
general: **por lo general** *usually*, I
la generosidad *generosity*, 7
generoso(a) *generous*, II
genial *great*, III6
el genio *genius*, 8
la gente *people*, III3; **Mucha gente ha venido de fuera.** *Many people have come from outside.*, III3
la gente mayor de edad *senior citizens*, 9
gentil *charming*, 9
la geografía *geography*, I
el gerente, la gerente *manager*, III12
el gigante *giant*, 9
gigante *giant (adj.)*, 10
gigantesco(a) *gigantic*, II
el gimnasio *gym*, I
girar *to turn around*, 9
el globo *balloon*, I
la gloria: **¡Estoy en la gloria!** *I'm in heaven!*, III7
el gobernador, la gobernadora *governor*, 11
la golosina *piece of candy*, 4
la goma de borrar *eraser*, I
gordo(a) *fat, overweight*, I; **Me cae gordo.** *It disagrees with me, I hate it.*, III4
la gota *drop (of liquid)*, 7
el goterón (pl. los goterones) *big drop (of liquid)*, 11
gozar *to enjoy*, 6
la grabación (pl. las grabaciones) *recording*, 9
el grabado *engraving*, 6
el grabador *tape recorder*, 8
Gracias. *Thanks.*, I; **gracias por** *thank you for*, II; **Gracias por invitarme, pero no puedo.** *Thanks for inviting me, but I can't.*, III6
gracioso(a) *funny*, 8
el grado *degree*, 5
el graduado, la graduada *graduate (student)*, 10
graduarse *to graduate*, III10;

Después de graduarnos... *After we graduate...*, III10
gran: **una gran persona** *a great person*, III1; **un gran tipo** *a great guy*, III1
grande *big*, I
el granito *granite*, 9
el grano *grain, seed*, 4; los granos germinados *sprouted grains*, 2
la grasa *fat (in food)*, III4; **Lleva mucha grasa.** *It has too much fat.*, III4
gratis *free*, II
grave *serious*, II
graznar *to squawk*, 12
el griego *Greek (language)*, 10
el grifo *faucet*, 9
el gringo, la gringa *United States citizen (impolite)*, 10
la gripe *flu*, I
gris *gray*, I
gritar *to shout*, 5
la grúa *derrick*, 3
grueso(a) *thick*, 12
¡Guácala! *Yuck!*, III4
el guacamole *dip made from mashed avocados*
el guante *glove*, 10
guapo(a) *good-looking*, III1
guardar *to keep*, III7; **no guardar los secretos** *not to keep secrets*, III7
guardarse *to protect oneself*, 5
el guardia *guard*, 5
guatemalteco(a) *Guatemalan*, II
Guatire *small city in Venezuela*, 8
el güero, la güera *blond or fair-skinned person*, 10
la guerra *war*, III5; **Espero que la guerra termine pronto.** *I hope the war ends soon.*, III5
el guerrero, la guerrera *warrior*, III5
el guía, la guía *guide*, II
guijarro *pebble*, 4
el guiñapo *rag, tatter*, 11
el güiro *Caribbean percussive instrument*, 6
el guisado *stew*, 4
guisado(a) *stewed*, 4
la guitarra *guitar*, I
el gusano *worm*, 4
gustar: A mí me (A ti te,...) gusta(n) + inf. I *(You,...) like (to)...*, I; **a quien le guste(n)** *who likes*, **Me (Te,...) gusta...** I *(You,...) like...*, I
el gusto *pleasure*, I; *taste*, III6; **¡Con mucho gusto!** *Gladly!*, I; **de muy mal gusto** *in very bad taste*, III6

ha (inf. **haber**) *has (auxiliary verb)*
haber *to have (auxiliary verb)*; **...ha**

cambiado mucho . . . *has changed a lot,* III3; **...ha empeorado bastante** . . . *has gotten quite a bit worse,* III3; **¿Has leído algo de?** *Have you read anything about . . .?,* III6; **¿Has oído hablar de…?** *Have you heard about . . .,* II; **¿Has pensado en?** *Have you thought of . . .?,* III6; **Han triunfado...** *They have succeeded . . .,* III10; **Mucha gente ha venido de fuera.** *Many people have come from outside.,* III3

haber que + inf. *to be necessary to +* verb, II; **Habrá que...** *It will be necessary to . . .,* III11; Hay que... *It's necessary to . . .,* III3

las **habichuelas** *beans*

la **habitación** (pl. las habitaciones) *room,* 3

el **habitante,** la **habitante** *inhabitant* **habitar** *to live (in),* 10

el **hábito** *habit,* III2; **tener buenos hábitos de alimentación** *to have good eating habits,* III2

habitual *habitual,* 9

el **habla** (f.) *speech;* de habla hispana *Spanish-speaking,* 11

hablar *to speak, to talk,* I; **dejar de hablarse** *to stop speaking to each other,* III7; **Hablando de...** *Speaking of . . .,* III6; **hablará** *will speak,* III3; **hablemos** *let's talk,* 1

Habrá que... *It will be necessary to . . .,* III11

hacer *to make, to do;* **¿Cuánto tiempo hace que...?** *How long have (has) . . . (been doing something)?,* II; **Hace diez años...** *Ten years ago . . .,* III12; **hace falta que busquemos** *we need to look for,* III6; **hace mucho frío (sol/calor/viento/fresco/buen tiempo/mal tiempo)** *it's very cold (sunny/hot/windy/cool/nice weather/bad weather),* I; **Hace mucho tiempo...** *A long time ago . . .,* II; hacer ejercicio *to exercise,* III2; **hacer esquí acuático** *to water-ski,* III1; hacer falta *to be necessary,* 9; hacer las paces *to make up with,* II; **hacer trabajos con la computadora** *to write papers on the computer,* III3; **hacerle un cumplido a alguien** *to compliment someone,* III7; **Hágame (Hazme) el favor de...** *Do me the favor of . . .,* III4; **Hagámoslo mañana.** *Let's do it tomorrow.,* III6; **Lo hice sin querer.** *I didn't mean to do it.,* III7; **No lo haré más.** *I won't do it anymore.,* III7; **No lo volveré a hacer.** *I won't do it again.,* III7; **Si no hacemos nada por...** *If we don't do anything about . . .,* III11

hacerse amigo(a) de alguien *to make friends with someone,* II

hacerse daño *to hurt oneself,* II

hacia *toward,* III9

el **hada** (f.) **madrina** *fairy godmother,* II

Hágame el favor de... *Do me the favor of . . .,* III4

Hagámoslo mañana. *Let's do it tomorrow.,* III6

la **hallaca** *tamale-like dish made of cornmeal stuffed with seasoned meat and vegetables, cooked in banana leaves*

el **hallazgo** *finding,* 2

el **hambre** (f.) *hunger,* III11; **tener (mucha) hambre** *to be (really) hungry,* I

la **hamburguesa** *hamburger,* I

Han triunfado... *They have succeeded . . .,* III10

harto(a) *fed up, sick and tired,* II

has (inf. **haber**) *you have (auxiliary verb),* III3; **¿Has leído algo de...?** *Have you read anything about . . .?,* III6; **¿Has pensado en...?** *Have you thought of . . .?,* III6

hasta *until, up to,* II; **Hasta cierto punto, sí, pero...** *Up to a point, yes, but . . .,* III5; **hasta que** *until (conj.),* III10

hay (special present tense of **haber**) *there is (there are),* I; **Hay que...** *It's necessary . . .,* III3; **No hay quien lo (la) aguante.** *Nobody can stand him (her).,* III1

la **hazaña** *deed,* 5

Hazme el favor de... *Do me the favor of . . .,* III4

el **hecho** *fact,* 10

hecho (past participle of **hacer**) *made, done,* III3

la **heladería** *ice cream store,* III4

el **helado** *ice cream,* I

helado(a) *freezing cold,* 6

hender (ie) *to split,* 9

heredar *to inherit,* 3

el **heredero,** la **heredera** *heir,* 8

la **herencia** *inheritance, heredity, heritage,* 6

herir (ie, i) *to wound,* 5

la **hermana** *sister,* I; **la media hermana** *half-sister,* I

la **hermanastra** *stepsister,* I

el **hermanastro** *stepbrother,* I

el **hermano** *brother,* I; **el medio hermano** *half-brother,* I

los **hermanos** *brothers, brothers and sisters,* I

hermoso(a) *beautiful,* III6

el **héroe** *hero,* III5

la **heroína** *heroine,* III5

hervir (ie, i) *to boil,* 4

el **hielo** *ice,* **patinar sobre hielo** *to ice-skate,* III1

la **hierba** *grass,* 5

el **hierro** *iron, steel,* 5

higiénico(a) *hygienic,* 11

la **hija** *daughter,* I

el **hijo** *son,* I; **¡Híjole!** *Oh my goodness!,* 4

los **hijos** *children,* I

el **hilo** *thread,* 9

la **hipertensión** *high blood pressure,* 2

la **hipótesis** *hypothesis,* 11

el **hispanohablante,** la **hispanohablante** *Spanish speaker,* 4

histérico(a) *stressed out,* III2

el **hogar** *home,* 10

la **hoja** *leaf,* 4; **la hoja de papel** *sheet of paper,* 2

¡Hola! *Hello!,* I

el **hombre** *man,* III5; **¡N'hombre!** *No way!*

el **hombro** *shoulder,* II

el **homicidio** *homicide,* III11

el **hondo** *depth,* 9

hondureño(a) *Honduran,* II

honesto(a) *honest,* II

honrado(a) *honest,* 5

honrar *to honor,* 1

la **hora** *hour, time (of day);* **¿A qué hora...?** *At what time . . .?,* I; **¿Qué hora es?** *What time is it?,* I

el **horario** *work hours, schedule,* III12

la **hormiga** *ant,* 4

el **horno** *oven,* III3; **cocinar en el horno de microondas** *to cook in the microwave oven,* III3; **el horno de microondas** *microwave oven,* III3

horrible *horrible,* I

hoy *today,* I; **hoy (en) día** *nowadays,* III3

el **huachinango** *red snapper (Mexico),* 4

hubiera (past subj. of **haber**): **Si hubiera paz...** *If there were peace . . .,* III11

la **hucha** *piggybank,* 12

hueco(a) *hollow,* 6

la **huella** *footprint,* 5

el **huésped,** la **huésped** *guest,* 9

los **huevos** *eggs,* I

la **huida** *escape,* 6

huir *to escape,* 5

humeante *smoky,* 5

la **humedad** *moisture,* 4

húmedo(a) *humid,* II

humilde *humble,* 5

el **humo** *smoke,* 2

el **humor** *mood, humor,* III1; **de buen (mal) humor** *in a good (bad) mood;* **tener un buen sentido del humor** *to have a good sense of humor,* III1

humorístico(a) *humorous,* 3

I

ida y vuelta *round trip*, II
la idea *idea*, I; **no tener la menor idea**
   not to have the slightest idea, III8;
   No tengo ni idea *I've no idea.*, II
ideal *ideal, best*, III12; **Lo ideal es...**
   The best thing is . . ., III12
idealizar *to idealize*, 5
idéntico(a) *identical*, 8
la identidad *identity*, 10
el idioma *language*, 1
la iglesia *church*, II
la ignorancia *ignorance*, III9
igual *the same*, III1; **Me da igual.** *It's*
   all the same to me., III1
Igualmente. *Same here.*, I
ilegal *illegal*, 10
ilógico(a) *illogical*, 1
la imagen *image*, 9
imaginativo(a) *imaginative*, III6
impaciente *impatient*, II
el impacto *impact*, 8
impecablemente *impeccably*, 6
imperdonable *unforgivable*, 7
el imperio *empire*, 4
implacable *relentless*, 11
implementar *to implement*, III11
implicar *to imply*, 4
la importación *importing*, 4
la importancia *importance*, 5
importante *important*, II; **Lo que es**
   importante es... *What's important*
   is . . ., III3
importar *to matter*, III1; **No me**
   importa. *It doesn't matter to me.*,
   III1
imposibilitar *to make impossible*, 6
la impresión (pl. **las impresiones**)
   impression, III9; **Tengo la**
   impresión de que... *I'm under the*
   impression that . . ., III9
impresionado(a) *impressed*, II
impresionante *impressive*
el impuesto *tax*, 12
impuesto (past participle of
   imponer) *imposed*, 6
inaceptable *unacceptable*, 3
inagotable *inexhaustible*, 5
la inauguración *unveiling*, 6
inaugurar *to inaugurate*, 11
incapaz (pl. incapaces) *incapable*, 10
incautarse *to confiscate*, 8
el incendio *fire*, 11
incinerar *to incinerate*, 3
incisivo(a) *biting (adj.)*, 6
incluir *to include*; **¿Está incluida?** *Is*
   it included?, I
inclusive *inclusively*, 4
incluso *included*, 3
incomprensible *incomprehensible*,
   III6
incontaminado(a) *uncontaminated*,
   11

el inconveniente *obstacle*, 11
incorporar *to incorporate*, 10
incurable *incurable*, 11
indemnizar *to indemnify*, 11
la independencia *independence*
indetenible *unstoppable*, 3
indicar *to show, to point out, to*
   indicate, 1
el indígena, la indígena *native,*
   Indian, 5
la indiferencia *indifference*, 1
el indio, la india *Indian*, 5
indispensable *indispensable*, 3
individualidad *individuality*, 10
indomable *untamable*, 6
inducir (zc) *to bring about*, 3
indudable *undoubtable*, 5
la industria petrolera *petroleum*
   industry, 3
inesperadamente *unexpectedly*, 4
inesperado(a) *unexpected*, 4
inestimable *priceless*, 11
inexperto(a) *inexperienced*, 5
infalible *infallible*, 11
inferido(a) *inferred*, 7
infiel *unfaithful*, III7
infinitamente *infinitely*, 11
la inflación *inflation*, 8
inflar *to blow up, to inflate*, I
la influencia *influence*
influenciar *to influence*, 8
influir *to influence*, 9
la información *information*, 2
informar *to inform*, III3
la informática *computer science*, 12
el informe *report*, 3
la ingeniería (agrónoma)
   (agricultural) engineering, 12
el ingeniero, la ingeniera *engineer,*
   III12
Inglaterra (f.) *England*, I
el inglés *English (language)*, I
inhóspito(a) *inhospitable*, 3
iniciar *to start, to initiate*, III11
la iniciativa *initiative*, III10; **tomar la**
   iniciativa *to take the initiative,*
   III10
inmediatamente *immediately*, II
inmenso(a) *huge*, 3
la inmigración *immigration*, 4
el inmigrante, la inmigrante
   immigrant, 10
inolvidable *unforgettable*
inquieto(a) *restless*, 8
inscribirse *to sign up, to enroll*, II
los insectos *insects*, II
insignificante *trivial*, III6
insistentemente *insistently*, 9
la insolencia *insolence*, 7
insoportable *unbearable*, III6
inspirar *to inspire*, 10
instalado(a) *installed*, 3
el instinto *instinct*, 11
las instrucciones *directions*, II
el instrumento *instrument*, I
insultar *to insult*, III7
el insulto *insult*, 3

intacto(a) *whole*, 7
inteligente *intelligent*, I
la intención (pl. **las intenciones**) *plan,*
   intention, III10; **con la intención**
   de *with the intention of*, III10;
   Tengo la intención de... *I intend*
   to . . ., III10
intenso(a) *intense*, 6
intentar *to try*, III6; **Intentaría...** *I*
   would try to . . ., III11
intercambiar *to exchange*, 2
interesante *interesting*, I
interesar *to interest*; **Me interesaría**
   estudiar para... *I'd be interested in*
   studying to be a . . ., III12; **No me**
   interesa para nada. *It doesn't*
   interest me at all., III1
interferir (ie, i) *to interfere*, 12
internacionalmente *internationally*
Internet *the Internet*, II
intimidar to *intimidate*, 4
íntimo(a) *intimate*, 6
la intolerancia *intolerance*, 10
inútil *useless*, 3
el invento *invention*, 3
la inversión (pl. las inversiones)
   investment, 3
invertir (ie, i) *to invest*, 10
la investigación (pl. las investigaciones)
   research, 12
el investigador, la investigadora
   researcher, 2
investigar *to investigate*, 4
el invierno *winter*, I
las invitaciones (sing. **la invitación**)
   invitations, I
los invitados *guests*, I
invitar *to invite; to offer to pay*, I;
   Gracias por invitarme, pero no
   puedo. *Thanks for inviting me, but*
   I can't., III6
involuntariamente *involuntarily*, 9
ir *to go*, I; *to get to*, II; **¿Cómo se va**
   a...? *How do you get to . . .?*, II; **ir a**
   la playa *to go to the beach*, III1; **ir**
   bien (mal) *to be going the right*
   way (the wrong way), II; **¡Qué va!**
   No way!, III5; **Voy a ser...** *I'm*
   going to be . . ., III12
ir a + inf. *to be going to (do*
   something), I
la ironía *irony*, 3
irremediable *incurable*, 3
irrigar *to irrigate*, 4
irse *to go away*, II
la isla *island*, I; la isla desierta *desert*
   island, 11
Italia (f.) *Italy*, I
italiano(a) *Italian*, I
izquierda: a la izquierda *to the*
   left, II

J

el jabón *soap,* II
jadear *to pant,* 11
jamás *never,* 6
el jamón *ham,* I
el jardín *garden,* I
el jazz *jazz,* I
el jefe, la jefa *boss, chief,* III12
joven (pl. jóvenes) *young,* I; **Cuando era joven...** *When I was young . . .,* III12
los jóvenes *young people,* 6
la joya *jewel,* 11
la joyería *jewelry store,* I
el juego *game, match;* **hacer juego con** *to match with,* II; **el juego de mesa** *(board) game,* I
el jueves *Thursday,* I
el juez, la juez (pl. los jueces) *judge,* 8
jugar (ue) *to play,* II; **jugar a las cartas** *to play cards,* III1; **jugar a los videojuegos** *to play videogames,* III1
el jugo *juice,* I; **el jugo de naranja** *orange juice,* I
la juguetería *toy store,* I
los juguetes *toys,* I
el juicio crítico *critical judgment,* 7
julio (m.) *July,* I
junio (m.) *June,* I
junto a *next to,* II
juntos(as) *together,* I
el juramento *oath,* 7
jurar *to swear,* 7
la justicia *justice,* 5
justo(a) *fair,* II
la juventud *youth,* 10
juzgar *to judge,* III9
juzgar mal *to misjudge,* 9

K

el kilómetro *kilometer,* 2; kilómetro cuadrado *kilometer²,* 1
el kiosco *newsstand,* 8

L

la (f. sing. article) *the,* I
la (f. sing. direct object pron.) *her (it),* I; **Lo (la) encuentro...** *I find him (her/it) . . .,* III6
La situación va a empeorarse. *The situation will get worse.,* III11
La solución que planteo es... *The solution I propose is . . .,* III11
La verdad es que... *The truth is that . . .,* III3
la labor *work,* 2
la ladera *hillside,* 4
el ladrón, la ladrona *thief,* III11
la lagartija *lizard,* 1
el lago *lake,* I
la lágrima *tear,* 10
la laguna *lagoon,* 6
lamentar *to mourn, to lament,* III5; **Lo lamentaremos.** *We'll regret it.,* III11
la lámpara *lamp,* I; **la lámpara de la calle** *streetlight,* II; la lámpara maravillosa *magic lamp,* 9
la lana *wool,* I
la lancha *boat,* II
el lápiz (pl. **los lápices**) *pencil,* I
largo(a) *long,* II
las (f. pl. article) *the,* I
las (f. pl. direct object pron.) *them,* I
la lástima *shame;* **¡Qué lástima!** *What a shame!,* I
lastimarse *to injure (oneself),* II
la lata *can,* II; **¡Qué lata!** *What a pain!,* 1
el latín *Latin (language)*
el latino, la latina *Latin American person,* 10
latinoamericano(a) *Latin American,* 8
los laureles *crown of laurel leaves given as reward,* 2
lavar *to wash,* I
lavarse los dientes *to brush your teeth,* II
le *to, for her/him/it/you (sing. formal),* I; **Le falta no sé qué.** *It needs something (I don't know what).,* III4; **Le falta sabor.** *It doesn't have enough flavor.,* III4; **Le falta sal.** *It needs (lacks, doesn't have enough) salt.,* III4
leamos *let's read,* 1
la leche *milk,* I
la lechería *dairy store,* III4
el lecho *bed,* 5
la lechuga *lettuce,* I
el lector, la lectora *reader,* 2
leer *to read,* I; **leer tiras cómicas** *to read comics,* III1
la legua *league, 5572 meters,* 9; a la legua *far away,* 11
las legumbres *vegetables,* I
lejano(a) *faraway, distant,* 8; el Lejano Oriente *Far East,* 1
lejos de *far from,* I
el lema *slogan,* 3
la lengua *tongue,* 10
el lenguaje *language,* 10
lentamente *slowly,* 5
los lentes *glasses,* I; **los lentes de sol** *sunglasses,* I
la leña *firewood,* II
les *to, for them/you* (pl.), I
el letrero *sign,* II
levantar *to lift,* I
levantarse *to get up,* II
la ley *law,* 10
la leyenda *legend,* 5
liberar *to free*
la libertad *liberty,* 9
el libertador *liberator*
la libra *pound,* 4
libre *free,* I; **un día libre** *a day off,* I
la librería *bookstore,* I
el libro *book,* I; **el libro de texto** *textbook,* 6
licenciarse *to get a degree,* 9
la licenciatura *bachelor's degree,* 12
la liga *league*
el líder, la líder *leader,* 10
ligeramente *quickly,* 12
ligero(a) *light,* I
los liliputienses *Lilliputians,* 9
limitar *to limit,* 9
la limonada *lemonade,* I
limpiar *to clean,* I
la limpieza *cleanliness,* 11
limpio(a) *clean,* I; **mantener limpio(a)** *to keep clean,* II
lindísimo(a) *really beautiful,* II
la línea *line,* I; **en línea** *online,* III8; **patinar en línea** *to in-line skate,* III1
lingüístico(a) *linguistic,* 10
el líquido *liquid,* 3
el lirón *dormouse;* **dormir tan bien como un lirón** *to sleep like a baby,* II
listo(a) (with **ser**) *clever, smart,* I; (with **estar**) *ready,* I
la litera *stretcher,* 5
el litro *liter,* 4
la llamada *telephone call,* 2
llamar *to call, to phone,* I
llamarse *to be named,* I; **Me llamo...** *My name is . . .,* I
los llaneros *people who live in the plains region,* 5
los llanos *plains,* 5
la llave *key,* 4
llegar *to arrive,* II; llegar a su meta *to achieve one's goal,* 3
llenar *to fill,* 6
lleno(a) *full,* 10
llevar *to take, to carry, to wear, to lead,* I; *to have,* III4; **Lleva mucha grasa.** *It has too much fat.,* III4; **llevar a cabo** *to carry out,* III10; **llevar gafas** *to wear glasses,* III1; **llevar una vida agitada** *to lead a hectic life,* III2; **¿Se las llevas?** *Will you take them to him (her)?,* III4
llevarse *to get along,* II
llorar *to cry,* III5; **Me dan ganas de llorar.** *It makes me feel like crying.,* III7
el llorón, la llorona *crybaby,* 5
llover (ue) *to rain,* I
la lluvia *rain,* 5
lo: lo de siempre *the usual,* I; **lo**

ideal *the best thing*, III12; **lo que**
what, that which, III3; **por lo**
general *generally*, I
lo (m. sing. direct object pron.)
it/him/you (formal), I;
Lo (la) encuentro... *I find him*
(her/it) . . ., III6; **Lo hice sin**
querer. *I didn't mean to do it.*, III7;
Lo lamentaremos. *We'll regret it.*,
III11; **Lo siento mucho, es que no**
sabía. *I'm very sorry, I just didn't*
know., III7; **Lo siento, pero ya**
tengo otros planes. *I'm sorry, but*
I already have other plans., III6
lo + adj. *the* (adj.) *thing*, II; **lo cual**
which, 12; **Lo ideal es...** *The best*
thing is . . ., III12; **lo menos** *at*
least, 12; **lo suficiente** *enough*, II
lo que *what*, III3; **Lo que es**
importante es... *What's important*
is . . ., III3; **Lo que noto es que...**
What I notice is that . . ., III3
localizar *to locate*, 7
loco(a) *crazy;* **estar loco(a) por** *to*
be crazy about, II; **Estoy loco(a)**
por... *I'm crazy about*, III1
la **locomotora** *locomotive*, 9
la **locura** *craziness*, 7
el **locutor, la locutora** *anchorperson*,
III8
el **lodo** *mud*, 3
lógico(a) *logical*, 1
lograr *to achieve, to manage to*,
III10; **Logró superar muchos**
obstáculos. *He (She) succeeded in*
overcoming many obstacles., III10
el **logro** *accomplishment*, 1
la **loma** *hill*, 3
la **lombriz** (pl. las lombrices) *worm;*
tan feliz como una lombriz *as*
happy as a lark, II
la **longitud** *length*, 9
el **loro** *parrot*, II
los (m. pl. article) *the*, I
los (m. pl. direct object pron.)
them, II
la **lucha** *struggle, fight*, 1
luchar *to struggle, to fight*, III5
luego *then, later*, I
el **lugar** *place;* **ningún lugar** *nowhere,*
not anywhere, I
luminoso(a) *luminous*, 8
la **luna** *moon*, 1
el **lunar** *mole*, 1
el **lunes** *Monday*, I
la **luz** (pl. **las luces**) *light*, II

la **madera** *wood*, 5
la **madrastra** *stepmother*, I
la **madre** *mother*, I
la **madrugada** *early morning hours*, 9

el **madrugador, la madrugadora** *early*
riser, 2
madrugar *to get up early*, 2
maduro(a) *ripe*, 4
el **maestro, la maestra** *teacher*, 2
magnífico(a) *great*, I; *magnificent*,
III6
el **maíz** *corn*, I
majo(a) *nice* (Spain), III1
el **mal** *evil*, 11; **No hay mal que cien**
años dure. *It won't last forever.*,
III7; **No hay mal que por bien no**
venga. *Every cloud has a silver*
lining., III7
mal *bad, badly*, I; **estar mal** *to feel*
poorly, I
la **maldad** *evil*, 10
maldito(a) *darned*, 3
el **malentendido** *misunderstanding*,
III7; **tener un malentendido** *to*
have a misunderstanding, III7
la **maleta** *suitcase*, I
el **maletero, la maletera** *baggage*
carrier, II
la **maleza** *weeds*, 9
el **malgenio** *bad temper*, 2
malhablado(a) *foul-mouthed*, 6
malo(a) *bad*, I
maltratar *mistreat*, 3
el **malvado, la malvada** *villain*, III5
la **mamá** *mom*, I
el **mancebo** *bachelor*, 7
la **mancha** *stain*, 7
el **mandado** *errand;* **hacer un**
mandado *to run an errand*, II
mandar *to send*, I
la **mandioca** *Brazilian name for yucca,*
a root vegetable, 3
manejar *to drive*, III3; *to manage*,
11; **manejar por la autopista** *to*
drive on the freeway, III3
la **manera** *way, manner*, 10
el **mango** *mango*, I
la **manía** *oddity*, 6
la **manipulación** *manipulation*, 10
la **mano** *hand*, I
mantener (ie) *to preserve, to keep*,
III10
mantenerse (ie) en forma *to stay in*
shape, III2
la **manzana** *apple*, I
la **maña** *skill*, 11
mañana (adv.) *tomorrow*, I;
Hagámoslo mañana. *Let's do it*
tomorrow., III6
la **mañana** *morning*, I; **por la mañana**
in the morning, I
maquillarse *to put on*
makeup, I
la **máquina** *machine*, 3; **la máquina de**
contestar *answering machine*, 3
el **mar** *sea*, II
el **maratón** *marathon*, 2
la **maravilla** *wonder, marvel;* **de**
maravilla *great*, II
maravilloso(a) *marvelous*, III6
marchar *to march*, 9

marcial *martial*, II; **practicar las**
artes marciales *to practice the*
martial arts, II
el **mariachi** *popular music originating*
in the Mexican state of Jalisco
el **marido** *husband*, 7
la **mariposa** *butterfly*, 9
los **mariscos** *shellfish*, III4
Marruecos *Morocco*, 9
el **martes** *Tuesday*, I
marzo (m.) *March*, I
más *more*, I; **más allá de** *beyond*, 9;
más o menos
so-so, I; **más... que** *more . . . than*, I
la **masa** *dough*, 4
la **masa humana** *mass of humanity*, 9
la **máscara** *mask*, II
masticar *to chew*, 12
el **mástil** *pole, mast*, 9
matar *to kill*, 7
el **mate** *Argentine and Paraguayan tea*
las **matemáticas** *mathematics*, I
la **materia** *school subject*, I
la **maternidad** *maternity*, 4
mayo (m.) *May*, I
mayor *greater, older*, I; **Cuando sea**
mayor *When I'm older . . .*, III10;
mayor que *older than*, II
el **mayordomo** *butler*, 5
la **mayoría de edad** *adulthood*, 5
la **mazmorra** *dungeon*, 5
me *(to, for) me*, I; **Me alegro que...**
I'm glad that . . ., III7; **Me cae**
gordo. *It disagrees with me.*, III4,
I hate it., III6; **Me da igual.** *It's all*
the same to me., III1; **Me da lo**
mismo. *It's all the same to me.*,
III1; **Me dan ganas de llorar.** *It*
makes me feel like crying., III7; **Me**
dedicaría a... *I would devote*
myself to . . ., III11; **Me deja**
frío(a). *It doesn't do anything for*
me., III6; **Me duele mucho que...**
It really hurts me that . . ., III7; **Me**
encanta que... *I'm delighted*
that . . ., III7; **Me encantaría ser...**
I'd love to be . . ., III12; Me es
indiferente. *I don't care one way or*
the other., 6; **Me gustaría ser...** *I'd*
like to be . . ., III12; **Me he fijado**
en... *I've noticed . . .*, III11; **Me**
imagino que... *I imagine that . . .*,
III3; **Me interesaría estudiar**
para... *I'd be interested in studying*
to be a . . ., III12; **Me la paso...**
I spend my time . . ., III1; **Me**
parece que... *It seems to me*
that . . ., III3; **Me parece un rollo.**
It seems really boring to me., III1;
Me siento frustrado(a). *I'm*
frustrated., III7; **Me suena a chino.**
It's Greek to me., III8
la **mecánica** *mechanics;* **trabajar en**
mecánica *to fix cars*, II
el **mecánico, la mecánica** *mechanic*,
III12
mecanizado(a) *mechanical*, 3

la **media hermana** *half-sister*, I

mediados: a mediados de *half way through*, 1

mediano(a) *medium*, II; **de estatura mediana** *of medium height*, III1

la medianoche *midnight*, 2

mediante *by means of, through*, 10

la medicina *medicine*, 5

medicinal *medicinal*, 11

el **médico, la médica** *doctor*, III12

la medida *moderation*, 2; *action*, 11; en cierta medida *in a certain way*, 3

medio(a) *medium, half* (adj.), I; **el medio hermano** *half-brother*, I; **medio tiempo** *part time, half time*, III12

el medio *middle*

el **medio ambiente** *environment*, II

los medios de comunicación *means of communication*, 8

medir (i, i) *to be . . . tall, to measure*, II

el mejillón (pl. los mejillones) *mussel*, 1

el **mejor, la mejor** *best*, II

Mejor... *Better . . .*, II; **mejor que** *better than*, II

mejorar *to improve*, II; **mejorará** *will improve*, III3

melancólico(a) *gloomy*, III9

el **melocotón** (pl. **los melocotones**) *peach*, III4

mencionar *to mention*, 4

el mendigo, la mendiga *beggar*, 8

menor *younger*, I; **menor que** *younger than*, II; **no tener la menor idea** *not to have the slightest idea*, III8

menos *less*, I; **... menos cuarto** *quarter to (the hour)*, I; **menos... que** *less . . . than*, I

el mensaje *message*, 5

la mente *mind*, 2

mentir (ie, i) *to lie*, III7; **...que nunca me mienta** *. . . who never lies to me*, III7

mentira: **Parece mentira...** *It's hard to believe . . .*, III8

el **menú** *menu*, I

menudo(a) *small*, 9

el **mercado** *market*, II

merecer (zc) *to deserve*, 1

merendar (ie) *to snack*, II

la merluza *hake*

el **mes** *month*, I

la **mesa** *table*, I

el **mesero, la mesera** *food server*, II

la meseta *plateau*, 4

la **meta** *goal*, III10

meter *to place, to put in*, 2

el **metiche, la metiche** *busybody*, II

el **metro** *subway*, II

mexicano(a) *Mexican*, I

méxicoamericano(a) *Mexican American*, 10

la mezcla *mixture*, 4

mi(s) *my*, I; **Mi más sentido pésame.** *My most heartfelt condolences.*, III7

mí (object of preposition) *me*, II

el miedo *fear*, 5

la miel *honey*, 11

mientras *while*, II

el **miércoles** *Wednesday*, I

migratorio(a) *migrant*, 10

mil *one thousand*, I

el milagro *miracle*, 6

la **milla** *mile*, I

millares *thousands*, 9

mimado(a) *pampered*, 7

mineral *mineral* (adj.), **el agua mineral** *mineral water*, I

el ministro, la ministra *minister*, 2

la **minoría** *minority*, III9

minoritario(a) *minority* (adj.), 9

mirar *to watch, to look at*, I

mirarse *to look at oneself*, II

el mirasol *hot pepper*, 4

la misa *mass (church service)*, 7

la miscelánea *miscellany*, 8

mismo(a) *same*, I; **Me da lo mismo.** *It's all the same to me.*, III1; él mismo (ella misma) *he himself (she herself)*, 6

misterioso(a) *mysterious*, 3

mítico(a) *mythical*, 9

el mito *myth*, 5

el mobiliario *furniture*, 3

la **mochila** *book bag, backpack*, I

la **moda** *fashion, style*; **de moda** *in style*, II; **la sección de moda** *fashion section*, III8

los modales *manners*, 9

el modelo, la modelo *model*, 6

moderno(a) *modern*, 5

el **modo** *manner, way*, II; **de todos modos** *anyway*, II; **el modo de ser** *nature, disposition*, III10

mohoso(a) *rusty*, 12

molestar *to bother*, II

el molino (generador) de viento *windmill, wind generator*, 3

momentáneo(a) *momentary*, 9

momentito: Un momentito. *Just a second.*, I

el **momento** *moment*, I

la **moneda** *coin*, II

el **mono** *monkey*, II

el **monopatín** *skateboard*, II

el monopolio *monopoly*, 3

monosílabo(a) *one-syllable* (adj.), 12

monstruoso(a) *monstrous*, 10

la **montaña** *mountain*, I; **escalar montañas** *to go mountain climbing*, III1; **la montaña rusa** *roller coaster*, II

la montañera *mountain bike*, 1

el **montañismo** *mountain climbing*, III1

montar *to ride*, I; **montar a caballo** *to go horseback riding*, III1; **montar en bicicleta** *to ride a bike*, I

el monte *mountain*, 1

el monumento *monument*

morado(a) *purple*, I

la moraleja *moral (of a story or fable)*, 5

morder (ue) *to bite*, 9

moreno(a) *dark-haired, dark-skinned*, III1

morir (ue, u) *to die*, III3

el mosaico *mosaic*

la mosca *fly*, 9

mostrar (ue) *to show*, 2

el motivo *reason*, 1

moverse (ue) *to move*, II

movible *moveable*, 9

el movimiento *movement*, 5; el movimiento nacionalista *nationalist movement*, 6

mucho(a) *a lot (of)*, I

muchos(as) *many, a lot of*, I

mudar *to move (something)*, 2

mudarse *to move (to change addresses)*, 7

los **muebles** *furniture*, 7

la mueca *grimace*, 11

la muerte *death*, 6

el muelle *pier*, 9

muerto (past participle of **morir**) *died*, III3; **quedar muerto(a)** *to be left dead*, III5

la **mujer** *woman, wife*, III5; **la mujer soldado** *soldier* (f.), III5

la multa *fine*, 11

multitudinarios(as) *multitudinous*, 6

mundial *worldwide*, 4

el mundo *world;* el mundo comercial *business world*, 8; **Todo el mundo sabe que...** *Everyone knows that . . .*, III8;

el municipio *municipality*, 11

la **muñeca** *wrist*, II

la muñeira *popular dance of Galicia*

el mural *mural*, 6

el muralismo mexicano *school of Mexican mural art*, 6

el muralista, la muralista *mural painter*

el **murciélago** *bat* (animal), II

el **museo** *museum*, I

la **música** *music*, I; **la música clásica/pop/rock** *classical/pop/rock music*, I

el **músico, la música** *musician*, III6

el **muslo** *thigh*, II

el nacatamal *cornmeal dough stuffed with meat, rice, potatoes, and tomatoes and cooked in plantain leaves*, 4

nacer (zc) *to be born*, 3

la nación (pl. las naciones) *country*, 9

la nacionalidad *nationality*, 8

nacionalizar *to nationalize*, 3

nada *nothing*, I; **¡Nada de eso!** *Of course not!*, III5; **nada más** *that's all*, I; **para nada** *at all*, I
nadar *to swim*, I
nadie *nobody, no one*, I; **No aguanto a nadie que sea descortés.** *I can't stand anyone who's rude.*, III7
la naranja *orange*, I; **el jugo de naranja** *orange juice*, I
la nariz (pl. **las narices**) *nose*, I
el **narrador**, la **narradora** *narrator*, 3
la natación *swimming*, I
nativo(a) *native*, 5
natural *natural*, II
la naturaleza *nature*, II
nauseabundo(a) *nauseating*, 11
náutico(a) *nautical*, I
la **nave** *nave (of a church)*
la nave espacial *spaceship*, II
el navegador *Web browser*, III8
el **navegante**, la **navegante** *sailor*, 5
navegar *to sail*, II; **navegar por Internet** *to surf the Internet*, III3; **navegar por la Red** *to surf the Net*, II
la Navidad *Christmas*, I
necesario(a) *necessary*, II
necesitar *to need*, I
el **néctar** *nectar*, 11
negar (ie) *to reject, to deny, to refuse*, III5
el **negocio** *business*, 2
negro(a) *black*, I
neoyorquino(a) *New York (adj.)*, 9
el **neoyorquino**, la **neoyorquina** *New Yorker*, 9
los **nervios** *nerves*, 7
nervioso(a) *nervous*, I
neutro *neutral*, 4
nevado(a) *snow-capped*
nevar (ie) *to snow*, I
la **nevera** *refrigerator*, 3
la **nevería** *ice cream store (Mexico)*, 4
¡N'hombre! *No way!*, II
ni *nor*, II; **no saber ni jota de** *to know absolutely nothing about*, III8; **no tener ni idea** *not to have the slightest idea*, II
nicaragüense (m./f.) *Nicaraguan*, II
la niebla *fog*, II
Niego haberme burlado... (inf. **negar**) *I deny having made fun of . . .*, III9
los **nietos** *grandchildren*, 2
la **nieve** *snow*, 5
ninguno(a) *none, no*, I; **ningún lugar** *nowhere, not anywhere*, I
la **niñera** *babysitter*, 5
la **niñez** *childhood*, 2
el niño, la niña *child*, II; **De niño, ... (De niña, ...)** *As a child . . .*, III12
el **nivel** *level, grade*, 2
no *no, not*, I; **¿no?** *isn't it?, right?*, I; **no aguanto...** *I can't stand . . .*, III7; **No cabe la menor duda.**

There's absolutely no doubt., III8; **no cabía en sí** *couldn't contain himself (herself)*, 11; **No creo que...** *I don't believe that . . .*, III8; **No debes** + inf. *You shouldn't . . .*, III2; **No es cierto que...** *It's not true that . . .*, III9; **No es ni fu ni fa.** *It's neither fish nor fowl.*, 6; **No es posible.** *It's not possible.*, III8; **No es verdad que...** *It's not true that . . .*, III9; **No estoy de acuerdo en que...** *I don't agree that . . .*, III9; **No estoy seguro(a) que...** *I'm not sure that . . .*, III8; **no guardar secretos** *not to keep secrets*, III7; **No hay mal que cien años dure.** *It won't last forever.*, III7; **No hay mal que por bien no venga.** *Every cloud has a silver lining.*, III7; **No hay quien lo (la) aguante.** *Nobody can stand him (her).*, III1; **No lo haré más.** *I won't do it anymore.*, III7; **No lo (la) soporto.** *I can't stand it (him/her)*, III6; **No lo volveré a hacer.** *I won't do it again.*, III7; **¡No me digas!** *You don't say!*, III8; **No me importa.** *It doesn't matter to me.*, III1; **No me interesa para nada.** *It doesn't interest me at all.*, III1; **No me lo esperaba.** *It caught me by surprise.*, III8; **No me lo puedo creer.** *I can't believe it.*, III8; **No olvides que...** *Don't forget that . . .*, III12; **¡No puede ser!** *It can't be!*, III8; **No puedo creer que...** *I can't believe that . . .*, III8; **no saber ni jota de** *to know absolutely nothing about*, III8; **No te conviene...** *It's not advisable that you . . .*, III6; **No te olvides de...** *Don't forget to . . .*, III6; **No te preocupes.** *Don't worry.*, III7; **no tener la menor idea** *not to have the slightest idea*, III8; no tener nada que ver con *to have nothing to do with*, 5; **No tengo ganas de** + inf. *I don't feel like . . .*, III6
la noche *night, evening*, I; **la Nochebuena** *Christmas Eve*, I; **la Nochevieja** *New Year's Eve*, I; **por la noche** *at night*, I
nombrar *to nominate*, 1
el **nombre** *name*, 6
normalmente *normally*, II
el norte *north*, II
nos *(to/for) us*, I; **Nos toca a nosotros...** *It's up to us . . .*, III3
nosotros mismos *we ourselves* 7
nosotros(as) *we; us (after preposition)*, I
nostálgico(a) *nostalgic*, 10
la nota *grade*, II
notable *remarkable*, 10
notar *to observe, to note*, III3; **Lo que noto es que...** *What I notice is that*

. . ., III3
las noticias *news*, II
el noticiero *news program*, III8
notorio(a) *notorious*, 6
novecientos(as) *nine hundred*, I
la novela *novel*, I; *soap opera*, 8
noventa *ninety*, I
la novia *girlfriend*, III7; *fiancée*, 5; *bride*, 5
noviembre (m.) *November*, I
el novio *boyfriend*, III7; *fiancé*, 5; *groom*, 5
la **nube** *cloud*, 2
nublado(a) *cloudy*, I
el núcleo *nucleus*, 4
nuestro(a) *our, ours*, I
nueve *nine*, I
nuevo(a) *new*, I
el número *number*, I; *(shoe) size*, II; *issue (of a magazine)*, 8
nunca *never, not ever*, I
nupcial *wedding (adj.)*, 7
nutrir *nourish*, 2

o *or*, I
obedecer (zc) *to obey*, 5
los obituarios *obituaries*, III8
el objetivo *goal, objective*, III10
la obligación *commitment*, 10
obligatorio(a) *obligatory*, 11
la obra: *work;* **la obra de teatro** *play (theater)*, 6; **la obra maestra** *masterpiece*, III6; **las obras públicas** *public works*, 12
el **obrero**, la **obrera** *worker*, 10
obsceno(a) *obscene*, 11
la **obsolencia** *being or becoming out of date*, 3
el obstáculo *obstacle*, III10; **Logró superar muchos obstáculos.** *He (She) succeeded in overcoming many obstacles.*, III10
obstinado(a) *obstinate*, 7
obtener (ie) *to get*, 9
occidental *western*
el océano *ocean*, II
ochenta *eighty*, I
ocho *eight*, I
ochocientos(as) *eight hundred*, I
el **ocio** *leisure*, 8; **la sección de ocio** *entertainment section*, III8
octubre (m.) *October*, I
ocupado(a) *busy*, I
ocupar *to occupy*, 11
ocuparse de *to look after*, 11
ocurrir *to happen*, 2; *to occur*, 12
odiar *to hate*, II
el **odio** *hatred*, 10

el oeste *west*, II
ofender (ie) *to offend*, 3
el ofendido, la ofendida *offended person*, 7
la oferta *offer, sale*, II
ofrecer (zc) *to offer*, II
el oído *(inner) ear*, I
oír *to hear, to listen*, II; **Oí que...,** *I heard that . . .*, III5; **¿Qué has oído de...?** *What have you heard about . . .?*, III6
ojalá que + subj. *hopefully . . .*, III5
la ojeada *brief survey*, 6
ojear *to skim*, 9
el ojo *eye*, I; **¡Ojo!** *Heads up!*, 2
la ola *wave*, 1
la olla *pot*, 1
olvidar *to forget*, II
olvidarse (de) *to forget (about), to forget (to)*, II; **No te olvides de...** *Don't forget to . . .*, III6; **¿Se te olvidó (olvidaron)...?** *Did you forget . . .?*, III4
omitir *to leave out, to omit*, 5
once *eleven*, I
el onoto *annatto (red food coloring)*, 4
opinar *to have an opinion*, III6; **¿Qué opinas de...?** *What's your opinion of . . .?*, III6
la opinión (pl. **las opiniones**) *opinion*, II
el optimista, la optimista *optimist*, 3
opuesto(a) *opposite*, 3
la oración *sentence*, 4
el orden *order, sequence*, 9
el ordenador *computer* (Spain), 3
ordenar *to tidy up*, II
la oreja *(outer) ear*, I
el orfanato *orphanage*
organizar *to organize*, I
el orgullo *pride*, III10
orgulloso(a) *proud*, III7; **Estoy orgulloso(a) de...** *I'm proud of . . .*, III7
el oriente *east*
el origen *origin*, 5
original *original*, III6
originar *to originate*, 4
el oro *gold*, 5
la orquesta *orchestra*, III6
oscuro(a) *dark*, 6
el oso *bear*, 11
las ostras *oysters*, III4
el otoño *fall* (season), I
otro(a) *another*, I
otros(as) *other, others*, I
el OVNI (Objeto Volante No Identificado) *UFO (Unidentified Flying Object)*, II
el oxígeno *oxygen*, 11

P

el pabellón criollo *Venezuelan dish with shredded beef, black beans, rice, and fried plantains*
la paciencia *patience*, 7
pacífico(a) *peaceful*, 7
pactar *to agree upon*, 7
el padrastro *stepfather*, I
el padre *father*, I
los padres *parents*, I
pagar *to pay*, 6
la página en blanco *blank page*
la página Web *Web page*, II
el país *country*, 10
el paisaje *landscape*
el pájaro *bird*, 11
la palabra *word*, 9
el palacio *palace*, 5
paladear *to relish*, 11
palidecer (zc) *to pale*, 11
la paliza *beating*; **¡Qué paliza!** *What a drag!*, III1
el palo *stick*, 6
las palomitas *popcorn*, 8
palpitante *throbbing*, 9
la palta *avocado* (southern cone of South America), 4
el pan *bread*; pan de jamón *loaf of bread baked with ham, olives, and spices*, 4; **el pan dulce** *sweet rolls*, I; **el pan tostado** *toast*, I
la panadería *bakery*, III4
panameño(a) *Panamanian*, II
el pánico *panic*, 3
la pantalla *screen*, 3
los pantalones *pants*; **los pantalones cortos** *shorts*, I
la pantorrilla *calf (of the leg)*, II
la papa *potato*, I; **las papas fritas** *french fries*, I
el papá *dad*, I
la papaya *papaya*, I
el papel *paper*, I; *dramatic role*, 3
las papitas *potato chips*, I
el paquete *package*, 3
el par *de pair of*, II
para *for, to, in order to, by*; **para** + inf. *in order to*, III10; para colmo *to top things off*, 8; **Para decir la verdad...** *To tell the truth . . .*, III6; **para que** *so that, in order that*, III10; **Para ser sincero(a)...** *To be honest . . .*, III6
el paracaídas *parachute*; **saltar en paracaídas** *to go skydiving*, I
la parada *stop*, II; **la parada del autobús** *bus stop*, II
la paradoja *paradox*, 10
la paráfrasis *paraphrasing*, 10
paraguayo(a) *Paraguayan*, II
el paraíso *paradise*, I
parar *to stop*, 2
parcial *partial*, 5

pardo(a) *brown*, I
parecer (zc) *to seem, to think*, I; **En efecto, parece ser así.** *Actually, it seems to be that way.*, III5; **Me parece que...** *It seems to me that . . .*, III3; **Me parece un rollo.** *It seems really boring to me.*, III1; **Parece mentira...** *It's hard to believe . . .*, III8; **¿Qué te parece?** *What do you think?*, III6
parecido(a) *like, alike*, 6
la pared *wall*, 2
la pareja *pair*, 4
el paréntesis *parenthesis*, 6
el pargo *red snapper*, III4
los parientes *relatives*, II
el paro forzoso *unemployment*, 11
el parque *park*, I; **el parque de atracciones** *amusement park*, I
el párrafo *paragraph*, 1
la parrillada *assortment of grilled meats*
la parte *part, behalf*; de mi parte *from me, on my behalf*, II; **¿De parte de quién?** *Who's calling?*, I
el partido de... *game of (sport)*, I
partir *to set out, to leave*, 5
pasado(a) de moda *out of style*, 3
pasado(a) *past, last* (with time), I
pasajero(a) *passing, temporary*, 8
el pasajero, la pasajera *passenger*, II
pasar *to happen, to pass*, I; **Esto pasará pronto** *This will soon pass*, III7; **Me la paso...** *I spend my time . . .*, III1; **pasar el rato** *to spend time*, I; **pasar por** *to drop by*, II; **pasarlo bien** *to have a good time*, I
el pasatiempo *pastime, hobby*, II
las Pascuas *Easter*, I
el paseaperros, la paseaperros *dog-walker*, 12
pasear en velero *to go sailing*, III1
el paseo *(social) walk, stroll*, I; **dar un paseo** *to take a walk*, I
el pasillo *hall*, 6
la pasión *passion*, 8
el paso *step*, 5
la pasta de dientes *toothpaste*, II
el pastel *cake*, I
la pastelería *pastry shop*, III4
la pata *paw*, 12
la patata *potato* (Spain)
la patilla *watermelon* (Venezuela), III4
el patinaje *skating*, III1
patinar *to skate*, I; **patinar en línea** *to go inline skating*, III1; **patinar sobre hielo** *to ice-skate*, III1; **patinar sobre ruedas** *to roller-skate*, III1
el pato *duck*; **tan aburrido como un pato** *a terrible bore*, II
el patrocinador, la patrocinadora *sponsor*, 1
patrocinar *to sponsor*, III6
el patrón, la patrona *boss*, 11
el pavimento *flooring, pavement*, 9
el pavor *terror*, 3

la paz (pl. **las paces**) *peace;* **acordar (ue) la paz** *to make peace,* III5; **hacer las paces** *to make up* (after a quarrel), III5

peatonal *pedestrian* (adj.), III3; **establecer una zona peatonal** *to set up a pedestrian zone,* III3

el **pecho** *chest,* 5

pedalear *to pedal,* 11

los **pedales** *pedals,* 11

el **pediatra, la pediatra** *pediatrician,* 12

el **pedido** *request,* 4

pedir (i, i) *to order, to ask for,* I

pedregoso(a) *stony,* 12

el **pegamento** *glue,* 4; el pegamento casero *homemade glue,* 4

peinarse *to comb your hair,* I

el **peine** *comb,* II

pelar *to peel,* 4

pelear *to fight,* II

pelearse *to have a fight,* III7

la **película** *movie, film,* I; **de película** *great* (colloquial), II

el **peligro** *danger,* III2; en peligro de extinción *endangered,* 3

peligroso(a) *dangerous,* II

pelirrojo(a) *red-headed,* III1

el **pelo** *hair,* I

la **pelusa** *fluff,* 5

la **pena** *sorrow, grief,* III7; **Comparto tu pena.** *I share your grief.,* III7; **Creo que vale la pena...** *I think it's worth it . . .,* III3; están que da pena *are such that it's painful,* 11

los **pensamientos** *thoughts,* 8

pensar (ie) *to think, to plan, to intend,* I; **Eso me hace pensar en...** *That brings to mind . . .,* III6; **¿Has pensado en...?** *Have you thought of . . .?,* III6; **¿Qué piensas de...?** *What do you think about . . .?,* III6

el **peor, la peor** *worst,* II

peor que *worse than,* II

pequeño(a) *small,* I

el **pequeño, la pequeña** *child;* **de pequeño(a)** *as a child,* II

los **percebes** *barnacles,* 1

la **percepción** *perception,* 8

percibir *to perceive,* 9

percusivo(a) *percussive,* 6

perder (ie) *to lose, to miss* (a class, an exam, and so on), II; **echado(a) a perder** *spoiled,* III4

perderse (ie) *to get lost,* II; **Se me perdió (perdieron)...** *I lost . . .,* III4

la **pérdida** *loss, waste,* 11

perdidamente *desperately,* 5

Perdón. *Excuse me.,* I

perdonar *to forgive, to excuse,* I; **Perdóname.** *Forgive me.,* III7

el **peregrino, la peregrina** *religious pilgrim*

perezoso(a) *lazy,* III9

perfectamente *perfectly,* 10

perfecto(a) *perfect,* I

el **periódico** *newspaper,* I

el **periodismo** *journalism,* 8

el **periodista, la periodista** *journalist,* III8

el **perjuicio** *injury,* 11

la **perla** *pearl*

la **permanente** *permanent wave,* 2

el **permiso** *permission;* **con permiso** *excuse me,* II

permitir *to allow,* 2

pero *but,* I; **Pero hay que tener en cuenta que...** *But you have to take into account that . . .,* III5; **pero por otro lado...** *but on the other hand . . .,* III3

perpetuo(a) *forever, perpetual,* 3

perplejo(a) *perplexed,* 5

el **perro** *dog,* I; **el perro caliente** *hot dog,* I; **tan noble como un perro** *as noble as a lion,* I

perseguir (i, i) *to chase,* 5

persistente *permanent, persistent,* 1

la **persona** *person,* I

el **personaje** *character,* 5

persuadir *to persuade,* 10

pertenecer (zc) *to belong,* 5

peruano(a) *Peruvian,* II

la **pesa** *(free)weight,* II

pesado(a) *annoying,* III1; *boring,* II

el **pésame** *condolences,* III7; **Mi más sentido pésame.** *My most heartfelt condolences.,* III7

pesar: a pesar de *in spite of,* 5

pesarse *to weigh oneself,* III2

la **pescadería** *fish market,* III4

el **pescado** *fish* (after being caught), I

pescar *to fish,* I

pese a *in spite of,* 10

el **pesimista, la pesimista** *pessimist,* 3

pésimo(a) *awful,* III6

el **peso** *weight,* III2; **cuidarse el peso** *to watch one's weight,* III2

la **petición** (pl. las peticiones) *request,* 7

el **petirrojo** *robin,* 11

el **petróleo** *petroleum,* II

petrolero(a) *petroleum*

el **pez** (pl. **los peces**) *fish* (before being caught), II

el **piano** *piano,* I

el **picadillo de arracache** *casserole with meat and vegetables*

picante *spicy,* I

el **pie** *foot,* I; al pie de la letra *to the letter, exactly,* 7

la **piedra** *stone,* 1

la **piel** *skin,* III2

Pienso + inf. *I intend to* + verb, III10

la **pierna** *leg,* I

la **pieza** *part,* 8

la **pimienta** *(black) pepper,* 4

el **pimiento** *pepper* (vegetable), 4

el **pincel** *paintbrush,* 6

pintar *to paint,* I; **Hace falta que pintemos...** *We need to paint . . .,* III6

pintoresco(a) *picturesque,* 3

la **pintura** *painting,* III6

la **piña** *pineapple,* III4

la **pirámide** *pyramid,* 10

la **piraña** *piranha,* 4

pisar *to step on,* 4

la **piscina** *swimming pool,* I

el **piso** *floor,* II

la **pista** *track,* I; **la pista de correr** *running track,* I; *runway,* 5

la **pistola** *gun,* 8

la **pizarra** *chalkboard,* 8

la **pizca** *pinch,* 4

pizpireta *cheerful,* 9

la **pizza** *pizza,* I

la **pizzería** *pizzeria,* I

el **placer** *pleasure,* 6

la **plana:** **la primera plana** *front page,* III8

la **plancha** *iron* (for ironing clothes), 1

planchar *to iron,* I

los **planes** *plans,* II

el **planeta** *planet,* II

plano(a) *smooth,* 6

la **planta** *plant,* I

plantado(a): **dejar plantado(a) a alguien** *to stand someone up,* III7

plantear *to state,* III11; **La solución que planteo es...** *The solution I propose is . . .,* III11

plasmar su pena *to capture her grief,* 6

el **plástico** *plastic,* II

la **plata** *silver, money,* 2

el **plátano** *banana,* I

plateado(a) *silver-plated,* 1

platicar *to chat,* II

el **platillo volador** *flying saucer,* 12

el **plato** *plate,* I; **el plato hondo** *bowl,* I; el plato principal *main dish,* 4

la **playa** *beach,* I

pleno(a) *full;* en plena forma *in good shape,* II

la **pluma** *feather,* 5

la **población** *population*

poblar *to populate,* 1

pobre *poor,* 5

el **pobretón, la pobretona** *poor thing,* 7

la **pobreza** *poverty,* 7

poco: un poco *a little,* 4

poco(a) *a little,* I

pocos(as) *few,* II

poder (ue) *to be able to, can,* I; **¿Podrías...?** *Could you . . .?,* III4; **¿Puedes darme algún consejo?** *Can you give me any advice?,* III2; **¿Qué puedo hacer por ti?** *What can I do for you?,* III7; **Si pudiera... viviría...** *If I could . . . I would live . . .,* III9; **Si pudieras... ¿adónde irías?** *If you could . . . where would you go?,* III9

poderoso(a) *mighty, powerful,* 5

¿Podrías...? *Could you . . . ?*, III4
la **poesía** *poetry*, 1
el **poeta**, la **poeta** *poet*, 1
polémico(a) *controversial*, 9
la **policía** *police*, 4; **la policía de tránsito** *traffic police*, 4
el policía, la policía *police officer*, III12
el pollo *chicken*, I; **el pollo frito** *fried chicken*, III4
el **polvo** *dust*, 10; **sacudir el polvo** *to dust*, II
ponderar *to mull over*, 7
poner *to put, to place, to set*, I; **Puse todo mi esfuerzo en...** *I put a lot of effort into . . .*, III10
ponerse *to put on*, I; *to become, to get*, II; **ponerse ansioso(a)** *to get anxious*, 2; **ponerse crema protectora** *to put on sunscreen*, III2; **ponerse en forma** *to get in shape*, II; **ponerse nervioso(a)** *to get nervous*, III2; **Se pusieron rojos.** *They blushed.*, III9
la **popularidad** *popularity*
por *at, along, by, for, in, through*, I; **por cable** *on cable*, III8; **por casualidad** *by coincidence*, 5; **por ciento** *percent*, II; **Por cierto.** *Certainly.*, III8; *by the way*, 6; **por consiguiente...** *consequently . . .*, III10; **por dentro** *on the inside*, 2; **por el hecho que** *due to the fact that*, 10; **por eso** *that's why*, I; **por favor** *please*, I; **Por favor, ayúdame con...** *Please help me with . . .*, III4; **por la mañana, tarde, noche** *in the morning, afternoon, night*, I; **por lo general** *in general*, I; **por lo tanto...** *therefore . . .*, III10; **por medio de** *by means of*, 10; **por otro lado** *on the other hand*, III3; **¿Por qué?** *Why?*, III1; **¿Por qué no...?** *Why don't . . . ?*, I; **¿Por qué no lo dejamos para...?** *Why don't we leave it for (another time)?*, III6; **Por supuesto.** *Of course.*, III5; **por tener...** *because I (you, . . .) have . . .*, III10; **por último** *finally*, II
el **pormenor** *detail*, 12
porque *because*, I
la **portada** *book or magazine cover*, 7
portarse *to behave*, 9
el **porteño**, la **porteña** *person from Buenos Aires*
el porvenir *future*, III3
posar *to pose*, 5
poseer *to possess*, 4
Posiblemente... *Possibly . . .*, III8
positivo(a) *positive*, 6
postal: la tarjeta postal *postcard*, I
postrado(a) *prostrate*, 6
el postre *dessert*, I
el pozo *(water) well*, II
el **pozole** *soup with hominy, meat, and chile*
prácticamente *practically*, 3

practicar *to practice, to participate in;* **practicar ciclismo** *to practice cycling*, III1
práctico(a) *practical*, 9
la **precaución** *precaution*, 1
el precio *price*, I
precioso(a) *lovely*
precisamente *precisely*, 6
preciso(a) *necessary*, II
precolombino(a) *pre-Columbian*, 10
predecir (i) *to foretell, to predict*, 3
la **predestinación** *predestination*, 5
la **predicción (pl. las predicciones)** *prediction*, 3
predilecto(a) *favorite*, 2
predominar *to predominate*, 4
las **preferencias** *preferences*, 6
preferir (ie, i) *to prefer*, I
la pregunta *question;* **hacer preguntas** *to ask questions*, II
preguntar *to ask*, 1
el prejuicio *prejudice*, III9
prejuzgar *to prejudge*, 9
preliminar *preliminary*, 3
el **premio** *prize, award*, 1
prender *to capture*, 12
la prensa *press*, III8
preocupado(a) *worried*, I
preocuparse *to worry*, I
preparar *to prepare*, I
la **presencia** *presence*, 7
presenciar *to watch, to witness*, 6
la **presentación oral** *oral presentation*, 9
presentar *to present, to introduce*, 1; **presentar un examen** *to take an exam*, 10
prestarse *to lend itself*, 7
la presión *pressure*, III2; **sufrir de presiones** *to be under pressure*, III2
presionados(as) por... *pressured to . . .*, III9
prestar *to lend*, 7; **prestar atención** *to pay attention*, II
el **prestigio** *prestige*, 8
presumido(a) *conceited*, III9
el **pretendiente** *suitor*, 5
el **pretérito** *preterite (tense)*, 4
prevenir (ie) *to warn*, 5
preventivo(a) *preventive*, 11
prever *to foresee*, 3
previo(a) *previous*, 8
la **primaria** *elementary school*, 11
la primavera *spring*, I
primaveral *spring-like*, 11
el primero *the first (of the month)*, I
primero(a) *first*, I; **primera categoría** *first class;* **la primera plana** *front page*, III8
el primo, la prima *cousin*, I
la princesa *princess*, II
el príncipe *prince*, II
principiar *to begin*, 6
el **principio** *the beginning*, 7
la prisa *hurry*, I; **darse prisa** *to hurry up*, I; **tener prisa** *to be in a hurry*, I

la **privacidad** *privacy*, 5
el probador *dressing room*, II
probar (ue) *to try, to taste*, 4
probarse (ue) *to try on*, II
el problema *problem*, I
procesar *to process*, 3
proclamar *to proclaim*, 9
procurar *to try*, 12
la **producción propia** *production for one's own use*, 4
el producto *product*, II; **los productos** *goods*, II; **los productos petroquímicos** *petrochemical products*
la **profecía** *prophecy*, 5
el profesor, la profesora *teacher, professor*, I
profundamente *deeply*, II
profundo(a) *deep*, 1
profusamente *profusely*, 7
el programa *program*, III8; **el programa de intercambio** *exchange program*, I
el programador, la programadora de computadoras *computer programmer*, III12
programar *to program*, 4
el **progresismo** *progressivism*, 11
el **promedio** *average*, 9
promover (ue) *to promote*, III11
el **pronombre** *pronoun;* **el pronombre de complemento directo/indirecto** *direct/indirect object pronoun*, 4
el **pronóstico** *forecast, prediction*, 3
pronto *soon*, II; **tan pronto como** *as soon as*, III10
la **propiedad** *property*, 11
la propina *tip, gratuity*, I
propio(a) *own*, 7
Propongo...(inf. proponer) *I propose . . .*, III11
el **propósito** *purpose*, 3; **A propósito, ¿qué has oído de...?** *By the way, what have you heard about . . . ?*, III6
la **prosa** *prose*, 1
prosperar *to thrive, to prosper*, 3
la **prosperidad** *prosperity*, 11
proteger *to protect*, II
provenir (ie) de *to come from*, 10
proyectar *to project*, 9
el **proyecto** *project*, 2
la **prueba** *quiz, test*, 5
la **publicación (pl. las publicaciones)** *publication*, 10
publicar *to publish*, 1
el **público** *audience*, 8
público(a) *public*, 11
el **puchero** *stew of meat, cabbage, carrots, and onions*
el **pueblo** *town*, 1; *people*, 10
Puede ser que... *It's possible that . . .*, III8
¿Puedes darme algún consejo? *Can you give me any advice?*, III2
el puente *bridge*, II
el puerco asado *roast pork*, III4

la puerta *door*, I

el puerto *port*

puertorriqueño(a) *Puerto Rican*, II

Pues... *Well . . .*, III3

el puesto (de trabajo) *position, job*, III12; **el puesto** *market stall*, 8

puesto (past participle of **poner**) *put*, III3

pulido(a) *polished*, 4

el pulmón *lung*, 9

el pulpo *octopus*, 1

la punta *tip, end*, 5

el puntal *pillar*, 9

el punto *point, dot*; **Depende de tu punto de vista.** *It depends on your point of view.*, III5; **en punto** *on the dot*, I; **Está en su punto.** *It's just right.*, III4; **Hasta cierto punto, sí, pero...** *Up to a point, yes, but . . .*, III5

puntuar *to punctuate*, 8

el puré (de papas) *mashed potatoes*, 4

Puse todo mi esfuerzo en... *I put a lot of effort into . . .*, III10

que *that, which, who, than*; **...que me apoye . . .** *that supports me*, III7; **...que nunca me mienta . . .** *who never lies to me*, III7; **...que respete mis sentimientos . . .** *that respects my feelings*, III7; **...que sea descortés . . .** *who is rude*, III7; **...que sepa . . .** *who knows*, III7; **que sí** *of course*, 7; **...que siempre me diga... . . .** *who always tells me . . .*, III7; **Que yo sepa...** *As far as I know . . .*, III8

¡Qué…! *How . . .!, What . . .!*, I; **¡Qué asco!** *How disgusting!*, III4; **¡Qué bueno (sabroso)!** *How good (tasty)!*, III4; **¡Qué paliza!** *What a drag!*, III1; **¡Qué sorpresa!** *What a surprise!*, III8; **¡Qué tontería!** *How silly!*, III5; **¡Qué va!** *No way!*, III5

¿Qué? *What? Which?*; **¿Qué debo hacer?** *What should I do?*, III2; **¿Qué has oído de...?** *What have you heard about . . .?*, III6; **¿Qué me aconsejas hacer?** *What do you advise me to do?*, III2; **¿Qué me cuentas de...?** *What can you tell me about . . .?*, III6; **¿Qué me recomiendas hacer?** *What do you recommend that I do?*, III2; **¿Qué opinas de...?** *What's your opinion of . . .?*, III6; **¿Qué piensas de...?** *What do you think about . . .?*, III6; **¿Qué puedo hacer por ti?** *What can I do for you?*, III7; **¿Qué sé yo?** *How should I know?*, III8; **¿Qué tal...?** *How is . . .?*, 4 **¿Qué te**

parece...? *What do you think of . . .?*, III6

el quebranto *breaking*, 6

los quechua *Quechuans, Indian people of Central Peru*, 4

quedar *to be left, to fit, to be located*, II; **quedar en** + inf. *to arrange to (do something)*, II; **quedar impresionado(a) con** *to think (something) is great*, II; **quedar muerto(a)** *to be left dead*, III5; **Te queda muy bien.** *It fits you very well.*, II

quedarse *to stay, to remain*, I; **quedarse frente a la tele** *to stay in front of the TV*, III2; **Se les quedó (quedaron)...**, *They left . . . behind.*, III4

los quehaceres *chores*, II

la queja *complaint*, 4

quejarse (de) *to complain*, II

quemar *to burn*, 5

quemarse *to get a sunburn, to get burned*, III2

la quena *Andean flute*, 6

querer (ie) *to want*, I; **Lo hice sin querer.** *I didn't mean to do it.*, III7; **Los dioses quieren que los guerreros acuerden la paz.** *The gods want the warriors to make peace.*, III5; **Quiero llegar a ser...** *I want to become . . .*, III12; **Quiero ser...** *I want to be . . .*, III12; **Quise...** *I wanted (tried) . . .*, III9

querido(a) *dear*, II

el quesillo *custard (Venezuela)*, III4

el queso *cheese*, I

quien(es) *who, whom*, I; **a quien le guste(n)...** *who likes . . .*, III7

¿Quién(es)? *Who?, Whom?*, III1

el químico, la químico *chemist*, 8

los químicos *chemicals*, II

quince *fifteen*, I

quinientos(as) *five hundred*, I

quinto(a) *fifth*

Quise... *I wanted (tried) . . .*, III9

quitar *to take away, to clear off*, II

quitarse *to take off (clothes)*, 2

Quizás... *Maybe . . .*, III8

rabelaisiano(a) *Rabelaisian*, 9

rabioso(a) *infuriated*, 7

la radio *radio*, I

las raíces (sing. **la raíz**) *roots*, III10

la rama *branch*, 12

el ramo (de rosas) *bouquet (of roses)*, 11

el rancho *dwelling that can range from a shanty to a small house (Venezuela)*, 3

rápidamente *quickly*, II

rápido(a) *fast*, 3

rapiña: ave de rapiña *bird of prey*, 1

raro(a) *rare*, 2

el rascacielos *skyscraper*, III3

raspar *to scrape*, 6

el rastro *trace*, 12

el rato *while, time*, I; **el rato libre** *free time*, II

rayas: de rayas *striped*, I

el rayo *bolt of lightning*, II; *ray of light*, 1

la raza *race (of people)*, 9

la razón (pl. las razones) *reason*, 6; **(no) tener razón** *to be right (wrong)*, II

reaccionar *to react*, III9; **reaccionaron** *they reacted*, III9

reacio(a) *stubborn*, 4

la realidad *reality*, 11

el realismo *realism*, 12

realista (m./f.) *realistic*, III6

la realización *fulfillment*, 11

realizar *to carry out*, III11; **realizar (un sueño)** *to fulfill (a dream)*, III10; **Si no realizamos...** *If we don't carry out . . .*, III11

rebajar el precio *lower the price*, II

la rebanada *slice*, 2

rebotar *to bounce*, 12

el recado *message*, I

recalcar *to emphasize*, 11

la recámara *bedroom (Mexico)*, 6

la receta *recipe*, 4; *prescription*, 12

recibir *to receive*, I

el reciclaje *recycling*, II

reciclar *to recycle*, II

recién *recent, recently*, 7

reclamar *to reclaim, to complain*, 4

el reclamo *claim, complaint*, 4

reclutar *to recruit*, 5

la recolección (pl. las recolecciones) *harvest*, 3

recodar *to twist, to turn*, 9

recoger *to pick up*, III3; **recogemos** *we pick up*, III3

recomendar (ie) *to recommend*, II; **¿Qué me recomiendas hacer?** *What do you recommend that I do?*, III2; **Te recomiendo que...** *I recommend that you . . .*, III6

recomenzar (ie) *to begin again*, 11

la recompensa *reward*, 6

reconciliarse *to make up, to reconcile*, III7

reconocer (zc) *to recognize*, III6; **Es importante que reconozcas...** *It's important for you to recognize . . .*, III6

recordar (ue) *to remind, to remember*, III6; **Eso me recuerda...** *That reminds me of . . .*, III6

recorrer *to go through, to travel through*

el recorrido *journey*, II

recrear *recreate*, 8

recreativo(a) *recreative*, 11

el recreo *recreation*

recubierto (past participle

of **recubrir**) *covered*, 6
recuerda (inf. **recordar**) *reminds*,
III6; **Eso me recuerda...** *That
reminds me of . . .*, III6
el **recuerdo** *memory, souvenir*, 6
la **recuperación** *recovery*, 6
recuperarse *to recover*, 10
recurioso(a) *very curious*, 8
los **recursos** *resources*, II
la **red** *web, net*, II; *trap*, 12; **navegar
por la Red** *to surf the Net*, II
redondo(a) *round*, 4
reemplazar *to replace*, 3
la **refacción: la tienda de refacciones**
parts store, III4
la **referencia** *reference*, 12
refinado(a) *refined*, 4
reflejar *to reflect*, 10
el **reflejo** *reflection*, 6
reflexionar *to consider, to reflect*, 2
el **refrán** *saying, proverb*, 5
el **refresco** *soft drink*, I
regalar *to give (as a gift)*, I; **Se lo
regalo por** *I'll let you have it for*, II
el **regalo** *gift, present*, I
regar (ie) *to water*, II
regatear *to bargain*, II
el **régimen** (pl. **los regímenes**) *diet*, II
registrar *to register, to check*, 3
registrarse *to register, to check in*, 10
la **regla** *ruler*, I; *rule*, 2
regocijarse *to rejoice*, III5
regresar *to return, to go back, to
come back*, I
Regular. *Okay.*, I
rehusar *to refuse*, 3
reírse (i, i) *to laugh*, III2; **se rieron**
they laughed, III9
reivindicar *to claim*, 4
relajarse *to relax*, III2
relampaguear *to flash (said
of lightning)*, 12
el **relato** *story, account, narration*, 4
rellenar *to fill, to stuff*, 4
el **reloj** *clock, watch*, I
remar *to row*, III1
el **remedio** *solution, remedy, help*, 3
el **remo** *rowing*, III1
la **remolacha** *beet*, 4
el **remolino** *whirlwind*, 10
remoto(a) *remote*, 4
renacentista *Renaissance;* estilo
renacentista, *Renaissance style*, 10
el **rencor** *resentment*, 7
rendido(a) *exhausted*, III2
la **rendija** *crack*, 12
rendir (i, i) *to yield*, 11
el **renglón** *line of writing*, 5
renunciar *to give up (something)*, 7
reparar *to fix*, 4
repasar *to review*, II
repletar *to cram full*, 9
repleto(a) *full*, 10
el **reportaje** *report*, III8
el **reportero, la reportera** *reporter*, III8
reposar *to rest*, 3
el **representante, la representante**

representative, 8
la **represión** *repression*, 9
reprimir *to repress*, 8
repugnante *disgusting*, 11
los **requisitos** *requirements*, III12
res: la carne de res *beef*, I; la falda de
res *skirt steak*, 4
resaltar *to emphasize*, 11
rescatar *to rescue*, 6
la **reseña** *review*, 6
reseñar *to review*, 8
el **reseñista, la reseñista** *reviewer*, 4
la **reserva** *reserve*, 9
reservado(a) *reserved*, 2
resfriado(a) *sick with a cold;* **estar
resfriado(a)** *to have a cold*, I
la **residencia** *dormitory*, 5
residir *to live*, 9
resignar *to resign*, 11
resolver (ue) *to solve*, II; **resolver un
problema** *to solve a problem*, III2
respecto a *with regard to*, 2
respetar *to respect*, III9; **...que
respete mis sentimientos**
. . . that respects my feelings, III7;
respetar sus sentimientos *to
respect someone's feelings*, III7
el **respeto** *respect*, III9; **respeto hacia**
respect for, III9
respirar *to breathe*, II
resplandecer (zc) *to shine*, 12
responder *to answer*, 3
responsable *responsible*, II
la **respuesta** *answer*, 2
restante *remaining*, 11
el **restaurante** *restaurant*, I
restaurar *to restore*, 4
restringir *to restrict*, 8
resuelto (past participle of **resolver**)
solved, III7; **El problema está
resuelto.** *The problem is solved.*,
III7
el **resultado** *result*, 5
resultar *to result*, III10; **resultaron
en** *resulted in*, III10
el **resumen** (pl. los **resúmenes**)
summary, 1
resumir *to sum up, to
summarize*, 1
retirar *to remove, to
withdraw*, 4
retirarse *to withdraw*, 3
el **reto** *challenge*, III10
retrasar *to delay*, 12
el **retrato** *portrait, photograph*, 5
la **reunión** (pl. las **reuniones**) *meeting*,
11
reunir *to bring together*, 10
reunirse *to get together*, II
revelar *to reveal*, 10
reventar *to blow up, to burst*, 6
la **revista** *magazine*, I
revolotear *to flutter*, 9
el **rey** *king*, 1
la **ría** *mouth of a river*, 1
rico(a) *rich, delicious*, I
el **riego** *irrigation*, 4

los **rieles** *tracks*, 9
rígido(a) *rigid*, 1
el **río** *river*, II
riquísimo(a) *delicious*, III4; **Sabe
riquísimo.** *It tastes delicious.*, III4
el **ritmo** *rhythm*, 10
rizado(a) *curly*, III1
robar *to steal*, 5
el **robo** *robbery*, III11; *rip-off*, I
la **roca** *rock*, 4
rodante *rolling*, 9
rodeado(a) de *surrounded by*, II
rodear *to surround*, 4
la **rodilla** *knee*, II
rogar (ue) *to plead*, 7
rojo(a) *red*, I
el **rollo: Me parece un rollo.** *It seems
really boring to me.*, III1
romántico(a) *romantic*, 3
romper con *to break up with*, III7
romperse *to break*, II; **Se le rompió
(rompieron)...** *He (She) broke . . .*,
III4
la **ropa** *clothes, clothing*, I; la ropa vieja
shredded beef with seasoning
roto (past participle of **romper**)
broken, III3
el **rótulo** *label*, 9
rubio(a) *blond, fair*, I
el **rubro** *item*, 4
la **rueda** *wheel;* **patinar sobre ruedas**
to roller-skate, III1; **la rueda de
Chicago** *Ferris wheel*, II
el **ruido** *noise*, II
ruidoso(a) *noisy*, II
el **ruiseñor** *nightingale*, 11
el **rumbo** *direction, way*, 1
el **rumor** *rumor*, III7
ruso(a) *Russian;* **la montaña rusa**
roller coaster, II
la **rutina** *routine*, 2

el **sábado** *Saturday*, I
saber *to know*, I; **Lo siento mucho,
es que no sabía.** *I'm very sorry, I
just didn't know.*, III7; **no saber ni
jota de...** *to know absolutely
nothing about . . .*, III8; **No sé.** *I
don't know.*, III5; **¿Qué sé yo?** *How
should I know?*, III8; **...que sepa
. . .** *who knows*, III7; **Que yo sepa...**
As far as I know . . ., III8; **Todo el
mundo sabe que...** *Everyone
knows that . . .*, III8; **Ya lo sé** *I
know.*, III8
saber *to taste*, III4; **Sabe riquísimo.**
It tastes delicious., III4
sabio(a) *sage, wise*, 5
el **sabor** *flavor*, III4; **Le falta sabor.** *It
doesn't have enough flavor.*, III4;
Tiene sabor a ajo. *It tastes like*

garlic., III4

sabroso(a) *tasty;* **¡Qué bueno (sabroso)!** *How good (tasty)!,* III4

sacar *to take out,* I; **sacar buenas notas** *to get good grades,* II; **sacar fotos** *to take pictures,* III1; sacarle provecho *to benefit from,* 6

sacudir *to shake;* **sacudir el polvo** *to dust,* II

sagrado(a) *sacred,* 5

la sal *salt,* I; **echarle mucha sal a la comida** *to put a lot of salt on food,* III2; **Le falta sal.** *It needs (lacks, doesn't have enough) salt.,* III4

la sala *living room,* I

salado(a) *salty,* I

el salario *salary,* III12

la salida *exit,* 9

salir *to go out, to leave,* I; **salir bien (mal)** *to do well, to turn out well (badly),* I

la salsa *musical style typical of the Caribbean,* 6

saltar *to jump,* II; **saltar a la cuerda** *to jump rope,* II; **saltar en paracaídas** *to go skydiving,* I

el salto *jump,* 9

el salto de agua *waterfall*

la salud *health,* II

saludar *to greet,* 7

el saludo *greeting, regards;* **dar un saludo a** *to give one's regards to,* II

salvadoreño(a) *Salvadoran,* II

salvaje *wild,* 11

salvar *to save,* 3

el salvavidas, la salvavidas *lifeguard,* 12

las sandalias *sandals,* I

la sandía *watermelon,* 4

el sándwich *sandwich,* I

la sangre *blood,* 5

sano(a) *healthy,* I

la sardina *sardine*

el sastre *tailor,* 8

la sátira *satire,* 3

satisfacer *satisfy,* 3

satisfecho(a) *satisfied,* 7

el saxofón *the saxophone,* III1

se *one, you, they, we,* III5; *self, selves,* I; *to him/her/it/you/them,* III4; **Se alegró mucho.** *He (She)was very happy.,* III9; **se burlaron** *they made fun of,* III9; se convirtieron en *they turned into,* 5; **Se cree el rey de Roma.** *He thinks he's a big shot.,* 9; Se cree la mamá de Tarzán. *She thinks she's a big shot.,* 9; **Se cree que...** *It's believed that . . .,* III5; **Se dice que...** *They say that . . .,* III5; **¿Se las llevas?** *Will you take them to him (her)?,* III4; Se le hizo tarde. *He (She) lost track of the time.,* 4; Se le nota que está enojado(a). *You can tell that he's (she's) angry.,* 4; **Se le rompió (rompieron)...** *He (She) broke . . .,* III4; **Se les quedó (quedaron)...**

They forgot . . ., They left . . . behind, III4; **Se me acabó (acabaron)...** *I ran out of . . .,* III4; **Se me hace que...** *It seems to me . . .,* III3; Se me hace un poco absurdo. *It seems a little absurd to me.,* 4; Se me pasó por alto. *It slipped my mind.,* 4; **Se me perdió (perdieron)...** *I lost . . .,* III4; **Se nos cayó (cayeron)...** *We dropped . . .,* III4; **Se nos descompuso (descompusieron)...** *. . . broke down on us.,* III4; Se nos fue el tren. *The train went off and left us.,* 4; **Se pusieron rojos.** *They blushed.,* III9; **se rieron** *they laughed,* III9; **Se siente orgulloso de haber...** *He (She) feels proud of having . . .,* III10; **¿Se te olvidó (olvidaron)...?** *Did you forget . . .?,* III4; **Si se encontrara una cura...** *If a cure were found . . .,* III11

la secadora de pelo *hair dryer,* II

secarse *to dry oneself,* II

la sección *section,* III8; **la sección de cocina** *food (cooking) section,* III8; **la sección de moda** *fashion section,* III8; **la sección de ocio** *entertainment section,* III8; **la sección de sociedad** *society section,* III8; **la sección deportiva** *sports section,* III8; **la sección financiera** *financial section,* III8

seco(a) *dry,* II; *cold, curt,* III9

secretamente *secretly,* 5

el sector industrial *industrial sector,* 11

secundario(a): estudios secundarios *high school,* 1

la sed *thirst;* **tener (mucha) sed** *to be (really) thirsty,* I

la seda *silk,* I

seguir (i, i) *to continue, to follow, to still be (doing something),* II; seguir adelante *to carry on,* 10

según *according to,* III5; **Según el gobierno...** *According to the government . . .,* III11

la seguridad *security,* 6

el seguro *insurance,* III12

seguro(a) *sure,* II; **Estoy seguro(a) que...** *I'm certain that . . .,* III8

seis *six,* I

seiscientos(as) *six hundred,* I

seleccionar *to choose*

el sello *stamp,* III1; **coleccionar sellos** *to collect stamps,* III1

la selva *jungle,* I; **la selva tropical** *rain forest,* II

el semáforo *traffic light,* II

la semana *week,* I

la Semana Santa *Holy Week,* 4

sembrar (ie) *to plant,* III3

semejante *similar,* 2

la semejanza *similarity,* 6

el semestre *semester,* I

la semilla *seed,* 4

el senador, la senadora *senator,* 11

sencillo(a) *simple,* II

el senderismo *hiking,* II

el sendero *path,* 12

la sensibilidad *sensitivity,* III11

sentar (ie) *to seat,* 9

sentarse (ie) *to sit down,* 3

el sentido *sense, feeling,* 10; **un buen sentido del humor** *a good sense of humor,* III1; los sentidos *the senses,* 6

sentido(a) *heartfelt,* III7; **Mi más sentido pésame.** *My most heartfelt condolences.,* III7

el sentimiento *feeling,* 2

sentir (ie, i) *to regret, to be sorry,* III7; **Lo siento mucho, es que no sabía.** *I'm very sorry, I just didn't know.,* III7; **Lo siento, pero ya tengo otros planes.** *I'm sorry, but I already have other plans.,* III7

sentirse (ie, i) *to feel,* I; **Me siento frustrado(a).** *I'm frustrated.,* III7; **sentirse muy solo(a)** *to feel very lonely,* III2; **sentirse orgulloso(a) de** *to feel proud of,* III10

la seña *sign,* 5

la señal *sign,* 2

señalar *to set,* 7; *to point out,* 8

el señor *sir, Mr.,* I

la señora *ma'am, Mrs.,* I

la señorita *miss,* I

septiembre (m.) *September,* I

la sequía *drought,* 10

ser *to be,* I; **Es cierto que...** *It's true that . . .,* III3; **Es difícil que...** *It's unlikely that . . .,* III8; **Es evidente que...** *It's evident that . . .,* III8; **Es fácil que...** *It's likely that . . .,* III8; **Es importante que** + subj. *It's important that . . .,* III6; **Es imposible que...** *It's impossible that . . .,* III8; **Es increíble que...** *It's unbelievable that . . .,* III8; **Es mejor que...** *It's better for . . . to . . .,* III6; **Es muy difícil de creer, pero es posible.** *That's very hard to believe, but it's possible.,* III5; **Es necesario que** + subj. *It's necessary for . . . to . . .,* III6; **Es nuestra responsabilidad...** *It's our responsibility . . .,* III3; **Es nuestro deber...** *It's our duty . . .,* III3; **Es obvio que...** *It's obvious that . . .,* III8; **Es posible que...** *It's possible that . . .,* III8; **Es probable que...** *It's probable that . . .,* III8; **Me encantaría ser...** *I'd love to be . . .,* III12; **Me gustaría ser...** *I'd like to be . . .,* III12; **...que sea descortés** *. . . who's rude,* III7; **ser desleal** *to be disloyal,* III7; **ser infiel** *to be unfaithful,* III7; **Sería buena (mala) idea...** *It would be a good (bad) idea to . . .,* III6; **Sería bueno** + inf. *It would be a good idea to . . .,*

III2; **¿Serías tan amable de dármela?** *Would you be so kind as to give it to me?*, III4; **Si yo fuera...** *If I were...*, III11; **Soy un(a) fanático(a) de...** *I'm a big fan of...*, III1; **Soy un(a) gran aficionado(a) a...** *I'm a big fan of...*, III1

el ser del espacio *being from outer space*, 5

el ser humano *human being*, 5

serenar *to calm down*, 2

la serie *series*, 8

la serigrafía *silk-screening*, 6

serio(a) *serious*, III1

serpear *to move like a snake*, 9

la serpiente *snake*, II

el servicio *service*, 11

el servicio financiero *financial services*

el servicio publicitario *advertising services*

el servidor, la servidora *faithful servant*, 11

la servilleta *napkin*, I

servir (i, i) *to serve, to help, to be of use*, II

sesenta *sixty*, I

los sesos *brains*, 11

setecientos(as) *seven hundred*, I

setenta *seventy*, I

severo(a) *severe*, 1

si *if*, I; **Si fueras rico(a)** *If you were rich...*, III9; **Si hubiera paz...** *If there were peace...*, III11; **Si no actuamos ahora...** *If we don't act now...*, III11; **Si no hacemos nada por...** *If we don't do anything about...*, III11; **Si no realizamos...** *If we don't carry out...*, III11; **Si pudiera... viviría...** *If I could... I would live...*, III9; **Si pudieras... ¿adónde irías?** *If you could... where would you go?*, III9; **Si se encontrara una cura...** *If a cure were found...*, III11; **Si tú pudieras...** *If you could...*, III11; **Si tuviera... compraría** *If I had... I would buy...*, III9; **Si tuvieras... ¿qué harías?** *If you had... what would you do?*, III9; **Si yo fuera...** *If I were...*, III11; **Si yo viviera...** *If I lived...*, III11

sí *yes*, I

siempre *always*, I; **lo de siempre** *the usual*, I

siete *seven*, I

el siglo *century*, III3

significar *to mean*, 8

el signo de puntuación *punctuation mark*, 8

siguiente *following*, 1

el silbido *whistle*, 5

el silencio *silence*, 5

silencioso(a) *quiet, silent*, 5

la silla *chair*, I

la silueta *silhouette*

el símbolo *symbol*

el símil *simile*, 9

la simpatía *sympathy*, 6

simpático(a) *nice*, I

sin *without*, II; **Sin duda alguna.** *Without a doubt.*, III8; sin embargo *nevertheless*, 5

sincero(a) *honest, sincere*, III6; **Para ser sincero(a)...** *To be honest...*, III6

la sinfonía *symphony*, 6

singular *unique*, 11

singularidad *uniqueness*, 10

siniestro(a) *left*; a diestra y a siniestra *right and left*, 9

sinónimo(a) *synonymous*, 10

sinuosamente *sinuously*, 3

síquico(a) *psychic*, 2

Sírvase. *Help yourself.*, 8

El sistema no funciona. *The system isn't working (doesn't work).*, II

el sitio *place*, 6; el sitio recreativo *recreation area*; **el sitio Web** *Web site*, III8

la situación *situation*, III11; **La situación va a empeorarse.** *The situation will get worse.*, III11

situar *to locate*, 11

el smog *smog*, II

sobrante *leftover* (adj.), 4

sobre *on, about, above*, 1

sobre sí *upon himself (herself)*, 12

sobregirado(a) *overdrawn*, 3

la sobremesa *after-dinner conversation*, 4

la sobrina *niece*, 7

el sobrino *nephew*, 7

sobrio(a) *sober*, 12

la sociedad *society*, III8; **la sección de sociedad** *society section*, III8

¡Socorro! *Help!*, 2

sofocar *suffocate*, 10

la soja *soybean*

el sol *sun*; **Hace sol.** *It's sunny.*, I; **tomar el sol** *to sunbathe*, I

solamente *only*, 4

el soldado, la mujer soldado *soldier*, III5

soleado(a) *sunny*, II

solemne *solemn*, 9

solicitar *to apply for, to request*, III12

la solicitud *application*, III12

el solista, la solista *soloist*, 6

solitario(a) *lonely, alone*, II

solo(a) *alone*, III2; **sentirse (i, i) muy solo(a)** *to feel all alone*, III2

sólo *only, just*, II

soltar (ue) *to let go of*, 9

el solterón *old bachelor*, 7

la solterona *old maid*, 7

la soltura *ease*, 8

la solución (pl. **las soluciones**) *solution*, III11; **La solución que planteo es...** *The solution I propose is...*, III11

solucionar *to solve*, 7

la sombra *shade, shadow*, 3

sombreado(a) *shaded*, 3

el sombrero *hat*, 5

sombrío(a) *somber*, 3

el sonido *sound*, 1

sonoro(a) *resounding*, 9

sonreír *to smile*, 5

la sonrisa *smile*, 7

soñar (ue) con + inf. *to dream of (doing something)*, III10

la sopa *soup*, I; la sopa negra *black bean soup*

soplar *to blow*, 6

soportar *to tolerate*, **No lo (la) soporto.** *I can't stand it (him/her).*, III6

sorber *to suck*, 11

sorprendente *surprising*, 2

sorprender *to surprise*, 7

el sorprendido, la sorprendida *surprised person*, 7

la sorpresa *surprise*; **la fiesta de sorpresa** *surprise party*, I; **¡Qué sorpresa!** *What a surprise!*, III8

el sótano *basement*, 3

su(s) *his, her, its, their, your*, I

subir *to go up*, II; **subir de peso** *to gain weight*, III2; **subir por** *to go up (a street or road)*, II

subirse *to get on (a bus, train...)*, II

súbito(a) *sudden*, 5

sublevar *to upset*, 7

el submarinismo *scuba diving*, 1

subrayado(a) *underlined*, 5

subterráneo(a) *underground*, 3

el suburbio *suburb*

suceder *to happen*, 6

sucio(a) *dirty*, I

sudar *to sweat*, II

Suecia (f.) *Sweden*, 6

el suegro *father-in-law*, 7

el sueldo *salary, pay*, 3

los suelos *ground*, 12

suena (inf. sonar): **Me suena a chino.** *It's Greek to me.*, III8

la suerte *luck*, 4

el suéter *sweater*, I

el sueño *dream*, I; **el sueño de mi vida** *my lifelong dream*, III5; **tener sueño** *to be sleepy*, I

suficiente *enough*, II

el sufrimiento *suffering*, 6

sufrir *to suffer*, III2; **sufrir de presiones** *to be under pressure*, III2; **sufrir de tensiones** *to suffer from tension*, III2

sugerir (ie, i) *to suggest*, III6; **Sugiero que...** *I suggest that...*, III6

el sujeto *subject*, 11

la suma *sum, entirety*, 2

supe (preterite of **saber**) *I found out*, III9

la superación *overcoming, excelling*, 10

superar *to overcome*, III10; **Logró superar muchos obstáculos.** *He

(She) succeeded in overcoming many obstacles., III10
superarse *to better oneself*, III10
superficial *superficial*, III6
el supermercado *supermarket*, I
el supervisor, la supervisora *supervisor*, 11
la supervivencia *survival*, 10
supiste (preterite of **saber**) *you found out*, III9
la súplica *request*, 5
suplicar *to beg, to implore*, 11
Supongo que... (inf. **suponer**) *I suppose that . . .*, III9
la supremacía *supremacy*, 4
supuestamente *supposedly*, III5
el sur *south*, II
el sureste *southeast*
surgir *to spring up*, 5
suspender *to fail (a test/a class)*, II; *to suspend*, 9
sustentar *to hold up*, 9
sustituir *to substitute*, 4
el susto *fright*, 5
susurrar *to whisper*, 5
sutil *subtle*, 11
suyo(a) *yours*, 5

la tabla de vela: montar en tabla de vela *to go windsurfing*, II
el tablero de control *control panel*, 11
la tajada *slice*, 4
tal *such*; **¿Qué tal?** *How's it going?*, I; **¿Qué tal si...?** *How about if . . .?*, I; **tal vez** *perhaps*, I; **Tal vez...** *Maybe . . .*, III8; **tal vez otro día** *perhaps another day*, I
talar *to cut down trees*, 3
talentoso(a) *talented*, 4
la talla: usar talla... *to wear size . . .*, II
el tallado en madera *woodworking*, 6
el taller *shop, workshop*, III4
el tamal *stuffed cornmeal steamed in cornhusks*
también *too, also*, I
el tambor *drum*, 5
tampoco *neither*, II
tan... como... *as . . . as . . .*, I
tan pronto como *as soon as*, III10
tanto(a) *as much*, I; **estar al tanto de** *to be well informed about*, III8; **por lo tanto...** *therefore . . .*, III10
tanto... como *both . . . and*
tantos(as) *as many*, I
la tapa *top, lid, cover*, 8
los tapatíos *people from the Mexican state of Jalisco*
la taquilla *ticket booth*, II
tardar *to delay, to take*

(time), 3
tarde (adv.) *late*, I
la tarde *afternoon*, I
la tarea *homework*, I
la tarjeta *greeting card*, I; **la tarjeta de crédito** *credit card*, 3; **la tarjeta postal** *postcard*, I
la tasa *rate*, 11
la taza *cup*, 4
el tazón *bowl*, I
te *(to, for) you*, I
el té frío *iced tea*, I
el teatro *theater*, I
el techado *roof*, 9
el techo *roof*, 3
la técnica *technique*, 1
el técnico, la técnica *technician, repair person*, 12
la tecnología *technology*, III3
tecnológico(a) *technological*, 3
el tejado *tile roof*, 12
tejer *to knit*, 11
el tejido *weaving, knitting*, 6
la tela *cloth*, 11
la Telaraña Mundial *World Wide Web*, II
las telecomunicaciones *telecommunications*, 10
el teléfono *phone*, I; **por teléfono** *on the phone*, I; **el teléfono celular** *cellular phone*, III3
el telégrafo *telegraph*, 9
el televidente, la televidente *television viewer*, 8
la televisión *television*, I
televisivo(a) *television (adj.)*, 8
el televisor *TV set*, I
el tema *theme, topic, subject*, III6; **Cambiando de tema, ¿qué me dices de...?** *Changing subjects, what can you tell me about . . .?*, III6
temblar *to tremble*, 8
el temblor *earthquake*, 5
temer *to fear*, III7; **Temo que...** *I'm afraid that . . .*, III7; **Temo que el deterioro continúe.** *I'm afraid the deterioration will continue.*, III11
la tempestad *storm*, 3
el templo *temple*, 10
Ten en cuenta que... *Keep in mind that . . .*, III3
la tendencia *tendency*, 10
tender (ie) *to tend*, 12; **tender la cama** *to make the bed*, II
el tenedor *fork*, I
tener (ie) *to have*, I; **Cuando tenía cinco años...** *When I was five . . .*, III12; **Lo siento, pero ya tengo otros planes.** *I'm sorry, but I already have other plans.*, III7; **no tener la menor idea** *not to have the slightest idea*, III8; **No tengo ganas de** + inf. *I don't feel like . . .*, III8; **por tener...** *because I (you,...) have...*, III10; **Si tuviera... compraría** *If I had . . . I would*

buy . . ., III9; **Ten en cuenta que...** *Keep in mind that . . .*, III3; **tener... años** *to be . . . years old*, I; **tener buenos hábitos de alimentación** *to have good eating habits*, III2; **tener celos de** *to be jealous of*, III7; **tener éxito** *to succeed*, III10; **tener ganas de** + inf. *to feel like (doing something)*, I; **tener que** + inf. *to have to (do something)*, I; **tener que ver con** *to have to do with*, 3; **tener un buen sentido del humor** *to have a good sense of humor*, III1; **tener un malentendido** *to have a misunderstanding*, III7; **Tengo entendido que...** *I understand that . . .*, III9; **Tengo la impresión de que...** *I'm under the impression that . . .*, III9; **tengo la intención de...** *I intend to . . .*, III10; **Tengo mucho que hacer. La próxima vez iré.** *I have a lot to do. Next time I'll go.*, III6; **Tenía muchas esperanzas de...** *I had high hopes of . . .*, III5; **Tiene sabor a ajo.** *It tastes like garlic.*, III4
el tenis *tennis*, I
el tenista, la tenista *tennis player*, 12
la tensión *tension*, III2; **sufrir de tensiones** *to suffer from tension*, III2
el tequeño *appetizer made of fried dough stuffed with cheese*
tercer(a) *third*
terco(a) *stubborn*, 7
terminar *to finish, to complete*, II; **Antes de terminar...** *Before finishing . . .*, III10; **Espero que la guerra termine pronto.** *I hope the war ends soon.*, III5
el término *term*, 5
la ternera *veal*, III4
las terrazas *terraces*, 4
el terremoto *earthquake*, 11
el terreno *terrain*, 1
la tesis *thesis*, 12
el tesoro *treasure*, 7
el testamento *will*, 8
el testimonio *testimony*, 9
los textiles *textiles, cloth*
ti *you* (object of preposition), I
la tía *aunt*, I; **una tía estupenda** *great girl*, III1
el tico, la tica *colloquial name for Costa Ricans*, 11
el tiempo *(concept of) time; weather; (verb) tense*, 3; **a tiempo** *on time*, II; **darse tiempo para pensar** *to give oneself time to think*, III7; **en aquellos tiempos** *in those times*, II; **en mis tiempos** *in my time*, II; **medio tiempo** *part time*, III12; **tiempo completo** *full time*, III12
la tienda *store, tent*, II; **la tienda de campaña** *tent*, 1; **la tienda de camping** *camping tent*, I; **la tienda**

de comestibles *grocery store*, I; **la tienda de refacciones** *parts store*, III4

tierno(a) *tender*, 2

la Tierra *Earth*, II

el tigre *tiger*, II

tilín: en un tilín *in a flash, quickly*, 2

la timidez *shyness*, 9

tímido(a) *shy*, III9

el timón *steering rod*, 5

tingo: del tingo al tango *from here to there (Mexico)*, 8

el tío *uncle*, I; **un tío estupendo, una tía estupenda** *great guy (girl)*, III1, I

típicamente *typically*, I

típico(a) *typical, traditional*, II

tirar *to throw out*, II

las tiras cómicas *comics*, III8; **leer tiras cómicas** *to read comics*, III1

los titulares *headlines*, III8

el título *title, degree*, 3

la tiza *chalk*, 8

la toalla *towel*, I

el tobillo *ankle*, II

tocar *to touch*, 12; **A mí me (A ti te) toca** + inf. *It's my (your) turn to . . .*, II; **Nos toca a nosotros...** *It's up to us . . .*, III3; **tocar (un instrumento)** *to play (an instrument)*, III1

el tocino *bacon*, I

todavía *still, yet*, I

todavía no *not yet*, II

todo(a) *all, every*, I; **Todo el mundo sabe que...** *Everyone knows that . . .*, III8

la tolerancia *tolerance*, 10

tolerar *to tolerate*, 5

tomar *to drink, to take, to eat*, I; tomar el papel de *to play the role of*, 2; **tomar el sol** *to sunbathe*, I; tomar en cuenta *to take into account*, 1; **tomar la iniciativa** *to take the initiative*, III10; **tomar las cosas con calma** *to take things calmly*, III2

el tomate *tomato*, I

las toneladas *tons*, 2

el tono *tone*, 1

la tontería *foolishness;* **¡Qué tontería!** *How silly!*, III5

tonto(a) *silly, foolish*, 9

el tope *end*, 9

el toque *touch*, 8

torcerse (ue) *to sprain*, II

la tormenta *storm*, II

tornar *to turn around*, 9

el torneo *tournament*, 4

el toro *bull;* **tan fuerte como un toro** *as strong as an ox*, II

la toronja *grapefruit*, I

torpe *slow, dull, clumsy*, III9

la torre *tower*, II

la torta *cake*, III4

la tortuga *turtle*, II

la tos *cough*, I

tostado(a) *toasted*, I; **el pan tostado** *toast*, I

tostar (ue) *to roast, to toast*, 4

el trabajador, la trabajadora *worker*, III12; **el trabajador, la trabajadora social** *social worker*, III12

trabajar *to work*, I

el trabajo *work, job*, I; *paper* (written assignment), III3; **el ambiente de trabajo** *workplace environment*, III12; **hacer trabajos con la computadora** *to write papers on the computer*, III3

traer *to bring*, I

el tráfico *traffic*, III3

la tragedia *tragedy*, 10

traicionar *to betray*, III5

el traje *suit*, I; **el traje de baño** *bathing suit*, I

trampas: sin trampas *no cheating*, 2

tranquilo(a) *calm*, II; *Tranquilo(a). Calm down.*, III7

el transeúnte, la transeúnte *passerby, temporary resident*, 4

transformar en *to change into*, 5

el tránsito *traffic*, II

transmitir *to pass on*, 5

el transporte público *public transportation*, 3

el tranvía *streetcar*, 6

tras *after*, 1

trasladar *to move*, 9

trasnochar *to stay up late*, 5

trastornar *to disturb*, 5

tratar *to treat*, III9

tratar con *to deal with*, 12

tratar de *try to*, 5; *to be about*, 3

el tratamiento *treatment*, 5

la travesura *trick;* **hacer travesuras** *to play tricks*, II

travieso(a) *mischievous*, III9

trece *thirteen*, II

treinta *thirty*, I

tremendo(a) *magnificent, ill-mannered*, 6

el tren *train*, II; **la estación de tren** *train station*, II

el trenzado *braid*, 9

trepar *to climb*, II

tres *three*, I

trescientos(as) *three hundred*, I

la tribu *tribe*, 5

el trigo *wheat*

el trillizo *triplet*, 9

triste *sad*, I

la tristeza *sadness*, 2

triunfar *to win out, to be successful;* III10; **Han triunfado...** *They have succeeded . . .*, III10

trocar *to change, to exchange*, 9

el trofeo *trophy*, 10

la trompa *proboscis, insect body part*

used for extracting nectar from flowers, 11

la trompeta *trumpet*, 6

el tronco *(tree) trunk*, 12

las tropas *troops*, 5

el trozo *piece*, 2

la trucha *trout*, III4

el truco *trick*, 8

el trueno *thunder*, II

tu(s) *your* (informal), I

tú *you* (informal), I; **¿Tú crees? No sé.** *Do you think so? I don't know.*, III5

el tubérculo *tuber*, 4

turbio(a) *muddy*, 9

el turismo *sightseeing;* **hacer turismo** *to go sightseeing*, I

el turista, la turista *tourist*, II

el turno *turn*, 1

tuviera (past subj. of **tener**): **Si tuviera... compraría...** *If I had . . ., I would buy . . .*, III9

Tuvo mucho éxito... *He (She) was very successful . . .*, III10

tuyo(a) *yours*, 3

u *or* (before words beginning with **o** or **ho**), II

la ubicación *location*, 1

ubicar *to orient*, 9

Ud. *abbreviation for* **usted,** *you*, 1

Uds. *abbreviation for* **ustedes,** *you*, 1

ufanarse *to be proud of*, 4

últimamente *recently*, 6

último(a) *final, last*, II; el último modelo *the latest style*, 6

un(a) *a, an*, I; **un poco** *a little*, I

la una *one o'clock*, I

uncir *to yoke, to tie together*, 9

único(a) *unique*, 10

unido(a) *close-knit*, I

unir *to unite*, 7

uno *one*, I

unos(as) *some, a few*, I

untarle la mano *to grease someone's palm*, 11

la uña *fingernail, toenail*, 12

la urbanización *neighborhood*, 4

urbano(a) *urban*

urgente *urgent*, II

uruguayo(a) *Uruguayan*, II

usar *to use, to wear*, II

usted *you* (formal), I

ustedes *you* (pl. formal), I

útil *useful*, 9

utilizar *to use*, 3

las uvas *grapes*, I

las **vacaciones** *vacation*, I
vaciar *to empty*, 12
vagar *to wander*, 5
la vaina *pod (of plant)*, 4
valer *to be worth;* **Creo que vale la pena...** *I think it's worth it . . .*, III3; **¿Cuánto vale?** *How much is it?*, II
valiente *brave*, III5
valioso(a) *valuable*
el **valle** *valley*, II
el valor *bravery*, 5; *value*, 5
el vampiro *vampire*, 6
el vapor *steamship*, 9
variar *to vary, to differ*, 4
la variedad *variety*, 4
varios(as) *some, several*, 2
la varita mágica *magic wand*, 9
el **vaso** *glass*, I
vasto(a) *huge*, 9
el vecino, la vecina *neighbor*, 4
veinte *twenty*, I
veinticincoavo *twenty-fifth*, 6
la vela: *sail;* **ir de vela** *to go sailing*, I; **montar en tabla de vela** *to go windsurfing*, II; la vela ligera *sailing*, 1
la velocidad *speed*, 11
velozmente *speedily*, 9
vencer *to defeat*, III5
el **vendedor, la vendedora** *salesperson*, III12
vender *to sell*, 8
venezolano(a) *Venezuelan*, II
venir (ie) *to come*, I; **el (la) ... que viene** *next (year, week, . . .)*, II
la venta *sale*, 11
la **ventaja** *advantage*, III3
la **ventana** *window*, I
ver *to see*, I
el **verano** *summer*, I
veras: de veras *really*, II
la **verdad** *truth*, II; **Para decir la verdad...** *To tell the truth . . .*, III6; **La verdad es que...** *The truth is that . . .*, III3; **de verdad** *to tell you the truth, really*, II; **¿verdad?** *don't you?, right?*
verdadero(a) *real, true*, 1
verde *green*, I
las verduras *vegetables*
la vergüenza *shame*, 4
verídico(a) *true*, 5

verificar *to verify*, 8
verse *to look, to appear;* **¿Cómo me veo?** *How do I look?*, II
verter (ie) *to pour out*, 4
el **vestido** *dress*, I
vestirse (i, i) *to get dressed*, II
el vestuario *wardrobe*, 3
la **vez** (pl. *las veces*) *time* (repetition); **a la vez** *at the same time*, III3; **a veces** *sometimes*, I; **alguna vez** *ever*, III3; **Érase una vez...** *Once upon a time . . .*, II
la **vía** *rail*, II; *path*, 11
el viaducto *elevated roadway*, 4
el viaje *trip;* **hacer un viaje** *to take a trip*, I
la víctima *victim*, 5
la **victoria** *victory*, III5
la **vida** *life*, I; **llevar una vida agitada** *to lead a hectic life*, III2; la vida actual *present life, nowadays*, 2; **la vida diaria** *daily life*, III3; la vida real *real life*, 8
la **videocasetera** *videocassette player*, III3
la videocinta *videotape*, 11
el **videojuego** *videogame*, I
el **vidrio** *glass*, II
viejo(a) *old*, I
la viera *scallop*, 1
el **viernes** *Friday*, I
vietnamita (m./f.) *Vietnamese*, 9
vigilar *to watch, to guard*, 5
vincular *to link, to connect*, 5
el vínculo *link*, 10
el vino *wine*, 2
la violencia *violence*, 6
violento(a) *violent*, 3
el virrey *viceroy*, 5
la virtud *virtue*, 11
la visión *vision*, 12
visitar *to visit*, I
la vista *view*
visto (past participle of **ver**) *seen*, 3
la **vitrina** *store window*, II; **mirar las vitrinas** *to window-shop*, II
vivir *to live*, I; **Si yo viviera...** *If I lived . . .*, III11
vivo(a) *bright, vivid, intense*, 6
vociferar *to shout*, 11
vocinglero(a) *loud-mouthed*, 9
volante *flying*, 9
volar (ue) *to fly*, 6
el volcán (pl. los volcanes) *volcano*, 5
el **voleibol** *volleyball*, I
el volumen *volume*, 1
la voluntad *will*, 12

volver (ue) *to go back, to return*, II; **No lo volveré a hacer.** *I won't do it again.*, III7
vos *you* (used in Argentina and other Latin American countries), 7
vosotros(as) *you* (pl., informal, Spain), I
la voz (pl. las voces) *voice*, 5
el **vuelo** *flight*, 5
vuestro(a) **your** (pl., informal, Spain), I
vuelto (past participle of **volver**) *returned*, 3

el **Web** *World Wide Web*, II

y *and;* **y cuarto** *quarter past (the hour);* **y media** *half past (the hour)*, I
ya *already*, I; **¡Ya lo sé!** *I know!*, III8, I
yo *I*, I
el **yoga** *yoga*, I

la zaga *rear (of car)*, 9
la **zanahoria** *carrot*, I
la **zapatería** *shoe store*, I
las **zapatillas de tenis** *tennis shoes* (Spain), I
los **zapatos** *shoes*, I
la **zona peatonal** *pedestrian zone*, III3; **establecer (zc) una zona peatonal** *to set up a pedestrian zone*, III3
el **zoológico** *zoo*, I
el zorro, la zorra *fox*, 11
la zozobra *anxiety*, 12

English-Spanish Vocabulary

This vocabulary includes all of the words presented in the **Vocabulario** sections of the chapters. These words are considered active—you are expected to know them and be able to use them. Expressions are listed under the first word and in some cases under a keyword in the phrase.

Spanish nouns are listed with the definite article and plural forms, when applicable. If a Spanish verb is stem-changing, the change is indicated in the parentheses after the verb: **dormir (ue)**. The number after each Spanish word or phrase refers to the chapter in which it becomes active vocabulary. Entries followed by the Roman numeral I indicate that the word became active in Level 1; entries followed by the Roman numeral II indicate the word was introduced in Level 2.

To be sure you are using Spanish words and phrases in their correct context, refer to the chapter and book in which they appear. You may also want to look up Spanish phrases in the Summary of Functions, pp. R2–R12.

a (an) *un, una,* I; **a few** *unos, unas,* I; **a little overweight** *un poco gordo(a),* I; **A long time ago . . .** *Hace mucho tiempo...,* II; **a lot (of)** *mucho(a), muchos(as),* I; **a terrible bore** *tan aburrido(a) como un pato,* II
absent-minded *distraído(a),* II
according to *según,* III5
accountant *el contador, la contadora,* III12
to **ache** *doler (ue),* I
to **achieve** *alcanzar,* III10; *lograr,* III10
to **act** *actuar,* III11
actually *en efecto,* III5
to **adapt** *adaptarse,* III3
to **admire** *admirar,* III6
to **admit a mistake** *admitir un error,* III7
advances *los adelantos,* III3
advantage *la ventaja,* III3
adventurous *aventurero(a),* II
advice *el consejo,* III2
advisable: It's not advisable that you . . . *No te conviene...,* III6
to **advise** *aconsejar,* III2
aerobics *los ejercicios aeróbicos,* I
affection *el cariño,* II
affectionate *cariñoso(a),* I
affectionately *con cariño,* II
afraid: I'm afraid that . . . *Temo que...,* III7
after *después,* I; *después de,* I; *después de que,* III10; **After we graduate, we . . .** *Después de graduarnos...,* III10
afternoon *la tarde,* I; **in the afternoon** *de la tarde,* I; *por la tarde,* I
afterwards *después,* II
again: I won't do it again. *No lo volveré a hacer.,* III7
against *contra,* III9
ago: a day (a week, a month,...) ago *hace un día (una semana, un mes, ...),* II; **A long time ago . . .** *Hace mucho tiempo...,* II
to **agree** *estar de acuerdo,* III5; **to agree to** *quedar en,* II
Agreed. *De acuerdo.,* I
air: air conditioning *el aire acondicionado,* II; **air quality** *la calidad del aire,* III3
alarm clock *el despertador,* II
all *todo(a); todos(as),* I; **All of a sudden . . .** *De repente...,* II; **All right.** *Está bien.,* I; *De acuerdo.,* II
almost *casi,* I; **almost always** *casi siempre,* I
alone *solo(a),* III2
along *por,* I; **along the beach** *por la playa,* I
alongside *al lado de,* II
already *ya,* I
also *también,* I
aluminum *el aluminio,* II
always *siempre,* I
ambition *la ambición,* III5; *la aspiración,* III10
American football *el fútbol norteamericano,* I
amusement park *el parque de atracciones,* I
amusing *divertido(a),* I
anchorperson *el locutor, la locutora,* III8
ancient *antiguo(a),* III6

and *y, e,* I; **And you?** *¿Y tú?,* I
angry *enojado(a),* III9; *enfadado(a),* III9
ankle *el tobillo,* II
anniversary party *la fiesta de aniversario,* I
to **announce** *anunciar,* III8
announcer *el locutor, la locutora,* III8
to **annoy** *fastidiar,* II
annoying *pesado(a),* III1
another *otro(a),* I
answering machine *el contestador,* III3
anthropology *la antropología,* I
anxious *ansioso(a),* III2
any *alguno(a),* I
anyway *de todos modos,* II
apple *la manzana,* I
application *la solicitud,* III12
to **apply for** *solicitar,* III12
appointment *la cita,* II
to **appreciate** *apreciar,* III9
April *abril (m.),* I
aquarium *el acuario,* I
architect *el arquitecto, la arquitecta,* III12
are: are due to *se deben a,* III10; **(people) are going to use** *(la gente) va a usar,* III3; **Are we going the right way to . . .?** *¿Vamos bien para...?,* II; **Are you still working?** *¿Sigues trabajando?,* II
Argentine *argentino(a),* II
arm (of the body) *el brazo,* I
army *el ejército,* III5
to **arrange to (do something)** *quedar en,* II
to **arrive** *llegar,* II
arrogant *arrogante,* III9
art *el arte, (pl. las artes),* I

article *el artículo*, III8
artist *el artista, la artista*, III6
artistic *artístico(a)*, II
as *tan*, II; **as a child** *de pequeño(a)*, II; *de niño(a)*, III12; **as a small child** *de chiquito(a)*, II; **as . . . as . . .** *tan... como ...*, I; **As far as I know . . .** *Que yo sepa...*, III8; **(as good as) a saint** *tan bueno(a) como un ángel*, II; **as happy as a lark** *tan feliz como una lombriz*, II; **as noble as a lion** *tan noble como un perro*, II; **as strong as an ox** *tan fuerte como un toro*, II
to ask for *pedir (i, i)*, I
to ask questions *hacer preguntas*, II
aspiration *la aspiración*, III10
to aspire to *aspirar a*, III10
to assimilate *asimilarse*, III10
at *a, por, en*, I; **at all** *para nada*, III7; **at home** *en casa*, II; **at last** *por fin*, I; **at night** *por la noche, en la noche*, I; **at the same time** *a la vez*, III3; **At what time?** *¿A qué hora?*, I
to attain *alcanzar*, III10
to attend *asistir a*, I
attitude toward *la actitud hacia*, III9
August *agosto (m.)*, I
aunt *la tía*, I
autumn *el otoño*, II
avocado salad *la ensalada de aguacate*, III4
to avoid *evitar*, II
awful *pésimo(a)*, III6

back (of the body) *la espalda*, I
back then *en aquel entonces*, II
backpack *la mochila*, I
bacon *el tocino*, I
bad *malo(a)*, I; *mal*, I, **it would be a good (bad) idea** *sería buena (mala) idea*, III6
baggage carrier *el maletero, la maletera*, II
bakery *la panadería*, III4
balanced *balanceado(a)*, II
bald *calvo(a)*, II
balloons *los globos*, I
ballpoint pen *el bolígrafo*, I
banana *el plátano*, I
band *la banda*, II
bank *el banco*, II
banker *el banquero, la banquera*, III12
bargain *la ganga*, II
to bargain *regatear*, II
baseball *el béisbol*, I
basketball *el baloncesto*, I
bat (animal) *el murciélago*, II
bathing suit *el traje de baño*, I

bathroom *el cuarto de baño*, II
to be *ser; estar*, I; **Be careful.** *Ten cuidado.*, II; **to be a cyclist** *practicar el ciclismo*, III1; **to be able** *poder (ue)*, I; **to be close to** *estar cerca de*, II; **to be crazy about** *estar loco(a) por*, II; **to be delighted** *encantarle*, III7; **to be disloyal** *ser desleal*, III7; **to be due to** *deberse a*, III10; **to be familiar with (something)** *conocer*, II; **to be far from** *estar lejos de*, II; **to be fed up (with)** *estar harto(a) (de)*, II; **to be frustrated** *frustrarse*, III7; **to be furious** *estar furioso(a)*, II; **to be glad** *alegrarse*, III7; **to be going to do something** *ir a + inf.*, I; **to be grateful for** *estar agradecido(a) por*, III10; **to be happy** *alegrarse*, III9; **To be honest . . .** *Para ser sincero(a)...*, III6; **to be hurt** *estar dolido(a)*, III7; **to be in a good (bad) mood** *estar de buen (mal) humor*, III7; **to be in a hurry** *tener (ie) prisa*, I; **to be in good shape** *estar en plena forma*, II; **to be interested in** *interesar(le)*, II; **to be jealous of** *tener (ie) celos de*, III7; **to be left dead** *quedar muerto(a)*, III5; **to be located** *encontrarse (ue)*, II; **to be named** *llamarse*, II; **to be near** *estar cerca de*, II; **to be on a diet** *hacer régimen*, II; *estar a dieta*, III2; **to be raised** *criarse*, III10; **to be ready** *estar listo(a)*, I; **to be situated** *quedar*, I; **to be sleepy** *tener (ie) sueño*, I; **to be under pressure** *sufrir de presiones*, II; **to be unfaithful** *ser infiel*, III7; **to be up to date on . . .** *estar al tanto de...*, III8; **to be well informed about . . .** *estar bien informado(a) sobre...*, III8; **to be worth** *valer*, I
beach *la playa*, I
beans *los frijoles*, I; *las caraotas (Venezuela)*, III4
beard *la barba*, III1
beautiful *hermoso(a)*, III6
because *porque*, I; **Because I have . . ., I . . .,** *Por tener..., yo...*, III10
to become: **I want to become** *quiero llegar a ser*, III12; **to become ill** *enfermarse*, II
bed *la cama*, I; **to go to bed** *acostarse (ue)*, II
beef *la carne de res*, I
before *antes de*, I; **Before classes begin . . .** *Antes de que empiecen las clases...*, III10; **Before finishing . . .** *Antes de terminar...*, III10
to begin *comenzar (ie)*, II; *empezar (ie)*, I; **to begin with** *para empezar*, II
behind *detrás de*, II
to believe *creer*, I; **I can't believe that . . .**

No puedo creer que..., III8; **I don't believe that . . .** *No creo que...*, III8; **It's very hard to believe, but it's possible.** *Es muy difícil de creer, pero es posible.*, III5; **It's hard to believe that . . .** *Parece mentira que...*, III8
belt *el cinturón*, I
beneath *debajo de*, I
benefits *los beneficios*, III12
besides *además*, I
best *el (la) mejor*, II; **the best thing is** *lo ideal es*, III12
to betray *traicionar*, III5
Better . . . *Mejor...*, II
to better oneself *superarse*, III10
better than *mejor que*, II
beverage *la bebida*, I
bicycle *la bicicleta*, I
big *grande*, I
bill *la cuenta*, I
bird *el ave, (pl. las aves)*, II
birthday party *la fiesta de cumpleaños*, I
black *negro(a)*, I
to blame someone *echarle la culpa*, III7
block: **city block** *la cuadra*, I
blond *rubio(a)*, I
blouse *la blusa*, I
to blow up balloons *inflar los globos*, I
blue *azul*, I
bluejeans *los bluejeans*, I
to blush *ponerse rojo(a)*, III9; **They blushed.** *Se pusieron rojos.*, III9
board game *el juego de mesa*, I
boat *la lancha*, II
body *el cuerpo*, I
Bolivian *Boliviano(a)*, II
book *el libro*, I
book bag *la mochila*, I
to bookmark *apuntar*, II
bookstore *la librería*, I
boots *las botas*, I
bore: **a terrible bore** *tan aburrido (a) como un pato*, II
bored *aburrido(a)*, II; **to be bored** *estar aburrido*, II
boring *aburrido(a)*, I; **It seems really boring to me.** *Me parece un rollo.*, III1; **to be boring** *ser (estar) aburrido(a)*, I
boss *el jefe, la jefa*, III12
botanical garden *el jardín botánico*, II
to bother *molestar*, II
bowl *el plato hondo*, I; *el tazón*, I
boy *el chico*, I
boyfriend *el novio*, III7
brave *valiente*, III5
bread *el pan*, I
break (rest period) *el descanso*, I
to break *romperse*, II; **He (She) broke . . .** *Se le rompió...*, III4
to break down *descomponer*, III4; **. . . broke down on us.** *Se nos descompuso (descompusieron).*, III4

to break up with someone *romper con*, III7

breakfast *el desayuno*, I; **to eat breakfast** *desayunar*, I

to breathe *respirar*, II

bridge *el puente*, II

to bring *traer*, I; **to bring the meal** *traer la comida*, II

broadcast network *la cadena*, III8

broken *roto(a)*, III3

brother *el hermano*, I; **brothers and sisters** *los hermanos*, I

brown *de color café*, I; *pardo*, I

brush *el cepillo*, II

to brush (one's hair, teeth, etc.) *cepillarse (el pelo, los dientes, etc.)*, II; **to brush your teeth** *lavarse los dientes*, I

to build *construir*, II

building *el edificio*, II

bumper cars *los carros chocones*, II

bus *el autobús*, I

bus stop *la parada del autobús*, II

business (firm) *la empresa*, III12

businessman, businesswoman *el (la) comerciante*, III12

busy *ocupado(a)*, I; **The line is busy.** *La línea está ocupada.*, I

busybody *el (la) metiche*, II

but *pero*, I; **but on the other hand . . .** *pero por otro lado...*, III3; **But you have to take into account that . . .** *Pero hay que tener en cuenta que...*, III5

butcher shop *la carnicería*, III4

to buy *comprar*, III7; **to buy someone a gift** *comprarle un regalo*, III7

by *por*, I; **by the end of** *para fines de*, II; **By the way . . .** *A propósito...*, III6

'Bye *Chao*, I

cable *el cable*, III8; **on cable** *por cable*, III8

cafeteria *la cafetería*, I

cake *la torta*, III4; *el pastel*, I

calculator *la calculadora*, I

calf (of the leg) *la pantorrilla*, II

to call *llamar*, I; **to call the guests** *llamar a los invitados*, I

calm *tranquilo(a)*, II

Calm down. *Tranquilo(a).*, III7

calmly *con calma*, III2

camera *la cámara*, I

to camp *acampar*, I

camping tent *la tienda de camping*, I

can *poder (ue)*, I; **Can I help?** *¿Puedo ayudar?*, II; **Can I help you . . .?** *¿Te ayudo a...?*, II; **Can you bring me . . .?** *¿Me puedes traer...?*, I; *¿Me traes...?*, I; **Can you**

bring us . . .? *¿Nos puede traer...?*, I; **Can you do me the favor of . . .?** *¿Me haces el favor de...?*, I; **Can you give me . . .?** *¿Puedes darme...?*, III2; **Can you help me?** *¿Me puede atender?*, II; **Can you help me to . . .?** *¿Me ayudas a...?*, I; *¿Puedes ayudarme a...?*, II; **Can you lower the price for me?** *¿Me puede rebajar el precio?*, II; **Can you pass me . . .?** *¿Me pasas...?*, I; **Can you tell me . . .?** *¿Me puede decir...?*, I; *¿Me podría decir...?*, II; **I can't.** *No puedo.*, I; **What can I bring you?** *¿Qué le puedo traer?*, I

candy *los dulces*, I; **candy store** *la dulcería*, I

canoe *la canoa*, I

cans *las latas*, II

car *el carro*, I

card *la tarjeta*, I; **playing cards** *las cartas*, III1

careful: to be careful *tener (ie) cuidado*, II

carpenter *el carpintero, la carpintera*, III12

carrot *la zanahoria*, I

to carry *llevar*, I

to carry out *llevar a cabo*, III10; *realizar*, III11

cash register *la caja*, II

cashier *el (la) cajero(a)*, II

cat *el gato*, I

to cause *causar*, III2

to celebrate *celebrar*, III5

cellular phone *el teléfono celular*, III3

century *el siglo*, III3

cereal *el cereal*, I

certain *seguro(a)*, III8

Certainly. *Por cierto.*, III8

chair *la silla*, I

challenge *el reto*, III10

to change *cambiar*, II; **Changing subjects, what can you tell me about . . .?** *Cambiando de tema, ¿qué me dices de...?*, III6

channel *el canal*, III8

to chat *platicar*, II

cheap (in price) *barato(a)*, I

Cheer up! *¡Ánimo!*, III7

cheese *el queso*, I

chemicals *los químicos*, II

chicken *el pollo*, I

child *el (la) niño(a)*, II; **as a child** *de pequeño(a), de niño(a)*, II; **as a small child** *de chiquito(a)*, II

children *los hijos*, I

Chilean *chileno(a)*, II

China *China (f.)*, I

Chinese food *la comida china*, I

chocolate *el chocolate*, I

chores *los quehaceres*, II; **household chores** *los quehaceres domésticos*, I

Christmas *la Navidad*, I; **Christmas Eve** *la Nochebuena*, I

church *la iglesia*, II

circus *el circo*, I

city *la ciudad*, I

city block *la cuadra*, II

clams *las almejas*, III4

clarinet *el clarinete*, III1

class *la clase*, I

classical music *la música clásica*, I

classified ads *los anuncios clasificados*, III8

classmate *el compañero, la compañera*, I

to clean *limpiar*, II; **to clean the kitchen** *limpiar la cocina*, I

clean *limpio(a)*, I

clear *despejado(a)*, II

to clear the table *quitar la mesa*, II

clever *listo(a)*, I

climate *el clima*, II

to climb *escalar*, I; **to climb trees** *trepar a los árboles*, II

clock *el reloj*, I

close to *cerca de*, II

close-knit *unido(a)*, I

closet *el armario*, I

clothing *la ropa*, I

cloud: Every cloud has a silver lining. *No hay mal que por bien no venga.*, III7

cloudy *nublado(a)*, I; **It's cloudy.** *Está nublado.*, I

clumsy *torpe*, III9

coast *la costa*, II

cod *el bacalao*, III4

coffee with milk *el café con leche*, I

coin *la moneda*, II

cold (personality) *seco(a)*, III9

cold (temperature) *frío(a)*, I; **It's cold** (weather). *Hace frío.*, I

cold (illness): to have a cold *estar resfriado(a)*, I

to collect *coleccionar*, II; **to collect stickers (stamps)** *coleccionar adhesivos (sellos)*, III1

Colombian *colombiano(a)*, II

color *el color*, I; **What color?** *¿De qué color?*, I

(color) photocopier *la fotocopiadora (a colores)*, III3

comb *el peine*, II

to comb your hair *peinarse*, I

to combat *combatir*, III9

to come *venir (ie)*, I; **come** (command) *ven*, I; **Come along!** *¡Ven conmigo!*, I

to come back *regresar*, I

comfortable *cómodo(a)*, I

comical *cómico(a)*, I

comics *las tiras cómicas*, III8

commentator *el (la) comentarista*, III8

commercial *el anuncio*, III8

to commit *cometer*, III11

commitment *el compromiso*, III10

compact disc *el disco compacto*, I

company (firm) *la empresa*, III12

competition *la competencia*, II

English-Spanish Vocabulary

to complain (about) *quejarse (de)*, II
to compliment someone *hacerle un cumplido a alguien*, III7
computer *la computadora*, III3
computer programmer *el (la) programador(a) de computadoras*, III12
computer science *la computación*, I
conceited *presumido(a)*, III9
concert *el concierto*, I
condolences *el pésame*, III7; **My most heartfelt condolences.** *Mi más sentido pésame.*, III7
condor *el cóndor*, II
congested *resfriado(a)*, I; **to be congested** *estar resfriado(a)*, I
consequently *por consiguiente*, III10
to conserve *conservar*, II
contemporary *contemporáneo (a)*, III6
to continue *seguir (i, i)*, II
to contribute *contribuir*, III2; *aportar*, III10
contribution *la aportación*, III10
conventional *convencional*, III6
convinced: to be convinced *estar convencido(a)*, III8
to cook *cocinar*, III3
cookie *la galleta*, I
cooking section *la sección de cocina*, III8
to copy *copiar*, II
corn *el maíz*, I
corner *la esquina*, II
Costa Rican *costarricense*, II
costume *el disfraz*, II
cotton (made of) *(de) algodón*, I
cough *la tos*, I
Could you . . .? *¿Podrías…?*, III4
to count on *contar (ue) con*, III7
country *el campo*, I
cousin *el primo, la prima*, I
crazy *loco(a)*, III1; **to be crazy about** *estar loco(a) por*, III1
creative *creativo(a)*, III6
crime *la delincuencia*, III11; *el crimen*, III11; **minor crime** *el delito*, III11
crime rate *la criminalidad*, III11
to cross (at . . .) *cruzar (en…)*, II
to cry *llorar*, III5
Cuban *cubano(a)*, II
cure *la cura*, III11
curly *rizado(a)*, III1
curt *seco(a)*, III9
custard *el flan*, I; *el quesillo (Venezuela)*, III4
custom *la costumbre*, III10
customer *el (la) cliente*, II
to cut the grass *cortar el césped*, I
cycling *el ciclismo*, II
cyclist: to be a cyclist *practicar el ciclismo*, III1

dad *el papá*, I
daily life *la vida diaria*, III3
dairy store *la lechería*, III4
dance (event) *el baile*, I
to dance *bailar*, I
dance (as an artform) *la danza*, III6
dancer *el bailarín, la bailarina*, III6
danger *el peligro*, III2
dangerous *peligroso(a)*, II
dark-haired, dark-skinned *moreno(a)*, III1
date (appointment) *la cita*, I
date (on calendar) *la fecha*, I
daughter *la hija*, I
day *el día*, I; **a free day** *un día libre*, I; **day before yesterday** *anteayer*, I; **every day** *todos los días*, I; **the day before** *el día anterior*, II; **(two, three, . . .) days later** *(dos, tres,…) días después*, II
dead *muerto(a)*, III5
dear *querido(a)*, II
December *diciembre (m.)*, I
to declare *declarar*, III5
to decorate *decorar*, II
decorations *las decoraciones*, I
to decrease *bajar*, III11
to dedicate *dedicar*, II
deeply *profundamente*, II
defeat (n.) *la derrota*, III5
to defeat *vencer*, III5
delicious *delicioso(a)*, I; *rico(a)*, I; *riquísimo(a)*, III4
delighted *encantado(a)*, III7
demanding *exigente*, II
to deny *negar (ie)*, III9; **I deny having made fun of . . .** *Niego haberme burlado de…*, III9
department store *el almacén*, I
to depend on *contar (ue) con*, III7; **It depends on your point of view.** *Depende de tu punto de vista.*, III5
depressed *deprimido(a)*, II
to design *diseñar*, III6
designer *el diseñador, la diseñadora*, III12
desk *el escritorio*, I
to despair *desesperarse*, II
dessert *el postre*, I
to destroy *destruir*, III3
destruction *la destrucción*, II
deterioration *el deterioro*, III11
to develop *desarrollar*, III3
dictionary *el diccionario*, I
did: Did you find out about . . .? *¿Te enteraste de…?*, II; **Did you forget . . .?** *¿Se te olvidó (olvidaron)…?*, III4; **Did you have a good time?** *¿Qué tal lo pasaste?*, II; **What did he (she/you) do?** *¿Qué hizo?*, I; **What did he (she)**

say? *¿Qué dijo?*, II; **What did they tell you?** *¿Qué te dijeron?*, II; **What did you do?** *¿Qué hiciste?*, II
diet *la dieta*, II; **to be on a diet** *hacer régimen*, II; *estar a dieta*, III2
difficult *difícil*, I
dining room *el comedor*, II
dinner *la cena*, I
directions *las instrucciones*, II
dirty *sucio(a)*, I
disadvantage *la desventaja*, III3
to disagree: It disagrees with me. *Me cae gordo.*, III4
disagreeable *antipático(a)*, I
disappointed *decepcionado(a)*, III7; *desilusionado(a)*, III7
discount *el descuento*, II
to discover *descubrir*, III3
discovered (past part.) *descubierto*, III3
discrimination *la discriminación*, III9
to discuss *discutir*, III7
disgusting: How disgusting! *¡Qué asco!*, III4
disease *la enfermedad*, III11
to dislike strongly *chocar(le)*, II
disloyal *desleal*, II
to do *hacer*, I; **do** *haz* (command), I; **do for you** *hacer por ti*, III7; **Do me the favor of . . .** *Hágame (Hazme) el favor de…*, III4; **Do you know (formal) . . .?** *¿Sabe Ud… ?*, II; **Do you know (informal) . . .?** *¿Sabes… ?*, II; **Do you know what you're going to order?** *¿Ya sabe(n) qué va(n) a pedir?*, II; **Do you (informal) like . . .?** *¿Te gusta(n)…?*, II; **Do you think so?** *¿Tú crees?*, III5; **Do you think that . . .?** *¿Crees que…?*, II; *¿Te parece que…?*, II; **Do you want to . . .?** *¿Quieres…?*, I; **Do you want to help me?** *¿Quieres ayudarme?*, II; **to do sit-ups** *hacer abdominales*, II; **to do something** *hacer algo*, II; **to do well** *salir bien*, II; **to do yoga** *hacer yoga*, I
doctor *el médico, la médica*, III12
documentary *el documental*, III8
dog *el perro*, I
dollar *el dólar*, I
dolphin *el delfín (pl. los delfines)*, II
Dominican (from the Dominican Republic) *dominicano(a)*, II
don't: Don't add salt. *No añadas sal.*, II; **Don't be . . .** *No seas…*, II; **Don't forget that . . .** *No olvides que…*, III12; **Don't forget to . . .** *No te olvides de…*, III6; **Don't smoke anymore.** *No fumes más.*, II; **Don't worry.** *No te preocupes.*, I; **don't you?** *¿verdad?*, I
door *la puerta*, I
doubt: There's absolutely no doubt. *No cabe la menor duda.*, III8; **Without a doubt.** *Sin duda*

R84 ENGLISH-SPANISH VOCABULARY

alguna., III8
to doubt *dudar,* III8; **I doubt that . . .** *Dudo que…,* III8
down: to go down (a street or road) *bajar por,* II
downpour *el aguacero,* II
downtown *el centro,* I; **Downtown, there is (are)…** *En el centro, hay…,* II
to draw *dibujar,* I
drawing *el dibujo,* III6
dream *el sueño,* III5; **my lifelong dream** *el sueño de mi vida,* III5
to dream of (doing something) *soñar (ue) con + inf.,* III10
dress *el vestido,* I
dressed: to get dressed *vestirse (i, i),* II
dressing room *el probador,* II
to drink *tomar, beber,* I; **to drink a soft drink** *tomar un refresco,* I
to drive *manejar,* III3
driver *el conductor, la conductora,* II
to drop: We dropped . . . *Se nos cayó (cayeron)…,* III4
to drop by and pick someone up *pasar por alguien,* II
drug addiction *la drogadicción,* III11
drums *la batería,* III1
dry *seco(a),* II
to dry one's hair *secarse el pelo,* II
to dry oneself *secarse,* II
due: are due to *se deben a,* III10
dull *torpe,* III9
dumb *bobo(a),* III9
during *durante,* I; **(during) free time** *(en) el tiempo libre,* I
to dust *sacudir el polvo,* II
duty *el deber,* III3
dwarf *el enano, la enana,* II

e-mail *la carta electrónica,* III3
eagle *el águila, (pl. las águilas),* II
ear: inner ear *el oído,* I; **outer ear** *la oreja,* I
to earn *ganar,* I
earring *el arete,* I
Earth *la Tierra,* II
east *el este,* II
Easter *las Pascuas,* I
easy *fácil,* I; **easy to** *fácil de,* III8
to eat *comer,* I; **to eat breakfast** *desayunar,* I; **to eat dinner** *cenar,* I; **to eat healthy food** *comer comida sana,* III2; **to eat ice cream** *tomar helado,* I; **to eat lunch** *almorzar (ue),* I; **to eat poorly** *alimentarse mal,* III2; **to eat well** *alimentarse bien,* III2
Ecuadorean *ecuatoriano(a),* II
editorials *los editoriales,* III8

education *la educación,* I
effects *los efectos,* II
effort *el esfuerzo,* III10; **I put a lot of effort into . . .** *Puse todo mi esfuerzo en…,* III10
eggs *los huevos,* I
Egypt *Egipto (m.),* I
eight *ocho,* I
eight hundred *ochocientos(as),* I
eighteen *dieciocho,* I
eighty *ochenta,* I
elbow *el codo,* I
electric appliance *el aparato eléctrico,* III3; **electric car** *el carro eléctrico,* III3
electricity *la electricidad,* II
electronic mail (e-mail) *el correo electrónico, el e-mail,* II
elegant *elegante,* II
eleven *once,* I
employee *el empleado, la empleada,* III12
end *el fin,* I
enemy *enemigo(a),* III5
energy *la energía,* II
engineer *el ingeniero, la ingeniera,* III12
England *Inglaterra (f.),* I
English (language) *el inglés,* I
to enjoy *disfrutar,* II
enough *lo suficiente,* II
to enroll *inscribirse,* II
entertaining *entretenido(a),* III6
entertainment section *la sección de ocio,* III8
enthusiastic *entusiasta,* II
entire *entero(a),* II
environment *el medio ambiente,* II
eraser *la goma de borrar,* I
errand *el mandado,* II
especially *especialmente,* I
evening *la noche,* I
event *el evento,* I
ever *alguna vez,* III3
every *todo(a), todos(as),* I; **Every cloud has a silver lining.** *No hay mal que por bien no venga.,* III7; **every day** *todos los días,* I
Everyone knows that . . . *Todo el mundo sabe que…,* III8
Everything turned out well. *Todo salió bien.,* II
exam *el examen, (pl. los exámenes),* I
excellent *excelente,* I
excited *emocionado(a),* II
Excuse me. *Perdón.,* I; *Perdóname.,* I; *Disculpe.,* II; *Con permiso.,* II
exercise *el ejercicio,* I
to exercise *hacer ejercicio,* III2
exhausted *agotado(a),* III2
exhibition *la exhibición,* III6
expensive *caro(a),* I
to explore *explorar,* I
extraordinary *de película,* II
extremely boring *aburridísimo(a) (with ser),* II
eyes *los ojos,* I

to face *enfrentar,* II
factory *la fábrica,* III3
to fail (a test, a class) *suspender,* II
fair (adj.) *justo(a),* II
fairy godmother *el hada (f.) madrina,* II
fairy tale *el cuento de hadas,* II
fall (season) *el otoño,* I
to fall asleep *dormirse (ue, u),* III2
to fall down *caerse,* II
to fall in love (with) *enamorarse (de),* II
family *la familia,* I
fan (enthusiast) *el fanático, la fanática,* III1; *el aficionado, la aficionada,* III1; **to be a fan of** *ser aficionado(a) a,* III1; *ser fanático(a) de,* III1
far *lejos,* II; **far away** *lejos,* II; **far from** *lejos de,* I
fashion section *la sección de moda,* III8
fat (in food) *la grasa,* III2
father *el padre,* I; **Father's Day** *el Día del Padre,* I
favorite *favorito(a),* I
to fear *temer,* III7
February *febrero (m.),* I
fed up *harto(a),* II
to feel *sentirse (ie, i),* I; **to feel hurt** *estar dolido(a),* III7; **to feel like (doing something)** *tener (ie) ganas de + inf.,* I; **to feel like crying** *darle ganas de llorar,* III7; **to feel lonely** *sentirse solo(a),* III2; **to feel poorly** *estar mal,* I; **to feel proud of** *sentirse orgulloso(a) de,* III10
feelings *los sentimientos,* III7
Ferris wheel *la rueda de Chicago,* II
festival *el festival,* II
fever *la fiebre,* I; **to have a fever** *tener (ie) fiebre,* I
few *pocos(as),* II
fifteen *quince,* I
fifty *cincuenta,* I
to fight *luchar,* III5; *pelear,* II; **to have a fight** *pelearse,* III7
film *la película,* I
finally *por último,* II; **Finally…** *Al final…,* II
financial section *la sección financiera,* III8
to find *encontrar (ue),* I; **If a cure were found . . .** *Si se encontrara una cura…,* III11 **to find a job** *encontrar (ue) un empleo,* II
to find out *averiguar,* II; **Did you find out about . . .?** *¿Te enteraste de…?,* II; **I found out** *supe,* III9; **you found out** *supiste,* III9

finger *el dedo*, I
to finish *terminar*, III10
firewood *la leña*, II
first *primero(a)*, I; **the first (of the month)** *el primero*, I
fish *el pescado*, I; *el pez*, *(pl. los peces)*, II
to fish *pescar*, I
fish market *la pescadería*, III4
to fit *quedar*, I; **It fits you very well.** *Te queda muy bien.*, I
to fit in *encajar*, III10
five *cinco*, I
five hundred *quinientos(as)*, I
to fix cars *trabajar en mecánica*, II
fixed prices *los precios fijos*, II
flavor *el sabor*, III4
float *la carroza*, II
floor *el piso*, II
flower shop *la florería*, I
flowers *las flores*, I
flu *la gripe*, I
flute *la flauta*, III1
to focus on *enfocarse en*, III10
fog *la niebla*, II
folder *la carpeta*, I
to follow directions *seguir (i, i) las instrucciones*, II
food *la comida*, I; **Chinese food** *la comida china*, I; **Italian food** *la comida italiana*, I; **Mexican food** *la comida mexicana*, I
food server *el mesero, la mesera*, II
food (cooking) section *la sección de cocina*, III8
foot *el pie*, I
football *el fútbol norteamericano*, I
for *para, por*, I; **for (a period of time)** *por*, II; **for me** *para mí*, II; **for that reason** *por eso*, I; **For whom?** *¿Para quién?*, I; **(for) her, him, you (sing.)** *le*, I; **(for) me** *me*, I
forest *el bosque*, I
forever: It won't last forever. *No hay mal que cien años dure.*, III7
to forget *olvidar*, II; **Did you forget . . . ?** *¿Se te olvidó (olvidaron)?*, III4; **Don't forget that . . .** *No te olvides que…*, III12; **They forgot . . .** *Se les quedó (quedaron)…*, III4; **to forget (about), to forget (to)** *olvidarse (de)*, II
Forgive me. *Discúlpame.*, III7; *Perdóname.*, III7
fork *el tenedor*, I
formal *formal*, I
forty *cuarenta*, I
four *cuatro*, I
four hundred *cuatrocientos(as)*, I
fourteen *catorce*, I
France *Francia* (f.), I
free *gratis*, II; **free day** *un día libre*, I; **free time** *el rato libre*, II; **(during) free time** *(en) el tiempo libre*, I
freeway *la autopista*, III3
French (language) *el francés*, I

French fries *las papas fritas*, I
fresh air *el aire puro*, II
Friday *el viernes*, I
fried chicken *el pollo frito*, III4
friend *el amigo* **(male)**, *la amiga* **(female)**, I; *el compañero* **(male)**, *la compañera* **(female)**, I
friendly *amigable*, III9
friendship *la amistad*, III7
from *de*, I; **from me** *de mi parte*, II; **from the** *del, de la*, I; **from the United States** *estadounidense* (m./f.), II
front page *la primera plana*, III8
fruit *la fruta*, I
fruit shop *la frutería*, III4
frustrated *frustrado(a)*, III7; **I'm frustrated.** *Me siento frustrado(a).*, III7; **We got frustrated.** *Nos frustramos.*, III9
fuel *el combustible*, II
to fulfill (a dream) *realizar (un sueño)*, III10
full time *tiempo completo*, III12
fun *divertido(a)*, I
fun: to have fun *divertirse (ie, i)*, II
funny *cómico(a)*, I
future *el porvenir*, III3

to gain weight *aumentar de peso*, II; *subir de peso*, III2
galaxy *la galaxia*, II
game *el juego*, I; **board game** *el juego de mesa*, I
game of . . . (sport) *el partido de…*, I
garbage *la basura*, II
garden *el jardín*, I
garlic *el ajo*, III4
gas *la gasolina*, II
gas station *la gasolinera*, II
generally *por lo general*, II
generous *generoso(a)*, II
geography *la geografía*, I
Germany *Alemania* (f.), I
to get: Get into shape. (command) *Ponte en forma.*, II; **to get a sunburn** *quemarse*, III2; **to get along** *llevarse bien*, II; **to get dressed** *vestirse (i, i)*, II; **to get enough sleep** *dormir (ue, u) lo suficiente*, III2; **to get good grades** *sacar buenas notas*, II; **to get lost** *perderse (ie)*, II; **to get married** *casarse*, II; **to get nervous** *ponerse nervioso(a)*, III2; **to get off the bus** *bajarse del autobús*, II; **to get on the bus** *subirse al autobús*, II; **to get (somewhere) on time** *llegar a tiempo*, II; **to get scared** *asustarse*, II; **to get tired** *cansarse*, II; **to get**

to know someone *conocer (zc)*, I; **to get together with friends** *reunirse con amigos*, II; **to get up** *levantarse*, II; **to get worse** *empeorar*, III3; *empeorarse*, III11
gift *el regalo*, III7; **to buy someone a gift** *comprarle un regalo*, III7; **to open gifts** *abrir los regalos*, I; **to receive gifts** *recibir regalos*, I
gigantic *gigantesco(a)*, II
girl *la chica*, I
girlfriend *la novia*, III7
to give *dar*, I; **to give (as a gift)** *regalar*, I; **to give one's regards to** *dar un saludo a*, II; **to give oneself** *darse*, III7; **to give permission** *dar permiso*, II; **to give someone a hug** *darle un abrazo*, III7
glad, to be *alegrarse*, III7
glass *el vidrio*, II; **glass of milk** *el vaso de leche*, I
glasses *las gafas*, III1
gloomy *melancólico(a)*, III9
to go *ir*, I; **go** *ve* (command), I; **go away** *vete* (command), I; **to go away** *irse*, II; **to go back** *regresar*, I; **to go by the bank** *pasar por el banco*, II; **to go by the pharmacy** *pasar por la farmacia*, II; **to go by the post office** *pasar por el correo*, II; **to go canoeing** *bajar el río en canoa*, I; **to go down (a street or road)** *bajar por*, II; **to go hiking** *dar una caminata*, I; **to go horseback riding** *montar a caballo*, III1; **to go inline skating** *patinar en línea*, III1; **to go mountain climbing** *escalar montañas*, III1; **to go out** *salir*, I; **to go sailing** *pasear en velero*, III1; **to go sightseeing** *hacer turismo*, I; **to go skydiving** *saltar en paracaídas*, I; **to go to bed** *acostarse (ue)*, II; **to go to the beach** *ir a la playa*, III1; **to go to the mall** *ir al centro comercial*, I; **to go up (a street or road)** *subir por*, II; **to go windsurfing** *montar en tabla de vela*, II; **to go with** *acompañar (a)*, II
goal *la meta*, III10
god *el dios*, III5
goddess *la diosa*, III5
going: Are we going the right way to . . . ? *¿Vamos bien para...?*, II; **I'm going to be . . .** *Voy a ser…*, III12; **people are going to use** *la gente va a usar*, III3
good *bueno(a)*, I; **Good afternoon.** *Buenas tardes.*, I; **Good evening.** *Buenas noches.*, I; **Good idea.** *Buena idea.*, I; **good mood** *buen humor*, III7; **Good morning.** *Buenos días.*, I; **Good night.** *Buenas noches.*, I; **good-looking** *guapo(a)*, III1; **Goodbye.** *Adiós.*, I; **in good shape** *en plena forma*, II

goods *los productos*, II
to **gossip** *chismear*, III7
gossip *el chisme*, II
gossip (person) *el chismoso, la chismosa*, II
gossipy *chismoso(a)*, III9
government *el gobierno*, III11
grades *las notas*, II
to **graduate** *graduarse*, III10
graduation party *la fiesta de graduación*, I
grandfather *el abuelo*, I
grandmother *la abuela*, I
grandparents *los abuelos*, I
grapefruit *la toronja*, I
grapes *las uvas*, I
grass *el césped*, I
grateful *agradecido(a)*, III10
gray *gris*, I; **gray hair** *las canas*, I
great *de maravilla*, II; *estupendo(a)*, I; *excelente*, I; *fenomenal*, III1; *genial*, III6; *magnífico(a)*, I; *¡Qué bueno!*, III4; **great guy** *un gran tipo*, III1; **great guy (girl)** *un(a) tío(a) estupendo(a)*, III1; **great person** *una gran persona*, III1
Greek: It's Greek to me. *Me suena a chino.*, III8
green *verde*, I
greeting *el saludo*, II
greeting card *la tarjeta*, I
grief *la pena*, III7
grilled *a la parrilla*, III4
grocery store *la bodega*, III4; *la tienda de comestibles*, I
to **grow** *crecer (zc)*, III3; *aumentar*, III11
to **grow up** *criarse*, III10
Guatemalan *guatemalteco(a)*, II
guests *los invitados*, I
guide *el (la) guía*, II
guitar *la guitarra*, I
gym *el gimnasio*, I

habit *el hábito*, II
hair *el pelo*, I; **He (She) has gray hair.** *Tiene canas.*, I
hair dryer *la secadora de pelo*, II
half past the hour *la(s)… y media*, I
half-brother *el medio hermano*, I
half-sister *la media hermana*, I
half time *medio tiempo*, III12
ham *el jamón*, I
hamburger *la hamburguesa*, I
hand *la mano*, I; **on the other hand** *por otro lado*, III3
to **hand in homework** *entregar la tarea*, II
handsome *guapo*, I
to **hang decorations** *colgar (ue) las decoraciones*, I

happy *contento(a)*, III7; *feliz*, II; **as happy as a lark** *tan feliz como una lombriz*, II; **He (She) was happy.** *Se alegró.*, III9; **I was happy** *estuve contento(a)*, III9
hard: It's hard to believe that… *Parece mentira que…*, III8
hardware shop *la ferretería*, III4
has (auxiliary verb): **has changed a lot** *ha cambiado*, III3; **has gotten worse** *ha empeorado*, III3
to **hate** *odiar*, II; **I hate it.** *Me cae gordo.*, III6
to **have** *tener (ie)*, I; **to have a cough** *tener tos*, I; **to have a cramp** *tener calambre*, II; **to have a fever** *tener fiebre*, I; **to have a fight** *pelearse*, III7; **to have a good time** *pasarlo bien*, I; **to have a misunderstanding** *tener un malentendido*, III7; **to have been (doing something) for (amount of time)** *hace… que…*, II; **to have breakfast** *desayunar*, I; **to have dinner (supper)** *cenar*, II; **to have fun** *divertirse (ie, i)*, II; **to have good eating habits** *tener (ie) buenos hábitos de alimentación*, III2; **to have the flu** *tener gripe*, I; **to have to (do something)** *tener que + inf.*, I; **to have to go** *tener que irse*, I
have (auxiliary verb): **Many people have come from outside.** *Mucha gente ha venido de fuera.*, III3; **Have you read anything about…?** *¿Has leído algo de…?*, III6; **Have you thought of…?** *¿Has pensado en…?*, III6
he *él*, I; **He (She) broke…** *Se le rompió…*, III4; **He (She) feels proud of having…** *Se siente orgulloso(a) de haber…*, III10; **He (She) has gray hair.** *Tiene canas.*, I; **He (She) has green (blue) eyes.** *Tiene (los) ojos verdes (azules).*, I; **he is** *él es*, I; **He (She/It) is from…** *Es de…*, I; **He (She) is late.** *Está atrasado(a).*, I; **he (she) is…tall** *mide…*, II; **He (She) is… years old.** *Tiene… años.*, II; **He (She) needs…** *Él (Ella) necesita*, III4; **He (She/They) need(s) to…** *Hace falta que + subj.*, III6; **he (she) said that** *dijo que*, II; **He (She) speaks… very well.** *Domina…*, III10; **he (she) wants** *quiere*, I; **He (She) was very happy.** *Se alegró mucho.*, III9; **He (She) was very successful…** *Tuvo mucho éxito…*, III10
head *la cabeza*, I
headlines *los titulares*, III8
health *la salud*, II
healthy *sano(a)*, I
to **hear** *oír*, II; *A propósito, ¿qué has oído de…?* **By the way, what**

have you heard about…?, III6; **I heard that…** *Oí que…*, III5
heat *el calor*, I; *la calefacción*, II
heaven: I'm in heaven! *¡Estoy en la gloria!*, III7
heavy *fuerte*, I
hectic life *la vida agitada*, III2
height *la estatura*, II
Hello. *Aló.*(when answering the phone), I; *Diga…*(when answering the phone), I; *¡Hola!*, I
to **help** *ayudar*, I; **Please help me with…** *Por favor, ayúdame con…*, III4; **to help at home** *ayudar en casa*, I
her (direct object) *la*, (object of preposition) *ella*, I; **Her name is…** *Se llama…*, I; **to (for) her** *le*, (possessive adj.) *su(s)*, I
here *aquí*, I
hero *el héroe*, III5
heroine *la heroína*, III5
high school *el colegio*, I
highway *la autopista*, III3
hiking *el senderismo*, II
him (direct object) *lo*, (object of preposition) *él*, **to (for) him** *le*, I
his *su(s)*, I; **His name is…** *Se llama…*, I
hobby *el pasatiempo*, II
holidays *los días festivos*, I
home *la casa*, I
homework *la tarea*, I
homicide *el homicidio*, III11
Honduran *hondureño(a)*, II
honest *honesto(a)*, II; **to be honest (with you)** *para ser sincero(a)*, III6
hope *la esperanza*, III5
to **hope (that)…** *esperar que + subj.*, III5; **to hope to…** *esperar + inf.*, III5
hopefully… *ojalá que + subj.*, III5
horrible *horrible*, I
horseback riding *la equitación*, III1; **to go horseback riding** *montar a caballo*, III1
hot *caliente*, I; **to be hot (weather)** *hacer calor*, I
hot dog *el perro caliente*, I
hour *la hora*, I
house *la casa*, I
household chores *los quehaceres domésticos*, I
How? *¿Cómo?*, III1; **How about if…?** *¿Qué tal si…?*, II; **How are you?** *¿Cómo estás?*, I; **How are you feeling?** *¿Cómo te sientes?*, II; **How can I help you?** *¿En qué le puedo servir?*, II; **How did it go?** *¿Cómo te fue?*, II; **How do I look?** *¿Cómo me veo?*, II; **How do you feel about…?** *¿Qué te parece si…?*, III6; **How do you get to…?** *¿Cómo se va a…?*, II; **How does it fit you?** *¿Cómo te queda?*, II; **How long have (has)…?** *¿Cuánto tiempo hace que…?*, II; **How many?**

¿Cuántos(as)?, III1; **How many people are in your family?** *¿Cuántas personas hay en tu familia?*, I; **How much?** *¿Cuánto(a)?*, III1; **How much does (do) ... cost?** *¿Cuánto cuesta(n)...?*, I; **How much is it?** *¿Cuánto es?*, I; *¿Cuánto vale?*, II; **How much will you let it go for?** *¿En cuánto lo deja?*, II; **How often?** *¿Con qué frecuencia?*, I; **How old are you?** *¿Cuántos años tienes?*, I; **How old is he (she)?** *¿Cuántos años tiene?*, I; **How should I know?** *¿Qué sé yo?*, III8; **How was it (were they)?** *¿Cómo estuvo (estuvieron)?*, *¿Qué tal estuvo (estuvieron)?*, II; **How's it going?** *¿Qué?*, I

How...! *¡Qué...!*, I; **How cheap!** *¡Qué barato(a)!*, I; **How disgusting!** *¡Qué asco!*, III4; **How expensive!** *¡Qué caro(a)!*, I; **How good!** *¡Qué bueno (sabroso)!*, III4; **How silly!** *¡Qué tontería!*, III5; **How tasty!** *¡Qué sabroso!*, III4

hug *el abrazo*, III7; **to give someone a hug** *darle un abrazo*, III7
humid *húmedo(a)*, II
humor: sense of humor *el sentido del humor*, III1
hundred *cien, ciento*, I
hunger *el hambre (f.)*, III11
hungry, to be (very) *tener (ie) (mucha) hambre*, I
hurry: Hurry up! *¡Date prisa!*, I; **I'm in a hurry.** *Tengo prisa.*, I
to hurt *doler (ue)*, I; **It really hurts me that ...** *Me duele mucho que...*, III7; **to be hurt** *estar dolido(a)*, III7; **to hurt (oneself)** *hacerse daño*, II
husband *el esposo*, I

I *yo*, I
I (emphatic) like to ... *A mí me gusta + inf.*, I
I achieved success in ... *Alcancé éxito en...*, III10
I admire very much ... *Admiro mucho...*, III6
I advise you to ... *Te aconsejo + inf.*, III2
I agree. *Estoy de acuerdo.*, III5
I already have (other) plans. *Ya tengo (otros) planes.*, III6
I already know. *Ya lo sé.*, II
I always have to do it. *Siempre me toca a mí.*, II
I am ... *Soy...*, I
I am fed up with ... *Estoy harto(a)*

de..., III1
I can't. *No puedo.*, III6
I can't believe it. *No me lo puedo creer.*, III8
I can't believe that ... *No puedo creer que...*, III8
I can't stand anyone ... *No aguanto a nadie...*, III7
I can't stand it (him/her). *No lo (la) soporto.*, III6
I deny having made fun of ... *Niego haberme burlado de...*, III9
I didn't know. *No sabía.*, III7
I didn't mean to do it. *Lo hice sin querer.*, III7
I disagree. *No estoy de acuerdo.*, II
I don't agree that ... *No estoy de acuerdo en que...*, III9
I don't believe it. *No lo creo.*, II
I don't believe that ... *No creo que...*, III8
I don't feel like ... *No tengo ganas de + inf.*, III6
I don't know. *No sé.*, III5
I don't like ... *No me gusta(n)...*, I
I don't think so. *Creo que no.*, I
I doubt it. *Lo dudo.*, II
I doubt that ... *Dudo que...*, III8
I feel ... *Me siento...*, II
I find it ... *Lo (La) encuentro...*, III6
I found out *supe*, III9
I generally eat (drink) ... *Por lo general tomo...*, I
I get along very well with ... *Me llevo muy bien con...*, II
I got angry *me enfadé*, III9; *me enojé*, III9
I got frustrated *me frustré*, III9
I had high hopes of ... *Tenía muchas esperanzas de...*, III5
I had to ... *Tenía que...*, II
I hate it. *Me cae gordo.*, III6
I have a lot to do. *Tengo mucho que hacer.*, III6
I have the impression that ... *Tengo la impresión que...*, III9
I have to go. *Tengo que irme.*, I
I heard that ... *Oí que...*, III5
I hoped to ... *Esperaba...*, II
I imagine that ... *Me imagino que...*, III9
I intend to ... *Pienso...*, III10; *Tengo la intención de...*, III10
I intend to work in ... *Pienso trabajar en...*, III12
I know! *¡Ya lo sé!*, III8
I like ... *Me gusta(n)...*, I
I like ... more *Me gusta más...*, I
I look for someone ... *Busco a alguien...*, III7
I lost ... *Se me perdió (perdieron)...*, III4
I plan to ... *Pienso...*, II
I planned to ... *Pensaba...*, II
I propose ... *Propongo...*, III11
I put a lot of effort into ... *Puse todo mi esfuerzo en...*, III10

I ran out of ... *Se me acabó (acabaron)...*, III4
I read that ... *Leí que...*, II
I really (don't) like ... *Me cae bien (mal)...*, II
I recommend ... *Recomiendo...*, II
I recommend that you ... *Te recomiendo + inf.*, III2
I spend my time ... *Me la paso...*, III1
I suggest that ... *Sugiero que...*, III6
I suppose that ... *Supongo que...*, III9
I think so. *Creo que sí.*, I
I think that ... *Me parece que...*, II; *Yo creo que...*, II
I think you're wrong. *Me parece que no tienes razón.*, II
I thought ... was great. *Quedé muy impresionado(a) con...*, II
I understand that ... *Tengo entendido que...*, III9
I want *quiero*, I
I want to be ... *Quiero ser...*, III12
I want to become ... *Quiero llegar a ser...*, III12
I wanted ..., *Quise...*, III9
I wanted to but couldn't. *Quería pero no pude.*, II
I was ... *estuve...*, III9
I was going to ... but I wasn't able. *Iba a... pero no pude.*, II
I wear size ... *Uso talla...*, II
I won't do it again. *No lo volveré a hacer.*, III7
I won't do it anymore. *No lo haré más.*, III7
I would devote myself to ... *Me dedicaría a...*, III11
I would like (to) *quisiera*, I
I would like ... *Me gustaría...*, I
I would start by ... *Yo empezaría por...*, III11
I would try to ... *Intentaría...*, III11
I'd be interested in studying to be a ... *Me interesaría estudiar para...*, III12
I'd like to be ... *Me gustaría ser...*, III12
I'd like to but I have to ... *Me gustaría, pero tengo que...*, II
I'd love to *Me encantaría*, II
I'd love to be ... *Me encantaría ser...*, III12
I'll call later. *Llamo más tarde.*, I
I'll give it to you for ... *Se lo doy por...*, II
I'll have ... (ordering food) *Para mí...*, II
I'll let you have it for ... *Se lo regalo por...*, II
I'll look for ... *Buscaré...*, III12
I'm afraid that *temo que*, III11
I'm certain that ... *Estoy seguro(a) que...*, III8
I'm convinced that ... *Estoy*

convencido(a) que..., III8

I'm delighted that ... *Me encanta que...*, III7

I'm from ... *Soy de...*, I

I'm going to be ... *Voy a ser...*, III12

I'm in a hurry. *Tengo prisa.*, I

I'm late. *Estoy atrasado(a).*, I

I'm not sure that ... *No estoy seguro(a) que...*, III8

I'm not sure. *No estoy seguro(a).*, II

I'm sick and tired of ... *Estoy harto(a) de...*, II

I'm sorry *lo siento*, III6

I'm sorry, but right now ... *Lo siento, pero en este momento...*, I

I'm sorry. I can't. *Lo siento. No puedo.*, I

I'm ... tall. *Mido...*, II

I'm ... years old. *Tengo... años.*, I

I'm (pretty) well, thanks. *Estoy (bastante) bien, gracias.*, I

I've already done it a thousand times. *Yo ya lo hice mil veces.*, II

I've no idea. *No tengo ni idea.*, II

I've noticed ... *Me he fijado en...*, III11

ice cream *el helado*, I

ice cream store *la heladería*, III4

to **ice-skate** *patinar sobre hielo*, III1

iced tea *el té frío*, I

idea *la idea*, I; **not to have the slightest idea** *no tener (ie) la menor idea*, III8

if *si*, I; **If I could ... I would live ...** *Si pudiera... viviría...*, III9; **If I had ... I would buy ...** *Si tuviera... compraría...*, III9; **If I lived ...** *Si yo viviera...*, III11; **If I were ...** *Si yo fuera...*, III11; **If there were ...** *Si hubiera...*, III11; **if we don't** *si no*, III11; **If ... were found ...** *Si se encontrara...*, III11; **If you could ...** *Si tú pudieras...*, III11; **If you could ... where would you go?** *Si pudieras... ¿adónde irías?*, III9; **if you want** *si quieres*, II; **If you were rich, what would you do?** *Si fueras rico(a), ¿qué harías?*, III9

ignorance *la ignorancia*, III9

ill *enfermo(a)*, II

imaginative *imaginativo(a)*, III6

to **imagine** *imaginarse*, III3

Imagine! *¡Fíjate!*, II

immediately *en seguida*, III3; *inmediatamente*, II

impatient *impaciente*, II

to **implement** *implementar*, III11

impression *la impresión*, III9; **I'm under the impression that ...** *Tengo la impresión de que...*, III9

to **improve** *mejorar*, III3

in *en, por*, I; **in a bad mood** *de mal humor*, II; **in a good mood** *de buen humor*, II; **in front of** *delante de*, II; **in my time** *en mis tiempos*,

II; **in order to ...** *para...*, III10; *con la idea de...*, III10; **In short ...** *En fin...*, II; **in such a way that ...** *de tal forma que...*, III10; **in the afternoon (p.m.)** *de la tarde, por la tarde*, I; **in the evening (p.m.)** *de la noche, por la noche*, I; **in the morning (a.m.)** *de la mañana, por la mañana*, I; **in those days** *en aquella época*, II; **in those times** *en aquellos tiempos*, II; **in very bad taste** *de muy mal gusto*, III6; **In your opinion ...** *En tu opinión...*, II

included *incluido(a)*, I

incomprehensible *incomprensible*, III6

Independence Day *el Día de la Independencia*, I

to **inflate** *inflar*, I

to **inform** *informar*, III3

informed: to be well informed about *estar bien informado(a) sobre*, III8

to **initiate** *iniciar*, III11

initiative: to take the initiative *tomar la iniciativa*, III10

to **injure (oneself)** *lastimarse*, II

insects *los insectos*, II

to **insult** *insultar*, III7

insurance *el seguro*, III12

intelligent *inteligente*, I

to **intend** *pensar + inf.*, I

to **interest** *interesar*, III1; **It doesn't interest me at all.** *No me interesa para nada.*, III1

interesting *interesante*, I

Internet *Internet*, III1

intersection *el cruce*, II

intolerable *insoportable*, III6

invitation *la invitación*, I

to **invite** *invitar*, I

to **iron** *planchar*, I

is going to be ... *va a estar...*, III3; *va a ser...*, III3

Is it (the tip) included? *¿Está incluida?*, I

Isn't it? *¿No?*, I

it (direct object) *lo, la*, II

It can't be! *¡No puede ser!*, III8

It caught me by surprise. *No me lo esperaba.*, III8

It depends on your point of view. *Depende de tu punto de vista.*, III5

It disagrees with me. *Me cae gordo.*, III4

It doesn't do anything for me. *Me deja frío(a).*, III6

It doesn't have enough ... *Le falta(n)...*, III4

it doesn't interest me *no me interesa*, III1

It doesn't matter to me. *No me importa.*, III1

It doesn't seem right to me. *No me parece.*, II

It fits you very well. *Te queda muy bien.*, I

It frustrates me that ... *Me frustra que...*, III7

It has too much ... *Lleva mucho(a)...*, III4

It is believed that ... *Se cree que...*, III5

it is going to *va a*, III11

It is true. *Es cierto.*, III3

It isn't true. *No es cierto.*, I

It lacks ... *Le falta(n)...*, III4

It needs ... *Le falta(n)...*, III4

it rains *llueve*, II

it seems *parece*, I; **It seems fine to me.** *Me parece bien.*, I; **It seems really boring to me.** *Me parece un rollo.*, III1; **it seems to be that way** *parece ser así*, III5; **It seems to me ...** *Se me hace que...*, III3; **It seems ... to me.** *Me parece...*, II; **It seems to me that ...** *Me parece que...*, III3

it snows *nieva*, II

It tastes ... *Sabe...*, III4

It was ... *Era*, III5

It was when ... *Fue cuando...*, II

It will be necessary to ... *Habrá que...*, III11

It won't last forever. *No hay mal que cien años dure.*, III7

It would be a good idea for you to ... *Sería bueno + inf.*, III2

It would be a good (bad) idea to ... *Sería buena (mala) idea...*, III6

It's a rip-off! *¡Es un robo!*, I

It's all the same to me. *Me da igual.*, III1; *Me da lo mismo.*, III1

It's better for ... to ... *Es mejor que...*, III6

It's (very) cold (weather). *Hace (mucho) frío.*, I

It's cool. *Hace fresco.*, I

It's evident that ... *Es evidente que...*, III8

It's Greek to me. *Me suena a chino.*, III8

It's hard to believe that ... *Parece mentira que...*, III8

It's hot. *Hace calor.*, I

It's important ... *Es importante...*, II

It's important that ... *Es importante que + subj.*, III6

It's impossible that ... *Es imposible que...*, III8

It's just right. *Está en su punto.*, III4

It's just that ... *Es que...*, II

It's late. *Es tarde.*, I

It's my treat. *Te invito.*, I

It's my turn. *Me toca a mí.*, II

It's necessary ... *Hay que...*, III3

It's necessary ... *Es necesario...*, II; *Es preciso...*, II

It's necessary for ... to ... *Es necesario que + subj.*, III6

It's not advisable that you ... *No te conviene...*, III6

It's not fair. *No es justo.*, II

It's not possible. *No es posible.*, III8

It's not true that ... *No es cierto*

que..., III9; **No es verdad que...**, III9

It's obvious that ... *Es obvio que...*, III8

It's one o'clock. *Es la una.*, I

It's our duty ... *Es nuestro deber...*, III3

It's our responsibility ... *Es nuestra responsabilidad...*, III3

It's possible that ... *Es posible que...*, III9; *Puede ser que...*, III8

It's probable that ... *Es probable que...*, III8

It's raining. *Está lloviendo.*, I; *Llueve.*, I

It's ruined. *Está echado(a) a perder.*, III4

It's separate. *Es aparte.*, I

It's snowing. *Está nevando.*, I; *Nieva.*, I

It's spoiled. *Está echado(a) a perder.*, III4

It's stylish. *Está de moda.*, II

It's sunny. *Hace sol.*, I

It's the (date) of the (month). *Es el ... de ...*, I

It's true that ... *Es cierto que...*, III8

It's (someone's) turn. *Le toca a...*, II

It's unlikely that ... *Es difícil que...*, III8

It's up to ... *Le toca a...*, II

It's up to all of us. *A todos nos toca.*, II

It's up to me. *Me toca a mí.*, II

It's up to us ... *Nos toca a nosotros...*, III3

It's up to you. *Te toca a ti.*, II

It's urgent ... *Es urgente...*, II

It's (very) windy. *Hace (mucho) viento.*, I

It's your turn. *Te toca a ti.*, II

Italian *italiano(a)*, I; **Italian food** *la comida italiana*, I

Italy *Italia (f.)*, I

J

jacket *la chaqueta*, I

January *enero (m.)*, I

jazz *el jazz*, I

jealous: someone who won't be jealous of *alguien que no tenga celos de*, III7; **to be jealous of** *tener celos de*, III7

jewelry store *la joyería*, I

job *el puesto (de trabajo)*, III12; *el trabajo*, I

joke *el chiste*, II

journalist *el (la) periodista*, III8

journey *el recorrido*, II

to **judge** *juzgar*, III9

juice *el jugo*, I

July *julio (m.)*, I

to **jump rope** *saltar a la cuerda*, II

June *junio (m.)*, I

jungle *la selva*, I

just *sólo*, II; **It's just right.** *Está en su punto.*, III4; **It's just that ...** *Es que...*, II; **Just a second.** *Un momentito.*, I; **No thanks, just the check.** *No gracias, sólo la cuenta.*, II

K

to **keep** *mantener (ie)*, III10; **Keep in mind that ...** *Ten en cuenta que...*, III3; **not to keep secrets** *no guardar los secretos*, III7

to **keep clean** *mantener (ie) limpio(a)*, II

kind *bondadoso(a)*, II; *amable*, III4

kitchen *la cocina*, I

knee *la rodilla*, II

knife *el cuchillo*, I

to **know (information)** *saber*, II; to **know (a person)** *conocer (zc) a*, II; **As far as I know ...** *Que yo sepa...*, III8; **I don't know.** *No sé.*, III5; **I know!** *¡Ya lo sé!*, III8; **I'm very sorry, I didn't know.** *Lo siento mucho, es que no sabía.*, III7; **someone who knows** *alguien que sepa*, III7; to **know absolutely nothing about ...** *no saber ni jota*

L

lack (of) *la falta (de)*, III9

to **lack: I (You, ...) lack** *Me (Te,...) falta(n)*, III4

lake *el lago*, I

to **lament** *lamentar*, III5

lamp *la lámpara*, I

last night *anoche*, I; **last Saturday** *el sábado pasado*, I; **last summer** *el verano pasado*, I; **last week** *la semana pasada*, I; **last year** *el año pasado*, III12

to **last: It won't last forever.** *No hay mal que cien años dure.*, III7

late *atrasado(a)*, I; *tarde*, I; **It's late.** *Es tarde.*, I; **to be late** *estar atrasado(a)*, I

later *más tarde*, I; *luego*, II

to **laugh** *reírse (i, i)*, III2

lawyer *el abogado, la abogada*, III12

lazy *flojo(a)*, II; *perezoso(a)*, III9

to **lead a healthy (hectic) life** *llevar una vida sana (agitada)*, I

to **learn (to do something)** *aprender a + inf.*, III6

leather (made of) *de cuero*, I

to **leave** *salir*, I; **They left ...** *Se les*

quedó..., III4; **to leave (behind)** *dejar*, II; **to leave a message** *dejar un recado*, I; **to leave the tip** *dejar la propina*, II

left *la izquierda*, II; **to the left** *a la izquierda*, II

leg *la pierna*, I

lemonade *la limonada*, I

less *menos*, I; **less ... than** *menos... que*, I

Let's do it tomorrow. *Hagámoslo mañana.*, III6

Let's see ... *A ver...*, III3; *Pues...*, III3

letter *la carta*, I

lettuce *la lechuga*, I

library *la biblioteca*, I

to **lie** *mentir (ie, i)*, III7; **someone who'll never lie to me** *alguien que nunca me mienta*, III7

life *la vida*, I

lifestyle *el estilo de vida*, II

to **lift weights** *levantar pesas*, I

light *la luz*, II

light (adj.) *ligero(a)*, I

lightning *el rayo*, II

to **like: I (You, ...) like ...** *Me (Te, ...) gusta(n)*, I; **I (You, ...) like (someone).** *Me (Te, ...) cae bien (alguien).*, II

to **listen to** *escuchar*, I; **Listen, have you heard about ...?** *Oye, ¿has oído hablar de...?*, II

to **listen to music** *escuchar música*, III1

to **live** *vivir*, I

living room *la sala*, I

lonely *solitario(a)*, II

long *largo(a)*, II; **A long time ago ...** *Hace mucho tiempo ...*, II

Look ... *Mira...*, II

to **look at oneself** *mirarse*, II

to **look for** *buscar*, I; **I'll look for ...** *Buscaré...*, III12

to **look young** *verse joven*, I

loose (clothes) *ancho(a)*, II

to **lose** *perder (ie)*, II

to **lose weight** *bajar de peso*, II

to **love: I (You, ...) love ...** *Me (Te,...) encanta(n)*, I; *Me (Te,...) fascina(n)*, II

to **lower the price** *rebajar el precio*, II

lunch *el almuerzo*, I

M

ma'am *señora*, I

made (past part.) *hecho*, III3

made of *de*, I

magazine *la revista*, I

magnificent *magnífico(a)*, III6

to **make** *hacer*, I; **make** *haz (command)*, I; **to make a mistake** *cometer un error*, III7; **to make a note of** *apuntar*, II; **to make an**

effort to *esforzarse (ue) por*, III10; **to make friends with someone** *hacerse amigo(a) de alguien*, II; **to make fun of** *burlarse de*, III9; **to make peace** *acordar (ue) la paz*, III5; **to make plans** *hacer planes*, II; **to make the bed** *hacer la cama*, I; *tender (ie) la cama*, II; **to make up** *hacer las paces*, II; *reconciliarse*, III7

mall *el centro comercial*, I
man *el hombre*, III5
to **manage to** *lograr*, III10
manager *el (la) gerente*, III12
mango *el mango*, I
many *muchos(as)*, I
to **march** *desfilar*, II
March (month) *marzo (m.)*, I
market *el mercado*, II
martial arts *las artes marciales*, II
marvelous *estupendo(a)*, I; *maravilloso(a)*, III6
mask *la máscara*, I
masterpiece *una obra maestra*, III6
to **match** *hacer juego con*, II
mathematics *las matemáticas*, I
to **matter** *importar*, III1
May (month) *mayo (m.)*, I
May I leave a message? *¿Puedo dejar un recado?*, I
Maybe . . . *Quizás...*, III8; *Tal vez...*, III8
Me too. *Yo también.*, I
meal *la comida*, I
meat *la carne*, I
mechanic *el mecánico, la mecánica*, III12
medium *mediano(a)*, II
medium height *de estatura mediana*, III1
to **meet (for the first time)** *conocer (zc) a*, I
to **meet up (with)** *encontrarse (ue) (con)*, II
to **memorize** *aprender de memoria*, II
memory *la memoria*, II
menu *el menú*, I
message *el recado*, I; **May I leave a message?** *¿Puedo dejar un recado?*, I
Mexican *mexicano(a)*, II
Mexican food *la comida mexicana*, I
microwave oven *el horno de microondas*, III3
mile *la milla*, I
milk *la leche*, I
milk shake *el batido*, I
mineral water *el agua* (f.) *mineral*, I
minority *la minoría*, III9
mirror *el espejo*, II
mischievous *travieso(a)*, III9
miss *la señorita*, I
to **miss (a class, an exam, etc.)** *perder (ie)*, II
to **miss (someone)** *echar (a alguien) de menos*, II
mistake *el error*, III7

misunderstanding *el malentendido*, III7
moment *el momento*, I; **one moment** *un momento*, I
Monday *el lunes*, I
money *el dinero*, I
monkey *el mono*, II
month *el mes*, I
mood: in a good (bad) mood *de buen (mal) humor*, III7
more *más*, I; **more . . . than** *más ... que*, I
morning *la mañana*, I
mother (mom) *la madre (mamá)*, I; **Mother's Day** *el Día de las Madres*, I
mountain *la montaña*, II; **mountain climbing** *el montañismo*, III1; **to go mountain climbing** *escalar montañas*, III1
to **mourn** *lamentar*, III5
moustache *el bigote*, III1
mouth *la boca*, I
to **move** *moverse (ue)*, II
movie *la película*, I
movie star *la estrella de cine*, II
movie theater *el cine*, I
Mr. *el señor*, I
Mrs. *la señora*, I
museum *el museo*, I
music *la música*, I; **classical music** *la música clásica*, I; **music by . . .** *la música de...*, I; **pop music** *la música pop*, I; **rock music** *la música rock*, I
musician *el músico, la música*, III6
must *deber*, II
my *mi*, I; *mis*, I
My city is . . . *Mi ciudad es...*, II
my last offer *mi última oferta*, II
my lifelong dream *el sueño de mi vida*, III5
My name is . . . *Me llamo...*, I

named, to be *llamarse*, I; **My name is . . .** *Me llamo...*, I
napkin *la servilleta*, I
natural resources *los recursos naturales*, II
nature *la naturaleza*, II
nature (disposition) *el modo de ser*, III10
near *cerca de*, I
necessary: It will be necessary to . . . *Habrá que..*, III11; **It's necessary to . . .** *Hay que...*, III3
neck *el cuello*, I
necklace *el collar*, I
to **need** *necesitar*, I; **He (She, . . .) needs to . . .** *Hace falta que ...*, III6
neither *tampoco*, II

network: (broadcast) network *la cadena*, III8
never, not ever *nunca*, I
new *nuevo(a)*, I; **new friends** *los nuevos amigos*, I; **New Year's Day** *el Año Nuevo*, I; **New Year's Eve** *la Nochevieja*, I
news *las noticias*, II
news program *el noticiero*, III8
newspaper *el periódico*, I
next *a continuación*, II; **next (day, year, . . .)** *al... siguiente*, II; *el (la)... que viene*, II; **Next time I'll go.** *La próxima vez iré.*, III6; **next to** *al lado de*, I; *junto a*, II
Nicaraguan *nicaragüense*, II
nice *buena gente*, III1; *majo(a)* (Spain), III1; *simpático(a)*, I
Nice to meet you. *Mucho gusto.*, I
night *la noche*, I; **Good night.** *Buenas noches.*, I; **last night** *anoche*, I; **the night before last** *anteanoche*, I
nine *nueve*, I
nine hundred *novecientos(as)*, I
nineteen *diecinueve*, I
ninety *noventa*, I
no *no*, I; *ninguno(a)* (adj.), I
no one *nadie*, I
No thanks, just the check. *No, gracias, sólo la cuenta.*, II
No way! *¡N'hombre!*, II; *¡Qué va!*, III5
nobody *nadie*, I
Nobody can stand him (her/it). *No hay quien lo (la) aguante.*, III1
noise *el ruido*, II
noisy *ruidoso(a)*, II
none *ninguno(a)*, II
nor *ni*, I
normally *normalmente*, II
north *el norte*, II; **to the north** *al norte*, II
nose *la nariz*, I
not: not anywhere *ningún lugar*, I; **not to have the slightest idea** *no tener (ie) la menor idea*, III8; **not to keep secrets** *no guardar los secretos*, III7; **not yet** *todavía no*, II
notes *los apuntes*, II
notebook *el cuaderno*, I
nothing *nada*, I
to **notice** *fijarse*, III11; **I've noticed . . .** *Me he fijado en...*, III11; **What I notice is that . . .** *Lo que noto es que...*, III3
novel *la novela* I
November *noviembre (m.)*, I
now *ahora*, I
nowadays *hoy (en) día*, III3
nowhere *ningún lugar*, I
nuclear energy *la energía nuclear*, III3
number *el número*, I
nurse *el enfermero, la enfermera*, III12
nutrition *la alimentación*, III2

O

obituaries *los obituarios,* III8
objective *el objetivo,* III10
obligated *obligado(a),* III3
obligation *el compromiso,* III10
obvious *obvio(a),* III8
ocean *el océano,* II
October *octubre* (m.), I
of *de,* I
of course *claro,* III8; *por supuesto,*
  III8; **Of course!** *¡Claro que sí!,*
  III5; *¡Cómo no!,* III5; *Desde*
  luego., III5; *¡Por supuesto!,* III5;
  Of course... *Claro que...,* III8;
  Of course not! *¡Claro que no!,*
  III5; *¡Nada de eso!,* III5
of the *del (de + el),* I
offer (n.) *la oferta,* II
often *muchas veces, con frecuencia,* I
Oh what a pain! *¡Ay, qué*
  pesado(a)!, II
okay *regular,* I
old *antiguo(a),* III6; *viejo(a),* I
older *mayor,* I; **older than**
  mayor que, II
on *en,* I; **on cable** *por cable,* III8;
  on my behalf *de mi parte,* II; **on**
  sale *en barata,* II; **On the**
  contrary. *Al contrario.,* III5; **on**
  the dot *en punto,* I; **on the (date)**
  of this month... *el... de este mes...,*
  I; **on the other hand** *por otro lado,*
  III3; **on top of** *encima de,* I
Once upon a time... *Érase una*
  vez..., II
one *uno(a),* I
one moment *un momento,* I
One must... *Hay que...,* II
onion *la cebolla* I
online *en línea,* III8
only *sólo,* I; **only when** *sólo cuando,* I
open *abierto(a),* III1
opened (past part.) *abierto,* III3
to **open gifts** *abrir los regalos,* I
open-air market *el mercado al aire*
  libre, II
orange (adj.) *anaranjado(a),* I
orange juice *el jugo de naranja,* I
orchestra *la orquesta,* III6
order: in order to *para,* I
to **order** *pedir (i, i),* I; **to order food**
  pedir (i, i) la comida, II
to **organize** *organizar,* I
original *original,* III6
other(s) *otros(as),* I
ought to *deber,* I
our *nuestro(a),* I
out: to find out *averiguar,* II;
  enterarse, II; *saber,* III9; **to go out**
  salir, I; **to run out of** *acabarse,*
  III4; **to take out** *sacar,* I
outside *fuera,* III3
to **overcome** *superar,* III10

overweight *gordo(a),* I; **a little**
  overweight *un poco gordo(a),* I
overwhelmed *agobiado(a),* III2
oysters *las ostras,* III4
ozone layer *la capa de ozono,* II

P

to **pack a suitcase** *hacer la maleta,* I
packaged goods *los productos*
  empacados, II
pain: Oh what a pain! *¡Ay, qué*
  pesado!, II
to **paint** *pintar,* I; **We need to paint...**
  Hace falta que pintemos..., III6
painting *la pintura,* III6
pair of *el par de,* II
pal *el compañero, la compañera,* I
Panamanian *panameño(a),* II
pants *los pantalones,* I
papaya *la papaya,* I
paper *el papel,* I
parade *el desfile,* II
to **parade** *desfilar,* II
paradise *el paraíso,* I
Paraguayan *paraguayo(a),* II
parents *los padres,* I
park *el parque,* I; **amusement park**
  el parque de atracciones, I
parking (space) *el estacionamiento,* II
parrot *el loro,* II
part time *medio tiempo,* III12
parts store *la tienda de refacciones,*
  III4
party *la fiesta,* I
to **pass** *pasar,* I; **to pass (an exam)**
  aprobar (ue) (un examen), II
passenger *el pasajero, la pasajera,* II
pastime *el pasatiempo,* II
pastry shop *la pastelería,* III4
to **pay attention** *prestar atención,* II
peace *la paz,* III5; **if there were peace**
  si hubiera paz, III11; **to make peace**
  acordar (ue) la paz, III5
peach *el melocotón,* III4
peanut butter *la crema de maní,* I
pedestrian zone *la zona peatonal,*
  III3
pencil *el lápiz,* I
people *la gente,* III3
percent *por ciento,* II
perfect *perfecto(a),* I
perhaps *tal vez,* I; **Perhaps...** *A lo*
  mejor..., III8; **perhaps another day**
  tal vez otro día, I
Peruvian *peruano(a),* II
petroleum *el petróleo,* II
pharmacist *el farmacéutico, la*
  farmacéutica, III12
pharmacy *la farmacia,* II
phone *el teléfono,* I; **on the phone**
  por teléfono, I
photocopier: (color) photocopier

  la fotocopiadora (a colores), III3
photography *la fotografía,* III1
physical education *la educación*
  física, I
piano *el piano,* I
to **pick up** *pasar por,* II; *recoger,* III3
pineapple *la piña,* III4
pizza *la pizza,* I
pizzeria *la pizzería,* I
place *el lugar,* I
to **place** *poner,* I; **place** *pon*
  (command), I
plaid *de cuadros,* I
plan *el plan,* I; **I already have plans.**
  Ya tengo planes., I
to **plan** *pensar + inf.,* I
planet *el planeta,* II
to **plant** *sembrar (ie),* III3
plant *la planta,* I
plastic *el plástico,* II
plate *el plato,* I
platform (in train station) *el andén,*
  (pl. los andenes), I
to **play** *jugar (ue),* II; **to play a**
  musical instrument *tocar un*
  instrumento, III1; **to play cards**
  jugar (ue) a las cartas, III1; **to**
  play sports *practicar deportes,* I;
  to play tricks *hacer travesuras,*
  II; **to play videogames** *jugar a*
  los videojuegos, III1
please *por favor,* I; **Please bring**
  me... *Por favor, me trae...,* II;
  Please help me., *Ayúdame, por*
  favor., II; **Please help me with...**
  Por favor, ayúdame con..., III4
police officer *el (la) policía,* III12
pollution *la contaminación,* II
pop music *la música pop,* I
pork: pork chops *las chuletas de*
  cerdo, III4; **roast pork** *puerco*
  asado, III4
position (job) *el puesto (de trabajo),*
  III12
Possibly... *Posiblemente...,* III8
post office *el correo,* I
postcards *las tarjetas postales,* I
poster *el cartel,* I
potato *la papa,* I
potato chips *las papitas,* I
to **practice** *practicar,* I
to **prefer** *preferir (ie, i),* I
prejudice *la prejuicio,* III9
premiere *el estreno,* II
to **prepare** *preparar,* I; **to prepare**
  dinner *preparar la cena,* I
to **preserve** *mantener (ie),* III10
press *la prensa,* III8
pressure: to be under pressure
  sufrir de presiones, III2
pressured to... *presionado(a) por...,*
  III9
pretty *bonito(a),* I
price *el precio,* I
price tag *la etiqueta,* II
pride *el orgullo,* III10
prince *el príncipe,* II

princess *la princesa*, II
probable *probable*, III8
problem *el problema*, III7
program *el programa*, III8
to **promote** *promover (ue)*, III11
to **propose** *plantear*, III11; *proponer*, III11
to **protect species** *proteger las especies*, II
proud *orgulloso(a)*, III7
psychologist *el sicólogo, la sicóloga*, III12
Puerto Rican *puertorriqueño(a)*, II
purple *morado(a)*, I
put (past part.) *puesto*, III8
to **put** *poner*, I; **put** *pon (command)*, I; **to put a lot of salt on food** *echarle mucha sal a la comida*, III2; **to put gas in the car** *poner gasolina al carro*, II; **to put on clothes** *ponerse la ropa*, II; **to put on make-up** *maquillarse*, I; **to put on sunscreen** *ponerse crema protectora*, III2; **to put on weight** *aumentar de peso*, II; *subir de peso*, III2

Q

quality *calidad*, III9
quarter past (the hour) *la(s)… y cuarto*, I
quarter to (the hour) *la(s)… menos cuarto*, I
quickly *rápidamente*, II
quiet *callado(a)*, III9
quite *bastante*, I

R

radio *la radio*, I
rail *la vía*, II
to **rain** *llover (ue)*, II
rain forest *la selva tropical*, II
raised, to be *criarse*, III10
to **react** *reaccionar*, III9
to **read** *leer*, I
ready *listo(a)*, I
realistic *realista*, III6
to **realize** *darse cuenta de*, III2
Really? *¿De veras?*, II
really beautiful *lindísimo(a)*, II
to **really like: I (You,…) really like …** *Me (Te,…) encanta(n)*, I
really nice (person) *buena gente*, II
to **recognize** *reconocer (zc)*, III6; **It's important for you to recognize …** *Es importante que reconozcas…*,

III6
to **recommend** *recomendar (ie)*, III2
to **reconcile** *reconciliarse*, III7
to **recycle** *reciclar*, II
recycling *el reciclaje*, II
red *rojo(a)*, I
red snapper *el pargo*, III4
red-headed *pelirrojo(a)*, III1
to **regret** *lamentar*, III11
to **rejoice** *regocijarse*, III5
relatives *los parientes*, II
to **relax** *relajarse*, III2
to **relieve** *aliviar*, III2
to **remain** *quedarse*, I
to **remember** *acordarse (ue) de*, II
report: news report *el reportaje*, III8
reporter *el reportero, la reportera*, III8
to **request** *solicitar*, III12
requirements *los requisitos*, III12
resources *los recursos*, II
to **respect** *respetar*, III7; **someone who'll respect …** *alguien que respete…*, III7
respect for *el respeto hacia*, III9
responsibility *la responsabilidad*, III3
responsible *responsable*, II
to **rest in the park** *descansar en el parque*, I
restaurant *el restaurante*, I
resulted in … *resultaron en…*, III10
résumé *el currículum (vitae)*, III12
to **return** *regresar*, I; *volver (ue)*, II
returned (past part.) *vuelto*, III3
to **review** *repasar*, II
rice *el arroz*, I
rich *rico(a)*, I
to **ride a bike** *montar en bicicleta*, I; **to ride a horse** *montar a caballo*, I
right *la derecha*, II; **to the right** *a la derecha*, II
right? *¿verdad?*, I; *¿no?*, I
right away *en seguida*, III3
rip-off *el robo*, I
river *el río*, II
roast pork *puerco asado*, III4
robbery *el robo*, III11
rock climbing *la escalada deportiva*, III1
rock music *la música rock*, I
roller coaster *la montaña rusa*, II
to **roller-skate** *patinar sobre ruedas*, III1
room *el cuarto*, I
roots *las raíces*, III10
round trip *ida y vuelta*, II
to **row** *remar*, III1
rowing *el remo*, III1
rude *descortés*, III9
ruined *echado(a) a perder*, III4
ruler *la regla*, I
rumor *el rumor*, III7
to **run** *correr*, I; **to run an errand** *hacer un mandado*, II
to **run out: I ran out of …** *Se me acabó (acabaron)…*, III4
running track *la pista de correr*, I
running water *el agua* (f.) *corriente*, II

S

sad *deprimido(a)*, II; *triste*, I
said (past part.) *dicho*, III3
sailing *la vela*, III1; **to go sailing** *pasear en velero*, III1
saint: (as good as) a saint *tan bueno(a) como un ángel*, II
salad *la ensalada*, I; **avocado salad** *l a ensalada de aguacate*, III4; **tossed salad** *la ensalada mixta*, III4
salary *el salario*, III12
sale *la oferta*, II
salesman, saleswoman *el vendedor, la vendedora*, III12
salt *la sal*, III4
salty *salado(a)*, I
Salvadoran *salvadoreño(a)*, II
same *mismo(a)*, I; **at the same time** *a la vez*, III3
Same here. *Igualmente.*, I
sandals *las sandalias*, I; *las chancletas*, I
sandwich *el sándwich*, I
satellite dish *la antena parabólica*, III3
Saturday *el sábado*, I
sausage *el chorizo*, III4
saxophone *el saxofón*, III1
to **say** *decir*, I; **He (She) says …** *Dice que…*, I; **to say goodbye (to)** *despedirse (i, i) (de)*, II
scared: to get scared *asustarse*, II
scarf *la bufanda*, I
schedule *el horario*, III12
science *las ciencias*, I
science fiction *la ciencia ficción*, II
scientist *el científico, la científica*, III12
scuba diving *el buceo*, III1; **to go scuba diving** *bucear*, I
sculptor *el escultor, la escultora*, III6
sculpture *la escultura*, III6
sea *el mar*, II
seasons (of the year) *las estaciones*, I
secrets *los secretos*, III7
to **see** *ver*, II
See you later. *Hasta luego.*, I
See you tomorrow. *Hasta mañana.*, I
to **seem** *parecer (zc)*, I; **It seems to me that …** *Me parece que…*, III3; *Se me hace que…*, III3; **to seem boring** *parecer pesado(a)*, II; *parecer un rollo*, III1
seen *visto*, III3
selfish *egoísta*, III9
semester *el semestre*, I
to **send** *enviar*, III3; **to send invitations** *mandar las invitaciones*, II
sense of humor *el sentido del humor*, III1
sensitivity *la sensibilidad*, III11

separate *aparte*, I
September *septiembre (m.)*, I
serious *grave*, II
to **serve** *servir (i, i)*, II; **to serve dessert** *servir (i, i) el postre*, II
to **set the table** *poner la mesa*, I
to **set up** *establecer (zc)*, III3
seven *siete*, I
seven hundred *setecientos(as)*, I
seventeen *diecisiete*, I
seventy *setenta*, I
shampoo *el champú*, II
shape *la forma*, II; **to be in good shape** *estar en plena forma*, II; **to stay in shape** *mantenerse (ie) en forma*, II
to **share with someone** *compartir con alguien*, III2
to **shave** *afeitarse*, I
she *ella*, I; **She is . . .** *Ella es...*, I; **She (He) looks young.** *Se ve joven.*, I **She (He) succeeded in overcoming many obstacles . . .** *Logró superar muchos obstáculos...*, III10
shellfish *los mariscos*, III4
shirt *la camisa*, I
shoe *el zapato*, I
shoe size *el número*, II
shoe store *la zapatería*, I
shop *el taller*, III4
to **shop: to window-shop** *mirar las vitrinas*, II
shopping mall *el centro comercial*, I
short (in height) *bajo(a)*, I; (in length) *corto(a)*, I
shorts *los pantalones cortos*, I
should *deber*, II
shoulder *el hombro*, II
show window *el escaparate*, II; *la vitrina*, II
shower: to take a shower *ducharse*, III2
shrimp *los camarones*, I
shy *tímido(a)*, III9
sick *enfermo(a)*, I
sightseeing: to go sightseeing *hacer turismo*, I
sign *el letrero*, II
silk (made of) *(de) seda*, I
silly *bobo(a)*, III9; **How silly!** *¡Qué tontería!*, III5
simple *sencillo(a)*, II
to **sing** *cantar*, I
singer *el cantante, la cantante*, III6
sir *señor*, I
sister *la hermana*, I
sit-ups *las abdominales*; **to do sit-ups** *hacer abdominales*, II
situation *la situación*, II
six *seis*, I
six hundred *seiscientos(as)*, I
sixteen *dieciséis*, I
sixty *sesenta*, I
size *la talla*, II; **shoe size** *el número*, II
to **skate** *patinar*, I; **to ice-skate** *patinar sobre hielo*, III1; **to roller-skate**

patinar sobre ruedas, III1
to **skateboard** *hacer monopatín*, II
skating *el patinaje*, III1; **to go inline skating** *patinar en línea*, III1
to **ski** *esquiar*, I
skin *la piel*, III2
skirt *la falda*, I
skis *los esquís*, I
skydiving: to go skydiving *saltar en paracaídas*, I
skyscraper *el rascacielos (pl. los rascacielos)*, III3
to **sleep** *dormir (ue, u)*, II2; **to get enough sleep** *dormir lo suficiente*, III2; **to sleep like a baby** *dormir tan bien como un lirón*, II
sleepy, to be *tener sueño*, I
slightest: not to have the slightest idea *no tener (ie) la menor idea*, III8
slippers *las chancletas*, I
slow *torpe*, III9
small *pequeño(a)*, I
smart *listo(a)*, I
smog *el smog*, II
to **smoke** *fumar*, II
to **snack** *merendar (ie)*, II
snake *la serpiente*, II
to **snow** *nevar (ie)*, II; **It's snowing.** *Nieva.*, I; **Está nevando.**, I
so . . . *así que...*, III10; *so that . . .* *para que...*, III10; **So that's how . . .** *Así (fue) que...*, II; **So, then . . .** *Entonces...*, II; **So what?** *Y eso, ¿qué?*, II
so-so *más o menos*, I; *más o menos bien*, II
soap *el jabón*, II
soccer *el fútbol*, I
soccer field *la cancha de fútbol*, I
social studies *las ciencias sociales*, I
social worker *el trabajador social, la trabajadora social*, III12
society section *la sección de sociedad*, III8
socks *los calcetines*, I
soft drink *el refresco*, I
solar energy *la energía solar*, III3
soldier *el soldado, la mujer soldado*, III5
solution *la solución*, III11
to **solve** *resolver (ue)*, II; **to solve a problem** *resolver (ue) un problema*, III2
solved (past part.) *resuelto*, III7
some *unos, unas*, I
Somebody told me that . . . *Alguien me dijo que...*, III5
someday *algún día*, II
someone (unknown) **who('ll)** *alguien que + subj.*, III7
something *algo*, I; **something (I don't know what)** *no sé qué*, III4
sometimes *a veces*, I
son *el hijo*, I
soon *pronto*, II
sorry, to be *sentir (ie, i)*, I; **I'm very**

sorry, I didn't know. *Lo siento mucho, es que no sabía.*, III7
soup *la sopa*, I
south *el sur*, II; **to the south** *al sur*, II
spaceship *la nave espacial*, II
Spanish *el español*, I
Spanish *español(a)* (adj.), II
to **speak** *hablar*, I; **Speaking of . . .** *Hablando de...*, III6; **to speak . . . very well** *dominar...*, III10
special effects *los efectos especiales*, II
specialty of the house *la especialidad de la casa*, II
to **spend** *gastar*, II; **I spend my time . . .** *Me la paso...*, III1; **to spend time with friends** *pasar el rato con amigos*, I
spicy *picante*, I
spoiled (person) *consentido(a)*, II; (food) *echado(a) a perder*, III4
to **sponsor** *patrocinar*, III6
spoon *la cuchara*, I
sports *los deportes*, I
sports section *la sección deportiva*, III8
to **sprain** *torcerse (ue)*, II
spring (season) *la primavera*, I
stadium *el estadio*, I
stamp *la estampilla*, II; *el sello*, III1
to **stand** *aguantar*, III7; **I can't stand anyone who . . .** *No aguanto a nadie que...*, III7; **Nobody can stand him (her/it).** *No hay quien lo (la) aguante.*, III1
to **stand in line** *hacer cola*, II
to **stand someone up** *dejar plantado(a) a alguien*, III7
star *la estrella*, II
to **start** *comenzar (ie)*, II; *empezar (ie)*, II
station (radio, TV) *la emisora*, III8
station (train) *la estación*, II
statue *la estatua*, III6
to **stay** *quedarse*, I; **to stay in front of the TV** *quedarse frente a la tele*, III2; **to stay in shape** *mantenerse (ie) en forma*, III2
steak *el bistec*, III4
stepbrother *el hermanastro*, I
stepfather *el padrastro*, I
stepmother *la madrastra*, I
stepsister *la hermanastra*, I
stereotype *el estereotipo*, III9
to **stereotype** *estereotipar*, III9
sticker *el adhesivo*, III1
still *todavía*, I; **to still be (doing something)** *seguir (i, i)*, II
stomach *el estómago*, I
to **stop** *dejar de*, II; **Stop smoking.** *Deja de fumar.*, II; **to stop speaking to each other** *dejar de hablarse*, III7
store *la tienda*, I
store clerk *el dependiente, la dependiente*, II

storm *la tormenta*, II
stove *la estufa*, II
straight *derecho (adv.)*, II
strawberry *la fresa*, I
streetlight *la lámpara de la calle*, II
stress *el estrés*, III2
stressed out *histérico(a)*, III2
to **stretch** *estirarse*, I
strict *estricto(a)*, I
striped *de rayas*, I
stroll *la caminata*, I; *el paseo*, I
strong *fuerte*, I; **as strong as an ox** *tan fuerte como un toro*, II
to **struggle for** *luchar por*, III5
studious *aplicado(a)*, II
to **study** *estudiar*, I
style *la moda*, II
subject *la materia*, I
subway *el metro*, II
to **succeed** *tener (ie) éxito*, III10; *triunfar*, III10; **He (She) succeeded in overcoming many obstacles.** *Logró superar muchos obstáculos.*, III10
success *el éxito*, III10; **I achieved success in . . .** *Alcancé éxito en...*, III10
sudden: All of a sudden . . . *De repente...*, II
to **suffer from tension** *sufrir de tensiones*, III2
sugar *el azúcar*, I
to **suggest** *sugerir (ie, i)*, III6
suit *el traje*, I; **bathing suit** *el traje de baño*, I
suitcase *la maleta*, I; **to pack the suitcase** *hacer la maleta*, I
summer *el verano*, I
sun *el sol*, II
to **sunbathe** *tomar el sol*, I
sunburn: to get a sunburn *quemarse*, II2
Sunday *el domingo*, I
sunglasses *los lentes de sol*, I
sunny *soleado(a)*, II; **to be sunny** *hacer sol*, I
sunscreen *el bloqueador*, I
to **suntan** *broncearse*, III2
superficial *superficial*, III6
supermarket *el supermercado*, I
to **support** *apoyar*, III7; **someone who'll support me** *alguien que me apoye*, III7
to **suppose** *suponer*, III9; **I suppose** *supongo*, III9
supposedly *supuestamente*, III5
sure *seguro(a)*, II
Sure! *¡Con mucho gusto!*, I
to **surf the Internet** *navegar por Internet*, III3; **to surf the Web** *navegar por la Red*, II
surprise *la sorpresa*, III8; **It caught me by surprise.** *No me lo esperaba.*, III8; **surprise party** *la fiesta de sorpresa*, I
surprised: Well, I'm not surprised. *Bueno, no me extraña.*, II

surrounded by *rodeado(a) de*, II
to **sweat** *sudar*, II
sweater *el suéter*, I
to **sweep** *barrer*, II
sweet *dulce*, I
sweet rolls *el pan dulce*, I
sweet shop *la pastelería*, I
to **swim** *nadar*, I
swimming *la natación*, I
swimming pool *la piscina*, I
system *el sistema*, II

T-shirt *la camiseta*, I
table *la mesa*, I
tag (price) *la etiqueta*, II
to **take** *tomar*, I; *llevar*, II; **to take a bath** *bañarse*, II; **to take a shower** *ducharse*, III2; **to take a trip** *hacer un viaje*, I; **to take care of** *cuidar*, I; **to take care of oneself** *cuidarse*, III2; **to take care of the cat** *cuidar al gato*, I; **to take care of your brother (sister)** *cuidar a tu hermano(a)*, I; **to take into account** *tener en cuenta*, III5; **to take notes** *tomar apuntes*, II; **to take out the garbage** *sacar la basura*, I; **to take pictures** *sacar fotos*, III1; **to take the bus** *tomar el autobús*, I; **to take the car to the gas station** *llevar el carro a la gasolinera*, II; **to take the car to the shop** *llevar el carro al taller*, II; **to take the initiative** *tomar la iniciativa*, III10; **to take the subway** *tomar el metro*, II; **to take things calmly** *tomar las cosas con calma*, III2; **Will you take them to him (her)?** *¿Se las llevas?*, III4
to **talk on the phone** *hablar por teléfono*, I
talkative *conversador(a)*, II
tall *alto(a)*, III1; **I'm . . . tall.** *Mido...*, II
taste *el sabor*, III4
to **taste: It tastes delicious.** *Sabe riquísimo(a).*, III4; **It tastes like garlic.** *Tiene sabor a ajo.*, III4
tasty *sabroso(a)*, III4; **How tasty!** *¡Qué sabroso(a)!*, III4
tea *el té*, I; **iced tea** *el té frío*, I
teacher *el profesor, la profesora*, I
technology *la tecnología*, III3
teeth *los dientes*, I; **to brush your teeth** *lavarse los dientes*, I; *cepillarse los dientes*, II
telephone *el teléfono*, I
television (medium) *la televisión*, I; **television set** *el televisor*, I

to **tell** *decir (i)*, II; **someone who'll always tell me . . .** *alguien que siempre me diga...*, III7; **Tell me.** *Dime.*, II; **Tell me about it!** *¡Cuéntamelo!*, II; **to tell jokes** *contar (ue) chistes*, II; **To tell the truth . . .** *Para decir la verdad...*, III6; **to tell you the truth** *de verdad*, II
ten *diez*, I
Ten years ago, . . . *Hace diez años,...*, III12
tennis *el tenis*, I
tennis court *la cancha de tenis*, I
tennis shoes *las zapatillas de tenis (Spain)*, I
thank you for *gracias por*, II
Thanks. *Gracias.*, I; **Thanks for inviting me.** *Gracias por invitarme.*, III6
Thanksgiving *el Día de Acción de Gracias*, I
that *que*, I
that *esa, ese, eso*, I; **That brings to mind . . .** *Eso me hace pensar en...*, III6; **That reminds me of . . .** *Eso me recuerda...*, III6; **That's all.** *Nada más.*, I; **That's it!** *¡Eso es!*, II; *Así es la cosa.*, II; **That's not so.** *No es así.*, II; **That's right.** *Así es.*, III5; *Eso es.*, III5; **That's very hard to believe, but it's possible.** *Es muy difícil de creer, pero es posible.*, III5; **That's very unlikely!** *¡Eso es muy difícil!*, III5; **That's why . . .** *Por eso...*, II
the *el, la, los, las*, I; **The bad thing is that . . .** *Lo malo es que...*, II; **The best thing is . . .** *Lo ideal es...*, III12; **The situation will get worse.** *La situación va a empeorarse.*, III11; **The solution I propose is . . .** *La solución que planteo es...*, III11; **The story goes that . . .** *Se cuenta que...*, II; **The system isn't working (doesn't work).** *El sistema no funciona.*, II; **The truth is that . . .** *La verdad es que...*, III3; **The usual!** *¡Lo de siempre!*, I
theater *el teatro*, I
their *su(s)*, I
them (direct object) *los (las)*, (after preposition) *ellos, ellas*, to (**for**) **them** *les*, II
then *luego*, I
there *allá*, I; **there are (there is)** *hay*, I; **There are five of us.** *Somos cinco.*, I; **There are more and more . . . and less and less . . .** *Cada vez hay más... y menos...*, II; **There is absolutely no doubt.** *No cabe la menor duda.*, III8; **There's going to be . . .** *Va a haber...*, III3
therefore *en consecuencia*, III10; *por lo tanto...*, III10
these *estas (adj.), estos (adj.), éstas*

(*pron.*), *éstos* (*pron.*), I

they *ellas, ellos,* I; **They are . . .** *Ellos (Ellas) son...,* I; **They blushed.** *Se pusieron rojos.,* III9; **They forgot . . .** *Se les quedó...,* III4; **They have succeeded . . .** *Han triunfado...,* III10; **they laughed** *se rieron,* III9; **They (You) like . . .** *Les gusta...,* I; **they made fun of** *se burlaron,* III9; **they reacted** *reaccionaron,* III9; **They say that . . .** *Cuentan que...,* III5; *Dicen que...,* III5; *Se dice que...,* III5; **they told me that** *me dijeron que,* II; **They're the same price.** *Son del mismo precio.,* I

thief *el ladrón, la ladrona,* III11
thigh *el muslo,* II
thin *delgado(a),* I
thing *la cosa,* I; **the + adj. + thing** *lo + adj.,* II
to **think** *pensar (ie),* I; *creer,* II; **Have you thought of . . .?** *Has pensado en...?,* III6; **to give oneself time to think** *darse tiempo para pensar,* III7; **to think (something) was great** *encontrar (ue) genial,* II; *quedar muy impresionado(a) con,* II
thirsty, to be (really) *tener (ie) (mucha) sed,* I
thirteen *trece,* I
thirty *treinta,* I
this *esta, este, esto,* I; *ésta,* II; *éste,* I; **This is (my friend) . . .** (to introduce a female) *Ésta es (mi amiga)...,* II; **This is (my friend) . . .** (to introduce a male) *Éste es (mi amigo)...,* II; **this morning** *esta mañana,* II; **This will soon pass.** *Esto pasará pronto.,* III7
those (adj.) *esas, esos,* I
thousand *mil,* I
three *tres,* I
three hundred *trescientos(as),* I
throat *la garganta,* I
to **throw out** *botar,* III3; **tirar,** II
thunder *el trueno,* II
Thursday *el jueves,* I
ticket *el boleto,* I
ticket booth *la taquilla,* II
to **tidy up** *ordenar,* II
tie *la corbata,* I
tiger *el tigre,* II
tight (clothes) *estrecho(a),* II
time (of day) *la hora,* I; (concept of) *el tiempo,* I; (repetition) *la vez,* III3; **at the same time** *a la vez,* III3; **At what time . . .?** *¿A qué hora...,* I; **I spend my time . . .** *Me la paso...,* III1; **to have a good time** *pasarlo bien,* II; **time to think** *tiempo para pensar,* III7
tip *la propina,* I
tired *cansado(a),* II
to **a,** *al (a + el), a la, para,* I; **to (for)**

her, (him/you) *le,* I; **to (for) me me,** I; **to the coast** *a la costa,* II; **to the east** *al este,* II; **to the left** *a la izquierda,* II; **to the north** *al norte,* II; **to the right** *a la derecha,* II; **to the south** *al sur,* II; **to the west** *al oeste,* II; **to them** *a ellos, a ellas,* I; **to (for) them, you (pl.)** *les,* I; **to (for) us** *nos,* I; **to you** (formal) *a ustedes,* I; **to (for) you** *te,* I
toast *el pan tostado,* I
today *hoy,* I
Today is the (date) of (month). *Hoy es el... de...,* I
toe *el dedo,* I
together *juntos(as),* I
tomato *el tomate,* I
tomorrow *mañana,* I
too *también,* I
too much *demasiado(a),* I
toothbrush *el cepillo de dientes,* II
toothpaste *la pasta de dientes,* II
tossed salad *la ensalada mixta,* III4
tourist *el turista, la turista,* II
toward *hacia,* III10
towel *la toalla,* II
tower *la torre,* II
town hall *el ayuntamiento,* III3
toy store *la juguetería,* I
toys *los juguetes,* I
track: running track *la pista de correr,* I; **train track** *la vía,* II
track and field *el atletismo,* II
traffic *el tráfico,* III3; *el tránsito,* II
traffic light *el semáforo,* II
train *el tren,* II; **train station** *la estación de tren,* II
to **train** *entrenarse,* II
trash *la basura,* II
trash can *el basurero,* III3
treat: It's my treat. *Te invito.,* I
to **treat** *tratar,* III9
tree *el árbol,* II
tremendous *formidable,* III6
trick *la travesura,* II
trivial *insignificante,* III6
trout *la trucha,* III4
true *cierto(a),* III3; **It's true that . . .** *Es cierto que...,* III3
to **trust** *confiar en,* III7
truth *la verdad,* II
truthfully *de verdad,* II
to **try** *intentar,* III6
to **try on** *probarse (ue),* II
Tuesday *el martes,* I
tuna *el atún,* I
turn: to be someone's turn *tocarle a alguien,* II
to **turn** *doblar,* II
to **turn off** *apagar,* II
to **turn out well** *salir bien,* II
turtle *la tortuga,* II
TV (set) *el televisor,* I; (medium) *la televisión,* I
twelve *doce,* I
twenty *veinte,* I
two *dos,* I; **two for one** *dos por uno,* II

two hundred *doscientos(as),* I
typical *típico(a),* II
typically *típicamente,* I

UFO (Unidentified Flying Object) *el OVNI (Objeto Volador No Identificado),* II
ugly *feo(a),* I
Uh . . . *Eh...,* III3
unbearable *insoportable,* III6
unbelievable *increíble,* III8
uncle *el tío,* I
under *debajo de,* I
to **understand** *entender (ie),* III9; **I understand that . . .** *Tengo entendido que...,* III9
unemployment *el desempleo,* III11
unfaithful *infiel,* III7
unlikely: It's unlikely that . . . *Es difícil que...,* III8
until *hasta,* II
up: to be up to someone *tocarle a alguien,* II; **to go up (a street)** *subir por,* II; **up to a certain point** *hasta cierto punto,* III5; **up to date** *al tanto de,* III8
to **update** *actualizar,* III12
urgent *urgente,* II
Uruguayan *uruguayo(a),* II
us (direct object) *nos,* I; **(object of preposition)** *nosotros(as),* I; **to (for) us** *nos,* I
to **use the computer** *usar la computadora,* II
usual: The usual! *¡Lo de siempre!,* I

vacation *las vacaciones,* I
to **vacuum** *pasar la aspiradora,* I
Valentine's Day *el Día de los Enamorados,* I
valley *el valle,* II
veal *la ternera,* III4
vegetables *las legumbres,* I
Venezuelan *venezolano(a),* II
very *muy,* I; *mucho,* II; **very bad** *muy mal,* I
victory *la victoria,* III5
videocassette player *la videocasetera,* III3
videogame *el videojuego,* I
villain *el malvado, la malvada,* III5
to **visit** *visitar,* I
volleyball *el voleibol,* I

waiter *el camarero*, I; *el mesero*, II
waitress *la camarera*, I; *la mesera*, II
to **wake up** *despertarse (ie)*, II
walk *la caminata*, I; *el paseo*, I
to **walk** *caminar*, I; **to walk the dog** *caminar con el perro*, I
wallet *la cartera*, I
to **want** *querer (ie)*, I
war *la guerra*, III5
warrior *el guerrero, la guerrera*, III5
to **wash oneself** *lavarse*, I; **to wash clothes** *lavar la ropa*, I; **to wash the car** *lavar el carro*, I
to **waste** *gastar*, II; *desperdiciar*, II
waste *el desperdicio*, II
watch *el reloj*, I
to **watch** *mirar*, I; **to watch one's weight** *cuidarse el peso*, III2; **to watch TV** *mirar la televisión*, I
water *el agua (f.)*, I; **mineral water** *el agua* **mineral**, I
to **water** *regar (ie)*, II
watermelon *la patilla* (Venezuela), III4
to **water-ski** *hacer esquí acuático*, III1
water skiing *el esquí acuático*, III1
way: No way! *¡N'hombre!*, II; *¡Qué va!*, II; **Actually, it seems to be that way.** *En efecto, parece ser así.*, III5; **to be going the right (wrong) way** *ir bien (mal)*, II
we *nosotros(as)*, I; **We don't have any more.** *No nos quedan.*, I; **We dropped . . .** *Se nos cayó (cayeron)...*, III4; **We have it in (color, size, etc.) . . .** *La tenemos en...*, II; **We like . . .** *Nos gusta(n)...*, I; **we pick up . . .** *recogemos...*, III3; **We should all . . .** *Todos deberíamos...*, II; **We'll regret it.** *Lo lamentaremos.*, III11; **We're obligated to . . .** *Estamos obligados a...*, III3
to **wear** *llevar*, I; **to wear (a size)** *usar*, II; **to wear glasses** *llevar gafas*, III1
weather *el tiempo*, I; **The weather is bad.** *Hace mal tiempo.*, I; **The weather is nice.** *Hace buen tiempo.*, I
Web page *la página Web*, II
Web site *el sitio Web*, III8
wedding *la boda*, III5
Wednesday *el miércoles*, I
week *la semana*, I
weekend *el fin de semana*, I
to **weigh oneself** *pesarse*, III2
weight *el peso*, II; **to gain weight** *aumentar de peso*, II; *subir de peso*, III2; **to lose weight** *bajar de peso*, III2
weights *las pesas*, I

well *el pozo*, II
Well . . . *Pues...*, III3; *Bueno...*, I; **Well, I have class now.** *Bueno, tengo clase.*, I; **Well, I'm not surprised.** *Bueno, no me extraña.*, II; **Well, that may be, but . . .** *Bueno, puede ser, pero...*, III5
well-being *el bienestar*, II
west *el oeste*, II; **to the west** *al oeste*, II
whale *la ballena*, II
what *lo que*, III3; **What I notice is . . .** *Lo que noto es...*, III3; **what's important** *lo que es importante*, III3;
What! *¡Qué!*, I; **What a bargain!** *¡Qué ganga!*, I; **What a drag!** *¡Qué paliza!*, III1; **What a shame!** *¡Qué lástima!*, I; **What a surprise!** *¡Qué sorpresa!*, III8
What? *¿Qué?*, III1; *¿Cómo?*, III1; *¿Cuál?*, I; **What are . . . like?** *¿Cómo son...?*, I; **What are you doing?** *¿Qué estás haciendo?*, I; **What can I bring you?** *¿Qué le puedo traer?*, I; **What can I do for you?** *¿Qué puedo hacer por ti?*, III7; **What can you tell me about . . .?** *¿Qué me cuentas de...?*, III6; **What classes do you have?** *¿Qué clases tienes?*, I; **What color is it (are they)?** *¿De qué color es (son)?*, I; **What did he (she/you) do?** *¿Qué hizo?*, I; **What did he (she) say?** *¿Qué dijo?*, II; **What did they tell you?** *¿Qué te dijeron?*, II; **What did you do?** *¿Qué hiciste?*, I; **What do you advise me to do?** *¿Qué me aconsejas hacer?*, III2; **What do you do after school?** *¿Qué haces después de clases?*, I; **What do you do on weekends?** *¿Qué hacen ustedes los fines de semana?*, I; **What do you eat for . . .?** *¿Qué tomas para...?*, I; **What do you like?** *¿Qué te gusta?*, I; **What do you like to do?** *¿Qué te gusta hacer?*, I; **What do you (emphatic) like to do?** *A ti, ¿qué te gusta hacer?*, I; **What do you prefer?** *¿Qué prefieres?*, I; **What do you recommend?** *¿Qué me recomiendas?*, II; **What do you recommend that I do?** *¿Qué me recomiendas hacer?*, III2; **What do you think about . . .?** *¿Qué te parece...?*, II; **What do you think of . . .?** *¿Qué opinas de...?*, III6; *¿Qué piensas de...?*, III6; **What do you want me to do?** *¿Qué quieres que haga?*, II; **What have you heard about . . .?** *¿Qué has oído de...?*, III6; **What if . . .?** *¿Qué tal si...?*, I; **What is the price?** *¿Qué precio tiene?*, II; **What is today's date?** *¿Cuál es la fecha?*, I; *¿Qué fecha es hoy?*, I; **What is your city like?** *¿Cómo es tu ciudad?*, II;

What shall I bring you . . .? *¿Qué le(s) traigo de...?*, II; **What should I do?** *¿Qué debo hacer?*, III2; **What time is it?** *¿Qué hora es?*, I; **What was . . . like?** *¿Cómo era...?*, II; **What would you like for . . .?** *¿Qué desea(n) de... ?*, II; **What's . . . like?** *¿Cómo es...?*, I; **What's in . . .?** *¿Qué hay en...?*, I; **What's the matter?** *¿Qué tienes?*, I; **What's the weather like?** *¿Qué tiempo hace?*, I; **What's there to drink?** *¿Qué hay para tomar?*, I; **What's wrong with . . .?** *¿Qué le pasa a...?*, I; **What's your name?** *¿Cómo te llamas?*, I
Whatever (you want). *Como quieras.*, III1
when *cuando*, I; **when . . . arrives** *cuando llegue...*, II; **when (I) finish classes** *cuando termine las clases*, II; **when (I) get a job** *cuando encuentre un empleo*, II; **when (I) get back to . . .** *cuando vuelva a...*, II; **when (I) have more money** *cuando tenga más dinero*, II; **When I turn 18 . . .** *Cuando cumpla los 18 años...*, III10; **when I was a child** *cuando era niño(a)*, II; **when I was five years old** *cuando tenía cinco años*, III12; **when I was young** *cuando era joven*, III12; **When I'm older . . .** *Cuando sea mayor...*, III10
When? *¿Cuándo?*, III1
where *donde*, I
Where? *¿Dónde?*, III1; *¿Adónde?*, I; **Where (to)?** *¿Adónde?*, I; **Where are you from?** *¿De dónde eres?*, I; **Where are you going?** *¿Adónde vas?*, I; **Where did you go?** *¿Adónde fuiste?*, I; **Where is it?** *¿Dónde queda?*, II; **Where is she (he) from?** *¿De dónde es?*, I
which *que*, I
Which? *¿Cuál?*, I; **Which is your favorite class?** *¿Cuál es tu clase favorita?*, I
white *blanco(a)*, I
white-haired *canoso(a)*, II
who *que*, I; **. . . who's rude.** *...que sea descortés.*, III7
who? *¿quién(es)?* III1; **Who likes . . .?** *¿A quién le gusta...?*, I; **Who's calling?** *¿De parte de quién?*, I
whole *entero(a)*, II
Whose turn is it? *¿A quién le toca?*, II
why: That's why . . . *Por eso...*, II
Why? *¿Por qué?*, III1; **Why don't . . .?** *¿Por qué no...*, I; **Why don't we leave it for . . .?** *¿Por qué no lo dejamos para...?*, III6; **Why don't you . . .?** *¿Por qué no...?*, II
wife *la esposa*, I
will: will continue *continuará*, III11; **will improve . . .** *mejorará...*, III3; **will speak . . .** *hablará...*, III3;

Will you take them to him (her)? *¿Se las llevas?*, III4
to **win** *ganar*, I
window *la ventana*, I
to **window-shop** *mirar las vitrinas*, II
windsurfing *la tabla de vela*, II; **to go windsurfing** *pasear en velero*, III1
winter *el invierno*, I
to **wish** *querer (ie)*, I
with *con*, I; **to go with** *acompañar (a)*, II; **with me** *conmigo*, I; **with the intention of** *con la intención de*, III10; **with you** *contigo*, I
within (a day, month, ...) *dentro de (un día, un mes,...)*, II
Without a doubt. *Sin duda alguna.*, III8
woman *la mujer*, III5
wool (made of) *de lana*, I
work *el trabajo*, I
to **work** *trabajar*, I; **to work in the garden** *trabajar en el jardín*, I
work hours *el horario*, III12
workplace environment *el ambiente de trabajo*, III12
workshop *el taller*, III4
World Wide Web *el Web, la Telaraña Mundial*, II
worn out *agobiado(a)*, III2; *rendido(a)*, III2
worried *preocupado(a)*, II; **to be worried (about something)** *estar preocupado(a) (por algo)*, I
to **worry** *preocuparse*, III7; **Don't worry.** *No te preocupes.*, I
worse *peor*, II; **to get worse**

empeorarse, III3; **worse than** *peor que*, II
worst *el peor, la peor*, II
worth it *vale la pena*, III3
would: Would you be so kind as to give it to me? *¿Sería(s) tan amable de dármela?*, III4; **Would you care for anything else?** *¿Se le(s) ofrece algo más?*, II; **Would you like ...?** *¿Te gustaría...?*, I; **Would you like anything else?** *¿Desean algo más?*, I
wrist *la muñeca*, II
to **write** *escribir*, I; **to write down** *apuntar*, II
to write papers on the computer *hacer trabajos con la computadora*, III3
writer *el escritor, la escritora*, III12
written *escrito*, III3
wrong: You're wrong! *¡Te equivocas!*, II

year *el año*, I; **last year** *el año pasado*, I; **New Year's Day** *El Día del Año Nuevo*, I; **New Year's Eve** *La Nochevieja*, I
yellow *amarillo(a)*, I
yes *sí*, I; **Yes, I like it.** *Sí, me gusta.*, I; **Yes, you're right.** *Sí, tienes razón.*, II
yesterday *ayer*, I

yet *todavía*, I
yoga *el yoga*, I
you *tú, vosotros(as)* **(informal)**, *usted, ustedes*, I; **you (informal) are** *eres*, I; **You are going the wrong way.** *Van mal.*, II; **You can't miss it.** *No se puede perder.*, II; **You don't say!** *¡No me digas!*, III8; **you found out** *supiste*, III9; **you have to** *hay que*, II; **you like** *te gusta(n)*, I; **You look very handsome (pretty).** *Te ves guapísimo(a).*, II; **You ought to ...** *Debes...*, II; **You should ...** *Debes...*, III12; *Deberías + inf.*, III2; **You shouldn't ...** *No debes + inf.*, III2; **You think so?** *¿Tú crees?*, II; **you (informal) want** *quieres*, I; **You're wrong!** *¡Te equivocas!*, II
young *joven*, I
younger *menor*, I; **younger than** *menor que*, II
your *tu, tus, su, sus, vuestro(a)*, I
youth hostel *el albergue juvenil*, II
Yuck! *¡Guácala!*, III4

zero *cero*, I
zone *la zona*, III3; **pedestrian zone** *la zona peatonal*, III3
zoo *el zoológico*, II

Grammar Index

This grammar index includes topics introduced in *¡Ven conmigo!* Levels 1, 2, and 3. The Roman numeral I preceding the page numbers indicates Level 1; the Roman numeral II indicates Level 2; and the Roman numeral III indicates Level 3. Page numbers in boldface type refer to **Gramática** and **Nota gramatical** presentations. Other page numbers refer to grammar structures presented in the **Así se dice, Nota cultural, Vocabulario, ¿Te acuerdas?** and **A lo nuestro** sections. Page numbers beginning with R refer to the Grammar Summary in this reference section (pages R100–R104).

a: I: 149, 269, 275, 334; after **conocer** II: 106; verbs followed by II: **231**, R30; with **alguien** and **nadie** II: 332; III: **205**; see also prepositions

accent marks: I: 5, **23**

adjectives: agreement—masculine and feminine I: 93; II: 10, **11**; III: 17, R24; singular and plural I: **58, 93**; II: 10, **11**; III: R24; demonstrative adjectives all forms I: 279; III: R24; possessive adjectives all forms I: **174**; III: R25; stressed possessive adjectives III: R25; with -**ísimo(a)** II: **225**; III: **101**, R26

adónde: I: **123**; see also question words

adverbs: adverbs ending in -**mente** II: **74**; III: R27; adverbs of frequency—**muchas veces, nunca, siempre, sólo cuando, todos los días** I: 145; **a menudo, cada día, de vez en cuando, todo el tiempo, una vez** I: 151; **a veces, normalmente, por lo general** II: 73; adverbs of place—**allí, aquí** II: **74**; adverbs of sequence—**después, luego, primero** I: 84, 361; **a continuación, para empezar, por último** II: 168; adverbs of time— **de la mañana, de la tarde, de la noche,** I: 88; **todavía** I: 145; **ya** I: 52, 85, 217; II: 42; **por la mañana, por la tarde, por la noche** I: 151; **anoche, ayer, la semana pasada** I: 307; **hoy, mañana** II: **74**

affirmative expressions: III: R25; **algo** I: 180, 246, 274, 334; **alguien** II: 332; **algún** II: 350; **alguna(s), o...o; sí** I: 32, 85; II: 21; **siempre** I: 145, 180; II: 73, 332; **también** I: 24; II: 134

al: contraction of **a** + **el** I: 114, 119, 123; III: R22; see also prepositions

algo: I: 180, 246, 274, 334

almorzar: I: **238, 362**; II: **46** see also stem-changing verbs

-**ando:** I: **299**; III: R31

articles: see definite articles, indefinite articles

caerse: II: **291**

calendar expressions: dates I: 154; days of the week I: 124

commands (imperatives): I: 90, 92; III: R35; formal command forms of verbs ending in -**gar**, -**car**, -**zar** II: **140, 260**; formal command forms of irregular verbs: **dar, estar, ir, saber, ser** II: **260**; formal command forms of reflexive verbs II: **260**; formal command forms of regular and irregular verbs II: **260**; informal commands, positive and negative: II: 138, **139**; III: **38**; introduction to informal commands I: **304**; irregular informal commands, positive: III: 38; irregular informal commands, positive and negative: **decir, hacer, ir, poner, salir, ser, tener, venir** II: 138, **140**; III: 38, R35; **nosotros** commands II: **334**; III: **172**, R35

cómo: I: **30**, 92, 178; III: 16

comparisons: comparing quality using **mejor/peor...que** II: 107; comparing age using **menor/mayor...que** II: 107; of inequality using adjectives with **más...que, menos...que** I: **277**; II: 107; III: 80, R26; of equality using adjectives with **tan...como** I: 277; II: 206, **207**; III: 80, R26; of equality using nouns with **tanto(s)...como** or **tanta(s)...como** II: **207**; III: 80, R26; see also superlatives

con: I: **104**; see also prepositions

conditional: III: 233, **313**, R28; hypothetical statements III: 232, 286; irregular stems III: 233; regular -**ar, -er, -ir** verbs III: **233**, 313, R28; uses III: **233, 313**; with the past subjunctive III: **287, 313**

conjunctions: **o** I: 132, 245, 247; II: **177**; use of **u** instead II: **177**; III: **18; pero** I: 32, 193; **porque** I: 87; **y** I: 193; II: 177; use of **e** instead II: **177**; III: **18**; subordinating conjunction: see **que**

conmigo: I: **116**

conocer: present tense all forms II: **106**; preterite III: 257; vs. **saber** II: **165**; III: **18**, R42

contigo: I: **116**

contractions: see **al** and **del**

creer: preterite tense all forms II: **291**

cuál(es): I: 95, 154, 277, 279; see also question words

cuando: I: 145

cuándo: II: **29**; III: 16; see also question words

cuánto(a): agreement with nouns I: **58**, 174, 246, 280; see also question words

cuántos(as): I: **30**, 280; see also question words

dar: preterite tense all forms II: **136**; III: R32; formal command forms II: 228

dates (calendar): I: **154**

days of the week: I: **124**

de: used in showing possession I: **89**; used with color I: **178**; used with material or pattern I: **275**; verbs followed by II: **231**; when expressing superlatives II: **227**

de dónde: I: **30**; III: 16; see also question words

deber: present tense all forms I: **184**; II: **101**

deberías vs. **debes:** II: **101**

decir: followed by the imperfect II: **236**; positive and negative **tú** commands II: **140**; preterite tense II: **236**; followed by the imperfect II: **236**; subjunctive III: 205

definite articles: all forms III: R22; **el, la** I: **33**; **los, las** I: **83** irregular use of III: **163**

del: contraction of **de + el** I: **89**; III: R22

demonstrative adjectives: all forms I: **279**; III: R24

demonstrative pronouns: see pronouns

diminutives: I: 187

direct object pronouns: see pronouns

doler: with parts of the body I: **336**; see also stem-changing verbs

dónde: I: 28, **30**, 118, 271; III: 16; see also question words

dormir: preterite tense all forms II: **134**; see also stem-changing verbs

durante: I: 145; see also prepositions

e: conjunction instead of **y:** II: 201; III: **18**

e → i stem-changing verbs: III: **11**, R37

e → ie stem-changing verbs: I: **209**, 362; II: **46**; III: **11**, R37; stem-changing verbs in the preterite: II: **174**; see also stem-changing verbs

el: I: 33; see also definite articles

empezar: I: **209**, 362; II: **46**; III: **11**; see also stem-changing verbs

en: as "on" I: **88**; as "at" I: 145; see also prepositions

encantar: I: 236

estar: contrasted with **ser** I: 240, 369; II: 105; III: R42; **estar +** present participle I: **299**; present tense all forms I: **118**; II: **39**, to ask how someone is and say how you are I: **24**, to talk about how things taste, look or feel I:**240**, to tell where people and things are located I: **118**; II: 49, **105**; preterite II: 225; III: 257, all forms III: **258**; see commands, formal command forms of irregular verbs

frequency: adverbs of—**muchas veces, nunca, siempre, sólo cuando, todavía, todos los días** I: 145; **a menudo, cada día, de vez en cuando, todo el tiempo, una vez** I: 151; **a veces, normalmente, por lo general** II: 73; see also adverbs

future plans: expressions in the present tense I: 362; III: 349

future tense: III: 78, **79**, 349, R33; irregular stems III: **79**, R33

gender of nouns: I: 33, **51**, **53**; III: R22

giving the date: I: **154**

gustar: all forms III: R41; likes and dislikes I: 32, 95, 113, 148; II: 21; telling what one would like I: 367

haber: future tense III: **79**; present subjunctive III: **198**; used with the present perfect tense III: **72**; see **hay**; see also imperfect tense

hacer: hace + amount of time + preterite III: 347; **hace** + amount of time + **que** + present tense to say how long someone has been doing something II: **82**; III: R29; **hacer** with weather I: 156, 157; III: R29; future tense III: **79**; past subjunctive III: **327**; present tense all forms (including irregular **yo** form) I: **180**; preterite I: 307, 340, 371

hay: I: 57, 174, 235; subjunctive III: **225**

iendo: I: **299**; III: R31

imperative mood: III: R35; see also commands

imperatives: see commands

imperfect tense: contrasted with the preterite II: **290**; III: 348; introduction II: **196**; irregular verbs: **ir, ver** II: **196**; III: 47 **ser** II: 202, **203**; III: 47 **haber** II: 204; regular verbs II: **196**, 198; III: **47**, R27; to say how people were feeling III: **258**; uses III: **348**; used to set the scene for a story II: 289; with the preterite to express an action in progress or describe the conditions of a particular event II: **290**; with the preterite to tell a story II: **296**

indefinite articles: all forms III: R23; **un, una** I: **51**, 53; unos, unas I: **53**

indicative mood: III: R31; after expressions of truth or certainty III: 232, **259**; in open-ended if clauses III: 327

indirect object pronouns: see pronouns

infinitives: I: **61**, 363; III: R30; after expressions of need III: 164; after prepositions III: **293**; definition of I: **61**; with expressions of feeling III: **196**; with recommendations III: **170**

informal commands: see commands

interrogatives: see question words

ir: commands, irregular informal II: **138**, **140**; formal II: **260**; imperfect tense all forms II: **197**; III: **47**; **ir** (in the imperfect) + **a** II: **232**; III: **81**; present tense all forms I: **123**; ir a + infinitive I: 208, **212**, 363; II: 17; III: 349; past subjunctive III: 327, 357; preterite tense all forms I: **342**, **371**; II: 45; R32

irregular verbs: III: R39–R41

-ísimo(a): II: **225**; III: 101; see also superlatives

ACKNOWLEDGMENTS

For permission to reprint copyrighted material, grateful acknowledgment is given to the following sources:

American Cancer Society, Inc.: Adaptation of "Quémate ahora, paga después" from the title page of American Cancer Society brochure, 1986. Copyright © by American Cancer Society, Inc.

Américas: From "Una causa picante" by Jack Robertiello from *Américas*, vol. 46, no. 1, January/February 1994. Copyright © 1994 by Américas, a bimonthly magazine published by the General Secretariat of the Organization of American States in English and Spanish.

Agencia Literaria Carmen Balcells, S.A.: "La tortuga" from *Las Piedras de Chile* by Pablo Neruda. Copyright © 1961 by the Fundación Pablo Neruda.

Bienestar: Adaptation from "17 Claves para manejar el estrés" (retitled "Cómo aliviar el estrés: 10 cosas esenciales") from *Bienestar*, no. 9. Copyright © by Bienestar: Organización Sanitas Internacional.

Maia A. Chávez: "Gringa/Chicana" by Maia Chávez from *Imagine*, no. 1, edited by Tino Villanueva.

Marco Denevi: Adapted from "Las abejas de bronce" by Marco Denevi.

Ediciones Destino, S.A.: From "El árbol de oro" from *Historias de Artámila* by Ana María Matute.

Editora Cinco, S.A.: Adapted from "Reír es bueno" from "Medicina noticias" from *En Forma*, año 6, no. 60, January 1993. Copyright © 1993 by Editora Cinco. S.A.

Editorial Armonía, S.A.: From "Cómo mantener vivas las buenas amistades" from *Kena Tips*, año 15, no. 10, 1991. Copyright © 1991 by Editorial Armonía, S.A.

Editorial Atlántida, S.A.: From "Superniña alpinista" from *Billiken*, no. 3740, September 16, 1991. Copyright © 1991 by Editorial Atlántida, S.A. Text and photograph from "Maratón a los 80" from *Billiken*, no. 3753, December 16, 1991. Copyright © 1991 by Editorial Atlántida, S.A. From "Historia del siglo XX" from *Billiken*, no. 3755, December 30, 1991. Copyright © 1991 by Editorial Atlántida, S.A. From "La escuela en la tele" de *Billiken*, no. 3765, March 9, 1992. Copyright © 1992 by Editorial Atlántida, S.A. From "Los chicos periodistas" from *Billiken*, no. 3789, August 24, 1992. Copyright © 1992 by Editorial Atlántida, S.A. "Cada pueblo, un desarrollo" from *Billiken*, no. 3795, October 5, 1992. Copyright © 1992 by Editorial Atlántida, S.A.

Editorial Atlántida, S.A.: From "La electricidad que viene del cielo" from *Conozca más*, año 4, no. 12, December 1, 1993. Copyright © 1993 by Editorial Atlántida, S.A. From "La 'tele' que le cambiará la vida" from *Conozca más*, año 4, no. 12, December 1, 1993. Copyright © 1993 by Editorial Atlántida, S.A.

Editorial Eres, S.A. de C.V.: Adapted from "Luis Miguel: 5 Años con Eres!" from *Eres*, Special Edition, año 6, no. 126, September 16, 1993. Copyright © 1993 by Editorial Eres, S.A. de C.V. Adaptation of "Maná" from *Somos*, año 4, no. 87, December 16, 1993. Copyright © 1993 by Editorial Eres, S.A. de C.V.

Editorial Televisa, S.A.: Adapted from "Para hacer las paces" from *Tú Internacional*, año 11, no. 11, November 1990. Copyright © 1990 by Editorial Televisa, S.A. From "El ejercicio, los alimentos..." from *Tú Internacional*, año 13, no. 10, October 1992. Copyright © 1992 by Editorial Televisa, S.A. "Mi 'escape' favorito..." from *Tú Internacional*, año 13, no. 12, December 1992. Copyright © 1992 by Editorial Televisa, S.A. "Estrategias para triunfar" from *Tú internacional*, año 14, no. 1, January 1993. Copyright © 1993 by Editorial Televisa, S.A. Adapted from "Test: ¿Equilibrada o descontrolada? from *Tú Internacional*, año 14, no. 7, July 1993. Copyright © 1993 by Editorial Televisa, S.A. Adapted from "Él te tiene loca...pero dudas si es fiel..." (retitled "Un novio infiel") from *Tú Internacional*, año 14, no. 11, November 1993. Copyright © 1993 by Editorial Televisa, S.A.

Espasa-Calpe, S.A., Madrid and Andrés Palma Michelson: From "La camisa de Margarita" from *Tradiciones Peruanas*, Tomo III, by Ricardo Palma. Copyright 1946 by Ricardo Palma.

G y J España Ediciones S.L., S. en C.: From "Claves para ver mejor la televisión" and from "La tele recrea situaciones idénticas a las de la vida real" from *Muy Interesante*, no. 197, October 1997. Copyright © 1997 by G y J España Ediciones S.L., S. en C.

Rodolfo Gonzales: From *I am Joaquín/Yo soy Joaquín: An Epic Poem* by Rodolfo Gonzales. Copyright © 1967 by Rodolfo Gonzales.

D.C. Heath and Company: "Signos de puntuación" by M. Toledo y Benito from *Repaso y composición*. Copyright 1947 by D.C. Heath and Company.

Seymour Menton: "El monopolio de la moda" by Luis Britto García from *El Cuento Hispanoamericano: Antología Crítico-Histórica* by Seymour Menton. Copyright © 1964, 1986 by Fondo de Cultura Económica, S.A. de C.V.

La Nación, San José, Costa Rica: From "Pedaleando por la vida" by Andrés Formoso from La Nación, April 4, 1994. Copyright © 1994 by La Nación.

National Textbook Co.: "Quetzal no muere nunca" from Leyendas Latinoamericanas by Genevieve Barlow. Copyright © 1970 by National Textbook Co.

Núcleo Radio Mil: From Radio schedule for "Radio 1000 AM" from Excelsior, November 3, 1994.

Sociedad Mixta de Turismo y Festejos de Gijón, S.A.: From "Festival Internacional de Cine de Gijón," from brochure, Gijón, Verano 88.

University of Oklahoma Press: From "The Viceroy and the Indian" from Of the Night Wind's Telling: Legends from the Valley of Mexico by E. Adams Davis. Copyright © 1946 by the University of Oklahoma Press.

Martha Zamora: Adapted from "Por qué se pintaba Frida Kahlo" by Martha Zamora from Imagine, vol. II, no. 1, 1985. Copyright © 1985 by Martha Zamora.

PHOTOGRAPHY CREDITS

Abbreviations used: (t), top, (b), bottom, (c), center, (l), left, (r), right, (bkgd) background. All other locations are noted with descriptor.

All photographs belong to Holt, Rinehart and Winston by Martha Granger/Edge Video Productions except:

vii (b), Sam Dudgeon/HRW; viii (t), Sam Dudgeon/HRW; ix (br), Daniel J. Schaefer; xii (bc), Sam Dudgeon/HRW; xv (tl), Michelle Bridwell/Frontera Fotos; 62-63 (bkgd), G. Martin/SuperStock; 64 (tr), Manley/SuperStock; 65 (tl), Luis Villota/Corbis Stock Market; 65 (tc), G. De Steinheil/SuperStock; 65 (cr), David J. Sams/Texas Inprint; 64 (bl), ©Robert Frerck/Odyssey/Chicago; viii (bc), Corbis Stock Market; ix (t), Stone/Jon Bradley; x (t), Manley/SuperStock; x (b), Michael Moody/D. Donne Bryant Photography; xii (cr), ©Robert Frerck/Odyssey/Chicago; xiii (cl), Francisco J. Rangel; xiv (t), S. Poulin/SuperStock; xiv (b), Chip & Rosa María de la Cueva Peterson; xv (t), ©Ricardo Carrasco-Stuparich; xvi (b), James Davis/International Stock Photography; xvii (t), Robert Brenner/PhotoEdit; xviii (t), Brenda Tharp/F-Stock, Inc.; xviii (b), NASA/GSFC/NOAA/USGS; xix (t), Leon Duque/Duque Múnera y Cia; xx (c), ©Robert Frerck/Odyssey/Chicago; xxii (c), David J. Sams/Texas Inprint; xvi (t), SuperStock; xvii (b), Bruce Laurance/Courtesy of Ballet Hispanico of New York; xxix (border), Joe Viesti/Viesti Collection, Inc.; 0-1 (bkgd), Robert Frerck/Corbis Stock Market; 2 (tr), ©Robert Frerck/Odyssey/Chicago; 2 (cr), Tibor Bognar/Corbis Stock Market; 2 (bl), P & G Bowater/The Image Bank; 2 (border), Joe Viesti/Viesti Collection, Inc.; 3 (tl), Tibor Bognar/Corbis Stock Market; 3 (tr), K. Gibson/SuperStock; 3 (bl), Charles Mahaux/Image Bank; 4-5 (bc), Stephen Frink/Corbis Stock Market; 5 (border), Joe Viesti/Viesti Collection, Inc.; 6 (bl), Compact disc cover from Puntos Cardiales by Ana Torroja © 1997 BMG Music, Spain, S.A., photos by Eddie Monsoon; 6 (tl), Michelle Bridwell/Frontera Fotos; 6 (cr), Tony Stone Images; 7 (br), Dennie Cody/FPG International; 7 (cr), Daniel J. Schaefer; 8 (c), Scott Markewitz/FPG International; 12 (tc), Kevin Syms/David R. Frazier Photolibrary; 14 (tr), R. Heinzen/SuperStock; 14 (bl), Robert Frerck/Corbis Stock Market; 14 (br), Kevin Syms/David R. Frazier Photolibrary; 17 (tl), Corbis Stock Market; 17 (l), Michelle Bridwell/Frontera Fotos; 17 (cl, r), Daniel J. Schaefer; 17 (cr), Michael Newman/Photo Edit; 22 (tr), N/S/Sovfoto/Eastfoto/PNI; 29 (tl), Tom Stewart/Corbis Stock Market; 29 (tc, tr), Michelle Bridwell/Frontera Fotos; 30 (br), Michelle Bridwell/Frontera Fotos; 32-33 (bkgd), Stone/Jon Bradley; 33 (border), Joe Viesti/Viesti Collection, Inc.; 35 (tl), Sam Dudgeon/HRW; 35 (tl), Tom and DeeAnn McCarthy/Corbis Stock Market; 35 (tr), Ronnie Kaufman/Corbis Stock Market; 35 (cr), Paul Barton/Corbis Stock Market; 35 (br, bl), Michael Heron/Corbis Stock Market; 35 (cl), P.R. Production/SuperStock; 37 (all), Michelle Bridwell/Frontera Fotos; 42 (all), John Langford/HRW; 46 (r), Bob Daemmrich Photo, Inc.; 46 (cl), Daniel J. Schaefer; 46 (cr), Michelle Bridwell/Frontera Fotos; 48 (tr), Michelle Bridwell/Frontera Fotos; 50 (tr, tl), Michelle Bridwell/Frontera Fotos; 50 (br), David R. Frazier Photolibrary; 51 (tl), Pictor Uniphoto; 56 (br), John Langford/HRW; 58 (all), Michelle Bridwell/Frontera Fotos; 60 (bl, br), Michelle Bridwell/Frontera Fotos; 60 (bc), David Madison; 62-63 (bkgd), Sam Dudgeon/HRW; 64 (border), Sam Dudgeon/HRW; 66-67 (all), Michael Moody/D. Donne Bryant Photography; 67 (border), Sam Dudgeon/HRW; 76 (cl), Robert Fried; 77 (tl), T. Rosenthal/SuperStock; 78 (tr), SuperStock; 78 (bl), Marty Granger/Edge Video Productions/HRW; 79 (all), Daniel J. Schaefer; 83 (bkgd), HRW Photo; 84 (br, tr), Sam Dudgeon/HRW; 84 (bl), Jeff Zaruba/Corbis Stock Market; 85 (mannequins), Bill Ross/Corbis; 85 (ties), Sam Dudgeon/HRW; 85 (phone), Digital imagery® copyright 2003 PhotoDisc, Inc.; 85 (women's shoes), Sam Dudgeon/HRW; 85 (blender), Digital imagery® copyright 2003 PhotoDisc, Inc.; 85 (car), Sam Dudgeon/HRW; 85 (athletic shoes, tv), Greg Geisler/HRW; 86 (diamonds), Index Stock Photography, Inc.; 86 (nail polish), Spencer Jones/FPG International; 86 (lipstick, watches), Sam Dudgeon/HRW; 86 (chairs), Ryo Konno/Photonica; 86 (toy 1, toy 2, toy 4), Ken Karp/HRW Photo; 86 (toy 3), J. Good/HRW Photo; 86 (table), Greg Geisler/HRW; 86 (cellular phone), Digital imagery® copyright 2003 PhotoDisc, Inc.; 91 (t), Sam Dudgeon/HRW; 94 (cl), Underwood & Underwood/Corbis-Bettmann; 94 (cr),

Photoworld/FPG International; 96-97 (bkgd), Sam Dudgeon/HRW; 97 (border), Sam Dudgeon/HRW; 102 (salad), HRW Photo; 102 (fish, trout, cake), ©Stockbyte; 102 (clams, carrot), Digital imagery® copyright 2003 PhotoDisc, Inc.; 102 (steak), Russell Dian/HRW; 102 (cantaloupe), Corbis Images; 104 (br), Bob Daemmrich/The Image Works; 105 (cr), Dirk Weisheit/D. Donne Bryant Photography; 105 (br), Branda J. Latvala/D. Donne Bryant Photography; 109 (pastelería), Arturo Salinas/HRW; 109 (la pescadería), Sam Dudgeon/HRW; 109 (el taller), Eric Beggs/HRW; 109 (all others), Digital imagery® copyright 2003 PhotoDisc, Inc.; 111 (c), M.L. Miller/Edge Video Productions/HRW; 111 (cl), Marty Granger/Edge Video Productions/HRW; 112 (c), G. Nieto/SuperStock; 114 (c), ©Robert Frerck/Odyssey/Chicago; 117 (br), Pictor Uniphoto; 119 (tr), David Phillips/Words & Images; 124 (border), ©Robert Frerck/Odyssey/Chicago; 124-125 (bkgd), John Mitchell/D. Donne Bryant Photography; 126 (tr), Tim Street-Porter; 126 (bl, br, border), ©Robert Frerck/Odyssey/Chicago; 127 (cr), Suzanne Murphy-Larronde/D. Donne Bryant Photography; 127 (tl), Rick Strange/Index Stock Imagery, Inc.; 127 (bl), Compact disc cover from Falta Amor by the group Maná, © Warner Music México S.A. de C.V.; 128-129 (bkgd), ©Robert Frerck/Odyssey/Chicago; 129 (border), ©Robert Frerck/Odyssey/Chicago; 132 (bl), ©Robert Frerck/Odyssey/Chicago; 135 (all), ©Robert Frerck/Odyssey/Chicago; 137 (bkgd), HRW Photo; 142 (b), John Neubauer/PhotoEdit; 150 (b), Sam Dudgeon/HRW; 152 (cl), Michelle Bridwell/Frontera Fotos; 156-157 (bkgd), Francisco J. Rangel; 157 (border), ©Robert Frerck/Odyssey/Chicago; 158 (tr), Porterfield/Chickering; 158 (br), ©Robert Frerck/Odyssey/Chicago; 158 (bl), Michelle Bridwell/Frontera Fotos; 159 (all), ©Robert Frerck/Odyssey/Chicago; 160 (bl), ©Robert Frerck/Odyssey/Chicago; 161 (bkgd), HRW Photo; 166 (tr), Alejandro Xul Solar, Uno, 1920, Watercolor and pencil on paper on card, 6-1/2 X 8-1/4 inches. Courtesy, Rachel Adler Gallery, New York.; 166 (cl), Fernando Botero, National Holiday, oil on canvas, 671/2 X 38 1/2 inches. Private Collection, Courtesy, Marlborough Gallery ; 166 (br), CORBIS/Christie's Images; 167 (c, cl), Suzanne Murphy-Larronde; 167 (tc), Sam Dudgeon/HRW; 167 (cr), James M. Mejuto; 167 (bkgd), HRW Photo; 168 (cl), Sam Dudgeon/HRW; 169 (tl), Larry Mulvehill; 171 (l), Nik Wheeler; 171 (cr, cl), ©Robert Frerck/Odyssey/Chicago; 171 (r), Porterfield/Chickering; 171 (br), Chuck Savage/Corbis Stock Market; 171 (bl, cl, cr), Michelle Bridwell/Frontera Fotos; 174 (br), Archive Photos; 175 (bl), Frida Kahlo. Frieda and Diego Rivera, 1931. San Francisco Museum of Modern Art/Albert M. Bender Collection. Gift of Albert M. Bender.; 176 (tc) Kahlo, Frida Fulang-Chang and I. 1937. Two-part ensemble (assembled after 1939) Part one: 1937, oil on composition board, 15 3/4 x 11" (39.9 x 27.9 cm), painted mirror frame (added after 1939), 22 1/4 x 17 3/8 x 1 3/4" (56.6 x 44.1 x 4.5 cm). Part two, (after 1939) mirror with painted mirror frame. 25 1/4 x 19 1/8 x 1 3/4" (64.1 x 48.5 x 4.4 cm), including frame. The Museum of Modern Art, New York. Mary Sklar Bequest. Photograph ©2001 The Museum of Modern Art, New York; 176 (br), Sam Dudgeon/HRW; 178 (bl), James M. Mejuto; 178 (br), Sam Dudgeon/HRW; 180 (cl), Steve Allen/Liaison Agency; 182 (br), Rick Reinhard/Impact Visuals; 184 (cr), Tim Street-Porter; 186-187 (bkgd), SuperStock; 186 (border), Beryl Goldberg Photography; 188 (tr), W. Woodworth/SuperStock; 188 (b), Joe Viesti /Viesti Collection; 188 (border), Beryl Goldberg Photography; 189 (cr), P.L. Raotoa/SuperStock; 189 (bl), SuperStock; 189 (tl), S. Poulin/SuperStock; 189 (br), Alejandro Xul Solar, horoscopo, 1927, watercolor on paper laid down on card, 6-5/8 x 9 inches. Courtesy Rachel Adler Gallery, New York.; 190-191 (bkgd), Chip & Rosa María de la Cueva Peterson; 191 (border), Beryl Goldberg Photography; 193 (tl), Jim Sparks/Tony Stone Images; 194 (c), Michael Newman/Photo Edit; 194 (cr), Joe Polillio/Liaison International; 200 (all), Michelle Bridwell/Frontera Fotos; 201 (tr), Michelle Bridwell/Frontera Fotos; 202 (cl), Lynn Sheldon Jr./D. Donne Bryant Photography; 202 (cr), D. Donne Bryant/D. Donne Bryant Photography; 215 (tr), Michelle Bridwell/Frontera Fotos; 215 (br), David Young-Wolff/PhotoEdit; 215 (bl), Josy Sturino/Allsport; 220-221 (bkgd), ©Ricardo Carrasco-Stuparich; 221 (border), Beryl Goldberg Photography; 222 (br), Michelle Bridwell/Frontera Fotos; 223 (tc), Bill Gallery/Stock Boston/PNI; 229 (bkgd), HRW Photo; 230 (tl), Nancy Humbach/HRW; 234 (l), Reuters/Enrique Marcarian/Archive Photos; 234 (cl), Steve Allen/Gamma Liaison; 234 (cr), Sichov/Sipa Press; 234 (r), V. Fernandez/Shooting Star International ; 235 (bl), Michelle Bridwell/Frontera Fotos; 235 (bc, br), Daniel J. Schaefer; 242 (bl), Michelle Bridwell/Frontera Fotos; 242 (br), Nancy Humbach/HRW; 243 (b), Michelle Bridwell/Frontera Fotos; 248-249 (bkgd), Corbis Images; 248 (girl), Suzanne Murphy-Larronde/D. Donne Bryant Photography; 248 (Statue of Liberty), Digital imagery® copyright 2003 PhotoDisc, Inc.; 248 (all others), Corbis Images; 250 (tr), Digital imagery copyright 2003 Photo Disc, Inc.; 250 (br), Charles Erickson/Courtesy of El Museo de Barrio; 250 (bl), Andrea Brizzi/Corbis Stock Market; 250 (girl), Suzanne Murphy-Larronde/D. Donne Bryant Photography; 250 (Statue of Liberty), Digital imagery® copyright 2003 PhotoDisc, Inc.; 250 (all others), Corbis Images; 251 (cl), E. Carle/SuperStock; 251 (tc), Sapinsky/Corbis Stock Market; 251 (cl), Alan Schein/Corbis Stock Market; 251 (br), David Hundley/Corbis Stock Market; 252-253 (bkgd), James Davis/International Stock Photography; 253 (girl), Suzanne Murphy-Larronde/D. Donne Bryant Photography; 253 (Statue of Liberty), Digital imagery® copyright 2003 PhotoDisc, Inc.; 253 (all others), Corbis Images; 254 (all), Nancy Humbach/HRW; 255 (all), Nancy Humbach/HRW; 261 (bkgd), HRW Photo; 269 (cr), Archive Photos; 273 (br), Sam Dudgeon/HRW; 277 (l),

Michael Newman/Photo Edit; 277 (c), Michelle Bridwell/ Frontera Fotos; 277 (r), Sam Dudgeon/HRW; 280-281 (bkgd), Robert Brenner/PhotoEdit; 281 (girl), Suzanne Murphy-Larronde/D. Donne Bryant Photography; 281 (Statue of Liberty), Digital imagery® copyright 2003 PhotoDisc, Inc.; 281 (all others), Corbis Images; 282 (all), Dora Villani/HRW; 283 (all), Dora Villani/HRW; 284 (Paul), Sam Dudgeon/HRW; 284 (all others), Dora Villani/HRW; 285 (br), Scarborough/Shooting Star International ; 286 (br), Albert Ortega Photography; 286 (tr), Wide World Photos; 286 (bl), Mitchell Layton/ Duomo Photography; 286 (bc), Steve Granitz/Retna, Ltd.; 286 (tc), Shooting Star International ; 286 (tl), Chris Trotman/Duomo Photography; 287 (cl), Mary Kate Denny/Photo Edit; 287 (cr), Bob Daemmrich/The Image Works; 287 (br), Bill Aron/Tony Stone Images; 288 (tr), Charles Erickson/Courtesy of El Museo del Barrio; 290 (tr), Michael Newman/PhotoEdit; 292 (border), HRW Photo; 292 (bkgd), HRW Photo; 292 (c), M.L.Miller/Edge Video Productions/HRW; 296 (cr), Richard Hutchings/ Photo Edit; 297 (l,r), Bruce Laurance/Courtesy of Ballet Hispanico of New York; 297 (bkgd), HRW Photo; 298 (cr), Mary Altier; 300 (tc), K. Kummels/SuperStock; 302 (bl), Sam Dudgeon/HRW; 302 (br), Michelle Bridwell/ Frontera Fotos; 305 (tr), SuperStock; 305 (b), Alan Schein/Corbis Stock Market; 310-311 (bkgd), Buddy Mays/Travel Stock; 310 (border), Robert Fried; 312 (cl), Buddy Mays/Travel Stock; 312 (tr), Max & Bea Hunn/D. Donne Bryant Photography; 312 (br), Buddy Mays/Travel Stock; 312 (border), Robert Fried; 313 (cr), Buddy Mays/ Travel Stock; 313 (tl), Trisha Buchhorn/Texas Inprint; 313 (cl), Brenda Tharp/F-Stock, Inc.; 313 (br), Roy Morsch/ Corbis Stock Market; 314-315 (bkgd), NASA/GSFC/ NOAA/USGS; 315 (border), Robert Fried; 316 (tr), Daniel Schaefer/HRW; 316 (cl), Bob Daemmrich/Stock Boston; 317 (cr), Daniel Schaefer/HRW; 318 (br), HRW; 321 (b), John Langford/HRW; 323 (bkgd), HRW Photo; 324 (tr), David Young-Wolff/Photo Edit; 325 (tr), Jeff Greenberg/ Photo Edit; 334 (cr), Jacques Jangoux/Tony Stone Images; 334 (cl), Hal Garb/Zephyr Pictures; 334 (b), Doug Bryant/ D. Donne Bryant Photography; 336 (br), AP/Wide World Photos; 336 (bl), SuperStock; 336 (bc), Culver Pictures, Inc.; 339 (c), Felicia Martinez/Photo Edit; 342-343 (bkgd), Leon Duque/Duque Múnera y Cia; 343 (border), Robert Fried; 344 (br), Robert W. Ginn/PhotoEdit; 345 (br), Michael Newman/Photo Edit; 346 (br), Robert Winslow; 352 (cr), Daniel J. Schaefer; 353 (br), Sam Dudgeon/ HRW; 358 (cl), ©Robert Frerck/Odyssey/Chicago; 358 (tl), David Young-Wolff/Photo Edit; 358 (tr), Tony Freeman/Photo Edit; 358 (br), Michelle Bridwell/Frontera Fotos; 359 (all), Sam Dudgeon/HRW; 366 (br), Sam Dudgeon/HRW; 368 (cr), Buddy Mays/Travel Stock; Backmatter images, Corbis Images, Digital imagery® copyright 2003 PhotoDisc, Inc., and HRW Photos.

ILLUSTRATION AND CARTOGRAPHY CREDITS

Abbreviated as follows: (t) top; (b) bottom; (l) left; (r) right; (c) center.

All art, unless otherwise noted, by Holt, Rinehart & Winston.

Front Matter: Page xxiii, MapQuest.com; xxiv, MapQuest.com; xxv, MapQuest.com; xxvi, MapQuest.com; xxvii, MapQuest.com; xxviii-xxix, MapQuest.com.

UNIT ONE: Page 2, MapQuest.com. **Chapter One:** Page 9, Edson Campos; 10, Meryl Henderson; 13, Meryl Henderson; 20, Walter Stuart; 21, Walter Stuart; 28, Edson Campos; 29, Bob McMahon. **Chapter Two:** Page 36, Aletha Reppel; 38, Bob McMahon; 39, Meryl Henderson; 40, Bob McMahon; 45, Fian Arroyo; 46, Fian Arroyo; 48, Edson Campos; 49, Eva Vagretti Cockrille.

UNIT TWO: Page 62, MapQuest.com. **Chapter Three:** Page 70, Michele Vrentas; 71, Elizabeth Brandt; 75, Edson Campos; 80, Edd Patton; 89, Edson Campos; 92, Bob McMahon. **Chapter Four:** Page 98, Fian Arroyo; 99, Fian Arroyo; 102, Fian Arroyo; 103, Edson Campos; 120, Eva Vagretti Cockrille; 122, Bob McMahon.

UNIT THREE: Page 124, MapQuest.com. **Chapter Five:** Page 130, Edson Campos; 131, Edson Campos; 138, Antonio Castro; 139, Antonio Castro; 140, Antonio Castro; 143, Meryl Henderson; 144, Catherine Huerta; 145, Catherine Huerta; 146, Catherine Huerta; 150, Eva Vagretti Cockrille; 152, Eva Vagretti Cockrille; 154, Eva Vagretti Cockrille. **Chapter Six:** Page 162, David Gothard; 163, Andrea Tachiera; 164, Meryl Henderson; 182, Edson Campos.

UNIT FOUR: Page 186, MapQuest.com. **Chapter Seven:** Page 201, Bob McMahon; 203 (t), Antonio Castro; 203 (b), Eva Vagretti Cockrille; 206, Fian Arroyo; 208, Edson Campos; 209, Edson Campos; 216, Fian Arroyo; 218, Bob McMahon. **Chapter Eight:** Page 222, Eva Vagretti Cockrille; 226, Eva Vagretti Cockrille; 233, Fian Arroyo; 234, Bob McMahon; 236, Guy Maestracci; 237, Guy Maestracci; 238, Guy Maestracci; 246, Edson Campos.

UNIT FIVE: Page 248, MapQuest.com. **Chapter Nine:** Page 257, Fian Arroyo; 260, Edson Campos; 266, Eva Vagretti Cockrille; 276, Bob McMahon. **Chapter Ten:** Page 286, MapQuest.com; 289, Edson Campos; 291, Meryl Henderson; 294, Edson Campos; 295, Eva Vagretti Cockrille; 306, Edson Campos; 308, Eva Vagretti Cockrille.

UNIT SIX: Page 310, MapQuest.com. **Chapter Eleven:** Page 319, Fian Arroyo; 320, Edson Campos; 326, Edson Campos; 328, Meryl Henderson; 330, Fian Arroyo; 331, Fian Arroyo; 332, Fian Arroyo; 335, Edson Campos. **Chapter Twelve:** Page 355, Edson Campos; 370, Fian Arroyo.